Frommer's®

W9-BFE-950

New England

15th Edition

by Matthew Barber, Leslie Brokaw,
Paul Karr, Herbert Bailey Livesey,
Marie Morris, Laura M. Reckford

WILEY
Wiley Publishing, Inc.

Published by:

WILEY PUBLISHING, INC.

111 River St.

Hoboken, NJ 07030-5774

ISBN 978-0-470-61434-1 (paper); ISBN 978-0-470-90643-9 (ebk); ISBN 978-0-470-93305-3 (ebk); ISBN 978-0-470-93306-0 (ebk);

Editor: Jennifer Moore, with Kathleen Warnock
Production Editor: Katie Robinson
Cartographer: Andrew Dolan
Photo Editor: Richard Fox
Production by Wiley Indianapolis Composition Services

Front cover photo: White picket fence and village church amid autumn colors at Fitzwilliam, New Hampshire ©Chad Ehlers / Alamy Images
Back cover photo: Pemaquid Point Lighthouse at sunrise ©Kenneth C. Zirkel / iStock Exclusive / Getty Images

For information on our other products and services or to obtain technical support, please contact our Customer Care Department within the U.S. at 877/762-2974, outside the U.S. at 317/572-3993 or fax 317/572-4002.

Wiley also publishes its books in a variety of electronic formats. Some content that appears in print may not be available in electronic formats.

Manufactured in the United States of America

5 4 3 2 1

CONTENTS

4 SUGGESTED NEW ENGLAND ITINERARIES 68

5 BOSTON & CAMBRIDGE 80

6 SIDE TRIPS FROM BOSTON 148

7 CAPE COD 195

8 MARTHA'S VINEYARD & NANTUCKET 269

14 MAINE 593

15 FAST FACTS: NEW ENGLAND 674

LIST OF MAPS

HOW TO CONTACT US

In researching this book, we discovered many wonderful places—hotels, restaurants, shops, and more. We're sure you'll find others. Please tell us about them, so we can share the information with your fellow travelers in upcoming editions. If you were disappointed with a recommendation, we'd love to know that, too. Please write to:

Frommer's New England, 15th Edition
Wiley Publishing, Inc. • 111 River St. • Hoboken, NJ 07030-5774
frommersfeedback@wiley.com

AN ADDITIONAL NOTE

Please be advised that travel information is subject to change at any time—and this is especially true of prices. We therefore suggest that you write or call ahead for confirmation when making your travel plans. The authors, editors, and publisher cannot be held responsible for the experiences of readers while traveling. Your safety is important to us, however, so we encourage you to stay alert and be aware of your surroundings. Keep a close eye on cameras, purses, and wallets, all favorite targets of thieves and pickpockets.

ABOUT THE AUTHORS

Matthew Barber (chapters 9–11) has lived in New England for 15 years. He helped author the restaurant chapters of *Frommer's Montréal & Québec City* and he writes about food and old-time cooking techniques at www.crispybits.com.

Leslie Brokaw (chapters 9–11) has been writing for Frommer's since 2006, authoring or contributing to *Frommer's Montréal & Québec City, Montréal Day by Day*, and *Frommer's Canada*. She lives in Boston and teaches at Emerson College.

Paul Karr (chapters 2–3 and 12–14) is an award-winning writer and editor and avid traveler. He is also the author of *Frommer's Nova Scotia, New Brunswick & Prince Edward Island; Frommer's Maine Coast;* and *Vancouver & Victoria For Dummies,* as well as a co-author of *Frommer's Canada.* His work has also appeared in the *New York Times, Sierra, Sports Illustrated,* and *Insight Guides* to Austria, Montreal, Switzerland, and Vienna. He divides his time between New York, New England, and Asia.

Herbert Bailey Livesey (chapters 9–11) has written about food and travel for over 30 years, authoring or contributing to *Frommer's Montréal & Québec City, Frommer's Europe,* and *Frommer's Canada.* He has been published in *Travel + Leisure, Food & Wine, Playboy, New York,* and *Yankee;* and he blogs about travel at www.akeyinthedoor.com.

Marie Morris (chapters 5–6) grew up in New York and graduated from Harvard, where she studied history. She has worked for the *Boston Herald, Boston* magazine, and the *New York Times.* She's the author of *Boston For Dummies, Irreverent Guide to Boston, Boston Day by Day,* and she covers Boston for *Frommer's New England.* She lives in Boston, not far from Paul Revere.

Laura M. Reckford (chapters 7–8) is the editor of *The Barnstable Enterprise* newspaper in the town of Barnstable on Cape Cod. Formerly the managing editor of *The Falmouth Enterprise* and *Cape Cod Life* magazine, she has also been on the editorial staffs of *Good Housekeeping* magazine and *Entertainment Weekly.* She co-authored the first edition of *France For Dummies.*

FROMMER'S STAR RATINGS, ICONS & ABBREVIATIONS

Every hotel, restaurant, and attraction listing in this guide has been ranked for quality, value, service, amenities, and special features using a **star-rating system.** In country, state, and regional guides, we also rate towns and regions to help you narrow down your choices and budget your time accordingly. Hotels and restaurants are rated on a scale of zero (recommended) to three stars (exceptional). Attractions, shopping, nightlife, towns, and regions are rated according to the following scale: zero stars (recommended), one star (highly recommended), two stars (very highly recommended), and three stars (must-see).

In addition to the star-rating system, we also use **seven feature icons** that point you to the great deals, in-the-know advice, and unique experiences that separate travelers from tourists. Throughout the book, look for:

special finds—those places only insiders know about

fun facts—details that make travelers more informed and their trips more fun

kids—best bets for kids and advice for the whole family

special moments—those experiences that memories are made of

overrated—places or experiences not worth your time or money

insider tips—great ways to save time and money

great values—where to get the best deals

The following **abbreviations** are used for credit cards:

AE	American Express	**DISC**	Discover	**V**	Visa
DC	Diners Club	**MC**	MasterCard		

TRAVEL RESOURCES AT FROMMERS.COM

Frommer's travel resources don't end with this guide. Frommer's website, **www.frommers. com**, has travel information on more than 4,000 destinations. We update features regularly, giving you access to the most current trip-planning information and the best airfare, lodging, and car-rental bargains. You can also listen to podcasts, connect with other Frommers. com members through our active-reader forums, share your travel photos, read blogs from guidebook editors and fellow travelers, and much more.

THE BEST OF NEW ENGLAND

One of the greatest challenges of traveling in New England is choosing from an abundance of superb restaurants, accommodations, and attractions. Where to start? Here's an entirely biased list of our favorite destinations and experiences. Over years of traveling through the region, we've discovered that these are places worth more than just a quick stop—they're all worth a major detour.

THE best OF SMALL-TOWN NEW ENGLAND

- **Marblehead** (MA): The "Yachting Capital of America" has major picture-postcard potential, especially in summer, when the harbor fills with boats of all sizes. From downtown, a short distance inland, make your way toward the water down the narrow, flower-dotted streets. The first glimpse of blue sea and sky is breathtaking. See "Marblehead," in chapter 6.
- **Provincetown** (Cape Cod, MA): At the far tip of the Cape's curl, in intensely beautiful surroundings, is Provincetown. Provincetown's history goes back nearly 400 years, and, in the last century, it's been a veritable headquarters of bohemia—a gathering place for famous writers and artists. It's also, of course, one of the world's top gay and lesbian resort areas. But Provincetown is a place for everyone who enjoys savory food, fun shopping, and fascinating people-watching. See "The Lower Cape," in chapter 7.
- **Nantucket** (MA): With grand 19th-century homes and cobblestone streets, it looks as though the whalers just left. Traveling to the island of Nantucket is like taking a trip to a parallel universe; you get historic charm but with 21st-century amenities. The island also has shops full of luxury goods, loads of historical sites open to the public, and miles of public beaches and bike paths. See "Nantucket," in chapter 8.
- **Oak Bluffs** (Martha's Vineyard, MA): Stroll down Circuit Avenue in Oak Bluffs with a Mad Martha's ice-cream cone, and then ride the Flying

Horses Carousel. This island harbor town is full of fun for kids and parents. Don't miss the colorful "gingerbread" cottages behind Circuit Avenue. Oak Bluffs also has great beaches, bike paths, and the Vineyard's best nightlife. See "Martha's Vineyard," in chapter 8.

o **Northampton** (MA): "Noho" is the cultural center of the Pioneer Valley, the north-south corridor in central Massachusetts that runs along the Connecticut River. Home to Smith College and within proximity of four other major liberal arts schools, Northampton boasts a large diversity of restaurants, lots of funky shopping, and some top music venues. See "Northampton," in chapter 9.

o **Stockbridge** (MA): Norman Rockwell made a famous painting of the main street of this, his adopted hometown in the southern Berkshires. Then as now, the sprawl of the Red Lion Inn and the other late-19th-century buildings make up the commercial district, with residential areas a beguiling mix of unassuming saltboxes and Gilded Age mansions. The Norman Rockwell Museum here gives an excellent overview of the artist, the town where he worked, and the social issues he addressed in his mid-20th-century art. See "Stockbridge," in chapter 9.

o **Washington** (CT): A classic, with a Congregational church facing a village green surrounded by clapboard Colonial houses—all of them with black shutters. See "Washington & Washington Depot," in chapter 10.

o **Essex** (CT): A walk past white-clapboard houses to the active waterfront on this narrow, unspoiled stretch of the Connecticut River rings all the right bells. You won't encounter an artificial note, a cookie-cutter franchise, or a costumed docent to muddy its near-perfect image. Be sure to take a ride on a 1920s steam locomotive or Mississippi-style riverboat. See "Essex & Ivoryton," in chapter 10.

o **Woodstock** (VT): Woodstock has a stunning village green, a whole range of 19th-century homes, woodland walks leading just out of town, and a settled, old-money air. This is a good place to explore on foot or by bike, or to just sit and watch summer unfold. See "Woodstock & Environs," in chapter 12.

o **Montpelier** (VT): This is the way all state capitals should be: slow paced, small enough so you can walk everywhere, and full of shops that still sell nails and strapping tape. Montpelier also shows a more sophisticated edge, with its Culinary Institute, an art-house movie theater, and several fine bookshops. But at heart, it's a small town, where you just might run into the governor at the corner store. See "Exploring Montpelier & Barre," in chapter 12.

o **Hanover** (NH): It's the perfect college town: the handsome brick buildings of Dartmouth College, a tidy green, a small but select shopping district, and a scattering of good restaurants. Come in the fall, and you'll be tempted to join in the touch football game on the green. See "Hanover," in chapter 13.

THE best PLACES TO SEE FALL FOLIAGE

o **Walden Pond State Reservation** (Concord, MA): Walden Pond sits surrounded by the woods where Henry David Thoreau built a small cabin and lived from 1845 to 1847. When the leaves are turning and the water reflects the colorful trees, it's hard to imagine why he left. See p. 159.

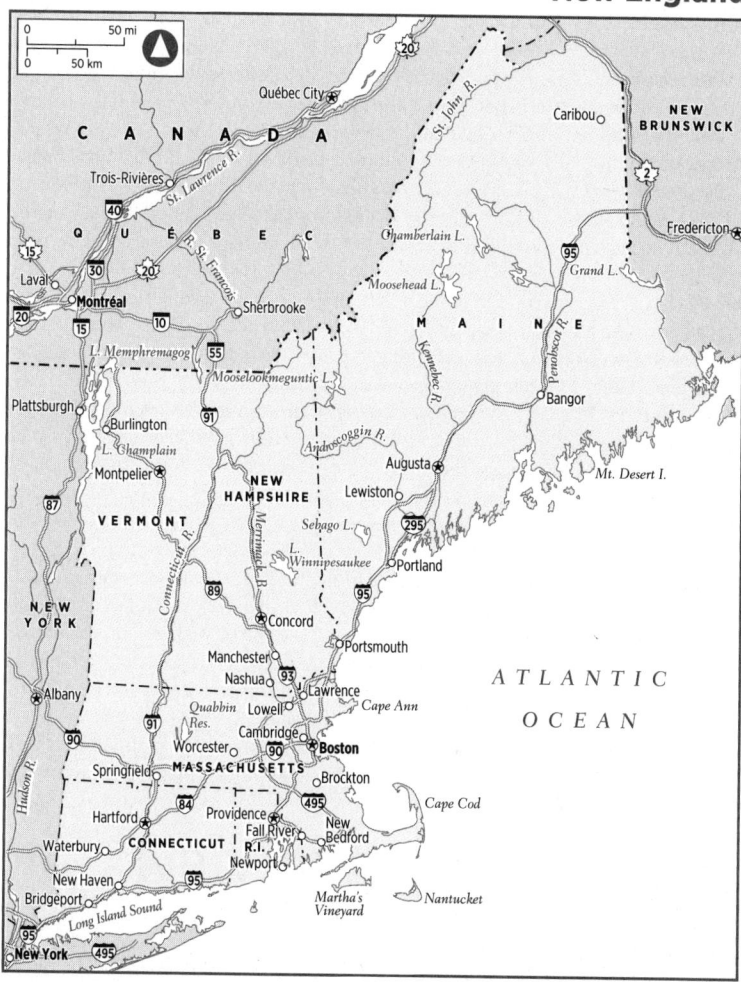

- **Mount Auburn Cemetery** (Cambridge, MA): More than 5,000 trees spread across Mount Auburn's 175 acres. Each deciduous specimen changes color on its own schedule, and, at the peak of foliage season, each seems to be a different shade of red, orange, or gold. See p. 130.
- **Bash-Bish Falls State Park** (South Egremont, MA): The comely village of South Egremont is surrounded by forested hills in this southwest corner of Massachusetts. The roads, which change from gravel to dirt and back, wind between crimson clouds of sugar maples and white birches feather-stroked against banks of black evergreens. The payoff is a three-state view from a promontory above a

50-foot cascade notched into a bluff, with carpets of russet and gold. The falls themselves are 80 feet high. See p. 339.

o **Ridgefield** (CT): No town in Connecticut has a grander, more imposing main street. Ridgefield's is 132 feet wide and lined with ancient elms, maples, and oaks. Impressive any time of the year, it is in its glory during the brief blaze of the October foliage season. Also here is the highly recommended Aldrich Contemporary Art Museum. See "Ridgefield," in chapter 10.

o **The Litchfield Hills** (CT): Rte. 7, running south to north through the rugged northwest corner of Connecticut, roughly along the course of the Housatonic River, explodes with color in the weeks before and after Columbus Day. Leaves drift down to the water and whirl away with the foaming river. See "The Litchfield Hills," in chapter 10.

o **I-91** (VT): An interstate? Don't scoff (the traffic can be terrible on narrow state roads). If you like your foliage viewing wholesale, cruise I-91 from Brattleboro to Newport. You'll be overwhelmed with gorgeous terrain, from the gentle Connecticut River Valley to the sloping hills of the Northeast Kingdom. See chapter 12.

o **Vermont Rte. 100** (VT): Rte. 100 winds the length of Vermont from Readsboro to Newport, plying the Mad River Valley for a stretch. It's the major north-south route through the center of the Green Mountains, and it's surprisingly undeveloped along most of its length. You won't have it to yourself along the southern stretches on autumn weekends, but as you head farther north, you'll leave the crowds behind. See chapter 12.

o **Crawford Notch** (NH): Rte. 302 passes through this scenic valley, where you can see the brilliant red maples and yellow birches high on the hillsides. In fall, Mount Washington, in the background, is likely to be dusted with an early snow. See "The White Mountains," in chapter 13.

o **Camden** (ME): The dazzling fall colors that cover the rolling hills are reflected in Penobscot Bay on the east side, and in the lakes on the west. Ascend the peaks for views out to the color-splashed islands in the bay. Autumn usually comes a week or so later on the coast, so you can stretch out your viewing pleasure. See "Penobscot Bay," in chapter 14.

THE best WAYS TO VIEW COASTAL SCENERY

o **Strolling Around Rockport** (MA): The town surrounds the small harbor and spreads out along the rugged, rocky coastline of Cape Ann. From the end of Bearskin Neck, the view is spectacular—fishing and pleasure boats in one direction, roaring surf in the other. The surf's the thing at Halibut Point State Park, at the tip of the peninsula. See "Cape Ann," in chapter 6.

o **Getting Back to Nature on Plum Island** (MA): The Parker River National Wildlife Refuge, in Newburyport, offers two varieties of coastal scenery: picturesque salt marshes packed with birds and other animals, and gorgeous ocean beaches that bear witness to the power of the Atlantic. See "Newburyport, Ipswich & Plum Island," in chapter 6.

o **Biking or Driving the Outer Cape** (MA): From Eastham through Wellfleet and Truro, all the way to Provincetown, Cape Cod's outermost towns offer dazzling ocean vistas and a number of exceptional bike paths, including the Province Lands, just outside Provincetown, that are bordered by spectacular swooping dunes. See "The Outer Cape," in chapter 7.

o **Heading "Up-Island" on Martha's Vineyard** (MA): Many visitors never venture beyond the port towns of Vineyard Haven, Oak Bluffs, and Edgartown. Though each has its charms, the scenery actually gets more spectacular "up-island," in such towns as Chilmark, where you'll pass moorlike meadows and family farms surrounded by stone walls. Follow State Road and the scenic Moshup Trail to the westernmost tip of the island, where you'll experience the dazzling colored cliffs of Aquinnah and the quaint fishing port of Menemsha. See "Martha's Vineyard," in chapter 8.

o **Cruising Newport's Ocean Drive** (RI): After a tour of the fabulously overwrought mansions—known as "cottages"—of the hyper-rich who are strung along Bellevue Avenue, continue by car or bike onto the shoreline road that dodges the spray of the Atlantic. It is a cleansing reminder of the power of nature over fragile monuments to the conceits of men. To extend the experience, take a 3.5-mile hike along the Cliff Walk that skirts the edge of the bluff commanded by the largest mansions. See p. 452.

o **Sitting in a Rocking Chair** (ME): The views are never better than when you're caught unaware—such as suddenly looking up from an engrossing book while you rock on the front porch of an oceanside inn. Throughout the Maine chapter, look for mention of inns right on the water, such as Beach House Inn (p. 609), Samoset Resort (p. 633), East Wind Inn, and The Claremont (p. 662).

o **Driving the Park Loop Road at Acadia National Park** (ME): This is the region's premier ocean drive. You'll start high along a ridge with views of Frenchman Bay and the Porcupine Islands, then dip down along the rocky shores to watch the surf crash against the dark rocks. Plan to do this 20-mile loop at least twice to get the most out of it. See p. 650.

THE best PLACES TO EXPLORE THE PAST

o **Paul Revere House** (Boston, MA): We often study the history of the American Revolution through stories of governments and institutions. At this little home in the North End, you'll learn about a real person. The self-guided tour is particularly thought-provoking, allowing you to linger on the artifacts that hold your interest. Revere had 16 children with two wives, supported them with his thriving silversmith's trade—and put the whole operation in jeopardy with his role in the events that led to the Revolution. See p. 123.

o **Old State House** (Boston, MA): Built in 1713, the once-towering Old State House is dwarfed by modern skyscrapers. It stands as a reminder of British rule (the exterior features a lion and a unicorn) and its overthrow—the Declaration of Independence was read from the balcony, which overlooks a traffic island where a circle of bricks represents the site of the Boston Massacre. See p. 123.

o **Faneuil Hall** (Boston, MA): Although Faneuil Hall is best known nowadays as a shopping destination, if you head upstairs, you'll be transported back in time. In the second-floor auditorium, park rangers talk about the building's role in the Revolution. Tune out the sound of sneakers squeaking across the floor, and you can almost hear Samuel Adams (his statue is out front) exhorting the Sons of Liberty. See p. 123.

o **"Old Ironsides"** (Boston, MA): Formally named the USS *Constitution*, the frigate was launched in 1797 and gained fame battling Barbary pirates and seeing action in the War of 1812. Last used in battle in 1815, it was periodically threatened with destruction until a complete renovation in the late 1920s started its career as a floating monument. The staff includes sailors on active duty who wear 1812 dress uniforms. See p. 123.

o **North Bridge** (Concord, MA): British troops headed to Concord after putting down the uprising in Lexington, and the bridge (a replica) stands as a testament to the Minutemen who fought here. The Concord River and its peaceful green banks give no hint of the bloodshed that took place. On the path in from Monument Street, placards and audio stations provide a fascinating narrative. See "Concord," in chapter 6.

o **Plymouth Rock** (Plymouth, MA): Okay, it's a fraction of its original size and looks like something you might find in your garden. Nevertheless, Plymouth Rock makes a perfect starting point for exploration. Close by is *Mayflower II,* a replica of the alarmingly small original vessel. The juxtaposition reminds you of what a dangerous undertaking the Pilgrims' voyage was. See "Plymouth," in chapter 6.

o **Sandwich** (MA): The oldest town on Cape Cod, Sandwich was founded in 1637. Glassmaking brought notoriety and prosperity to this picturesque town in the 19th century. Visit the Sandwich Glass Museum for the whole story, or tour one of the town's glassblowing studios. Don't leave without visiting the 76-acre Heritage Museums and Gardens, which has a working carousel, a sparkling antique-car collection, and a wonderful collection of Americana. See "The Upper Cape," in chapter 7.

o **Nantucket** (MA): It looks as though the whalers just left, leaving behind their grand houses, cobbled streets, and a gamut of enticing shops offering luxury goods from around the world. The Nantucket Historical Association owns more than a dozen properties open for tours, and the Whaling Museum is one of the most fascinating sites in the region. Tourism may be rampant, but not its tackier side effects, thanks to stringent preservation measures. See "Nantucket," in chapter 8.

o **Old Sturbridge Village** (Sturbridge, MA): With authentic buildings and costumed staff, this is a re-created rural settlement of the 1830s. Visitors stroll through the village, which is spread across more than 200 acres, to see working versions of a saw mill, a blacksmith shop, a school, and a cooperage. Lazy boat rides are popular, as is a hands-on craft center. In summertime, a horse-drawn stagecoach traverses the dirt lanes, and, when there's snow, guests can take horse-drawn sleigh rides. See p. 319.

o **Emily Dickinson Museum: The Homestead and The Evergreens** (Amherst, MA): The "Belle of Amherst" was born at the Homestead in 1830 and spent much of her life here. The museum has a bookshop, an exhibit hall, and guided tours. See p. 331.

- **Historic Deerfield** (Deerfield, MA): Arguably the best-preserved Colonial village in New England. The historic section of this town has more than 80 houses dating back to the 17th and 18th centuries, with none of the clutter of modernity. Ten museum houses on the main avenue can be visited through tours conducted by the organization known as Historic Deerfield. See p. 333.
- **Hancock Shaker Village** (Pittsfield, MA): By the time "Mother" Ann Lee died in 1784, the austere Protestant sect she founded, known as the Shakers, had fanned out across the country to form communal settlements from Maine to Indiana. Hancock, edging the Massachusetts–New York border, was one of the most important. The village presents restored buildings, engaging exhibits, and a selection of Shaker crafts, including furniture and home accessories. See p. 356.
- **Mark Twain House & Museum** (Hartford, CT): This museum and the adjacent Harriet Beecher Stowe Center explore the lives of two of America's finest authors and their roles in exploring African-American history. See p. 398.
- **College Hill** (Providence, RI): Here, on the east side of Providence, is the site of the former Rhode Island College, which started in 1764 and was later renamed Brown University. College Hill is now a National Historic District and has several square miles of 18th- and 19th-century houses, Colonial to Victorian, lining its streets, with the Brown campus in the middle. See p. 430.
- **Bristol** (RI): This small town south of Providence and north of Newport is best known as home to the nation's oldest 4th of July parade, which has run annually here since 1785. It draws up to 200,000 spectators every year. The main boulevard, Hope Street, has a red, white, and blue band instead of a double yellow line down the middle, marking the 1.8-mile parade route. See "Bristol," in chapter 11.
- **Newport** (RI): Newport retains abundant recollections of its storied maritime past. In addition to its great harbor—clogged with tugs, ferries, yachts, and majestic sloops—the City by the Sea has preserved three distinctive enclaves: the waterside homes of Colonial seamen, the hillside Federal houses of port-bound merchants, and the ostentatious mansions of America's post–Civil War industrial and financial grandees. See "Newport," in chapter 11.
- **Shelburne Museum** (Shelburne, VT): Think of this sprawling museum as New England's attic. Located on the shores of Lake Champlain, the Shelburne features not only the usual exhibits of quilts and early glass, but also whole buildings preserved like specimens in formaldehyde. Look for the lighthouse, the railroad station, and the stagecoach inn. This is one of northern New England's "don't miss" destinations. See p. 540.
- **Portsmouth** (NH): Portsmouth is a salty coastal city that just happens to boast some of the most impressive historic homes in New England. Start at Strawbery Banke, a historic compound of 42 buildings dating from 1695 to 1820. Then visit the many other grand homes in nearby neighborhoods, such as the house John Paul Jones occupied while building his warship during the Revolution. See "Portsmouth," in chapter 13.
- **Victoria Mansion** (Portland, ME): The Donald had nothing on the Victorians when it came to excess. You'll see Victorian decorative arts at their zenith in this Italianate mansion built during the Civil War years by a prosperous hotelier. It's open to the public for tours in summer and also puts on outstanding Christmas-season programs. See p. 617.

THE best FAMILY ACTIVITIES

o **Exploring the Museum of Fine Arts** (Boston, MA): Parents hear "magnificent Egyptian collections." Kids think: "Mummies!" Even the most hyper youngster manages to take it down a notch in these quiet, refined surroundings, and the collections at the MFA simultaneously tickle visitors' brains. See p. 120.

o **Experimenting in the Museum of Science** (Boston, MA): Built around demonstrations and interactive displays that never feel like homework, this museum is wildly popular with kids—and adults. Explore the exhibits, then take in a show at the planetarium or the Mugar Omni Theater. Before you know it, everyone will have learned something, painlessly. See p. 120.

o **Catching a Free Friday Flick at the Hatch Shell** (Boston, MA): Better known for the Boston Pops' 4th of July concert, the Esplanade is also famous for family films (such as *Bee Movie* or *Madagascar*) shown on Friday nights in summer. The lawn in front of the Hatch Shell turns into a giant, carless drive-in as hundreds of people picnic and wait for dark. See p. 139.

o **Visiting the Heritage Museums and Gardens** (Cape Cod, MA): This site with museum buildings spread over 76 acres will delight both children and adults. Kids will especially love the gleaming antique cars, the collections of soldiers and Native American clothing, and the 1912 carousel that offers unlimited rides. Outdoor concerts free with admission take place most Sunday afternoons in season. See p. 199.

o **Whale-Watching off Provincetown** (Cape Cod, MA): Boats leave MacMillan Wharf for the 8-mile journey to Stellwagen Bank National Marine Sanctuary, a rich feeding ground for several types of whales. Nothing can prepare you for the thrill of spotting these magnificent creatures feeding, breaching, and even flipper-slapping. See p. 257.

o **Romping Around the Higgins Armory Museum** (Worcester, MA): Harry Potter fans will be in heaven in this Gothic museum of suits of armor, especially if the trip coincides with one of the days featuring combat demonstrations. See p. 316.

o **Deep-Sea Fishing:** Charter fishing boats these days usually have high-tech fish-finding gear—imagine how your kids will react to reeling in one big bluefish after another. The top spots to mount such an expedition are Barnstable Harbor and Rock Harbor in Orleans, on Cape Cod, and the Maine coast. See chapters 7 and 14, respectively.

o **Riding the Flying Horses Carousel in Oak Bluffs** (Martha's Vineyard, MA): Some say this is the oldest carousel in the country, but your kids might not notice the genuine horsehair, sculptural details, or glass eyes. They'll be too busy trying to grab the brass ring to win a free ride. After your ride, stroll around the town of Oak Bluffs. Children will be enchanted with the "gingerbread" houses, a carryover from the 19th-century revivalist movement. See p. 270.

o **Biking Nantucket** (MA): Short, flat trails crisscross the island, and every one leads to a beach. The shortest rides lead to Children's Beach, with its own playground, and Jetties Beach, with a skate park and watersports equipment for rent; older kids will be able to make the few miles to Surfside and Madaket. See "Nantucket," in chapter 8.

o **Exploring the Connecticut Science Center** (Hartford, CT): Open since July 2009, this kid-centric center is adjacent to Hartford's Riverfront Plaza and revitalized

Connecticut River waterfront, part of a major freshening up designed to attract visitors. The area looks good, and the center has 150 exhibits, mostly interactive, and a 3D theater. See p. 396.

o **Visiting Mystic Seaport and Mystic Aquarium** (Mystic, CT): The double-down winner in the family-fun sweepstakes has to be this combination: a visit to the waterfront settlement of the Seaport, which captures the look and feel of a 19th-century seafaring village, and a trip to the Aquarium, with performing white whales and sea lions. These are the kinds of G-rated attractions that have no age barriers. See p. 416 and 416, respectively.

o **Taking in a Triple-A Baseball Game** (Pawtucket, RI): McCoy Stadium is home to the Pawtucket Red Sox, a baseball team that is the stop right before players get to the Boston Red Sox. A night here is an inexpensive way to see good baseball in a low-key venue. The stadium is 6 miles from downtown Providence. See p. 431.

o **Setting Up along the Providence Rivers for WaterFire** (Providence, RI): This has become the city's exclamation point: On at least a dozen nights from spring through fall, thousands of people descend to the riverfront to see a free nighttime installation of bonfires right on the water. See p. 432.

o **Swimming in the Ocean** (Newport, RI): There are good beaches all along the New England coast. In this city, the best is Easton's Beach, near the engaging Cliff Walk. See p. 452.

o **Ice skating on Outdoor Rinks:** New Englanders don't take to the outdoors in winter with quite the enthusiasm as, say, the Québécois, but they give it a good shot with outdoor skating. Family-friendly rinks are set up in Boston Common; downtown Providence, RI; and downtown Newport, RI. See p. 136, 431, and 453.

o **Visiting the Ben & Jerry Ice Cream Factory** (Waterbury, VT): Kids and ice cream are a great combination, and the half-hour tours that leave every 10 minutes in summer won't tax anybody's patience. Browse the small ice-cream museum, enjoy the playground and cow-viewing area, and make sure to save room for the free samples. See p. 525.

o **Exploring the Shelburne Museum** (Shelburne, VT): This museum contains one of the nation's most singular collections of American decorative, folk, and fine art. Kid favorites include the Circus Building, with a 35,000-piece three-ring miniature circus; an operating vintage carousel; a collection of dolls and dollhouses; and automata, large (sometimes 3 ft. tall), often comical wind-up toys. See p. 540.

o **Riding the Mount Washington Cog Railway** (Crawford Notch, NH): It's fun! It's terrifying! It's a great glimpse into history. Kids love this ratchety climb to the top of New England's highest peak aboard trains that were specially designed to scale the mountain in 1869. As a technological marvel, the railroad attracted tourists by the thousands a century ago. They still come to marvel at the sheer audacity of it all. See p. 588.

THE best COUNTRY INNS

o **Hawthorne Inn** (Concord, MA; ✆ **978/369-5610**): Everything here—the 1870 building, the garden setting a stone's throw from the historic attractions, the antiques, the eclectic decorations, the accommodating innkeepers—is top of the line. See p. 160.

o **Coonamessett Inn** (Falmouth, MA; ☎ **508/548-2300**): Picture windows overlooking a pond and 7 verdant acres make this former (from 1796) homestead a very special place to stay. Separate sitting rooms and knotty pine walls add to its comfort and charm. Plus, Sunday brunch is a real treat. See p. 206.

o **Captain's House Inn** (Chatham, Cape Cod, MA; ☎ **800/315-0728**): An elegant country inn dripping with good taste, this is among the best small inns in the region. Most rooms have fireplaces, elegant paneling, and antiques; they're sumptuous yet cozy. Your British hostess serves a stupendous high tea. This could be the ultimate spot to enjoy Chatham's Christmas Stroll festivities. See p. 238.

o **Charlotte Inn** (Edgartown, Martha's Vineyard, MA; ☎ **508/627-4751**): Edgartown tends to be the most formal enclave on Martha's Vineyard, and this compound of exquisite buildings is by far the fanciest address in town. The rooms are distinctively decorated: One boasts a baby grand, another its own thematic dressing room. The restaurant, **Catch at the Terrace,** is also top-notch. See p. 283.

o **The Old Inn on the Green** (New Marlborough, MA; ☎ **413/229-7924**): This former stagecoach stop from 1760 has five rooms in the main inn and six in an adjacent 18th-century house. What really recommends this venue, though, are the good in-house meals. The intimate dining area has fireplaces, and the only illumination at dinner is from candles. Menus are sophisticated, and there often are good package deals in the off season and midweek. See p. 341.

o **The Porches** (North Adams, MA; ☎ **413/664-0400**): The Porches may stretch the definition of the "country inn" category, but this is too much fun to ignore. It was put together with six 19th-century workmen's houses lined up opposite the Massachusetts Museum of Contemporary Art (MASS MoCA), a new veranda running across their length. The wit of the innkeepers is evident in the use of paint-by-the-numbers pictures and sublimely kitschy accessories, but DVD players and free Wi-Fi ensure no 21st-century deprivation.See p. 362.

o **Mayflower Inn & Spa** (Washington, CT; ☎ **860/868-9466**): Not a tough call at all for this part of the region: Immaculate in taste and execution, the Mayflower is as close to perfection as any such enterprise is likely to be. Rooms start at $1,040 a night. See p. 380.

o **Griswold Inn** (Essex, CT; ☎ **860/767-1776**): "The Gris" has been accommodating sailors and travelers as long as any inn in the country, give or take a decade. In all that time, it has been a part of life and commerce in the lower Connecticut River Valley, always ready with a mug of suds, a haunch of beef, and a roaring fire. The walls are layered with nautical paintings and memorabilia, and they've even gotten up the nerve to add a wine bar to the mix. See p. 408.

o **The Equinox Resort & Spa** (Manchester Village, VT; ☎ **800/362-4747**): This is southern Vermont's grand resort, with nearly 200 rooms in a white-clapboard compound that seems to go on forever. The rooms are pleasant enough, but the real draws are the grounds and the resort's varied activities—it's set on 2,300 acres with pools, tennis courts, an 18-hole golf course, and even its own mountainside. Tried everything on vacation? How about a falconry class? See p. 484.

- **Windham Hill Inn** (West Townshend, VT; ✆ 800/944-4080): Welcome amenities such as air-conditioning in the rooms and a conference room in the barn have been added, while preserving the charm of this 1823 farmstead. It's at the end of a remote dirt road in a high upland valley, and guests are welcome to explore 160 private acres on a network of walking trails. See p. 492.

- **The Pitcher Inn** (Warren, VT; ✆ 802/496-6350): Even though this place was built in 1997, it's possessed of the graciousness of a longtime, well-worn inn. It combines traditional New England form and scale with modern and luxe touches, plus a good dollop of whimsy. See p. 522.

- **Basin Harbor Club** (Vergennes, VT; ✆ 800/622-4000): Established in 1886, this waterside gem is a classic family resort, with golf, tennis, and boating on Lake Champlain, jackets-required dining, stunning views, and evening lectures on the arts. Bring books and board games, and relearn what summer's all about. See p. 541.

- **White Barn Inn** (Kennebunkport, ME; ✆ 207/967-2321): The White Barn's staff hail from all over, and guests are treated with a Continental graciousness that's hard to match anywhere else in New England. The setting is lovely, too. Rooms, suites, and cottages here are all a delight, and the meals (served in the barn) are among the best in Maine. See p. 610.

- **The Claremont** (Southwest Harbor, ME; ✆ 800/244-5036): The 1884 Claremont is a Maine classic. This waterside lodge has everything a Victorian resort should, including sparely decorated rooms, creaky floorboards in the halls, great views of water and mountains, and a perfect croquet pitch. See p. 662.

THE best MODERATELY PRICED ACCOMMODATIONS

- **Newbury Guest House** (Boston, MA; ✆ 800/437-7668): This lovely property would be a good deal even if it weren't ideally located on Newbury Street, Boston's version of Rodeo Drive. Rates even include breakfast. See p. 101.

- **Pilgrim Sands Motel** (Plymouth, MA; ✆ 800/729-7263): The ocean views and two pools (indoor and outdoor) make this a great deal, whether you're immersing yourself in Pilgrim lore or passing through on the way from Boston to Cape Cod. See p. 193.

- **White Horse Inn** (Provincetown, Cape Cod, MA; ✆ 508/487-1790): The very embodiment of Provincetown funkiness, this inn has hosted such celebrities as filmmaker John Waters and poet laureate Robert Pinsky. Rooms are short on amenities but long on artiness. The apartments, cobbled together by innkeeper Frank Schaefer, are highly original and a lot of fun.

- **Nauset House Inn** (East Orleans, Cape Cod, MA; ✆ 800/771-5508): This romantic 1810 farmhouse is like a sepia-toned vision of old Cape Cod. Recline in a wicker divan surrounded by fragrant flowers while the wind whistles outside. Better yet, stroll to Nauset Beach and take a quiet walk as the sun sets. Your genial hosts also prepare one of the finest breakfasts in town. See p. 243.

- **Hopkins Inn** (New Preston, CT; ✆ 860/868-7295): This yellow farmhouse bestows the top view of Lake Waramaug, and is at its best on soft summer days when robust Alpine dishes can be taken out on the terrace. The somewhat spartan rooms don't tempt winding-down guests with either phones or TVs. The Hopkins Vineyard is adjacent. See p. 381.

o **Inn at the Mad River Barn** (Waitsfield, VT; ✆ 800/631-0466): It takes a few minutes to adapt to the spartan rooms and no-frills accommodations here. But you'll soon discover that the real action takes place in the living room and dining room, where skiers relax and chat after a day on the slopes, and share heaping helpings at mealtime. See p. 521.

THE best RESTAURANTS

o **Legal Sea Foods** (Boston, MA, and other locations; ✆ 617/266-6800): Newcomers ask where to go for fresh seafood, then react suspiciously when we recommend a world-famous restaurant instead of a local secret. No, it's no secret—but it's a wildly successful chain for a reason. See p. 105.

o **Mamma Maria** (Boston, MA; ✆ 617/523-0077): The best restaurant in the restaurant-choked North End is a far cry from the spaghetti-and-meatballs workhorses that crowd this Italian-American neighborhood. The Northern Italian cuisine at this elegant town house is something to write home about. See p. 108.

o **902 Main** (South Yarmouth, Cape Cod, MA; ✆ 508/398-9902): With fabulous service, an elegant atmosphere, and to-die-for food, this is the place to go for fine dining in the Mid-Cape. Such entrees as filet mignon with portobello mushrooms, rack of lamb with truffle mashed potatoes, and haddock with organic beets will set you swooning.

o **Atria** (Edgartown, Martha's Vineyard, MA; ✆ 508/627-5840): This fine-dining restaurant set in an 18th-century sea captain's home gets rave reviews for its gourmet cuisine and its high-quality service. This is one of those places where you can just relax and have a fantastic and memorable meal, because the staff knows exactly what they are doing. See p. 288.

o **Centre Street Bistro** (Nantucket, MA; ✆ 508/228-8470): Two of the best chefs on the island, Ruth and Tim Pitts, combine their talents at this cozy little hole-in-the-wall restaurant. The best part is that this place features wonderful, creative cuisine at fairly reasonable prices, compared to other island fine-dining restaurants. See p. 312.

o **Zinc** (Lenox, MA; ✆ 413/637-8800): Setting the Berkshires culinary standard, this stylish, contemporary bistro impresses on every repeat visit. It looks great, for starters, with its zinc bar, buffed woods, and flowers everywhere. Most everything that arrives on a plate is supremely satisfying, joining familiarity with the French repertoire with cunning twists in execution. Try one of the 24 wines by the glass and the irresistible five-cheese tasting. See p. 355.

o **Bespoke** (New Haven, CT; ✆ 203/562-4644): The preeminent newish restaurant in Connecticut, Bespoke has been open since 2006. Food arrives in one dazzling display after another: seafood chowder in a coconut milk broth; roasted sea bass in a carrot-curry broth; and "Two-Way" duck, an Asian-style leg confit and breast with rhubarb-celery salad. See p. 392.

o **Union League Café** (New Haven, CT; ✆ 203/562-4299): The august setting of arched windows and high ceilings is more than 150 years old and was long the sanctuary of an exclusive club. It still looks good, but the tone has been lightened into an approximation of a Lyonnais brasserie. See p. 393.

o **Fluke Wine, Bar & Kitchen** (Newport, RI; ✆ **401/849-7778**): The third floor of this venue, with a small bar and a few tables, is a cozy find, with views of the harbor and a convivial crowd to enjoy them. The chef has a New Orleans background, so spicy flavors are to be expected. You can make a meal of the small plates. See p. 459.

o **Chantecleer** (Manchester Center, VT; ✆ **802/362-1616**): Swiss chef Michel Baumann has been turning out dazzling dinners here since 1981, and the kitchen hasn't gotten stale in the least. The dining room in an old barn is magical, the staff helpful and friendly. It's a great spot for those who demand top-notch Continental fare but don't like the fuss of a fancy restaurant. See p. 487.

o **T. J. Buckley's** (Brattleboro, VT; ✆ **802/257-4922**): This tiny diner on a dark side street serves up outsize tastes prepared by a talented chef. Forget about stewed-too-long diner fare; get in your mind big tastes blossoming from the freshest of ingredients prepared just right. See p. 497.

o **Hemingway's** (Killington, VT; ✆ **802/422-3886**): Killington seems an unlikely place for a serious culinary adventure, yet Hemingway's will meet the loftiest expectations. The menu changes frequently to ensure only the freshest of ingredients. If it's available, be sure to order a bowl of the wild mushroom and truffle soup. See p. 511.

o **Arrows** (Ogunquit, ME; ✆ **207/361-1100**): The emphasis at this elegant spot is on local fare—often drawing on ingredients from nearby organic vegetable gardens. Prices are not for the fainthearted, but the experience is top-rate, from the cordial service to the silver and linens. Expect New American cuisine informed by an Asian sensibility. See p. 606.

o **White Barn Inn** (Kennebunkport, ME; ✆ **207/967-2321**): The setting in an ancient, rustic barn is magical. The tables are set with floor-length tablecloths, and the chairs feature imported Italian upholstery. The food? To die for. Start with lobster spring rolls, then enjoy entrees such as roasted duck with juniper sauce or Maine lobster over fettuccine with a cognac coral butter sauce. See p. 612.

o **Fore Street** (Portland, ME; ✆ **207/775-2717**): Fore Street is one of northern New England's most celebrated restaurants. The chef's secret? Simplicity, and lots of it. Some of the most memorable meals are prepared over an applewood grill. See p. 620.

o **Hugo's** (Portland, ME; ✆ **207/774-8538**): Chef Rob Evans has performed a CPR job on this once-proud bistro that's been nothing short of amazing; it now stands among Maine's finest restaurants. The tasting menus are especially wonderful, and there's an affiliated Belgian-fries shop just down the street for guilty-pleasure dining as well. See p. 620.

THE best LOCAL DINING EXPERIENCES

o **Durgin-Park** (Boston, MA; ✆ **617/227-2038**): Your favorite thing here might be the famous cornbread, the equally famous baked beans, the super-fresh seafood, the gigantic prime rib, the luscious strawberry shortcake, the historic setting, or even the smart-mouthed service. In any case, Durgin-Park has been a magnet for Bostonians and visitors since 1827. See p. 110.

o **Woodman's of Essex** (Essex, MA; ✆ **800/649-1773**): This busy North Shore institution is not for the faint of heart—or the hard of artery, unless you like eating corn and steamers while everyone around you is gobbling fried clams and onion rings. The food at this glorified clam shack is fresh and delicious, and a look at the organized pandemonium behind the counter is worth the (reasonable) price. See p. 173.

o **Black Eyed Susan's** (Nantucket, MA; ✆ **508/325-0308**): This is extremely exciting food in a funky bistro atmosphere. The place is small, popular with locals, and packed. Sitting at the diner counter and watching the chef in action is a show in itself. No credit cards, no reservations, and no liquor license are all inconvenient, but if you can get past all that, you're in for a top-notch dining experience. See p. 312.

o **Judie's** (Amherst, MA; ✆ **413/253-3491**): Don't leave the Pioneer Valley without trying the upbeat, bustling Judie's. The house specialty is stuffed popovers—there are five varieties, from gumbo to shrimp scampi. See p. 332.

o **Louis' Lunch** (New Haven, CT; ✆ **203/562-5507**): Not a lot of serious history has happened in New Haven, but boosters claim it was here at Louis' Lunch that hamburgers were invented in 1900. True or not, this little luncheonette lives on, moved from its original site in order to save it. The patties are freshly ground daily, thrust into vertical grills, and served on white toast. Garnishes are tomato, onion, and cheese. No ketchup and no fries, so don't even ask. See p. 394.

o **Pizza** (New Haven, CT): New Haven's claim to America's first pizza is a whole lot shakier than its claim to the first burgers (see above), but the city excels in the ultrathin, charred variety of what they still call "apizza" in these parts, pronounced "ah-peetz." Old-timer **Frank Pepe's,** 157 Wooster St. (✆ **203/865-5762**), is usually ceded top rank among the local parlors, but it is joined by such contenders as **Sally's,** 237 Wooster St. (✆ **203/624-5271**), and **Modern Apizza,** 874 State St. (✆ **203/776-5306**). See p. 394.

o **The Place** (Guilford, CT; ✆ **203/453-9276**): The Place cooks its food over outdoor open wood fires. You sit on tree stumps (and can buy a T-shirt that confirms that you "Put Your Rump On A Stump") and dig into what's essentially a clambake—clams, corn on the cob, and lobster. See p. 402.

o **Abbott's Lobster in the Rough** (Noank, CT; ✆ **860/536-7719**): Places like this frill-free lobster restaurant abound along more northerly reaches of the New England coast, but here's a little bit o' Maine a few miles from the heart of Mystic. Shore dinners rule, so roll up sleeves, tie on napkins, and dive into platters of boiled shrimp and steamed mussels, and dunk hot lobster chunks in pots of drawn butter. See p. 419.

o **Johnnycakes and Stuffies** (RI): Most worthy regional food faves eventually become known to the wider world (witness Buffalo wings). But the Ocean State still has some taste treats that are mysteries beyond its borders. "Johnnycakes" are flapjacks made with cornmeal, which come small and plump or wide and lacy, depending upon family tradition. "Stuffies" are the baby-fist-size *quahog* (*KWAH*-og or *KOE*-hog) clams barely known elsewhere in New England. The flesh is chopped up, combined with minced bell peppers and bread crumbs, and packed back into both halves of the shell. See p. 435.

o **Blue Benn Diner** (Bennington, VT; ✆ 802/442-5140): This 1945 Silk City diner has a barrel ceiling, acres of stainless steel, and a vast menu. Don't overlook specials scrawled on paper and taped all over the walls. And leave room for a slice of delicious pie, such as blackberry, pumpkin, or chocolate cream. See p. 479.

o **Bove's** (Burlington, VT; ✆ 802/864-6651): A Burlington landmark since 1941, Bove's is a classic red-sauce-on-spaghetti joint that's a throwback to a lost era. The red sauce is rich and tangy, and the garlic sauce packs enough garlic to knock you clear out of your booth. See p. 544.

o **Al's French Frys** (South Burlington, VT; ✆ 802/862-9203): This is where Ben and Jerry go to eat french fries—as does every other potato addict in the state. See p. 543.

o **Lou's** (Hanover, NH; ✆ 603/643-3321): Huge crowds flock to Lou's, just down the block from the Dartmouth campus, for breakfast on weekends. Fortunately, breakfast is served all day here, and the sandwiches on fresh-baked bread are huge and delicious. See p. 571.

o **Silly's** (Portland, ME; ✆ 207/772-0360): Hectic and fun, this tiny, informal, kitschy restaurant serves up delicious finger food, such as pita wraps, hamburgers, and pizza. The milkshakes alone are worth the detour. See p. 623.

THE best OF THE PERFORMING ARTS (WINTER)

o **Boston Symphony Orchestra** (Boston, MA; ✆ 617/266-1492): One of the "Big Five" top North American orchestras, the BSO is worth scheduling a trip around. See p. 140.

o **Symphony Hall** (Boston, MA; ✆ 617/266-1492): When the BSO is out of season or on the road, the Boston Pops and other local and visiting groups and performers take over the orchestra's acoustically perfect home. See p. 139.

o **The Nutcracker** (Boston, MA; ✆ 617/695-6955 [box office]): New England's premier family-oriented holiday event is Boston Ballet's extravaganza. When the Christmas tree grows through the floor, even fidgety preadolescents forget that they think they're too cool to be here. See p. 140.

o **The Comedy Connection at the Wilbur Theatre** (Boston, MA; ✆ 617/248-9700): Even in the Athens of America, it's not all high culture. The biggest national names and some regional up-and-comers take the stage at this historic theater, which occasionally books musical acts. See p. 142.

o **Gloucester Stage Company** (Gloucester, MA; ✆ 978/281-4433): Founded in 1979, the Gloucester Stage presents contemporary dramas and the occasional comedy. It's known as an important developer of new American theater, and some of its productions have won awards and been produced off and on Broadway. See p. 177.

o **Iron Horse Music Hall** (Northampton, MA; ✆ 413/586-8686): The premiere honky-tonk music venue of central Massachusetts has folk, bluegrass, and rock music every night, from touring artists to local musicians. There's decent dining, too. See p. 330.

o **Trinity Repertory Company** (Providence, RI; ☎ **401/351-4242**): Right in the central area of downtown, close to some of the best restaurants and hotels of the city, is this estimable theater company. See p. 438.

o **Long Wharf Theatre** (New Haven, CT; **203/787-4282**): This is a prestigious company, known for its success in producing new plays that often make the jump to Off-Broadway and even Broadway itself. The season runs from October to June. See p. 395.

o **Vermont Symphony Orchestra** (Burlington, VT; ☎ **800/876-9205**): This is Vermont's top classical music outfit, with a year-round schedule that includes outdoor performances in the hills and on the town greens of the state during warm summer weather.

o **Portland Stage Company** (Portland, ME; ☎ **207/774-0465**): This is one of the outstanding regional theaters in the Northeast. Their season runs October through May, with an eclectic schedule of classic and modern shows such as *Noises Off* and *Much Ado About Nothing,* and also a track record of developing and producing new American work. See p. 616.

o **Portland Symphony Orchestra** (Portland, ME; ☎ **207/842-0800**): They'll knock your socks off from September through May in their series of pops and classical concerts at the Merrill Auditorium. See p. 616.

THE best OF THE PERFORMING ARTS (SUMMER)

o **The Cape Cod Playhouse** (Dennis, MA; ☎ **877/385-3911** or 508/385-3911) is the oldest continuously active straw-hat theater in the country, and still one of the best. A parade of stars from Humphrey Bogart to Julie Harris has trod the boards in the decades since the 1920s. Performances are staged from mid-June to early September. See p. 229.

o **Hatch Shell** (Boston, MA; ☎ **617/626-1250**): This amphitheater on the Charles River Esplanade plays host to free music, dance performances, and films almost all summer. Around the 4th of July, the Boston Pops provides the entertainment. Bring a blanket to sit on. See p. 139.

o **Shakespeare on the Common** (Boston, MA; ☎ **617/426-0863**): Boston Common makes a surprisingly perfect backdrop for Commonwealth Shakespeare Company's top-notch interpretations of the Bard. See p. 142.

o **The Berkshire Theatre Festival** (Stockbridge, MA; ☎ **413/298-5576**): An 1887 "casino" and converted barn are homes to the stages where both new and classic plays are mounted from June to late August, here in one of the prettiest towns in the Berkshires. Name artists on the order of Kevin Kline and Al Pacino are often listed as actors and directors in the annual playbill. See p. 344.

o **Jacob's Pillow Dance Festival** (Becket, MA; ☎ **413/243-0745**): Celebrated dancer/choreographer Martha Graham made this her summertime performance space for decades, and today its guest troupes are among the world's best, often including the Mark Morris Dance Group, Les Grands Ballets Canadiens, and Twyla Tharp. The growing campus includes a store, pub, dining room, and tent restaurant. See p. 346.

- **Shakespeare & Company** (Lenox, MA; ☎ 413/637-3353): Sprawled across a bucolic 63-acre property, this theater company presents most of its summer season of works outdoors, on a large tented stage. A night here is one of the many civilized ways to enjoy a summer evening in the Berkshires. See p. 350.
- **Tanglewood Music Festival** (Lenox, MA; ☎ 617/266-1492): By far the most dominating presence on New England's summer cultural front, the classical music festival that takes place on this magnificent Berkshires estate is the summer playground for the Boston Symphony Orchestra. Room is also made for such guest soloists as Itzhak Perlman and Yo-Yo Ma, as well as popular jazz artists Diana Krall and Wynton Marsalis. See p. 350.
- **Williamstown Theatre Festival** (Williamstown, MA; ☎ 413/597-3400): Classic, new, and avant-garde plays are all presented during the July-through-August season at this venerable festival. There are two stages, one for works by established playwrights, the smaller second venue for less mainstream or experimental plays. See p. 361.
- **Newport Folk Festival and Jazz Festival Newport** (RI): From Memorial Day to Labor Day, only a scheduling misfortune will deny visitors the experience of an outdoor musical event. The highlights are the folk and jazz festivals. A waterfront Irish Festival takes place in September. See p. 446.
- **Ogunquit Playhouse** (Ogunquit, ME; ☎ 207/646-2402) is Summer Stock. The 750-seat theater has been showcasing good plays since the 1930s (and it looks it); famous actors from Bette Davis, Tallulah Bankhead, and Sally Struthers (though not all at the same time!) trod the boards each summer. Performances usually run from mid-May through mid-October. See p. 603.
- **New London Barn Playhouse** (New London, NH; ☎ 603/526-6710) is the place to head in New Hampshire if you like some musical theater on your summer vacation. Drawing on the local pool of acting talent, shows like *Hairspray*, *Hello, Dolly!*, and *Carousel* take over the house from June through August. See p. 571.
- **Marlboro Music Festival** (Marlboro, VT; ☎ 802/254-2394 [summer] or 215/569-4690 [winter]) is one of the great summer music festivals in the U.S. Renowned classical artists and the stars of tomorrow head to this small town for a sort of "summer camp," where you can hear them at work and play from mid-July through mid-August. See p. 490.

THE best DESTINATIONS FOR ANTIQUES HOUNDS

- **Charles Street** (Boston, MA): Beacon Hill is one of the city's oldest neighborhoods, and at the foot of the hill is a thoroughfare that's equally steeped in history. Hundreds of years' worth of furniture, collectibles, and accessories jam the shops along its five blocks. River Street, which runs parallel to Charles (follow Chestnut St. 1 block), is worth a look, too. See p. 137.
- **Main Street, Essex** (MA): The treasures on display in this North Shore town run the gamut, from "one step above yard sale" to "one step below nationally televised auction." Follow Rte. 133 west of Rte. 128 through downtown and north almost all the way to the Ipswich border. See "Cape Ann," in chapter 6.

o **Rte. 6A: The Old King's Highway** (Cape Cod, MA): Antiques buffs, as well as architecture and country-road connoisseurs, will have a field day along scenic Rte. 6A. Designated a Regional Historic District, this former stagecoach route winds through a half-dozen charming villages and is lined with scores of antiques shops. The largest concentration is in Brewster, but you'll find good pickings all along this meandering road, from Sandwich to Orleans. See chapter 7.

o **Brimfield Antique and Collectible Shows** (Brimfield, MA): The otherwise sleepy town west of Sturbridge erupts with three monster antiques shows every summer, in mid-May, mid-July, and early September. Upward of 5,000 dealers set up tented and tabletop shops in fields around town. See p. 319.

o **Sheffield** (MA): This southernmost town in the Berkshires is home to at least two dozen dealers in collectibles, Americana, military memorabilia, English furniture of the Georgian period, and silverware. Most are strung along Rte. 7, also known as Main Street or Sheffield Plain. See p. 338.

o **Woodbury** (CT): More than 40 high-end dealers along Main Street offer a diversity of precious treasures, near-antiques, and simply funky old stuff. American and European furniture and other pieces are most evident, but there are forays into crafts and assorted whimsies as well. Pick up the directory of the Woodbury Antiques Dealers Association (www.antiqueswoodbury.com), available in most shops. See p. 378.

o **Portsmouth** (NH): Picturesque downtown Portsmouth is home to a half-dozen or so antiques stores and some fine used-book shops. For more meaty browsing, head about 25 miles northwest on Rte. 4 to Northwood, where a dozen good-size shops flank the highway. See "Portsmouth," in chapter 13.

o **Rte. 1, Kittery to Scarborough** (ME): Antiques scavengers delight in this 37-mile stretch of less-than-scenic Rte. 1. Antiques minimalls and high-class junk shops alike are scattered all along the route, though there's no central antiques zone. See "The Southern Maine Coast," in chapter 14.

NEW ENGLAND IN DEPTH

by Paul Karr

Most of this book is intended to lead you toward the best or most interesting historical attractions, museums, eating and drinking places, shops, and lodgings in the six New England states. But this chapter is different: In these pages, I try to capture something of the elusive character of New England and its famously short-spoken, resourceful residents. I tell you how the region came to be formed geologically, how it was populated by people and animals, what kind of foods are most popular and distinctive here today, and how to recognize when you've moved across some invisible divide from one imagined "region" to another. And I tell you about some of the best books, music, and films written in or about these states. Ready? Buckle up: Here comes your crash course.

The Regions in Brief

On a map, New England might look like one big patch of scrubby woods—with a few cities thrown in for good measure—bordered by a single coastline. Yet it's anything but homogenous. The various states (and parts of states) here have carved out distinct identities, shaped by human history, geology, weather, fish, the quality of trees or soils in the area—you name it. Here are the key micro-regions to keep in mind as you travel through the region. Remember them; they're how New England talks about itself.

Boston Oliver Wendell Holmes dubbed Boston the "hub of the solar system," and the label stuck. Today, "the Hub" is the region's largest and most vibrant city. This alluring metropolis of historic and modern buildings, world-class museums, and top-notch restaurants is an important stop for travelers on any trip to New England. Cambridge, across the Charles River, is an equally appealing destination.

Cape Cod & The Islands The ocean is writ large on Cape Cod, a low peninsula with miles of sandy beaches and grassy dunes that whisper in the wind. The carnival-like atmosphere of Provincetown is a draw, as are the genteel charms of Martha's Vineyard and Nantucket, two islands just offshore.

The Pioneer Valley Extending through Massachusetts along the Connecticut River, the area takes its name from the early settlers who arrived here in the 17th century. Among the many picturesque towns is unspoiled Historic Deerfield.

The Berkshires Massachusetts's rolling hills at the state's western edge are home to historic old estates, graceful villages, and an abundance of festivals and cultural events, including the Tanglewood Music Festival and Jacob's Pillow Dance Festival.

The Litchfield Hills The historic northwest corner of Connecticut has sleepy villages, hidden hiking trails, and a surfeit of New England charm—all just a couple of hours from New York City.

The Connecticut Coast The eastern coast is home to the historic towns of Mystic and New London, where you can get a glimpse of the shipbuilding trade at the Mystic Seaport museum and the Navy submarine base in nearby Groton.

Newport, Rhode Island Area The life-styles of the truly rich and famous are on parade in Newport, once home to the likes of the Astors and Vanderbilts. A tour of the oceanfront mansions never fails to astonish.

Green Mountains Extending the length of Vermont from Massachusetts to Canada, this mostly gentle chain of forested hills and low mountains allows for great hiking, scenic back-road drives, fantastic inns, and superb bicycling. The apples and the maple syrup here taste pretty good, too; be sure and stock up.

Lake Champlain Pastoral and scenic, the region of Vermont that forms half the lake-shore of Lake Champlain has idyllic drives and a sense of gracious openness—along with a lot of dairy cows and great views of New York's Adirondacks.

Northeast Kingdom This is Vermont at its most remote and lost-in-time best. The state's northeastern counties are rugged, hilly, and unpolished, but there are some improbable grace notes such as the little city of St. Johnsbury: It has not one but *two* excellent museums. You can also find great cheddar cheese right at the source.

Coastal New Hampshire Yes, New Hampshire *does* have a coastline—though only 18 miles of it—and packed into this tiny area you'll find plenty of sand, surf, honky-tonk beach boardwalks, and sailboat views. As a bonus, there's also the historic and entertaining little city of Portsmouth: a smaller (possibly even better) version of Boston, a great place to shop and drink a beer or a cup of coffee.

The Upper Valley The Connecticut River Valley dividing Vermont and New Hampshire is a world unto itself, full of villages, rolling hills, covered bridges, river views, and small-town bakeries. It's got smarts, too: Dartmouth College is here.

Lakes Region Lake Winnipesaukee is the crown jewel of New Hampshire's Lakes Region, but other lakes and ponds scattered in the area also add in charm what they lack in size. *On Golden Pond* was filmed on one of them, though this region's fame and beauty long predate Hollywood's recent discovery of them.

White Mountains Since the mid-1800s, New Hampshire's towering White Mountains have drawn travelers magnetically with their rugged, windswept peaks, forests dotted with glacial boulders, and clear, rushing streams. You can find New England's best backcountry hiking and camping here . . . but also its wildest weather. Keep a radio and a cellphone handy.

Western Maine This oft-overlooked region—centered on Bethel, but taking in a wide swath of territory north and south of that village—is as different from nearby

North Conway as could be. It's home to brawny hills, wide fast rivers, unbelievably scenic lakes, great foliage, and endless opportunities for quiet hiking and skiing. You might even see a moose.

Coastal Maine Maine's rocky coast is the stuff of legend, art, and poetry. The southern coast has the best beaches; to the north, the Down East region offers spectacular rocky headlands and huge Acadia National Park. Great views, lighthouses, lobster shacks, and local color abound.

Maine's North Woods The mostly uninhabited North Woods of Maine are still almost entirely owned by timber companies, yet there are some spectacular places tucked within them. One of Maine's hidden jewels is worth a visit: big, wild Baxter State Park, home to the state's largest peak, impressive Mount Katahdin.

NEW ENGLAND TODAY

As recently as a few decades ago, people in New England often lived off the land. They might have fished for cod, harvested timber in the back 40, managed gravel pits, or worked in general stores. Or they worked in New England's many mills. Of course, some still do these things.

But hardscrabble work is no longer the only economic engine in the region. Today, a New Englander might be a displaced editor from Boston or New York; a farmer who grows organic produce for gourmet restaurants in the big city; a banking or PR consultant who handles business in her slippers by e-mail. You'll also find *lots* of folks whose livelihood depends on tourism—the tour guide, the family selling honey and maple syrup by the side of a Vermont highway, the math teacher moonlighting as a motel owner, the high school kid working summers in the T-shirt shop, the repair-shop guy fixing out-of-towners' sports cars when they break down on mountain roads. (Not that that's ever happened to me. No way. Never.)

New England's economy is slowly changing, from one that was strictly "blue collar" to something that's much more diverse, if still unclear. This is no longer the province of dairy farms and woolen mills, though those places still exist in pockets. It's a place of light industry, technology, arts and crafts, world-class cuisine—still all informed by a self-sufficiency, flexibility, and creativity rarely seen elsewhere. (People tend to double up on jobs around here.) And they *all* manage to deal with the awful weather.

As a region of humble means, the place's new value as a tourist drive-through and a place to buy a second home has ruffled some feathers. That process has also begun homogenizing a place that had been somewhat of a cultural holdout from the mall-ification of America. Once a region of distinctive villages, green commons, and prim courthouse squares, New England's landscape in certain places has begun to resemble suburbs anywhere else—strip malls dotted with fast-food chains, big-box discount stores, and home-improvement emporia. While undeniably convenient to locals, they aren't doing much for tourism.

Yes, strip malls have arrived in Portland, Burlington, Kittery, Freeport, North Conway, and along Maine's Rte. 1. Elsewhere, too. Some locals love 'em, and some hate 'em; it's a mixed blessing, because this region has always taken pride in its low-key, practical approach to life. In many smaller communities, town meetings are still the preferred form of government. Residents gather in public spaces to speak out—sometimes rather forcefully—on the issues of the day: funding for local schools, road repairs, fire trucks, and declarations of their towns as pro-America or antinuclear. "Use it up, wear it out, make do, or do without" still works here, but it's the polar opposite of the outlet-shopping ethos gradually filtering into the region. And therein lies the rub: This region is trying to have it both ways, Norman Rockwell *and* Relais & Châteaux.

Development is a related issue, even if tough economic times have cooled it off for the moment. Many old-timers (and some blow-ins) believe development shouldn't be ushered in regardless of the cultural cost. Others feel that the natural landscape isn't sacred, though, and the region has seen a surge of new town houses of late, covering ski slopes and hillsides throughout these six states. *Nobody's* happy about the rising property taxes and real estate values here—except those already landed in prime locations.

No, development hasn't exploded here. Not yet. But if it ever *does,* many of the characteristics that make New England so unique—and attract those tourist dollars—could disappear. The brick mills and churches, cow pastures, big old maple trees, and whitewashed homes might slowly be replaced by a grayish blanket of condo associations, Banana Republics, outlet malls, and upscale B&Bs. Would the Green Mountains and the Maine coast still draw tourists if they began to look like any other place in America? Yes, of course, but maybe not as many; people like novelty. So it's a tricky balance to maintain.

Then there's the question of those new arrivals I mentioned earlier. The rise of the information age is drawing telecommuters and entrepreneurs to these pristine villages, because they can run entire businesses and move equities around the world wirelessly in a flash. These folks bring big-city sophistication (and appetites for gourmet dining) with them. So how will these affluent newcomers adapt to the ticky-tacky lawn ornaments on their neighbors' property; clear-cutting and moose hunting in the countryside nearby; and increasing numbers of tour buses cruising their village greens? Nobody knows.

Change has never come quickly in New England, and this one, too, will take time to play itself out. The question won't be resolved anytime in the near future. Residents' kids and grandkids will still be hashing out the exact same issues, years later.

But you're just visiting, right? So here's what to expect when you get here. Some say New England's character is still informed by its Calvinist history, which decrees that nothing can change one's fate and hard work is practically the only true virtue. That is partly true: Just take a walk down the main streets of such towns as Bellows Falls, Rockland, Westbrook, and Newport.

On the other hand, look again: It's not *all* rock-hard mattresses, tasteless meals, and hunting licenses. There might even be art galleries and microbreweries in that old canning factory or shoe mill. Be sure to visit these places: They're great. But then also set aside time to spend an afternoon rocking and reading on the broad porch of an older inn or general store (if you can find one), or to wander around on some abandoned county road with no particular destination in mind.

Because if you crave great homemade pie, some of the best foliage in the world, quiet two-lanes and lovely 19th-century inns and bed-and-breakfasts, this is *the* place for you to visit—one of my very favorite places in North America. Yes, it's becoming modern; you can now sleep in luxury inns (a pretty recent development) and dine on gourmet fare that wouldn't have had a chance of being accepted here a generation ago, food that's the equal of anything in Manhattan or San Francisco. The mix of new and old is *working,* so far, and that's why I love coming here—and you will, too.

Finally, Mother Nature has the last word: This is a sparsely populated place, enduringly quiet and lovely no matter whether it's sparkling with white powdery snow, brilliant autumn leaves, or reflections from a quiet New Hampshire pond at the dead center of summer. The chief export products here are indolence and self-reflection—increasingly rare commodities these days. Take time to savor them.

MASSACHUSETTS The Bay State has always been the place in New England with the most drama and intrigue. (Remember the Boston Tea Party and Paul Revere's Ride?) And it still is. The place that brought you the Kennedys hit the news wires hard again in early 2010 when state voters elected (the horrors) a *Republican* senator—the first time that had happened in ages. A few years previous, Bay Staters had elected the state's first black governor, former Attorney General Deval Patrick, to office. And Massachusetts political figures continue to make waves nationally, such as Senator John Kerry, who narrowly lost the nation's Presidential election to incumbent George W. Bush in 2004.

Boston's technology economy is still booming, but outside that sector and that city, things have, frankly, been better. The fishing and farming economies, once the state's mainstay, are something less than robust. **Cape Cod** and the **Berkshires**—the two glorious landscapes that bookend this state and do a good deal of its touristic trade—each experienced visitation drops during the economic downturn of 2008–09. And even previously untouchable institutions of higher learning, such as Harvard University in **Cambridge,** could not escape the crisis: Harvard's endowment lost a staggering $8 billion in the market downtown.

Still, through it all, there are always the Red Sox—the single most unifying force in the six New England states. Two recent World Series titles (in 2004 and 2007) brought unspeakable joy to the entire region—followed by a return to the usual grousing about the Yankees—while the New England Patriots and Boston Celtics won Super Bowls and an NBA Championship, cementing the city's claim as America's new "Titletown."

CONNECTICUT The state of Connecticut, quite frankly, for many years, was basically one big plot of farmland with a strip of shipbuilders on its fringe of a coast. You can still find the odd tobacco barn, boatyard, naval base, or orchard here and there, but otherwise those days are long gone; today the state has found some interesting new niches in which to sustain itself. The city of **Hartford** is the nation's unquestioned insurance powerhouse, for instance, while its suburb of **Bristol** has found a surprising second life as the world headquarters for ESPN, the planet's largest sports broadcasting network.

Meanwhile, the southwestern coast—such towns as **Greenwich** and **Fairfield**—has become one of the most expensive places in the entire country to purchase a home, thanks to its location within commuting distance of New York City. Hedge funds are particularly fond of setting up shop in these parts. Yale University continues to breathe erudite life into **New Haven; Stamford** is experiencing a minirevival as an alternate business center to high-rent Manhattan; and the many quiet byways stretching into forested hills continue to attract leaf-peepers, second-home buyers, and vacationers just as they have always done.

RHODE ISLAND   Pretty little Rhode Island just goes about its business, staying out of the news and seemingly immune to all the barbs about its size. Quick, what's the top industry in America's smallest state? Tourism? No. Manufacturing? Not. Try "health services" (chain pharmacy CVS is based here, among other companies). There's also a smattering of light industry and business and insurance services, plus tourism as visitors come to gawk at the lovely mansions of **Newport** or enjoy the capital city of **Providence** (home to Brown University). The state *did* hit the news briefly for all the wrong reasons when longtime Providence mayor Buddy Cianci did time behind bars after a racketeering conspiracy conviction. But otherwise, this state only shows up on Hollywood big screens when local sons make movies and TV shows about it (see "New England in Popular Culture," p. 31).

VERMONT   Change is afoot in the Green Mountains. Of course, this has always been a place of gorgeous hiking and ski trails, Robert Frostian walks, scenic back-road drives, and wonderful inns. It's both the fall-foliage and the maple syrup capital of the Western world. Yet something else is up: Hotshot gourmet chefs are pouring into the place at what seems like a breakneck pace. Even quite small towns—**Manchester, Essex, Warren, Wilmington,** and **Vergennes,** to name just a few—have Michelin-worthy restaurants. It's somehow all appropriate for the U.S. state with the smallest capital (**Montpelier,** pop. 8,000). And the Ben & Jerry's ice-cream factory in **Waterbury** is a must-visit for the kids.

Meanwhile, **Lake Champlain** still beckons with its lovely sunsets; and **Burlington** is slowly changing from a hippie town (though it still has a progressive-party mayor) into a sophisticated little place of light industry, technology, and gourmet eats. The city regularly wins quality-of-life-in-the-nation awards for its combination of fresh air, lake views, bike trails, a compact walkable downtown, and a mixture of bookstores, bars, restaurants, and university students.

But life in Vermont's **Northeast Kingdom** *isn't* changing. The region *still* isn't exactly a "kingdom" (or, if it is, black flies and cows are its subjects); instead, it is Vermont at its most primeval and lost-in-time. You'll find few emerald meadows or fancy inns up here; the place is rugged and unpolished as a stone.

NEW HAMPSHIRE   Like Vermont, tough and historic New Hampshire is also changing. In a state where it was unthinkable to vote anything but Republican, the state has elected Democratic governors, senators, and representatives in recent years—though it still stubbornly resists a state sales tax. Southern New Hampshire, in particular, is experiencing a sharp demographic shift as leftward-leaning Bostonians filter into the state and use it as a bedroom community. You see this most strongly in places such as **Exeter** and **Portsmouth,** but also in cities such as **Nashua** and **Manchester,** where tech and business enterprises are sprouting up.

Some things remain unchanged, thankfully: Portsmouth is still an odd amalgam of pierced baristas, antique homes and inns, fishermen, folk musicians, and good restaurants. **Hanover** still stars Dartmouth College. **Lake Winnipesaukee** is still a huge, lovely, placid body of water ringed with quiet towns (such as **Wolfeboro**) and honky-tonk attractions (see: **Weirs Beach**). Finally, the **White Mountains** will *never* change. New England's best backcountry hiking and camping are still found here, and always will be.

MAINE   Maine is holding its own. You can still see a loon here, or horror author Stephen King walking down a road. You can still eat lobsters and fresh-caught fish, and photograph some of the world's most famous lighthouses. The economy isn't going great runs, but it's not at rock-bottom, either. **Portland** remains one of New England's best places to visit and dine in, with architecture and restaurants that rival anywhere else, while the **Kennebunks** and the **Yorks** offer choice beaches for summer lazing and strolls plus plenty of souvenir shops. Maine's rocky coast is still the stuff of legend, art, and poetry—a list of quaint towns and drives would fill an entire book and then some.

An uncomfortable divide is starting to develop in places. As you get upcountry, for instance, you can feel a difference between affluence (huge summer mansions on Mount Desert Island or around Penobscot Bay) and the hard-working locals who fish, lobster, or wait tables in summer, then tow cars or shovel and plow snow the rest of the year to get by. Land values have shot up in these lovely regions. Regardless, they're some of my favorite places to visit in New England: towns such as **Freeport, Camden,** and **Blue Hill,** plus the natural wonders of amazing **Acadia National Park.** Finally, the big Woods of Maine pose a future battleground—for now, timber and paper companies, forest activists, and developers maintain a standoff. But one day, when the economy kicks upward again, values may clash. Meanwhile, **Mount Katahdin** and **Moosehead Lake** will *always* be worth a visit, no matter what.

LOOKING BACK AT NEW ENGLAND

Viewed from a distance, New England's history mirrors that of its namesake, England. The region rose from nowhere to gain tremendous historical prominence, captured a good deal of overseas trade, and became an industrial powerhouse and center for creative thought. And then the party ended relatively abruptly, as commerce and culture sought more fertile grounds to the west and south.

To this day, New England remains entwined with its past. Walking through Boston, layers of history are evident at every turn, from the church steeples of Colonial times (dwarfed by glass-sided skyscrapers) to verdant parklands that bespeak the refined sensibility of the late Victorian era.

History is even more inescapable in off-the-beaten-track New England. Travelers in Downeast Maine, northern New Hampshire, Connecticut's Litchfield Hills, the Berkshires, and much of Vermont will find clues to what Henry Wadsworth Longfellow called "the irrevocable past" everywhere they turn, from stone walls running through woods to Federal-style homes.

Here's a brief overview of some historical episodes and trends that shaped New England.

Indigenous Culture

Native Americans have inhabited New England since about 7000 B.C. While New York's Iroquois Indians had a presence in Vermont, New England was inhabited chiefly by Algonquins who lived a nomadic life. Connecticut was home to some 16 Algonquin tribes, who dubbed the region Quinnetukut.

After the arrival of the Europeans, French Catholic missionaries succeeded in converting many Native Americans, and most tribes sided with the French in the French and Indian Wars in the 18th century. Afterward, the Indians fared poorly at the hands of the British, and were quickly pushed to the margins. Today, they are found in greatest concentration at several reservations in Maine. The Pequots have established a thriving gaming industry in Connecticut. Other than that, the few clues left behind by Indian cultures have been more or less obliterated by later settlers.

2 | The Colonists

Viking explorers from Newfoundland may or may not have sailed southward into New England—stories abound—but what's certain is the European colonists arrived in the very early 17th century and eventually displaced entirely the Native American culture that existed in the region.

It began in 1604, when some 80 French colonists spent a winter on a small island on what today is the Maine–New Brunswick border. They did not care for the harsh weather of their new home and left in spring to resettle in present-day Nova Scotia. In 1607, 3 months after the celebrated Jamestown, Virginia, colony was founded, another group of 100 settlers (this time from England) established a community at Popham Beach in present-day Phippsburg, Maine. The Maine winter demoralized these would-be colonists as well, and they returned to England the following year.

The colonization of the region began in earnest with the arrival of the Pilgrims at Plymouth Rock in 1620. The Pilgrims—a religious group that had split from the Church of England—established the first permanent colony, although it came at a hefty price: Half the group perished during the first winter. But the colony began to thrive over the years, in part thanks to helpful Native Americans.

The success of the Pilgrims lured other settlers from England, who established a constellation of small towns outside of Boston that became the Massachusetts Bay Colony. Roger Williams was expelled from the colony for his religious beliefs; he founded the city of Providence, Rhode Island. Other restless colonists expanded their horizons in search of lands for settlement. Throughout the 17th century, colonists from Massachusetts pushed northward into what are now New Hampshire and Maine, and southward into Connecticut. The first areas to be settled were lands near protected harbors along the coast and on navigable waterways.

The more remote settlements came under attack in the 17th and early 18th centuries in a series of raids by Indians, conducted both independently and in concert with the French. These proved temporary setbacks; colonization continued throughout New England into the 18th century.

The American Revolution

Starting around 1765, Great Britain launched a series of ham-handed economic policies to reign in the increasingly feisty colonies. These included a direct tax—the Stamp Act—to pay for a standing army. The crackdown provoked strong resistance. Under the banner of "No taxation without representation," disgruntled colonists engaged in a series of riots, resulting in the Boston Massacre of 1770, when five protesting colonists were fired upon and killed by British soldiers.

In 1773, the most infamous protest took place in Boston. The British had imposed the Tea Act (the right to collect duties on tea imports), which prompted a group of colonists dressed as Indians to board three British ships and dump 342 chests of tea into the harbor. This incident was dubbed the Boston Tea Party.

Hostilities reached a peak in 1775, when the British sought to quell unrest in Massachusetts. A contingent of British soldiers was sent to Lexington to seize military supplies and arrest two high-profile rebels—John Hancock and Samuel Adams. The militia formed by the colonists exchanged gunfire with the British, thereby igniting the Revolution ("the shot heard round the world").

Notable battles in New England included the Battle of Bunker Hill outside Boston, which the British won but at tremendous cost; and the Battle of Bennington in Vermont, in which the colonists prevailed. Hostilities formally ended in February 1783, and in September, Britain recognized the United States as a sovereign nation.

Farming & Trade

As the new republic matured, economic growth in New England followed two tracks. Residents of inland communities survived by farming and trading in furs. Vermont in particular has always been an agrarian state, and remains a prominent dairy producer to this day.

On the coast, boatyards sprang up from Connecticut to Maine, and ship captains made fortunes trading lumber for sugar and rum in the Caribbean. Trade was dealt a severe blow following the Embargo Act of 1807, but commerce eventually recovered, and New England ships could be encountered around the globe.

The growth of the railroad in the mid–19th century was another boon. The train opened up much of the interior. The rail lines allowed local resources—such as the fine marbles and granites from Vermont—to be shipped to markets to the south.

An Industrial Revolution Arrives

New England's Industrial Revolution found seed around the time of the embargo of 1807. Barred from importing English fabrics, Americans built their own textile mills. Other common household products were also manufactured domestically, especially shoes. Towns such as Lowell, Massachusetts; Lewiston, Maine; and Manchester, New Hampshire, became centers of textile and shoe production. In Connecticut, the manufacture of arms and clocks emerged as major industries. Industry no longer plays the prominent role it once did—manufacturing first moved to the South, then overseas.

Tourism Boom, Economic Bust

In the mid- and late 19th century, New Englanders discovered a new cash crop: the tourist. All along the Eastern Seaboard, it became fashionable for the gentry and eventually the working class to set out for excursions to the mountains and the shore. Regions such as the Berkshires, the White and Green mountains, and Block Island were lifted by the tide of summer visitors. The tourism wave crested in the 1890s in Newport, Rhode Island, and Bar Harbor, Maine, both of which were flooded by the affluent. Several grand resort hotels from tourism's golden era still host summer travelers in the region.

But this economic rebirth would not last long. While railways allowed New England to thrive in the mid–19th century, the trains also eventually played a pivotal role in undermining the region's prosperity. The driving of the Golden Spike in 1869 in Utah, linking America's Atlantic and Pacific coasts by rail, was heard loud and clear in New England, and it had a discordant ring. Transcontinental rail meant farmers and manufacturers could ship goods from the fertile Great Plains and California to faraway markets, making it harder for New England's hardscrabble farmers to survive. Likewise, the coastal shipping trade was dealt a fatal blow by this new transportation network. And the tourists set their sights on the Rockies and other stirring destinations in the West.

Beginning in the late 19th century, New England lapsed into an extended economic slumber. Families walked away from their farmhouses (there was no market for resale) and set off for regions with more promising opportunities. The abandoned, decaying farmhouse almost became an icon for New England, and vast tracts of open farmland were reclaimed by forest. With the rise of the automobile, the grand resorts further succumbed, and many closed their doors as inexpensive motels siphoned off their business.

Tourism & Tech: A Second Wind

During the last 2 decades of the 20th century, much of New England rode an unexpected wave of prosperity. A real-estate boom shook the region in the 1980s, driving land prices sky-high as prosperous buyers from New York and Boston acquired vacation homes or retired to the most alluring areas. In the 1990s, the sudden rise of high-tech companies in the Boston area, riding the Internet wave, sent ripples from Boston out into the hinterlands of Maine and New Hampshire. New York City's rebound as a world-class tourism destination brought fresh jobs, money, and homeowners pouring into Connecticut, Rhode Island, and Vermont. Tourism experienced a resurgence as the urbanites of the Eastern Seaboard opted for shorter, more frequent vacations closer to home during economic dips.

Though the recent boom has been welcome news to many long-term residents, those in the most remote regions of New England never benefited from this boom. Especially hard-hit were such places as northeastern Vermont and far Downeast Maine, where many residents still depend on local resources—timber, fisheries, and farmland—to eke out a living, though land prices have begun rising even here, as city dwellers seek ever-quieter places to recreate or retire.

ART & ARCHITECTURE IN NEW ENGLAND

Architecture

You can often trace the evolution of a town by its architecture, as styles evolve from basic structures to elaborate Victorian mansions. The primer below should aid with basic identification.

- **Colonial** (1600–1700): The New England house of the 17th century was a simple, boxy affair, often covered in shingles or rough clapboards. Don't look for ornamentation; these homes were designed for basic shelter from the elements, and are often marked by prominent stone chimneys. You can see examples at Plimoth Plantation and in Salem, near Boston.

- **Georgian** (1700–1800): Ornamentation comes into play in the Georgian style, which draws heavily on classical symmetry. Georgian buildings were in vogue in England at the time, and were embraced by affluent colonists. Look for Palladian windows, formal pilasters, and elaborate projecting pediments. Deerfield (in the Pioneer Valley of MA) is a good destination for seeing early Georgian homes; and Providence, Rhode Island, and Portsmouth, New Hampshire, have abundant examples of later Georgian styles.

- **Federal** (1780–1820): Federal homes (sometimes called Adams homes) may best represent the New England ideal. Spacious yet austere, they are often rectangular or square, with low-pitched roofs and little ornament on the front, although carved swags or other embellishments are frequently seen near the roofline. Look for fan windows and chimneys bracketing the building. Excellent Federal-style homes are found throughout the region in towns such as Kennebunkport, Maine.

- **Greek Revival** (1820–60): The most easy-to-identify Greek Revival homes feature a projecting portico with massive columns, like a part of the Parthenon grafted onto an existing home. The less dramatic homes may simply be oriented such that the gable faces the street, accenting the triangular pediment. Greek Revival didn't catch on in New England the way it did in the South, but some fine examples exist, notably in Newfane, Vermont.

- **Carpenter Gothic** and **Gothic Revival** (1840–80): The second half of the 19th century brought a wave of Gothic Revival homes, which borrowed their aesthetic from the English country home. Aficionados of this style and its later progeny featuring gingerbread trim owe themselves a trip to Oak Bluffs at Martha's Vineyard in Massachusetts, where cottages are festooned with scrollwork and exuberant architectural flourishes.

- **Victorian** (1860–1900): This is a catchall term for the jumble of mid- to late-19th-century styles that emphasized complexity and opulence. Perhaps the best-known Victorian style—almost a caricature—is the tall and narrow Addams Family–style house, with mansard roof and prickly roof cresting. You'll find these scattered throughout the region. The Victorian style also includes squarish **Italianate** homes with wide eaves and unusual flourishes, such as the outstanding Victoria Mansion in Portland, Maine.

  Stretching the definition of Victorian a bit is the **Richardsonian Romanesque** style, which was popular for railroad stations and public buildings. The classic Richardsonian building, designed by H. H. Richardson himself in 1872, is Trinity Church, in Boston.

- **Shingle** (1880–1900): This uniquely New England style quickly became preferred for vacation homes on Cape Cod and the Maine coast. They're marked by a profusion of gables, roofs, and porches, and are typically covered with shingles from roofline to foundation.

- **Modern** (1900–present): Outside of Boston, New England has produced little in the way of notable modern architecture. In the 1930s, Boston became a center for the stark **International Style** with the appointment of Bauhaus veteran Walter Gropius to the faculty at Harvard. Some intriguing experiments in this style are found on the M.I.T. and Harvard campuses, including Gropius's Campus Center and Eero Saarinen's Kresge Auditorium.

Visual Arts

New England is also justly famous for the **art** it has produced, particularly the seascapes painted on Cape Cod, along the coast of Maine, and by **Hudson River School** artists such as Thomas Cole and his student Frederic Church. Some of the other artists who have memorably painted New England landscapes and seascapes include **Winslow Homer** (1836–1910), **Fairfield Porter** (1907–75), **John Marin** (1870–1953), **Neil Welliver** (1929–2005), and **Andrew Wyeth** (born 1917), he of the iconic *Christina's World,* painted in a coastal Maine field.

To showcase these works, and the works of other local and traveling artists, there are a surprising number of excellent art museums and galleries throughout New England, even in such unlikely places as Williamstown, Massachusetts; St. Johnsbury, Vermont; and Portland and Rockland, Maine. Consult individual chapters for more details on local art offerings.

THE LAY OF THE LAND

The human history of New England is usually thought of as beginning at a fixed point: in 1492, when Columbus sailed the ocean blue. But the clock actually winds *much* farther back than that—beginning thousands of years ago, when Native American tribes fished Atlantic shores and hunted these hills. And even they were here for only a sliver of the long period of time required to create this place; situations like this call for the word *eons*. The rocks upon which you climb, sun yourself, and picnic are old—staggeringly old.

Before arriving, then, it's a good idea to acquaint yourself with the natural history of the place. Armed with a little respect and appreciation for the landscape before you, you just might treat it more reverently while you're here—and help ensure that it remains for future generations to behold.

Rocky Road: Geology Sets the Table

The beginnings of New England are perhaps a half-billion years old. That's right: *billion*, with a B.

Deep wells of liquid rock known as magma were moving upward through the earth's mantle, exploding in underground volcanoes, then hardening—still underground, mind you—into granite-like rocks. Much later, natural forces, such as wind and water, wore away and exposed the upper layers of these rocks. Their punishment was only beginning, however; soon enough (geologically speaking, that is), what is now eastern North America and most of Europe began to shove up against each other, slowly but inexorably.

This "collision" (which was more like an *extremely* slow-motion car wreck) heated, squeezed, transformed, and thrust up the rocks that now form the backbone of the coastline. Ice ages came and went, but the rocks remained; the successive waves of glaciation and retreat scratched up the rocks like old vinyl records, and the thick tongues of pressing ice cut deep notches out of them. The ice swept up huge boulders and deposited them in odd places.

When the glaciers finally retreated for the last time, tens of thousands of years ago, the water melting from the huge ice sheet covering North America swelled the level of the Atlantic high enough to submerge formerly free-flowing river valleys and bays, giving the coastline and such places as **Acadia National Park** and Vermont's **Smuggler's Notch** their distinctively rocky, knuckled faces. The melting ice sheets also laid down tons of silt and sand in their wake, leaving the sandy barrens and gentle hills of central and western Massachusetts.

Life Sets In: Plants & Animals

Once the bones of this landscape were established, next came the flesh: plants and animals. After each ice age, conifers such as spruce and fir trees—alongside countless grasses and weeds—began to reform, then decompose and form soils. It was tough work: Much of New England is a rocky, acidic place, inhospitable to farming. Yet a few plants persevered (as plants tend to do), and spruces, firs, and hemlocks soon formed an impenetrable thicket covering much of the bedrock. When those evergreen trees died of old age, were struck by lightning and caught on fire, or were cut down by settlers (or beavers), different kinds of trees—beeches, birches, brilliant sugar maples—rushed in to replace them.

As the trees and flowers and fruits became reestablished, animals wandered back, too—some now extinct, but some still thriving today in the fields, hills, and woods of the region. As temperatures warmed, deer and songbirds eventually followed, and polar bears and caribou were no longer regular features of New England—though caribou and moose still wander the northern stretches of this region.

New England's unique position, near the warm Gulf Stream without quite touching it, has also bequeathed the region with an amazing variety of marine life. The warm offshore Gulf current passes over a high, shallow undersea plateau known as the Georges Bank, then collides with the much colder waters of the North Atlantic. This collision creates swirls and upwelling currents from the sea floor, bringing loads of microscopic food particles up toward the surface—food that sustains an astonishingly complex variety of microorganisms, the bottom rungs in a ladder of marine life.

The food chain culminates in migrating whales, who make for a wonderful spectacle off the New England coast twice per year. Seabirds make similar passages, lighting upon the rocks, fields, and lakes here in spring and fall. The coast also teems (though not as much as it once did) with codfish, lobsters, crabs, and other sea creatures.

The region's coastal tide pools are also worth exploring. This precarious zone, where land and rock meet ocean, is an ever-changing world of seaweed, snails, barnacles, darting water bugs, clams, shellfish, mud-burrowing worms, and other creatures. Interestingly, creatures live in distinct, well-marked "bands" as you get closer to the water. Rocks that are always submerged contain one mixture of seaweed, shellfish, and marine organisms, while rocks that are exposed and then resubmerged each day by the tides have a different mix.

And that's just a sampling of what's out there. Whether you explore New England on foot, by bicycle, by kayak, by horse-drawn carriage, or by charter boat, you're certain to see something you've never seen before. Be attentive, and you'll come away with a deeper respect for all things natural—not only here, but everywhere.

NEW ENGLAND IN POPULAR CULTURE

Books

New Englanders have generated entire libraries, from the earliest days of hellfire-and-brimstone Puritan sermons to Stephen King's horror novels set in fictional Maine villages.

Among the more enduring writings from New England's earliest days are the poems of Massachusetts Bay Colony resident **Anne Bradstreet** (ca. 1612–72) and the sermons and essays of **Increase Mather** (1639–1723) and his son, **Cotton Mather** (1663–1728).

After the American Revolution, Hartford dictionary writer **Noah Webster** (1758–1843) issued a call to American writers: "America must be as independent in literature as she is in politics, as famous for arts as for arms." He struck an early blow for pragmatism by taking the "u" out of British words like "labour" and "honour."

The tales of **Nathaniel Hawthorne** (1804–64) captivated a public eager for a native literature. His most famous story, *The Scarlet Letter,* is a narrative about morality set in 17th-century Boston, but he wrote numerous other books that wrestled with themes of sin and guilt, often set in the emerging republic.

Henry Wadsworth Longfellow (1807–82), the Portland poet who settled in Cambridge, caught the attention of the public with evocative narrative poems focusing on distinctly American subjects. His popular works included "The Courtship of Miles Standish," "Paul Revere's Ride," and "Hiawatha." Poetry in the mid–19th century was the equivalent of Hollywood movies today—Longfellow could be considered his generation's Steven Spielberg (apologies to literary scholars).

The zenith of New England literature occurred in the mid– and late 19th century with the Transcendentalist movement. These writers and thinkers included **Ralph Waldo Emerson** (1803–82), **Bronson Alcott** (1799–1888), and **Henry David Thoreau** (1817–62). They fashioned a way of viewing nature and society that was uniquely American. They rejected the rigid doctrines of the Puritans, and found sustenance in self-examination, the glories of nature, and a celebration of individualism. Perhaps the best-known work to emerge from this period was Thoreau's *Walden.*

Among other regional writers who left a lasting mark on American literature was **Emily Dickinson** (1830–86), a native of Amherst, Massachusetts, whose precise and enigmatic poems placed her in the front rank of American poets. **James Russell Lowell** (1819–91), of Cambridge, was an influential poet, critic, and editor. Later poets were imagist **Amy Lowell** (1874–1925), from Brookline, Massachusetts, and **Edna St. Vincent Millay** (1892–1950), from Camden, Maine.

The bestselling *Uncle Tom's Cabin,* the book Abraham Lincoln half-jokingly accused of starting the Civil War, was written by **Harriet Beecher Stowe** (1811–86) in Brunswick, Maine. She lived much of her life as a neighbor of **Mark Twain** (himself an adopted New Englander) in Hartford, Connecticut. Another bestseller was the children's book *Little Women,* written by **Louisa May Alcott** (1832–88), whose father, Bronson, was part of the Transcendentalist movement.

New England's later role in the literary tradition may best be symbolized by the poet **Robert Frost** (1874–1963). Though born in California, he lived his life in Massachusetts, New Hampshire, and Vermont. In the New England landscape and community, he found a lasting grace and rich metaphors for life. (Among his most famous lines: "Two roads diverged in a wood, and I—I took the one less traveled by, / And that has made all the difference.")

New England continues to attract writers drawn to the noted educational institutions and the privacy of rural life. Prominent contemporary writers and poets who live in the region at least part of the year include **John Updike, Nicholson Baker, Christopher Buckley, P. J. O'Rourke, Bill Bryson, John Irving,** and **Donald Hall.**

Film & TV

New England is frequently captured through the lens of Hollywood, thanks in equal parts to its natural beauty; its Calvinist, slightly spooky history; and the unusual number of star actors, actresses, and directors who were raised here and continue to push forward projects incorporating local storylines or landscapes.

Lillian Gish's 1920 silent film *Way Down East* was perhaps the first movie to bring cinematic attention to the region, and films now regularly depict Boston's grimy underbelly (in films such as *The Departed* and *Mystic River*); local Red Sox–mania (the engine for such films as *Fever Pitch*); working-class struggle and identity crises (in such films as *Good Will Hunting*); and a host of horror films written by Maine's Stephen King—from *Carrie*, *Cujo*, and *The Dead Zone* down through to a welter of TV miniseries—that make it sometimes seem like the only inhabitants of small New England towns are supernatural forces. However, King also penned the story upon which the lovely film *The Shawshank Redemption*, which also purports to take place in Maine, was based.

Rhode Island has hit the big screen in a big way, thanks to three famous director/writers who were born in the state: brothers Peter and Bobby Farrelly, who depict the state in such films as *Me, Myself & Irene* and *Dumb and Dumber*; and Seth MacFarlane, whose series Family Guy is set in Quahog, RI.

Several other television series have been based in New England through the years, such as this wildly popular trifecta: *Cheers* (1982–93), set in a chummy Boston bar (which is still there beside Boston Common); *Newhart* (1982–90), in which actor Bob Newhart comically attempted to run a Vermont bed-and-breakfast inn; and *Murder, She Wrote* (1984–96), which saw crime novelist Angela Lansbury stumbling across and solving real-life crimes, with seeming ease, from her perch in fictional Cabot Cove, Maine. *Wings* (1990–97) was a TV program, set at a small airstrip on Massachusetts's Nantucket Island, that propelled several actors on to further fame.

More recently, *Boston Public*, *The Practice*, and *Boston Legal* explored facets of public schools and legal practice in that city.

Music

New England musicians have contributed mightily to the American music scene. An exhaustive list of stars is impossible here, but I'll note a few highlights.

Folk-pop singer **James Taylor** was born in Boston, long ensconced on Martha's Vineyard, and now resides in his beloved Berkshires. The Hall of Fame rock band **Aerosmith** also has roots in Boston (and first played together in a barn in NH). Crooner **Rudy Vallee** was born in Vermont and raised in Westbrook, Maine. The wildly popular '70s rock group **Boston** was fronted by residents of that city.

Pop stars **Michael Bolton** and **John Mayer** were both born in Connecticut, while jam-band **Phish** was formed in Burlington, Vermont, by college friends. Texas-based country-folk musician **Slaid Cleaves** was raised in western Maine. Nashville singer-songwriter **Patty Griffin** was also born and raised in Maine.

And Boston has cranked out decades' worth of alternative-rock bands such as **The Pixies,** the **J. Geils Band,** and **The Cars,** to name just three.

IMPRESSIONS

The woods are lovely, dark and deep. / But I have promises to keep, / And miles to go before I sleep, / And miles to go before I sleep.

—Robert Frost, "Stopping by Woods on a Snowy Evening"

EATING AND DRINKING IN NEW ENGLAND

New England got a late start in the food game—for a while, it was basically fish, vegetables, simple soup, and whatever was dragged home from a hunt, and updated versions of that—but it has caught up, in spades. Today, you can eat really well in this region, thanks to some unusually crafty producers, importers, and chefs, using local ingredients to create such things as curried pumpkin soup, seared local day boat scallops, venison medallions with shiitake mushrooms, and wild boar with juniper berries.

Along the coastline, live lobsters can be bought literally off the boat at **lobster pounds.** You can buy fried fish and fried clams at **fish and clam shacks** almost anywhere on the coast, too. More upscale seafood eateries in sea towns serve the local catch of the day grilled or sautéed with an array of sauces.

Inland, take time to sample local farm products such as the sweet maple syrup, sold throughout northern New Hampshire and Vermont; it's the best in the world. Look also for Vermont's famous cider; Maine's tiny, tasty wild blueberries; and Berkshire apples in western Massachusetts.

Every summer, small farmers across the region set up stands at the ends of driveways selling fresh produce straight from the garden. You can find berries, fruits, and sometimes home-baked breads here. These stands are rarely tended; just leave what you owe, and maybe a bit of a tip, in the coffee can. Also watch for the appearance of **"U-pick" farms** in summertime. For a fee that's much less than what you pay in a store for the packaged fruit, you fill up bags of strawberries or blueberries and take 'em home. Kids love this.

Restaurateurs haven't overlooked New England's bounty, either. Big-city chefs flock here every year to hang up new shingles and test themselves with the local ingredients; some restaurants maintain their own herb and vegetable gardens. Some of these places stretch the budget a bit, but plenty of others fall squarely into the "road food" category. Here's an abbreviated field guide to New England's distinctively local eats.

o **Apples:** Maine, Vermont, and Massachusetts are all well-known for their fall apple harvests. Look for orchards in foothills, such as those in central and western Maine, the Champlain Valley, and the Berkshire Hills. Cold Hollow Cider Mill in **Waterbury** (near **Stowe,** VT) is probably the most famous cider purveyor in the U.S.

o **Baked beans:** Boston will be forever linked with baked beans (hence the nickname "Beantown"), but the dish remains extremely popular in parts of Maine, too. Saturday-night church dinners (also known as "bean hole" suppers) usually consist

... AND ROCKABYE SWEET BABY JAMES

Now the first of December was covered with snow;
and so was the turnpike from Stockbridge to Boston;
Lord, the Berkshires seemed dream-like, on account of that frosting . . .

—James Taylor, "Sweet Baby James"

of baked beans and brown bread, plus pasta salads and the like. There's also a famous B&M baked-bean plant still operating in **Portland.**

o **Blueberries:** One sometimes gets the feeling that Downeast Maine's economy would collapse without the humble blueberry. To taste it, look for roadside stands and diners from the midcoast north, selling pies made with fresh berries from mid- until late summer. These tiny blueberries (which grow on low shrubs on wind-swept rocks or hilltops) are much tastier than the bigger, commercial variety. You can even pick your own pail of berries, for free, high on the slopes of certain hills such as **Blue Hill** and **Pleasant Mountain.** Look for the bush's oval, leathery, tealike leaves.

o **Cheese:** Cheese is a Vermont specialty: Cheddar is the most common variety (you can buy a huge "wheel" of cheddar at any country store worth its salt), but goat cheeses are starting to make a serious run, too. The Northeast Kingdom and Connecticut Valley are especially rich in cheese. Take a cheese-factory tour in **Cabot, Grafton,** or **Plymouth Notch** to see what goes into your cheddar, or scour the local natural-foods store (often called a "co-op" in Vermont) for the most local version of cow and goat cheese.

o **Clam chowder:** The obligatory Boston dish of choice, clam chowder consists simply of chopped clams, milk, and some butter, flour and/or salt pork to thicken the mixture into soup form. Rhode Islanders eat a reddish version incorporating tomatoes or tomato soup in lieu of the milk. It's not for everyone.

o **Fish chowder:** My favorite coastal dish is also the simplest one: fish chowder, which in its purest form consists of the day's catch of chopped-up white fish (cod, haddock), enough milk to satisfy a small animal, peeled potatoes, and nice big chunk of butter. No thickener, cornstarch, or flour—*please*. This dish is best enjoyed with an ocean view, a square of blueberry cake, and a cup of bad coffee. And in the fishing villages of coastal Maine, that's exactly how it's still served to legions of tired and hungry local fisherman as they trundle in after long, cold days out on the water hauling nets or traps.

o **Johnnycakes:** A Colonial recipe largely lost to time, the Johnnycake still survives in the odd Rhode Island wayside diner. These heavy pancakes are made from cornmeal and molasses rather than the usual wheat flour and sugar.

o **Lobster:** You can buy freshly steamed lobsters at pounds in most Maine fishing towns, usually from a shack right on the main fishing pier. The setting is usually as rustic it gets—maybe a couple of picnic tables on a slab of concrete, plus a shed where huge vats of water are kept at a boil. Lobster *rolls* consist of lobster meat plucked from the shell, mixed with just enough mayonnaise to hold it all together, then served on a buttered hot-dog roll. (No celery, please!) You'll find them everywhere along the Maine coast; expect to pay $9 to $15 per roll, more in lean lobster-harvest years.

o **Maple syrup:** Nothing says New England like maple syrup. You can buy the stuff in any of the New England states, but the best is made in New Hampshire and Vermont. Visit in late spring (the first week of Mar is recommended) to get a close look at the process at the local sap houses. Sugarmakers boil up the sweet stuff and ladle it onto pancakes, ice cream, or snow to let you sample before you buy. And you *will* buy.

o **Moxie:** Early in the 20th century, the Maine soda known as Moxie actually outsold Coca-Cola. Part of its allure was the fanciful story behind its 1885 creation: A traveler named Moxie was said to have observed South American Indians consuming the sap of a native plant, which gave them extraordinary strength. The drink was then "re-created" by Maine native Dr. Augustin Thompson. Okay, that's a bunch of malarkey. But it's still quite popular in Maine, even if some outsiders liken the taste to a combination of cough medicine and dirt. I happen to like it a lot.

o **NECCO wafers:** The New England Confectionery Company (hence the name) in Cambridge, Massachusetts, has been making these powdery wafers since 1847. The candies are widely available throughout New England.

o **Shellfish:** Mussels, oysters, clams, and scallops can all be bought at fish markets up and down the Maine coast—or at restaurants in said towns and cities—raw (if you're renting a cottage), steamed, or fried. Take your pick. Be sure to know how to choose fresh bivalves at the market if you're cooking for yourself; a single bad one can make a person mighty sick.

o **Smoked fish:** Fish-smoking isn't a huge industry in New England, but it does exist, especially in Downeast Maine. That's not really surprising, given the huge supply of smokeable fish living just offshore.

Finally, no survey of food and drink in New England would be complete without serious mention of the **beer.** New England has more microbreweries than any other region outside the Pacific Northwest; in fact, it might outrank that region by now in quality (and maybe quantity).

The beers of Vermont and Maine, especially, are legion—and they're often in the places you'd least expect to find them: little towns such as dour **Middlebury** (Otter Creek Brewing) and **Morrisville** (Rock Art Brewing), in Vermont; august **Kennebunkport,** Maine (Federal Jack's); and the former mill town of **Topsham** (Sea Dog Brewing Co.), also in Maine. Once you get to the city, the situation gets even better.

The concentration of minibreweries in both **Burlington,** Vermont, and **Portland,** Maine, actually staggers the mind: There are a half-dozen distinct brewing operations in both of those small cities, all making great beer and all (so far) making profits. For a closer look at some of these craft brewers, pick up my *Frommer's Coastal Maine: Day by Day;* I have organized a special tour of Portland's area breweries for hopheads like me.

Other standouts include Sam Adams Brewing in **Boston** (not micro anymore); the Great Providence Brewing Co. in **Providence;** and the Commonwealth Brewing Co. (Boston's first brewpub). But there are literally *hundreds* more. Go to any gourmet or natural-foods store—or even a local gas station—anywhere you travel and check the refrigerator section for local finds.

PLANNING YOUR TRIP TO NEW ENGLAND

For such a small area, New England is a surprisingly diverse region; you can do anything from deep-sea fish to leaf-peep on mountaintops, and dine on anything from flapjacks with real maple syrup (at 6am, preferably wearing flannels) to world-class restaurant fare. Yet all six states can be reached in roughly an hour or less by either plane or car from New York City.

As such, it's a wonderful destination for both the family and the peripatetic traveler. In most of the region, crime is nonexistent to low. In fact, your primary worries involve choosing the right time of year to visit; determining the most efficient way to get from point A to point B (New England is still a bit mass-transit challenged); and choosing from among the many natural treasures, roadside diners, and historical tours and walks available here. In this chapter, many of the critical aspects of planning your trip are covered.

For additional help in planning your trip and for more on-the-ground resources in New England, please turn to Chapter 15, "Fast Facts," on p. 674.

WHEN TO GO

The Seasons

The well-worn joke about the climate in New England is that it has just two seasons—winter and August. Though this bromide might have originated as a ploy to keep outsiders from moving up here (and it worked, partly), there's also a kernel of truth to it. But don't worry. The ever-shifting seasons here are precisely what make New England so distinctive, and three of the four are genuinely enjoyable. The fourth (which is not the one you might have guessed) is, well, tolerable.

SUMMER   The peak summer season in New England runs from 4th of July weekend until Labor Day weekend. That's a pretty slim sandwich, only about 8½ weeks. But, wow, does the population of each of these states ever swell between the starting line and summer's checkered flag! Vast crowds surge into New England on each of these two holiday weekends, and a constant stream also moves northward daily in between them.

It's no wonder. Summers here are exquisite, particularly because the daylight lasts so long—until 9 or 9:30pm in late June and early July. Forests are verdant and lush; the sky is a deep blue, the cumulus clouds puffy and almost painfully bright white. In the mountains, warm days are the rule, followed by cool nights. On the coast, ocean breezes keep temperatures down even when it's triple-digit steaming in the big cities. (Of course, these sea breezes sometimes also produce thick, soupy fogs that linger for days.) In general, expect moderation: In Portland, Maine, the thermometer tops 90°F (32°C) for only 4 or 5 days each year, at most.

Local weather in this region is largely determined by the winds. Summer's southwesterly winds bring haze, heat, and humidity (to everywhere except the seashore); northwesterly winds bring cool bright weather and knife-sharp views. These systems tend to alternate during the summer, the heat and humidity building slowly and stealthily for a few days—then swiftly getting kicked out on their ears by stiff, cool winds pressing down from Canada. Then the pattern repeats. Rain is rarely far away in summer—some days it's in the form of an afternoon thunderstorm, sometimes a steady drizzle that brings a 3- or 4-day soaking. On average, about 1 day in 3 here will bring some rain. But hey, that's what keeps the Green Mountains green.

For most of this region (we'll get to VT in a moment), midsummer is prime time. Expect to pay premium prices at hotels and restaurants. (The exception is around the empty ski resorts, where you can often find bargains.) Also be aware that early summer brings out scads of biting black flies and mosquitoes, a state of affairs that has spoiled many north-country camping trips. Come prepared for these guys.

What to do? Play some golf. Go hiking in the woods. Swim in the ocean. Catch a minor-league baseball game. Or indulge in one of our favorite activities: rocking in a chair on a screened porch, reading a book, playing guitar, or just listening intently to the sounds of loons or crickets and watching the night sky for stars you never knew existed.

AUTUMN   Don't be surprised to smell the tang of fall approaching even as early as mid-August, when you'll also begin to notice a few leaves turning blaze-orange on the maples at the edges of wetlands or highways. Fall comes early to New England, puts its feet up on the couch, and stays for some time. The foliage season begins in earnest in the northern part of the region by the third week in September; in the southern portions, it reaches its peak by mid-October. But it's beautiful everywhere.

Fall in New England is one of the great natural spectacles in the world. When the region's rolling hills tart up in brilliant reds and stunning oranges, grown men pull to the sides of roads and fall to their knees weeping (and snapping, and taking video; the scenery is garish in a way that seems deviously designed to tease and embarrass shy, understated New England). The best part? This spectacle is nearly as regular as clockwork, with only a few years truly "bad" for foliage (due to oddly warm or wet weather).

Keep in mind, however, that autumn is the most popular time of year to travel—bus tours flock like migrating geese to New England in early October. As a result, hotels are invariably booked solid at that time. (Local radio stations have been known to put out calls for residents to open up their doors to travelers who otherwise might have to sleep in their cars.) Reservations are essential. Don't be surprised if you're assessed a foliage surcharge of $10 to $50 or more per room at your inn or hotel. Deal with it; you can't buy scenery like this.

Some states maintain seasonal **foliage hotlines and/or websites** to let you know when the leaves are at their peak: **Vermont** (© **800/VERMONT** [837-6668]; www.travel-vermont.com/seasons/report.asp), **Maine** (© **888/624-6345;** www.mainefoliage.com), and **New Hampshire** (© **800/258-3608**). The **U.S. Forest Service** also maintains a foliage hotline at © **800/354-4595,** updating conditions within the White Mountain National Forest in New Hampshire.

WINTER   New England winters are like wine—some years are good, some are lousy. During a good season, mounds of light, fluffy snow blanket the deep woods and fill the ski slopes. A "good" winter offers a profound peace and tranquillity as the fresh snow muffles all noise and brings such a thunderous silence to the entire region that the hiss and pop of a wood fire at a country inn can seem noisome. During these sorts of winters, exploring the forest on snowshoes or cross-country skis is an experience bordering on the magical.

During the *other* winters, though—the yucky ones—the weather fairies instead bring a nasty melange of rain, freezing rain, and sleet (um, frozen rain). The woods become filled with crusty snow, the cold is damp and bone-numbing, and it's bleak, bleak, bleak as gunpowder-gray clouds lower and linger for weeks.

There are some cures for this malaise. The higher in elevation you go into the mountains of northern New England, or the farther north you head (to such places as Jay, VT), the better your odds of finding snow.

On the other hand, meteorologically speaking, the coast in winter is a crapshoot, at best, more likely to yield rain (or sticky, heavy "snowball" snow) than powdery snow. Yes, winter vacations on the ocean can be spectacular—think Winslow Homerian waves crashing savagely onto an empty beach—but after a day or two of trying to navigate your car around big, gray, slushy snow banks, you too will soon be heading for Stowe.

Ski areas get crowded during the winter months. Some of them get *very* crowded. Expect maximum pricing, so-so food, and a herd mentality; this is the price you must pay for enjoying great skiing. The resorts get especially packed during school vacations, which is just when many resorts choose to employ the rather mercenary tactic of jacking up rates at hotels *and* on the slopes.

By the way, if you visit a small town in this region during winter, there is another pleasure to enjoy during deepest winter: public ice skating and ice hockey. You'll find locals skating on town greens, lakes, ponds, rivers, and probably on top of swimming pools, for all we know—anywhere that will hold a little water. How do you find these spots? Easy. Look for a clump of cars beside an iconic little warming hut with a wood-burning or oil-burning stove inside, sending up smoke puffs like a signal to the masses.

SPRING   After the long, long winter, spring in New England is a tease. She promises a lot and comes dressed in impressive finery (see: delicate purple lilacs, which blossom for just a week). But in many years, spring lasts only a week, sometimes less than that (we're not kidding), "occurring" around mid-May but sometimes as late as

June. There's a reason New Englanders hardly ever use the word *spring* in conversation with peers. They just call this time of year "mud season."

It happens fast. One morning the ground is muddier than muddy, the trees are barren, and gritty snow is still collected in shady hollows. The next day, it's in the 80s and humid, maple trees are blooming with little red cloverlike buds; kids are swimming in the lakes where the docks have just been put in; and somewhere in New Hampshire, a blue cover is being ripped off an aboveground pool.

Travelers need to be awfully crafty to experience spring in New England—and, once they get here, they often have trouble finding a room. That's because a good number of innkeepers and restaurateurs close up for a few weeks for repairs or to venture someplace warm. The upside? Rates are never cheaper than they are in spring. It's simply jaw-dropping how little you can pay in March for the same room that would cost 3 to 10 times *more* in the middle of summer or October.

Boston Average Temperatures & Rainfall

	JAN	FEB	MAR	APR	MAY	JUNE	JULY	AUG	SEPT	OCT	NOV	DEC
Temp. (°F)	30	31	38	49	59	68	74	72	65	55	45	34
Temp. (°C)	-1	-1	3	9	15	20	23	22	18	13	7	1
Rainfall (in.)	3.8	3.5	4.0	3.7	3.4	3.0	2.8	3.6	3.3	3.3	4.4	4.2

Burlington, Vermont Average Temperatures & Rainfall

	JAN	FEB	MAR	APR	MAY	JUNE	JULY	AUG	SEPT	OCT	NOV	DEC
Temp. (°F)	25	27	38	53	66	76	80	78	69	57	44	30
Temp. (°C)	-4	-3	3	12	19	24	27	26	21	14	7	-1
Rainfall (in.)	2.2	1.7	2.3	2.9	3.3	3.4	4.0	4.0	3.8	3.1	3.1	2.2

New England Calendar of Events

For an exhaustive list of events beyond those listed here, check http://events.frommers.com, where you'll find a searchable, up-to-the-minute roster of what's happening in cities all over the world.

FEBRUARY

U.S. National Toboggan Championships, Camden, ME. This is a raucous and lively athletic event where being overweight is actually an advantage. Held at the toboggan chute of the Camden Snow Bowl. Call ☏ 207/236-3438. Early February.

Dartmouth Winter Carnival, Hanover, NH. Huge, elaborate ice sculptures grace the village green during this festive celebration of winter, which includes numerous sporting events. Call ☏ 603/646-3399. Mid-February.

Stowe Derby, Stowe, VT. The oldest downhill/cross-country ski race in the nation pits racers who scramble from the wintry summit of Mount Mansfield into the village on the Stowe Recreation path. Call ☏ 802/253-7704. Late February.

MARCH

Maine Boatbuilders Show, Portland, ME. More than 200 exhibitors and 9,000 boat aficionados gather, as winter fades, to make plans for the coming summer. A great place to meet boat builders and get ideas for your dream craft. Call ☏ 207/774-1067. Mid-March.

APRIL

Patriots Day, Boston area (Paul Revere House, Old North Church, Lexington Green, Concord's North Bridge), MA. The events of April 18 and 19, 1775, which signified the start of the Revolutionary War, are commemorated and reenacted. Participants dressed as

Paul Revere and William Dawes ride to Lexington and Concord to warn the Minutemen. Battle reenactments take place at Lexington and Concord. Call the **Lexington Chamber of Commerce** (© 781/862-1450; www.lexington chamber.org) or the **Concord Chamber of Commerce** (© 978/369-3120; www. concordchamberofcommerce.org). Claiming to be the "world's oldest" marathon (except perhaps the original), the **Boston Marathon** (www.bostonmarathon.org) is an annual feature of Patriots Day. Third Monday in April; a state holiday in Massachusetts and Maine.

Daffodil Festival, Nantucket, MA. Spring's arrival is trumpeted with masses of yellow blooms adorning everything in sight, including a cavalcade of antique cars. Call © 508/228-1700. Late April.

Independent Film Festival of Boston, various locations. Features, shorts, and documentaries by international filmmakers make up the schedule for this increasingly buzz-worthy event. Check ahead (**www. iffboston.org**) for the schedule. Late April.

MAY

Brimfield Antique and Collectibles Show, Brimfield, MA. Up to 6,000 dealers fill several fields near this central Massachusetts town, with similar fairs in July and September. Call © 800/628-8379 or go to **www.brimfieldshow.com**. Mid-May, also mid-July and early Sept.

Cape Maritime Week, Cape Cod, MA. A multitude of cultural organizations mount special events—such as lighthouse tours—highlighting the region's nautical history. Call © 508/362-3828. Mid-May.

Annual Basketry Festival, Stowe, VT. A week-long event with displays and workshops by talented artisans. Call © 802/253-7223. Mid-May.

Spring Shearing, Woodstock, VT. A celebration of spring and an educational event. Learn all about what happens on a traditional farm, from sowing to shearing. Events take place at the Billings Farm Museum. Call © 802/457-2355. Late May.

Figawi Sailboat Race, Hyannis (on Cape Cod) to Nantucket, MA. The largest and wildest sailboat race on the East Coast. Intensive partying in Hyannis and on Nantucket surrounds this popular event. Call © 508/362-5230. Late May.

JUNE

Old Port Festival, Portland, ME. A block party in the heart of Portland's historic district with live music, food vendors, and activities for kids. Call © 207/772-6828. Early June.

Yale-Harvard Regatta, on the Thames River in New London, CT. One of the oldest collegiate rivalries in the country. Check the schedule for the heavyweight men's crew at **http://yalebulldogs.cstv.com**. Early June.

Taste of Hartford, Hartford, CT. One of New England's largest outdoor festivals, where many area restaurants serve up their specialties. You'll also get a "taste" of local music, dance, magic, and comedy. Call © 860/728-3089. Early June.

Boston Pride March, Back Bay to Beacon Hill, Boston. The largest LGBT pride parade in New England is the highlight of a week-long celebration of diversity. The parade, on the second Sunday of the month, starts at Copley Square and ends on Boston Common. Call © 617/262-9405 or go to **www.bostonpride.org**. Early June.

Market Square Day, Portsmouth, NH. This lively street fair attracts 300 vendors and revelers from throughout southern New Hampshire and Maine into downtown Portsmouth to dance, listen to music, sample food, and enjoy summer's arrival. Call © 603/436-3988. Mid-June.

Nantucket Film Festival, Nantucket, MA. This annual event focuses on storytelling through film and includes showings of short and feature-length films, documentaries, staged readings, panel discussions, and screenplay competitions. You may see a celebrity or two. Call © 508/228-1700. Mid-June.

Provincetown Film Festival, Provincetown, MA. Focusing on alternative film, this fete has brought out celebrities such as John Waters and Lily Tomlin. Call ✆ **508/487-FILM [3456].** Mid-June.

Annual Windjammer Days, Boothbay Harbor, ME. For nearly 4 decades, windjammers have gathered in Boothbay Harbor to kick off the summer sailing season. Expect music, food, and a parade of magnificent sailboats. Call ✆ **207/633-2353.** Late June.

Vermont Quilt Festival, Essex and Colchester. Displays are only part of the allure of New England's largest quilt festival. Attend classes and have your heirlooms appraised. Class and event descriptions can be found at **www.vqf.org**, or call ✆ **802/872-0034.** Late June through early July.

Jacob's Pillow Dance Festival, Becket, MA. The oldest dance festival in America features everything from ballet to modern dance and jazz. For a season brochure, call ✆ **413/243-0745,** or go to **www.jacobspillow.org**. Late June through August.

Williamstown Theater Festival, Williamstown, MA. This nationally distinguished festival presents everything from the classics to comedies and contemporary works. Scattered among the drama are readings and cabarets. Call ✆ **413/597-3400** or go to **www.wtfestival.org**. Late June through August.

JULY

Tanglewood Music Festival, near Lenox, MA. The Boston Symphony Orchestra makes its summer home at this fine estate, bringing symphonies, chamber groups, and soloists to the Berkshire Hills. Call the orchestra's home base in Boston at ✆ **617/266-1492,** or go to **www.tanglewood.org**. July through August.

Boston Harborfest, downtown Boston, along Boston Harbor, and the Boston Harbor Islands, MA. The city puts on its Sunday best for the 4th of July, which has become a gigantic weeklong celebration of Boston's maritime history. Events include concerts, tours, cruises, fireworks, the Boston Chowderfest, and the annual turnaround of the USS *Constitution*. Contact **Boston Harborfest** (✆ **617/227-1528;** www.bostonharborfest.com). First week in July.

Boston Pops Concert and Fireworks Display, Hatch Memorial Shell on the Esplanade, Boston. The big day culminates in the famous Boston Pops' 4th of July concert. People wait from dawn 'til dark for the music to start. Visit **www.july4th.org.** July 4th.

Wickford Art Festival, Wickford, RI. More than 200 artists gather in this quaint village for one of the East Coast's oldest art festivals. Call ✆ **401/294-6840,** or go to **www.wickfordart.org**. Mid-July.

Barnstable County Fair, East Falmouth (on Cape Cod), MA. An old-time county fair complete with rides, food, and livestock contests. Call ✆ **508/563-3200.** Late July.

Marlboro Music Festival, Marlboro, VT. This is a popular 6-week series of classical concerts featuring talented student musicians and seasoned artists performing in the peaceful hills outside of Brattleboro. Call ✆ **802/254-2394** (or 215/569-4690 in winter) for information. Weekends from mid-June to mid-August.

Maine Lobster Festival, Rockland, ME. Fill up on the local harvest and a boiled lobster or two at this event marking the importance and delectability of Maine's favorite crustacean. Call ✆ **800/LOB-CLAW [562-2529]** or 207/596-0376. Late July to early August.

Greater Hartford Festival of Jazz, downtown Hartford, CT. Join locals for free performances at the pavilion in Bushnell Park. Visit **www.hartfordjazz.com**. Late July.

AUGUST

Craftsman's Fair, Sunapee, New Hampshire. Quality crafts from several hundred New Hampshire artisans are displayed and sold at this weeklong festival in Sunapee State Park, held each year on the first Saturday of August. Call ✆ **603/763-2416.**

Italian-American Feasts, Boston, MA. These weekend street fairs in Boston's North End begin in July and end in late August with the two biggest: the Fisherman's Feast and the Feast of St. Anthony. The sublime (fresh seafood prepared while you wait, live music, dancing in the street) mingles with the ridiculous (carnival games, tacky T-shirts, fried-dough stands) to leave a lasting impression of fun and indigestion. Visit **www.fishermansfeast. com** or **www.saintanthonysfeast.com** for a preview. Weekends throughout August.

Southern Vermont Art & Craft Fair, Manchester, VT. More than 200 artisans show off their fine work at this popular festival, which also features creative food and good music. Held on the grounds of Hildene, a grand historic home. Call ✆ **802/425-3399.** Early August.

Newport Folk Festival, Newport, RI. Thousands of music lovers congregate at Fort Adams State Park for a heavy dose of performances on an August weekend. It's one of the nation's premier festivals. Go to **www.newportfolk.com.** Early August.

Annual Star Party, St. Johnsbury, VT. The historic Fairbanks Museum and Planetarium hosts special events and shows, including night-viewing sessions during the Perseid Meteor Shower. Call ✆ **802/748-2372.** Mid-August.

Wild Blueberry Festival, Machias, ME. A festival marking the harvest of the region's wild blueberries. Call ✆ **207/255-4402** or 207/255-6665. Mid-August.

JVC Jazz Festival, Newport, RI. This 3-day jazz festival brings together some of the best in the music industry to play for a sizzling weekend at Fort Adams State Park. Go to **www.festivalnetwork.com.** Mid-August.

Martha's Vineyard Agricultural Fair, West Tisbury, MA. An old-fashioned country fair featuring horse pulls, livestock shows, musicians, and woodsman contests, along with plenty of carnival action. Call ✆ **508/693-4343.** Third weekend in August.

Pops Goes the Summer, Barnstable County Fairgrounds, Falmouth, MA. Cape Cod Symphony Orchestra concert followed by a huge fireworks display. Call ✆ **508/ 548-8500.** Late August.

SEPTEMBER

Blue Hill Fair, Blue Hill, ME. This classic country fair is held outside one of Maine's cutest little villages on Labor Day weekend. Call ✆ **207/374-3701.** Labor Day weekend.

Windjammer Weekend, Camden, ME. Come visit Maine's impressive fleet of old-time sailing ships, which host open houses throughout the weekend at this scenic harbor. Call ✆ **207/236-4404.** Labor Day weekend.

Norwalk Seaport Oyster Festival, Norwalk, CT. This waterfront festival celebrates Long Island Sound's seafaring past. Highlights include oyster-shucking and slurping contests, harbor cruises, concerts, and fireworks. Call ✆ **203/838-9444,** or go to **www.sea port.org.** Weekend after Labor Day.

Vermont State Fair, Rutland, VT. All of Vermont seems to show up for this grand event, with a midway, live music, and plenty of agricultural exhibits. Call ✆ **802/775-5200.** Early to mid-September.

Eastern States Exhibition, West Springfield, MA. "The Big E" is New England's largest agricultural fair, with a 4-H horse show, ox pulling, carnival food, a midway, and entertainment from the likes of Joan Jett. Call ✆ **413/737-2443,** or go to **www. thebige.com.** Mid- to late September.

Provincetown Arts Festival, Provincetown, MA. One of the country's oldest art colonies celebrates its past and present with local artists opening their studios. Call ✆ **508/487-3424.** Late September.

Common Ground Country Fair, Unity, ME. A sprawling, old-time state fair with a twist: The emphasis is on organic foods, recycling, crafts, and wholesome living. Call ✆ **207/568-4142.** Late September.

OCTOBER

Fryeburg Fair, Fryeburg, ME. Cotton candy, tractor pulls, live music, and huge vegetables and barnyard animals can all be found at Maine's largest agricultural fair. Call ☏ **207/985-3268.** Early to mid-October.

Mystic Seaport Chowderfest, Mystic, CT. A festival of soup ("chowda" in these parts) served from bubbling cauldrons set on wood fires. Call ☏ **860/572-5315,** or visit **www.mysticseaport.org**. Mid-October.

Head of the Charles Regatta, Boston and Cambridge, MA. High school, college, and post-collegiate rowing teams and individuals—some 4,000 in all—race in front of hordes of fans along the Charles River's banks and bridges. Call ☏ **617/868-6200,** or visit **www.hocr.org**. Late October.

Salem Haunted Happenings, Salem, MA. Parades, parties, fortune-telling, cruises, and tours lead up to a ceremony on Halloween. Contact **Destination Salem** (☏ **877/SALEM-MA** [725-3662]), or check the website (www.hauntedhappenings. org) for specifics. All month.

NOVEMBER

Northampton Independent Film Festival, Northampton, MA. The cultural center of the state's Pioneer Valley hosts a creative film fest and brings in guests from the region. Visit **www.niff.org** for details. Early November.

Thanksgiving Celebration, Plymouth, MA. The town observes the holiday that put it on the map with a "stroll through the ages," showcasing 17th- and 19th-century Thanksgiving preparations in historic homes. Nearby Plimoth Plantation, where the colony's first years are re-created, wisely offers a Victorian Thanksgiving feast (reservations required). Call **Destination Plymouth** (☏ **800/872-1620;** www. visit-plymouth.com) or **Plimoth Plantation** (☏ **800/262-9356** or 508/746-1622; www.plimoth.org). Week including Thanksgiving Day.

DECEMBER

Black Nativity, Converse Hall, Tremont Temple Baptist Church, 88 Tremont St., Boston, MA. (☏ **617/723-3486;** www. blacknativity.org). Poet Langston Hughes wrote the "gospel opera," and a cast of more than 100 brings it to life. Most weekends in December.

Christmas Prelude, Kennebunkport, ME. This scenic coastal village greets Santa's arrival in a lobster boat and marks the coming of Christmas with street shows, pancake breakfasts, and tours of the town's splendid inns. Call ☏ **207/967-0857.** Early December.

Christmas Stroll, Nantucket, MA. The island briefly stirs from its winter slumber for one last shopping/feasting spree, attended by costumed carolers and Santa in a horse-drawn carriage. The weekend event is the pinnacle of Nantucket Noel, a month of festivities starting in late November. Call ☏ **508/228-1700.** Early December.

Candlelight Stroll, Portsmouth, NH. Historic Strawbery Banke gets in a Christmas way with old-time decorations and more than 1,000 candles lighting the 10-acre grounds. Call ☏ **603/433-1100.** First 3 weekends in December.

Boston Tea Party Reenactment, Old South Meeting House and Congress Street Bridge, Boston, MA. A lively, all-ages audience-participation happening re-creates the events of December 16, 1773. Call ☏ **617/482-6439,** or visit **www.oldsouth meetinghouse.org**. Mid-December.

Christmas Season Festivities, Newport, RI. The whole city collaborates to use only clear bulbs to illuminate the harbor and wharves, the restored Colonials, and the Victorian splendor of Bellevue Avenue. It's all designed to simulate the glow of candlelight and the atmosphere of olden days. There also are wreath sales, a blessing of the fleet, caroling evenings, holiday concerts, gingerbread-house viewings, and more. Visit **www.christmasinnewport.org**. Every day in December.

Christmas Eve and Christmas Day, festivities throughout New England. Nantucket, MA, features carolers in Victorian garb, art exhibits, and tours of historic homes. December 24 and 25.

First Night, Boston. The original arts-oriented, no-alcohol, citywide New Year's Eve celebration includes a parade, ice sculptures, art exhibitions, theatrical performances, and indoor and outdoor entertainment. Fireworks light up the sky above Boston Common at 7pm and over Boston Harbor at midnight. For details, contact **First Night** (✆ **617/542-1399;** www.firstnight.org) or check the newspapers when you arrive. December 31.

New Year's Eve, regionwide. Portland, ME; Providence, RI; Hartford, CT; Portsmouth, NH; Burlington, VT; and many other cities and towns celebrate the coming of the New Year. Check with local chambers of commerce for details. December 31.

ENTRY REQUIREMENTS
Passports

Virtually every air traveler entering the U.S. is required to show a passport. All persons, including U.S. citizens, traveling by air between the United States and Canada, Mexico, Central and South America, the Caribbean, and Bermuda are required to present a valid passport. *Note:* U.S. and Canadian citizens entering the U.S. at land and sea ports of entry from within the western hemisphere must now also present a passport or other documents compliant with the Western Hemisphere Travel Initiative (WHTI; see **www.getyouhome.gov** for details). Children 15 and under may continue entering with only a U.S. birth certificate, or other proof of U.S. citizenship.

It is advised to always have at least one or two consecutive blank pages in your passport to allow space for visas and stamps that need to appear together. It is also important to note when your passport expires. Many countries require your passport to have at least 6 months left before its expiration in order to allow you into the destination.

Visas

For information on obtaining a visa, see chapter 15, "Fast Facts."

The U.S. Department of State has a **Visa Waiver Program (VWP)** allowing citizens of the following countries to enter the United States without a visa for stays of up to 90 days: Andorra, Australia, Austria, Belgium, Brunei, Czech Republic, Denmark, Estonia, Finland, France, Germany, Hungary, Iceland, Ireland, Italy, Japan, Latvia, Liechtenstein, Lithuania, Luxembourg, Malta, Monaco, the Netherlands, New Zealand, Norway, Portugal, San Marino, Singapore, Slovakia, Slovenia, South Korea, Spain, Sweden, Switzerland, and the United Kingdom. *Note:* This list was accurate at press time; for the most up-to-date list of countries in the VWP, consult http://travel.state.gov/visa. Even though a visa isn't necessary, in an effort to help U.S. officials check travelers against terror watch lists before they arrive at U.S. borders, visitors from VWP countries must register online through the Electronic System for Travel Authorization (ESTA) before boarding a plane or a boat to the U.S. Travelers must complete an electronic application providing basic personal and travel eligibility information. The Department of Homeland Security recommends filling out the form at least 3 days before traveling. Authorizations will be valid for up to 2 years or until the traveler's passport expires, whichever comes first. Currently, there is no fee for the online application. **Note:** Any passport issued on or after October 26, 2006, by a VWP country must be an **e-Passport** for VWP travelers to be eligible to enter the U.S. without a visa. Citizens of these nations also need to present a round-trip air or cruise ticket upon arrival. E-Passports contain computer chips capable of storing biometric information, such as the required digital photograph of the holder. If your passport doesn't have this feature, you can still travel without a visa if the valid passport was issued before October 26, 2005, and includes a machine-readable zone; or if the valid passport was issued between October 26, 2005, and October 25, 2006, and includes a digital photograph. For more information, go to **http://travel.state.gov/visa**. Canadian citizens may enter the United States without visas, but will need to show passports and proof of residence.

Citizens of all other countries must have (1) a valid passport that expires at least 6 months later than the end of their visit to the U.S.; and (2) a tourist visa.

Customs

WHAT YOU CAN BRING INTO THE U.S.

Every visitor 21 years of age or older may bring in, free of duty, the following: (1) 1 U.S. quart of alcohol; (2) 200 cigarettes, 50 cigars (but not from Cuba), or 3 pounds of smoking tobacco; and (3) $100 worth of gifts. These exemptions are offered to travelers who spend at least 72 hours in the United States and who have not claimed them within the preceding 6 months. It is forbidden to bring into the country almost any meat products (including canned, fresh, and dried meat products such as bouillon, soup mixes, and so forth). Generally, condiments including vinegars, oils, pickled goods, spices, coffee, tea, and some cheeses and baked goods, are permitted. Avoid rice products, as rice can often harbor insects. Bringing fruits and vegetables is prohibited since they may harbor pests or disease. International visitors may carry in or out up to $10,000 in U.S. or foreign currency with no formalities; larger sums must be declared to U.S. Customs on entering or leaving, which includes filing form CM 4790. For details regarding U.S. Customs and Border Protection, consult your nearest U.S. embassy or consulate, or **U.S. Customs** (www.customs.gov).

WHAT YOU CAN TAKE HOME FROM THE U.S.

For information on what you're allowed to bring home if you're visiting from an international destination, contact one of the following agencies:

Canadian Citizens: Canada Border Services Agency, Ottawa, Ontario, K1A 0L8 (✆ **800/461-9999** in Canada, or 204/983-3500; www.cbsa-asfc.gc.ca).

U.K. Citizens: HM Revenue & Customs, Crownhill Court, Tailyour Road, Plymouth, PL6 5BZ (✆ **0845/010-9000;** from outside the U.K., 020/8929-0152; www.hmce.gov.uk).

Australian Citizens: Australian Customs Service, Customs House, 5 Constitution Ave., Canberra City, ACT 2601 (✆ **1300/363-263;** from outside Australia, 612/6275-6666; www.customs.gov.au).

New Zealand Citizens: New Zealand Customs, The Customhouse, 17–21 Whitmore St., Box 2218, Wellington, 6140 (✆ **04/473-6099** or 0800/428-786; www.customs.govt.nz).

Medical Requirements

Unless you're arriving from an area known to be suffering from an epidemic (particularly cholera or yellow fever), inoculations or vaccinations are not required for entry into the United States.

GETTING THERE & AROUND

Getting to New England

BY PLANE

Nearly all the major airlines fly into Boston's **Logan International Airport** (airport code: BOS), your likely hub of arrival or connection if you're coming by air. You'll find a complete list of airlines servicing New England in chapter 15. For more information about Logan, contact the airport at ℭ **800/235-6426** or check the airport's website at www.massport.com/logan.

Commercial carriers serve other important locales in the region as well, such as Bradley International Airport (airport code: BDL), in Hartford, Connecticut; and in places such as **Burlington,** Vermont (code BTV); **Manchester,** New Hampshire (code MHT); **Portland,** Maine (code PWM); and **Providence,** Rhode Island (code PVD). Airlines most commonly fly to these airports from New York or Boston, although direct connections from other cities, such as Chicago, Cincinnati, and Philadelphia, are available.

Even smaller towns and cities are served by feeder airlines and charter companies, including those flying into air strips in **Rutland,** Vermont (code RUT); **Rockland,** Maine (code RKD); and **Trenton,** Maine (code BHB), near Bar Harbor. Just remember that many of the scheduled flights to these smaller New England cities are aboard small turboprop (propeller-driven) planes; ask the airline or your travel agent if that makes you nervous.

While flights into smaller airports are convenient, they're usually pricey. It's almost always cheaper to fly into Logan, and then rent a car and drive (or take a bus) to your final destination. Boston is about 1 hour by car from the beaches of southern Maine, 2 hours from Portland, and 3 hours or less from the White Mountains and most points in Vermont. On the other hand, Logan can become congested, security lines are long, delayed flights are endemic, and traffic can be nightmarish—so the increased expense of flying into smaller hubs might be offset by the speedier check-ins, departures, and arrivals.

Discount airfares aren't easy to find in northern New England, but progress has been made. Over the last decade, for instance, the airport in Manchester, New Hampshire, has grown by leaps and bounds thanks largely to the arrival of **Southwest Airlines** (ℭ **800/435-9792;** www.southwest.com), which has brought competitive, low-cost airfares and improved service. Manchester has gone from a sleepy backwater airport to a bustling destination. Travelers looking for good deals to this region do well to check with the airline first before pricing bigger gateways.

Discount airline **JetBlue** also offers direct service from Burlington, Vermont, to New York City's LaGuardia Airport with onward connections. For more information, call ℭ **800/538-2583,** or check online at **www.jetblue.com**. Also check the "Getting There" section at the beginning of each chapter in this book for the latest details

WHO FLIES WHERE

Here's a breakdown of which airlines fly where in the region (I am skipping over Boston's Logan airport, because nearly every airline flies into it):

o **Cape Air's** routes include Cessnas from Boston to Rutland, Vermont.

o **Continental** flies into Bangor and Portland, Maine, and Manchester, New Hampshire, from Newark Liberty International Airport (near New York City). It also flies into Providence from such places as Cleveland and Newark.

o **Delta** flies into Providence from Atlanta, Detroit, and Minneapolis.

o **JetBlue** flies into Portland, Maine, and Burlington, Vermont, from New York City's John F. Kennedy International Airport.

o **Northwest** flies into Burlington and Portland.

o **Southwest** flies nonstop into Logan and Manchester from numerous airports, and into Providence from quite a few, as well—even Chicago, Houston, and the West Coast. It also flies into Hartford from Chicago and Denver.

o **United** flies into Burlington, Portland, Manchester, and Hartford from various points.

o **US Airways** and its commuter subsidiaries fly from Boston, Philadelphia, and New York's LaGuardia to Burlington, Manchester, and Portland, as well as some smaller airports in Maine, such as Bar Harbor and Presque Isle.

on local airports, and my primer "Flying into Northern New England: The Skinny" in the box below.

Overseas visitors may want to take advantage of the APEX (Advance Purchase Excursion) reductions offered by all major U.S. and European carriers. In addition, some large airlines offer transatlantic or transpacific passengers special discount tickets under the name **Visit USA,** which allows mostly one-way travel from one U.S. destination to another at very low prices. Unavailable in the U.S., these discount tickets must be purchased abroad in conjunction with your international fare. This system is the easiest, fastest, cheapest way to see the country.

BY CAR

Coming from the New York City area by car (your most likely entry point, unless you're coming from Canada), several interstate highway corridors serve New England. **I-91** heads more or less due north from Hartford, Connecticut, through Massachusetts, and along the Vermont–New Hampshire border. **I-95** parallels the Atlantic coast through Boston, after which it strikes northeast across New Hampshire and along the southern Maine coast before heading north toward the Canadian border. The Massachusetts Turnpike **(I-90)** makes a wandering east-west jaunt from Boston to the lovely Berkshire hills (for a price—it's a toll road).

From Boston, you head south on I-95 to reach Rhode Island, north on I-95 for Maine, northwest up **I-93** for New Hampshire and the White Mountains, or southwest on **I-84** directly into the heart of Connecticut. Most of these highways flow smoothly through rural countryside, except on summer weekends or at rush hour around the big metro areas. In Concord, New Hampshire, **I-89** splits off from I-93 and heads into Vermont. Stay on I-89 if you want to reach Montpelier and Burlington; exit northward onto **I-91** at White River Junction if you want to visit St. Johnsbury and the Northeast Kingdom.

If scenery is your priority, the most picturesque way to enter New England is from the west. Drive through New York's scenic Adirondack Mountains to Port Kent, New York, on Lake Champlain, then catch the car ferry across the lake to Burlington.

Note that travel times may be longer than you think because there are few fast roads in New England and lots of local ones. From Boston to Portland takes about 2 hours, and to Bar Harbor about 5 hours.

Your EZPass will also work on the MassPike, where the transponder system is called FastLane.

For listings of the major car rental agencies in New England, please see the "Fast Facts," in chapter 15.

International visitors should note that insurance and taxes are almost never included in quoted rental car rates in the U.S. Be sure to ask your rental agency about additional fees for these. They can add a significant cost to your car rental.

Many rental-car agencies have non-negotiable age requirements, both minimum-age limits (generally 25 or older) and upper-age requirements (often 70–75 for certain vehicles).

BY TRAIN

From Boston and New York City, commuter train lines radiate out to the suburbs (which include locales in southern New Hampshire and coastal Connecticut, respectively), but elsewhere train service in northern New England is basically limited to three **Amtrak** (© **800/872-7245;** www.amtrak.com) lines: two running to Vermont and one to Maine.Amtrak's *Vermonter* service departs from Washington, D.C., once a day (currently at 8:10am weekdays, 40 min. earlier Sat–Sun), with stops in Baltimore, Philadelphia, and New York City (at 11:30am) before following the Connecticut River northward, mostly through Vermont. The train calls at Brattleboro, Bellows Falls, Claremont (in NH), White River Junction, Randolph, Montpelier, Waterbury, and Essex Junction (near Burlington), finally arriving in St. Albans some 10 hours after leaving Manhattan.

The *Ethan Allen Express* departs New York's Penn Station once daily at 3:15pm (except Fri, when it leaves at 5:45pm) and travels somewhat more quickly, moving north along the Hudson River before veering northeast into Vermont, stopping at Fair Haven (near Castleton) and terminating in Rutland after about 5½ hours.

Amtrak relaunched rail service to Maine in late 2001, restoring a line that had been idle since the 1960s. The *Downeaster* service operates five times daily between North Station in Boston and Portland, Maine; if you're coming from elsewhere on the East Coast, you will need to change train stations in Boston—a slightly frustrating exercise requiring either a taxi ride through congested streets or a ride and transfer on Boston's aging subway system. The *Downeaster* makes stops in Haverhill, Massachusetts; Exeter, Durham, and Dover, New Hampshire; and Wells, Saco, and Old Orchard Beach, Maine. Travel time is about 2 hours and 25 minutes between Boston and Portland. Bikes are allowed to be on- or off-loaded at Boston, Wells, and Portland. The one-way fare from Boston to Portland is $24.

International visitors might want to buy a **USA Rail Pass,** good for 15, 30, or 45 days of unlimited travel on **Amtrak** (© **800/USA-RAIL** [872-7245]; www.amtrak. com). The pass is available online or through many overseas travel agents. See the Amtrak website for the cost of travel within the western, eastern, or northwestern United States. Reservations are generally required and should be made as early as possible. Regional rail passes are also available.

Also note that all **AAA members** get a 10% discount on Amtrak tickets if they're booked at least 3 days in advance. Bring your membership card to the station or train when you ride.

BY BUS

Coming from anywhere outside the Northeast, you'll probably take a **Greyhound** (© **800/231-2222;** www.greyhound.com) bus to Boston's big depot at South Station first, then switch to a regional carrier. International visitors can obtain information about the **Greyhound North American Discovery Pass.** The pass can be obtained from travel agents outside the U.S. or at **www.discoverypass.com,** for unlimited travel and stopovers in the U.S. and Canada.

BY "CHINATOWN" BUSES

Thanks to the so-called **Chinatown shuttles,** busing to and from Boston (and some other New England cities) from every major East Coast city has become an extremely cost-effective way to get into the region. These bus services, originally created by Chinese-Americans as a means of getting between New York City and the cities of Boston, Philadelphia, and Washington, D.C., are open to everyone and offer rock-bottom prices. From New York, the average ride ranges from $15 to $18; but there are times when specials reduce the fares to just $1. There are now nearly a dozen smaller bus companies operating along these routes, and fare information plus bookings can be made on one well-designed agency site called **BusJunction** (www. busjunction.com), which searches the major discount sites, Chinese bus companies, as well as Greyhound and Peter Pan.

You will probably wait for the bus to pick you up, or depart from a street corner, rather than a bus station, which some people might count as a bonus if you're not fond of bus stations.

The Chinatown bus companies essentially gave birth to a more cushy set of cheap bus lines, whose coaches are newer, often offer Wi-Fi, and their drivers are more likely to speak English, such as:

o **Megabus** (© **877/GO2-MEGA** [462-6342]; www.megabus.com)
o **Boltbus** (© **877/BOLTBUS** [265-8287]; www.boltbus.com)
o **Vamoose** (© **877/393-2828;** www.vamoosebus.com)

Getting Around
BY CAR

If you're visiting from abroad and plan to rent a car in the United States, you probably won't need the services of an additional automobile organization. If you're planning to buy or borrow a car, automobile-association membership is recommended. **AAA,** the **American Automobile Association** (© **800/222-4357;** http://travel. aaa.com), is the country's largest auto club and supplies its members with maps, insurance, and, most important, emergency road service.

New England Driving Distances

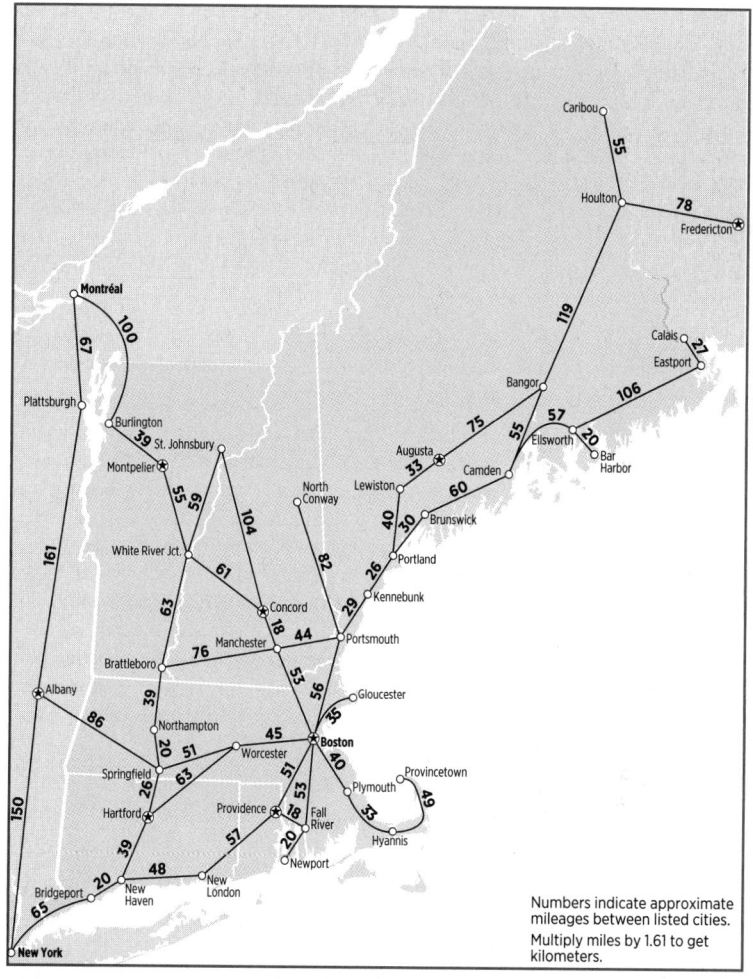

Numbers indicate approximate mileages between listed cities.
Multiply miles by 1.61 to get kilometers.

The major airports in New England (see "Getting to New England," earlier in this chapter) all host national car-rental chains.

Travel can be confusing in this region at times, as there are few straight roads; it's good to have someone adept at map reading in the car. North-and-south travel is relatively straightforward, thanks to the **four major interstates** crisscrossing the region. But traveling east and west sometimes involves a zigzagged route stitching together state, federal, and county roads.

On the other hand, New England is of a size that touring by car can usually be done comfortably—so long as you're not determined to see all six states in a week (see chapter 4 for some of our suggested itineraries). Note that **Maine is a lot bigger** than all the other New England states; when making travel plans, beware of road maps that don't fully convey the state's size. (By driving time, Portland is closer to New York City than it is to Baxter State Park.)

Traffic is generally light compared to that of most urban and suburban areas along the East Coast, but there's a big exception: Traffic anywhere in or around **Boston** can be sluggish anytime, and Friday afternoons and evenings in the summer are positively infuriating; the tentacles of Beantown traffic now extend all the way to I-495, which you may need to use to get from the New York area to, say, coastal Maine. Come prepared for unexpected delays, if you'll be anywhere near Boston. Other choke points, such as Rte. 1 along the Maine coast (during summer weekends) or attractive New England back-road routes (during the height of foliage season), can also back up for miles at certain times of the year.

To avoid the worst of the tourist traffic, **travel smart.** Try to avoid being on the road during big summer holidays or foliage weekends; if your schedule allows it, travel on weekdays rather than on weekends, and hit the road early or late in the day to avoid the midday crunch.

International visitors should note that insurance and taxes are almost never included in quoted rental car rates in the U.S. Be sure to ask your rental agency about additional fees for these. They can add a significant cost to your car rental. Also keep in mind that foreign driver's licenses are usually recognized in the U.S., but you may want to consider obtaining an **international driver's license.**

Finally, if you're a connoisseur of back roads, get a **DeLorme atlas** of the region. These Maine-made atlases offer an extraordinary level of detail, right down to logging roads and public boat launches. DeLorme's headquarters and map store (© **800/561-5105** or 800/642-0970; www.delorme.com) are in Yarmouth, Maine, but their products are available at bookstores, rest stops, and gas stations throughout the region.

BY BUS

Once you're in northern New England, **bus service can be spotty**—though it's gotten somewhat better lately. You'll be able to reach the major cities by bus, but few of the smaller towns or villages. Tickets range from about $25, one-way for Boston to Portland, to $45 for Boston to Burlington. Buses require no advance planning or reservations, though buses can fill up on Fridays, Sundays, and around major holidays or holiday travel times.

Greyhound (© **800/231-2222;** www.greyhound.com) operates in all six states—though mostly just along the interstate highways—with frequent departures from Boston.

Concord Coach Lines (© **800/639-3317** or 603/228-3300; www.concord coachlines.com) serves Maine and New Hampshire, including Midcoast Maine and some smaller towns in the Lake Winnipesaukee, Upper Valley, and White Mountains areas. Buses on the Maine routes play (PG-13 rated or below) movies en route.

C&J (© **800/258-7111** or 603/430-1100; www.ridecj.com;) connects Boston with Portsmouth, Durham, and Dover, New Hampshire, on buses that promise Wi-Fi access.

BY TRAIN

As noted above, **Amtrak** provides limited rail travel to and from the region. But it's not really a valid option for getting around, as Amtrak is quite expensive in the region compared to the short distances it covers. See "By Train," under "Getting There," earlier in this chapter, for full details about train service to *northern* New England, where fares do sometimes rival or beat those of airlines.

In coastal Connecticut, the frequent **MTA Metro North Railroad** commuter trains to and from New York City and within the state are a *much* cheaper option than Amtrak. A trip between New York City and New Haven, for instance, costs $13 to $25 one-way on the Metro North, versus $30 (and 20 min. longer, with far fewer departures) on Amtrak. Check the system's website at **http://mta.info/mnr** for schedules and fares.

MONEY & COSTS

THE VALUE OF $1 VS. OTHER POPULAR CURRENCIES

US$	C$	UK£	Euro (€)	A$	NZ$
1	.99	.65	.74	1.07	1.40

Frommer's lists prices in the local currency. The currency conversions quoted above were correct at press time. However, rates fluctuate, so before departing consult a currency exchange website such as **www.oanda.com/convert/classic** to check up-to-the-minute rates.

Here's a scene I've seen repeated many times around New England. A couple has driven up from the city, just for the day, in great weather to sightsee and grab dinner before returning. But something magical has happened. They've fallen in love with each other all over again, and with the quaint loveliness of (insert town name or beach here). They've decided to sleep for the night in a feather bed, eat a nice meal, and maybe watch the sun set over the (ocean/mountains/lake), then head home in the morning.

Except that here they stand, in front of a tourist information center staff member (or hanging off a pay phone), looking despondent.

"Isn't there *anything* cheaper?" pleads one of the lovebirds. "No, and that's a good price," comes back the answer, as nicely as possible. "You won't find anything better this time of year."

It's true. Travelers are in for some **sticker shock** in New England during peak travel seasons. From June through August, and again in October, there's simply no such thing as a cheap motel room here. Even no-frills mom-and-pop motels can (and do) happily charge $100 a night or more for a bed that might rate just a notch above camping in a tent. Bland business hotels at the mall or airport, miles from sights or good restaurants, charge even more. A *lot* more.

To be fair, innkeepers here need to charge more in summer: Most of their annual income comes during a 2- or 3-month stretch. (Peak foliage season in October and holiday weekends are their only other chances to make money, and many places close down for the season from Oct through early May.)

WHAT THINGS COST IN NEW ENGLAND	US$
Small cup of coffee at Capitol Grounds in Montpelier, VT	1.40
1 ride on the "T" subway in Boston	2.00
Cheeseburger at Louis' Lunch in New Haven, CT	6.00
Weekend admission to the Vermont State Fair in Rutland	10.00
Adult admission to the Portland (ME) Museum of Art	10.00
Haddock boat at Two Lights Lobster Shack, Cape Elizabeth, ME	13.00
Adult admission to the Boston Museum of Fine Arts, Boston	17.00
3-course dinner (no alcohol) at The Terrace at the Hanover Inn, NH	57.00
1 night at Hampton Inn Portland Airport (ME), plus tax	145.00
Dinner (with wine, tax, and tip) at The White Barn Inn, Kennebunk, ME	153.00
1 night at The Liberty Hotel, Boston	417.00

So if you're coming to this region in summer, fall, or ski season (and I'll bet that you are), **lodging** will occupy a bigger chunk of your budget than you expected.

Luckily, however, the cost of meals, gas, and day-to-day expenses is generally **more affordable** here than you'd pay in a major city elsewhere in the country. You can find excellent entrees at upscale, creative restaurants for around $20, comparing favorably with similar dishes at big-city restaurants that would top $30.

Beware of hidden credit card fees while traveling. Check with your credit or debit card issuer to see what fees, if any, will be charged for overseas transactions.

Recent reform legislation in the U.S., for example, has curbed some exploitative lending practices. But many banks have responded by increasing fees in other areas, including fees for customers who use credit and debit cards while out of the country—even if those charges were made in U.S. dollars. Fees can amount to 3% or more of the purchase price. Check with your bank before departing to avoid any surprise charges on your statement.

The easiest and best way to get cash away from home is from an **ATM** (automated teller machine). ATMs are easy to find in New England's populated areas and regions that cater to tourists. Machines are also making their way into the smallest villages, but don't count on finding them in every last town; stock up on cash when you can.

STAYING HEALTHY

New Englanders, by and large, consider themselves a healthy bunch, which they ascribe to clean living, brisk northern air, vigorous exercise (leaf raking, snow shoveling, and so on), and few excesses other than the stresses and strains of being a Red Sox fan (now greatly alleviated, thank goodness). You shouldn't face any serious health risks when traveling in the region.

Regional Health Concerns

Exceptions to the above statement? Well, yes—you may find yourself at higher risk when exploring the outdoors, particularly in the backcountry. A few things to watch for when venturing off the beaten path:

o **Poison ivy:** This shiny, three-leafed plant is common throughout the region. If you touch it, you could develop a nasty, itchy rash that might seriously erode further enjoyment of your vacation. Some people experience a dangerously bad reaction, while others are barely affected. If you're unfamiliar with what poison ivy looks like, ask at a ranger station or visitor information booth. Many have posters or books to help you with identification.

o **Giardia:** That crystal-clear stream coursing down a backcountry peak might look pure, but it could be contaminated with animal feces. Disgusting, yes, and also dangerous. When ingested by humans, *Giardia* cysts can cause serious diarrhea and loss of weight. The symptoms might not surface until well after you've left the backcountry and returned home. Carry your own water for day trips, or bring a small filter (available at any camping or sporting goods store) to treat backcountry water. Failing that, at least boil your water or treat it with iodine pills before using it—even for cooking, drinking, or washing. If you feel diarrhea coming on, see a doctor immediately.

o **Lyme disease:** Lyme disease has been a growing problem in New England since 1975, when it was identified in the town of Lyme, Connecticut; thousands of cases are reported nationwide annually, and the disease is no trifling matter: Left untreated, Lyme disease can damage the heart. The disease is transmitted by tiny deer ticks, which are difficult to see—but check your socks and body daily anyway (ideally with a partner). If you spot a bull's-eye-shaped rash, 3 to 8 inches in diameter (the rash may feel warm but usually doesn't itch), see a doctor right away. Lyme disease is more easily treated in early phases than later. Other symptoms may include muscle and joint pain, fever, or fatigue.

o **Rabies:** Since 1989, rabies has increasingly been spreading northward into New England. The disease is transmitted through animal saliva and is especially prevalent in skunks, raccoons, bats, and foxes. **It is always fatal if left untreated** in humans. Infected animals tend to display erratic and aggressive behavior; the best advice is to keep a safe distance between yourself and any wild animal you might encounter. If you're bitten, wash the wound as soon as you can and immediately seek medical attention. Treatment is no longer as painful as it used to be, but still involves a series of shots.

If you're planning a long hike into the backcountry, bring a small first-aid kit of basic medicines and bandages. Towns and villages in all six states are well stocked with pharmacies, chain grocery stores, and Walmart-type stores where you can stock up on common medicines (such as calamine lotion, aspirin, and painkillers) to cope with minor ailments along the way.

If You Get Sick

Hospitals are easy to find in even small cities around New England; **health care is excellent here.** In rural areas, however, you might need to depend on regional health centers or walk-in clinics. Check the phone book or ask your hotel concierge upon check-in to learn what the best, nearest option is.

If you suffer from a chronic illness, consult your doctor before your departure. Pack **prescription medications** in your carry-on luggage, and carry them in their original containers, with pharmacy labels—otherwise, they won't make it through airport security.

Visitors from outside the U.S. should carry the generic names of their prescription drugs. Foreign visitors may also need to pay all medical costs upfront in an emergency and seek reimbursement later. For U.S. travelers, most health-care plans provide coverage if you get sick away from home—but check. If it doesn't, try to buy a temporary **travel insurance policy** for in-country travel from a reliable company such as **Travel Guard** (© **800/826-4919;** www.travelguard.com).

We list additional **emergency numbers** in chapter 15.

CRIME & SAFETY

New England—with the exception of Boston—boasts some of the lowest crime rates in the entire country. Northern New England is even safer; the odds of anything really bad happening during your visit here are extremely slim. But travelers should still take all the usual precautions against theft, robbery, and assault when on the road.

Avoid any unnecessary public displays of wealth, for instance. Don't bring out fat wads of cash from your pocket, and save your best jewelry for private occasions. If you are approached by someone who demands money, jewelry, or anything else, hand it over. Don't argue or negotiate. Just comply. Afterward, contact police right away by dialing © **911.**

The crime you're statistically most likely to encounter here (as with anywhere in the U.S.) is the theft of items from your car. Don't leave anything of value in plain view, and lock valuables out of sight in your trunk. If you have an electronic security system, use it.

Also take the usual precautions against leaving cash, laptops, or valuables in your hotel room (or at least lying around in the open) whenever you're out of your room. Many hotels have safe-deposit boxes; use them. Smaller inns and hotels often do not offer any kind of safe, but it can't hurt to check.

Finally, when traveling late at night, look for a well-lighted area if you need to gas up or step out of your car for any reason.

SPECIALIZED TRAVEL RESOURCES

In addition to the destination-specific resources listed below, please visit Frommers. com for other specialized travel resources.

LGBT Travelers

New England has a strong gay and lesbian presence, though some parts are friendlier to gays and lesbians than others. As elsewhere in the country, larger cities tend to be more accommodating to gay travelers than smaller towns. A number of hotels and inns in the region, from small B&Bs to large resorts, welcome gay and lesbian travelers, and a growing number of these inns are owned by gay or lesbian couples. Check ads and advertisements in gay and lesbian community newspapers and magazines for more information.

Connecticut, Massachusetts, New Hampshire, and Vermont permit same-sex marriage (and many gay and lesbian couples choose to have a wedding in one of these states). Rhode Island recognizes same-sex marriages, but does not perform them.

Boston has the region's largest gay population, many concentrated in the **South End** neighborhood; in fact, many locals credit gays and lesbians with transforming "Southie" from a downtrodden, working-class 'hood into its current incarnation as home to many of the city's quirkiest antiques shops, restaurants, and B&Bs.

Provincetown, Massachusetts (at the very end of Cape Cod), without a doubt, is the gay-friendliest town in New England, and draws gay and lesbian travelers from all over the world. Rainbow flags fly proudly throughout the town, and it's safe to say this is a must-visit place for any gay or lesbian first-time traveler to the region.

Northampton, Massachusetts—home to Smith College—boasts a substantial and thriving lesbian community and is a must-stop for travelers of that ilk.

Vermont has traditionally been one of the most open-minded in New England— and a major destination for gay and lesbians since 2000, when state law acknowledged civil unions. A local backlash (marked by TAKE BACK VERMONT signs) has arisen in response to passage of the law, but opponents have so far failed to get the law repealed. For information on Vermont civil unions, consult the state-run website **http://www.sec.state.vt.us/municipal/civil_mar.htm.**

Ogunquit, on the southern Maine coast, is a hugely popular destination among gay travelers and features a lively beach and bar scene in the summer. In winter, it's mellower. One place to learn more about the local and tourist community is at the website **www.gayogunquit.com**, which has good information on gay-owned inns, restaurants, and nightclubs around town.

For a more detailed directory of gay-oriented enterprises in New England, including coverage of northern New England, check out the *Pink Pages* (**www.pinkweb. com**), a useful website based in Boston.

Travelers with Disabilities

Most disabilities shouldn't stop anyone from traveling to New England. There are more options and resources out there than ever before—even if some older parks and small inns still have ancient stairs that can prove difficult for the mobility-challenged. Check ahead if this is an issue for you.

Public transit in all New England's major cities—Portland, Boston, Providence, Manchester, Burlington, and so forth—is special-accessible, and so are buses that connect some smaller towns and cities. All chain business hotels and resorts can be assumed to be special-accessible, but smaller inns (even luxury inns) and bed-and-breakfasts sometimes aren't; it depends on the age and architecture of the individual property, and whether ownership has renovated. If this is a critical factor for you, call the property in advance of booking and ask.

The free **America the Beautiful** national parks pass (formerly known as **Golden Access Passport**) gives visually impaired or persons with permanent disabilities (regardless of age) **free lifetime entrance to federal recreation sites** administered by the National Park Service (which includes the Fish and Wildlife Service, Forest Service, Bureau of Land Management, and Bureau of Reclamation). It's especially useful here because the bearer gains entry into **Acadia National**

Park, the **White Mountain National Forest,** and the **Green Mountain National Forest.** Other monuments, historic sites, recreation areas, and national wildlife refuges are also covered by the pass.

The pass can be obtained only in person, at any Park Service facility that charges an entrance fee. You need to show proof of medically determined disability. Besides free entry, the pass also offers a 50% discount on some federal-use fees charged for such facilities as camping, swimming, parking, boat launching, and tours. For more information, go to the **Park Service** website at **www.nps.gov/fees_passes.htm,** or call ℭ **888/467-2757.**

Family Travel

Families have little trouble finding fun, low-key things to do with kids in New England. The natural world seems to hold tremendous wonder for the younger set—an afternoon exploring mossy banks and rocky streambeds can be a huge adventure. Older kids may like the challenge of climbing a mountain peak or learning to paddle a canoe in a straight line, and the beach is always good for hours of afternoon diversion.

Be sure to ask about **family discounts** when visiting attractions. Many places offer a flat family rate that is less than paying for each ticket individually. Some parks and beaches charge by the car rather than the head.

Also, when planning your trip be aware that certain small inns cater only to couples and prefer that families not stay there, or at least request that children be a certain **minimum age.** This guidebook notes the recommended age for children where restrictions apply, but it's always best to ask first, just to be safe. At any rate, if you mention that you're traveling with kids when making reservations, often you'll get accommodations nearer the game room or the pool, making everyone's life a bit easier.

Recommended destinations in New England for families include **Lake Winnipesaukee** and **Lake Sunapee** in New Hampshire (for splashing around and kid-friendly attractions); **York Beach** and **Acadia National Park** in Maine (ditto); **Waterbury,** Vermont, for its famous ice-cream factory; and **Cape Cod,** for its splendiferous beaches. **North Conway,** New Hampshire, and **Freeport,** Maine, also make good bases for families with young kids; each town has a supply of hotels and motels with swimming pools, plus great shopping and—in the case of North Conway—such attractions as minitrain rides, streams for splashing around in, easy hikes, and the kid-friendly attraction Story Land.

To locate accommodations, restaurants, and attractions that are particularly kid-friendly, look for the "Kids" icon throughout this guide.

Senior Travel

New England is well suited to older travelers, with a wide array of activities for seniors and very low crime rates. Mention the fact that you're a senior whenever you make your travel reservations. Throughout the region, travelers over the age of 60 qualify for reduced or free admission to theaters, museums, ski resorts, and other attractions, as well as discounted fares on public transportation.

The U.S. National Park Service offers an **America the Beautiful Senior Pass** (formerly the **Golden Age Passport**), which gives seniors 62 years or older lifetime entrance to all properties administered by the National Park Service—including Acadia National Park, the White Mountain and Green Mountain national forests, monuments, historic sites, recreation areas, and national wildlife refuges—for a one-time processing fee of $10. The pass must be purchased in person at any NPS facility that charges an entrance fee. Besides free entry, the American the Beautiful Senior Pass also offers a 50% discount on some federal-use fees charged for such facilities as camping, swimming, parking, boat launching, and tours. For more information, go to **www.nps.gov/fees_passes.htm**, or call 🕾 **888/467-2757.**

Members of **AARP,** 601 E St. NW, Washington, DC 20049 (🕾 **888/687-2277;** www.aarp.org), get discounts on hotels, airfares, and car rentals. AARP offers members a wide range of benefits, including *AARP The Magazine* and a monthly newsletter. Anyone 50 or older can join.

Traveling with Pets

Some places allow pets, some don't. This guide notes inns that allow pets, but even so, you shouldn't show up anywhere with a pet in tow unless you've cleared it with the innkeeper ahead of time. Note that many establishments have only one or two rooms (often a cottage or room with exterior entrance) set aside for guests traveling with pets, and they won't be quite so happy to see Fido if the "pet room" is already occupied. Also, it's common for a surcharge (usually $10–$20 per pet, per night) to be added to your bill to cover the extra cleaning effort made by housekeeping staff.

Several websites dispense tips and list animal-friendly lodgings and campgrounds: **www.petswelcome.com**, **www.pettravel.com**, and **www.travelpets.com** together contain thousands of listings. Also note that all **Motel 6** hotel properties accept leashed, "well-behaved" pets.

Keep in mind that dogs are prohibited on most hiking trails, and must be leashed at all times on federal lands administered by the National Park Service (which includes **Acadia National Park** in ME). Pets are allowed to hike off-leash in the **White Mountains National Forest** in New Hampshire and the **Green Mountain National Forest** in Vermont, but you must be able to control yours by voice. No pets are allowed at any time (leashed or unleashed) at **Baxter State Park** in Maine. Some other Maine state parks do allow pets on a leash.

RESPONSIBLE TOURISM

Parts of New England are so wild and unpopulated that any travel in those regions (the White Mountains, ME's North Woods and Baxter State Park, and certain passes in the Green Mountains) automatically qualifies as "ecotravel"; you can't be among icy peaks and bears and *not* be ecotouring. But is this travel responsible? Is it "green"?

Local Resources

In New England, I've found that local statewide chapters of the National Audubon Society and The Nature Conservancy turn out to be some of the very best resources. Each of these offices runs education programs and tours and maintains trail systems and nature preserves.

In Maine, the **Maine Audubon Society** (20 Gilsland Farm Rd., Falmouth; 🕾 **207/781-2330;** www.maineaudubon.org) maintains an impressive nature center and extensive grounds just 10 miles north of Portland. It's a good spot to bird-watch. The Maine chapter of **The Nature Conservancy** (14 Main St., Brunswick; 🕾 **207/729-5181;** www.nature.org) has a small office in a Brunswick mill complex but maintains a *huge* selection of parks, preserves, and other natural areas through-out the state—absolutely consult them on places to go.

In New Hampshire, contact the **Society for the Preservation of New Hampshire Forests** (54 Portsmouth St., Concord; ✆ **603/224-9945;** www.spnhf.org) and **New Hampshire Audubon** (84 Silk Farm Rd., Concord; ✆ **603/224-9909;** www.nhaudubon.org). In Massachusetts, the **Massachusetts Audubon Society** (208 S. Great Rd., Littleton; ✆ **781/259-9500;** www.massaudubon.org.) must be one of the nation's most active chapters, maintaining everything from island beaches holding rare birds to a farm converted into an education center. Its headquarters are a quick drive or train ride from downtown Boston.

In Connecticut, the **Connecticut Audubon Society** (2325 Burr St., Fairfield; ✆ **203/259-6305;** www.ctaudubon.org) maintains impressive bird-watching and hiking areas plus a kid-friendly headquarters and nature center. In Rhode Island, it's the **Audubon Society of Rhode Island** (12 Sanderson Rd., Smithfield; ✆ **401/949-5454;** asri.org) you want to see.

If you *really* want to travel responsibly, consider a hiking or inn-to-inn bike tour. Boston cycling maps and tips are available from the **Massachusetts Bicycle Coalition** (171 Milk St., Boston ✆ **617/542-2453;** www.massbike.org). In New Hampshire, get in touch with the club known as the **Granite State Wheelmen** (www.granitestatewheelmen.org).

Also ask about "green" ecotour outfits that take care to leave only small footprints on the landscapes they're traveling through. These sorts of outfitters bring small groups into the wilderness, and they usually use "light" transportation methods (kayaks, sailboats, snowshoes, bicycles, what-have-you) while traveling in them. They might also contribute a portion of their profits to wildlife organizations or land trusts, or pay for carbon "credits" to offset the fuel they use.

New England's six state tourism offices can point you to these sorts of outfitters and many additional resources. So can the various local tourism offices dotting the region's villages, towns, and cities. All you need to do is ask.

IT'S EASY BEING GREEN

We can all help conserve fuel and energy when we travel. Here are a few simple ways you can help preserve your favorite destinations:

o Whenever possible, choose non-stop flights; they generally require less fuel than those that must stop and take off again.

o If renting a car is necessary, ask the rental agent for the most fuel-efficient model available. Not only will you use less gas, but you'll also save money at the pump.

o At hotels, request that your sheets and towels not be changed daily. You'll save water and energy by not washing them as often, and you'll prolong the life of the towels, too. (Many hotels already have programs like this in place.)

o Turn off the lights and air-conditioner or heater when you exit your hotel room.

o info on volunteer travel, visit **www.volunteerabroad.org** and **www.idealist.org**.

General Tips

Every time you take a flight or drive a car, carbon dioxide is released into the atmosphere. Although one could argue that any vacation that includes an airplane flight or use of a car can't be truly called "green," you can still contribute positively to the environment while on vacation. Choose forward-looking companies that embrace responsible development practices and help preserve destinations for the future. An increasing number of sustainable tourism initiatives can help you plan a family trip and leave as small a "footprint" as possible.

Responsibletravel.com, run by a spokesperson for responsible tourism in the travel industry, contains a great source of sustainable travel ideas.

You can find eco-friendly travel tips, statistics, and touring companies and associations—listed by destination under "Travel Choice"—at the International Ecotoursm Society (TIES) website, **www.ecotourism.org**. Also check out **Conservation International** (www.conservation.org), which, with *National Geographic Traveler,* annually presents **World Legacy Awards** to those travel tour operators, businesses, organizations, and places that have made a significant contribution to sustainable tourism. **Ecotravel.com** is part online magazine and part eco-directory that lets you search for touring companies in several categories (water-based, land-based, spiritually oriented, and so on).

Whale-watching is popular from some parts of the Maine coast. For information about the whales you'll be glimpsing (and how to respect them), visit the **Whale and Dolphin Conservation Society** (www.wdcs.org). For info on traveling lightly in general, see **Tread Lightly** (www.treadlightly.org) online.

SPECIAL-INTEREST & ESCORTED TRIPS

Outdoors-Oriented Trips

One rewarding way to spend a vacation is to learn a new outdoor skill or add to your knowledge. You can find plenty of options in New England, ranging from formal weeklong classes to 1-day workshops. Here are three of the best:

o **Learn to fly-fish on New England's fabled rivers.** Among the region's most respected schools are the two offered on-site by the region's outdoor equipment powerhouses: **Orvis** (© 888/235-9763 for retail, © 866/531-6213 for fly-fishing classes) in Manchester, Vermont; and **L.L.Bean** (© 800/441-5713) in Freeport, Maine. L.L.Bean also offers a number of workshops on many *other* outdoor skills through its outstanding **Outdoor Discovery Program;** call © 888/552-3261 for information about the program.

o **Learn about birds and coastal ecosystems in Maine.** Budding and experienced naturalists can expand their understanding of marine wildlife while residing on 333-acre Hog Island in Maine's wild and scenic Muscongus Bay through the **Maine Audubon Society,** 20 Gilsland Farm Rd., Falmouth, ME 04105 (© 207/781-2330; www.maineaudubon.org). Famed birder Roger Tory Peterson once taught birding classes here, and I can personally vouch for Maine Audubon's educational programs. Call or visit their lovely headquarters just north of Portland.

o **Sharpen your outdoor skills.** The **Appalachian Mountain Club,** 5 Joy St., Boston, MA 02108 (© **800/372-1758** or 617/523-0636; www.outdoors.org), offers a full roster of outdoor adventure classes, many taught at the club's Pinkham Notch Camp at the base of New Hampshire's Mount Washington. You could learn outdoor photography, wild mushroom identification, or backcountry orienteering. In winter, ice-climbing and telemark-skiing lessons are taught in the White Mountains. Course fees often include accommodations, and most are reasonably priced. Call or write for a catalog.

New England also especially lends itself to outdoorsy adventures that combine fresh air and exercise with Mother Nature as your instructor in a vast, beautiful classroom. For special-interest trips of an even more active type, see "The Active Traveler," below.

Historic Tours

Historic New England is a nonprofit foundation that owns and operates 36 historical properties around New England, ranging from places built in the 17th century to the present, including a number of properties profiled in this book.

Members get into all of the organization's properties for free and receive a number of other benefits, including a subscription to *Historic New England* magazine; a guide to the group's properties; and invitations to members-only events and other perks. Memberships cost $45 per year for individuals or $55 for an entire household.

For more information on Historic New England and its properties, visit the group's website at **www.historicnewengland.org**, or call the organization's Boston headquarters at © **617/227-3956.**

Escorted General-Interest Tours

Escorted tours are structured group tours, with a group leader. The price usually includes everything from airfare to hotels, meals, tours, admission costs, and local transportation.

Despite the fact that these tours require big deposits and predetermine nearly all of your hotels, restaurants, and itineraries, many people crave the sort of structure they offer. And it's true—they do let you sit back and enjoy a trip without having to drive *or* worry about the little details. They take you to a maximum number of sights, in the minimum amount of time, usually with the least amount of hassle. They're particularly convenient for people with limited mobility, and they can be a great way to make new friends.

On the downside, though, you get little opportunity for interaction with locals. Escorted tours are generally jam-packed with activities, leaving little room for individual whims. And they often focus on only the most heavily touristed sites, so you might miss out on some off-the-beaten-track gems.

Still, if you're interested, dozens of companies operate bus and van tours of New England. **Tauck World Discovery** in Norwalk, CT (© **800/788-7885;** www. tauck.com), is just one of the many outfits offering fall foliage tours of New England, for instance—they even have a resident "foliologist" (and no, that isn't really a word) on staff to monitor the peak leaf color in various spots. Tauck's "Grand Autumn in New England" tour covers four of the six states in this book, and sleeps overnight in hotels and inns in the region for most of its 11 nights.

Consult your travel agent for additional options. And, for even more information on escorted tours—including a list of useful questions to ask before booking your trip—see our own website at **www.frommers.com/planning**.

THE ACTIVE TRAVELER

New England is a superb destination for those who don't consider a vacation to be a vacation unless it takes place far, far away from buildings and cars. Hiking, canoeing, and skiing are among the most popular outdoor activities here, but you can also try rock climbing, sea kayaking, mountain biking, road biking, sailing, winter mountaineering, and snowmobiling.

The farther north you go in this region, the more remote and wild the terrain becomes. For pointers on where to head, see the section "Enjoying the Great Outdoors" in the subsequent chapters, where you'll also find detailed information on local services and outfitters, when appropriate.

General Advice

The ideal way to enjoy the outdoors here is to head for public lands where the natural landscape has been best preserved. The wildest areas in New England include the Green Mountain National Forest in Vermont, the White Mountain National Forest in New Hampshire, and Baxter State Park and Acadia National Park in Maine. Use this book to help pick the best area for what you want to experience. You can often find adventure-travel outfitters and suppliers in towns around the fringes of these parks.

Once you've zeroed in the area you will visit, a bit of advice: Stay put. I've run across too many gung-ho travelers who try to bite off too much—some biking in Vermont, a little hiking in the White Mountains or Berkshire Hills, and then maybe some kayaking and lobsters in Maine. All in a week! That's a good formula for developing a close personal relationship with the highway, not relaxation. I advise you to pick one area, settle in for a few days or a week, and explore locally by foot, canoe, or kayak. This will give you time to enjoy an extra hour lounging at a remote lake or camping in the backcountry. You'll also learn a lot more about the area. In my experience, few travelers regret planning to do too little on their vacations to New England, but plenty of visitors regret having tried to do too much.

Travelers used to hire guides just to ensure that they would later be able to find their ways back *out* of the woods. With development encroaching on so many once-pristine areas of New England, it's now sometimes useful to have guides help you find your way *into* the woods and away from civilization's long reach. Clear-cuts, second-home developments, and trails teeming with weekend hikers are obstacles to be avoided—and a good dose of local knowledge is the cure; it's the best way I know to find the most alluring (and least congested) spots.

Basically, you've got three options: Hire a guide, sign up for a guided trip, or dig up the essential information yourself.

Guided Tours

The phenomenon of guided tours in New England has exploded in recent years, in both number and variety. These range from 2-night guided inn-to-inn hiking trips to weeklong canoe and kayak expeditions, camping each night along the way. Below are a few reputable outfitters to get you started.

- **Allagash Canoe Trips,** P.O. Box 932, Greenville, ME 04441 (☏ **207/237-3077;** www.allagashcanoetrips.com), leads 5- to 7-day canoe trips down Maine's noted and wild Allagash River and other local rivers. You provide a sleeping bag and clothing; they take care of everything else.
- **BattenKill Canoe Ltd.,** 6328 Historic Rte. 7A, Arlington, VT 05250 (☏ **800/421-5268** or 802/362-2800; www.battenkill.com), runs guided canoeing and walking excursions in Vermont (as well as abroad). Nights are spent at quiet inns.
- **Bike the Whites,** P.O. Box 1785, North Conway, NH 03865 (☏ **800/421-1785;** www.bikethewhites.com), offers self-guided biking tours between three inns in the White Mountains, with each day requiring about 20 miles of biking. Luggage is shuttled from inn to inn.
- **Country Walkers,** P.O. Box 180, Waterbury, VT 05676 (☏ **800/464-9255** or 802/244-1387; www.countrywalkers.com), has a glorious color catalog (more like a wish book) outlining supported walking trips around the world. Among the offerings: walking tours in coastal Maine and north-central Vermont. Trips generally run 4 to 5 nights and include all meals and lodging at appealing inns.
- **Maine Island Kayak Co.,** 70 Luther St., Peaks Island, ME 04108 (☏ **207/766-2373;** www.maineislandkayak.com), has a fleet of seaworthy kayaks for camping trips up and down the Maine coast, as well as to such places as Canada and Belize. The firm has a number of 2- and 3-night expeditions every summer and plenty of experience in training novices.
- **New England Hiking Holidays,** P.O. Box 1648, North Conway, NH 03860 (☏ **800/869-0949** or 603/356-9696; www.nehikingholidays.com), has an extensive inventory of trips, including weekend trips in the White Mountains, as well as more extended excursions to the Maine coast, Vermont, and overseas. Trips typically involve moderate day hiking coupled with nights at comfortable lodges.
- **Vermont Bicycle Touring,** P.O. 614 Monkton Rd., Bristol, VT 05443 (☏ **800/245-3868;** www.vbt.com), is one of the more established and well-organized touring operations, with an extensive bike tour schedule in North America, Europe, and New Zealand. VBT offers several trips apiece in both Vermont and Maine, including a 6-day Acadia trip with some overnights at the grand Claremont Hotel.

For More Information

Guidebooks to the region's backcountry are plentiful and diverse. **L.L.Bean**'s headquarters in Freeport, Maine (plus a half-dozen outlet stores scattered through the region), as well the **Green Mountain Club**'s head office in Waterbury, Vermont (see below), each stock excellent selections of local guidebooks, as do bookshops throughout the region. An exhaustive collection of New England outdoor guidebooks for sale may be found online at **www.mountainwanderer.com**, a company based right in the White Mountains of New Hampshire. The **Appalachian Mountain Club,** 5 Joy St., Boston, MA 02108 (☏ **800/262-4455** or 617/523-0636; www.outdoors.org), publishes a number of definitive guides to hiking and boating in the region.

Map Adventures, P.O. Box 15214, Portland, ME 04112 (☏ **207/879-4777**), is a small firm that publishes a growing line of good recreational maps covering popular New England areas, including the Stowe and Mad River Valley areas, the Camden Hills of Maine, Acadia National Park, and the White Mountains. See what they offer online at **www.mapadventures.com**.

Local outing clubs are also a good source of information, and most offer trips to nonmembers. The largest of the bunch is the Appalachian Mountain Club, whose chapters run group trips almost every weekend throughout the region, with northern New Hampshire especially well represented. Another active group is the **Green Mountain Club,** 4711 Waterbury–Stowe Rd., Waterbury Center, VT 05677 (✆ **802/244-7037;** www.greenmountainclub.org).

STAYING CONNECTED

Mobile Phones

Just because your cellphone works at home doesn't mean it'll work deep in the woods of northern Maine—or even at that rustic country B&B, thanks to our nation's (and the region's) fragmented and competing cellphone coverage systems. You may or may not be within your roaming area, even if you have a national calling plan. It's a good bet that your phone will work in the region's major cities, but look over your wireless company's coverage map on its website before heading out to be sure; T-Mobile, Sprint, and Nextel are particularly weak at covering rural areas here.

If you're not from the U.S., you'll be appalled at the poor reach of the **GSM wireless network** (which is used by much of the rest of the world) here. Your phone will probably work in most cities and interstate corridors in New England, and along much of the southern Maine coast; but it definitely *won't* work in most of the rural areas, which means nearly all the rest of the region. You also may or may not be able to send SMS (text messages) home.

You can **rent a cellphone** at any major airport in this region, and *buy* a cellphone (without a long-term contract, in most cases) in the downtown districts of towns and cities as well as at airports.

Internet & E-mail

Cities in New England of all sizes, from Boston and Hartford to Portland and Burlington, always have a couple of **cybercafes;** in small towns and rural areas, though, it's often hit-or-miss (usually miss).

Most **airports** in the region either have **Internet kiosks** that provide basic Web access for a per-minute fee, or **Wi-Fi access** free or for a charge. (In first-class lounges, it's almost always free.)

Starbucks coffee shops, which are spreading ever deeper into the region, offer free, unlimited access to Wi-Fi in their many (many) outlets.

New England's **public libraries** are also surprisingly generous about offering Internet access, nearly always for free; you may need to submit a driver's license or library card or other piece of identification as a deposit.

Business hotels and a surprising number of New England's inns, motels, and even campgrounds are also offering Wi-Fi hotspot access, often free (the more expensive the hotel, the more likely it is that there will be a charge).

Newspapers & Magazines

Almost every small city and town in New England has a daily or weekly newspaper covering local happenings. The largest **daily papers** include the *Boston Globe* (Massachusetts), *Hartford Courant* (Connecticut), *Portland Press Herald* (Maine), *Manchester Union Leader* (New Hampshire), and the *Burlington Free Press* (Vermont).

Boston, Burlington, Portland, and a few other cities also offer **free alternative weekly papers** that are handy sources of information on concerts and shows at local clubs.

The *Wall Street Journal* and the *New York Times* are distributed widely throughout New England, though they can be difficult to find in some small or remote towns.

Telephones

Generally, hotel surcharges on long-distance and local calls are astronomical, so you're better off using your **cellphone** or a **public pay phone.** Most convenience stores in New England sell **prepaid calling cards** in denominations of up to $50; for international visitors, these can be the least expensive way to call home. Many public pay phones at airports now accept American Express, MasterCard, and Visa credit cards directly. Local calls made from a pay phone in most of New England cost from 25¢ to 50¢ each; pennies aren't accepted.

Most long-distance and international calls can be dialed directly from any phone. **For calls within the United States and to Canada,** dial 1 followed by the area code and the seven-digit number. **For other international calls,** dial 011 followed by the country code, city code, and the number you are calling.

For **collect** or person-to-person calls, dial the number 0 then the area code and number; an operator will come on the line, and you should specify whether you are calling collect, person-to-person, or both. If your operator-assisted call is international, ask for the overseas operator.

For **local directory assistance** ("information") in most towns in New England, dial ℂ **411;** for long-distance information, dial 1, plus the appropriate area code, plus ℂ **555-1212.**

Calls to area codes **800, 888, 877,** and **866** are toll-free. However, calls to area codes **700** and **900** (chat lines, bulletin boards, "dating" services, and so on) can be expensive—charges of 95¢ to $3 or more per minute. Some numbers have minimum charges that can run $15 or more.

TIPS ON ACCOMMODATIONS

"The more we travel," said an unhappy couple one morning at a New Hampshire inn, "the more we realize why we go back to our old favorites time and again." The reason for their grumpiness? They had been forced to switch rooms at 2 o'clock in the morning because rain began dripping onto them through the ceiling.

They're hardly the first victims. New England is famous for its plethora of country inns and bed-and-breakfasts (B&Bs), which offer a wonderful alternative to the sort of cookie-cutter, chain-hotel rooms that line most U.S. highways from coast to coast. But (as this unhappy couple learned) there are *reasons* why some people prefer the cookie-cutter hotels. In a chain hotel, you can be reasonably sure that water won't drip through your ceiling in the middle of the night. At the inns, you sometimes get drips, creaks, and quirks with the territory. (Stick to two- and three-star recommendations in this book if you want to avoid such quirkiness.)

Still, every **inn** and **B&B** listed in this guide yields a decent—often a high-quality—experience. Just keep in mind that every place is different, and you need to match the personality of the place with your own. Some inns are more polished than others. Even those calling themselves "resorts" might lack the luxury-hotel amenities to which business travelers have grown accustomed in chain hotels, such as in-room phones, air-conditioning, and Wi-Fi access. If you need these things, call the hotel ahead and ask about them—and read our listings carefully (including the listings details at the end of each write-up).

*A **note on hotel smoking policies:*** Most hotels in New England still maintain separate smoking and nonsmoking rooms and/or floors. If you're sensitive to cigarette smoke, be sure to book a nonsmoking room. Inns and bed-and-breakfasts generally ban smoking completely within, though some (not many) allow it on outdoor patios, in yards, or in other restricted areas.

SUGGESTED NEW ENGLAND ITINERARIES

Getting to know New England requires equal amounts of patience and persistence. Your most memorable experience might come at a roadside lobster pound marked only with a scrawled paper sign, at the end of a hiking trail that overlooks a peaceful lake, or while exploring a cobblestone alley that's not on any map.

Racing around with a checklist and a beat-the-clock attitude is a recipe for disaster. The happiest visitors to New England are those who stay awhile in one spot, getting to know a manageable area through well-crafted day trips. Read on for strategies that can help you organize your time.

BOSTON & VICINITY IN 1 WEEK

Basing yourself in Boston or Cambridge is a good way to get to know eastern Massachusetts while not limiting yourself to one destination. On this itinerary, you'll get a taste of Boston and Cambridge, then set out on day trips to the history-rich suburbs. You'll go in roughly chronological order: Start in Plymouth with the Pilgrims; move on to Lexington and Concord to learn about the rebellious colonists; and finally, visit the North Shore, which flourished after the Revolution. If you're renting a car, note that you don't need it for the full week—pick it up on (and don't start paying for it until) Day 4.

Days 1 & 2: Boston ★★★

Begin exploring downtown Boston by walking at least part of the 2.5-mile **Freedom Trail** (p. 121). The whole shebang can be an all-day affair, but I suggest concentrating on the first two-thirds of the trail, from **Boston Common** through **Faneuil Hall.** Break for lunch at **Faneuil Hall Marketplace** (p. 118), then head into the

Suggested New England Itineraries

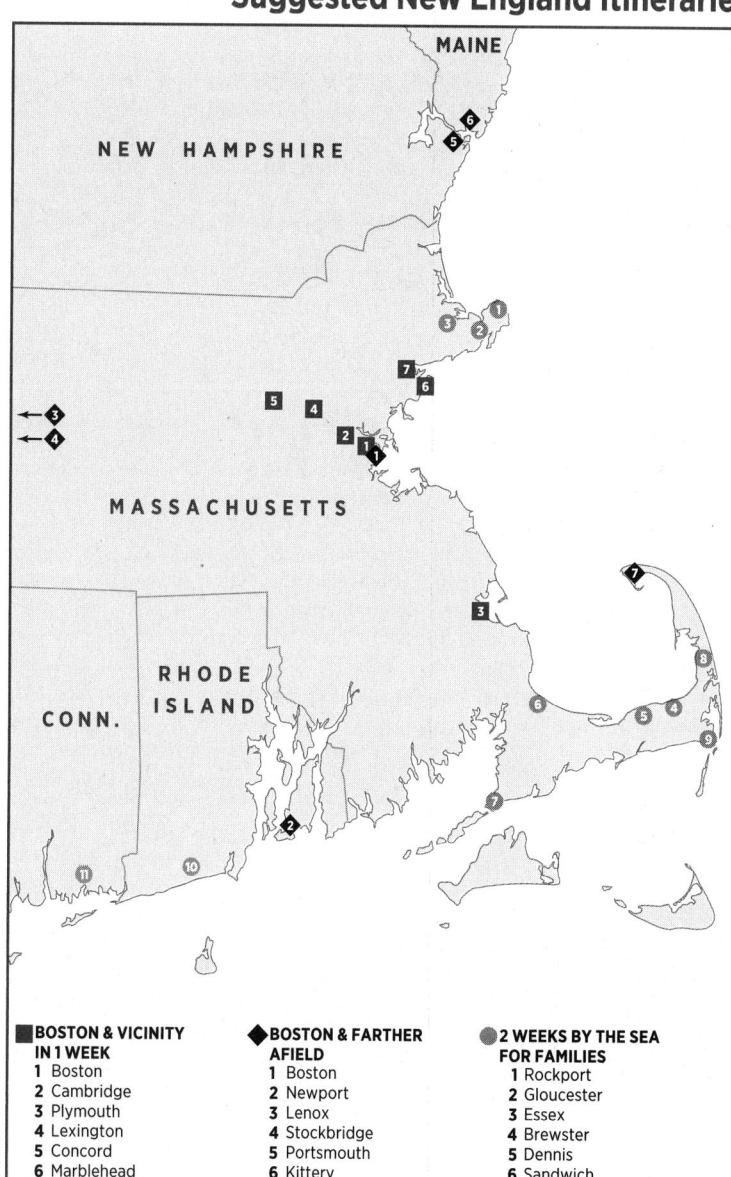

■ BOSTON & VICINITY IN 1 WEEK
1 Boston
2 Cambridge
3 Plymouth
4 Lexington
5 Concord
6 Marblehead
7 Salem

◆ BOSTON & FARTHER AFIELD
1 Boston
2 Newport
3 Lenox
4 Stockbridge
5 Portsmouth
6 Kittery
7 Provincetown

● 2 WEEKS BY THE SEA FOR FAMILIES
1 Rockport
2 Gloucester
3 Essex
4 Brewster
5 Dennis
6 Sandwich
7 Woods Hole
8 Cape Cod National Seashore
9 Chatham
10 South County
11 Mystic

North End for a stroll on the main drag, **Hanover Street,** and a visit to the **Paul Revere House** (p. 123), one of my favorite Boston attractions. From there, it's an easy walk to Long Wharf or Rowes Wharf, where you can take a **sightseeing cruise** (p. 125) or, if you want to save time and money, a **ferry ride** (p. 88) to the Charlestown Navy Yard and back. Have dinner at **Legal Sea Foods** (p. 105) on Long Wharf, or return to the North End for Italian food.

On Day 2, prearrange tickets for a **Boston Duck Tour** (p. 126), ideally one that leaves from the Prudential Center in the early afternoon. Be at the **Museum of Fine Arts** (p. 120) when it opens; consider taking a tour to give you an overview before you explore on your own. Head to the Back Bay for lunch and your Duck Tour, then make a beeline for the retail delights of **Newbury Street.** Newbury dead-ends at the **Public Garden** (p. 124), where you can unwind and perhaps go for a spin on a **Swan Boat** (p. 124). For dinner, check out Boston's take on French cuisine at **Brasserie Jo** (p. 113) or **Petit Robert Bistro**.

Day 3: Cambridge ★★

Start in **Harvard Square** (p. 127) with a student-led or self-guided tour of the main Harvard campus. Up next are the treasures of the **Harvard Art Museum,** currently under one roof at the Sackler Museum as the complex's other two buildings undergo extensive renovations (p. 129); you may prefer the **natural history museums,** especially if children are along. Then head to lovely Brattle Street and the **Longfellow National Historic Site** (p. 130). From there, walk along Massachusetts Avenue toward Porter Square, a route with some excellent shopping opportunities. In fact, this whole day represents a fantastic chance to mix shopping and snacking with sightseeing. Have dinner at **Mr. Bartley's Burger Cottage** (p. 116), then hit a bookstore or two.

Day 4: Plymouth ★★

Spend a day with the Pilgrims. Start with a 17th-century reality check at **Plimoth Plantation** (p. 191), which opens at 9am. The hands-on activities are almost as much fun as mingling with the "settlers," who stay in character as they chat with visitors. In downtown Plymouth, have lunch at the **Lobster Hut** (p. 194), where the deck overlooks the harbor, then explore a bit, starting at **Plymouth Rock** (p. 190). Take in some historic attractions—the *Mayflower II* (p. 190) is next to the Rock, and the **Pilgrim Hall Museum** (p. 190) is nearby—before returning to Boston or Cambridge for dinner.

Day 5: Lexington ★ & Concord ★★★

Spend most of the morning in **Lexington** (p. 150), acquainting yourself with the earliest events of the Revolutionary War and visiting the historic **Buckman Tavern** (p. 152). Have lunch in Concord and explore the beautiful town, choosing the destinations and events that particularly interest you. I suggest starting with the **Concord Museum** (p. 156), touring **Orchard House** (p. 156), and stopping at **Walden Pond** (p. 159) on the way back into town, perhaps for a picnic dinner.

Day 6: Boston & Cambridge

After 2 days on the road, stick close to "home." Head to Dorchester and the **John F. Kennedy Library and Museum** (p. 119), which is accessible by public transit and offers free parking (you're paying for that rental car, so you might as well get some use out of it). Spend the afternoon at the **Museum of Science** (p. 120), allowing enough time for an IMAX film, if that appeals to you.

Day 7: Marblehead ★★★ & Salem ★★

Begin your day on the picturesque streets of Old Town **Marblehead** (p. 162), a top destination for both sightseeing and shopping. If your hotel room rate doesn't include breakfast, arrive hungry and make a dent in a stack of pancakes at the **Driftwood Restaurant** (p. 165). The **Jeremiah Lee Mansion** (p. 163) is a must if you enjoy house tours. Spend the afternoon in **Salem** (p. 165), where the can't-miss destination is the **Peabody Essex Museum** (p. 165); if time allows, also visit the **Salem Witch Museum** (p. 169). This itinerary leaves you in a handy location for returning to Boston or for heading out to explore the wonders of northern New England.

BOSTON & FARTHER AFIELD

The 10-towns-in-6-days bus tours that clog the highways and byways of the Northeast every fall miss the point: The goal of a savvy traveler to New England is an experience that's deeper than it is wide. But even I'll admit to a fondness for day trips that take me just a bit out of my comfort zone. Each of these excursions is about as long as you'd want a day trip to be—and can easily work as an overnight journey. Tackle this itinerary before or after a visit to Boston and Cambridge, or as a tune-up for another of the trips in this chapter. On the first 3 days, an extra driver will come in handy; on the 4th day, there's no driving at all.

Day 1: Newport ★★★

If you don't hit traffic, you can cover the 75 or so miles between Boston and Newport in a little over an hour. The city's top attractions are the "cottages"—Newport-speak for "mansions"—that line Bellevue Avenue along the magnificent shore. Don't attempt to tour more than two **cottages** (p. 446) in a day, partly because they all start to run together, and partly because you'll want to leave time for exploring the picturesque downtown area. Between the glorious scenery and the serendipitous shopping, Newport is a perfect place to while away an afternoon. Linger into the evening for a drink or dinner near the water.

Day 2: The Berkshires ★★

Try to schedule this trip to coincide with a morning rehearsal or afternoon concert by the **Boston Symphony Orchestra** at **Tanglewood** (p. 350), in Lenox. It's a long ride (at least 2 hr.) from Boston, so you'll want to get an early start, especially if you're attending a rehearsal. Spread out a blanket, picnic on the lawn, and enjoy the scene, one of the hallmarks of summer in New England. After rehearsal or before and after a concert, select one western Massachusetts town to explore, but just one—crowds and traffic dictate that you not try to get too ambitious. My choice is **Stockbridge** (p. 343), because I'm a sucker for the **Norman Rockwell Museum** (p. 345).

Day 3: Portsmouth ★★ & Kittery ★

A little over an hour from Boston is a gem of historic architecture, maritime sights and sounds, funky shops and cafes, and beautiful scenery. Portsmouth is worth a trip just for **Strawbery Banke** (p. 558), where the historic buildings *are* the displays. Build in some time to explore the cobblestone downtown area, then cross the Piscataqua River for some serious shopping at the **Kittery** outlets and a bite to eat at **Bob's Clam Hut** (p. 600).

Day 4: Provincetown ★★★

Ferries (conventional and high-speed) connect Boston to **Provincetown** (p. 253) every day in the summer and on weekends in the spring and fall. The trip by car is absolutely punishing, especially on a busy weekend, but an ocean voyage is always a good idea. On a day trip, you'll have time for world-class people-watching, strolling along **Commercial Street,** perusing the novelty shops and art galleries, lunching on seafood, and—if you're quick—a trip to one of the famous beaches. However, you'll have to forgo the hopping gay nightlife scene unless you've planned a longer excursion.

A WEEK BY THE SEA FOR FAMILIES

A family can easily spend a pleasant week or so exploring the beaches, boats, cobblestones, shops, museums, and attractions of coastal Maine and New Hampshire.

Days 1 & 2: Portland ★★★

Portland is a joy for families. The **Children's Museum of Maine** (p. 615) is almost exactly in the center of town, making it a good jumping-off point for a city tour. The excellent **Portland Museum of Art** (p. 617), right next door, provides teens and college-age family members with something different to do.

In the historic **Old Port** (p. 615), Exchange Street is the key shopping address. Kids will enjoy the ice-cream shops, boats, and quirky gift stores. The city tourist office is on Commercial Street.

The **Maine Narrow Gauge Railroad Co. & Museum** (p. 616) combines a short train ride to the foot of the cliffs framing Portland's east end with a museum.

Another great experience is a cruise on the **Casco Bay Ferry** (p. 615) lines. You can take anything from a 20-minute run to a half-day "mail boat" cruise. Two good destinations are **Peaks Island**—a favorite among parents pushing strollers, with easy-to-cruise streets and Portland views—and **Long Island,** which has an excellent beach.

For baseball fans, an outing to Hadlock Field to watch the **Portland Sea Dogs** (p. 618) can't be beat; it's one of our favorite minor-league parks.

Finally, young and old alike enjoy the sunsets, picnics, sailboat views, and swing sets of the park along the **Eastern Promenade** (p. 615).

Day 3: Cape Elizabeth ★★

Plan to spend at least one afternoon hitting the string of beaches and light-houses off Rte. 77 in the quiet town of **Cape Elizabeth** and surrounds, just 15 minutes from Portland.

Kids will especially enjoy the **Portland Head Light** (p. 616) and romping around in the sand and surf on **Crescent, Scarborough,** and **Willard beaches.**

Day 4: Old Orchard Beach ★

Drive 20 minutes south of Portland and you come to **Old Orchard Beach.** This place may strike you as corny at first, but it rarely fails to entertain. On the pier out over the water, you can find cotton candy, french fries, and arcade games. There's also a long beach to stroll along.

Day 5: Ogunquit ★★

About 40 minutes south of Old Orchard is **Ogunquit** (p. 602), which offers enough distractions for a few days. In addition to a main street full of shops, restaurants, and cafes, it has a main beach that's a vast stretch of powdery sand at low tide and has some of Maine's warmest ocean water (which isn't saying much!). **Perkins Cove** (p. 602) has sea views, ice-cream and candy shops, an excellent small bookstore, and lots of souvenirs for sale.

Day 6: York ★★★ and Kittery ★

Only a 10-minute drive south, these twin towns offer a lot for families. **York** (p. 594) has a dynamite lighthouse (with homemade ice cream nearby), an amusement arcade, several excellent beaches, and the **Goldenrod** (p. 600), a candy store where kids can watch taffy being pulled. You can buy boxes to take home—half the fun is deciding which candies to buy. **Kittery** (p. 594) is more for adults, but its extensive set of outlet stores also appeals to teen shopaholics.

Day 7: Portsmouth ★★

Portsmouth (p. 554) is a good base for exploring local parks and beaches. Be sure to visit New Castle Island for its historic streets; the outstanding collection of oceanside state parks lining Rte. 1A in Rye; and **Strawbery Banke** (p. 558) by the downtown Portsmouth waterfront, with its historic buildings and restora-tions. Near the historic complex is lovely **Prescott Park** with its harbor views, abundant flower gardens, green lawns, and food vendors. In town, there are plenty of shops and restaurants—begin hunting in **Market Square.**

2 WEEKS BY THE SEA FOR FAMILIES

Spend your first week in New Hampshire and Maine, as described above, then head south. The water off Massachusetts and Rhode Island is warmer than the northern New England surf (though it's all relative), but the attractions and distractions are just as enjoyable.

Days 8 & 9: Cape Ann ★★

Use your first day in Cape Ann to explore this lovely peninsula. Visit downtown **Rockport** (p. 180) for souvenirs and fudge. Push on to **Halibut Point State Park** (p. 182), at the tip of Cape Ann, which boasts spectacular views and plenty of room to run around. In **Gloucester** (p. 173), walk the waterfront boulevard that extends north from **Stage Fort Park,** and let the children blow off some steam by exploring the park itself. Before or after, head west on Rte. 133 for fried clams at the legendary **Woodman's of Essex** (p. 173).

On Day 9, head to the beach early, before the parking lots fill up. The rocky coast yields to welcoming strips of sand at several inviting spots. A good destination for families is Gloucester's **Wingaersheek Beach** (p. 174), where kids will happily while away the day. Plan on an early dinner, because you have a long drive ahead of you tomorrow.

Days 10, 11 & 12: Cape Cod ★★★

Base yourselves in **Brewster** (p. 230) or **Dennis** (p. 224); they're convenient but not in the heart of the tourist frenzy. On your first day, stick close to your home base and the child-friendly beaches that front Cape Cod Bay. On Day 11, venture to Falmouth by way of Sandwich. Be at the **Heritage Museums and Gardens** in Sandwich (p. 199) at 9am, and don't expect to get away without a carousel ride. Push on to the **Woods Hole Aquarium** (p. 202). Mix and match your routes in each direction, combining the speed and boredom of Rte. 6 with the pokey pace and abundant distractions of routes 6A and 28 to accommodate the level of interest in the back seat. Day 12 may just be another local beach day, but a fun option is **Cape Cod National Seashore** (p. 206) in the Outer Cape, followed by a stroll around lovely downtown **Chatham** (p. 234).

Let the family energy level dictate how you fill out your days. This area abounds with options for outdoor fun; depending on your kids' ages and interests, you might try biking, kayaking, or fishing. Just be sure to allow for some quality beach time and that timeless Cape combo, miniature golf and soft-serve ice cream. If it's summer, sports fans will want to take in a **Cape Cod Baseball League** game (p. 232). Starting times are in the afternoon as well as the evening, a boon for parents who are working around naps.

Days 13 & 14: South County & Mystic

Work your way west from Cape Cod along the Rhode Island coast, taking advantage of a good excuse to experience relatively undiscovered **South County** (p. 460). You'll reach Connecticut in time to explore the **Mystic Aquarium** (p. 416). That leaves a full day for a visit to **Mystic Seaport** (p. 416); fuel up first with a hearty breakfast at **Kitchen Little** (p. 420).

THE BEST OF VERMONT IN 1 WEEK

You can enjoy a good taste of Vermont in less than a week. This trip involves about 2 or 3 hours of driving daily, if you don't linger (though I wholeheartedly recommend it). You can also scout out places to which you'd like to return and explore in depth.

More Suggested New England Itineraries

☆ FOUR DAYS AFOOT IN THE WHITE MOUNTAINS
1 Kancamagus Highway
2 Jackson
3 Pinkham Notch
4 Tuckerman Ravine
5 Wildcat Ski Area
6 Crawford Notch
7 Mount Washington
8 Franconia Notch

● THE BEST OF VERMONT IN 1 WEEK
1 Burlington
2 Shelburne
3 Middlebury
4 Proctor
5 Dorset
6 Manchester
7 Arlington
8 Woodstock
9 Plymouth
10 Killington
11 Warren
12 Waitsfield
13 Montpelier
14 Barre
15 Waterbury

■ A WEEK BY THE SEA FOR FAMILIES
1 Portland
2 Cape Elizabeth
3 Old Orchard Beach
4 Ogunquit
5 York
6 Kittery
7 Portsmouth

◆ EXPLORING THE MAINE COAST
1 York
2 Portland
3 Freeport
4 Brunswick
5 Bath
6 Pemaquid Peninsula
7 Rockland
8 Rockport
9 Camden
10 Stonington
11 Blue Hill
12 Brooklin
13 Bar Harbor
14 Acadia National Park

Days 1 & 2: Burlington ★★

Check in to the hotel and head out to explore **Burlington** (p. 536). Depending on the weather, rent bikes or in-line skates, or just put on some comfortable walking shoes—this is a great destination for pedestrians.

Budget plenty of time for exploring the pedestrian-only **Church Street Marketplace** (p. 538)—keep an eye out for the popcorn guy hawking sugared kettle corn in summer—as well as the University of Vermont campus.

Each night, have dinner at one of Burlington's many excellent midpriced restaurants. In the evening, you can check out the **Vermont Mozart Festival**.

Day 3: Shelburne ★★ & Middlebury ★

Head south to **Shelburne** (p. 439) in the morning, and spend most of the day exploring the remarkable **Shelburne Museum** (p. 540).

Afterward, drive south to the classic town of **Middlebury** (p. 514) and spend the night at a country inn. The historic **Otter Creek** district, set on a steep hillside by the rocky creek, is well worth exploring and has some great crafts for sale. If you're an art lover, explore the campus and art museum of little **Middlebury College** (p. 516). For dinner, we like **American Flatbread** (p. 523), though it's open only 2 nights a week.

Day 4: In & Around Dorset ★★ & Manchester ★★

From Middlebury, drive south on Rte. 7 and then west on Rte. 4 almost to the New York border, then go south on Rte. 30 through **Dorset** (p. 480) and **Manchester** (p. 480), both classic Vermont small towns with scenic vistas. If you're a history fan, you'll love **Hildene** (p. 481), the former estate of Robert Todd Lincoln, son of the assassinated president.

Spend the night in Manchester, Dorset, or Arlington (p. 483)—being sure to leave time late in the day for **outlet shopping** (p. 489) in Manchester and a stop at the flagship **Orvis** outdoors shop.

Day 5: Woodstock ★★★

Today head east on Rte. 30 into the Green Mountains, then follow Rte. 35 north to the town of **Woodstock** (p. 499). Break out those maps if you crave back roads.

Be sure to sit a spell on Woodstock's lovely town green, taking some photographs of the covered bridge. You can walk from the center of town to the underrated **Billings Farm and Museum** (p. 500). Drop in to a local pub or coffee shop for a pint or a cup, and try to stay overnight here or nearby.

Day 6: The Mad River Valley

After exploring Woodstock in the morning, head west on Rte. 4 with a detour to **Plymouth** to visit the **President Calvin Coolidge State Historic Site** (p. 508).

Continue through **Killington** and up scenic Rte. 100 to the **Mad River Valley** (p. 519). If it's winter and you're a skier, you may be in heaven; the ski hill here is Vermont's most laid-back.

Overnight in **Warren** or **Waitsfield**—dropping in to the cute **Warren General Store** (p. 523) for souvenirs—and, if time permits, rent a bike.

Day 7: Back to Burlington ★★

Spend your final day of this tour working your way back to Burlington.

On the way, spend an hour or two in the lovely little capital city of **Montpelier.** If you're interested, check out the immense working quarries in **Barre.**

You may be pressed for time, but your kids won't let you miss the **Ben & Jerry's factory tour** (p. 525) in Waterbury. There's plenty of shopping around here, too, so give in.

End your trip with dinner in **Burlington** (p. 536), at one of the restaurants you missed on your first visit—even if it's just **Al's** (p. 543).

4 DAYS IN THE WHITE MOUNTAINS

New Hampshire's White Mountains reveal extraordinary natural grandeur from the roadside, and they provide the opportunity to explore mountain crags and crystalline streams.

Day 1: The "Kanc" ★★★

Start at the town of Lincoln, at exit 32 of I-93, and drive to North Conway via the scenic **Kancamagus Highway** (p. 572), stopping for some short hikes or a picnic. Indulge in a few shopping forays in town, and savor the views of the Mount Washington Valley. Head to the village of **Jackson** (p.581) for the night.

Relax before dinner at **Jackson Falls,** or take a bike ride up **Carter Notch Road** or other back roads in the hills above the village.

Day 2: Pinkham Notch ★★

Stay another night in Jackson, and spend the day exploring by foot around **Pinkham Notch** (p. 58). Stop at **Glen Ellis Falls** (p. 582) en route to the base of Mount Washington. Park at Pinkham Notch and hike to dramatic **Tuckerman Ravine** (p. 582) for a picnic lunch.

Return to your car and continue north to **Wildcat Ski Area** (p. 584). Take the chairlift to the summit for spectacular views of Mount Washington, the Presidential Range, and the Carter Range. Return to Jackson for the night.

Day 3: Mount Washington ★★★

Retrace your path down Rte. 16 and back to Rte. 302, turn right, and drive through **Crawford Notch** (p. 586). If weather and time allow, hike to one of the scenic waterfalls.

Go to the **Mount Washington Cog Railway** (p. 588) on the far side of the Notch. Take the train ride to the summit of **Mount Washington** (dress warmly). On your return, stop by the grand **Mount Washington Hotel** (p. 588) for a celebratory snack.

Day 4: Franconia Notch ★★

Continue west on Rte. 302 to Rte. 3. Turn left (south) onto I-93, then drive through scenic **Franconia Notch** (p. 589). Visit some of the scenic attractions (such as the **Flume Gorge** [p. 590] or the **tram ride to Cannon Mountain** [p. 590]) as time permits.

EXPLORING THE MAINE COAST

The inlets and peninsulas of the Maine coast make it impossible to plot a straight course. This trip takes you a little more than halfway up (really, across) the coast, allowing time for serendipitous detours and delays. Tack on some extra time at the end to really explore Acadia.

Day 1: York ★★

Drive into Maine from the south on I-95, and head immediately for **York Village** (p. 594; the first exit). Spend some time snooping around the historic homes of the **Old York Historical Society** (p. 598), and stretch your legs on a walk through town or the woods.

Drive north through **York Beach,** stock up on saltwater taffy at the **Goldenrod** (p. 600), and spend the night near the beach.

Days 2 & 3: Portland ★★★

Using the right route, getting to Portland can be as fun as being there. You can hit the antiques shops along parts of Rte. 1 as you drive north. If you're in a hurry or traveling in summer, avoid the crowds on Rte. 1 by taking I-95.

In **Portland** (p. 612) by afternoon, collect tourism information and devise a schedule. Plan to stay in the city or on a nearby beach, shopping for jewelry, souvenirs, or even kites; taste-testing chowder and microbrewed beer; and just soaking up the salty air and atmosphere. Don't forget a walk along the **Eastern Promenade** (p. 615) or a **day cruise** (p. 615) on a local ferry.

Day 4: Freeport ★★★, Brunswick ★ & Bath ★★

Head north early to beat the shopping crowds at the outlet haven of Freeport. You can't leave too early for **L.L.Bean** (p. 625)—it never closes!

From Freeport, continue north to **Wiscasset,** the so-called "Prettiest Village in Maine," or to the **Boothbay** region (p. 623). Spend a relaxing night in a picturesque B&B.

Days 5 & 6: Camden ★★★ & Penobscot Bay

Heading north from the Bath-Brunswick area, detour down to **Pemaquid Point** (p. 628) for a late picnic as you watch the surf roll in. Then head back to Rte. 1 and set your sights on the heart of Penobscot Bay.

Rockland (p. 630), which you'll reach first, is the workaday part of the equation. The best places here are the arty cafes and the excellent museum and restaurants. Nearby **Rockport** (p. 636) is a tiny harbor town with excellent views and a small main street.

Finally, head a few miles north to wander around downtown **Camden** (p. 635), poking into shops and galleries. Hike up one of the impressive hills at **Camden Hills State Park** (p. 636), hop a **ferry** to an island (North Haven and Isleboro are both great for biking), or sign up for a daylong sail on a **windjammer.** We also like getting ice cream and hot dogs down by the harbor.

Day 7: Blue Hill ★★★ & Deer Isle

From Camden, drive up and around the head of Penobscot Bay and then down the bay's eastern shore. The roads here are great for aimless drives, but head for **Stonington** (p. 642), far down at the end of the peninsula on **Deer Isle** (p. 641).

Next, head to scenic **Blue Hill** (p. 641) for dinner and lodging. You'll love the views from here, and the combination of a Maine fishing town and new-blood bookshops and restaurants is quite appealing. Also take a spin around the peninsula to smaller towns such as **Blue Hill Falls** and **Brooklin,** where you'll see boatyards, old-fashioned general stores (post offices included), and ingenuity holding it all together. *This* is the real Maine.

Days 8, 9, 10 & 11: Bar Harbor ★★ & Acadia National Park ★★★

Bar Harbor is a great base for exploring **Mount Desert Island,** which is well worth 4 (or more) days on a Maine itinerary. You may want to stay at least 2 nights in Bar Harbor, especially if you have kids along. It provides access to comforts and services such as a movie theater, souvenir shops, bike and kayak rentals, free shuttle buses all over the island, and numerous restaurants. Yes, it's a lot more developed (perhaps too much so) than the rest of the island, but think of it as a supply depot.

Hike, bike, boat, or do whatever you must to explore the island and **Acadia National Park** (p. 646), one of America's finest. What it lacks in size, it makes up for through intimate contact with nature. Investigate the island at your own pace: Take a beginner's **kayak trip** down the eastern shore, a **hike** out to **Bar Island,** or a **mountain-bike trip** along one of the many **carriage roads** built by the Rockefeller family. Only bicycles and horses are allowed on these roads, making them a tranquil respite from the island's highways, which—almost unbelievably—do get crowded in summer.

The scenic **Park Loop Road** is a great introduction to what's in store for you later (crashing waves, big mountains, drop-dead gorgeous views). Make sure to get a park pass that lasts more than a day.

While exploring the rest of the island, be sure to hit some of the nonpark towns, too. **Northeast Harbor and Southwest Harbor** are fishing towns that tourism has partly transformed into tiny centers of art, music, and shopping. However, they still have small stores where fishermen shop for slickers and Wonder bread.

What about those things you wanted to do but didn't have time for? Do them on your last day in Acadia: Watch a sunrise from the top of **Cadillac Mountain** (p. 652); cap off your visit with a cold-water dip at **Sand Beach** (p. 651) and tea and popovers at **Jordan Pond House** (p. 654); take a quick last hike up **The Bubbles** (p. 653); or just enjoy one last lobster atop a wooden pier.

BOSTON & CAMBRIDGE

by Marie Morris

Boston looks better today than it has in many years. The $15-billion highway-construction project known as the "Big Dig" wrapped up in 2007, and downtown has been transformed. Where a grim elevated expressway once stood, the Rose Kennedy Greenway now parallels the waterfront. The long, narrow park, dotted with diverse plantings, engaging public art, and irresistible fountains, is the crown jewel of a system of new green spaces, inviting plazas, surface roads, and buildings.

A subterranean highway now carries traffic through Boston, a modern metropolis that's also steeped in history. Rich in Colonial lore and 21st-century technology, it's a living landmark that changes every day.

Cambridge and Boston are so close that many people believe they're the same—a notion both cities' residents and politicians are happy to dispel. Cantabrigians are often considered more liberal and better educated than Bostonians, which is another idea that's sure to get you involved in a heated discussion. Harvard University dominates Cambridge's history and geography, but there's more to the city than just the school.

Take a few days (or weeks) to get to know the Boston area, or use it as a gateway to the rest of New England. Here's hoping your experience is memorable and delightful.

ORIENTATION

Arriving

BY PLANE Most major domestic carriers serve Boston's Logan International Airport, usually just called "Logan." Many major international carriers fly into Boston. Major carriers also serve New Hampshire's **Manchester–Boston Regional Airport** (✆ **603/624-6556;** www.flymanchester.com; airport code MHT) and **T. F. Green Airport,** in the Providence suburb of Warwick, Rhode Island (✆ **888/268-7222;** www.pvdairport.com; airport code PVD). **Flight Line** (✆ **800/245-2525;** www.flightlineinc.com) van service connects the Manchester airport to destinations in Massachusetts, including the Sullivan Square Orange Line T stop and suburban Woburn; one-way fares start at $19. In addition, **Greyhound** (✆ **800/231-2222;** www.greyhound.com) runs buses to Boston's South Station and Logan Airport. The trip takes 60 to 90 minutes; the fare is $19 one-way, $37 round-trip. To and from T. F. Green, **Peter Pan/Bonanza** (✆ **800/343-9999;** www.peterpanbus.com) runs buses; fares start at $13 one-way, $26 round-trip. You can also take a cab or local bus to downtown Providence and transfer to either the MBTA commuter rail or Amtrak. Allow at least 2 hours. A direct rail link is scheduled to open in late 2010.

   Logan International Airport (✆ **800/23-LOGAN** [235-6426]; www.massport.com/logan; airport code BOS) is in East Boston at the end of the Sumner, Callahan, and Ted Williams tunnels, 3 miles across the harbor from downtown. Each of the four terminals has ATMs, Internet kiosks, pay phones with dataports, fax machines, and information booths (near baggage claim). Wireless Internet access is free all over the airport. Terminals C and E have bank branches that handle currency exchange; A and C have children's play spaces.

   A **cab** from the airport to downtown or the Back Bay costs about $20 to $35 and can be as high as $45 in bad traffic. The ride into town takes 10 to 45 minutes, depending on traffic and the time of day. If you must travel during rush hour or on Sunday afternoon, allow extra time, or plan to take the subway or water shuttle (and pack accordingly).

   The Logan Airport website (**www.massport.com/logan**) lists numerous companies that operate **shuttle-van service** to local hotels. One-way prices start at $14 per person and are subject to fuel surcharges as gas prices fluctuate.

   The trip from Logan to the downtown waterfront (near cabstands and several hotels) in a weather-protected **boat** takes 7 minutes and costs $10 one-way. Service runs from early morning through early evening daily, year-round; hours are shorter on weekends and in the winter. The free no. 66 shuttle bus connects all terminals to the Logan ferry dock; call ahead from the dock for water taxi pickup. Three on-call water taxi operators serve the downtown waterfront and other points around Boston Harbor: **City Water Taxi** (✆ **617/422-0392;** www.citywatertaxi.com), **Rowes Wharf Water Transport** (✆ **617/406-8584;** www.roweswharfwatertransport.com), and **Boston Harbor Water Taxi** (✆ **617/593-9168;** www.bostonharborwatertaxi.com). The MBTA (✆ **800/392-6100** or 617/222-3200; www.mbta.com) contracts out scheduled ferry service to **Harbor Express,** which runs to Long Wharf, behind the Marriott Long Wharf hotel.

   Some hotels have **limousines** or **shuttle vans;** ask when you make your reservations. To arrange private service, call ahead for a reservation, especially at busy times. Your hotel can recommend a company, or try **Boston Coach** (✆ **800/672-7676;** www.bostoncoach.com) or **Carey Limousine Boston** (✆ **800/336-4646** or 617/623-8700; www.carey.com). **PlanetTran** (✆ **888/756-8876;** www.planettran.com) uses only hybrid vehicles.

BY CAR Boston is 218 miles from New York City; driving time is about 4½ hours. From Washington, D.C., it takes about 8 hours to cover the 468 miles; the 992-mile drive from Chicago takes around 21 hours.

Driving to Boston is not difficult, but between the cost of parking and the hassle of traffic, the savings on airfare may not be worth the aggravation. If you're thinking of using the car to get around town, think again—you won't need one to explore Boston and Cambridge, but you almost certainly will have to pay for parking.

The major highways are **I-90,** the Massachusetts Turnpike ("Mass. Pike"), an east-west toll road that runs from Logan Airport to the New York State Thruway; **I-93/U.S. 1,** which extends north to Canada; and **I-93/Rte. 3,** the Southeast Expressway, which connects with the south, including Cape Cod. **I-95** (MA Rte. 128) is a beltway about 11 miles from downtown that connects to I-93 and to highways to Rhode Island, Connecticut, and New York to the south and New Hampshire and Maine to the north. **Note:** The Mass. Pike's **FastLane** program is compatible with some out-of-state toll-collection systems, including New York's **EZPass.**

To reach Cambridge, take **Storrow Drive** or **Memorial Drive** (on either side of the Charles River). The Mass. Pike's Allston/Cambridge exit connects with Storrow Drive. It has a Harvard Square exit; cross the Anderson Bridge to John F. Kennedy Street to reach the square. Memorial Drive intersects with Kennedy Street; turn away from the bridge to reach the square.

AAA (© 800/AAA-HELP [4357]; www.aaa.com) provides members with maps, itineraries, and other information, and arranges free towing if you break down. To reach the state police, who patrol the state's highways, call © **911** from your cellphone.

BY TRAIN Boston has three rail centers: **South Station,** on Atlantic Avenue; **Back Bay Station,** on Dartmouth Street across from the Copley Place mall; and **North Station,** on Causeway Street. **Amtrak** (© **800/USA-RAIL** [872-7245] or 617/482-3660; www.amtrak.com) serves all three. Each train station is also a subway station. See the "Boston Transit & Parking" map on p. 87.

Amtrak serves Boston from the south and from Portland, Maine. **Acela Express** high-speed service, when it's on time, reaches Boston from New York in just under 4 hours and from Washington, D.C., in about 6 hours. Standard Northeast Corridor service takes 4 to 5 hours and 8 hours, respectively.

South Station is a stop on the Red Line, which runs to Cambridge by way of Park Street, the hub of the **subway** (© **800/392-6100** or 617/222-3200; www.mbta.com). At Park Street you can connect to the Green and Orange lines. The Orange Line links Back Bay Station with Downtown Crossing (where there's a walkway to Park St. station) and other points. The **commuter rail** serves Ipswich, Rockport, and Fitchburg from North Station, and points south and west of Boston, including Plymouth, Massachusetts, and Providence, Rhode Island, from South Station.

BY BUS The **South Station Transportation Center** (© **617/737-8040;** www.south-station.net), on Atlantic Avenue next to the train station, is the city's bus-service hub. It's served by regional and national lines, including **Greyhound** (© **800/231-2222** or 617/526-1800; www.greyhound.com) and the affiliated companies **Peter Pan** (© **800/343-9999;** www.peterpanbus.com) and **Bonanza** (© **888/751-8800**).

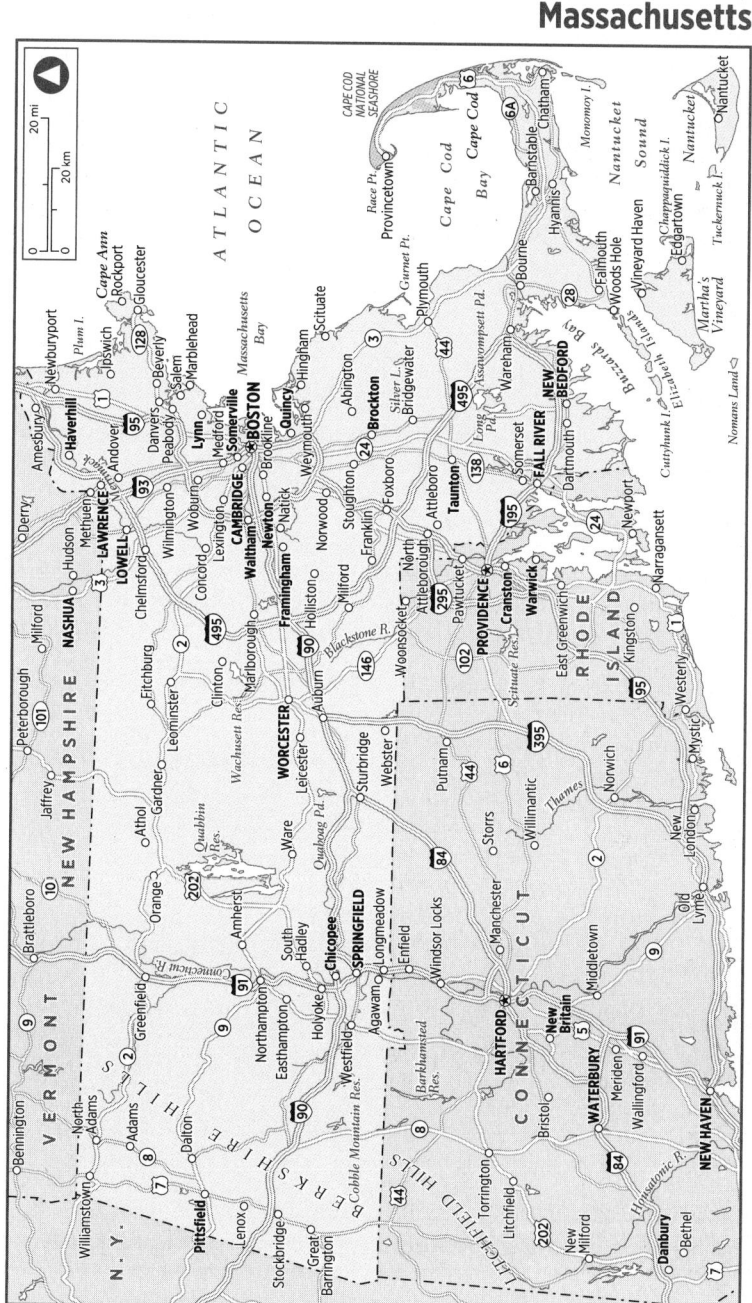

Visitor Information

BEFORE YOU LEAVE HOME The **Greater Boston Convention & Visitors Bureau** (📞 888/SEE-BOSTON [733-2678] or 617/536-4100; www.bostonusa.com) offers a comprehensive information kit ($10) with a planner, guidebook, map, and information about discounts, and a separate *Kids Love Boston* guide ($5). Free smaller planners for specific seasons or events are often available. The **BostonUSA** iPhone app (99¢) allows users to buy e-tickets for attractions and tours and enter by just showing the screen.

The **Cambridge Office for Tourism** (📞 800/862-5678 or 617/441-2884; www.cambridge-usa.org) distributes information about Cambridge.

The **Massachusetts Office of Travel and Tourism** (📞 800/227-6277 or 617/973-8500; www.massvacation.com) distributes the *Getaway Guide*, a free magazine with information on attractions and lodgings statewide, a map, and a seasonal calendar.

An excellent resource for travelers with disabilities is **VSA Arts Massachusetts** (📞 617/350-7713; TTY 617/350-6536; www.vsamass.org).

IN PERSON The **Boston National Historical Park Visitor Center,** 15 State St. (📞 617/242-5642; www.nps.gov/bost), across the street from the Old State House and the State Street T, is a good place to start exploring. Park rangers staff the center and lead seasonal free tours of the Freedom Trail. The center is wheelchair accessible and has restrooms; it's open daily from 9am to 5pm. The ranger-staffed center at the **Charlestown Navy Yard** (📞 617/242-5601) keeps the same hours.

The Freedom Trail begins at the **Boston Common Information Center,** 148 Tremont St., on the Common. The center is open Monday through Friday from 8:30am to 5pm, Saturday from 9am to 5pm. The **Prudential Information Center,** on the main level of the Prudential Center, is open Monday through Friday from 9am to 5:30pm, Saturday and Sunday from 10am to 6pm. The **Greater Boston Convention & Visitors Bureau** (📞 888/SEE-BOSTON [733-2678] or 617/536-4100) operates both centers.

The outdoor information booth at **Faneuil Hall Marketplace,** between Quincy Market and the South Market Building, is staffed in the spring, summer, and fall from 10am to 6pm Monday through Saturday, noon to 6pm Sunday.

In Cambridge, there's an **information kiosk** (📞 617/497-1630) in the heart of Harvard Square, near the T entrance at the intersection of Mass. Ave., John F. Kennedy Street, and Brattle Street. It's open Monday through Friday from 9am to 5pm, Saturday and Sunday from 9am to 1pm.

City Layout

Parts of Boston reflect the city's original layout, a seemingly haphazard plan that can disorient even longtime residents. Old Boston abounds with alleys, dead ends, one-way streets, streets that change names, and streets named after extinct geographical features. On the plus side, every "wrong" turn **downtown,** in the **North End,** or on **Beacon Hill** is a chance to see something you might otherwise have missed.

Boston Neighborhoods in Brief

See the map on p. 87 to locate these areas. When Bostonians say **"downtown,"** they usually mean the first six neighborhoods below. With a couple of exceptions (noted here),

Boston is generally safe, but you should take the same precautions as in any large city, especially at night.

The Waterfront This narrow area along **Atlantic Avenue** and **Commercial Street,** once filled with wharves and warehouses, now boasts luxury condos, marinas, restaurants, offices, and hotels. Most of the **Rose Kennedy Greenway** is here, as are the New England Aquarium and docks for harbor cruises and whale watches.

The North End One of the city's oldest neighborhoods was an immigrant stronghold for much of its history. It's now less than half Italian-American, but you'll still hear Italian spoken and find many Italian restaurants, *caffès*, and shops. **Hanover Street** and **Salem Street** are the main streets of the North End, which adjoins Faneuil Hall Marketplace and the Waterfront. Clubs and restaurants cluster on and near **Causeway Street** in the **North Station** area (btw. N. Washington St. and Beacon Hill), where you shouldn't wander the side streets alone late at night.

Faneuil Hall Marketplace & Haymarket Employees aside, Boston residents tend to be scarce at Faneuil Hall Marketplace (also called Quincy Market). An irresistible draw for out-of-towners and suburbanites, the cluster of restored market buildings adjacent to the North End is the city's most popular attraction. **Haymarket,** along Blackstone Street, is home to an open-air produce market on Friday and Saturday.

Government Center Here, modern design breaks up Boston's traditional red-brick facade. Across **Cambridge Street** from Beacon Hill, Government Center is home to state and federal office towers, Boston City Hall, and a central T stop.

Financial District In the city's banking, insurance, and legal center, skyscrapers surround the landmark Custom House Tower. This area is frantic during the day, busy after work on weekdays, and nearly empty at night. **State Street** separates it from Faneuil Hall Marketplace.

Downtown Crossing The Freedom Trail runs through this shopping and business district adjacent to Boston Common, which hops during the day and slows at night. The intersection that gives Downtown Crossing its name is where Winter Street becomes Summer Street at **Washington Street,** the most "main" street downtown.

Beacon Hill Narrow, tree-lined streets and architectural showpieces make up this largely residential area near the State House. **Charles Street** is the main drag of "the Hill." Two of the city's loveliest and most exclusive spots are here: Mount Vernon Street and Louisburg (pronounced "Lewis-burg") Square. Massachusetts General Hospital is off **Cambridge Street.** On the south side, **Beacon Street** borders Boston Common.

Charlestown One of the oldest areas of Boston is where you'll see the Bunker Hill Monument and USS *Constitution* ("Old Ironsides"). Yuppification has brought some diversity to the mostly white residential neighborhood, but pockets remain that have earned their reputation for insularity. To get here, follow **North Washington Street** from the North End.

South Boston Waterfront/Seaport District Across **Fort Point Channel** from downtown, you'll find the Boston Convention & Exhibition Center, Seaport Boston World Trade Center, Institute of Contemporary Art, a federal courthouse, Museum Wharf, and one end of the Ted Williams Tunnel.

Chinatown One of the largest Chinese communities in the country abounds with Asian restaurants, groceries, and other businesses. The "Combat Zone," or red-light district, has nearly disappeared, and Chinatown has expanded to fill the area between Downtown Crossing and the Mass. Pike extension. Its main street is **Beach Street.** The tiny **Theater District** is here, extending about 1½ blocks in each direction from the intersection of Tremont and Stuart streets; be careful here at night.

South End Cross **Huntington Avenue** or **Stuart Street** to reach this landmark district packed with Victorian row houses and little parks. The South End has a large gay community and some of the city's best restaurants. Main thoroughfares include **Tremont** and **Washington streets** and **Harrison Avenue,** which originate downtown, and **Columbus Avenue.** *Note:* The South End is not South Boston, the residential neighborhood across I-93.

Back Bay Fashionable since its creation out of landfill in the mid–19th century, the Back Bay overflows with gorgeous architecture and chic shops. It extends from **Arlington Street,** in the plush area near the **Public Garden,** to the student-dominated sections near Massachusetts Avenue, or **Mass. Ave.** Unlike downtown, it's laid out in a grid. The main streets include the prime shopping areas of **Boylston** and **Newbury streets** and largely residential Commonwealth Avenue, or **Comm. Ave.,** and **Beacon Street.** The cross streets go in alphabetical order.

Kenmore Square The landmark white-and-red Citgo sign above the intersection of **Comm. Ave., Beacon Street,** and **Brookline Avenue** tells you you're approaching Kenmore Square. Boston University students throng its shops, bars, restaurants, and clubs. The college-town atmosphere goes out the window when the Red Sox are in town and baseball fans flock to Fenway Park, 3 blocks away.

The Fenway Here, between Kenmore Square and the Longwood Medical Area, you'll find Fenway Park, the Museum of Fine Arts, the Isabella Stewart Gardner Museum, and innumerable students. The southern border is Huntington Avenue, the honorary "Avenue of the Arts" (or, with a Boston accent, "Otts"), home to Symphony Hall (at the corner of **Mass. Ave.**) and the MFA. Parts of Huntington can be a little risky; if you're leaving the museum at night, grab a cab or the Green Line, and try to travel in a group.

Cambridge The backbone of Boston's neighbor across the Charles River is **Mass. Ave.,** which originates in Roxbury and extends as far as Lexington. The Red Line subway parallels Mass. Ave. in the areas you're likeliest to visit, around the **Kendall/MIT, Central, Harvard,** and **Porter** T stops.

GETTING AROUND

It's impossible to say this often enough: When you reach your hotel, *leave your car in the garage and walk or use public transportation.* If you must drive in Boston or Cambridge, ask at the front desk for the quickest route (which may not be obvious from a map or mapping website).

By Public Transportation

The Massachusetts Bay Transportation Authority, or **MBTA** (© **800/392-6100** or 617/222-3200; www.mbta.com), is known as the "T," and its logo is the letter in a circle. It runs subways, trolleys, buses, and ferries in Boston and many suburbs, as well as the commuter rail. Its website includes maps, schedules, and other information.

Newer stations on the Red, Blue, and Orange lines are wheelchair accessible; the Green Line is being converted. All T buses have lifts or ramps. To learn more, contact the **Office for Transportation Access** (© **800/533-6282** within Massachusetts, or 617/222-5123; TTY 617/222-5415).

Boston Transit & Parking

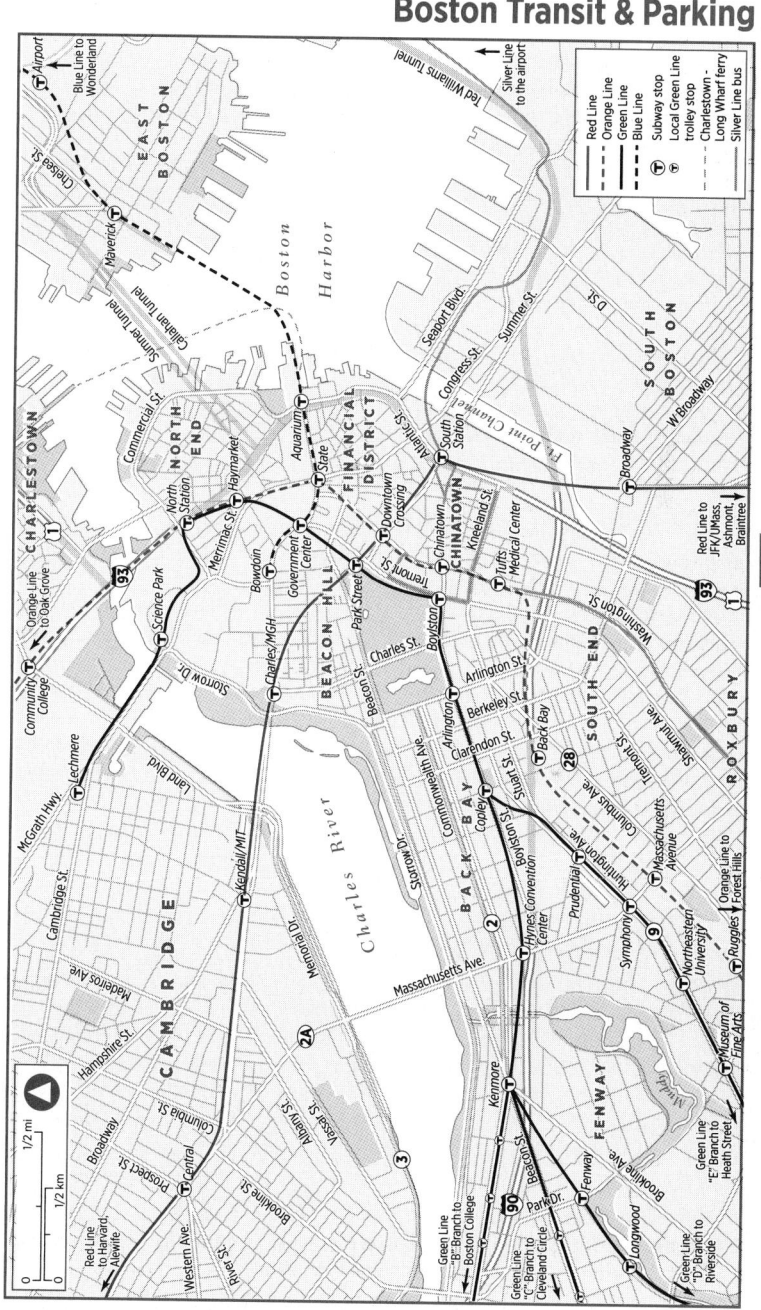

The T's Fare-Collection System

MBTA (☏ **800/392-6100** or 617/222-3200; www.mbta.com) passengers pay their fares with stored-value Charlie-Tickets or CharlieCards. Buses and trolleys also accept cash. Fares are lower if you pay with a CharlieCard than if you use a CharlieTicket or cash. The **CharlieCard** (a plastic "smart card" with an embedded chip) registers when you hold it in front of the rectangular fare reader; the **CharlieTicket** (heavy paper with a magnetic strip) goes into and pops out of a slot on the turnstile or fare box. Self-service kiosks at the entrance to each subway station and in each airport terminal allow you to add value to CharlieTickets and Charlie-Cards, using cash or a credit or debit card. They dispense CharlieTickets but not CharlieCards. To get a CharlieCard, ask a T employee, order one in advance, or visit a retail location (check the website for a list of convenience stores, newsstands, and other outlets). Consider ordering CharlieCards or CharlieTickets online before you leave home; at press time, shipping is free, and you won't have to buy one immediately upon arriving.

BY SUBWAY & TROLLEY   Red, Blue, and Orange line trains and Green Line trolleys make up the **subway** system, which runs partly aboveground. The commuter rail to the suburbs is purple on system maps and is sometimes called the Purple Line. The Silver Line is a fancy name for a bus line; route **SL1** runs from South Station to the airport via the South Boston waterfront, including the convention center and the World Trade Center (the SL2 serves the cruise ship terminal area). The fare on the subway and Silver Line routes SL1 and SL2 is $1.70 with a CharlieCard, $2 with a CharlieTicket or cash. Transfers to local buses are free. Service begins around 5:15am and ends around 12:30am. On New Year's Eve, closing time is 2am and service is free after 8pm. A sign on the token booth in every station gives the time of the last train in either direction.

The oldest system in the country, the T dates to 1897. The Green Line is the most unpredictable—leave early if you're taking it to a vital appointment, and bring cab fare in case you have to jump off. Note that downtown stops are so close together that walking is often faster. The system is generally safe, but always watch out for pickpockets, especially during the holiday season.

BY BUS   T buses and "trackless trolleys" (buses with electric antennae) provide service around town and to and around the suburbs. The fare for local buses and Silver Line routes SL4 and SL5 is $1.25 with a CharlieCard (transferring to the subway costs 45¢), $1.50 with a CharlieTicket or cash. Express-bus fares are higher. Important local routes include **no. 1** (Mass. Ave. from Dudley Sq. in Roxbury through the Back Bay and Cambridge to Harvard Sq.), **nos. 92** and **93** (btw. Haymarket and Charlestown), **no. 77** (Mass. Ave. from Harvard Sq. north to Porter Sq. and Arlington), and **SL4** and **SL5** of the Silver Line (which connect South Station and Downtown Crossing to Dudley Station via the South End).

BY FERRY   The MBTA Inner Harbor ferry connects **Long Wharf** (near the New England Aquarium) with the **Charlestown Navy Yard**—it's a good way to get back downtown from "Old Ironsides" and the Bunker Hill Monument. The fare is $1.70. Visit www.mbta.com or call ✆ **617/227-4321** for information.

By Taxi

Taxis are expensive and not always easy to flag—find a cabstand or call a dispatcher. Stands are usually near hotels. There are also busy taxi stands at Faneuil Hall Marketplace (on North St. and in front of 60 State St.), South Station, Back Bay Station, and on Mass. Ave. in Harvard Square, near the Coop and in front of Au Bon Pain.

To call ahead, try the **Independent Taxi Operators Association** (✆ 617/426-8700; www.itoataxi.com), **Boston Cab** (✆ 617/536-5100), **Top Cab/City Cab** (✆ 617/536-5100; www.topcab.us), or **Metro Cab** (✆ 617/782-5500; www.boston-cab.com). In Cambridge, call **Ambassador Brattle/Yellow Cab** (✆ 617/492-1100 or 617/547-3000; www.brattlecourier.com). Boston Cab can dispatch a wheelchair-accessible vehicle; advance notice is recommended. If you want to report a problem or have lost something in a Boston cab, contact the police department's **Hackney Unit** (✆ **617/343-4475;** www.cityofboston.gov/police/hackney).

The Boston fare structure is as follows: the first ½ mile (when the flag drops), $2.60; each additional ½ mile, 40¢. Wait time is extra, and the passenger pays tolls as well as a total of $7.50 in fees on trips leaving Logan Airport. Charging a flat rate in the city is not allowed; the police department maintains a list (available at www.massport.com/logan) of flat rates for trips to the suburbs.

BY WATER TAXI Three companies operate daily year-round; one-way fares from and to various points around the harbor start at $10. Reservations are recommended but not required; you can call from the dock for pickup. The companies are **City Water Taxi** (✆ **617/422-0392;** www.citywatertaxi.com), **Rowes Wharf Water Taxi** (✆ **617/406-8584;** www.roweswharfwatertransport.com), and **Boston Harbor Water Taxi** (✆ **617/593-9168;** www.bostonharborwatertaxi.com).

By Car

If you plan to visit only Boston and Cambridge, you do not need a car. Construction, expensive parking, awful drivers, and confusing geography make Boston, in particular, a motorist's nightmare. If you arrive by car, park at the hotel and walk or use public transit. For day trips, you'll probably want a car.

RENTALS The major car-rental firms have offices at Logan Airport and in Boston; most have other area branches. Boston levies a $10 convention center surcharge on car rentals. If you're traveling at a busy time, especially during foliage season, reserve well in advance. Most agencies offer shuttle service from the airport to their offices. *Note:* If you're a **Zipcar** member, your card works in the Boston area.

PARKING It's difficult to find your way around Boston and practically impossible to park in some areas. Most spaces on the street are metered (and vigorously patrolled until 6pm or later Mon–Sat), have strict time limits, or both. Parking downtown usually costs $1 an hour; bring plenty of quarters. On some streets, mostly in the Back Bay, you pay at a nearby machine and affix the receipt to the inside of the driver's-side window. Time limits range from 15 minutes to 2 hours. The penalty is a $45 ticket, but should you blunder into a tow-away zone, retrieving the car will take at least $100 and a lot of running around. The city tow lot is at 200 Frontage Rd., South Boston (✆ **617/635-3900;** T: Red Line to Andrew, then grab a cab).

It's best to leave the car in a garage or lot and walk. A full day at most lots costs no more than $30, but some downtown facilities charge as much as $45. Some restaurants offer discounts at nearby garages; ask when you make reservations.

The city-run **Boston Common Garage,** off Charles Street (✆ **617/954-2096;** www.mccahome.com/bcg.html), accepts vehicles under 6 feet, 3 inches tall. Enter the garage in the state **Transportation Building/CityPlace,** 10 Park Plaza (✆ **617/973-7054;** www.pilgrimparking.com), from Charles Street South. The **Prudential Center Garage** (✆ **617/236-3060;** www.prudentialcenter.com) has entrances on Boylston Street, Huntington Avenue, and Exeter Street, and at the Sheraton Boston Hotel. Parking is discounted if you buy something at the Shops at Prudential Center and have your ticket validated. The **Copley Place Garage,** off Huntington Avenue (✆ **617/375-4488;** www.simon.com), offers a similar deal. Many businesses in Faneuil Hall Marketplace validate parking at the **75 State St. Garage** (✆ **617/742-7275;** www.75statestreetgarage.com).

Good-size garages downtown are at **Government Center,** off Congress Street (✆ **617/227-0385;** www.governmentcentergarage.com); **New Sudbury Street** off Congress Street (✆ **617/973-6954**); and **Zero Post Office Square,** in the Financial District (✆ **617/423-1500;** www.posquare.com). In the Back Bay, there's a large garage near the Hynes Convention Center, on **Dalton Street** (✆ **617/421-9484;** www.pilgrimparking.com).

DRIVING RULES   When traffic permits, you may turn right at a red light after stopping, unless a sign says otherwise. Seat belts are mandatory for adults and children, children under 12 may not ride in the front seat, and infants and children under 8 must be in car seats. Text-messaging while behind the wheel is illegal for drivers of all ages. Except in an emergency, motorists under 18 may not use cellphones while driving. Pedestrians in the crosswalk and vehicles already in a rotary (traffic circle or roundabout) have the right of way.

[FastFACTS] BOSTON & CAMBRIDGE

Area Codes Boston proper, **617** and **857;** immediate suburbs, **781** and **339;** northern and western suburbs, **978** and **351;** southern suburbs, **508** and **774.** *Note:* To complete a local call, you must dial all 10 digits.

Car Rentals See "Getting Around," above.

Drinking Laws The legal drinking age is 21. In many bars, particularly near college campuses, and at sporting events, you will probably be asked for ID. Last call typically is 30 minutes before closing time (1am in bars, 2am in clubs).

Embassies & Consulates See "Embassies & Consulates," in chapter 15, "Fast Facts."

Emergencies Call ✆ **911** for fire, ambulance, or police. For the state

police, call ✆ **617/523-1212** or, from a cellphone, ✆ **911.** The Boston police direct emergency number is ✆ **617/343-4911.**

Hospitals Massachusetts General Hospital, 55 Fruit St. (✆ **617/726-2000;** www.massgeneral.org), and **Tufts Medical Center,** 750 Washington St. (✆ **617/636-5000;** www. tuftsmedicalcenter.org), are closest to downtown. In Cambridge is **Mount**

Auburn Hospital, 330 Mt. Auburn St. (☎ **617/492-3500;** www.mountauburn hospital.org).

Internet Access Visit **www.wififreespot.com** to find public Wi-Fi hotspots. For wired access, the ubiquitous **FedEx Office** charges 10¢ to 20¢ a minute at locations including 2 Center Plaza, Government Center (☎ **617/973-9000**); 187 Dartmouth St., Back Bay (☎ **617/262-6188**); and 1 Mifflin Place, off Mount Auburn Street near Eliot Street, Harvard Square (☎ **617/497-0125**). In the Back Bay, **Tech Superpowers,** 252 Newbury St., 3rd floor (☎ **617/267-9716;** www. newburyopen.net), offers access by the hour ($5/ hour; $3/15 min. minimum) with or without a computer.

Newspapers & Magazines The daily papers are the *Boston Globe* and *Boston Herald.* The daily *Globe* and the Friday *Herald* contain cultural listings. The weekly arts-oriented *Boston Phoenix,* published on Thursday, has entertainment and restaurant listings.

Where, a free monthly magazine, contains information on shopping, nightlife, attractions, museums, and galleries. Newspaper boxes around Boston and Cambridge dispense the free weekly

Phoenix and *Weekly Dig,* and the biweekly *Improper Bostonian* and *Stuff@Night. Boston* magazine is a lifestyle-oriented monthly.

Pharmacies The **CVS** (www.cvs.com) locations at 587 Boylston St., off Copley Square in the Back Bay (☎ **617/437-8414**), and at the Porter Square Shopping Center, off Mass. Ave. in Cambridge (☎ **617/876-5519**), are open 24/7, as are their pharmacies. The **CVS** at 155–157 Charles St. (☎ **617/523-1028**), next to the Charles/MGH Red Line T stop on Beacon Hill, is open 24/7, but the pharmacy closes at 8pm. Some emergency rooms can fill your prescription at the hospital's pharmacy.

Police Call ☎ **911** for emergencies. For the state police, call ☎ **617/523-1212** or, from a cellphone, ☎ **911.**

Restrooms The visitor center at 15 State St. has public restrooms, as do most tourist attractions, hotels, department stores, shopping centers, coffee bars, and public buildings. Free-standing, self-cleaning pay toilets (25¢) are scattered around downtown, but check carefully before using them; despite regular patrols, IV-drug users have been known to take

advantage of the generous time limits.

Safety On the whole, Boston and Cambridge are safe cities for walking. As in any urban area, stay out of parks (including Boston Common, the Public Garden, the Rose Kennedy Greenway, the Esplanade, and Cambridge Common) at night unless you're in a crowd. Areas to avoid at night include Boylston Street between Tremont and Washington, and Tremont Street from Stuart to Boylston. Try not to walk alone late at night in the Theater District and around North Station. Public transportation is busy and safe, but service stops between 12:30 and 1am.

Smoking Massachusetts prohibits smoking in all workplaces, including clubs, bars, and restaurants. The city of Boston bans smoking in all hotels, inns, and B&Bs.

Taxes The 6.25% sales tax does not apply to food, prescription drugs, newspapers, or clothing that costs less than $175. In Boston and Cambridge, the tax on meals and takeout food is 7% and the lodging tax is 14.45%.

Taxis See "Getting Around," earlier in this chapter.

WHERE TO STAY

With enough flexibility, you probably won't have too much difficulty finding a suitable place to stay in or near the city. Year-round, it's always a good idea to **make a reservation,** and the earlier you book, the better your chances of landing a (relative) bargain. Definitely book ahead if you plan to travel **between April and November,** when conventions, college graduations, and vacations increase demand. During **foliage season,** the busiest and priciest time of year—even more expensive than the summer—plan early or risk staying far from Boston.

The average Boston and Cambridge hotel room rate in recent years has been around $200. Rates at most downtown hotels are lower on weekends than on weeknights, when business and convention travelers fill rooms; leisure hotels offer discounts during the week. If you don't mind cold and the possibility of snow, aim for January through March, when you'll find great deals, especially on weekends.

Before you rule out a hotel because of its location, consult a map. Downtown neighborhoods are so small that the borders are somewhat arbitrary. The division to consider is **downtown vs. the Back Bay vs. Cambridge** and not, say, Downtown Crossing vs. the adjacent Financial District. For example, if your interests lie primarily in Cambridge, the Back Bay is not the most convenient place to stay.

The state **hotel tax** is 5.7%. Boston and Cambridge (like Worcester and Springfield) add a 2.75% convention-center tax to the 6% city tax, bringing the total tax to 14.45%.

BED & BREAKFASTS   Most lodgings require a minimum stay of at least 2 nights. The following organizations can help you find a B&B:

o **Bed & Breakfast Agency of Boston** (✆ **800/248-9262,** 0800/89-5128 from the U.K., or 617/720-3540; fax 617/523-5761; www.boston-bnbagency.com)

o **Bed & Breakfast Reservations North Shore/Greater Boston/Cape Cod** (✆ **800/832-2632,** 617/964-1606, or 978/281-9505; fax 978/281-9426; www.bbreserve.com)

o **Bed and Breakfast Associates Bay Colony** (✆ **888/486-6018** or 781/449-5302; fax 781/455-6745; www.bnbboston.com)

o **Host Homes of Boston** (✆ **800/600-1308** or 617/244-1308; fax 617/244-5156; www.hosthomesofboston.com)

The Waterfront & Faneuil Hall Marketplace

These areas are convenient to the Financial District and other downtown destinations, but not as handy if you plan to spend a lot of time in the Back Bay or Cambridge.

VERY EXPENSIVE

Boston Marriott Long Wharf ★   The landmark Marriott occupies a great location a stone's throw from the New England Aquarium. It attracts business travelers with its proximity to the Financial District and families with its pool and easy access to downtown and waterfront attractions. Rooms are large, with plenty of natural light (the standalone building has no close neighbors), and units close to the harbor afford good views of the wharves and the waterfront.

296 State St. (at Atlantic Ave.), Boston, MA 02109.© **800/228-9290** or 617/227-0800. Fax 617/227-2867. www.marriottlongwharf.com. 400 units. Apr–Nov $249–$629 double; Dec–Mar $159–$369 double; year-round $450–$800 suite. AE, DC, DISC, MC, V. Parking $44. T: Blue Line to Aquarium. **Amenities:** Restaurant; lounge; concierge; exercise room; Jacuzzi; indoor pool; room service. *In room:* A/C, TV, fridge, hair dryer, Wi-Fi ($13/day).

InterContinental Boston ★   With top-notch service and amenities, InterConti-nental consistently earns repeat business from its predominantly corporate clientele. The 21-story glass-sheathed building (the hotel occupies the bottom 12 floors) faces the Rose Kennedy Greenway, practically in the Financial District and near the con-vention center and Boston Harbor. Guest rooms on the east (back) side have lovely water views. All are large, with oversize work desks and huge bathrooms. The spa, health club, dining options, and upper-story condos amplify the residential feel, making the InterContinental a worthy competitor for the nearby Boston Harbor Hotel.

510 Atlantic Ave., Boston, MA 02210.© **800/424-6835** or 617/747-1000. Fax 617/747-5190. www.inter continentalboston.com. 424 units. $299–$600 double; from $800 suite. Extra person $35. Children 17 and under stay free in parent's room. AE, DC, DISC, MC, V. Valet parking $39. T: Red Line to South Station. Pets under 25 lb. accepted ($100 fee). **Amenities:** Restaurant; 2 bars; babysitting; concierge; 24-hr. health club & spa; 45-ft. lap pool; room service. *In room:* A/C, TV, hair dryer, minibar, Wi-Fi ($15/day).

MODERATE

Harborside Inn ★★   The Harborside Inn offers an unbeatable combination of location and value. The renovated 1858 warehouse is near Faneuil Hall Market-place, the harbor, and the Financial District. The nicely appointed guest rooms, renovated in 2008, are furnished in contemporary style, with subtle nautical touches and enough room for a table and chairs. Accommodations on the top floors have lower ceilings and better views. Rooms that face the street are more expensive but can be noisier; reserve an interior unit if that's a concern.

185 State St. (btw. Atlantic Ave. and the Custom House Tower), Boston, MA 02109.© **888/723-7565** or 617/723-7500. Fax 617/670-6015. www.harborsideinnboston.com. 98 units. $109–$299 double. Extra person $15. Rates may be higher during special events. AE, DC, DISC, MC, V. Off-site parking $29; res-ervation required. T: Blue Line to Aquarium or Orange Line to State. **Amenities:** Concierge; access to nearby health club ($15). *In room:* A/C, TV/DVD, hair dryer, Wi-Fi (free).

At the Airport
EXPENSIVE

The **Embassy Suites Hotel Boston at Logan Airport,** 207 Porter St., Boston, MA 02128 (© **800/EMBASSY** [362-2779] or 617/567-5000; www.bostonlogan airport.embassysuites.com), is a 273-unit hotel with an indoor pool, exercise room, and business center. Each suite in the 10-story hotel has a living room with a pullout couch. Room rates, which start at $199, include breakfast, high-speed Internet access, and shuttle service to the airport and the Airport T stop.

Hilton Boston Logan Airport ★★   This hotel, smack in the middle of the air-port, draws most of its guests from meetings, conventions, and canceled flights. It's convenient and well equipped for business travelers, and an excellent fallback for vacationers who don't mind commuting to downtown. Guest rooms are large; the best

Boston Accommodations

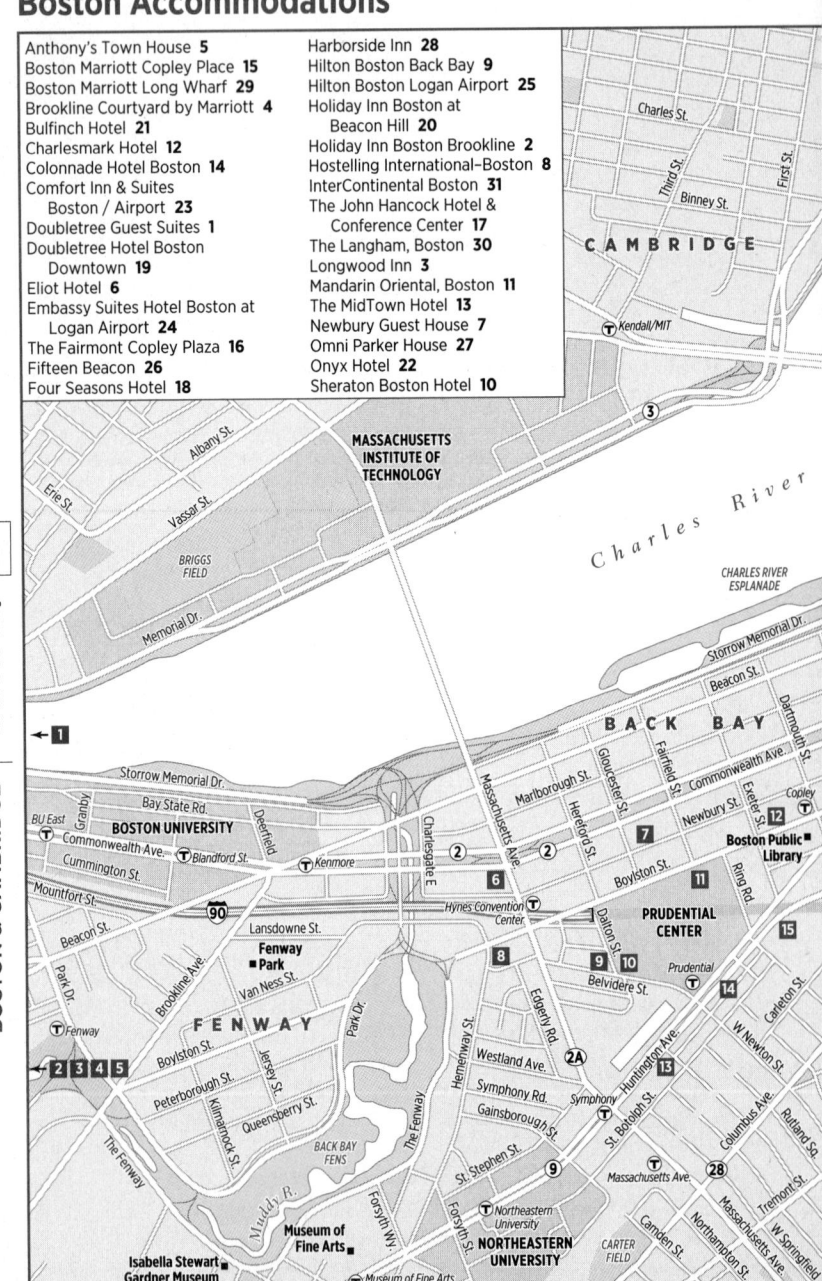

Anthony's Town House **5**
Boston Marriott Copley Place **15**
Boston Marriott Long Wharf **29**
Brookline Courtyard by Marriott **4**
Bulfinch Hotel **21**
Charlesmark Hotel **12**
Colonnade Hotel Boston **14**
Comfort Inn & Suites
　Boston / Airport **23**
Doubletree Guest Suites **1**
Doubletree Hotel Boston
　Downtown **19**
Eliot Hotel **6**
Embassy Suites Hotel Boston at
　Logan Airport **24**
The Fairmont Copley Plaza **16**
Fifteen Beacon **26**
Four Seasons Hotel **18**

Harborside Inn **28**
Hilton Boston Back Bay **9**
Hilton Boston Logan Airport **25**
Holiday Inn Boston at
　Beacon Hill **20**
Holiday Inn Boston Brookline **2**
Hostelling International–Boston **8**
InterContinental Boston **31**
The John Hancock Hotel &
　Conference Center **17**
The Langham, Boston **30**
Longwood Inn **3**
Mandarin Oriental, Boston **11**
The MidTown Hotel **13**
Newbury Guest House **7**
Omni Parker House **27**
Onyx Hotel **22**
Sheraton Boston Hotel **10**

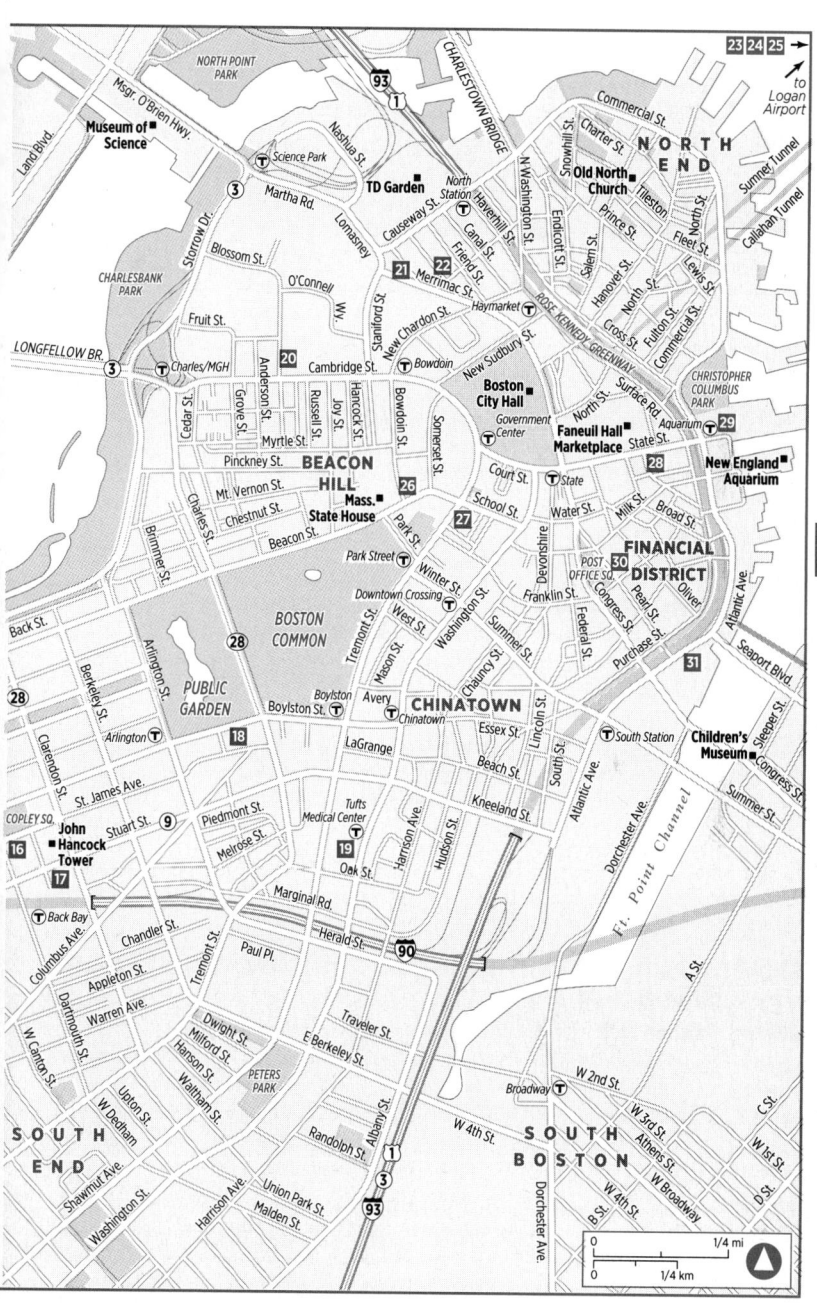

units, on higher floors of the 10-story building, afford sensational views. Soundproofing throughout the hotel is excellent. Walkways lead directly to Terminals A and E.

1 Hotel Dr., Logan International Airport, Boston, MA 02128. © **800/HILTONS** (445-8667) or 617/568-6700. Fax 617/568-6800. www.hiltonfamilyboston.com. 599 units. $139–$399 double; from $500 suite. Children 17 and under stay free in parent's room. AE, DC, DISC, MC, V. Valet parking $38; self-parking $32. T: Blue Line to Airport, then take shuttle bus. Pets accepted ($25/night). **Amenities:** Restaurant; Irish pub; coffee counter; concierge; health club; Jacuzzi; 40-ft. lap pool; room service; sauna. *In room:* A/C, TV, hair dryer, Wi-Fi ($10/day).

MODERATE

Comfort Inn & Suites Logan Airport   The airport lies about 3½ miles south of the well-equipped, eco-conscious Comfort Inn. The eight-story hotel offers large rooms, an attentive staff, an indoor pool, and a good range of features for business and leisure travelers. The somewhat inconvenient location translates to reasonable rates, and the North Shore is easily accessible if you plan to take a day trip.

85 American Legion Hwy. (Rte. 60), Revere, MA 02151. © **877/485-3600** or 781/485-3600. Fax 781/485-3601. www.comfortinnboston.com. 208 units. $109–$239 double; $139–$279 suite. Rates include continental breakfast. Children 17 and under stay free in parent's room. AE, DC, DISC, MC, V. Free parking. T: Blue Line to Airport; take airport shuttle bus to terminal, then hotel shuttle. Pets accepted ($25/night). **Amenities:** Restaurant; lounge; exercise room; indoor pool; room service. *In room:* A/C, TV, hair dryer, Wi-Fi (free).

Financial District

VERY EXPENSIVE

The Langham, Boston ★★   This is one of the best business hotels in the city, with a busy weekend clientele of vacationers attracted by excellent rates for luxurious accommodations and amenities, including a pool. Elegantly decorated and large enough to hold a generous work area, the luxurious guest rooms have 153 configurations. The most desirable units in the nine-story building overlook the lovely park in Post Office Square (buildings surround the other three sides).

250 Franklin St. (at Post Office Sq.), Boston, MA 02110. © **800/791-7761** or 617/451-1900. Fax 617/423-2844. http://boston.langhamhotels.com. 318 units. $185–$495 double; suites from $545 and way up. Extra person $35. AE, DC, DISC, MC, V. Valet parking $39 Sun–Thurs, $25 Fri–Sat. T: Blue or Orange Line to State, or Red Line to Downtown Crossing or South Station. Pets accepted ($50 fee). **Amenities:** Restaurant and lounge; cafe w/Sun brunch and Sat "Chocolate Bar Buffet" (Sept–June); concierge; state-of-the-art health club & spa; Jacuzzi; 40-ft. indoor pool; room service; sauna. *In room:* A/C, TV, hair dryer, Internet ($10/day), minibar, MP3 docking station.

Downtown Crossing/Beacon Hill/North Station

VERY EXPENSIVE

Fifteen Beacon ★★   Nonstop pampering, high-tech appointments, and outrageously luxurious rooms make this Boston's premier boutique hotel. The 10-story property has attracted demanding travelers, especially businesspeople, since it opened in 2000. Management bends over backward to keep them returning, with attentive service and lavish perks. The guest rooms, individually decorated in austere but plush style that's more SoHo than Beacon Hill, contain king- and queen-size beds with Frette linens, surround-sound stereo systems, gas fireplaces, 42-inch flatscreens, and 4-inch TVs in the bathroom. "Studio" units have a sitting area.

15 Beacon St. (1 block from the State House), Boston, MA 02108. © **877/XV-BEACON** (982-3226) or 617/670-1500. Fax 617/670-2525. www.xvbeacon.com. 62 units (some with shower only). From $295

double; from $1,200 suite. AE, DISC, MC, V. Valet parking $42. T: Red or Green Line to Park St., or Blue Line to Government Center. Dogs accepted ($25 fee); refundable deposit required. **Amenities:** Restaurant; bar; babysitting; concierge; exercise room; access to nearby health club ($15); room service. *In room:* A/C, TV, CD player, fax/copier/printer, hair dryer, minibar, MP3 docking station, Wi-Fi (free).

EXPENSIVE

The **Holiday Inn Boston at Beacon Hill,** 5 Blossom St., at Cambridge Street (© **800/HOLIDAY** [465-4329] or 617/742-7630), offers all the features you'd expect of the international chain and has a heated outdoor pool.

Omni Parker House ★ The Parker House offers a great combination of over 150 years of history (since 1855!) and extensive renovations. Regular interior and exterior renovations keep the property in excellent shape. Guest rooms, a patchwork of more than 50 configurations, aren't huge, but they are thoughtfully laid out and nicely appointed. Business travelers can book a room with an expanded work area; sightseers can economize by requesting a smaller, less expensive unit. *Tip:* Sign up (free) for the frequent-guest program, and the hotel waives the in-room Internet access fee.

60 School St. (at Tremont St.), Boston, MA 02108. © **800/843-6664** or 617/227-8600. Fax 617/742-5729. www.omniparkerhouse.com. 551 units, some with shower only. $159–$189 economy room; $189–$289 double; $249–$399 suite. Children 17 and under stay free in parent's room. AE, DC, DISC, MC, V. Valet parking $40. T: Green or Blue Line to Government Center, or Red or Green Line to Park St. Pets accepted; deposit required. **Amenities:** Restaurant; 2 bars; concierge; exercise room; room service. *In room:* A/C, TV, hair dryer, Internet ($10/day), minibar, MP3 docking station.

Onyx Hotel ★ This plush boutique hotel half a block from TD Garden is convenient to Beacon Hill, the North End, and downtown. The 10-story hotel is contemporary in style, with high ceilings that make the decent-size rooms feel even bigger. Each unit holds a large work desk and has a well-appointed bathroom. The best accommodations are the top-floor suites, but any room with a floor-to-ceiling window feels like a minipalace. This rapidly changing neighborhood grows more desirable by the day, but it's a zoo before and after big events at the Garden.

155 Portland St. (btw. Causeway St. and Anthony Valenti Way), Boston, MA 02114. © **866/660-6699** or 617/557-9955. Fax 617/557-0005. www.onyxhotel.com. 112 units. $209–$349 double. Extra person $25. Children 17 and under stay free in parent's room. Rates include evening cocktail reception. AE, DC, DISC, MC, V. Valet parking $40. T: Green or Orange Line to North Station. Pets accepted (free). **Amenities:** Lounge; exercise room; access to nearby health club; room service. *In room:* A/C, TV, hair dryer, minibar, MP3 docking station, Wi-Fi (free).

MODERATE

Bulfinch Hotel ★ One block from North Station, the Bulfinch is a leisure-traveler magnet that also attracts thrifty businesspeople. Rooms are on the small side, but custom furnishings create the illusion of more space. Plush fabrics, flatscreen TVs, and marble bathrooms set off the contemporary, uncluttered design. The best units are junior suites—oversize doubles—known as "nose rooms" because they're in the pointed end of the triangular building.

107 Merrimac St. (at Lancaster St., 1 block from Causeway St.), Boston, MA 02114. © **877/267-1776** or 617/624-0202. Fax 617/624-0211. www.bulfinchhotel.com. 80 units, most with shower only. $169–$399 double; $199–$489 executive king. Children 17 and under stay free in parent's room. AE, DC, DISC, MC, V. Parking $30 in nearby garage. T: Green or Orange Line to North Station. Pets accepted ($50 fee). **Amenities:** Restaurant and lounge; concierge; exercise room; room service. *In room:* A/C, TV, hair dryer, Internet (free).

Chinatown/Theater District

MODERATE

Doubletree Hotel Boston Downtown ★ 🍴   Within walking distance of both downtown and the Back Bay, the Doubletree is a better deal than most competitors in either neighborhood. The six-story building is a former high school with high ceilings and compact, well-designed rooms. Ask for a unit that faces away from busy Washington Street, and your view will be of a cityscape rather than of the hospital across the street. Don't confuse this hotel with its all-suite corporate sibling near Cambridge (p. 101). This Doubletree adjoins the Wang YMCA of Chinatown, and room rates include access to its extensive facilities.

821 Washington St. (at Oak St., 1 block from Stuart St.), Boston, MA 02111. ℂ **800/222-8733** or 617/956-7900. Fax 617/956-7901. www.hiltonfamilyboston.com. 267 units, some with shower only. $139–$299 double; $189–$359 suite. Extra person $10. Children 17 and under stay free in parent's room. AE, DC, DISC, MC, V. Valet parking $38. T: Orange Line to New England Medical Center. **Amenities:** Restaurant and lounge; coffee shop; concierge; executive-level rooms; access to adjoining YMCA w/Olympic-size pool; room service. *In room:* A/C, TV, hair dryer, minibar, Wi-Fi ($10/day).

Back Bay/South End

VERY EXPENSIVE

Eliot Hotel ★★★   This exquisite hotel combines the flavor of Yankee Boston with European-style service and amenities. On tree-lined Comm. Ave., it feels more like a classy apartment building than a hotel, with a romantic atmosphere that belies the top-notch business features. Almost every unit is a spacious suite (16 rooms are standard doubles) furnished with antiques. French doors separate the living rooms and bedrooms, and bathrooms are outfitted in Italian marble. The 1925 building is near Boston University and MIT (across the river), and the atmosphere contrasts pleasantly with the bustle of Newbury Street, a block away.

370 Comm. Ave. (at Mass. Ave.), Boston, MA 02215. ℂ **800/443-5468** or 617/267-1607. Fax 617/536-9114. www.eliothotel.com. 95 units, 8 with shower only. $235–$395 double; $355–$545 1-bedroom suite; $580–$890 2-bedroom suite. Extra person $30. Children 17 and under stay free in parent's room. AE, DC, MC, V. Valet parking $36. T: Green Line B, C, or D to Hynes Convention Center. Pets accepted (free). **Amenities:** Restaurant; sashimi bar; babysitting; concierge; free access to nearby health club; room service. *In room:* A/C, TV, hair dryer, minibar, Wi-Fi ($5/day).

The Fairmont Copley Plaza Hotel ★★   The "grande dame of Boston" is a true grand hotel with a well-earned reputation for excellent service. Built in 1912, the six-story Renaissance Revival building holds spacious guest rooms that have a residential feel. Plush draperies and upholstery and custom-made traditional furnishings, including oversize desks, make the well-heeled leisure and business clientele feel at home. Rooms that face the lovely square afford better views than those overlooking busy Dartmouth Street. *Tip:* Members of Fairmont's frequent-guest program, which is free to join, don't pay for Internet access.

138 St. James Ave. (btw. Dartmouth St. and Trinity Pl.), Boston, MA 02116. ℂ **800/441-1414** or 617/267-5300. Fax 617/267-7668. www.fairmont.com/copleyplaza. 383 units. From $289 double; from $899 suite. Extra person $30. AE, DC, MC, V. Valet parking $42. T: Green Line to Copley or Orange Line to Back Bay. Pets accepted ($25/night). **Amenities:** Restaurant; lounge (Oak Bar, p. 146); concierge; concierge-level rooms; access to nearby health club ($20); exercise room; room service. *In room:* A/C, TV, hair dryer, minibar, MP3 docking station, Wi-Fi ($15/day).

Four Seasons Hotel ★★★   Many hotels offer top-notch guest rooms, public areas, fitness facilities, service, and restaurants in a beautiful location. But no other hotel in Boston—indeed, in New England—combines every element of a luxury hotel as seamlessly as the Four Seasons. If I were traveling with someone else's credit cards, I'd head straight here. The 16-story brick-and-glass building (the hotel occupies eight floors) blends traditional and contemporary style. The best units overlook the Public Garden; city views from the back of the hotel aren't as desirable. The staff is famously accommodating to businesspeople, families, and celebrities.

200 Boylston St. (at Hadassah Way, btw. Arlington St. and Charles St. S.), Boston, MA 02116.© **800/819-5053** or 617/338-4400. Fax 617/423-0154. www.fourseasons.com/boston. 273 units. $495 double weekdays, $425 double weekends; from $895 1-bedroom suite; from $1,545 2-bedroom suite. AE, DC, DISC, MC, V. Valet parking $46. T: Green Line to Arlington. Pets under 25 lb. accepted (free). **Amenities:** Restaurant and bar (Bristol Lounge, p. 113); babysitting; concierge; health club; Jacuzzi; 24-hr. 44-ft. pool overlooking the Public Garden; room service. *In room:* A/C, TV/DVD, CD player, hair dryer, minibar, MP3 docking station, Wi-Fi ($10/day).

Mandarin Oriental, Boston ★★   The Hong Kong–based luxury chain's first New England property (opened in 2008) offers devoted shoppers and international business travelers a great location, sublime service, and top-notch amenities, including an excellent spa. The hotel, a block from Newbury Street, connects directly to the Prudential Center, Hynes Convention Center, and Copley Place. Guest rooms are large and luxurious, with Frette linens and peaceful color palettes. The Mandarin Oriental's closest competitors—the Four Seasons (above) and the InterContinental (p. 93)—have superior fitness facilities, but the your-wish-is-my-command service and access to shopping and dining here may tip the scales for you.

776 Boylston St. (at Fairfield St.), Boston, MA 02199.© **866/526-6567** or 617/535-8888. Fax 617/535-8889. www.mandarinoriental.com/boston. 148 units. Apr–Nov from $625 double, from $1,995 suite; Nov–Mar from $305 double, from $775 suite. Children 16 and under stay free in parent's room. AE, DC, DISC, MC, V. Valet parking $45. T: Green Line to Copley or Green Line E to Prudential. Pets accepted (free). **Amenities:** Restaurant; lounge; babysitting; concierge; exercise room; access to nearby health club ($35); room service; 16,000-sq.-ft. spa; airport transfers ($110). *In room:* A/C, TV/DVD, hair dryer, minibar, MP3 docking station, Wi-Fi ($15/day).

EXPENSIVE

The largest convention hotels in New England adjoin the Prudential Center–Copley Place complex, which incorporates the Hynes Convention Center. The 1,147-unit **Boston Marriott Copley Place,** 110 Huntington Ave. (© **800/228-9290** or 617/236-5800; www.copleymarriott.com), is at the Copley Place side and has a good-size pool. Off Boylston near the Hynes, the **Sheraton Boston Hotel,** 39 Dalton St. (© **800/325-3535** or 617/236-2000; www.sheraton.com/boston), offers 1,215 guest rooms and one of the best pools in town.

Colonnade Hotel Boston ★★ ☺   The centrally located, independently owned Colonnade is a luxurious spot of European-style calm in the Back Bay's retail frenzy. The attentive, gracious staff caters to an international clientele of businesspeople, sightseers, shoppers, and families. The 11-story concrete-and-glass hotel has large guest rooms, decorated in muted earth tones, with pillow-top beds, marble-clad bathrooms, and sleek residential-style furnishings. Floor-to-ceiling windows face the bustling Prudential Center or the South End's urban patchwork. The seasonal "rooftop resort" and swimming pool are a welcome change of pace in warm weather.

120 Huntington Ave. (at Garrison St., 1 block from W. Newton St.), Boston, MA 02116. ☎ **800/962-3030** or 617/424-7000. Fax 617/424-1717. www.colonnadehotel.com. 285 units. $229–$459 double; $575 and way up suite. Children 11 and under stay free in parent's room. AE, DC, DISC, MC, V. Parking $38. T: Green Line E to Prudential. Pets accepted (free). **Amenities:** Restaurant (Brasserie Jo, p. 113); bar; babysitting; concierge; well-equipped exercise room; heated outdoor rooftop pool; room service. *In room:* A/C, TV/DVD, hair dryer, minibar, MP3 docking station, Wi-Fi ($14/day).

Hilton Boston Back Bay ★★ Across the street from the Prudential Center complex, the Hilton is primarily a business hotel, but families also find it comfortable. The carefully maintained rooms in the 26-story tower are large, soundproof, and furnished in modern style. The weekend packages, especially in winter, can be a great deal. The closest competitor is the Sheraton, across the street. It's three times the Hilton's size (which generally means less personalized service), has a better pool, and books more vacation and function business.

40 Dalton St. (at Belvidere St., off Boylston St.), Boston, MA 02115. ☎ **800/874-0663,** 800/445-8667, or 617/236-1100. Fax 617/867-6104. www.hiltonfamilyboston.com. 390 units, 66 with shower only. $149–$399 double; from $450 suite. Extra person $20. Rollaway $25. Children 17 and under stay free in parent's room. AE, DC, DISC, MC, V. Self-parking $39. T: Green Line B, C, or D to Hynes Convention Center. Pets accepted ($75 fee). **Amenities:** Restaurant; bar; concierge; well-equipped exercise room; indoor pool; room service. *In room:* A/C, TV, hair dryer, minibar, Wi-Fi ($15/day).

MODERATE

Charlesmark Hotel ★★ 🎁 In the heart of the Back Bay, the Charlesmark has a boutique feel and great prices. Its amenities are more than sufficient for most business or leisure travelers. Rooms are small, but ingenious design uses custom furnishings to maximize space. Beds have pillow-top mattresses, and the lobby holds two computers and a printer for guests' use. Rates include breakfast, light refreshments such as bottled water and fruit, and local phone calls, all part of management's policy not to pad your bill with incidentals.

655 Boylston St. (btw. Dartmouth and Exeter sts.), Boston, MA 02116. ☎ **617/247-1212.** Fax 617/247-1224. www.thecharlesmark.com. 40 units, most with shower only. $129–$249 double. Rates include continental breakfast. Children stay free in parent's room. AE, DC, DISC, MC, V. Self-parking $27 in nearby garage. T: Green Line to Copley. **Amenities:** Lounge; access to nearby health club ($10). *In room:* A/C, TV/DVD, CD player, fridge, hair dryer, Wi-Fi (free).

The John Hancock Hotel & Conference Center 📦 This eight-story hotel near Back Bay Station is a limited-service lodging that's popular with groups that use the abundant meeting space. The compact, comfortable guest rooms aren't fancy, but they're well maintained and big enough not to feel claustrophobic; bathrooms, however, are tiny. Winter rates here are fantastic. The eponymous insurance firm books the whole place in the weeks before the Boston Marathon.

40 Trinity Place (off Stuart St.), Boston, MA 02116. ☎ **617/933-7700.** Fax 617/933-7709. www.jhcenter.com. 64 units. $189 double. Rates include continental breakfast. Extra person $15. Children 17 and under stay free in parent's room. AE, DC, DISC, MC, V. Parking $27 in nearby garage. Closed to the public 1st 3 weeks of Apr. T: Orange Line to Back Bay or Green Line to Copley. *In room:* A/C, TV, hair dryer, Wi-Fi (free).

The MidTown Hotel ★ 😊 🎁 Popular with families, budget-conscious business-people, and tour groups, this centrally located hotel is a good deal, and its parking fee is the lowest around. On a busy street opposite the Prudential Center, the two-story establishment was most recently renovated in 2008. Guest rooms are large, bright, and attractively outfitted, although bathrooms are on the small side. Some units have connecting doors that allow families to spread out. The best rooms are on the side of the building that faces away from Huntington Avenue.

220 Huntington Ave. (at Cumberland St., 1 long block from Mass. Ave.), Boston, MA 02445. ☎ **800/343-1177** or 617/262-1000. Fax 617/262-8739. www.midtownhotel.com. 159 units. $119–$259 double; $139–$279 suite. Extra person $15. Children 17 and under stay free in parent's room. AE, DC, DISC, MC, V. Parking $18. T: Green Line E to Prudential or Orange Line to Massachusetts Ave. Dogs accepted ($30 fee). **Amenities:** Concierge; access to nearby health club ($5–$10); heated outdoor pool. *In room:* A/C, TV, hair dryer, Wi-Fi ($10/day).

Newbury Guest House ★★ ✦   After just a little shopping in the Back Bay, you'll appreciate what a find this cozy place is: a bargain on Newbury Street. The comfortably furnished, nicely appointed guest rooms take up three 1880s brick town houses. The largest are the bay-window units, which overlook the lively street. This place operates near capacity all year, prompting my only caveat: Reserve early.

261 Newbury St. (btw. Fairfield and Gloucester sts.), Boston, MA 02116. ☎ **800/437-7668** or 617/670-6000. Fax 617/670-6100. www.newburyguesthouse.com. 32 units, some with shower only. $139–$279 double. Extra person $25. Rates include continental breakfast. Minimum 2 nights on Fri-Sat. AE, DC, DISC, MC, V. Parking $20 (reservation required). T: Green Line B, C, or D to Hynes Convention Center. **Amenities:** Access to nearby health club ($25). *In room:* A/C, TV, fridge, hair dryer, Wi-Fi (free).

INEXPENSIVE

Hostelling International–Boston   This hostel near the Berklee College of Music caters to students, youth groups, and other travelers in search of comfortable, no-frills lodging. Accommodations are dorm-style, with six beds per room; a couple of private units sleep one or two. Shared rooms have lockers. The air-conditioned hostel has two kitchens, 29 bathrooms, and a large common room. It provides linens, or you can bring your own; sleeping bags are not permitted. The enthusiastic staff organizes free and inexpensive cultural, educational, and recreational programs. Check ahead if you're traveling in late 2011; a move to the Theater District is in the works.

12 Hemenway St. (off Boylston St.), Boston, MA 02115. ☎ **888/999-4678** or 617/536-9455. Fax 617/424-6558. www.bostonhostel.org. 205 beds. Members of Hostelling International–American Youth Hostels $28–$45 per bed, nonmembers $31–$48 per bed; members $80–$130 per private unit, nonmembers $83–$133 per private unit. Children 3–12 half-price, children 2 and under free. Rates include continental breakfast. MC, V. T: Green Line B, C, or D to Hynes Convention Center. **Amenities:** Access to nearby health club ($6); Wi-Fi (free). *In room:* A/C, no phone.

Outskirts & Brookline

Staying in this area means commuting to downtown Boston. Because of the unwieldy public transit connections, it's not a great choice if your destination is Cambridge.

EXPENSIVE

Doubletree Guest Suites ★★ ✦   This hotel is one of the best deals in town— every unit is a two-room suite. It's near Cambridge and the bike path along the Charles River—not in a real neighborhood and not near the T, but there's shuttle service to local destinations. The large suites, which were renovated in 2007, surround a 15-story atrium. Most bedrooms have a king-size bed and writing desk. Each living room contains a sofa bed and dining table. The Hyatt Regency Cambridge, the hotel's nearest rival, is more convenient but generally more expensive.

400 Soldiers Field Rd. (at Cambridge St.), Boston, MA 02134. ℭ **800/222-8733** or 617/783-0090. Fax 617/783-0897. www.hiltonfamilyboston.com. 308 units. $129–$309 double. Extra person $10. Children 17 and under stay free in parent's room. AE, DC, DISC, MC, V. Valet parking $30; self-parking $25. Pets accepted with prior approval ($250 deposit). **Amenities:** Restaurant; lounge; excellent Scullers Jazz Club (p. 143); concierge; well-equipped exercise room; Jacuzzi; indoor pool; room service. *In room:* A/C, TV, fridge, hair dryer, MP3 docking station, Wi-Fi ($10/day).

MODERATE

Options in this price range and area are chain hotels, including the **Brookline Courtyard by Marriott,** 40 Webster St., Brookline (ℭ **866/296-2296,** 800/321-2211, or 617/734-1393), and the **Holiday Inn Boston Brookline,** 1200 Beacon St., Brookline (ℭ **800/HOLIDAY** [465-4329] or 617/277-1200).

INEXPENSIVE

Anthony's Town House Many patrons at this four-story brownstone guest-house, a family business since 1944, are Europeans accustomed to homey accommodations with shared bathrooms, and budget-minded Americans won't be disappointed. Each floor has three high-ceilinged rooms furnished in Queen Anne or Victorian style, plus a shared bathroom with enclosed shower; the staff will supply a VCR, DVD player, hair dryer, or iron on request. The large front rooms have bay windows, and two family units hold as many as five comfortably. The guesthouse is about 15 minutes from downtown by T.

1085 Beacon St., Brookline, MA 02446. ℭ **617/566-3972.** Fax 617/232-1085. www.anthonystownhouse. com. 10 units, none with private bathroom. $78–$108 double; from $125 family room. Extra person $10. Weekly rates available. No credit cards. Limited free parking. T: Green Line C to Hawes St. *In room:* A/C, TV, Wi-Fi (free), no phone.

Longwood Inn In a residential area near the Boston-Brookline border, this three-story guesthouse offers comfortable, regularly updated accommodations at modest rates. Guests have the use of a full kitchen, dining room, and patio with tables and chairs. The apartment has its own bathroom and kitchen. Tennis courts, a running track, and a playground at the school next door are open to the public. Public transit is within easy reach, and the Longwood Medical Area and Coolidge Corner are a short walk away.

123 Longwood Ave. (at Marshall St., 1 block from Kent St.), Brookline, MA 02446. ℭ **617/566-8615.** Fax 617/738-1070. www.longwood-inn.com. 22 units, 4 with shower only. Apr-Nov $124–$149 double; Dec-Mar $89–$114 double. Extra person $5–$10. 1-bedroom apt (sleeps 4-plus) $124–$159. Weekly rates available. AE, DISC, MC, V. Free parking. T: Green Line D to Longwood or C to Coolidge Corner. *In room:* A/C, TV, Wi-Fi (free).

Cambridge

VERY EXPENSIVE

The Charles Hotel ★★★ This nine-story brick hotel, a block from Harvard Square, has been *the* place for business and leisure travelers in Cambridge since it opened in 1985. Much of its fame derives from its excellent restaurants, jazz bar, day spa, and service. In the posh guest rooms, the style is contemporary country, with custom adaptations of Shaker furniture. The austere design contrasts with the indulgent amenities, which include down quilts and Bose Wave radios; bathrooms hold phones and TVs.

1 Bennett St. (at Eliot St., 1 block from Mount Auburn St.), Cambridge, MA 02138. ℭ **800/882-1818** or 617/864-1200. Fax 617/864-5715. www.charleshotel.com. 294 units. $299–$599 double; $409 and way up suite. AE, DC, MC, V. Valet or self-parking $34. T: Red Line to Harvard. Pets accepted ($50 fee).

Cambridge Accommodations & Dining

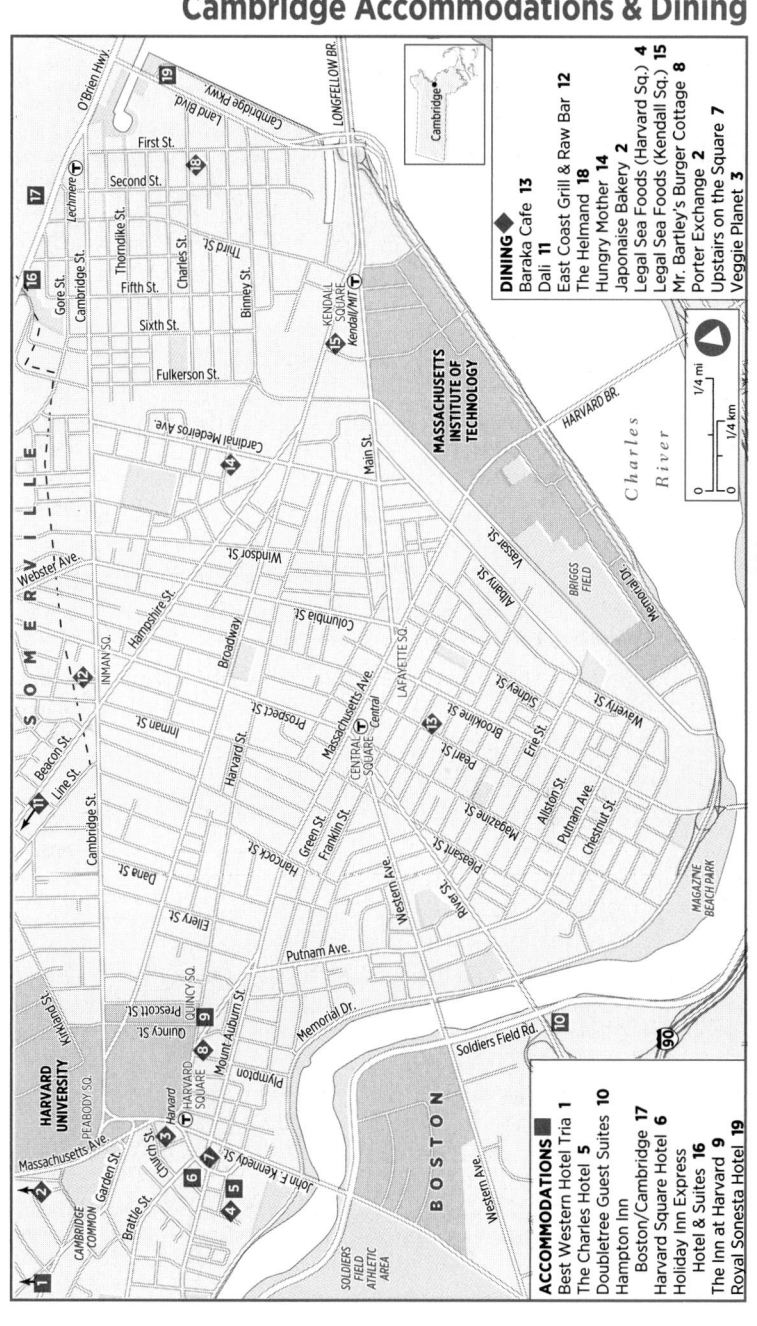

DINING ◆
Baraka Cafe **13**
Dali **11**
East Coast Grill & Raw Bar **12**
The Helmand **18**
Hungry Mother **14**
Japonaise Bakery **2**
Legal Sea Foods (Harvard Sq.) **4**
Legal Sea Foods (Kendall Sq.) **15**
Mr. Bartley's Burger Cottage **8**
Porter Exchange **2**
Upstairs on the Square **7**
Veggie Planet **3**

ACCOMMODATIONS ■
Best Western Hotel Tria **1**
The Charles Hotel **5**
Doubletree Guest Suites **10**
Hampton Inn
Boston/Cambridge **17**
Harvard Square Hotel **6**
Holiday Inn Express
Hotel & Suites **16**
The Inn at Harvard **9**
Royal Sonesta Hotel **19**

Amenities: 2 restaurants; 2 bars; Regattabar jazz club (p. 143); concierge; free access to adjacent health club w/pool, Jacuzzi, and sauna; room service; adjacent spa. *In room:* A/C, TV/DVD, hair dryer, minibar, Wi-Fi (free).

Royal Sonesta Hotel ★★ ☺   This luxurious hotel is close to only a few things but convenient to everything. Features both for businesspeople and families, such as the business center and indoor/outdoor pool with retractable roof, are excellent. The CambridgeSide Galleria mall and the Museum of Science are nearby, and Kendall Square is 10 minutes away on foot. Most of the spacious rooms have lovely views of the river or the city. (Higher prices are for better views.) Everything is custom designed in modern yet comfortable style. The closest competition is Hotel Marlowe, across the street, which offers less extensive fitness options and fewer river views.

40 Edwin H. Land Blvd. (at CambridgeSide Place), Cambridge, MA 02142. ✆ **800/766-3782** or 617/806-4200. Fax 617/806-4232. www.sonesta.com/boston. 400 units, some with shower only. $239–$279 standard double; $259–$299 superior double; $279–$319 deluxe double; $339 and up suite. Extra person $25. Children 17 and under stay free in parent's room. AE, DC, DISC, MC, V. Valet or self-parking $27. T: Green Line to Lechmere, then a 10-min. walk. **Amenities:** Restaurant; cafe w/seasonal outdoor seating; bike rental; concierge; well-equipped 24-hr. health club & spa; heated indoor/outdoor pool w/retractable roof; room service. *In room:* A/C, TV, hair dryer, minibar, Wi-Fi (free).

EXPENSIVE

Rates at the **Hampton Inn Boston/Cambridge,** 191 Msgr. O'Brien Hwy., East Cambridge (✆ **800/426-7866** or 617/494-5300; www.bostoncambridge. hamptoninn.com), include parking, buffet breakfast, and high-speed Internet in the guest rooms (with Wi-Fi in the lobby area).

The Inn at Harvard ★★   The Inn at Harvard is adjacent to Harvard Yard, and its Georgian-style architecture would fit nicely on campus. The elegant hotel is popular with business travelers and university visitors. The decent-size guest rooms have pillow-top beds, and each has a work area with an Aeron chair. The four-story skylit atrium holds the "living room," a well-appointed lounge that's suitable for a meeting if you don't want to conduct business in your room.

1201 Massachusetts Ave. (at Quincy St.), Cambridge, MA 02138. ✆ **800/458-5886** or 617/491-2222. Fax 617/520-3711. www.hotelsinharvardsquare.com. 111 units, some with shower only. $159–$269 double; $1,500 presidential suite. AE, DC, DISC, MC, V. Valet parking $30. T: Red Line to Harvard. **Amenities:** Restaurant (breakfast only); dining privileges at the nearby Harvard Faculty Club; exercise room; room service. *In room:* A/C, TV, hair dryer, Wi-Fi ($10/day).

MODERATE

The **Holiday Inn Express Hotel & Suites,** 250 Msgr. O'Brien Hwy., East Cambridge (✆ **888/887-7690** or 617/577-7600; fax 617/354-1313; www.hiexpress. com/boscambridgema), is 10 minutes from the Green Line on a busy street. Room rates include parking, Wi-Fi, and breakfast.

Best Western Hotel Tria ★ 🍴   The Tria gained 55 rooms in a 2009 renovation that overhauled the existing 66 units. Because of the borderline-suburban location, it usually beats other Cambridge hotels on price and has standard rooms as large as some properties' suites. The building is set back from the busy road, which cuts down on traffic noise. The walking/jogging path and golf course at Fresh Pond, a shopping center, and Whole Foods and Trader Joe's markets are nearby. The T is about 10 minutes away on foot or 5 minutes on the hotel shuttle; Lexington and Concord are less than a half-hour by car.

220 Alewife Brook Pkwy. (at Concord Ave.), Cambridge, MA 02138. © **866/333-8742** or 617/491-8000. Fax 617/491-4932. www.hoteltria.com. 121 units. Mid-Mar to Oct $149–$299 double; Nov to mid-Mar $119–$179 double. Rates include breakfast. Children 16 and under stay free in parent's room. AE, DC, MC, V. Parking $12. T: Red Line to Alewife, then a 10-min. walk. Pets accepted; reservation required ($25 fee and $100 deposit). **Amenities:** Restaurant; bar; coffee shop; bikes; exercise room. *In room:* A/C, TV, fridge, hair dryer, Wi-Fi (free).

Harvard Square Hotel   At busy times, including pretty much every night in the fall, rates for the modest accommodations here seem high—but you really can't beat the location. Smack in the middle of "the Square," the six-story brick hotel is a favorite with visiting parents and budget-conscious business travelers. The unpretentious, well-maintained guest rooms are relatively small but comfortable and neatly decorated in contemporary style. Each has a flatscreen TV (important when every inch counts), and some overlook Harvard Square.

110 Mount Auburn St. (at Eliot St.), Cambridge, MA 02138. © **800/458-5886** or 617/864-5200. Fax 617/492-4896. www.hotelsinharvardsquare.com. 73 units, some with shower only. $99–$229 double. Extra person $10. Children 16 and under stay free in parent's room. AE, DC, DISC, MC, V. Parking $30. T: Red Line to Harvard. **Amenities:** Dining privileges at the Harvard Faculty Club; free access to nearby health club. *In room:* A/C, TV, fridge, hair dryer, Wi-Fi ($10/day).

WHERE TO DINE

Travelers from around the world relish the variety of skillfully prepared seafood available in the Boston area. Lunch is an excellent, economical way to check out a fancy restaurant without breaking the bank. At restaurants that accept reservations, it's always a good idea to make them, particularly for dinner.

Waterfront
EXPENSIVE

Legal Sea Foods ★★★ SEAFOOD   This well-known chain may not be the secret insider tip you were expecting, but trust me. The family-owned business enjoys an international reputation because it serves only the freshest, best-quality fish and shellfish, which it processes at its own state-of-the-art plant. The menu includes regular selections plus whatever looked good at the market that morning, prepared in every imaginable way, and it's all splendid. The chowders—both clam and fish—are justly famous. Entrees run from grilled fish served plain or with Cajun spices (try the arctic char) to *cioppino* (an aquarium's worth of seafood in tomato broth) to mammoth lobsters. And a wine journalist friend tells me the wine list here is the best at any restaurant chain in the country.

255 State St. © **617/742-5300.** www.legalseafoods.com. Reservations recommended. Main courses $11–$19 at lunch, $14–$35 at dinner; lobster market price. AE, DC, DISC, MC, V. Mon–Thurs 11am–10pm; Fri–Sun 11am–11pm. T: Blue Line to Aquarium. Also at the Prudential Center, 800 Boylston St., btw. Fairfield and Gloucester sts. (© **617/266-6800;** T: Green Line B, C, or D to Hynes Convention Center, or E to Prudential); 26 Park Sq., btw. Columbus Ave. and Stuart St. © **617/426-4444;** T: Green Line to Arlington); Copley Place, 2nd level (© **617/266-7775;** T: Orange Line to Back Bay or Green Line to Copley); in the courtyard of the Charles Hotel, 20 University Rd., off Bennett St., Cambridge (© **617/491-9400;** T: Red Line to Harvard); 5 Cambridge Center, off Main St., Cambridge (© **617/864-3400;** T: Red Line to Kendall/MIT); and in the three domestic terminals at Logan Airport.

Boston Dining

Artú **28**
Boston Public Library **5**
Brasserie Jo **6**
The Bristol Lounge **9**
Café Jaffa **2**
Caffè dello Sport **26**
Caffè Vittoria **24**
Chacarero **19, 20**
Chau Chow City **13**
China Pearl **15**
Davio's Northern Italian
  Steakhouse **8**
Durgin-Park **33**
The Elephant Walk **1**
Fajitas & 'Ritas **18**
Galleria Umberto Rosticceria **27**
Gigi Gelateria **23**
Giacomo's Ristorante **29**

Hamersley's Bistro **12**
Hei La Moon **17**
La Summa **30**
Legal Sea Foods (Copley Place) **7**
Legal Sea Foods (Park Square) **10**
Legal Sea Foods (Prudential) **4**
Legal Sea Foods (Waterfront) **35**
Mamma Maria **31**
Market **11**
McCormick & Schmick's **34**
Mike's Pastry **25**
Neptune Oyster **22**
Peach Farm **16**
Pizzeria Regina **21**
Tapéo **3**
Xinh Xinh **14**
Ye Olde Union Oyster House **32**

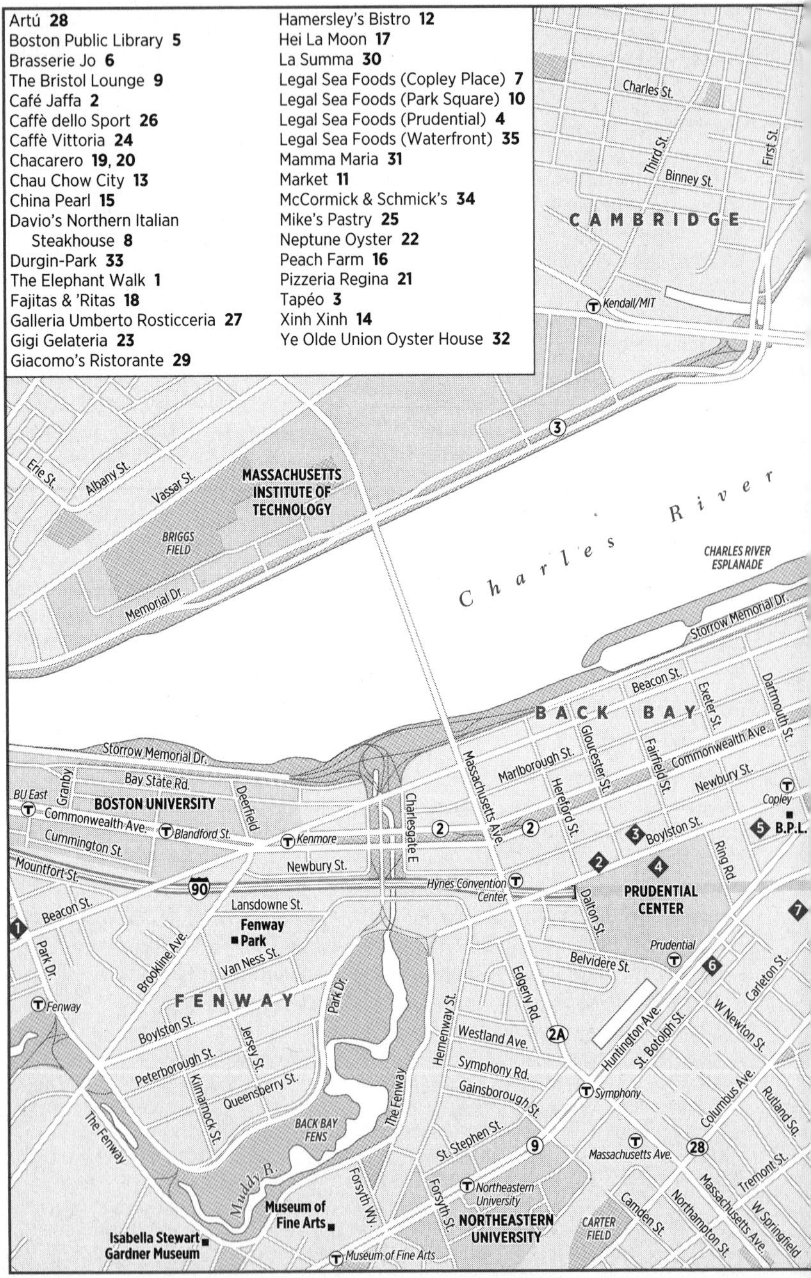

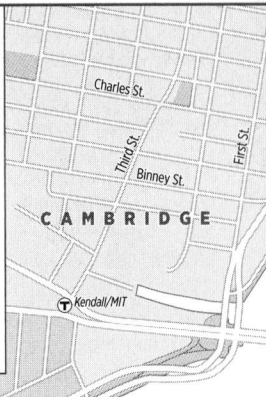

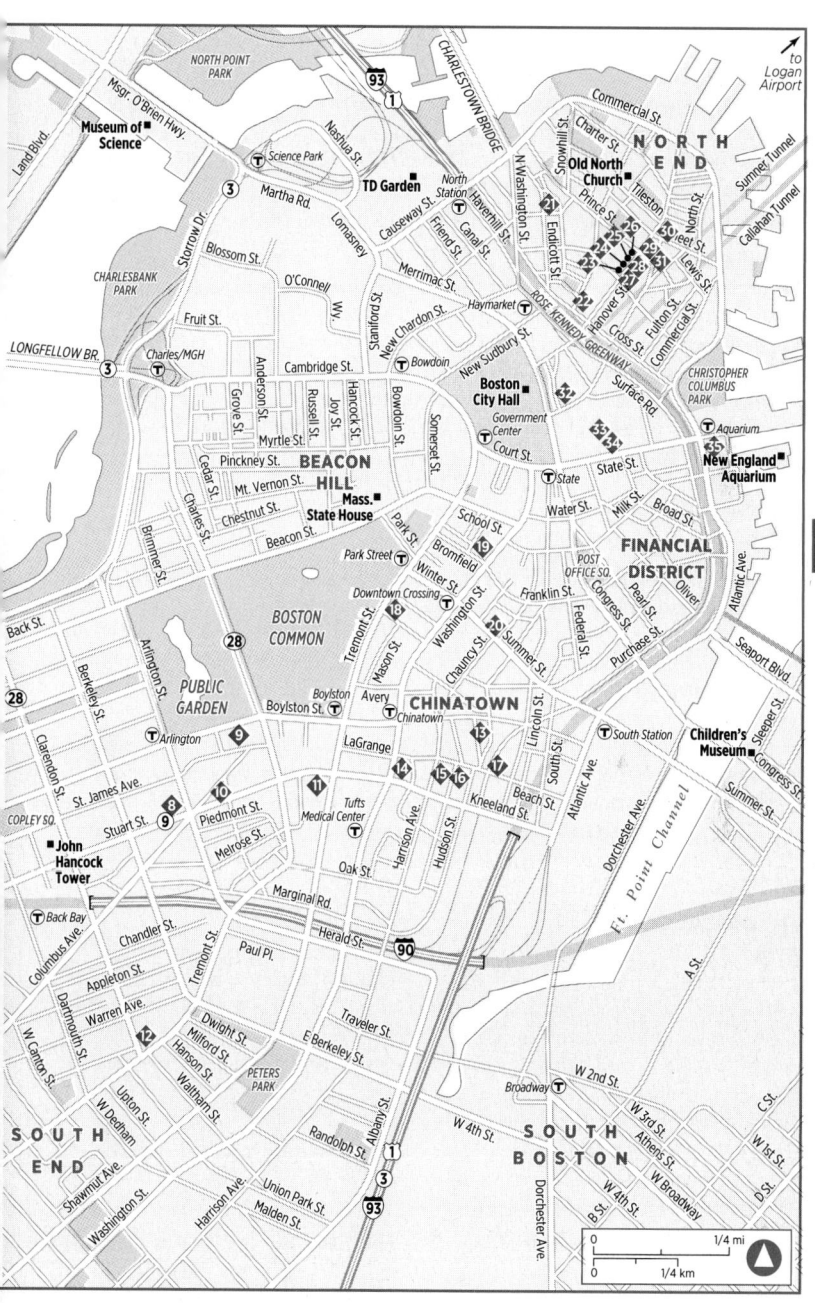

The North End

Many North End restaurants don't serve dessert, but you can satisfy your sweet tooth at a *caffè*. Favorites include **Caffè Vittoria,** 296 Hanover St. (© **617/227-7606**), and **Caffè dello Sport,** 308 Hanover St. (© **617/523-5063**). At **Mike's Pastry,** 300 Hanover St. (© **617/742-3050**), order at the counter and go, or find what you want in the cases, then take a seat and order from a server. For gelato, head to **Gigi Gelateria,** 272 Hanover St. (© **617/720-4243**), which serves 50 flavors of the Italian version of ice cream.

VERY EXPENSIVE

Mamma Maria ★★★ NORTHERN ITALIAN In a town house overlooking North Square and the Paul Revere House, the best restaurant in the North End offers innovative seasonal cuisine in a sophisticated yet comfortable setting. The menu changes seasonally, and portions are more than generous. Fork-tender *osso buco* is almost enough for two, but you'll want it all for yourself. You can't go wrong with main-course pastas, either, and the fresh seafood specials are uniformly marvelous. The pasta, bread, and desserts are homemade, and the wine list is excellent.

3 North Sq. © **617/523-0077.** www.mammamaria.com. Reservations recommended. Main courses $26–$40. AE, DC, DISC, MC, V. Sun–Thurs 5–9:30pm; Fri–Sat 5–10:30pm. Valet parking available. T: Green or Orange Line to Haymarket.

EXPENSIVE

Neptune Oyster ★ SEAFOOD Tiny and cramped, Neptune feels like one of those off-the-radar places out-of-towners fantasize about—or it would, if it weren't so crowded. Superfresh, inventively prepared seafood keeps this restaurant busy and loud almost all the time; even in winter, I suggest planning for lunch or an early dinner on a weekday if you don't enjoy waiting. Check out the daily specials, then start with oysters, comparing specimens from both coasts. Main courses include some menu standards, at least two of which aren't seafood, and dishes that make good use of whatever's fresh that day. Neptune is just off the Freedom Trail and easy to find: Look for the oysters on a bed of ice in the front window and the crowd inside.

63 Salem St. © **617/742-3474.** www.neptuneoyster.com. Reservations not accepted. Main courses $14–$34; lobster market price. AE, MC, V. Sun–Thurs 11:30am–9:30pm; Fri–Sat 11:30am–10:30pm. Raw bar closes 1 hr. after kitchen. T: Green or Orange Line to Haymarket.

MODERATE

Artú ITALIAN Artú is a neighborhood favorite as well as a good stop for Freedom Trail walkers. It's known for superb roasted meats and veggies as well as home-style pasta dishes. Roast lamb, penne alla puttanesca, and chicken stuffed with ham and cheese are all terrific. Panini are big in size and flavor—prosciutto, mozzarella, and tomato is sublime, and chicken parmigiana is tender and filling. Artú isn't great for quiet conversation, especially during dinner in the noisy main room, but it's one of the most reliably satisfying restaurants in the North End.

6 Prince St. © **617/742-4336.** www.artuboston.com. Reservations recommended at dinner. Main courses $8–$14 at lunch, $14–$23 at dinner; sandwiches $6–$8. AE, MC, V. Daily 11am–11pm; bar menu until 1am. T: Green or Orange Line to Haymarket.

Giacomo's Ristorante ★★ ITALIAN/SEAFOOD The line snakes down the street, especially on weekends. No reservations, cash only, a tiny dining room with an open kitchen—what's the secret? Terrific food, plenty of it, and the "we're all in this together" atmosphere. To start, try fried calamari or mozzarella with excellent marinara sauce. Take the chef's advice or put together your own main dish from the list of daily ingredients on a board on the wall; the best suggestion is salmon and sun-dried tomatoes in tomato cream sauce over fettuccine. Nonseafood offerings such as butternut squash ravioli are equally memorable. Service is friendly but incredibly swift. (Those hungry people want your seat.) After a 40-minute dinner, dessert at a *caffè* is practically a necessity.

355 Hanover St. © **617/523-9026.** Reservations not accepted. Main courses $14–$18; specials market price. No credit cards. Mon–Thurs 5–10pm; Fri–Sat 5–10:30pm; Sun 4–10pm. T: Green or Orange Line to Haymarket.

La Summa ★ SOUTHERN ITALIAN   Away from the restaurant rows of Hanover and Salem streets, La Summa maintains a cozy neighborhood atmosphere. It's worth seeking out for wonderful homemade pasta and desserts; more elaborate entrees are scrumptious, too. Try any seafood special, lobster ravioli, *pappardelle e melanzane* (eggplant strips tossed with ethereal fresh pasta), or the house special—veal, chicken, sausage, shrimp, artichokes, pepperoncini, olives, and mushrooms in white-wine sauce. Desserts, especially ricotta cheesecake, are terrific.

30 Fleet St. © **617/523-9503.** www.lasumma.com. Reservations recommended on Fri–Sat. Main courses $12–$24. AE, DC, DISC, MC, V. Mon–Wed 4–10:30pm; Thurs–Sat noon–10:30pm; Sun noon–9:30pm. T: Green or Orange Line to Haymarket.

INEXPENSIVE

An excellent eat-and-run spot just off the Freedom Trail is the cafeteria-style **Galleria Umberto Rosticceria,** 289 Hanover St. (© **617/227-5709**). Join the line for tasty pizza, *arancini* (a rice ball filled with ground beef, peas, and cheese), potato croquettes, or calzones. Lunch is served Monday through Saturday; cash only.

Pizzeria Regina ★★ PIZZA   In business since 1926, Regina's looks like a movie set, but it's the real thing. The line stretches up the street at busy times; even during off hours, business is seldom slow. Busy waitresses weave through the boisterous dining room, delivering peerless pizza hot from the brick oven. The list of toppings includes nouveau ingredients such as sun-dried tomatoes, but that's not authentic. House-made sausage, maybe some pepperoni, and a couple of beers—now, *that's* authentic.

11½ Thacher St. © **617/227-0765.** www.pizzeriaregina.com. Reservations not accepted. Pizza $13–$19. AE, MC, V. Mon–Thurs 11:30am–10pm; Fri–Sat 11:30am–11pm; Sun noon–10pm. T: Green or Orange Line to Haymarket.

Faneuil Hall Marketplace & Financial District

The **food court in Quincy Market,** at the center of Faneuil Hall Marketplace, is a great place to pick up picnic fare. Eat here, or cross Atlantic Avenue and dine in Christopher Columbus Waterfront Park.

EXPENSIVE

The national chain **McCormick & Schmick's Seafood Restaurant** has a branch at Faneuil Hall Marketplace in the North Market Building (© **617/720-5522**).

Ye Olde Union Oyster House ★ NEW ENGLAND/SEAFOOD   America's oldest restaurant in continuous service, the Union Oyster House opened in 1826. Its tasty New England fare is popular with tourists on the adjacent Freedom Trail as well as savvy locals. They're not here for anything fancy; the best bets are simple, classic preparations. Try oyster stew or a cold seafood sampler of oysters, clams, and shrimp. Follow with a broiled or grilled dish such as scrod or salmon, or perhaps fried seafood or grilled pork loin. A "shore dinner" (chowder, steamers, lobster, corn, and dessert) is an excellent introduction to local favorites. *Tip:* A plaque marks John F. Kennedy's favorite booth (no. 18), where he often read the Sunday papers.

41 Union St. (btw. North and Hanover sts.). *℃* **617/227-2750.** www.unionoysterhouse.com. Reservations recommended. Main courses $10–$24 (most under $17) at lunch, $17–$29 at dinner; lobster market price. Children's menu $5–$12. AE, DC, DISC, MC, V. Sun–Thurs 11am–9:30pm (lunch menu until 5pm); Fri–Sat 11am–10pm (lunch until 6pm). Union Bar daily 11am–midnight (lunch until 3pm, late supper until 11pm). Validated and valet parking available. T: Green or Orange Line to Haymarket.

MODERATE

Durgin-Park ★★ ☺ NEW ENGLAND   For huge portions of delicious food and a rowdy atmosphere where CEOs share tables with students, Bostonians have flocked to Durgin-Park since 1827. The line stretches down the stairs to the first floor of Faneuil Hall Marketplace's North Market building, and many diners are here as part of a tour group. Come here for prime rib the size of a hubcap, piles of fried seafood, fish dinners broiled to order, and bounteous portions of roast turkey. Steaks and chops are broiled on an open fire over wood charcoal. This is the place to try Boston baked beans. For dessert, strawberry shortcake is justly celebrated.

340 Faneuil Hall Marketplace. *℃* **617/227-2038.** www.durgin-park.com. Reservations recommended at dinner. Main courses $8–$16 at lunch, $11–$40 at dinner; lobster market price. Children's menu $8–$9. AE, DC, DISC, MC, V. Mon–Sat 11:30am–10pm; Sun 11:30am–9pm. Validated parking available. T: Green or Blue Line to Government Center, Green or Orange Line to Haymarket, or Blue Line to Aquarium.

INEXPENSIVE

Sultan's Kitchen ★ TURKISH/MIDDLE EASTERN   The flavorful, reasonably priced food accounts for the long lunchtime lines at the Sultan's Kitchen. The Turkish cuisine is like nothing else in downtown Boston, and the Middle Eastern options have unusual twists (orange zest in the tabbouleh, fava beans in the falafel). I recommend ordering a combination of *meze* (appetizers), salads, and kabobs, available with sandwiches and as part of a plate with rice pilaf and salads. Most of the businesspeople who flock here are either heading back to the office or eating in the small table area. Lucky you can have everything packed up for a picnic on the Rose Kennedy Greenway or at Christopher Columbus Waterfront Park.

116 State St. (at Broad St.). *℃* **617/570-9009.** www.sultans-kitchen.com. Sandwiches $6–$9; main courses $9–$12. AE, DC, MC, V. Mon–Fri 11am–8:30pm; Sat 11am–4pm. T: Orange or Blue Line to State.

Chinatown/Theater District

The best way to sample Chinese food is by trying **dim sum,** the traditional midday meal featuring a variety of appetizer-style dishes. It's especially popular on weekends, when the variety of offerings is greatest. My favorite destination is **Hei La Moon** ★★, 88 Beach St. (*℃* **617/338-8813;** www.heilamoon.com). Not quite as good, but close, are **China Pearl,** 9 Tyler St., 2nd floor (*℃* **617/426-4338;** www.chinapearlrestaurant.com), and **Chau Chow City,** 83 Essex St. (*℃* **617/338-8158;** http://chauchowcity.net).

The Lunch Line

The lines are so long at **Chacarero**, 26 Province St., between School and Bromfield streets (📞 **617/367-1167**; www.chacarero.com; T: Blue or Orange Line to State), and 101 Arch St., off Summer Street (📞 **617/542-0392**; T: Red or Orange Line to Downtown Crossing), because of the scrumptious Chilean sandwiches, served on house-made bread. Order chicken, beef, or vegetarian "with everything"—tomatoes, cheese, avocado, hot sauce, and (unexpected but delicious) green beans—and dig in. For less than $8, you feel like a savvy Bostonian.

VERY EXPENSIVE

Market ★★★ FUSION   The brainchild of culinary megastar Jean-Georges Vongerichten, Market boasts an inventive menu, exotic and local ingredients, impeccable service, exceptional wine list, even a superb burger. The food demonstrates why chefs have groupies. Main courses show off those local ingredients, with seafood from New England waters bathing in emulsions of Asian spice, citrus, and soy alongside seasonal vegetables, and expertly prepared meat dishes reminding you that you're in a hotel restaurant. I enlisted the pickiest diners I know to help me evaluate Market, and their biggest criticism was that the glass-walled dining room gets somewhat noisy—it's the buzz of happy, satisfied diners.

In the W Boston hotel, 100 Stuart St. (at Tremont St.). 📞 **617/310-6790**. www.marketbyjgboston.com. Reservations recommended. Lunch main courses $21–$24, 3-course prix fixe $26; dinner main courses $15–$39 (most $19–$29), 5-course prix fixe $58 (whole tables only). AE, DC, DISC, MC, V. Mon–Fri 7–10:30am, Sat–Sun 8–11am; daily (Sat–Sun brunch) 11:45am–2:30pm; Sun–Thurs 5–10pm, Fri–Sat 5–11pm. Valet parking available. T: Green Line to Boylston.

MODERATE

Peach Farm ★ SEAFOOD/CANTONESE/SZECHUAN   Chinatown's go-to place for fresh seafood is a subterranean hideaway with no decor to speak of and service so fast that just saying "calamari" seems to make spicy dry-fried salted squid appear on your table. Gobble it up while it's hot, then explore: delicious, messy clams with black-bean sauce; braised chicken or beef hot pot; emerald-green stir-fried pea-pod stems. Spicy salt shrimp—you can eat them whole, shells, heads, and all—is addictive; my favorite is that same spicy salt preparation applied to scallops. Fresh fish steamed with ginger and scallions, a Cantonese classic, comes to your table thrashing in a plastic bucket and reappears moments later, perfectly cooked.

4 Tyler St. 📞 **617/482-3332**. Reservations recommended for large groups at dinner. Main courses $5–$34 (most items less than $15); fresh seafood market price. MC, V. Daily 11am–3am. T: Orange Line to Chinatown.

INEXPENSIVE

Xinh Xinh ★★ VIETNAMESE   One of the best Vietnamese restaurants in the Boston, Xinh Xinh (say "sin sin") offers close to 200 dishes, from fresh spring rolls to specialties that include various animal parts. If you can't find something appealing or need help deciding, the helpful staff will step in. The menu includes wonderful appetizers (try the fried spring rolls), numerous vegetarian options, and an extensive beverage selection. My favorite options are *bun*—shredded lettuce, cooked vermicelli, fresh mint, and other toppings with your choice of hot protein, all mixed together—anything with lemon-grass chicken, and an exceptional version of traditional beef noodle soup, or *pho*.

7 Beach St. (at Knapp St., 1 block from Washington St.). ✆ **617/422-0501.** Main courses $6–$14 (most less than $11). MC, V. Daily 10am–10pm. T: Orange Line to Chinatown.

Fajitas & 'Ritas ★ TEX-MEX   This colorful, entertaining restaurant serves nachos, quesadillas, burritos, and fajitas, exactly the way you want them. Mark your food and drink selections on a checklist, and your busy server quickly returns with big portions of tasty food. Everything is superfresh, because this place is so popular that nothing sits around for very long. As the name indicates, 'ritas (margaritas) are a house specialty. Primarily a casual business destination at lunch, it's livelier at dinner (probably thanks to the 'ritas) and a perfect stop before or after a movie at the nearby AMC Loews Boston Common theater.

25 West St. (btw. Washington and Tremont sts.). ✆ **617/426-1222.** www.fajitasandritas.com. Reservations accepted only for parties of 8 or more. Main dishes $5–$9 at lunch, $6–$14 at dinner. AE, DC, DISC, MC, V. Mon–Tues 11:30am–9pm; Wed–Thurs 11:30am–10pm; Fri–Sat 11:30am–11pm; Sun noon–8pm. T: Red or Green Line to Park St., or Orange Line to Downtown Crossing.

South End

VERY EXPENSIVE

Hamersley's Bistro ★★★ BISTRO   This is the place that put the South End on Boston's culinary map, a pioneering restaurant that manages to be classic *and* contemporary. It's both a top special-occasion restaurant and a neighborhood hangout. The seasonal menu offers entrees noted for their emphasis on local ingredients and classic techniques. Deceptively simple roast chicken with garlic, lemon, and parsley is deservedly famous, and the inventive seafood dishes and flavorful meat preparations are uniformly superb. The wine list and desserts are excellent, and there's seasonal outdoor seating.

553 Tremont St. ✆ **617/423-2700.** www.hamersleysbistro.com. Reservations recommended. Main courses $24–$39; 3-course prix-fixe dinner $38–$42. AE, DISC, MC, V. Sun–Thurs 5:30–9:30pm; Fri–Sat 5:30–10pm. Sun brunch 11am–2pm. Closed 1st week of Jan. Valet parking available. T: Orange Line to Back Bay.

Back Bay

VERY EXPENSIVE

Davio's Northern Italian Steakhouse ★★★ STEAKS/NORTHERN ITALIAN   Robust cuisine in a business-chic setting makes this excellent restaurant a hit with diners in search of top-notch Northern Italian cuisine, picture-perfect steakhouse offerings, and inventive-comfort-food sides. Davio's is a great compromise for Italophiles (the lobster risotto is the best in town) dining with hard-core carnivores. The exceptional wine list includes some rare Italian vintages, and the excellent breads and desserts are made in-house. Despite the open kitchen, the bar in the middle of the room, and the lively lounge area, the noise level allows for conversation, even at busy times. *Tip:* When the Yankees are in town to play the Red Sox, you can often see at least a few of the players here.

75 Arlington St. ✆ **617/357-4810.** www.davios.com. Reservations recommended. Main courses $9–$43 at lunch (most less than $25), $17–$51 at dinner; 4-course tasting menu $75. AE, DC, DISC, MC, V. Mon–Fri

11:30am–3pm; Sun–Tues 5–10pm (lounge menu until 11pm); Wed–Sat 5–11pm (lounge menu until midnight). Validated and valet parking available. T: Green Line to Arlington.

EXPENSIVE

The excellent tapas restaurant **Tapéo,** 266 Newbury St. (② **617/267-4799;** www. tapeo.com), is owned by the same family who owns **Dalí** (p. 114).

Brasserie Jo ★★ REGIONAL FRENCH   The Boston branch of this Chicago favorite serves food that's classic—house-made pâtés, fresh baguettes, superb shellfish, salade Niçoise, Alsatian onion tart, coq au vin—but never boring. The casual, all-day brasserie and bar fits well in this neighborhood, where shoppers can always use a break but might not want a full meal. It's also a good bet before or after a Boston Symphony or Pops performance, and it's popular for business lunches. The noise level can be high when the spacious room is full—have your tête-à-tête at a table near the bar.

In the Colonnade Hotel, 120 Huntington Ave. ② **617/425-3240.** www.brasseriejoboston.com. Reservations recommended at dinner. Main courses $10–$23 (most under $17) at lunch, $17–$33 at dinner; *plats du jour* $18–$32. AE, DC, DISC, MC, V. Mon–Fri 6:30am–11pm; Sat 7am–11pm; Sun 7am–10pm; late-night menu daily until 1am. Valet and garage parking available. T: Green Line E to Prudential.

The Bristol Lounge ★★ AMERICAN   The Bristol Lounge is to a regular restaurant as the Four Seasons is to a regular hotel: It looks about the same, but everything is just *better.* The all-day menu extends from pricey breakfast items to tasty bar bites to sophisticated versions of classic dishes. The juicy burgers are famous, the soups and salads depend on what's fresh and seasonal, and the main courses are top-of-the-line comfort food (roasted chicken, hand-rolled pastas). Desserts are inventive versions of traditional favorites. In keeping with every other element of a meal here, the service is fantastic.

In the Four Seasons Hotel, 200 Boylston St. ② **617/338-4400.** www.fourseasons.com/boston. Reservations recommended. Main courses $18–$33 at lunch, $20–$35 at dinner; bar menu $8–$27. AE, DC, DISC, MC, V. Mon–Thurs 6:30am–11:30pm; Fri 6:30am–12:30am; Sat 7am–12:30am; Sun 7am–11:30pm. Valet parking available. T: Green Line to Arlington.

INEXPENSIVE

In the Boston Public Library, 700 Boylston St. (② **617/859-2251;** www.thecateredaffair.com/bpl), the **Courtyard** restaurant serves weekday lunch and afternoon tea Wednesday through Friday, and the self-service **MapRoom Café** serves meals and snacks Monday through Saturday from 9am to 5pm.

Café Jaffa MIDDLE EASTERN   A long, narrow brick room with a glass front, Café Jaffa looks more like a snazzy pizza place than the excellent Middle Eastern restaurant it is. Reasonable prices, high quality, and large portions draw crowds for traditional dishes such as falafel, baba ghanoush, and hummus, as well as burgers and steak tips. For dessert, try the baklava if it's fresh (give it a pass if not).

48 Gloucester St. ② **617/536-0230.** www.cafejaffa.net. Main courses $8–$19; sandwiches and salads $5–$10. AE, DC, DISC, MC, V. Mon–Thurs 11am–10:30pm; Fri–Sat 11am–11pm; Sun noon–10pm. T: Green Line B, C, or D to Hynes Convention Center.

Kenmore Square

EXPENSIVE

The Elephant Walk ★★ FRENCH/CAMBODIAN   France meets Cambodia on the menu at this madly popular spot 4 blocks from Kenmore Square. Many Cambodian dishes have part-French names, such as *curry de crevettes* (shrimp curry with picture-perfect vegetables) and *mee siem au poulet,* a tangle of rice noodles, sliced omelet, tofu, chicken, and vegetables. Or try *loc lac,* fork-tender beef cubes in addictively spicy sauce. On the French side, you'll find classics such as roasted chicken and pan-seared tuna. Vegetarians, vegans, and diners who can't have gluten are well taken care of, and the pleasant staff will help out if you need guidance.

900 Beacon St. ☏ **617/247-1500.** www.elephantwalk.com. Reservations recommended. Main courses $10–$20 at lunch (most items less than $12), $15–$20 at dinner; 3-course tasting menu $17 at lunch, $30 at dinner. AE, DC, DISC, MC, V. Mon–Fri 11:30am–2:30pm; Sun–Thurs 5–10pm; Fri–Sat 5–11pm; Sun brunch 11am–2:30pm. Valet parking available at dinner. T: Green Line C to St. Mary's St.

Cambridge

The Red Line runs from downtown Boston to Harvard Square. Many of the restaurants listed here can be reached on foot from there. To go in search of inexpensive ethnic food, head for Central and Inman squares.

Note: See the "Cambridge Accommodations & Dining" map, on p. 103, for the locations of the restaurants reviewed below.

VERY EXPENSIVE

Upstairs on the Square ★★ AMERICAN   Overlooking a park off Harvard Square, Upstairs on the Square is the perfect combination of comfort food and fine dining. It consists of two lovely spaces; I prefer the more casual Monday Club Bar, a dining room where firelight flickers on jewel-toned walls. The food—unusual salads and sandwiches, satisfying soups, fried chicken, inventive pastas, steak with ever-changing versions of potatoey goodness—is homey and satisfying, and the bar is a tweedy Cambridge scene. The top-floor **Soirée Room,** a jewel box of pinks and golds under a low, mirrored ceiling, is the place for that big anniversary dinner. In both rooms, you'll find outstanding wine selections and desserts.

91 Winthrop St. (at John F. Kennedy St.). ☏ **617/864-1933.** www.upstairsonthesquare.com. Reservations recommended. Monday Club Bar main courses $13–$28, prix-fixe lunch $20. Soirée Room main courses $23–$34, tasting menus $50–$95. AE, DC, DISC, MC, V. Monday Club Bar Mon–Sat 11am–3pm; Sun–Thurs 5–10pm, Fri–Sat 5–11pm (bar until 1am); Sun brunch 10am–3pm; afternoon tea Sat 3–5pm. Soirée Room Tues–Thurs 5–10pm; Fri–Sat 5:30–11pm. Validated and valet parking available. T: Red Line to Harvard.

EXPENSIVE

Legal Sea Foods has branches in Harvard Square and in Kendall Square; see "Waterfront," above.

Dalí ★★ SPANISH   This festive restaurant casts an irresistible spell—people wait an hour or more for a table and hardly complain. The authentic Spanish fare includes excellent paella, but most diners come in a group and explore the tapas offerings, all perfect for sharing. They include delectable garlic potatoes, salmon balls with not-too-salty caper sauce, pork tenderloin with blue goat cheese, and delicious sausages, plus monthly specials. The staff sometimes seems rushed but never fails to supply bread for sopping up juices and sangria for washing it all down. I like to finish with "ubiquitous flan" or *tarta de chocolates.*

415 Washington St., Somerville. ☏ **617/661-3254.** www.DaliRestaurant.com. Reservations accepted only Sun–Thurs until 6:30pm, Fri until 6pm, Sat for parties of 6 or more until 6pm. Tapas $4.50–$16 (most $10 or less); main courses $20–$25; late-night menu $4.50–$9. AE, DC, MC, V. Daily 5:30–11pm; bar serves food until 12:30am. T: Red Line to Harvard; follow Kirkland St. to intersection of Washington and Beacon sts. (20-min. walk or $5 cab ride).

East Coast Grill & Raw Bar ★★★ SEAFOOD/BARBECUE   Huge portions, a dizzying menu, and funky decor have made the East Coast Grill incredibly popular since 1985. The kitchen handles fresh seafood (an encyclopedic variety), barbecue, and grilled fish and meats with authority and imagination. The influence of founder Chris Schlesinger, a national expert on grilling and spicy food, is apparent in the exuberant menu descriptions ("super fresh catch o' the moment," "wings of mass destruction"). More than at perhaps any other restaurant in town, it's imperative to check the specials board here—thank me later.

1271 Cambridge St., Inman Sq. ⓒ **617/491-6568.** www.eastcoastgrill.net. Reservations accepted only for parties of 5 or more Sun–Thurs. Main courses $15–$30; fresh seafood market price. AE, DISC, MC, V. Sun–Thurs 5:30–10pm; Fri–Sat 5:30–10:30pm; Sun brunch 11am–2:30pm. Validated parking available. T: Red Line to Central, 10-min. walk on Prospect St., or Red Line to Harvard, then bus 69 (Harvard-Lechmere) to Inman Sq.

Hungry Mother ★ SOUTHERN/CONTEMPORARY AMERICAN   French technique transforms Southern food at this casual little place, one of Boston's most reliable neighborhood restaurants. Hungry Mother's menu changes with the season, emphasizing local and sustainable ingredients. That translates to an unforgettable appetizer of Maine shrimp and grits with chunks of house-made tasso ham, super-crispy cornmeal crusts on green tomatoes and delectable catfish, pork shoulder stewed in bourbon and served with one chewy rib. Desserts are more Southern than French; if sweets aren't your thing, consider something from the inventive drinks menu.

233 Cardinal Medeiros Ave. (at Bristol St., 1 block from Hampshire St.), Kendall Sq. ⓒ **617/499-0090.** www.hungrymothercambridge.com. Reservations recommended. Main courses $17–$25; late-night menu $3–$11. AE, DC, DISC, MC, V. Tues–Sun 5–10pm, late-night menu 10pm–12:30am. Validated parking available. T: Red Line to Kendall/MIT, then 10-min. walk.

MODERATE

Baraka Café ★ ALGERIAN/TUNISIAN/MEDITERRANEAN   A tiny, aromatic destination for adventurous diners, Baraka Café specializes in flavorful, highly spiced (not necessarily hot) cuisine. Locals talk about it as though it's a secret, but one look at the line that forms on weekend evenings will tell you it's not. The drawbacks—no alcohol, cash only, tiny dining room, deliberate service—are insignificant when the food is this good. It's easy to fill up on house-made breads and appetizers, but save room for the likes of fork-tender lamb chops and eggplant stuffed with a tasty concoction of olives, spinach, scallions, and two cheeses. Daily specials show off the kitchen's considerable abilities better than the limited regular menu.

80½ Pearl St., Central Sq. ⓒ **617/868-3951.** www.barakacafe.com. Reservations not accepted. Main courses $5–$9 at lunch, $9–$16 at dinner. No credit cards. Tues–Sat 11:30am–3pm; Tues–Sun 5:30–10pm. T: Red Line to Central.

The Helmand ★★ AFGHAN   The unusual cuisine, elegant setting, and reasonable prices make this spacious spot near the CambridgeSide Galleria mall the worst-kept secret in Cambridge. The delectable flavors and textures evoke Middle Eastern, Indian, and Pakistani cuisine. Many dishes are vegetarian, and meat is often one element of a dish rather than the centerpiece. Every meal comes with delectable bread made fresh in a wood-fired brick oven near the entrance. The grilled entrees are fine, but I prefer homier dishes such as pastas and stews. For dessert, don't miss the Afghan version of baklava.

143 First St. ☎ **617/492-4646.** www.helmandrestaurantcambridge.com. Reservations recommended. Main courses $13–$23. AE, MC, V. Sun–Thurs 5–10pm; Fri–Sat 5–11pm. T: Green Line to Lechmere.

INEXPENSIVE

The food court on the lower level of the **Porter Exchange** mall, 1815 Mass. Ave., Porter Square, is home to half a dozen or so Japanese businesses that attract expats from all over the Boston area. They all open in the late morning and close by 9pm. The superauthentic dining options are mostly fast-food counters with small seating areas; regardless of where you eat, finish up with French- and Japanese-style pastries at **Japonaise Bakery** (☎ 617/547-5531).

Mr. Bartley's Burger Cottage ★★ AMERICAN   Great burgers and phenomenal onion rings make Bartley's a perennial favorite with a cross-section of Cambridge. Founded in 1960, this family business is a high-ceilinged, crowded room plastered with memorabilia. Anything you can think of to put on ground beef is available, from American cheese to grilled pineapple. Good dishes that don't involve meat include veggie burgers and creamy, garlicky hummus.

1246 Mass. Ave. ☎ **617/354-6559.** www.bartleysburgers.com. Burgers $10–$14; main courses, salads, and sandwiches $5–$9. No credit cards. Mon–Sat 11am–9pm. Closed Dec 25–Jan 1. T: Red Line to Harvard.

Veggie Planet ★ PIZZA/VEGETARIAN/VEGAN   Don't let the virtuous slant of Veggie Planet's menu put you off—this is tasty, flavorful food that happens to be (mostly) good for you. The subterranean restaurant in the legendary coffeehouse and folk club has an unusual specialty: your choice of organic pizza dough, brown rice, or coconut rice, topped with combinations of ingredients. Some—tomatoes, spinach, and cheese—you'd expect to see on pizza; others, such as zesty peanut curry or black beans, salsa, and pepper jack cheese, you might not. There's no meat, and dairy only if you want it. Salads, soups, and delectable desserts round out the menu, which features natural and fair-trade soft drinks in addition to beer and wine.

In Club Passim, 47 Palmer St. (at Church St., 1 block from Mass. Ave.). ☎ **617/661-1513.** www.veggie planet.net. Main courses $7–$11; children's menu $3–$6. No credit cards. Mon–Sat 11:30am–10:30pm, Sun 11am–10:30pm (brunch until 3pm). T: Red Line to Harvard.

SEEING THE SIGHTS IN BOSTON

At press time, the **Boston Tea Party Ship & Museum** (☎ 617/269-7150; www. bostonteapartyship.com), which closed after a fire in 2001, was scheduled to reopen in 2011. Check at your hotel or call ahead before setting out.

DISCOUNT PASSES   As you plan your sightseeing, consider these money-saving options. Check their respective websites for info about buying each pass.

If you concentrate on the included attractions, a **Boston CityPass** (☎ 888/330-5008; www.citypass.com) offers great savings. It's a booklet of tickets to the Museum of Fine Arts, Museum of Science, New England Aquarium, Skywalk Observatory at the Prudential Center, and either the Kennedy Library or Harvard Museum of Natural History. The price (at press time, $46 for adults, $29 for children 3–11) represents a 46% savings for adults who visit all six attractions, and having a ticket means you can go straight to the entrance without waiting in line. The passes, good for 9 days from first use, include discounts good at other local businesses.

Boston Attractions

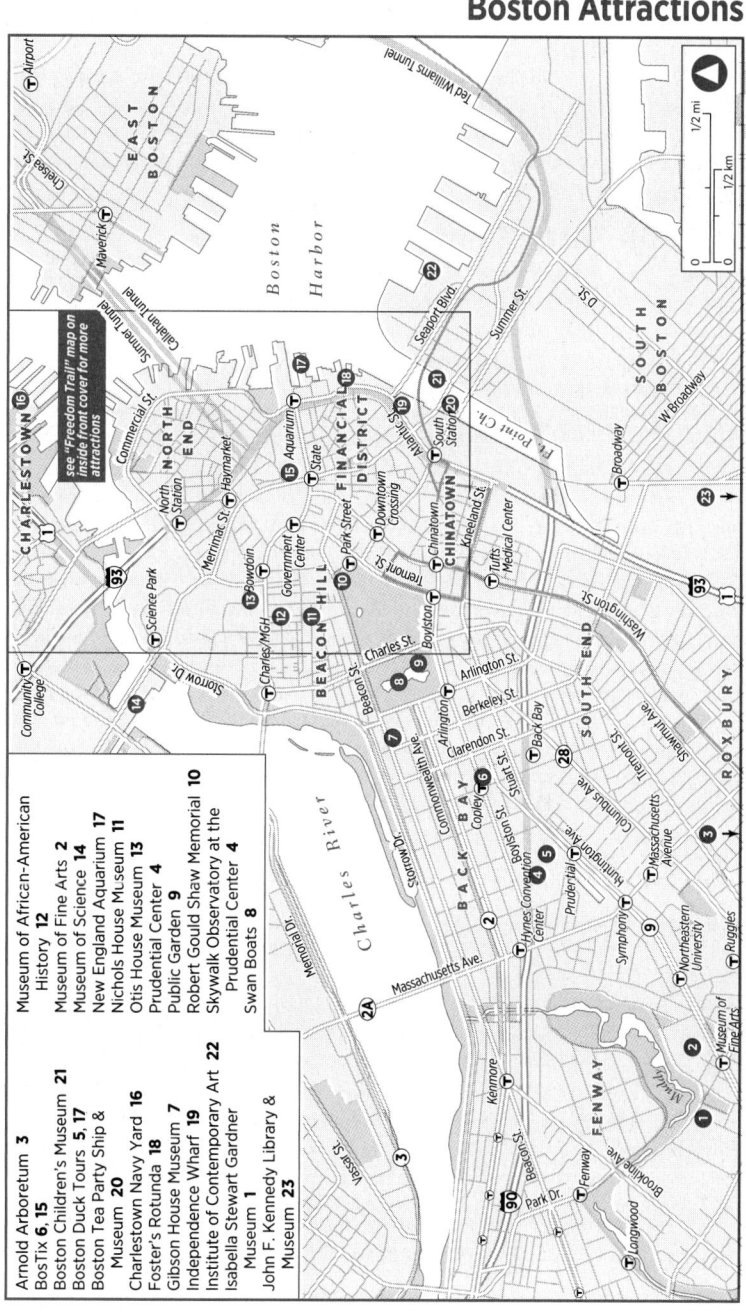

Arnold Arboretum **3**
BosTix **6, 15**
Boston Children's Museum **21**
Boston Duck Tours **5, 17**
Boston Tea Party Ship &
  Museum **20**
Charlestown Navy Yard **16**
Foster's Rotunda **18**
Gibson House Museum **7**
Independence Wharf **19**
Institute of Contemporary Art **22**
Isabella Stewart Gardner
  Museum **1**
John F. Kennedy Library &
  Museum **23**

Museum of African-American
  History **12**
Museum of Fine Arts **2**
Museum of Science **14**
New England Aquarium **17**
Nichols House Museum **11**
Otis House Museum **13**
Prudential Center **4**
Public Garden **9**
Robert Gould Shaw Memorial **10**
Skywalk Observatory at the
  Prudential Center **4**
Swan Boats **8**

see "Freedom Trail" map on
inside front cover for more
attractions

CityPass's main competition is the **Go Boston Card** (© **800/887-9103;** www. gobostoncard.com). It includes admission to 70 Boston-area and New England attractions, a guidebook, dining and shopping discounts, and a 2-day trolley pass. If you strategize wisely, this card can be a great value. It costs $50 for 1 day, $75 for 2 days, $96 for 3 days, $135 for 5 days, and $165 for 7 days, with discounts for children and winter travelers. A spin-off, the Explorer Pass, lets you select 3 of the 25 included attractions and is good for 30 days. It costs $45 for adults and $29 for children—a potentially good deal, but do the math.

The Top Attractions

Faneuil Hall Marketplace ★★ ☺ Since Boston's most popular attraction opened in 1976, cities all over the country have imitated the "festival market" concept. The complex of shops, food counters, restaurants, bars, and public spaces is such a magnet for tourists and suburbanites that you might understandably think the only Bostonians here are employees.

The five-building complex incorporates brick-and-stone plazas that teem with crowds shopping, eating, performing, watching performers, and people-watching. In warm weather, it's busy from just after dawn until well past dark. **Quincy Market** (you'll hear the whole complex called by that name) is the central Greek Revival–style building; its central corridor is an enormous food court. On either side, glass canopies cover restaurants, bars, and pushcarts that hold everything from crafts created by New England artisans to hokey souvenirs. Here you'll also see a bar that exactly replicates the set of the TV show *Cheers.* In the plaza between the **South Canopy** and the South Market building is an **information kiosk,** and throughout the complex you'll find a mix of chain stores and unique shops. One constant since the year after the original market opened (1826) is **Durgin-Park,** a traditional New England restaurant (p. 110). **Faneuil Hall ★** itself—nicknamed the "Cradle of Liberty"—sometimes gets overlooked, but it's well worth a visit. National Park Service rangers give free 20-minute talks every half-hour from 9am to 5pm in the second-floor auditorium.

Btw. North, Congress, and State sts. and John F. Fitzgerald Surface Rd. © **617/523-1300.** www.faneuilhall marketplace.com. Marketplace Mon–Sat 10am–9pm; Sun noon–6pm. Food court opens earlier; some restaurants and bars close later. T: Green Line to Government Center, Orange Line to Haymarket or State, or Blue Line to Aquarium or State.

Institute of Contemporary Art ★★ The city's first new art museum in nearly a century, the ICA is a blast. The cantilevered building juts out above the harbor, affording views of the water, the waterfront, and the airport. Besides being an irresistible draw, the architecture reflects the institution's curatorial philosophy that art is inseparable from everyday life. The ICA showcases 20th- and 21st-century art in every imaginable medium, including film and video, music, literature, and dance. Opened in 2006, the 65,000-square-foot museum gives the institution the space it needs to create a permanent collection for the first time since its founding (under a different name) in 1936. Visitors have already enjoyed works by Louise Bourgeois and Anish Kapoor that wouldn't have fit in (literally or figuratively) elsewhere in Boston, and the schedule of events, concerts, films, and other activities seemingly can't expand quickly enough. The cafe overlooks the water and offers outdoor seating in fine weather, and the gift shop, the **ICA Store,** is spectacular.

100 Northern Ave. © **617/478-3100.** www.icaboston.org. Admission $15 adults, $10 seniors and students, free for children 17 and under and those visiting only the cafe. Free to all Thurs after 5pm and to families (up to 2 adults with children 12 and under) last Sat of month Jan–Oct. Sat–Sun, Tues–Wed, and some Mon holidays 10am–5pm; Thurs–Fri 10am–9pm. T: Red Line to South Station, then Silver Line bus to World Trade Center.

Isabella Stewart Gardner Museum ★★ Isabella Stewart Gardner (1840–1924) was an incorrigible individualist long before such behavior was acceptable for a woman in polite Boston society, and her legacy is a treasure for art lovers. "Mrs. Jack" designed her exquisite home in the style of a 15th-century Venetian palace and filled it with European, American, and Asian painting and sculpture. You'll see works by Titian, Botticelli, Raphael, Rembrandt, Matisse, and Mrs. Gardner's friends James McNeill Whistler and John Singer Sargent. Titian's magnificent *Europa* is one of the most important Renaissance paintings in the United States.

The building holds a hodgepodge of furniture and architectural details imported from European churches and palaces. The *pièce de résistance* is the magnificent skylit courtyard, filled year-round with fresh flowers from the museum greenhouse. A special exhibition gallery features two or three changing shows a year, often by contemporary artists in residence, and a new wing designed by internationally renowned architect Renzo Piano is under construction and scheduled to open in 2012.

280 The Fenway. © **617/566-1401.** www.gardnermuseum.org. Admission $12 adults, $10 seniors, $5 college students. Free for children 17 and under, adults named Isabella with ID, and adults on their birthdays. Tues–Sun and some Mon holidays 11am–5pm. T: Green Line E to Museum of Fine Arts.

John F. Kennedy Library and Museum ★★ ☺ The Kennedy era springs to life at this dramatic complex overlooking Dorchester Bay. It captures the 35th president's accomplishments in video and audio recordings as well as fascinating displays of memorabilia and photos. Far from being a static experience, it changes regularly, with temporary shows and reinterpreted displays that highlight and complement the permanent exhibits. A visit begins with a 17-minute film about Kennedy's early life. The exhibits start with the 1960 campaign and end with a tribute to Kennedy's legacy. There's a film about the Cuban Missile Crisis, along with displays on Attorney General Robert F. Kennedy, the civil rights movement, the Peace Corps, the space program, First Lady Jacqueline Bouvier Kennedy, the Kennedy family, and JFK's assassination and funeral.

Columbia Point. © **866/JFK-1960** or 617/514-1600. www.jfklibrary.org. Admission $12 adults, $10 seniors and students with ID, $9 youths 13–17; free for children 12 and under. Surcharges may apply for special exhibitions. Daily 9am–5pm (last film at 3:55pm). T: Red Line to JFK/UMass, then free shuttle bus (every 20 min.). By car, take Southeast Expwy. (I-93/Rte. 3) south to exit 15 (Morrissey Blvd./JFK Library), turn left onto Columbia Rd., and follow signs to free parking lot.

Museum of African American History ★★ ☺ The final stop on the **Black Heritage Trail** (p. 121) offers a comprehensive look at the history and contributions of blacks in Boston and Massachusetts. Changing and permanent exhibits incorporate art, artifacts, documents, historic photographs, and other objects—including many family heirlooms. The museum occupies the **Abiel Smith School** (1834), the first American public grammar school for African-American children, and the **African Meeting House,** 8 Smith Ct. The oldest standing black church in the United States, the meetinghouse opened in 1806. Once known as the "Black Faneuil Hall," it also schedules lectures, concerts, and church meetings.

46 Joy St. ✆ **617/725-0022.** www.maah.org. Admission $5 adults, $3 seniors and youths 13–17; free for children 12 and under. Mon–Sat 10am–4pm. T: Red or Green Line to Park St. or Red Line to Charles/MGH.

Museum of Fine Arts ★★★ ☺   One of the world's great museums, the MFA works constantly to become even more accessible and interesting. Every installation reflects a curatorial attitude that makes even those who go in with a feeling of obligation leave with a sense of discovery and wonder. That includes children, who can launch a scavenger hunt, admire the mummies, or participate in family-friendly programs scheduled year-round. At press time, the museum was completing its new **Art of the Americas Wing,** the heart of a quarter-million-square-foot expansion project that was scheduled to open in November 2010.

The MFA is especially noted for its **Impressionist paintings ★★★** (including dozens of Monets), Asian and Old Kingdom Egyptian collections, classical art, Buddhist temple, and fashion arts. The American and European paintings and sculpture are a remarkable assemblage of timeless works that may seem as familiar as the face in the mirror or as unexpected as a comet. There are also magnificent holdings of prints, photography, furnishings, and decorative arts, including the finest collection of Paul Revere silver in the world. The museum has a cafeteria, cafe, and fine-dining restaurant as well as an excellent gift shop. Pick up a floor plan (available in eight languages) at the Sharf Information Center, or take a free **guided tour** (weekdays except Mon holidays at 10:30am–3pm; Wed at 6:15pm; Sat–Sun 11am–3pm).

The MFA's adult admission fee, which covers two visits within 10 days, is among the highest in the country. A Boston CityPass or Go Boston Card (see the introduction to this section) is a great deal if you plan to visit enough of the other included attractions.

465 Huntington Ave. ✆ **617/267-9300.** www.mfa.org. Admission $20 adults, $18 seniors and students; $7.50 children 7–17 on school days until 3pm, otherwise free. Admission good for 2 visits within 10 days. Voluntary contribution ($20 suggested) Wed 4–9:45pm. Free admission to museum shop, library, and restaurants. Sat–Tues 10am–4:45pm; Wed–Fri 10am–9:45pm. T: Green Line E to Museum of Fine Arts or Orange Line to Ruggles.

Museum of Science ★★★ ☺   For the ultimate pain-free educational experience, head to the Museum of Science. The demonstrations, experiments, and interactive displays introduce facts and concepts so effortlessly that everyone learns something. Take a couple of hours or a whole day to explore the permanent and temporary exhibits, most of them hands on and all of them great fun. Among the hundreds of exhibits, you might find out how much you'd weigh on the moon, battle urban traffic (in a computer model), or climb into a space module. Activity centers focus on individual and interdisciplinary fields of interest—natural history (with live animals), computers, and the human body. Temporary exhibits change regularly, and just about any time you hear about a national or international touring show, this is one of its stops.

The separate-admission theaters are worth planning for, even if you're skipping the exhibits. Buy all your tickets at once, because shows sometimes sell out. The **Mugar Omni Theater ★★★**, which shows IMAX movies on a five-story screen, is an intense experience. Check ahead for information about science and rock-music laser shows at the **Charles Hayden Planetarium,** which was under renovation at press time.

Science Park, off O'Brien Hwy. on bridge btw. Boston and Cambridge. © **617/723-2500.** www.mos. org. Admission to exhibit halls $20 adults, $18 seniors, $17 children 3–11; to Butterfly Garden or 3-D Digital Cinema (available only with exhibit hall admission) $4.50 adults, $4 seniors, $3.50 children 3–11. Mugar Omni Theater $9 adults, $8 seniors, $7 children 3–11. Discounted combination tickets available. July 5 to Labor Day Sat–Thurs 9am–7pm, Fri 9am–9pm; day after Labor Day to July 4 Sat–Thurs 9am–5pm, Fri 9am–9pm. Extended hours during school vacations. T: Green Line to Science Park.

New England Aquarium ★ ☺ This entertaining complex is home to more than 15,000 fish and aquatic mammals. At busy times, it seems to contain at least that many people. You'll want to spend at least half a day, and afternoon crowds can make getting around painfully slow, so try to make this your first stop of the day, especially on weekends. Also consider buying a Boston CityPass or Go Boston Card (p. 116) and skipping the ticket line. The **Simons IMAX Theatre** ★★★, which has its own hours and admission fees, is worth planning ahead for, too. It shows 3-D films that concentrate on the natural world. Discounts are available when you combine a visit to the aquarium with an IMAX film or a whale watch (see "Organized Tours," below).

The focal point of the main building is the four-story, 200,000-gallon **Giant Ocean Tank.** It holds a replica of a Caribbean coral reef, a vast assortment of sea creatures, and, twice a day, scuba divers who feed the sharks. Other exhibits focus on freshwater and tropical specimens, the Amazon, jellyfish, and the ecology of Boston Harbor. The hands-on **Edge of the Sea** exhibit contains a tide pool with sea stars, sea urchins, and horseshoe crabs; and the **Medical Center** is a working veterinary hospital.

Central Wharf (Milk St. and Old Atlantic Ave.). © **617/973-5200.** www.newenglandaquarium.org. Admission $21 adults, $19 seniors, $13 children 3–11. Free admission for outdoor exhibits, cafe, and gift shop. July to Labor Day Sun–Thurs 9am–6pm, Fri–Sat and holidays 9am–7pm; day after Labor Day to June Mon–Fri 9am–5pm, Sat–Sun and holidays 9am–6pm. Simons IMAX Theatre: © **866/815-4629.** Tickets $10–$13 adults, $8–$11 children 3–11. Daily from 9:30am. T: Blue Line to Aquarium.

The Freedom Trail ★★★

A line of red paint or red brick down the center of the sidewalk, the 2½-mile Freedom Trail links 16 historic sights. Markers identify the stops, and plaques point the way from one to the next. The trail begins at **Boston Common,** where the Information Center, 148 Tremont St., distributes pamphlets that describe a self-guided tour.

A 2-hour narrative commissioned by the Freedom Trail Foundation (© **617/357-8300;** www.thefreedomtrail.org) includes interviews, sound effects, and music, and allows visitors to tour the trail at their own pace. It costs $15 (credit cards only); buy it as an MP3 download, or rent a handheld digital audio player, for use with or without headphones, that can be picked up at the Boston Common Visitor Center and dropped off there or at several other locations. The foundation's costumed **Freedom Trail Players** lead 90-minute tours ($13 adults, $11 seniors and students, $7 children 12 and under) on two different, overlapping routes around downtown and the North End. Make reservations online, allowing time to explore the interactive website.

You can also explore the 1.5-mile **Black Heritage Trail** ★★ from here. Two-hour guided tours start at the **Robert Gould Shaw Memorial,** on Beacon Street across from the State House. They're available Monday through Saturday from Memorial Day to Labor Day and by request at other times; contact the visitor center (© **617/742-5415;** www.nps.gov/boaf) for starting times or to make a reservation. Or go on your own, using a brochure (available at the Museum of African American History and the Boston Common and State Street visitor centers) that includes a map and descriptions of the buildings. The trail includes stations on the Underground Railroad and homes of famous citizens. The only stops that are open to the public are the **African Meeting House** and the **Abiel Smith School,** which make up the **Museum of African American History** (p. 119).

As you follow the Freedom Trail, you'll come to the **Boston National Historical Park Visitor Center,** 15 State St. (© **617/242-5642;** www.nps.gov/bost). From here, rangers lead free tours from Patriots Day through November; check ahead for the schedule. The first-come, first-served tours are limited to 30 people and not offered in bad weather. The wheelchair-accessible center has restrooms and a bookstore. It's open daily from 9am to 5pm.

The hard-core history fiend who peers at every artifact and reads every plaque along the trail will wind up at Bunker Hill some 4 hours later, weary but rewarded. The family with restless children will probably appreciate the enforced efficiency of the 90-minute ranger-led tour.

Space doesn't permit detailing every stop on the trail, but here's a concise listing:

o **Boston Common.** In 1634, when their settlement was just 4 years old, the town fathers paid the Rev. William Blackstone £30 for this property. In 1640, it was set aside as common land. Be sure to stop at Beacon and Park streets, where a **memorial ★★★** designed by Augustus Saint-Gaudens celebrates Col. Robert Gould Shaw and the Union Army's 54th Massachusetts Colored Regiment, who fought in the Civil War. You may remember the story of the first American army unit made up of free black soldiers from the movie *Glory.*

o **Massachusetts State House** (© **617/727-3676;** www.mass.gov/statehouse). Charles Bulfinch designed the "new" State House, and Gov. Samuel Adams laid the cornerstone of the state capitol in 1795. Take a self-guided tour or call ahead to schedule a conducted tour (weekdays 10am–3:30pm).

o **Park Street Church,** 1 Park St. (© **617/523-3383;** www.parkstreet.org). The plaque at the corner of Tremont Street describes this Congregational church's storied past. From mid-June through August, it's open for tours Tuesday through Friday from 9am to 4pm, Saturday 9am to 3pm. Year-round Sunday services are at 8:30 and 11am, and 4 and 6pm.

o **Old Granary Burying Ground.** This cemetery, established in 1660, contains the graves of Samuel Adams, Paul Revere, John Hancock, and the wife of Isaac Vergoose, believed to be the "Mother Goose" of nursery-rhyme fame. It's open daily from 9am to 5pm (until 3pm in winter).

o **King's Chapel,** 58 Tremont St. (© **617/523-1749;** www.kings-chapel.org). Completed in 1754, this church was built by erecting the granite edifice around the existing wooden chapel. The **burying ground** (1630), facing Tremont Street, is the oldest in Boston. It's open daily from 8am to 5:30pm (until 3pm in winter).

o **Site of the First Public School.** A colorful mosaic in the sidewalk on (of course) School Street honors the school, founded in 1634. Inside the fence that surrounds adjacent Old City Hall is the 1856 **Benjamin Franklin statue,** the first portrait statue erected in Boston.

o **Old Corner Bookstore Building,** 3 School St. Built in 1718, it's on a plot of land that was once home to the religious reformer Anne Hutchinson.

o **Old South Meeting House ★**, 310 Washington St. (© **617/482-6439;** www. osmh.org). Originally built in 1670 and replaced by the current structure in 1729, it was the starting point of the Boston Tea Party. It's open daily, April to October from 9:30am to 5pm, November to March from 10am to 4pm. Admission is $6 for adults, $5 for seniors, and $1 for children 6 to 18.

- **Old State House Museum** ★, 206 Washington St. (✆ **617/720-1713;** www. bostonhistory.org). Built in 1713, this building was the seat of Colonial government in Massachusetts before the Revolution, and the state capitol until 1798. The fascinating exhibits spotlight city history. The museum is open daily from 9am to 6pm in July and August, until 4pm in January, and until 5pm the rest of the year. Admission is $7.50 for adults, $6 for seniors and students, and $3 for children 6 to 18.

- **Boston Massacre Site.** On a traffic island in State Street, across from the T station under the Old State House, a ring of cobblestones marks the place where the skirmish took place on March 5, 1770.

- **Faneuil Hall** ★ (✆ 617/242-5642; www.nps.gov/bost). Built in 1742, and enlarged using a Charles Bulfinch design in 1805, it was a gift to the city from the merchant Peter Faneuil. National Park Service rangers give free 20-minute talks every half-hour from 9am to 5pm in the second-floor auditorium.

- **Paul Revere House** ★★★, 19 North Sq. (✆ **617/523-2338;** www.paulrevere house.org). The oldest house in downtown Boston (built around 1680) presents history on a human scale. It's open April 15 through October daily from 9:30am to 5:15pm, November through April 14 from 9:30am to 4:15pm (closed Mon Jan–Mar). Admission is $3.50 for adults, $3 for seniors and students, and $1 for children 5 to 17.

- **Old North Church** ★, 193 Salem St. (✆ **617/523-6676;** www.oldnorth.com). Paul Revere saw a signal in this church's steeple and set out on his "midnight ride." Officially named Christ Church, this is the oldest church building in Boston (1723). It's open daily June through October from 9am to 5pm, with shorter hours the rest of the year; a $3 donation is requested. Free tours of the church begin every 15 minutes. The 50-minute behind-the-scenes tour ($8 adults, $6 seniors and students, $5 children 16 and under; buy tickets online) includes visits to the steeple and the crypt; it's available daily from July through October, on weekends in June, and the rest of the year by appointment. Sunday services (Episcopal) are at 9 and 11am.

- **Copp's Hill Burying Ground,** off Hull Street. The second-oldest cemetery (1659) in the city, it contains the graves of Cotton Mather and Prince Hall, who established the first black Masonic lodge. It's open daily from 9am to 5pm (until 3pm in winter).

- **USS Constitution** ★★, Charlestown Navy Yard (✆ **617/242-5670;** www. history.navy.mil/ussconstitution). Active-duty sailors wearing 1812 dress uniforms give free tours of "Old Ironsides." They begin every half-hour between 10am and 3:30pm in summer Tuesday through Sunday, and in winter Thursday through Sunday. The **USS *Constitution* Museum** ★ (✆ **617/426-1812;** www.uss constitutionmuseum.org) is open daily May through October 15 from 9am to 6pm, October 16 through April from 10am to 5pm. Admission is free; donations are encouraged. National Park Service rangers staff the adjacent **Charlestown Navy Yard Visitor Center** (✆ **617/242-5601**) and give free 1-hour guided tours of the base.

○ **Bunker Hill Monument** (☎ **617/242-5641**; www.nps.gov/bost), Charlestown. The 221-foot granite obelisk honors the memory of the men who died in the Battle of Bunker Hill on June 17, 1775. A punishing flight of 294 stairs leads to the top. National Park Service rangers staff the monument, which is open daily from 9am to 5pm (climbing stops at 4:30pm). Admission to the monument and to the **Bunker Hill Museum ★**, across the street, is free.

House Museums

The most fascinating historic home in Boston is the **Paul Revere House** (p. 123). To see three other interesting residences, you must take a guided tour. Check ahead for open days and hours.

Out to Sea

A fun way to return to downtown from Charlestown is on the **ferry** that connects the Navy Yard to Long Wharf (near the Aquarium). It costs $1.70.

On Beacon Hill, you'll find two houses as notable for their Charles Bulfinch architecture as for their occupants. Tours of the 1796 **Otis House Museum ★★**, 141 Cambridge St. (☎ **617/994-5920**; www.historic-newengland.org), home of a young lawyer who was later mayor of Boston, discuss post-Revolutionary social, business, and family life. Tours cost $8. The 1804 **Nichols House Museum ★**, 55 Mount Vernon St. (☎ **617/227-6993**; www.nicholshousemuseum.org), holds beautiful antique furnishings collected by several generations of the Nichols family. Tours cost $7.

Nearby, in the Back Bay, the **Gibson House Museum,** 137 Beacon St. (☎ **617/267-6338;** www.thegibsonhouse.org), is a lavishly decorated 1859 brownstone that embodies the word *Victorian*. Tours cost $9.

Parks & Gardens

The best-known park in Boston is the spectacular **Public Garden ★★★**, bordered by Arlington, Boylston, Charles, and Beacon streets. Something lovely is in bloom at the country's first botanical garden at least half of the year. For 5 months, the lagoon is home to the celebrated **Swan Boats** (☎ **617/522-1966**; www.swanboats.com). The pedal-powered vessels—the attendants pedal, not the passengers—come out of hibernation on the Saturday before Patriot's Day (the 3rd Mon of Apr). They operate in summer daily from 10am to 5pm; in spring daily from 10am to 4pm; and from Labor Day to mid-September Monday through Friday from noon to 4pm and Saturday and Sunday from 10am to 4pm. The 15-minute ride costs $2.75 for adults, $2 for seniors, and $1.25 for children 2 to 15.

Even more spectacular is the **Arnold Arboretum ★★**, 125 Arborway, Jamaica Plain (☎ **617/524-1718;** www.arboretum.harvard.edu). One of the oldest parks in the United States, founded in 1872, it is open daily from sunrise to sunset. Admission is free. The 265-acre Frederick Law Olmsted design contains more than 15,000 ornamental trees, shrubs, and vines from all over the world. Lilac Sunday, in May, is the only time picnicking is allowed. To get here, take the Orange Line to Forest Hills and follow signs to the entrance.

Organized Tours

WALKING TOURS ★★   From May to October, the nonprofit **Boston by Foot ★★** (© 617/367-2345; www.bostonbyfoot.org) conducts excellent historical and architectural tours that focus on neighborhoods or themes. The rigorously trained volunteer guides encourage questions. The guides sell tickets ($12 adults, $8 children 6–12; Boston Underfoot tour of the city's infrastructure $14 per person, including subway fare); reservations are not required. The 90-minute tours take place rain or shine.

Historic New England ★ (© 617/994-5920; www.historicnewengland.org) offers a 2-hour walking tour of Beacon Hill and other excursions that concentrate on particular areas or topics—surf their site for specifics and schedules. Most tours begin at the Otis House Museum, 141 Cambridge St. Prices start at $12, which includes a tour of the museum; reservations are recommended.

TROLLEY TOURS   Because Boston is so pedestrian friendly, a trolley tour isn't the best choice for the able-bodied and unencumbered making a long visit. But if you're short on time, unable to walk long distances, or traveling with children, a trolley tour can be worth the money. The narrated tour can give you an overview before you focus on specific attractions, or you can use your all-day pass to hit as many places as possible in 8 hours or so.

The various companies cover the major attractions and offer informative narratives in their 90- to 120-minute tours. Most offer free reboarding if you want to visit the sites. Tickets cost $35 to $43 for adults, $16 or less for children (subject to fuel surcharges). Boarding spots are at hotels, historic sites, and tourist information centers. Each company paints its cars a different color. They include orange-and-green **Old Town Trolley Tours** (© 617/269-7150; www.trolleytours.com); **Beantown Trolleys** (© 800/343-1328 or 617/720-6342; www.grayline.com), which say "Gray Line" but are red; silver **CityView Trolleys** (© 617/363-7899; www.cityviewtrolleys.com); and yellow-and-green **Upper Deck Trolley Tours** (© 617/742-1440; www.bostonsupertrolleytours.com).

SIGHTSEEING CRUISES ★★   The season runs from April to October, with spring and fall offerings often restricted to weekends. Check websites for discount coupons before you leave home. If you're prone to seasickness, check the size of the vessel (larger equals more comfortable) before buying tickets.

Boston Harbor Cruises, 1 Long Wharf (© 877/733-9425 or 617/227-4321; www.bostonharborcruises.com), is the largest company. Ninety-minute historic sightseeing cruises depart daily at 11am, 1, 3, and 6 or 7pm (the sunset cruise), with extra excursions at busy times. Tickets are $21 for adults, $19 for seniors, and $17 for children 4 to 12; sunset-cruise tickets are $1 more. The 45-minute USS *Constitution* cruise schedule gives you time to visit Old Ironsides. Tours leave Long Wharf hourly from 10:30am to 4:30pm, and on the hour from the Navy Yard from 11am to 5pm. Tickets are $16 for adults, $14 for seniors, and $12 for children.

The **Charles Riverboat Company** (© 617/621-3001; www.charlesriverboat.com; T: Green Line to Lechmere) offers 60-minute narrated cruises around the lower Charles River basin five times daily, a daily tour of the Charles River lock system and Boston Harbor, and a daily sunset cruise (call for times). Boats leave

The most unusual and enjoyable way to see Boston is with **Boston Duck Tours** ★★★ (© 800/226-7442 or 617/267-DUCK; www.bostonducktours. com). The tours, offered from late March to November and the first three weekends of December, are pricey but great fun. Sightseers board a "duck," a reconditioned World War II amphibious landing craft, behind the Prudential Center on Huntington Avenue or at the Museum of Science. The 80-minute narrated tour begins with a quick but comprehensive jaunt around the city. Then the duck lumbers down a ramp, splashes into the Charles River, and takes a spin around the basin. Tickets cost $32 for adults, $28 for seniors and students, $22 for children 3 to 11, and $9 for children 2 and under. Tours run every 30 to 60 minutes from 9am to a half-hour before sunset. Discounted (by $3 or $4) 55-minute tours leave from the New England Aquarium starting at 3pm daily from June through August and on weekends in April, May, September, and October. You can buy tickets online or in person (at the Prudential Center, the Museum of Science, and the New England Aquarium). Try to buy same-day tickets early in the day, or ask about the limited number of tickets available starting 30 days in advance. Reservations are not accepted (except for groups of 20 or more). No tours late December through mid-March.

from the CambridgeSide Galleria mall, and tickets cost $14 to $16 for adults, $12 to $14 for seniors, and $8 to $10 for children.

WHALE-WATCHING ★★ For information on Cape Ann excursions, see "A Whale of an Adventure," in chapter 6.

The **New England Aquarium** (p. 121) runs whale-watching trips (© 617/973-5200 for information, 617/973-5206 for tickets; www.newenglandaquarium.org) daily from May to mid-October and on weekends in April and late October. They travel several miles out to Stellwagen Bank, the feeding ground for whales as they migrate from Newfoundland to Provincetown. Allow 3 to 4 hours. Tickets are $40 for adults, $32 for children 3 to 11. Children must be at least 3 years old and 30 inches tall. Reservations are strongly recommended; you can buy tickets online.

With its onboard exhibits and vast experience, the Aquarium offers the best whale watches in Boston. If they're booked, try **Boston Harbor Cruises** (© 877/SEE-WHALE [733-9425] or 617/227-4321; www.bostonharborcruises.com), which operates high-speed catamarans, or **Massachusetts Bay Lines** (© 617/542-8000; www.massbaylines.com).

Especially for Kids

Destinations with something for every family member include **Faneuil Hall Marketplace** (p. 118) and the **Museum of Fine Arts** (p. 120), which offers special weekend and after-school programs. Hands-on exhibits and large-format films are the headliners at the **New England Aquarium** (p. 121) and the **Museum of Science** (p. 120). A **Red Sox game** (see "Spectator Sports," later in this chapter) is another sure-fire kid pleaser.

The allure of seeing people the size of ants draws young visitors to the **Prudential Center Skywalk** (© 617/236-3318). They can see actual ants—though they might prefer dinosaurs—at the Museum of Comparative Zoology, part of the **Harvard Museum of Natural History** (see "Exploring Cambridge," below).

Older children who have studied American history will enjoy a visit to the **John F. Kennedy Library and Museum** (p. 119). Middle-schoolers who enjoyed Esther Forbes's *Johnny Tremain* might get a kick out of the **Paul Revere House** (p. 123). Young visitors who have read Robert McCloskey's children's classic *Make Way for Ducklings* will relish a visit to the **Public Garden,** as will fans of E. B. White's *The Trumpet of the Swan,* who certainly will want to ride on the **Swan Boats.** Considerably less tame and much longer are **whale watches** (see "Organized Tours," above, and "A Whale of an Adventure," in chapter 6); **sightseeing cruises** fall somewhere in the middle.

The **Boston Tea Party Ship & Museum** (© 617/338-1773; www.boston teapartyship.com) closed after a fire in late 2001. It's currently renovating, expanding, and planning to reopen in 2011. It makes an entertaining stop on the way to or from the Children's Museum.

The walking-tour company **Boston by Foot ★★** (© 617/367-2345; www. bostonbyfoot.org) has a special program, **Boston by Little Feet,** geared to children 6 to 12. The 1-hour walk gives a child's-eye view of the architecture along the Freedom Trail and of Boston's role in the American Revolution. Children must be accompanied by an adult. Tours ($8 per person) run May through October and meet at the statue of Samuel Adams on the Congress Street side of Faneuil Hall Friday and Saturday at 10am, Sunday at 2pm, rain or shine.

Boston Children's Museum ★★ ☺ A delightful destination for kids under 11, the Children's Museum is great fun for adults, too. Children can stick with the family or wander on their own. The centerpiece of the renovated warehouse is a three-story-high maze that incorporates motor skills and problem-solving. The hands-on exhibits include, among many others, **Johnny's Workbench,** a souped-up version of puttering in the garage; physical experiments (such as creating giant soap bubbles); and the **Japanese House,** a 2-story residence from Kyoto, one of Boston's sister cities. A special room, **PlaySpace,** is packed with toys and activities for children 3 and under and their caregivers. Check ahead for information on traveling exhibitions and special programs.

300 Congress St. (Museum Wharf). © **617/426-8855.** www.bostonchildrensmuseum.org. Admission $12 adults, $9 seniors and children 1–15, free for children under 1; Fri 5–9pm $1 for all. Sat–Thurs 10am– 5pm; Fri 10am–9pm. T: Red Line to South Station, walk north on Atlantic Ave. 1 block (past Federal Reserve Bank), turn right onto Congress St., walk 2 blocks; or Silver Line to Courthouse, walk toward downtown and turn left at the Fort Point Channel. Call for information on discounted parking.

EXPLORING CAMBRIDGE

Harvard Square ★★ is a people-watching paradise of students, instructors, commuters, shoppers, and sightseers. Restaurants and stores pack the three streets that radiate from the center of the square and the streets that intersect them. On weekend afternoons and evenings year-round, you'll hear music and see street performers. To get away from the urban bustle, stroll down to the paved paths along the Charles River.

WELCOME TO THE NORTH END

The Paul Revere House and the Old North Church are the best-known buildings in the **North End ★★★**, Boston's "Little Italy" (although it's *never* called that). Home to natives of Italy and their assimilated children, numerous Italian restaurants and private social clubs, and many historic sights, this is one of the oldest neighborhoods in the city. It was home in the 17th century to the **Mather family** of Puritan ministers, who certainly would be shocked to see the merry goings-on at the festivals and street fairs that take over different areas of the North End on weekends in July and August.

The Italians (and their yuppie neighbors who have made inroads since the 1980s) are only the latest immigrant group to dominate the North End. In the 19th century, this was an Eastern European Jewish enclave and later an Irish stronghold. In 1890, President Kennedy's mother, Rose Fitzgerald, was born on Garden Court Street and baptized at St. Stephen's Church.

Modern visitors might be more interested in a Hanover Street *caffè,* the perfect place to have coffee or a soft drink and feast on sweets. **Mike's Pastry ★★★**, 300 Hanover St. (© **617/742-3050;** www.mikespastry.com), is a bakery that does a frantic takeout business and has tables where you can sit down and order one of the confections on display in the cases. The signature item is cannoli (tubes of crisp-fried pastry filled with sweetened ricotta cheese); the cookies, cakes, and other pastries are excellent, too. You can also sit and relax at **Caffè dello Sport** or **Caffè Vittoria,** on either side of Mike's.

Before you leave the North End, stroll toward the water and see whether there's a **bocce** game going on at the courts on Commercial Street near Hull Street. The European pastime is both a game of skill and an excuse to hang around and shoot the breeze—in Italian and English—with the locals (mostly men of a certain age). It's so popular that the neighborhood has courts both outdoors, in the Langone Playground at Puopolo Park, and indoors, at the back of the adjacent Steriti Rink, 561 Commercial St.

From Boston, take the Red Line toward Alewife. In Cambridge, the subway stops at Kendall/MIT, and Central, Harvard, and Porter squares. If you're staying in or visiting the Back Bay, a more interesting route is the no. 1 bus (Harvard–Dudley), which runs along Mass. Ave.

By car from Boston, follow Mass. Ave., or take Storrow Drive along the south bank of the river to the Harvard Square exit. Memorial Drive runs along the north side of the river near MIT, Central Square, and Harvard. Traffic in and around Harvard Square is almost as bad as in downtown Boston. After you reach Cambridge, park and walk.

Harvard University

Harvard is the oldest college in the country, and if you suggest aloud that it's not the best, you may encounter the attitude that inspired the saying "You can always tell a Harvard man, but you can't tell him much." The university encompasses the college and 10 graduate and professional schools in more than 400 buildings around Boston and Cambridge. Free student-led tours of the main campus leave from the **Events & Information Center,** in Holyoke Center, 1350 Mass. Ave. (© **617/495-1573;**

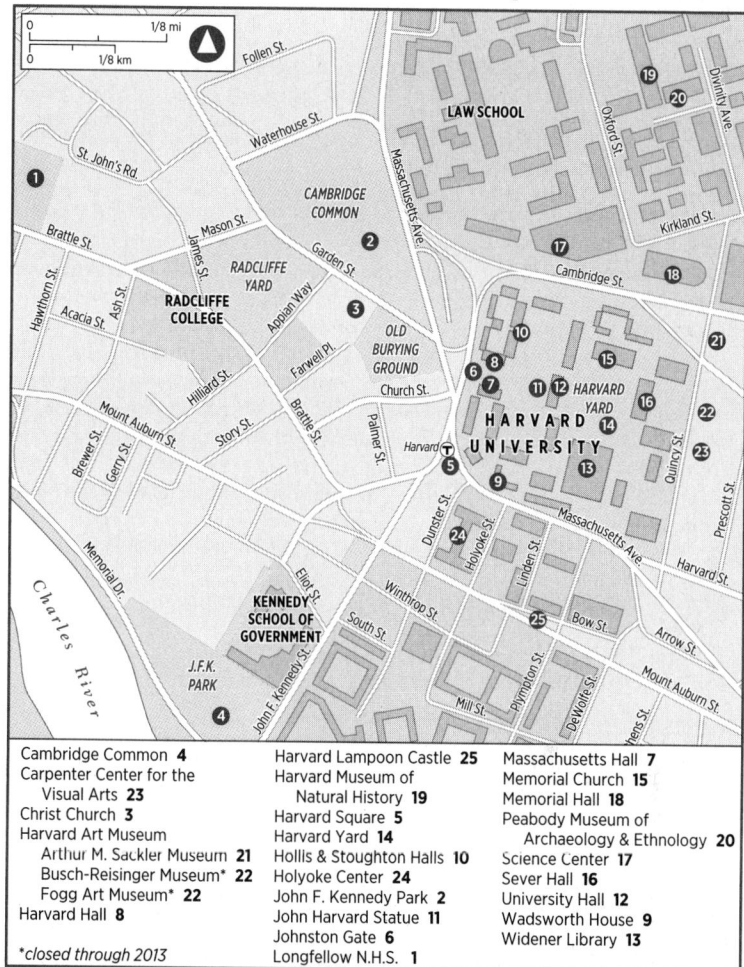

Cambridge Common **4**
Carpenter Center for the
    Visual Arts **23**
Christ Church **3**
Harvard Art Museum
    Arthur M. Sackler Museum **21**
    Busch-Reisinger Museum* **22**
    Fogg Art Museum* **22**
Harvard Hall **8**

*closed through 2013

Harvard Lampoon Castle **25**
Harvard Museum of
    Natural History **19**
Harvard Square **5**
Harvard Yard **14**
Hollis & Stoughton Halls **10**
Holyoke Center **24**
John F. Kennedy Park **2**
John Harvard Statue **11**
Johnston Gate **6**
Longfellow N.H.S. **1**

Massachusetts Hall **7**
Memorial Church **15**
Memorial Hall **18**
Peabody Museum of
    Archaeology & Ethnology **20**
Science Center **17**
Sever Hall **16**
University Hall **12**
Wadsworth House **9**
Widener Library **13**

www.harvard.edu/visitors), during the school year twice a day weekdays and once on Saturday (except during vacations), and during the summer four times a day Monday through Saturday. Check ahead for exact times; reservations aren't necessary. You're also free to wander on your own. The center has maps, illustrated booklets, and self-guided walking-tour directions.

Harvard Art Museum   This internationally renowned museum consists of three institutions, two of which are closed for renovations scheduled to last through 2013. While the Fogg and Busch-Reisinger museums are under wraps, the **Arthur M. Sackler Museum** is showing highlights drawn from the quarter-million works in the museum's collections, which include everything from ancient sculptures to contemporary photos. The exhibit, *Re-View*, features a selection of some 600 objects; check ahead to see which themes the curators have chosen to focus on during your visit.

485 Broadway. © **617/495-9400.** www.harvardartmuseum.org. Admission $9 adults, $7 seniors, $6 students, free for children 17 and under; free to MA residents before noon Sat. Tues–Sat 10am–5pm. Closed major holidays. T: Red Line to Harvard, cross Harvard Yard diagonally from the T station and exit onto Quincy St., turn left, and walk to the next corner; or turn your back on the Coop and follow Mass. Ave. to Quincy St., then turn left and walk 1 long block.

Harvard Museum of Natural History and Peabody Museum of Archaeology & Ethnology ★ ☺   These fascinating museums house the university's collections of items and artifacts related to the natural world. Parents and kids alike will find something interesting here, be it a dinosaur skeleton, the largest turtle shell in the world, a Native American artifact, or the world-famous Glass Flowers.

The **Glass Flowers** ★★★ are 3,000 models of more than 840 plant species devised between 1887 and 1936 by the German father-and-son team of Leopold and Rudolph Blaschka. You may have heard about them, and you may be skeptical, but it's true: They look real. Children love the **zoological collections** ★★, where dinosaurs share space with preserved and stuffed insects and animals that range in size from butterflies to whales. The **Peabody Museum** ★ boasts the **Hall of the North American Indian,** which displays 500 artifacts representing 10 cultures. Photographs, textiles, pottery, and art and crafts of all ages and descriptions fill the galleries.

Museum of Natural History: 26 Oxford St. © **617/495-3045.** www.hmnh.harvard.edu. Peabody Museum: 11 Divinity Ave. © **617/496-1027.** www.peabody.harvard.edu. Admission to both $9 adults, $7 seniors and students, $6 children 3–18; free to MA residents Sun until noon year-round and Wed 3–5pm Sept–May. Daily 9am–5pm. T: Red Line to Harvard. Cross Harvard Yard, keeping John Harvard statue on right, and bear right before Science Center. First left is Oxford St. Check website for parking info.

A Historic House

Longfellow National Historic Site ★   The books and furniture inside the yellow mansion have remained intact since the poet Henry Wadsworth Longfellow died here in 1882. During the siege of Boston in 1775–76, the house served as the headquarters of Gen. George Washington, with whom Longfellow was fascinated. On the absorbing tour—the only way to see the house—you'll learn about the history of the building and its famous occupants.

105 Brattle St. © **617/876-4491.** www.nps.gov/long. Guided tours $3 adults, free for children 15 and under. Call ahead to confirm hours and tour times. June–Oct Wed–Sun 10am–4:30pm. Tours 10:30 and 11:30am and 1, 2, 3, and 4pm. Closed Nov–May. T: Red Line to Harvard, then follow Brattle St. about 7 blocks; house is on the right.

A Celebrated Cemetery

Dedicated in 1831, **Mount Auburn Cemetery** ★, 580 Mt. Auburn St. (© **617/547-7105;** www.mountauburn.org), was the first of America's rural, or garden, cemeteries. Since the day it opened, Mount Auburn has been a popular place to retreat and reflect. The graves of Henry Wadsworth Longfellow, Oliver Wendell Holmes, Mary Baker Eddy, Winslow Homer, and many other prominent New Englanders are here. In season, you'll see gorgeous flowering trees and shrubs. Stop at the **visitor center** in Story Chapel (daily 9am–4pm Apr–Oct except during burials; closed Sun Nov–Mar) for an overview and a look at the changing exhibits, or ask at the office or front gate for brochures and a map. You can rent 60-minute driving or 75-minute walking audio tours ($7; a $15 deposit is required) and listen in your car or on a portable player. The **Friends of Mount Auburn Cemetery** conducts workshops and lectures and coordinates walking tours; call the main number for topics, schedules, and fees. The cemetery is open daily from 8am to 5pm October through April, 8am to 7pm May through September; admission is free. Pets, picnicking, biking, and jogging are not allowed. Bus route nos. 71 and 73 start at Harvard station and stop near the gates; they run frequently on weekdays, less often on weekends. From Harvard Square by car (5 min.) or on foot (30 min.), take Mount Auburn Street or Brattle Street west; just after they intersect, the gate is on the left.

A Stroll Around Cambridge

To explore Harvard and the surrounding area, begin your walk in **Harvard Square.** Town and gown meet at this lively intersection, where you'll get a taste of the improbable mix of people drawn to the crossroads of Cambridge.

Start at the Harvard T station, with the **Harvard Coop** at your back. Walk half a block, crossing Dunster Street. To your right is **Holyoke Center,** an administration building designed by the Spanish architect Josep Luis Sert, the dean of the university's Graduate School of Design from 1953 to 1969, and a disciple of Le Corbusier.

Across the street is **Wadsworth House,** 1341 Mass. Ave., a yellow wood structure built in 1726 as a residence for Harvard's fourth president. Its claim to fame is a classic: George Washington slept here. Turn left and follow the outside of the brick wall along Mass. Ave. to another T entrance. Pass through **Johnston Gate,** which guards the oldest part of **Harvard Yard.** "The Yard" was just a patch of grass with grazing animals when Harvard College was established in 1636 to train young men for the ministry. The Continental Army, under Washington's command, spent the winter of 1775–76 here.

With Johnston Gate at your back, to your right is **Massachusetts Hall** (1720), the university's oldest surviving building. It houses the president's office and rooms for first-year students. To your left is **Harvard Hall** (1765), a classroom building. The matching side-by-side buildings behind Harvard Hall are **Hollis** and **Stoughton halls.** Hollis dates to 1763 and has been home to many students who went on to great fame, among them Ralph Waldo Emerson, Henry David Thoreau, and Charles Bulfinch.

Across the Yard is **University Hall,** the college's main administration building, designed by Bulfinch and constructed in 1812–13. It's the backdrop of the **John Harvard statue ★★**, one of the most photographed objects in the Boston area. Designed by Daniel Chester French in 1884, it's known as the "Statue of Three Lies" because the inscription reads "John Harvard—Founder—1638." In fact, the college was established in 1636; Harvard (one of many people involved) wasn't the founder, but donated money and his library; and this isn't John Harvard, anyway. No portraits of him survive, so the model was, according to various accounts, either his nephew or a student. Walk over to the statue and join the throng of tourists posing for pictures with the benevolent-looking gentleman.

Walk around University Hall into the adjoining quadrangle; you're leaving the "Old Yard" for the "New Yard," where commencement and other university-wide ceremonies take place. On your right is **Widener Library,** the centerpiece of the world's largest university library system. It was built in 1913 as a memorial to Harry Elkins Widener, a 1907 Harvard graduate who died when the *Titanic* sank in 1912. Legend has it that he was unable to swim 50 yards to a lifeboat, and his mother donated $2 million for the library on the condition that every undergraduate pass a 50-yard swimming test.

Facing the library is **Memorial Church,** built in 1931 and topped with a tower and weather vane 197 feet tall. You're welcome to look around this Georgian Revival–style edifice unless services are going on. The entrance is on the left. The south wall, toward the Yard, lists the names of Harvard graduates who died in World War I, World War II, Korea, and Vietnam. One is Joseph P. Kennedy, Jr. ('38), the president's older brother.

Continue across the Yard onto Quincy Street. To your right is the curvilinear **Carpenter Center for the Visual Arts,** 24 Quincy St. Designed by the Swiss-French architect **Le Corbusier** and completed in 1963, it's the only Le Corbusier building in North America.

Facing the Carpenter Center, turn left and follow Quincy Street, crossing Broadway (the architect Norman Foster once called this area an "architectural zoo"), and walk another block. To your left is **Memorial Hall,** a massive Victorian structure built from 1870–74. The hall of memorials (enter from Kirkland or Cambridge sts.) is a transept where you can read the names of the Harvard men who died fighting for the Union during the Civil War—but not those who died for the Confederacy. Next door is the **Science Center,** Zero Oxford St., a 10-story monolith that supposedly resembles a Polaroid camera. (Edwin H. Land, founder of Cambridge-based Polaroid Corporation, was one of its main benefactors.) Sert also designed this structure, which was built in 1970–72.

Keep "Mem Hall" and the Science Center to your right and follow the walkway for the equivalent of a block and a half as it curves around toward Mass. Ave. The **Harvard Law School** campus is on your right. Carefully cross Mass. Ave. to **Cambridge Common.** Memorials and plaques dot this well-used plot of greenery and bare earth. Turn left and head back toward Harvard Square; after a block or so, you'll walk near or over **horseshoes** embedded in the concrete. This is the path William Dawes, Paul Revere's fellow alarm-sounder, took from Boston to Lexington on April 18, 1775.

Turn right onto Garden Street and find **Christ Church,** Zero Garden St. The oldest church in Cambridge, it was designed by Peter Harrison of Newport, Rhode Island (also the architect of King's Chapel in Boston), and opened in 1761. Note the square wooden tower. In the vestibule, you can still see bullet holes made by British muskets.

With the church at your back, turn right and return to Mass. Ave. Turn right again, then walk 2 blocks into the middle of the square and 1 more block on John F. Kennedy Street. Turn left onto Mount Auburn Street. Stay on the left side of the street as you cross Dunster, Holyoke, and Linden streets.

The corner of Mount Auburn and Linden streets is a good vantage point for viewing the **Harvard Lampoon Castle,** designed by Wheelwright & Haven in 1909. Listed on the National Register of Historic Places, this is the home of Harvard's undergraduate humor magazine, the *Lampoon.* The main tower looks like a face, with windows as the eyes, nose, and mouth, topped by what looks like a miner's hat. All five of the building's addresses have been mentioned on *The Simpsons,* which draws many of its writers from the staff.

Cross Mount Auburn Street and walk south (away from Holyoke Center) on Holyoke Street or Dunster Street to get a sense of some of the rest of the campus. Turn right on Winthrop Street or South Street, continue to John F. Kennedy Street, and turn left. Cross the street at some point, and follow it toward the Charles River, almost to Memorial Drive, passing the Graduate School of Government. On your right is **John F. Kennedy Park.** Walk away from the street to the fountain, engraved with excerpts from the president's speeches. This is an excellent place to take a break and plan the rest of your day.

SPECTATOR SPORTS & GETTING OUTSIDE

Spectator Sports

Boston enjoys a well-deserved reputation as a great sports town. The Red Sox, Celtics, and New England Patriots (who play in suburban Foxboro) have been more successful and popular than the Bruins recently, but local fans are nothing if not loyal—just ask all those Celtics fans who waited 22 years between NBA championships. Fans are also passionate about college sports, particularly hockey, in which the Division I schools are fierce rivals.

BASEBALL No other experience in sports matches watching the **Red Sox** play at **Fenway Park ★★★**, which they do from April to early October, and later if they make the playoffs. The quirkiness of the oldest park in the major leagues (1912) only adds to the mystique, and the euphoria that accompanied the team's 2004 and 2007 World Series titles has hardly abated. Tickets are wildly expensive, but one of the most imaginative management teams in baseball strives to make visiting Fenway worth big bucks. Yawkey Way turns into a sort of carnival midway for ticket holders before games, with concession stands, live music, and other diversions.

The **ticket office** (*C* **877/REDSOX-9** [733-7699]; www.redsox.com) is at 4 Yawkey Way, off Brookline Avenue. Tickets go on sale in December; order early. They're the most expensive in the majors—a few upper bleacher seats go for $12, but most are in the $28-to-$95 range. Forced to choose between tickets for a grandstand section numbered 10 or below and bleacher seats, go for the bleachers and the better view. A limited number of same-day standing-room tickets ($20–$30) are available before each game, and fans sometimes return presold tickets, especially if a rainout causes rescheduling. It can't hurt to check, particularly if the team isn't playing well; visit the website and navigate to "Red Sox Replay." *Tip:* The Game Day Ticket Sales office, near Gate E on Lansdowne Street, offers tickets that went unsold for some reason. The doors open 2 hours before game time; lining up is permitted 3 hours before that (but not earlier).

Tours (*C* **617/236-6666**) start on the hour daily from 9am to 4pm (or 3 hr. before game time, whichever is earlier), in the summer; winter hours are shorter and tours may be truncated because of construction. No tours are offered on holidays or before day games. The cost is $12 for adults, $11 for seniors, and $10 for children 3 to 15.

BASKETBALL The Boston Celtics' faithful are still savoring their 2008 run to the title. The season runs from early October to April or May. Especially when a top contender is visiting, you may have trouble getting tickets. Prices are as low as $10 for some games and top out at around $300. For information, call **TD Garden** (℡ 617/624-1000; www.nba.com/celtics); for tickets, contact **Ticketmaster** (℡ 617/931-2000; www.ticketmaster.com). To reach the Garden, take the Green or Orange Line to North Station. *Note:* Spectators may not bring any bags, including backpacks and briefcases, into the arena.

FOOTBALL The **New England Patriots** (℡ 800/543-1776; www.patriots.com) were playing to sellout crowds even before they won three Super Bowls in 4 years (2002, 2004, and 2005) and famously fizzled out in 2008. The Pats play from August to December or January at Gillette Stadium on Rte. 1 in Foxboro, about 45 minutes south of the city. Tickets ($65–$169) sell out well in advance. Call or check the website for information on individual ticket sales and public-transit options.

HOCKEY Tickets to see the **Boston Bruins** are expensive ($33–$172) but worth it for serious fans. For information, call **TD Garden** (℡ 617/624-1000; www.bostonbruins.com); for tickets, call **Ticketmaster** (℡ 617/931-2000; www.ticketmaster.com). To reach the Garden, take the Green or Orange Line to North Station. *Note:* Spectators may not bring any bags, including backpacks and briefcases, into the arena.

Economical fans will be pleasantly surprised by the quality of local **college hockey ★**. Even for sold-out games, standing-room tickets are usually available shortly before game time. Local teams include **Boston College,** Conte Forum, Chestnut Hill (℡ 617/552-GOBC [4622]; www.bceagles.com); **Boston University,** Agganis Arena, 928 Commonwealth Ave. (℡ 617/353-3838; www.goterriers.com); **Harvard University,** Bright Hockey Center, North Harvard Street, Allston (℡ 877/GO-HARVARD [464-2782] or 617/495-2211; www.gocrimson.com); and **Northeastern University,** Matthews Arena, St. Botolph Street (℡ 617/373-4700; www.gonu.com).

THE MARATHON Every year on Patriot's Day (the 3rd Mon in Apr), the **Boston Marathon ★★★** rules the roads from Hopkinton to Copley Square in Boston. An especially nice place to watch is tree-shaded Comm. Ave. between Kenmore Square and Mass. Ave., but you'll be in a crowd wherever you stand, particularly near the finish line in front of the Boston Public Library. For information about qualifying, contact the **Boston Athletic Association** (℡ 617/236-1652; www.bostonmarathon.org).

ROWING In late October, the **Head of the Charles Regatta ★** (℡ 617/868-6200; www.hocr.org) attracts some 4,000 oarsmen and oarswomen. The largest crew event in the country draws hundreds of thousands of spectators who socialize and occasionally even watch the action.

Getting Outside

The **Department of Conservation & Recreation** (www.state.ma.us/dcr) oversees activities on the state's public lands. The website describes properties and activities, and has a planning area to help you make the most of your time.

BEACHES The beaches in Boston, with their icy water and periodic safety-related closings, are not worth the trouble. If you want to swim, book a hotel with a pool. If you want sand between your toes, hit the beach on the North Shore or at Walden Pond in Concord. See chapter 6 for information on suburban beaches.

A VACATION IN THE ISLANDS

Majestic ocean views, hiking trails, historic sights, rocky beaches, nature walks, campsites, and picnic areas abound in New England. The **Boston Harbor Islands** ★★ (✆ **617/223-8666;** www. bostonislands.com) have them all. The unspoiled beauty of the national park area is a welcome break from the urban landscape, but even many longtime Bostonians haven't visited. Bring a sweater or jacket, and note that fresh water is available only on Georges and Spectacle islands. (Management strongly suggests that you bring your own.)

Thirty-four islands dot the Outer Harbor, and at least a half-dozen are open to the public. Ferries run to the **Georges Island,** home of Fort Warren (1834), which held Confederate prisoners during the Civil War. You can investigate on your own or take a ranger-led tour. The island has a visitor center, refreshment area, fishing pier, picnic area, and wonderful view of Boston's skyline. **Spectacle Island** has 5 miles of hiking trails, a beach, and an eco-friendly visitor center.

Allow at least half a day, longer if you plan to take the water shuttle ($3/day) to **Lovell, Bumpkin,** or **Grape Island;** all have picnic areas and campsites.

Boston's Best Cruises (✆ **617/222-6999;** www.bostonsbestcruises.com) operates the ferry from Long Wharf to Georges Island (30 min. or less) and Spectacle Island (15 min.); round-trip tickets are $14 for adults, $10 for seniors, $8 for children 3 to 11, and $42 for families (2 adults, 2 kids). Cruises depart daily on the hour (every 30 min. Fri-Sun) from 9am to 5pm from early May through Columbus Day weekend. In the off season, check ahead for winter wildlife excursions (scheduled occasionally).

A public-private National Park Partnership administers the Boston Harbor Islands National Recreation Area (www. nps.gov/boha). For more information, visit the website, consult the staff at the **kiosk on Long Wharf,** or contact the **Friends of the Boston Harbor Islands** (✆ **617/740-4290;** www.fbhi.org).

BIKING Even expert cyclists who feel comfortable with Boston's layout will be better off in Cambridge, which has more and better bike lanes, or on the area's many bike paths. The 18-mile **Dr. Paul Dudley White Charles River Bike Path** follows the river from the Museum of Science to Watertown and back. You can enter and exit at many points along the way. Bikers share the path with lots of pedestrians, joggers, and in-line skaters. On warm-weather Sundays from 11am to 7pm, **Memorial Drive** from Central Square to west Cambridge is closed to cars.

State law requires that children 11 and under wear helmets. Bicycles are forbidden on buses and the Green Line, and on other subway lines during rush hours.

Rental shops charge $30 to $50 per day. They include **Urban AdvenTours,** 103 Atlantic Ave. (✆ **617/670-0637;** www.urbanadventours.com), which delivers to hotels; **Back Bay Bicycles,** 366 Comm. Ave., near Mass. Ave. (✆ **617/247-2336;** www.backbaybicycles.com); and **Cambridge Bicycle,** 259 Mass. Ave. (✆ **617/876-6555;** www.cambridgebicycle.com). For more information, contact **MassBike** (✆ **617/542-2453;** www.massbike.org).

GOLF The **Massachusetts Golf Association** (✆ **800/356-2201** or 774/430-9100; www.mgalinks.org) represents more than 400 courses around the golf-mad

5

BOSTON & CAMBRIDGE

Spectator Sports & Getting Outside

state; the website has a searchable database. Given a choice, play on a weekday, when you'll find lower prices and smaller crowds than on weekends.

One of the best public courses in the area, **Newton Commonwealth Golf Course,** 212 Kenrick St., Newton (© **617/630-1971;** www.sterlinggolf.com), is a challenging 18-hole Donald Ross design. It's 5,305 yards from the blue tees, par is 70, and greens fees are $30 weekdays, $37 weekends. Within the city limits is the legendary 6,009-yard **William J. Devine Golf Course,** in Franklin Park, Dorchester (© **617/265-4084;** www.cityofboston.gov/parks). As a Harvard student, Bobby Jones sharpened his game on the 18-hole, par-70 course. Greens fees are $38 weekdays, $45 weekends. Less challenging but with more of a neighborhood feel is 9-hole, par-35 **Fresh Pond Golf Course,** 691 Huron Ave., Cambridge (© **617/349-6282;** www.freshpondgolf.com). The 3,161-yard layout adjoins the Fresh Pond Reservoir (there's water on four holes) and charges $22, or $32 to go around twice, on weekdays; $26 and $38 on weekends.

GYMS   Your concierge can recommend a health club and perhaps arrange a discounted visit. Hotels with good health clubs (see "Where to Stay," earlier in this chapter) include the Four Seasons Hotel, the InterContinental Boston, the Royal Sonesta Hotel, and the Charles Hotel. The best combination of facilities and value is at the **Wang YMCA of Chinatown,** 8 Oak St. W., off Washington Street (© **617/426-2237;** www.ymcaboston.org). A day pass costs $10.

ICE SKATING   The rink at the Boston Common **Frog Pond** (© **617/635-2120;** www.cityofboston.gov/parks) is an extremely popular cold-weather destination. It's an open surface with an ice-making system and a clubhouse. Admission is $4 for adults, free for children 13 and under; skate rental costs $8 for adults, $5 for kids. Try to go on a weekday; huge crowds descend on weekends.

IN-LINE SKATING   Unless you're confident of your ability and your knowledge of Boston traffic, stay off the streets. A favorite car-free spot is the **Esplanade,** between the Back Bay and the Charles River. It continues onto the bike path that runs to Watertown and back, but once you leave the Esplanade, the pavement in many spots is in disrepair. Your best bet is to wait for a spring, summer, or fall Sunday, when **Memorial Drive** in Cambridge closes to cars. It's a perfect surface. The **InLine Club of Boston** offers event and safety information on its website (**www.sk8net.com**).

Expect to pay about $15 for rentals. Try the **Beacon Hill Skate Shop,** 135 Charles St. S. (© **617/482-7400**), or one of the vendors who set up shop on Memorial Drive on warm-weather Sundays.

JOGGING   The **Dr. Paul Dudley White Charles River Bike Path** (see "Biking," above) is the area's busiest jogging trail. It's so popular because it's car-free (except at intersections), scenic, and generally safe. The bridges along the river allow for circuits of various lengths, but be careful around abutments, where you can't see far ahead. Don't jog at night, and try not to go alone. Visit the DCR website (www. state.ma.us/dcr) to view a map that gives distances. If the river's not convenient, check with the concierge or desk staff at your hotel for a map with suggested routes.

SAILING   The best deal in town is **Community Boating, Inc.,** 21 David Mugar Way, on the Esplanade (© **617/523-1038;** www.community-boating.org). It's open April through November, and the fleet includes 13- to 23-foot sailboats as well as windsurfers and kayaks. Visitors pay $75 for a day of sailing in the Charles River basin, $35 for a day's use of a kayak.

SHOPPING

Boston-area shopping represents a tempting blend of classic and contemporary. Boston and Cambridge boast tiny boutiques and sprawling malls, esoteric bookshops and national chain stores, classy galleries, and snazzy secondhand-clothing outlets.

Note: Massachusetts has no sales tax on clothing priced below $175 or on food. All other items are taxed at 6.25% (as are restaurant meals and takeout food). The state no longer prohibits stores from opening Sunday morning, but many still wait until noon or don't open at all—call ahead before setting out.

BACK BAY   This is New England's premier shopping district. Dozens of upscale galleries, shops, and boutiques make **Newbury Street ★★★** a world-famous destination. Nearby, an enclosed walkway across Huntington Avenue links **Copley Place** (✆ 617/262-6600) and the **Shops at Prudential Center** (✆ 800/SHOP-PRU [746-7778]). This is where you'll find the tony department stores **Barneys New York** (✆ 617/385-3300), **Lord & Taylor** (✆ 617/262-6000), **Neiman Marcus** (✆ 617/536-3660), and **Saks Fifth Avenue** (✆ 617/262-8500). At press time, the Back Bay is home to the only open Boston location of **Filene's Basement,** 497 Boylston St (✆ 800/843-8474).

If you're passionate about art, set aside a couple of hours for strolling along **Newbury Street.** Besides being a prime location for upscale boutiques, it boasts an infinite variety of styles and media in the dozens of art galleries at street level and on the higher floors. (Remember to look up.) Most galleries are open Tuesday through Sunday from 10 or 11am to 5:30 or 6pm. For specifics, pick up a copy of the free monthly *Gallery Guide* at businesses along Newbury Street.

DOWNTOWN   **Faneuil Hall Marketplace** (✆ 617/523-1300; www.faneuil hallmarketplace.com) is the busiest attraction in Boston, not only for its smorgasbord of food outlets, but also for its shops, boutiques, and pushcarts. Although it has more upscale chain outlets than only-in-Boston shops, it's a fun experience.

If the hubbub here is too much for you, stroll over to **Charles Street,** at the foot of Beacon Hill. A short but commercially dense (and picturesque) street, it's home to perhaps the best assortment of gift and antiques shops in the city. Be sure to check out the contemporary home accessories at **Koo De Kir,** 65 Chestnut St., just off Charles (✆ **617/723-8111;** www.koodekir.com); the well-edited selection at **Upstairs Downstairs Antiques,** 93 Charles St. (✆ **617/367-1950**); and the engagingly funky gifts at **Black Ink,** 101 Charles St. (✆ **617/723-3883;** www. blackinkboston.com).

One of Boston's oldest shopping areas is **Downtown Crossing.** Now a traffic-free pedestrian mall along Washington, Winter, and Summer streets near Boston Common, it's home to **Macy's;** tons of smaller clothing, shoe, and music stores; food and merchandise pushcarts; and a branch of **Borders.** At press time, the original **Filene's Basement ★★★**, 426 Washington St. (✆ **617/542-2011**), is closed. Check ahead to see whether this location has reopened, or hit the Back Bay location (see above).

The tourist-magnet **North End** has a limited but fun retail scene. Venture beyond the main drag, Hanover Street, and you'll find worthwhile stops on Salem, Parmenter, and Richmond streets. The **Velvet Fly,** 28 Parmenter St. (✆ **617/557-4359;** www.thevelvetfly.com), carries women's fashions that are either genuine

BY THE BOOK

Bookworms flock to Cambridge; Harvard Square in particular caters to general and specific audiences. Check out the basement of the **Harvard Book Store,** 1256 Mass. Ave. (© **800/542-READ** [7323], or 617/661-1515; www.harvard. com), for great deals on remainders and used books. **Curious George & Friends,** 1 John F. Kennedy St. (© **617/498-0062;** www.curiousg.com), specializes in children's merchandise. Jammed shelves line the tiny **Grolier Poetry Book Shop,** 6 Plympton St. (© **617/547-4648;** www. grolierpoetrybookshop.com). Barnes & Noble runs the book operation at the **Harvard Coop,** 1400 Mass. Ave. (© **617/499-2000;** www.thecoop.com), which stocks textbooks, academic works, and a large general selection.

One T stop away is the excellent independent shop **Porter Square Books,** in the Porter Square Shopping Center, 25 White St. (© **617/491-2220;** www. portersquarebooks.com). And there's a **Borders** (© **617/679-0887**) at the CambridgeSide Galleria mall.

In Boston, you'll find a huge selection of used and rare titles at the **Brattle Book Shop,** 9 West St. (© **800/447-9595** or 617/542-0210; www.brattlebook shop.com), near Downtown Crossing. Downtown Crossing has a **Borders,** 24 School St. (© **617/557-7188;** www. borders.com), and the Back Bay has both a **Barnes & Noble** (© **617/247-6959;** www.barnesandnoble.com), in the Shops at Prudential Center, and a **Borders,** 511 Boylston St. (© **617/236-1444**).

vintage or in the vintage spirit; **Shake the Tree,** 67 Salem St. (© **617/742-0484;** www.shakethetreeboston.com), is a gift shop and boutique that specializes in arty jewelry, clothing, and home accessories.

CAMBRIDGE The bookstores, boutiques, and T-shirt shops of **Harvard Square** lie about 15 minutes from downtown Boston by subway. Despite the neighborhood association's efforts, chain stores have swept across the Square. You'll find a mix of national and regional outlets, and more than a few persistent independent retailers. They include **Colonial Drug,** 49 Brattle St. (© 617/864-2222; www.colonial drug.com), which stocks hard-to-find perfume and other high-end cosmetics; another branch of **Black Ink,** 5 Brattle St. (© 617/497-1221); and **Oona's,** 1210 Mass. Ave. (© 617/491-2654; www.oonasexperiencedclothing.com), a trove of lovely "experienced" clothing and accessories.

For a less generic experience, walk north along **Mass. Ave.** to the next T stop, in Porter Square. The stroll takes about an hour. Check out **WardMaps.com,** 1735 Mass. Ave. (© 617/497-0737; www.wardmaps.com), which carries maps and map-imprinted gifts; eco-aware **Greenward,** 1776 Mass. Ave. (© 617/395-1338; www.greenwardshop.com); and **Joie de Vivre,** 1792 Mass. Ave. (© 617/864-8188; www.joiedevivre.net), a top-notch gift shop.

And if you just can't manage without a trip to a mall, head to East Cambridge. Take the Green Line to Lechmere, or the Red Line to Kendall/MIT and the free shuttle bus to the **CambridgeSide Galleria,** 100 CambridgeSide Place (© 617/621-8666; www.cambridgesidegalleries.com).

BOSTON & CAMBRIDGE AFTER DARK

For up-to-date entertainment information online, start at **http://events.frommers. com.** The *Boston Globe* offers suggestions at www.boston.com/thingstodo/nightlife and as @bostoncalendar on Twitter. The *Boston Herald*'s Hotline blog (www. bostonherald.com) covers nightlife. For 3-D entertainment listings, consult the daily *Globe* or the Friday *Herald.* Four free publications, available at newspaper boxes around town, publish nightlife listings: the *Boston Phoenix*, the *Improper Bostonian, Stuff@Night* (a *Phoenix* offshoot), and the *Weekly Dig.* The *Phoenix* website (www. bostonphoenix.com) archives the paper's season preview issues; especially before a summer or fall visit, it's a worthwhile planning tool.

GETTING TICKETS Some companies and venues sell tickets over the phone or online; many will refer you to a ticket agency. The major agencies that serve Boston are **Ticketmaster** (© 800/745-3000 or 617/931-2000; www.ticketmaster.com) and **Telecharge** (© 800/432-7250; www.telecharge.com). Many smaller venues use independent companies that don't charge as much. To avoid fees—and possible losses if your plans change and you can't get your money back—visit the box office in person. If you wait until the day before or day of a performance, you'll sometimes have access to tickets that were held back and have just gone on sale.

DISCOUNT TICKETS Visit a **BosTix** (© 617/482-2849; www.bostix.org) booth, at Faneuil Hall Marketplace (on the south side of Faneuil Hall) or in Copley Square (at the corner of Boylston and Dartmouth sts.), where same-day tickets to musical and theatrical performances are half-price, subject to availability. Credit cards are not accepted, and there are no refunds or exchanges. Check the board or the website for the day's offerings. The booths, which are also Ticketmaster outlets, are open Tuesday through Saturday from 10am to 6pm (half-price tickets go on sale at 11am), Sunday from 11am to 4pm. The Copley Square location is also open Monday from 10am to 6pm. *Tip:* Sign up for e-mail updates (you can always unsubscribe later).

The Performing Arts

The city's premier classical performance venue is **Symphony Hall,** 301 Mass. Ave. (© 617/266-1492; www.bso.org). It plays host to other notable groups and artists when the Boston Symphony Orchestra and the Boston Pops are away. The **Hatch Shell** on the Esplanade (© 617/727-5215; www.mass.gov/dcr) is an amphitheater best known as the home of the Pops' 4th of July concerts. On summer nights, crowds turn out for free music and dance performances and films.

Other venues that attract big-name visitors include the **Berklee Performance Center,** 136 Mass. Ave. (© 617/747-2261; www.berkleebpc.com); the **Boston Center for the Arts,** 539 Tremont St. (© 617/426-5000; www.bcaonline.org); the **Cutler Majestic Theatre,** 219 Tremont St. (© 617/824-8000; www.maj. org); and **Sanders Theatre,** 45 Quincy St., Cambridge (© 617/496-2222; www. fas.harvard.edu/~memhall).

THE MAJOR COMPANIES

In addition to the companies below, the **Boston Lyric Opera** (☎ **617/542-6772;** www.blo.org) performs classical and contemporary works. The season runs from November to May. Performances are at the **Shubert Theatre,** 265 Tremont St.

Boston Ballet ★★ One of the top dance companies in the country, Boston Ballet performs *The Nutcracker* from Thanksgiving to New Year's and an eclectic mix of classic story ballets and contemporary works during the rest of the season (Oct–May). Performing at the Boston Opera House, 539 Washington St. ☎ **617/695-6955.** www.bostonballet.org. Tickets $25–$135. Senior, student, and child rush tickets (2 hr. before curtain) $20, except for The Nutcracker. T: Orange Line to Chinatown or Green Line to Boylston.

Boston Pops ★★ From May to early July, tables and chairs replace Symphony Hall's floor seats, and drinks and light refreshments are served. The Pops play a range of music from light classical to show tunes to popular music, often with celebrity guest stars. Performances are Tuesday through Sunday evenings. Special holiday performances in December ($32–$122) usually sell out well in advance, but it can't hurt to check. The regular season ends with two **free outdoor concerts** at the Hatch Shell on the Esplanade along the Charles River: the July 3 rehearsal and the traditional 4th of July concert. Symphony Hall, 301 Mass. Ave. (at Huntington Ave.). ☎ **617/266-1492** or 617/CONCERT (266-2378; program information). SymphonyCharge ☎ **888/266-1200** (outside 617) or 617/266-1200. www.bso.org. Tickets $40–$99 for tables; $20–$63 for balcony seats. T: Green Line E to Symphony, or Orange Line to Mass. Ave.

Boston Symphony Orchestra ★★★ The Boston Symphony, one of the world's greatest, was founded in 1881. James Levine is the music director. You might want to schedule your trip to coincide with a particular performance, or with a visit by a celebrated guest artist or conductor. The season runs from October to April, with performances most Tuesday, Thursday, and Saturday evenings; Friday afternoons; and some Friday evenings. Explanatory talks (included in the ticket price) begin 75 minutes before the curtain. If you can't get tickets in advance, check at the box office for returns from subscribers 2 hours before showtime. A limited number of rush tickets are available on the day of the performance for Tuesday and Thursday evening and Friday afternoon programs. Some Wednesday evening and Thursday morning rehearsals are open to the public. Symphony Hall, 301 Mass. Ave. (at Huntington Ave.).

Dessert Alert

Finale is a "desserterie" that serves a mouth-watering variety of glorious desserts in elegant, romantic surroundings with lots of velvet and soft lighting. Yes, it's a tad expensive. No, this is not a balanced meal. But the sweet tooths (sweet teeth?) who flock here don't care. The original is at 1 Columbus Ave., in the pointy end of the Park Plaza Building (☎ **617/423-3184;** www.finale desserts.com), with branches at 30 Dunster St., Harvard Square (☎ **617/441-9797**), and 1306 Beacon St., Coolidge Corner, Brookline (☎ **617/232-3233**). Finale also serves real food, such as salads and pizzas, but the desserts are the real draw.

© **617/266-1492** or 617/CONCERT (266-2378; program information). SymphonyCharge © **888/266-1200** (outside 617) or 617/266-1200. www.bso.org. Tickets $29–$115. Rush tickets $9 (on sale 10am Fri, 5pm Tues and Thurs). Rehearsal tickets $19. T: Green Line E to Symphony, or Orange Line to Mass. Ave.

THEATER & PERFORMANCE ART

Boston is one of the last cities for pre-Broadway tryouts, allowing an early look at a classic (or classic flop) in the making. It's also a popular destination for touring companies of established hits. You'll find most of the shows headed to or coming from Broadway in the **Theater District,** at the **Colonial Theatre,** 106 Boylston St. (© **617/426-9366;** www.broadwayacrossamericaboston.com); the **Boston Opera House,** 539 Washington St. (© **617/259-3400;** www.bostonopera-houseonline.com); and the two venues that make up the Citi Performing Arts Center (© **617/482-9393;** www.citicenter.org), the **Shubert Theatre,** 265 Tremont St., and the **Wang Theatre,** 270 Tremont St. The promoter often is **Broadway Across America** (© 866/523-7469; www.broadwayacrossamerica.com).

The excellent local theater scene boasts the **Huntington Theatre Company,** which performs at the Boston University Theatre, 264 Huntington Ave. (© **617/266-0800;** www.huntington.org), and the **American Repertory Theatre (ART),** which makes its home at Harvard University's Loeb Drama Center, 64 Brattle St., Cambridge (© **617/547-8300;** www.americanrepertorytheater.org). The ART also books **Club Oberon,** a "theatrical club space"—think performance art, cabaret, and liquor—at 2 Arrow St. (at Mass. Ave.; © 617/496-8004; www.cluboberon.com).

The off-Broadway performance-art sensation **Blue Man Group** is a trio of cobalt-colored entertainers who use music, percussion, food, and audience participants—props include social commentary, Twinkies, marshmallows, breakfast cereal, toilet paper, and lots of blue paint. Older children and teenagers enjoy the mayhem as much as adults. Shows are at the **Charles Playhouse,** 74 Warrenton St. (© **617/426-6912;** www.blueman.com), in the Theater District. Tickets are $69 and $48 at the box office and through Ticketmaster (© **800/982-2787;** www.ticketmaster.com).

The Club & Music Scene

The Boston-area club scene changes constantly, and there is a good time for everyone somewhere—or at least every early bird. Bars close at 1am, clubs at 2am. The subway shuts down between 12:30 and 1am. Check the *Globe,* the *Phoenix,* the Friday *Herald, Stuff@Night,* or the *Improper Bostonian.*

The drinking age is 21; a valid driver's license or passport is required as proof of age. The law is strictly enforced, especially near college campuses—in other words, practically everywhere. Even if you're not drinking, many clubs require patrons to be 21 (or, in some cases, 18 or 19). Wherever you go, be prepared to show ID if you appear to be younger than 35 or so.

Big-name rock and pop artists play **TD Garden,** 100 Legends Way (Causeway St.; © **617/624-1000;** www.tdgarden.com), when it's not in use by the Bruins (hockey), the Celtics (basketball), the circus (in Oct), or touring ice shows. Concerts are in the round or on the arena stage.

COMEDY

The Comedy Studio ★★   Nobody here is a sitcom star—yet. With a stellar reputation for searching out undiscovered talent, the no-frills Comedy Studio draws connoisseurs, students, and network scouts. Sketches and improv spice up the standup. Shows are Tuesday (magicians) through Sunday at 8pm. At the Hong Kong restaurant, 1238 Mass. Ave., Cambridge. ☏ **617/661-6507**. www.thecomedystudio.com. Cover $8–$10. T: Red Line to Harvard.

Wilbur Theatre This historic Theater District venue holds 1,200 for performances by big-name standup comics and lower-profile musical acts. 246 Tremont St. (at Stuart St.). ☏ **617/248-9700** or 617/931-2000 (Ticketmaster). www.thewilburtheatre. com. T: Green Line to Boylston or Orange Line to New England Medical Center.

DANCE CLUBS

The *Improper Bostonian* and the *Phoenix* club listings are good resources for info about this ever-changing scene, but a savvy concierge is even better. *Tip:* Most club websites let you put your name on the VIP list. Can't hurt, might help.

Royale Boston ★★ This onetime hotel ballroom boasts excellent house and techno DJs, a huge dance floor, and a U-shaped balcony that's perfect for checking out the action below. Live shows, booked by a New York–based promoter noted for its rock acts, take good advantage of the sight lines. Royale opened in March 2010 in the space that formerly held the Roxy; check the website for a current schedule. In the Courtyard Boston Tremont hotel, 279 Tremont St. (½ block from Stuart St.). ☏ **617/338-7699**. www.royaleboston.com. Cover $15–$20. T: Green Line to Boylston or Orange Line to New England Medical Center.

FOLK & ECLECTIC

Club Passim ★★★ Joan Baez, Suzanne Vega, and Tom Rush all started out in this legendary basement coffeehouse. There's live music nightly, and coffee, food (by Veggie Planet; p. 116), beer, and wine until 10:30pm. Open Sunday through Thursday from 11am to 11pm, Friday and Saturday until midnight. 47 Palmer St., Cambridge. ☏ **617/492-7679**. www.passimcenter.org. Cover $5–$40; most shows $20 or less. T: Red Line to Harvard.

Johnny D's Uptown Restaurant & Music Club ★★★   This family-owned establishment draws a congenial, low-key crowd for performers on international tours as well as local acts. The music ranges from zydeco to rock, blues to ska. It's only two stops past Harvard Square on the Red Line (about a 15-min. ride at night).

Open Monday 12:30pm to 1am, Tuesday through Saturday 11am to 1am, weekends 9am to 1am. Lunch is served Tuesday through Friday until 6pm; dinner is served Tuesday through Thursday from 6 to 9pm and Friday and Saturday from 6 to 10pm (a dinner reservation guarantees you a seat for the show); lighter fare is served Tuesday through Saturday until midnight. A jazz brunch takes place Saturday and Sunday from 9am to 2:30pm, and there's a blues jam Sunday from 4:30 to 8pm. 17 Holland St., Davis Sq., Somerville. ✆ **617/776-2004** or 617/776-9667 (concert line). www.johnnyds. com. Cover $3–$20, usually $8–$12. T: Red Line to Davis.

JAZZ & BLUES

On summer Thursdays at 6pm, the **Boston Harbor Hotel** (✆ **617/439-7000**) stages performances on the "Blues Barge," which floats in the water behind the hotel. The theater at the Cambridge Multicultural Arts Center, 41 Second St., Cambridge (✆ **617/577-1400;** www.cmacusa.org; T: Green Line to Lechmere), becomes a jazz club at least a couple of times a month year-round.

Regattabar ★★   The Regattabar's lineup of local and international artists is often considered the best in the area, but be sure to check the lineup at Scullers (see below). Nellie McKay and McCoy Tyner have appeared recently. The third-floor room holds about 200 and can get a little noisy. Buy tickets in advance or try your luck at the door an hour before showtime. In the Charles Hotel, 1 Bennett St., Cambridge. ✆ **617/661-5000,** or 617/395-7757 for tickets. www.regattabarjazz.com. Tickets $12–$35. T: Red Line to Harvard.

Scullers Jazz Club ★★★   Overlooking the Charles River, Scullers books top singers and instrumentalists—recent notables include Mose Allison, Herb Alpert, and Diane Schuur. Patrons tend to be more hard-core and quieter than the crowds at the Regattabar, but it depends on who's performing. The box office is open Monday through Saturday from 11am to 6pm. Ask about dinner and overnight packages. In the Doubletree Guest Suites hotel, 400 Soldiers Field Rd. ✆ **617/562-4111.** www.scullersjazz.com. Tickets $18–$50. Validated parking available.

Wally's Cafe ★★   This Boston institution, near a busy corner in the South End, opened in 1947. Its New Orleans–style all-about-the-music atmosphere draws a notably diverse crowd—black, white, straight, gay, affluent, indigent—for nightly live music by local ensembles, students and instructors from the Berklee College of Music, and the occasional international star. 427 Mass. Ave. ✆ **617/424-1408.** www. wallyscafe.com. 1-drink minimum. T: Orange Line to Mass. Ave.

ROCK & ALTERNATIVE

House of Blues ★★   Yes, it's part of a chain—but save the smart remarks until after you check out the top-notch talent the House of Blues books. Across the street from Fenway Park, it keeps this neighborhood busy year-round, not just during baseball season. Like the other locations, it serves above-average Southern food and draws a crowd for the Sunday gospel brunch. 15 Lansdowne St. ✆ **888/693-2583** or 617/960-8358. www.houseofblues.com. T: Green Line B, C, or D to Kenmore.

The Middle East ★★★   One of the best rock clubs in New England books an impressive variety of progressive and alternative acts in two rooms (upstairs and downstairs) every night. Showcasing top local talent as well as bands with international reputations, it's a popular hangout that gets crowded, hot, and *loud*. In the

Cocktail Culture: Get Your Drink On

Like a lot of other trends, the cocktail craze arrived in Boston late and quickly took off. A nationally renowned example of the hard-core cocktail bar is **Drink ★★**, 348 Congress St. (✆ 617/695-1806; www.drinkfortpoint.com; T: Red Line to South Station). Don't take my word for it—high-profile amateur mixologist Rachel Maddow of MSNBC says it's the best bar in Boston, if not the country. Drink has no menu, just bartenders who chat with you about what you're in the mood for and create something on the spot. Sounds crazy, works perfectly. It's pricey, but you're paying for an evening's entertainment and an enthusiastic guide. Open daily at 4pm.

same complex are the **Corner,** a former bakery that features acoustic artists and belly dancers, and **ZuZu** (✆ 617/492-9181), a Middle Eastern restaurant with its own music schedule. 472–480 Mass. Ave., Central Sq., Cambridge. ✆ **617/864-EAST** [3278], or 800/745-3000 (Ticketmaster). www.mideastclub.com. Cover $8–$25 (ZuZu cover $5 Fri–Sat only). T: Red Line to Central.

Toad ★★ 🍸 Essentially a bar with a stage, this narrow space attracts a savvy three-generation clientele with big local names and no cover. Toad enjoys good acoustics but not much elbow room—a plus when restless musicians wander into the crowd. 1912 Mass. Ave., Cambridge. ✆ **617/497-4950** (info line). www.toadcambridge.com. T: Red Line to Porter.

T. T. the Bear's Place ★ A mainstay of the Central Square live-music scene since it opened in 1985, "T. T.'s" has an uncanny knack for booking hot new talent. You might see cutting-edge alternative and roots music or up-and-coming indie rockers. New bands predominate early in the week, with more established artists on weekends. 10 Brookline St., Cambridge. ✆ **617/492-0082,** or 617/492-BEAR (2327; concert line). www.ttthebears.com. Cover $3–$17. T: Red Line to Central.

Bars & Lounges

Bleacher Bar ★ This place is under the center-field bleachers at Fenway Park. The most coveted seats—there's a time limit on game days—face a window that overlooks the outfield (it's covered with one-way glass during games). The unimaginative beer menu and decent food are reasonably priced, all things considered. 82A Lansdowne St. ✆ **617/262-2424.** www.bleacherbarboston.com. T: Green Line B, C, or D to Kenmore.

The Black Rose Purists might sneer at the Black Rose's touristy location, but performers don't. Sing along with the authentic entertainment at this jam-packed pub and restaurant at the edge of Faneuil Hall Marketplace. 160 State St. ✆ **617/742-2286.** www.irishconnection.com. Cover $3–$5. T: Orange or Blue Line to State.

The Bristol Lounge ★★★ An elegant room with cushy seating and a fireplace, the Bristol Lounge is an oasis anytime, and it features a fabulous dessert buffet on

weekend nights. There's live jazz every evening, and food until 11:30pm (12:30am Fri–Sat). In the Four Seasons Hotel, 200 Boylston St. ✆ **617/351-2037.** T: Green Line to Arlington.

Casablanca ★★   Students and professors crowd this legendary Harvard Square watering hole, especially on weekends. It offers an excellent jukebox, excellent food, and excellent eavesdropping. 40 Brattle St., Cambridge. ✆ **617/876-0999.** T: Red Line to Harvard.

Cask 'n Flagon ★   A long fly ball away from Fenway Park, "the Cask," which opened in 1969, is one of the best-known sports bars in this sports-mad city. It's much bigger than it looks from Brookline Avenue, but lines on game days are still comically long. The crowds watching major events on numerous TVs in the memorabilia-drenched bar are large and enthusiastic year-round. 62 Brookline Ave. ✆ **617/536-4840.** www.casknflagon.com. T: Green Line B, C, or D to Kenmore.

Cheers (Beacon Hill)   This one-time neighborhood bar has embraced its status as a TV icon. A copy of the bar from the set of the long-running sitcom makes a good photo backdrop for the legions of out-of-towners who flock here. 84 Beacon St. ✆ **617/227-9605.** www.cheersboston.com. T: Green Line to Arlington.

Cheers (Faneuil Hall Marketplace)   Blatantly but good-naturedly courting fans of the sitcom, this bar exactly replicates the set of the TV show. You know you want to. Quincy Market Building, South Canopy. ✆ **617/227-7532.** www.cheersboston.com. T: Green or Blue Line to Government Center, or Orange Line to Haymarket.

DeLux Cafe ★   Ultracool but never obnoxious about it, the DeLux is one of the classiest dives around. The funky decor (check out the Elvis shrine), selection of microbrews, and veggie-friendly ethnic menu attract a cross-section of the South End, from off-duty chefs to yuppies. 100 Chandler St. ✆ **617/338-5258.** T: Orange Line to Back Bay.

Eastern Standard   A cavernous brasserie with a mile-long marble bar, Eastern Standard is an all-things-to-all-people destination. It serves food from early morning to late night, offers outdoor seating, and has a hopping bar scene every night during the week and almost all day on weekends. The specialty cocktails are numerous and diverse, and the bartenders know their way around the wine list. On Red Sox game nights, be ready to spend a lot of time on your feet. In the Hotel Commonwealth, 528 Commonwealth Ave. ✆ **617/532-9100.** www.easternstandardboston.com. T: Green Line B, C, or D to Kenmore.

Flat Top Johnny's ★★   A spacious, loud room with a bar and 12 red-topped pool tables, Flat Top Johnny's has a casual neighborhood feel despite being in a rather sterile office-retail complex. Open Monday to Wednesday from 4pm to 1am and Thursday to Sunday from noon to 1am. 1 Kendall Sq., Cambridge. ✆ **617/494-9565.** www.flattopjohnnys.com. T: Red Line to Kendall/MIT.

The Fours   One of Boston's best and best-known sports bars, the Fours is about one football field away from TD Garden. Festooned with sports memorabilia and TVs, it's a madhouse before Celtics and Bruins games—and a promising place to pick up an extra ticket. 166 Canal St. ✆ **617/720-4455.** T: Green or Orange Line to North Station.

Grendel's Den ★   A vestige of prefranchise Harvard Square, this cozy subterranean space is *the* place to celebrate turning 21. Recent grads and grad students dominate, but Grendel's has been so popular for so long that it also gets its share of Gen Y's parents. 89 Winthrop St., Cambridge. ✆ **617/491-1050.** www.grendelsden.com. T: Red Line to Harvard.

Hard Rock Cafe ☺   This link in the chain is a fun one—just ask the other tourists. The gigantic space across the street from Faneuil Hall Marketplace abounds with memorabilia of Nirvana, Madonna, local favorites Aerosmith and the Cars, and others. 24 Clinton St. ✆ **617/424-ROCK** (7625). www.hardrock.com. T: Orange Line to Haymarket, or Green or Blue Line to Government Center.

Jacques Cabaret ★   The only drag venue in town, Jacques draws a friendly crowd of gay and straight patrons who mix with the "girls" and sometimes engage in a shocking activity—that's right, disco dancing. The eclectic entertainment includes live music (on weekends), performance artists, and, of course, drag shows. Open daily from noon to midnight; no credit cards. 79 Broadway, Bay Village. ✆ **617/426-8902.** www.jacquescabaret.com. Cover $6–$10. T: Green Line to Arlington.

Jerry Remy's Sports Bar & Grill ★   As a player and a broadcaster, Jerry Remy has made his living at Fenway Park for years. This cavernous establishment is on the expensive side, but the food is tasty, and the sheer number of TVs means you won't miss a play. There's patio seating in good weather. 1265 Boylston St. ✆ **617/236-7369.** www.jerryremys.com. T: Green Line B, C, or D to Kenmore, then 10-min. walk.

John Harvard's Brew House ★★   This subterranean Harvard Square hangout pumps out terrific English-style brews in a clublike setting and prides itself on its food. 33 Dunster St., Cambridge. ✆ **617/868-3585.** www.johnharvards.com. T: Red Line to Harvard.

Mr. Dooley's Boston Tavern ★★   Sometimes an expertly poured Guinness is all you need. If one of the nicest bartenders in the city pours it, so much the better. This Financial District spot offers many imported beers on tap, live music, and a menu of pub favorites. 77 Broad St. ✆ **617/338-5656.** www.somerspubs.com. Cover $3–$5 Fri–Sat. T: Orange Line to State or Blue Line to Aquarium.

Oak Bar ★★   This room feels like an old-fashioned men's club—but one that embraces women. The lighting is muted, the leather seating soft and welcoming, and the raw bar picture-perfect. There's live entertainment on weekends. Proper dress (no shorts or sneakers) is required. Open Sunday through Thursday until midnight, Friday and Saturday until 1am. In the Fairmont Copley Plaza Hotel, 138 St. James Ave. ✆ **617/267-5300.** www.theoakroom.com. T: Green Line to Copley or Orange Line to Back Bay.

The Plough & Stars ★   Although it's comically small, the Plough is a huge presence on the local pub and live-music scenes. A neighborhood hangout during the day, it's a hipster magnet at night. The kitchen serves lunch, dinner, and weekend brunch. 912 Mass. Ave., Cambridge. ✆ **617/576-0032.** www.ploughandstars.com. T: Red Line to Central or Harvard.

Silvertone Bar & Grill ★   One of the few real hangouts in the Downtown Crossing area, this tiny subterranean bar attracts an incredibly loud after-work crowd. The dining room is noted for reasonably priced comfort food (try the sublime macaroni and cheese). Closed Sunday. 69 Bromfield St. © **617/338-7887.** www.silvertonedowntown.com. T: Red or Green Line to Park Street.

Top of the Hub ★★★   The 52nd-story view of greater Boston from this appealing lounge is especially lovely at sunset. There's music and dancing nightly. Dress is casual but neat. Prudential Center, 800 Boylston St. © **617/536-1775**. T: Green Line E to Prudential.

6 | SIDE TRIPS FROM BOSTON

by Marie Morris

Besides being, in the words of Oliver Wendell Holmes, "the hub of the solar system," Boston is the hub of a network of wonderful day trips and longer excursions. The destinations in this chapter are lively communities where you'll find sights and attractions of great beauty and historical significance. Exploring can take as little as half a day or as long as a week or more.

WEST OF BOSTON   If time is short, combine a visit to Cambridge (see chapter 5) with a trip to Lexington and Concord for a hefty dose of American history. The route that Paul Revere took out of Boston on April 18, 1775, is tough to follow—he started by crossing the harbor in a rowboat, for one thing—but his fellow rider, William Dawes, cut through Harvard Square. Both proceeded to warn the colonists that British troops were on the march.

NORTH OF BOSTON   Great prosperity came to eastern Massachusetts after the Revolution, as the new nation took advantage of the lifting of British trade barriers. Today the spoils of the China trade adorn mansions and public edifices in seaside locales such as Marblehead, Salem, and Cape Ann. Fishing is still an important industry, but these days the area caters more to commuters and tourists than to those who make their living from the sea. A worthwhile detour from the north or west is Lowell, a once-decrepit mill town where tourism is now the largest industry.

SOUTH OF BOSTON   The communities between Boston and Cape Cod are mostly commuter suburbs. The area's prime sightseeing destination is Plymouth, one of the oldest permanent European settlements

 Follow the Leader

If you lack the time or inclination to make your own arrangements, consider an escorted tour. One reliable company is Gray Line's **Brush Hill Tours,** 435 High St., Randolph (📞 **800/343-1328** or **617/720-6342**; www.brushhilltours. com), which offers a wide variety of half- and full-day excursions.

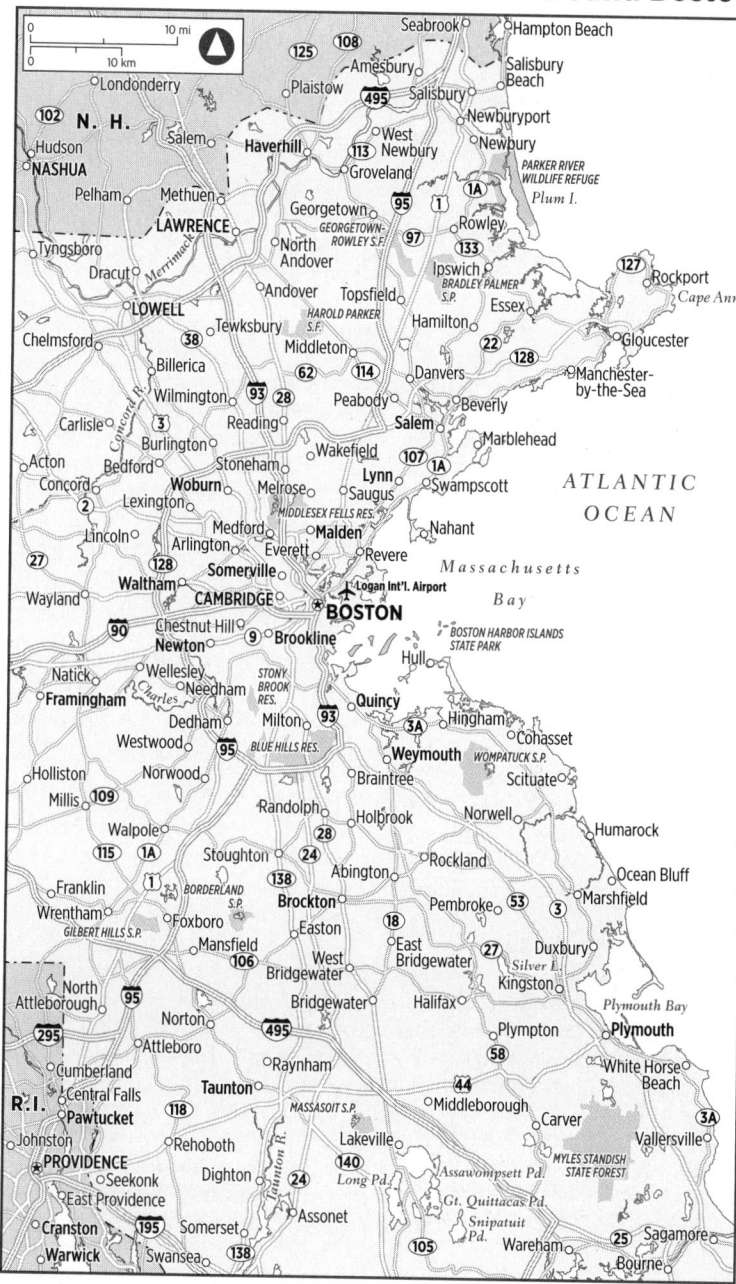

in North America. It's a pleasant place where you can walk in the footsteps of the Pilgrims—and of the countless out-of-towners who flock here in summer and at Thanksgiving. Farther south, the old whaling port of New Bedford makes an interesting detour.

LEXINGTON ★

9 miles NW of downtown Boston; 6 miles NW of Cambridge; 6 miles E of Concord

A country village turned prosperous suburb, Lexington takes great pride in its history. It's a pleasant town with some engaging destinations, but it lacks the atmosphere and abundant attractions of nearby Concord. Being sure to leave time for a tour of the Buckman Tavern, you can schedule as little as a couple of hours to explore downtown Lexington, possibly en route to Concord. A visit can also fill a half- or full day. The town contains part of Minute Man National Historical Park, which is definitely worth a visit.

The shooting phase of the Revolutionary War started here, with a skirmish on the town common, now called the Battle Green. It began when British troops clashed with local militia members, who were known as "Minutemen" for their ability to assemble on short notice. British soldiers marched from Boston to Lexington late on April 18, 1775. Tipped off, Paul Revere and William Dawes rode ahead to sound the warning. They did their job so well that the alarm came long before the advancing forces. The Lexington Minutemen, under the command of Capt. John Parker, got the word shortly after midnight, but the redcoats were still several hours away. The colonists repaired to their homes and the Buckman Tavern. Five hours later, some 700 British troops under Major Pitcairn arrived.

A tense standoff ensued. Three times Pitcairn ordered them to disperse, but the patriots—fewer than 100, and some accounts say 77—refused. Parker called: "Stand your ground. Don't fire unless fired upon, but if they mean to have a war, let it begin here!" Finally the captain, perhaps realizing as the sky grew light how badly outnumbered his men were, gave the order to fall back.

As the Minutemen began to scatter, a shot rang out. One British company charged into the fray, and the colonists attempted to regroup as Pitcairn tried unsuccessfully to call off his troops. Nobody knows who started the shooting, but when it was over, 8 militia members, including a drummer boy, lay dead, and 10 were wounded.

Essentials

GETTING THERE   From downtown Boston, take Storrow Drive or Memorial Drive to Rte. 2. Follow Rte. 2 from Cambridge through Belmont, exit at Rte. 4/225, and follow signs to downtown Lexington. Or take Rte. 128 (I-95) to exit 31A and follow signs. If it's not rush hour, allow about 35 minutes. **Massachusetts Avenue** (the same "Mass. Ave." you saw in Boston and Cambridge) runs through the center of town. There's metered parking on the street and in several municipal lots, and free parking at the National Heritage Museum and the National Historical Park.

The **MBTA** (© **800/392-6100** or 617/222-3200; www.mbta.com) runs bus routes no. 62 (Bedford) and 76 (Hanscom) to Lexington from Alewife station, the last stop on the Red Line. The one-way fare is $1.25 with a CharlieCard or $1.50 with a CharlieTicket, and the trip takes about 25 minutes. Buses leave every hour

Lexington

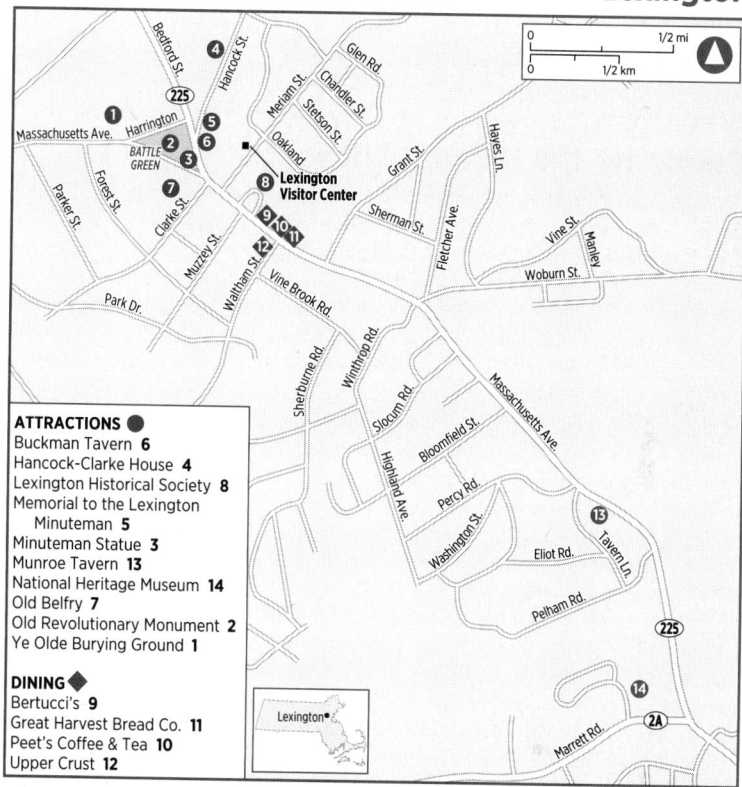

ATTRACTIONS ●
Buckman Tavern **6**
Hancock-Clarke House **4**
Lexington Historical Society **8**
Memorial to the Lexington
    Minuteman **5**
Minuteman Statue **3**
Munroe Tavern **13**
National Heritage Museum **14**
Old Belfry **7**
Old Revolutionary Monument **2**
Ye Olde Burying Ground **1**

DINING ◆
Bertucci's **9**
Great Harvest Bread Co. **11**
Peet's Coffee & Tea **10**
Upper Crust **12**

during the day and every half-hour during rush periods Monday through Saturday, with no service on Sunday. The seasonal Liberty Ride tour connects Lexington and Concord (see "Getting Around," below).

VISITOR INFORMATION   The Chamber of Commerce **Visitors Center,** 1875 Mass. Ave. (℃ **781/862-2480;** www.lexingtonchamber.org), distributes maps and information. The **Greater Merrimack Valley Convention & Visitors Bureau** (℃ **800/443-3332** or 978/459-6150; www.merrimackvalley.org) covers Lexington.

GETTING AROUND   Downtown Lexington is easily negotiable on foot, and most attractions are within walking distance. If you prefer not to walk to the Munroe Tavern and the National Heritage Museum (see below), bus nos. 62 and 76 pass by on Mass. Ave.

The **Liberty Ride** (℃ **781/862-0500,** ext. 702; www.libertyride.us) is a 90-minute narrated trolley tour that connects the attractions in Lexington and Concord. It operates from 10am to 4pm Saturday and Sunday of Patriot's Day weekend and daily from Memorial Day weekend through late October; check ahead to confirm the schedule. The fare (good for 24 hrs.) is $25 for adults, $10 for children 5 to 17, free for children 4 and under. There's free parking at the National Heritage Museum and the national park visitor center, and your ticket entitles you to discounts at local businesses.

SPECIAL EVENTS   **Patriot's Day,** a state holiday observed on the third Monday in April, commemorates the start of the Revolution. Celebrations include a reenactment of the battle and other festivities. Visit **www.battleroad.org** for information.

Exploring the Historic Sites

Minute Man National Historical Park is in Lexington, Concord, and Lincoln. At the Lexington end of the park is the **Minute Man Visitor Center ★**, off Rte. 2A, about one-half mile west of I-95 exit 30B (© **781/674-1920;** www.nps.gov/ mima). This area of the park includes the first 4 miles of the Battle Road, the route the defeated British troops took as they left Concord. Begin your visit here by watching "The Road to Revolution," a multimedia program that explains Paul Revere's ride and the events of April 19, 1775. (Winter visitors can start in Concord.) Also here are informational displays and a 40-foot mural illustrating the battle. On summer weekends, rangers lead tours of the park; check ahead for times. The **Battle Road Trail,** a 5-mile interpretive path, carries pedestrian, wheelchair, and bicycle traffic. Panels and granite markers along the trail explain the military, social, and natural history of the area. In season (Mar–Nov), this center is open daily from 9am to 5pm, but schedules vary. Surf online or call ahead (try the North Bridge Visitor Center, © **978/369-6993,** if there's no answer at the main number) for open days and hours. For more information, see "Concord," below.

Start your visit to downtown Lexington at the **visitor center,** on the town common or Battle Green. It's open daily from 9am to 5pm (10am–4pm Dec–Mar). A diorama and accompanying narrative illustrate the Battle of Lexington. The **Minuteman statue** (1900) on the green is of Capt. John Parker, who commanded the militia. The **Old Revolutionary Monument** (1799) marks the grave of seven of the eight colonists who died in the conflict, which the **Line of Battle Boulder** commemorates. The **Memorial to the Lexington Minutemen** bears the names of the men who fell in the battle. Across Mass. Ave., near Clarke Street, is the **Old Belfry,** a reproduction of the free-standing bell that sounded the alarm the day of the battle. **Ye Olde Burying Ground,** at the west end of the green, dates to 1690 and contains Parker's grave. A stop at the visitor center and a walk around the monuments takes about half an hour and gives a good sense of what went on here and why the participants are still held in such high esteem.

Lexington Historical Society ★★ ☺   The historical society's signature properties were among the country's first **historic houses** when restoration of the three buildings began around the turn of the 20th century. A guided tour (30–45 min. each) is the only way to see the houses.

Across from the Battle Green is the **Buckman Tavern ★★**, 1 Bedford St., built around 1710. If time is short and you have to pick just one house to visit, make it this one. The interior of the tavern has been restored to approximate its appearance on the day of the battle. The colonists gathered here to await word of British troop movements, and they brought their wounded here after the conflict. The tour of the tavern, by guides in period dress, is educational and entertaining.

Not far away, the **Hancock-Clarke House,** 36 Hancock St., is where Samuel Adams and John Hancock were staying when Paul Revere arrived. They fled to nearby Woburn. Visit the 1737 house, which contains some original furnishings as well as artifacts of the Battle of Lexington, to see an orientation film about the town.

The British took over the 1690 **Munroe Tavern ★**, 1332 Mass. Ave. (about 1 mile from the Green), to use as their headquarters and, after the battle, field hospital. Here you'll learn more about the royal troops and see furniture carefully preserved by the Munroe family, including the table and chair President George Washington used when he dined here in 1789. The historically accurate gardens in the rear (free admission) are beautifully planted and maintained.

The historical society makes its headquarters downtown in the 1846 Lexington Depot, where changing exhibits on local history are open to the public.

Depot Sq. (off Mass. Ave., near the Battle Green). ② **781/862-1703** or 781/862-5598 for information about group tours, offered by appointment only. www.lexingtonhistory.org. **Buckman Tavern:** Daily Apr–Oct. Tours every 30 min. 10am–4pm. Closed Nov–Mar. **Hancock-Clarke House:** Daily Apr–Oct. Tours on the hour 10am–4pm. Closed Nov–Mar. **Munroe Tavern:** Daily Apr–Oct. Tours on the hour noon–4pm. Closed Nov–Mar. Admission to all 3 houses $10 adults, $6 children 6–16; to each individual house, $6 adults, $4 children.

National Heritage Museum ★★ ☺ ✦   This fascinating museum explores history through popular culture. It makes an entertaining complement to the Colonial focus of the rest of the town. The installations in the six exhibition spaces change regularly; you can start with another dose of the Revolution, the permanent exhibit *Sowing the Seeds of Liberty.* Other topics have ranged from George Washington to postcards to Jim Henson and the Muppets. Lectures, concerts, and family programs are also offered, and the cafe serves lunch (Tues–Fri). The Scottish Rite of Freemasonry sponsors the museum.

33 Marrett Rd., Rte. 2A (at Mass. Ave.). ② **781/861-6559.** www.nationalheritagemuseum.org. Free admission. Tues–Sat and some Mon holidays 10am–5pm; Sun noon–5pm. Bus: 62 or 76 from downtown Lexington to Rte. 2A.

Shopping

Mass. Ave. near the center of town is a retail hub. Check out **Catch a Falling Star,** 7 Depot Sq. (② 781/674-2432; www.catchafallingstartoys.com); **Sweet Beads,** 1792 Mass. Ave. (② 781/860-7727; www.sweetbeads.us); **Signature Stationers,** 1800 Mass. Ave. (② 781/863-2777; www.signaturestationers.com); and the **Crafty Yankee,** 1838 Mass. Ave. (② 781/863-1219; www.craftyyankee.com). By car, the sprawling **Burlington Mall** (② 978/272-8667; www.burlington-mall.com) is about 10 minutes away, off I-95/128.

Where to Stay

Aloft Lexington (② **877/GO-ALOFT** [462-5638] or 781/861-1391; www.aloft lexington.com) and **Element Lexington** (② **877/ELEMENT** [353-6368] or 781/761-1750; www.elementlexington.com) are side-by-side locations of Starwood's newest brands. Aloft rooms have 9-foot ceilings that make the good-size units feel even larger; the hotel has a pool and a 24-hour restaurant. Rates start at $219 on weekdays, with weekend and off-season discounts. The extended-stay Element brand targets business travelers; units have full kitchens and Westin's signature Heavenly Beds. High-season weekday rates start at $259. The newly built hotels are on the same property at 727 Marrett Rd. It's just off I-95/Rte. 128 exit 30B, far enough from the interstate that traffic noise isn't a serious problem.

Where to Stay Nearby

Bedford is 15 minutes from downtown Lexington on Rte. 4/225, across I-95. The **Boston/Bedford Travelodge,** 285 Great Rd., Bedford (🕐 **781/275-6120;** www. travelodge.com), is an affordable motel with an outdoor pool. Rates for a double room in high season start around $69.

Doubletree Hotel Boston/Bedford Glen ★   The sights in Lexington and Concord are convenient to this three-story hotel, which neatly makes the transition from a weekday business destination to a weekend family resort. It's an excellent base for day-tripping, and there's plenty to do without leaving the attractively land-scaped 24-acre property. Rooms are large, with Doubletree's signature cushy beds. The hotel shuttle transports guests to destinations within 5 miles, including the Burlington Mall.

44 Middlesex Tpk., Bedford, MA 01730. 🕐 **800/222-TREE** [8733] or 781/275-5500. Fax 781/275-8956. www.doubletree.com. 284 units. Sun–Thurs $139–$249 double; Fri–Sat $99–$229 double. Extra person $15. Children 18 and under stay free in parent's room. AE, DC, DISC, MC, V. Pets accepted ($25 fee). **Amenities:** Restaurant; lounge; concierge; fitness center; Jacuzzi; indoor pool; room service; indoor/outdoor tennis courts. *In room:* A/C, TV, fridge, hair dryer, Wi-Fi (free).

Where to Dine

If you're not continuing to Concord, which has more interesting dining options, Lexington offers some pleasant choices. The fresh soups and sandwiches at the cafe at the **National Heritage Museum** (see above) make it a popular spot for lunch Tuesday through Friday. You'll find excellent pizza at **Bertucci's,** 1777 Mass. Ave. (🕐 **781/860-9000;** www.bertuccis.com), and the **Upper Crust,** 41 Waltham St. (🕐 **781/247-0089;** www.theuppercrustpizzeria.com). Other reliable chain outlets serving soups and sandwiches include **Peet's Coffee & Tea,** 1749 Mass. Ave. (🕐 **781/357-2090;** www.peets.com), and **Great Harvest Bread Co.,** 1736 Mass. Ave. (🕐 **781/861-9990;** www.greatharvest.com).

CONCORD ★★★

18 miles NW of Boston; 15 miles NW of Cambridge; 6 miles W of Lexington.

Concord (say "conquered") revels in its legacy as a center of groundbreaking thought and its role in the country's political and intellectual history. A visit can easily fill a day; if your interests are specialized or time is short, a half-day excursion is reasonable. For an excellent overview of town history, start your visit at the **Concord Museum.**

After just a little time in this lovely town, you may find yourself adopting the local attitude toward two of its most famous residents: Ralph Waldo Emerson, a well-respected uncle figure, and Henry David Thoreau, everyone's favorite eccentric cousin. Long before they wandered the countryside, the first official battle of the Revolutionary War took place at the **North Bridge,** now part of Minute Man National Historical Park. By the mid–19th century, Concord was the center of the Transcendentalist movement. Homes of **Emerson, Thoreau, Nathaniel Hawthorne,** and **Louisa May Alcott** are open to visitors, as is the authors' final resting place, **Sleepy Hollow Cemetery.**

Concord

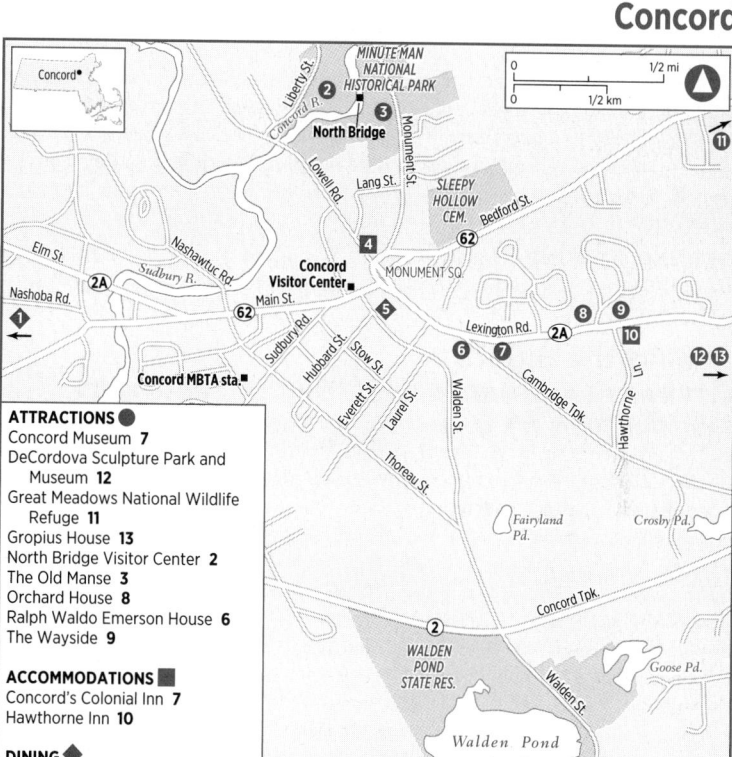

ATTRACTIONS ●
Concord Museum **7**
DeCordova Sculpture Park and
 Museum **12**
Great Meadows National Wildlife
 Refuge **11**
Gropius House **13**
North Bridge Visitor Center **2**
The Old Manse **3**
Orchard House **8**
Ralph Waldo Emerson House **6**
The Wayside **9**

ACCOMMODATIONS ■
Concord's Colonial Inn **7**
Hawthorne Inn **10**

DINING ◆
Concord Cheese Shop **5**
Nashoba Brook Bakery & Cafe **1**

Essentials

GETTING THERE   From Lexington (10 min. by car), take Rte. 2A west from Mass. Ave. (Rte. 4/225) at the National Heritage Museum; follow the BATTLE ROAD signs. From Boston and Cambridge (30–40 min.), take Rte. 2 into Lincoln and stay in the right lane. Where the main road makes a sharp left, go straight onto Cambridge Turnpike, and follow signs to HISTORIC CONCORD. To go directly to Walden Pond, use the left lane, take what's now Rte. 2/2A another mile or so, and turn left onto Rte. 126. There's parking throughout town and at the attractions.

The **commuter rail** (© **800/392-6100** or 617/222-3200; www.mbta.com) takes about 45 minutes from North Station in Boston, with a stop at Porter Square in Cambridge. The round-trip fare is $13. The station is about ¾ of a mile over flat terrain from the town center. There is no bus service from Boston to Concord. For information about **Liberty Ride** tours of Concord and Lexington, see "Getting Around," p. 151.

VISITOR INFORMATION   The **Chamber of Commerce,** 15 Walden St., Ste. 7 (✆ **978/369-3120;** www.concordchamberofcommerce.org), maintains a visitor center at 58 Main St., next to Middlesex Savings Bank, 1 block south of Monument Square. It's open daily 10am to 4pm from April through October; public restrooms in the same building are open year-round. Guided walking tours are available. Group tours are offered by appointment. The town website (www.concordma.gov) includes visitor information. You can also contact the **Greater Merrimack Valley Convention & Visitors Bureau** (✆ **800/443-3332** or 978/459-6150; www.merrimack valley.org).

GETTING AROUND   Major attractions are within walking distance of downtown. If you're trying to stop everywhere in a day or are visiting Walden Pond or Great Meadows, you'll need a car.

Seeing the Sights
LITERARY LANDMARKS & HISTORIC ATTRACTIONS

Concord Museum ★★ ☺   Just when you're (understandably) suspecting that everything interesting in this area started on April 18, 1775, and ended the next day, this superb museum sets you straight. It's a great place to start your visit to the town. The **History Galleries** ★★ explore the question "Why Concord?" Artifacts, murals, films, maps, documents, and other presentations illustrate the town's role as a Native American settlement, Revolutionary War battleground, 19th-century intellectual center, and focal point of the 20th-century historic preservation movement. One of the lanterns that signaled Paul Revere from the Old North Church is on display. You'll also see the contents of Ralph Waldo Emerson's study and a large collection of Henry David Thoreau's belongings. Pick up a **Family Explorer Kit** ★ as you enter and use the activities to get a hands-on feel for life in the past.

53 Cambridge Tpk. (at Lexington Rd.). ✆ **978/369-9609** (recorded info) or 978/369-9763. www. concordmuseum.org. Admission $10 adults, $8 seniors and students, $5 children 6–17. June–Aug daily 9am–5pm; Apr–May and Sept–Dec Mon–Sat 9am–5pm, Sun noon–5pm; Jan–Mar Mon–Sat 11am–4pm, Sun 1–4pm. Follow Lexington Rd. out of Concord Center and bear right at museum onto Cambridge Tpk.; entrance is on left. Parking allowed on road.

The Old Manse ★   The engaging history of this home touches on the military and the literary, but it's mostly the story of a family. The Rev. William Emerson built the Old Manse in 1770 and watched the Battle of Concord from his yard. For almost 170 years, the house was home to his widow, her second husband, their descendants, and two famous friends. Newlyweds Nathaniel Hawthorne and Sophia Peabody moved here in 1842 and stayed for 3 years. As a wedding present, Henry David Thoreau sowed the vegetable garden (re-created today). William's grandson Ralph Waldo Emerson wrote the essay "Nature" here. Today you'll see mementos and memorabilia of the Emerson and Ripley families and of the Hawthornes, who scratched notes on two windows with Sophia's diamond ring.

269 Monument St. (at North Bridge). ✆ **978/369-3909.** www.oldmanse.org. Guided tour $8 adults, $7 seniors and students, $5 children 6–12, $25 families. Apr 19–Oct Mon–Sat 10am–5pm, Sun and holidays noon–5pm (last tour at 4:30pm); check ahead for winter hours. From Concord Center, follow Monument St. ½ mile to North Bridge parking lot (on right); Old Manse is on left.

Orchard House ★★★ ☺   *Little Women* (1868), Louisa May Alcott's best-known and most popular work, was written and set at Orchard House. Seeing the family home brings the Alcotts to life for legions of female visitors and their pleasantly surprised male companions. Fans won't want to miss the excellent tour, copiously illustrated with heirlooms. Serious buffs can check in advance for information on special events and holiday programs, some of which require reservations.

Louisa's father, the writer and educator Amos Bronson Alcott, created Orchard House by joining and restoring two homes. Bronson and his wife, the social activist Abigail May Alcott, and their family lived here from 1858 to 1877, socializing in the same circles as Emerson, Thoreau, and Hawthorne. Models for the characters in *Little Women* included Anna ("Meg"), an amateur actress, and May ("Amy"), a talented artist. Elizabeth ("Beth"), a gifted musician, died before the family moved to this house, which opened to the public in 1911. Check ahead for info about centennial events in 2011.

399 Lexington Rd. ℂ **978/369-4118.** www.louisamayalcott.org. Guided tour $9 adults, $7 seniors and students, $5 children 6-17, $25 families. Apr-Oct Mon-Sat 10am-4:30pm, Sun 1-4:30pm; Nov-Mar Mon-Fri 11am-3pm, Sat 10am-4:30pm, Sun 1-4:30pm. Closed Jan 1-15. Follow Lexington Rd. out of Concord Center and bear left at Concord Museum; house is on left. Overflow parking across the street.

Ralph Waldo Emerson House   This house offers a taste of the days when a philosopher could attain the status we now associate with rock stars. Emerson, also an essayist and poet, lived here from 1835 until his death, in 1882. He moved here after marrying his second wife, Lydia Jackson, whom he called Lydian; she called him Mr. Emerson, as the staff still does. The tour gives a good look at his personal side and at the fashionably ornate interior decoration of the time. You'll see original furnishings and some of Emerson's personal effects.

28 Cambridge Tpk. ℂ **978/369-2236.** www.rwe.org/emersonhouse. Guided tours $8 adults, $6 seniors and children 7-17. Call to arrange group tours (10 people or more). Patriot's Day weekend to late Oct Thurs-Sat 10am-4:30pm, Sun 1-4:30pm. Closed late Oct to mid-Apr. Follow Cambridge Tpk. out of Concord Center; just before Concord Museum, house is on right.

Sleepy Hollow Cemetery ★   Follow the signs for AUTHOR'S RIDGE and climb the hill to the graves of some of the town's literary lights, including the Alcotts, Emerson, Hawthorne, and Thoreau. Emerson's bears no religious symbols, just an uncarved quartz boulder. Thoreau is buried nearby; at his funeral, in 1862, his old friend Emerson concluded his eulogy with these words: " . . . wherever there is knowledge, wherever there is virtue, wherever there is beauty, he will find a home."

Entrance on Rte. 62 W. ℂ **978/318-3233.** www.concordma.gov. Free admission. Daily 7am to dusk, weather permitting. No buses allowed.

The Wayside ★   The Wayside was Nathaniel Hawthorne's home from 1852 until his death, in 1864. The Alcotts also lived here (the girls called it "the yellow house"), as did Harriett Lothrop, who wrote the *Five Little Peppers* books under the pen name Margaret Sidney and owned most of the current furnishings. The Wayside is part of Minute Man National Historical Park, and the fascinating 45-minute ranger-led tour illuminates the occupants' lives and the house's crazy-quilt architecture. The exhibit in the barn (free admission) consists of audio presentations and figures of the authors. Call ahead to double-check hours, which are subject to change.

455 Lexington Rd. ℂ **978/318-7863.** www.nps.gov/mima. Guided tour $5 adults, free for children 17 and under. May-Oct; days and hours vary. Closed Nov-Apr. Follow Lexington Rd. out of Concord Center past Concord Museum and Orchard House. Parking across the street.

MINUTE MAN NATIONAL HISTORICAL PARK ★★

This 970-acre park preserves the scene of the first Revolutionary War battle, on April 19, 1775. After the skirmish at Lexington, the British continued to Concord in search of stockpiled arms (which militia members had already moved). Warned of the advance, the colonists crossed the North Bridge, evading the "regulars" standing guard, and awaited reinforcements. The British searched nearby homes and burned any guns they found, and the Minutemen, seeing the smoke, mistakenly thought the soldiers were burning the town. The gunfire that ensued, the opening salvo of the Revolution, is remembered as "the shot heard round the world."

The park is open daily, year-round. A visit can take as little as half an hour, for a jaunt to the North Bridge (a reproduction), or as long as half a day or more, if you stop at both visitor centers and perhaps participate in a ranger-led program. Park management suggests beginning your visit at the Minute Man Visitor Center (see "Lexington," above), which is closed in the winter. Alternatively, start at the **North Bridge Visitor Center ★**, 174 Liberty St., off Monument Street (© **978/369-6993;** www.nps.gov/mima), which overlooks the Concord River and the bridge. A diorama and video illustrate the battle; exhibits include uniforms, weapons, and tools of Colonial and British soldiers. Rangers lead programs and answer questions. Outside, picnicking is allowed, and the scenery (especially the fall foliage) is lovely. The center is open daily from 9am to 5pm (11am–3pm in winter).

To go straight to the bridge, follow Monument Street until you see the parking lot on the right. Walk a short distance to the bridge, stopping along the unpaved path to read and hear the narratives. On one side of the bridge is a plaque marking the grave of the British soldiers who died here. On the other side is Daniel Chester French's **Minute Man** statue, engraved with a stanza of the poem Emerson wrote for the dedication ceremony in 1876.

NEARBY SIGHTS

DeCordova Sculpture Park + Museum ★★   Outdoors and in, this institution shows the work of American contemporary and modern artists, with an emphasis on living New England residents. The main building, on a leafy hilltop, overlooks a pond and the sculpture park. Exhibits center on imaginative themes as well as the work of individual artists. Picnicking is allowed in the sculpture park; bring your lunch or buy it at the cafe (Tues–Fri 11am–3pm, Sat–Sun 11am–4pm). Free tours of the main galleries start at 1pm Thursday and 2pm Sunday year-round; sculpture-park tours run May through October on weekends at 1pm.

51 Sandy Pond Rd., Lincoln. © **781/259-8355.** www.decordova.org. Museum: $12 adults; $10 AAA members; $8 seniors, students, and children 6–12. Tues–Sun and Mon holidays 10am–5pm. Sculpture park: Free admission when museum is closed. Daily daylight hours. From Rte. 2 east, take Rte. 126 south to Baker Bridge Rd. (1st left after Walden Pond). When it ends, go right onto Sandy Pond Rd.; museum is on left. From I-95, take exit 28B, follow Trapelo Rd. 2½ miles to Sandy Pond Rd., then follow signs.

Gropius House ★   Architect Walter Gropius (1883–1969), founder of the Bauhaus school of design, built this hilltop home for his family in 1938 after accepting a job at the Harvard Graduate School of Design. He used traditional materials such as clapboard, brick, and fieldstone, with components then seldom seen in domestic architecture, including glass blocks and chrome (on the banisters). Marcel Breuer designed many of the furnishings, which were made for the family at the Bauhaus.

Decorated as it was in the last decade of Gropius's life, the house affords a revealing look at his life, career, and philosophy.

68 Baker Bridge Rd., Lincoln. (**C** **781/259-8098.** www.historicnewengland.org. Admission $10 adults, $9 seniors, $5 students and children. Tours on the hour June–Oct 15 Wed–Sun 11am–4pm; Oct 16–May Sat–Sun 11am–4pm. From Rte. 2 east, take Rte. 126 south to left on Baker Bridge Rd. (1st left after Walden Pond); house is on right. From I-95, take exit 28B, follow Trapelo Rd. to Sandy Pond Rd., go left onto Baker Bridge Rd.; house is on left.

WILDERNESS RETREATS

The titles of Henry David Thoreau's first two published works can serve as starting points: *A Week on the Concord and Merrimack Rivers* (1849) and *Walden* (1854).

To see the area from water level, there's no need to take a week; 2 hours or so should suffice. Rent a **canoe or kayak** ★ at the **South Bridge Boat House,** 496–502 Main St. (**C** **978/369-9438;** www.canoeconcord.com), just over half a mile west of the center of town, and paddle to the North Bridge and back. Rates are about $16 per hour on weekends, less on weekdays.

At **Walden Pond State Reservation** ★★, 915 Walden St., Rte. 126 (**C** **978/ 369-3254;** www.mass.gov/dcr), a pile of stones marks the site of the cabin where Thoreau lived from 1845 to 1847. Today the picturesque reservation is an extremely popular destination for walking (a path circles the pond), swimming, and fishing. Although crowded, it's well preserved and insulated from development, making it less difficult than you might expect to imagine Thoreau's experience. Call for the schedule of interpretive programs. No dogs or bikes are allowed. Parking costs $5. In good weather, the lot fills early every day—call before setting out, because the rangers turn away visitors if the park has reached capacity (1,000). From Concord Center, take Walden Street (Rte. 126) south, cross Rte. 2, and follow signs to the parking lot.

Another Thoreau haunt, an especially popular destination for birders, is **Great Meadows National Wildlife Refuge** ★, 73 Weir Hill Rd., Sudbury (**C** **978/443-4661;** www.fws.gov/northeast/greatmeadows). The Concord portion of the 3,800-acre refuge includes 2.7 miles of walking trails around man-made ponds that attract abundant wildlife. More than 200 species of native and migratory birds have been recorded. The refuge is open daily from sunrise to sunset; admission is free. Dogs are not allowed. Follow Rte. 62 (Bedford St.) east out of Concord Center for 1⅓ miles, then turn left onto Monsen Road and look for the entrance on the left.

Shopping

Downtown Concord, off **Monument Square,** is a terrific shopping destination. Here you'll find the **Toy Shop of Concord,** 4 Walden St. (**C** **978/369-2553;** www.concordtoys.com); the **Grasshopper Shop,** 36 Main St. (**C** **978/369-8295**), which carries women's clothing and accessories; and the **Concord Bookshop,** 65 Main St. (**C** **978/369-2405;** www.concordbookshop.com). In West Concord, check out the old-school **West Concord 5 & 10,** 106 Commonwealth Ave. (**C** **978/369-9011**), which carries everything from light bulbs to rubber duckies.

Where to Stay

The **Best Western at Historic Concord,** 740 Elm St. (**C** **800/780-7234** or 978/369-6100; www.bestwestern.com), is just off Rte. 2, about 2 miles from the center of town. The motel has a fitness room and a seasonal outdoor pool. Doubles in high season start at $139, which includes continental breakfast and Wi-Fi.

Concord's Colonial Inn ★   The main building of the Colonial Inn has overlooked Monument Square since 1716. Like many historic inns, it's not luxurious, but it is comfortable and centrally located. Additions since it became a hotel in 1889 have left the inn large enough to offer modern conveniences and small enough to feel friendly. It's popular with businesspeople as well as vacationers, especially during foliage season. The 15 original guest rooms—one of which (no. 24) supposedly is haunted—are in great demand. Reserve early if you want to stay in the main inn, which is decorated in Colonial style. Rooms in the 1970 Prescott House have country-style decor, and four free-standing buildings hold one-, two-, and three-bedroom suites suitable for long-term stays.

Two lounges serve light meals; outdoor tables afford a front-row seat for the action on Monument Square. The restaurant serves salads, sandwiches, and pasta at lunch, and traditional American fare at dinner. Afternoon tea is served on weekends; reservations required (✆ **978/369-2373**).

48 Monument Sq., Concord, MA 01742. ✆ **800/370-9200** or 978/369-9200. Fax 978/371-1533. www.concordscolonialinn.com. 56 units (some with shower only). Apr to early Sept $179–$249 main inn, $149–$199 Prescott House; mid-Sept to Oct $199–$249 double main inn, $169–$219 double Prescott House; Nov–Mar from $159 double main inn, from $129 double Prescott House. Long-term discounts available. AE, DC, DISC, MC, V. **Amenities:** Restaurant; 2 lounges; bar w/live music on Fri–Sat; concierge; executive-level rooms; access to nearby health club ($10). *In room:* A/C, TV/DVD, hair dryer, Wi-Fi (free).

Hawthorne Inn ★★   This is the quintessential country inn. Built around 1870, it sits on a tree-shaded property across the street from Nathaniel Hawthorne's home, the Wayside. Antiques and handmade quilts enhance the rooms, which aren't huge but are meticulously maintained and gorgeously decorated. My favorite is the Walden Room, which has black wallpaper, but they're all delightful. Original art is on display throughout, and there's a small pond in the peaceful garden. Personable innkeepers Gregory Burch and Marilyn Mudry, who have operated their eco-conscious inn for more than 3 decades, acquaint interested guests with the philosophical, spiritual, military, and literary aspects of Concord's history.

462 Lexington Rd., Concord, MA 01742. ✆ **978/369-5610.** Fax 978/287-4949. www.concordmass.com. 7 units (some with shower only). $179–$319 double. Rates include full breakfast. Extra person $30. Off-season discounts available. AE, DISC, MC, V. From Concord Center, take Lexington Rd. ¼ mile east; inn is on right. *In room:* A/C, hair dryer, Wi-Fi (free).

Where to Dine

See also the **Colonial Inn,** above. For picnic provisions, visit the **Concord Cheese Shop,** 29 Walden St. (✆ **978/369-5778;** www.concordcheeseshop.com).

Nashoba Brook Bakery & Café ★ AMERICAN   The enticing variety of artisan breads, baked goods, pastries, and made-from-scratch soups, salads, and sandwiches makes this airy cafe a popular destination throughout the day. The industrial-looking building off West Concord's main street backs up to little Nashoba Brook, which is visible through the glass back wall. Order and pick up at the counter, then grab a seat along the window or near the children's play area. Or order takeout—this is great picnic food.

152 Commonwealth Ave., West Concord. ✆ **978/318-1999.** www.slowrise.com. Sandwiches $7; other menu items $2–$8. MC, V. Mon–Fri 7am–5:30pm; Sat 7am–5pm; Sun 8am–5pm. From Concord Center,

North of Boston: Planning Pointers

For convenience and flexibility, drive to destinations north of Boston if you can. Renting a car may be cheaper than the commuter rail, if your group is large enough; even if it isn't, flexibility is priceless. The trip from Boston to Cape Ann on I-93 and Rte. 128 by car takes about an hour. A more leisurely excursion on routes 1A, 129, and 114 takes you through Marblehead to Salem. You can also follow Rte. 1 to I-95 and Rte. 128, but don't attempt it during rush hour. To take Rte. 1A, leave downtown through the Callahan or Ted Williams Tunnel. If you miss the entrance and wind up on I-93, follow signs to Rte. 1 and pick up Rte. 1A in Revere. The **North of Boston Convention & Visitors Bureau** (© 800/742-5306 or 978/977-7760; www.north ofboston.org) publishes a visitor guide that covers many destinations in this chapter. The website of the **Essex National Heritage Area** (© 978/740-0444; www.essexheritage.org) is another good resource.

follow Main St. (Rte. 62) west, across Rte. 2; bear right at traffic light in front of train station and go 3 blocks. For overflow parking, turn right onto Commonwealth Ave. and right onto Winthrop St.

MARBLEHEAD ★★★

15 miles NE of Boston; 4 miles SE of Salem

Like an attractive person with a great personality, Marblehead has it all. Scenery, history, architecture, and shopping combine to make it one of the area's most popular day trips for both locals and visitors. The narrow streets of historic "Old Town" lead down to the magnificent harbor that helps make Marblehead the self-proclaimed "Yachting Capital of America." Plaques on many homes give the dates of construction as well as the names of the builders and original occupants—a history lesson without any studying.

Many of the houses have stood since before the Revolutionary War, when Marblehead was a center of merchant shipping. Two historic homes are open to visitors. Allow at least a full morning to visit Marblehead, but be flexible, because you may want to hang around.

Essentials

GETTING THERE From Boston, take Rte. 1A north until you see signs in Lynn for Swampscott and Marblehead. Take Lynn Shore Drive to Rte. 129, and follow it into Marblehead. Or take I-93 or Rte. 1 to Rte. 128, then Rte. 114 through Salem into Marblehead. Except at rush hour, allow 35 to 40 minutes. Parking is tough, especially in Old Town—grab the first spot you see.

MBTA (© **800/392-6100** or 617/222-3200; www.mbta.com) bus no. 441/442 runs from Haymarket (Orange or Green Line) in Boston to downtown Marblehead on weekdays; on weekends service is from Wonderland station at the end of the Blue Line. During weekday rush hours, bus no. 448/449 connects Marblehead to Downtown Crossing. The trip takes about an hour; the one-way fare is $2.80 with a CharlieCard, $3.50 with a CharlieTicket.

VISITOR INFORMATION   The **Marblehead Chamber of Commerce,** 62 Pleasant St. (© **781/631-2868;** www.visitmarblehead.com), is open weekdays from 9am to 5pm. The **information booth** (© **781/639-8469**) on Pleasant Street near Spring Street is open mid-May through October, weekdays from noon to 5pm, weekends from 10am to 6pm. Before you visit, download a description of a walking tour from the chamber website.

GETTING AROUND   Wear good walking shoes—the car or bus can get you to Marblehead, but it can't negotiate many of the narrow streets of Old Town. The downtown area is fairly compact and moderately hilly.

SPECIAL EVENTS   Sailing regattas take place all summer. The National Off-shore One Design (NOOD) Regatta, or **Race Week,** falls in mid- to late July and attracts yachting enthusiasts from all over the country. During the **Christmas Walk,** on the first weekend in December, Santa Claus arrives by lobster boat.

Exploring the Town

A stroll through the winding streets of **Old Town ★★★** invariably leads to shopping, snacking, or gazing at something picturesque, be it the harbor or a beautiful home. Be sure to spend some time in **Crocker Park ★★**, on the water off Front Street. Especially in warm weather, when boats jam the harbor, the view is breathtaking. The park has benches and allows picnicking. The view from **Fort Sewall,** at the other end of Front Street, is just as mesmerizing. The ruins of the fort, built in the 17th century and rebuilt late in the 18th, are another excellent picnic spot.

Just inland, the **Lafayette House** is a private home at the corner of Hooper and Union streets. Legend has it that one corner of the first floor was chopped off in 1824 to allow Lafayette's carriage to negotiate the turn. In Market Square, on Washington Street near State Street, is the **Old Town House,** a public meeting and gathering place since 1727.

By car or bicycle, the swanky residential community of **Marblehead Neck ★** is worth a look. Follow Ocean Avenue across the causeway. Here you can visit the Massachusetts Audubon Society's **Marblehead Neck Wildlife Sanctuary** (© **800/AUDUBON** [283-8266] or 781/259-9500; www.massaudubon.org); look for the tiny sign at the corner of Risley Avenue. Admission is free. Afterward, continue to the end of "the Neck," at Harbor and Ocean avenues, where **Chandler Hovey Park** has a (closed) lighthouse and a panoramic view. Many inns and B&Bs provide bikes for guests' use; to rent, visit **Marblehead Cycle,** 25 Bessom St., 1 block off Pleasant Street (© **781/631-1570;** www.marbleheadcycle.com). Bikes rent for $25 a day.

Abbot Hall   A 5-minute stop here (look for the clock tower) is just the ticket if you want to be able to say you did some sightseeing. The town offices and historical commission share Abbot Hall with Archibald M. Willard's iconic painting *The Spirit of '76* ★, on display in the Selectmen's Meeting Room. The thrill of recognizing the ubiquitous drummer, drummer boy, and fife player is the main reason to stop here. Display cases in the halls contain artifacts from the Historical Society's collections.

Washington Sq. © **781/631-0528.** www.marblehead.org. Free admission. Year-round Mon-Tues and Thurs 8am-5pm, Wed 7:30am-7:30pm, Fri 8am-1pm; check ahead for summer hours. From the historic district, follow Washington St. up the hill.

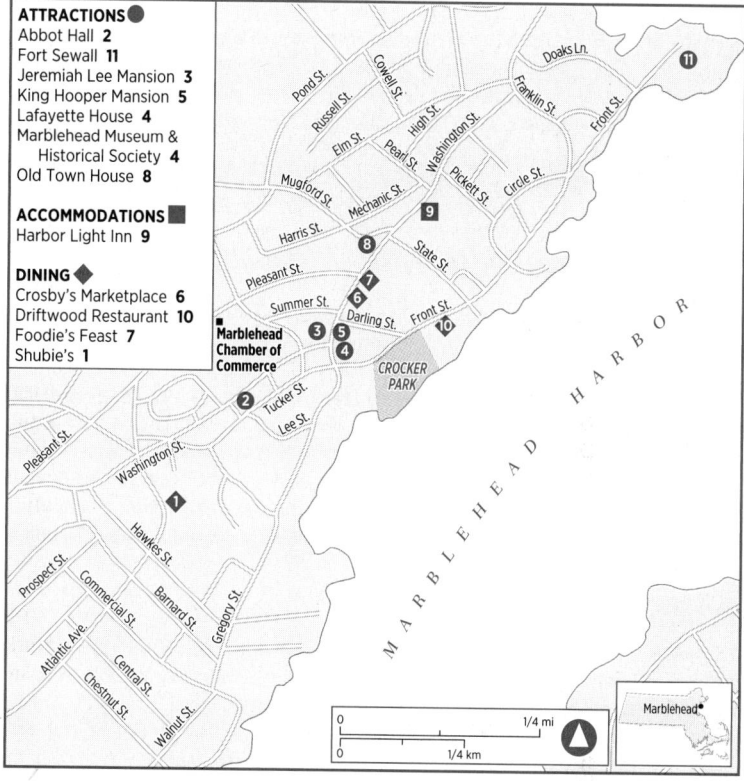

ATTRACTIONS●
Abbot Hall **2**
Fort Sewall **11**
Jeremiah Lee Mansion **3**
King Hooper Mansion **5**
Lafayette House **4**
Marblehead Museum &
   Historical Society **4**
Old Town House **8**

ACCOMMODATIONS ■
Harbor Light Inn **9**

DINING ◆
Crosby's Marketplace **6**
Driftwood Restaurant **10**
Foodie's Feast **7**
Shubie's **1**

Jeremiah Lee Mansion/Marblehead Museum & Historical Society ★★

Built in 1768 for a wealthy merchant, the Lee mansion is an extraordinary example of pre–Revolutionary Georgian architecture. Rococo woodcarving and other details complement historically accurate room arrangements; the most exciting feature for aficionados is the original hand-painted wallpaper. Ongoing restoration and interpretation by the Marblehead Museum & Historical Society place the 18th- and 19th-century furnishings and artifacts in context. The friendly guides welcome questions and are well versed in the history of the home. The lawn and gardens are open to the public.

Across the street in the society's offices are two galleries; one shows changing exhibits, and the other paintings by the noted folk artist J. O. J. Frost, a Marblehead native. Call ahead for the schedule of **summer walking tours.**

161 Washington St. ✆ **781/631-1768.** www.marbleheadmuseum.org. Guided tours $5 adults, $4.50 seniors and students. June-Oct Tues-Sat 10am-4pm. Closed Nov-May. Galleries: 170 Washington St. Free admission; donations appreciated. Tues-Sat 10am-4pm (closed Sat Nov-May). From Abbot Hall, follow Washington St. down the hill; mansion is on left.

King Hooper Mansion/Marblehead Arts Association & Gallery   Shipping tycoon Robert Hooper got his nickname because he treated his sailors so well, but it's easy to think he was called "King" because he lived like royalty. Around the corner from the home of Jeremiah Lee (whose sister-in-law was the second of Hooper's four wives), the 1728 mansion gained a Georgian addition sometime after 1745. The **Marblehead Arts Association** stages exhibits in four galleries, schedules special events, and sells members' work in the gift shop. The mansion has a lovely garden; enter through the gate at the right of the house.

8 Hooper St. © **781/631-2608.** www.marbleheadarts.org. Free admission. Summer Sun and Tues–Wed noon–5pm, Thurs–Sat 10am–5pm; winter Tues–Fri noon–5pm, Sun 1–5pm. Where Washington St. curves at the foot of hill near Lee Mansion, look for the colorful sign.

Shopping ★★

One of Marblehead's claims to fame is its excellent retail scene. Shops, boutiques, and galleries abound in **Old Town** and on **Atlantic Avenue** and the east end of **Pleasant Street.** Good stops include **Arnould Gallery & Framery,** 111 Washington St. (© **781/631-6366**); **Artists & Authors,** 108 Washington St. (© **781/639-0400;** www.artists-authors.com), which carries rare books and fine art; **Cargo Unlimited,** 82 Washington St. (© **781/631-1112;** www.cargounlimited.com), for home furnishings and accessories; **Mud Puddle Toys,** 1 Pleasant St. (© **781/631-0814;** www. mudpuddletoys.com); and the excellent **St. Michael's Thrift Shop,** behind the Episcopal church at 20 Pleasant St. (© **781/631-0657;** www.stmichaels1714.org; no credit cards).

Where to Stay

The accommodations listings of the **Chamber of Commerce** (© **781/631-2868;** www.marbleheadchamber.com) include many of the town's innumerable inns and B&Bs. Contact the chamber or consult one of the agencies listed in chapter 5, under "Where to Stay."

Harbor Light Inn ★★   Two Federal-era mansions make up this gracious inn, a stone's throw from the Old Town House. From the wood floors to the 1729 beams (in a third-floor room) to the pool, it's both historic and relaxing. Rooms are comfortably furnished in period style, with some lovely antiques; most have canopy or four-poster beds. Eleven have working fireplaces, and five have double Jacuzzis. The best rooms, on the top floor at the back of the building (away from the street), have distant harbor views. The undeniably romantic inn also attracts business travelers.

58 Washington St., Marblehead, MA 01945. © **781/631-2186.** Fax 781/631-2216. www.harborlightinn. com. 21 units (7 with shower only). $145–$335 double; $195–$375 suite. Rates include breakfast and afternoon refreshments. 2- to 3-night minimum Fri–Sat and holidays. AE, MC, V. Free parking. **Amenities:** Tavern; concierge; access to nearby health club ($5); Jacuzzi; heated outdoor pool; airport shuttle. In room: A/C, TV/DVD, hair dryer, Wi-Fi (free).

A SEASIDE INN NEARBY

Diamond District Bed & Breakfast ★★   This comfortable Georgian-style mansion, built in 1911 as a private home, attracts both business and leisure travelers. The Atlantic is a block away; the 3-mile public beach (a good place to burn off the inn's generous breakfast) is popular for jogging, skating, and biking as well as swimming. It's visible from many of the good-size rooms, tastefully decorated with elaborate Victorian touches. The best are third-floor units with ocean views and Jacuzzi tubs. Two rooms have cozy electric fireplaces. The large living room and porch overlook houses on Lynn Shore Drive and, just past them, the ocean. The Jacuzzi, on the back lawn, also has a water view.

142 Ocean St., Lynn, MA 01902. © **800/666-3076** or 781/595-2200. Fax 781/599-5122. www.diamond districtinn.com. 11 units (some with shower only). $165–$295 double. Rates include breakfast. Extra person $20. 2-night minimum on busy weekends. AE, DC, DISC, MC, V. Take Rte. 1A north to signs for Swampscott/Marblehead; after rotary, take Lynn Shore Dr. north, past 2 lights and Christian Science church. Turn left onto Wolcott Rd., then right onto Ocean St.; inn is on the right. **Amenities:** Jacuzzi. *In room:* A/C, TV, Internet (free).

Where to Dine

Marblehead has a number of dining options, plus bars that serve decent food. The tavern at the **Harbor Light Inn** (see listing above) offers a limited bar menu in a cozy 18th-century setting. In good weather, I prefer a picnic. Stock up at **Crosby's Marketplace,** 115 Washington St. (© **781/631-1741;** www.crosbysmarkets.com); **Foodie's Feast,** 114 Washington St. (© **781/639-1104;** www.foodiesfeast.com); or **Shubie's,** 16 Atlantic Ave. (© **781/631-0149;** www.shubies.com).

Driftwood Restaurant ★ DINER/SEAFOOD   At the foot of State Street next to Clark Landing (the town pier) is an honest-to-goodness local hangout. Join the crowd at a table or the counter for generous portions of breakfast (served all day) or lunch. Try pancakes or hash, chowder, or a seafood "roll" (a hot-dog bun filled with, say, fried clams or lobster salad). The house specialty, served on weekends and holidays, is fried dough, a sort of New England beignet. At busy times, you may have to wait outside for a table.

63 Front St. © **781/631-1145.** Main courses $3–$12; breakfast items under $7. No credit cards. Daily 5:30am–2pm.

SALEM ★★

16 miles NE of Boston; 4 miles NW of Marblehead

Settled in 1626, 4 years before Boston, Salem later enjoyed international renown as a center of merchant shipping. Today it's known around the world because of a 7-month episode in 1692. The **witchcraft trial** hysteria led to 20 deaths, 3-plus centuries of notoriety, countless lessons on the evils of prejudice, and innumerable bad puns ("Stop by for a spell" is a favorite slogan). But there's much more to the city, which embraces its history as a thriving seaport, a literary inspiration, and a vital partner in the post–Revolutionary War China trade.

The city abounds with witch-associated attractions, plus nearly as many reminders of its seagoing legacy. Salem's merchant vessels circled the globe in the 17th and 18th centuries, returning laden with treasures. One reminder of that era, a replica of the 1797 East Indiaman tall ship *Friendship,* is anchored near the Salem Maritime National Historic Site. Locations associated with **Nathaniel Hawthorne** complement the sorceresses and sailors. And one of the finest cultural institutions in New England, the **Peabody Essex Museum,** is a must-see for lovers of art and artifacts. Salem is a family-friendly destination that's worth at least a half-day visit, perhaps after a stop in Marblehead; it can easily fill a day.

Essentials

GETTING THERE   From Marblehead, take Rte. 114 west into downtown Salem. From Boston, take I-93 or Rte. 1 to Rte. 128, then Rte. 114 east. Or take Rte. 1A north from Boston, being careful in Lynn, where the road turns left and immediately right. There's metered street parking and a reasonably priced garage opposite the visitor center.

From Boston, the **MBTA** (© **800/392-6100** or 617/222-3200; www.mbta.com) runs commuter trains from North Station and bus no. 450 from Haymarket (Orange or Green Line). The train is more comfortable but runs less frequently. It takes 30 to 35 minutes; the round-trip fare is $11. The station is about 5 blocks from the downtown area. The one-way fare for the 35- to 55-minute bus trip is $2.80 with a CharlieCard, $3.50 with a CharlieTicket.

The **Salem Ferry** (© **978/741-0220;** www.salemferry.com) operates daily from Memorial Day weekend through October. The 50-minute catamaran trip connects Central Wharf, next to Boston's New England Aquarium (Blue Line) to the Blaney Street Wharf, off Derby Street, a 15-minute walk or quick hop on the Salem Trolley (see "Getting Around," below) from downtown. The peak adult fare (before 4pm from late June to early Sept) is $13 one-way, $24 round-trip, with discounts for seniors, children, families, and evening passengers. The one-way off-season fare is $10 for all.

VISITOR INFORMATION   Start at the **National Park Service Regional Visitor Center,** 2 New Liberty St. (© **978/740-1650;** www.nps.gov/sama), open daily from 9am to 5pm. Exhibits highlight early settlement, maritime history, and the leather and textiles industries. The center distributes brochures and pamphlets—including one that describes a walking tour of the historic district—and shows a free film on Essex County that provides a good overview.

The city tourism office, **Destination Salem** (© **877/SALEM-MA** [725-3662] or 978/744-3663; www.salem.org), produces a free visitor guide that includes a good map and posts a calendar of events on its website. The **Salem Chamber of Commerce,** 265 Essex St. (© **978/744-0004;** www.salem-chamber.org), maintains a rack of brochures and pamphlets. It's open weekdays 9am to 5pm. The municipal website (www.salem.com) and an excellent community website (www.salemweb.com) offer information for out-of-towners.

GETTING AROUND   In the congested downtown area, walking is the way to go. If it's hot or you plan lots of sightseeing, you might prefer to ride. **Salem Trolley ★** (© **508/744-5469;** www.salemtrolley.com) offers a 1-hour narrated tour and unlimited reboarding at any of its 13 stops. The tour starts at the Essex Street side of the visitor center. It operates from 10am to 5pm (last tour at 4pm) daily April through October; check ahead for off-season hours. Tickets ($15 adults, $14 seniors, $5 children 6–14) are good all day.

SPECIAL EVENTS   The city's month-long Halloween celebration, **Haunted Happenings ★★** (www.hauntedhappenings.org), includes parades, parties, tours, and a ceremony on the big day. In August, the 2-day **Salem Maritime Festival** fills the area around the Salem Maritime National Historic Site (see listing below) with live music, food, and demonstrations of nautical crafts. The festival kicks off **Heritage Days,** a weeklong event that celebrates Salem's multicultural history with

Salem

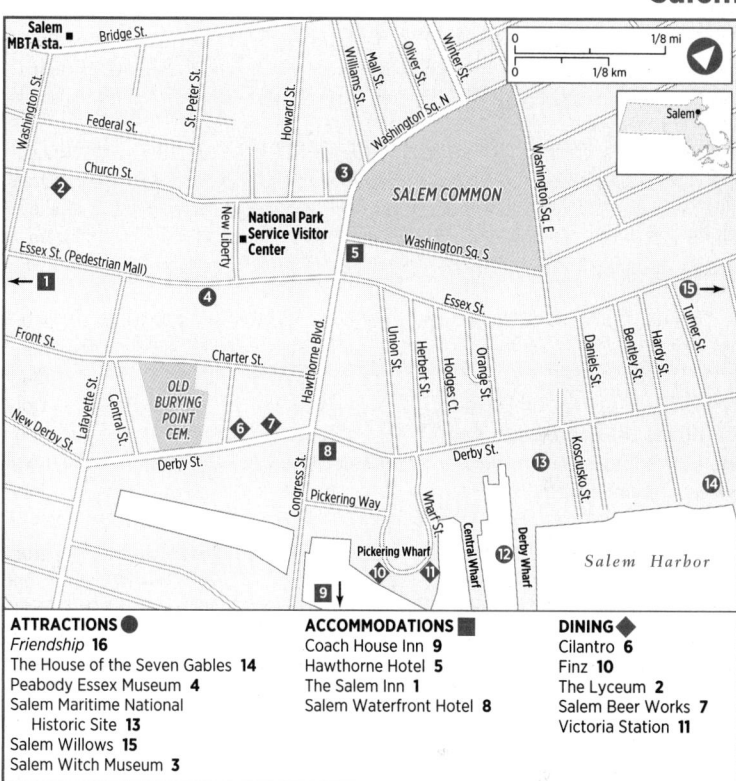

Salem MBTA sta.
Bridge St.
Washington St.
St. Peter St.
Howard St.
Mall St.
Williams St.
Oliver St.
Winter St.
Washington Sq. N.
Federal St.
Church St.
New Liberty
National Park Service Visitor Center ■
3
SALEM COMMON
Washington Sq. E
Washington Sq. S
5
Essex St. (Pedestrian Mall)
← **1**
2
4
Essex St.
15 →
Front St.
Charter St.
Hawthorne Blvd.
Union St.
Herbert St.
Hodges Ct.
Orange St.
Daniels St.
Bentley St.
Hardy St.
Turner St.
New Derby St.
Lafayette St.
Central St.
OLD BURYING POINT CEM.
6 7
8
Derby St.
13
Kosciusko St.
14
Derby St.
Congress St.
Pickering Way
Wharf St.
Central Wharf
Derby Wharf
Salem Harbor
Pickering Wharf
10 **11**
12
9 ↓

0   1/8 mi
0   1/8 km
Salem●

ATTRACTIONS ●
Friendship **16**
The House of the Seven Gables **14**
Peabody Essex Museum **4**
Salem Maritime National Historic Site **13**
Salem Willows **15**
Salem Witch Museum **3**

ACCOMMODATIONS ■
Coach House Inn **9**
Hawthorne Hotel **5**
The Salem Inn **1**
Salem Waterfront Hotel **8**

DINING ◆
Cilantro **6**
Finz **10**
The Lyceum **2**
Salem Beer Works **7**
Victoria Station **11**

musical and theatrical performances, a parade, and fireworks. Contact Destination Salem (see "Visitor Information," above) or **Escapes North** (www.escapesnorth. com) for details.

Exploring Salem

The **historic district** extends well inland from the waterfront; ask at the visitor center for the walking-tour pamphlet. Many 18th-century houses, some with original furnishings, still stand. Ship captains lived near the water at the east end of downtown, in relatively small houses crowded close together. The captains' employers, the shipping-company owners, built their homes away from the water (and the accompanying aromas). Many lived on the grand thoroughfare of **Chestnut Street ★★**, now a National Historic Landmark.

By car or trolley, the **Salem Willows** (© **978/745-0251;** www.salemwillows. com) amusements are 5 minutes away; many signs point the way. The strip of rides and snack bars has a honky-tonk air, and the waterfront park is a good place to picnic and wander along the shore. Admission is free; metered parking is available. To enjoy the great view without the arcades and rides, have lunch one peninsula over at **Winter Island Park.**

The House of the Seven Gables ★ ☺

Nathaniel Hawthorne's cousin lived here, and stories and legends of the house and its inhabitants inspired his 1851 book. If you don't know the eerie tale, don't let that keep you away—begin with the audiovisual program, which tells the story. The house, built by Capt. John Turner in 1668, holds six rooms of period furniture, including pieces referred to in the book, and a secret staircase. Tours include a visit to Hawthorne's birthplace and descriptions of what life was like for the house's 18th-century inhabitants. The costumed guides are helpful and eager to answer questions. Also on the grounds, overlooking Salem Harbor, are period gardens, the Retire Beckett House (1655), and a counting house (1830).

54 Turner St. ℂ **978/744-0991.** www.7gables.org. Guided tour of house and grounds $13 adults, $12 seniors and AAA members, $7.50 children 5-12. Surcharges may apply for special exhibitions. July–Oct daily 10am–7pm (until 11pm Oct Fri–Sat); Nov–June daily 10am–5pm. Closed 1st 2 weeks of Jan. From downtown, follow Derby St. east 3 blocks past Derby Wharf.

Peabody Essex Museum ★★ ☺

A local favorite since 1799, the Peabody Essex has grown into a national presence. All by itself, this captivating museum is reason enough to visit Salem.

Impressive collections of art from New England and around the world are the museum's calling card, but they're just part of the story. The museum owns 22 historic houses, including a well-preserved 18th-century Qing dynasty house, **Yin Yu Tang ★**, which was shipped here from China and reassembled. The only example of Chinese domestic architecture outside that country, the house captures 2 centuries of rural life. It's part of a huge wing designed by Moshe Safdie that opened in 2003.

The 854,000 items in the permanent collections blend contemporary acquisitions with "the natural and artificial curiosities" Salem's sea captains and merchants brought back from around the world to the Peabody Museum (1799) and local and domestic objects collected by the Essex Institute (1821), the county historical society. The displays help you understand the significance of each object, and interpretive materials (including interactive and hands-on activities) let children get involved. Noteworthy collections include American, African, Indian, Asian, and East Asian art and objects; photography; and the practical arts and crafts of East Asian, Pacific Island, and Native American peoples. Portraits of area residents include Charles Osgood's omnipresent rendering of Nathaniel Hawthorne.

East India Sq. ℂ **800/745-4054** or 978/745-9500. www.pem.org. Admission $15 adults, $13 seniors, $11 students, free for children 16 and under. Yin Yu Tang admission $4 with museum admission. Tues–Sun and Mon holidays 10am–5pm. Take Hawthorne Blvd. to Essex St., following signs for visitor center. Enter on Essex St. or New Liberty St.

Salem Maritime National Historic Site ★ ☺

An entertaining introduction to Salem's seagoing history, this complex includes an exciting attraction: a real live ship. The *Friendship* ★★ is a full-size replica of a 1797 East Indiaman merchant vessel, a three-masted 171-footer that disappeared during the War of 1812. The guided ranger tour includes a tour of the ship.

Central Wharf holds a warehouse (ca. 1800) that houses the orientation center. Tours, which vary seasonally, expand on Salem's maritime history. Yours might include the **Derby House** (1762), a wedding gift to shipping magnate Elias Hasket

THE SALEM WITCH HYSTERIA

The Salem witch trials took place in 1692, a product of old-world superstition, religious control of government, and plain old boredom.

The crisis began quietly in Salem Village (now the town of Danvers). The Rev. Samuel Parris's household included his 9-year-old daughter, Elizabeth; her cousin Abigail; and a West Indian slave named Tituba, who told stories to amuse the girls during the long, harsh winter. Entertained by tales of witchcraft, sorcery, and fortunetelling, the girls and their friends began to act out the stories, claiming to be under a spell, rolling on the ground and wailing. The settlers, aware that thousands of people in Europe had been executed as witches in the previous centuries, took the behavior seriously.

At first, only Tituba and two other women were accused of casting spells. The infighting typical of the Puritan theocracy surfaced soon enough, and an accusation of witchcraft became a handy way to settle a score. Anyone "different" was a potential target, from the elderly to the deaf to the poor. A special court convened in Salem proper, and although the girls recanted, the trials began. Defendants had no counsel, and pleading not guilty or objecting to the proceedings was considered equivalent to confessing. From March 1 to September 22, the court convicted 27 of the more than 150 people accused.

In the end, 19 people went to the gallows, and one man who refused to plead, Giles Corey, was pressed to death by stones piled on a board on his chest. Finally, cooler heads prevailed. Leading cleric Cotton Mather and his father, Harvard president Increase Mather, led the call for tolerance. With the jails overflowing, the court called off the trials and freed the remaining prisoners, including Tituba.

The episode's lessons about openmindedness and tolerance have echoed through the years. Salem was the backdrop for Arthur Miller's 1953 play *The Crucible,* a story about the witch trials as well as an allegory about the McCarthy Senate hearings—another kind of witch hunt in a time when those lessons needed to be taught again.

Derby from his father. Legend (myth, really) has it that Nathaniel Hawthorne was working at the 1819 Custom House when he found an embroidered scarlet "A." If you prefer to explore on your own, you can see a free film and wander around Derby Wharf, the West India Goods Store, the Bonded Warehouse, the Scale House, and Central Wharf.

174 Derby St. ☎ **978/740-1660.** www.nps.gov/sama. Free admission. Guided tour $5 adults, $3 seniors and children 6–16. Daily 9am–5pm. Take Derby St. east; just past Pickering Wharf, Derby Wharf is on the right.

Salem Witch Museum ★★ ☺   This is one of the most memorable attractions in eastern Massachusetts—it's both interesting and scary. The main draw of the museum (a former church) is a three-dimensional audiovisual presentation with life-size figures. The show takes place in a huge room lined with displays that are lighted in sequence. The 30-minute narration (translations are available) tells the tale of the witchcraft trials and the accompanying hysteria. The well-researched presentation recounts the story accurately, if somewhat overdramatically. One of the victims was crushed to death by rocks piled on a board on his chest—smaller kids may need a reminder that he's not real.

19½ Washington Sq., on Rte. 1A. ✆ **978/744-1692.** www.salemwitchmuseum.com. Admission $8 adults, $7 seniors, $5.50 children 6-14. Daily July–Aug 10am–7pm; Sept–June 10am–5pm; check ahead for Oct hours. Follow Hawthorne Blvd. to the northwest corner of Salem Common.

SHOPPING

Pickering Wharf, at the corner of Derby and Congress streets (✆ **978/740-6990;** www.pickeringwharf.com), is a waterfront complex of shops, boutiques, restaurants, and condos. It's popular for strolling, snacking, and shopping, and the central location makes it a local landmark. The retail-rich **Essex Street pedestrian mall** is a block from a cluster of shops that cater to crafters. I especially like **Seed Stitch Fine Yarn,** 21 Front St. (✆ **978/744-5557;** www.seedstitchfineyarn.com), and **Beadworks,** 10 Front St. (✆ **978/741-2323;** www.beadworkssalem.com).

Several shops specialize in witchcraft accessories. Bear in mind that Salem is home to many practicing witches who take their beliefs very seriously. The **Broom Closet,** 3–5 Central St. (✆ **978/741-3669;** www.broomcloset.com), and **Crow Haven Corner,** 125 Essex St. (✆ **978/745-8763;** www.crowhavencorner.net), stock everything from crystals to clothing.

Shops throughout New England sell the chocolate confections of **Harbor Sweets ★★**, Palmer Cove, 85 Leavitt St., off Lafayette Street (✆ **978/745-7648;** www.harborsweets.com). The retail store overlooks the floor of the factory; tours begin Tuesday and Thursday at 11am (call ahead to confirm). The deliriously good sweets are expensive, but candy bars and small assortments are available. It's closed Sunday.

Where to Stay

The busiest and most expensive time of year is **Halloween week;** reserve well in advance if you plan to travel anytime in October. The **Salem Waterfront Hotel,** 225 Derby St., at Pickering Wharf (✆ **888/337-2536** or 978/740-8788; www. salemwaterfronthotel.com), is a large, modern establishment with an indoor pool. Double rates in high season start at $179, which includes Wi-Fi and parking.

In nearby **Danvers,** on or near Rte. 1 north of I-95, many of the major motel chains have locations that lie 30 minutes or less from downtown Salem.

Coach House Inn Built in 1879 for a ship's captain, this welcoming inn is 2 blocks from the harbor and 9 blocks from downtown. The three-story mansion, set back from the street by a well-kept lawn, is tastefully furnished in just-frilly-enough style. The good-size guest rooms have high ceilings and four-poster beds, and most have (nonworking) fireplaces. Breakfast arrives at your door in a basket. The inn is 15 to 20 minutes on foot or 5 minutes by car on Lafayette Street (which in Salem is also rtes. 1A and 114) from the center of town, up the street from Salem State College.

284 Lafayette St. (at Ocean Ave.), Salem, MA 01970. ✆ **800/688-8689** or 978/744-4092. Fax 978/745-8031. www.coachhousesalem.com. 11 units (9 with private bathroom; 2 with shower only). $130–$189 double; $198–$280 2-room suite. Rates include continental breakfast. 2- to 3-night minimum Fri–Sat and holidays. AE, DISC, MC, V. Free parking. *In room:* A/C, TV, fridge, Wi-Fi (free).

Hawthorne Hotel ★ This historic hotel, built in 1925, is both convenient and comfortable. It attracts vacationers and business travelers, and is popular for functions. The six-story building is centrally located and well maintained, with a traditional atmosphere. The attractively furnished guest rooms vary in size from snug to spacious, and some bathrooms are small. The best units, on the Salem Common (north) side of the building, have better views than rooms that face the street. Ask to be as high up as possible, because the neighborhood is busy.

18 Washington Sq. W. (at Salem Common), Salem, MA 01970. © **800/729-7829** or 978/744-4080. Fax 978/745-9842. www.hawthornehotel.com. 89 units (30 with shower only). $140–$220 double; $209–$344 suite. Extra person $12. Children 15 and under stay free in parent's room. 2-night minimum May-Oct weekends. AE, DC, DISC, MC, V. Limited self-parking. Pets accepted ($10/night; $100 deposit). **Amenities:** Restaurant (American); tavern; concierge; exercise room; access to nearby heath club; room service. *In room:* A/C, TV, hair dryer, Wi-Fi (free).

Salem Inn ★★   The Salem Inn occupies the comfortable niche between too-big hotel and too-small B&B. Rooms in its three buildings are large and tastefully decorated; some have fireplaces, canopy beds, and whirlpool tubs. The best units are the honeymoon and family suites in the 1874 Peabody House. The variety allows the innkeepers to match accommodations with guests, whether they're honeymooners, sightseers, or families. The peaceful rose garden at the rear of the main building is open to all guests.

7 Summer St. (Rte. 114), Salem, MA 01970. © **800/446-2995** or 978/741-0680. Fax 978/744-8924. www.saleminnma.com. 41 units (some with shower only). Mid-Apr to Sept $139–$199 double, $199–$259 suite; Oct $190–$245 double, $260–$350 suite; Nov to mid-Apr $119–$169 double, $169–$229 suite. Rates include continental breakfast. Extra person $15–$25. 2- to 3-night minimum during holidays and special events. AE, DC, DISC, MC, V. Free parking. Pets accepted by prior arrangement ($15–$25/ night). **Amenities:** Access to nearby health club. *In room:* A/C, TV, hair dryer, Wi-Fi (free).

Where to Dine

Pickering Wharf has a food court as well as several restaurants with outdoor seating overlooking the marina. **Victoria Station** (© **978/744-7644;** www.victoriastation inc.com) serves seafood and traditional American dishes and has a huge salad bar. Innovative seafood preparations and creative drinks are the draw at **Finz** (© **978/744-8485;** www.hipfinz.com). Nearby, **Cilantro,** 282 Derby St. (© **978/745-9436;** www.cilantrocilantro.com), earns raves for its Mexican cuisine; it's closed Monday. The cafe at the **Peabody Essex Museum** (p. 168) serves lunch.

The Lyceum ★★ NEW ENGLAND/MEDITERRANEAN   The wonderful food attracts local businesspeople as well as out-of-towners to this elegant spot. The kitchen is especially skillful with seafood, often from local waters; be sure to check out the raw bar options. Bounteous chicken salad with unusual slaw or the inventive risotto of the day makes a substantial but not incapacitating lunch in the middle of sightseeing. At dinner, bistro style prevails, with the likes of delectable steak frites and pan-seared cod with saffron-tomato broth. Sunday brunch here is a treat, with superb egg dishes and tasty choices for the breakfast-averse.

43 Church St. (at Washington St.). © **978/745-7665.** www.thelyceum.com. Reservations recommended. Main courses $10–$16 at lunch, $15–$27 at dinner. AE, DISC, MC, V. Mon–Fri 11:30am-2:30pm; daily 5:30-9:30pm; Sun brunch 11am-3pm. Validated parking available.

Salem Beer Works PUB GRUB   Beer is the headliner at this popular downtown restaurant, but the food is also worth mentioning. Piled-high burgers, salads, sandwiches, and buckets of fried delicacies such as onion rings, jalapeño poppers, and pickles (that's right, fried pickles) complement the house-made brews.

278 Derby St. © **978/745-BEER** (2337). www.beerworks.net. Main courses $8–$16. AE, DISC, MC, V. Sun-Thurs 11:30am-midnight; Fri-Sat 11:30am-1am.

MILLING AROUND: A TRIP TO LOWELL

A 19th-century textile center that later fell into disrepair, Lowell is a 21st-century success story. A city built around restored mills and industrial canals will never be a glamorous vacation spot, but thousands of visitors a year find Lowell a fascinating and rewarding destination. The sights concentrate on the history of the Industrial Revolution and the textile industry. They include boardinghouses where the "mill girls" lived; the workers, some as young as 10, averaged 14-hour days weaving cloth on power looms.

Start at the **Lowell National Historical Park Visitor Center,** 246 Market St. (✆ **978/970-5000;** www.nps.gov/lowe), open daily from 9am to 5pm (until 4:30pm in winter). Rangers lead free programs and tours, and canal cruises and free trolley tours operate in

summer. Ask for a map of the area, and use it to find your way around downtown. Two interesting museums are within walking distance: the **American Textile History Museum,** 491 Dutton St. (✆ **978/441-0400;** www.athm.org), and the **New England Quilt Museum ★**, 18 Shattuck St. (✆ **978/452-4207;** www.nequiltmuseum.org). For more information, consult the **Greater Merrimack Valley Convention & Visitors Bureau** (✆ **800/443-3332** or 978/459-6150; www.merrimackvalley.org).

To drive to Lowell, take Rte. 3 or I-495 to the Lowell Connector and follow signs north to exit 5B and the historic district. The **commuter rail** (✆ **800/392-6100** or 617/222-3200; www.mbta.com) from Boston's North Station takes about 45 minutes and costs $14 round-trip.

CAPE ANN

Gloucester, Rockport, Essex, and Manchester-by-the-Sea make up Cape Ann, a rocky peninsula so enchantingly beautiful that when you hear the slogan "Massachusetts's *Other* Cape," you may forget what the first one was. Cape Ann and Cape Cod do share some attributes—scenery, shopping, seafood, and traffic. The smaller cape's proximity to Boston and manageable scale make it a wonderful day trip and a good choice for a longer stay.

With the decline of the fishing industry that brought great prosperity to the area in the 19th century, Cape Ann has played up its long-standing reputation as a haven for artists. Along with galleries and crafts shops, you'll find historical attractions, beaches—and oh, that scenery!

Although all four towns have large year-round populations, this is hardly a four-season destination. Many establishments close in fall or early winter through April or May; some open on weekends in December.

The **Cape Ann Transportation Authority** (✆ **978/283-7916;** www.canntran.com) runs buses from town to town on Cape Ann and operates special summer routes (except Sun).

The **Cape Ann Chamber of Commerce,** 33 Commercial St., Gloucester (✆ **800/321-0133** or 978/283-1601; www.capeannvacations.com), and the **North of Boston Convention & Visitors Bureau** (✆ **800/742-5306** or 978/977-7760; www.northofboston.org) provide abundant visitor information.

Manchester-by-the-Sea

The scenic route to Gloucester from points south is Rte. 127, which runs through Manchester-by-the-Sea, a lovely village incorporated in 1645. Now a prosperous suburb, Manchester is probably best known for **Singing Beach** (see "Life's a Beach . . . with Very Cold Water!" below). The **commuter rail** (© **800/392-6100** or 617/222-3200; www.mbta.com) from Boston costs $14 and stops in the center of the compact downtown area, where there are many shops and restaurants. Nearby **Masconomo Park** overlooks the harbor.

The home of the Manchester Historical Society is the **Trask House,** 10 Union St. (© **978/526-7230;** www.manchesterhistorical.com), a 19th-century sea captain's residence. Tours show off the period furnishings, including pieces produced in Manchester, and the society's costume collections. It's specialized but intriguing to devotees of house tours. The society also operates the **Seaside No. 1 Fire House Museum,** which holds two antique engines and memorabilia of the town fire and police departments. Both buildings are open Saturdays in July and August from noon to 3pm, and by appointment.

Magnolia

Pay close attention as you head north from Manchester or south from Gloucester on Rte. 127—Magnolia is easy to miss, but the village (technically, part of Gloucester) is worth a detour. Notable for its lack of waterfront commercial property, the village center is unremarkable. The homes surrounding it, many of them former summer residences now occupied year-round, are magnificent.

Essex ★

West of Gloucester on Rte. 133 lies a beautiful little town known for Essex clams, salt marshes, a long tradition of shipbuilding, a plethora of antiques shops, and one celebrated restaurant.

Legend has it that **Woodman's of Essex ★★★**, 121 Main St. (© **800/649-1773** or 978/768-6057; www.woodmans.com), was the birthplace of the fried clam in 1916. Today the thriving family business is a great spot to join legions of locals and visitors from around the world for lobster "in the rough," chowder, steamers, corn on the cob, onion rings, and superb fried clams. The line is usually long, even in winter, but it moves quickly and offers a view of the regimented commotion in the food-prep area. Eat in a booth, upstairs on the deck, or out back at a picnic table. You'll want to be well fed before you explore the numerous antiques shops along Main Street. Open daily at 11am.

The water views in town are of the Essex River, a saltwater estuary. The offerings of **Essex River Cruises ★**, Essex Marina, 35 Dodge St. (© **800/748-3706** or 978/768-6981; www.essexcruises.com) include narrated 90-minute tours of the lovely salt marshes that put you in prime birding territory. They run daily mid-May through mid-October. The pontoon boat, which allows for excellent sightseeing, is screened and has restrooms. Tickets cost $25 adults, $22 seniors, $10 children 4 to 12; reservations are suggested.

Gloucester ★★

The ocean has been Gloucester's lifeblood since long before the first European settlement in 1623. The most urban of Cape Ann's communities, Gloucester (which

LIFE'S A BEACH . . . WITH VERY COLD WATER!

Paradoxically, Cape Ann is almost as well known for its sandy beaches as for its rocky coastline. Things to know: First, the water is *cold*. Second, parking can be scarce, especially on weekends, and pricey—as much as $25. If you can't set out before breakfast, wait until midafternoon and hope that the early birds have had enough. During the summer, lifeguards are on duty from 9am to 5pm at larger public beaches. Surfing is generally permitted outside of those hours. The beaches listed here all have bathhouses and snack bars. Swimming or not, watch out for greenhead flies in July and August. They don't sting—they take little bites of flesh. Bring or buy insect repellent.

The best-known North Shore beach is **Singing Beach ★★**, off Masconomo Street in Manchester-by-the-Sea. Because it's accessible by public transportation, it attracts the most diverse crowd—carless singles, local families, and other beach bunnies of all ages. From the train station, they walk about half a mile on Beach Street to find sparkling sand and lively surf. Take the commuter rail (© **800/392-6100** or

617/222-3200; www.mbta.com) from Boston's North Station.

Nearly as famous and popular is **Crane Beach ★**, off Argilla Road in Ipswich, part of a 1,400-acre barrier beach reservation. Fragile dunes and a white-sand beach lead down to Ipswich Bay. The chilly surf is calmer than at less sheltered Singing Beach. Pick up Argilla Road south of Ipswich Center near the intersection of rtes. 1A and 133. or take the Ipswich Essex Explorer bus (see "Ipswich," p. 185). Also on Ipswich Bay is Gloucester's **Wingaersheek Beach ★**, on Atlantic Street off Rte. 133. From exit 13 off Rte. 128, the beach is about 15 minutes away (mind the speed limits). Wingaersheek has beautiful white sand and a glorious view. Because these beaches are harder to get to, they attract more of a local crowd, as well as lots of day-tripping families.

Most other good beaches in Gloucester have almost no nonresident parking. Two exceptions are **Half Moon Beach** and **Cressy's Beach,** at Stage Fort Park, off Rte. 127 near Rte. 133 and downtown. The sandy beaches and the park snack bar are popular local hangouts.

rhymes with "roster") is a working city, not a cutesy tourist town. Miles of gorgeous coastline surround the densely populated downtown area. Gloucester is home to one of the last commercial fishing fleets in New England, an internationally celebrated artists' colony, a large Portuguese-American community, and just enough historic attractions. Allow at least half a day, perhaps combined with a visit to the tourist magnet of Rockport; a full day would be better, especially if you plan a whale watch.

ESSENTIALS

GETTING THERE   From Boston, the quickest route is I-93 (or Rte. 1, if it's not rush hour) to Rte. 128, which ends at Gloucester. From Salem, a slower but prettier approach is Rte. 1A across the bridge at Beverly to Rte. 127. It runs through Manchester to Gloucester. The Manchester exits from Rte. 128 allow access to Rte. 127. There's street parking and a free lot on the causeway to Rocky Neck. Gloucester is 33 miles northeast of Boston, 16 miles northeast of Salem, and 7 miles north of Rockport.

Gloucester

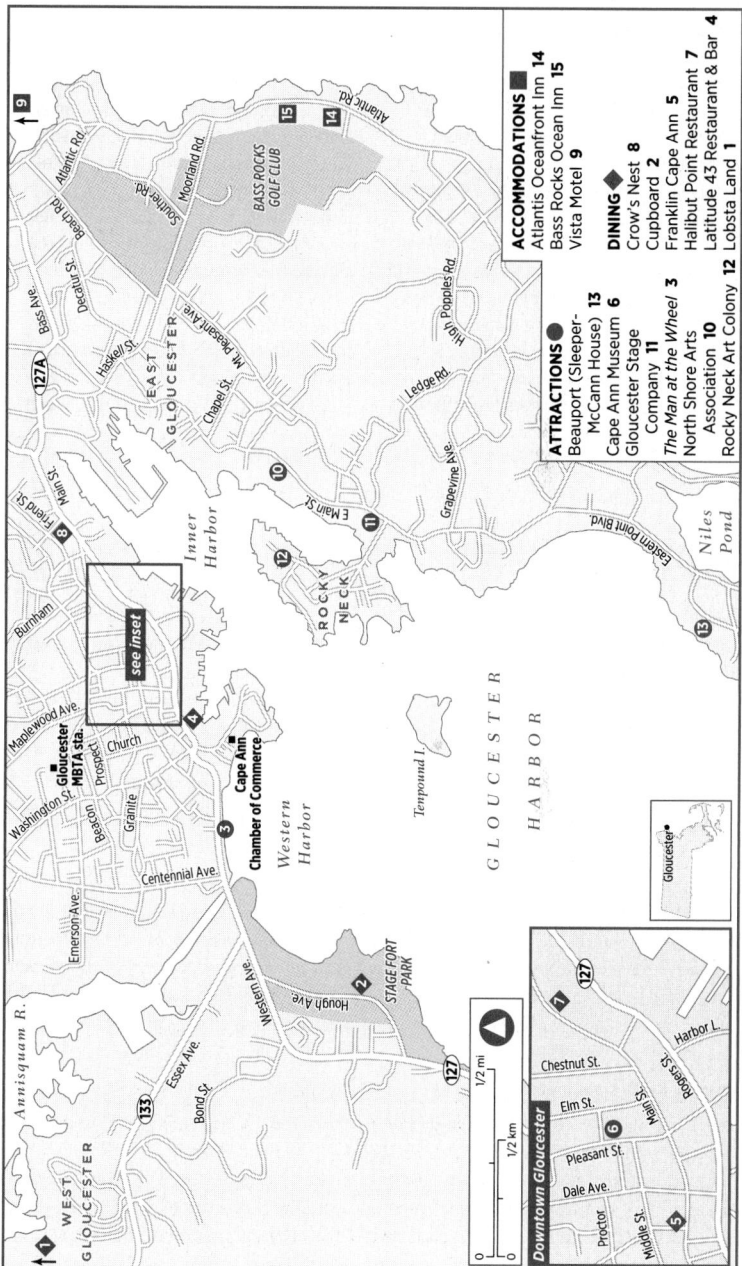

ACCOMMODATIONS ■
Atlantis Oceanfront Inn **14**
Bass Rocks Ocean Inn **15**
Vista Motel **9**

DINING ◆
Crow's Nest **8**
Cupboard **2**
Franklin Cape Ann **5**
Halibut Point Restaurant **7**
Latitude 43 Restaurant & Bar **4**
Lobsta Land **1**

ATTRACTIONS ●
Beauport (Sleeper-McCann House) **13**
Cape Ann Museum **6**
Gloucester Stage Company **11**
The Man at the Wheel **3**
North Shore Arts Association **10**
Rocky Neck Art Colony **12**

Downtown Gloucester

175

The Real Hometown of . . . *The Perfect Storm*

Long after the release of the blockbuster movie, Sebastian Junger's bestselling book *The Perfect Storm* remains a popular reason to visit Gloucester. The thrilling but tragic nonfiction account of the "no-name storm" of 1991 centers on the ocean and a neighborhood tavern. The **Crow's Nest,** 334 Main St. (✆ **978/281-2965;** www.crowsnest gloucester.com), is a no-frills place with a horseshoe-shaped bar and a crowd of regulars who seem amused that their hangout is a tourist attraction. The Crow's Nest plays a major role in Junger's story, but its ceilings aren't high

enough for it to be a movie set, so the film crew built an exact replica nearby. If you admired the movie's wardrobe design, check out the shirts and caps at **Cape Pond Ice ★,** 104 Commercial St., near the Chamber of Commerce (✆ **978/283-0174;** www.capepondice. com). "The Coolest Guys Around" offer 40-minute tours of their industrial facility, which is famous for its ice sculptures; bring (or buy) a sweatshirt. The price is $10 for adults, $6 for seniors and children under 12, and reservations are recommended.

The **commuter rail** (✆ **800/392-6100** or 617/222-3200; www.mbta.com) runs from Boston's North Station. The trip takes about 1 hour; the round-trip fare is $15. The station is about 8 blocks from the waterfront. The **Cape Ann Transportation Authority** (✆ **978/283-7916;** www.canntran.com) runs buses from town to town, as well as special summer routes (except Sun).

VISITOR INFORMATION The city's **Visitors Welcoming Center** (✆ **800/649-6839** or 978/281-8865; www.gloucesterma.com) is at Stage Fort Park, off Rte. 127 at Rte. 133. It's open in summer daily from 9am to 5pm. The **Cape Ann Chamber of Commerce,** 33 Commercial St. (✆ **800/321-0133** or 978/283-1601; www.capeannvacations.com), is open year-round (summer Mon–Fri 9am–5pm, Sat 10am–5pm, Sun 10am–4pm; winter Mon–Fri 9am–5pm).

GETTING AROUND Downtown is fairly compact and walkable, but there's more to Gloucester than that. If you can manage it, travel by car. You'll be able to make the best use of your time, especially if you plan several stops. The **Cape Ann Transportation Authority** (see above) serves Gloucester.

SPECIAL EVENTS Gloucester holds festivals and street fairs on weekends all summer. The best known is **St. Peter's Fiesta,** a colorful 4-day event at the end of June. The Italian-American fishing colony's festival includes parades, carnival rides, music, food, sporting events, and the blessing of the fleet. The **Schooner Festival,** a floating party with plenty of land-based revelry, takes place over Labor Day weekend.

EXPLORING THE TOWN

Start at the water, as visitors have done for centuries. The French explorer Samuel de Champlain called the harbor "Le Beauport" in 1604—some 600 years after the Vikings first visited—and its configuration and proximity to good fishing gave it the reputation it enjoys to this day. Fishing and tourism are Gloucester's leading industries. The city is exceptionally welcoming—residents seem genuinely happy to see out-of-towners and to offer directions and insider info.

On Stacy Boulevard (west of downtown) is a reminder of the sea's danger. Leonard Craske's bronze statue of the **Gloucester Fisherman,** known as "The Man at the Wheel," bears the inscription "They That Go Down to the Sea in Ships 1623–1923." To the west is a memorial to the women and children who waited at home. As you take in the glorious view, consider this: More than 10,000 fishermen lost their lives during the city's first 300 years.

Stage Fort Park, off Rte. 127 near the intersection with Rte. 133, offers an excellent view of the harbor and has a busy seasonal snack bar, the **Cupboard** (✆ **978/281-1908**). The park is a good spot for picnicking, swimming, or playing on the cannons in the Revolutionary War fort.

To reach **East Gloucester,** follow signs as you leave downtown or go directly from Rte. 128, exit 9. On East Main Street, you'll see signs for the world-famous **Rocky Neck Art Colony** ★★, in the Rocky Neck Gallery, 53 Rocky Neck Ave. (✆ **978/282-0917;** www.rockyneckartcolony.org), the oldest continuously operating art colony in the country. Park in the lot on the tiny causeway and head west along Rocky Neck Avenue, which abounds with studios, galleries, restaurants, and people. The attraction is the presence of working artists, not just shops that happen to sell art. In summer, most galleries are open daily from 10am to 10pm. The prestigious **North Shore Arts Association,** 11 Pirates Land, off East Main Street (✆ **978/283-1857;** www.north shoreassoc.org), founded in 1922, is open from May through October Monday through Saturday from 10am to 5pm, Sunday from noon to 5pm. Admission is free.

Also in East Gloucester, the **Gloucester Stage Company** ★, 267 E. Main St. (✆ **978/281-4099;** www.gloucesterstage.org), is one of the best repertory troupes in New England. It schedules six plays a season (late May to early Sept).

Beauport (Sleeper-McCann House) ★★ Aficionados of house tours will want to build their schedules around a visit to this magnificent property on the stylish Back Shore, the product of a uniquely creative mind. Interior designer and antiquarian Henry Davis Sleeper accumulated vast collections of American and European decorative arts and antiques in his summer home. From 1907 to 1934, he decorated the 40-plus rooms to illustrate literary and historical themes. The entertaining tour concentrates more on the house in general than on the countless objects. You'll see architectural details from other buildings, magnificent arrangements of colored glassware, the "Red Indian Room" (with a majestic view of the harbor), and even the kitchen and servants' quarters.

75 Eastern Point Blvd. ✆ **978/283-0800.** www.historicnewengland.org. Guided tour $10 adults, $9 seniors, $5 students and children 6–12. Tours on the hour. June to mid-Oct Tues–Sat 10am–4pm. Closed mid-Oct to May. Take E. Main St. south to Eastern Point Blvd. (a private road), continue ½ mile to house, park on left.

Cape Ann Museum ★ This meticulously curated museum makes an excellent introduction to Cape Ann's history and artists. It devotes an entire gallery to the extraordinary work of **Fitz Henry Lane** ★★★ (formerly known as Fitz Hugh Lane), the Luminist painter whose light-flooded canvases show off his native Gloucester. The nation's single largest collection of his paintings and drawings is here. Other galleries feature works on paper by 20th-century artists, work by other contemporary artists, and granite-quarrying tools and equipment. There's also an outdoor sculpture court. The maritime and fisheries galleries display entire vessels, exhibits on the fishing industry, ship models, and historic photographs and models of the Gloucester waterfront. Check ahead for information about touring the historic houses: The adjacent **Capt. Elias Davis House** (1804), decorated and furnished in Federal style, and the newly restored 1710 **White-Ellery House,** a rare example of First Period architecture about a mile away at 244 Washington St.

27 Pleasant St. ☎ **978/283-0455.** www.capeannmuseum.org. Admission $8 adults, $6 seniors and students, free for children 11 and under. Mar–Jan Tues–Sat 10am–5pm, Sun 1–4pm. Closed Feb. Follow Main St. west through downtown and turn right onto Pleasant St.; the museum is 1 block up on right. Metered parking on street or in lot across street.

SCHOONER ADVENTURES

The 65-foot schooner *Thomas E. Lannon* ★ (☎ **978/281-6634;** www.schooner. org) is a lovely reproduction of a Gloucester fishing vessel. The tall ship sails from Seven Seas Wharf downtown; 2-hour excursions ($38 for adults, $33 for seniors, $25 for children 16 and under) leave about four times a day from mid-June to mid-September, less often on weekends from mid-May to mid-June and mid-September to mid-October. Reservations are recommended. The company offers music and dining cruises, including sunset lobster bakes.

The two-masted schooner *Adventure* ★ (☎ **978/281-8079;** www.schooner-adventure.org), a 122-foot fishing vessel built in Essex in 1926, has been extensively restored and resumed scheduled public sailing in 2010. The "living museum," a National Historic Landmark, is docked downtown at Rowe Square, off Rogers Street; check ahead for information.

SHOPPING

Rocky Neck (see "Exploring the Town," above) offers great browsing. Downtown, Main Street between Pleasant and Washington streets is a good destination. Agreeable stops include **Mystery Train,** 21 Main St. (☎ **978/281-8911;** www.mystery trainrecords.com), which carries used music and films; **Ménage Gallery,** 134 Main St. (☎ **978/283-6030;** www.menagegallery.com), which shows work by artists and artisans; and the **Dogtown Book Shop,** 132 Main St. (☎ **978/281-5599;** www. dogtownbooks.com), noted for its used and antiquarian selection.

WHERE TO STAY

Gloucester abounds with B&Bs; for guidance, check with the Cape Ann Chamber of Commerce (☎ **978/283-1601**). The 40-unit **Vista Motel,** 22 Thatcher Rd. (Rte. 127A), Gloucester (☎ **866/VISTA-MA** [847-8262] or 978/281-3410; www. vistamotel.com), is a comfortable establishment on a hilltop near the Rockport border. Summer rates range from $135 for standard rooms to $180 for efficiencies and include Wi-Fi access and continental breakfast.

Atlantis Oceanfront Motor Inn Across the street from the water, the Atlantis enjoys stunning views from every window. The well-maintained, good-size guest rooms are decorated in comfortable, contemporary style, and every unit has a terrace or balcony. The view from second-floor accommodations is a little better. The Atlantis doesn't have the resort feel of its pricier neighbor, the Bass Rocks Ocean Inn (see below), but the million-dollar views are the same.

125 Atlantic Rd., Gloucester, MA 01930. ☎ **800/732-6313** or 978/283-0014. Fax 978/281-8994. www. atlantisoceanfrontinn.com. 40 units (7 with shower only). Late June to Labor Day $170–$215 double; spring and fall $140–$180 double. Extra person $10. Rollaway or crib $15. Children 12 and under stay free in parent's room. Minimum stay may be required. AE, MC, V. Closed Nov to late Apr. Take Rte. 128 to the

A WHALE OF AN ADVENTURE

The waters off the Massachusetts coast are prime **whale-watching ★★** territory, and Gloucester is a center of cruises. Stellwagen Bank, which runs from Gloucester to Provincetown about 27 miles east of Boston, is a rich feeding ground for the magnificent mammals. The whales often perform by jumping out of the water, and dolphins occasionally join the show. Naturalists on board narrate the trip for the companies listed here, pointing out the whales and describing birds and fish that cross your path.

The season runs from April or May to October. Bundle up—it's much cooler at sea than on land—and wear a hat and rubber-soled shoes. Pack sunglasses, sunscreen, and a camera. If you're prone to motion sickness, take precautions, because you'll be at sea for 3½ to 5 hours.

This is an extremely competitive business—they'd deny it, but the companies are virtually indistinguishable. Most guarantee sightings, offer morning and afternoon cruises and deep-sea fishing excursions, honor other firms' coupons, and offer Internet, AARP, and AAA discounts. Check ahead for sailing times, prices (at least $45 for adults, slightly less for seniors and children), and reservations, which are strongly recommended. In downtown Gloucester, **Cape Ann Whale Watch** (✆ **800/877-5110** or 978/283-5110; www.seethewhales.com) is the best-known operation. Also downtown are **Capt. Bill & Sons Whale Watch** (✆ **800/33-WHALE** [339-4253] or 978/283-6995; www.captbillandsons.com) and **Seven Seas Whale Watch** (✆ **888/238-1776** or 978/283-1776; www.7seas-whalewatch.com). At the Cape Ann Marina, off Rte. 133, is **Yankee Whale Watch** (✆ **800/WHALING** [942-5464] or 978/283-0313; www.yankeefleet.com). If your schedule allows, plan to visit the **Whale Center of New England**, in the Gloucester Maritime Heritage Center, 24 Harbor Loop (✆ **978/271-6351**; www.whalecenter.org), before or after your trip. Admission is free.

---

end (exit 9, E. Gloucester), turn left onto Bass Ave. (Rte. 127A), and follow it ½ mile. Turn right and follow Atlantic Rd. **Amenities:** Cafe (breakfast only); heated outdoor pool. *In room:* A/C, TV, fridge, hair dryer, Wi-Fi (free).

Bass Rocks Ocean Inn The Bass Rocks offers gorgeous views and modern accommodations in a traditional setting. The spacious guest rooms take up a sprawling, comfortable two-story motel across the road from the rocky shore. An 1899 Colonial Revival mansion known as the "wedding-cake house" holds a handful of one-bedroom suites and the public areas. The inn has an old-fashioned resort feel that distinguishes it from the neighboring Atlantis (see above). Each motel room has a balcony or patio; second-floor rooms have slightly better views. In the afternoon, the staff serves coffee, tea, lemonade, and cookies.

107 Atlantic Rd., Gloucester, MA 01930. ✆ **888/802-7666** or 978/283-7600. Fax 978/281-6489. www.bassrocksoceaninn.com. 51 units. Summer $249–$350 double; $450 suite. Spring and fall $169–$249 double, $300–$350 suite. Children 12 and under stay free in parent's room. Extra person $10; rollaway or crib $12. Rates include continental breakfast. 3-night minimum summer weekends, some spring and fall weekends. Closed Nov to late Apr. AE, DC, DISC, MC, V. Follow Rte. 128 to the end (exit 9, E. Gloucester), turn left onto Bass Ave. (Rte. 127A), and follow it ½ mile; turn right and follow Atlantic Rd. **Amenities:** Bikes; heated outdoor pool. *In room:* A/C, TV/VCR, fridge, hair dryer, Wi-Fi.

WHERE TO DINE

See "Essex" (p. 173) for information on the celebrated **Woodman's of Essex,** which is about 20 minutes from downtown Gloucester. The Stage Fort Park snack bar, the **Cupboard,** 41 Hough Ave. (✆ **978/281-1908**), serves excellent fried seafood and blue-plate specials in the summer. **Lobsta Land,** 10 Causeway St., near exit 12 off Rte. 128 (✆ **978/281-0415**), is a summer-only destination for familiar and unusual seafood dishes and amazing french fries.

The Franklin Cape Ann ★★ BISTRO   A sophisticated offshoot of a neighborhood favorite in Boston's South End, the Franklin is a welcome addition to the fried-seafood-focused local dining scene. It does serve seafood, but in inventive preparations such as chili-glazed salmon and grilled garlic calamari. Meat dishes are equally creative. The two-story restaurant also offers fabulous martinis and live jazz at least 1 night a week, making it a popular late-evening destination.

118 Main St. ✆ **978/283-7888.** www.franklincafe.com. Reservations recommended. Main courses $15-$21. AE, MC, V. Daily 5–10:30pm (Fri–Sat until midnight); bar daily 4:30pm–1am.

Halibut Point Restaurant SEAFOOD/AMERICAN   Halibut Point is a friendly tavern that serves generous portions of good food. The "Halibut Point Special"—a cup of chowder, a burger, and a beer—hits the high points. The clam chowder is terrific, and some people come to Gloucester just for the spicy Italian fish chowder. There's also a raw bar. Main courses are simple (mostly sandwiches) at lunch, more elaborate at dinner. Be sure to check the specials board—you didn't come all this way to a fishing port not to have fresh fish, did you?

289 Main St. ✆ **978/281-1900.** Main courses $7–$14 lunch, $11–$20 dinner. AE, DISC, MC, V. Daily 11:30am–11pm.

Latitude 43 Restaurant & Bar ★ SEAFOOD/CREATIVE AMERICAN/ SUSHI   A funky, laid-back place that isn't coasting on its waterfront location, "Lat 43" is popular year-round, which means the picky locals eat here, too. The menu offers something for everyone: Clam and fish chowder, greaseless fried seafood, and tasty burgers and lobster rolls for traditionalists, plus sophisticated dishes, such as salads overflowing with local produce, and bistro favorites such as braised lamb shank. You can even get sushi, an option inexplicably absent from many New England seaports. There's seating on the pleasant deck in good weather.

25 Rogers St. (½ block from Washington St.). ✆ **978/281-0223.** www.latfortythree.com. Reservations recommended at dinner. Main courses $7–$16 at lunch, $17–$25 at dinner; lobster market price. AE, DISC, MC, V. Sun–Thurs 11:30am–9pm, Fri–Sat 11:30am–10pm; tavern until 1am daily.

Rockport

This lovely little town at the tip of Cape Ann was settled in 1690. Over the years, it has been a fishing port, a center of granite excavation, and a thriving summer community whose specialty seems to be selling fudge and refrigerator magnets to out-of-towners. But there's more to Rockport than just gift shops. It's home to a lovely state park, and it's popular with photographers, sculptors, jewelry designers, and painters. Winslow Homer, Fitz Henry Lane, and Childe Hassam are among the famous artists who have captured the local color. At times, especially on summer weekends, you'll be hard pressed to find much local color in this tourist-weary destination. But for every year-round resident who seems genuinely startled when people waving cameras descend each June, there are dozens who are proud to show off their town.

Rockport makes an entertaining half-day trip, perhaps combined with a visit to Gloucester. Out of season, from January to mid-April, Rockport is pretty but somewhat desolate. The year-round population is large enough that some businesses stay open and keep reduced hours.

ESSENTIALS

GETTING THERE   Rockport is north of Gloucester along Rte. 127 or 127A. At the end of Rte. 128, turn left at the signs for Rockport to take 127, which is shorter but more commercial. To take 127A, continue on 128 to the sign for East Gloucester and turn left. Parking is tough, especially on summer Saturdays, but metered spots are available throughout downtown. Make one loop around downtown and then head to the free parking lot on Upper Main Street (Rte. 127). The shuttle bus to downtown costs $1. Rockport is 40 miles northeast of Boston and 7 miles north of Gloucester.

The **commuter rail** (📞 800/392-6100 or 617/222-3200; www.mbta.com) runs from Boston's North Station. The trip takes 60 to 70 minutes; the round-trip fare is $16. The station is about 6 blocks from the downtown waterfront. **Cape Ann Transportation Authority** (📞 978/283-7916; www.canntran.com; no Sun service) buses serve Rockport.

VISITOR INFORMATION   The **Rockport Chamber of Commerce,** 170 Main St. (📞 978/546-6575; www.rockportusa.com), is part of the Cape Ann Chamber of Commerce (📞 978/283-1601; www.capeannvacations.com; see "Gloucester," earlier in this chapter). The chamber operates an information booth on Upper Main Street (Rte. 127) daily from July 1 through Labor Day and on weekends from mid-May to June and early September through mid-October. It's about a mile from the town line and a mile from downtown—look for the WELCOME TO ROCKPORT sign.

GETTING AROUND   For traffic and congestion, Boston has nothing on Rockport on a summer weekend afternoon. If you can schedule only one weekday trip, make it this one. When you arrive, park and walk, especially downtown. The Cape Ann Transportation Authority (see above) serves the town.

SPECIAL EVENTS   The **Rockport Chamber Music Festival** (📞 978/546-7391; www.rcmf.org) takes place in June at the **Shalin Liu Performance Center,** 37 Main St., which opened in 2010. Events include performances, family concerts, and lectures. The annual **Christmas pageant,** on Main Street in early December, is a kid-friendly event with carol singing and live animals.

EXPLORING THE TOWN

The most famous sight in Rockport has something of an "Emperor's New Clothes" aura—it's a wooden fish warehouse on the town wharf, or T-Wharf, in the harbor. The barn-red shack known as **Motif No. 1** is the most frequently painted and photographed object in a town filled with lovely buildings and surrounded by rocky coastline. The color certainly catches the eye in the neutrals of the surrounding seascape, but you may find yourself wondering what the big deal is. Originally constructed in 1884 and destroyed during the blizzard of 1978, Motif No. 1 was rebuilt using donations from residents and visitors. It stands again on the same pier, duplicated in every detail, reinforced to withstand storms.

Nearby is **Bearskin Neck,** named after an unfortunate ursine visitor who washed ashore in 1800. It holds perhaps the highest concentration of gift shops anywhere. The narrow peninsula has one main street (South Rd.) and several alleys crammed with galleries, snack bars, antiques shops, and ancient houses. The peninsula ends in a plaza with a magnificent water view.

Throughout town, more than two dozen **art galleries** ★ display the work of local and nationally known artists. The **Rockport Art Association,** 12 Main St. (✆ 978/546-6604; www.rockportartassn.org), sponsors exhibitions and special shows. It's open daily in the summer, Tuesday through Sunday in the winter.

The 1922 **Paper House,** 52 Pigeon Hill St., Pigeon Cove (✆ 978/546-2629), is an unusual experience. Everything in it (including the furniture) was built entirely out of 100,000 newspapers. Every item is made from papers of a different period. It's open April through October, daily from 10am to 5pm. Admission is $1.50 for adults, $1 for children. Follow Rte. 127 north from downtown about 1½ miles until you see signs at Curtis Street pointing to the left.

SHOPPING

Bearskin Neck boasts dozens of little shops that carry clothes, gifts, toys, jewelry, souvenirs, inexpensive novelties, and expensive handmade crafts and paintings. Another enjoyable stroll is along **Main** and **Mount Pleasant streets.** Good stops include the nonprofit **Toad Hall Bookstore,** 47 Main St. (✆ 978/546-7323; www.toadhallbooks.org); **Tidal Edge Gallery,** 3 School St., off Main Street (✆ 978/546-3196; www.tidaledgegallery.com); and **Willoughby's,** 20 Main St. (✆ 978/546-9820), a women's clothing and accessories shop.

Two favorite stops are retro delights. Downtown, you can watch taffy being made at **Tuck's Candy Factory,** 7 Dock Sq. (✆ 800/569-2767 or 978/546-6352; www.tuckscandy.com), a local landmark since 1929. Near the train station, **Crackerjacks,** 27 Whistlestop Mall, off Railroad Avenue (✆ 978/546-1616), is an old-fashioned variety store with a great crafts department.

A Trip to the Edge of the Sea

The tip of Cape Ann is accessible to the public and well worth the 2½-mile trip north on Rte. 127 to **Halibut Point State Park** ★★ (✆ 978/546-2997; www.mass.gov/dcr). The surf-battered point got its name not from the fish, but because sailing ships heading for Rockport and Gloucester must "haul about" when they reach the jutting promontory. This is a great place to wander around and admire the scenery. On a clear day, you can see Maine.

About 10 minutes from the parking area, you'll come to a huge water-filled quarry (swimming is absolutely forbidden) and a visitor center, where staffers dispense information, brochures, and bird lists. There are walking trails, tidal pools, a World War II observation tower, and a rocky beach where you can climb around on giant boulders. To take a self-guided tour, pick up a brochure at the visitor center or the Chamber of Commerce. Check ahead for information about guided tours and other special programs; good resources include the park **blog** (www.halibutpoint.wordpress.com) and the website of the **Friends of Halibut Point State Park** (www.halibutpointfriends.org). The park is open daily from Memorial Day to Labor Day, 8am to 8pm; otherwise daily dawn to dusk. Parking costs $2 from Memorial Day to Columbus Day.

WHERE TO STAY

When Rockport is busy, it's very busy, and when it's not, it's practically empty. The town's dozens of **B&Bs** fill in good weather and empty or even close in the winter. If you haven't made summer reservations well in advance, cross your fingers and call the Chamber of Commerce to ask about cancellations. Most innkeepers will pick guests up at the train station; if you're not driving, be sure to ask when you reserve.

In Town

Captain's Bounty Motor Inn   This modern, well-maintained motor inn is on the water. In fact, it's almost *in* the water, and nearly as close to the center of town as to the harbor. Each rather plain unit in the three-story building overlooks the water and has its own balcony. Rooms are spacious and soundproof, with good cross-ventilation but no air-conditioning. The best units are on the adults-only top floor. Although the inn is hardly plush, the staff is welcoming, and you can't beat the location.

1 Beach St., Rockport, MA 01966. ✆ **978/546-9557.** Fax 978/546-9993. www.captainsbounty motorinn.com. 24 units. Late May to late Sept $165 double, $175 efficiency, $205 efficiency suite; spring and fall $120–$140 double, $130–$145 efficiency, $150–$160 efficiency suite. Extra adult $10; $5 for each child. 2-night minimum Fri–Sat and holidays. MC, V. Closed Nov–Mar. Pets accepted ($10/night). *In room:* TV/DVD, fridge, Wi-Fi (free).

Inn on Cove Hill (Caleb Norwood Jr. House) ★   This attractive Federal-style inn was built in 1771 using the proceeds of pirates' gold found nearby. Although it's just 2 blocks from the town wharf, the inn is set back from the road and has a hide-away feel. Guest rooms are decorated in period style; most have Colonial furnishings and handmade quilts, and some have canopy beds. Innkeeper Betsy Eck overhauls one room each winter. Water views from the back of the house are worth the climb to the third floor. The generous breakfast is served in the dining room or, in good weather, in the pleasant garden. A harbor-view apartment across the street is available for long-term (1 week or more) stays.

37 Mount Pleasant St., Rockport, MA 01966. ✆ **888/546-2701** or 978/546-2701. Fax 978/546-1095. www.innoncovehill.com. 7 units (some with shower only). $125–$165 double. Extra person $25. Rates include continental breakfast. 2-night minimum mid-May to mid-Oct and most Fri–Sat. MC, V. *In room:* A/C, TV, no phone.

On the Outskirts

Emerson Inn by the Sea ★★   Somewhere in an old guest register, you might find Ralph Waldo Emerson's name—the philosopher stayed at the original (1840) inn. The building expanded in 1912, and innkeepers Bruce and Michele Coates have transformed it into a miniresort with an outdoor pool and sweet views of the Atlantic and the rocky shore. The place retains a relaxing old-fashioned feel. Traditional furnishings such as four-poster beds grace the rooms, which are nicely appointed but not terribly large. If you can manage the stairs, the view from the top floor is worth the exertion. The best units have private balconies, fireplaces, or hot tubs. Two three-bedroom cottages nearby each rent for $1,800 to $4,500 a week. The **Grand Café** restaurant (✆ **978/546-9500**) enjoys a good reputation for contemporary American cuisine. It serves dinner daily in the summer and on weekends in the off season; reservations are required.

1 Cathedral Ave., Rockport, MA 01966. ✆ **800/964-5550** or 978/546-6321. Fax 978/546-7043. www. emersoninnbythesea.com. 35 units (some with shower only). May–Oct $299–$379 "best" double; $229–$229 oceanview double; $159–$179 double without view. Off-season discounts available. Extra

person $25; cot $25. Rates include full breakfast May–Oct, continental breakfast Nov–Apr. 2- or 3-night minimum weekends May–Oct. AE, DC, DISC, MC, V. Follow Rte. 127 north from the center of town for 2 miles; turn right at sign on Phillips Ave. **Amenities:** Dining room; outdoor pool; sauna. *In room:* A/C, TV, hair dryer, Wi-Fi (free).

WHERE TO DINE

A good way to experience the town is to arrive before the tourist hordes descend and enjoy a hearty breakfast. **Flav's Red Skiff,** 15 Mount Pleasant St. (© **978/546-7647**), is a welcoming local hangout.

The Rockport dining scene isn't nearly as varied or sophisticated as Gloucester's; if you're not ravenous, consider going there or to **Woodman's of Essex** (p. 173), or make a reservation at the Grand Café, the public dining room at the **Emerson Inn by the Sea** (see above).

Roy Moore Lobster Company ★ ❦ SEAFOOD   This little fish market is the only reason some locals will agree to visit Bearskin Neck during the summer. It serves ultrafresh lobster cooked in seawater and served with drawn butter and plenty of paper towels. The luscious crustaceans and a limited selection of other dishes (including clam chowder) are available to stay or go. Prices are exceptionally reasonable, thanks in part to the lack of atmosphere—the small dining area is outdoors, drinks are from the soda machine. The service at the counter is efficient and friendly.

39 Bearskin Neck. © **978/546-7808.** Reservations not accepted. Seafood market price. MC, V. Apr–Nov daily 11:30am–9:30pm.

NEWBURYPORT, PLUM ISLAND & IPSWICH

The area between Cape Ann and the New Hampshire border is magnificent, with outdoor sights and sounds that can only be described as natural wonders, and enough impressive architecture to keep any city slicker happy.

In a part of the world where the word *charming* is used almost as often as *hello,* Newburyport is a singular example of a picturesque waterfront city. Downtown Newburyport is on the Merrimack River. On the town's Atlantic coast, Plum Island contains one of the country's top nature preserves. On the other side of Ipswich Bay, Ipswich is a lovely town that's home to Crane Beach, part of another wildlife reservation.

Newburyport ★★

To get here directly from Boston, take I-93 (or Rte. 1 if it's not rush hour) to I-95—*not* Rte. 128, as for most other destinations in this chapter—and follow it to exit 57, a solid 45-minute ride. Signs point to downtown, where you can park and explore. The **commuter rail** (© **800/392-6100** or 617/222-3200; www.mbta.com) from North Station takes about 75 minutes and costs $16 round-trip.

Newburyport has a substantial year-round population that lends it a less touristy atmosphere than its appearance might suggest. Start your visit at the **Greater Newburyport Chamber of Commerce and Industry,** 38R Merrimac St. (© **978/462-6680;** www.newburyportchamber.org), in the red-brick downtown shopping district. It also runs a seasonal information booth on Merrimac Street near Green Street. The website includes copious information and an events calendar, as well as a downloadable map of a walking tour.

Market Square, at the foot of State Street near the waterfront, is the center of a neighborhood packed with boutiques, gift shops, plain and fancy restaurants, and antiques stores. You can also wander to the water, take a stroll on the boardwalk, and enjoy the action on the river. Architecture buffs will want to climb the hill to High Street, where the **Charles Bulfinch**–designed building (1805) that houses the Superior Court is only one of several Federal-era treasures.

If you haven't gone out to sea yet, now is a good time, and here's a good place: **Newburyport Whale Watch ★★**, Hilton's Dock, 54 Merrimac St. (© **800/848-1111** or 978/499-0832; www.newburyportwhalewatch.com), offers 4½-hour cruises on a 100-foot boat with onboard marine biologists as guides. Ticket prices are competitive with rates at the Gloucester outfits (see "A Whale of an Adventure," p. 179), and reservations are recommended.

Or head to the ocean using an inland route: From downtown, take Water Street south until it becomes Plum Island Turnpike and follow it to the Parker River National Wildlife Refuge.

Parker River National Wildlife Refuge ★★

The 4,662-acre refuge on **Plum Island** is a complex of barrier beaches, dunes, and salt marshes, one of the few remaining in the Northeast. The refuge is flat-out breathtaking, whether you're exploring the marshes or the seashore. More than 800 species of plants and animals (including more than 300 bird species) visit or make their home on the narrow finger of land between Broad Sound and the Atlantic Ocean. Get your bearings at the **visitor center**, 6 Plum Island Tpk. (© **978/465-5753;** http://parkerriver.fws.gov), which houses interactive displays and other exhibits. It's open daily 11am to 4pm.

The refuge offers some of the best **birding ★★★** anywhere, as well as observation of mammals and plants. Wooden boardwalks with observation towers and platforms wind through marshes and along the shore—most lack handrails, so this isn't an activity for rambunctious children. Birders come from around the world hoping to see native and migratory species such as owls, hawks, martins, geese, warblers, ducks, snowy egrets, swallows, and Canada geese. Other visitors and residents include monarch butterflies, foxes, beavers, and harbor seals.

The ocean beach closes April 1 to allow piping plovers, listed by the federal government as a threatened species, to nest. The areas not being used for nesting reopen July 1; the rest open in August, when the birds are through. The currents are strong and can be dangerous, and there are no lifeguards—swimming is allowed but not encouraged. Surf fishing is popular, though; striped bass and bluefish are found in the area. A permit is required for night fishing and vehicle access to the beach.

The refuge is open from dawn to dusk year-round. The daily entrance fee is $5 for motorists, $2 for bikers and pedestrians. The seven parking lots fill quickly on weekends when the weather is good, so plan to arrive early. South of lot 4 (Hellcat Swamp), the access road is flat and well maintained but not paved.

Ipswich ★

Across Ipswich Bay from Plum Island is the town of Ipswich. It's accessible from Rte. 1A (which you can pick up in Newburyport or at Rte. 128 in Hamilton) and from Rte. 133 (which intersects with Rte. 128 in Gloucester and I-95 in

MORE WHALE TALES: A TRIP TO NEW BEDFORD

The masses that flock to eastern Massachusetts aren't yet swarming the cobblestone streets of New Bedford, which makes it a good destination for families on the verge of crowd-phobia. The **New Bedford Whaling National Historical Park,** which encompasses the downtown historic district, commemorates the city's past as the world's leading whaling port.

The downtown area near the waterfront has been restored, and the attractions are reasonably close together. Start your visit at the **National Park Service Visitor Center,** 33 William St. (© **508/996-4095;** www.nps.gov/nebe), open daily from 9am to 5pm. The exhibits include a film about whaling and the city's history. Take a guided walking tour (daily in summer, some off-season weekends) or pick up a brochure that describes self-guided excursions around the historic district.

The centerpiece of the Historical Park is the **New Bedford Whaling Museum ★,** 18 Johnny Cake Hill (© **508/997-0046;** www.whalingmuseum.org). It's the world's premier whaling museum, which sounds terribly specialized but is actually quite absorbing. On display in the lobby is the skeleton of a 65-foot juvenile blue whale. Admission to the lobby is free, but the rest of the museum is worth a visit. Children love the half-scale model of the whaling bark *Lagoda,* the world's largest ship model. The museum is open June to December daily from 9am to 5pm, until 9pm one Thursday a month; winter hours are Monday through Saturday 9am to 4pm, Sunday noon to 4pm. Admission is $10 for adults, $9 for seniors and students, and $6 for children 6 to 14.

The **Seamen's Bethel,** 15 Johnny Cake Hill (© **508/992-3295**), a nondenominational chapel described in Herman Melville's classic novel *Moby-Dick,* is across the street. It's open weekdays in the summer from 10am to 5pm; admission is free, and donations are appreciated. Up the hill from the water, the **Rotch-Jones-Duff House & Garden Museum,** 396 County St. (© **508/997-1401;** www.rjdmuseum.org), is an 1834 Greek Revival mansion with magnificent formal gardens. Admission is $5 for adults; $4 for seniors, students, and AAA members; $2 for children 12 and under.

To get to New Bedford, take the Southeast Expressway south to I-93 (Rte. 128), then Rte. 24 south. Follow signs to Rte. 140 south to I-195. From Plymouth, take Rte. 44 west to Rte. 24 south. **Dattco** (© **800/229-4879;** www.dattco.com) buses take 75 minutes from Boston's South Station ($24 round-trip). For more information, contact the **New Bedford Office of Tourism** (© **508/979-1745;** www.destinationnewbedford.org) or the **Bristol County Convention & Visitors Bureau** (© **800/288-6263** or 508/997-1250; www.bristol-county.org).

Georgetown). The **MBTA** (© **800/392-6100** or 617/222-3200; www.mbta.com) commuter rail serves Ipswich; the round-trip fare is $14, and the trip from Boston takes about an hour. On weekends and holidays in the summer, the Cape Ann Transportation Authority operates the **Ipswich Essex Explorer** bus (© **978/283-7916** or 978/356-8540; www.ipswichessexexplorer.com), which connects the station to the attractions, including Crane Beach. The fare is $1.50; an all-day pass costs $5.

The **Ipswich Visitor Information Center,** in the Hall Haskell House, 36 S. Main St., Rte. 133 (℃ **978/356-8540**), is open weekends in May and daily from Memorial Day weekend through October. The **Ipswich Chamber of Commerce** (℃ **978/356-9055;** www.ipswichma.com) supports the center and offers abundant information on its website.

Settled in 1630, Ipswich is dotted with **17th-century or "First Period" houses ★**—reputedly the largest concentration in the United States. Many are private homes; ask at the visitor center for a map of a tour that passes three dozen of them, or rent the audio version ($8). The **Iswich Historical Society & Museums** (℃ **978/356-2811;** www.ipswichmuseum.org) offers tours of the **John Whipple House,** 1 South Village Green, and the **Heard House Museum,** 54 S. Main St. Tours ($5 each, or $7 for both houses) run Wednesday through Saturday from Memorial Day weekend through Columbus Day weekend; check ahead for schedules.

Ipswich is also known for two more contemporary structures. The **Clam Box ★★**, 246 High St., Rte. 1A/133 (℃ **978/356-9707;** www.ipswichma.com/clambox), is a restaurant shaped like—what else?—a red-and-white-striped takeout clam box. It's a great place to try Ipswich clams, and not easy to sneak past if you have children in the car. Heading south from Newburyport, it's on the right. The place is closed December through February.

South of Ipswich Center, near the intersection of rtes. 1A and 133, look carefully for the Argilla Road sign (on the east side of the street). If you're traveling west on Rte. 133 from Gloucester and Essex, watch for a sign on the right pointing to Northgate Road, which intersects with Argilla Road. Follow it east to the end, where you'll find the 1,400-acre **Crane Estate.**

The property is home to **Crane Beach** (see "Life's a Beach . . . with Very Cold Water!" on p. 174), the **Crane Wildlife Refuge ★★**, a network of hiking trails, and **Castle Hill on the Crane Estate,** 290 Argilla Rd. (℃ **978/356-4351;** www. thetrustees.org). One of the Boston area's most popular wedding locations, the exquisite Stuart-style seaside mansion known as the Great House was built by Richard Teller Crane, Jr., who made his fortune in plumbing and bathroom fixtures early in the 20th century. You have several options for seeing the property; guided tours run late May to mid-October. One-hour house tours ($10 for adults, $5 for children 8–18) take place Wednesday and Thursday from 10am to 3pm, Friday and Saturday 10am to 1pm. Ninety-minute landscape tours of Castle Hill ($5) start at 10am Thursday and Saturday. Year-round, you can explore the estate ($8 per car on summer weekends, otherwise $5 per car) without entering the house.

Children who can't get excited about a tour might be pacified by a stop just before Castle Hill. **Russell Orchards Store and Winery ★**, 143 Argilla Rd. (℃ **978/356-5366;** www.russellorchards.com), is open daily May through November. It has a picnic area, farm animals, and an excellent country store. Depending on the season, you might go on a hayride or taste fruit wines. Be sure to try some cider and doughnuts.

PLYMOUTH ★★

45 miles SE of Boston

Everyone educated in the United States knows at least a little of the story of Plymouth—about how the Pilgrims, fleeing religious persecution, left Europe on the *Mayflower* and landed at Plymouth Rock in 1620. Many also know that the Pilgrims endured disease and privation, and that just 53 people from the original group of 102 celebrated what we now call "the first Thanksgiving" in 1621 with Squanto, a Pawtuxet Indian associated with the Wampanoag people, and his cohorts.

What you won't know until you visit is how small everything was. The *Mayflower* (a reproduction) seems perilously tiny, and when you contemplate how dangerous life was at the time, it's hard not to marvel at the settlers' accomplishments. The *Mayflower* passengers weren't even aiming for Plymouth. They originally set out for what they called "Northern Virginia," near the mouth of the Hudson River. On November 11, 1620, rough weather and high seas forced them to make for Cape Cod Bay and anchor at Provincetown. The captain then announced that they had found a safe harbor and refused to continue to their original destination. On December 16, Provincetown having proven an unsatisfactory location, the weary travelers landed at Plymouth.

Plymouth is in many ways a model destination, where the 17th century coexists with the 21st, and most historic attractions are both educational and fun. Visitors jam the downtown area and waterfront in summer, but the year-round population is so large that Plymouth feels more like the working community it is than like a touristy day-trip destination. It's a manageable excursion from Boston, particularly enjoyable if you're traveling with children. It also makes a good stop between Boston and Cape Cod.

Essentials

GETTING THERE   By car, follow the Southeast Expressway (I-93) from Boston to Route 3. From Cape Cod, take Rte. 3 north. Take exit 6A to Rte. 44 east, and follow signs to the historic attractions. The trip from Boston takes 45 to 60 minutes if it's not rush hour. Take exit 5 to the **Regional Information Complex** for maps, brochures, and information. Take exit 4 to go directly to **Plimoth Plantation.** Metered parking is available throughout town.

The **commuter rail** (© **617/222-3200;** www.mbta.com) serves Cordage Park, on Rte. 3A north of downtown, from South Station. The round-trip fare is $16. Plymouth and Brockton **buses** (© **508/746-0378;** www.p-b.com) take about an hour from South Station. They run more often than the train, but they cost more ($14 one-way, $24 round-trip) and drop off and pick up passengers at the park-and-ride lot at Rte. 3, exit 5. The **Plymouth Area Link** bus (© **800/483-2500** or

---

 THE ADAMS FAMILY

A worthwhile detour en route to Plymouth is the **Adams National Historical Park** in Quincy, about 10 miles south of Boston. The park preserves the birthplaces of Presidents John Adams and John Quincy Adams, the house where four generations of the family lived, and other buildings associated with the political dynasty. A trolley connects the buildings, which are open for guided tours daily from 9am to 5pm in season

(Apr 19–Nov 10). Admission is $5 for adults, free for children under 16. The grounds and the visitor center, 1250 Hancock St. (© **617/770-1175;** www.nps.gov/adam), are open in the winter Wednesday through Friday from 10am to 4pm. The center is across the street from the Quincy Center stop on the Red Line; call or check their website for driving directions.

Plymouth

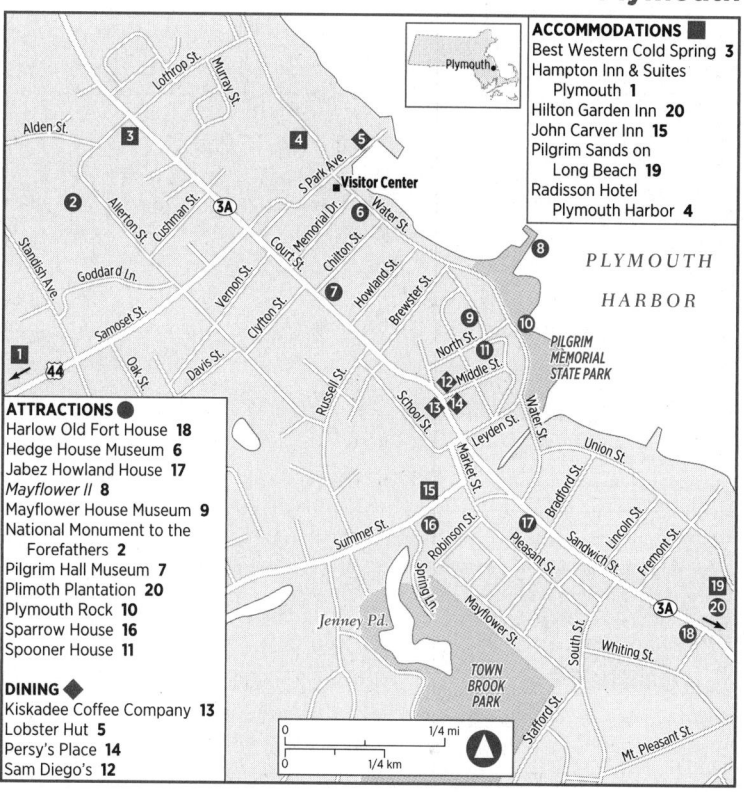

ACCOMMODATIONS ■
Best Western Cold Spring **3**
Hampton Inn & Suites
Plymouth **1**
Hilton Garden Inn **20**
John Carver Inn **15**
Pilgrim Sands on
Long Beach **19**
Radisson Hotel
Plymouth Harbor **4**

PLYMOUTH

HARBOR

PILGRIM
MEMORIAL
STATE PARK

ATTRACTIONS ●
Harlow Old Fort House **18**
Hedge House Museum **6**
Jabez Howland House **17**
Mayflower II **8**
Mayflower House Museum **9**
National Monument to the
Forefathers **2**
Pilgrim Hall Museum **7**
Plimoth Plantation **20**
Plymouth Rock **10**
Sparrow House **16**
Spooner House **11**

DINING ◆
Kiskadee Coffee Company **13**
Lobster Hut **5**
Persy's Place **14**
Sam Diego's **12**

508/747-1819; www.gatra.org/pal.html) connects the train station and bus stop with downtown. The fare is $1, free for children 6 and under.

VISITOR INFORMATION   If you haven't visited the Regional Information Complex (see above), pick up a map at the **Visitor Information Center** (☏ **508/747-7525**), open seasonally at 130 Water St., across from Town Pier. To plan ahead, contact Plymouth Visitor Information, known as **Destination Plymouth** (☏ **800/USA-1620** [872-1620] or 508/747-7533; www.visit-plymouth.com). The **Plymouth County Convention & Visitors Bureau** (☏ **800/231-1620** or 508/747-0100; www.seeplymouth.com) publishes a vacation planner.

GETTING AROUND   The downtown attractions are accessible on foot. A shallow hill slopes from the center of town to the waterfront. **America's Hometown Shuttle** (☏ **508/746-0378**; www.p-b.com/ahs.html) runs throughout the town in a loop from late June through Labor Day weekend, daily from 10am to 5pm. The fare ($15 adults, $7.50 children 6–11) includes a narrated tour and unlimited reboarding. Check ahead for the schedule and route.

Exploring the Historic Sites

No matter how many times you suffered through elementary-school pageants wearing a big black hat and paper buckles on your shoes, you can still learn something about Plymouth and the Pilgrims. The logical place to begin (good luck talking children out of it) is where the Pilgrims first set foot—at **Plymouth Rock ★★**, on the waterfront in **Pilgrim Memorial State Park** (⌂ 508/747-5360; www.mass.gov/dcr), the smallest state park in Massachusetts. The rock, accepted as the landing place of the *Mayflower* passengers, was originally 15 feet long and 3 feet wide. It was moved on the eve of the Revolution and several times thereafter. In 1867, it assumed its present position at tide level. The Colonial Dames of America commissioned the portico around the rock, designed by McKim, Mead & White and erected in 1920. The rock isn't much to look at, but the accompanying descriptions are interesting, and the atmosphere curiously inspiring.

The park south of the Rock is **Brewster Gardens,** a lovely space that traces Town Brook. This is a good shortcut to **Jenney Pond,** in Town Brook Park, across Summer Street from the John Carver Inn. A short distance from the bustle of the waterfront, the park has plenty of room to run around as well as a pond populated by ducks and geese.

A short distance from the waterfront is the **National Monument to the Forefathers,** a granite behemoth inscribed with the names of the *Mayflower* passengers. Heading away from the harbor on Rte. 44, look carefully on the right for the turn onto Allerton Street, and climb the hill. The 81-foot-high monument is elaborately decorated with figures representing moral and political virtues and scenes of Pilgrim history. The monument is incongruous in its little park in a residential neighborhood, but it's also quite impressive. The view from the hilltop is excellent.

Mayflower II ★ ☺   Berthed a few steps from Plymouth Rock, *Mayflower II* is a full-scale reproduction of the type of ship that brought the Pilgrims from England to America in 1620. Even at full scale, the 106½-foot vessel, constructed in England from 1955 to 1957, seems remarkably small. Although little technical information about the original *Mayflower* survives, the designer of *Mayflower II* incorporated the few references in Governor Bradford's account of the voyage with other research to re-create the ship as authentically as possible. Costumed guides provide interesting first-person narratives about the vessel and voyage. Displays describe and illustrate the journey and the Pilgrims' experience, including 17th-century navigation techniques.

State Pier. ⌂ **508/746-1622.** www.plimoth.org. Admission $10 adults, $9 seniors, $7 children 6–12. Plimoth Plantation and *Mayflower II* admission (good for 2 consecutive days) $28 adults, $26 seniors and students, $18 children 6–12, $110 families (2 adults and up to 4 children 6–17; not available online). Late Mar to late Nov daily 9am–5pm. Closed Dec to mid-Mar.

Pilgrim Hall Museum ★   This is a great place to get a sense of the day-to-day lives of Plymouth's first European residents. Many original possessions of the early Pilgrims and their descendants are on display, including Myles Standish's sword, Governor Bradford's Bible, and an uncomfortable chair (you can sit in a replica) that belonged to William Brewster. Regularly changing exhibits explore the early settlers' lives, and hands-on activities such as treasure hunts get kids interested.

75 Court St. ⌂ **508/746-1620.** www.pilgrimhall.org. Admission $8 adults, $7 seniors, $6 AAA members, $5 children 5–17, $25 families. Feb–Dec daily 9:30am–4:30pm. Closed Jan. From Plymouth Rock, walk north on Water St. and up the hill on Chilton St.

Plimoth Plantation ★★ ☺ Allow at least half a day to explore this re-creation of the 1627 village, which children and adults find equally interesting. Enter by the hilltop fort and walk down to the farm area, visiting homes and gardens along the way. The "Pilgrims" are actors who, in speech, dress, and manner, assume the personalities of members of the original community. You can watch them framing a house, splitting wood, shearing sheep, preserving foodstuffs, or cooking stew over an open hearth, all as it was done in the 1600s. Wear comfortable shoes—you'll be walking a lot.

The plantation is as accurate as research can make it, constructed with careful attention to historical detail. The planners combined accounts of the original colony with archaeological research, old records, and the history written by the Pilgrims' leader, William Bradford (who often used the spelling "Plimoth"). There are daily militia drills with matchlock muskets that are fired to demonstrate the community's defense system. In fact, little defense was needed, because the Native Americans were friendly. Local tribes included the Wampanoags, who are represented near the village at a replica of a homesite (included in plantation admission). Museum staffers show off native foodstuffs, agricultural practices, and crafts.

At the main entrance are two modern buildings that house exhibits, a gift shop, a bookstore, a cafeteria, and an auditorium that shows a film produced by the History Channel. There's also a picnic area. Call or surf online ahead for information on special events, lectures, tours, workshops, theme dinners, and family programs.

137 Warren Ave. (Rte. 3). ✆ **508/746-1622.** www.plimoth.org. Admission (good for 2 consecutive days) $24 adults, $22 seniors, $14 children 6-12. Plimoth Plantation and *Mayflower II* admission $28 adults, $26 seniors and students, $18 children 6-12, $110 families (2 adults and up to 4 children 6-17; not available online). Late Mar to late Nov daily 9am–5pm. Closed Dec to mid-Mar. From Rte. 3, take exit 4, Plimoth Plantation Hwy.

The Historic Houses

Plymouth's historic houses are worth a visit to see the changing styles of architecture and furnishings since the 1600s. Costumed guides explain the homemaking and crafts of earlier generations. When they're not undergoing renovation, most of the houses are open Memorial Day through Columbus Day, during Thanksgiving celebrations, and around Christmas; call for schedules and pay close attention to open days, which are limited.

Tip: Unless you have a sky-high tolerance for house tours, pick just one or two from eras that you find particularly interesting. This advice applies especially if you're sightseeing with children.

Six homes are usually open to visitors. The 1640 **Sparrow House,** 42 Summer St. (✆ **508/747-1240;** www.sparrowhouse.com; admission $2 adults, $1 children), and the 1667 **Jabez Howland House,** 33 Sandwich St. (✆ **508/746-9590;** www. pilgrimjohnhowlandsociety.org; $4 adults, $1 children), are most engaging for those curious about the original settlers. Other houses that are open to the public include the 1677 **Harlow Old Fort House,** 119 Sandwich St. ($5 adults, $2 children), the 1754 **Mayflower House Museum,** 4 Winslow St. (✆ **508/746-2590;** www. themayflowersociety.com; $4), and the 1809 **Hedge House Museum,** 126 Water St. (✆ **508/746-0012;** $5 adults, $2 children). The **Plymouth Antiquarian Society** (✆ **508/746-0012;** www.plymouthantiquariansociety.org) owns the Harlow Old Fort House and the Hedge House Museum as well as the 1749 **Spooner**

House, 27 North St., which was closed for renovation at press time. Contact the society for updates.

Organized Tours & Cruises

To walk in the Pilgrims' footsteps, take a **Colonial Lantern Tour ★** (© 774/454-8126; www.lanterntours.com). Participants carry pierced-tin lanterns on a 90-minute walking tour of the original settlement under the direction of a knowledgeable guide. Tours—of Pilgrim history or "Ghosts & Legends"—run nightly April through Thanksgiving, rain or shine. Tickets are $12 for adults, $10 for seniors and children 6 to 16; check the meeting place when you call for reservations. The company offers special tours for Halloween and Thanksgiving.

Narrated cruises run from April or May through October or November. They leave from State Pier or Town Wharf. **Pilgrim Belle Cruises** (© 508/747-3434; www.pilgrimbellecruises.com) offers 75-minute narrated tours of the harbor on a paddle-wheeler ($16 adults, $14 seniors, $11 children 2–12), as well as dining and entertainment cruises and ferry service to Provincetown (p. 253). **Capt. John Boats** (© 800/242-2469 or 508/747-2400; www.captjohn.com) offers whale watches ($40 adults, $34 seniors, $28 children) and deep-sea fishing excursions. **Lobster Tales** (© 508/746-5342; www.lobstertalesinc.com) offers **pirate cruises** ($18 per person), which allow kids ages 4 to 11 to don hats and face paint and "defend" the boat against marauding buccaneers, and **lobster excursions** ($15 adults, $13 seniors, $11 children 11 and younger), which give passengers the chance to haul up traps and observe marine life.

Shopping

Water Street, on the harbor, boasts an inexhaustible supply of souvenir shops. A less kitschy destination, just up the hill, is Rte. 3A, known as Court, Main, and Warren Street as it runs through town. **Lily's Apothecary,** 6 Main St. Extension, in the old post office (© 508/747-7546; www.lilysapothecary.com), carries a big-city-style selection of skin- and hair-care products. **Main Street Antiques,** 46 Main St. (© 508/747-8887), is home to dozens of dealers. **Pilgrim's Progress,** 13 Court St. (© 508/746-6033; www.pilgrimsprogressclothing.com), carries women's and men's clothing. **British Imports,** 1 Court St. (© 877/264-8586 or 508/747-2972; www.britishsupplies.com), attracts homesick Marmite fans from miles around.

Where to Stay

On busy summer weekends, it's not unusual for every room in town to be taken; make reservations well in advance.

The 175-unit **Radisson Hotel Plymouth Harbor,** 180 Water St. (© 800/395-7046 or 508/747-4900; www.radisson.com/plymouthma), is the only chain hotel downtown. On a hill across the street from the waterfront, it offers the usual amenities, including a pool in the atrium lobby, and Sleep Number beds in most guest rooms. Rates for doubles in high season start at $139 and include Wi-Fi.

Less than 10 minutes from the downtown attractions is the **Hampton Inn & Suites Plymouth,** 10 Plaza Way (© 800/HAMPTON [426-7866] or 508/747-5000; www). The 122-unit property is near two shopping centers and has an indoor pool. High-season double rates start at $139 and include breakfast and Wi-Fi.

The **Hilton Garden Inn,** 4 Home Depot Dr. (© **877/782-9444** or 508/830-0200; www.hiltongardeninn.com), is at Rte. 3 exit 5, about 10 minutes from downtown. The hotel has an exercise room, an indoor pool, and extensive business features; doubles in high season go for $149 and up, including high-speed Internet access.

Best Western Cold Spring ★★ Convenient to downtown and the historic sites, this fastidiously maintained Cold Spring hotel and the adjacent cottages surround nicely landscaped lawns. Rooms are pleasantly decorated and big enough for a family to spread out; if you want privacy, book a two-bedroom cottage. The tolerable distance from the water makes this place a good deal: The two-story complex is 1 long block inland, set back from the street in a quiet part of town.

188 Court St. (Rte. 3A), Plymouth, MA 02360. © **800/678-8667** or 508/746-2222. Fax 508/746-2744. www.bwcoldspring.com. 58 units (10 with shower only), 2 2-bedroom cottages. Apr–Nov $99–$159 double; $139–$199 suite; $109–$159 cottage. Extra person $10. Rollaway $10. Crib $5. Children 11 and under stay free in parent's room. Rates include continental breakfast. AE, DC, DISC, MC, V. Closed Dec–Mar. Pets accepted ($10 fee). **Amenities:** Outdoor pool. *In room:* A/C, TV, hair dryer, Wi-Fi (free).

John Carver Inn ☺ A three-story Colonial-style building with a landmark portico, this hotel offers comfortable, modern accommodations and plenty of amenities. It's within walking distance of the main attractions on the edge of the downtown business district. The indoor "theme pool," a big hit with families, has a large water slide and a model Pilgrim ship. Business features, including meeting space, make this the Radisson's main competition for corporate travelers. The good-size guest rooms are decorated in Colonial style. The best units are the lavish suites with private Jacuzzis; "four-poster" rooms contain king-size beds.

25 Summer St., Plymouth, MA 02360. © **800/274-1620** or 508/746-7100. Fax 508/746-8299. www.johncarverinn.com. 80 units. Early Apr to mid-June and mid-Oct to Nov $119–$219 double; $259–$299 suite; mid-June to mid-Oct $159–$249 double; $299–$329 suite; Dec to early Apr $109–$199 double, $239–$279 suite. Extra person $20; rollaway $20; crib free. Children 18 and under stay free in parent's room. AE, DC, DISC, MC, V. **Amenities:** Restaurant; concierge; fitness center; Jacuzzi; indoor pool; room service. *In room:* A/C, TV, hair dryer, Wi-Fi (free).

Pilgrim Sands on Long Beach ★★ ☺ This attractive motel sits on its own beach 3 miles south of town, within walking distance of Plimoth Plantation. If you want to avoid the bustle of downtown and still be near the water, it's an excellent choice. The well-maintained property also has an indoor and an outdoor pool. Prices for the good-size rooms vary with the view; if you can swing it, book a beachfront unit—the scenery is worth the money, especially when the surf is rough.

150 Warren Ave. (Rte. 3A), Plymouth, MA 02360. © **800/729-7263** or 508/747-0900. Fax 508/746-8066. www.pilgrimsands.com. 64 units. Summer $155–$195 double; spring and early fall $114–$169 double; Apr and late fall $94–$134 double; Dec–Mar $84–$99 double. $159–$309 suite year-round. Extra person $6–$8 (suite $10–$15). Up to 2 children ages 6 and under stay free in parent's room. Rates include continental breakfast. 2-night minimum holiday weekends. AE, DC, DISC, MC, V. **Amenities:** Coffee shop; indoor and outdoor pools; access to nearby health club ($10); Jacuzzi. *In room:* A/C, TV, fridge, hair dryer, Internet or Wi-Fi (free).

Where to Dine

Plimoth Plantation (p. 191) has a cafeteria and a picnic area, and occasionally schedules theme dinners. **Sam Diego's** (© **508/747-0048**), 51 Main St., is a lively Tex-Mex restaurant. **Kiskadee Coffee Company,** 18 Main St. (© **508/830-1410;** www.kiskadeecoffee.com), is a good place for a snack and a caffeine boost.

Lobster Hut ★ SEAFOOD   A busy self-service restaurant with a great view, the Lobster Hut is popular with locals and sightseers alike. Order and pick up at the counter, then head to an indoor table or out onto the deck overlooking the bay. To start, try clam chowder or lobster bisque. The seafood "rolls" (hot-dog buns with your choice of filling) are excellent. The many fried seafood options include clams, scallops, shrimp, and haddock. The menu also includes boiled and steamed seafood, burgers, chicken tenders—and lobster, of course. Beer and wine are served, but only with meals.

25 Town Wharf. ℂ **508/746-2270.** Reservations not accepted. Lunch specials (Mon–Fri until 4pm) $8–$11; main courses $7–$19; sandwiches $3–$11 (most under $8); clams and lobster market price. MC, V. Summer daily 11am–9pm; winter daily 11am–7pm. Closed Jan.

Persy's Place AMERICAN   Persy's Place is part of a small chain known for its menu, reputedly the largest in New England. Breakfast options, served all day, range from a dozen variations on eggs Benedict to a broad selection of pancakes—try Cape Cod style, with cranberries and walnuts, for a taste of local flavor. The magic here is in throwback dishes, such as baked beans (yes, for breakfast) and finnan haddie (smoked haddock cooked in cream), and such oddities as biscuits and gravy. The diner-style restaurant is a good choice for lunch, too, which is why it's often packed, especially on weekends.

35A Main St. (at Middle St.). ℂ **508/732-9876.** www.persysplace.com. Breakfast items $4–$16; lunch items $6–$16. AE, MC, V. Daily 7am–3pm.

CAPE COD

by Laura M. Reckford

Only 75 miles long, Cape Cod is a curving peninsula that encompasses miles of beaches, hundreds of freshwater ponds, more than a dozen richly historic New England villages, scores of classic clam shacks and ice-cream shops—and it's just about everyone's idea of the perfect summer vacation spot.

More than 13 million visitors flock to the Cape to enjoy summertime's nonstop carnival. In full swing, the Cape is, if anything, perhaps a bit too popular for some tastes. Connoisseurs are discovering the subtler appeal of the off season, when prices plummet along with the population. For some select travelers, the prospect of sunbathing en masse on sizzling sand can't hold a candle to a long, solitary stroll on a windswept beach with only the gulls as company. Come Labor Day, the crowds clear out—even the stragglers are gone by Columbus Day—and the whole place hibernates until Memorial Day weekend, the official start of "the season."

I've listed mostly summer rates for the accommodations in this chapter, because that's when the vast majority of travelers plan their trips, but if you decide to explore the Cape off season, you'll get the added benefit of lower prices everywhere you go.

The **Cape Cod Chamber of Commerce,** 5 Patti Page Way, exit 6 (Rte. 132) off Rte. 6, Hyannis (© **888/332-2732** or 508/862-0700; fax 508/362-2156; www.capecodchamber.org), is a clearinghouse of information.

THE UPPER CAPE

Because the Upper Cape towns are so close to Boston by car (just over an hour), they've become bedroom as well as summer communities. They are perhaps a bit more staid than those towns farther east, but they are also spared some of the fly-by-night qualities that come with a transient populace. Shops and restaurants tend to stay open year-round.

Sandwich ★★

Sandwich is both the oldest town on the Cape and the most quaint. Towering oak trees, 19th-century churches, and historic houses line its winding Main Street. A 1640 gristmill still grinds corn beside bucolic Shawme Pond. Farther east, Sandy Neck, one of the Cape's most beautiful beaches, extends out into Cape Cod Bay.

Cape Cod

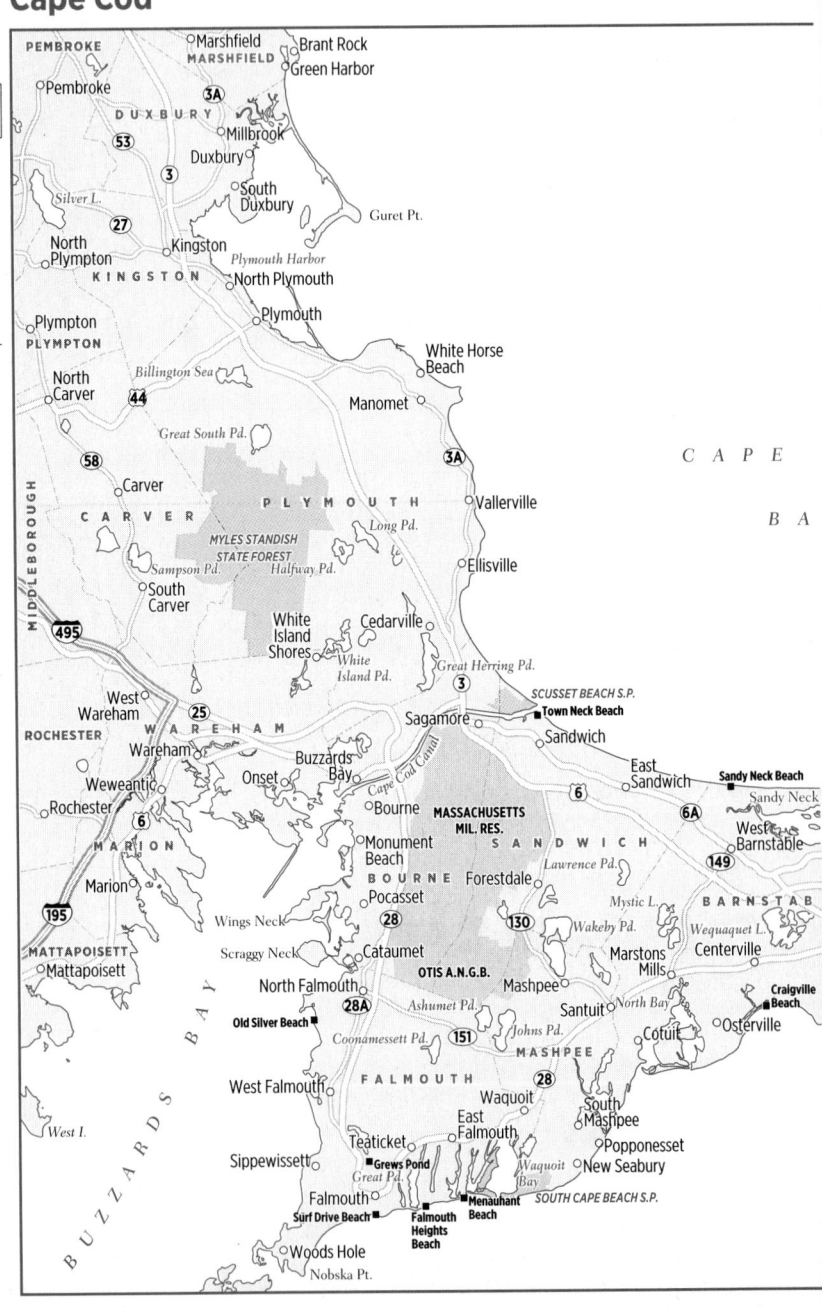

PROVINCETOWN

Race Point Beach
Race Pt.
Herring Cove Beach
Provincetown
Provincetown Har.
Long Pt.

Pilgrim L.
Head of the Meadow
Truro
Corn Hill Beach
TRURO

A T L A N T I C

O C E A N

CAPE COD NATIONAL SEASHORE

WELLFLEET
Wellfleet
Mayo Beach
Cahoon Hollow Beach
White Crest Beach
Marconi Beach
Wellfleet Harbor
Lieutenant I.
Jeremy Pt.

C O D

Y

North Eastham
EASTHAM
Eastham

Rock Harbor
Skaket Beach
East Brewster
Breakwater Beach
Paines Creek Beach
Linnells Landing Beach
Flax Pond
Brewster
Corporation Beach
Mayflower Beach
Chapin Beach
Dennis
Scargo Lake
East Dennis
6A
NICKERSON S.P.
124
South Brewster
BREWSTER
Cliff Pd.
ORLEANS
Orleans
Nauset Beach
Pilgrim Beach
South Orleans

Grays Beach
Yarmouth Port
Barnstable Har.
Barnstable
Yarmouth
YARMOUTH
DENNIS
Upper Mill Pd.
Long Pd.
134
6
39
137
28
East Harwich
Pleasant Bay
Chatham Port
North Beach
HARWICH
CHATHAM
West Harwich
Harwich
Harwich Port
Oyster Pond
Chatham
Chatham Light Beach

Barnstable Mun. Airport
132
West Yarmouth
Hyannis
28
Veterans Beach
Kalmus Beach
South Yarmouth
West Dennis Beach
West Dennis
Bass River Beach
Parker's River Beach
Seagull Beach
Dennis Port
South Dennis
West Chatham
Forest Beach
Hardings Beach
South Beach

Hyannis Port
Orrin Keyes Beach
Pt. Gammon

N A N T U C K E T

S O U N D

Monomoy I.
MONOMOY NATIONAL WILDLIFE REFUGE
Monomoy Pt.

0   5 mi
0   5 km

Sandwich's claim to fame is its prominence as the home to the nation's first glass factories in the early to mid–19th century. The town still supports a number of highly skilled glassmakers.

The town is popular with families and nature buffs who find excellent spots for hiking, biking, and canoeing. Sandwich also makes a convenient base for exploring other parts of the Cape that may offer more lively activities, such as the nightlife of Hyannis or the ocean beaches of Wellfleet.

ESSENTIALS

GETTING THERE   Cross the Cape Cod Canal on either the Bourne or Sagamore Bridge. At the Bourne Bridge rotary, take Sandwich Road along the canal; it turns into Rte. 6A as it nears Sandwich Center. If you cross the Sagamore Bridge, take exit 1 or 2, and follow Sandwich Road/Rte. 6A or Rte. 130, respectively, to Sandwich Center. Sandwich is 3 miles east of the Sagamore Bridge, 16 miles northwest of Hyannis.

VISITOR INFORMATION   The **Cape Cod Canal Region Chamber of Commerce,** 70 Main St., Buzzards Bay (© **508/759-6000;** fax 508/759-6965; www.capecodcanalchamber.org), is open year-round, daily 9am to 5pm. The chamber's **Sandwich Information Center** (© **508/833-1632**) is located on Rte. 130 (exit 2, off Rte. 6, the Mid-Cape Hwy.). In-season hours are 10am to 5pm.

BEACHES & GETTING OUTSIDE

BEACHES   For the beaches listed below, nonresident parking stickers—$90 for the length of your stay—are available at **Sandwich Town Hall Annex,** 145 Main St. (© **508/833-8012**). Note that there's no swimming allowed within the Cape Cod Canal—the currents are much too swift and dangerous.

- **Sandy Neck Beach ★★★**, off Sandy Neck Road in East Sandwich: This 6-mile stretch of silken barrier beach with low, rounded dunes is one of the Cape's most beautiful beaches; in summer, its parking lot tends to fill up early. It's also popular with endangered piping plovers—and their nemesis, off-road vehicles (ORVs). That means that ORV trails are closed for some of the summer while the chicks hatch. ORV permits ($140 per season for nonresidents) can be purchased at the gatehouse (© **508/362-8300**). ORV drivers must be equipped with such supplies as a spare tire, jack, shovel, and tire-pressure gauge. Parking costs $15 per day in season. Up to 3 days of camping in self-contained vehicles is permitted at $10 per night plus an ORV permit.

- **Town Neck Beach,** off Town Neck Road in Sandwich: A bit rocky but ruggedly pretty, this narrow beach offers a busy view of passing ships, plus restrooms and a snack bar. Parking costs $10 per day, or you can hike from town (approx. 1½ miles) via the boardwalk spanning the salt marsh.

- **Wakeby Pond,** Ryder Conservation Area, John Ewer Road (off S. Sandwich Rd. on the Mashpee border): The beach, on the Cape's largest freshwater pond, has lifeguards, restrooms, and parking ($10 per day).

BICYCLING   The **Cape Cod Canal bike path ★★★** is actually two flat 7-mile paths on each side of the canal, maintained by the U.S. Army Corps of Engineers (© **508/759-5991** for recreation hotline). For easy access to the path on the Cape side of the canal, park free at the Bourne Recreation Area, north of the Bourne Bridge, on the Cape side. You can also park free at the Sandcatcher Recreation Area at the end of Freezer Road in Sandwich. For the path on the mainland side of the canal, you can park at the **Cape Cod Canal Region Chamber of Commerce** parking lot at 70 Main St., in Buzzards Bay.

CANOEING   To explore by canoe, rent one in Falmouth (see below) and paddle around Old Sandwich Harbor, out to Sandy Neck, or through the salt-marsh maze of Scorton Creek, which leads out to Talbot Point.

FISHING   Sandwich has eight fishable ponds; for licenses, inquire at **Town Hall** in the center of town (✆ **508/888-0340**). No permit is required to fish from the banks of the Cape Cod Canal. Call the **Army Corps of Engineers** (✆ **508/759-5991**) for canal tide and fishing information.

NATURE & WILDLIFE AREAS   The **Shawme-Crowell State Forest,** off Rte. 130 in Sandwich (✆ **508/888-0351**), offers 298 campsites and 742 acres to roam. Entrance is free; parking costs $2. Camping costs $12 for Massachusetts residents; $14 for nonresidents. The **Sandwich Boardwalk** links the town and Town Neck Beach by way of salt marshes that attract many birds, including great blue herons.

The 57-acre **Green Briar Nature Center & Jam Kitchen ★**, 6 Discovery Hill Rd., off Rte. 6A (✆ **508/888-6870;** www.thorntonburgess.org), has a mile-long path crossing marsh and stands of white pine.

MUSEUMS

Heritage Museums and Gardens ★★★ ☺ ⛟   This is one of those rare museums that appeals equally to adults and children. The 76 beautifully landscaped acres are crisscrossed with walking paths and riotous with color in late spring, when the museum's famous collection of towering rhododendrons are in bloom. Scattered buildings house a wide variety of collections, from Native American artifacts to Cape Cod Baseball League memorabilia. The high point for most kids will be a ride on the 1912 carousel. There's also a replica Shaker round barn packed with gleaming antique automobiles. Outdoor summer concerts are usually held Sunday around 2pm.

Grove and Pine sts. (approx. ½ mile southwest of the town center). ✆ **508/888-3300.** www.heritage museumsandgardens.org. Admission $12 adults, $10 seniors, $6 children 6-16, free for children 5 and under. AE, DISC, MC, V. Apr-Oct Fri-Wed 10am-5pm; Thurs 9am-8pm. Closed Nov-Mar.

Sandwich Glass Museum ★★ ⛟   Even if you don't consider yourself a glass fan, make an exception for this fascinating museum, which captures the history of the town above and beyond its legendary industry. A brief video introduces Deming Jarves's brilliant 19th-century endeavor to bring glassware—a hitherto rare commodity available only to the rich—within reach of the middle classes. All went well until Midwestern factories undercut Jarves by using coal to fire their furnaces. Unable to keep up with their level of mass production, Jarves switched back to hand-blown techniques just as his workforce was ready to revolt. An excellent little gift shop stocks Sandwich glass replicas and original glassworks. In summer, volunteers demonstrate glassblowing techniques.

129 Main St. (in the center of town). ✆ **508/888-0251.** www.sandwichglassmuseum.org. Admission $5 adults, $1.25 children 6-14, free for children 5 and under. Apr-Dec daily 9:30am-5pm; Feb-Mar Wed-Sun 9:30am-4pm. Closed Jan, Thanksgiving, and Christmas.

WHERE TO STAY

Many motels line Rte. 6A in Sandwich, but the one with the best location is **Sandy Neck Motel,** at 669 Rte. 6A, East Sandwich (✆ **800/564-3992** or 508/362-3992; www.sandyneck.com), which sits at the entrance to the road leading to Sandy Neck, the best beach in these parts. Rates are $129 for a double, $199 to $299 for one- and two-room efficiencies. The motel is closed November to mid-April.

The Belfry Inne and Bistro ★★   This inn comprises three buildings in the center of Sandwich Village. The turreted 1879 rectory, called The Drew House, is a Victorian "painted lady," done up in shades of pink. The rooms are romantic, with queen-size retrofitted antique beds, a claw-foot tub (or Jacuzzi), and a scattering of fireplaces and private balconies. A casual restaurant called the Painted Lady Café is in this building. Next door is the Abbey, a former church that owner Chris Wilson has converted into six unique deluxe guest rooms, and one fine restaurant called the **Belfry Bistro** (see below). The Abbey rooms are painted vivid colors and tucked cleverly into sections of the old church. All the Abbey rooms have Jacuzzis. Mr. Wilson also owns the Village House, next door, which has eight rooms decorated in a French country style.

8 Jarves St. (in the center of town), Sandwich, MA 02563. ✆ **800/844-4542** or 508/888-8550. Fax 508/888-3922. www.belfryinn.com. 22 units (in 3 buildings). Summer $149–$315 double. Rates include full breakfast. AE, MC, V. **Amenities:** 2 restaurants (New American bistro and casual cafe). *In room:* TV, Wi-Fi (free).

The Dan'l Webster Inn and Spa ★★   This large, popular inn is a dependable bet for a comfortable stay or a hearty meal. The main building sits on the site of a Colonial tavern favored by Daniel Webster, the famous orator and Boston lawyer. Guest rooms are ample and nicely furnished with reproductions. Deluxe suites, some in nearby historic houses, offer such perks as balconies, gas fireplaces, oversize whirlpool tubs, and heated tile bathroom floors. The inn's common spaces are convivial, if bustling; the restaurant is a tour-bus lunch spot that turns out surprisingly sophisticated fare.

149 Main St. (in the center of town), Sandwich, MA 02563. ✆ **800/444-3566** or 508/888-3622. Fax 508/888-5156. www.danlwebsterinn.com. 46 units. Summer $199–$249 double; $289–$399 suite. Off-season rates include full breakfast. AE, DC, DISC, MC, V. **Amenities:** Restaurant (New American); tavern/bar; small outdoor heated pool; access to health club (2 miles away); room service; spa. *In room:* A/C, TV, hair dryer, Wi-Fi (free).

Isaiah Jones Homestead ★   Of the many B&Bs in Sandwich Center, this one is a particularly good value, though the fancier rooms tend to be more expensive (and more elegant) than those at other small B&Bs in town. The innkeepers have carefully appointed this courtly 1849 Victorian with fine antiques and reproductions. Many rooms have additional romantic touches such as fireplaces and oversized whirlpool baths. Two minisuites in the Carriage House have sitting alcoves. The room named for industrial magnate Deming Jarves boasts an inviting floral-curtained half-canopy bed and a whirlpool tub. A gourmet three-course breakfast is served daily.

165 Main St. (in the center of town), Sandwich, MA 02563. ✆ **800/526-1625** or 508/888-9115. Fax 508/888-9648. www.isaiahjones.com. 7 units. Summer $175–$275 double. Rates include full breakfast. AE, DC, DISC, MC, V. No children 11 or under. *In room:* A/C, TV/DVD, hair dryer, Wi-Fi (free), no phone.

Spring Hill Motor Lodge ★   This motel boasts all sorts of amenities, such as night-lit tennis court and a large pool. The interiors are cheerfully contemporary, the grounds beautifully landscaped. In addition to the motel rooms, there are four cottages that are light, airy, and comfortable.

351 Rte. 6A (approx. 2½ miles east of the town center), East Sandwich, MA 02537. ✆ **800/657-2514** or 508/888-1456. Fax 508/833-1556. www.springhillmotorlodge.com. 24 units; 4 cottages (shower only).

Summer $125–$165 double; $225–$275 efficiency; $185–$265 1-bedroom cottage; $235–$350 2-bedroom cottage. AE, DC, DISC, MC, V. **Amenities:** Heated outdoor pool; night-lit tennis court. *In room:* A/C, TV, fridge, Wi-Fi (free).

Wingscorton Farm Inn ★★ ☺ 👔 This Colonial farmhouse on 7 acres will delight youngsters and animal lovers of all ages. It's been a working farm since 1758 and still houses a brood of sheep, goats, dogs, cats, chickens, a pet turkey, and a potbellied pig. The paneled guest rooms have canopy beds, working fireplaces, and braided rugs. Modernists might prefer the carriage house, with its skylight-suffused loft bedroom, kitchen (with woodstove), and private deck. A private bay beach is a short walk down a country lane.

11 Wing Blvd. (off Rte. 6A, about 5 miles east of the town center), East Sandwich, MA 02537. ℂ **508/888-0534.** Fax 508/888-0545. http://wingscortonfarm.com. 5 units. Summer $225 suite; $250 carriage house. Rates include full breakfast. AE, MC, V. Pets accepted ($10 per night). *In room:* A/C, TV, fridge, no phone.

WHERE TO DINE

Aqua Grille ★ SEAFOOD Overlooking the town's picturesque marina and not-so-picturesque power plant, this place wants to be the premier spot for fish in Sandwich. The towering lobster salad, with *haricot verts,* tomato, avocado, chives, and crème fraîche, is the perfect antidote to a steamy summer night. Those with larger appetites may want to try the baby-back pork spare ribs with peach barbecue sauce, which comes with—what else?—potato salad and Boston baked beans. Ask for a table that doesn't face the power plant.

14 Gallo Rd. (next to Sandwich Marina). ℂ **508/888-8889.** www.aquagrille.com. Reservations recommended. Main courses $8–$20. AE, DC, MC, V. Apr–Oct Mon–Fri 11:30am–9pm, Sat–Sun noon–9pm; call for off-season hours.

The Bee-Hive Tavern ★ AMERICAN A cut above the rather characterless restaurants clustered along this stretch of Rte. 6A, the Bee-Hive employs atmospheric old-time touches: Green-shaded banker's lamps illuminate the dark wood booths, and vintage prints convey a clubby feel. The food is straightforward but tasty and well priced, too. Steaks, chops, and fresh fish are among the pricier choices, while burgers, sandwiches, and salads cater to lighter appetites (and wallets). At lunch, try the lobster roll, one of the Cape's best.

406 Rte. 6A (approx. ½ mile east of the town center), East Sandwich. ℂ **508/833-1184.** Main courses $7–$16. MC, V. Mon–Sat 11:30am–3pm, 5–9pm; Sun 8am–3pm and 5–9pm.

The Belfry Bistro ★★ 👔 NEW AMERICAN Sandwich's most upscale dining option is in a renovated abbey, formerly a Catholic church. The menu changes seasonally, but among the appetizers you might find a Thai crab and baby shrimp cake or mini barbecue pork empanadas, which are braised and wrapped in pastry. The entrees run from an unusual black grouper roasted in a banana leaf to the traditional grilled filet of beef over whipped potatoes with green beans. Because this restaurant hosts many weddings and other events, it is sometimes closed to the public, so be sure to call ahead. While the Belfry Bistro serves dinner only, the more casual **Painted Lady Café** next door serves lighter, less expensive fare ($8–$25), such as brie-cheese burgers and chicken potpie, from 11:30am to 9pm.

8 Jarves St. (in the center of town). ℂ **508/888-8550.** Reservations recommended. Main courses $20–$32. AE, MC, V. Feb–Dec Tues–Sat 5–10pm; call for off-season hours. Closed Jan.

The Dan'l Webster Inn ★★ AMERICAN   You have a choice of four main dining rooms—from a casual, Colonial-motif tavern to a skylight-topped conservatory fronting a splendid garden. The atmospheric Tavern at the Inn, with its own pub-style menu, is the most popular. A restaurant on this scale could probably get away with ho-hum food, but the output is on par with that of the Cape's best boutique restaurants. Try a classic dish such as the *fruits de mer* in white wine.

149 Main St. (in the center of town). © **508/888-3622.** Reservations recommended. Main courses $18–$29; Tavern menu $7–$14. AE, DC, DISC, MC, V. Daily 8am–9pm; call for off-season hours.

Marshland Restaurant on 6A 🔥 DINER   Locals have been digging this diner for 2 decades. This is home-cooked grub, slung fast and cheap. You'll gobble up the hearty breakfast and be back in time for dinner.

109 Rte. 6A. (near the intersection with Rte. 130). © **508/888-9824.** www.marshlandrestaurant.com. Most items under $10. AE, MC, V. Daily 6am–8:30pm.

Falmouth & Woods Hole ★★★

Falmouth is a classic New England town, complete with church steeples encircling the town green and a walkable and bustling Main Street. With over 32,000 year-round residents, it's the second-largest town on the Cape, after Barnstable.

Woods Hole ★★★, one of eight villages in Falmouth, has been a world-renowned oceanic research center since 1871, when the U.S. Commission of Fish and Fisheries set up a primitive seasonal collection station. Today the various scientific institutes—the National Marine Fisheries Service, the Marine Biological Laboratory, and the Woods Hole Oceanographic Institute—employ thousands of scientists. They offer a unique opportunity to get in-depth—and often hands-on—exposure to marine biology. Woods Hole is also one of the hipper communities on the Cape, with a number of restaurants, bars, and shops making crowded Water Street (don't even think of parking here in summer) a very pleasant place to stroll.

Falmouth Heights ★★★, a cluster of shingled Victorian summer houses on a bluff east of Falmouth's harbor, is as popular as it is picturesque; its narrow ribbon of beach is a magnet for all, especially families.

ESSENTIALS

GETTING THERE   After crossing the Bourne Bridge, take Rte. 28 south. Falmouth is 18 miles south of the Bourne Bridge, 20 miles southwest of Hyannis.

Falmouth's bus station near the center of town is serviced by **Bonanza Bus Lines** (59 Depot Ave.; © **508/548-7588;** www.bonanzabus.com). Daily buses to Falmouth run from Boston, Logan Airport, Providence, and New York.

GETTING AROUND   To get around Falmouth and Woods Hole (where parking in summer is impossible due to ferry traffic to Martha's Vineyard), use the **Whoosh Trolley,** which makes a circuit every 20 minutes down Falmouth's Main Street to Woods Hole. You can flag it down anywhere along the route.

The **Sea Line Shuttle** (© **800/352-7155**) connects Woods Hole and Falmouth with Hyannis year-round (except holidays). The fare ranges from $1 to $3.50, depending on distance.

VISITOR INFORMATION   Contact the **Falmouth Chamber of Commerce,** Academy Lane, Falmouth, MA 02541 (© **800/526-8532** or 508/548-8500; fax 508/548-8521; www.falmouthchamber.com).

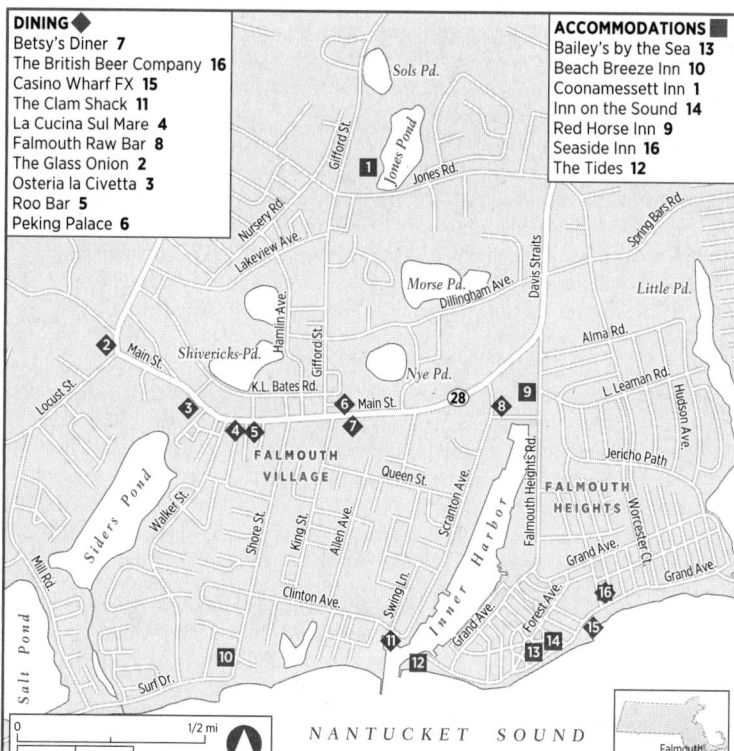

DINING◆
Betsy's Diner **7**
The British Beer Company **16**
Casino Wharf FX **15**
The Clam Shack **11**
La Cucina Sul Mare **4**
Falmouth Raw Bar **8**
The Glass Onion **2**
Osteria la Civetta **3**
Roo Bar **5**
Peking Palace **6**

ACCOMMODATIONS■
Bailey's by the Sea **13**
Beach Breeze Inn **10**
Coonamessett Inn **1**
Inn on the Sound **14**
Red Horse Inn **9**
Seaside Inn **16**
The Tides **12**

SPECIAL EVENTS

The **Falmouth Road Race** (www.falmouthroadrace.com), on the second Sunday in August, is a 7.3-mile run from the Captain Kidd Bar in Woods Hole to The British Beer Company in Falmouth Heights. It all started nearly 30 years ago when two buddies decided to race from one bar to the other. Now the race attracts 10,000 participants from all over the world. Those who want to run need to apply to a lottery in April.

BEACHES & GETTING OUTSIDE

BEACHES   While Old Silver Beach, Surf Drive Beach, and Menauhant Beach will sell a day pass, most other Falmouth public beaches require a parking sticker. Day passes to Old Silver are $20 and passes to Surf Drive and Menauhant are $10. If you're renting a cottage in the area, you can obtain a temporary beach parking sticker for $60 per week or $70 for two weeks at **Falmouth Town Hall,** 59 Town Hall Sq. (© **508/548-7611**), or at the **Surf Drive Beach Bathhouse** in season

(© **508/548-8623**). The town beaches, for which a parking fee is charged, all have lifeguards, restrooms, and concession stands. Falmouth's public shores include:

○ **Falmouth Heights Beach** ★★★, off Grand Avenue in Falmouth Heights: Once a rowdy spot, this is now primarily a family beach. Parking is sticker-only. This neighborhood supported the Cape's first summer colony, and the grand Victorian mansions still overlook the beach.

○ **Grews Pond** ★★, in Goodwill Park off Palmer Avenue in Falmouth: This freshwater pond in a large town forest stays fairly uncrowded, even in the middle of summer. While everyone else is trying to find parking at Falmouth's popular saltwater beaches, here you can park for free and wander shady paths around the pond. It has a playground, picnic tables, barbecue grills, lifeguard, and restrooms.

○ **Menauhant Beach** ★, off Central Avenue in East Falmouth: A bit off the beaten track, Menauhant is a little less mobbed than Falmouth Heights Beach and better protected from the winds. Parking costs $10.

○ **Old Silver Beach** ★★★, off Rte. 28A in North Falmouth: Western-facing (great for sunsets) and relatively calm, this warm Buzzards Bay beach is a popular, often crowded, choice. It's the chosen spot for the college crowd. Families with young children cluster on the opposite side of the street where a shallow pool formed by a sandbar is perfect for toddlers. Parking costs $20.

○ **Surf Drive Beach** ★★★, off Shore Street in Falmouth: About a half-mile from downtown, this is an easy-to-get-to choice. The tidal beach between the jetties is a shallow, calm area called "the kiddie pool." Parking is limited and costs $10.

BICYCLING   Considered a top attraction for visitors to Falmouth, the newly expanded **Shining Sea Bicycle Path** ★★★ (© **508/548-8500**) is a 12-mile mostly flat beauty skirting Vineyard Sound from North Falmouth to Woods Hole with views of cranberry bogs, farmland, ponds, and the Great Sippewissett Marsh as you head along Vineyard Sound to Woods Hole. (Unfortunately, most of the beach along this stretch is rocky.) You can park at the trail head off County Road in North Falmouth, off Old Dock Road in West Falmouth, off Depot Avenue or Locust Street in Falmouth center, or at any spot in town (parking in Woods Hole is scarce). The closest bike shop is **Corner Cycle,** at Palmer Avenue and North Main Street (© **508/540-4195**) near the Village Green, which rents hybrids for about $20 a day.

BOATING   **Patriot Party Boats,** 227 Clinton Ave. (at Scranton Ave. on the harbor), Falmouth (© **800/734-0088** or 508/548-2626; www.patriotpartyboats.com), offers scenic cruises around Vineyard Sound aboard the three-masted schooner *Liberté* ★★. Two-hour sails cost $20 to $30 for adults and $15 to $20 for children 12 and under. Also offered in July and August are 2-hour sunset cruises on the *Patriot Too.*

   Cape Cod Kayak (1270 Rte. 28A, Cataumet, just north of North Falmouth © **508/563-9377;** www.capecodkayak.com) rents kayaks and offers lessons and eco-tours. A fun kayak excursion begins at the boat ramp next to Edward's Boat Yard in Waquoit. It takes about 15 minutes paddling south down the Child's River to reach Waquoit Bay and **Washburn Island** ★★★, a protected reserve with wooded trails. Another half-hour of paddling will get you to the pristine beaches on either the east or north side of Washburn.

FISHING   Falmouth has six fishable ponds. A free guide is available from the Falmouth Chamber of Commerce. Freshwater fishing and shellfishing licenses can be obtained at **Falmouth Town Hall,** 59 Town Hall Sq. (© **508/548-7611,** ext. 219). Freshwater fishing licenses can also be obtained at **Eastman's Sport & Tackle,** 150 Main St. (© **508/548-6900**).

Surf Drive Beach is a great spot for surf-casting, once the crowds have dispersed. Other good locations are the jetties off Nobska Point in Woods Hole and Bristol Beach on Menauhant Road in East Falmouth.

To go after bigger prey, head out with a group on one of the **Patriot Party Boats** (© **800/734-0088** or 508/548-2626; www.patriotpartyboats.com), which leave twice daily in season. The clunky *Patriot Too,* with an enclosed deck, is ideal for family-style "bottom fishing" (4-hr. trips $40 adults, $25 children 11 and under; equipment provided).

NATURE & WILDLIFE AREAS Ashumet Holly and Wildlife Sanctuary ★★, operated by the Massachusetts Audubon Society at 186 Ashumet Rd., off Rte. 151 (© **508/362-1426**), is an intriguing 49-acre collection of more than 1,000 holly trees, along with over 130 species of birds and a kettle pond that's covered with a carpet of Oriental lotus blossoms in summer. The trail fee is $3 for adults and $2 for seniors and children under 16.

Near the center of Falmouth (follow Depot Rd. to the end) are the 650-acre **Beebe Woods ★★,** a treasure for hikers and dog walkers. From here, you can wend your way to the 90-acre **Peterson Farm ★★** (entrance off Woods Hole Rd.; take a right at the Quisset farm stand), with paths through woods and fields, as well as a flock of sheep and a llama grazing in a meadow. Bluebird boxes (special birdhouses for bluebirds) line the path on the way to a quiet pond.

The 2,250-acre **Waquoit Bay National Estuarine Research Reserve (WBNERR),** at 149 Waquoit Hwy. in East Falmouth (© **508/457-0495;** www.waquoitbayreserve.org), maintains a 1-mile nature trail. Also inquire about the 20-minute boat ride to **Washburn Island ★★★,** where naturalist-led guided walks are offered. The boat ride/guided walks are offered Saturday in season by reservation. Washburn Island is a unique site with many intact ecosystems, including a dense forest and a barrier beach open for exploring (and sunbathing!). Amazingly, in the middle of summer you may have this beautiful, unspoiled beach to yourself.

WATERSPORTS Falmouth is something of a sailboarding mecca, prized for its unflagging southwesterly winds. While Old Silver Beach in North Falmouth is the most popular spot for windsurfing, the sport is allowed there only prior to 9am and after 5pm. The Trunk River area on the west end of Falmouth's Surf Drive Beach and a portion of Chapoquoit Beach are the only public beaches where windsurfers are allowed during the day.

SEA SCIENCE

Woods Hole Oceanographic Institution Exhibit Center and Gift Shop

This world-class research organization—locally referred to by its acronym, WHOI (pronounced "Hooey")—is dedicated to the study of marine science. Kids might enjoy looking through microscopes at organisms or listening to sounds of marine animals on a computer. *Titanic* fans might be interested in the brief video, displays, and life-size model of the submersible that discovered the wreck. Walking tours of WHOI are offered twice a day on weekdays in July and August (reservations required; call © **508/289-2252**).

15 School St. (off Water St.), Woods Hole. ☎ **508/289-2663.** www.whoi.edu. $2 donation requested. Late May to early Sept Mon–Sat 10am–4:30pm, Sun noon–4:30pm; call for off-season hours. Closed Jan–Mar.

Woods Hole Science Aquarium ★ ☺ A little beat up after more than a century of service, this aquarium—the first such institution in the country—may not be state-of-the-art, but it's a treasure nonetheless. The displays, focusing on local waters, might make you think twice before taking a dip. Children show no hesitation, though, in getting up to their elbows in the "touch tanks." A key exhibit illuminates the effect of plastic trash on the marine environment. A state-of-the-art seal tank is located out front. There are usually two seals in rehabilitation here, and they are fed at 11am and 4pm.

Albatross St. (off the western end of Water St.), Woods Hole. ☎ **508/495-2001.** http://aquarium.nefsc. noaa.gov. Donations accepted. June–Aug Tues–Sat 11am–4pm; Sept–May Mon–Fri 11am–4pm. Adults need a picture ID to enter.

WHERE TO STAY
Moderate

Bailey's by the Sea ★ 🎒 If you love the beach, the location of this charming bed-and-breakfast, a few steps from Falmouth Heights Beach, is liable to make you swoon. Bailey's has a casual feel, with whitewashed walls and views of Vineyard Sound from all seven of the inn's rooms. Everything about this inn feels very summery, from the sheer curtains, full with breezes, the rocking chairs, even the waffle robes provided in each room. Falmouth Heights, one of the Cape's first summer communities, is a wonderful place to stroll and gaze at Victorian homes or simply walk for miles along the beach, with views of Martha's Vineyard in the distance. Two restaurants, a family-style tavern and a fine-dining establishment, are a short walk away.

321 Grand Ave., Falmouth Heights, MA 02540. ☎ **866/548-5748** or 508/548-5748. www.baileysbythe sea.com. 6 units. Summer $205–$310 double; off season $155–$235. Rates include full breakfast. MC, V. *In room:* A/C, TV, hair dryer, Wi-Fi (free).

Beach Breeze Inn ★ This inn has a great location, just steps from Surf Drive Beach and a short and pleasant stroll to Main Street, with its many shops and restaurants. Guests here beat the summer traffic blues, because with beach and town within walking distance, you never need to use your car! Rooms are sunny and spacious, with motel-style privacy; many of them have separate entrances. The inn was built in 1858 and spent many years as a run-down boardinghouse. In recent years, it has been thoroughly freshened up and is now a terrific lodging option, particularly for families.

321 Shore St. (approx. ¼ mile south of Main St.), Falmouth, MA 02540. ☎ **800/828-3255** or 508/548-1765. www.beachbreezeinn.com. 20 units. Summer $179–$289 double; $1,500–$1,700 weekly efficiencies. MC, V. **Amenities:** Unheated pool. *In room:* TV, fridge, hair dryer, Wi-Fi (free).

Coonamessett Inn ★★ A gracious inn built around the core of a 1796 homestead, the Coonamessett Inn is Falmouth's most traditional lodging choice. Set on 7 lush acres overlooking a pond, the inn is known for its comfortable rooms, which are decorated in what might be called "Cape Cod modern"—knotty pine walls jazzed up with colorful curtains, for example. The units with the best light are nos. 1 through 6 of the Village Rooms; they have large picture windows overlooking a pond. Most rooms have a separate sitting room attached with an overstuffed couch. On-site is a restaurant featuring a tavern. The buffet brunch here on Sunday draws people from all over town.

Jones Rd. and Gifford St. (approx. ½ mile north of Main St.), Falmouth, MA 02540. © **508/548-2300.** Fax 508/540-9831. www.capecodrestaurants.org. 27 units, 1 cottage. Summer $170–$250 double; $220 2-bedroom suite; $280 cottage. Rates include continental breakfast. AE, MC, V. **Amenities:** Restaurant. *In room:* A/C, TV, hair dryer.

Inn on the Sound ★★ 🗒

The ambience here is as breezy as the setting, high on a bluff beside Falmouth's premier sunning beach, with a sweeping view of Vineyard Sound from the large front deck. There's none of the usual frilly/cutesy stuff in these well-appointed guest rooms, most of which have ocean views, several with their own private decks. The focal point of the inn's living room is a handsome boulder hearth (nice for those chilly winter nights). Most guests enjoy having their breakfast, which features lots of home-baked goodies, on the front deck.

313 Grand Ave., Falmouth Heights, MA 02540. © **800/564-9668** or 508/457-9666. Fax 508/457-9631. www.innonthesound.com. 10 units (6 shower only). Summer $195–$345 double. Rates include full breakfast. AE, DISC, MC, V. No children 15 or under. *In room:* TV, hair dryer, Wi-Fi (free), no phone.

Sands of Time Motor Inn & Harbor House ★

This property, across the street from the ferry terminal for Martha's Vineyard and a short walk to the village of Woods Hole, consists of a two-story motel in front of a shingled 1879 Victorian mansion. The motel rooms feature crisp, above-average decor, plus private balconies overlooking the harbor. The rooms in the Harbor House mansion are more lavish—some with four-poster beds and working fireplaces.

549 Woods Hole Rd., Woods Hole, MA 02543. © **800/841-0114** or 508/548-6300. Fax 508/457-0160. www.sandsoftime.com. 35 units (2 with shared bathroom). Summer $150–$200 double. Rates include continental breakfast. AE, DC, DISC, MC, V. Closed mid-Nov to mid-Apr. **Amenities:** Small heated pool. *In room:* A/C, TV.

Woods Hole Inn ★★

Located in the heart of the colorful village of Woods Hole, this is the place to stay for people who want to be in the thick of it. The ferry terminal is just steps from the back door, so expect to hear the horn announcing its departure beginning at the crack of dawn. For putting up with the noise and hurly-burly of this setting, you are rewarded with beautiful views of Vineyard Sound and Martha's Vineyard from the rooms. Rooms are stylishly decorated with high-end amenities and the innkeepers are committed to staying "green." A burrito shack, called **Quick's Hole,** is in the back of the building.

28 Water St., Woods Hole, MA 02543. © **508/495-0248.** www.woodsholeinn.com. 6 units. Summer $150–$295 double. Rates include continental breakfast. MC, V. Pets accepted in 1 unit (free). Closed mid-Nov to mid-Apr. **Amenities:** Restaurant (burrito shack). *In room:* TV/DVD, Wi-Fi (free).

Inexpensive

For a basic motel with a great location, try the **Tides Motel** (© **508/548-3126**), at the west end of Grand Avenue in Falmouth Heights. The 1950s-style no-frills (no air-conditioning, no phone) motel is a good value. It sits on the beach at the head of Falmouth Harbor, facing Vineyard Sound. Rates in season are $165 to $175 for a double, $220 for a suite. The Tides is closed late October to mid-May.

The **Red Horse Inn ★**, 28 Falmouth Heights Rd., (© **508/548-0053;** www.redhorseinn.com) is a family-friendly option just a short walk from Falmouth Harbor in Falmouth Heights. The 22 rooms are priced from $175 to $275. It's closed November through March.

The **Seaside Inn,** at 263 Grand Ave., Falmouth Heights (© **800/827-1976** or 508/540-4120; www.seasideinnfalmouth.com), is a reasonably priced motel in a superb location, across the street from Falmouth Heights Beach and next to the British Beer Company, a family-style restaurant and pub. The 23 rooms with air-conditioning, TVs, and phones with free local calls are priced at $149 to $194 for a double, $194 to $319 for a deluxe room. It's open year-round.

WHERE TO DINE
Expensive
Casino Wharf FX ★ SEAFOOD   This two-story restaurant located right on Falmouth Heights Beach has a sublime location. A quibble is that the Marriot-style decor is not very Cape-y. Both levels of the restaurant have soaring ceilings and large outdoor decks set above the beach. I recommend coming here for lunch and ordering either the delicious Cape Cod Reuben (a fried cod sandwich with cheese) or yummy swordfish kabobs. Dinner is somewhat pricey, with traditional grilled seafood and steak entrees.

286 Grand Ave. (next to Falmouth Heights Beach), Falmouth Heights. © **508/540-6160.** http://casinowharf.weebly.com. Reservations accepted. Main courses $18–$40. AE, MC, V. Daily Mon-Thurs 11:30am–3pm and 5:30–10pm; Fri-Sun 8:30–11am, 11:30am–3pm, and 5–10pm; call for off-season hours.

Falmouth Raw Bar ★ SHELLFISH   If what you crave is a giant lobster roll, which consists of chunks of lobster and mayo on a big hotdog bun, this stylish bar overlooking Falmouth Inner Harbor is the place to get it. It costs $25 but is enough for two people if you throw in some chowder and appetizers. The drinks menu is about twice as long as the food menu, with frozen drinks a specialty.

56 Scranton Ave. (at the corner of Robbins Rd., next to Falmouth Inner Harbor), Falmouth.© **508/548-7729.** www.falmouthrawbar.com. Reservations not accepted. Main courses $17–$45. AE, MC, V. Daily 11:30am–10pm; call for off-season hours. Closed mid-Oct to Apr.

Fishmonger's Cafe ★ AMERICAN/MIDDLE EASTERN/THAI   This cafe jutting out into the harbor attracts local young people, scientists, and tourists for an array of imaginatively prepared dishes, with vegetarian choices a specialty. Lunch could be a tempeh burger or a regular beef version. The eclectic, changing dinner menu includes some Middle Eastern and Thai-style entrees. Regulars sit at the counter to enjoy a bowl of the fisherman's stew, while newcomers usually go for the tables by the window, where you can watch boats come and go from Eel Pond.

56 Water St. (at the Eel Pond drawbridge), Woods Hole. © **508/540-5376.** www.fishmongercafe woodshole.com. Reservations not accepted. Main courses $15–$25. AE, MC, V. Mid-June to Oct daily 8am–9pm; call for off-season hours. Closed mid-Dec to mid-Feb.

The Glass Onion ★★★ NEW AMERICAN   Taking its cues from long-vanished local fine dining establishments such as the Regatta of Falmouth, this newest restaurant in Falmouth's fine-dining scene is destined for great success. Preferred seating in this handsome establishment are the large booths along the walls. Service manages to be both big-city efficient and small-town friendly, the kind of place where the owner greets you at the door. But it's the memorable food that brings customers back. Local ingredients, such as Barnstable little neck clams and Chatham day boat scallops, highlight a menu that relies mainly on local provender, especially fresh fish. This is one of those rare restaurants where ordering is a can't-lose proposition.

37 N. Main St. (in Queens Buyway plaza), Falmouth. ☎ **508/540-3730.** www.theglassoniondining.com. Reservations for parties of 6 or more only. Main courses $16–$33. AE, MC, V. Tues–Sat 5-10pm.

La Cucina Sul Mare ★★ ITALIAN   Locals and tourists alike line up outside this popular Main Street restaurant, craving its hearty Italian fare. The interior features cheerful murals and a tin ceiling, and large picture windows overlook Main Street. Chef/owner Mark Ciflone's signature dishes include classic Italian specialties such as lasagna, braised lamb shanks, *osso buco*, lobster *fra diablo* over linguine, *zuppa de pesce*, rigatoni a la vodka, chicken Parmesan, and veal piccata, among others. The desserts here are homemade and truly delicious.

237 Main St., Falmouth. ☎ **508/548-5600.** www.lacucinasulmare.com. Reservations not accepted, but you can call a half-hour before arrival to put your name on the list. Main courses $15–$25. AE, MC, V. Tues–Sun 11:30am-3pm and 5-10pm.

Osteria La Civetta ★★★ 📖 NORTHERN ITALIAN   Run by the Toselli family of Bologna, Italy, this restaurant features European-style dining and service. Courses are ordered a la carte. Meat is not served on the same plate as pasta; even vegetables are ordered separately. Because diners are expected to have multiple courses, servings are smaller than at the average American restaurant. But diners can share courses for a moderately priced fine-dining experience. The food here is exquisite. Homemade pasta makes the lasagna al la bolognese a great choice. Another favorite is the handmade *tagliatelle al funghi e tartufo nero,* which has mushrooms, porcini, and black truffle oil. Desserts are also made on-site—my favorite is the chocolate salami; don't ask, just order and eat.

133 Main St. (across from the post office) Falmouth. ☎ **508/540-1616.** www.osterialacivetta.com. Reservations recommended. Main courses $15–$25. MC, V. Wed–Sun 11:30am-2pm and 6-10pm.

Phusion Grille ★ NEW AMERICAN/ASIAN   Because of its innovative menu and terrific location on Eel Pond in Woods Hole, Phusion Grille has the potential to be one of Falmouth's best restaurants. But there tends to be a different chef every summer, and the food can be a bit inconsistent; sometimes it is wonderful, sometimes underwhelming. The interior is all blond wood and Asian screens, but nothing blocks the water views out the wraparound floor-to-ceiling windows. The menu changes nightly depending on the catch of the day, but keep an eye out for the bouillabaisse and the sautéed sea scallops tossed with artichokes and a lobster sherry cream sauce. There's also a sushi bar.

71 Water St., Woods Hole. ☎ **508/457-3100.** www.phusiongrille.com. Reservations not accepted. Main courses $21–$27. AE, MC, V. Tues–Sun 11am-2pm and 5-10pm; call for off-season hours. Closed mid-Oct to Apr.

RooBar ★ NEW AMERICAN   In a town with a surfeit of restaurants, RooBar has consistently good food and service and the hippest atmosphere. It has an intriguing menu with lots of creative dishes; you can have a three-course gourmet meal with such items as Thai wontons and snapper pie, which is braised snapper in a puff pastry. Or you can have a simple, inexpensive meal: just a cheeseburger or wood-oven grilled pizza with unusual toppings such as scallops and prosciutto. The arty decor of this stylish bistro features hand-blown glass lamps over the bar and metal sconce sculptures on the walls. They don't take reservations, but if you call a half-hour ahead, you can put your name on the waiting list.

285 Main St. (at Cahoon Ct.). ℂ **508/548-8600.** www.theroobar.com. Reservations not accepted. Main courses $11–$26. AE, MC, V. Daily 5–10pm; call for off-season hours.

Moderate

Chapoquoit Grill ★★ NEW AMERICAN   The only dining spot in sleepy West Falmouth, this little roadside bistro has Californian aspirations: wood-grilled slabs of fish accompanied by trendy salsas, and crispy personal pizzas delivered straight from the brick oven. People drive here from miles around for the consistently good, flavorful food. A no-reservations policy means long waits nightly in season and weekends year-round.

410 Rte. 28A, West Falmouth. ℂ **508/540-7794.** www.chapoquoitgrill.com. Reservations not accepted. Main courses $10–$18. MC, V. Daily 5–10pm.

Landfall ★ AMERICAN   A waterfront location steps from the ferry to Martha's Vineyard, terrific decor, and good service make this restaurant a fun choice when you are in Woods Hole, though note that Landfall also has steep prices. Besides the usual fish and pasta dishes, there's "light" fare—the best choice—which includes burgers and fish and chips. This is a good place to bring the kids; a children's menu comes with games and crayons. Or come for a drink at the half-dory bar to enjoy this massive wooden building constructed of salvage.

Luscombe Ave. (½ block south of Water St.), Woods Hole. ℂ **508/548-1758.** www.woodshole.com/landfall. Reservations recommended. Main courses $7–$26. AE, MC, V. Mid-May to Sept daily 11:30am–9pm; call for off-season hours. Closed late Nov to mid-Apr.

Peking Palace ★★ CHINESE/JAPANESE/THAI   This popular restaurant serves three regional Chinese cuisines (Cantonese, Mandarin, and Szechuan), as well as Japanese, Thai, and Polynesian food. The decor is modern and sophisticated. Sip a fanciful drink to give yourself time to take in the menu, and be sure to solicit your server's opinion: That's how I encountered some heavenly, spicy chilled squid.

452 Main St. (a few blocks east of the center of town), Falmouth. ℂ **508/540-8204.** www.peking palacefalmouth.com. Reservations for parties of 6 or more only. Main courses $5–$15. AE, MC, V. Daily 11:30am–midnight.

Inexpensive

Betsy's Diner ★ ☺ 🍴 AMERICAN   This is hearty food like your mother used to make, if your mother was a variation of June Cleaver. The menu features turkey dinner, breakfast all day, and homemade pies. Some say the fried clams here are the best in town. Kids love that each red vinyl booth is equipped with its own jukebox with retro hits.

457 Main St. (in the center of town). ℂ **508/540-0060.** Reservations not accepted. All items under $11. AE, MC, V. Mon–Sat 6am–9pm, Sun 6am–2pm; call for off-season hours.

The British Beer Company ★ PUB FARE/PIZZA   The view is great at this faux British pub across the street from Falmouth Heights beach. The best choices are the fish and chips, burgers, and pizzas. The lobster bisque is also good and has won local awards. Of course, they serve beer—23 draft selections, including Guinness and John Courage, as well as bottled brews.

263 Grand Ave. (across from the beach), Falmouth Heights. ℂ **508/540-9600.** www.britishbeer.com/local/falmouth. Reservations not accepted. All items under $15. AE, DC, DISC, MC, V. Daily noon–10pm.

Dining in Nearby Mashpee

Starfish Restaurant ★★ (© 508/539-0025; www.capecodrestaurants.org) is an upscale but moderately priced bistro with a contemporary and hip atmosphere with curving walls and cozy sitting areas. The menu, which concentrates on seafood, varies with the seasons; main courses run between $20 and $30. Starfish Restaurant is at 20 Joy St. (off Rte. 28, in South Cape Village plaza across from Mashpee Commons), Mashpee, and is open year-round every evening 4:30pm to closing and for Sunday brunch. Also appealing in the large shopping plaza known as Mashpee Commons are **Wicked Fire Kissed Pizza** at 36 South St. (© 508/477-7422; www.wicked restaurant.com), which has excellent gourmet pizza and an urban swank atmosphere; and **Trevi Café and Wine Bar** at 25 Market St. (© 508/477-0055; www.trevicafe.com), a European-style wine bar.

The Clam Shack ★ ☺ SEAFOOD   This classic clam shack at the head of Falmouth harbor offers steaming plates of fried seafood that you carry to a picnic table inside, outside, or up on the roof deck. It's basic fare, but the fish is fresh and you can't beat the view. Kids will love eating on the roof-top deck.

227 Clinton Ave. (off Scranton Ave., about 1 mile south of Main St.). © **508/540-7758.** Reservations not accepted. Main courses $5–$15. No credit cards. Daily 11:30am–7:45pm. Closed early Sept to late May.

Moonakis Cafe ★★ DINER   This place serves the best breakfast in town, with a large list of special omelets and pancakes every morning, which you can wolf down at a table or sitting on a stool at the counter. Many people rave about the homemade corned-beef hash. If you're lucky, owner Paul Rifkin will wander over to your table and strike up a conversation, or even better, a debate. Lunch highlights are the quahog chowder and pastrami sandwich.

460 Waquoit Hwy./Rte. 28, Waquoit. © **508/457-9630.** Reservations not accepted. All items under $10. MC, V. Mon–Sat 7am–1:30pm, Sun 7am–noon.

FALMOUTH AFTER DARK

The Boathouse (© **508/548-7800;** www.boathousefalmouth.com), at 88 Scranton Ave. on Falmouth Inner Harbor, features live bands in season, from classic rock to jazz, and dancing is popular here. God knows whom you'll meet in the rough-and-tumble old **Cap'n Kidd ★**, 77 Water St., in Woods Hole (© **508/548-9206;** www.the captainkidd.com): maybe a lobsterwoman, maybe a Nobel Prize winner. You'll find good grub, too. Everyone heads to **Liam Maguire's Irish Pub ★**, on 273 Main St. in Falmouth (© **508/548-0285;** www.liammaguire.com), for a taste of the Emerald Isle. There's live music on weekends year-round, often by Liam himself. **Grumpy's,** at 29 Locust St. (© **508/540-3930;** www.grumpyspub.net), is a good old bar/shack with live music (rock, blues, and jazz) Thursday to Saturday nights. Cover is $2 to $10.

THE MID-CAPE

Visitors who want to be centrally located on Cape Cod choose the Mid-Cape, which is just over an hour from Boston (without traffic), an easy (less than an hour) drive to the Outer Cape, and an hour ferry ride from Nantucket. This is the Cape's most populous area and also the prime location for its cheapest motels, which line Rte. 28 from Hyannis to Dennis.

Hyannis is the Cape's unofficial capital. Rte. 132 is a sprawling concrete jungle of strip malls and chain stores. But nearby is Hyannis's bustling Main Street and harbor, not to mention the famous summer community of Hyannisport. Hyannis is the area of the Cape perhaps most affected by the Kennedy mystique of the 1960s, which had the unfortunate side effect of spurring heedless development over the ensuing decades—a period during which the Cape's year-round population doubled to more than 200,000. The summer population on Cape Cod is about three times that, and you'd swear every single person had daily errands to run in Hyannis. And yet this overrun town still has plenty of pockets of charm, especially the waterfront area and Main Street.

The real beauty of the Mid-Cape lies in its smaller places: old-money hideaways, such as **Osterville** ★ to the west, and charming villages, such as **Barnstable Village, West Barnstable** ★★, and **Yarmouth Port** ★★, which can be found along the **Old King's Highway (Rte. 6A)** ★★★ on the northern bay side of the Cape. A drive along this winding two-lane road reveals the early architectural history of the region, from humble Colonial saltboxes to ostentatious captains' mansions. Scores of intriguing antiques shops subtly compete to draw a closer look, and each village seems a throwback to a kinder, gentler era.

Hyannis & Environs ★

Hectic Hyannis is the commercial center and transportation hub of the Cape, with the large Cape Cod Mall and busy Barnstable Municipal Airport. It also has a diverse selection of restaurants, bars, and nightclubs. But if you were to confine your visit to the major roads of this one town, you'd get a warped view of the Cape. Along routes 132 and 28, you could be visiting Anywhere, USA: The roads are lined with the standard chain stores and mired with maddening traffic.

Hyannis's hotels and motels have more beds at better prices than anywhere else on the Cape, and several of them near the harbor have great water views and are good choices if you happen to have missed the last ferry out to Nantucket. For a quieter vacation, I recommend heading due north to Barnstable Village, where you'll find myriad charming B&Bs along the scenic Old King's Highway/Rte. 6A. (See "Barnstable Village & Environs," below.) Once you're settled, you can visit Hyannis to sample some of the Cape's best restaurants and nightlife.

ESSENTIALS

GETTING THERE   After crossing the Sagamore bridge, head east on Rte. 6 or 6A. Rte. 6A passes through Barnstable Village; Rte. 132 (exit 6 off Rte. 6) leads to Hyannis. You can also fly into Hyannis, and there is good bus service from Boston and New York.

VISITOR INFORMATION   Contact the **Hyannis Area Chamber of Commerce,** 397 Main St., Hyannis, MA 02601 (© **877/HYANNIS** [492-6647] or 508/775-2201; fax 508/790-1970; www.hyannis.com).

BEACHES & GETTING OUTSIDE

BEACHES   Most of the Nantucket Sound beaches are fairly protected and offer little in the way of surf. Parking costs $15 a day, usually payable at the lot; for a week-long parking sticker ($50), visit the Recreation Department at the **Hyannis Youth &**

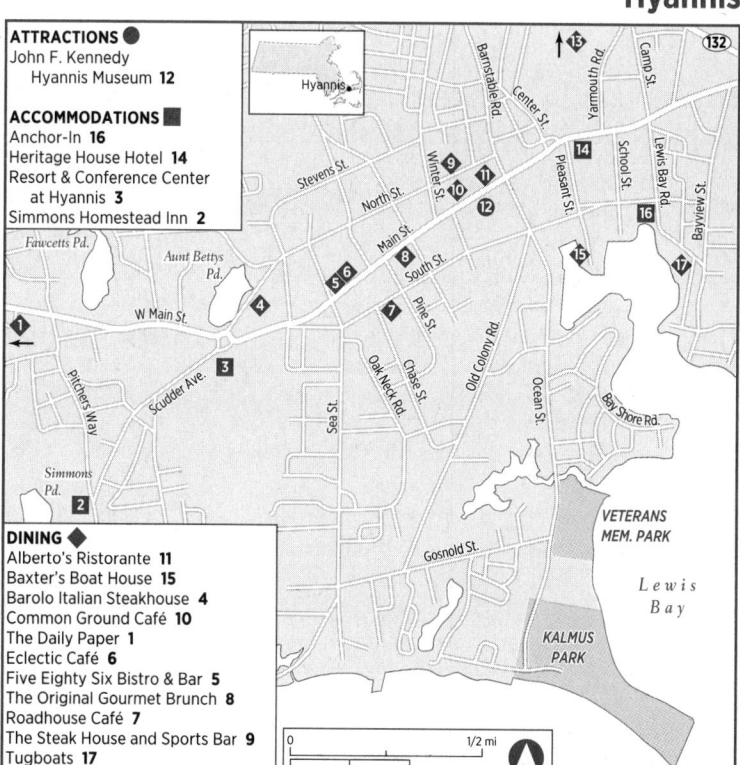

ATTRACTIONS ●
John F. Kennedy
Hyannis Museum **12**

ACCOMMODATIONS ■
Anchor-In **16**
Heritage House Hotel **14**
Resort & Conference Center
at Hyannis **3**
Simmons Homestead Inn **2**

DINING ◆
Alberto's Ristorante **11**
Baxter's Boat House **15**
Barolo Italian Steakhouse **4**
Common Ground Café **10**
The Daily Paper **1**
Eclectic Café **6**
Five Eighty Six Bistro & Bar **5**
The Original Gourmet Brunch **8**
Roadhouse Café **7**
The Steak House and Sports Bar **9**
Tugboats **17**
Wianno Grille **13**

Community Center, 141 Bassett Lane (☎ **508/790-6345**). This impressive new year-round community center also offers two year-round ice skating rinks, two basketball courts, a skateboard park, a cafe, and a teen center. Day passes can be purchased for $5, or you can buy an annual pass for $40. Public skating costs $7 adults, $5 kids, and $5 for skate rentals.

○ **Craigville Beach** ★★★, off Craigville Beach Road in Centerville: This broad expanse of sand has lifeguards and restrooms. A destination for the bronzed and buffed, it's known as "Muscle Beach." A short walk up a hill takes you to Craigville Village, a former Methodist camp meeting site with Carpenter Gothic–style cottages.

○ **Kalmus Beach** ★★, off Gosnold Street in Hyannisport: This 800-foot spit of sand stretching toward the mouth of the harbor makes an ideal launching site for windsurfers. The surf is tame, the slope shallow, and the conditions ideal for young kids. There are lifeguards, a snack bar, and restrooms.

○ **Orrin Keyes Beach** ★★, also known as Sea Street Beach, located at the end of Sea Street in Hyannis: This little beach at the end of a residential road is popular with families.

o **Veterans Beach,** off Ocean Street in Hyannis: A small stretch of harborside sand adjoining the John F. Kennedy Memorial, this spot is not tops for swimming. Parking is usually easy, though, and it's walkable from town. A snack bar, restrooms, and playground are on site.

FISHING Among the charter boats berthed in Barnstable Harbor is the 36-foot *Drifter* (© 508/398-2061), offering half- and full-day trips. **Hy-Line Cruises** offers seasonal sonar-aided "bottom" or blues fishing on boats leaving from its Ocean Street dock in Hyannis (© 508/790-0696). **Helen H Deep-Sea Fishing** at 137 Pleasant St., Hyannis (© 508/790-0660), offers year-round expeditions aboard a 100-foot boat with a heated cabin and full galley.

GOLF The **Hyannis Golf Club,** Rte. 132 (© 508/362-2606), offers a 46-station driving range and an 18-hole championship course. Smaller but scenic is the 9-hole **Cotuit High Ground Country Club,** 31 Crockers Neck Rd., Cotuit (© 508/428-9863).

WATERSPORTS **Eastern Mountain Sports,** 1513 Iyannough Rd./Rte. 132 (© 508/362-8690; www.ems.com), offers rental kayaks—as well as tents and sleeping bags—and sponsors free clinics and walks, including a full-moon hike. Kayaks rent for about $50 a day.

SIGHTSEEING TOURS BY "STEAMER"

Hy-Line Harbor Cruises For a fun and informative introduction to the harbor and its residents, take a leisurely 1-hour tour aboard one of Hy-Line's 1911 steamer replicas. The Sunday 3pm "Ice Cream Float" includes a design-your-own Ben & Jerry's sundae.

Ocean St. Dock, Hyannis. © **508/790-0696.** www.hy-linecruises.com. Tickets $16 adults, free to $8 children 12 and under. Parking is $5 per car. Late June to Sept departures daily; call for schedule. Closed Nov to mid-Apr.

THE KENNEDY LEGACY

Don't even bother trying to track down the Kennedy Compound in Hyannisport; it's effectively screened from view. You'll see more at the following museum. Or, if you absolutely must satisfy your curiosity, take a harbor cruise (see "Sightseeing Tours by 'Steamer,'" above).

John F. Kennedy Hyannis Museum This display of blown-up photographs captures the Kennedys during the glory days from 1934 to 1963. A special display added in 2009 is devoted to the legacy of Senator Edward M. Kennedy, who died in August of that year.

397 Main St., Hyannis. © **508/790-3077.** http://jfkhyannismuseum.org. Admission $5 adults, $2.50 children 10–16 and seniors. Mid-Apr to Oct Mon–Sat 9am–5pm; Sun and holidays noon–5pm; last admission at 3:30pm; call for off-season hours.

SHOPPING

Hyannis is undoubtedly the commercial center of the Cape, and you can find most anything you could want on Main Street. Art enthusiasts will want to check out the seven **Harbor Your Arts** artist shacks (www.harboryourarts.com) along the harbor off Ocean Street and several more artist studios on **Pearl Street.** The first Thursday of every month in summer is an **arts stroll** with gallery openings from 6 to 8pm. Head to the wealthy enclaves west of Hyannis, such as Osterville, and in West

Barnstable and Barnstable Village along the Old King's Highway (Rte. 6A) to the north, to locate more unusual shops and galleries.

Two very hip clothing stores just off Main Street in Hyannis are **Shaunna Clothier** (478 South St., Hyannis; © **508/771-8009;** www.shaunnaclothier.net), which specializes in bold and very modern outfits and accessories, and **Shift Boutique** (535 South St., Hyannis; © **508/775-2652;** www.shiftboutique.com), an eco-conscious boutique.

For one-of-a-kind gifts, look no farther than **Red Fish, Blue Fish,** 374 Main St., Hyannis (© **508/775-8700;** http://redfishbluefish.com), across from Barnstable Town Hall.

Books By The Sea, 846 Main St., Osterville (© **508/420-9400**), is a wonderful independent bookstore specializing in local authors and books about the region.

Kindred's Antiques and Folk Art, 845 Main St., Osterville (© **508/420-7390;** www.kindredsantiquesandfolkart.com), offers an appealing selection of gifts with crafts by local artists.

Tao Water Art Gallery, 1989 Rte. 6A, West Barnstable (© **508/375-0428;** www.taowatergallery.com), is a former garage converted into a very Zen-like space. It features paintings by Chinese artists as well as museum reproductions of Chinese antiques and jade.

It's worth a special trip to see the salvaged antique lumber that is turned into cupboards, tables, and chairs at **West Barnstable Tables,** 2454 Meetinghouse Way (off Rte. 149, near the intersection of Rte. 6A), West Barnstable (© **508/362-2676;** www.westbarnstabletables.com).

WHERE TO STAY

Hyannis has a variety of large, generic but convenient hotels and motels.

The **Anchor-In,** 1 South St. (alongside Hyannis Harbor), Hyannis (© **508/775-0357;** www.anchorinn.com), stands above other hotels by virtue of its harborfront location and attention to detail by the property's hosts/owners. The 43 rooms are divided into traditional, deluxe, and executive (the latter with large decks and Jacuzzis) categories. Many have water-view balconies, and there is an outdoor heated pool. Summer rates including continental breakfast are $219 to $225 traditional, $239 to $289 deluxe, and $389 to $429 executive.

Heritage House Hotel, 259 Main St., Hyannis (© **800/352-7189** or 508/775-7000; www.heritagehousehotel.com), is ideally located in the center of town, walking distance from restaurants, shops, and the ferries to Nantucket and Martha's Vineyard. The hotel has an indoor and an outdoor pool, hot tub and saunas, and a restaurant/lounge on-site. The 130 rooms are priced at $129 on weekdays and $149 on weekends for double occupancy.

If you prefer more amenities, there's the **Resort & Conference Center at Hyannis,** at the West End Circle just off Main Street (© **866/828-8259;** www.capecodresort andconference.com). Summer rates are $200 to $230 double. Out the back door is an 18-hole, par-3 executive golf course. The resort lays claim to indoor and outdoor pools, two restaurants, and a fitness center.

A great choice for families is the **Cape Codder Resort and Spa,** 1225 Iyannough Rd./Rte. 132 (at the intersection of Bearse's Way), Hyannis (© **888/297-2200** or 508/771-3000; www.capecodderresort.com). It features two restaurants (Grand Cru Wine Bar and Hearth 'n Kettle for families), and a spa (massage and other body treatments). Kids love the indoor wave pool with two water slides. Summer rates for the 261 rooms are $198 for a double, $350 to $382 for a suite.

Long Dell Inn ★★ 🗡 This handsome 1850s former sea captain's home, which is on the National Register of Historic Places, has been welcoming guests for 80 years. The current innkeepers are the types with real know-how, serving up three-course gourmet breakfasts and providing great advice on things to do. Rooms are comfortable and charmingly decorated in classic New England style; two have private decks and one has a minifridge and microwave. But perhaps the best part about the inn is its location, just a short walk to Craigville Beach, one of the best beaches on Cape Cod.

436 S. Main St., Centerville, MA 02632. © **508/775-2750.** www.longdellinn.com. 7 units. Summer $155–$180 double. Rates include full breakfast. AE, DISC, MC, V. *In room:* A/C, TV, hair dryer, Wi-Fi (free).

Simmons Homestead Inn ★★ 🎁 The first thing passersby notice is all the classic red sports cars: 50 at last count. A former ad exec and race-car driver, innkeeper Bill Putman likes to collect. He's made his sports-car collection into a small museum, open to the public, called **Toad Hall** (© **508/778-4934;** www.toadhall cars.com) after *The Wind in the Willows.* Admission is $8 adults, $4 children; free for guests. Each room in this rambling 1820s house has an animal theme represented by stuffed toys, sculptures, even needlepoint and wallpaper. Guests who prefer privacy may book the spiffily updated "servants' quarters," a spacious wing with its own deck. This is the kind of place where you'll find everyone milling around the hearth sipping complimentary wine while they compare notes and nail down dinner plans. To help his guests plan their days, Putman has typed up extensive notes on day trips, bike routes, and his own quirky restaurant reviews.

288 Scudder Ave. (approx. ¼ mile west of the West End rotary), Hyannisport, MA 02647. © **800/637-1649** or 508/778-4999. Fax 508/790-1342. www.simmonshomesteadinn.com. 14 units. Summer $180–$240 double; $300 2-bedroom suite. Rates include full breakfast. AE, DISC, MC, V. Dogs accepted ($25 fee). **Amenities:** Bikes; billiards parlor. *In room:* A/C ($10/night charge), hair dryer, Wi-Fi (free), no phone.

WHERE TO DINE IN HYANNIS, CENTERVILLE & COTUIT
Expensive

Alberto's Ristorante ★★ ITALIAN What makes this place a sure bet is consistency. You always know you'll get a great meal here. Owner/chef Felisberto Barreiro's most popular dishes are his treatments of lobster, rack of lamb, and beef tenderloin. Hand-cut pasta is also a specialty, including the ultrarich seafood ravioli cloaked in saffron-cream sauce.

360 Main St., Hyannis. © **508/778-1770.** www.albertos.net. Reservations recommended. Main courses $14–$27. AE, DC, DISC, MC, V. Daily 11:30am–9:30pm.

Barolo Italian Steakhouse ★★ NORTHERN ITALIAN Under new ownership in 2010, this restaurant is one of the best in town. Located inside a brick office complex, this place does everything right, from offering flavored extra-virgin olive oil for dunking the crusty bread to getting those pastas perfectly al dente. Entrees include a number of tempting veal choices, as well as such favorites as *Linguine al Frutti di Mare,* with littlenecks, mussels, shrimp, and calamari. The desserts are baked on premises.

1 Financial Place (297 North St., just off the West End rotary), Hyannis. © **508/778-4200.** www.barolo italiansteakhouse.com. Reservations recommended. Main courses $10–$27. AE, DC, MC, V. June–Sept Sun–Thurs 4:30–10pm, Fri–Sat 4:30–11pm; call for off-season hours.

Eclectic Cafe ★★ 📷 NEW AMERICAN   This small restaurant hidden down an alley off Hyannis's Main Street is creating quite a buzz. The setting is intimate, with a cozy dining room, a small bar, and seating on the outdoor patio. Be adventurous when ordering. If the striped bass with chutney is on the menu, go for it (it's award-winning). Otherwise, look for the halibut stuffed with horseradish butter.

606 Main St. (in the west end of town), Hyannis. 📞 **508/771-7187.** http://eclecticcafecapecod.com. Reservations recommended. Main courses $19–$28. AE, DISC, MC, V. Apr–Oct daily 5–9:30pm.

Five Eighty Six Bistro and Bar ★★ BISTRO   For a hopping bar scene and good eats, this is a solid choice. Your best bet on the small menu is the selection of wood-fire-grilled gourmet pizzas, though the menu also includes standard bistro fare, such as steak frites, as well as pasta, meat, and seafood dishes. In season on the weekends, live music starts at 9:30pm.

586 Main St., Hyannis. 📞 **508/778-6515.** www.fiveeightysixbistro.com. Reservations recommended. Main courses $13–$24. AE, DC, MC, V. Daily 5–9:30pm. Bar until 1am.

Naked Oyster Bistro and Raw Bar ★★ NEW AMERICAN   Overlook the fact that this fun bistro is located in an office complex and enjoy the experience. The specialty here is fresh local seafood, and oyster fans will be fascinated by the selection of "dressed oysters," from the traditional Rockefeller to a more exotic baked *oishi* with wasabi and soy. On the menu are spicy options like sautéed Thai shrimp and blackened Cajun swordfish, as well as hearty dishes like grilled filet mignon with garlic mashed potatoes. Portions are large and service is professional and cheerful. On weeknights, a young-professionals scene lines up at the long mahogany bar, and some say the bartenders serve the best martinis in town.

20 Independence Dr., Hyannis (off Rt. 132 at Park Place). 📞 **508/778-6500.** www.nakedoyster.com. Reservations recommended. Main courses $14–$24. AE, MC, V. Apr–Oct Tues–Sat 11:30am–9:30pm, Sun 2–8pm.

The Regatta of Cotuit ★★★ NEW AMERICAN   Under chef/owner Weldon Fizell, this remains one of the best restaurants on Cape Cod. In addition to fine-dining cuisine in the Federal-era rooms of this 1790 house, there is a less expensive "tap room" menu and a more casual bar room. The food and service are always top-notch here. Specials might include roasted buffalo tenderloin with blackberry Madeira sauce served with braised fresh greens and a Stilton sage bread pudding.

4631 Rte. 28 (near the intersection of Rte. 130), Cotuit. 📞 **508/428-5715.** www.regattarestaurant.com. Reservations recommended. Main courses $24–$34; tap room menu $10–$27. AE, MC, V. Apr–Dec daily 5–10pm; Jan–Mar Wed–Sun 5–10pm.

Roadhouse Café ★★ AMERICAN/NORTHERN ITALIAN   This is neither a roadhouse nor a cafe, but it is a solid entry in the Hyannis dining scene. The menu is split between American standards and real Italian cooking. Among the appetizers are beef carpaccio with fresh-shaved Parmesan, and vine-ripened tomatoes and buffalo mozzarella drizzled with balsamic vinaigrette. The vinaigrette also makes a tasty marinade for native swordfish headed for the grill. A less expensive, lighter-fare menu, including what some have called "the best burger in the world," is served in the snazzy bistro in back, which also features live jazz Monday nights (see "Hyannis & Environs After Dark," below).

488 South St. (off Main St., near the West End rotary), Hyannis. 📞 **508/775-2386.** www.roadhouse cafe.com. Reservations recommended. Main courses $15–$26. AE, DC, DISC, MC, V. Daily 4–10:30pm.

The Steak House and Sports Bar ★ STEAKHOUSE   One of the few places in town where you can count on getting a good steak, the Steak House has an upscale sports bar-type atmosphere with 32 high-def TVs. The appetizer menu is loaded with hearty fare like ribs, and you can also order big, juicy burgers and pastrami sandwiches. The steak menu is all about the cut: porterhouse, filet mignon, T-bone, sirloin. After you choose your cut, you order your potato (fried, baked, mashed, garlic) and vegetable.

72 North St., Hyannis. ℂ **508/775-7100.** www.steakhousecapecod.com. Reservations recommended. Main courses $10–$27. AE, DC, MC, V. Daily 4:30–11pm; call for off-season hours.

Moderate

Tugboats ★ ☺ AMERICAN   Yet another harborside perch for munching and ogling, this one's especially appealing. Forget fancy dining and chow down on blackened-swordfish bites (topping a Caesar salad, perhaps) or lobster fritters. Among the desserts is a Key lime pie purportedly lifted straight from Papa's of Key West.

21 Arlington St. (at the Hyannis Marina, off Willow St.), Hyannis. ℂ **508/775-6433.** www.capecod restaurants.com. Reservations not accepted. Main courses $11–$18. AE, DC, DISC, MC, V. Late May to Oct daily 11:30am–10:30pm; Apr to mid-May Tues–Sun 11:30am–10:30pm. Closed Nov–Mar.

Inexpensive

Baxter's Boat House ★ ☺ 🍴 SEAFOOD   A shingled shack on a jetty jutting out into the harbor, Baxter's caters to the boating crowd with fried clams and fish virtually any way you like it, served on paper plates at picnic tables.

177 Pleasant St. (near the Steamship Authority ferry), Hyannis. ℂ **508/775-7040.** www.baxterscapecod. com. Main courses $8–$14. AE, MC, V. Late May to early Sept Mon–Sat 11:30am–10pm, Sun 11:30am–9pm; mid-Apr to mid-May and mid-Sept to mid-Oct Thurs–Sun 11:30am–9pm. Closed mid-Oct to early Apr.

Centerville Pie Company ★ 🏛 AMERICAN   Located on busy Rte. 28 across the street from the Bell Tower Mall is a breakfast and lunch diner that doubles as the number one place in the region to get pies: apple, blueberry, Tollhouse, chicken potpie, and Guinness beef pies—all homemade. The place achieved 15 minutes (at least) of fame when Oprah discovered the pies while in town for Eunice Kennedy's funeral in August 2009. It's been non-stop busy here since then.

1671 Falmouth Rd./Rte. 28, Centerville. ℂ **774/470-1406.** http://centervillepies.com. Most items under $10. MC, V. Daily 8am–2pm.

Common Ground Cafe ★ 🍴 AMERICAN   They serve really good sandwiches here at this New Age-y cafe run by a commune. The barn-board walls and wide-board floors surround alcoves with private booths containing amorphous tree-stump tables. But enough about atmosphere; this place makes the best iced tea on Cape Cod (the house blend—a mixture of mint teas and lemon). Besides yummy sandwiches, you can order delicious salads, and the burrito with turkey is a winner.

420 Main St., Hyannis. ℂ **508/778-8390.** Most items under $10. AE, DC, DISC, MC, V. Mon–Thurs 10am– 9pm; Fri 10am–3pm.

The Daily Paper ★ ☺ 🍴 DINER   The newest diner in town has all the expected accoutrements, like red banquets and a long diner counter with plenty of swivel stools, but you'll also find excellent grub here, including what one diner called "the best toast I've ever had." Breakfast is served to 11:30am Monday through Saturday and all day on Sunday. There is also a kids' menu.

644 West Main St., Hyannis. ℂ **508/790-8800.** www.dailypapercapecod.com. Most items under $10. MC, V. Mon–Sat 6am–2pm; Sun 7am–1pm.

The Original Gourmet Brunch ★ 🎁 AMERICAN   Though the name feels very 1970s, this classic breakfast joint hearkens back to the 1950s, when small, quirky family-owned restaurants were all that Cape Cod had to offer. When you travel the narrow red-brick path off Main Street into this humble low-ceilinged establishment, you may first notice the oddly slanted floors. Next you'll see the walls covered with autographed photos of celebrities who have rubbed elbows with owner Joe Cotellessa, the man who probably seated you. The menu offers over 100 combinations of omelets, from peanut butter and jelly to bacon and asparagus. You can also order Belgian waffles, quiche, and award-winning chili.

517 Main St., Hyannis. 🕿 **508/771-2558.** Reservations not accepted. All items under $11. MC, V. Daily 7am–2pm.

HYANNIS & ENVIRONS AFTER DARK

From July to early September, try to catch a show at the **Cape Cod Melody Tent ★★**, West End rotary, Hyannis (🕿 **508/775-9100**). Built as a summer theater in 1950, this billowy big top proved even better suited to variety shows. A nonprofit venture since 1990, the Melody Tent has hosted the major performers of the past 50 years, from jazz greats to comedians and crooners to rockers. The tent offers children's theater every Wednesday at 11am.

For a hip hangout for grown-ups (Hyannis nightlife tends to attract mostly 20-somethings), check out **Island Merchant** (302 Main St., Hyannis; 🕿 **508/771-1337;** www.theislandmerchant.com), where there is nightly entertainment, whether DJ or live—blues, rock, funk, or soul. You can order great "island-influenced" sandwiches (think smoked pulled pork) and desserts like Key lime pie. Island Merchant is open Wednesday to Monday 4pm to 1am. There's no cover.

Embargo (453 Main St., Hyannis; 🕿 **508/771-9700;** capecodbar.com), the new hot spot in Hyannis, specializes in martinis and tapas. This is a popular place for happy hour, which takes place from 4:30 to 6pm nightly. On Tuesday, tapas are half-price all night. Dinner at Embargo is served 4:30 to 11pm daily. There's live music Tuesday and Thursday, and a DJ on Friday and Saturday nights. Embargo is open year-round, and there's no cover.

The congenial **Baxter's Boat House,** 177 Pleasant St. (see "Where to Dine," above), Hyannis (🕿 **508/775-7040**), with low-key blues piano, draws an attractive crowd. And a good place for after-dinner entertainment is **Roadhouse Café ★**, 488 South St. (see "Where to Dine," above), Hyannis (🕿 **508/775-2386**), a dark-paneled bar that stocks 48 boutique beers. Insiders show up Monday nights to hear local jazz great Dave McKenna.

The cramped dance floor makes for instant camaraderie at **Harry's ★★**, 350 Stevens St. (at the corner of Main St.), Hyannis (🕿 **508/778-4188**), which features live blues and rockabilly nightly in season, and about 5 nights a week the rest of the year. The cover is $3 to $4 Thursday through Saturday.

Barnstable Village & Environs ★★

Just a couple of miles from Hyannis, the bucolic village of Barnstable houses the county courthouse and government offices for the region. In this peaceful setting are some of the most charming B&Bs around. The bay area along historic Rte. 6A, the Old King's Highway, unfolds in a blur of greenery and well-kept Colonial houses.

BEACHES & GETTING OUTSIDE

BEACHES Barnstable's primary bay beach is **Sandy Neck,** accessed through East Sandwich (see "The Upper Cape," earlier in this chapter).

CANOEING You can rent a canoe from **Eastern Mountain Sports** (see "Watersports," under "Hyannis & Environs," earlier in this chapter) and paddle around Scorton Creek, Sandy Neck, and Barnstable Harbor.

WHERE TO STAY

Ashley Manor Inn ★ A lovely country inn along the Old King's Highway, this 1699 mansion retains many of its original features, including a hearth with beehive oven and wide-board floors, many of them brightened with Nantucket-style splatter paint. The rooms, all but one with working fireplace, are spacious and inviting. A deluxe unit has a separate entrance, whirlpool bath, and canopy bed. The 2-acre property includes a Har-Tru tennis court. Breakfast on the brick patio is worth waking up for.

3660 Rte. 6A (just east of Hyannis Rd.), Barnstable, MA 02630. ✆ **888/535-2246** or 508/362-8044. Fax 508/362-9927. www.ashleymanor.net. 6 units. Summer $175 double; $235 suite. Rates include full breakfast. AE, DISC, MC, V. **Amenities:** Bikes; Har-Tru tennis court. In room: A/C, hair dryer, Wi-Fi (free).

Beechwood Inn ★★ 👔 Look for a butterscotch-colored 1853 Queen Anne Victorian all but enshrouded in weeping beech trees. Admirers of late-19th-century decor are in for a treat: The interior is dark with a red-velvet parlor and a tin-ceilinged dining room. Two of the upstairs bedrooms embody distinctive period styles from the 1860s and 1880s. Each affords a distant view of the bay. Rooms range from quite spacious (Lilac) to romantically snug (Garret).

2839 Rte. 6A (about 1½ miles east of Rte. 132), Barnstable, MA 02630. ✆ **800/609-6618** or 508/362-6618. Fax 508/362-0298. www.beechwoodinn.com. 6 units (2 with shower only). Summer $185–$210 double. Rates include full breakfast. AE, DISC, MC, V. In room: A/C, TV/VCR, fridge, hair dryer, Wi-Fi (free), no phone.

Lamb and Lion Inn ★ This is an unusual property: part B&B, part motel. From the roadside, it's one of those charming old Cape Cod cottages (ca. 1740) along the Old King's Highway. Inside it's a motel-like space with units encircling a pool and hot tub. The rooms are all individually decorated, and six rooms have kitchenettes. All rooms in the main inn building are air-conditioned. The multilevel barn suite, with three loft-type bedrooms, is a funky historic space (built in 1740), filled with rustic nooks and crannies.

2504 Main St. (Rte. 6A), Barnstable, MA 02630. ✆ **800/909-6923** or 508/362-6823. Fax 508/362-0227. www.lambandlion.com. 10 units (4 with shower only). Summer $189–$275 double. Rates include continental breakfast. MC, V. Well-behaved pets accepted (40-lb. limit; $25 per night; free after 4 nights). **Amenities:** Jacuzzi; outdoor solar-heated pool. In room: A/C, TV/DVD, Wi-Fi (free).

WHERE TO DINE

Barnstable Restaurant and Tavern ★★ NEW AMERICAN/PUB Talk about atmosphere: This 200-year-old former stagecoach stop has it in spades. But it is also a place for the kind of high-quality dining you might not expect at a "ye olde pub." Chef Rob Calderone has put together a menu of sophisticated options such as roast lamb with mustard sauce, roast duck with orange liqueur sauce, and sole piccata. A raw bar spotlights local oysters and clams. Families looking for a reasonably priced meal will be pleased by the prices for burgers, sandwiches, and fried seafood. On sunny days, sitting outside on the terrace across the street from the old granite courthouse is a great option, particularly for Sunday brunch.

3176 Main St./Rte 6A (in the center of town), Barnstable Village. © **508/362-2355.** www.barnstable restaurant.com. Main courses $9–$25. AE, DC, MC, V. Daily 11:30am–9pm.

Dolphin Restaurant ★★ NEW AMERICAN Never mind the corny decor in what looks like just another run-of-the-mill eatery. The finesse is found in the menu, where, amid the more typical fried fish, you'll find such delicacies as Chilean sea bass with roasted corn salsa and lime vinaigrette, and roast duck served with the glaze of the evening, perhaps mango.

3250 Rte. 6A (in the center of town), Barnstable. © **508/362-6610.** www.dolphinrestaurantcapecod. Main courses $17–$23. AE, MC, V. May–Oct Mon–Sat 11:30am–3pm and 5–9:30pm, Sun 5–9:30pm. Nov–Apr 5–9pm.

Mattakeese Wharf ★ SEAFOOD This place, with great views and average food, is always packed; don't even bother on summer weekends. The outdoor seating fills up first, and no wonder, with Sandy Neck sunsets to marvel over. The bouillabaisse is always good, and you can't go wrong if you stick to the varied combinations of pasta, seafood, and sauce—from Alfredo to *fra diablo.* There's live piano music most nights in season.

271 Mill Way (approx. ½ mile north of Rte. 6A), Barnstable. © **508/362-4511.** www.matakeese.com. Reservations recommended. Main courses $14–$28. AE, DC, DISC, MC, V. Mid-May to mid-Oct daily 11:30am–10pm; call for off-season hours. Closed mid-Oct to mid-May.

Yarmouth ★★

Yarmouth represents the Cape at its best—and its worst. **Yarmouth Port ★★**, on Cape Cod Bay, is an enchanting village, whereas the sound-side villages of West and South Yarmouth are a lesson in unbridled development run amuck. This section of Rte. 28 is a nightmarish gauntlet of mostly tacky accommodations and attractions.

ESSENTIALS

GETTING THERE After crossing the Sagamore bridge, head east on Rte. 6 or 6A. The section of Rte. 6A north of Rte. 6's exit 7 passes through the village of Yarmouth Port. The villages of West Yarmouth, Bass River, and South Yarmouth are located along Rte. 28, east of Hyannis; to reach them from Rte. 6, take exit 7 (Yarmouth Rd.) or exit 8 (Station St.) south.

VISITOR INFORMATION Contact the **Yarmouth Area Chamber of Commerce,** 657 Rte. 28, West Yarmouth, MA 02673 (© **800/732-1008** or 508/778-1008; fax 508/778-5114; www.yarmouthcapecod.com).

BEACHES & GETTING OUTSIDE

BEACHES Yarmouth boasts 11 saltwater and 2 pond beaches open to the public. The body-per-square-yard ratio can be pretty intense along the sound, but so is the social scene, and no one seems to mind. The beachside parking lots charge $12 to $15 a day, with weeklong stickers going for $45.

o **Bass River Beach ★**, off South Shore Drive in Bass River (South Yarmouth): At the mouth of the largest tidal river on the eastern seaboard, this sound beach offers restroom facilities and a snack bar, plus a wheelchair-accessible fishing pier.

The beaches along the south shore (Nantucket Sound) tend to be clean and sandy with comfortable water temps, but they can also be crowded.

○ **Grays Beach,** off Center Street in Yarmouth Port: This isn't much of a beach, but tame waters make this tiny spit of dark sand good for young children. It adjoins the Callery–Darling Conservation Area with a 2.5-mile trail. The Bass Hole boardwalk offers one of the most scenic walks in the Mid-Cape. Parking is free, and there's a picnic area.

○ **Parker's River Beach,** off South Shore Drive in Bass River: The usual amenities are available, such as restrooms and a snack bar, plus there's a gazebo for the sun-shy.

○ **Seagull Beach** ★, off South Sea Avenue in West Yarmouth: Rolling dunes, a boardwalk, and all the necessary facilities, like restrooms and a snack bar, attract a young crowd. Bring bug spray, though: Greenhead flies get the munchies in July.

FISHING Of the five fishing ponds in the Yarmouth area, Long Pond near South Yarmouth is known for its largemouth bass and pickerel; for details and a license (shellfishing is another option), visit **Town Hall,** at 1146 Rte. 28 in South Yarmouth (© **508/398-2231**), or **Riverview Bait and Tackle,** at 1273 Rte. 28 in South Yarmouth (© **508/394-1036**). Full-season licenses for out-of-state residents cost $39. You can cast for striped bass and bluefish off the pier at Bass River Beach (see "Beaches," above).

NATURE & WILDLIFE AREAS For a pleasant stroll, follow the 2 miles of trails maintained by the **Historical Society of Old Yarmouth.** Park behind the post office. The in-season trail fee (50¢ adults, 25¢ children) includes a trail guide. Your path will cross the 1873 Kelley Chapel, said to have been built by a Quaker grandfather to comfort his daughter after the death of her child.

MUSEUMS

The Edward Gorey House ★★ 🎁 The Cape's newest attraction is a museum devoted to the life and works of whimsically mischievous illustrator Edward Gorey, whose best-known work may be the animated opening to the television series *Mystery!* on PBS. He was also the author of many illustrated books, including *The Doubtful Guest* and *The Gashlycrumb Tinies*. Gorey died in the spring of 2000, and his home on the Yarmouth Port Common off Rte. 6A (the Old Kings Hwy.) has been converted into an intimate museum displaying original artworks, photographs, and first editions from his career as an author, playwright, illustrator, and costume and set designer. Gorey's passion for animals is also a focus of the collection.

8 Strawberry Lane (off Rte. 6A, on the Common), Yarmouth Port. © **508/362-3909.** www.edward goreyhouse.org. Admission $5 adults, $3 students and seniors, $2 children 6–12, free for children 5 and under. Wed–Sat 11am–4pm, Sun noon–4pm. Closed Feb.

Winslow Crocker House ★★ The only property on the Cape currently preserved by the prestigious Society for the Preservation of New England Antiquities, this house, built around 1780, deserves every honor. Not only is it a lovely example of the shingled Georgian style, but it's also packed with outstanding antiques collected in the 1930s by Mary Thacher, a descendant of the town's first land grantee. Anthony Thacher and his family had a rougher crossing than most: Their ship foundered off Cape Ann in 1635, and though their four children drowned, Thacher and his wife were able to make it to shore, clinging to the family cradle. You'll come across a 1690 replica in the parlor.

250 Rte. 6A (approx. ½ mile east of the town center), Yarmouth Port. ℂ **617/227-3957,** ext. 256. www. spnea.org. Admission $4 adults, $4 seniors, $2.50 children 6–12, free to Yarmouth Port residents and SPNEA members. June–Oct 1st Sat each month, tours hourly 11am–5pm (last tour at 4pm). Closed Nov–May.

SHOPPING

Driving Rte. 6A, the Old King's Highway, in Yarmouth Port, you'll pass a number of antiques stores and shops for the home. The most colorful bookshop on the Cape is **Parnassus Books,** 220 Rte. 6A, Yarmouth Port (ℂ **508/362-6420;** www.parnassus books.com), housed in an 1858 Swedenborgian church. New stock, including the Cape-related reissues published by Parnassus Imprints, is offered alongside the older treasures. The outdoor racks, maintained on an honor system, are open 24 hours a day.

WHERE TO STAY

There are so many hotels and motels lining Rte. 28 and along the shore in West and South Yarmouth that it can be hard to make sense of the choices. For those staying on Rte. 28, the town runs frequent beach shuttles in season. Families looking for a reasonably priced beach vacation may want to consider one of the following options, all near or on the beach.

The attractive 101-unit white clapboard **Tidewater Motor Lodge,** 135 Main St. (Rte. 28), West Yarmouth (ℂ **800/338-6322** or 508/775-6322; www.tidewater-capecod.com), has indoor and outdoor pools. Double rates go for $140 to $160 in summer. The 114-unit **Clarion Inn,** 1199 Main St. (Rte. 28), South Yarmouth (ℂ **800/527-0359** or 508/394-7600; www.clarioncapecod.com), has a game room and indoor and outdoor heated pools. Summer rates are $169 to $189 for a double room.

Captain Farris House ★★ Sumptuous is the only way to describe this 1845 inn, improbably set a block off bustling Rte. 28. Fine antiques and striking contemporary touches elevate the interiors beyond the average B&B decor. Some suites are apartment-size, with fireplaces and whirlpool tubs. Welcoming touches include chocolates, fresh flowers, and plush robes. Next door, the Elisha Jenkins House contains an additional suite with its own deck.

308 Old Main St. (just west of the Bass River Bridge), Bass River, MA 02664-4530. ℂ **800/350-9477** or 508/760-2818. Fax 508/398-1262. www.captainfarris.com. 10 units (1 with shower only). Summer $175–$215 double; $225 suite. Rates include full breakfast. AE, DISC, MC, V. *In room:* A/C, TV/VCR, hair dryer, Wi-Fi (free).

Red Jacket Beach Resort ★★ ☺ Of the huge resort motels lining Nantucket Sound in South Yarmouth, Red Jacket has the best location. It's at the end of the road and borders Parker's River on the west, so sunsets are particularly fine. Families who want all the fixings—including an ice-cream shop and a putting green—will find them, though the atmosphere can be a bit impersonal. All rooms have a balcony or private porch.

1 S. Shore Dr. (P.O. Box 88), South Yarmouth, MA 02664. ℂ **800/672-0500** or 508/398-6941. Fax 508/398-1214. www.redjacketresorts.com. 170 units, 14 cottages. Summer $285–$450 double; $550–$1,025 cottages ($3,000–$5,500 weekly). MC, V. Closed Nov to mid-Apr. **Amenities:** Restaurant; bar/lounge; children's program (Mon–Fri July–Aug); concierge; exercise room; Jacuzzi; indoor and outdoor heated pools; sauna; spa; tennis court; watersports equipment rental. *In room:* A/C, TV/VCR, fridge, hair dryer, Wi-Fi (free).

WHERE TO DINE

At **Hallett's**, 139 Rte. 6A, Yarmouth Port (📞 **508/362-3362**), an 1889 drugstore, you can get a float from the original marble soda fountain.

Expensive

Lyric ★★ MEDITERRANEAN This fairly new establishment strives to deliver a more sophisticated cuisine that's a cut above most of the New England-y fare you'll find around these parts. While the exterior is a modest 18th-century Cape, the contemporary interior features a stylish bar area and cozy smaller rooms lined with banquets. Highlights here are the establishment's own foie gras; the potato and leek bisque topped with a scallop, and the half lobster over homemade pasta. All entrees are served with organic vegetables. The wine list offers reasonably priced choices and a number of options by the glass. A singer and piano player add to the evening ambience.

43 Main St./Rte. 6A (near the Cummaquid border), Yarmouth Port. 📞 **508/362-3501.** www.lyriccape cod.com. Reservations recommended. Main courses $18–$34. AE, MC, V. Thurs–Sat 11:30am–2:30pm; Thurs–Tues 4:30–9:30pm; Sun 11:30am–3pm.

Inaho ★★ 🍴 JAPANESE What better application of the Cape's oceanic bounty than fresh-off-the-boat sushi? From the front, Inaho is a typical Cape Cod cottage, but park in the back so you can enter through the Japanese garden. The decor is minimalist with traditional shoji screens and crisp navy-and-white banners softened by tranquil music and service. On chilly days, opt for the tempura or a steaming bowl of shabu-shabu.

157 Main St./Rte. 6A (in the village center), Yarmouth Port. 📞 **508/362-5522.** www.inahocapecod. com. Reservations recommended. Main courses $13–$23; sushi pieces and rolls $3–$7. MC, V. Tues–Sun 5–10pm; call for off-season hours.

Old Yarmouth Inn NEW ENGLAND If a traditional Cape Cod atmosphere is what you are looking for, you can't do much better than this old stagecoach inn serving Yankee basics like prime rib and baked scrod. The food is fresh and hearty and the preparations are tasty. There's also a lighter-fare menu. One of the most requested dishes is the deluxe lobster roll, with big chunks of fresh lobster. The Sunday brunch, a combination buffet and a la carte meal, is popular. This place can be crowded on weekends in season.

223 Rte. 6A (in the center of Yarmouth Port). 📞 **508/362-9962.** www.oldyarmouthinn.com. Reservations recommended. Main courses $14–$25. AE, DC, DISC, MC, V. June–Oct Tues–Sat 11:30am–2:30pm, Sun 10am–1:30pm, daily 4:30–9pm; call for off-season hours.

Dennis ★★

In Dennis, as in Yarmouth, virtually all the good stuff—pretty drives, inviting shops, and restaurants with real personality—is in the north, along Rte. 6A. Rte. 28, on the other hand, is chockablock with generic motels and strip malls.

ESSENTIALS

GETTING THERE After crossing the Sagamore Bridge, head east on Rte. 6 or 6A. Rte. 6A passes through the villages of Dennis and East Dennis (which can also be reached via northbound Rte. 134 from exit 9 off Rte. 6). Rte. 134 South leads to South Dennis; if you follow Rte. 134 all the way to Rte. 28, the village of West Dennis is a couple of miles to your west, and Dennis Port a couple of miles east. If you're coming by plane, you will fly into Hyannis.

VISITOR INFORMATION Contact the **Dennis Chamber of Commerce,** 242 Swan River Rd., West Dennis, MA 02670 (© **800/243-9920** or 508/398-3568; www.dennischamber.com).

BEACHES & RECREATIONAL PURSUITS

BEACHES Dennis harbors more than a dozen saltwater and two freshwater beaches open to nonresidents. The bay beaches are charming and a big hit with families. The beaches on the Sound tend to be packed wall-to-wall with families, but the parking lots are usually not too crowded because many beachgoers stay within walking distance. The lots charge $15 to $20 per day; for a 1-week permit ($60), visit **Town Hall** on Main Street in South Dennis (© **508/394-8300**).

o **Chapin Beach ★★**, off Rte. 6A in Dennis: Surrounded by dunes, this is a nice, long bay beach with occasional boulders. No lifeguard is on duty, but there are restrooms.

o **Corporation Beach ★★**, off Rte. 6A in Dennis: This bay beach boasts a wheelchair-accessible boardwalk, lifeguards, snack bar, restrooms, and a children's play area.

o **Mayflower Beach ★★**, off Rte. 6A in Dennis: This 1,200-foot bay beach has the necessary amenities, plus an accessible boardwalk. The tide pools attract lots of children.

o **Scargo Lake,** a large kettle-hole pond (formed by a melting fragment of a glacier) has two pleasant beaches: Scargo Beach, accessible right off Rte. 6A; and Princess Beach, with restrooms and a picnic area, located off Scargo Hill Road.

o **West Dennis Beach ★★**, off Rte. 28 in West Dennis: This long (half-mile) but narrow beach along the Sound has lifeguards, a playground, a snack bar, restrooms, and a special kite-flying area. The eastern end is reserved for residents; in any case, the western end tends to be less packed.

BICYCLING The 25-mile **Cape Cod Rail Trail ★★★** (© **508/896-3491**) starts here, on Rte. 134, a half-mile south of Rte. 6, exit 9. Once a Penn Central track, this paved bikeway extends all the way to Wellfleet (with a few on-road lapses), passing through woods, marshes, and dunes. At the trail head is **Bob's Bike Shop,** 430 Rte. 134, South Dennis (© **508/760-4723**), which rents bikes and in-line skates and does repairs. Rates are $10 for a couple of hours and up to $22 for the full day. Another bike path runs along Old Bass Road, 3.5 miles north to Rte. 6A.

FISHING Fishing is allowed in Fresh Pond and Scargo Lake; for a license (shellfishing is also permitted), visit **Town Hall,** on Main Street in South Dennis (© **508/394-8300**), or **Riverview Bait and Tackle,** at 1273 Rte. 28 in South Yarmouth (© **508/394-1036**). Plenty of people drop a line off the Bass River Bridge along Rte. 28 in West Dennis. Several charter boats, including the *Albatross* (© **508/385-3244**), operate out of the Northside Marina in East Dennis's Sesuit Harbor.

NATURE & WILDLIFE AREAS Behind the town hall parking lot on Main Street in South Dennis, a half-mile walk along the **Indian Lands Conservation Trail** leads to the Bass River, where blue herons and kingfishers often take shelter. Dirt roads off South Street in East Dennis, beyond the Quivet Cemetery, lead to Crow's Pasture, a patchwork of marshes and dunes bordering the bay; this circular trail is about a 2.5-mile round-trip.

Theater Especially for Kids at The Cape Playhouse

If the kids get sick of all the miscellaneous go-cart and minigolf concessions on Rte. 28, take them to a show. On Friday mornings in season, the **Cape Playhouse** ★★ (© 508/385-3911; www.capeplayhouse.com), 820 Rte. 6A, Dennis, hosts visiting companies that mount theater geared toward children 4 and up. Shows are at 9:30 and 11:30am, and at only $9, tickets go fast.

MUSEUMS

Cape Cod Museum of Art ★★   Part of the prettily landscaped Cape Playhouse complex, this museum has done a great job of acquiring hundreds of works by area artists dating back to the early 20th century.

60 Hope Lane (off Rte. 6A in the center of town). © 508/385-4477. www.cmfa.org. Admission $8 adults, free for children 17 and under, admission by donation Wed 10am–1pm and Thurs 5–8:30pm. MC, V. Mon–Sat 10am–5pm (Thurs until 8:30pm); Sun noon–5pm.

SHOPPING

Dennis Port has a growing cluster of flea market–style antiques shops, but you may want to save your time and money for the better shops along Rte. 6A, where you'll also find fine contemporary crafts.

More than 136 dealers stock the co-op **Antiques Center of Cape Cod,** 243 Rte. 6A, about 1 mile south of Dennis Village center, Dennis (© **508/385-6400;** www.antiquescenterofcapecod.com); it's the largest such enterprise on the Cape.

Dennis along Rte. 6A has become a magnet for interesting small galleries. Among the finest is **Scargo Stoneware Pottery and Art Gallery,** 30 Dr. Lord's Rd. S. (off Rte. 6A, about 1 mile east of the town center), Dennis (© **508/385-3894;** www.scargopottery.com).

WHERE TO STAY

Corsair & Cross Rip Resort Motels ★ ☺   Of the many family-oriented motels lining this part of Nantucket Sound, these two neighbors are among the nicest, with fresh contemporary decor, two beach-view pools, and their own chunk of sand. As a rainy-day backup, there are an indoor pool, a game room, and a toddler playroom equipped with toys.

41 Chase Ave. (off Depot St., 1 mile southeast of Rte. 28), Dennis Port, MA 02639. © **800/201-1072** or 508/398-2279. Fax 508/760-6681. www.corsaircrossrip.com. 47 units. Summer $225–$300 double. Special packages and family weekly rates available. AE, MC, V. Closed mid-Oct to Apr. **Amenities:** Jacuzzi; 2 outdoor pools; indoor pool. *In room:* A/C, TV w/HBO, fax, fridge, hair dryer, Wi-Fi (free).

Isaiah Hall B&B Inn ★★   This inn's location on a quiet side street in a residential neighborhood bodes well for a good night's sleep, but it's also just a short walk to restaurants, entertainment options, and Corporation Beach. Breakfasts are served at the long plank table that dominates the 1857 country kitchen. Room styles range from 1940s knotty pine to spacious and spiffy.

152 Whig St. (1 block northwest of the Cape Playhouse), Dennis, MA 02638. © **800/736-0160** or 508/385-9928. Fax 508/385-5879. www.isaiahhallinn.com. 10 units (5 with shower only). Summer $150–$199 double; $375 suite. Rates include full breakfast. AE, DISC, MC, V. Closed mid-Oct to late Apr. No children 6 or under. *In room:* A/C, TV/VCR, hair dryer, Wi-Fi (free).

Lighthouse Inn ★★ ☺ Set on placid West Dennis Beach on Nantucket Sound, this resort has been welcoming families for over 60 years. In 1938, Everett Stone acquired a decommissioned 1855 lighthouse and built an inn and a 9-acre cottage colony around it. With amusements such as miniature golf and shuffleboard right on the premises, as well as a heated outdoor pool and tennis courts, there's plenty to do. The rooms aren't what you'd call fancy, but some have great views. Lunch is served on the deck overlooking Nantucket Sound, a delightful setting in which to enjoy a club sandwich. **The Sand Bar,** a classic bar with cabaret-style entertainment, serves as the on-site nightspot.

1 Lighthouse Inn Rd. (off Lower County Rd., ½ mile south of Rte. 28), West Dennis, MA 02670. ℂ **508/398-2244.** Fax 508/398-5658. www.lighthouseinn.com. 44 units, 24 cottages. Summer $255–$280 double; $500–$600 2-bedroom cottage; $543–$624 3-bedroom cottage. MC, V. Rates include full breakfast and all gratuities. Closed mid-Oct to mid-May. **Amenities:** 2 restaurants (large dining room, pool snack bar); bar; children's program (July–Aug); outdoor heated pool; outdoor tennis court. *In room:* A/C, TV, fridge, hair dryer, Wi-Fi (free).

WHERE TO DINE

For a time-travel treat, visit **Sundae School** ★, 381 Lower County Rd., at Sea Street, about a half-mile south of Rte. 28, Dennis Port (ℂ **508/394-9122;** www. sundaeschool.com). The spacious barn has been retrofitted with a turn-of-the-20th-century marble soda fountain and other artifacts from the golden age of ice cream.

Expensive

Blue Moon Bistro ★★ MEDITERRANEAN Beautiful presentations of innovative cuisine are the hallmarks at this Dennis Village venue, one of the newer eateries in the Cape's fine-dining roster. The restaurant's deep blue ceiling and dark wood floors contribute to the warm and inviting atmosphere; crisp, white tablecloths hint at the elegant dining to come. Chef/owner Peter Hyde, who was trained in Europe, gives a twist to traditional recipes. Instead of a crab cake, his is a crab and cod cake with spicy red peppers. His Mediterranean fish soup includes chorizo for added pizzazz. A couple of vegetarian options are always on the menu in addition to fish and meat entrees, which include the luscious grilled beef tenderloin wrapped in house-smoked bacon. Don't miss the house-made desserts.

605 Main St./Rte 6A (in the center of town), Dennis Village. ℂ **508/385-7100.** www.bluemoonbistro. net. Reservations recommended. Main courses $16–$30. AE, MC, V. June to late Aug Wed–Sat 11:30am–3pm and 4:30–11pm, Tues and Sun 5–9:30pm; Apr–May and late Aug to Nov Wed–Sun 4–11pm. Closed Dec–Mar.

Gracie's Table ★ SPANISH/TAPAS Just steps from the Cape Playhouse and Cape Cinema, Gracie's Table offers something different on Cape Cod: Spanish-style dining. Preparations by chef/owner Ann Austin are inspired by cuisine from the Basque region as well as southwest France. While there are plenty of full meals to choose from, the specialty here is tapas, the Spanish term for small unusual dishes. The best way to enjoy tapas is for each diner to choose several smaller dishes and share the different tastes with dining companions. Tapas choices include hot lobster roll, sushi style; potato and chorizo tortilla; and tuna carpaccio with horseradish sorbet. The dining room is sleek and sophisticated, and is staffed by professional servers, pleased to recommend their favorite tapas.

800 Main St./Rte 6A (at Theatre Marketplace in front of the Cape Playhouse complex), Dennis Village. © **508/385-5600.** www.graciestablecapecod.com. Reservations recommended. Tapas $5–$15; main courses $15–$30. AE, MC, V. Daily 5–9pm; call for off-season hours.

The Ocean House New American Bistro and Bar ★★ 🍴 NEW AMERI-CAN   This restaurant set on the beach overlooking Nantucket Sound has long had a stellar reputation, and now it's better than ever. There's a buzz around the creative cuisine served here, making this oceanfront restaurant a must-visit location. One appealing thing about the Ocean House is that you can come for a multicourse fine-dining meal or just nibble on some appetizers. Favorites are the lemongrass-battered gray sole and the grilled beef tenderloin with Maytag blue cheese. With the dining room's large arches framing the beach beyond, this is a wonderful place to spend the evening. A special $25 three-course fall dinner is a boon for bargain hunters.

3 Chase Ave. (at Depot St., on the beach), Dennis Port. © **508/394-0700.** www.oceanhouserestaurant. com. Reservations strongly recommended. Main courses $18–$34. MC, V. June–Sept Tues–Sun 5–10pm; call for off-season hours. Closed Jan to mid-Mar.

The Red Pheasant Inn ★★ CONTEMPORARY AMERICAN   An enduring Cape favorite since 1977, this handsome space—an 18th-century barn-turned-chandlery—has managed not only to keep pace with trends, but also to remain a front-runner. Popular dishes include roast rack of lamb, sole meunière, and, in the fall, game specials like venison. Two massive brick fireplaces tend to be the focal point in the off season. In fine weather, you'll want to sit outside in the lovely shade garden.

905 Main St. (approx. ½ mile east of the town center). © **508/385-2133.** www.redpheasantinn.com. Reservations required. Main courses $18–$30. DISC, MC, V. Apr–Dec daily 5–9pm; Jan–Mar Wed–Sun 5–9pm.

Moderate

Gina's by the Sea ★★ ITALIAN   A landmark amid Dennis's "Little Italy" beach community since 1938, this intimate restaurant specializes in traditional Italian comfort food. Save room for Mrs. Riley's Chocolate Rum Cake, made daily by the owner's mother. This popular place fills up fast, so if you want to eat before 8:30pm, arrive before 5:30pm.

134 Taunton Ave. (approx. 1½ miles northwest of Rte. 6A; turn north across from the Public Market and follow the signs). © **508/385-3213.** www.ginasbythesea.com. Reservations not accepted. Main courses $10–$23. AE, MC, V. June to late Aug daily 5–10pm; Apr–May and late Aug to Nov Thurs–Sun 5–10pm. Closed Dec–Mar.

Norabella ★★ SOUTHERN ITALIAN   This charming chef-owned establishment is a slice of Olde Cape Cod. It's a tiny hole-in-the-wall shack that you would drive right by if we didn't tell you about it. Chef Jeff Wilson's specialty is authentic Italian—similar to what you might find in Boston's North End—but without the overwhelming garlic. The menu includes such favorites as penne Bolognese and veal Milanese. This is also the type of place where the chef pokes his head out of the kitchen and asks you how the meal was. The chef's special dessert is the chocolate hazelnut fritters, but I prefer the tiramisu; it's light and sumptuous.

702 Rte. 28. © **508/398-6672.** http://norabella.com. Reservations recommended. Main courses $15–$22. MC, V. Take exit 9 off Rte. 6; after several traffic lights, take a right onto Rte. 28. Daily 4:30–10pm.

Scargo Cafe ★ INTERNATIONAL   Formerly a sea captain's house, this lively bistro has a menu split into "traditional" and "adventurous" categories. Traditionalists will find surf and turf, and the popular grilled lamb loins served with mint jelly (talk about traditional!); adventurous dishes include "wildcat chicken" (a sauté of sausage, mushrooms, and raisins, flambéed with apricot brandy). Serving food until 11pm, Scargo is one of only a couple of options in the neighborhood to go to after a show at the Cape Playhouse across the street.

799 Main St./Rte. 6A (opposite the Cape Playhouse). (**508/385-8200.** www.scargocafe.com. Reservations accepted for parties of 6 or more. Main courses $19–$31. AE, DISC, MC, V. Mid-June to mid-Sept daily 11am–3pm and 4:30–11pm; mid-Sept to mid-June daily 11am–10pm.

Inexpensive

Chapin's Restaurant ★ AMERICAN   Located just a few steps from Chapin Beach in Dennis, this year-round establishment with a big outdoor deck is a hit with families looking for reasonably priced fare. A new bar area overlooking the beach has made it popular with a nighttime crowd as well. Specialties include lobster quesadilla, cobb salad, and lobster pie. A range of Italian specialties also appears on the menu. The seasonal Raw Bar is stocked from the East Dennis Oyster Farm.

85 Taunton Ave., Dennis. (**508/385-7000.** www.chapinsrestaurant.com. Reservations not accepted. Main courses $7–$17. MC, V. Take exit 8 off Rte. 6, right on Rte. 6A to New Boston Rd. to Beach St. to Taunton Ave. Mon–Fri 4–8:30pm, Sat–Sun 11:30am–9pm.

DENNIS AFTER DARK

The oldest continuously active straw-hat theater in the country, and still one of the best, the **Cape Cod Playhouse ★★**, 820 Rte. 6A ((**877/385-3911** or 508/385-3911; www.capeplayhouse.com), was the 1927 brainstorm of Raymond Moore, who'd spent a few summers as a playwright in Provincetown and quickly tired of the strictures of "little theater." Salvaging an 1838 meetinghouse, he plunked it amid a meadow and got his New York buddy, designer Cleon Throckmorton, to turn it into a proper theater. It was an immediate success, and a parade of stars has trod the boards in the decades since, from Humphrey Bogart to Julie Harris. Not all of today's headliners are quite as impressive, but the theater can be counted on for a varied season of polished work. Performances are staged from mid-June to early September. Tickets range from $25 to $45.

The **Cape Cinema ★★**, 36 Hope Lane, off Rte. 6A in the center of town ((**508/385-22503** or 508/385-5644; www.capecinema.com), is an Art Deco surprise, with a Prometheus-themed ceiling mural. The setting and seating—black leather armchairs—may spoil you forever.

THE LOWER CAPE

The Lower Cape has fewer year-rounders than the Mid- and Upper Cape towns, so the communities on this part of Cape Cod are more summer-oriented. Several upscale and expensive resorts and restaurants also call this area home.

Along the easternmost portion of historic Rte. 6A, **Brewster** still enjoys much the same cachet that it had as a high roller in the maritime trade. But for the cars, it looks much as it might have in the late 19th century, with its general store still serving as a social center. Perhaps because excellence breeds competition, Brewster has spawned several fine restaurants and has become something of a magnet for gourmands.

Realtors tout **Chatham,** the Cape's most chichi town, as "the Nantucket of the Cape." Its Main Street offers appealing shops and eateries, complemented by a scenic lighthouse and plentiful beaches nearby.

As the gateway to the Outer Cape, where all roads merge, **Orleans** is a bustling town in the summer. The village of East Orleans is a destination itself, offering a couple of fun restaurants and—best of all—a good chunk of magnificent, unspoiled Cape Cod National Seashore.

7 Brewster ★★

With miles of placid Cape Cod Bay beaches and acres of state park land, Brewster is an attractive place for families. Rte. 6A, the Old King's Highway, becomes Brewster's Main Street and is the address for a bevy of B&Bs, pricey restaurants, and the Cape's finest antiques shops. The town has managed to absorb a huge development within its borders, the 380-acre condo complex known as Ocean Edge. Brewster also welcomes the tens of thousands of campers and day-trippers headed for Nickerson State Park.

ESSENTIALS

GETTING THERE After crossing the Sagamore Bridge, head east on Rte. 6 or 6A. Rte. 6A on the north side of the Cape passes through the villages of West Brewster, Brewster, and East Brewster. You can also reach Brewster by taking Rte. 6 to exit 10 north, along Rte. 124.

VISITOR INFORMATION Contact the **Brewster Chamber of Commerce Visitor Center,** behind Brewster Town Hall, 2198 Main St./Rte. 6A, Brewster (© **508/896-3500;** fax 508/896-1086; www.brewstercapecod.org).

BEACHES & GETTING OUTSIDE

BEACHES Brewster's eight bay beaches have minimal facilities. When the tide is out, the beach extends as much as 2 miles, leaving behind tide pools to splash in and explore. On a clear day, you can see the whole curve of the Cape, from Sandwich to Provincetown. Purchase a beach parking sticker ($15 per day, $50 per week) at the **Visitor Center** behind Town Hall, at 2198 Main St. (Rte. 6A; © **508/896-4511**).

○ **Breakwater Beach ★★**, off Breakwater Road, Brewster: Only a brief walk from the center of town, this calm, shallow beach (the only one with restrooms) is ideal for young children.

○ **Flax Pond ★★** in Nickerson State Park (see "Nature & Wildlife Areas," below): This freshwater pond has a bathhouse and offers watersports rentals. The park contains two more ponds with beaches—Cliff and Little Cliff. Access and parking are free.

○ **Linnell Landing Beach ★**, on Linnell Road in East Brewster: This is a half-mile, wheelchair-accessible bay beach.

○ **Paines Creek Beach ★**, off Paines Creek Road, West Brewster: With 1½ miles to stretch out on, this bay beach has something to offer sun lovers and nature lovers alike. Your kids will love it if you arrive when the tide's coming in—the current will give an air mattress a nice little ride.

BICYCLING The **Cape Cod Rail Trail ★★★** (www.mass.gov/dcr/parks/southeast/ccrt.htm) intersects with the 8-mile **Nickerson State Park** trail system at the park entrance, where there's plenty of free parking; you could follow the Rail Trail back to Dennis (about 12 miles) or onward toward Wellfleet (13 miles). In season, **Idle Times** (© **508/255-8281;** www.idletimesbikes.com) provides rentals

BIKING THE CAPE COD RAIL TRAIL

The 25-mile **Cape Cod Rail Trail ★★★** is one of New England's longest and most popular bike paths. Once a bed of the Penn Central Railroad, the trail is relatively flat and straight. On weekends in summer, you'll have to contend with dogs, in-line skaters, families, and bikers who whip by you on their way to becoming the next Lance Armstrong. Still, if you want to venture away from the coast and see some of the Cape's countryside without having to deal with motorized traffic, this is one of the best ways to do it.

The trail starts in South Wellfleet on Lecount Hollow Road or in South Dennis on Rte. 134, depending on which way you want to ride. Beginning in South Wellfleet, the path cruises by purple wildflowers, flowering dogwood, and small maples, where red-winged blackbirds and goldfinches nest. In Orleans, you'll have to ride on West Road until the City Council decides to complete the trail. Fortunately, the roads provide a good view of the boats lining Rock Harbor. Clearly marked signs lead back to the Rail Trail. You'll soon enter Nickerson State Park bike trails, or continue straight through Brewster to a series of swimming holes—Seymour, Long, and Hinckleys ponds. A favorite picnic spot is the Pleasant Lake General Store in Harwich. Shortly afterward, you'll cross over Rte. 6 on Rte. 124 before veering right through farmland, soon ending in South Dennis.

—*Stephen Jermanok*

within the park. Another good place to jump in is on Underpass Road about a half-mile south of Rte. 6A. Here you'll find **Brewster Bicycle Rental,** 442 Underpass Rd. (© **508-896-8149;** www.brewsterbike.com).

FISHING   Brewster offers more ponds for fishing than any other town: 14 in all. Among the most popular are Cliff and Higgins ponds (within Nickerson State Park). For a license, visit the town clerk at **Town Hall,** 2198 Rte. 6A (© **508/896-3701**).

GOLF   The 18-hole championship **Ocean Edge Golf Course,** 832 Villages Dr. (© **508/896-5911;** www.oceanedge.com), is Brewster's most challenging, followed closely by **Captain's Golf Course,** 1000 Freemans Way (© **508/896-5100;** www.captainsgolfcourse.com).

NATURE & WILDLIFE AREAS   Admission is free to the two trails maintained by the Cape Cod Museum of Natural History (see below). The **South Trail,** covering a .75-mile round-trip south of Rte. 6A, crosses a natural cranberry bog beside Paines Creek to reach a hardwood forest of beeches and tupelos; toward the end of the loop, you'll come upon a "glacial erratic," a huge boulder dropped by a receding glacier. Before heading out on the .25-mile **North Trail,** stop in at the museum for a free guide describing the local flora. Also accessible from the museum parking lot is the **John Wing Trail,** a 1.5-mile network traversing 140 acres of preservation land, including upland, salt marsh, and beach. (**Note:** This can be a soggy trip. Heed the posted warnings about high tides, especially in spring, or you might very well find yourself stranded.)

As it crosses Rte. 6A, Paines Creek Road becomes Run Hill Road. Follow it to the end to reach **Punkhorn Park Lands,** an undeveloped 800-acre tract popular with mountain bikers; it features several kettle ponds, a "quaking bog," and 45 miles of dirt paths.

The short jaunt around the **Stony Brook Grist Mill** is especially scenic. In spring, you can watch the alewives (freshwater herring) vaulting upstream to spawn, and, in the summer, the millpond is surrounded and scented by honeysuckle.

The 1,955-acre **Nickerson State Park,** at Rte. 6 and Crosby Lane (© **508/896-3491;** www.mass.gov/dcr/parks/southeast/nick.htm), encompasses 418 campsites (reservations pour in a year in advance, but some are held open for new arrivals willing to wait a day or two), eight kettle ponds, and 8 miles of bicycle paths.

WATERSPORTS   Sailboats, kayaks, canoes, and more are available seasonally at **Jack's Boat Rentals** (© **508/896-8556**), on Flax Pond in Nickerson State Park. You can also rent a canoe from **Goose Hummock ★** in Orleans (© **508/255-2620;** www.goose.com) and paddle around Paines Creek and Quivett Creek, as well as Upper and Lower Mill ponds.

A BREWSTER MUSEUM

Cape Cod Museum of Natural History ★★★ ☺   Long before *ecology* became

a buzzword, noted naturalist writer John Hay helped found a museum dedicated to Cape Cod's unique landscape. The children's exhibits include a "live hive"—like an ant farm, only with busy bees—and marine-room tanks. The bulk of the museum is outdoors, where 85 acres invite exploration (see "Nature & Wildlife Areas," above). There's an on-site archaeology lab on Wing Island, thought to have sheltered one of Brewster's first settlers—the Quaker John Wing, driven from Sandwich in the mid–17th century by religious persecution—and before him, native tribes dating back 10 millennia. The museum sponsors lectures, concerts, marsh cruises, bike tours, seal cruises, and "eco-treks"—including a sleepover on uninhabited Monomoy Island, off Chatham.

869 Rte. 6A (approx. 2 miles west of the town center). © **800/479-3867** (eastern MA only) or 508/896-3867. www.ccmnh.org. Admission $8 adults, $7 seniors, $3.50 children 3-12. June–Sept daily 10am–4pm; Oct–Mar Wed–Sun 11am–3pm; Apr–May Wed–Sun 10am–4pm.

SHOPPING

No one should miss **The Brewster Store,** 1935 Main St./Rte. 6A, in the center of town (© **508/896-3744;** www.brewsterstore.com), built as a church in 1852. You'll find everything from penny candy to comics to the bestselling Brewster Store coffee. Neighbors meet on the wide front porch to catch up on village gossip.

WHERE TO STAY

Michael's Cottages and Bed and Breakfast ★ 🛍   These cottages on an

immaculately groomed compound are small yet centrally located. Across the street is Brewster's Drummer Boy Park, which has a playground, historic windmill, and antique house. Brewster's summer band concerts are held there as well. The closest beach is Paines Creek, about a mile away. In July and August, rentals are available by the week only.

618 Main St./Rte. 6A, Brewster, MA 02631. © **800/399-2967** or 508/896-4025. Fax 508/896-3158. www.michaelsinbrewster.com. 7 units (5 with shower only). Summer $150–$160 double ($850–$915 weekly); $1,200–$2,100 3-bedroom weekly. B&B rooms include continental breakfast. AE, DISC, MC, V. *In room:* A/C, TV, fridge, hair dryer.

Ocean Edge Resort & Club ★   Looking like an enormous seaside estate, Ocean Edge offers numerous amenities, including a beach, 8 swimming pools, 11 tennis courts, and a championship 18-hole golf course. Replete with New England–style charm—lovely quilts, sliding glass doors that lead to patios or balconies—hotel rooms off the mansion are large and comfortable. Spread across the 400-acre property, one-to three-bedroom villas offer the freedom of a private residence (full kitchens, washer/dryers, and fireplaces in some) and the convenience of not having to drive (shuttle buses run all over the property). However, you might want to go out for groceries or to a local restaurant once in a while; the food served here is fine but not impressive.

2907 Main St./Rte. 6A, Brewster, MA 02631. © **800/896-9000.** Fax 508/896-9123. www.oceanedge. com. 335 units. Summer $265–$445 hotel room (double), $800–$1,800 2- to 3-bedroom villa ($2,400–$7,500 weekly). Minimum-stay restrictions may apply during peak periods. AE, DISC, MC, V. **Amenities:** 4 restaurants; babysitting; bikes; children's program; concierge; exercise room; golf course; 8 pools (2 indoor, 4 outdoor, 2 for toddlers); room service; 11 tennis courts. *In room:* A/C, TV, hair dryer, full kitchen or kitchenette (in villas), Wi-Fi (free).

Old Sea Pines Inn ★★ ☺ 🍴   This reasonably priced, large historic inn is a great spot for families. The inn's former days as the Sea Pines School of Charm and Personality for Young Women can still be seen in the handful of rather minuscule boarding school–scale rooms on the second floor. These bargain rooms, with shared bathrooms, are the only ones in the house without air-conditioning, but at $110 per night in season, who cares? The annex rooms are downright playful, with colorful accouterments, such as pink TVs. Sunday evenings from mid-June through mid-September, Old Sea Pines is the site of a dinner/theater performance by the Cape Cod Repertory Theatre.

2553 Main St. (approx. 1 mile east of the town center), Brewster, MA 02631. © **508/896-6114.** Fax 508/632-0084. www.oldseapinesinn.com. 24 units (5 with shared bathroom). Summer $85 double with shared bathroom, $110–$165 double with private bathroom; $155–$175 suite. Rates include full breakfast and afternoon tea. AE, DC, DISC, MC, V. Closed Jan–Mar. *In room:* TV, hair dryer, Wi-Fi.

WHERE TO DINE

The Bramble Inn Restaurant ★★★ NEW AMERICAN   Often named among the best restaurants on Cape Cod, the Bramble Inn is also one of the most expensive—but worth it for a special night out. A less pricey a la carte bistro menu is available Sunday to Thursday in the Hunt Room bar and in the courtyard garden. Fortunately, no matter which menu you order from, you'll be able to enjoy Ruth Manchester's extraordinary cuisine. Her assorted seafood curry (with lobster, cod, scallops, and shrimp in a light curry sauce with grilled banana, toasted almonds, coconut, and chutney) and her rack of lamb (with deep-fried beet-and-fontina polenta, pan-seared zucchini, and mustard port cream) have been written up in the *New York Times.*

2019 Main St. (approx. ½ mile east of Rte. 124). © **508/896-7644.** www.brambleinn.com. Reservations required for fine dining, not for bistro. Fixed-price dinner $44–$64; bistro $18–$32. AE, DISC, MC, V. June to early Sept daily 5:30–9pm; call for off-season hours. Closed Jan–Mar.

Chillingsworth ★★★ FRENCH   This longtime contender for the title of fanci-est restaurant on the Cape has two dining options: formal dinner, with jackets rec-ommended for men, and the more casual bistro. The dining room contains antique appointments dating back several centuries and a six-course Francophiliac table d'hôte menu that will challenge the most shameless gourmands. Specialties include steamed lobster over spinach and fennel with sea beans and lobster-basil butter sauce. Finish with warm chocolate cake with pistachio ice cream and chocolate drizzle. Or try the moderately priced bistro, which serves Sunday brunch and lunch and dinner daily in season in the adjoining greenhouse or on the shady lawn. Chill-ingsworth has three deluxe guest rooms on the premises.

2449 Main St. (approx. 1 mile east of the town center). ℂ **800/430-3640** or 508/896-3640. www. chillingsworth.com. Reservations required for fine-dining; recommended for bistro. Fixed-price meals $60–$70; bistro $17–$32. AE, DC, MC, V. Mid-June to Aug Thurs–Sun 11:30am-2:30pm and Mon–Sun 6–9:30pm (bistro opens for dinner at 5:30pm). On Mon seating only for fine dining (7-7:30pm); call for off-season hours. Closed Dec to mid-May.

Moderate

The Brewster Fish House ★★ NEW AMERICAN   Spare and handsome as a Shaker refectory, this small restaurant bills itself as "nonconforming" and delivers on the promise. Its approach to seafood borders on genius: Consider, for instance, squid delectably tenderized in a marinade of soy and ginger; or silky-tender, walnut-crusted ocean catfish accompanied by kale sautéed in Marsala. Beef and vegetarian options are always available as well. Better get there early (before 7pm) if you want to get in.

2208 Main St. (about ½ mile east of the town center). ℂ **508/896-7867.** http://brewsterfish.com. Reservations not accepted. Main courses $17–$29. MC, V. May–Aug Mon–Sat 11am-3pm and 5-9:30pm, Sun noon-3pm and 5–9:30pm; call for off-season hours. Closed mid-Dec to Apr.

Inexpensive

Brewster Inn & Chowder House ★ NEW AMERICAN   To get the gist of the expression "chow down," just observe the early-evening crowd happily doing so at this century-old restaurant. The draw is hearty staples at prices geared to ordinary people rather than splurging tourists. This place also makes the best martinis in town, and there's a good old bar, **The Woodshed,** out back.

1993 Rte. 6A (in the center of town). ℂ **508/896-7771.** Main courses $12–$18. AE, DISC, MC, V. Late May to mid-Oct daily 11:30am-2:30pm, Sun–Thurs 5–9:30pm, Fri-Sat 5–10pm; call for off-season hours.

Cobie's ★ AMERICAN   Accessible to cars whizzing along Rte. 6A and within collapsing distance for cyclists exploring the Rail Trail, this picture-perfect clam shack has been dishing out exemplary fried clams, lobster rolls, foot-long hot dogs, black-and-white frappés, and all the other beloved summer staples since 1948.

3260 Rte. 6A (approx. 2 miles east of Brewster center). ℂ **508/896-7021.** www.cobies.com. Most items under $15. No credit cards. Late May to early Sept daily 11am–9pm. Closed mid-Sept to mid-May.

Chatham ★★★

Chatham (pronounced "Chatt-um") is small-town America the way Norman Rock-well imagined it. Roses climb white picket fences in front of shingled Cape cottages, all within a stone's throw of the ocean. The Cape's fanciest town is also its prettiest. As a result, inn rooms are pricier here and rentals are snapped up more quickly. But those looking for a picture-perfect New England town will love Chatham's winding

Chatham

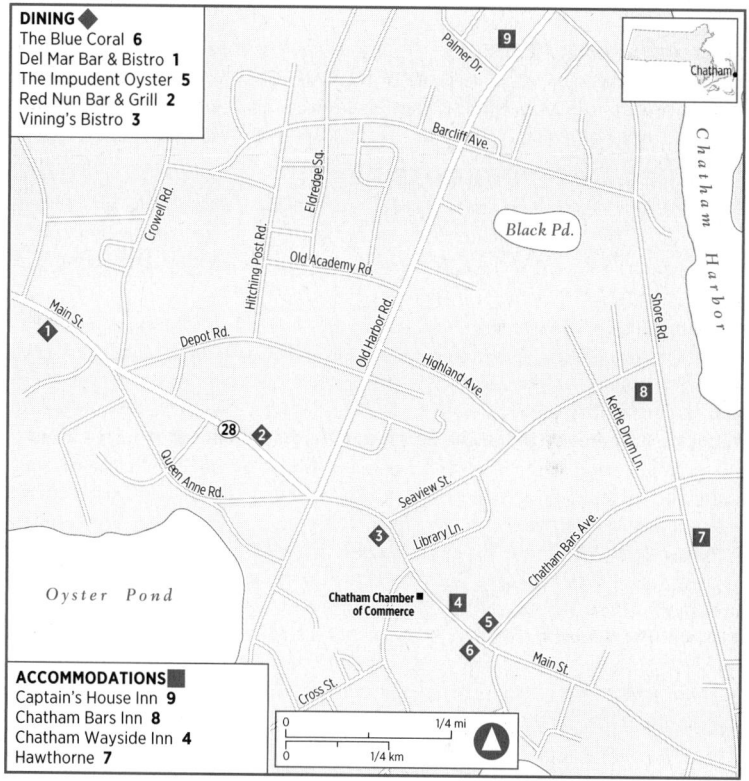

DINING ◆
The Blue Coral **6**
Del Mar Bar & Bistro **1**
The Impudent Oyster **5**
Red Nun Bar & Grill **2**
Vining's Bistro **3**

Black Pd.

Chatham Harbor

Palmer Dr. **9**

Barcliff Ave.

Crowell Rd.

Eldredge Sq.

Hitching Post Rd.

Old Academy Rd.

Old Harbor Rd.

Shore Rd.

Main St. **1**

Depot Rd.

Highland Ave.

Kettle Drum Ln.

8

28 **2**

Queen Anne Rd.

Seaview St.

Chatham Bars Ave.

3

Library Ln.

7

Oyster Pond

Chatham Chamber ■
of Commerce

4

5

6

Main St.

ACCOMMODATIONS■
Captain's House Inn **9**
Chatham Bars Inn **8**
Chatham Wayside Inn **4**
Hawthorne **7**

Cross St.

0   1/4 mi
0   1/4 km

Main Street, which is filled with pleasing shops and leads to a beautiful beach with a lighthouse.

Sticking out along the coast like a sore elbow, Chatham was one of the first spots to attract early explorers. Samuel de Champlain stopped by in 1606 but got into a tussle with the prior occupants and then left in a hurry. The first colonist to stick around was William Nickerson of Yarmouth, who befriended a local *sachem* (tribal leader) and built a house beside his wigwam in 1656. To this day, listings for Nickersons occupy a half-page in the Cape Cod phone book.

Chatham is one of the few areas on the Cape to support a commercial fishing fleet—against increasing odds. Over-fishing has resulted in closely monitored limits to give the stock time to bounce back. Boats must now go out as far as 100 miles to catch their fill. Despite the difficulties, it's a way of life few locals would willingly relinquish.

ESSENTIALS

GETTING THERE After crossing the Sagamore Bridge, head east on Rte. 6 and take exit 11 south (Rte. 137) to Rte. 28. From this intersection, South Chatham is about a half-mile west, and West Chatham is about 1½ miles east. Chatham itself is about 2 miles farther east on Rte. 28. The town lies 32 miles east of Sandwich, 24 miles south of Provincetown.

VISITOR INFORMATION   Visit the **Chatham Chamber of Commerce,** 533 Main St., Chatham, MA 02633 (© **800/715-5567** or 508/945-5199; www.chatham info.com); or the new **Chatham Chamber booth** at the intersection of routes 137 and 28 (no phone).

BEACHES & GETTING OUTSIDE

BEACHES   Chatham has an unusual array of beach styles, from the peaceful shores of the Nantucket Sound to the treacherous, shifting shoals along the Atlantic. For beach stickers ($15 per day, $60 per week), call the **Permit Department** on George Ryder Road in West Chatham (© **508/945-5180**).

○ **Chatham Light Beach ★★**: Located directly below the lighthouse parking lot (where stopovers are limited to 30 min.), this narrow stretch of sand is easy to get to: Just walk down the stairs. Currents here can be tricky and swift, though, so swimming is discouraged.

○ **Cockle Cove Beach, Ridgevale Beach, and Hardings Beach ★★**: Lined up along the Sound, each at the end of its namesake road south of Rte. 28, these family-pleasing beaches offer gentle surf and full facilities. Ridgevale Beach also has kayak and sailboat rentals.

○ **Forest Beach ★**: No longer an officially recognized town beach (there's no life-guard), this Sound landing near the Harwich border is still popular, especially among surfboarders.

○ **Oyster Pond Beach,** off Rte. 28: Only a block from Chatham's Main Street, this sheltered saltwater pond (with restrooms) swarms with children.

○ **South Beach ★★**: A former island jutting out slightly to the south of the Chatham Light, this glorified sandbar can be dangerous, so heed posted warnings and content yourself with strolling.

○ **North Beach ★★**: Extending all the way south from Orleans, this 5-mile barrier beach is accessible from Chatham only by boat; you can take the **Beachcomber** (© **508/945-5265**), a water taxi, which leaves from the fish pier. The round-trip costs $12 for adults, $8 for children 12 and under.

BICYCLING   Though Chatham has no recreational paths per se, a demarcated biking/skating lane makes a scenic 8-mile circuit of town, heading south onto "The Neck," east to the Chatham Light, up Shore Road all the way to North Chatham, and back to the center of town. A brochure prepared by the **Chatham Chamber of Commerce** (© **800/715-5567** or 508/945-5199) shows the route.

FISHING   Chatham has five ponds and lakes that permit fishing; Goose Pond off Fisherman's Landing is among the top spots. For saltwater fishing without a boat, try the fishing bridge on Bridge Street at the southern end of Mill Pond. First, though, get a license at **Town Hall,** 549 Main St., in Chatham (© **508/945-5101**). If you hear the deep sea calling, sign on with the *Headhunter* (© **508/430-2312;** www.capecodfishingcharters.com). Sport-fishing rates average around $650 for 5 hours. Shellfishing licenses are available at the **Permit Department,** on George Ryder Road in West Chatham (© **508/945-5180**).

NATURE & WILDLIFE AREAS   Heading southeast from the Hardings Beach parking lot, the 2-mile-round-trip **Seaside Trail** offers beautiful parallel panoramas of Nantucket Sound and Oyster Pond River. Access to 40-acre **Morris Island,** southwest of the Chatham Light, is easy: Walk or drive across and start right in on a marked .75-mile trail. Heed the high tides, as advised, though—they can come in surprisingly quickly, leaving you stranded.

The **Beachcomber ★★** (✆ **508/945-5265;** www.sealwatch.com) runs **seal-watching cruises** out of Stage Harbor. Parking is behind the former Main Street School, on the left before the rotary. The cruises cost $22 for adults, $20 for seniors, $16 for children 3 to 15, and are free for children 2 and under.

The uninhabited **Monomoy Islands ★★**, 2,750 acres of brush-covered sand favored by some 285 species of migrating birds, are the perfect pit stop along the Atlantic Flyway. Harbor and gray seals are catching on, too: Hundreds now carpet the coastline from late November through May. The **Wellfleet Bay Wildlife Sanctuary,** operated by the Audubon Society (✆ **508/349-2615**), offers guided trips. The Audubon's trips take place April through November; the cost is $30 to $60.

SHOPPING

Chatham's tree-shaded Main Street offers a terrific opportunity to shop and stroll. Headed for such prestigious outlets as Neiman Marcus, the hand-blown glassworks of James Holmes originate at **Chatham Glass Company,** 758 Main St., just west of the Chatham rotary (✆ **508/945-5547;** www.chathamglass.com), where you can literally look over their shoulders as the pieces take shape. At **Chatham Pottery,** 2058 Rte. 28, east of the intersection with Rte. 137 (✆ **508/430-2191;** http://store.chathampottery.com), striking graphics characterize the collaborative work of Gill Wilson (potter) and Margaret Wilson-Grey (glazer).

WHERE TO STAY

Chatham's accommodations tend to be more expensive than those of neighboring towns, but you can also find several good inexpensive motel options.

Practically across the street from the Chatham Bars Inn, the very basic **Hawthorne,** 196 Shore Rd. (✆ **508/945-0372;** www.thehawthorne.com), boasts one of the best locations in town: right on the water, with striking views of Chatham Harbor, Pleasant Bay, and the Atlantic Ocean. An additional perk here is the free phone calls (both local and long distance) and Wi-Fi access. Rates for the 26 rooms are $290 to $320 double.

Chatham Seafarer, 2079 Rte. 28 (about a half-mile east of Rte. 137), West Chatham (✆ **800/786-2772** or 508/432-1739; www.chathamseafarer.com), is a well-run motel on Rte. 28. It's about a half-mile from Ridgevale Beach and also has a pool. Rates are $165 to $215 double.

Another inexpensive option is **The Chatham Motel,** 1487 Main St./Rte. 28, Chatham (✆ **800/770-5545** or 508/945-2630; www.chathammotel.com), 1½ miles from Hardings Beach. It has an outdoor pool, and summer rates in the 32 rooms are $165 double, $225 suites.

Very Expensive

Chatham Bars Inn ★★ ☺   Set majestically above the beach in Chatham with commanding views out to a barrier beach and the Atlantic Ocean beyond is the grand Chatham Bars Inn. The colonnaded 1914 brick building is surrounded by

26 shingled cottages on 20 acres. This resort also has a heated outdoor pool, tennis courts, and four restaurants. Take in the sweeping ocean views from the breezy veranda, where you can order a drink and recline in an Adirondack chair. Many guest rooms have balconies with views of the beach or the landscaped grounds. Cottage rooms are cheery with painted furniture and Waverly fabrics.

Shore Rd. (off Seaview St., approx. ½ mile northwest of the town center), Chatham, MA 02633. © **800/ 527-4884** or 508/945-0096. Fax 508/945-5491. www.chathambarsinn.com. 205 units. Summer $425–$630 double; $720–$980 1-bedroom suite; $790–$1,600 2-bedroom suite. AE, DC, MC, V. **Amenities:** 4 restaurants (the formal Main Dining Room, the Chef's Table and Wine Cellar, the Tavern, and the seasonal Beach House Grill located right on the beach); babysitting; children's program (ages 4 and over in summer); concierge; exercise room; putting green (Seaside Links, a 9-hole course open to the public; guests play for $18); outdoor heated pool; room service; spa; 3 tennis courts ($15 an hour). *In room:* A/C, TV/VCR/DVD, fridge, hair dryer, Wi-Fi (free).

In Nearby Harwich

Wequassett Inn Resort and Golf Club ★★★ ☺ Fans of golf, sailing, and tennis will enjoy this 22-acre resort occupying its own little peninsula sticking out on Pleasant Bay. Though advertised as in Chatham, the resort is actually just over the town line in Harwich. Adjacent is the private Cape Cod National Golf Club, where inn guests enjoy exclusive privileges. The resort's restaurant, **28 Atlantic** is one of the Cape's top dining spots. Tucked amid the woods along the shore, 15 buildings, built in the 1940s, harbor roomy quarters done up in a country style. They cost a bit more than the 56 more modern "villa" rooms because of their beachfront locations. All units have either a balcony or a patio. Beach-loving guests can choose the calm private bay beach just steps from the rooms or Chatham's North Beach, a 15-minute ride via the inn's Power Skiff ($12).

2173 Rte. 28 (approx. 5 miles northwest of Chatham center, on Pleasant Bay), Chatham, MA 02633. © **800/225-7125** or 508/432-5400. Fax 508/432-5032. www.wequassett.com. 104 units. Summer $475–$825 double; $600–$1,365 suites. AE, DC, DISC, MC, V. Closed Dec–Mar. **Amenities:** 2 restaurants (28 Atlantic for fine dining; Outer Bar and Grille for casual fare); babysitting; bikes; children's program; concierge; exercise room; golf club nearby; ($105 for a round, $20 for a cart); heated outdoor pool; room service; 4 tennis courts ($15 an hour per person) plus a pro shop; watersports equipment (sailboards, Sunfish, Daysailers, and Hobie Cats) rentals; free horseshoes, basketball, and volleyball equipment; yoga and Pilates classes for $15. *In room:* A/C, TV, hair dryer, minibar, MP3 docking station, Wi-Fi (free).

Expensive

Captain's House Inn ★★★ 🏫 This 1839 Greek Revival house—along with a cottage and a carriage house—set on 2 meticulously maintained acres is a shining example of 19th-century style. The hospitality and amenities here make this one of the top B&Bs on Cape Cod. Guest rooms are richly furnished, with atmospheric touches like canopied four-poster beds, beamed ceilings, and brick hearths. The inn provides a wonderful array of extras, like robes, bottled water, newspapers, early-morning coffee, and room service. Many rooms have fridges and Jacuzzi tubs. The window-walled breakfast room is also the site of a traditional tea. Light lunches can be enjoyed poolside for an extra charge.

369–377 Old Harbor Rd. (approx. ½ mile north of the rotary), Chatham, MA 02633. © **800/315-0728** or 508/945-0127. Fax 508/945-0866. www.captainshouseinn.com. 16 units (2 with shower only). Summer $260–$475 double. Rates include full breakfast and afternoon tea. AE, DISC, MC, V. **Amenities:** Exercise room; outdoor heated pool; room service. *In room:* A/C, TV/DVD and/or VCR, hair dryer, Wi-Fi (in most; free).

Chatham Wayside Inn ★★   Centrally located on Chatham's Main Street, this 1860 stagecoach stop has undergone a thoroughly modern renovation. Don't expect any musty antique trappings: It's all lush carpeting, Waverly fabrics, and polished reproductions. The prize rooms have patios or balconies overlooking the town bandstand. The restaurant serves three meals a day and is open to the public.

512 Main St. (in the center of town), Chatham, MA 02633. ⓒ **800/391-5734** or 508/945-5550. Fax 508/945-3407. www.waysideinn.com. 56 units. Summer $265–$325 double, $400–$475 suite. DISC, MC, V. **Amenities:** Restaurant/bar; outdoor heated pool. *In room:* A/C, TV/DVD, hair dryer, Wi-Fi (free).

Pleasant Bay Village ★★   Across the street from Pleasant Bay, a few minutes' walk from a bay beach, this is one fancy motel. Over the past 25 years, the owner has transformed the property into a Zen-like paradise, where waterfalls cascade through colorful rock gardens into a stone-edged pool surrounded by whimsical Oriental gardens. Guest rooms, done up in pastels, are unusually pleasant. Many bathrooms feature marble countertops and stone floors. The suites have fully equipped kitchens, including microwave ovens, as well as two televisions, one with a DVD player. In summer, the restaurant serves three meals a day. You can order lunch from the grill without having to leave your place at the heated pool.

1191 Orleans Rd./Rte. 28 (approx. 3 miles north of Chatham center), Chatham Port, MA 02633. ⓒ **800/547-1011** or 508/945-1133. Fax 508/945-9701. www.pleasantbayvillage.com. 58 units. Summer $185–$265 double; $265–$525 1- or 2-bedroom suite (for 4 occupants). AE, MC, V. Closed Nov–Apr. **Amenities:** Restaurant (breakfast May–Oct; lunch and dinner July–Aug only); Jacuzzi; heated pool. *In room:* A/C, TV, fridge, hair dryer, Wi-Fi (free).

WHERE TO DINE
Very Expensive

28 Atlantic ★★★ NEW AMERICAN   This restaurant, on the grounds of the Wequassett Inn resort (see above) in nearby Harwich, is one of the top places to eat on Cape Cod. The elegant, spacious dining room overlooks Pleasant Bay through immense floor-to-ceiling glass panels. Service is professional and stylish. And the food stands out as superb, from the *amuse bouche* (a little taste teaser) offered at the start of the meal to the exceptional desserts served at the end. Menu items use local provender as much as possible, but also make use of delicacies from around the world. You might start with the Cape lobster and roasted corn bisque with sherried Devonshire cream; move on to the composed salad of mâche, melon, prosciutto, grapes, goat-cheese mousse, and tawny port syrup; and then get to your main course, perhaps skillet-seared local bluefish with saffron smoked mussel risotto, wilted Swiss chard, and lobster oil. You're in for a treat here; it's all exquisite. For more casual dining, the Wequassett has a poolside cafe, the **Outer Bar** ★★, open to the public from 11:30am to 10pm; it's a stylish place to grab a drink or a light meal while listening to live jazz and basking in views of Pleasant Bay.

2173 Rte. 28 (at the Wequassett Inn, approx. 5 miles northwest of Chatham center, on Pleasant Bay). ⓒ **508/430-3000.** www.wequassett.com. Reservations recommended. Main courses $21–$44. AE, DC, DISC, MC, V. May–Nov daily 7am–10pm; call for off-season hours. Closed Dec–Mar.

Expensive

The Blue Coral ★ NEW AMERICAN   This restaurant features "seaside cuisine" on an outdoor courtyard just off Main Street. Specialties include a 3-pound lobster dinner with all the fixin's, and sushi-grade blue-fin tuna, pan seared with balsamic demi-glaze. One of the most popular dishes is the lobster ravioli, served with a brandy cream sauce. There's live jazz and blues on Thursday through Sunday nights in season.

483 Main St., Chatham. ✆ **508/348-0485.** www.thebluecoral.com. Reservations accepted. Main courses $18–$40. AE, DISC, MC, V. Daily 11:30am–2:30pm and 5–10pm. Closed late Sept to late June.

Del Mar Bar & Bistro ★ BISTRO/PIZZA   Wood-fired thin crust pizza—try the fig and prosciutto—is a specialty at this urban-flavored bistro a 2-mile drive from Chatham center. There is entertainment—reggae, steel drums, jazz—Wednesday to Sunday in season.

907 Main St., Chatham. ✆ **508/945-9988.** http://delmarchatham.com. Reservations accepted. Main courses $17–$28. AE, MC, V. Daily 5–10pm.

Moderate

Buca's Tuscan Roadhouse ★★ 🏨 NORTHERN ITALIAN   This popular Harwich restaurant is very close to the Chatham border and well worth the drive for anyone staying in the lower Cape. It's got a great atmosphere—somehow romantic and festive at the same time; wonderful food; and superior service. The only problem is getting a reservation, even in January. But once you do, you can relax and enjoy homemade pastas, fresh-off-the-boat fish, and tender cuts of meat—it doesn't get much better than this. From basics like eggplant parmigiana to cacciucco, a melange of seafood in a garlic-y broth, the food is delicious. Wines by the glass are also exceptional.

4 Depot Rd. (on the corner of Rte. 28, close to the Chatham border), Harwich. ✆ **508/432-6900.** www.bucasroadhouse.com. Reservations recommended. Main courses $18–$25. AE, MC, V. June–Aug daily 5–10pm; call for off-season hours.

The Impudent Oyster ★ INTERNATIONAL   All but hidden off the main drag, this perennially popular eatery cooks up fabulous fish in exotic guises, ranging from Mexican to Szechuan, but mostly Continental. The flavorful specialties of the house are the *sole piccata* (native sole with lemon, fresh herb, and caper butter sauce), the steak *au poivre,* and the *pesca fra diablo* (local littlenecks, lobster, and other seafood served in a spicy sauce over fettuccine). A tavern menu is served at the bar from 3 to 5pm, featuring soup, salads, raw bar, chicken fingers, and burgers. This place is very busy in the summer, and if you don't make a reservation, you may be out of luck.

15 Chatham Bars Ave. (off Main St., in the center of town). ✆ **508/945-3545.** Reservations recommended. Main courses $14–$20. AE, MC, V. Mon–Thurs 11:30am–3pm and 5–9:30pm; Fri–Sat 11:30am–3pm and 5–10pm; Sun noon–3pm and 5–9:30pm.

Vining's Bistro ★★ 🏨 FUSION   If you're looking for cutting-edge cuisine, venture upstairs at Chatham's minimall and into this ineffably cool cafe. The menu offers compelling juxtapositions such as the warm lobster tacos with salsa fresca and crème fraîche, or the spit-roasted chicken suffused with achiote-lime marinade and sided with a salad of oranges and jicama.

595 Main St. (in the center of town). ✆ **508/945-5033.** http://viningsbistro.net. Reservations not accepted. Main courses $16–$24. AE, DC, MC, V. June to mid-Oct daily 5:30–9:45pm; call for off-season hours. Closed Jan–Mar.

Inexpensive

Red Nun Bar & Grill 🍴 DINER   Casual little hole-in-the-wall places like this used to be plentiful on the Cape; now there are precious few. With just five tables and some bar seats, this is a good place to go early, late, or off season. They serve comfort food, like Mama's meatloaf, cheeseburgers, and a fish sandwich made from the morning's catch that was probably brought in by one of the guys bellied up to the bar. There's a good selection of beers on tap, too.

746 Main St. (near Monomoy Theatre and Veterans Field). ☎ **508/348-0469.** www.rednun.com. All items under $11. No credit cards. May–Sept Mon–Thurs 4pm–1am, Fri–Sun noon–1am; call for off-season hours. Closed Jan 15–Apr 1.

CHATHAM AFTER DARK

Chatham's free **band concerts** ★★ are arguably the best on the Cape and attract crowds in the thousands. This is small-town America at its most nostalgic, as the band plays standards of yesteryear that never go out of style. Held in Kate Gould Park (off Chatham Bars Ave.) from July to early September, the concerts kick off at 8pm every Friday. Come early to claim your square of lawn, which is already checked with blankets by late afternoon. Call ☎ **508/945-5199** for information.

A great leveler, the **Chatham Squire** ★, 487 Main St. (☎ **508/945-0942**; http://thesquire.com), attracts CEOs, seafarers, and collegians alike. They serve great pub grub here, too.

Orleans ★★

Orleans is where the "Narrow Land" (the early Algonquin name for the Cape) starts to get very narrow indeed: From here on up—or "down," in paradoxical local parlance—the Cape is never more than a few miles wide from coast to coast. This is also where the oceanside beaches open up into a glorious expanse some 40 miles long, framed by dramatic dunes and serious surf.

The Cape's three main roads (routes 6, 6A, and 28) converge here, too, so on summer weekends, it acts as a rather frustrating funnel. Nevertheless, Main Street boasts some appealing restaurants and shops. The village of East Orleans, near the entrance to Nauset Beach, may be the best place to base yourself. The 10-mile beach, which is the southernmost stretch of the Cape Cod National Seashore preserve, is a magnet for families and young folks.

ESSENTIALS

GETTING THERE   After crossing the Sagamore Bridge, head east on Rte. 6 or 6A (the long but scenic route); both converge with Rte. 28 in Orleans. The town is 35 miles east of Sandwich, 25 miles south of Provincetown.

VISITOR INFORMATION   Contact the **Orleans Chamber of Commerce,** 44 Main St. (P.O. Box 153), Orleans, MA 02653 (☎ **800/865-1386** or 508/255-1386; www.capecod-orleans.com). There's an **information booth** at the corner of Rte. 6A and Eldredge Parkway (☎ **508/240-2484**).

BEACHES & GETTING OUTSIDE

BEACHES   From here all the way to Provincetown on the Cape's eastern side, you're dealing with the wild Atlantic Ocean. Current ocean conditions are clearly posted at the entrance to Nauset Beach. Purchase 1-week parking permits ($50 for renters) from **Town Hall** on School Road (☎ **508/240-3775**). Day passes for Nauset Beach and Skaket Beach are $15 per car. Day-trippers who arrive early enough—better make that before 10am on weekends in July and August—can pay at the gate (☎ **508/240-3780**).

o **Crystal Lake ★**, off Monument Road about ¾ mile south of Main Street: Parking—if you can find a space—is free, but there are no facilities here.

o **Nauset Beach ★★★**, in East Orleans (☎ **508/240-3780**): Stretching southward all the way past Chatham, this barrier beach, which is part of the Cape Cod National Seashore but is managed by the town, has long been one of the Cape's gonzo beach scenes—good surf, big crowds, lots of young people. Full facilities, including a terrific snack bar, can be found within the 1,000-car parking lot. The in-season parking fee is $15 per car, which is also good for same-day parking at Skaket Beach (see below). Substantial waves make for good surfing and boogie-boarding in the special section to the far left reserved for that purpose. In July and August, concerts are held from 7 to 9pm in the gazebo.

o **Pilgrim Lake ★**, off Monument Road about 1 mile south of Main Street: This small freshwater beach is covered by a lifeguard in season. You must have a beach parking sticker.

o **Skaket Beach ★**, off Skaket Beach Road to the west of town: This peaceful bay beach is a better choice for families. When the tide recedes, little kids will enjoy splashing about in the tide pools left behind. Parking costs $15, and you'd better turn up early.

BICYCLING   Orleans presents the one slight gap in the 26-mile **Cape Cod Rail Trail ★★★** (☎ **508/896-3491;** www.mass.gov/dcr/parks/southeast/ccrt.htm): Just east of the Brewster border, the trail merges with town roads for about 1½ miles. The best way to avoid vehicular aggravation and fumes is to zigzag west to scenic Rock Harbor. Bike rentals are available at **Orleans Cycle** at 26 Main St. (☎ **508/255-9115;** www.orleanscyclecapecod.com).

BOATING   **Arey's Pond Sailing School,** off Rte. 28 in South Orleans (☎ **508/255-7900;** www.areyspondboatyard.com), offers sailing lessons on Little Pleasant Bay. Individual lessons are $65 per hour; weekly group lessons are around $189. The **Goose Hummock Outdoor Center** at 15 Rte. 6A, south of the rotary (☎ **508/255-2620;** www.goose.com), rents out canoes, kayaks, and more, and the northern half of Pleasant Bay is the perfect place to use them.

FISHING   Fishing is allowed in Baker Pond, Pilgrim Lake, and Crystal Lake. For licenses, visit **Town Hall,** at Post Office Square in the center of town (☎ **508/240-3700,** ext. 305), or **Goose Hummock** (see above). Surf-casting—no license needed—is permitted on Nauset Beach South, off Beach Road. **Rock Harbor ★★**, a former packet landing on the bay (about 1¼ miles northwest of the town center), shelters New England's largest sport-fishing fleet: some 18 boats at last count. One call (☎ **800/287-1771** in MA, or 508/255-9757) will get you information on them all—or go look them over in person. Rock Harbor charter prices range from $550 for 4 hours to $750 for 8 hours. Individual prices are also available.

WATERSPORTS   The **Pump House Surf Co.,** at 9 Rte. 6A (☎ **508/240-2226;** http://pumphousesurf.com), rents and sells wet suits, body boards, and surfboards. Stop by for up-to-date reports on where to find the best waves. **Nauset Surf Shop** at Jeremiah Square, Rte. 6A at the rotary (☎ **508/255-4742;** www.nausetsports.com), also rents surfboards, boogie boards, skim boards, kayaks, and wet suits.

SHOPPING

Though shops are somewhat scattered, Orleans is full of great finds for browsers. You'll find some 400 vintage light fixtures at **Continuum Antiques,** 7 S. Orleans Rd., Rte. 28, south of the junction with Rte. 6A (ⓒ **508/255-8513**). Stop by **Kemp Pottery,** 9 Rte. 6A, just south of the rotary (ⓒ **508/255-5853;** www.kemppottery. com), and check out the turned and slab-built creations from soup tureens to fanciful sculptures.

WHERE TO STAY
Moderate

The Cove ★   Ask for a water-view room at this motel complex, on busy Rte. 28, that also fronts placid Town Cove. The interiors are adequate, if not dazzling, and a small heated pool and a restful gazebo overlook the waterfront. Some rooms have kitchenettes and balconies with cove views.

13 S. Orleans Rd. (Rte. 28, north of Main St.), Orleans, MA 02653. ⓒ *800/343-2233* or 508/255-1203. Fax 508/255-7736. www.thecoveorleans.com. 47 units. Summer $157–$196 double; $207–$234 suite. AE, DC, DISC, MC, V. **Amenities:** Small heated pool. *In room:* A/C, TV/DVD, fridge, hair dryer, Wi-Fi (free).

A Little Inn on Pleasant Bay ★★ 🎐   Sitting on a hill overlooking the bay, this is a lovely property. The four rooms in the peaceful main house, which dates to 1798, are decorated warm tiles, light woods, and subtle colors. An adjacent building, called the "Paddock," has three additional rooms. Breakfast served outside is an extravagant affair they call a "European buffet," with a spread of pastries, yogurt, muesli, cereals, fresh fruits, and assorted meats and cheeses.

654 S. Orleans Rd., South Orleans, MA 02662. ⓒ *888/332-3351* or 508/255-0780. www.alittleinnon pleasantbay.com. 9 units. Summer $245–$315 double. Rates include continental breakfast and evening sherry. AE, MC, V. No children 9 or under. *In room:* A/C, hair dryer, Wi-Fi (free), no phone.

Nauset Knoll Motor Lodge ★★ 🗡   Overlooking Nauset Beach, one of Cape Cod's most popular beaches, this nothing-fancy motel with picture windows will suit beach lovers to a T. The simple, clean rooms are well maintained, and by staying here, you'll save on daily parking charges at Nauset Beach. The whole complex is owned by Uncle Sam and is under the supervision of the National Park Service.

237 Beach Rd. (at Nauset Beach, approx. 2 miles east of the town center), East Orleans, MA 02643. ⓒ **508/255-2364.** www.capecodtravel.com/nausetknoll. 12 units. Summer $175 double. MC, V. Closed late Oct to early Apr. *In room:* TV, no phone.

The Orleans Inn ★   You can't miss this mansard-roofed beauty, perched right on the edge of Town Cove. Try to get one of the rooms facing the water. Built in 1875, the inn has been lovingly restored and maintains its central place in the community. The simple rooms, some with twin beds or sleeper sofas, are cheerful with modern amenities and extra touches like a box of chocolates on the bureau. Downstairs is a bar and restaurant with wonderful views of the cove.

3 Old County Rd./Rte. 6A (just south of the Orleans rotary), Orleans, MA 02653. ⓒ **508/255-2222.** Fax 508/255-6722. www.orleansinn.com. 11 units. Summer $175–$250 double; $250–$325 suite. Rates include continental breakfast. AE, MC, V. **Amenities:** Restaurant/bar. *In room:* TV, fridge.

Inexpensive
Nauset House Inn ★★ 🗡   Just a half-mile from Nauset Beach, this reasonably priced country inn is a cozy setting for those seeking a quiet retreat. Several of the

rooms in greenery-draped outbuildings feature such romantic extras as a sunken tub or private deck. The most romantic hideaway here, though, is a 1907 conservatory appended to the 1810 farmhouse inn. It's the perfect place to lounge when the rain pounds down, prompting the camellias to waft their heady perfume. Breakfast would seem relatively workaday, were it not for the setting—a pared-down, rustic refectory—and innkeeper Diane Johnson's memorable muffins and pastries.

143 Beach Rd. (approx. 1 mile east of the town center), East Orleans, MA 02643. ⓒ **800/771-5508** or 508/255-2195. Fax 508/240-6276. www.nausethouseinn.com. 14 units (6 with shared bathroom; 4 with shower only). Summer $80 single with shared bathroom; $89–$99 double with shared bathroom; $120–$185 double with private bathroom. Rates include full breakfast. DISC, MC, V. Closed Nov–Mar. No children 11 or under. *In room:* No phone.

WHERE TO DINE
Expensive

Abba ★★ INTERNATIONAL/FUSION   Abba continues to earn raves for its fresh take on fine dining in the Lower Cape. Tables are closely packed inside, so I prefer the covered outdoor dining area behind the restaurant. Chef/co-owner Erez Pinhas of Israel creates what can only be described as fusion cuisine: a little Middle Eastern, a little European, a little New American, plus some Thai and New England thrown in. Where else can you start with a falafel, move on to a steaming plate of shrimp pad Thai, and then end with chilled melon soup? And everything is delicious.

90 Old Colony Way (at West Rd., 2 blocks from Main St., toward Skaket Beach). ⓒ **508/255-8144.** www.abbarestaurant.com. Reservations recommended. Main courses $18–$27. AE, MC, V. June–Aug Tues–Sun 5–10pm; call for off-season hours.

Moderate

Joe's Beach Road Bar & Grille at the Barley Neck Inn ★ NEW AMERICAN   This 1857 captain's house with adjoining tavern is a favorite with locals. While the front room has a more traditional ambience, the tavern space features a huge fieldstone fireplace and World War II posters. With denim tablecloths and bandannas serving as napkins, the atmosphere is casual. The 28-foot mahogany bar is a popular meeting place. The menu varies from such fancy dishes as grilled Atlantic salmon filet with a red-pepper coulis and basil vinaigrette to Joe's pizza (with goat cheese, roasted peppers, and spinach) or highfalutin fish and chips—beer-battered, with saffron aioli.

At the Barley Neck Inn, 5 Beach Rd. (approx. ½ mile east of the town center), East Orleans. ⓒ **508/255-0212.** www.barleyneck.com. Reservations accepted. Main courses $10–$25. AE, DC, MC, V. June to early Sept daily 5–10pm; call for off-season hours.

The Lobster Claw Restaurant ★ ☺ SEAFOOD   This sprawling family-owned business has been serving up quality seafood for almost 30 years. Get the baked stuffed lobster with all the fixings. This place is very casual, with picnic tables and paper plates, so kids can't get into too much trouble here.

Rte. 6A (just south of the rotary), Orleans. ⓒ **508/255-1800.** www.lobsterclaw.com. Main courses $10–$19. AE, DC, DISC, MC, V. Daily 11:30am–9pm. Closed Nov–Mar.

Mahoney's Atlantic Bar & Grill ★ NEW AMERICAN   Seafood is the specialty at this casual restaurant. Dishes like tuna sashimi, grilled sea bass, and pan-seared lobster are why you came to Cape Cod. You can also order poultry, meat, pasta, and vegetarian dishes. In season, some nights there's live jazz and blues.

28 Main St. (in the center of town). ⓒ **508/255-5505.** www.mahoneysatlantic.com. Reservations recommended. Main courses $16–$25. AE, MC, V. May–Sept daily 5–10pm; Oct–Apr Tues–Sun 5–10pm.

Inexpensive

Cap't Cass Rock Harbor Seafood SEAFOOD   Most tourists figure that a silvered shack sporting this many salvaged lobster buoys has an inside track on the freshest of seafood. The supposition makes sense, but the stuff here is about par for the area and the preparations are basic. Nevertheless, it's fun to eat in a joint left untouched for decades as time—and dining fads—marched on.

117 Rock Harbor Rd. (on the harbor, approx. 1½ miles northwest of the town center). No phone. Most main courses under $12. No credit cards. Late June to mid-Oct Tues–Sun 11am–2pm and 5–9pm. Closed mid-Oct to late June.

ORLEANS AFTER DARK

Joe's Beach Road Bar & Grille ★, at the Barley Neck Inn (✆ **508/255-0212;** see "Where to Dine," above), is a big old barn of a bar that might as well be town hall: It's where you'll find all the locals exchanging juicy gossip and jokes. On Sunday evenings in season, there's live "Jazz at Joe's."

Land Ho! ★★ (✆ **508/255-5165;** www.land-ho.com/orleans/home/html), the best pub in town, features lives music year-round Thursday through Saturday evenings as well as Monday and Tuesday nights during high season. There's usually no cover charge.

THE OUTER CAPE

It's only on the Outer Cape that the landscape and even the air feel really beachy. You can smell the seashore just over the horizon—in fact, everywhere you go, because you're never more than a mile or two away from sand and surf. You won't find any high-rise hotels or tacky amusement arcades along the shoreline—just miles of pristine beaches and dune grass rippling in the wind. That's because in the early 1960s, 27,000 acres here became the federally protected Cape Cod National Seashore.

Wellfleet ★★★

With the well-tended look of a classic New England village and surrounded by beaches, Wellfleet is the chosen destination for artists, writers, off-duty psychiatrists, and other contemplative types who hope to find more in the landscape than mere quaintness or rusticity. Such distinguished literati as Edna St. Vincent Millay and Edmund Wilson put this rural village on the map in the 1920s, in the wake of Provincetown's bohemian heyday.

To this day, Wellfleet remains remarkably unspoiled. Once you leave Rte. 6, commercialism is kept to a minimum, though the town boasts plenty of appealing shops, distinguished galleries, and a couple of very good New American restaurants. It's hard to imagine any other community on the Cape supporting so sophisticated an undertaking as the Wellfleet Harbor Actors' Theatre, or hosting such a wholesome event as public square dancing on the adjacent Town Pier. And where else could you find a thriving drive-in movie theater right next door to an outstanding nature preserve?

ESSENTIALS

GETTING THERE   After crossing the Sagamore Bridge, head east on Rte. 6 to Orleans, and after the rotary, continue north on Rte. 6 to Wellfleet. Wellfleet is 42 miles northeast of Sandwich, 14 miles south of Provincetown.

VISITOR INFORMATION Contact the **Wellfleet Chamber of Commerce,** off Rte. 6, Wellfleet, MA 02663 (© **508/349-2510;** fax 508/349-3740; www.wellfleet chamber.com).

BEACHES & GETTING OUTSIDE

BEACHES Wellfleet's fabulous ocean beaches tend to sort themselves demographically: Lecount Hollow is popular with families, Newcomb Hollow with high-schoolers, White Crest with the college crowd, and Cahoon Hollow with 30-somethings. Only the latter two permit parking by nonresidents ($15 per day). To enjoy the other two, as well as Burton Baker Beach on the harbor at Indian Neck and Duck Harbor on the bay, plus three freshwater ponds, you'll have to walk or bike in, or see if you qualify for a sticker ($70 per week for renters). Bring proof of residency to the seasonal Beach Sticker Booth on the Town Pier, or call the **Wellfleet Recreation Department** (© **508/349-9818**). Parking is free at all beaches and ponds after 4pm.

○ **Marconi Beach ★★,** off Marconi Beach Road in South Wellfleet: A National Seashore property, this cliff-lined beach (with restrooms) charges an entry fee of $15 per day, or $45 for the season. *Note:* The bluffs are so high that the beach lies in shadow by late afternoon.

○ **Mayo Beach,** Kendrick Avenue (near the Town Pier): Right by the harbor, facing south, this warm, shallow bay beach (with restrooms) is hardly secluded but will please young waders. Parking is free. You could grab a bite (and a paperback) at The Bookstore Restaurant across the street.

○ **White Crest & Cahoon Hollow Beaches ★★★,** off Ocean View Drive in Wellfleet: These two town-run ocean beaches—big with surfers—are open to all. Both have snack bars and restrooms. Parking costs $15 per day, $45 for the season.

BICYCLING In addition to serving as the final destination of the 25-mile **Cape Cod Rail Trail ★★★** (© **508/896-3491;** www.mass.gov/dcr/parks/southeast/ ccrt.htm), Wellfleet is also among its more desirable destinations: A country road off the bike path leads right to Lecount Hollow Beach. The deli at the adjoining **South Wellfleet General Store** (© **508/349-2335**) can see to your snacking needs.

BOATING **Jack's Boat Rentals,** located on Gull Pond off Gull Pond Road, about a half-mile south of the Truro border (© **508/349-9808;** www.jacksboatrental.com) rents out canoes, kayaks, sailboards, and Sunfish, as well as sea cycles and surf bikes. Gull Pond connects to Higgins Pond by way of a placid, narrow channel lined with red maples and choked with water lilies. It's a great place to paddle. If you'd like a canoe for a few days, you'll need to go to the Jack's Boat Rentals location on Rte. 6 in Wellfleet (next to the Cumberland Farms).

 The **Chequessett Yacht & Country Club,** on Chequessett Neck Road in Wellfleet (© **508/349-0198;** www.cycc.net), offers group sailing lessons. For experienced sailors, **Wellfleet Marine Corp.,** on the Town Pier (© **508/349-2233;** www.welfleetmarine.com), rents sailboats in season.

FISHING For a license to fish at Long Pond, Great Pond, or Gull Pond, visit **Town Hall** at 300 Main St. (© **508/349-0301**). Surf-casting, which doesn't require a license, is permitted at the town beaches. Shellfishing licenses—Wellfleet's oysters are world-famous—can be obtained from the **Shellfish Department,** on the Town Pier off Kendrick Avenue (© **508/349-0300**).

In season, heading out from Wellfleet Harbor is the 60-foot party fishing boat *Navigator* (℃ **508/349-6003**). Charter boats include the *Erin-H* (℃ **508/349-9663**; www.virtualcapecod.com/erinh).

NATURE & WILDLIFE AREAS　Right in town, the short, picturesque board-walk known as **Uncle Tim's Bridge,** off East Commercial Street, crosses Duck Creek to access a tiny island crisscrossed by paths.

The Cape Cod National Seashore maintains two spectacular self-guided trails. The 1.25-mile **Atlantic White Cedar Swamp Trail ★★**, off the parking area for the Marconi Wireless Station (see "Cape Cod National Seashore," later in this chapter), shelters a rare stand of the lightweight species prized by Native Americans as wood for canoes; the moss-choked swamp is a magical place, refreshingly cool even at the height of summer. A boardwalk will see you over the muck, but the return trip does entail a calf-testing half-mile trek through deep sand. Consider it a warm-up for magnificent **Great Island,** jutting 4 miles into the bay (off the western end of Chequessett Neck Rd.) to cup Wellfleet Harbor. Before attaching itself to the main-land in 1831, Great Island harbored a busy whaling post. Be sure to cover up, wear sturdy shoes, bring water, and venture to Jeremy Point—the very tip—only if you're sure the tide is going out.

You'll find 6 miles of very scenic trails lined with lupines and bayberries within the **Wellfleet Bay Wildlife Sanctuary ★★★**, off Rte. 6 north of the Eastham border, in South Wellfleet (℃ **508/349-2615**; www.wellfleetbay.org). A spiffy, eco-friendly visitor center serves as both introduction and gateway to this 1,000-acre refuge, maintained by the Massachusetts Audubon Society. Passive solar heat and composting toilets are just a few of the waste-cutting elements incorporated into the seemingly simple building. You might see red-winged blackbirds and osprey as you follow the looping trails through pine forests, salt marsh, and moors. The sanctuary offers naturalist-guided tours and workshops for children. Inquire about canoeing, birding, and seal-watching excursions. Trail use is free for Massachusetts Audubon Society members; otherwise, the fee is $5 for adults and $3 for seniors and children 3 to 12. Trails are open July through August from 8am to 8pm, and September through June from 8am to dusk. The visitor center is open from Memorial Day to Columbus Day daily from 8:30am to 5pm; off season, it's closed Monday.

WATERSPORTS　Surfing is restricted to White Crest Beach, and sailboarding to Burton Baker Beach at Indian Neck during certain tide conditions; ask for a copy of the regulations at the Beach Sticker Booth on the Town Pier. **Eric Gustavson** (℃ **508/349-1429**; www.funseekers.org) offers windsurfing and surfing lessons ($120 for 2 hr.) and, for the more adventurous, kiteboarding ($250 for 3 hr.) and stand-up paddleboarding ($60 per hour).

SHOPPING

A stroll from Main Street down Bank Street and then along Commercial Street will take you past a dozen galleries worth a look. Crafts make a strong showing, too, as do contemporary women's clothing and eclectic home furnishings. But unlike Provincetown, which has something to offer virtually year-round, Wellfleet pretty much closes up come Columbus Day.

The **Cove Gallery,** 15 Commercial St., by Duck Creek (℃ **508/349-2530**; www.covegallery.com)—with a waterside sculpture garden—carries the paintings and prints of many well-known artists, including Barry Moser and Leonard Baskin. John Grillo's work astounds every summer during his annual show in July. **Jules Besch Stationers,** 15 Bank St. (© **508/349-1231**), specializes in stationery products, including papers, gift cards, handmade journals, and unusual gift items.

WHERE TO STAY

Even'tide ★ ☺   Set back from busy Rte. 6, this well-run motel is a good base for families. In case of rain, there's a 60-foot heated indoor pool—a rarity in this part of the Cape. There are seven cottages on the property with one-, two-, and three-bedroom units. In the pines are a barbecue and a picnic area. The Rail Trail goes right by, and a 1-mile footpath through the woods leads to Marconi Beach.

650 Rte. 6 (approx. 1 mile north of the Eastham border), South Wellfleet, MA 02663. © **800/368-0007** in MA only, or 508/349-3410. Fax 508/349-7804. www.eventidemotel.com. 40 units (1 with shower only). Summer $155–$180 double, $185–$220 efficiency. AE, DISC, MC, V. **Amenities:** Large heated indoor pool. In room: A/C, TV, fridge.

The Inn at Duck Creeke   This historic complex is set on 5 woodsy acres overlooking a tidal creek and salt marsh. The 1880s captain's house features wide-board floors and charming but basic rooms, many with shared bathrooms; the carriage house contains a few light and airy cabin-style rooms; and the 1715 saltworks building has smaller rooms with antique decor. In the main building, each shared bathroom adjoins two rooms, which might not suit those in search of privacy. All rooms have fans, and those on the third floor have air-conditioning. The carriage house and saltworks building are quieter and can be downright romantic. But there's definitely a no-frills quality to this place—towels are thin, and so are walls. A big plus is that there are two good restaurants on-site: **Sweet Seasons** (see "Where to Dine," below) and the **Duck Creeke Tavern,** with live entertainment in season.

70 Main St., Wellfleet, MA 02667. © **508/349-9333.** Fax 508/349-0234. www.innatduckcreeke.com. 27 units (8 with shared bathroom, 5 with shower only). Summer $95–$115 double with shared bathroom; $125–$140 double with private bathroom. Rates include continental breakfast. AE, MC, V. Closed Nov–Apr. **Amenities:** 2 restaurants. In room: No phone, Wi-Fi (free).

Surfside Cottages ★★ ☺   This is where you want to be: smack dab on a spectacular beach with 50-foot dunes, within biking distance of Wellfleet Center and a short drive from Provincetown. All of the one-, two-, or three-bedrooms have kitchens, fireplaces, barbecues, outdoor showers, and screened porches. Some even have roof decks. From mid-May to mid-October, the cottages rent weekly. Bring your own sheets and towels; renting a set costs $10 per person.

Ocean View Dr. (at Lecount Hollow Rd.), South Wellfleet, MA 02663. ©/fax **508/349-3959.** www.surfsidecottages.com. 18 cottages (all with showers only). Summer $1,200–$1,500 weekly; off season $95–$175 per day. MC, V. Closed Nov to early Apr. Pets accepted in some cottages off season ($50 fee). In room: Fridge.

WHERE TO DINE

Hatch's Fish & Produce Market ★, 310 Main St., behind Town Hall (© **508/349-6734** for produce, 508/349-2810 for fish market; www.hatchsfishmarket.com), is the unofficial heart of Wellfleet. You'll find the best local bounty, from fresh-picked corn to fruit-juice popsicles to steaming lobsters. Virtually no one passes through without picking up a little something, including the latest town gossip. It's closed from late September until May.

Mac's Seafood Market and Harbor Grill Restaurant ★ ☺ 👔 SEAFOOD   On the town pier, this takeout shack with picnic tables features fresh local seafood unloaded from the boats just steps away. Besides grilled fish dinners, Mac's serves homemade chowders, sushi, and a raw bar. The same owners also have **Mac's Shack** (☎ **508/349-6333**), a traditional clam shack open for dinner in season, located at 91 Commercial St., just east of town center, and featuring fried seafood with all the fixings served on paper plates at picnic tables.

Wellfleet Town Pier. ☎ **508/349-9611.** www.macsseafood.com. Main courses $10–$20. MC, V. Daily 7:30am–10pm. Closed mid-Oct to late May.

Moby Dick's Restaurant ★ ☺ SEAFOOD   This is your typical clam shack. Order your meal at the register, sit at a picnic table, and a cheerful college student brings it to you. The fried fish, clams, scallops, and shrimp are all good; try the Moby's Seafood Special—a heaping platter of all of the above, plus coleslaw and fries. Then there's the clambake special with lobster, steamers, and corn on the cob. Bring the family and chow down.

Rte. 6, Wellfleet. ☎ **508/349-9795.** www.mobydicksrestaurant.com. Reservations not accepted. Main courses $8–$20. MC, V. Mid-June to early Sept daily 11:30am–10pm; call for off-season hours. Closed mid-Oct to Apr.

Sweet Seasons Restaurant/Duck Creeke Tavern ★ NEW AMERICAN   Chef-owner Judith Pihl's Mediterranean-influenced fare is still appealing after more than 2 decades, as is this dining room's peaceful pond view. Some of the dishes can be a bit heavy by contemporary standards, but there's usually a healthy alternative: Wellfleet littlenecks and mussels in a golden, aromatic tomato-and-cumin broth, for instance, as opposed to Russian oysters with smoked salmon, vodka, and sour cream. Specialties of the house include creamy sage-and-asparagus ravioli, and Seasons shrimp with feta and ouzo.

At The Inn at Duck Creeke, 70 Main St. (approx. ⅛ mile west of Rte. 6). ☎ **508/349-6535.** www.innat duckcreeke.com. Reservations recommended. Main courses $19–$30. AE, MC, V. July–Sept Tues–Sun 5:30–10pm. Closed Oct–June.

The Wicked Oyster ★★ NEW AMERICAN   This old warehouse-style building houses a cool and casual year-round restaurant. There are several sections: an enclosed front porch, an ample dining room, and a large bar area. With a busy to-go area for coffee and pastries, this place definitely has a bustling atmosphere. You'll see families with small children, 20-something couples, and older folks enjoying this comfortable and convenient restaurant. Breakfast is popular and features a multitude of omelets plus very strong coffee. At lunch, sandwiches and fried fish appear on the menu. Dinner choices range from burgers to more refined options, like pan-fried sole with lemon caper butter, spring risotto with mushrooms and asparagus, or, for large appetites, grilled angus tenderloin.

50 Main St. (just off Rte. 6, close to Wellfleet Center). ☎ **508/349-3455.** www.thewickedo.com. Reservations recommended. Main courses $16–$26. MC, V. June–Aug daily 7am–2pm and 5:30–10pm; call for off-season hours.

Winslow's Tavern ★★ BISTRO   This new upscale bistro offers summertime treats like grilled lobster and bistro classics like steak frites in a contemporary setting. Of course, they have Wellfleet oysters, the town's world-famous bivalve. But they also have wonderful salads and light meals.

316 Main St. (in the center of town). © **508/349-6450.** www.winslowstavern.com. Reservations for parties of 6 or more only. Main courses $13–$23. AE, MC, V. July–Aug daily noon–3pm and 5:30–10pm; call for off-season hours. Closed late Oct to mid-May.

WELLFLEET AFTER DARK

The **Beachcomber** ★, 1220 Old Cahoon Hollow Rd., off Ocean View Drive (© **508/349-6055;** www.thebeachcomber.com), arguably the best dance club on Cape Cod, is definitely the most scenic. It's right on Cahoon Hollow Beach—so close, in fact, that late beachgoers on summer weekends can count on a free concert of reggae, blues, ska, or rock. Cover varies. It's closed early September to late May.

The **Wellfleet Drive-In Theater,** 51 Rte. 6, just north of the Eastham border (© **800/696-3532** or 508/349-2520; www.wellfleetdrivein.com), built in 1957, is the only drive-in left on Cape Cod and one of a scant half-dozen surviving in the state. The rituals are as unbending and endearing as ever: the playtime preceding the cartoons, the countdown plugging the allures of the snack bar, and finally, two full first-run features. It's open daily from late May through mid-September; show time is at dusk. Call for off-season hours.

The principals behind the **Wellfleet Harbor Actors' Theatre** ★, 2357 Rte. 6 (next to the post office) and 1 Kendrick Ave., near the Town Pier (© **508/349-6835;** www.what.org), aim to provoke—and usually succeed, even amid this very sophisticated, seen-it-all summer colony. Performances are given from late May through October daily at 8pm.

Truro ★★

With only 1,600 year-round residents (fewer than it boasted in 1840, when Pamet Harbor was a whaling and shipbuilding port), Truro amounts to little more than a smattering of stores and public buildings, and lots of low-profile houses hidden away in the woods and dunes. Edward Hopper lived in contented isolation in a South Truro cottage for nearly 4 decades. If you find yourself craving cultural stimulation or other kinds of excitement, head to Provincetown, which is only a 10-minute drive away.

ESSENTIALS

GETTING THERE   After crossing the Sagamore Bridge, head east on Rte. 6 or 6A to Orleans and north on Rte. 6.

VISITOR INFORMATION   Contact the **Truro Chamber of Commerce,** Rte. 6A (at Head of the Meadow Rd.), Truro, MA 02666 (© **508/487-1288;** www.trurochamberofcommerce.com). Truro is 46 miles east of Sandwich, 10 miles south of Provincetown.

BEACHES & GETTING OUTSIDE

BEACHES   Parking at all of Truro's exquisite Atlantic beaches, except for one Cape Cod National Seashore access point (Corn Hill Beach), is reserved for residents and renters. To obtain a sticker ($30 for 1 week; $60 for 2 weeks), inquire at the beach-sticker office at 14 Truro Center Rd., behind the post office in Truro Center (© **508/487-3635**).

o **Corn Hill Beach** ★★, off Corn Hill Road: Offering restrooms, this bay beach—near the hill where the Pilgrims found the seed corn that ensured their survival—is open to nonresidents for a parking fee of $10 per day.

○ **Head of the Meadow ★★★**, off Head of the Meadow Road: Among the more remote National Seashore beaches, this spot (equipped with restrooms) is known for its excellent surf. A parking lot connected by a short boardwalk to the beach makes this beach more easily accessible than other National Seashore beaches. It is also connected by a short bike path to Pilgrim Heights (see "Bicycling," below). Parking costs $15 per day, or $45 per season.

BICYCLING Although it has yet to be linked up to the Cape Cod Rail Trail, Truro does have a stunning 2-mile bike path of its own: the **Head of the Meadow Trail ★**, off the road of the same name (look for a right turn about a half-mile north of where routes 6 and 6A intersect). Part of the old 1850 road toward Provincetown, it skirts the bluffs, passing Pilgrim Lake and ending at High Head Road.

FISHING Great Pond, Horseleech Pond, and Pilgrim Lake—flanked by parabolic dunes carved by the wind—are all fishable; for a freshwater fishing license, visit **Town Hall** on Town Hall Road (📞 **508/487-2702**). You can also call the town hall for a shellfishing license. Surf-casting is permitted at Highland Light Beach, off Highland Road.

GOLF North Truro has the most scenic—and historic—9-hole course on the Cape. Created in 1892, the minimally groomed, Scottish-style **Highland Links,** at 10 Lighthouse Rd., off South Highland Road (📞 **508/487-9201;** www.truro-ma. gov), shares a lofty bluff with the 1853 Highland Light.

NATURE TRAILS The Cape Cod National Seashore, which makes up 70% of Truro's land, offers three self-guided nature trails. The .5-mile **Pamet Trail ★**, off North Pamet Road, leads you past an old cranberry-bog building and bogs that have reverted to marshland. Park in the lot to the left of the Little America youth hostel and walk back to the fire road entrance about 500 feet down North Pamet Road. The **Pilgrim Spring Trail ★** and **Small Swamp Trail ★** (each a .75-mile loop) head out from the National Seashore parking lot just east of Pilgrim Lake. Both paths overlook Salt Meadow, a freshwater marsh favored by hawks and osprey.

A MUSEUM & LIGHTHOUSE

Highland House Museum and Highland Lighthouse Built as a hotel in 1907, the Highland House is a perfect repository of the odds and ends collected by the Truro Historical Society: ship's models, harpoons, primitive toys, a pirate's chest, and so on. In 1996, Highland Lighthouse was moved back from its perilous perch above a rapidly eroding dune. Now the lighthouse is within 800 feet of the museum and is also operated by the Truro Historical Society. Lighthouse tours run May through October. Unfortunately, a 48-inch height requirement means little ones can't climb up the tower.

27 Highland Light Rd. (off S. Highland Rd., 2 miles north of the town center on Rte. 6). 📞 **508/487-1121.** www.trurohistorical.org. Admission to both museum and lighthouse $5 adults, free for children 11 and under. Admission to museum or lighthouse $4. Museum June–Sept Mon–Sat 10am–4:30pm; Sun 1–4:30pm. Last ticket sold at 3:30pm. Lighthouse mid-June to mid-Oct daily 10am–5:30pm. Closed mid-Oct to mid-June.

WHERE TO STAY

Days Cottages ★ 🍴 Lined up along the bay beach in North Truro, these identical cottages—named after flowers—are all white clapboard with sea-foam green shutters. Although lacking frills, each has a living room, two small bedrooms, a kitchen, and a bathroom. The downside is that these accommodations are somewhat rough: The bedrooms are minuscule, and in some of the cottages, the fireplace has about 10 years' worth of graffiti written on the brick chimney. There is also the noise of passing cars on this busy stretch of road to contend with. The upside is miles of bay beach for walking and swimming, with views of Provincetown's quirky skyline in the distance. In season, beginning June 1, the cottages are rented only by the week, and they usually book up far in advance.

Rte. 6A (a couple of miles south of the Provincetown border), North Truro, MA 02652. © **508/487-1062.** Fax 508/487-5595. www.dayscottages.com. 23 cottages (all with shower only). Summer $1,250 weekly. No credit cards. Closed mid-Oct to Apr. *In room:* Fridge.

Kalmar Village ★★ ☺ 💰 Spiffier than many of the motels and cottages between Pilgrim Lake and Pilgrim Beach, this 1940s complex features little white cottages shuttered in black. Amenities include picnic tables, grills, and daily maid service. Some cottages have air-conditioning. The clientele—mostly families—can splash the day away in the 60-foot freshwater pool or on the 400-foot private beach.

674 Shore Rd. (Rte. 6A, approx. ¼ mile south of the Provincetown border), North Truro, MA 02652. © **508/487-0585.** Fax 508/487-5827. www.kalmarvillage.com. 16 units, 40 cottages. Summer $125–$300 double, $655–$1,065 efficiency; $1,485–$2,600 cottages weekly. DISC, MC, V. Closed mid-Oct to late May. **Amenities:** Outdoor pool. *In room:* TV, fridge.

WHERE TO DINE

Babe's Mediterranean Bistro ★ MIDDLE EASTERN Babe's is the Outer Cape's newest place for ethnic cuisine. Chef/owner Peter Thrasher takes his inspiration from the Eastern Mediterranean and North Africa in preparing his cuisine. The menu, which uses vegetables from the chef's garden, changes often. Flavors taste wonderfully different, making this a perfect place for diners unafraid to explore. Dishes to try include *Muhammara,* a hummuslike spread served as an appetizer with special bread; chickpea and asparagus soup; Turkish lamb kabobs; *Izmiri Krofte,* a type of meatball dish with figs and peppers; and Moroccan chicken served in a clay pot with fresh herbs.

69 Shore Rd. (Rte. 6A), North Truro. © **508/487-9955.** www.babestruro.com. Reservations recommended. Main courses $14–$20. MC, V. June–Sept daily 5:30–10pm. Closed Oct–May.

Blackfish Restaurant ★ NEW AMERICAN If you hear people whispering about a restaurant in Truro, it is probably this one, considered a secret place that only insiders know about. Set in the former Blacksmith Shop Restaurant, this place

---

 A Vineyard in the Dunes

This pastoral property just off Rte. 6 in Truro is one of the last working farms in the Outer Cape and the site of an honest-to-goodness vineyard. Horticulturists Kathy Gregrow and Judy Wimer of **Truro Vineyard of Cape Cod** (11 Shore Rd./Rte. 6A, North Truro; © 508/487-6200; www.trurovineyardsofcapecod.com) uncorked their first homegrown chardonnay and Cabernet Franc in the fall of 1996, the muscadet in 1997, the merlot in 1998. Inside the main house, the living room, with its exposed beams, is decorated with interesting oenological artifacts. Late May through October, free wine tastings are held daily from noon to 5pm. Guided tours of the property take place at 1 and 3pm.

still has the rustic, casual feel of the old place, but the cuisine—featuring such delicacies as foie gras, duck prosciutto, and Wellfleet mussels—gives it away as a spot for fine dining. Burgers are also a specialty and come with such fancy toppings as goat cheddar and Worcestershire aioli.

17 Truro Center Rd. (Rte. 6A), Truro. ℂ **508/349-3399.** Reservations recommended. Main courses $19–$24, burgers $9–$13. MC, V. Late May to mid-Oct daily 5–10pm. Closed mid-Oct to late May.

Terra Luna ★ FUSION   This serene restaurant, a '70s throwback, specializes in using organic and locally grown ingredients. It may be the only restaurant on the Cape serving pine-nut ricotta vegan lasagna (or vegan anything, for that matter). On the menu are well-priced Pacific Rim and/or neo-Italian fare, such as penne prosciutto sautéed with garlic, black pepper, and a splash of vodka. Main courses include roasted local cod with homemade gnocchi and free-range chicken with savory bread pudding.

104 Shore Rd. (Rte. 6A), North Truro. ℂ **508/487-1019.** www.theterraluna.com. Reservations recommended. Main courses $17–$28. AE, MC, V. Late May to mid-Oct daily 5:30–10pm. Closed mid-Oct to late May.

SWEETS & TAKEOUT

Jams 🛍️   Seeing as this deli/bakery/grocery is basically the whole enchilada in terms of downtown Truro, and seasonal to boot, it's good that it's so delightful. It's full of tantalizing aromas: fresh, creative pizzas (from pesto to pupu); rotisseried fowl sizzling on the spit; or cookies straight from the oven. The pastry and deli selections deserve their own four-star restaurant but are all the more savory as part of a picnic.

14 Truro Center Rd. (off Rte. 6, in the center of town). ℂ **508/349-1616.** Call for hours. Closed early Sept to late May.

Provincetown ★★★

You made it all the way to the end of the Cape, to one of the most interesting spots on the eastern seaboard. Explorer Bartholomew Gosnold must have felt much the same thrill in 1602, when he and his crew happened upon a "great stoare of codfysshes" here. The Pilgrims, of course, were overjoyed when they slogged into the harbor 18 years later. Never mind that they'd landed several hundred miles off course.

And Charles Hawthorne, the painter who "discovered" this near-derelict fishing town in the late 1890s and introduced it to the Greenwich Village intelligentsia, was besotted by this "jumble of color in the intense sunlight accentuated by the brilliant blue of the harbor."

He'd probably be aghast at the commercial circus his enthusiasm has wrought—though pleased, no doubt, to find the Provincetown Art Association & Museum, which he helped found in 1914, still going strong. The whole town, in fact, is dedicated to creative expression, both visual and verbal. The general atmosphere of open-mindedness plays a pivotal role, allowing a varied assortment of individuals to explore their creative urges.

That same open-mindedness may account for Provincetown's ascendancy as a gay and lesbian resort. In peak season, the streets are a celebration of the individual's freedom to be as "out" as imagination allows. But the street life also includes families, art lovers, and gourmands. In short, Provincetown has something for just about everyone.

Provincetown

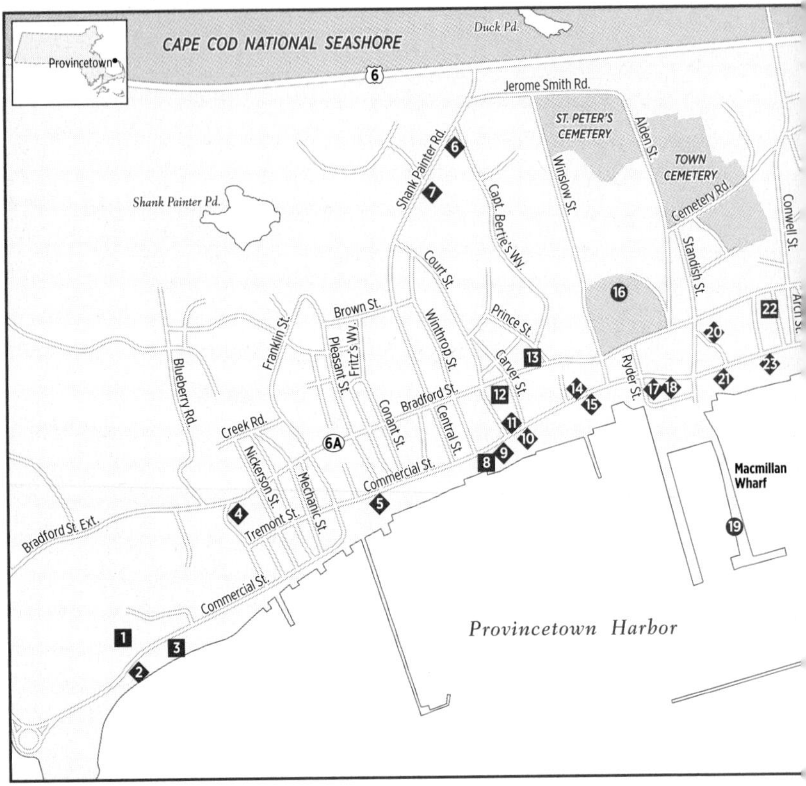

CAPE COD NATIONAL SEASHORE

Duck Pd.

Provincetown

Jerome Smith Rd.

6

Shank Painter Rd.

ST. PETER'S
CEMETERY

Alden St.

TOWN
CEMETERY

Cemetery Rd.

Winslow St.

6

7

Shank Painter Pd.

Capt. Bertie's Wy.

Standish St.

Conwell St.

22

Court St.

Prince St.

16

Arch St.

Franklin St.

Brown St.

Winthrop St.

Carver St.

20

Blueberry Rd.

Pleasant St.

W. S. Fitz.

13

Bradford St.

Central St.

12

14

15

Ryder St.

17 18

23

Creek Rd.

Conant St.

11

21

Nickerson St.

6A

Commercial St.

8 9

10

Macmillan
Wharf

Bradford St. Ext.

Mechanic St.

Tremont St.

4

5

19

Commercial St.

Provincetown Harbor

1

3

2

ESSENTIALS

GETTING THERE   After crossing the Sagamore Bridge, head east on Rte. 6 or 6A to Orleans, then continue north on Rte. 6 to Provincetown. Provincetown is 56 miles northeast of Sandwich, 42 miles northeast of Hyannis.

If you plan to spend your entire vacation in Provincetown, you won't need a car—everything is within walking or biking distance. And because parking is a hassle, consider leaving your car at home and taking a boat from Boston or Plymouth. You'll get to skip the horrendous Sagamore Bridge traffic jams and arrive by sea like the Pilgrims did.

Bay State Cruises (© **617/748-1428;** www.provincetownfastferry.com) makes round-trips from Boston, daily from late June through September. The high-speed ***Provincetown Express*** boat takes 90 minutes and makes three round-trips daily from mid-May to mid-October. It leaves Boston's World Trade Center at 8:30am, 1, and 5:30pm. On the return trip, it leaves Provincetown at 10:30am, 3, and 7:30pm. Tickets on the high-speed boat cost $49 one-way, $73 round-trip for adults. Children 3 to 12 are $32 one-way, $58 round-trip. Reservations are recommended. The regular 3-hour boat, called ***Provincetown II,*** leaves Boston's Commonwealth Pier

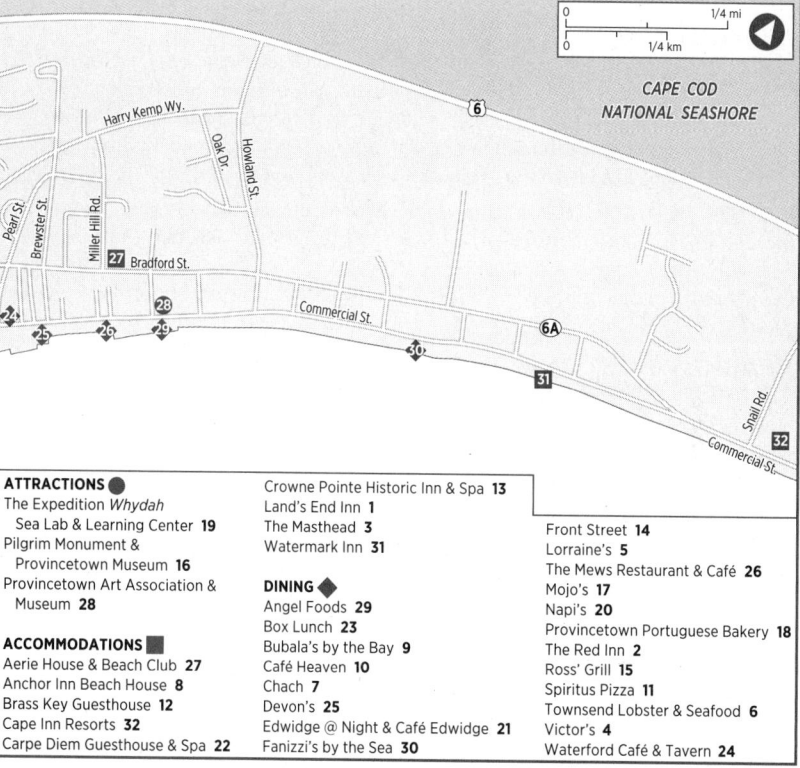

| 0 | | | | 1/4 mi |
| 0 | | 1/4 km | | |

Harry Kemp Wy.

Oak Dr.

Howland St.

6

CAPE COD
NATIONAL SEASHORE

Pearl St.

Brewster St.

Miller Hill Rd.

27 Bradford St.

28

24
25 26 29

Commercial St.

6A

30

31

Snail Rd.

32

Commercial St.

ATTRACTIONS ●
The Expedition *Whydah*
  Sea Lab & Learning Center **19**
Pilgrim Monument &
  Provincetown Museum **16**
Provincetown Art Association &
  Museum **28**

ACCOMMODATIONS ■
Aerie House & Beach Club **27**
Anchor Inn Beach House **8**
Brass Key Guesthouse **12**
Cape Inn Resorts **32**
Carpe Diem Guesthouse & Spa **22**

Crowne Pointe Historic Inn & Spa **13**
Land's End Inn **1**
The Masthead **3**
Watermark Inn **31**

DINING ◆
Angel Foods **29**
Box Lunch **23**
Bubala's by the Bay **9**
Café Heaven **10**
Chach **7**
Devon's **25**
Edwidge @ Night & Café Edwidge **21**
Fanizzi's by the Sea **30**

Front Street **14**
Lorraine's **5**
The Mews Restaurant & Café **26**
Mojo's **17**
Napi's **20**
Provincetown Portuguese Bakery **18**
The Red Inn **2**
Ross' Grill **15**
Spiritus Pizza **11**
Townsend Lobster & Seafood **6**
Victor's **4**
Waterford Café & Tavern **24**

on Friday, Saturday, and Sunday at 9:30am and arrives in Provincetown at 12:30pm. At 3:30pm, the boat leaves Provincetown, arriving in Boston at 6:30pm. On the slow boat, round-trip fare is $44; free for children to age 12.

Boston Harbor Cruises (© **617/227-4321;** www.bostonharborcruises.com) runs fast ferries from Long Wharf in Boston to Provincetown's MacMillan's Wharf. It's a 90-minute trip. In high season, there are three round-trips a day, leaving at 9am, 2, and 6:30pm from Boston, and leaving from Provincetown at 11am, 4, and 8:30pm. In the shoulder season, late May to mid-June and from early September to mid-October, there are one or two trips a day. Ferry tickets cost $79 round-trip for adults. Tickets for seniors cost $69 round-trip; and tickets for children cost $58 round-trip. Bikes cost $6 each way. Reservations are a must on this popular boat.

Capt. John Boats (© **508/747-2400;** www.provincetownferry.com) connects Plymouth and Provincetown daily mid-June through August; Tuesday, Wednesday, Saturday, and Sunday in September; and weekends only from late May to mid-June. The 90-minute boat ride leaves the state pier in Plymouth at 10am; it leaves Provincetown at 4:30pm. The adult round-trip fare is $40, seniors $35, children under 12 $30; bikes are $5 extra.

You can also fly into Provincetown. **Cape Air** (℅ **800/352-0714**; www.fly capeair.com) offers flights from Boston and from Nantucket in season. Both trips take about 25 minutes.

GETTING AROUND

Parking is at a premium. Illegally parked cars are ticketed (even on Sun), and repeat offenders will be towed. If your inn provides parking, you may want to keep your car there and get around on foot, bicycle, or shuttle. **Provincetown's Summer Shuttle** (℅ **508/487-3424**) loops through town and to the beach daily from late June through October. You can also contact the **Mercedes Cab Company** (℅ **508/487-3333**).

VISITOR INFORMATION   Contact the **Provincetown Chamber of Commerce,** 307 Commercial St., Provincetown, MA 02657 (℅ **508/487-3424;** fax 508/487-8966; www.ptownchamber.com), or the gay-oriented **Provincetown Business Guild,** 115 Bradford St., P.O. Box 421, Provincetown, MA 02657 (℅ **800/637-8696** or 508/487-2313; fax 508/487-1252; www.ptown.org).

BEACHES & GETTING OUTSIDE

BEACHES   With nine-tenths of its territory (basically, all but the downtown area) protected by the Cape Cod National Seashore, Provincetown has miles of beaches. The 3-mile bay beach that lines the harbor, though certainly swimmable, is not all that inviting compared with the magnificent ocean beaches overseen by the National Seashore. The two official access areas (see below) tend to be crowded; however, you can always find a less densely populated stretch if you're willing to hike down the beach a bit.

○ **Herring Cove ★★★**: This popular west-facing National Seashore beach is known for its spectacular sunsets. The long stretches of pristine sand front a calmer beach than Race Point (see below) because Herring Cove faces Cape Cod Bay. This is a haven for same-sex couples, who tend to gather to the far left side of the beach. Parking costs $15 per day, $45 per season.

○ **Long Point:** Trek out over the breakwater at the far west end of Commercial Street and walk about 1½ miles over sand—or catch a water shuttle—$8 one-way, $12 round-trip—from Flyer's Boat Rental (see "Boating," below) to visit this very last spit of land, capped by an 1827 lighthouse. Locals call it "the end of the earth." Shuttles run hourly in July and August.

○ **Race Point ★★★**: Facing the Atlantic Ocean, Race Point offers rougher surf than Herring Cove, and you might actually spot whales. Parking costs $15 per day, $45 per season.

BICYCLING   North of town, nestled amid the Cape Cod National Seashore preserve, is one of the more spectacular bike paths in New England, the 7-mile **Province Lands Trail ★★**, a heady swirl of steep dunes anchored by wind-stunted scrub pines. With its free parking, the **Province Lands Visitor Center ★** (℅ **508/487-1256;** www.nps.gov/caco) is a good place to start: You can survey the landscape from the observation tower to try to get your bearings before setting off amid the dizzying maze. Follow signs to a spur path leading to one of the beaches, Race Point or Herring Cove, lining the shore. Rentals are offered in season by **Arnold's Where You Rent The Bikes** (℅ **508/487-0844**), 329 Commercial St., and **Gale Force Bikes,** 144 Bradford St. (℅ **508/487-4849;** www.galeforcebikes.com), in the West End. There's also **Ptown Bikes,** 42 Bradford St. (℅ **508/487-8735;** www.ptownbikes. com); reserve several days in advance.

WHALE-WATCHING IN P-TOWN

Stellwagen Bank, 8 miles off Province-town, is a rich feeding ground for whales. The **Dolphin Fleet/*Portuguese Princess*** ★★★, MacMillan Wharf (☎ **800/826-9300** or 508/240-3636; www.provincetownwhalewatch.com), offers naturalist-led whale-watching trips to Stellwagen and is partnered with the Center for Coastal Studies, a local group that studies the endangered right whale.

Tickets for the 3½-hour trips are $39 for adults, $33 for seniors, $31 for children 7 to 12, and free for children under 7. Call to reserve. Trips aren't offered from late October through March.

Tips for first-timers: Dress very warmly, in layers, and take along a waterproof windbreaker. If you're prone to seasick-ness, consider taking a motion-sickness pill at the start of the trip. (They are pro-vided free as you board the vessel.)

BOATING   In addition to operating a Long Point shuttle from its own dock (see "Beaches," above), **Flyer's Boat Rental,** 131 Commercial St., in the West End (☎ **508/487-0898;** www.flyersboats.com), offers all sorts of craft, from kayaks and dinghies to sailboats of varying sizes; sailing lessons and fishing-gear rentals are also available.

FISHING   Surf-casting is permitted at Herring Cove Beach (off Rte. 6) and Race Point Beach (near the Race Point Coast Guard Station); many people drop a hand-line or light tackle right off the West End breakwater. For low-cost deep-sea fishing from a party boat, board the ***Cee Jay*** (☎ **800/675-6724** or 508/487-4330; www.ceejayfishing.com).

NATURE TRAILS   Within the Province Lands (off Race Point Rd., a half-mile north of Rte. 6), the National Seashore maintains the 1-mile **Beech Forest Trail ★**, a shaded path that circles a shallow freshwater pond blanketed with water lilies before heading into the woods. You can see the shifting dunes gradually encroaching on the forest.

A walk along the **West End breakwater ★★** out to the end of **Long Point** is about 5 miles round-trip. Walking just to the end of the wide breakwater, located at the end of Commercial Street next to the Provincetown Inn, is quite popular and takes about 30 minutes each way. You'll see all ages maneuvering the layered boulders. If you want to continue to Long Point, the very tip of Cape Cod, it's about a 1½-hour walk across soft sand. At low tide, the distance can be shortened by cutting across the salt flats. **Wood End Lighthouse** is directly across the spit of sand near the breakwater. **Long Point Lighthouse** is at the end of the point. Hikers determined to reach the end of Long Point will want to bring a hat, water, and sunscreen. The inside of the arm has views of Provincetown and Provincetown Harbor and a couple of shipwrecks.

ORGANIZED TOURS & CRUISES

Art's Dune Tours ★★ is at the corner of Commercial and Standish streets (☎ **800/894-1951** or 508/487-1950; www.artsdunetours.com). In 1946, Art Costa started driving sightseers out to ogle the decrepit "dune shacks" where such transient luminaries as Eugene O'Neill, Jack Kerouac, and Jackson Pollock found their respective muses. The park service wanted to raze these eyesores, but luckily saner heads prevailed: They're now National Historic Landmarks. The tours typically take about 1 to 1½ hours. Tickets are $25 for adults, $17 for children 6 to 11. Additional tours offered include a sunset clambake dune tour ($85) and a barbecue tour ($75).

A recommended boat tour is aboard the **Bay Lady II** ★ (📞 **508/487-9308;** www.sailcapecod.com), which leaves from MacMillan Wharf. The sunset trip on this 73-foot reproduction gaff-rigged Grand Banks schooner is especially spectacular. Tickets cost $20 to $25 for adults, $12 to $20 for children under 12. Four 2-hour sails run daily from mid-May to mid-October.

MUSEUMS

The Expedition *Whydah* Sea Lab & Learning Center ✋   Though the subject matter is fascinating, this site is a bit of a tourist trap. Cape Cod native Barry Clifford made headlines in 1984 when he tracked down the wreck of the 17th-century pirate ship *Whydah* (pronounced *Wid*-dah, Yankee-speak for "widow") 1,500 feet off the coast of Wellfleet, where it had lain undisturbed since 1717. Only 10% excavated to date, it has already yielded over 100,000 artifacts. In this museum/lab, visitors can supposedly observe the reclamation work being done, though it's unusual to actually see scientists or scholars at work.

MacMillan Wharf (just past the whale-watching fleet). 📞 **508/487-8899.** www.whydah.com. Admission $10 adults, $8 children 6–12. June–Aug daily 10am–8pm; Apr–May and Sept–Oct daily 10am–5pm. Closed Nov–Mar.

Pilgrim Monument & Provincetown Museum ★★   Anywhere you go in town, this granite tower looms, ever ready to restore your bearings. Climb up the 60 gradual ramps interspersed with 116 steps—a surprisingly easy lope—and you'll get a gargoyle's-eye view of the spiraling coast and, in the distance, Boston against a backdrop of New Hampshire's mountains. Definitely devote some time to the curious exhibits in the museum chronicling P-town's checkered past as both fishing port and arts nexus. Among the memorabilia, you'll find polar bears brought back from the expeditions of Arctic explorer and Provincetown native Donald MacMillan as well as early programs for the Provincetown Players.

High Pole Hill Rd. (off Winslow St., north of Bradford St.). 📞 **508/487-1310.** www.pilgrim-monument. org. Admission $7 adults, $5 seniors and students, $3.50 children 4–12. July–Aug daily 9am–7pm; off season daily 9am–5pm. Last admission 45 min. before closing. Closed Dec–Mar.

Province Lands Visitor Center of the Cape Cod National Seashore ★   Though much smaller than the Salt Pond Visitor Center, this satellite does a good job of explicating this special environment, where plant life must fight a fierce battle to maintain its hold amid shifting sands buffeted by salty winds. Be sure to circle the observation deck for great views. Inquire about special events, such as guided walks, family campfires, and canoe programs (reservations required).

Race Point Rd. (approx. 1½ miles northwest of the town center). 📞 **508/487-1256.** www.nps.gov/caco. Free admission. Mid-Apr to late Nov daily 9am–5pm. Closed late Nov to mid-Apr.

Provincetown Art Association & Museum ★★★   This remarkable cache of 20th-century American art—now in an extraordinary modern building—began with five paintings donated by local artists, including Charles Hawthorne, the charismatic teacher who first "discovered" this picturesque outpost. Founded in 1914, only a year after New York's revolutionary Armory Show, the museum was the site of innumerable "space wars," as classicists and modernists vied for square footage. In today's less competitive atmosphere, it's not unusual to see a tame still life next to an unrestrained abstract. The museum sponsors a full schedule of concerts, lectures, readings, and classes.

460 Commercial St. (in the East End). ℭ **508/487-1750.** www.paam.org. Admission $7 adults. July–Aug daily noon–5pm and 8–10pm; call for off-season hours.

SHOPPING

ART GALLERIES   Of the several dozen galleries in town, only a handful are reliably worthwhile. In season, most of the galleries and even some of the shops open around 11am, then close from around 5 to 7pm, reopening and greeting visitors up to as late as 10 or 11pm. Shows usually open on Friday evenings, prompting a "stroll" tradition spanning the many receptions.

Berta Walker is a force to be reckoned with, having nurtured many top artists through her association with the Fine Arts Work Center before opening her own gallery in 1990, the **Berta Walker Gallery ★**, 208 Bradford St., in the East End (ℭ **508/487-6411;** www.bertawalker.com). Closed from late October to late May.

DNA (Definitive New Art) Gallery ★, 288 Bradford St., above the Provincetown Tennis Club in the East End (ℭ **508/487-7700**), has attracted such talents as photographer Joel Meyerowitz, Provincetown's favorite portraitist, known for such tomes as *Cape Light;* sculptor Conrad Malicoat, whose free-form brick chimneys and hearths can be seen around town; and local conceptualist/provocateur Jay Critchley. Readings by cutting-edge authors add to the buzz. Closed from mid-October to late May.

Julie Heller started collecting early P-town paintings as a child—and a tourist, at that. She chose so incredibly well, her roster at **Julie Heller Gallery ★**, 2 Gosnold St., on the beach in the center of town and 465 Commercial St., across from the art association (ℭ **508/487-2169;** www.juliehellergallery.com), reads like a who's who of local art. Hawthorne, Avery, Hofmann, Lazzell, Hensche—all the big names from Provincetown's past are here, as well as some contemporary artists. Closed weekdays January to April.

DISCOUNT SHOPPING   **Marine Specialties,** 235 Commercial St., in the center of town (ℭ **508/487-1730;** www.ptownarmynavy.com), is packed to the rafters with useful stuff, from discounted Doc Martens to cut-rate Swiss Army knives. Hung from the ceiling are some real antiques, including several carillons' worth of ship's bells.

FASHION   **Giardelli/Antonelli Studio Showroom,** 417 Commercial St., in the East End (ℭ **508/487-3016**), is filled with Jerry Giardelli's unstructured clothing elements in vibrant colors and inviting textures. They demand to be mixed and matched with Diana Antonelli's statement jewelry.

Mad as a Hatter, 360 Commercial St. (ℭ **508/487-4063**), has hats to suit every style and inclination. It's closed January to mid-February.

Moda Fina, 349 Commercial St. (ℭ **508/487-6632;** www.shopmodafina.com), specializes in women's clothing and accessories, including shoes, lingerie, and unique summer dresses.

WHERE TO STAY
Very Expensive
Anchor Inn Beach House ★★   This waterfront property centrally located on Commercial Street underwent a multimillion-dollar face-lift in 2001. Many rooms

feature deluxe showers, whirlpool baths, and fireplaces. Sixteen guest rooms have balconies overlooking the harbor. Four have separate entrances through private porches. Some of the rooms, called "yacht cabins," are quite small but have fabulous views. Others are large suites with king-size beds, two-person whirlpool baths, and French doors leading to a private balcony. Breakfast is an elaborate affair that could include quiche or eggs Benedict.

175 Commercial St. (in the center of town), Provincetown, MA 02657. ✆ **800/858-2657** or 508/487-0432. Fax 508/487-6280. www.anchorinnbeachhouse.com. 23 units. Summer $275–$385 double; $400 suite. Rates include continental breakfast. AE, MC, V. Closed Jan–Mar. *In room:* A/C, TV/VCR, CD player, fridge, hair dryer.

Brass Key Guesthouse ★★★ Brass Key is the fanciest place to stay in Provincetown. With Ritz-Carlton–style amenities and service in mind, the innkeepers have created a paean to luxury. They've thought of everything: down pillows, jetted showers, and free iced tea and lemonade delivered poolside. Rooms in the 1828 Federal-style Captain's House and the Gatehouse are decorated in a playful country style, while the Victorian-era building is classically elegant, with materials like mahogany, walnut, and marble. Most deluxe guest rooms have gas fireplaces and oversize whirlpool tubs. In high season, the clientele here is primarily gay men, though all are made to feel welcome.

67 Bradford St. (in the center of town), Provincetown, MA 02657. ✆ **800/842-9858** or 508/487-9005. Fax 508/487-9020. www.brasskey.com. 41 units, 4 cottages. Summer $319–$399 double; $399–$659 suite and cottage. Rates include continental breakfast and afternoon wine-and-cheese hour. AE, DISC, MC, V. Closed late Nov to early Apr. No children 17 or under. **Amenities:** Bar, 17-ft. Jacuzzi; outdoor heated pool. *In room:* A/C, TV/DVD, fridge, hair dryer, Wi-Fi (free).

Crowne Pointe Historic Inn ★★ This property, Provincetown's newest luxury inn with a pool and a spa, is perched high on Bradford Street and features deluxe commons areas and attractive gardens. The staff is accommodating and professional. Rooms are spacious, and some of the deluxe rooms and suites have fireplaces, wet bars, and Jacuzzis. Buffet breakfast is served in the large living room, which has plenty of overstuffed couches for lounging while you plan your day.

82 Bradford St. (in the center of town), Provincetown, MA 02657. ✆ **877/CROWNE1** (276-9631) or 508/487-6767. Fax 508/487-5554. www.crownepointe.com. 35 units. Summer $299–$529 double. Rates include continental breakfast and wine-and-cheese hour. AE, MC, V. **Amenities:** Bar, 10-person Jacuzzi; heated outdoor pool; sauna; steam room. *In room:* A/C, TV/DVD, hair dryer, Wi-Fi (free).

Expensive

Land's End Inn ★★★ 🏨 Enjoying a prime perch atop Gull Hill in the far West End of Commercial Street, this whimsical 1907 bungalow is bursting with outlandish antiques. There are three deluxe rooms that make use of the inn's soaring towers. Some of the other rooms are small, but all are filled with kitschy Victorian and Art Deco *objets*. The view from the lounge over the bay and town below, is spectacular. The breakfast, an elaborate continental spread, features fresh fruits and homemade baked goods.

22 Commercial St. (in the West End), Provincetown, MA 02657. ✆ **800/276-7088** or 508/487-0706. Fax 508/487-0755. www.landsendinn.com. 16 units. Summer $305–$420 double; $430–$480 tower rooms. Rates include continental breakfast and wine-and-cheese hour. AE, MC, V. Closed Nov–Apr. *In room:* A/C, no phone, Wi-Fi (free).

The Masthead ★★ ☺ This is one of the few places in town, other than the impersonal motels, that actively welcomes families, and the placid 450-foot private beach will delight young splashers. The cottages are fun, some with wicker furniture and antiques. In the water-view rooms perched above the surf, with their 7-foot picture windows overlooking the bay and Long Point, you may feel as though you're onboard a ship.

31–41 Commercial St. (in the West End), Provincetown, MA 02657. ✆ **800/395-5095** or 508/487-0523. Fax 508/487-9251. www.themasthead.com. 21 units (2 with shared bathroom, 16 with shower only), 4 cottages. Summer $99 double with shared bathroom; $125–$312 double; $213–$333 efficiency; $489 2-bedroom apt; $2,541–$2,919 cottage weekly. AE, DC, DISC, MC, V. *In room:* A/C, TV, fridge.

Watermark Inn ★★ ☺ If you'd like to experience P-town without being stuck in the thick of it (the carnival atmosphere can get tiring at times), this contemporary inn at the peaceful edge of town is the perfect choice. This beachfront hotel contains dazzling suites; the prize ones, on the top floor, have picture windows and sweeping deck views. Handmade quilts brighten up clean, monochromatic rooms. A plus for families: The calm harbor beach is right out the back door, so no need to lug everything across town (unless you crave bigger waves).

603 Commercial St. (in the East End), Provincetown, MA 02657. ✆ **508/487-0165.** Fax 508/487-2383. www.watermark-inn.com. 10 units. Summer $205–470 suite. From mid-May to mid-Sept suites rent by the week only ($1,310–$2,300 per week). AE, MC, V. *In room:* TV, fridge.

Moderate

Aerie House & Beach Club ★★ 🐾
This place is a good candidate for the all-things-for-all-people award. You can have one of four deluxe rooms on the beach at the Beach Club building (425 Commercial St.), each with waterfront deck and kitchen, or a very comfortable bargain-priced room (there are even a few with shared bathrooms) in the Bradford Street building. The continental breakfast here is among the best you'll find locally, with special egg preparations and homemade baked goods. Your hosts Steve Tait and Dave Cook are knowledgeable and accommodating.

184 Bradford St. (in the East End), Provincetown, MA 02657. ✆ **800/487-1197** or 508/487-1197. www. aeriehouse.com. 11 units (3 with shared bathroom). Summer $135–$145 double with shared bathroom; $150–$320 double with private bathroom. MC, V. Well-behaved dog allowed with prior permission ($10 per night). **Amenities:** Bikes; Jacuzzi. *In room:* A/C, TV/DVD, fridge, Wi-Fi (free).

Cape Inn ★
This no-surprises motel on the waterfront at the far eastern edge of town is a good choice for first-timers not quite sure what they're getting into. Guests in waterfront rooms get a nice view of town. In season, free movies are shown in the restaurant/lounge on a 100-foot screen, and dinner is served in the restaurant. There's also a poolside bar and grill. Though this motel is a bit of a hike from the town's center, an in-season shuttle will whisk you down Commercial Street or to the beaches.

698 Commercial St. (at Rte. 6A, in the East End), Provincetown, MA 02657. ✆ **800/422-4224** or 508/487-1711. Fax 508/487-3929. www.capeinn.com. 78 units. Summer $140–$200 double. Rates include continental breakfast. AE, DC, DISC, MC, V. Closed Nov–Apr. Dogs accepted ($15 per night). **Amenities:** Restaurant; outdoor pool. *In room:* A/C, TV, fridge, hair dryer.

Carpe Diem Guesthouse & Spa ★★
The newest of the two buildings comprising this stylish B&B in the center of town features four suites and a deluxe Namaste spa (with massage, P-town's largest steam room, Finnish dry sauna, and hydrojet spa tub). Guest rooms are exquisitely decorated with European antiques and brightly painted walls and wallpaper. All rooms have down comforters and pillows, as well as bathrobes. Deluxe garden suites have private entrances, Jacuzzis, and fireplaces. The full breakfast features homemade pastries served at the dining-room table.

12 Johnson St. (in the center of town), Provincetown, MA 02657. ☎ **800/487-0132** or ☎/fax 508/487-4242. www.carpediemguesthouse.com. 22 units. Summer $225–$245 double, $305–$365 suites. Rates include full breakfast and wine-and-cheese hour. AE, DISC, MC, V. **Amenities:** Spa (steam room, sauna, Jacuzzi). *In room:* A/C, TV/VCR, fridge (in most), Wi-Fi (free).

WHERE TO DINE

Spiritus Pizza, 190 Commercial St. (☎ **508/487-2808;** www.spirituspizza.com), is an extravagant pizza parlor that stays open until 2am. The pizza's good, as are the fruit drinks and premium ice cream. For a peaceful morning repast, check out the little garden in back. Or peruse the scrumptious meat pies and pastries at **Provincetown Portuguese Bakery,** 299 Commercial St. (☎ **508/487-1803**). Both establishments are closed November to early April.

Very Expensive

The Red Inn ★★ NEW AMERICAN   Located at the far west end of Commercial Street, this picture-perfect establishment has wraparound floor-to-ceiling windows and great beach views. The refined atmosphere makes this a favorite for special occasions, when your dinner might begin with a glass of champagne and end with a soufflé. This is fine dining on the calorie-rich side, with entrees like grilled thick pork chops with tomatillo salsa and pepper-crusted filet mignon with truffle mashed potatoes and Jack Daniel's sauce. Fresh fish and vegetarian main courses are always on the menu. There are also four beautiful guest rooms on site.

15 Commercial St. ☎ **508/487-7334.** Reservations required. www.theredinn.com. Main courses $21–$38. AE, DC, DISC, MC, V. Mid-June to early Sept daily 5:30–10pm, Sat–Sun 10am–2:30pm; call for off-season hours.

Expensive

Devon's ★★★ NEW AMERICAN   You can tell who Devon is: He's the one seating people, acting as line cook, busing tables, taking reservations, and chatting with customers. The force behind Devon's is a multitalented restaurateur with a great attitude. The tiny restaurant itself, a former boat shack, has fewer than 10 tables inside, all next to the open kitchen. In good weather, the choice seats are on the patio out front. Service is professional and the food elegantly prepared and nicely presented. The menu changes often but features wonderful fish, steak, chicken, and vegetarian meals. One favorite is sole with a simple *beurre blanc* sauce. This is a romantic option, but you definitely need a reservation. It's also a good breakfast choice for those staying in the far East End of town.

401½ Commercial St. (in the East End). ☎ **508/487-4773.** www.devons.org. Reservations recommended. Main courses $18–$25. DISC, MC, V. June–Sept Thurs–Tues 8am–1pm and 6–10pm; call for off-season hours. Closed Nov–Apr.

Edwidge @ Night and Café Edwidge ★★ NEW AMERICAN   Breakfast and dinner are run by two different teams at this second-floor restaurant, long a favorite with locals. For seating, you have a choice: inside where wooden booths, rafters, and close-set tables provide a casual feel; or outside on a narrow, breezy patio that offers more private dining. Outstanding menu items for dinner include tuna tartare or lobster dumplings as appetizers, and for the main course, filet mignon with a blue cheese fritter or *moqueta,* a Brazilian seafood dish. If you want to have breakfast here, you must arrive early in order to get a table.

333 Commercial St. (in the center of town). ☎ **508/487-4020.** Reservations recommended. Main courses $18–$29. MC, V. June–Sept daily 8–11am and 6–10pm; call for off-season hours. Closed Nov–Apr.

Front Street ★★ MEDITERRANEAN FUSION/ITALIAN For years, this restaurant has delivered high-quality food and service, and locals consider it a cherished locale. Located in a belowground space on Commercial Street, this cozy restaurant feels most comfortable on the chilly days. Chef Donna Aliperti is constantly improving her menu, inspired by trips to Italy and southern France. The fusion menu, available in season, has creative items like soft-shell crabs with corn-studded risotto and Chinese five-spice grilled duckling. The traditional Italian menu features pastas.

230 Commercial St. ℂ **508/487-9715.** www.frontstreetrestaurant.com. Reservations recommended. Main courses $18–$25. DISC, MC, V. June–Sept daily 6–10pm; call for off-season hours.

Lorraine's ★★ MEXICAN/NEW AMERICAN Long heralded by year-rounders as a spot for creative food and a festive atmosphere, Lorraine's is on the far west end of Commercial Street. Even those who shy away from Mexican restaurants should try the truly unique food here. Maryland soft-shell crabs are lightly dusted in flour seasoned with Chimayo chili powder, pan-sautéed, and served with a jalapeño aioli. For a main course, consider *viere verde*—sea scallops sautéed with tomatillos, flambéed in tequila, and cloaked in a green-chili sauce. For a treat, check out the extensive tequila menu; shots are served with a wonderful tomato juice–based chaser.

133 Commercial St. (in the West End). ℂ **508/487-6074.** www.lorrainesrestaurant.com. Reservations recommended. Main courses $17–$26. DISC, MC, V. June–Sept daily 6–10pm; call for off-season hours. Closed mid-Dec to Mar.

The Mews & Cafe Mews ★★ INTERNATIONAL/AMERICAN FUSION Bank on fine food and suave service at this beachfront restaurant, an enduring favorite since 1961. Upstairs is the cafe with its century-old mahogany bar and lighter menu. The dining room downstairs sits right on the beach. The best soup in the region is the Mews's scrumptious summertime special, chilled cucumber-miso bisque with curry shrimp timbale. Among the showier entrees is "captured scallops": prime Wellfleet specimens enclosed with a shrimp-and-crab mousse in a crisp wonton pouch and served atop a petite filet mignon with chipotle aioli. Desserts and coffees—take them upstairs in the cafe, to the accompaniment of soft-jazz piano—are delectable.

429 Commercial St. ℂ **508/487-1500.** www.mews.com. Reservations recommended. Main courses $18–$29. AE, DC, DISC, MC, V. Mid-June to early Sept daily 6–10pm, Sun 11am–2:30pm; late Sept to mid-June daily 6–10pm only.

Ross' Grill ★★★ 🍴 NEW AMERICAN BISTRO Tucked on the second floor in the back of the Whaler's Wharf, Ross' may be hard to find, but you won't forget it once you've tried what some consider the best food in Provincetown. This is the place to go when you are in the mood for a very special, intimate dinner. The dining room, with subdued lighting and decorated with an urban feel, has large windows overlooking the waterfront. With 75 wines available by the glass, this is also the place to come for wine aficionados. Menu items of note include the steak frites with hand-cut french fries; the roasted free-range chicken with panzanella salad; and the shellfish risotto, a delightful mixture of fresh provender from the sea.

237 Commercial St. (in the Whaler's Wharf). ℂ **508/487-8878.** www.rossgrillptown.com. Reservations recommended. Main courses $22–$40. MC, V. May–Sept Mon and Wed–Sat 11:30am–3pm and 5:30–9:30pm, Sun noon–3pm and 5:30–9pm; Apr and Oct Thurs–Mon 5:30pm to close; call for off-season hours.

Moderate

Bubala's by the Bay ★ ECLECTIC   This trendy bistro promises "serious food at sensible prices." And that's what it delivers: from buttermilk waffles to creative focaccia sandwiches to fajitas, Cajun calamari, and pad Thai. This is a big operation for Provincetown, and the huge outdoor patio facing Commercial Street is particularly popular in the morning. In season, there's entertainment nightly from 10pm to 1am.

183 Commercial St. (in the West End). ℂ **508/487-0773.** www.bubalas.com. Main courses $10–$21. AE, DISC, MC, V. Apr to mid-Oct daily 8am–11pm. Closed late Oct to Apr.

Café Heaven ★ AMERICAN   Prized for its leisurely country breakfasts (served until mid-afternoon to accommodate reluctant risers), this modern storefront—adorned with big, bold paintings by acclaimed Wellfleet artist John Grillo—also turns out substantial sandwiches, such as avocado and goat cheese on a French baguette.

199 Commercial St. (in the center of town). ℂ **508/487-9639.** Reservations not accepted. Most items $11–$15. No credit cards. July-Aug daily 8am–3pm; call for off-season hours. Closed Feb–May.

Fanizzi's By The Sea ★ 🍴 ITALIAN/SEAFOOD   This waterfront restaurant in the far East End of town is the perfect place to get away from all the hustle and bustle in the town center. The beauty of this casual restaurant is that you can have a burger and fries, order comfort food like Mom's meatloaf, or splurge on shrimp scampi, and it's all very reasonably priced. The view from the large wraparound plate glass windows is among the best in town. The $13 buffet brunch, served until 2pm on Sunday, is a good deal.

539 Commercial St. (in the far east end of town). ℂ **508/487-1964.** www.fanizzisrestaurant.com. Reservations accepted. Main courses $9–$21. AE, MC, V. Mid-June to mid-Sept Mon–Sat 11:30am–10pm, Sun 10am–9pm; call for off-season hours.

Napi's ★★ INTERNATIONAL   Restaurateur Napi Van Dereck can be credited with bringing P-town's restaurant scene up to speed—back in the early 1970s. His namesake restaurant still reflects that zeitgeist, with its rococo-hippie carpentry, select outtakes from his sideline in antiques, and some rather outstanding art. The cuisine is a lot less granola than it was, or maybe we've just caught up—hearty peasant fare never really goes out of style. And these peasants really get around, culling dumplings from China, falafel from Syria, and, from Greece, shrimp feta flambéed with ouzo and Metaxa. This restaurant has its own parking lot (around back), which is unusual in Provincetown.

7 Freeman St. (at Bradford St.). ℂ **800/571-6274** or 508/487-1145. www.napis-restaurant.com. Reservations recommended. Main courses $14–$26. DISC, MC, V. May to mid-Sept daily 5–10pm; mid-Sept to Apr daily 11:30am–4pm and 5–9pm.

Victor's ★★ NEW AMERICAN/TAPAS   One of Provincetown's newest restaurants, this gem is getting very good word of mouth. Though it is a bit out of the way, at the far west end of Bradford Street, people are making the trek. The dining room is modern with a cathedral ceiling and large stone fireplace. The special tapas are designed portion-wise so that two people can order three plates (for about $15 apiece) and feel full. The raw bar is open 3 to 10pm with fresh shellfish.

175 Bradford St. Ext. (in the west end, near W. Vine St.) ℂ **508/487-1777.** www.victorsptown.com. Reservations recommended. Tapas (small plates) $9–$15. MC, V. Mid-June to mid-Sept daily 8am–4pm and 5:30-10:30pm; call for off-season hours. Closed Nov–Mar.

Waterford Café & Tavern ★★ NEW AMERICAN Formerly the Commons, this centrally located cafe has a number of dining atmospheres: There's a sidewalk cafe, an upper level cafe, a street level tavern, a garden dining area, a second-floor deck, and the Daily Dose juice bar. No matter where you end up, you'll get to partake of tasty and creative fare. The establishment boasts the only wood-fired oven in town, which comes in handy in preparing the popular gourmet pizzas with unique toppings. A 13-room inn is located behind the restaurant.

386 Commercial St. ℂ **508/487-6400.** www.thewaterfordinn.com. Reservations recommended. Main courses $10–$26. AE, MC, V. Mid-June to mid-Sept daily 8am–4pm and 5:30–10:30pm; call for off-season hours. Closed Nov–Mar.

Inexpensive

Chach ★★ 🏠 DINER A diner run by a chef instead of a cook means the omelets are divine, the BLTs are heavenly, and the menu holds all kinds of little surprises, like Mexican specials. It's a little off the beaten track, but it's worth seeking out Chach's for reasonably priced dining without the crowds you find on Commercial Street.

73 Shankpainter Rd. (off Bradford St., a few blocks south of town). ℂ **508/487-1530.** All items under $10. No credit cards. Apr–Feb Thurs–Tues 7am–3pm. Closed Mar.

Townsend Lobster & Seafood ★★ ☺ 🏠 SEAFOOD Insiders know to head off the beaten track, down Shankpainter Road, to find the best seafood platter deals in town. This is off-the-boat seafood, the freshest in town, caught by Capt. Chris, who is also the owner of the restaurant. His goal is a family-friendly place to get good seafood, and he has succeeded on both counts.

87 Shankpainter Rd. (off Bradford St., a few blocks south of town). ℂ **508/487-5161.** Reservations not accepted. Main courses $10–$23. MC, V. Apr–Oct daily 11am–8pm. Call for off-season hours.

TAKEOUT & PICNIC FARE

Mojo's ★, 5 Ryder St. Extension (ℂ **508/487-3140**), is a seafood shack known for its lightly breaded fried fish and hand-cut fries. You can also order veggie burgers, burritos, and chicken tenders. Eat at one of the six picnic tables on the patio or take it to the beach. Closed mid-Oct to early May.

The best gourmet shop is **Angel Foods,** 467 Commercial St., in the East End (ℂ **508/487-6666;** www.angelfoods.com), which offers Italian specialties and other prepared foods.

The rollwiches—pita bread packed with a wide range of fillings—at **Box Lunch,** 353 Commercial St., in the center of town (ℂ **508/487-6026;** www.boxlunch. com), are ideal for a strolling lunch.

PROVINCETOWN AFTER DARK

Perhaps the nation's premier gay bar, **The Atlantic House** ★, 6 Masonic Place, off Commercial Street (ℂ **508/487-3821;** www.ahouse.com), is open year-round. The "A-House" also welcomes straights, except in the leather-oriented Macho Bar upstairs. In the Little Bar, check out the Tennessee Williams memorabilia, including a portrait *au naturel.*

Come late afternoon, if you're wondering where all the beachgoers went, it's a safe bet that a number are attending the gay-lesbian tea dance held daily in season from 4 to 6:30pm on the pool deck at the **Boatslip Beach Club** ★, 161 Commercial St. (ℂ **508/487-1669;** www.boatslipresort.com). Closed November through April.

Crown & Anchor ★, 247 Commercial St. (© **508/487-1430;** www.thecrown andanchor.net), houses a number of bars spanning leather, disco, comedy, drag shows, and cabaret. Facilities include a pool bar and game room. It's closed November through April.

You can depend on the **Post Office Café and Cabaret,** 303 Commercial St. (© **508/487-3892**), for amusing drag and comedy shows. Despite its cramped size, it's one of P-towns most popular clubs. In recent years, the B-Girlz (Hard Kora, Barbie-Q, and Belle Bottom) have been the featured act. The cover is $20. It's closed November to April.

The chic women's bar, **Vixen,** at the Pilgrim House, 336 Commercial St. (© **508/487-6424;** http://ptownvixen.com), features local and national jazz, blues, and comedy acts, including such favorites as Lea DeLaria and Melissa Ferrick a couple of times per season. There are also pool tables. It's closed November to April.

Governor Bradford, 312 Commercial St. (© **508/487-2781**), is a good old bar, featuring pool tables, drag karaoke (summer nights at 9:30pm), and disco.

Cape Cod National Seashore ★★★

No trip to Cape Cod would be complete without a visit to the **Cape Cod National Seashore** on the Outer Cape. Take an afternoon barefoot stroll along the "The Great Beach" and see why the Cape attracts so many artists and poets. On August 7, 1961, President John F. Kennedy signed a bill designating 27,000 acres in the 40 miles from Chatham to Provincetown as the Cape Cod National Seashore. However, as early as the 1930s, the National Park Service had been interested in Cape Cod's ocean beach; back then, the land would have cost taxpayers about $10 an acre! Unusual for a national park, the Seashore includes 500 private residences, the owners of which lease land from the park service. Convincing residents that a National Seashore would be a good thing for Cape Cod was an arduous task back then, and Provincetown still grapples with Seashore officials over town land issues.

ESSENTIALS

GETTING THERE   Take Rte. 6, the Mid-Cape Highway, to Eastham; it's about 50 miles from the Sagamore Bridge.

VISITOR INFORMATION   Pick up a map of the National Seashore at the **Salt Pond Visitor Center,** in Eastham (© **508/225-3421;** www.nps.gov/caco). It's open daily: late May to early September from 9am to 5pm (until 4:30pm the rest of the year). A $3-million rehab of the visitor center was completed in 2005. The smaller **Province Lands Visitor Center** (p. 258), is located in Provincetown. Both centers have ranger activities, gift shops, and restrooms. Seashore beaches are all clearly marked off Rte. 6. Additional beaches along this stretch are run by individual towns; you must have a sticker or pay a fee to park.

BEACHES & GETTING OUTSIDE

BEACHES   The Seashore's claim to fame is its spectacular beaches—in reality, one long beach—with dunes 50 to 150 feet high. This is the Atlantic Ocean, so the surf is rough (and cold), but a number of the beaches have lifeguards. A $45 pass will get you into all of them for the season, or you can pay a daily rate of $15. Most of the Seashore beaches have large parking lots, but you'll need to arrive early (before 10am) on busy summer weekends to claim a spot. If the beach you want to go to is full, try the one next door—most of the beaches are 5 to 10 miles apart. Don't forget your beach umbrella—the sun can get intense.

Coast Guard Beach ★★★ and **Nauset Light Beach ★★★**, off Ocean View Drive, Eastham: Connected to outlying parking lots by a free shuttle, these pristine beaches have lifeguards and restrooms. With the old Coast Guard building on one and the striped lighthouse on the other, these two strands are among the most scenic in the Seashore.

Head of the Meadow Beach ★★, off Head of the Meadow Road, Truro: Among the more remote National Seashore beaches, this spot (with restrooms) is known for its excellent surf. Because beachgoers don't have to traverse steep dunes to get here, Head of the Meadow is easier for seniors and those with disabilities to access.

Marconi Beach ★★, off Marconi Beach Road in South Wellfleet: The bluffs are so high here that the beach lies in shadows by late afternoon. Restrooms are available.

Race Point Beach ★★★ and **Herring Cove Beach ★★★**, off Rte. 6, Provincetown: Race Point has rough surf, and you might even spot a whale on its way to Stellwagen Bank, a breeding ground. Herring Cove, with much calmer waters, is a good place to watch sunsets and is popular with same-sex couples.

BICYCLING Some say the best bike path on Cape Cod is the **Province Lands Trail ★★★**, 5 swooping and invigorating miles at Race Point Beach. There is also a 2-mile relatively flat path linking Head of the Meadow Beach to High Head Beach in Truro.

FISHING Surf-casting is allowed from the ocean beaches. Race Point is a popular spot.

NATURE TRAILS The Seashore has a number of walking trails—all free, all picturesque. In Eastham, **Fort Hill ★★★**, off Rte. 6, has one of the best scenic views on Cape Cod, as well as a popular boardwalk trail through a red maple swamp. Following the trail markers around Fort Hill, you'll pass "Indian Rock" (bearing the marks of untold generations who used it to sharpen their tools) and enjoy scenic vantage points overlooking the channel-carved marsh and out to sea. The Fort Hill Trail hooks up with the .5-mile Red Cedar Swamp Trail, offering boardwalk views of an ecology that's otherwise inaccessible.

The **Nauset Marsh Trail ★** is accessed from the Salt Pond Visitor Center, on Rte. 6 in Eastham. **Great Island ★★**, on the bay side in Wellfleet, is one of the finest places to have a picnic; you could spend the day hiking the trails. On **Pamet Trail ★**, off North Pamet Road in Truro, hikers pass the decrepit old cranberry-bog building on the way to a trail through the dunes. Don't try the old boardwalk trail over the bogs here; it has flooded and is no longer in use. The **Atlantic White Cedar Swamp Trail ★★** is located at the Marconi Wireless Station site (described below). **Small Swamp ★** and **Pilgrim Spring ★** trails are found at Pilgrim Heights Beach. **Beech Forest Trail ★★** is located at Race Point in Provincetown.

SEASHORE SIGHTS The **Old Harbor Lifesaving Station ★**, Race Point Beach off Race Point Road, Provincetown (ⓒ **508/487-1256;** www.nps.gov/caco), was 1 of 13 lifesaving stations mandated by Congress in the late 19th century. This shingled shelter with a lookout tower was part of a network responsible for saving some 100,000 lives. Before the U.S. Lifesaving Service was founded in 1872 (it became part of the Coast Guard in 1915), shipwreck victims lucky enough to be washed ashore were still doomed unless they could find a "charity shed"—a hut supplied with firewood—maintained by the Massachusetts Humane Society. The six valiant "Surfmen" manning each lifesaving station took a more active approach, patrolling the beach at all hours and rowing out into the surf to save all they could. Their old equipment is on view at this museum. Admission is free; there's a parking fee for Race Point Beach (see "Beaches," above). It's open daily from 3 to 5pm in July and August; call for off-season hours. It's closed November through April.

The **Marconi Wireless Station,** on Marconi Park Site Road (off Rte. 6), South Wellfleet (© **508/349-3785;** www.nps.gov/caco), tells the story of the birth of international telegraphic communication. It's from this spot that inventor Guglielmo Marconi sent the world's first wireless communiqué: "Cordial greetings from President Theadore [sic] Roosevelt to King Edward VII in Poldhu, Wales." It was also here, in 1912, that news of the *Titanic* first reached these shores. There's scarcely a trace left of this extraordinary feat of technology (the station was dismantled in 1920); still, the outdoor displays convey the leap of imagination that was required.

The **Captain Edward Penniman House ★** at Fort Hill, off Rte. 6 in Eastham, is a grandly ornate 1868 Second Empire mansion. It's open for tours in season, but the exterior far outshines the interior. Call the visitor center (© **508/255-3421**) for times. Check out the huge whale jawbone gate before crossing the street to the trails (see "Nature Trails," above).

Five lighthouses, all automated now, dot the Seashore. In 1996, both Nauset Light, in Eastham, and Highland Light, in Truro, were successfully moved from precarious positions on the edge of dunes in order to save the beloved lighthouses. **Nauset Light ★**, with its cheerful red stripe, was originally moved to Eastham from Chatham in 1923. The lighthouse flashes an alternating red and white light that can be seen for 23 miles.

Highland Light ★★, also known as **Cape Cod Light,** is the site of the first light in this area, dating back to 1798. The present structure was built in 1857. Follow signs from Rte. 6 in North Truro to the end of Highland Road. This lighthouse, set high on a cliff, was the first light seen by ships traveling from Europe. Now that the structure has been moved back from the eroding cliff, visitors are allowed to climb the staircase to the top with a guide. *Note:* There's a minimum 4-foot height requirement for climbing the lighthouse. Nearby is the 1907 **Highland House ★★**, home of the collections of the Truro Historical Society. Admission to both lighthouse and museum is $5 for adults, free for children under 12. Both are open June through September, daily from 10am to 5pm.

Wood End Light, on Long Point in Provincetown, is an unusual square lighthouse built as a "twin" to Long Point Light in 1873. Hearty souls can hike first across the breakwater at the west end of Commercial Street and then about a half-mile over soft sand to see this lighthouse.

Long Point Light, established in 1827, is isolated at the very tip of Cape Cod. It's about a 1½-hour walk from the breakwater, or a short boat ride from the center of Provincetown. Its fixed green light can be seen for 8 miles. This lighthouse was once the center of a thriving fishing community in the 1800s. Storms and erosion led the community to float their houses across the bay to Provincetown's West End, where a couple of the houses—some of the oldest in town—are still standing.

MARTHA'S VINEYARD & NANTUCKET

by Laura M. Reckford

Megastars and CEOs, vacationing families and penniless students all seek refuge on Martha's Vineyard and Nantucket, two picturesque islands off the coast of Cape Cod. Both islands have much to offer families with children and couples seeking a romantic getaway. Their fame as summer resorts doesn't begin to take into account their rich history, diverse communities, and artistic traditions. But the popularity of these islands means that if you must go in the middle of summer, expect crowds and even—yikes!—traffic jams.

While only about 25 nautical miles apart, each island has a distinct personality. Martha's Vineyard, large enough to support a year-round population spanning a broad socioeconomic spectrum, is not quite as rarefied as Nantucket. Vineyarders pride themselves on their liberal stances. True, a prime oceanside estate might fetch millions here, but the residents still dicker over the price of zucchini at the local farmers' market.

Nantucket, flash-frozen in the mid–19th century through zealous zoning, has long been considered a Republican haven. It's rich and traditional. Social scene aside, Nantucket has more pristine public shores than the Vineyard, as well as the best upscale shopping in the region. But there's something for everyone on both islands, and an island vacation is bound to be one that's cherished for many years.

MARTHA'S VINEYARD ★★★

With 100 square miles, Martha's Vineyard is New England's largest island, yet each of its six communities is blessed with endearing small-town charm. When the former First Family vacationed here, locals joked that the Clintons tested their reputed nonchalance toward famous faces.

But don't visit the Vineyard for the celebrities. Instead, savor the decidedly laid-back pace of this unique place.

Most visitors don't take the time to explore the entire island, staying in the "down-island" towns of **Vineyard Haven ★** (officially called Tisbury), **Edgartown ★★★**, and **Oak Bluffs ★★★**. The "up-island" towns—**West Tisbury ★★**, Chilmark ★ (including the fishing village of **Menemsha ★★★**), and **Aquinnah ★** (formerly known as Gay Head)—tend to be less touristy.

By all means, admire the regal sea captains' homes in Edgartown. Stroll down Circuit Avenue in Oak Bluffs with a Mad Martha's ice-cream cone, then ride the Flying Horses Carousel, said to be the oldest working carousel in the nation. Check out the cheerful "gingerbread" cottages behind Circuit Avenue, where the echoes of 19th-century revival meetings still ring out from the imposing tabernacle.

But don't forget to journey "up-island" to marvel at the red-clay cliffs of Aquinnah, a national historic landmark. Or bike the country roads of West Tisbury and Chilmark. Buy a lobster roll in the fishing village of Menemsha. There's a surprising degree of diversity here, for those who take the time to discover it.

Essentials
GETTING THERE
By Ferry

Most visitors take a ferry from the mainland to the Vineyard. You'll most likely catch the ferry from the village of Woods Hole in the town of Falmouth on Cape Cod; boats also run from Falmouth Inner Harbor, Hyannis, New Bedford, Rhode Island, and Nantucket. It's easy to get a passenger ticket on almost any of the ferries, but space for cars is extremely limited, especially on summer weekends, when reservations must be made months in advance. Unless you absolutely must have your car with you, leave it on the mainland. Traffic and parking on the island can be brutal in summer, and it's easy to take shuttle buses (see below) from town to town or simply bike around.

FROM WOODS HOLE IN FALMOUTH The state-run **Steamship Authority** (© **508/477-8600** or 508/693-9130 for reservations and information; Apr 4–Sept 7 daily 7am–9pm, reduced hours the rest of the year; www.steamshipauthority.com) operates daily, year-round, weather permitting.

The cost of a round-trip passenger ticket on the ferry to Martha's Vineyard is $15 for adults and $8 for children 5 to 12. Bringing a bike costs an extra $6 round-trip. You do not need a reservation on the ferry if you're traveling without a car, and no reservations are needed for parking.

The Steamship Authority has the only ferries to Martha's Vineyard that accommodate cars. These large ferries make the 45-minute trip to Vineyard Haven throughout the year; some boats go to Oak Bluffs from late May to late October (call or check the website for seasonal schedules). The cost of a round-trip car passage from mid-May to mid-October is $135 to $155; in the off season, it drops to $85 to $105. The higher rates are for vehicles more than 17 feet long. Car rates do not include drivers or passengers. Although you can buy tickets over the phone, it's much faster to purchase them online at the boat line's website, **www.steamshipauthority.com**.

Many people prefer to leave their cars on the mainland, take the ferry, and then travel around the island by shuttle bus or taxi, or rent a bicycle, car, or jeep on the

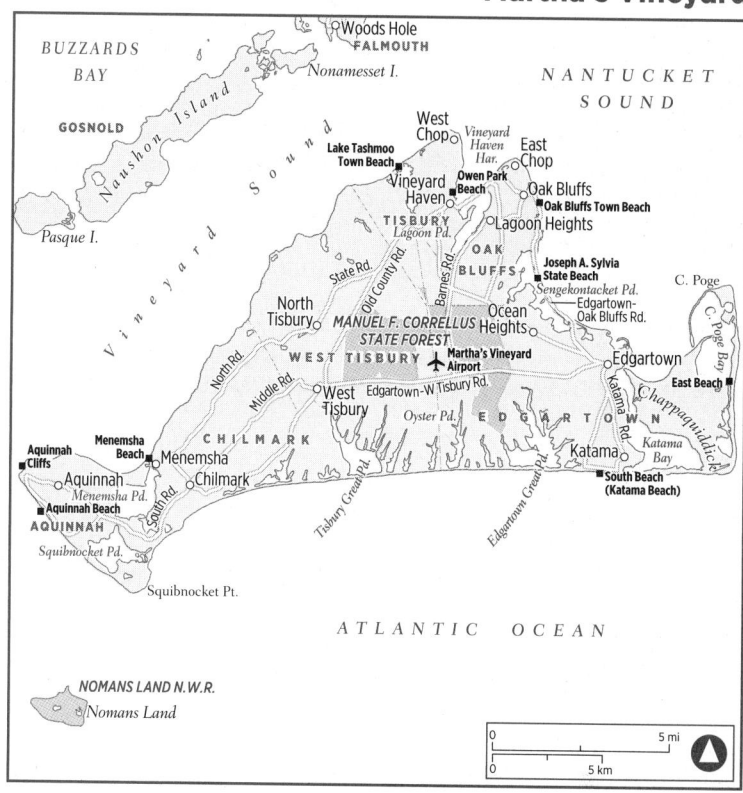

island. You can park your car at the Woods Hole lots (always full in the summer) or at one of the many lots in Falmouth and Bourne that absorb the overflow of cars. Parking costs $10 to $12 per day. Free shuttle buses (some equipped for bikes) run regularly from the outlying lots to the Woods Hole ferry terminal. If you're leaving your car on the mainland, plan to arrive at the parking lots at least an hour before sailing time to allow for parking, taking the free shuttle bus to the ferry terminal, and buying your ferry ticket.

FROM FALMOUTH INNER HARBOR You can board the *Island Queen* (© **508/548-4800;** www.islandqueen.com) for a 35-minute cruise to Oak Bluffs (passengers only). The boat runs from late May to mid-October; round-trip fare is $18 for adults, $9 for children under 13, and an extra $6 for bikes. There are seven crossings a day in season (eight on Fri and Sun), and no reservations are needed. Parking runs $15 a day. Credit cards are not accepted.

The **Falmouth–Edgartown Ferry Service,** 278 Scranton Ave. (© **508/548-9400;** www.falmouthferry.com), operates a 1-hour passenger ferry, called the *Pied Piper,* from Falmouth Harbor to Edgartown. The boat runs from late May to

CAR PASSAGE TO MARTHA'S VINEYARD

Reservations are required to bring your car to Martha's Vineyard on Friday, Saturday, Sunday, and Monday from mid-June to mid-September, plus Memorial Day weekend. During these months, standby is in effect only on Tuesday, Wednesday, and Thursday. Technically, vehicle reservations can be made up to 1 hour in advance of ferry departure, but in summer ferries are almost always full. Be aware that your space may be forfeited if you have not checked into the ferry terminal 30 minutes prior to sailing time. Reservations may be changed to another date and time with at least 24 hours' notice; otherwise, you will have to pay for an additional ticket for your vehicle.

If you arrive without a reservation on a day that allows standby travel, come early and be prepared to wait in line for hours. Your passage is guaranteed if you're in line by 2pm on designated standby days. For up-to-date **Steamship Authority** information, check out their website (**www.steamshipauthority.com**).

mid-October; reservations are required. In season, there are five crossings a day (six on Fri). Round-trip fares are $40 to $50 for adults (weekends are more expensive) and $25 to $30 for children under 12. Bicycles are $10 round-trip. Parking is $25 per day.

FROM HYANNIS   Early June through late September, **Hy-Line,** Ocean Street Dock (© **508/778-2600;** www.hy-linecruises.com), operates a conventional ferry from the Ocean Street dock to Oak Bluffs on Martha's Vineyard. It runs three trips a day; travel time is about 1 hour and 45 minutes. A round-trip costs $43 for adults and $22 for children 5 to 12 ($10 extra for bikes). It's a good idea to reserve a parking spot in Hyannis; the all-day fee is $10.

Hy-Line also operates a year-round **fast ferry** from Hyannis to Martha's Vineyard. It departs five to six times daily in season and takes 55 minutes. Round-trip tickets cost $69 for adults, $48 for children.

FROM NANTUCKET   From early June to mid-September, **Hy-Line,** Ocean Street Dock (© **508/778-2600;** www.hy-linecruises.com), runs three passenger ferries to Oak Bluffs on Martha's Vineyard. There is no car-ferry service between the islands. The trip time is 1 hour and 10 minutes. The one-way fare is $34 for adults, $21 for children 5 to 12, and $5 extra for bikes.

FROM NEW BEDFORD   The fast ferry M/V *Whaling City Express* travels to Martha's Vineyard in 1 hour. It makes six trips a day in season and is in service year-round, 7 days a week. A ticket costs $35 one-way and $70 round-trip for adults; $31 one-way and $62 round-trip for seniors; and $20 one-way, $40 round-trip for children under 12. Bikes cost $12 round-trip. Contact **New England Fast Ferry** for details (© **866/453-6800;** www.nefastferry.com).

FROM NORTH KINGSTOWN, RHODE ISLAND   From mid-June through October **Vineyard Fast Ferry** (© **401/295-4040;** www.vineyardfastferry.com) runs the high-speed catamaran *Millennium* to Oak Bluffs two to three round-trips daily. The trip takes 90 minutes. The ferry leaves from Quonset Point, about 10 minutes from Rte. I-95, 15 minutes from T. F. Green Airport in Providence, and 20 minutes from the Amtrak station in Kingston. Rates are $69 round-trip for adults, $46 round-trip for children 4 to 12, free for children under 4, and $12 round-trip for bikes. Parking next to the ferry port is $10 per day.

By Plane

You can fly into **Martha's Vineyard Airport** (airport code: MVY), also known as Dukes County Airport (© **508/693-7022**), in West Tisbury, about 5 miles outside Edgartown.

Airlines serving the Vineyard include **Cape Air/Nantucket Airlines** (© **800/352-0714** or 508/771-6944; www.flycapeair.com), which connects the island year-round with Boston (trip time 34 min.; hourly shuttle service in summer costs about $240 round-trip), Hyannis (trip time 20 min., $86), Nantucket (15 min., $88), and New Bedford (20 min., $84); and **US Airways** (© **800/428-4322**), which flies from Boston for about $215 round-trip and also has seasonal weekend service from La Guardia (trip time 1 hr., 15 min.), which costs approximately $400 round-trip.

Year-round charter service is offered by **Direct Flight** (© **508/693-6688**).

By Bus

Peter Pan Bus Lines (© **888/751-8800** or 508/548-7588; www.bonanzabus. com) connects the Woods Hole ferry port with Boston (from South Station), New York City, and Providence, Rhode Island. The trip from South Station in Boston takes about 1 hour and 35 minutes and costs about $26 one-way, $50 round-trip; from Boston's Logan Airport the cost is $30 one-way, $55 round-trip; from New York, the bus trip to Woods Hole takes about 6 hours and costs approximately $73 one-way or $121 round-trip.

By Limo

Falmouth Taxi (© **508/548-3100**) also runs limo service from Boston and the airport to the Woods Hole ferry terminal. It charges $195, including gratuity.

GETTING AROUND

BY BICYCLE & MOPED   The best way to explore the Vineyard is on two wheels. There's a little of everything for cyclists, from paved paths to hilly country roads (see "Exploring the Vineyard on Two Wheels," later in this chapter, for details on where to ride).

Mopeds, which you need a driver's license to rent and a helmet to ride, are also a way to navigate Vineyard roads, but be aware they are considered quite dangerous on the island's busy, winding, and sandy roads—the number of accidents involving mopeds seems to rise every year. Also, islanders tend to feel quite negative about mopeds.

Bike-rental shops are clustered in all three down-island towns. Scooter- and moped-rental shops are only in Oak Bluffs and Vineyard Haven. Bike rentals cost around $20 a day, scooters and mopeds $46 to $85. For bike rentals in Vineyard Haven, try **Martha's Bike Rentals,** Lagoon Pond Road (© 508/693-6593). For mopeds, try **Adventure/Thrifty Rentals,** Beach Road (© 508/693-1959; www. islandadventuresmv.com). In Oak Bluffs, there's **Anderson's,** Circuit Avenue Extension (© 508/693-9346), which rents bikes only; and **Sun 'n' Fun,** Lake Avenue (© 508/693-5457; www.sunnfunrentals.com). In Edgartown, you'll find bike rentals at **R. W. Cutler Bike,** 1 Main St. (© 508/627-4052; www.edgartownbikerentals. com); **Edgartown Bicycles,** 190 Upper Main St. (© 508/627-9008); and **Wheel Happy,** 204 Upper Main St. and 8 S. Water St. (© 508/627-5928).

BY CAR If you're here for a long visit or if you want to do some exploring up-island, you may want to bring a car or rent one on the island. Keep in mind that car-rental rates can soar during peak season, and gas is also much more expensive on the island. Representatives of national car-rental chains are located at the airport and in Vineyard Haven and Oak Bluffs. Local agencies also operate out of all three port towns, and many of them rent jeeps, mopeds, and bikes in addition to cars. The national chains include **Budget** (© **800/527-0700** or 508/693-1911; www.budget. com) and **Hertz** (© **800/654-3131**; www.hertz.com).

For local agencies, in Vineyard Haven, you'll find **Adventure Rentals,** Beach Road (© **508/693-1959;** www.islandadventuresmv.com); and in Edgartown, **AAA Island Rentals,** 141 Main St. (© **508/627-6800**).

BY SHUTTLE BUS In season, shuttle buses run often enough to make them a practical means of getting around. They are also cheap, dependable, and easy.

The **Martha's Vineyard Regional Transit Authority** (© **508/693-9440;** www. vineyardtransit.com) operates shuttle buses year-round on about a dozen routes around the island. The buses, which are white with purple logos, cost about $2 to $5, depending on distance. The pricing formula is $1 per town. For example, Vineyard Haven to Oak Bluffs is $2, but Vineyard Haven to Edgartown (passing through Oak Bluffs) is $3. A 1-day pass is $6; a 3-day pass is $15. The Edgartown Downtown Shuttle and the South Beach buses circle throughout town or out to South Beach every 20 minutes in season. They also stop at the free parking lots just north of the town center—this is a great way to avoid circling the streets in search of a vacant spot on busy weekends. The main down-island stops are Vineyard Haven (near the ferry terminal), Oak Bluffs (near the Civil War statue in Ocean Park), and Edgartown (Church St., near the Old Whaling Church). From late June to early September, they run from 6am to midnight every 15 minutes or half-hour; hours are reduced in spring and fall. Buses also go out to Aquinnah (via the airport, West Tisbury, and Chilmark), leaving every couple of hours from down-island towns and looping about every hour through up-island towns.

For bus tours of the island, call **Island Transport** (© **508/693-0058;** www. mvtour.com) or hop on one of the Island Transport buses that are stationed at the ferry terminals in Vineyard Haven and Oak Bluffs in the summer.

BY TAXI Upon arrival, you'll find taxis at all ferry terminals and at the airport, and there are permanent taxi stands in Oak Bluffs (at the Flying Horses Carousel) and Edgartown (next to the Town Wharf). Most taxi outfits operate cars as well as vans for larger groups and travelers with bikes. Cab companies on the island include **Adam Cab** (© **800/281-4462** or 508/693-3332), **Accurate Cab** (© **888/557-9798** or 508/627-9798; the only 24-hr. service), **All Island Taxi** (© **800/693-TAXI** [8294] or 508/693-2929), and **Patti's Taxi** (© **508/693-1663**). Rates from town to town in summer are generally flat fees based on where you're headed and the number of passengers on board. A trip from Vineyard Haven to Edgartown would probably cost around $23 for two people. Late-night revelers should keep in mind that rates double after midnight until 7am.

BY CHAPPAQUIDDICK FERRY From June to mid-October, the **On-Time ferry** (© **508/627-9427;** www.chappyferry.net) runs the 5-minute trip from Memorial Wharf on Dock Street in Edgartown to Chappaquiddick Island. It leaves every 5 minutes from 7am to midnight. Passengers, bikes, mopeds, dogs, and cars (three at a time) are all welcome. The one-way cost is $3 per person, $10 for one car/one driver, $6 for one bike/one person, and $5 for one moped or motorcycle/one person.

VISITOR INFORMATION

Contact the **Martha's Vineyard Chamber of Commerce** at Beach Road, Vineyard Haven (P.O. Box 1698 Vineyard Haven, MA 02568; ☎ **508/693-0085;** fax 508/693-7589), or visit their website at **www.mvy.com**. There are also information booths at the ferry terminal in Vineyard Haven, across from the Flying Horses Carousel in Oak Bluffs, and on Church Street in Edgartown. For information on current events, check the two local newspapers, the *Vineyard Gazette* (www.mvgazette. com) and the *Martha's Vineyard Times* (www.mvtimes.com).

In case of an **emergency,** call ☎ **911** and/or head for the **Martha's Vineyard Hospital,** Linton Lane, Oak Bluffs (☎ **508/693-0410**), which has a 24-hour emergency room.

A Stroll Around Edgartown ★★★

A good way to acclimate yourself to the pace and flavor of the Vineyard is to walk the streets of Edgartown. This walk starts at the Dr. Daniel Fisher House and meanders along for about a mile; it takes about 2 to 3 hours.

If you're driving, park at the free lots at the edge of town (you'll see signs on the roads from Vineyard Haven and West Tisbury) and bike or take the shuttle bus (it costs only 50¢) to the Edgartown Visitor Center on Church Street.

The **Dr. Daniel Fisher House ★**, 99 Main St. (☎ **508/627-8017;** www. mvpreservation.org/fisher.html), is a prime example of Edgartown's trademark Greek Revival opulence. A key player in the 19th-century whaling trade, Dr. Fisher amassed a fortune sufficient to found the Martha's Vineyard National Bank. Built in 1840, his proud mansion boasts such classical elements as colonnaded porticos and a delicate roof walk.

Note: The only way to view the interior (now headquarters for the Martha's Vineyard Preservation Trust) is with a guided **Vineyard Historic Walking Tour** (☎ **508/627-8619**). This tour, which also takes in the neighboring Old Whaling Church, originates next door at the Vincent House Museum. Tours are offered June through September Monday through Saturday from noon to 3pm. The cost is $7 to $10 for adults, free for children 12 and under.

The **Vincent House Museum ★**, off Main Street between Planting Field Way and Church Street, is a transplanted 1672 full Cape and is considered the oldest surviving dwelling on the island. The **Old Whaling Church ★★**, 89 Main St., is a magnificent 1843 Greek Revival edifice designed by local architect Frederick Baylies, Jr., and was built as a whaling boat would have been, out of massive pine beams; it boasts 27-foot windows and a 92-foot tower. Maintained by the Preservation Trust and still supporting a Methodist parish, the building is now primarily used as a performance venue.

Continuing down Main Street and turning right onto School Street, you'll pass another Baylies monument, the 1839 **Baptist Church,** which, having lost its spire, was converted into a private home with a rather grand, column-fronted facade. Two blocks farther is the **Vineyard Museum ★★**, 59 School St. (☎ **508/627-4441;** www.mvmuseum.org), a fascinating complex assembled by the Dukes County Historical Society. This cluster of buildings contains exhibits of Native American crafts, an entire 1765 house, an extraordinary array of maritime art, and the Gay Head Light Tower's decommissioned Fresnel lens.

Give yourself enough time to explore the museum's curiosities before heading south 1 block on Cooke Street. Cater-cornered across South Summer Street, you'll spot the first of Baylies's impressive endeavors, the 1828 **Federated Church.** One block left are the offices of the *Vineyard Gazette,* 34 S. Summer St. (𝄐 **508/627-4311;** www.mvgazette.com). Operating out of a 1760 house, this exemplary small-town newspaper has been going strong since 1846.

Walk down South Summer Street to Main Street and take a right toward the water, stopping at any inviting shops along the way. Veer left on Dock Street to reach the **Old Sculpin Gallery,** 58 Dock St. (𝄐 **508/627-4881**), open from late June to mid-September. The output of the Martha's Vineyard Art Association is displayed. The real draw is the stark old building itself, which started out as a granary and spent the better part of the 20th century as a boat-building shop.

Cross the street to survey the harbor from the second-floor deck at Town Wharf. You can watch the tiny On-Time ferry make its 5-minute crossing to **Chappaquiddick Island ★★.** Don't bother looking for the original **Dike Bridge,** infamous scene of the Kennedy/Kopechne scandal; it has been dismantled and, at long last, replaced.

Stroll down North Water Street to admire the many formidable captain's homes, several of which have been converted into inns. Each has a tale to tell. The 1750 **Daggett House** (no. 59), which is now a private home, started out as a 1660 tavern, and the original beehive oven is flanked by a "secret" passageway. Nathaniel Hawthorne holed up at the **Edgartown Inn** (no. 56) for nearly a year in 1789, while writing *Twice Told Tales*—and, it is rumored, romancing a local maiden who inspired *The Scarlet Letter.* On your way back to Main Street, you'll pass the **Gardner–Colby Gallery** (no. 27), filled with beautiful island-inspired paintings.

After all that walking, stop for a drink at **The Newes from America,** 23 Kelley St., off North Water Street 𝄐 **508/627-4397;** www.kelley-house.com/dining_news_from_america.asp). This Colonial basement pub serves up specialty beers and the best French onion soup on the island (see "Where to Dine," later in this section).

Beaches & Outdoor Pursuits

BEACHES Most down-island beaches in Vineyard Haven, Oak Bluffs, and Edgartown are open to the public and are just a walk or a short bike ride from town. In season, shuttle buses make stops at **State Beach,** between Oak Bluffs and Edgartown. Most of the Vineyard's magnificent up-island shoreline is privately owned or restricted to residents, and thus off-limits to visitors. Renters in up-island communities, however, can obtain a beach sticker (around $35–$50 for a season sticker) for those private beaches by applying with a lease at the relevant **town hall:** West Tisbury, 𝄐 **508/696-0147;** Chilmark, 𝄐 **508/645-2100;** or Aquinnah, 𝄐 **508/645-2300.** Also, many up-island inns offer the perk of temporary passes to the beautiful up-island beaches. In addition to the public beaches listed below, you might track down a few hidden coves by requesting a map of conservation properties from the **Martha's Vineyard Land Bank** (𝄐 **508/627-7141**). Below is a list of visitor-friendly beaches:

○ **Aquinnah Beach ★★★** (Moshup Beach), off Moshup Trail: Parking costs $20 a day in season at this peaceful half-mile beach just east (Atlantic side) of the colorful cliffs. Although they've violating the law, nudists tend to gravitate toward this beach.

Edgartown

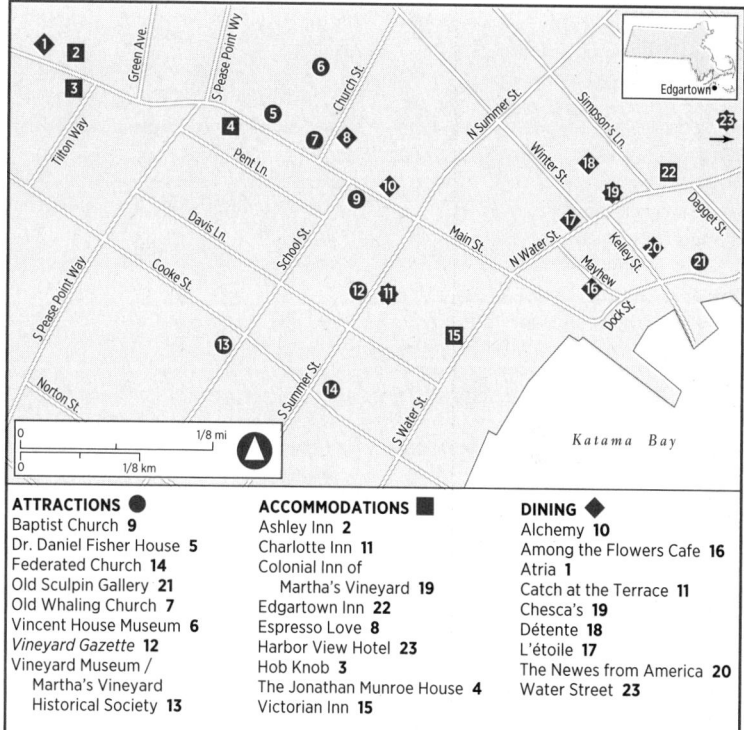

ATTRACTIONS ●
Baptist Church **9**
Dr. Daniel Fisher House **5**
Federated Church **14**
Old Sculpin Gallery **21**
Old Whaling Church **7**
Vincent House Museum **6**
Vineyard Gazette **12**
Vineyard Museum /
    Martha's Vineyard
    Historical Society **13**

ACCOMMODATIONS ■
Ashley Inn **2**
Charlotte Inn **11**
Colonial Inn of
    Martha's Vineyard **19**
Edgartown Inn **22**
Espresso Love **8**
Harbor View Hotel **23**
Hob Knob **3**
The Jonathan Munroe House **4**
Victorian Inn **15**

DINING ◆
Alchemy **10**
Among the Flowers Cafe **16**
Atria **1**
Catch at the Terrace **11**
Chesca's **19**
Détente **18**
L'étoile **17**
The Newes from America **20**
Water Street **23**

Because of rapid erosion, climbing the cliffs or taking clay for a souvenir is forbidden. Restrooms are near the parking lot, which is a 10-minute walk from the beach.

○ **East Beach ★★,** Wasque (pronounced *Way*-squee) Reservation, Chappaquiddick: Relatively few people bother biking or hiking (or four-wheel-driving) this far, so you should be able to find all the privacy you crave. Take the On-Time Ferry to Chappaquiddick, then go straight 2½ miles and continue straight for another half-mile on a dirt road. Biking on Chappaquiddick is one of the great Vineyard experiences, but the roads can be quite sandy and are best suited to a mountain bike. Along the dirt road, you'll pass **Mytoi,** a 14-acre Japanese garden open to the public, which is an oasis of flora and fauna. Because of its exposure on the east shore of the island, the surf here is rough. Pack a picnic; there are no stores on Chappy. There is a portable toilet in the parking lot. Most people park their car near the Dike Bridge and walk the couple of hundred yards out to the beach. Admission is $3 per person.

○ **Joseph A. Sylvia State Beach ★★★**, midway between Oak Bluffs and Edgartown: Stretching a mile and flanked by a paved bike path, this placid beach has views of Cape Cod and Nantucket Sound and is prized for its gentle and (relatively) warm

EXPLORING THE VINEYARD ON TWO WHEELS

Biking on the Vineyard is a memorable experience, not only for the smooth, well-maintained paths, but also for the long stretches of virtually untrafficked up-island roads that reveal breathtaking country landscapes and sweeping ocean views.

A triangle of paved bike paths, roughly 8 miles to a side, links the down-island towns of Oak Bluffs, Edgartown, and Vineyard Haven. The Vineyard Sound portion along Beach Road, flanked by water on both sides, is especially enjoyable. From Edgartown, you can also follow the bike path to South Beach. For a more woodsy ride, there are paved paths and mountain-biking trails in the **Manuel F. Correllus State Forest** (© **508/693-2540;** www.mass.gov/dcr/parks/south east/corr.htm), a vast spread of scrub oak and pine in the middle of the island. The bike paths are accessible off Edgartown–West Tisbury Road.

The up-island roads leading to West Tisbury, Chilmark, Menemsha, and Aquinnah are a cyclist's paradise, with unspoiled pastureland, old farmhouses, and brilliant sea views reminiscent of Ireland's countryside. But keep in mind that the terrain is often hilly, and the roads are narrow and a little rough around the edges. From West Tisbury to Chilmark Center, try **South Road**— about 5 miles—which passes stone walls rolling over moors, clumps of pine and wildflowers, verdant marshes and tidal pools, and, every once in a while, an Old Vineyard farmhouse. **Middle Road** is another lovely ride with a country feel and will also get you from West Tisbury to Chilmark. (It's usually less trafficked, too.)

waves, which make it perfect for swimming. The drawbridge is a local landmark, and visitors and islanders alike have been jumping off it for years. Be aware that State Beach is one of the Vineyard's most popular; in midsummer, it's packed. The shuttle bus stops here, and roadside parking is also available—but it fills up fast, so stake your claim early. Located on the eastern shore of the island, this is a Nantucket Sound beach, so waters are shallow and rarely rough. There are no restrooms, and only the Edgartown end of the beach, known as Bend-in-the-Road Beach, has lifeguards.

- **Lake Tashmoo Town Beach** ★, off Herring Creek Road, Vineyard Haven: The only spot on the island where lake meets ocean, this tiny strip of sand is good for swimming and surf-casting but is somewhat marred by limited parking and often brackish waters. Nonetheless, this is a popular spot, as beachgoers enjoy a choice between the Vineyard Sound beach, with mild surf, or the placid lake beach. Bikers will have no problem reaching this beach from Vineyard Haven; otherwise, you have to use a car to get here.

- **Menemsha Beach** ★★, next to Dutchers Dock in Menemsha Harbor: The gentle surf of this small but well-trafficked strand, with lifeguards and restrooms, is popular with families. In season, it's virtually wall-to-wall umbrellas. Nearby food vendors in Menemsha—selling everything from ice cream and hot dogs to shrimp cocktail—are a plus here.

- **Oak Bluffs Town Beach,** Seaview Avenue: This sandy strip extends from both sides of the ferry wharf, which makes it a convenient place to linger while waiting

My favorite up-island route is the 6-mile stretch from Chilmark Center out to Aquinnah via **State Road** and **Moshup Trail** ★. The ocean views along this route are spectacular. Don't miss the **Quitsa Pond Lookout,** about 2 miles down State Road, which provides a panoramic vista of Nashaquitsa and Menemsha ponds, beyond which you can see Menemsha, Vineyard Sound, and the Elizabeth Islands. A bit farther, just over the Aquinnah town line, is the Aquinnah spring, a roadside iron pipe where you can refill your water bottle with the freshest and coldest water on the island. At the fork after the spring, turn left on Moshup Trail—in fact, a regular road— and follow the coast, which offers gorgeous views of the ocean and the sweeping sand dunes. You'll soon wind up in Aquinnah, where you can explore the red-clay cliffs and pristine beaches. On the return trip, you can take the handy bike ferry ($7 round-trip) from Aquinnah to Menemsha. It runs daily in summer and on weekends in May.

There are lots of bike-rental operations near the ferry landings in Vineyard Haven and Oak Bluffs, as well as a few rental shops in Edgartown. For information on rentals, see "Getting Around," earlier in this chapter.

A very good outfitter out of Boston, called **Backroads** (**©** **800/462-2848;** www.backroads.com), runs 6-day island-hopping tours of Martha's Vineyard and Nantucket. Stays are at various inns on the islands. It's a perfect way to experience both islands.

for the next boat. This is an in-town beach, within walking distance for visitors staying in Oak Bluffs. The surf is consistently calm and the sand smooth, so it's also ideal for families with small children. Public restrooms are available at the ferry dock, but there are no lifeguards.

o **Owen Park Beach,** off Main Street in Vineyard Haven: A tiny strip of harborside beach adjoining a town green with swings and a bandstand will suffice for young children, who, by the way, get lifeguard supervision. There are no restrooms, but this is an in-town beach, which is probably a quick walk from your Vineyard Haven inn.

o **South Beach (Katama Beach)** ★★★, about 4 miles south of Edgartown on Katama Road: If you have time for only one trip to the beach and you can't get up-island, go with this popular 3-mile barrier strand that boasts heavy wave action (check with lifeguards for swimming conditions), sweeping dunes, and, most important, relatively ample parking space. It's also accessible by bike path or shuttle. Lifeguards patrol some sections of the beach, and there are sparsely scattered toilet facilities. The rough surf here is popular with surfers. *Tip:* As you face the water, families tend to head to the left, college kids to the right.

A word about Aquinnah: Almost every visitor to the Vineyard finds his way to the cliffs, and with all the tour buses lined up in the huge parking lot and the rows of tacky concession stands and gift shops, this can seem like a rather outrageous tourist trap. You're right; it's not the Grand Canyon. But the observation deck, with its view of the colorful cliffs, the adorable brick lighthouse, and the Elizabeth Islands beyond, will make you glad you made the effort. Instead of rushing away, stop for a cool drink and a clam roll at the snack bar with the deck overlooking the ocean.

FISHING For shellfishing, get information and a permit from the appropriate town hall (for the telephone numbers, see "Beaches," above). Popular spots for surf-casting include **Wasque Point** on Chappaquiddick, South Beach, and the jetty at Menemsha Pond.

The party boat *Skipper* (© 508/693-1238) offers half-day trips out of Oak Bluffs harbor in season. The cost is $35 for adults, $25 for children 12 and under. Deep-sea excursions can be arranged aboard **Summer's Lease** (© 508/693-2880) out of Oak Bluffs. Up-island, there is **North Shore Charters** (© 508/645-2993; www.bassnblue.com).

Cooper Gilkes III, proprietor of **Coop's Bait & Tackle,** at 147 W. Tisbury Rd. in Edgartown (© 508/627-3909; http://coopsbaitandtackle.com), which offers rentals as well as supplies, is another acknowledged authority. He's available as an instructor or charter guide.

GOLF The 9-hole **Mink Meadows Golf Course,** off Franklin Street in Vineyard Haven (© 508/693-0600; www.minkmeadowsgc.com), is open to the general public, while the championship-level 18-hole **Farm Neck Golf Club,** off Farm Neck Road in Oak Bluffs (© 508/693-3057), is semiprivate.

NATURE TRAILS About a fifth of the Vineyard's landmass has been set aside for conservation, and it's all accessible to bikers and hikers. The **West Chop Woods,** off Franklin Street in Vineyard Haven, comprise 85 acres with marked walking trails. Midway between Vineyard Haven and Edgartown, the **Felix Neck Wildlife Sanctuary** ★★ includes a 6-mile network of trails over varying terrain, from woodland to beach.

The 633-acre **Long Point Wildlife Refuge** ★★, off Waldron's Bottom Road in West Tisbury (© 508/693-7392 for the gatehouse; www.thetrustees.org), offers heath and dunes, freshwater ponds, a popular family-oriented beach, and interpretive nature walks for children.

Up-island, along the sound, the **Menemsha Hills Reservation,** off North Road in Chilmark (© 508/693-7662), encompasses 210 acres of rocks and bluffs, with steep paths, lovely views, and even a public beach. **The Cedar Tree Neck Sanctuary,** off Indian Hill Road southwest of Vineyard Haven (© 508/693-5207), offers some 300 forested acres that end in a stony beach. Swimming and sunbathing are prohibited.

Some remarkable botanical surprises can be found at the 20-acre **Polly Hill Arboretum** ★★, 809 State Rd., West Tisbury (© 508/693-9426; www.polly hillarboretum.org). The late legendary horticulturist Polly Hill developed this property over the past 40 years, and a trust now allows the public to wander the grounds Thursday to Tuesday from 7am until 7pm. This is a magical place, particularly mid-June to July, when the Dogwood Allée is in bloom. Wanderers will pass old stone walls on the way to The Tunnel of Love, an arbor of hornbeam. You'll also see witch hazels, camellias, magnolias, and rhododendrons. To get there from Vineyard Haven, go south on State Road, bearing left at the junction of North Road. The arboretum entrance is about a half-mile down, on the right. There is a requested donation of $5 for adults.

WATERSPORTS **Wind's Up,** 199 Beach Rd., Vineyard Haven (© 508/693-4252; www.windsupmv.com), rents out canoes, kayaks, and various sailing craft, including windsurfing boards, and offers instruction on a placid pond; it also rents surfboards and boogie boards. Canoes and kayaks rent for $20 per hour.

Museums & Historic Landmarks

Cottage Museum ★   This little museum, a cottage in the center of Oak Bluffs' famous "campground," displays 19th-century artifacts, like bulky black bathing costumes and a melodeon used for informal hymnal sing-alongs. The campground consists of a 34-acre circle with more than 300 multicolored, elaborately trimmed Carpenter Gothic cottages, which look very much the way they might have more than a hundred years ago. These adorable little houses were loosely modeled on the revivalists' canvas tents that inspired them. In the 1860s, when many of the cottages were built, campers typically attended three lengthy prayer services daily. Opportunities for worship remain at the 1878 Trinity Methodist Church within the park or, just outside, on Samoset Avenue, at the nonsectarian 1870 Union Chapel, a magnificent octagonal structure with superb acoustics.

At the very center of the Camp Meeting Grounds is the striking **Trinity Park Tabernacle** ★★. Built in 1879, the open-sided chapel is the largest wrought-iron structure in the country. Thousands can be accommodated on its long wooden benches, which are usually filled to capacity for the Sunday-morning services in summer, as well as for community sings (Wed in July–Aug) and occasional concerts.

1 Trinity Park (within the Camp Meeting Grounds), Oak Bluffs. © 508/693-7784. www.mvcma.org. Admission $2 (donation). Mid-June to Sept Mon–Sat 10am–4pm. Closed Oct to mid-June.

Flying Horses Carousel ★★ ☺   You don't have to be a kid to enjoy what is considered to be the oldest working carousel in the country. Built in 1876 at Coney Island, this National Historic Landmark predates the era of horses that "gallop." Lacking the necessary gears, these mounts merely glide smoothly in place to the joyful strains of a calliope. Take a moment to admire the intricate hand carving and real horsehair manes, and gaze into the horses' glass eyes for a surprise: tiny animal charms glint within.

33 Circuit Ave. (at Lake Ave.), Oak Bluffs. © 508/693-9481. Tickets $1.50 per ride, or 8 rides for $10. Late May to early Sept daily 10am–10pm; call for off-season hours. Closed mid-Oct to mid-Apr.

The Martha's Vineyard Museum ★   All of Martha's Vineyard's colorful history is captured in this compound of historic buildings. To acclimate yourself chronologically, start with the pre-Colonial artifacts—from arrowheads to colorful Gay Head clay pottery—displayed in the 1845 **Captain Francis Pease House.** The **Gale Huntington Reference Library** houses rare documentation of the island's history, from genealogical records to whaling-ship logs. Some extraordinary memorabilia, including scrimshaw and portraiture, are on view in the adjoining **Francis Foster Maritime Gallery.**

To get a sense of daily life during the era when the waters of the East Coast were the equivalent of a modern highway, visit the **Thomas Cooke House,** a shipwright-built Colonial, built in 1765, where the Customs collector lived and worked. The Fresnel lens on display outside the museum was lifted from the Gay Head Lighthouse in 1952, after nearly a century of service. Though it no longer serves to warn ships of dangerous shoals (that light is automated now), it still lights up the night every evening in summer, just for show.

59 School St. (corner of Cooke St., 2 blocks southwest of Main St.), Edgartown. ☏ **508/627-4441.** www.mvmuseum.org. Admission in season $7 adults, $4 children 6-15. Mid-June to mid-Oct Tues–Sat 10am–5pm; mid-Oct to late Dec and mid-Mar to mid-June Wed–Fri 1–4pm, Sat 10am–4pm; early Jan to mid-Mar Wed–Fri by appointment, Sat 10am–4pm.

Organized Tours & Cruises

The Trustees of Reservations, a statewide land conservation group, offers fascinating 2½-hour **Natural History Tours ★★★** (☏ **508/627-3599;** www.thetrustees.org) by safari vehicle or kayak around Cape Poge on Chappaquiddick Island. The kayak tour on Poucha Pond and Cape Poge Bay is designed for all levels. The cost for the safari tour is $35 for adults, $15 for children 15 and under. The cost for the kayak tour is $40 for adults, $18 for children 15 and under. A tour of the Cape Poge lighthouse costs $25 for adults and $12 for children.

Shopping ★

ARTS & CRAFTS Oak Bluff's little art gallery cluster, called the Art District, is worth a visit. Just beyond the "gingerbread" cottage colony on Dukes County Avenue, are six interesting shops: **Periwinkle Studio** (☏ 508/696-8304, an intriguing gallery; **Alison Shaw Gallery** (☏ 508/696-7429; www.alisonshaw.com), featuring the exquisite photographs of this former newspaper photographer; **Pik Nik Art & Apparel** (☏ 508/693-1366; www.piknikmv.com), a funky array of crafts, gifts, and clothing; **Dragonfly Gallery** (☏ 508/693-8877; www.mvdragonfly.com), offering a range of mediums; **Red Mannequin** (☏ 508/693-2858), with clothing, gifts, and artwork; and **Lucinda's Enamels** (☏ 508/696-7863; www.lucindasheldon.com), showcasing fine-art jewelry.

No visit to Edgartown would be complete without a peek at the wares of scrimshander Thomas J. DeMont, Jr., at **Edgartown Scrimshaw Gallery,** 43 Main St. (☏ **508/627-9439**). All the scrimshaw in the gallery is hand-carved using ancient mammoth ivory or antique fossil ivory.

The Field Gallery, State Road (in the center of town), West Tisbury (☏ **508/693-5595;** www.fieldgallery.com), is where Marc Chagall meets Henry Moore and where Tom Maley's playful figures have enchanted locals and passersby for decades. You'll also find paintings by Albert Alcalay and drawings and cartoons by Jules Feiffer. The Sunday-evening openings are high points of the summer social season. Closed from mid-October to mid-May.

Don't miss the **Granary Gallery at the Red Barn,** Old County Road (off Edgartown–West Tisbury Rd., about one-quarter mile north of the intersection), West Tisbury (☏ **508/693-0455;** www.granarygallery.com), which displays astounding prints by the late longtime summerer Alfred Eisenstaedt and dazzling color photos by local luminary Alison Shaw.

Another unique local artisans' venue is **Martha's Vineyard Glass Works,** State Road, North Tisbury (☏ **508/693-6026;** www.mvglassworks.com). The three resident artists—Andrew Magdanz, Susan Shapiro, and Mark Weiner—have shown nationwide to considerable acclaim. Their output is decidedly avant-garde and may not suit all tastes, but it's an eye-opening array and all the more fascinating once you've witnessed a work in progress.

GIFTS/HOME DECOR   Craftworks, 149 Circuit Ave. (☎ **508/693-7463**), is filled to the rafters with whimsical, contemporary American crafts.

Carly Simon's **Midnight Farm,** 18 Water-Cromwell Lane, Vineyard Haven (☎ **508/693-1997;** www.midnightfarm.net), offers high-end, imaginative gift items from candles to children's clothes to furniture and glassware.

Where to Stay

When deciding where to stay on Martha's Vineyard, you'll need to consider the type of vacation you prefer. The down-island towns of Vineyard Haven, Oak Bluffs, and Edgartown provide shops, restaurants, beaches, and harbors within walking distance, and frequent shuttles to get you all over the island. But all three can be overly crowded on busy summer weekends. Vineyard Haven is the gateway for most of the ferry traffic; Oak Bluffs is a raucous town with most of the Vineyard's bars and nightclubs; and many visitors make a beeline to Edgartown's manicured Main Street. Up-island inns provide more peace and quiet, but you'll probably need a car to get around. Also, you may not be within walking distance of the beach.

I've provided only summer rates below because the Vineyard is so seasonal. If you do visit in the off-season, you may find substantial discounts at the establishments that remain open year-round.

EDGARTOWN
Very Expensive

Charlotte Inn ★★★   Ask anyone to recommend the best inn on the island, and this is the name you're most likely to hear. It's one of only two Relais & Châteaux properties on the Cape and islands. Linked by formal gardens, each of the 18th- and 19th-century houses has a distinctive look and feel, though the predominant mode is English country. All but one of the rooms have TVs; some have VCRs. The bathrooms are luxurious, and some are bigger than most standard hotel rooms. **Il Tesoro** (☎ **508/939-3840;** www.iltesoro.net) is the on-site fine-dining restaurant.

27 S. Summer St. (in the center of town), Edgartown, MA 02539. ☎ **508/627-4751.** Fax 508/627-4652. www.charlotteinn.net. 25 units. Summer $395–$695 double; $895–$1,000 suite. Rates include continental breakfast; full breakfast offered for extra charge ($15). AE, MC, V. No children 13 and under. **Amenities:** Fine-dining restaurant. *In room:* A/C, TV, hair dryer.

Harbor View Hotel ★★   This once-grand 19th-century hotel is looking to regain its former glory by undergoing a multiyear $77-million renovation. Among the changes, 21 smaller hotel rooms have been converted into 13 luxury suites, some with private gardens and outdoor showers. The shingle-style complex started out as two Gilded Age waterfront hotels, later joined by a 300-foot veranda that overlooks Edgartown Harbor and the lighthouse. Behind the hotel is a large pool surrounded by newer annexes, where some rooms and suites have kitchenettes. The hotel is just far enough from "downtown" Edgartown to avoid the traffic, but close enough for a pleasant walk past regal captain's houses. **Water Street** (p. 289) serves three meals in an elegant setting and **Henry's** is a cozy barroom.

131 N. Water St. (approx. ½ mile northwest of Main St.), Edgartown, MA 02539. ☎ **800/225-6005** or 508/627-7000. Fax 508/627-8417. www.harbor-view.com. 124 units. Summer $369–$625 double; $1,200 1-bedroom suite; $1,500 2-bedroom suite; $1,800–$2,100 3-bedroom suite. Call for off-season rates. AE, DC, MC, V. **Amenities:** 2 restaurants (fine dining; more casual bar daily for lunch and dinner); babysitting; concierge; fitness center; heated outdoor pool; room service (seasonal only). *In room:* A/C, TV/DVD, fridge, hair dryer, Wi-Fi (free).

The Hob Knob ★★   Owner Maggie White's 19th-century Gothic Revival inn is an exquisite destination that vies for top honors as one of the Vineyard's best places to stay. Her style is peppy/preppy, with crisp floral fabrics and striped patterns creating a clean and comfortable look. The farm breakfast is a delight and is served at beautifully appointed individual tables in sunny, brightly painted dining rooms. An agrarian theme is a decorative touch throughout the inn. The attentive staff will pack a splendid picnic basket or plan a charter fishing trip on Maggie's 27-foot *Boston Whaler*.

128 Main St. (on upper Main St., in the center of town), Edgartown, MA 02539. © **800/696-2723** or 508/627-9510. Fax 508/627-4560. www.hobknob.com. 17 units. Summer $420–$545 double. Rates include full breakfast and afternoon tea. AE, MC, V. No children 6 and under. **Amenities:** Bikes ($20 per day); exercise room; room service; sauna. *In room:* A/C, TV/DVD, fridge, hair dryer, Wi-Fi (free).

The Winnetu Inn & Resort ★★★   This large luxury hotel loaded with on-site activities sits on 11 acres overlooking South Beach in Katama. Guests can walk down a 250-yard path to get to the private beach, which is next to South Beach on the Atlantic Ocean. A 3-mile bike path links the inn to Edgartown, but the inn also runs a shuttle service that can pick up inn guests at the Edgartown ferry. Most rooms are two- and three-bedroom suites with kitchenettes, and there is one deluxe cottage with a four-person hot tub and a roof deck. Some guest rooms have ocean views and washer/dryers. Many have private decks or patios. The fine-dining restaurant, **Lure,** is a treat.

South Beach, Edgartown, MA 02539. © **866/335-1133** or 508/310-1733. www.winnetu.com. 48 units. Summer $320 double; $770–$1,200 1-bedroom suite; $920 2-bedroom suite; $1,600 3-bedroom suite. AE, MC, V. Closed Nov to mid-Apr. **Amenities:** Fine-dining restaurant; children's program (late June to early Sept); concierge; exercise room; outdoor heated pool; putting green; tennis courts (6 Har-Tru, 4 all-weather). *In room:* A/C, TV/DVD, kitchenette, Wi-Fi (free).

Expensive

Ashley Inn ★ 🍴   On Upper Main Street in Edgartown, this attractive B&B is just a short walk to the many shops and restaurants on Main Street and picturesque Edgartown Harbor. Innkeepers Fred and Janet Hurley have decorated the bedrooms in the 1860 captain's house with period antiques and quilts, and some rooms have canopy or four-poster beds. Thoughtful extras at this B&B include a little box of Chilmark Chocolates left on your pillow. A carriage house offers suites with a kitchen and a whirlpool tub. In the morning, breakfast is served at individual tables in the dining room.

129 Main St., Edgartown, MA 02539. © **508/627-9655.** Fax 508/627-6629. www.ashleyinn.net. 10 units. Summer $255–$285 double; $310–$315 1-bedroom suites; $575–$600 2-bedroom suite. Rates include full breakfast. MC, V. *In room:* A/C, TV.

Colonial Inn of Martha's Vineyard ★★ ☺   This 1911 inn in the center of Edgartown has been transformed into a fine modern hotel, and recent extensive renovations have elevated it to what can accurately be described as "affordable luxury." Its lobby serves as a conduit to the Nevins Square shops beyond. The guest rooms are decorated in soothing, contemporary tones with pine furniture, crisp fabrics, hardwood floors, and beadboard wainscoting. Suites have VCRs (complimentary videos) and kitchenettes. Many rooms have gas fireplaces. Be sure to visit the roof deck, ideally around sunset or, if you're up for it, sunrise.

38 N. Water St., Edgartown, MA 02539. © **800/627-4701** or 508/627-4711. Fax 508/627-5904. www.colonialinnmvy.com. 28 units. Summer $245–$425 double; $595 and up suite or efficiency. Rates include continental breakfast and afternoon tea. AE, MC, V. Closed Dec–Mar, except for luxury suites in Residence Club, which are open year-round. Pets accepted in 2 designated suites ($30/night). **Amenities:** Restaurant (Chesca's, p. 290); exercise room; spa. *In room:* A/C, TV, hair dryer.

The Jonathan Munroe House ★★ 🎁 With its graceful wraparound, colon-naded front porch, the Jonathan Munroe House stands out from the other inns and captain's homes on this stretch of upper Main Street. Inside, the formal parlor has been transformed into a comfortable gathering room with European flair. Guest rooms are immaculate, antique-filled, and dotted with clever details. Many rooms have fireplaces. At breakfast, don't miss the homemade waffles and pancakes, served on the sunny porch. Request the garden cottage if you're in a honeymooning mood.

100 Main St., Edgartown, MA 02539. 🅒 **877/468-6763** or 🅒/fax 508/627-5536. www.jonathan munroe.com. 7 units, 1 cottage. Summer $215–$250 double; $325 cottage. Rates include full breakfast and wine-and-cheese hour. AE, MC, V. No children 11 and under. *In room:* A/C, hair dryer, Wi-Fi (free).

Victorian Inn ★★ Do you long to stay at a quaint, reasonably priced inn that is bigger than a B&B but smaller than a Marriott? The Victorian Inn is a freshened-up version of those old-style hotels that used to inhabit every New England town. There are enough rooms here so you don't feel as if you are trespassing in someone's home, yet there's a personal touch. With three floors of long, graceful corridors, the Victorian could serve as a stage set for a 1930s romance. Several rooms have canopy beds and balconies. The innkeepers are always quick to dispense helpful advice with good humor.

24 S. Water St. (in the center of town), Edgartown, MA 02539. 🅒 **508/627-4784.** www.thevic.com. 14 units. Summer $245–$425 double. Rates include full breakfast and afternoon tea. MC, V. Dogs accepted late Sept to May ($25 fee). *In room:* A/C, TV, hair dryer, no phone, Wi-Fi (free).

Moderate

Edgartown Inn ★ 🍴 This lovely, centrally located 1798 Federal manse, a show-place even here on captain's row, offers perhaps the best value on the island. Nathaniel Hawthorne holed up here for nearly a year, and Daniel Webster also spent time here. The rooms are no-frills but pleasantly traditional; some have TVs and harbor views. Modernists may prefer the two cathedral-ceilinged quarters in the annex out back, which offer lovely light and a sense of seclusion. Service is excellent; be sure to say hello to Henry King, who has been on the staff for over 50 years.

56 N. Water St., Edgartown, MA 02539. 🅒 **508/627-4794.** Fax 508/627-9420. www.edgartowninn. com. 20 units (4 with shared bathroom). Summer $125 double with shared bathroom; $170–$275 double with private bathroom. No credit cards. Closed Nov–Mar. No children 6 and under. *In room:* A/C, TV (some), no phone.

OAK BLUFFS

Those looking for a basic motel with a central location can try **Surfside Motel,** across from the ferry dock on Oak Bluffs Avenue (🅒 **800/537-3007** or 508/693-2500; www.mvsurfside.com). Summer rates are $160 to $215 for doubles, $250 to $310 for suites. It is open year-round and well-behaved pets are allowed.

Expensive

Isabelle's Beach House ★ This grand 19th century home, across the street from the ocean in Oak Bluffs, has been recently renovated. Some of the rooms are on the small side, but they are light and airy, with attractive and comfortable bedding. You'll love sitting on a rocking chair out on the veranda.

83 Seaview Ave. (on the sound), Oak Bluffs, MA 02557. 🅒 **800/674-3129** or 508/693-3955. Fax 508/693-2729. www.isabellesbeachhouse.com. 11 units. Summer $275 double; $300–$395 suite. Rates include continental breakfast. AE, DISC, MC, V. Closed late Oct to early May. *In room:* A/C, TV, fridge, hair dryer.

Moderate

The Dockside Inn ★ Set close to the harbor, the Dockside is perfectly located for exploring the town of Oak Bluffs. The welcoming exterior, with its colonnaded porch and balconies, duplicates the inns of yesteryear. Inside, the whimsical Victorian touches will transport you into the spirit of this rollicking town. Most of the cheerfully decorated rooms have either garden or harbor views; some have private decks. Location, charm, and flair make this a popular place, so book early.

9 Circuit Ave. Ext. (Box 1206), Oak Bluffs, MA 02557. ℂ **800/245-5979** or 508/693-2966. Fax 508/696-7293. www.vineyardinns.com. 22 units. Summer $200–$250 double; $350 suite. Rates include continental breakfast. AE, DISC, MC, V. Closed late Oct to early Apr. Dogs under 28 lbs. accepted ($25 fee). *In room:* A/C, TV, hair dryer.

The Oak Bluffs Inn ★ This homey Victorian inn has a fun location at the top of Circuit Avenue, Oak Bluffs's main drag. The inn stands out with its colorful Victorian paint scheme and its prominent cupola, from which guests can enjoy a 360-degree view of Oak Bluffs. A 2-minute stroll from the inn gets you to all the Oak Bluffs attractions, like the gingerbread cottages, the tabernacle, the Flying Horses Carousel, the waterfront park, and the ferries. Some of the rooms are a tad on the small side, but others are spacious and even have comfortable seating areas.

64 Circuit Ave. (at the corner of Pequot Ave.), Oak Bluffs, MA 02557. ℂ **800/955-6235** or 508/693-7171. Fax 508/693-8787. www.oakbluffsinn.com. 9 units. Summer $215–$300 double. Rates include continental breakfast. AE, MC, V. Closed Nov–Apr. *In room:* A/C, hair dryer, no phone.

Wesley Hotel ★ 🍴 Formerly one of the grand hotels of Martha's Vineyard, this imposing 1879 property, right on the harbor, is now a solid entry in the good-value category, especially with its low off-season rates. It occupies a terrific location in Oak Bluffs, across the street from the harbor, in the center of the action. The only drawback here can be the noise from revelers on the boats in the harbor, or traffic on busy Lake Avenue. Most of the rooms are fairly compact and basic, though some are spacious with harbor views. The Wesley Arms, behind the main building, contains 33 air-conditioned rooms accessible by elevator. Eight suites and executive suites have kitchenettes. Reserve early to specify harbor views, which do not cost more than regular rooms. This is one of the few Vineyard hotels that does not require a minimum stay in season.

70 Lake Ave. (on the harbor), Oak Bluffs, MA 02557. ℂ **800/638-9027** or 508/693-6611. Fax 508/693-5389. www.wesleyhotel.com. 95 units, all with shower only. Summer $230–$260 double; $310 suite. AE, DISC, MC, V. Closed late Oct to Apr. *In room:* A/C, TV, no phone.

VINEYARD HAVEN (TISBURY)
Expensive

The Mansion House Inn ★★ 🎁 After a fire burned down the 200-year-old Tisbury Inn several years ago, the owners decided to rebuild, making this one of the island's most full-service inns. The building, occupying a prominent corner location in Vineyard Haven, is a community hub, with a restaurant, health club, and shops. The three-story hotel is comfortable, with generous amenities. The rooms range in size from cozy to spacious, and prices vary accordingly. Many have kitchenettes, flatscreen TVs, and extra-large bathtubs. Some have harbor views. All the rooms are equipped with high-speed Internet service. One of the most unusual features of the inn is the 75-foot mineral-spring (no chlorine) pool in the health club in the inn's basement. The restaurant, **Zephrus,** is open to the public for lunch and dinner, and also supplies room service for guests until late in the evening.

9 Main St., Vineyard Haven, MA 02568. © **888210-4504** or 508/693-2200. Fax 508/693-4095. www.mvmansionhouse.com. 40 units. $299–$309 double; $399–$559 suite. Rates include full buffet breakfast. AE, MC, V. **Amenities:** Restaurant (Zephrus, a fine-dining New American–style restaurant); health club and spa w/75-ft. pool. *In room:* A/C, TV, fridge, Wi-Fi (free).

CHILMARK (INCLUDING MENEMSHA), WEST TISBURY & AQUINNAH
Very Expensive

Beach Plum Inn ★★ 🎁 This country inn is set on 8 lush acres, with a lawn sloping gracefully down to Vineyard Sound. The room decor is predominantly cottage-y, though some rooms lean toward elegance. All but one room have decks or patios, some with views of Menemsha Harbor; and all have high-thread-count bed linens and Egyptian cotton towels. Some units have canopied beds and are quite romantic. Five of the rooms have a whirlpool tub. The inn's restaurant is one of the best fine-dining spots on the island (see "Where to Dine," later).

Beach Plum Lane (off North Rd., ½ mile northeast of the harbor), Menemsha, MA 02552. © **877/645-7398** or 508/645-9454. Fax 508/645-2801. www.beachpluminn.com. 11 units. Summer $425–$575 double or cottage. Rates include full breakfast in season; continental breakfast off season. AE, DC, DISC, MC, V. Closed Nov–Apr. **Amenities:** Restaurant (fine dining); babysitting; tennis court; croquet court. *In room:* A/C, TV, fridge, hair dryer.

Expensive

Lambert's Cove Inn ★★ Set far off the main road and surrounded by apple trees and lilacs, this secluded estate suggests an age when time was measured in generations. In recent years, owners have upgraded the rooms and the decor, all done up in a sumptuous English country style. Some rooms have extras like Jacuzzi tubs, and all have luxurious bedding. You'll find an all-weather tennis court on the grounds, a pool and hot tub, and the namesake beach 1 mile away. The inn's **restaurant** is known for skillfully prepared New American dinners.

Lambert's Cove Rd. (off State Rd., approx. 3 miles west of Vineyard Haven), West Tisbury, MA 02568. © **866/526-2466** or 508/693-2298. Fax 508/693-7890. www.lambertscoveinn.com. 15 units. Summer $225–$550 double. Rates include full breakfast. AE, MC, V. Dogs under 35 lbs. accepted by prior arrangement ($25/night). **Amenities:** Restaurant (dinner only); Jacuzzi; outdoor pool; tennis court. *In room:* A/C, TV/DVD, CD player, hair dryer, Internet access (free).

Menemsha Inn and Cottages ★★ Set in the pines near Menemsha Harbor, the Menemsha Inn is a place to revel in the outdoors (on 11 seaside acres) without distractions. The property is about a half-mile walk through a wooded path to the beach. There's no restaurant—just a restful breakfast room. Cottages have hair dryers, TVs, VCRs, DVDs, dataports, outdoor showers, barbecue grills, and kitchenettes. The most luxurious suites are located in the Carriage House, which has a spacious common room with a fieldstone fireplace. All rooms have private decks; most have water views. Guests have access to complimentary passes and shuttle bus service to the Lucy Vincent and Squibnocket private beaches.

Off North Rd. (approx. ½ mile northeast of the harbor), Menemsha, MA 02552. © **508/645-2521.** Fax 508/645-9500. www.menemshainn.com. 15 units, 12 cottages. Summer $355–$385 double; $450–$815 suite; $4,800/week 2-bedroom cottage. Rates include continental breakfast for rooms and suites. AE, MC, V. Closed Nov–Apr. **Amenities:** Exercise room; tennis court. *In room:* TV/DVD, hair dryer.

Moderate

The Captain R. Flanders House ★ 🎁 Set amid 60 acres of rolling meadows crisscrossed by stone walls, this late-18th-century farmhouse has remained much the same for 2 centuries. The living room, with its broad-plank floors, is full of astonishing antiques. Two countrified cottages overlook the pond. The owners will provide you with a coveted pass to nearby Lucy Vincent Beach.

North Rd. (approx. ½ mile northeast of Menemsha), Chilmark, MA 02535. ✆ **508/645-3123.** www. captainflanders.com. 5 units (2 with shared bathroom); 2 cottages. Summer $190 double with shared bathroom; $225 double with private bathroom; $300 cottage. Rates include continental breakfast. AE, MC, V. Closed Nov to early May. *In room:* No phone.

Where to Dine

Outside Oak Bluffs and Edgartown, all of Martha's Vineyard is "dry," including Vineyard Haven, so bring your own bottle; some restaurants charge a small corkage fee.

EDGARTOWN
Very Expensive

Atria ★★★ NEW AMERICAN   This fine-dining restaurant, set in an 18th-century sea captain's house, gets rave reviews for its gourmet cuisine and high-caliber service. Pronounced with the emphasis on the second syllable (ah-TRE-ah), the name refers to the brightest of three stars forming the Southern Triangle constellation. You can sit in the elegant dining room, on the rose-covered wraparound porch, or at the brick cellar bar downstairs for more casual dining. The menu offers a variety of creative dishes with influences from around the country and the globe, with stops in the Mediterranean, the Middle East, and Asia. It features organic island-grown produce, just-off-the-boat seafood, local shellfish, and aged prime meats. Two popular starters are the miso soup with steamed crab dumplings and the Thai lemongrass mussels. Unusual main courses include wok-fried Martha's Vineyard lobster or cracklin' pork shank with Southern collard greens. On weekends, in the bar, there is live entertainment along the lines of acoustic guitar. *Tip:* It's not on the menu, but this place makes the best burger and fries on the island. If you order it, they'll make it.

137 Main St. (a short walk from the center of town). ✆ **508/627-5850.** www.atriamv.com. Reservations recommended. Main courses $30–$48. AE, MC, V. June–Sept daily 5:30–10pm; call for off-season hours.

L'étoile ★★★ CONTEMPORARY FRENCH   The famous L'étoile has moved out of the Charlotte Inn and is now several blocks away, in the building that formerly housed the Tuscany Inn. Chef Michael Brisson is still in charge here, and he creates an ever-evolving menu devoted to local produce and seafood, along with delicacies flown in from the four corners of the earth. The menu changes often, but a typical meal here might begin with spice-crusted duck foie gras, then truffled beets with greens, and a main course of étuvée of native lobster with scallop and corn fritters. A small, less expensive bar menu ($15–$19) with items like spinach salad and roasted Cornish game hen is available in the bar nightly. A three-course chef's tasting menu is $95.

22 N. Water St. (off Main St.). ✆ **508/627-5187.** www.letoile.net. Reservations recommended. Main courses $36–$49, chef's tasting menu $95. MC, V. July to mid-Sept daily 6–10pm; call for off-season hours. Closed late Nov to mid-Feb.

Lure Grill ★★★ NEW AMERICAN   Though a bit out of the way—it's at the Winnetu Oceanside Resort, near Katama Beach—this restaurant does everything right. Those fortunate enough to get a window seat or a spot on the deck can watch the sun set as they enjoy the fine cuisine and professional service. Menu selections make the most of local produce and seafood. You might begin with Katama oysters, for example. As for main courses, unique choices include poached lobster with pea ravioli or wild king salmon with crabmeat-and-artichoke risotto. Homemade desserts like the caramelized apple charlotte, are inspired.

At the Winnetu Oceanside Resort, Katama (South Beach). ℂ **508/627-3663.** www.luremv.com. Reservations recommended. Main courses $24–$37. MC, V. July–Aug daily 5:30–9:30pm; call for off-season hours. Closed Dec to mid-Apr.

Expensive

Alchemy ★★ FRENCH BISTRO   This spiffy restaurant is a slice of Paris on Main Street. Such esoteric choices as oyster brie soup and Burgundy Vintners salad share the bill with escargot-and-chanterelle fricassee. As befits a true bistro, there's a large selection of cocktails, liqueurs, and wines. In addition to lunch and dinner, a bar menu is served from 2:30 to 11pm. This choice isn't for everyone, but sophisticated diners will enjoy the Continental flair.

71 Main St. (in the center of town). ℂ **508/627-9999.** http://alchemymv.com. Main courses $22–$33. AE, MC, V. Apr–Nov daily noon–2:30pm and 5:30–10pm; call for off-season hours.

Water Street ★★ NEW AMERICAN   With its exquisite view of Edgartown Harbor and the lighthouse, this is a terrific place to have a drink or to dine. The long and elegant bar is particularly smashing. The menu is simple but stylish. To start, there's soft-shell crab with arugula and teardrop tomatoes. As a main course, try the caramelized sea scallops with a salad of Asian pear and apple. Service is excellent; these are trained waiters, not your usual college surfer dudes. At the end of your meal, you may want to sit on the rockers on the Harbor View Hotel's wraparound porch and watch the lights twinkling in the harbor.

At the Harbor View Hotel (p. 283), 131 N. Water St. ℂ **508/627-7000.** www.harbor-view.com/dining_Water_Street.asp. Reservations recommended. Main courses $22–$30. AE, MC, V. Mon–Sat 7–11am, noon–2pm, and 6–10pm; Sun 8am–2pm and 6–10pm; call for off-season hours.

 THE QUINTESSENTIAL LOBSTER DINNER

When the basics—a lobster and a sunset—are what you crave, head to the **Home Port,** on North Road in Menemsha (ℂ **508/645-2679;** www.homeportmv. com), a favorite of locals and visitors alike. In addition to the usual seafood fare, Chef Johnny Graham has added ribs and fish tacos. At first glance, prices for the lobster dinners may seem a bit high, but note that they include an appetizer of your choice (go with the stuffed quahog), salad, amazing fresh-baked breads, a nonalcoholic beverage (remember, it's BYOB in these parts), and dessert. Locals not keen on summer crowds prefer to order their lobster dinners for pickup (less than half-price) at the restaurant door, then head down to Menemsha Beach for a private sunset supper. A delivery cart stationed at the pick-up window will ferry your dinner out to you on the beach. For those who prefer to sit inside the restaurant, reservations are required. Fixed-price platters range from $26 to $60. The Home Port is open mid-June to Labor Day daily at 5pm, with last reservations at 9pm. Call for off-season hours. It's closed mid-September to mid-May.

Détente ★★ NEW AMERICAN   Taking the French word for *relaxation* and *good relations,* this small Edgartown restaurant is working to be the choice for fine dining on the Vineyard. Fans of this intimate establishment cite the sophisticated wine bar and creative fine-dining cuisine. The menu is based on seasonal specials, featuring foods from local farms and markets. For starters, you can go light, with a spring watercress and spiced pecan salad, or heavy, with island lobster ravioli. The main courses are similarly varied, from pesto-marinated rack of lamb to orange curry–crusted monkfish. The wine list is extensive, with more choices available by the glass than anywhere else on the island.

Off Winter St. (in Nevins Sq., behind the Colonial Inn). © **508/627-8810.** www.detentewinebar.com. Reservations recommended. Main courses $29–$35. AE, MC, V. June–Aug Mon–Sat 5:30–10pm, Sun 11am–2pm and 5:30–10pm; call for off-season hours.

Moderate

Among the Flowers Cafe ★★ 🍴 AMERICAN   Everything's fresh and appealing at this small outdoor cafe near the dock. The breakfasts are the best around, and the comfort-food dinners are among the most affordable options in this pricey town. There's almost always a wait, not just because it's so picturesque, but because the food is homey, hearty, and kind on the wallet.

Mayhew Lane. © **508/627-3233.** www.mvol.com/menu/amongtheflowers. Main courses $10–$18. Reservations not accepted. AE, DC, DISC, MC, V. July–Aug daily 8am–9:30pm; May–June and Sept–Oct daily 8am–4pm. Closed Nov–Apr.

Chesca's ★★ 🎁 ITALIAN   This modern-decor restaurant at the Colonial Inn (p. 284) is a solid entry, with yummy food at reasonable prices. You're sure to find favorites like paella (with roasted lobster and other choice seafood), risotto (with roasted vegetables), and ravioli (with portobello mushrooms and asparagus). Smaller appetites can fill up on homemade soup and salad.

At the Colonial Inn, 38 N. Water St. © **508/627-1234.** www.chescasmv.com. Reservations accepted for parties with 6 or more only. Main courses $22–$36. AE, MC, V. Late May to mid-Oct daily 5:30–10pm; Apr to late May Thurs–Sun 5:30–9:30pm; call for off-season hours. Closed mid-Oct to Mar.

Inexpensive

Espresso Love ★★ 🎁 AMERICAN   Hidden behind a parking lot, this little gem is not only a great place to stop for breakfast (blueberry scones, fresh-baked muffins) and lunch (big sandwiches), but for dinner as well. The wholesome recipes of Carol McManus, the owner, rule the evening. Ms. McManus has even written a cookbook with her favorite recipes, and you'll find many of them, including the sumptuous lobster cakes, on the menu here.

17 Church St. (off Main St., behind the courthouse). © **508/627-9211.** http://espressolove.com. Main courses $12–$18; breakfast items and sandwiches $10 or less. AE, MC, V. July–Aug daily 6:30am–10pm; off season 6:30am–6pm.

The Newes from America ★★ 🎁 PUB GRUB   The food is better than average at this subterranean tavern, built in 1742. Beers are a specialty here. Try a rack of five esoteric brews, or let your choice of food—from a wood-smoked oyster "Island Poor Boy" sandwich with linguiça (Portuguese-style sausage) relish to an 18-ounce porterhouse steak—dictate your draft. The menu comes handily annotated with recommendations. Don't miss the seasoned fries.

At the Kelley House, 23 Kelley St. © **508/627-4397.** www.kelley-house.com/dining_newes_from_america. Main courses $9–$16. AE, MC, V. Daily 11:30am–11pm.

OAK BLUFFS
Expensive

Oyster Bar Grill ★★ NEW AMERICAN Occupying a large space on Circuit Avenue, new owners have reinvented and reinvigorated this spot into a hip venue for the 30-something crowd. Specializing in seafood and—unusual for Martha's Vineyard—steak, the food preparations at the Oyster Bar are not fussy and are a bit less expensive than similar island venues. The decor is also more casual. The huge oak bar is the site of a hopping scene, with live music on weekends year-round. The Sunday brunch buffet attracts a large following.

67 Circuit Ave. ℂ **508/693-6600.** Reservations recommended. Main courses $16–$28. AE, MC, V. May–Nov Mon–Sat 4–11pm; Sun 11–3pm and 4–11pm; call for off-season hours.

Sweet Life Cafe ★★★ FRENCH/AMERICAN Locals are crazy about this pearl of a restaurant set in a restored Victorian house on upper Circuit Avenue. In season, the most popular seating is outside in the gaily lit garden. Fresh island produce is featured, and the seafood specials are particularly enticing. If the roasted lobster with potato-Parmesan risotto, roasted yellow beets, and smoked-salmon chive fondue is offered, order it.

63 Circuit Ave. ℂ **508/696-0200.** www.sweetlifemv.com. Reservations recommended. Main courses $18–$35. AE, DISC, MC, V. Mid-May to Aug daily 5:30–10pm; Apr to mid-May and Sept–Nov Thurs–Mon 5:30–9:30pm. Closed Dec to mid-May.

Inexpensive

Coop de Ville ★ SEAFOOD Of the several open-air harbor-front choices in Oak Bluffs, Coop de Ville has the best service and food. This outdoor fried-seafood shack serves up tasty beer-battered shrimp, grilled swordfish, lobster salad, and "world famous" chicken wings. It's a fun place to people-watch on sunny summer days as boaters cruise around the harbor.

Dockside Market Place, alongside Oak Bluffs Harbor. ℂ **508/693-3420.** www.coopdevillemv.com. Most items $9–$20. MC, V. June–Aug daily 11am–10pm; call for off-season hours. Closed mid-Oct to Apr.

Sharky's Cantina ★ MEXICAN This swinging Mexican joint right on Circuit Avenue is the new hot spot in Oak Bluffs. Stretching from one end of the restaurant to the other, the large bar is packed five deep (with mostly young people) in the summer. It's within yelling distance of the dining area, where the margaritas wash down a standard array of quesadillas, tacos, enchiladas, and burritos. Although typical for a Mexican restaurant, the menu is an inexpensive rarity on the Vineyard. An unusual touch, the full menu is served until 12:30am.

31 Circuit Ave. ℂ **508/693-7501.** www.sharkyscantina.com. Most items $6–$18. MC, V. Daily 11am–12:30am.

Slice of Life 🎁 DELI This deli at the upper end of Circuit Avenue is the place to head for gourmet sandwiches, salads, and wholesome soups. The eclectic menu also includes burgers and pizza. All the food is very wholesome. The deli also sells wine, beer, and specialty coffees.

50 Circuit Ave. ℂ **508/693-3838.** www.sliceoflifemv.com. Reservations not accepted. Most items under $10. MC, V. June–Aug daily 8am–8pm; call for off-season hours.

VINEYARD HAVEN (TISBURY)

Just around the corner from the Black Dog Tavern on Water Street, near the ferry terminal, is the **Black Dog Bakery** (ℂ **508/693-4786;** www.theblackdog.com).

The doors open at 5am, and from midmorning on, it's elbowroom only as customers line up for freshly baked breads, muffins, and desserts that can't be beat. Don't forget some homemade doggy biscuits for your pooch.

Expensive

Black Dog Tavern ★ NEW AMERICAN How does a humble harbor shack come to be a national icon? Location helps. So do cool T-shirts. Soon after *Shenandoah* Capt. Robert Douglas decided, in 1971, that this hardworking port could use a good restaurant, influential vacationers stuck waiting for the ferry began to wander into this saltbox to tide themselves over with a bit of "blackout cake" or peanut-butter pie. The food is still home-cooking good, especially the seafood, and the blackout cake has lost none of its appeal. Though the lines grow ever longer, nothing much has changed at this beloved spot. Eggs Galveston for breakfast at the Black Dog Tavern is still one of the ultimate Vineyard experiences—go early, when it first opens, and sit on the porch, where the views are perfect.

Beach St. Extension (on the harbor), Vineyard Haven. ✆ **508/693-9223.** www.theblackdog.com. Reservations not accepted. Main courses $14–$27. AE, MC, V. June to early Sept daily 7–11am, noon–4pm, and 5–10pm; call for off-season hours.

Saltwater ★ NEW AMERICAN With big picture windows, this restaurant takes full advantage of its very pretty location overlooking the Lagoon Pond in Vineyard Haven. With this view, seafood is, of course, a specialty—try the day-boat scallops with curry coconut broth—but there are a number of special island-inspired dishes on the menu, particularly among the salads, made with island-grown produce.

79 Beach Rd. (at Tisbuy Marketplace, a 10-min. walk from Main St.). ✆ **508/338-4666.** www.saltwaterrestaurant.com. Reservations recommended. Main courses $25–$35. MC, V. July–Aug Mon-Sat 11:30am–3pm, 5:30–9:30pm; Sun 10am–3pm and 5:30–9:30pm. Call for off-season hours.

Le Grenier ★★ FRENCH If Paris is the heart of France, Lyons is its belly—and that's where chef-owner Jean Dupon grew up on his *Maman*'s hearty cuisine. Dupon has the Continental moves down, as evidenced by such classics as steak au poivre; calf's brains Grenobloise with beurre noir and capers; and lobster Normande flambéed with Calvados, apples, and cream. Despite the fact that *Le Grenier* means (and, in fact, is housed in) "an attic," the restaurant is quite romantic, especially when aglow with hurricane lamps. Remember, you BYOB here.

96 Main St. (in the center of town). ✆ **508/693-4906.** www.legrenierrestaurant.com. Reservations suggested. Main courses $22–$32. AE, DC, DISC, MC, V. Daily 5:30–9pm.

Zephrus at the Mansion House Inn ★ INTERNATIONAL This hip restaurant is a great place to go for casual fine dining. Seating is at the sidewalk cafe on Main Street or inside by the hearth in view of the open kitchen. Main-course winners are pan-roasted pork tenderloin served with sweet 'tater tots, and shrimp and farfalle pasta. Though the menu is in constant flux, there is always a good vegetarian choice like the delicious vegetable risotto with truffle vinaigrette. Bring your favorite wine; the corkage fee is $5 per table.

9 Main St., Vineyard Haven ✆ **508/693-3416.** www.zephrus.com. Reservations recommended. Main courses $9–$20. AE, DC, DISC, MC, V. July–Aug daily 11:30am–3pm and 5:30–9pm; call for off-season hours.

Inexpensive

Art Cliff Diner ★ ECLECTIC DINER Expect the best diner food you've ever had at this quirky establishment. It's a short walk from the center of Vineyard Haven.

Be aware that the hours are a little unreliable, and you should call to be sure it is open before making the trek. The food here is really scrumptious, whether you are having the just-caught fish of the day served with herbs from the chef's garden, or a simple burger, cooked just right. Desserts are homemade, of course.

39 Beach Rd. (a short walk from Main St.). © **508/693-1224.** Reservations not accepted. Main courses all under $15. No credit cards. July–Aug daily 7am–2pm; call for off-season hours. Closed Nov–Apr.

CHILMARK (INCLUDING MENEMSHA) & WEST TISBURY
Very Expensive

The Beach Plum Inn Restaurant ★★★ INTERNATIONAL   This jewel of a restaurant is on a bluff overlooking the fishing village of Menemsha. Attention to quality has made this one of the island's top dining venues. Guests can dine inside in the spare but elegant dining room, or outside on the tiled patio. Chef James McDonough's most popular dishes include hazelnut-encrusted halibut with Marsala wine beurre blanc sauce. The most winning appetizer is the elaborate blackened lobster tips, served with mango cream sauce and house-cured gravlax with home-made wild rice and corn pancakes. For dessert, you'll flip for the chocolate quadru-ple-layer cake made with white and dark chocolate mousse and Chambord. In the spring and fall, there is usually an ethereal soufflé on the menu, either Grand Mar-nier or chocolate.

At the Beach Plum Inn, 50 Beach Plum Lane (off North Rd.), Menemsha. © **508/645-9454.** www. beachpluminn.com. Reservations required. Main courses $32–$42; 4-course fixed-price menu $68; off season only fixed-priced menu $50. AE, MC, V. Mid-June to early Sept daily seatings 5:30–6:45pm and 8–9:30pm; call for off-season hours. Closed Dec–Apr.

Lambert's Cove Inn Restaurant ★★ 📕 NEW AMERICAN   One of the Vine-yard's favorite chefs, Joe Silva, runs the kitchen at this romantic country inn. If you are staying in one of the down-island towns such as Edgartown or Oak Bluffs, driv-ing through the wooded countryside to this secluded inn feels like an expedition to an earlier time. The interior of the restaurant is set up with crisp white tablecloths and antique furniture. In good weather, you can dine alfresco on a deck surrounded by flowering trees and shrubs. The menu features fresh seafood and island produce and meats. You might start with a crab and asparagus napoleon, or a simple but lus-cious cream-of-mushroom soup. Special dinner entrees include grilled, marinated duck-breast casserole baked in a sherry lobster cream sauce. Desserts are home-made delicacies. Don't forget, the town of West Tisbury is "dry," so you must bring your own alcoholic beverages.

Lamberts Cove Rd. (off State Rd., approx. 3 miles west of Vineyard Haven), West Tisbury. © **508/693-2298.** www.lambertscoveinn.com/restaurant.html. Reservations recommended. Main courses $24–$32. AE, MC, V July–Aug daily 6–9pm; call for off-season hours.

Moderate

The Bite ★★ 📕 SEAFOOD   It's usually places like the Bite that you crave when you think of New England. This is your quintessential "chowdah"-and-clam shack, flanked by picnic tables. The Bite makes superlative chowder, potato salad, fried fish, and so forth.

Basin Rd. (off North Rd., approx. ¼ mile northeast of the harbor), Menemsha. © **508/645-9239.** Main courses $18–$30. No credit cards. July–Aug daily 11am–8pm; call for off-season hours. Closed late Sept to Apr.

Martha's Vineyard After Dark

All towns except Oak Bluffs and Edgartown are dry, and last call at bars and clubs is at midnight. Hit Oak Bluffs for the rowdiest bar scene and best nighttime street life. In Edgartown, you may have to hop around before you find the evening's most happening spot.

The Vineyard's top nightclub is at the airport, of all places. **Nectar's** (formerly Hot Tin Roof) features comedy, rock, reggae, Latin, and blues from spring through fall. For schedules and more information, call ✆ **508/693-1137;** or check out their website at www.nectarsmv.com.

Young and loud are the buzzwords at the **Lamppost** and the **Dive Bar,** 111 Circuit Ave., Oak Bluffs (✆ **508/696-9352**), a pair of clubs in the center of town. The Lamppost features live bands and a dance floor; the Dive Bar, acoustic acts. This is where the young folk go, and the performers could be playing blues, reggae, R&B, or '80s. The cover is $1 to $5.

The Vineyard's first and only brewpub, **Offshore Ale Company,** 30 Kennebec Ave., Oak Bluffs (✆ **508/693-2626;** www.offshoreale.com), is an attractively rustic place, with oak booths and peanut shells strewn on the floor. Local acoustic performers entertain 6 nights a week in season. The cover is $5.

The Ritz Cafe, 1 Circuit Ave., Oak Bluffs (✆ **508/693-9851**), is a down-and-dirty hole-in-the-wall that features live music nightly in season and on weekends year-round. The cover is $2 to $3.

Performing Arts

The magnificent 1843 **Whaling Church,** 89 Main St., Edgartown (✆ **508/627-4442;** www.mvpreservation.org/whale.html), functions primarily as a 500-seat performing-arts center offering lectures and symposia, films, plays, and concerts. Ticket prices vary; call for a schedule.

The Vineyard Playhouse, 24 Church St., Vineyard Haven (✆ **508/696-6300** or 508/693-6450; www.vineyardplayhouse.org), is an intimate black-box theater, where Equity professionals put on a rich season of favorites and challenging new work, followed, on summer weekends, by musical or comedic cabaret in the gallery/lounge. Children's theater selections are performed on Saturday at 10am. Townspeople often get involved in the outdoor Shakespeare production, a 3-week run starting in mid-July at the Tashmoo Overlook Amphitheatre, about a mile west of town.

NANTUCKET ★★★

Once the whaling capital of the world, this tiny island, 30 miles off the coast of Cape Cod, still counts its isolation as a defining characteristic. At only 3½×14 miles in size, Nantucket is smaller and more insular than Martha's Vineyard. But charm-wise, Nantucket stands alone—21st-century amenities wrapped in an elegant 19th-century package.

Sophisticated Nantucket Town features bountiful stores, quaint inns, cobblestone streets, interesting historic sites, and pristine beaches. The rest of the island is mainly residential, but for a couple of notable villages. **Siasconset** (nicknamed 'Sconset), on the east side of the island, is a tranquil community with picturesque, rose-covered cottages and a handful of businesses, including a pricey French restaurant. Sunset aficionados head to **Madaket,** on the west coast of the island, for the evening spectacular.

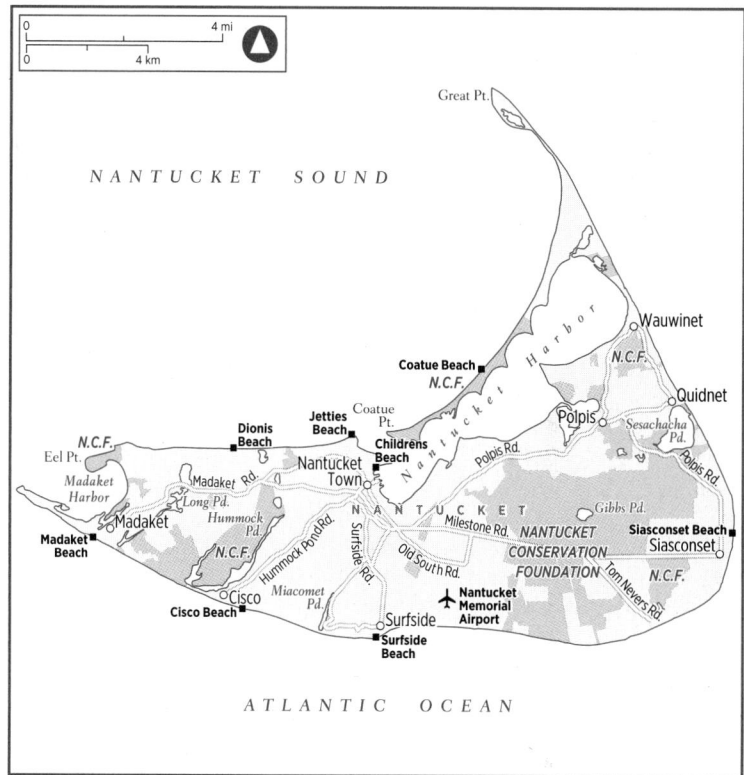

The lay of the land on Nantucket is rolling moors, cranberry bogs, and miles of exquisite public beaches. The vistas are honeymoon-romantic: an operating windmill, three lighthouses, and a skyline dotted with church steeples.

Essentials

GETTING THERE
By Ferry

FROM HYANNIS   Ferry service to Nantucket is fairly hassle-free, unless you're bringing a car in summer. But first-time visitors will find a car more a nuisance than a convenience, unless they're staying outside Nantucket Town.

From Hyannis (South St. Dock, take exit 7 off Rte. 6 and follow signs), the **Steamship Authority** (© **508/477-8600** in Hyannis, or 508/228-3274 in Nantucket; www.steamshipauthority.com) operates year-round ferry service for cars, passengers, and bicycles to Steamship Wharf on Nantucket using both high-speed and conventional ferries.

The Steamship Authority's **high-speed ferry** to Nantucket, *Iyanough* (© **508/495-3278**), is for passengers only. It takes 1 hour and runs five times a day in season.

Tickets cost $33 one-way ($65 round-trip) for adults, $25 one-way ($49 round-trip) for children 5 to 12. Parking costs $12 to $15 per day. Watch for the ferry parking signs on Rte. 6; if lots next to the dock are full, you may need to take exit 6 for a satellite lot, instead of exit 7 for the main lot. Satellite lots are on Lewis Bay Road, which is walking distance to the ferry terminal, and Yarmouth Road, from which you take a shuttle bus to the terminal. Passenger reservations are highly recommended on the high-speed ferry.

Total trip time on the **conventional ferry** that carries cars is 2 hours and 15 minutes. There are six slow ferry trips a day in season. A round-trip fare for a car costs $380 to $430 from mid-May to mid-October, $260 to $300 the rest of the year. The higher rates are charged for vehicles more than 17 feet long. Car rates do not include drivers or passengers. Passenger tickets are $17 one-way ($33 round-trip) for adults, $8.50 one-way ($17 round-trip) for children 5 to 12; bikes cost $12 round-trip. Parking costs $12 to $15 per day; you don't need to make parking reservations.

No advance reservations are needed for passengers traveling without their cars on the conventional ferry. But if you bring your car in summer, you must reserve *months in advance*—only six boats make the trip daily, and they fill up fast. Arrive at least 1 hour before departure to avoid having your space given away. There is a $10 fee for canceling a reservation.

Hy-Line Cruises, Ocean Street Dock (✆ **888/778-1132** or 508/778-2600; for high-speed ferry reservations, call ✆ **800/492-8082** or 508/778-0404; www. hy-linecruises.com), offers two types of passenger-only ferries from the Ocean Street Dock in Hyannis to Nantucket's Straight Wharf.

The Grey Lady, a year-round **high-speed** passenger ferry, makes the trip in 1 hour. The cost is $39 one-way ($75 round-trip) for adults, $29 one-way ($51 round-trip) for children 5 to 12, and $6 ($12 round-trip) for bicycles. The boat seats 260 and makes five to six round-trips daily in season; reserve in advance.

From early May through October, Hy-Line runs its standard 1-hour-and-50-minute **conventional ferry** service three times a day. Round-trip tickets are $43 for adults, $22 for children ages 5 to 12, and $10 extra for bikes. On busy holiday weekends, the slow ferry fills up, too, so order tickets in advance; buy or pick up your tickets at least half an hour before sailing time.

 ## Parking on the Mainland (Recommended!)

Because you won't need a car on Nantucket, consider parking your car in Hyannis before boarding the ferry to the island. If you are taking the **Hy-Line** ferry service from Ocean Street Dock (✆ **888/778-1132** or 508/778-2602) in July or August, it's a good idea to not only reserve tickets in advance, but also reserve a parking spot ahead of time. The all-day parking fee is $17 in season, and the lots are off Ocean Street, a short walk from the terminal. Travelers on **Steamship Authority** (✆ **508/477-8600**) vessels do not need a parking reservation. Parking at the Steamship Authority lots is $12 to $15 per day, depending on the season. Free shuttle buses take passengers to the Steamship terminal from off-site lots. The Hy-line and Steamship Authority ferry terminals are on opposite ends of Hyannis Harbor.

The standard ferry also has a **first-class section** with a private lounge, restrooms, a bar, and a snack bar; a continental breakfast or afternoon cheese and crackers is also served onboard. No pets are allowed in the first-class section. Tickets in the first-class section are $56 round-trip for all ages.

Hy-Line's **"Around the Sound" cruise** is a 1-day round-trip excursion from Hyannis with stops on Nantucket and Martha's Vineyard. It runs from early June to late September. The price is $84 for adults, $54 for children 5 to 12, and $18 extra for bikes.

FROM MARTHA'S VINEYARD   From Oak Bluffs on Martha's Vineyard, Hy-Line runs three passenger-only ferries to Nantucket from early June to mid-September (there is no car-ferry service btw. the islands). The trip time is 1 hour and 10 minutes. The one-way fare is $34 for adults, $21 for children 5 to 12, and $6 extra for bikes.

FROM HARWICH PORT   You can avoid the summer crowds in Hyannis by boarding a passenger-only ferry with **Freedom Cruise Line,** 702 Rte. 28 in Harwich Port, across from Brax Landing (✆ **508/432-8999;** www.nantucketislandferry.com). From mid-May to mid-October, boats leave from Saquatucket Harbor in Harwich Port; the trip takes 1½ hours. Round-trip tickets are $68 for adults, $51 for children ages 2 to 11, $6 for children under 2, and $12 extra for bikes. Parking is free if you pick up your car the same day, but it's $15 for each night thereafter. Reservations are highly recommended.

By Plane

You can fly into **Nantucket Memorial Airport** (airport code: ACK; ✆ **508/325-5300**), which is about 3 miles south of Nantucket Road on Old South Road. The flight to Nantucket takes 30 to 40 minutes from Boston, 15 minutes from Hyannis, and a little more than an hour from New York City airports.

Airlines providing service to Nantucket include **Cape Air/Nantucket Airlines** (✆ **800/352-0714;** www.flycapeair.com) year-round from Hyannis ($109 round-trip), Boston (about $300 round-trip), Martha's Vineyard ($88 round-trip), and New Bedford ($160 round-trip); **Continental Express** (✆ **800/525-0280;** www.continental.com) from Newark, seasonally (about $520 round-trip); **Island Airlines** (✆ **508/228-7575;** www.islandair.net) year-round from Hyannis ($94 round-trip); and **Colgan/US Airways Express** (✆ **800/428-4322;** www.colganair.com) year-round from Boston ($383 round-trip) and New York ($479 and up round-trip).

Island Airlines and Nantucket Airlines both offer year-round charter service to the island.

GETTING AROUND

Nantucket is easily navigated on bike, moped, or foot, and also by shuttle bus or taxi. The Chamber of Commerce strongly suggests that visitors leave their cars behind in order to minimize congestion and environmental impact. If you're staying outside Nantucket Town, however, or if you plan to explore the outer reaches of the island, you might want to bring your car or rent one here. Keep in mind that if you do opt to travel by car, in-town traffic can reach gridlock in the peak season, and parking can be a nightmare.

BY BICYCLE & MOPED   Biking is a great way to get around Nantucket. The island is relatively flat, and paved bike paths abound—they'll get you from Nantucket Town to Siasconset, Surfside, and Madaket. There are also many unpaved back roads to explore, which makes mountain bikes a wise choice. Mopeds are also available, but be aware that local rules and regulations are strictly enforced. Mopeds are not allowed on sidewalks or bike paths. You'll need a driver's license to rent a moped, and state law requires that you wear a helmet.

You can bring your own bike over on the ferries for an additional charge. Otherwise, shops that rent bikes and mopeds (all within walking distance of the ferries) include **Cook's Cycle Shop, Inc.,** 6 S. Beach St. (© **508/228-0800**); **Nantucket Bike Shops,** at Steamboat Wharf and Straight Wharf (© **508/228-1999;** wwwnantucketbikeshop.com); and **Young's Bicycle Shop,** at Steamboat Wharf (© **508/228-1151;** www.youngsbicycleshop.com), which also does repairs. Bike rentals average $20 to $30 for 24 hours.

BY SHUTTLE BUS From June through September, inexpensive shuttle buses, with bike racks and wheelchair lifts, make a loop through Nantucket Town and to outlying spots; for routes and stops, contact the **Nantucket Regional Transit Authority** (© **508/228-7025;** www.nantucket.net/trans/nrta) or pick up a schedule at the visitor center on Federal Street or the chamber of commerce office on Main Street. The cost is $1 to $2, and exact change is required. A 3-day pass can be purchased at the visitor center for $10. Dogs are allowed on the bus as long as they are relatively clean and dry.

BY CAR & JEEP I recommend a car, if you'll be here for more than a week or if you're staying outside Nantucket Town. Remember, though, there are no in-town parking lots; parking, although free, is limited.

Rental agencies on the island include **Affordable Rentals of Nantucket,** 6 S. Beach Rd. (© 508/228-3501); **Budget,** at the airport (© 800/527-0700 or 508/228-5666); **Hertz,** at the airport (© 800/654-3131 or 508/228-9421); **Nantucket Windmill Auto Rental,** at the airport (© 800/228-1227 or 508/228-1227); and **Young's 4×4 & Car Rental,** Steamboat Wharf (© 508/228-1151). A standard car costs about $100 per day in season; a four-wheel-drive rental costs about $185 per day (including an Over-Sand Permit).

BY TAXI You'll find taxis (many are vans that can accommodate large groups or those traveling with bikes) waiting at the airport and at all ferry ports. During the busy summer months, I recommend reserving a taxi in advance to avoid a long wait upon arrival. Rates are flat fees, based on one person riding before 1am, with surcharges for additional passengers, bikes, and dogs. A taxi from the airport to Nantucket Town hotels will cost about $10. Reliable cab companies include **Canty's Cab** (© 508/228-2888), **Chief's Cab** (© 508/284-8497), **Bev's Taxi** (© 508/228-7874), **Lisa's Taxi** (© 508/228-2223), and **Val's Cab Service** (© 508/228-9410).

VISITOR INFORMATION

For information, contact the **Nantucket Island Chamber of Commerce,** at 48 Main St., Nantucket, MA 02554 (© **508/228-1700;** www.nantucketchamber.org). When you arrive, you should also stop by the **Nantucket Visitors Service and Information Bureau,** 25 Federal St. (© **508/228-0925**). It's open daily from June to September, and Monday to Saturday from October to May. There are also information booths at Steamboat Wharf and Straight Wharf. Always check the island's newspaper, the *Inquirer & Mirror* (known locally as "The Inky"), for information on events and activities around town.

Nantucket Accommodations, P.O. Box 217, Nantucket, MA 02554 (© **508/228-9559;** fax 508/325-7009; www.nantucketaccommodation.com), a 30-year-old private service, arranges advance reservations for inns, cottages, guesthouses, bed-and-breakfasts, and hotels; it has access to 95% of the island's lodging, in addition to houses and cottages available by the night or week (as opposed to most realtors, who will handle rentals for only 2 weeks or more). The charge for the service is $15, assessed only when a reservation is made. Last-minute travelers should keep in mind the **Nantucket Visitors Service and Information Bureau** (© 508/228-0925), a daily referral service for available rooms provided free by the town. It's not a booking service, but it always has the most updated list of accommodations availability and cancellations.

ATMs can be difficult to locate on Nantucket. **Nantucket Bank** (© 508/228-0580) has five locations: 2 Orange St., 104 Pleasant St., Amelia Street, the Hub on Main Street, and the airport lobby, all open 24 hours. **Pacific National Bank** has four locations: A&P Supermarket (next to the wharves), the Stop & Shop (open 24 hr. seasonally), the Steamship Wharf Terminal, and Pacific National Bank lobby (open during bank hours only).

In case of a **medical emergency,** the **Nantucket Cottage Hospital,** 57 Prospect St. (© 508/228-1200;** www.nantuckethospital.org) is open 24 hours.

Beaches & Outdoor Pursuits

BEACHES   In distinct contrast to Martha's Vineyard, virtually all of Nantucket's 110-mile coastline is open to the public.

○ **Children's Beach:** This small beach is a protected cove just west of busy Steamship Wharf. Appealing to families, it has a park, a playground, restrooms, lifeguards, a snack bar, and even a bandstand for free weekend concerts.

○ **Cisco Beach ★★**: About 4 miles from town, in the southwestern quadrant of the island (from Main St., turn onto Milk St., which becomes Hummock Pond Rd.), Cisco enjoys vigorous waves—great for the surfers who flock here, not so great for the waterfront homeowners. Restrooms and lifeguards are available.

○ **Coatue Beach ★**: This fishhook-shaped barrier beach, on the northeastern side of the island at Wauwinet, is Nantucket's outback, accessible only by four-wheel-drive vehicles, watercraft, or the very strong-legged. Swimming is strongly discouraged because of fierce tides.

○ **Dionis Beach ★★★**: About 3 miles out of town (take the Madaket bike path to Eel Point Rd.) is Dionis, which enjoys the gentle Nantucket Sound surf and steep, picturesque bluffs. It's a great spot for swimming, picnicking, and shelling, and you'll find fewer children than at Jetties or Children's beaches. Stick to the established paths to prevent further erosion. Lifeguards patrol here, and restrooms are available.

○ **Jetties Beach ★★★**: Located about a half-mile west of Children's Beach on North Beach Street, Jetties is about a 20-minute walk, or an even shorter bike ride, shuttle bus ride, or drive, from town (there's a large parking lot, but it fills up early on summer weekends). It's another family favorite for its mild waves, lifeguards, bathhouse, and restrooms. Facilities include the town tennis courts, volleyball nets, a skate park, and a playground; watersports equipment and chairs are also available to rent. In August, Jetties hosts an intense sand-castle competition, and the 4th of July fireworks are held here.

○ **Madaket Beach ★★★**: Accessible by Madaket Road, by the 6-mile bike path that runs parallel to it, and by shuttle bus, this westerly beach is narrow and subject to pounding surf and sometimes serious crosscurrents. Unless it's a fairly tame day, you might content yourself with wading. It's the best spot on the island for admiring the sunset. Facilities include restrooms, lifeguards, and mobile food service.

o **Siasconset ('Sconset) Beach ★★**: The easterly coast of 'Sconset is as pretty as the town itself and rarely, if ever, crowded, perhaps because of the water's strong sideways tow. You can reach it by car, by shuttle bus, or via the Polpis or Milestone bike paths, about an 8-mile trip. Lifeguards are usually on duty, but the closest facilities (restrooms, grocery store, and cafe) are back in the center of the village.

o **Surfside Beach ★★★**: Three miles south of town via a popular bike/skate path, broad Surfside—equipped with lifeguards, restrooms, and a surprisingly accomplished little snack bar—is appropriately named and very popular. It draws thousands of visitors a day in high season, from college students to families, but the free-parking lot can fit only about 60 cars—you do the math, or better yet, ride your bike or take the shuttle bus.

BICYCLING ★★★   Several paved bike paths radiate out from the center of town to outlying beaches. The **bike paths** run about 6 miles west to Madaket, 3.5 miles south to Surfside, and 8 miles east to 'Sconset. To avoid backtracking from 'Sconset, continue north through the charming village, and return on the **Polpis Road bike path ★★**. Strong riders could do a circuit of the entire island in a day, but most will be content to combine a single route with a few hours at a beach.

For a free map of the island's bike paths, stop by **Young's Bicycle Shop,** at Steamboat Wharf (© **508/228-1151;** www.youngsbicycleshop.com). It's definitely the best place for bike rentals. See "Getting Around," above, for more bike-rental shops.

FISHING   For shellfishing, you'll need a permit from the **harbormaster's office,** at 34 Washington St. (© **508/228-7261**). Deep-sea charters heading out of Straight Wharf include Capt. Bob DeCosta's *The Albacore* (© **508/228-5074;** www.albacore charters.com), Capt. Josh Eldridge's *Monomoy* (© **508/228-6867;** www.monomoy chartersnantucket.com), and Capt. David Martin's *Absolute* (© **508/325-4000;** http://absolutesportfishing.com).

NATURE TRAILS   Through preservationist foresight, about one-third of Nantucket's shoreline is protected from development. Contact the **Nantucket Conservation Foundation,** at 118 Cliff Rd. (© **508/228-2884;** www.nantucketconservation. com), for a map of its holdings ($4), which include the 205-acre **Windswept Cranberry Bog** (off Polpis Rd.), where bogs are interspersed amid hardwood forests; and a portion of the 1,100-acre **Coskata–Coatue Wildlife Refuge ★★**, comprising the barrier beaches beyond Wauwinet (see "Organized Tours & Cruises," below). **The Maria Mitchell Association** (see "Museums & Historic Landmarks," below) sponsors guided birding and wildflower walks in season.

WATERSPORTS   **Jetties Sailing Center** manages the concession at **Jetties Beach** (© **508/228-5358**), which offers lessons and rents out kayaks, sailboards, sailboats, and more. **Sea Nantucket,** on tiny Francis Street Beach off Washington Street (© **508/228-7499**), also rents kayaks; it's a quick sprint across the harbor to beautiful Coatue.

Museums & Historic Landmarks

Hadwen House ★★   During Nantucket's most prosperous years, whaling merchant Joseph Starbuck built the "Three Bricks" (nos. 93, 95, and 97 Main St.) for

Nantucket Town

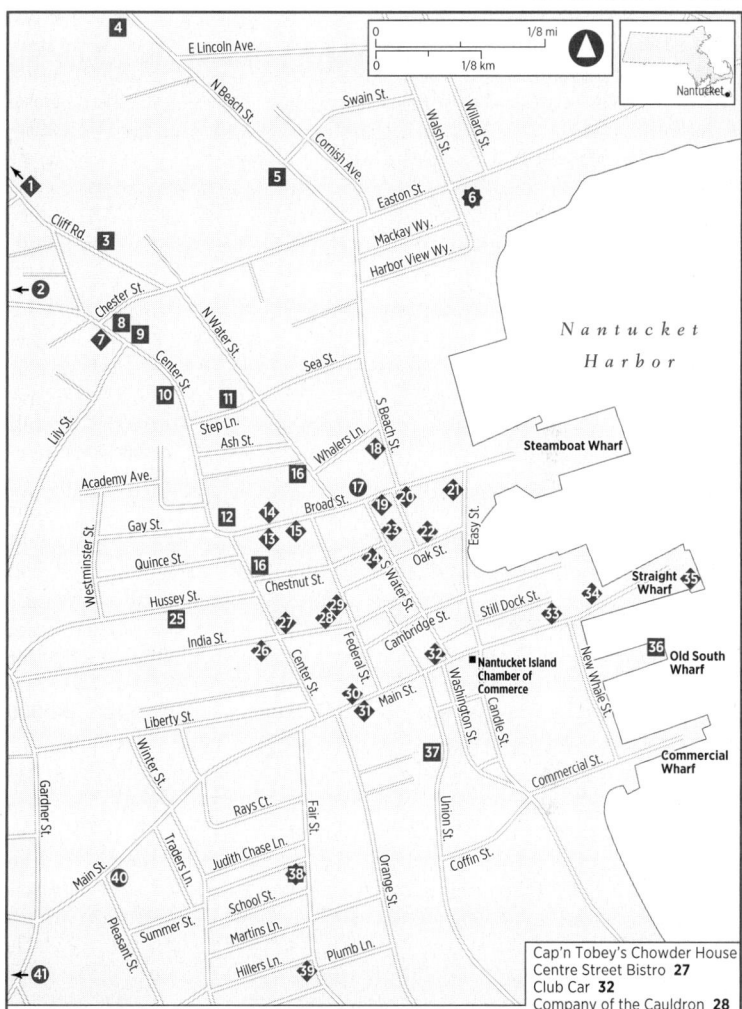

ATTRACTIONS ●
Hadwen House **40**
Jethro Coffin House **2**
Maria Mitchell Association **41**
Whaling Museum **17**

ACCOMMODATIONS ■
Anchor Inn **10**
Beachside at Nantucket **4**
Brant Point Inn **5**
Centerboard Guest House **8**
Cliff Lodge **3**
The Cottages/Woof Cottages **36**
Jared Coffin House **12**
Martin House Inn **9**

Nantucket Whaler Guest House **16**
The Pineapple Inn **25**
The Ships Inn **38**
Union Street Inn **37**
Vanessa Noel Hotel & Hotel Green **16**
The Veranda House **11**
White Elephant **6**

DINING ◆
American Seasons **7**
Arno's **30**
Black Eyed Susan's **26**
Boarding House **29**
Brant Point Grill **6**
The Brotherhood of Thieves **14**

Cap'n Tobey's Chowder House
Centre Street Bistro **27**
Club Car **32**
Company of the Cauldron **28**
Corazon del Mar **23**
Dune **15**
Easy Street Cantina **21**
The Even Keel Café **31**
Figs at 29 Fair **39**
The Juice Bar **19**
Le Languedoc Bistro **13**
LoLa Burgers **20**
Òran Mór **18**
Queequeg's **22**
Ropewalk **35**
Ships Inn Restaurant **38**
Something Natural **1**
Straight Wharf **34**
Town **24**

his three sons. His daughter married successful businessman William Hadwen, owner of the candle factory that is now the Whaling Museum, and Hadwen built this grand Greek Revival home across the street from his brothers-in-law in 1845. Although locals (mostly Quakers) were scandalized by the opulence, the local outrage spurred Hadwen on, and he decided to make the home even grander than he had originally intended. It soon became a showplace for entertaining the Hadwens' many wealthy friends. The home has been furnished with period pieces, and the gardens have been maintained in period style.

96 Main St. (at Pleasant St., a few blocks southwest of the town center). ✆ **508/228-1894.** www.nha. org. Admission included in Nantucket Historical Association's History Ticket ($18 adults, $9 children 15 and under). AE, MC, V. June–Sept Mon–Sat 10am–5pm, Sun noon–5pm; call for off-season hours. Closed Dec–Mar.

Jethro Coffin House ★ This 1686 saltbox is the oldest building left on the island. A National Historical Landmark, the brick design on its central chimney has earned it the nickname "The Horseshoe House." It was struck by lightning and severely damaged (in fact, nearly cut in two) in 1987, prompting a long-overdue restoration. It's filled with period furniture such as a trundle bed on wooden wheels.

Sunset Hill Rd. (off W. Chester Rd., approx. ½ mile northwest of the town center). ✆ **508/228-1894.** www. nha.org. Admission included in Nantucket Historical Association's History Ticket ($18 adults, $9 children). AE, MC, V. Late May to mid-Oct Mon–Sat 10am–5pm; Sun noon–5pm. Closed mid-Oct to late May.

The Maria Mitchell Association ★★ ☺ This is a group of six buildings organized and maintained in honor of distinguished astronomer and Nantucket native Maria Mitchell (1818–89). The science center consists of astronomical observatories, with a lecture series, children's science seminars, and stellar observation opportunities (when the sky is clear) from the **Loines Observatory,** 59 Milk St. Ext. (✆ 508/228-8690), and the **Vestal Street Observatory,** 3 Vestal St. (✆ **508/228-9273**).

The **Hinchman House Natural Science Museum** (✆ 508/228-0898), 7 Milk St., houses a visitor center and offers lectures, bird-watching, wildflower and nature walks, and discovery classes for children and adults. The **Mitchell House** (✆ **508/228-2896**), 1 Vestal St., the astronomer's birthplace, features a children's history series and adult-artisan seminars, and has wildflower and herb gardens. The **Science Library** (✆ **508/228-9219**) is at 2 Vestal St., and the tiny, child-oriented aquarium (✆ **508/228-5387**) is at 28 Washington St.

4 Vestal St. (at Milk St., approx. ½ mile southwest of the town center). ✆ **508/228-9198.** www.mmo. org. Admission to each site: $5 adults, $4 children. Museum pass (for birthplace, aquarium, science museum, and Vestal St. Observatory) $10 adults, $8 children ages 6–14. MC, V. Early June to late Aug Tues–Sat 10am–4pm; call for off-season hours.

Nantucket Life-Saving Museum ★★ 🎁 Housed in a replica of the Nantucket Life-Saving Station, the museum has loads of interesting exhibits, including historic photos and newspaper clippings, as well as one of the last remaining Massachusetts Humane Society surf boats and its horse-drawn carriage.

158 Polpis Rd. (2½ miles east of town) ✆ **508/228-1885.** www.nantucketlifesavingmuseum.com. Admission $5 adults, $2 children. Mid-June to mid-Oct daily 9:30am–4pm.

Whaling Museum ★★★ ☺ Reopened in 2005 after a grand multimillion-dollar renovation, this museum is a showpiece in the region. Appropriately, it is housed in a former spermaceti-candle factory (candles used to be made from a waxy fluid extracted from sperm whales). Kids will love the awe-inspiring skeleton of a whale (stranded in the 1990s), and adults will be fascinated by the exceptional collections of scrimshaw and nautical art. (Check out the action painting, *Ship Spermo of Nantucket in a Heavy Thunder-Squall on the Coast of California 1876*, executed by a captain who survived the storm.) A wall-size map depicts the 'round-the-world meanderings of the *Alpha*, accompanied by related journal entries. The admission price includes daily lectures on the brief and colorful history of the industry, like the beachside "whalebecue" feasts that natives and settlers once enjoyed. Don't miss the gift shop on the way out.

13 Broad St. (in the center of town). *℗* **508/228-1894.** www.nha.org. Admission $15 adults, $8 children 5–14. Admission is also included in the Nantucket Historical Association's History Ticket ($18 adults, $9 children). AE, MC, V. Apr–Nov Mon–Wed and Fri–Sat 10am–5pm; Thurs 10am–9pm; Sun noon–5pm. Closed Dec–Mar.

Organized Tours & Cruises

The Trustees of the Reservations, a statewide conservation organization, runs the 3-hour **Coskata–Coatue Wildlife Refuge Natural History Tour ★★★** (*℗* **508/228-6799**). The trip via Ford Expedition takes you over sand dunes and through rare habitat out to the **Great Point Lighthouse,** a replica of the 1818 original. On the way, you might spot snowy egrets, ospreys, and terns. Tours are offered mid-May to mid-October, daily at 9:30am and 1:30pm. The cost is $40 for adults and $15 for children 12 and under; call to reserve.

Endeavor **Sailing Excursions ★★**, at Slip 15 on Straight Wharf (*℗* **508/228-5585;** www.endeavorsailing.com), offers jaunts around the harbor on the *Endeavor,* a 31-foot replica of a historic Friendship sloop. Skipper James Genthner will gladly drop you off at one the beaches for a bit of sunbathing or beachcombing. Rates are $25 to $35 for a 1½-hour sail; reservations are recommended. No sailings November through April.

Shopping

Nantucket is home to dozens of upscale shops specializing in everything from woven sweaters to golden Nantucket basket necklaces. All the shops listed below are right in the center of Nantucket Town.

ART & CRAFTS The Artists' Association of Nantucket has the widest selection of work by locals, and the gallery at 19 Washington St. (*℗* **508/228-0294;** www.nantucketarts.org) is impressive. It's open April through January and by appointment only February and March.

Exquisite art glass, as well as ceramics, jewelry, and basketry, can be found at **Dane Gallery,** 28 Centre St. (*℗* **508/228-7779;** http://danegallery.com).

FASHION Martha's Vineyard may have spawned "Black Dog" fever, but this island boasts the inimitable "Nantucket reds"—cotton clothing that starts out tomato-red and washes out to salmon-pink. The fashion originated at **Murray's Toggery Shop,** 62 Main St. (*℗* **800/368-2134** or 508/228-0437; www.nantucketreds.com).

Nantucket Looms, 26 Federal St. (*℗* **508/228-1908;** www.nantucketlooms. com), sells hand-woven cashmere, mohair, and cotton sweaters, as well as scarves, throws, and rugs crafted in the workshop upstairs.

JEWELRY Diana Kim England, Goldsmiths, 56 Main St. (*℗* **508/228-3766;** www.dianakimengland.com), is a team of five goldsmiths who have over 70 years of combined experience in making jewelry. You'll find gold baskets and pearls, as well as unique custom pieces.

Where to Stay

As with Martha's Vineyard, I give only summer rates here, because Nantucket is so seasonal. However, if you do visit in the off-season, you can find substantial discounts at any of the places that remain open. Note, though, that lodging rates on Nantucket are at high-season levels during the popular **Christmas Stroll** in December and **Daffodil Festival** in April.

VERY EXPENSIVE

Cliffside Beach Club ★★★ 🎒 Right on the beach and a 15-minute walk from town, this is the premier lodging on the island. It may not be as fancy as some, but there's a sublime beachy-ness to the whole setup, from the simply decorated rooms and the cheerful, youthful staff to the colorful umbrellas lined up on the beach. All guest rooms have such luxuries as French milled soaps, thick towels, and exceptional linens. Lucky guests on the 4th of July get a front-row seat for the fireworks staged at Jetties Beach nearby.

46 Jefferson Ave. (approx. 1 mile from town center), Nantucket, MA 02554. © **800/932-9645** or 508/228-0618. Fax 508/325-4735. www.cliffsidebeach.com. 25 units, 1 cottage. Summer $450–$710 double; $875–$2,500 suite; $900 3-bedroom apt; $1,085 cottage. There is a 5.3% service charge in addition to taxes. Rates include continental breakfast. AE. Closed mid-Oct to late May. **Amenities:** Restaurant (the Galley, an elegant French bistro; p. 308); babysitting; concierge; exercise room; steam saunas; hydrotherapy spa. *In room:* A/C, TV/DVD, fridge, hair dryer.

Nantucket Whaler Guesthouse ★★ This 1850s sea captain's house is unique, in that each room is a suite with its own entrance and kitchen facilities. Compared to other B&Bs on the island, the Nantucket Whaler Guesthouse has a particularly private feel, almost like having your own apartment. All rooms are comfortably outfitted with cottage-y furnishings, including overstuffed couches and stacks of games and books.

8 N. Water St. (in the center of town), Nantucket, MA 02554. © **800/462-6882** or 508/228-6597. Fax 508/228-6291. www.nantucketwhaler.com. 12 units (4 with shower only). Summer $325–$460 double; $650–$795 2-bedroom suite. AE, DC, MC, V. Closed mid-Dec to late Apr. No children 11 and under. *In room:* A/C, TV/VCR/DVD, CD player, hair dryer.

Vanessa Noel Hotel and Hotel Green ♨ Shoe designer Vanessa Noel owns two centrally located inns side by side. VNH has eight rooms with boutique hotel features like Philippe Starck fixtures, feather beds with custom Frette linens, Bulgari toiletries, 15-inch flatscreen televisions, and minibars stocked with the hotel's bottled water. But most of the rooms are tiny (particularly given the prices), though two units, including a fun attic space, are fairly spacious. Next door, the **Vanessa Noel Hotel Green** (© **508/228-5300**) boasts an ecological theme, using organic cottons on the bedding and eco-friendly toiletries.

5 Chestnut St. (in the center of town), Nantucket, MA 02554. © **508/228-5300.** Fax 508/228-8995. www.vanessanoelhotel.com. 8 units. Summer $300–$480 double. AE, DISC, MC, V. *In room:* A/C, TV, hair dryer, minibar.

The Wauwinet ★★ This beachfront retreat is Nantucket's only Relais & Châteaux property. It is also one of the few inns not within walking distance of town, though a shuttle bus offers fairly convenient service. The inn is situated next to a wildlife sanctuary and is nestled between the Atlantic Ocean and Nantucket Bay. Each lovely room is individually decorated, with pine armoires, plenty of wicker, exquisite Audubon prints, and handsome fabrics, though some are on the small side. Extras include robes, bottled water, and a personalized set of engraved note cards. The staff goes to great lengths to please, ferrying you into town, for instance, or dispatching you on a 21-foot launch across the bay to your own private strip of beach in season.

120 Wauwinet Rd. (P.O. Box 2580), approx. 8 miles east of Nantucket center, Nantucket, MA 02554. ℂ **800/426-8718** or 508/228-0145. Fax 508/325-0657. www.wauwinet.com. 25 units, 10 cottages. Summer $680–$1,250 double; $1,020–$1,450 cottage. Rates include full breakfast and afternoon wine and cheese. AE, DC, MC, V. Closed Nov to mid-May. **Amenities:** Restaurant (fine dining); mountain bikes; concierge; room service; 2 clay tennis courts w/pro shop and teaching pro; watersports equipment (rowboats, sailboats, sea kayaks)/rentals. *In room:* A/C, TV/DVD and movie library, CD player, hair dryer, Wi-Fi (free).

White Elephant ★★★   This luxury property, right on the harbor, is the ultimate in-town lodging. Guest rooms (distributed among one building and 12 cottages) are big and airy—the most spacious on Nantucket—with country-chic decor. About half the rooms have working fireplaces, and most have harbor views. The same company owns Breakers, a 25-room hotel next door that offers a less bustling atmosphere. **The Brant Point Grill,** the pricey restaurant on-site, serves three meals a day. A brand-new **spa** offers a range of services.

50 Easton St. (P.O. Box 1139), Nantucket, MA 02554. ℂ **800/445-6574** or 508/228-2500. Fax 508/325-1195. www.whiteelephanthotel.com. 53 units (2 with shower only). Summer $615–$775 double; $680 1-bedroom cottage, $1,300 2-bedroom cottage, $1,430 3-bedroom cottage. Rates include full breakfast. AE, DC, DISC, MC, V. Closed Dec–Mar. **Amenities:** Restaurant (lobster and steakhouse serving lunch and dinner daily, plus an afternoon raw bar); concierge; exercise room; room service; spa. *In room:* A/C, TV/DVD and movie library, CD player, fridge, hair dryer.

EXPENSIVE

Beachside at Nantucket ★   No ordinary motel, the Beachside has 90 guest rooms that have been lavished with Provençal prints and handsome rattan and wicker furniture; the patios and decks overlooking the central courtyard with its heated pool have been prettified with French doors and latticework. Note that the Beachside has very reasonable off-season rates—$110 a night in the spring.

30 N. Beach St. (approx. ¾ mile west of the town center), Nantucket, MA 02554. ℂ **800/322-4433** or 508/228-2241. Fax 508/228-8901. www.thebeachside.com. 90 units. Summer $355–$505 double; $425–$750 suite. Rates include continental breakfast. AE, DC, DISC, MC, V. Closed late Oct to late Apr. Pets accepted ($25 fee). **Amenities:** Heated outdoor pool. *In room:* A/C, TV, fridge, hair dryer, Wi-Fi (free).

The Cottages/Woof Cottages ★★   These small apartments have the best location on the island, stacked up on a wharf that juts out into Nantucket Harbor. If you are looking for a place on Nantucket where you can bring your pooch, these one- and two-bedroom cottages are the perfect choice. All cottages are fresh and sparkling—floors polished, walls painted—and each has an eat-in kitchen and cozy living-room area. Dogs get a welcome basket of treats and a Nantucket bandana. Guests have privileges at the **White Elephant spa,** a sister property.

One Old South Wharf (in the center of town), Nantucket, MA 02554. ℂ **866/838-9253** or 508/325-1499. Fax 508/325-1173. www.harborviewcottages.com. 33 units. Summer $490–$750 studio and 1-bedroom; $750–$1,145 2-bedroom; $910–$1,240 3-bedroom. AE, MC, V. Closed mid-Oct to May. Dogs accepted in Woof Cottages with prior approval ($60 for 1–3 nights; $75 for 4 or more nights). *In room:* TV/VCR, CD player, kitchenette, hair dryer, Wi-Fi (free).

Jared Coffin House ★★ ☺   This grand brick manse built in 1845 is the social center of town. Accommodations in three historic buildings range from well-priced singles to spacious doubles. The central location does have a drawback: Front rooms can be quite noisy. Inn guests get spa privileges and a discount on breakfast and lunch at the Brant Point Grill, the inn's sister property on the harbor. This property is currently undergoing a multimillion-dollar renovation, but buildings not under renovation remain open.

29 Broad St. (at Centre St.), Nantucket, MA 02554. © **800/248-2405** or 508/228-2400. Fax 508/228-8549. www.jaredcoffinhouse.com. 60 units (8 with shower only). Summer $155–$175 single; $290–$470 double. AE, DC, DISC, MC, V. **Amenities:** Restaurant (Chinese); concierge. *In room:* TV, fridge, hair dryer, Wi-Fi (free).

The Pineapple Inn ★★
This beautifully renovated historic inn is one of the premier places to stay on the island. The graceful Quaker entrance of the 1838 home leads to spacious guest rooms decorated with fine reproductions and antiques, Oriental rugs, marble bathrooms, and many four-poster canopy beds. The continental breakfast here is extra deluxe with fresh baked goods, espresso, cappuccino, and freshly squeezed orange juice. Inn guests can use the pool and private Atlantic Ocean beach at one of the inn's sister properties in 'Sconset.

10 Hussey St. (in the center of town), Nantucket, MA 02554. © **508/228-9992.** Fax 508/325-6051. www.pineappleinn.com. 12 units (4 with shower only). Summer $230–$375 double. Rates include continental breakfast. AE, MC, V. Closed early Dec to mid-Apr. No children 7 and under. *In room:* A/C, TV, hair dryer.

Union Street Inn ★★ 🎁
Innkeepers Deborah and Ken Withrow have a terrific location for their 1770s property, a quiet residential section just steps from Main Street. Ken's experience in big hotels shows in the full concierge service offered here. Many guest rooms have canopied or four-poster beds; half have working wood-burning fireplaces. All are outfitted with antique furniture and fixtures. Unlike many Nantucket inns forbidden by zoning laws to serve a full breakfast, this inn's location allows for a superb complete breakfast.

7 Union St. (in the center of town), Nantucket, MA 02554. © **800/225-5116** or 508/228-9222. Fax 508/325-0848. www.unioninn.com. 12 units (11 with shower only). Summer $295–$575 double; $545 suite. Rates include full breakfast. AE, MC, V. Closed Jan to mid-Apr. *In room:* A/C, TV, CD player, hair dryer, Wi-Fi (free), no phone.

The Veranda House ★★ 🎁
This "retro chic" hotel is located in a quiet neighborhood a short walk from the center of town. It is perched on a hill, so rooms on the third floor have distant harbor views. Some of the most deluxe rooms have private balconies. All rooms have deluxe amenities like Frette linens and goose down comforters on the beds. Breakfast, which features such delicacies as artisan cheeses and fresh-baked pastries, is served on the ample front porch.

Three Step Lane (a few blocks from town center), Nantucket, MA 02554. © **877/228-0695** or 508/228-0695. Fax 508/374-0406. www.theverandahouse.com. 18 units. Summer $309–$449 double; $589 suite. Rates include continental breakfast. AE, MC, V. Closed Nov to late May. *In room:* A/C, TV/DVD, hair dryer, Wi-Fi (free).

MODERATE

Anchor Inn ★ 🦪
This historic gem, an 1806 captain's home, is next to the Old North Church. Another property, 72 Centre St., is three doors down from the inn. Authentic details can be found throughout both houses, in the antique hardware and paneling, wide-board floors, and period furnishings. The five rooms in the 72 Centre St. house are a particularly good value; they are smaller and less expensive.

66 Centre St. (P.O. Box 387, in the center of town), Nantucket, MA 02554. © **508/228-0072.** www. anchor-inn.net. 9 units (all with shower only). Summer $195–$229 double; $250–$285 suite. Rates include continental breakfast. AE, MC, V. Closed Jan–Feb. *In room:* A/C, TV, hair dryer, Wi-Fi (free).

Brant Point Inn ★

Thea and Pete Kaiser's two inn buildings, Brant Point and Atlantic Mainstay next door, offer relatively affordable accommodations in a good location, in between town and Jetties Beach. The inns are traditional post-and-beam style with country furnishings (think quilts on the beds). The guest living room has exposed oak beams and a massive Belgian block fireplace. Pete is an experienced fisherman and can arrange fishing trips for guests.

6 N. Beach St. (a few blocks west of the center of town), Nantucket, MA 02554. © **508/228-5442.** Fax 508/228-8498 www.brantpointinn.com. 8 units. Summer $245 double, $225–$345 suite. Rates include continental breakfast. AE, MC, V. Closed Nov–Apr. *In room:* A/C, TV, fridge, hair dryer.

Centerboard ★★

This updated 1886 home boasts parquet floors, Oriental rugs, lavish fabrics, plush feather mattresses, and lace-trimmed linens. Of the inn's seven bedrooms, the first-floor suite is perhaps the most romantic, with a green-marble Jacuzzi and a private living room with fireplace. Other rooms and bathrooms are on the compact side, as befits a Victorian-era building.

8 Chester St. (in the center of town), Nantucket, MA 02554. © **508/228-9696.** Fax 508/325-4798. www.centerboardguesthouse.com. 7 units. Summer $275–$450 double; $435 suite. Rates include continental breakfast. AE, MC, V. Closed Nov–Apr. *In room:* A/C, TV, fridge, hair dryer, Wi-Fi (free).

Cliff Lodge ★★ 🛏️

This charming 1771 whaling captain's house has a country casual style. The cheerful guest rooms feature colorful quilts and splatter-painted floors. Rooms range from a first-floor beauty with king-size bed, paneled walls, and fireplace to the tiny third-floor rooms tucked into the eaves. The spacious apartment in the rear of the house is a sunny delight. Climb up to the widow's walk for a bird's-eye view of the town and harbor.

9 Cliff Rd. (a few blocks from the center of town), Nantucket, MA 02554. © **508/228-9480.** Fax 508/228-6308. www.clifflodgenantucket.com. 12 units. Summer $155 single; $195–$320 double; $395 apt. Rates include continental breakfast. MC, V. No children 11 and under. *In room:* A/C, TV.

Martin House Inn ★★ 🐟

This is one of the lower-priced B&Bs in town, but also one of the most stylish, with a formal parlor and a spacious side porch, complete with hammock. Some guest rooms in this historic 1803 mariner's home have four-poster beds and working fireplaces. The four garret singles with a shared bathroom are a bargain.

61 Centre St. (btw. Broad and Chester sts.; a couple of blocks from town center), Nantucket, MA 02554. © **508/228-0678.** Fax 508/325-4798. www.martinhouseinn.net. 13 units (5 with shower only, 4 with shared bathroom). Summer $125 single with shared bathroom; $195 double with shared bathroom; $220–$385 double; $405 suite. Rates include continental breakfast. AE, MC, V. *In room:* A/C, no phone.

The Ship's Inn ★ 🐟

This pretty, historic inn is on a quiet side street, just slightly removed—3 blocks—from Nantucket's center. Rooms are comfortable and spacious, considering the house was built in 1831. The decor has a homey touch. The fine dining restaurant downstairs holds its own (see "Where to Dine," below).

13 Fair St. (a few blocks from town center), Nantucket, MA 02554. © **888/872-4052** or 508/228-0040. Fax 508/228-6524. www.shipsinnnantucket.com. 12 units (2 with shared bathroom). Summer $135 single with shared bathroom; $275 double. No children 7 and under. Rates include continental breakfast. AE, MC, V. Closed late Oct to mid-May. **Amenities:** Restaurant (fine dining; p. 311) located in the basement. *In room:* A/C, TV, fridge, hair dryer.

Where to Dine

VERY EXPENSIVE

Brant Point Grill ★ ♨ NEW AMERICAN   For the high prices, you can probably do better than this harborside eatery, though it does have some interesting features. Specializing in lobster, steak, and chops, the chef prepares some dishes on a Fire Cone grill, a 21st-century interpretation of a Native American technique that cooks food by radiant heat and imparts it with a smoky mesquite flavor. Two specialties are tenderloin beef Wellington and an exotic mushroom risotto. If you can't sit on the terrace, try to snag a seat near one of the windows, where you can watch the twilight fade over the harbor. The raw bar is open July through Labor Day from 4 to 7pm for light snacks.

At the White Elephant Hotel (Easton and Willard sts.). ✆ **508/325-1320.** www.whiteelephanthotel. com/restaurant. Collared shirt and long pants requested for gentlemen. Reservations strongly recommended. Main courses $26–$39; 3-course prix fixe meal $45. AE, DISC, MC, V. Mid-Apr to early Dec daily noon–2:30pm and 6–10pm. Closed mid-Dec to mid-Apr.

Chanticleer Inn ★★★ MODERN FRENCH   The Chanticleer, in the signature rose-covered cottage in 'Sconset, is the place everyone wants to go for special occasions. Co-owners Susan Handy and Chef Jeff Worster, who also own Black Eyed Susan's (see below), run this charming place as a *brasserie moderne*. Wonderful inventions like cod beignets and traditional appetizers like *moules frites*, share the menu with creative versions of steak au poivre and seared Nantucket sea scallops. Tart au citron is among the stellar desserts, but you can also end your meal with a *plats fromage* with three types of succulent cheeses. How French!

9 New St., Siasconset. ✆ **508/257-4499.** www.thechanticleer.net. Reservations strongly recommended. Jacket preferred for men. Main courses $21–$43. AE, DC, MC, V. July–Aug Tues–Sun noon–2pm and 6–10pm; call for off-season hours. Closed Nov–Apr.

Cinco Restaurant and Bar ★ INTERNATIONAL TAPAS   This exquisite restaurant specializes in tapas, those popular little Spanish-style plates of food. This is not the place to come with a big appetite, but it's a great place for a light meal and to enjoy the lively atmosphere. There are about two dozen choices on the menu; three or four per person would make a small meal, but you'll want to share. The preparations and tastes are unusual and sophisticated, making use of cured meats, marinated vegetables, grilled fish, and other delicacies—for example, cornmeal-crusted soft-shell crab and Nantucket fluke ceviche.

5 Amelia Dr. (¼ mile from the rotary, just off South Rd.). ✆ **508/325-5151.** www.cinco5.com. Reservations recommended. Tapas $11–$31. MC, V. Mid-June to Sept daily 6–10:30pm; call for off-season hours.

Club Car ★★ CONTINENTAL   For decades, one of the top restaurants on Nantucket, this posh venue is popular with locals. The menu has classic French influences. Popular offerings include a first course of octopus in the style of Bangkok with mint and hot peppers, and the classic entree of roast rack of lamb Club Car (with fresh herbs, honey-mustard glaze, and minted Madeira sauce). Some nights, seven-course tasting menus are available for $65 per person. The lounge area/piano bar, set in an antique car from the old Nantucket railroad, attracts a lively scene.

1 Main St. ✆ **508/228-1101.** www.theclubcar.com. Reservations recommended. Main courses $24–$45. MC, V. July–Aug daily 11am–3pm and 6–10pm; call for off-season hours. Closed early Dec to late May.

Galley Beach ★★★ NEW AMERICAN   Come to this beachfront restaurant with the coolest bar decor on the island if you want to feel like you are in a *Travel &*

Leisure fashion spread. Part of the Cliffside Beach Club (p. 304)—the Galley offers a particularly deluxe fine-dining experience. Given the setting, it's no surprise that the specialty is seafood, caught locally by island fishermen. Produce comes from the restaurant's own organic garden. The menu changes often, but noteworthy options include either the signature New England clam chowder with smoked bacon or the lobster spring rolls. As a main course, choose between a Nantucket flounder meunière, native halibut with parsley potatoes and green beans, Black Angus filet, or a 2-pound local lobster with truffle butter and all the fixings.

54 Jefferson Ave., Nantucket. © **508/228-9641.** www.galleybeach.net. Reservations recommended. Main courses $29–$39. AE, MC, V. Daily noon–2pm and 5–10pm. Closed Oct to late May.

Straight Wharf ★★★ NEW AMERICAN   Straight Wharf, on the waterfront in the center of town, has long been known for its creative cuisine. The two chefs here like to feature playful takes on old favorites. A starter might be pear celery salad with a main course of wild striped bass with fried green tomatoes. A more affordable "summer grill" menu, served in the bar area, features simpler fare. Make your reservation for 8pm on the deck so you can watch the sun set over the harbor.

Straight Wharf. © **508/228-4499.** www.straightwharfrestaurant.com. Reservations recommended. Main courses $34–$38; summer grill menu $16–$22. AE, MC, V. July–Aug Tues–Sun 6–9:30pm; call for off-season hours. Closed late Sept to late May.

The Summer House ★★ 🛎 FUSION   The classic 'Sconset-style atmosphere distinguishes this fine-dining experience from others on the island: wicker and wrought-iron, roses, and honeysuckle. A pianist plays nightly—often Gershwin standards, and the pounding Atlantic Ocean is just over the bluff. Though this is one of the few restaurants not in the center of town, it is worth a trip to the far side of the island for the atmosphere and cuisine inspired by Mediterranean cultures. Though the menu changes often, a three-course meal here might begin with sherry lobster bisque. Homemade pastas like chestnut ravioli caprese are not to be missed. One of the specialty entrees is the veal chop stuffed with asparagus and fontina. If it's blueberry season, end your meal with a slice of blueberry pie. **The Beachside Bistro** is a casual poolside venue open for lunch during summer.

17 Ocean Ave., Siasconset. © **508/257-9976.** www.thesummerhouse.com. Reservations recommended. Main courses $33–$39. AE, MC, V. July–Aug daily noon–4pm (at the Beachside Bistro late June to early Sept) and 6–10pm; mid-May to June and Sept to mid-Oct Wed–Sun 6–10pm. Closed mid-Oct to Apr.

Topper's at The Wauwinet ★★ REGIONAL/NEW AMERICAN   This 1850 restaurant—part of a secluded resort—is a tastefully subdued knockout, with wicker armchairs, splashes of chintz, and a two-tailed mermaid to oversee a chill-chasing fire. Try to sit at one of the cozy banquettes, if you can. This is Nantucket's most formal restaurant. The menu, a three-course prix fixe with numerous choices, features the finest regional cuisine: Lobster is a major event (it's often sautéed with champagne *beurre blanc*), and be on the lookout for specials like arctic char. Desserts, like the toasted brioche with poached pears and caramel sauce, are fanciful and fabulous. Topper's is well known for its superlative wine menu. In season, the Wauwinet Inn runs a complimentary launch service to the restaurant for lunch and dinner; it leaves from Straight Wharf at 11am and 5pm, takes 1 hour, and also makes the return trip.

120 Wauwinet Rd. (off Squam Rd.), Wauwinet. © **508/228-8768.** www.wauwinet.com/restaurant.php. Reservations required for dinner and the launch ride over. 3-course prix fixe $85. AE, DC, MC, V. May–Oct daily noon–2pm and 6–9:30pm. Closed Nov–Apr.

EXPENSIVE

American Seasons ★★ REGIONAL AMERICAN   This romantic little restaurant has a great theme: Choose your region (New England, Pacific Coast, Wild West, or Down South) and select creative offerings. Start, for instance, with Louisiana crayfish risotto with fire-roasted onion and fried parsnips in a sweet corn purée from Down South; then move on to the Pacific Coast's aged beef sirloin with caramelized shallot and Yukon potato hash. A lighter tapas menu is available throughout the evening.

80 Centre St. (2 blocks from the center of town). ⓒ **508/228-7111.** www.americanseasons.com. Reservations recommended. Main courses $24–$30. AE, MC, V. Mid-Apr to Dec daily 6–9pm. Closed Jan to mid-Apr.

Boarding House ★★ NEW AMERICAN   This centrally located fine-dining restaurant doubles as one of the most popular bars in town. You can dine in the romantic lower-level dining room or upstairs in the hopping bar area. But on clear summer nights, you'll want to get one of the tables outside on the patio. The menu has definite Asian and Mediterranean influences, but the signature dish is the classic grilled lobster tails with grilled asparagus, mashed potatoes, and champagne beurre blanc. The award-winning wine list offers a range of prices.

12 Federal St. ⓒ **508/228-9622.** www.boardinghouse-pearl.com. Reservations recommended. Main courses $26–$36. AE, MC, V. July–Aug daily 6–10pm; call for off-season hours.

Company of the Cauldron ★★★ CONTINENTAL   Considered the most romantic restaurant on the island, this candlelit dining room features a classical harpist in season. The menu is unusual, in that there is a single three- to four-course fixed-price meal each night, so would-be patrons must check the menu out front or call ahead to see which night to go. Dietary preferences can be accommodated with advance notice. The meal might start with a red beet and lobster risotto, then on to pepper-crusted Chateaubriand, and ending with a rustic apple tart. There are just two seatings nightly.

5 India St. (btw. Federal and Centre sts.). ⓒ **508/228-4016.** www.companyofthecauldron.com. Reservations required. Fixed-price dinner $50–$55. MC, V. Early July to early Sept Tues–Sun, 2 seatings at 6:45 and 8:45pm; call for off-season hours. Closed mid-Oct to mid-Apr, except Thanksgiving weekend and the first 2 weeks of Dec.

Corazon del Mar ★★ LATIN   This Latin kitchen features a ceviche and raw bar, unusual and authentic tacos, and a tequila bar. You'll find exciting taste sensations that you can't get anywhere else on island. Octopus glazed with olive oil is served with crushed potatoes and pepper; crispy codfish tacos come with an avocado and cabbage chili. But the portions are on the small side and, with these prices, that means not a lot of bang for your buck.

21 S. Water St. ⓒ **508/228-0815.** www.corazonnantucket.com. Main courses $22–$32. AE, MC, V. July–Aug daily 5:30–10pm; call for off-season hours.

Dune ★★ NEW AMERICAN   This chic bistro is one of the island's newer restaurants. The chef/owner, Michael Getter, who also started the restaurant American Seasons, is considered one of the island's most creative chefs. The interior is very modern, all sleek lines and neutral earth-tone colors. The food is made up of seasonal local produce and fish and meats from area farms. High-season choices that are light and summery might include a yellowfin tuna Niçoise and a wonderful pan-seared striped bass with cucumber gazpacho.

20 Broad St. (in the center of town). ℂ **508/228-5550.** www.dunenantucket.com. Reservations recommended. Main courses $28–$38. AE, MC, V. July to mid-Sept daily noon–2pm and 5:30–9:30pm. Call for off-season hours.

Fifty-Six Union ★★ NEW AMERICAN   This understated restaurant offers fine dining without pretensions: just good service, a pleasing contemporary atmosphere, and wonderful food. Diners can sit in the bar area, which tends to be loud and lively, in the quieter Garden Room, or on the outdoor patio. Intriguing appetizers include a Bosc pear salad and crab Rangoon with a spicy sauce. Main-course choices range from Javanese fried rice with shrimp and chicken, to a rack of Colorado lamb with mustard crust.

56 Union St. (½ mile from Main St.). ℂ **508/228-6135.** www.fiftysixunion.com. Reservations recommended. Main courses $23–$44. AE, MC, V. Early July to early Sept daily 6–10pm, Sun 10am–1pm; call for off-season hours.

Òran Mór ★★ NEW AMERICAN   Chef/owner Chris Freeman brings his stellar reputation to this popular upscale restaurant, an intimate second-floor space that has an aura of romance. Chef Freeman specializes in native seafood and local produce. You will always find Nantucket lobster on the menu, but you'll also encounter unusual appetizers like grilled quail with wild mushrooms. As for entrees, try the local roasted striped bass with littleneck clams or the Peking duck breast with peach ginger salsa.

2 S. Beach St. (in the center of town). ℂ **508/228-8655.** www.oranmorbistro.com. Reservations recommended. Main courses $22–$34. AE, MC, V. July–Aug daily 6–10pm; Sept–June Thurs–Sat and Mon–Tues 6–9pm; Sun noon–9pm.

Ropewalk ★ SEAFOOD   This open-air restaurant, which sits at the end of Straight Wharf, doubles as Nantucket's only outdoor raw bar, and it's where the yachting crowd hangs out after a day on the boat. While the food is a bit overpriced, the location is prime. This is a good place to enjoy a light meal or appetizers, such as fried calamari, crab cakes, or fried oysters. The dinner menu includes pineapple-glazed swordfish and bourbon peach barbecue breast of chicken.

1 Straight Wharf. ℂ **508/228-8886.** www.theropewalk.com. Reservations not accepted. Main courses $23–$33. MC, V. May–Oct daily 11am–10pm. Closed Nov–Apr.

Ship's Inn Restaurant ★★ NEW AMERICAN   This intimate restaurant in the brick-walled basement of a historic inn is one of the island's most romantic dining options. The waitstaff here is professional and entertaining, a real treat. The menu features a variety of fresh fish, meat, and pasta dishes, including several lighter options made without butter or cream. A flavorful starter here is the Roquefort and walnut terrine with Asian pear. Popular main dishes include the pan-roasted Muscovy duck breast and the grilled yellowtail flounder. For a festive dessert, there's always the Grand Marnier soufflé.

In the Ship's Inn, 13 Fair St. ℂ **508/228-0040.** www.shipsinnnantucket.com. Reservations recommended. Main courses $19–$34. AE, MC, V. July–Sept Wed–Mon 5–10pm; call for off-season hours. Closed Nov–Apr.

Trattoria Sfoglia ★★★ NORTHERN ITALIAN   This unpretentious eatery ranks at the top of many people's "my favorite" lists for Nantucket. Dining is in the European style, where you order several courses, beginning with an antipasto, like clams, salami, tomato, and fennel; next, perhaps a corn risotto with lobster and zucchini and a roasted sausage with *contorni* (tasty preparations of farm-fresh vegetables, like beets or eggplant). Light eaters can ask for a half-order of the house-made pasta, which is enough to satisfy the average appetite. The kitchen turns out home-baked bread that some call the island's best, and its own gelato. The only catch: The restaurant is not in the center of town, so visitors without cars will have to take a taxi.

130 Pleasant St. (across from Stop & Shop). (C) **508/325-4500.** www.sfogliarestaurant.com/nantucket. Reservations recommended. Main courses $14–$29. No credit cards. Apr to mid-Oct Mon–Sat 6–10pm; call for off-season hours.

MODERATE

Black Eyed Susan's ★★★ 🎁 INTERNATIONAL   This is supremely exciting food in a funky diner-style atmosphere. Reservations are accepted for the 6pm seating only, and they go fast. Others must line up outside; the line starts forming around 5:30pm. The menu is in constant flux, as Chef Jeff Worster's mood and influences change every 3 weeks. I always enjoy the spicy Thai fish cake and the tandoori chicken with green mango chutney. There's usually a Southwestern touch, like the Dos Equis–beer-battered catfish quesadilla with mango slaw, hoppin' john, and jalapeño. There's no liquor license, but you can BYOB. It's also cash only.

10 India St. (in the center of town). (C) **508/325-0308.** www.black-eyedsusans.com. Reservations accepted for 6pm seating only. Main courses $15–$25. No credit cards. Apr–Oct daily 7am–1pm, Mon–Sat 6–10pm; call for off-season hours. Closed Nov–Mar.

The Brotherhood of Thieves ★ PUB GRUB   A recent renovation and expansion has taken away most of the former grittiness of this classic whaling bar, but it is still popular. In July and August, tourists line up for tables in the dark tavern downstairs to chow down on burgers and hand-cut curly fries. A new upstairs dining room also has an outside raised terrace. In the fall and winter, locals sit beside the cozy brick hearths downstairs for dinner offerings like fisherman's stew or surf 'n' turf. This place serves food later than anyone else in town; you can order off the late-night menu until midnight.

23 Broad St. (C) **508/228-2551.** http://brotherhoodofthieves.com. Reservations accepted for parties of 6 or more. Main courses $7–$25. MC, V. Mar–Jan Mon–Sat 11:30am–midnight; Sun noon–10pm. Closed Feb.

Centre Street Bistro ★★★ NEW AMERICAN   This tiny fine-dining restaurant in the center of Nantucket town is owned and operated by Ruth and Tim Pitts, who are considered top chefs on the island. It gets top ratings by doing everything right, from atmosphere to service, to the memorable food. This cozy place features wonderful, creative cuisine at reasonable prices, especially compared with other island fine-dining restaurants. The menu changes often, but high points have included the warm goat-cheese tart or the smoked salmon taco to start, and the sesame-encrusted bistro shrimp with mango relish as a main course. Desserts, like the white-chocolate banana tart, are knock-outs.

29 Centre St. (C) **508/228-8470.** www.nantucketbistro.com. Reservations not accepted. Main courses $19–$25. MC, V. Wed–Sun noon–2:30pm and 6–10pm.

Figs at 29 Fair by Todd English MEDITERRANEAN   Celebrity chef Todd English created the menu at this historic restaurant, formerly known as the Woodbox. The ambience remains the same: ancient rafters, exposed beams, and antique tables and lit by very romantic candlelight. Mr. English calls his cuisine "rustic Mediterranean," and in this case that means an array of pasta, such as spaghettini with large Tuscan meatballs, and pizzas with such unusual toppings as figs (of course) and prosciutto.

29 Fair St. © **508/228-7800.** www.thesummerhouse.com/29. Reservations accepted. Main courses $17–$27. AE, MC, V. Apr–Dec Mon–Sat 6:30–9:30pm, Sun 10am–2pm and 6:30–9:30pm. Closed Jan–Mar.

Le Languedoc Cafe ★★ NEW AMERICAN   Nantucket's most authentic French cafe offers a cozy atmosphere and reasonable prices. An expensive dining room is upstairs, but locals prefer the casual bistro atmosphere downstairs and out on the terrace. Soups are superb, as are the Angus-steak burgers with garlic french fries, which is on the small but lower-priced bar menu. More elaborate dishes include the roasted tenderloin of pork stuffed with figs and pancetta.

24 Broad St. © **508/228-2552.** www.lelanguedoc.com. Reservations not accepted for cafe; reservations for dining room at 5:30 or 6pm only; others on wait list. Bar menu $14–$22. Dining room $24–$44. AE, MC, V. June–Sept daily 5:30–9:30pm, Tues–Sun 11:30am–2pm; call for off-season hours. Closed Jan to mid-Apr.

Queequeg's ★ NEW AMERICAN/SEAFOOD   A cozy bistro atmosphere and good value are the hallmarks of this small restaurant, which is tucked along a side street behind the Athenaeum. Outside seating is available on the patio in good weather. As befits the *Moby Dick* reference in the name, the specialty here is sea-food. The menu offers a range from basics to fancier fare. For example, as an appetizer, you could have the New England clam chowder or Prince Edward Island mussels. The rich and flavorful pan-seared halibut with Parmesan risotto is a favorite with locals. Meat-lovers may enjoy Yankee pot roast or beef tenderloin. Light eaters take note: Several entrees are available in half-portions at almost half the price.

6 Oak St. © **508/325-0992.** www.queequegsnantucket.com. Reservations recommended. Main courses $23–$28. MC, V. June–Sept daily 5–10:30pm; call for off-season hours.

Town ★ INTERNATIONAL   Chef Neil Hudson's twist at this restaurant is bringing international cooking styles from Africa, India, South America, and Asia to Nantucket's signature seafood dishes. For instance, the lobster tandoori gives an Indian flavor to the classic seared-lobster dish. You can dine outside or in the dining room, but many people prefer to sit at the bar, which is manned by Graeme Fleming, one of the island's more well-known bartenders.

4 E. Chestnut St. © **508/325-TOWN** (8696). www.townnantucket.com. Main courses $24–$32. AE, MC, V. July–Aug daily 5:30–10pm; Sept–June daily 6–9pm.

INEXPENSIVE

Arno's ☺ BISTRO   A storefront facing the passing parade of Main Street, this institution packs a surprising amount of style between its bare-brick walls. The internationally influenced menu yields tasty, bountiful platters for breakfast, lunch, and dinner. Specialties include grilled sirloin steaks and fresh grilled fish. Arno's has a family-friendly atmosphere, and there is a children's menu. Inside the restaurant is a new wine bar called **the 41.**

41 Main St. © **508/228-7001.** www.arnos.net. Reservations recommended. Main courses $12–$23. AE, MC, V. Apr–Dec daily 8am–2pm and 5–9pm. Closed Jan–Mar.

Cap'n Tobey's Chowder House ★ SEAFOOD   The specialty at this convenient eatery close to the harbor is seafood, obtained daily from local fishermen. Diners can choose among halibut, yellowfin tuna, and haddock, and have it grilled, baked, or blackened. The raw bar features oysters, littlenecks, and shrimp. Upstairs, **Off Shore at Cap'n Tobey's** has live music in season. Downstairs attracts a sports-bar crowd.

20 Straight Wharf. ☎ **508/228-0836.** Main courses $10–$22. AE, DC, DISC, MC, V. Late June to Sept daily 11:30am–10pm; call for off-season hours. Closed Jan–Apr.

The Even Keel Café AMERICAN   This low-key cafe in the heart of town serves breakfast, lunch, and dinner both indoors, at tables or the long counter, and outside, on the patio in the back. Unlike with much of Nantucket's dining scene, you'll find reasonable prices and nonexotic fare here, like burgers, pizza, and sandwiches, as well as Mexican and Italian choices. Other menu items include barbecue baby back ribs, chicken breast in coconut curry sauce, and lobster risotto. There's a kids' menu, as well as high-speed Internet access. On Sunday, they serve a hearty brunch. A small martini bar faces the front window.

40 Main St. ☎ **508/228-1979.** www.evenkeelcafe.com. Reservations not accepted. Main courses $10– $22. AE, MC, V. July–Aug daily 7am–10pm; call for off-season hours.

Take-Out & Picnic Fare

You can get fresh-picked produce right on Main Street from the traveling truck from **Bartlett's Ocean View Farm ★**, 33 Bartlett Farm Rd. (☎ **508/228-9403;** www. bartlettsfarm.com), or head out to this seventh-generation farm where, in June, you get to pick your own strawberries. They also sell sandwiches, quiches, pastries, pies, and more. They're closed January through March.

At **Easy Street Cantina ★★**, 2 Broad St. (☎ **508/228-5418**), you'll find cheap and yummy street food, including hearty fish tacos and cheese enchiladas. There are a couple of stand-up tables and booths here, but the better option is to take your meal to a bench on Main Street and people-watch while eating the best bargain meal on the island.

A terrific value on pricey Nantucket, **Something Natural,** 50 Cliff Rd. (☎ **508/228-0504;** www.somethingnatural.com), turns out gigantic sandwiches with fresh ingredients piled atop fabulous bread. Save room for their addictive chocolate-chip cookies. Something Natural is closed mid-October to March.

The **Juice Bar ★★**, 12 Broad St. (☎ **508/228-5799**), is a humble hole in the wall that dishes out some of the best homemade ice cream and frozen yogurt around, complemented by superb homemade hot fudge. It's closed from mid-October to mid-April.

Lola Burger, 10 Broad St. (☎ **508/325-0282**), is the street-food version of the overpriced bistro down the street, and this place serves up some fine burgers. Take yours over to the harbor and watch the yachting crowd come and go.

Nantucket After Dark

The **Chicken Box,** 12 Dave St. (☎ **508/228-9717;** www.thechickenbox.com), is the rocking spot for the 20-something crowd. It sometimes seems as if the entire population of the island is shoving its way in here. Jimmy Buffett shows up late at night about once a summer, unannounced, and jams with the band. The cover runs from $4 to $15. The **Rose and Crown,** 23 S. Water St. (☎ **508/228-2595;** www. theroseandcrown.com), draws all ages with its loud dance music. The cover for live bands on weekends is $3 to $5. It's closed January through March.

Theater buffs will want to spend an evening at the **Theatre Workshop of Nantucket,** Methodist Church, 2 Centre St. (☎ **508/228-4305;** www.theatreworkshop. com), which now has Emmy Award–winning actor John Shea at the helm. The year-round slate of live theater includes the work of Broadway-quality writers and composers.

CENTRAL & WESTERN MASSACHUSETTS

by Herbert Bailey Livesey, Leslie Brokaw & Matthew Barber

While Boston and its maritime appendage Cape Cod face the sea and embrace it, inland Massachusetts turns in upon itself. Countless ponds and lakes shimmer in its folds and hollows, often hidden by deep forests and granite outcroppings. Farms and vestiges of industrial buildings speckle the north-south valleys of the Connecticut and Housatonic rivers.

9

The heartland Pioneer Valley, enclosing the Connecticut River, earned its name in the early 18th century, when European trappers and farmers first began to push west from the colonies clinging to the edges of Massachusetts Bay. They were followed by ambitious capitalists who erected redbrick mills along the river for the manufacture of textiles and paper. Most of those enterprises failed or faded in the post–World War II movement to the milder climate and cheaper labor of the South, leaving a miasma of economic hardship that has yet to be completely resolved. But those industrialists also helped fund many of the distinguished colleges for which the valley is now known, and the educated populations that come out of these schools provide the region with youthful energy and a rich cultural life.

Roughly the same pattern applied in the Berkshires, the twin ranges of rumpled hills that define the western band of the state. The development of this region in the 19th century was prompted mainly by the construction of the railroad from New York and Boston. Artistic and literary folk made a favored summer retreat of it, followed by wealthy urbanites attracted by the region's reputation for creativity and bohemianism. Many of their extravagant mansions, dubbed "Berkshire Cottages," still survive, and the region continues to attract the town-and-country crowd, who support a vibrant summer schedule of the arts and then steal away as the crimson leaves fall and the Berkshires grow quiet beneath 6 months of snow.

WORCESTER

44 miles W of Boston; 52 miles NE of Springfield

Massachusetts's second-largest city, Worcester (pronounced *Wuss*-ter, or, locally, *Woos*-tah) has its dilapidated edges, but so, too, do many of the region's urban areas, most of which reached their apogees in the late 19th century. Still, the city has its charms and a surprising number of good museums and eating venues. There are enough attractions here to justify a stopover or to fill an overnight.

The student population draws from over a dozen schools, including Clark University, Worcester Polytechnic Institute, and College of the Holy Cross.

Two years after the 1848 Seneca Falls Woman's Rights Convention, Worcester was the site of the first National Women's Rights Convention. The history of that event is online at the National Park Service website, www.nps.gov.

Essentials

GETTING THERE   Worcester is 2 miles north of the east-west Massachusetts Turnpike (I-90) via I-290, which bisects the city. Driving can be tricky in Worcester, with the convergence of highways and its one-way streets, so get detailed directions to your destination. **Amtrak** (✆ **800/USA-RAIL** [872-7245]; www.amtrak.com) stops here daily each way on its route between Boston and Chicago.

VISITOR INFORMATION   The **Visitor Center** is on the second floor of the Worcester Historical Museum, 30 Elm St. (✆ **508/755-7400;** www.centralmass. org). A PDF of the **Central Massachusetts Visitors Guide** is at the website.

What to See & Do

EcoTarium ☺   This family-oriented institution is set on a woodsy campus crossed by meandering nature trails. Primarily directed at young children, the complex includes an indoor planetarium and a museum with interactive displays about ecology and conservation, and live and taxidermied animals. Outside, there are bald eagles, otters, owls, and a polar bear, and a one-third-scale model of an 1860s steam engine takes a 12-minute loop through the grounds. Adults and children 7 and older can play amid the canopies of oak and hickory trees 40 feet above ground on the **Tree Canopy Walkway** (summer only). In June and July, outdoor jazz concerts welcome the sunset.

222 Harrington Way. (✆ **508/929-2700.** www.ecotarium.org. General admission $10 adults, $8 seniors, students, and ages 3–18. Additional fees: Planetarium $5, Explorer Express Train $2.50, Tree Canopy Walkway $10. Tues–Sat 10am–5pm; Sun noon–5pm. From I-90 west, exit 11, north on Rte. 122 (Grafton St.) for 3 miles, right on Plantation St., right on Franklin St., right on Harrington Way. From I-90 east, exit 10, east on Rte. 209, exit 21 and right on Plantation St., left on Franklin, right on Harrington Way.

Higgins Armory Museum ★ ☺   Here's where you'll find your knight in shining armor—or at least the armor. This steel-and-glass-framed museum has medieval tapestries, stained-glass windows, and—in the Great Hall, which is fashioned after Gothic castles of yore—dozens of suits of armor, a posed jousting match, and swords and daggers. There's even a suit for a dog. The substantial collection comes from John W. Higgins, president (1912–50) of a Worcester company that processed steel and clearly possessed a keen interest in Renaissance armor and heraldry. Combat demonstrations and family "OverKnight" sleepovers are periodically hosted here; Harry Potter fans will be in heaven.

100 Barber Ave. ℂ **508/853-6015.** www.higgins.org. Admission $10 ages adults, $7 children 4-16, audio tour $2. Tues–Sat 10am-4pm; Sun noon-4pm. From I-190 north, exit 1 onto Rte. 12 north; after a small bridge, take a sharp right (nearly a U-turn) at the first light onto unmarked Barber Ave.

Worcester Art Museum ★★ WAM boasts an unexpectedly impressive collection of artworks, from 2nd-century Buddhist pieces to 20th-century American photos. Special exhibits of contemporary work give some fizz and pop to the hushed classical setting, which features a beautiful interior courtyard. Particular strengths are the American wing, with canvases by Cassatt, Sargent, and Whistler; some memorable works by anonymous Colonial artists; and silver by Paul Revere. The Europeans on the second floor include Gauguin, Monet, Dürer, and Gainsborough. There's a 12th-century Gothic chapter house, once used by Benedictine monks, transported from France and said to be the first medieval room to come to the U.S. A cafe offers soups and sandwiches from 11:30am to 2pm, with an outdoor courtyard in warm months.

55 Salisbury St. (corner of Tuckerman St.) ℂ **508/799-4406.** www.worcesterart.org. Admission $10 adults, $8 seniors, free 17 and under and for all Sat 10am-noon. Wed–Sun 11am-5pm (from 10am Sat, 8pm on 3rd Thurs of the month).

Getting Outside

The chasm at **Purgatory Chasm State Park,** Purgatory Road, Sutton (ℂ **508/234-3733;** www.mass.gov/dcr/parks/central/purg.htm), is a quarter-mile-long gap between massive granite walls. A **family hike** ☺ here is good for both adults and children of moderate-to-good condition. (Bonus if you're slender: You'll be able to explore the narrowest nooks and crannies.) The main trail runs down the middle of the gap with several return options including the .5-mile Chasm Loop. It's one of several family hikes recommended by the state's Department of Conservation and Recreation; you can find the entire list online at www.mass.gov/dcr/recreate/central_self-guided_hikes.pdf.

Where to Stay

Most of the accommodations in and around the city are chain motels. **Sturbridge,** 21 miles away, has an atmospheric option in its **Publick House** (p. 320).

Beechwood Hotel ★ The eye-catching feature of this redbrick boutique hotel is its round core structure, which resembles a medieval keep. Public spaces and guest rooms are agreeably furnished; and executive-level rooms and suites have skyline views. Sunday brunches in the **Harlequin Restaurant** receive local notice. The hotel is located across the street from the University of Massachusetts Medical School and Medical Center complex.

363 Plantation St. (at Rte. 9), Worcester, MA 01605. ℂ **800/344-2589** or 508/754-5789. Fax 508/752-2060. www.beechwoodhotel.com. 73 units. $169–$224 double. Rates include continental breakfast. AE, DC, DISC, MC, V. Free parking. **Amenities:** Restaurant; bar; exercise room; room service. *In room:* A/C, TV, hair dryer, Wi-Fi (free).

Crowne Plaza Along with its desirable location in the downtown business district, this outlet of the well-known chain delivers on most points of expected conveniences. With room options suitable for leisure and business travelers alike, the clientele is as varied as the bustle of activity happening in the seminar, meeting, and convention spaces. Amenities include an in-house bar, a restaurant and pizzeria, an on-site theater that becomes a comedy club on weekends, an indoor/outdoor pool, and a small exercise room. Guest rooms on the fifth through ninth floors were renovated in early 2009 (ask for one of them), and all rooms have triple-sheeted bedding. Executive level rooms are available for $20 over the rack rate and feature a private lounge with concierge on weekdays, a complimentary continental breakfast, and hors d'oeuvres in the evening. A quiet zone on the eighth floor is an option for those seeking a peaceful visit.

10 Lincoln Sq. (corner of Rte. 9 and Maj. Taylor Blvd.), Worcester, MA 01608. ✆ **888/444-0401** or 508/791-1600. Fax 508/791-1796. www.crowneplaza.com. 243 units. $119–$179 double; suites from $249. AE, DC, DISC, MC, V. Self-parking $6. Pets under 50 lb. accepted ($20/night). **Amenities:** Restaurant; bar; exercise room; heated indoor/outdoor pool w/Jacuzzi; room service. *In room:* A/C, TV, CD player, hair dryer, MP3 docking station, Wi-Fi (free).

Where to Dine

Just a few blocks east of the downtown train station, a strip of restaurants and cafes line Shrewsbury Street. Among them are the Italian **VIA,** 89 Shrewsbury St. (✆ **508/754-4842;** www.viaitaliantable.com), and a handsome steakhouse, **111 Chop House,** 111 Shrewsbury St. (✆ **508/799-4111;** www.111chophouse.com), both run by the same group behind Sole Proprietor (see below). Also, **Bocado,** 82 Winter St. (✆ **508/797-1011;** www.bocadotapasbar.com), is a tapas and wine bar a few blocks south of Shrewsbury Street that gets good local notice.

Armsby Abbey ★ PUB FARE   This popular gastropub opened in 2008 to much acclaim, evidenced by wins in an unprecedented 13 categories in *Worcester Magazine*'s Best of 2009 awards—including Best New Restaurant and Best Chef. With candlelit tables, exposed brick walls, and a long mahogany bar, the Armsby's coziness is infectious. The menu focuses on artisanal items, with a preference for local ingredients, and an enticing cheese plate, the regionally sourced Baystate Slate ($20), is one of the big winners. Patrons are mainly 20- and 30-somethings who appreciate the wallet-friendly menu, which changes frequently but always features gourmet sandwiches, stone-baked pizzas, and a small but mouth-watering selection of entrees. A large chalkboard details beers available that day (more than 20 on tap), and there are lots of creative cocktails. This is not a spot for a quick drink before heading elsewhere. It's a hangout, a place to settle in for the night.

144 N. Main St., Worcester. ✆ **508/795-1012.** www.armsbyabbey.com. Main courses $9–$20. AE, DISC, MC, V. Mon–Thurs 11:30am–midnight; Fri 11:30am–2am (kitchen until 11pm); Sat 11am–2am (kitchen until 11pm); Sun 11am–midnight (kitchen until 10pm). After 6pm, must be 21 to enter.

Sole Proprietor ★★ SEAFOOD   A chummy, well-run act, from the congenial staff to the long wine card (over 30 available by the glass). Fish preparations range from bare-bones simple to entrancingly complex: One side of the large rectangular bar is given over to a sushi and raw bar, while the kitchen produces such worthy inventions as tuna steak Barcelona—the fish coated with cracked peppercorns, grilled medium rare, and laid over a bed of feta cheese, sun-dried tomatoes, scallions, and basil leaves. Lunch specials run from $9 to $12, and portions are generous. We loved the bowl piled high with fat scallops, penne pasta, root vegetables, and bacon.

118 Highland St. (Rte. 9) ✆ **508/798-3474.** www.thesole.com. Main courses $16–$40; sushi rolls $7–$12. AE, DISC, MC, V. Mon–Thurs 11:30am–10pm; Fri–Sat 11:30am–11pm; Sun 4–9:30pm; bar open and serving bar food until 1:30am daily.

STURBRIDGE & OLD
STURBRIDGE VILLAGE ★★★

59 miles W of Boston; 22 miles SW of Worcester; 35 miles E of Springfield

Sturbridge is a quiet New England town of 7,837 residents that offers two reasons to visit. The first is **Old Sturbridge Village,** a living outdoor/indoor museum sprawled across over 200 acres with costumed "residents" who demonstrate the pursuits of the period (see below). It's one of the top tourist destinations in central Massachusetts and deservedly popular. The other reason to visit is an antiques show that sets up three times a year in the adjacent town of Brimfield.

Essentials

GETTING THERE Sturbridge is at the intersection of the Massachusetts Turnpike (I-90) and I-84. Rtes. 20 and 131 are the main roads in town. Note that some "Main Street" addresses are on Rte. 20 and others are on Rte. 131.

VISITOR INFORMATION The **Sturbridge Area Tourist Association Visitor Center** is at 380 Main St. (Rte. 20 directly at the exit for Old Sturbridge Village; ✆ **800/628-8379** or 508/347-2761; www.sturbridgetownships.com).

SPECIAL EVENTS Brimfield is a sleepy village just to the west of Sturbridge, but three times a year more than 5,000 dealers gather along a one-mile stretch of Rte. 20, the main drag through town, for the **Brimfield Antique and Collectible Shows ★** (www.brimfield.com and www.brimfieldexchange.com). Shows run for 6 days (Tues–Sun) in mid-May, mid-July, and early September. Most of the dealers and collectors stay in Sturbridge, so you'll need to reserve a room at least 6 months in advance of show periods.

In March, the state's maple syrup farms are deep into production, and **maple-sugaring demonstrations** are available at sugar shacks and other venues. Check the events calendar at Old Sturbridge Village (below), which sells maple syrup made by the teeny family operation **K. E. Farm,** 317 Leadmine Rd. (✆ **508/347-9323;** www.maplesugarhouse.com), a few miles away. Farmers Karen and Ernie and their old wooden sugar shack transform gallons of sap into pints of liquid gold.

What to See & Do

Expect crowds in the area when the Brimfield Antique show is on and during summer holiday weekends and October foliage season.

Old Sturbridge Village ★★★ ☺ Spread across 200 acres, Old Sturbridge Village uses authentic 19th-century buildings to re-create a rural settlement of the 1830s. On the large property are a saw mill, a country store, a blacksmith shop, a school, a cooperage, a printing office, and a parson's home. At the edges of the village are a working farm and an herb garden. Lazy boat rides are popular, as is a hands-on craft center. In summertime, a horse-drawn stagecoach traverses the dirt lanes, and when there's snow guests can take horse-drawn sleigh rides.

Visitors stroll through the village, where costumed docents demonstrate heirloom gardening, clothes dying, musketry, barrel-making, and more, generally using language true to the period. Special events take place on the 4th of July and during the Christmas season. On winter weekends, the participatory **Dinner in a Country Village** is great fun: Guests stay after-hours to pitch in and make a typical meal of the times on a massive hearth by candlelight, and then gather around a single table to enjoy the fruits of their labor—roast chicken, "beef olives," gourd soup, trifle, fresh-roasted coffee.

1 Old Sturbridge Village Rd. ☎ **800/733-1830** or 508/347-3362. www.osv.org. Admission (2-day pass) $20 adults, $18 seniors, $7 children 3–17, free for children 2 and under. Apr 1–Oct 24 daily 9:30am–4pm (sometimes until 5pm); Oct 25–Mar 31 reduced days and hours; please confirm before visiting. From I-84, take exit 3B onto Rte. 20 west, and follow signs to village.

Where to Stay

Familiar chains include the **Comfort Inn & Suites,** 215 Charlton Rd. (Rte. 20; ☎ **508/347-3306;** www.sturbridgecomfortinn.com) and **Hampton Inn of Sturbridge,** 328 Main St. (Rte. 131; ☎ **508/347-6466;** www.myhamptoninn.com). The **Heritage Corridor Bed & Breakfast Group** (www.HeritageCorridorBB. com) has links to some of the quainter accommodations in the area.

Publick House ★   This is the high-profile lodging in the Sturbridge area. The most desirable rooms are the 17 in the main **Historic Inn.** Built in 1771, it's heavy on atmosphere, with Colonial reproduction pieces, quilts on some beds, and floors and ceilings that long ago settled into not-quite-right angles. A downstairs **tavern** with fireplace, used mainly by guests, is a jovial venue. Suites in the adjacent **Chamberlain House** are larger and somewhat more contemporary. The **Country Motor Lodge,** on the back side of the property, lacks any 18th-century personality whatsoever but has rooms that start at just $69. Meals are available in the tavern and the more refined **Tap Room** (they share the same menu). A small "bake shoppe" does brisk business throughout the day.

277 Main St. (Rte. 131), P.O. Box 187, Sturbridge, MA 01566. ☎ **800/782-5425** or 508/347-3313. www. publickhouse.com. 115 units. $99–$160 double in the Historic Inn; $135–$199 suite in the Chamberlain House; $69–$139 double in Motor Lodge. AE, DISC, MC, V. Pets accepted in some rooms of Country Motor Lodge ($10 fee). **Amenities:** 2 restaurants (American); bar; outdoor pool. *In room:* A/C, TV, hair dryer, Wi-Fi (free).

Where to Dine

B.T.'s Smokehouse ★ BARBECUE   This teeny tiny barbeque joint in a former hot dog stand in a strip mall uses apple wood to slow cook pulled pork, beef brisket, and pork ribs, and they're imbued with a rich, dusky taste. The $3 pulled-pork mini, the size of an apple, is a perfect snack, but you can load up on brisket chili, hot dogs, corn bread, or potato salad, too. In warm weather, patrons flock to the outdoor benches. A slightly larger B.T.'s outlet is located 4 miles away in Brimfield, at 227 Sturbridge Rd. (also Rte. 20).

376 Main St. (Rte. 20). ☎ **508/433-6537.** www.btsmokehouse.com. Main courses under $10. MC, V. Mon–Tues 11am–6pm; Wed–Sat 11am–8pm; Sun noon–6pm. B.T.'s is located in a strip mall off of Rte. 20 next to Yankee Spirits.

Cedar Street Restaurant ★★ AMERICAN   Tucked into the first floor of a house on a residential street, Cedar Street is nothing but right notes every step of the way. The decor is traditional with modern touches, and the volume on a crowded night is buzzy without being overwhelming. But we're here for the food, and it doesn't fail to impress. Duck with juniper honey drizzle and toasted pistachio dust, and buttermilk fried chicken with red-eye gravy and braised Swiss chard are as good as you'd find in a big city. Good thing, given the prices, which are at the high end for this region. The experience is worth it. If it's available, close with the strawberry molasses bread pudding with cinnamon gelato and a sugar cookie spoon.

12 Cedar St., just off of Rte. 20. © **508/347-5800.** www.cedarstreetrestaurant.com. Main courses $17–$32. AE, MC, V. Daily from 5pm.

SPRINGFIELD

90 miles W of Boston; 26 miles N of Hartford; 5 miles S of I-90

This once-prosperous manufacturing city on the east bank of the Connecticut River shows signs of redevelopment throughout downtown, with recycled loft and factory buildings standing beside modern glass towers. Vacationers can pass a few hours or a night here, but Springfield is primarily a stopover city.

Essentials

GETTING THERE   Springfield is located at the juncture of the east-west Massachusetts Turnpike (I-90) and north-south I-91.

   Bradley International (© **860/292-2000;** www.bradleyairport.com; airport code BDL), the primary airport serving Springfield, is located in Windsor Locks, Connecticut, about 20 miles to the south. Rent a car here from any of the major companies, or catch a bus, cab, or limo into Springfield. Major airlines serving Bradley are **American** (© 800/433-7300), **Continental** (© 800/523-3273), **Delta** (© 800/221-1212), **United** (© 800/864-8331), and **US Airways** (© 800/428-4322).

   Amtrak (© **800/USA-RAIL** [872-7245]; www.amtrak.com) trains running both east-west and north-south stop in Springfield.

VISITOR INFORMATION   The **Greater Springfield Convention and Visitors Bureau** (© **800/723-1548;** www.valleyvisitor.com) has downloadable maps of Springfield and other nearby cities at its website. Visitor centers are at 1441 Main St. (© **413/787-1548**), and inside the Basketball Hall of Fame (see below). The centers offer brochures, maps, and discount tickets to local attractions.

SPECIAL EVENTS   During the last 2 weeks in September, **"The Big E"—the Eastern States Exposition** (© **413/737-2443;** www.thebige.com) is held in West Springfield. It's a huge old-fashioned agricultural fair with a 4-H horse show, ox-cart pulling, such carnival food as deep-fried cheesecake, games, a midway, and entertainment from the likes of disco star Thelma Houston and country band Sugarland. Also on the grounds is **Storrowton Village,** an authentic re-creation of a 19th-century village. It's open from mid-June through Labor Day, Tuesday through Saturday 11am to 3pm.

What to See & Do

Naismith Memorial Basketball Hall of Fame ★★ ☺   A feast for fans, the Basketball Hall of Fame celebrated its 50th anniversary in 2009 with the induction class that included Michael Jordan. The complex has an Honors Ring with biographies of everyone enshrined—women finally began making the list in 1985—and there are interactive displays with vast quantities of memorabilia of the sport, which was invented by Dr. James Naismith in Springfield in 1891 (early teams included the Philadelphia Hebrews and the Chicago Studebakers). On the ground floor is a basketball court where clinics and shootings contests are held. A large gift shop sells T-shirts, jerseys, and the like. Seven chain restaurants occupy the complex and an adjacent Hilton hotel.

1000 W. Columbus Ave. (at Union St.). ℭ **877/446-6752.** www.hoophall.com. Admission $17 adults, $14 seniors, $12 children 5–15, free for children 4 and under. Daily 10am–4pm (until 5pm Sat). The facility is located on a sliver of land adjacent to I-91.

Six Flags New England ☺ The big amusement park of Massachusetts gets mixed reactions. It has about 60 rides of varying excitement quotients, and everyone raves about the 3½-minute Bizarro roller coaster (formerly called Superman—Ride of Steel), which features fog and flame effects, loud music, a 221-foot drop, and speeds up to 77 mph. When the park isn't crowded (weekdays and early on weekends), little ones like Wiggles World and Thomas Town, the strolling *Looney Tunes* characters from *Looney Toons* Movie Town, and the Mr. Six's Splash Island water park. On the downside, there are few shaded areas, parking is a hike, the park can get packed with teens, lines get very long, and you'll need a small bank loan to feed a family on the $9 hot dogs and $13 souvenir refill cups (no outside food is allowed). Six Flags filed for bankruptcy in mid-2009 but planned to reorganize and continue operations. *Tip:* You can purchase discounted tickets on their website.

1623 Main St. (Rte. 159), Agawam. ℭ **413/786-9300.** www.sixflags.com. $42 general admission, $31 anyone under 5'4," free for children ages 2 and under. Parking $15. Mid-June through Aug daily 10:30am to at least 8pm most days; limited days and hours mid-Apr to mid-June and Sept–Nov; check website for exact hours. Closed Nov to mid-Apr. The park is 6 miles south of Springfield.

Springfield Museums at the Quadrangle ★ ☺ A library and five museums— one new since 2009, one temporarily closed—surround a small grassy quadrangle and constitute this worthwhile, appealing resource. Start at the Welcome Center (daily 10am–5pm) to purchase tickets, which cover all five museums. The newest venue is the **Museum of Springfield History,** which details the city's manufacturing roots and the products, from motorcycles to Milton Bradley board games, made here.

The **Museum of Fine Arts** ★ is the most important of the lot, with over a dozen galleries. A permanent **Currier & Ives gallery** ★ features new exhibits every 6 months of work by the printmakers. Other galleries have Colonial paintings from Gilbert Stuart and John Copley of the Revolutionary period all the way up to 20th-century abstract expressionists such as Frank Stella and Helen Frankenthaler.

On the end of the quad near the library is the **George Walter Vincent Smith Art Museum,** housed in an 1896 Italian Renaissance–style mansion. Upstairs are largely sentimental pastoral scenes, with a few small landscapes by George Inness, Thomas Cole, and Albert Bierstadt. The main floor displays Japanese samurai weaponry surrounding a carved 1805 Shinto shrine. An **Art Discover Center** here has costumes and armor for kids to play dress-up. The other prime spot for children is the **Springfield Science Museum,** which features a planetarium, dioramas of African animals, and a small Dinosaur Hall.

The **Connecticut Valley Historical Museum,** which housed a replica 1780s kitchen with a hearth for cooking, is closed for reinstallation.

The Quad itself is a peaceful respite, with marble benches throughout the small park. On the library end is the **Dr. Seuss National Memorial Sculpture Garden,** with sculptures of the author himself (who was born in Springfield), the Cat in the Hat, the Grinch, Thing One and Thing Two, and other creations of his fertile mind. The one blemish is that overhanging trees are favorites for birds, with the unfortunate results below.

DR. SEUSS'S NEIGHBORHOOD

Author and illustrator Theodor Seuss Geisel, better known as Dr. Seuss, grew up in Springfield and is a much beloved native son. In 1937, he named the first of his books, *And to Think That I Saw It on Mulberry Street,* after the Springfield avenue where his grandparents lived. (The book was rejected by 27 publishers before finding a home at Vanguard Press.)

Classics such as *The Cat in the Hat* and *How the Grinch Stole Christmas* followed. Hundreds of millions of copies of his dozens of books have been sold, and they've been translated into 15 languages.

Geisel spent most of his adult life in California, but much of his inspiration can be traced to Springfield. Bartholomew Cubbins's castle bears a strong resemblance to the Howard Street Armory, and some of his landscapes look as if they were recalled from his playtime in Forest Park, near his boyhood home at 74 Fairfield St.

Mulberry Street is about a half-mile from the **Dr. Seuss National Memorial Sculpture Garden** (p. 322) and still has glimpses of the charm of its august years, with Victorian manses and undistinguished apartment buildings along its length.

21 Edwards St. (℗ **800/625-7738** or 413/263-6800. www.springfieldmuseums.org and www.catinthe hat.org. Combined admission for all museums: $13 adults, $9 seniors and college students, $6.50 children 3-17; planetarium $3 adults, $2 children. Sculpture garden free. Tues–Sun 11am–4pm, with slightly longer hours for the Science Museum.

Where to Stay

If the Marriott is full, the atrium-style **Sheraton Springfield Monarch Place,** 1 Monarch Place (℗ **800/325-3535;** www.sheraton-springfield.com), is directly across the street and has 325 rooms and comparable prices.

Springfield Marriott ★★ Guest rooms are on the seventh floor or higher, and the hotel feels well appointed and trim. Rooms have dark wood and marble bathroom floors and sinks, and some corner rooms have particularly large bathrooms. Pay a little extra to stay on one of the concierge-level floors, and you'll get complimentary breakfast and hors d'oeuvres and access to an honor bar. An in-house sports bar has a 10-foot television screen. A newly renovated lobby presents a sparkling introduction. The entire hotel is smoke-free.

2 Boland Way, Springfield, MA 01105. (℗ **800/228-9290** or 413/781-7111. Fax 413/731-8932. www.marriott hotels.com. 262 units. $103–$214 double. Parking $14. AE, DISC, MC, V. **Amenities:** 2 restaurants; 2 bars; health club; heated indoor pool; room service; sauna. *In room:* A/C, TV, fridge, hair dryer, Wi-Fi ($13/day).

Where to Dine

Also keep in mind the excellent ribs and other BBQ available at **Theodore's Booze, Blues & BBQ** (below, in "Springfield After Dark").

Student Prince (The Fort) ★ GERMAN/AMERICAN Year in, year out, Student Prince remains a top go-to place in Springfield. It was opened in 1935 by German immigrants serving schnitzels and sauerbraten. That year might not have seemed the precise historical moment to ensure the success of such an enterprise, but somehow the restaurant thrived. Today it can seat 248. Waitresses rush about in sensible shoes, slapping plates down and tolerating no lip. Monster portions are the rule, with veal shanks as thick as a linebacker's forearm. Weiner schnitzel, roulade, and sauerbraten are obvious choices and tasty. Be sure to take a peek at the enormous stein collection in the bar, which fills shelves all the way to the high ceiling.

8 Fort St. ✆ **413/788-6628**. www.studentprince.com. Main courses $11–$26. AE, DISC, MC, V. Mon-Wed 11am–9pm; Thurs–Sat 11am–10pm; Sun noon–8pm.

Springfield After Dark

Symphony Hall, 34 Court St., at East Columbus Avenue (✆ **413/788-7033;** www.symphonyhall.com), is a venue for touring musicals such as *Hairspray* and *Chicago,* children's shows, and the **Springfield Symphony Orchestra** (✆ **413/733-2291;** www.springfieldsymphony.org). The orchestra's main season runs October through May, with Pops and other programs throughout the year. The box office is around the corner at 1350 Main St.

Downtown is eerily quiet at night (it can feel dodgy, too, so travel with a friend if possible). There's an ever-changing collection of beer-and-pool joints, music bars, and eateries on Worthington and Bridge streets near our two recommended hotels. The most popular is **Theodore's Booze, Blues & BBQ,** 201 Worthington St. (✆ **413/736-6000;** www.theobbq.com), which showcases blues bands Friday and Saturday and offers up killer barbecue.

THE PIONEER VALLEY ★★

South Hadley: 5 miles N of I-90; Northampton: 17 miles N of I-90; Amherst: 24 miles N of I-90; Deerfield: 34 miles N of I-90; Turners Falls: 43 miles N of I-90 and 91 miles NW of Boston (via Rte. 2)

Low hills and quilted fields channel the Connecticut River as it runs south toward Long Island Sound, forming the Pioneer Valley. The earliest European settlers came here in the mid-1600s for what proved to be uncommonly fertile soil, and they were followed in the 19th century by men who harnessed the power of the river and became wealthy textile and paper manufacturers.

These industrialists took the lead in funding the prestigious institutions of higher learning that are now the pride of the region: Smith, Mount Holyoke, Amherst, and Hampshire colleges. The town of Amherst also is home to the sprawling main campus of the University of Massachusetts, with its 27,016 students. All five schools contribute mightily to the cultural life of the valley and the towns of **South Hadley, Northampton,** and **Amherst.**

In the north, closer to Vermont, the old section of the village of **Deerfield** preserves the architecture and atmosphere of Colonial New England, while **Turners Falls** is a town-that-time-forgot now being remade by an infusion of new artists.

I-91 and the smaller Rte. 5 traverse the valley from south to north, more or less parallel to each other. On the interstate, the region takes less than an hour to drive from bottom to top. Rte. 5 offers a better peek at pastoral vistas and old mill towns.

The website of the **Massachusetts Office of Travel & Tourism** (✆ **800/227-6277** or 617/973-8500; www.massvacation.com/lodging) has an easy-to-use search function for lodgings. Note that room rates rise considerably at graduation time (early May) and when parents come through to drop off students (late Aug and early Sept).

The Pioneer Valley

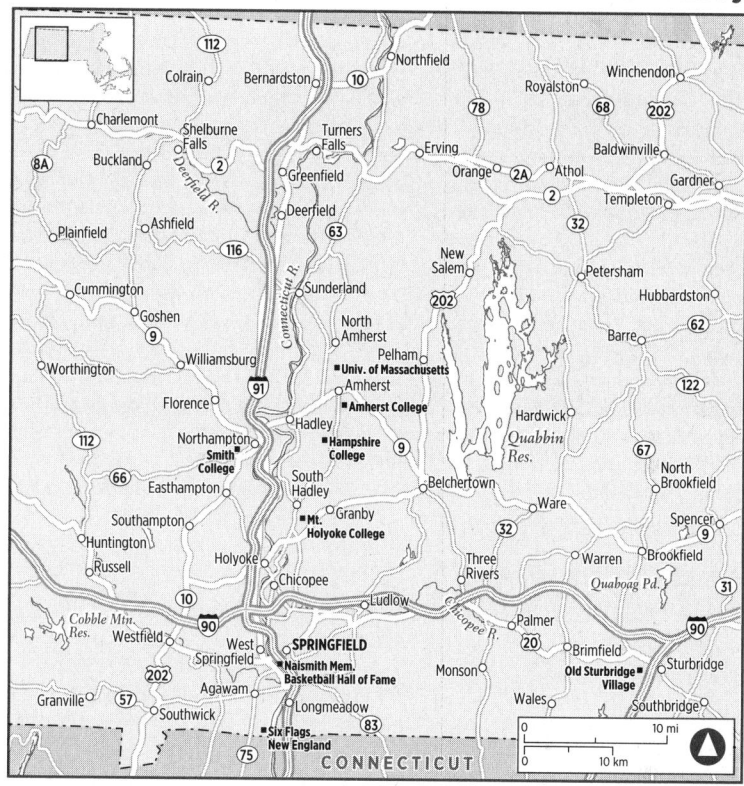

Essentials

GETTING THERE   From Boston and upstate New York, take the Massachusetts Turnpike (I-90) to Springfield, then I-91 or Rte. 5 north. While there are local buses, you really need a car to explore this area.

The nearest major airport is **Bradley International** (© 860/292-2000; www. bradleyairport.com; airport code BDL), in Windsor Locks, Connecticut. (See "Springfield," earlier in this chapter, for a list of airlines that serve Bradley.) **Valley Transporter** (© 800/872-8752; www.valleytransporter.com) offers van shuttles between the airport and the towns and schools of the Pioneer Valley. Reservations are recommended.

The north-south **Amtrak** (© 800/USA-RAIL [872-7245]; www.amtrak.com) *Vermonter* route stops in Amherst. It runs from St. Albans, Vermont, in the north to Washington, D.C., in the south, traveling through New York City, Philadelphia, and Baltimore.

Peter Pan Bus Lines (© 800/343-9999; www.peterpanbus.com) has buses that connect the towns of the Valley.

Downloadable maps of the Pioneer Valley overall, Northampton, and Amherst are at **www.valleyvisitor.com/view-maps.html**. You can also request, through the website, a hard copy of the Pioneer Valley Visitor's Guide.

South Hadley

This stately town pops up on Rte. 116 alongside farming and working-class communities because of **Mount Holyoke College.** Pioneer educator Mary Lyon founded the school, then a seminary, in 1837, and the college is the oldest of the "Seven Sisters" colleges for women (Barnard, Bryn Mawr, Radcliffe, Smith, Vassar, and Wellesley are the other six.)

The campus is home to a worthy **Art Museum ★** (✆ **413/538-2245;** www.mtholyoke.edu/artmuseum), which focuses on works from Asia, Egypt, and contemporary America. Renovation and expansion have brought more of the collection into regular view. Hours are Tuesday through Friday from 11am to 5pm, Saturday and Sunday from 1 to 5pm. Admission is free.

J. A. Skinner State Park (✆ **413/586-0350;** www.mass.gov) straddles the border between South Hadley and Hadley. On its 400 acres are picnic grounds, miles of trails, and the historic **Summit House** (May to mid-Oct Sat–Sun 10am–5pm), a former hotel, with panoramic views of the valley. The 1½-mile road to the summit is open to cars from mid-April to mid-November and to walkers year-round. The park entrance is on Mountain Road, off Rte. 47, in Hadley.

Northampton ★★

Known locally as "Noho," Northampton is the cultural center of the valley. The diversity of restaurants (and overall number) is far greater than most cities its size can flaunt, and its many stores are as kicky as any devout shopper could hope. Events range from chamber music to art exhibitions to an **independent film festival** (www.niff.org) held each November. Try to allow at least an overnight or a long day in the area.

Smith College, the largest liberal arts college for women in the United States, is Northampton's dominating physical and spiritual presence. Its campus sprawls along Main Street just west of the commercial center.

The city has a large gay and lesbian population, and a **Pride March** is held every May (**www.northamptonpride.org**). A well-received book by Tracy Kidder, *Home Town* (Random House, 1999), profiled Northampton and a number of its citizens.

Tip: The city has a strong tradition of *crosswalk courtesy:* Once a pedestrian puts a toe into a crosswalk, cars in both directions stop. Take note when you're driving.

WHAT TO SEE & DO

The popular U.S. President Calvin Coolidge practiced law in Northampton both before and after his occupancy of the Oval Office (1923–29). The White House website notes this vignette about Coolidge: "Both his dry Yankee wit and his frugality with words became legendary. His wife, Grace Goodhue Coolidge, recounted that a young woman sitting next to Coolidge at a dinner party confided to him she had bet she could get at least three words of conversation from him. Without looking at her he quietly retorted, 'You lose.'" Coolidge lived in houses at 21 Massasoit St. and on Hampton Terrace, but these are not open to the public. The **Forbes Library,** 20 West St. (✆ **413/587-1011;** www.forbeslibrary.org), maintains the Calvin Coolidge

Presidential Library & Museum, the only presidential collection hosted by a public library in the United States. It's open just to researchers, although a number of Coolidge photos and links to Coolidge information are posted at the library website.

Historic Northampton Museum & Education Center   This museum used to allow visitors to tour the three 18th- and early-19th-century homes on its property, but no more (there's a chance the 1719 Parsons House might reopen at some point). For now, a small museum displays items such as photographs, cradles, and carved chests from the 1700s; Calvin Coolidge memorabilia; and silk dresses from 19th century.

46 Bridge St. (Rte. 9, east of the railroad bridge). (© **413/584-6011.** www.historic-northampton.org. Admission $3. Mon–Sat 10am–5pm; Sun noon–5pm.

Smith College ★   Equal parts tranquil and heady, the Smith campus is a bucolic melange of rolling hills, broad lawns, and architecture in the Gothic, Greco-Roman, Renaissance, and medieval traditions. Visitors are as likely to hear an undergrad chirp, "See you in glee club!" as they are to see the phrase "Patriarchy Sux!" written in chalk. Frederick Law Olmsted, who designed New York's Central Park, laid out much of the original landscaping, and the campus contains wooded walks and botanic gardens.

Elm St. (© **413/584-2700.** www.smith.edu.

Smith College Museum of Art ★★   With a $35-million renovation and expansion in 2003, this facility stepped up to claim equal footing with New England's finest college art museums, including those at Williams, Harvard, and Yale. It already had an impressive permanent collection of paintings by Degas, Monet, Picasso, and Winslow Homer, among many 19th- and 20th-century Europeans and Americans. Now there is not only more space to show them, but also ample room for an ambitious program of temporary exhibitions. Third-floor galleries have fine views of the campus and allow abundant light for canvases. A **cafe** serves drinks and snacks. There's no parking lot specifically for the museum, so look for a metered street spot.

Elm St. and Bedford Terrace. (© **413/585-2760.** www.smith.edu/artmuseum. Admission $5 adults, $4 seniors, $3 students, $2 children ages 6–12. Tues–Sat 10am–4pm; Sun noon–4pm; 2nd Fri of the month until 8pm, with free admission 4–8pm.

GETTING OUTSIDE

The **Arcadia Wildlife Sanctuary,** 127 Combs Rd., Easthampton (© **413/584-3009;** www.massaudubon.org), is a preserve operated by the Massachusetts Audubon Society. Bordering the Connecticut River, the sanctuary contains marshes, woods, trails, and a nature center. **Evening canoe rides** are offered in summer. Admission is $4 for adults, $3 for seniors and children ages 2 to 12. It's located 3 miles southwest of Northampton on Rte. 10 and is open daily.

   Look Memorial Park, 300 N. Main St., Florence (© **413/584-5457;** www. lookpark.org), is just northwest of Northampton on Rte. 9. The park has woods, a lake, pedal boats, miniature golf, a small steamer train, tennis courts, and picnic grounds. The park hosts frequent special events for children and families. Parking is $4 April to October, $2 November to March, with per-person fees for activities.

SHOPPING

Northampton enjoys the most diverse shopping in the valley. Its half-mile-long Main Street, from Bridge Street at the eastern end to the Smith College campus on the western end, is rich with upscale restaurants, art galleries, acupuncture clinics, buskers, and jewelry and clothing boutiques. Downtown has segued from funky to nearly chic over the past 20 years, and it's as easy to find vegan chocolate and organic egg omelets as it is Ugg boots and expensive glass artworks.

Thorne's Marketplace, 150 Main St. (www.thornesmarketplace.com), is a former department store reconfigured into two dozen boutiques and casual eating places. **Scandihoovians,** 22 Strong Ave. (© **413/586-0002;** www.scandihoovians. com), features Scandinavian housewares, jewelry, and clothes. Burnishing the city's reputation as a small town with an unusually vigorous arts community is the prestigious **R. Michelson Gallery,** 132 Main St. (© **413/586-3964;** www.rmichelson. com), which occupies a grand former bank and puts on shows that range from the photography of Leonard Nimoy to the colorful sketches of Dr. Seuss. **Essentials,** 88 Main St. (© **413/584-2327**), sells hip housewares, including kitschy "Japanistic" items, French ware (Tintin, the Little Prince, and the like), and shoulder bags of all sizes.

And there are **bookstores.** "The Pioneer Valley is arguably the most author-saturated, book-cherishing, literature-celebrating place in the nation," wrote the *New York Times* in 2007. A half-dozen independent bookstores in downtown continue to vouch for that claim. They are listed at **www.ravenusedbooks.com,** the website of **Raven Used Books,** 4 Old South St. (© **413/584/9868**).

WHERE TO STAY

As central as Northampton is to the Pioneer Valley, there aren't many options for accommodations here. Rte. 9, which runs between Noho and Amherst, has some chain options including **Knights Inn Hadley,** 208 Russell St. (Rte. 9; © **413/585-1552;** www.knightsinn.com), **Holiday Inn Express Amherst-Hadley,** 400 Russell St. (Rte. 9; © **413/582-0002;** www.ichotelsgroup.com), and **Courtyard By Marriott Hadley Amherst** (p. 332). Anticipate higher rates and limited vacancies during graduation and homecoming periods as well as the usual holiday weekends.

Hotel Northampton ★ Built in 1927, the main brick building of this hotel is a grand focal point at the center of town and close to restaurants and evening activities. Classical music and a large spray of flowers greet guests in the lobby. Rooms vary considerably (ask about options when booking and ask to see several, if possible, when checking in) and contain Colonial reproductions, feather duvets, and assorted Victoriana. A newer building behind the driveway, called Gothic Gardens, offers the most updated rooms with bigger TVs and better bedding. The hotel's **Wiggins Tavern** is an atmospheric watering hole with dark beams and three stone fireplaces; the **Coolidge Park Café** has an outdoor terrace in warm weather and a good-looking bar.

36 King St. (Rte. 5 at Rte. 9), Northampton, MA 01060. © **800/547-3529** or 413/584-3100. Fax 413/584-9455. www.hotelnorthampton.com. 106 units. $165–$230 double. Rates include continental breakfast. AE, DC, DISC, MC, V. Limited free parking (first come, first served). **Amenities:** 2 restaurants; bar; exercise room; room service. *In room:* A/C, TV, hair dryer, Wi-Fi ($10/day).

WHERE TO DINE

For a sweet treat, keep in mind **Herrell's,** 8 Old South St. (© **413/586-9700;** www. herrells.com), a celebrated New England super-premium ice-cream emporium. It scoops a huge variety of flavors, including Malted Vanilla and Heath Bar Crunch.

Eastside Grill ★★ AMERICAN This white-clapboard building with a nautical look is particularly appealing to the over-40 set looking for refuge from the prevailing collegiate tone of Northampton. A third of the entrees involve beef, such as the delicious tenderloin with Gorgonzola and fried leeks, but the seafood choices are impressive, too, especially the sweat pea seafood risotto made with lobster broth and topped with fistfuls of fat scallops, shrimp, and PEI mussels. The grill is noisy and can border on raucous, and service can be slow; it's the place for a good, generous, and fairly priced meal, not a romantic one.

19 Strong Ave. (1 block south of Main St.). ℂ **413/586-3347.** www.eastsidegrill.com. Reservations recommended. Main courses $9–$22. AE, DISC, MC, V. Mon–Thurs 5–10pm; Fri 5–10:30pm; Sat 4–10:30pm; Sun 4–9pm.

Fitzwilly's AMERICAN   Occupying an 1898 building, this ingratiating pub makes the most of its atmospheric stamped-tin ceilings and ample space. Copper brewing kettles signal an intriguing selection of beers, and patrons dive into pub faves such as nachos, burgers, pastas, and crab cakes. Food is available until midnight every day.

23 Main St. (near the bridge). ℂ **413/584-8666.** www.fitzwillys.com. Main courses $7–$20. AE, DC, DISC, MC, V. Daily 11:30am–midnight; bar until 1am.

Green Street Café ★ FRENCH   Tucked on a side street behind the Smith College campus, Green Street is a colorful and cozy venue: Collegiate, yes, but with a touch of Europe. The hand-written menu includes lots of small plates such as leek and gruyere tart, omelet of the day, and house-smoked bluefish. A short list of mains includes duck breast with lemon and whiskey sauce. An attached wine bar offers a more casual dining option. The restaurant grows its own vegetables in season.

64 Green St. ℂ **413/586-5650.** www.greenstreetcafenorthampton.com. Reservations recommended. Main courses $17–$26. MC, V. Mon–Sat noon–2pm and 5–10pm; Sun 10am–2pm and 5–10pm. Wine bar daily 5pm–midnight. Follow Main St. toward the Smith campus, bear left onto West St., turn right onto Green St.

Osaka ★ JAPANESE   Sushi *and* steak? They're rarely paired together, but, at the ever inventive Osaka, the blend regularly wins the local readers' favorite awards. The menu lists 59 kinds of makizushi (rolls) with such nutty names as Foxy Lady and Treasury Island, and over two dozen selections of a la carte nigirizushi and sashimi. Then it takes a deep breath before adding soups, chef's specials, teriyaki, and hibachi dinners. The eel and avocado roll, spicy red snapper, and ebi tempura have all been good. Decor includes lots of blond wood, with a sushi bar at the entrance.

7 Old South St. (1 block off Main St.). ℂ **413/587-9548.** www.osakanorthampton.com. Rolls $3.95–$14; sushi a la carte $3–$14; main courses $5.95–$28. AE, DC, DISC, MC, V. Mon–Sat 11:30am–11pm (Fri–Sat until midnight); Sun 12:30–11pm.

Spoleto ★ 🍴 ITALIAN   With high ceilings, Tuscan-orange walls, and red banquettes ringing the edges of the room, Mediterranean-rich Spoleto has an upscale-casual Euro flair that fits right into this academic town with its well-traveled populace. The bolognese is justifiably popular: It's a large bowl piled high with pasta and a thick sauce of ground sausage, beef, and veal, and paired with a local ale from the Berkshire Brewing Company, it's as hearty a meal as one could ask for. Keep in mind the 3-course dinner for $20 (most of the main courses on the menu plus nearly any appetizer and dessert), which is a good bargain. The visual center of the restaurant is a bar that juts into the main room, and it's a comfortable perch for solo eaters to dine.

50 Main St. ℂ **413/586-6313.** www.spoletorestaurants.com. Main courses $15–$26; 3-course prix fixe $20. AE, DC, DISC, MC, V. Mon–Thurs 5–10pm; Fri 5–11pm; Sat 4:30–11pm; Sun 4–9pm.

NORTHAMPTON AFTER DARK

Northampton is the nightlife magnet of the valley. For a rundown of what's happening, look for the free *Valley Advocate* (www.valleyadvocate.com).

An old favorite, the **Iron Horse Music Hall ★★**, 20 Center St. (*©* **413/586-8686;** www.iheg.com), is a New England honky-tonk that hosts a wide variety of artists nearly nightly, including Evan Dando, the Magnetic Fields, and regional folk-singers. Cover is typically between $10 and $23. There's also decent food here. A sister venue, the larger **Calvin Theatre and Performing Arts Center,** 19 King St. (*©* **401/586-8686;** www.iheg.com), offers performers such as Rufus Wainwright and the David Grisman Quintet.

Open since 1891, the **Academy of Music,** 274 Main St. (*©* **413/584-9032;** www.academyofmusictheatre.com), is the granddaddy of the region. It shows art-house and foreign films and provides a venue for symphony concerts, children's shows, and local theater. Classical and chamber music is the customary fare at Smith's **Sweeney Concert Hall** (*©* **413/586-8686;** www.smith.edu/smitharts/calendar.html).

Diva's, 492 Pleasant St. (*©* **413/586-8161;** www.divasofnoho.com), is a lesbian nightclub. It was named Best Gay Bar in the *Valley Advocate*'s 2009 Reader's Poll.

Pleasant Street Theater, 27 Pleasant St. (*©* **413/584-5848;** www.amherst cinema.org), is an independent art movie house.

Amherst

Another Pioneer Valley town defined by its educational institutions, this one has an even larger student population than most, with distinguished **Amherst College** occupying much of its center, the large **University of Massachusetts** campus to its immediate northwest, and **Hampshire College** off South Pleasant Street.

 ## SOUNDTRACK OF THE VALLEY

The Pioneer Valley is home to a rich variety of folk and jazz music. When you're driving the area, consider these CDs and radio DJs for local sounds:

- Chris Smither, "Time Stands Still" (2009): Smither has been making guitar picking, raspy-blues-sounding music for over 40 years. He relocated to Amherst in 2009, the same year he released his 13th record.
- Young at Heart Chorus: Based in Northampton, this senior chorus has performers in their 70s and 80s. A 2006 documentary brought their work to a broader audience, and the 2008 CD "Mostly Live" features their

renditions of the Rolling Stones' "You Can't Always Get What You Want" and "Ruby Tuesday," U2's "One," and The Clash's "Should I Stay Or Should I Go."

- Kris Delmhorst, "Shotgun Singer" (2008): Delmhorst recorded this countrified folk CD in a rural cabin in the area, playing all the parts herself.
- DJs Tom Reney and Kari Njiiri: Popular presences for over 25 years on the Valley's public radio station, WFCR 88.5 FM, Reney hosts the Jazz à la Mode program weeknights from 8–11pm and Njiiri the Jazz Safari mix Saturdays from 8pm to midnight.

WHAT TO SEE & DO

The best strolling is within a few blocks any direction of the town green. At the northeast corner of the green is the **Town Hall,** a fortresslike Romanesque Revival creation of Boston's H. H. Richardson.

Amherst College   Named for Baron Jeffery Amherst, a British general during the last of the French and Indian Wars, the illustrious liberal-arts college was founded in 1821. Robert Frost was a member of the faculty for more than a decade. Amherst's campus cuts through the heart of the town and makes for a pretty stroll. Its **Mead Art Museum ★**, rtes. 116 and 9 (✆ 413/542-2335), specializes in American art, including Hudson River School landscapes and modern works by Robert Henri and Frank Stella. Admission is free, and it's open daily except Monday.

S. Pleasant and College sts. ✆ **413/542-2000.** www.amherst.edu.

Emily Dickinson Museum: The Homestead and The Evergreens ★   Designated a National Historic Monument, the Homestead is where Emily Dickinson was born in 1830 and where she lived until her family moved in 1840, and the Evergreens was the next-door home of her brother Austin and his wife. Dickenson and her family returned in 1855, and the famous poet stayed here until her death 31 years later. The "Belle of Amherst" was the granddaughter and daughter of local movers and shakers, the source of her support while she produced the poetry that was increasingly celebrated even as she withdrew into near-total seclusion. The two buildings now make up Emily Dickinson Museum, with a free Tour Center, bookshop, and exhibit space in the Homestead, and guided tours (for fees) of both homes.

280 Main St. (2 blocks east of the Town Hall). ✆ **413/542-8161.** www.emilydickinsonmuseum.org. Free to visit the center and bookshop. Entrance to Homestead and Evergreens by guided tour only: $8 adults, $7 seniors and students, $5 ages 6–17, free for children 5 and under. Center Mar–Dec Wed–Sun 11am–5pm, guided tours 1–3:30pm. Closed the rest of the year. Reservations recommended.

National Yiddish Book Center   This airy complex on the Hampshire College campus is devoted to rescuing and redistributing Yiddish-language books and to celebrating Yiddish culture through films, lectures, and other public events. In addition to a large book depository, the center has four exhibition galleries, a bookstore, the last Yiddish linotype machine used to publish the *Jewish Daily Forward* newspaper, a library, and a theater—be sure to see the spectacular chandelier here. The center is located in an apple orchard, and there are gardens and picnic tables.

1021 West St. (Rte. 116). ✆ **413/256-4900.** www.yiddishbookcenter.org. Free admission. Mon–Fri 10am–4pm; Sun 11am–4pm.

University of Massachusetts Fine Arts Center   On a sprawling 1,450-acre campus north of the town center, UMass Amherst's FAC books a variety of dance, flamenco, jazz, and choral groups. The foremost of the campus's six galleries is here, too: The **University Gallery ★** focuses on 20th-century work. Park in the metered public lot behind the visitor center, across the street.

151 Presidents Dr., on the UMass campus (follow signs to CONCERT HALL). ✆ **413/545-2511.** www.umass.edu/fac. Free admission to Gallery. Tues–Fri 11am–4:30pm; Sat–Sun 2–5pm.

GETTING OUTSIDE

The **Norwottuck Rail Trail** (✆ **413/586-8706,** ext. 12; www.mass.gov/dcr/parks/central/nwrt.htm) is a bike path that connects Hadley, Northampton, and Amherst.

It follows the former Boston and Maine rail bed for 11 miles and travels more or less parallel to Rte. 9. In the midsection, it passes through open farmland.

SHOPPING

Clay's, 32 Main St. (℃ **413/256-4200**), has funky, flowing women's clothes in natural fibers, and a small sign next to the dressing rooms that says, "You are radiant & beautiful." **Amherst Typewriter & Computer,** 41 N. Pleasant St. (℃ **413/253-7122**), has a gorgeous collection of antique and just old typewriters on display. **Newbury Comics,** 50 Main St. (℃ **413/256-8840;** www.newburycomics.com), is a CD and tchotchke store (T-shirts, Ugly Dolls, Crazy Cat Lady Action Figures), which is part of a chain of 28 stores in New England.

WHERE TO STAY

The prettiest hotel in Amherst, the **Lord Jeffery Inn,** is closed for major restoration and expansion, and scheduled to reopen in spring 2011 at the earliest.

Courtyard By Marriott Hadley Amherst ★ Newly built in 2007, this chain hotel has a sleek decor befitting more expensive properties: rooms are equipped with cherrywood work desks, two telephones, and flatscreen TVs. Located on the main drag, Rte. 9, just at the Hadley/Amherst border, it's convenient to the UMass campus and set back enough from the road to be quiet inside. There's a well-appointed fitness room, and the hotel is entirely smoke-free.

423 Russell St. (Rte. 9), Hadley, MA 01035. ℃ **413/256-5454.** Fax 413/256-5422. www.marriott.com/bdlhd. 96 units. $120–$160 double. Free parking. AE, DC, DISC, MC, V. **Amenities:** Breakfast cafe; bar; 24-hr. exercise room; Jacuzzi; small indoor pool. *In room:* A/C, TV, fridge, hair dryer, Wi-Fi (free).

WHERE TO DINE

Additional options include the venues listed in "Amherst After Dark," below.

Amherst Coffee CAFE/COFFEEHOUSE If you're looking for the perfect cappuccino, come here: The coffee is strong and it's capped with a thick foam that the baristas often swirl into decorative leaf patterns. Pair it with a pear-pecan muffin and chill out in the bright room and sea of laptops. There's a large, shared wooden table down the center, and wine and nibbles at a small bar area after 3pm.

28 Armory St. ℃ **413/256-8987.** www.amherstcoffee.com. Mon–Sat 6:30am–12:30am; Sun 8am–11pm.

Chez Albert ★ FRENCH Copper-top tables and large picture windows give a Euro touch to this bistro overlooking the town green. For a light lunch, the Chez Salad is fresh with a tang, pairing mesclun greens and dried cherries with duck confit and chopped egg. Paired with the peppery white bean paste that's served with a rustic bread, you'll feel taken care of *and* as if you're following the dining habits of skinny French women. Other lunch options, which are about half the price of dinner main courses, include beef tartine and seafood stew.

27 S. Pleasant St. ℃ **413/253-3811.** www.chezalbert.net. Main courses $22–$25. AE, DISC, MC, V. Tues–Fri 11:30am–2pm; daily 5–9pm (until 10pm Thurs–Sat).

Judie's ★★ AMERICAN Don't leave Amherst without eating at the upbeat, bustling Judie's. The place has an infectious good cheer, and the vivacious owner does do her best to suit every taste. Throughout the day, folks drop by for a cup of seafood bisque or one of the trademark popovers (basil pesto chicken, for example). Dinner entrees include the vegetarian risotto cakes with black bean sauce, and the seafood gumbo with shrimp, sausage, scallops, salmon, and lobster. This being a college town, portions run from really big to immense, the better to assuage raging young metabolisms.

51 N. Pleasant St. (📞 **413/253-3491.** www.judiesrestaurant.com. Main courses $9–$20. AE, DISC, MC, V. Daily 11:30am–10pm (Fri–Sat until 11pm).

AMHERST AFTER DARK

Students and other young adults tend to gravitate toward the livelier music scene in Northampton, but Amherst does offer some nighttime entertainment. **The Black Sheep,** 79 Main St. (📞 **413/253-3442;** www.blacksheepdeli.com), has music every Friday from 6 to 8pm and Sunday afternoons to go along with its sandwiches and scrumptious desserts. **Amherst Brewing Company,** 24 N. Pleasant St. (📞 **413/253-4400;** www.amherstbrewing.com), features good homemade beer and vittles.

Amherst College's **Buckley Recital Hall** (📞 **413/542-2195**) hosts chamber music performances that include classical quartets and solo pianists. Also check out the schedule of the **University of Massachusetts Fine Arts Center** (p. 331).

Old Deerfield ★★★

Meadows cleared and plowed more than 330 years ago still surround this historic town between the Connecticut and Deerfield rivers. Follow the signs to "Old Deerfield" or "Historic Deerfield," a turn-off of Rte. 5. This small neighborhood has more than 80 homes built in the 17th, 18th, and 19th centuries. Most are private, but 10 can be visited mid-April through November on tours conducted by **Historic Deerfield,** a local tourism organization (see below). Also on the main street is the distinguished prep school, **Deerfield Academy,** founded in 1797.

Deerfield is an invaluable fragment of American history and has been designated a National Historic Landmark village. Massacres of Deerfield's English settlers by the French and Indian enemies of the British nearly wiped out the town in 1675 and again in 1704. In the latter raid, 47 people were killed and another 112 were taken prisoner and marched north to French Quebec.

Special **celebrations** in the town are held on Patriot's Day (the third Mon in Apr), President's Day, Thanksgiving, and the Christmas holidays.

WHAT TO SEE & DO

The main thoroughfare of Old Deerfield, simply called **The Street,** is a mile long. The museum houses are located a few blocks either direction of the visitor center.

Historic Deerfield Neighborhood Walking Tour ★★★ To stroll the main street and visit the 10 properties open for viewing, park behind the Historic Deerfield visitor center (located across the street from squat little post office) or at the nearby Flynt Center of Early American Life. (Stop into the post office, too, for a step back in time.) Begin at **the visitor center,** where tickets for guided tours are sold. While there are no charges for walking the neighborhood, the only way to get inside most of the houses during the mid-April to November tour season is with a guide. If you want to stroll on your own, the visitor center sells walking tour booklets—or just download an itinerary from the website.

The 10 houses currently on the tour were constructed between 1730 and 1850. They contain furnishings, textiles, ceramics, silver, and pewter as well as implements used from the mid–17th century to 1850. Included are items made in the Connecticut River Valley during its prominence as an industrial center.

CENTRAL & WESTERN MASSACHUSETTS

The Pioneer Valley

The **Flynt Center of Early American Life ★** has galleries for changing exhibitions of textiles, paintings, and decorative arts relevant to the local history. Call ahead for hours, which vary throughout the year.

A free attraction is the **Channing Blake Meadow Walk.** The trail begins beside the Rev. John Farwell Moors House, a Historic Deerfield holding on the west side of The Street. It goes through a working farm, past the playing fields of Deerfield Academy, and through pastures beside the Deerfield River. Along the trail, sheep and cattle are seen up close; for that reason, dogs aren't allowed.

A **museum store** (ℭ **413/775-7170**) across the street from the visitor center sells a judicious selection of evocative items such as weather vanes, hand-dipped candles, and reproductions of household items found in the village houses.

80 Old Main St. ℭ **413/775-7214.** www.historic-deerfield.org. Tours $12 adults, $5 ages 6–21, free for 5 and under. Daily 9:30am–4:30pm mid-Apr through Nov. No tours Dec–Apr. Flynt Center Sat–Sun 9:30am–4:30pm in winter.

9

Yankee Candle Village ☺ This emporium is outside the Old Deerfield neighborhood, back on Rte. 5. The Yankee Candle Company is a kingdom built on Americans' insatiable need for candles that are scented like cider donuts or vanilla cupcakes. This huge flagship complex is more than just a store, though: In addition to miles of candles, it features a toy store, home furnishings, an old-fashioned candle-dipping demonstration area, a flavored popcorn stand, a year-round Bavarian Christmas Village, and indoor snow showers every 4 minutes.

25 Greenfield Rd. (Rte. 5), South Deerfield. ℭ **877/636-7707.** www.yankeecandle.com. Free admission. Daily 10am–6pm.

WHERE TO STAY & DINE

Deerfield Inn ★ Built in 1884, this inn in the middle of Old Deerfield is one of the best-known stopping places in the valley. The innkeepers have restlessly scoured the establishment, replacing bathroom fixtures, refinishing the older furniture, and installing new carpeting and flatscreen TVs. Antiques and reproductions are carefully mixed throughout. With blazes in the several fireplaces and an atmospheric tavern in which to linger, this is as pleasant a setting as you'll find in the area. The main restaurant is closed Tuesday and Wednesday, but the tavern serves food every day. The rates here are deeply discounted during nonpeak periods.

81 Old Main St., Deerfield, MA 01342. ℭ **800/926-3865** or 413/774-5587. Fax 413/775-7221. www.deerfieldinn.com. 23 units. $170–$260 double. Rates include breakfast. AE, MC, V. **Amenities:** Restaurant; bar. *In room:* A/C, TV/DVD, hair dryer, Wi-Fi (free).

Turners Falls

The village of Turners Falls was built in the 1860s as a mill town along the Connecticut River, and immigrants from Germany, French Canada, Lithuania, and Ireland all came to chase their dreams. As with other spots in the region, the village began a long economic slide when the mills started closing in the 1940s.

The profile of Turners Falls has risen in recent years, thanks to artistic programming and an active partnership among cultural and commercial groups. They've pumped some new life into a town that still looks much like it must have 70 years ago. It still has a bit of the feel of a ghost town, but it is worth a stop.

The Pioneer Valley

CENTRAL & WESTERN MASSACHUSETTS

WHAT TO SEE & DO

A brochure produced by **Turners Falls River Culture** (www.turnersfallsriver culture.org) lays out a 20-site walking tour that takes in the 19th-century brick buildings that still line the old-fashioned main street, Avenue A. It's available at area businesses or can be downloaded from the website.

If you don't have a map, start your visit at the **Great Falls Discovery Center,** 2 Ave. A (✆ **413/863-3221;** www.greatfallsma.org). It has dioramas of the shoreline and birding culture along the Connecticut River. It's open daily May through mid-October, Friday and Saturday the rest of the year. Bicyclists can park here and take a ride along the new **Franklin County Bikeway's Canalside Trail,** a 4-mile path that opened in 2008. It starts a block closer to the canal and heads off to the left, to Deerfield.

The **Gallery at Hallmark,** 85 Ave. A (✆ **413/863-0085;** http://gallery.hallmark. edu), offers upscale shows of photography, paintings, and sculpture by both local and established artists such as William Wegman. The gallery is affiliated with the **Hallmark Institute of Photography** (www.hallmark.edu), which offers a 10-month in-residence program in Turners Falls. The **Shea Theater,** 71 Ave. A (✆ **413/863-2281;** www.theshea.org), in the Colle Opera House building, hosts music and community theater.

For snacks and light lunch, the **2nd Street Baking Co.,** 69 2nd St. (✆ **413/863-4455;** www.2ndstreetbakingco.com), makes its own whoopie pies, rustic breads, vegan cookies, and sandwiches. It's open Tuesday through Saturday from 7am to 6pm.

The jewel of the area is about 5 miles away. The **Montague Mill,** ★ 440 Greenfield Rd. (Rte. 47), Montague, is a red gristmill from 1834 that has been repurposed into a half-dozen small businesses. They include the rambling and comfortable **Montague Book Mill** (✆ **413/367-9206;** www.montaguebookmill.com), whose tagline is "Books you don't need in a place you can't find"; CD and LP store **Turn It Up** (✆ **413/367-0309;** www.turnitup.com), which features a selection of local artists; and **The Lady Killigrew Cafe** (✆ **413/367-9666;** www.theladykilligrew. com), a cozy oasis of healthy snacks (brown rice salad, peanut-ginger udon noodles), a choice of wines, and free Wi-Fi (no espresso drinks, however). Its nine tables are perched nearly on top of the small Sawmill River and have spectacularly lovely views, although all the people pecking away on laptop computers barely seem to notice. It's open daily from 8am to 10pm. From Turners Falls, head out on Third Street about a mile and take the right fork; that road turns into Rte. 47 and the mill comes up on your right after 4½ miles. (If you continue south on Rte. 47, you'll reach Amherst and Northampton.)

Finally, from April through late fall, consider a drive 14 miles west of Turners Falls to Shelburne Falls for a stroll across the **Bridge of Flowers** (www.bridgeofflowers mass.org). A 1908 trolley bridge over the Deerfield River was converted in 1929 into an eye-popping garden pathway that has been maintained ever since by the Shelburne Falls Area Women's Club Bridge of Flowers Committee. Gladiolus, peonies, Echinacea, roses, clematis, daisies, snapdragons, wisteria, and more weave together to form an ever-changing quilt of color. To get there, follow Rte. 2 west into Shelburne Falls center.

If you continue 27 miles on Rte. 2 from Shelburne Falls, you'll reach North Adams (p. 362), the northern end of the Berkshires.

THE BERKSHIRES ★★★

Sheffield: 119 miles N of New York City and 143 miles W of Boston; Great Barrington: 6 miles N of Sheffield; Stockbridge: 8 miles N of Great Barrington; Lee: 4 miles NE of Stockbridge; Lenox: 6 miles north of Stockbridge; Pittsfield: 7 miles north of Lenox; Williamstown and North Adams: 21 miles N of Pittsfield, 202 miles N of New York City, and 131 miles NW of Boston

More than hills but less than mountains, the Taconic and Hoosac ranges that define this region at the western end of Massachusetts go by the collective name "The Berkshires." The hamlets, villages, and two small cities have long drawn sustenance from the region's kindly Housatonic River and its tranquil tributaries, and are as New England as can be.

Mohawk and Mohegan lived and hunted here, and while white missionaries established settlements at Stockbridge and elsewhere in an attempt to Christianize the native tribes, the Indians eventually moved west. Farmers, drawn to the narrow but fertile flood plains of the Housatonic, were increasingly supplanted in the 19th century by manufacturers, who erected the brick mills that drew their power from the river.

At the same time, artists and writers were attracted by the mild summers and seclusion that these hills and lakes offered. Nathaniel Hawthorne, Herman Melville, and Edith Wharton were among those who put down temporary roots. By the late 19th century and the arrival of the railroad, wealthy New Yorkers and Bostonians had discovered the region and begun to erect extravagant summer "cottages." With their support, culture and the performing arts found a hospitable reception. By the 1930s, theater, dance, and music performances had established themselves as regular summer fixtures. Tanglewood, Jacob's Pillow, and the Berkshire and Williamstown Theatre festivals draw tens of thousands of visitors every summer.

Note that many inns routinely stipulate minimum 2- or 3-night stays in summer and over holiday weekends, and often require advance deposits.

Essentials

GETTING THERE The **Massachusetts Turnpike** (I-90) runs east-west from Boston to the Berkshires, with an exit near Lee and Stockbridge. From New York City, the scenic **Taconic State Parkway** connects with I-90 not far from Pittsfield. To reach the southern end of the county, exit the Taconic at Rte. 20 heading toward Hillsdale, New York, and Great Barrington, Massachusetts.

Amtrak (© **800/USA-RAIL** [872-7245]; www.amtrak.com) operates the *Lake Shore Limited* daily between Boston and Chicago, stopping in Pittsfield each way.

VISITOR INFORMATION The **Berkshire Visitors Bureau,** 3 Hoosac St., Adams, MA (© **800/237-5747** or 413/443-9186; www.berkshires.org), can assist with questions and lodging reservations. Local chambers of commerce and visitor centers maintain information booths at central locations in Great Barrington, Lee, Lenox, Pittsfield, and Stockbridge (see the sections that follow).

A free weekly newspaper, the *Advocate* (**www.advocateweekly.com**), has an online calendar of events in the northern and southern Berkshires.

Sheffield ★

The first settlement of any size encountered when approaching from Connecticut on Rte. 7, Sheffield occupies a flood plain beside the Housatonic River, 11 miles south of Great Barrington, with the Berkshires rising to the west.

The Berkshires

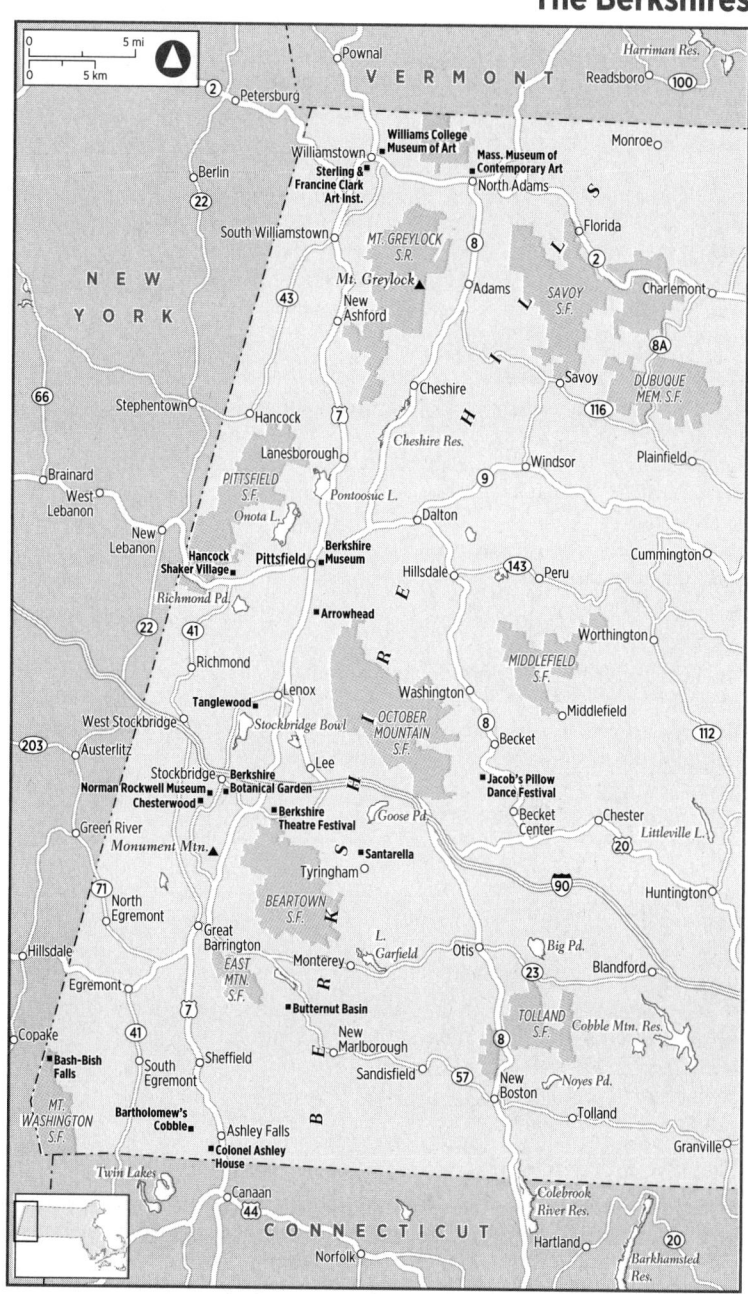

Agriculture has long been the principal occupation of its residents and still is, to a degree. Everyone else sells antiques, or so it might seem driving along Rte. 7 (also known as Main St. or Sheffield Plain). The meticulously maintained houses cultivate an impression of prosperous tranquillity.

Memorial Day to Columbus Day, stop by the **Ashley House,** Cooper Hill Road, in Ashley Falls (© **413/298-3239;** www.thetrustees.org). Built by Colonel Ashley himself in 1735, this modified saltbox is believed to be the oldest house in Berkshire County. Ashley was a person of considerable repute in Colonial western Massachusetts: a pioneer settler, an officer during one of the French and Indian Wars, and later a lawyer and a judge. The house is open from 10am to 5pm on Saturday and Sunday. Admission to the grounds is free; tours of the house are $5 for adults and $3 for children 6 to 12. To find it, drive south from Sheffield on Rte. 7, then veer onto Rte. 7A toward Ashley Falls. Bear right on Rannapo Road. At the Y intersection, turn right on Cooper Hill Road.

GETTING OUTSIDE

The 278-acre nature reservation called **Bartholomew's Cobble ★**, on Rte. 7A (© **413/229-8600;** www.thetrustees.org), lies beside an oxbow bend in the Housatonic River. A "cobble," by local definition, is a "scenic, rocky eminence rising from the valley floor." These 6 miles of trail cross pastures, penetrate forests, and provide vistas of the river valley from the area's high point, Hurlburt's Hill. Picnicking is permitted. Birders should take binoculars. Trails are open from sunrise to sunset, and the small natural-history museum is open daily from 9am to 4:30pm. Admission is $5 for adults and $1 for children 6 to 12.

ANTIQUING

Sheffield lays justifiable claim to the title of "Antiques Capital of the Berkshires"— no small feat, given what seems to be an effort by half the population of the Berkshires to sell collectibles, oddities, and true antiques to the other half. These are canny, knowledgeable dealers who know exactly what they have, so expect high quality and few bargains.

Darr Antiques and Interiors, 34 S. Main St. (© **413/229-7773**), specializes in 18th- and 19th-century English and American furniture. Farther north along Rte. 7, **Dovetail Antiques,** 440 Sheffield Plain (© **413/229-2628**), features American clocks. Continuing along Rte. 7, on the left at the edge of town, is **Susan Silver,** 755 N. Main St. (© **413/229-8169;** www.susansilverantiques.com), with meticulously restored 18th- and 19th-century English library furniture (desks, reading stands) and French accessories.

There are at least two dozen other dealers along this route. Most of them stock the **free directory** of the Berkshire County Antiques Dealers Association (**www.bcaada.com**), which lists member dealers from Sheffield to Cheshire and across the border in Connecticut and New York. The association will mail out its free map and guide of the region.

South Egremont

If you're coming to the Berkshires from the Taconic Parkway in New York, you can't help but drive through the town of Egremont. Its larger, busier half is South Egremont, once a stop on the stagecoach route between Hartford and Albany. It retains many structures from that era, including mills that utilized the stream that still rushes by. Those circumstances make it a magnet for antiques dealers and restaurateurs.

GETTING OUTSIDE

HIKING   Scenic **Bash-Bish Falls State Park ★★**, on Rte. 23 (*©* **413/528-0330;** www.mass.gov), makes a rewarding outing for a day of hiking, birding, and fishing (no picnicking, though). To get here, drive west on Rte. 23 from town, turning south on Rte. 41, and immediately right on Mount Washington Road. Watch for signs directing the way to Mount Washington State Forest and Bash-Bish Falls. After 8 miles, a sign indicates a right turn toward the falls; look for it opposite a church with an unusual steeple. The road begins to follow the course of a mountain stream, going downhill. In about 3 miles is a large parking place next to a craggy promontory.

The sign also points off to a trail down to the falls, which should be negotiated only by reasonably fit adults. First, mount the promontory for a splendid view across the plains of the Hudson Valley to the pale-blue ridgeline of the Catskill Mountains. You'll be able to hear, but not yet see, the falls, which are down to the left. If this trail seems too steep, continue driving down the road to another parking area, on the left. From here, a gentler trail, a little over a mile long, leads to the falls. The falls themselves are quite impressive, crashing down from more than 80 feet. The park is open from dawn to dusk. It has 15 campsites, but there are no services inside the park, and alcoholic beverages aren't permitted.

SKIING   At the western edge of the township, touching the New York border, is the **Catamount Ski Area,** on Rte. 23 (*©* **413/528-1262;** www.catamountski.com). Only about 2 hours from Manhattan, it is understandably popular with New Yorkers. It has over 30 trails, including the daunting double-diamond Catapult (the steepest run in the Berkshires), and seven chairlifts, as well as a 400-foot half-pipe for snowboarders. Night skiing and rentals are available. On weekends, full-day lift tickets cost $56 for adults, $45 for seniors and children 7 to 13, and $25 for children 6 and under.

WHERE TO STAY

Weathervane Inn   An affectionate cat welcomes new arrivals to a building that began as a 1786 farmhouse but was renovated in Greek Revival style in 1835. Many guest rooms have four-poster beds with quilts; fireplaces have been added to two units. In summer, a 3-night stay is required on weekends. Yoga classes are held Monday through Saturday either at the barn at the inn or around the corner at the Berkshire Breathing Project. A public golf course is next door to the inn.

Rte. 23, South Egremont, MA 01258. *©* **800/528-9580** or 413/528-2111. Fax 413/528-1713. www.weathervaneinn.com. 10 units. $115–$165 double; $225–$275 suite. Rates include breakfast and afternoon tea. AE, DC, MC, V. **Amenities:** Outdoor pool. *In room:* A/C.

Great Barrington ★

Even with a population barely over 7,500, this pleasant retail center, 7 miles south of Stockbridge, is the largest town in the southern part of the county. Rapids in the Housatonic provided power for a number of mills in centuries past, most of which are now gone; and, in 1886, this was one of the first communities in the world to have electricity on its streets and in its homes.

Great Barrington has no sights of particular significance, leaving time to browse its many antiques galleries and specialty shops. Convenient as a home base for excursions to such nearby attractions as Monument Mountain, Bash-Bish Falls, Butternut Basin, Tanglewood concerts, and the historic houses of Stockbridge, it has a number of unremarkable but entirely adequate motels north of the center along or near Rte. 7 that tend to fill up more slowly on weekends than the better-known inns in the area. Great Barrington is something of a dining destination, too, with 55 eating places, including, at last count, *four* sushi bars!

A **farmer's market** is held on Saturday from 9am to 1pm in season at the train station on Castle Street.

The **Southern Berkshire Chamber of Commerce** maintains an information booth at 362 Main St. (© **413/528-1510;** www.southernberkshires.com), near the town hall. It's open Tuesday through Sunday from 10am to 5pm.

GETTING OUTSIDE

The **Egremont Country Club,** on Rte. 23 (© **413/528-4222;** www.egremont countryclub.com), is open to the public. Its facilities include a scenic 18-hole golf course, tennis courts, and an Olympic-size pool. Greens fees are $45 on weekends and $25 on weekdays for visitors; tee times required.

Butternut Basin, on Rte. 23, 2 miles east of town (© **413/528-2000;** www. skibutternut.com), is known for its strong family ski programs, including three programs for children of varying levels of experience and Learn to Ski and Learn to Snowboard programs for first-timers. A five-lane tubing park provides another downhill option. There's also a children's center for nonskiers ages 6 months to 8 years. On weekends, full-day lift tickets cost $55 for adults, $45 for seniors and children 7 to 13, and $20 for children 6 and under.

Four miles north of town, west of Rte. 7, is **Monument Mountain,** with two hiking trails to the summit. The easier route is the Indian Monument Trail, about an hour's hike to the top; the more difficult one, the Hickey Trail, isn't much longer but takes the steep way up. The summit, called Squaw Peak, offers splendid views.

SHOPPING

Head straight for Railroad Street, the town's best shopping strip. Start on the corner with Main Street, at **T. P. Saddle Blanket & Trading Co.** (© **413/528-6500**). An unlikely emporium that looks as if it was lifted whole from the Rockies, it's packed with boots, hats, Indian jewelry, blankets, and jars of salsa.

Mistral's, 6 Railroad St. (© **413/528-1618;** www.mistralshome.com), stocks Gallic tableware, linens, fancy foods, and furniture. **Church Street Trading Company,** 4 Railroad St. (© **413/528-6120**), defies easy categorization, with walking sticks, dog collars, and candles all on display. Primary wares are sturdily stylish North Country sweaters, shirts, and pants.

The Chef's Shop, 31 Railroad St. (© **413/528-0135;** www.thechefsshop.net), features a bounty of gadgets and cookbooks, as well as cooking classes. Across the street, **La Pace,** 313 Main St. (© **413/528-1888**), is an upmarket housewares store with an Italian tilt.

Stay on Rte. 7, going north of the center, and you'll pass a large mall with an anchoring Kmart. In that unlikely location is one of the best bookstores in the area: **The Bookloft,** Barrington Plaza (© **413/528-1521;** www.thebookloft.com).

WHERE TO STAY

Several acceptable motels are situated north of town on Rte. 7, the most desirable being the **Holiday Inn Express,** 415 Stockbridge Rd. (℃ **413/528-1810;** www. ichotelsgroup.com), which has an indoor pool, Jacuzzi, small fitness room, and rooms with Jacuzzi tubs and/or fireplaces; rates include breakfast. The **Chamber of Commerce** operates a lodging hotline at ℃ **800/269-4825** or 413/528-4006.

The Old Inn on the Green ★★ This former stagecoach stop from 1760 and the adjacent 18th-century Thayer House are under the ownership of the chef and his wife. The five rooms in the main inn are authentically restored and evocative of their original years, with wide floorboards and period latches; several include access to a second-story veranda. Rooms in Thayer House are larger, with a combination of fireplaces, VCRs, and whirlpool tubs. The intimate dining rooms in the pre-Revolutionary tavern have fireplaces, and the only other illumination at dinner is from candles. Menus are sophisticated, often featuring sweetbreads and diver scallops, and closing with a large selection of regional cheeses (consider the glorious tasting menu for $70). Reservations are strongly advised, especially on summer weekends and off-season. There is outdoor dining in warmer weather.

Rte. 57, New Marlborough, MA 01230. ℃ **413/229-7924.** www.oldinn.com. 11 units. $235–$395 double. Rates include breakfast. AE, MC, V. Take Rte. 23 east from Great Barrington, picking up Rte. 57 after 3½ miles. After 5¾ miles, the Old Inn is on the left. **Amenities:** Restaurant; courtyard pool. *In room:* AC, hair dryer, Wi-Fi (free).

Windflower Inn A roadside lodging built in the middle of the last century in Federal style, the Windflower commands a 10-acre plot of land opposite the Egremont Country Club, on Rte. 23 between Great Barrington and South Egremont. The gracious family that has owned and operated the inn through two generations makes everyone welcome. Six rooms have fireplaces; four have canopy beds.

684 S. Egremont Rd. (P.O. Box 25), Great Barrington, MA 01230. ℃ **800/992-1993** or 413/528-2720. Fax 413/528-5147. www.windflowerinn.com. 13 units. $100–$225 double. Rates include full breakfast and afternoon tea. Children 15 and under stay in parent's room for $25. AE. **Amenities:** Outdoor pool. *In room:* A/C, TV, Wi-Fi (free).

WHERE TO DINE

In addition to the places listed below, consider the excellent dining room at **The Old Inn on the Green** (above).

Expensive

Aegean Breeze ★ GREEK   Readers who associate Greek cuisine with roadside diners or dingy blue-and-white storefronts in strip malls will have their preconceptions swept away by this commendable taverna. Almost hidden on the heavily commercial street leading north from Great Barrington to Stockbridge, it occupies a building with an enclosed porch, an open terrace, and three dining rooms. The menu is laid out in the traditional manner, with sections for *mezedes* (appetizers), *salates,* and *thalasina* (seafood), along with pastas, poultry, and lamb. Execution counts here, elevating such standards as *moussaka* (potatoes, eggplant, and ground beef with béchamel) and lamb *plaki* (with mushrooms, Vidalia onions, and feta baked in a clay pot). Especially appealing are the fish and shellfish—16 varieties of them—utterly fresh and simply prepared. *Opa!*

327 Stockbridge Rd. ℃ **413/528-4001.** www.aegean-breeze.com. Reservations recommended on Fri-Sat. Main courses $15–$32. AE, MC, V. Daily 11am-10pm.

Allium NEW AMERICAN   This offshoot of a growing northern Berkshire chainlet has the best of intentions. While the kitchen professes to use local and seasonal ingredients whenever possible, reality insists that the menu includes items imported well distant from the immediate region. That doesn't alter the fact that the salad of Garroxta cheese, Serrano ham, and roasted almonds—all ingredients from Spain—is a tasty start, along with crusty bread dipped in fruity olive oil (European, as well). Most entrees are sizeable in portion, if variable in execution. Squash-filled ravioli didn't impress, but the cod fritters—crisp outer shells enclosing a creamy *brandade* with a drizzle of aioli—was as good a dish as comes. With care and a little luck, an entirely satisfactory meal can be had.

42 Railroad St. ℂ **413/528-2118.** www.mezzeinc.com. Reservations recommended. Main courses $18–$30. AE, DC, MC, V. Sun–Thurs 5–9pm; Fri–Sat 5–10pm.

Bizen ★ JAPANESE   Pronounced "bee-*zen*," this was one of the first sushi restaurants to be introduced to the Berkshires. Its worn interior makes a wan effort to evoke a Japanese *ryokan*, with faux ceiling beams, paper lanterns, and blond wood tables and chairs. There are four main rooms, the largest occupied by a three-sided sushi bar. Two skilled chefs occupy that arena, fabricating enormously creative combo rolls rarely seen in lesser establishments. These are not your routine supermarket sushi and sashimi. Throw caution aside and order one of the *omasake* meals, handing over responsibility to the chef's whim. The several categories range in price from $30 to $110—the least expensive will be sufficient for most appetites. They claim to use only organic veggies and artisan sakes.

17–21 Railroad St. ℂ **413/528-4343.** www.bizensushi.com. Main courses $15–$34. AE, MC, V. Daily noon–10pm (until 10:30pm Fri–Sat).

Castle Street Cafe ★★ NEW AMERICAN   This storefront bistro has ruled the Great Barrington roost for some time now, along the way installing what it calls a "Celestial Bar" in the next building, with live jazz Fridays and Saturdays most of the year, more often in summer. "Berkshire-grown" three-course dinners for $30 are served Sunday, Monday, and Wednesday. While a Francophilic inclination is apparent in the main room (hello, steak *au poivre*), it isn't overpowering—warm duck on Asian slaw and tortilla-crusted sole with citrus salsa are other possibilities. Have a drink at the bar while considering the night's specials, or stay there for such casual eats as burgers, pizzas, and cheese plates. An award-winning wine list is another reason to stop in.

10 Castle St. (near the Town Hall). ℂ **413/528-5244.** www.castlestreetcafe.com. Reservations recommended on Fri–Sat. Main courses $16–$29. AE, DISC, MC, V. Sun–Thurs 5–9pm; Fri–Sat 5–10pm (until 10:30pm in the Celestial Bar).

Napa NEW AMERICAN   Self-described as a "wine bar and eatery," this new entry helps fill in the space left empty by the closing of Pearl's and Café Helsinki. It enhances its value by staying open daily for both lunch and dinner (many local restaurants do not) and diminishes it by charging a little too much for food that is too often less than memorable. A good strategy might be to have a couple of appetizers at the bar with a glass or two from the substantial wine list. Fried calamari with fennel pollen and spiced tomatoes were reliable, as were the crispy oysters and red lentil and chorizo soup. Jazz combos play here some weekends.

293 Main St. (opposite Railroad St.). ℂ **413/528-4311.** www.napagb.com. Reservations recommended on Fri–Sat. Main courses $15–$37. AE, MC, V. Daily 11:30am–3pm and 5–10pm.

Moderate

Aroma ✦ INDIAN Evidence of a long departed spaghetti joint has finally been erased. Focus on the menu: Apart from especially good deals at lunch, when all items are under $9, choice is what it's all about. Dinner has over 80 a la carte possibilities, plus 16 breads baked on premises. That can be daunting, especially for those unaccustomed to Indian cuisine, but the menu provides useful descriptions. It's hard to go wrong with a couple of vegetable or meat *samosas* (crispy turnovers), chicken or fish *tikka* (marinated chunks cooked on skewers), sides of basmati rice and mango chutney, and spinach *nan* (leavened flatbread stuffed with fresh spinach). **A *warning*:** When the menu says "spicy," believe it. They'll tone down the heat on request.

485 Main St. ☎ **413/528-3116.** www.aromabarandgrill.com. Main courses $12–$17. AE, DC, MC, V. Tues–Sun noon–3pm and 5–10:30pm, Mon–Sun 5–10.

Inexpensive

Rubiner's ★ DELI A former neoclassical bank building has been transformed into a true (not ersatz) gourmet shop. The imposing inner space displays dozens of cheeses of both American and European origin, along with such related products as freshly baked breads, charcuterie, pickles, condiments, and platters of prepared foods. Around back, at the edge of a parking lot, is a smaller attached cafe called **Rudi's** (same address) serving espresso drinks and a selection of foods in the French manner—pâté and cornichons and sandwiches *jambon et fromage* among them. On occasional Fridays and Saturdays from 4 to 7pm, oysters on the half shell are featured. With a glass or two of sauvignon blanc, that's a happy hour.

264 Main St. ☎ **413/528-0488.** Most items under $12. MC, V. Daily 10am–6pm (until 4pm Sun); variably later in Rudi's cafe.

GREAT BARRINGTON AFTER DARK

A grand old downtown cinema, the **Mahaiwe Performing Arts Center,** 14 Castle St. (☎ **413/528-0100;** www.mahaiwe.org), has been restored to some of its century-old glory, and stages a surprising variety of music, dance, and drama. The **Aston Magna Festival** features classical music performed on period instruments. Concerts are held at irregular intervals throughout the year at St. James Church, Main Street, and Taconic Avenue (☎ **800/875-7156** or 413/528-3595; www.astonmagna.org).

Live jazz is often presented at the **Castle Street Café** and **Napa** (see "Where to Dine," p. 342). The **Triplex Cinema,** 70 Railroad St. (☎ **413/528-8886**), shows a mixed bag of independent and foreign flicks as well as major studio releases.

Stockbridge ★★

Readily accessibility from Boston and New York (about 2½ hr. from each and reachable by rail since the mid–19th century), Stockbridge has been transformed from the original frontier settlement into a Gilded Age summer retreat for the rich. One of the Berkshires' hottest destinations, Stockbridge is inevitably jammed on warm weekends and during foliage season.

Along and near Main Street are a number of historic homes and other attractions, enough to fill up a long weekend, even without a Tanglewood concert.

The town has long been popular with artists and writers. Illustrator Norman Rockwell, who lived here for 25 years, rendered the Main Street of his adopted town in a famous painting. A prominent event is the Christmas celebration on the first Sunday in December, when antique cars are parked along Main Street to re-create a scene painted by Rockwell decades ago (**www.stockbridgechamber.org/christmas.html**).

Stockbridge lies 7 miles north of Great Barrington and 6 miles south of Lenox. The **Stockbridge Chamber of Commerce** (✆ **413/298-5200;** www.stockbridge chamber.org) maintains an information booth opposite the row of stores depicted by Rockwell. It's open May through October.

WHAT TO SEE & DO

Berkshire Botanical Garden   Recently celebrating its 75th anniversary, these 15 acres of flower beds, ponds, and vegetable and herb gardens are an inviting destination for strollers and picnickers. The first weekend in October features a harvest festival.

Rtes. 102 and 183. ✆ **413/298-3926.** www.berkshirebotanical.org. Admission $7 adults, $5 seniors, $3 students, free for children 11 and under. May–Oct daily 10am–5pm. Tours offered Sat–Sun June–Aug. Drive west from downtown on Main St., picking up Church St. (Rte. 102) northwest for 2 miles.

The Berkshire Theatre Festival ★★   From June to August, and on a smaller scale into December, the Berkshire Theatre Festival holds its season of classic and new plays, often with marquee names starring or directing. Kevin Kline and Al Pacino are among the many film and theater names who have been participants. Its main stage is in a "casino" built in 1887 to plans by architect Stanford White. A second venue, the Unicorn Theatre, opened in 1996.

P.O. Box 797, Main St. ✆ **413/298-5576.** www.berkshiretheatre.org. Tickets: Main Stage $38–$69, Unicorn Theatre $36–$45.

Chesterwood ★   Sculptor Daniel Chester French, best known for the Lincoln Memorial in Washington, D.C., used this estate as his summer home for more than 30 years. His Minute Man statue at the Old North Bridge in Concord, completed in 1875 when the artist was 25 years old, launched his highly successful career. The 122-acre grounds are used for an annual show of contemporary sculpture. Visitors can take self-guided tours of the studio, residence, and grounds. Guided tours are sometimes offered at 10:30am, 1:30pm, or 3:30pm, but times and dates should be confirmed, so call ahead. Bring a lunch for picnicking on the lovely grounds.

4 Williamsville Rd. ✆ **413/298-3579.** www.chesterwood.org. Admission $15 adults, children free. May–Oct daily 11am–4pm. Drive west on Main St., south on Rte. 183 approx. 1 mile to the CHESTERWOOD sign.

Mission House   The Rev. John Sergeant had benevolent, if paternalistic, intentions in the 1730s: He sought to build a house among the members of the Housatonic tribe to convert them to "civilized" ways through proximity to his godly self and small band of settlers. The weathered Mission House, built in 1739, was the site of this Christianizing process. History buffs will enjoy the 45-minute guided tour.

Main and Sergeant sts. (Rte. 102). ✆ **413/298-3239.** www.thetrustees.org. Admission $6 adults, $3 children 6–12. Memorial Day to Columbus Day daily 10am–5pm. Visits are by guided tour only.

Naumkeag ★   In 1886, Stanford White designed this 26-room summer house for Joseph Hodge Choate, who served as U.S. ambassador to the Court of St. James. The client dubbed it Naumkeag, a Native American name for Salem, Massachusetts, his childhood home. His house of many gables and chimneys is largely of the New England shingle style, surrounded by impressive gardens with fabulous views to the west. Admission is by guided tour only, worth it for the glimpses of the rich interior, which features extensive use of mahogany and California redwood. One oddity is the chandelier of Murano glass in the shape of a badminton shuttlecock. Tucked away in a dark corner upstairs are several original Goya etchings.

Prospect Hill. ℂ **413/298-3239.** www.thetrustees.org. Admission $10 adults, $3 ages 6–12. Memorial Day to Columbus Day daily 10am–5pm. From the Cat & Dog Fountain in the intersection next to the Red Lion Inn, drive north on Pine St. to Prospect Hill Rd., approx. ½ mile.

Norman Rockwell Museum ★★   This striking building opened in 1993, at a cost of $4.4 million, to house the works of Stockbridge's favorite son. The illustrator used both his neighbors and the town where he lived to tell stories about an America now rapidly fading from memory. Most of Rockwell's paintings adorned covers of the *Saturday Evening Post:* warm and often humorous depictions of homecomings, first proms, and visits to the doctor. He addressed serious concerns, too, notably with his poignant portrait of a little African-American girl being escorted by U.S. marshals into a previously segregated school. Critics long derided his paintings as saccharine and sentimental, but today a revision of sorts has led to widespread appreciation for his deft brushwork. The lovely 36-acre grounds also contain Rockwell's last studio (closed Nov–Apr). The museum and grounds remain open year-round.

9 Rte. 183. ℂ **413/298-4100.** www.nrm.org. Admission $15 adults, $14 seniors, $10 students, free for children 18 and under. May–Oct daily 10am–5pm; Nov–Apr Mon–Fri 10am–4pm, Sat–Sun 10am–5pm. Take Main St. (Rte. 102) west to the junction with Rte. 183, then left (south) at the traffic signal. In about ½ mile, you'll see the entrance to the museum on the left.

WHERE TO STAY

Inn at Stockbridge ★   A little over a mile north of Stockbridge center, the main 1906 building has a grandly columned porch set well back from the road on 12 acres. The innkeepers are eager to please, serving full breakfasts by candlelight and afternoon spreads of wine and cheese. Several bedrooms have fireplaces and whirlpool tubs, and there are four suites in a remodeled barn.

30 East St. (Rte. 7), Stockbridge, MA 01262. ℂ **888/466-7865** or 413/298-3337. Fax 413/298-3406. www.stockbridgeinn.com. 16 units. June–Oct $195–$375 double; Nov–May $199–$280 double. Rates include full breakfast and afternoon refreshments. AE, DISC, MC, V. No children 11 and under. **Amenities:** Exercise room; heated outdoor pool. *In room:* A/C, TV/VCR, hair dryer, Wi-Fi (free).

The Red Lion Inn ★★   So well known that it serves as a symbol of the Berkshires, this busy inn had its origins as a stagecoach tavern in 1773. The rocking chairs on the porch are the place to while away an hour reading or people-watching. An ancient birdcage elevator carries guests up to halls and rooms filled with antiques ranging in styles that span 2 centuries. Floors creak and tilt, as might be expected, but modern comforts are provided. Six satellite buildings are within 3 miles of the inn. Dining choices include the pricey traditional dining room, the casual and atmospheric **Widow Bingham Tavern,** the **Lion's Den** pub, and, in good weather, the courtyard out back. The pub has nightly live entertainment, usually of the folk-rock variety. Book your room far in advance.

30 Main St. (PO Box 954), Stockbridge, MA 01262. ℂ **413/298-5545.** Fax 413/298-5130. www.redlioninn. com. 108 units (14 with shared bathrooms). Jan to late May $95–$260 double; $180–$410 suite; late May to late Oct $160–$315 double, $330–$490 suite; late Oct to Dec $130–$275 double, $180–$415 suite. 2-night minimum stay Memorial Day through Oct, Dec, and holidays. AE, DC, DISC, MC, V. Pets accepted ($40 per pet per night). **Amenities:** 3 restaurants; 2 bars; babysitting; exercise room; Jacuzzi; heated outdoor pool; room service; tennis and golf privileges nearby. *In room:* A/C, TV, fridge (in suites), hair dryer, Wi-Fi (free).

Taggart House ★★   Ordinarily, an inn with only four guest rooms wouldn't merit space here. But what rooms! The decor of this outwardly sedate 1850 Victorian/Colonial mansion provides guests with a breathtaking immersion in the Gilded Age. Start with the theatrical main floor—the inlaid mahogany dining table was once a centerpiece in an Argentine palace. There's a paneled library, a ballroom, a harpsichord, and nine beguiling fireplaces. And upstairs, beds are decorated with fur throws, East Indian silk coverlets, and velvet canopies. Breakfast is served at 9:30am.

18 Main St. (1 block west of the Red Lion), Stockbridge, MA 01262. © **800/918-2680.** www.taggart house.com. 4 units. May–Oct $250–$350 double; Nov–Apr $175–$250 double. Rates include breakfast. 2-night minimum stay Fri–Sat May–Oct. AE, DISC, MC, V. Young children not accepted. *In room:* A/C, hair dryer, Wi-Fi (free).

WHERE TO DINE

Once Upon A Table 🔖 NEW AMERICAN   Find this place down an alley off Main Street, east of the Red Lion Inn. Walls with pictures of French waiters constitute most of the decor. In high season, a line of hungry patrons often forms outside. The kitchen's aptitude has wavered over its decade of existence, but has rarely been less than satisfactory and often considerably better. That depends who happens to be shaking the skillets back there, of course, but the trend has been up. Start with the woodsy mushroom soup or the "chowdah" in which the clam chunks outnumber the potatoes. More venturesome tastes might prefer the escargot potpie or the vegetable dumplings with spicy soy vinaigrette. Eggplant ravioli, sautéed gnocchi with pesto, or pecan-crusted trout with herb-roasted, organic potatoes are other possibilities.

34 Main St. © **413/298-3870.** www.onceuponatablebistro.com. Reservations recommended in high season. Main courses $18–$27. MC, V. Mon–Sat 11am–3pm and 5–9pm; Sun 11am–6pm (shorter hours in winter).

Lee/Becket

While Stockbridge and Lenox were developing into luxurious recreational centers for the upper crust of Boston and New York, Lee was a thriving paper-mill town. That meant that it was shunned by the wealthy summer people and thus remained essentially a blue-collar town of workers and merchants. It has a somewhat raffish—though not unappealing—aspect, with its center bunched with shops and offices and few of the stately homes that characterize neighboring communities.

The area's contribution to the Berkshire cultural calendar is Jacob's Pillow Dance Festival in Becket, which first thrived as "Denishawn," a fabled alliance between founders Ruth St. Denis and Ted Shawn.

Lee is 5 miles east of Stockbridge, and Becket is 11 miles east of Lee. In summer and early fall, the **Lee Chamber of Commerce** (© **413/243-0852;** www.lee chamber.org) operates an **information center** on the town common, Rte. 20 (© **413/243-4929**). The folks there can help you find lodging, often in guesthouses and B&Bs—rarely as grand as those in neighboring Lenox, but nearly always cheaper. That's something to remember when every other place near Tanglewood is either booked or quoting prices of $300 a night.

WHAT TO SEE & DO

Jacob's Pillow Dance Festival ★★★   In 1933, Ted Shawn decided to put on a show in the barn, and so Jacob's Pillow was born. After decades of advance and retreat and evolution, Jacob's Pillow is now to dance what Tanglewood is to classical music. Once a regular summer venue for Shawn and famed dancer and choreographer Martha Graham, one of his early disciples, the theater has long welcomed troupes of international reputation, including the Mark Morris Dance Group, Les Grands Ballets Canadiens, Twyla Tharp, and the Paul Taylor Dance Company. The season runs from late June to late August, and tickets go on sale April 1; the schedule is usually available by March 1.

Prominent companies are seen in the main Ted Shawn Theatre, while other troupes are assigned to the Doris Duke Studio Theatre. Admission is free to Inside/Out, an outdoor stage. The growing campus includes a store, pub, dining room, tent restaurant, and exhibition space. Picnic lunches can be preordered 24 hours in advance.

P.O. Box 287, George Carter Rd., Becket. (℃) **413/243-0745.** www.jacobspillow.org. Tickets $10–$58. From Lee, take Rte. 20 east approx. 9 miles, then turn north on Rte. 8 toward Becket.

Santarella ★   With no obligatory historic homes or museums to see in Lee, visitors often make the short excursion to a fairy-tale structure called Santarella, known by most as the "Gingerbread House." Conical turrets top towers, while the shingled roof rolls like waves on the ocean. It served as a studio for sculptor Henry Hudson Kitson from 1930 to 1947 and now is used only for weddings and other special events. The garden is also open to visitors.

75 Main Rd., Tyringham. (℃) **413/243-2819.** www.santarella.us. Take Rte. 20 south from Lee to Rte. 102, near the no. 2 interchange of the Mass. Pike. Following the signs through the complicated intersection, pick up Tyringham Rd. on the other side, and drive south approx. 4 miles.

GETTING OUTSIDE

October Mountain State Forest (℃ **413/243-1778;** www.mass.gov) offers 50 campsites (with showers) and more than 16,000 acres for hiking, canoeing, cross-country skiing, and snowmobiling. Camping season is from mid-May to mid-October; reservations are suggested. To get there, drive northwest on Rte. 20 into town, turn right on Center Street, and follow the signs.

WHERE TO STAY

Applegate ★   This B&B utilizes a gracious 1920s Georgian Colonial manse to full advantage. The nicest unit has a canopy bed, Queen Anne reproductions, sunlight filtering through gauzy curtains, a steam shower, and a fireplace (with real wood). All rooms have stoves or fireplaces, and most have wet bars, TVs, and/or Jacuzzis. Chocolates and brandy await guests at bedside. Breakfast is by candlelight, and the innkeepers set out wine and cheese in the afternoon. They are "flexible" on children.

279 W. Park St., Lee, MA 01238. (℃) **800/691-9012** or 413/243-4451. www.applegateinn.com. 10 units plus a 2-bedroom cottage. June–Oct $270–$395 double; Nov–May $175–$295 double. MC, V. From Stockbridge, drive north on Rte. 7 approx. ½ mile; take a right on Lee Rd. The inn is 2¼ miles ahead. **Amenities:** Bikes; access to nearby health club; heated outdoor pool; tennis court. *In room:* A/C, hair dryer, Wi-Fi (free).

Chambéry Inn ★   This was the Berkshires' first parochial school (1885), named for the French hometown of the nuns who ran it. That accounts for the extra-large bedrooms, about 500 square feet each, which were formerly classrooms. Six of them, with 13-foot ceilings and the original woodwork and blackboards, are equipped with whirlpool tubs and gas fireplaces. Some rooms have TV/VCRs, CD players, and fridges. A breakfast basket is delivered to your door each morning.

199 Main St., Lee, MA 01238. ☏ **800/537-4321** or 413/243-2221. Fax 413/243-0039. www.chamberyinn. com. 9 units. $80–$170 double. Rates include breakfast. AE, DISC, MC, V. No children 15 and under. **Amenities:** Room service. *In room:* A/C, TV, hair dryer, Wi-Fi (free).

Devonfield   From the road, there's no way to tell what this place is. The sign out front reads only DEVONFIELD, and the large house standing on a rise amid tall hemlocks and 29 acres could as easily be a yoga retreat or a conference center. But an inn it is, of the comfy-casual variety, verging on elegant. When FDR and Queen Wilhemina stayed here decades ago, they were probably given the house on the other side of the pool, with its large sitting room with fireplace, kitchen, Jacuzzi, and king bedroom. Five rooms have fireplaces. Several common rooms invite guests inclined to cocooning. New owners have put a great deal of effort into upgrading bathrooms, enclosing two porches, adding new furniture, and installing flatscreen TVs.

85 Stockbridge Rd., Lee, MA 01238. ☏ **800/664-0880** or 413/243-3298. Fax 413/243-1360. www. devonfield.com. 10 units. June–Oct $200–$325 double; Nov–May $165–$300 double. Rates include full breakfast. 3-night minimum stay on weekends July–Aug, 2-night minimum Oct. MC, V. No children 12 and under. **Amenities:** Heated outdoor pool; tennis court. *In room:* A/C, TV/VCR, hair dryer.

Lenox ★★ & Tanglewood ★★★

Stately homes and fabulous mansions mushroomed in this former agricultural settlement from the 1890s until 1913, when the 16th Amendment, authorizing income taxes, put a severe crimp in that impulse. But Lenox remains a repository of extravagant domestic architecture surpassed only in such fabled resorts of the wealthy as Newport and Palm Beach. And because many of the cottages have been converted into inns and hotels, it is possible to get inside some of these beautiful buildings, if only for a cocktail or a meal.

The reason for so many lodgings in a town with a population of barely 5,000 is Tanglewood, a nearby estate where a series of concerts by the Boston Symphony Orchestra is held every summer.

Lenox lies 7 miles south of Pittsfield. The **Lenox Chamber of Commerce** (☏ **413/637-3646;** www.lenox.org) provides visitor information and lodging referrals.

WHAT TO SEE & DO

Berkshire Scenic Railway Museum ★   This museum rolls: It's a long train of vintage engines, passenger coaches, and even a caboose that makes 90-minute trips between Lenox and Stockbridge. The 1903 Lenox station is open to visitors on the weekend days the nostalgic excursions take place. Uniformed conductors narrate the trips, half of them along the Housatonic River and often within sight of some of the grand "cottages" of the Gilded Age wealthy.

Willow Creek Rd. (Housatonic St.). ☏ **413/637-2210.** www.berkshirescenicrailroad.org. Admission $15 adults, $14 seniors, $8 children ages 4–14. Sat–Sun, and holidays only, Memorial Day weekend to Oct.

Frelinghuysen Morris House & Studio ★   Built on 46 acres next to the Tanglewood property in the early 1940s, this Bauhaus-influenced house was the home of abstract artists Suzy Frelinghuysen and George L. K. Morris. Their chosen style was Cubism, which they pursued long after it had been abandoned by better-known practitioners. Works by some of those artists—Braque, Léger, Gris, and Picasso— can be viewed alongside the canvases of the owners. Visits are by tour only.

92 Hawthorne St. ☏ **413/637-0166.** www.frelinghuysen.org. Admission $12 adults, $11 seniors, $6 students, free for children 11 and under. Late June to Labor Day Thurs–Sun 10am–3pm; Sept to Columbus

Lenox

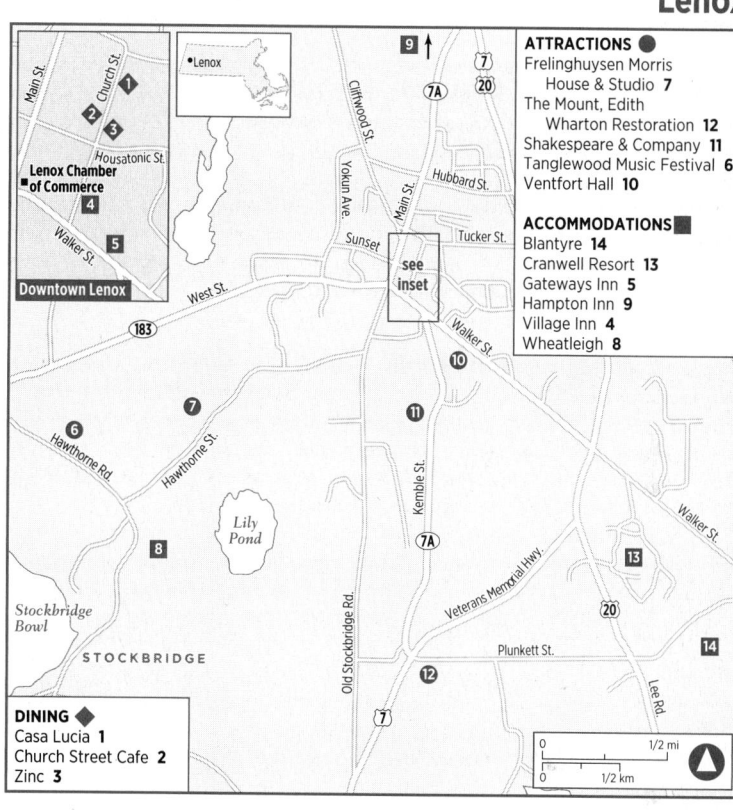

ATTRACTIONS ●
Frelinghuysen Morris
  House & Studio **7**
The Mount, Edith
  Wharton Restoration **12**
Shakespeare & Company **11**
Tanglewood Music Festival **6**
Ventfort Hall **10**

ACCOMMODATIONS ■
Blantyre **14**
Cranwell Resort **13**
Gateways Inn **5**
Hampton Inn **9**
Village Inn **4**
Wheatleigh **8**

DINING ◆
Casa Lucia **1**
Church Street Cafe **2**
Zinc **3**

Lenox Chamber of Commerce

Downtown Lenox

Lily Pond

Stockbridge Bowl

STOCKBRIDGE

see inset

0   1/2 mi
0   1/2 km

Day Thurs–Sat 10am–3pm. Drive south from Tanglewood on Rte. 183, turn left on Hawthorne Rd., then left again on similarly named Hawthorne St.

The Mount, Edith Wharton Restoration ★   Wharton, who won a Pulitzer for her novel *The Age of Innocence,* was singularly equipped to write that deftly detailed examination of the upper classes of the Gilded Age and the first decades of the 20th century. She was born into that stratum of society in 1862 and traveled in the circles that made the Berkshires a regular stop on their restless movements between New York, Florida, Newport, and the Continent. Wharton had her villa built on this 130-acre lakeside property in 1902 and lived here 10 years before leaving for France, never to return. She took an active hand in the creation of the Mount, which makes the mansion a notable rarity—it's one of the few designated National Historic Landmarks designed by a woman. A terrace cafe overlooks the lovely grounds. The facility was in dire financial straits and danger of foreclosure in 2008, but appears to be on more steady footing after an aggressive "Save the Mount" campaign.

2 Plunkett St. (at the intersection of rtes. 7 and 7A). ☎ **413/551-5111.** www.edithwharton.org. Admission $10 adults, $8 students, free for children 11 and under. May–Dec 10am–4pm.

Shakespeare & Company ★★ The repertory company had long used buildings and amphitheaters on the grounds of the Mount (see above) to stage its May-to-December season of plays by the Bard, works by Chekhov and George Bernard Shaw, and efforts by new American and English playwrights. After increasingly bitter conflict with the custodians of the Wharton property, officials of the company purchased a 63-acre property on Kemble Street, closer to downtown Lenox. With construction of a Founder's Theatre, the Spring Lawn Theatre, the tented Rose Footprint Theatre, an administration building, and planned rehabilitation of other existing buildings, the Company enjoys its very own campus devoted to the dramatic arts. (It also has more than $10 million in debt, making the future uncertain.) Walking trails have been developed on the grounds, and a cafe in the theater lobby serves drinks and light fare. Picnickers are welcome.

70 Kemble St. ℰ **413/637-3353.** www.shakespeare.org. Tickets $15–$60.

Tanglewood Music Festival ★★★ Lenox is filled with music every summer, and the undisputed headliner is the **Boston Symphony Orchestra (BSO),** directed by James Levine. Concerts are given at the famous Tanglewood estate, usually beginning in July and ending the weekend before Labor Day. The estate is on West Street (actually in Stockbridge township, although it's always associated with Lenox). From Lenox, take Rte. 183 1½ miles southwest of town.

While the BSO is Tanglewood's 800-pound cultural gorilla, the program features a menagerie of other performers and musical idioms. These run the gamut from popular artists (James Taylor and Bonnie Raitt) and jazz musicians (including Diana Krall and Wynton Marsalis) to such classical soloists as Itzhak Perlman and Yo-Yo Ma.

The **Koussevitzky Music Shed** is an open auditorium that seats 5,000, surrounded by a lawn where an outdoor audience lounges on folding chairs and blankets. Chamber groups and soloists appear in the smaller **Ozawa Hall.** Major performances are on Friday and Saturday nights and Sunday afternoon.

Tentative programs are available after January 1, and tickets usually go on sale in February and can sell out quickly (you can buy them online). To go at the last minute, take a blanket or lawn chair and get tickets for lawn seating, which is almost always available. You can also attend open rehearsals during the week, as well as the rehearsal for the Sunday concert on Saturday morning.

The estate itself (ℰ **413/637-5165;** June–Aug), with more than 500 acres of lawns and gardens, much of it overlooking the lake called Stockbridge Bowl, was put together starting in 1849 by William Aspinwall Tappan. Admission to the grounds is free when concerts aren't scheduled.

In 1851, a structure on the property called the Little Red Shanty was rented to Nathaniel Hawthorne, who stayed here long enough to write a children's book, *Tanglewood Tales,* and meet Herman Melville, who lived in nearby Dalton. The existing Hawthorne Cottage is a replica (closed to the public). On the grounds is the original Tappan mansion, with fine views.

West St., Stockbridge. ℰ **617/266-1492.** www.tanglewood.org. Tickets $28–$99 Shed and Ozawa Hall, $19–$25 lawn. Lawn tickets for children 11 and under are free; children 4 and under not allowed in the Shed or Ozawa Hall. Higher prices for opening nights and some special appearances.

Ventfort Hall ★ The painstaking, ongoing renovation of this Gilded Age mansion continues while visitors are welcomed to view those parts of the impressive "cottage" partially or fully restored. (To view the work still ahead of them, take a peek through the window in the bookshop at a room in early stages of the effort.) The Elizabethan Revival manse was originally constructed at the behest of a sister of J. P. Morgan in 1893. One of its most striking features is the collection of 61 29-inch porcelain dolls modeling elaborate women's fashions of the period 1855 to 1914; creator John Burbidge used to design wedding dresses for such prominent brides as the daughters of Presidents Johnson and Nixon. The exterior was used in the film, *The Cider House Rules*.

104 Walker St. (© **413/637-3206.** www.gildedage.org. Admission $12 adults, $5 children 5–17, free 4 and under. Guided tours daily in summer, Sat–Sun Nov–May.

GETTING OUTSIDE

Pleasant Valley Wildlife Sanctuary, 472 West Mountain Rd. (© **413/637-0320;** www.massaudubon.org), has a small museum and 7 miles of hiking and snowshoeing trails crossing its 1,300 acres. Beaver lodges and dams can be glimpsed from a distance, and waterfowl and other birds are found in abundance—bring binoculars. The nature center is open Tuesday through Friday from 9am to 5pm, Saturday and Sunday 10am to 4pm; admission is $4 adults, $3 seniors and children 3 to 15. To get here, drive north about 6½ miles on rtes. 7 and 20 and turn left on West Dugway Road.

More extensive trails can be found at **October Mountain State Forest** (see "Getting Outside," under the section on Lee, p. 346) or at **Beartown State Forest,** 69 Blue Hill Rd., in nearby Monterey (© **413/528-0904;** www.mass.gov). The **Appalachian Trail,** which runs from Maine to Georgia, connects here with a loop trail around a small pond with a nice swimming area. Take Rte. 7 south for 3½ miles, then turn left onto West Road. After 2½ miles, turn left at the T intersection onto Rte. 102 east. Turn right over the bridge onto Meadow Street, then turn right onto Pine Street and follow the signs.

SHOPPING

The Bookstore, 11 Housatonic St. (© **413/637-3390;** www.bookstoreinlenox.com), with author signings and poetry readings, helps fill a yawning gap in the Berkshires, which are curiously short on comprehensive bookstores. Those in pursuit of art and antiques, on the other hand, cannot easily exhaust the possibilities—there are over a half dozen galleries on the 2-block-long Church Street in the center of town, just for starters. For fashion-forward clothing for men and women, much of it Italian-made, check in at **Casablanca,** 21 Housatonic St. (© **413/637-2680**). L.L.Bean, it isn't. Out on Rte. 7, heading toward Pittsfield, serious cooks should watch for **Different Drummer's Kitchen,** 374 Pittsfield Rd. (© **413/637-0606;** www.differentdrummerskitchen.com).

WHERE TO STAY

Most area lodgings can accommodate only small numbers of guests. Because the Tanglewood concert season is a powerful draw, prices are highest in summer, as well as during the brief foliage season in mid-October. Rates are set according to wildly varying combinations of seasons and days of the week as well as facilities offered. Minimum 2- or 3-night stays are usually required during the Tanglewood weeks, foliage season, weekends, and holidays. **Note:** For visits during the Tanglewood season, reserve far in advance—February isn't too soon.

Some inns here are so rule-ridden and facility-free that they come off as crabby— no kids, no pets, no phones, no credit cards, no breakfast before 9am, shared bathrooms—while costing twice as much as nearby motels that have all those conveniences.

Rtes. 7 and 20 north and south of town harbor a number of motels, including the **Mayflower Motor Inn** (☏ 413/443-4468), the **Days Inn** (☏ 413/637-3560), the **Lenox Motel** (☏ 413/499-0324), and the **Comfort Inn** (☏ 413/443-4714).

Very Expensive

Blantyre ★★★   This sumptuous 1902 Tudor-Norman mansion used to open only during the warmer months. Now it cossets its guests year-round in its undeniably luxurious public rooms, dining areas, and bedchambers. A long drive curls up through 100 acres to the main manor, where guests enter a baronial lobby packed with imposing antique furniture, a massive fireplace, stuffed animal heads, and a carved and beamed ceiling suitable for the country home of a 19th-century blueblood. Elsewhere, decor is beholden to no uniform decorative style, the rooms by turn heavily masculine and airily feminine. Dining is of the highest order, as dictated by the prestigious Relais & Châteaux hotel association. Coat and tie are required at dinner. If any place is worth these breathtaking tariffs, it's this one.

16 Blantyre Rd. (Rte. 20), Lenox, MA 01240. ☏ **413/637-3556.** Fax 413/637-4282. www.blantyre.com. 24 units. $550–$950 double, suites from $750. Rates include full breakfast. 2-night minimum stay Fri-Sat, 3-night minimum on holidays. AE, DC, MC, V. Pets accepted in 2 units ($75/night). No children 12 and under. **Amenities:** Restaurant; exercise room w/sauna; heated outdoor pool; room service; 4 tennis courts. *In room:* TV/DVD, fridge, hair dryer, Wi-Fi (free).

Cranwell Resort ★★★   The main building of this all-season resort looks like a castle in the Scottish Highlands, but no 17th-century laird lived this well. That's where the most expensive rooms are; the rest are in four smaller outlying buildings. Accommodations are outfitted with less concern for adherence to a particular style than for surrounding guests in immediate comfort. In addition to the lovely grounds (serving as cross-country ski trails in winter), there is a 60-acre golf school. Three dining rooms range from formal to pubby, and live jazz is featured Friday and Saturday nights. An enormous 35,000-square-foot spa includes an indoor pool, lounges with fireplaces, and 17 spa treatment rooms.

55 Lee Rd. (Rte. 20), Lenox, MA 01240. ☏ **800/272-6935** or 413/637-1364. Fax 413/637-4364. www.cranwell.com. 107 units. May–Oct $295–$445 double, Nov to mid-May $195–$345 double. AE, DC, DISC, MC, V. **Amenities:** 4 restaurants; bar; babysitting; bikes; golf course; extensive health club & spa; heated outdoor and indoor pools; room service; 4 tennis courts. *In room:* A/C, TV/VCR, fridge, hair dryer, Wi-Fi (free).

Wheatleigh ★★   A fountain out front and a lobby fireplace with deeply carved garlands and cherubim set the tone. Beyond, glamorous urbanites often drape themselves in Gatsbyesque poses around the lavishly appointed great hall. Much of the time, they look elaborately bored, no easy feat in this persuasive 1893 replica of a 16th-century Tuscan *palazzo*, which aspires to the highest standards of the moneyed Berkshires. Happily, the interior decor is muted, not florid, utilizing neutral colors and restrained shapes. Wheatleigh has always been very expensive, even though the "superior" rooms average only 10×14 feet. But other places are catching up, and the manager is striving to give requisite value. The dining room rounds out the experience, with painstakingly conceived food presented superbly.

Hawthorne Rd., Lenox, MA 01240. ☏ **413/637-0610.** Fax 413/637-4507. www.wheatleigh.com. 19 units. $715–$2,100 double. Rates include daily wine tastings. AE, DC, MC, V. **Amenities:** 2 restaurants; lounge; babysitting; bikes; concierge; exercise room; heated outdoor pool; tennis court. *In room:* A/C, TV/DVD, fax, hair dryer, Wi-Fi (free).

Expensive

Gateways Inn ★★ Harley Procter, who hitched up with a man called Gamble and made a bundle, had this house built in 1912. Its most impressive feature is the staircase that winds down into the lobby. Designed by McKim, Mead, and White, it's a stunner, just the thing for a grand entrance. Equally impressive is the suite named for conductor Arthur Fiedler, with not one but two fireplaces and a big four-poster on the sun porch. Eight rooms have working fireplaces. Dining in the creative Italian restaurant is one of Lenox's greater pleasures. The bar features 140 grappas and 225 single-malt scotches. A terrace is available for light meals and desserts. Lunch is offered on summer weekends, with light fare after dinner to midnight.

51 Walker St., Lenox, MA 01240. © **888/492-9466** or 413/637-2532. Fax 413/637-1432. www.gateways inn.com. 12 units. June–Oct $240–$345 double; Nov–May $150–$200 double. Rates include breakfast. 2-night minimum stay in high season. AE, DC, DISC, MC, V. No children 11 and under. **Amenities:** Restaurant; lounge. *In room:* A/C, TV, hair dryer, Wi-Fi (free).

Moderate

Hampton Inn What to say about a local entry of a familiar chain that isn't all that different from its midlevel competitors? Accept it for what it is: new, fresh, clean, staffed with young people eager to please. The business center has two computers and one printer (no charge). Complimentary coffee, tea, and hot chocolate are available 24/7 in the lobby. A laundry room is available (for free) to guests. *USA Today* is free in the breakfast room; the *New York Times* and *Boston Globe* are available at the front desk. If you crave the charm of a Lenox bed-and-breakfast, don't book here. If you want modern conveniences at reasonable tariffs and a chance to find a room in peak Tanglewood and foliage seasons, give a long look here.

445 Pittsfield Rd., Lenox, MA 01240. © **413/499-1111.** Fax 413/499-4444. www.berkshirehampton.com. 79 units. $110–$149 double. Rates include breakfast. AE, DC, DISC, MC, V. **Amenities:** Small exercise room; heated indoor pool. *In room:* A/C, TV, hair dryer, high-speed Internet (free).

Village Inn An inn off and on since 1775, this place hasn't a whiff of pretense. Its rooms come in considerable variety and are categorized as Deluxe, Superior, Standard, or Economy. That means four-posters in the high-end rooms, some of which have fireplaces, and constricted quarters with smaller beds and no extras at the lower prices. Claw-foot tubs are common. The third floor was most recently renovated. Afternoon tea and dinner are served in the restaurant, with prices lower than the town average, and light meals are available in the tavern, where there is jazz on summer weekends.

16 Church St., Lenox, MA 01240. © **800/253-0917** or 413/637-0020. Fax 413/637-9756. www.village inn-lenox.com. 32 units. Summer–fall $165–$304 double; winter–spring $122–$181 double. Discount 30% during midweek in winter/spring. Rates include breakfast. AE, DC, DISC, MC, V. No children 5 and under. **Amenities:** Restaurant; bar. *In room:* A/C, TV/VCR, hair dryer.

Yankee Inn ☺ Of the several motels strung along Rte. 20 east of Lenox center, this is arguably the most desirable, and a place to remember when the area's inns are filled. It is also more congenial for families; children are welcome, as they are not in most B&Bs. Housekeeping is of a reasonably high standard, and furnishings, while routine in design, are as fresh-looking as might be expected in a city hotel. Some rooms have gas fireplaces and unstocked fridges. Long, empty corridors don't enhance the experience, but the indoor/outdoor pool, convenient location, and moderate prices (for the Berkshires) compensate.

461 Pittsfield Rd. (Rte. 20), Lenox, MA 01240. ℂ **800/835-2364** or 413/499-3700. Fax 413/499-3634. www.berkshireinns.com. 96 units. $109–$149 double. Rates include breakfast. AE, DC, DISC, MC, V. **Amenities:** Lounge; modest exercise room; heated indoor/outdoor pool, Wi-Fi (free, in lobby). *In room:* A/C, TV, hair dryer.

WHERE TO DINE

See also "Where to Stay," above, as many inns have dining rooms. In particular, **Blantyre** (ℂ **413/637-3556**) is worth a splurge. Most of the restaurants recommended below serve lunch, in a region where many don't open until evening. On the other hand, restaurants here are apt to close for weeks or months in winter, so always call ahead.

Chocoholics will want to check out the **Chocolate Springs Café,** 55 Pittsfield Lenox Rd. (Rte. 7; ℂ **413/637-9820;** www.chocolatesprings.com). The entire spectrum of the dark confection is explored, from bonbons to truffles to pastries. There is live music Saturday afternoons.

Casa Lucia ★ ITALIAN   Here at the far end of Lenox's restaurant row, the post-preppie crowd of regulars and weekend refugees from the city is attired in country cashmere and tweed, a taste no doubt honed at campuses of the Ivy League and Seven Sisters. The waitresses display a professionalism rarely experienced in these hills, bringing satisfying starters—carpaccio, grilled calamari with peppers and anchovies, and the like—followed by superior renditions of *osso bucco con risotto* (the most expensive), *bistecca alla Fiorentina,* and six pastas, such as rabbit *tagliatelle.* Dine out on the broad deck in warmer months. Be aware that the restaurant often closes from January to spring; call ahead.

80 Church St. ℂ **413/637-2640.** Reservations recommended. Main courses $25–$39. AE, DC, DISC, MC, V. Tues–Sun 5:30–10pm (also Sun in summer; winter hours fluctuate).

Church Street Cafe ★★ NEW AMERICAN   Lenox's most popular eating place delivers fanciful combinations that please the eye and pique the taste buds. Menus change with the seasons, but past options have included chicken marinated in Latin spices with polenta cake and black beans, braised leg and thigh and seared breast of duck in a red wine reduction, and sake-marinated sea bass with shrimp dumplings and shiitakes simmered in soy-ginger broth. Lunch is a busy time here, with rich, earthy gumbo, red chili roasted chicken quesadillas, and crab cake sandwiches among the long-standing favorites. The decor is rudimentary, the service friendly but rushed. A large covered deck fills up whenever the weather allows.

65 Church St. ℂ **413/637-2745.** www.churchstreetcafe.biz. Reservations recommended on Fri–Sat. Main courses $24–$30. MC, V. May–Oct daily 11:30am–2pm and 5:30–9pm; Nov–Feb Tues–Sat 11:30am–2pm and 5:30–8:30pm. Closed Feb–Apr.

Viva SPANISH   While it doesn't qualify for hosannas, the virtues of this roadside farmhouse in the hamlet of Glendale include the fact it is a straight 10-minute shot to Tanglewood and even closer to the Norman Rockwell Museum. It also honors the Spanish tapas invention, with a long menu of those hot and cold saucer-sized savories. Some of these hew to tradition, others drift off into pan-oceanic riffs with little concern for authenticity. They are generally well-executed, as with the *pulpo gallego,* meaty octopus tentacles dusted with smoked paprika. Four or five tapas should be adequate for two people to share. If not, on offer are three *paellas* and a Catalan fish stew called *zarzuela.* Ignore the bullfight posters and the wandering guitarist, clichés that should have passed away along with Generalissimo Franco.

14 Glendale Rd. (Rte. 183). ℂ **413/298-4433.** www.vivaberkshires.com. Reservations recommended on Fri–Sat. Main courses $15–$30. MC, V. Wed–Sat 11:30am–2pm; Sun 5–9pm.

Zinc ★★ BISTRO   Zinc occupies the upper echelon of Berkshires. For one thing, it is the best-looking restaurant in town, with its eponymous zinc bar, stamped-tin ceiling, flowers, lacquered woods, and butcher paper over white tablecloths. The cuisine and wine list adhere with some rigor to the French-bistro canon. Past menus have listed such toothsome entrees as lamb loin with spinach and chickpea fries, diver scallops with sweet potato and andouille hash, and yellowfin tuna with black rice and coconut chili emulsion. Otherwise, standards duck confit, coq au vin, and steak frites are done well. A remarkable 24 wines are available by the glass, most going quite well with the five-cheese tasting ($15). The owner has the admirable philosophy of staying open year-round—you can always find a meal here.

56 Church St. ℂ **413/637-8800.** www.bistrozinc.com. Reservations recommended. Main courses $18–$30. AE, MC, V. Daily 11:30am–3pm and 5:30–9pm (bar until 1am).

Pittsfield

Berkshire County's largest city (pop. 44,285) routinely gets little attention in most tourist literature. A commercial and industrial center, it has little of the charm that marks such popular destinations as Stockbridge and Lenox. Something is afoot, though. Always a convenient base for day excursions to other parts of the central Berkshires, this blue-collar city is reinventing itself, with attractions, more worthwhile restaurants, and an ever livelier nightlife. Emblematic of this shift was the 2006 reopening of the **1903 Colonial Theatre,** once again home to dance, comedy, and music from classical to country (**www.thecolonialtheatre.org**).

A document discovered in 2004 that banned the playing of baseball within 80 yards of the main church in 1791 suddenly gave Pittsfield claim to the invention of the game, 48 years before Cooperstown, New York.

Pittsfield lies 137 miles west of Boston, 7 miles north of Lenox. The **Berkshire Visitors Bureau** (ℂ **800/237-5747** or 413/443-9186; www.berkshires.org) is in the same block of buildings as the Crowne Plaza Hotel, on Berkshire Common.

WHAT TO SEE & DO

Arrowhead   Herman Melville bought this 18th-century house in 1850 and lived here until 1863. It was during this time that he wrote *Moby-Dick*. A nature trail and shop are on-site. In truth, however, the house is of limited interest to visitors other than literature students and avid readers.

780 Holmes Rd. ℂ **413/442-1793.** www.mobydick.org. Admission $12 adults, $5 students 15 and older, $3 children 6–14. From Memorial Day to Columbus Day daily 9:30am–4pm; rest of year by appointment only. Visits are by guided tour only, given on the hour 10am–3pm. Drive east from Park Sq. on East St., turn right on Elm St., and turn right on Holmes Rd.

Barrington Stage Company   At intervals throughout the year, but with concentrations from late June to October, this nonprofit theater group mounts musicals, comedies, and dramas at the **Mainstage** on Union Street and three smaller venues.

30 Union St. ℂ **413/526-8888.** www.barringtonstageco.org. Tickets $15–$35 adults (discounts for seniors), $10 students.

Berkshire Museum ★   It began in 1903 as the "Museum of Natural History and Art," words chiseled in stone above the entrance. Holdings bounce from Babylonian cuneiform tablets to tanks of live fish to archaeological artifacts such as a delicate necklace from Thebes, dating to at least 1500 B.C. Included in the permanent collections are works by such 19th-century portraitists and landscapists as George Inness, Edwin Church, and Albert Bierstadt. Temporary exhibitions are frequent and professionally mounted. An auditorium seating 300 serves as the "Little Cinema," which shows art and foreign films during the warmer months.

39 South St. (Rte. 7, 1 block south of Park Sq.). *C* **413/443-7171.** www.berkshiremuseum.org. Admission $11 adults, $6 ages 3–18. Mon–Sat 10am–5pm; Sun noon–5pm.

Hancock Shaker Village ★★★   The serenity of the setting, among low hills and meadows, and the carefully considered placement of the buildings and their relationships with each other, are the essence of Shaker philosophy, "Order is Heaven's law." Twenty restored buildings make up the village, which explores the religious practices and lifestyle habits of the austere Protestant sect. Its signature structure is the **1826 round stone barn:** The Shaker preoccupation with functionalism joined with purity of line and respect for materials has never been clearer than it is in the design of this building. Its round shape expedited the chores of feeding and milking livestock by arranging cows in a circle, and the precise joinery of the roof beams and support pillars is a joy to observe.

The other must-see is the brick dwelling that contained the village's communal dining room, kitchens, and sleeping quarters. Sexes were separated at meals, work, and religious services, and there are staircases leading to male and female "retiring rooms."

While artisans and docents demonstrate Shaker crafts and techniques, only some dress in period clothing to portray Shaker inhabitants. All are knowledgeable about their subject, though, and dispense nuggets about the Shaker discipline such as the requirement to dress the right side first and to step with the right foot first. Special programs include sustainable gardening workshops and Shaker-inspired candlelight dinners in autumn ($65, reservations essential). The museum shop is excellent, and a **cafe** serves lunches in summer and fall, with some dishes based on Shaker recipes.

Rtes. 20 and 41, Pittsfield. *C* **800/817-1137** or 413/443-0188. www.hancockshakervillage.org. Admission $17 adults, $8 children 13–17, free 12 and under. Mid-Apr to mid-Oct daily 10am–5pm; rest of year, call ahead for hours and events.

GETTING OUTSIDE

Plaine's Bike, Ski & Snowboard, 55 W. Housatonic St., at Center Street (*C* **413/499-0294;** www.plaines.com), rents bikes and carries equipment for all the sports its name suggests. It's on Rte. 20, west of downtown.

Pittsfield State Forest, entered on Cascade Street (*C* **413/442-8992;** www.mass.gov), is a little over 3 miles west of the center of town. It includes 65 acres of wild azalea fields that explode in pink blossoms in June. There's also camping, boating, fishing, hiking, biking, and cross-country skiing here. Open daily from 8am to 8pm. Admission is $5 per car from early May to mid-Oct.

BOATING   **Onota Boat Livery,** 463 Pecks Rd. (*C* **413/442-1724**), rents canoes and motorboats on Onota Lake, conveniently located at the western edge of the city. It's open Monday through Saturday from 7am to 5:30pm.

SKIING   South of the city center, off Rte. 7 near the Pittsfield city limits, is the **Bousquet Ski Area,** Dan Fox Drive (*C* **413/442-8316;** www.bousquets.com). Bousquet (pronounced *Bos*-kay) has 22 trails, with a vertical drop of 750 feet, two

MOVERS & SHAKERS IN MASSACHUSETTS

The former Ann Lee, once imprisoned in England for her excess of religious zeal, arrived in New York with eight disciples in 1774, just as the disgruntled American colonies were about to burst into open rebellion. She had anointed herself leader of the United Society of Believers in Christ's Second Coming and was known as Mother Ann. The austere Protestant sect was dedicated to simplicity, equality, and celibacy. They were popularly known as "the Shakers" for their spastic movements when in the throes of religious ecstasy.

By the time Mother Ann died in 1784, the Shakers had many converts, who then fanned out across the country to form communal settlements from Maine to Indiana. One of the most important Shaker communities, **Hancock,** edged the Massachusetts–New York border, near Pittsfield.

Shaker society produced dedicated, highly disciplined farmers and craftspeople whose products were much in demand in the outside world. They sold seeds, invented early agricultural machinery and hand tools, and erected large buildings of several stories and exquisite simplicity. Their spare, clean-lined furniture and accessories anticipated the so-called Danish Modern style by a century and in recent years have drawn astonishingly high prices at auction.

All of these accomplishments required a verve owed at least in part to sublimation of sexual energy, for a fundamental Shaker tenet was total celibacy for its adherents. The society grew through converts and adoption of orphans (who were free to leave, if they wished). But, by the 1970s, the movement had a bare handful of believers. The string of Shaker settlements and museums that remain testify to their dictum, "Hands to work, hearts to God."

double lifts, and two rope tows. Night skiing is available Monday through Saturday. Rentals and lessons are offered. Lift tickets cost $20 to $37; snow tubing costs $15.

Jiminy Peak ★, in Hancock (© **413/738-5500;** www.jiminypeak.com), aspires to four-season activity, so skiing and snowboarding on 28 trails (18 open at night) with seven lifts is supplemented the rest of the year by horseback riding, trapshooting, fishing in a stocked pond, a rock-climbing wall, tennis, mountain biking, pools, and golf at the nearby Waubeeka Springs course. There's lodging right at the resort (see The Country Inn at Jiminy Peak, below), with lift tickets included in the room rates. For day-trippers, all-day tickets cost $45 for adults and $33 for juniors on the weekend, $39 for adults and $29 for juniors during the week.

WHERE TO STAY

The Country Inn at Jiminy Peak ☺   This is one of the better lodging deals in the Berkshires, if your idea of luxury is space. The units, all 1- to 3-bedroom suites with full kitchens and sofa beds, are perfect for families. Also great for kids are the on-site downhill skiing and snowboarding (see "Getting Outside," above). In summer, there's downhill mountain-biking for the adventurous, plus bobsled rides on an alpine slide, a bungee-trampoline, a climbing wall, a giant swing, trout fishing, and minigolf. A convenience store on the property has groceries, wine, beer, and a post office.

Brodie Mountain Rd. (near Rte. 43), Hancock, MA 01237. ✆ **800/882-8859** or 413/738-5500. Fax 413/738-5513. www.jiminypeak.com. 105 units. $129–$909 1–3 bedroom suite. Winter rates include lift tickets. Children 17 and under stay free in parent's room. AE, DC, DISC, MC, V. **Amenities:** 2 restaurants; 2 bars; babysitting; children's programs; exercise room; heated outdoor and indoor pools; 6 tennis courts. *In room:* A/C, TV/VCR, hair dryer, kitchenette, Wi-Fi (free).

Crowne Plaza ☺ The tallest building in town at 14 stories, this former Hilton isn't hard to find (although it may take a little 'round-the-block maneuvering to get to the front door). It has the bells and whistles expected of upper-middle chain hotels and is more family-friendly than many smaller lodgings in the region. Kids are welcome, and readily occupied with the heated indoor pool and PlayStations in every room. With 179 rooms, there's also a good chance of copping a bed on Tanglewood weekends.

1 West St., Pittsfield, MA 01201. ✆ **877/227-6963** or 413/499-2000. Fax 413/442-0449. www.berkshire crowne.com. 179 units. $117–$169 double. AE, DISC, MC, V. Free self-parking in garage. **Amenities:** Restaurant; bar; babysitting; exercise room w/Jacuzzi; heated indoor pool; room service. *In room:* A/C, TV; hair dryer, Wi-Fi (free).

Thaddeus Clapp House The eponymous Mr. Clapp was ahead of his time, incorporating central heating and indoor plumbing in his 1871 manse. He also rejected the excesses of High Victorian design, stripping his home to what amounted—at the time—to near-minimalism. Restoration brought gas fireplaces and high-speed Internet to the extra-large rooms. The owner/manager is a fervent Pittsfield booster and a font of information about the local dining and cultural scenes.

74 Wendell Ave., Pittsfield, MA 01201. ✆ **888/499-6840** or 413/499-6840. Fax 413/499-6842. www. clapphouse.com. 8 units. $125–$295 double. Rates include breakfast. AE, DISC, MC, V. *In room:* A/C, TV, fridge, high-speed Internet (free), hair dryer.

WHERE TO DINE

Brix Wine Bar ★ BISTRO What a refreshing antidote to the largely forlorn Pittsfield dining landscape. The enthusiasm of the owners and staff for their 34-seat enterprise is infectious, the kind that brings patrons back again and again. Brix is named for the inventor of a device used to measure the sugar content of grapes, and wine, obviously, is a priority, with every effort made to instruct newbies and cosset sophisticates. An extraordinary 50 pressings are available by the glass, and flights of four wines cost only $10. The eats are tantalizing, geared to the smallest or largest of appetites, running from unusual sandwiches to plates of charcuterie, cheese, and savory tarts—simply keep ordering until sated. Don't miss the perfectly salted *frites*, fried in duck fat and served with a ramekin of garlic mayo.

40 West St. (opposite Crown Plaza Hotel). ✆ **413/236-9463.** www.brixwinebar.com. Main courses $12–$26. AE, MC, V. Tues–Thurs 5–10pm; Fri–Sat 5–10:30pm; Sun 10am–2pm and 5–10pm.

Jae's Spice ★ PAN-ASIAN Pittsfield can use the ministrations of more entrepreneurs, but the presence of the eponymous owner Jae is an encouraging sign. This is the latest of a string of similar enterprises originating in Boston. Do hope Jae succeeds here, so we can return for the exceptional scallion and seafood pancakes, the *mandoo* (fried meat dumplings), and the grilled squid stuffed with smoked salmon. The cranky reviews on some food websites to the contrary (who *are* those people?), this is a most pleasurable stop.

297 North St. (btw. Summer & Union sts.). ✆ **413/443-1234.** Main courses $17–$34. AE, MC, V. Daily 11:30am–2:30pm and 5:30–9pm (bar and kitchen open later).

Williamstown ★★

This community and its prestigious liberal-arts college were both named for Col. Ephraim Williams, who was killed in 1755 in one of the French and Indian Wars. He bequeathed the land for creation of a school and a town. Williams College grew, spreading east from the central common along both sides of Main Street (Rte. 2). Over Williamstown's long history, buildings have been erected in styles of the times, making Main Street a virtual museum of institutional architecture, with representatives of the Georgian, Federal, Gothic Revival, Romanesque, and Victorian styles (and a few yet to be labeled). Inserted into this diverting display is the '62 Center for Theatre and Dance, a thoroughly contemporary structure that opened in September 2005 (p. 361). It stands at dignified distances from the older buildings, so what might have been a tumultuous visual hodgepodge is instead a stately lesson in historical design. The impressive Sterling and Francine Clark Art Institute is the best reason to make a special trip, perhaps in conjunction with a performance at the ambitious Williamstown Theatre Festival.

WHAT TO SEE & DO

Sterling and Francine Clark Art Institute ★★★

Within these walls are canvases by Renoir (34 of them), Degas, Gauguin, Toulouse-Lautrec, Pissarro, and Corot, their predecessor. Look for Turner's splendid seascape, *Rockets and Blue Lights.* Also on display is the famed Degas sculpture *Little Dancer,* believed to be his only three-dimensional piece and a signature work of the Institute. In addition to these standouts, you'll find works by 15th- and 16th-century Dutch portraitists, European genre and landscape painters, and Americans Sargent and Homer, as well as fine porcelain, silver, and antiques. The Clarks were more disciplined in their acquisitions than most wealthy collectors, and their museum qualifies as one of the great cultural resources of the Berkshires and of the state.

Apart from the collection itself, the Clarks' farsighted endowment funded the modern wing added to the original neoclassical building and has covered all acquisitions, upkeep, and renovations. Their stipulation that there be no admission fee was finally breached, but the charge applies only to adults and only 5 months a year. A substantial bookstore in the lobby has been joined by a snack counter and an attractive cafe. An additional wing is under construction, and the separate Stone Hill Center, primarily an art conservation facility, makes room for two galleries for temporary exhibitions. The terrace offers fine views of the surrounding hills.

Discount ticket packages are available for admission to the Clark and MASS MoCA in North Adams (p. 362) or the Norman Rockwell Museum in Lenox (p. 345).

225 South St., Williamstown. ⓒ **413/458-2303.** www.clarkart.edu. Admission June–Oct $15 adults, free for students and children; free to all Nov–May. Tues–Sun 10am–5pm (daily July–Aug).

Williams College Museum of Art ★

The second leg of Williamstown's two prominent art repositories exists in large part thanks to the college's collection of almost 400 paintings by the American modernists Maurice and Charles Prendergast. The museum also has works by Gris, Léger, Whistler, Picasso, Warhol, and Hopper. Increasingly important among its holdings is its African collection, containing ceremonial vessels, dolls, masks, fetish figures, and agricultural implements, most of them from East Africa. The museum hosts frequent special exhibitions and lecture series.

15 Lawrence Hall Dr., Williamstown. ⓒ **413/597-2429.** www.wcma.org. Free admission. Tues–Sat (and some Mon holidays) 10am–5pm; Sun 1–5pm.

GETTING OUTSIDE

Mount Greylock State Reservation ★ contains the highest peak (3,491 ft.) in Massachusetts, as well as a section of the Appalachian Trail. A long, narrow, bumpy road allows cars almost to the summit, where the War Memorial Tower affords vistas of the Taconic and Hoosac ranges, far into Vermont and New York (parking $2). The ride down is very popular with mountain bikers. Trails radiate from the parking lot near the reservation's **Bascom Lodge** (✆ 413/743-1591; www.bascomlodge.net), a grandly rustic creation of the Civilian Conservation Corps in the New Deal 1930s. Simple dormitory beds and four private rooms accommodating a total of 32 guests are available for rent from mid-May to October, and family-style meals are available (reservations required for breakfast and dinner; no reservations needed for lunch). The lodge has stone fireplaces for lounging after a hike and an enclosed porch with expansive views of the mountain range.

SHOPPING

In the small downtown shopping district, **Library Antiques,** 70 Spring St. (✆ 413/458-3436; www.libraryantiques.com), is filled with a wealth of English chess sets, African carvings, Peruvian alpaca sweaters, Polish stoneware, and antique American fishing lures and creels. Slightly south of town on Rte. 7, **Collectors Warehouse,** 105 North St. (✆ 413/458-9686), has a little bit of everything—jewelry, books, dolls, furniture, and glassware. Farther south on Rte. 7, **Saddleback Antiques,** 1395 Cold Spring Rd. (✆ 413/458-5852), features country, wicker, and Victorian furniture.

WHERE TO STAY

This is a college town, so in addition to the usual peak periods of July, August, and the October foliage season, accommodations fill up during graduation and on football weekends. The largest lodging in town is the **Williams Inn,** 1090 Main St. (✆ 800/828-0133 or 413/458-9371; www.williamsinn.com). Despite the name, it is a standard motel, with a dining room, tavern, and indoor pool. Also consider accommodations in nearby North Adams (p. 362).

Field Farm Guesthouse After an extended vacation of B&B-hopping, there may come a time when one more tilted floor or wobbly Windsor chair will send even a devout inn-lover over the edge. Here's an antidote. This pristine example of postwar modern architecture rose in 1948 on a spectacular 296-acre estate with 4 miles of trails. Most guest rooms look over meadows to Mount Greylock. The Scandinavian Modern furniture was made to order for the house, and three guest rooms have decks while two have fireplaces. Don't expect TV or phones, but there is Wi-Fi. Breakfasts are hearty meals of waffles and five-cheese omelets making use of fruits, herbs, and vegetables grown on the property. The inn is open Thursday through Sunday only in the winter months.

554 Sloan Rd., Williamstown, MA 01267. ✆/fax **413/458-3135.** Fax 413-458-3144. www.thetrustees.org/field-farm. 5 units. $150–$295 double. Rates include breakfast. DISC, MC, V. Follow Rte. 7 to Rte. 43 and turn west, then make an immediate right on Sloan Rd. Continue 1 mile to the Field Farm entrance, on the right. Closed Mon–Wed Nov–Apr. **Amenities:** Heated outdoor pool; tennis court. *In room:* Hair dryer, Wi-Fi (free).

The Orchards ★★ A sedate choice just right for visiting Williams alumni and parents, the Orchards has an upscale country-club atmosphere; it's the sort of place where afternoon tea is an event. Each of its public and private rooms enjoys a mix of antique and reproduction English-style furniture. Even standard units are size-able, all with separate dressing cubicles, and those with working fireplaces have chaise longues and deeply padded chairs. Some have fridges with soft drinks; safes are hidden in places we can't divulge. There is live piano in the lounge on weekends.

222 Adams Rd., Williamstown, MA 01262. © **800/225-1517** or 413/458-9611. Fax 413/458-3273. www.orchardshotel.com. 49 units. $139–$209 double. AE, DC, DISC, MC, V. **Amenities:** Restaurant; bar; exercise room w/sauna and Jacuzzi; heated outdoor pool. *In room:* A/C, TV/VCR, hair dryer, MP3 docking station, Wi-Fi (free).

WHERE TO DINE

Mezze BISTRO   Meals here are entirely competent, if less than dazzling. The enthusiasm for small plates is addressed in the name and on the menu, with tapas-type starters like marcona almonds, duck rillette, house-cured olives, and pickled vegetables. Among the more ambitious dishes are sea scallops with cauliflower purée, hen-of-the-woods mushrooms with a truffle dressing, and braised rabbit joined with house-made pasta, leeks, and oyster mushrooms. Less esoteric choices are roast chicken with risotto, and grilled steak. The clientele seems to be composed primarily of professors, administrators, and students with visiting parents in tow.

16 Water St. © **413/458-0123.** www.mezzeinc.com. Main courses $13–$28. AE, DISC, MC, V. Sun–Thurs 5–9pm; Fri–Sat 5–10pm.

Spice Root ✦ INDIAN   Catch an irresistible whiff of this Indian eatery from several storefronts away, and thoughts of anything but food vanish. Students like it for the student-only $13 dinner special, and the a la carte menu is rewarding, with 11 starters, five breads, several curries, nine vegetarian dishes, tandoor specialties, and a half-dozen dishes from Bombay. Standouts are the curried salmon, chicken or lamb tikka masala, fiery shrimp vindaloo, and a veggie delight that involves bell peppers stuffed with mashed potatoes, paneer cheese, and spinach accompanied by yellow lentils. Breads are baked on-site, and the *nan* filled with cheese, nuts, and raisins is a particular treat.

23 Spring St. © **413/458-5200.** www.spiceroot.com. Main courses $10–$22. AE, DISC, MC, V. Tues–Sun 11:30am–2:30pm; daily 5–10pm.

WILLIAMSTOWN AFTER DARK

The Williams College Department of Music sponsors concerts and recitals. Call its **Concertline** (© 413/597-3146) for information on upcoming events. In addition, the **Clark Art Institute** (p. 359) hosts frequent classical-music events.

The '62 Center for Theatre and Dance ★★   Williamstown has long hosted one of the Berkshires' premier summer attractions, the **Williamstown Theatre Festival** (© 413/597-3400; www.wtfestival.org), and now it has a facility that provides a proper showcase. This ambitious center opened in the fall of 2005 (the year in its name is for the class that graduated in 1962), providing three performance venues as well as studios, classrooms, and rehearsal spaces. Dramatic productions, dance, music, and related cultural events, involving students, alumni, and professionals, are mounted all year. Staging classic and new plays during its season from late June to late August, the festival attracts many top actors and directors. The MainStage Theatre presents works by major playwrights, while the CenterStage often features more experimental productions. It's not too difficult to get tickets; even if a performance is said to be sold out, there are often cancellations in the

30 minutes before curtain. Tickets to the Festival itself range from about $20 to $55, while admission to other events is often free, and no more than $10. 1000 Main St. (P.O. Box 517). ✆ **413/597-2425.** www.williams.edu/go/62center.

North Adams

In the mid-1990s, it seemed impossible that this comatose mill town could recover. Its unemployment rate was the highest in the state, and over two-thirds of its storefronts were empty. A land developer once even suggested that the town be flooded to create lakefront property.

However, North Adams experienced a whiplash turnaround, and today many of those once-abandoned storefronts are taken up with restaurants, galleries, and high-tech start-ups. The unlikely reason, to almost everyone's agreement, is an art museum that opened in 1999. An abandoned industrial complex has been converted, despite early hoots of derision, into a center for the visual and performing arts. It is called the **Massachusetts Museum of Contemporary Art,** nicknamed MASS MoCA, and it has strikingly altered the socioeconomic dynamic of North Adams.

The first Sunday of October is **Fall Foliage Day** (www.fallfoliageparade.com), with a parade of fire engines, marching bands, and Clydesdales; and balloons, hot dogs, and cotton candy on sale at sidewalk stands.

WHAT TO SEE & DO

About 27 miles east of North Adams on Rte. 2 is Shelburne Falls, home of the **Bridge of Flowers** (p. 335). It's open April through late autumn and is a good place for a stroll if you're road-tripping or driving to the Pioneer Valley (p. 324).

Massachusetts Museum of Contemporary Art ★★ A lot of excitement and anticipation surrounded this ambitious project, the conversion of an empty 27-building textile factory into a center for the arts. Even before its official opening, it had a nickname—MASS MoCA—and hosted performances by David Byrne, Patti Smith, and the Merce Cunningham Dance Company. Works on display are often outsized, crossing traditional aesthetic boundaries to marry elements of both performing and visual arts. Its chief virtue—from the standpoint of those contemporary artists who choose to work on a grand scale—is the vastness of the spaces available. The museum has also hosted a variety of musical events, experimental films, even dance parties, and is attracting small tenant companies working the vineyards of technology, including software, video, and e-commerce. MASS MoCA has attracted hundreds of thousands of visitors and is certainly worth the short detour east from neighboring Williamstown.

The snacky **Lickety Split** (✆ **413/663-3372**) occupies a space on the ground floor of the museum, serving coffee, ice cream, and light fare.

87 Marshall St. ✆ **413/662-2111.** www.massmoca.org. Admission $15 adults, $10 students, $5 children 6–16, free children 5 and under. Wed–Mon 11am–5pm.

WHERE TO STAY

The Porches ★★ "Retro-rural chic" might describe this row of six detached 19th-century workingmen's houses stitched together by an uninterrupted streetside veranda, the spaces in between roofed over and fitted with indoor catwalks and patios. Rooms are witty tributes to the past, with kitschy lamps and paint-by-numbers pictures on the walls, but are also equipped with DVD players and Wi-Fi.

A computer is provided for guests' use, and laptop rentals are available. Down duvets, bathrobes, and cushy sofas make things even cozier. Ask for one of the second-floor king rooms with balcony. Coffee, croissant, and a newspaper in a rocking chair on the porch on a warm autumn morning is a singular pleasure. Evening cocktails are available, too.

231 River St., North Adams, MA 01247. ℂ **413/664-0400.** Fax 413/664-0401. www.porches.com. 47 units. Mid-May to early Nov $180–$335 double; mid-Nov to early May $130–$195 double. Rates include breakfast. 2-night minimum stay Fri–Sat May–Nov and holidays. AE, DC, MC, V. Located behind the MASS MoCA complex, ½ block west of Marshall St. Pets accepted ($50/night). **Amenities:** Exercise room; Jacuzzi; year-round heated outdoor pool; sauna. *In room:* A/C, TV/DVD, hair dryer, minibar, Wi-Fi (free).

WHERE TO DINE

Gramercy Bistro ★ NEW AMERICAN   This quiet bistro rules the North Adams culinary roost. On the menu, organic and local meet creative and global. Sea scallops with potato hash and roasted poblano sauce. Sweetbreads with caper sauce, mushrooms, and carmelized cauliflower. Thai mussels bathed in a spicy red curry broth. Much of it works, although some amount to good impulses that fall short. Fair prices compensate for the overall lack of wonder. It all takes place in a fairly small space with vintage photos of city scenes.

24 Marshall St. ℂ **413/663-5300.** www.gramercybistro.com. Main courses $18–$26. Mon, Wed–Thurs 5–9pm; Fri–Sat 5pm–10pm; Sun 10am–1pm and 5–9pm.

Jack's Hot Dog Stand 🏷 DINER   What a hoot is Jack's! There's its history—on this site, a narrow street in downtown North Adams, since 1917, still operated by the grandson of the founder. There is the crush—12 stools at the counter with room for a single file of eager eaters against the wall, sitters and standees politely making room for families and old people. And there is the frenzy—counter people shouting orders and making jokes: "Got two here! What's waitin'? Three cheese!" Patrons are avidly loyal: One driver of an 18-wheeler parked outside to run in for his takeout, stacking traffic down the block, and no one honked—they just understood. Of course, Jack's also hosts hot dog-eating contests. A recent winner ate 88 in an hour. Two dogs, two burgers, two fries, and two Cokes cost $9.80. Take that, Golden Arches.

12 Eagle St. (near Main St.). ℂ **413/664-9006.** www.jackshotdogstand.com. All items under $3. No credit cards. Mon–Fri 10am–7pm; Sat 10am–4pm.

CONNECTICUT

by Herbert Bailey Livesey, Leslie Brokaw & Matthew Barber

Connecticut resists generalization. It doesn't rank at the top or bottom of any important chart of virtues or liabilities. It boasts no dramatic geographical feature. It's the nation's third-smallest state—only 90 miles wide and 55 miles top to bottom—and while parts of it are clogged with humanity, some corners are as undeveloped as inland Maine.

10

Established in 1635 by disgruntled English settlers who didn't like the way things were going at Plymouth Colony, Connecticut has long seemed spiritually divorced from the rest of New England—a place to be traversed when traveling between New York and Boston. But a closer look reveals an abundance of reasons to slow down and linger.

To a great extent, Connecticut's personality derives from the presence of water. In addition to having Long Island Sound along its entire southern coast, its hills and coastal plain are sliced through by significant rivers and their tributaries: the Housatonic, Naugatuck, Quinnipiac, Connecticut, and Thames. These waterways provided power for mills and the towns that grew around them.

While many of these industrial localities are only shells of their prosperous 19th-century selves, Connecticut has preserved scores of classic Colonial villages, from the Litchfield Hills in the northwest to the Mystic coast in the opposite corner to the wildly scenic towns of the Connecticut River Valley in between. These areas are as placid and timeless as they have been since the 1700s—while, at the same time, as polished and sophisticated as transplanted urbanites can make them. A salty maritime heritage is palpable in the old boat-building and fishing villages at the mouths of its rivers, especially those east of New Haven.

Connecticut is New England's front porch. Pull up a chair and stay awhile.

THE GOLD COAST: FAIRFIELD COUNTY

Stamford: 40 miles NE of New York City; Norwalk: 50 miles NE of New York City; Westport: 53 miles NE of New York City; Ridgefield: 61 miles NE of New York City

Mansions, marinas, and luxury apartment blocks nudge up against each other along the deeply indented Long Island Sound shoreline in the

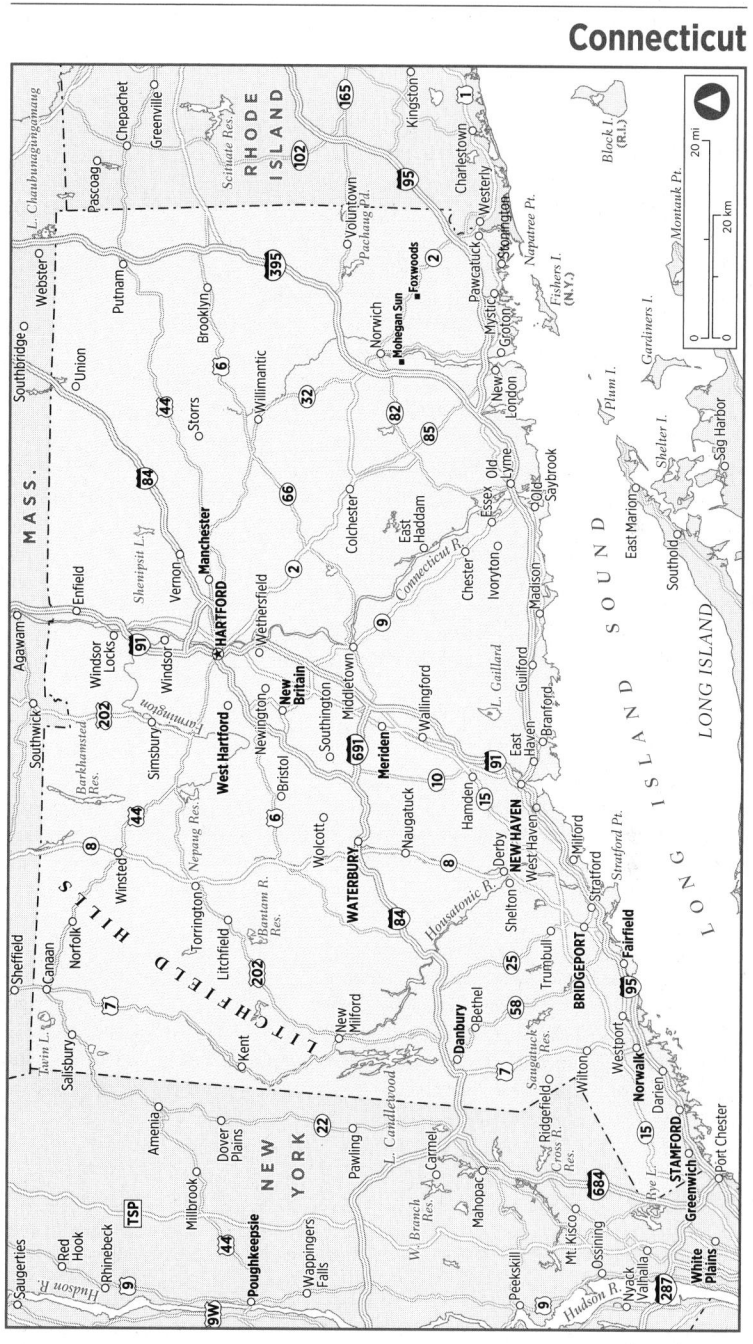

southwestern corner of the state. This is one of the most heavily developed stretches of the coast and, in terms of family income, one of the wealthiest. Coastal Fairfield County has long been known as the "Gold Coast," especially to real estate agents. As the land rises slowly inland from the water's edge, woods thicken, roads narrow, and pockets of New England unfold. Yacht country becomes horse country.

The first suburbs began to form in the middle of the last century, when train rails started radiating north and east from New York's Grand Central Terminal into the countryside. This part of the state was made accessible for summertime refugees from the big city, and eventually weekend houses became permanent dwellings. Corporate executives liked the life of the gentry, so after World War II, they started moving their companies closer to their new homes. Stamford became a city; Greenwich, New Canaan, Darien, and Westport were the bedroom communities of choice—pricey, haughty, and redolent of the good life. (Of course, Fairfield County also contains Bridgeport, a depressed city that once considered filing for bankruptcy and has a penchant for political scandal.)

But for visitors, the fashionable "exurbs" (beyond suburban) and their beaches, restaurants, and upscale shops are the draw, along with the villages farther north, especially Ridgefield, that hint of Vermont, all within 1½ hours of Times Square.

Essentials

GETTING THERE   From New York and points south, take I-95 or, preferably, the Hutchinson and Merritt parkways. From eastern Massachusetts and northern Connecticut, take I-84 south to Danbury, then Rte. 7 south into Fairfield County.

The **Metro North** (© **800/METRO-INFO** [638-7646] or 212/532-4900; www.mta.nyc.ny.us/mnr) commuter line has many trains daily from New York's Grand Central Terminal, with stops at Greenwich, Stamford, Darien, Norwalk, Westport, and additional stations all the way to New Haven. Express trains make the trip in 45 to 65 minutes.

VISITOR INFORMATION   Information on the northern part of the county is available at www.litchfieldhills.com, while the **Coastal Fairfield County Convention and Visitor Bureau** (© **800/866-7925;** www.coastalCT.com) can provide materials on the coastal towns.

Stamford

A trickle of corporations started moving their headquarters from New York 38 miles northeast to Stamford in the 1960s. That flow became a stream by the 1980s, and today more than a dozen Fortune 500 companies, including General Electric and Xerox, direct their operations from here. They have erected shiny midrise towers that give the city of 117,000 residents an appearance more like the new urban centers of the Sun Belt than those of the Snow Belt.

One result is a lively downtown that other, less prosperous, Connecticut cities surely envy. Roughly contained by Greylock Place, Tresser Boulevard, and Atlantic and Main streets, it has two theaters, tree-lined streets with many shops and a large mall, pocket parks and plazas, and a number of stylish restaurants, sidewalk cafes, and clubs patronized by the city's large cohort of young single professionals.

For further information, check **www.coastalCT.com**.

WHAT TO SEE & DO

Stamford Museum & Nature Center ★ ☺   About 5 miles north of the city center is this fine family-oriented resource. The center has a large lake, an open pen with a pair of frolicking river otters, and a 10-acre working farm with goats, sheep, cattle, peacocks, and a maple sugaring house. May and June mark the arrival of newborn chicks, kids, calves, and lambs. On the grounds are a country store, nature trails, a small planetarium, and an oddball Tudor-Gothic house with galleries of art, natural history, and Indian lore.

39 Scofield Town Rd. (at High Ridge Rd.). © **203/322-1646.** www.stamfordmuseum.org. Admission $8 adults, $6 seniors and students 18 and over, $4 children 4–17. Bendel Mansion & Galleries Mon-Sat and holidays 9am–5pm, Sun 11am–5pm; Heckscher Farm daily 9am–5pm (until 4pm Nov–Mar). Feeding time is 9am. The center is 1 mile north of exit 35 off the Merritt Pkwy. (Rte. 15).

SHOPPING

United House Wrecking, 535 Hope St. (© **203/348-5371;** www.unitedhouse wrecking.com), is a find for dedicated antiques hounds, who will want to make time for this sprawling emporium of oddments. The name may not sound promising, but the company got its start selling architectural remnants salvaged from building demolitions. For years, it featured such items as 1930s gas pumps, stone pigs, and pagodas. Now it showcases far less bizarre imported antiques and reproductions in over 36,000 square feet of display space. It's open Monday through Saturday from 9:30am to 5:30pm, Sunday from noon to 5pm. It's also tough to find. From exit 9 of I-95, pick up Rte. 1, then Rte. 106 north; make a left on Glenbrook Road, which becomes Church Street, and turn right on Hope Street. Be sure you have a map or detailed directions.

WHERE TO STAY

Courtyard by Marriott ★★   Pushing its customary midlevel template upward, this perky young entry adds a touch of plush to the standards of its chain. Apart from its central downtown location, it adds value by housing one of the best restaurants in town, **Napa & Co.** (see "Where to Dine," below). That's rare for a Courtyard, which usually offers only breakfast and vending machines. Some suites have Jacuzzi tubs and/or terraces. The hotel is smoke-free.

275 Summer St. (at Broad St.), Stamford, CT 06901. © **800/321-2211** or 203/358-8822. Fax 203/358-8811. www.marriott.com. 115 units. $209–$224 double. Packages available. AE, DC, DISC, MC, V. Valet parking $18; self-parking $12. **Amenities:** Restaurant; lounge; room service. *In room:* A/C, TV, hair dryer, Wi-Fi (free).

Stamford Marriott ★★   A couple of significant steps above its sibling Courtyard by Marriott (above), this upper-crust chain entry piles on the extras. Most notable is the Agora day spa, with six treatment rooms for facials, body wraps, and waxing, among other services. Steam rooms and 13-head full-body showers are additional attractions. What's more, the hotel has an indoor golf training center with its own staff pro. There is a concierge floor, with lounge. The hotel is smoke-free.

243 Tresser Blvd. (exit 7, I-95), Stamford, CT 06901. © **800/732-9689** or 203/357-9555. Fax 203/324-6897. www.marriottstamford.com. 506 units. $189–$279 double. AE, DC, DISC, MC, V. Valet parking $18; self-parking $12. **Amenities:** 2 restaurants; lounge; concierge; exercise room; heated indoor/outdoor pool; room service; spa. *In room:* A/C, TV, hair dryer, Wi-Fi ($10/day).

WHERE TO DINE

Dragonfly Lounge CONTEMPORARY INTERNATIONAL   More a bar than a restaurant, that doesn't mean some good eats can't be had at this popular gathering place. It looks like a baronial *bierstube,* thanks to faux rough-hewn beams and the leaded panes of neo-Gothic windows. Because booze-fueled mingling is the prevailing activity, food is admittedly ancillary. Still, the small plates card ($8–$16) offers such possibilities as General Tso's Calamari, Wagyu carpaccio, and lobster nachos, dishes that are nearly always satisfying, tasty, and not uncommonly pricey. Satays and grilled pizzas are additional bar offerings. Patrons intent on actual meals can order from the "coursed dining" page, which include entrees along the lines of gin-marinated boar chop, roasted Artic char, and bleu cheese and squash ravioli. Come for live jazz Thursday through Saturday.

488 Summer St. (at Spring St.). ℰ **203/357-9800.** www.dragonf1yloungect.com. Main courses $20–$36. AE, MC, V. Tues–Thurs 5pm–midnight (Fri–Sat until 1am).

Coromandel ★ INDIAN   This restaurant is part of a chainlet of Indian winners striving to make diners aware that Indian eaters don't have to be harshly illuminated, feebly decorated dives with sullen waiters. Here are white tablecloths and lustrous woods as setting for food that tantalizes all the senses before a fork even touches it. Standouts are *dahi dhani jhinga* (prawns cooked with yogurt and coriander) and *mamsam koora* (lamb in a chili-fired gravy), and just about anything from the tandoor oven. Brunch/lunch buffets are a good deal ($11 weekdays, $14 weekends) and don't seem to be comprised entirely of yesterday's leftovers, too often the rule at lesser competitors.

68 Broad St. (at Summer St.). ℰ **203/964-1010.** www.coromandelcuisine.com. Main courses $15–$26. MC, V. Mon–Fri noon–2:30pm and 5–10pm (until 11pm Fri); Sat noon–3pm and 5–11pm; Sun noon–9pm.

Layla's Falafel ◢ MIDDLE EASTERN   Along gaudy, traffic-frantic Rte. 137, this looks like just another strip-mall-ethnic joint. Walking through the door, the handful of tables, plastic laminate, and bad paintings of Arabian street scenes do little to alter the original impression. But the welcome is cordial, especially for the regulars who pile in after work for takeout. Choose from an enticing menu to put together bountiful one-plate meals. One such is the Arabic lamb *shawarma,* the central ingredient rolled in flatbread and briefly grilled, then joined with a tossed green salad and a thick puddle of perfect hummus (a chick-pea dip/spread, for the uninitiated). Another is the special deal of five falafel balls in a wrap with hummus and fries for only $9.

936 High Ridge Rd. (Rte. 137). ℰ **203/461-8004.** www.laylasfalafel.com. Most items under $10. MC, V. Daily 11am–9:30pm.

Napa & Co. ★ NEW AMERICAN   Multiple props are lavished on this, the city's most honored restaurant, especially by the activists of the locavore-sustainable-organic-farm-to-table crowd. What it has done is simplify its recipes, cutting back from those towering stacks of baroque ingredients and presentations one dares not disturb. It also hasn't pretended that every component on every plate was raised in the garden out back. Realism prevails. The appetizer charcuterie board contains four meats, none of them likely produced within 500 miles. Cheese is showcased, and some of them *are* from the region. Wines are featured, stacked high on two walls of the 20-foot main room. The efficient staff is not given to extraneous chatter with diners.

75 Broad St. (at Summer St., in the Courtyard Marriott). ℰ **203/353-3319.** www.napaandcompany. com. Main courses $16–$34. AE, DC, DISC, MC, V. Mon–Fri 6:30–10am, 11:30am–3pm, and 5:30–10pm; Sat–Sun 7:30–10:30am; Sat 5:30–10pm.

Smokey Joe's BARBECUE   Smack on the Stamford–Darien line, this wouldn't pass a Fort Worth authenticity test, but it's close enough. Upstairs is a down-and-dirty bar with pool table; downstairs, a classic barbecue joint. Stand in the cafeteria line and select from confusing lists of ribs, brisket, pulled pork, sausage, and birds, supplemented with some Tex-Mex specialties. Then retire to the unadorned dining room to gorge.

1308 E. Main St. (Rte. 1). *(C)* **203/406-0605.** www.smokeyjoesribs.com. Main courses $11–$28. AE, MC, V. Mon–Thurs 11:30am–9:30pm; Fri–Sat 11:30am–10:30pm; Sun 11:30am–9pm; bar daily until 1:30am.

STAMFORD AFTER DARK

The **Stamford Center for the Arts,** Atlantic Street and Tresser Boulevard (*(C)* **203/325-4466;** www.stamfordcenterforthearts.org), has three venues. The **Rich Forum** is the best known, presenting professional productions, with boldface name actors, of successful Broadway and off-Broadway plays as well as musical and dance presentations. The **Palace Theatre,** 61 Atlantic St., offers musicals; rotating appearances by the Stamford Symphony Orchestra, the Connecticut Grand Opera and Orchestra, and the Connecticut Ballet; and one-night stands by solo acts and such traveling troops as B. B. King, Dave Barry, and the Alvin Ailey Dance Theater. Smaller, often experimental plays and related performances are given in the **Leonhardt Studio** at Rich Forum.

Norwalk

Given the despair that pervades many New England cities, the continuing betterment of this city's once notorious South Norwalk neighborhood gladdens the heart. The rehabilitation of several blocks of 19th-century row houses is transforming the waterfront into a trendy precinct that has come to be called, inevitably, "SoNo." The **Norwalk Seaport Oyster Festival** (*(C)* **203/838-9444;** www.seaport.org), held in early September, attracts over 50,000 visitors to its tall ships, oyster boats, crafts show, and food booths. There are even skydivers.

Bounded roughly by Washington, Water, and North and South Main streets, SoNo is readily accessible from the South Norwalk railroad station.

WHAT TO SEE & DO

Lockwood-Mathews Mansion Museum   Erected in 1864, this granite mansion in the Second Empire style is covered with peaked and mansard slate roofs, and has 62 rooms arranged around a stunning sky-lit octagonal rotunda. Marble, gilt, marquetry, and frescoes were commissioned and incorporated with abandon. Visits are by guided tour. The mansion has been designated a National Historic Landmark.

295 West Ave. *(C)* **203/838-9799.** www.lockwoodmathewsmansion.org. Admission $10 adults, $8 seniors and students, $6 ages 8–18, free for children 7 and under. Wed–Sun noon–4pm. From I-95 southbound, take exit 15; from I-95 northbound, take exit 14.

The Maritime Aquarium at Norwalk ★★   This facility remains the centerpiece of revitalized SoNo. The present name isn't inclusive, as part of the complex incorporates a section of boat-builders at work as well as exhibits of model ships and full-size vessels, including the *Tango,* which was *pedaled* across the Atlantic. While they don't call it a thrill ride, a submarine simulator takes 18 passengers at a time down to the ocean depths, shaking and shuddering all the way; the climax is a battle between a whale and a giant squid. The main attractions, though, are the marine creatures and mammals on view. Five harbor seals are fed at 11:45am, 1:45, and 3:45pm, when they wriggle up on the rocks and even rest their heads in their handler's lap. Additional exhibits include a pair of river otters, an open petting pool of three species of rays, and tanks alive with swimmers and other creatures, including sea turtles and sharks. Although the exhibits mostly focus on the waters of Long Island Sound, some cover Africa and the tropics, as well. A giant six-story IMAX screen shows nature films that aren't necessarily confined to the seven seas.

10 N. Water St. (℃ **203/852-0700.** www.maritimeaquarium.org. Admission (aquarium only) $11 adults, $10 seniors, $9 children ages 2–12; IMAX $9 adults, $8 seniors, $6.50 children; combination packages (aquarium plus IMAX movie) $17 adults, $15 seniors, $13 children. July–Aug daily 10am–6pm; Sept–June daily 10am–5pm.

CRUISES

Excursions by 49-passenger ferry to **Sheffield Island** and its historic 1868 lighthouse are offered by the **Norwalk Seaport Association,** 132 Water St. (℃ **203/838-9444;** www.seaport.org). The boat departs from Hope Dock, near the Maritime Aquarium. Weather permitting, the boat sets out two to three times daily, on Saturday and Sunday from Memorial Day weekend to late September as well as Monday through Friday from late June to late September. The round-trip takes about 2½ hours, with a 15-minute layover on the island. Fares are $20 for adults, $18 for seniors (Mon–Wed), $12 for ages 4 to 12, and $5 for ages 3 and under. Thursday evenings from 6 to 9:30pm in season bring clambakes to the island. Other outings include sunset cruises, occasional Sunday picnics, and Thursday night dinner cruises in summer. Always call ahead for schedules.

Similarly, the research vessel *Oceanic* has "creature cruises" on weekends from September to April as well as daily in July and August to spot seals and bird life, as well as marine study cruises at other times, a service of the Maritime Aquarium. Fares are $21 per person. Reserve ahead by calling ℃ **203/852-0700,** ext. 2206.

SHOPPING

Serious shoppers have several choices, primarily among the boutiques and galleries along Washington and Main streets. **Cow's Outside,** 81 Washington St. (**203/866-2668**), specializes in custom-made leather goods, including jackets, cowboy boots, shoes, hats, and handbags; it's closed Monday and Tuesday. Nearby is **A Taste of Holland,** 83 Washington St. (℃ **203/838-6161;** www.kaasnco.com), run by Dutch expatriates, which features all manner of goods from their homeland, including ceramics, herring, cheese, wooden shoes, candies, and Dutch girl dolls. **And Company, Inc.,** 127 Washington St. (℃ **203/831-8855**), offers bedding, bath products, furniture, lamps, tabletop fashions, and personal care items. Its success spawned additional stores across the street, at #104 and #108, which sell stylish clothing for men and women.

WHERE TO DINE

For a break from shopping and strolling, drop into **SoNo Caffeine,** 133 Washington St. (℃ **203/857-4224;** www.sonocaffeine.com), which sells wraps and panini, offers live jazz and pop some nights—check their website for schedules—and sticks a price tag on virtually every piece of furniture in the place.

Barcelona ★ MEDITERRANEAN   Tapas are the featured attraction here, one of five such outposts in western Connecticut. The kitchen isn't doctrinaire about recipes, which range all over the Mediterranean and even down to South America for inspiration. Two or three tapas per person make a meal, and sharing is inevitable. Start, perhaps, with *charcuteria,* either an assortment of Spanish cheeses, which changes daily, or of cured meats and sausages, usually including nutty Serrano ham. The day's additional delectables might be *chorizo* with sweet and sour figs, garlic shrimp, or *piquillo* peppers (a type of chili pepper) stuffed with potato-cod *brandade* (puree of potato, salt cod, olive oil, and milk). Paella and *parrillada* (mixed grill) "for the table" are main course options. The enclosed patio is open year-round.

63-65 N. Main St. (north of Washington St.). ℂ **203/899-0088.** www.barcelonawinebar.com. Reservations recommended on Fri-Sat. Tapas $3.50-$14; main courses $20-$27. AE, DC, DISC, MC, V. Daily 5pm-1am (Fri-Sat until 2am).

Kazu JAPANESE   The bountiful bento box displayed near the entrance mesmerizes diners awaiting seats. It typically contains a crispy shrimp and calamari salad, salmon skin roll, two vegetable dumplings, a tofu salad, and a chicken *katsu* pizza. At lunch, it's easily enough for two. And given the indifferent decor of plastic room dividers and skimpy representations of irises and lotus blossoms, it's a good thing the focus is on the food to come. Three or four chefs operate at the sushi bar in back, employing truly fresh fish to turn out dumplings and rolls both traditional and cross-cultural in character. In the latter category are jalapeño shrimp with *ponzu* sauce and the duck spring roll with celery, shiitake, sweet pepper, and mango sauce. Odd or conventional, most items work to happy satisfaction.

64 North Main St. (near West Ave.). ℂ **203/866-7492.** www.kazuono.com. Reservations recommended at dinner. Main courses $16-$24. AE, DC, MC, V. Mon-Fri noon-10pm (Fri until 11pm); Sat 5:30-11pm; Sun 5-9:30pm.

Match ★★ NEW AMERICAN   You know a restaurant is hot when the patrons are as young and good-looking as the staff. Match makes every "Best Of" list in the state, and those tributes are justified. Don't expect elegance: Most of the walls are bare brick, the ceiling is exposed wood joists, and industrial lamps provide most of the lighting. There is the expected martini menu, including pineapple and white chocolate versions for those who don't like the taste of alcohol. Five different kinds of designer pizza emerge from the brick oven at the back, delivered to the counter that surrounds it. As much eating as drinking goes on at the steel-topped main bar, with happy diners making the most of such *mmm*-inducing edibles as truffled fried oysters, and "8-hour" veal osso bucco with risotto, fried sage, and scallions.

98 Washington St. (btw. Broad and Main sts). ℂ **203/852-1088.** www.matchsono.com. Reservations strongly recommended on Fri-Sat. Main courses $22-$38. AE, DC, MC, V. Daily 5-10pm (Fri-Sat until 11pm).

SOUTH NORWALK AFTER DARK

Several of SoNo's restaurants offer musical entertainment on unpredictable schedules. **SoNo Caffeine,** mentioned above, has presented folkies, Brazilian bands, and pop singer-songwriters. Taking up the space of three storefronts, the **Black Bear Saloon,** 80 Washington St. (ℂ **203/299-0711;** www.blackbearsono.com), delves into karaoke and brings on cover bands of various enthusiasms; it's open every day from lunch through late evening. **Rain SoNo,** 112 Washington St. (ℂ **203/866-0800;** www.rainsono.com), is a two-level lounge and dance club with DJs on Thursday and Friday nights, live bands on Saturday. It attempts to reproduce the club vibe of larger cities, with men in jeans and polo shirts and women who make no effort to disguise their gender. Bottle service and "unique martinis" fuel the merriment.

Westport

After World War II, the housing crunch had young couples scouring the metropolitan area for affordable housing along the three main routes of what is now known as the Metro North transit system. Some of them wound up in this pretty village beside the Saugatuck River, a couple of miles inland from Long Island Sound (47 miles northeast of New York City, 29 miles southwest of New Haven). Most of the new commuter class found Westport to be too far away from Manhattan (1–1½ hr. each way on the train), and it was deemed the archetype of the far-out bedroom communities that were dubbed the exurbs.

Notable for its large contingent of people in the creative crafts, primarily commercial artists, advertising copywriters, art directors, and their fellows, the town also appealed to CEOs and higher-level executives, many of whom solved their commuting problem by moving their offices to nearby Stamford. (The food company Newman's Own, founded by the late actor Paul Newman, is based here, too.) The result is a bustling community with surviving elements of its rural New England past wrapped in a sheen of Big Apple panache.

For more information, check out **www.coastalCT.com.**

GETTING OUTSIDE

Sherwood Island State Park, Green Farms (© **203/566-2305;** www.ct.gov), was the state's first park. It has two long swimming beaches separated by a grove of trees sheltering dozens of picnic tables with grills. Surf fishing is a possibility from designated areas, and the park has concession stands, restrooms, and a new nature center. The park is open from Memorial Day to Labor Day, daily from 8am to sunset. Pets are not allowed. By car, take exit 18 off I-95 or U.S. 1, following the road called the Sherwood Island Connector. Admission for out-of-state cars from Memorial Day to September is $10 Monday through Friday, $15 Saturday and Sunday.

You can get to Sherwood Island by taking a train to Westport and a taxi from the station to the park. If you don't have a car, you might also prefer to use that method to get to **Compo Beach,** the long municipal strand not far from downtown.

West of the town center is **Earthplace** (formerly called the Nature Center for Environmental Activities), 10 Woodside Lane (© **203/227-7253;** www.earthplace. org). Its 62 acres offer walking trails, a wildlife rehab center, and a building with live animals and an aquarium. The center is open Monday through Saturday from 9am to 5pm, Sunday from 1 to 4pm; the grounds are open daily from 7am to dusk. Admission is $7 adults, $5 for children 12 and under.

Rent a sailboat or kayak or arrange a lesson at the **Longshore Sailing School,** Longshore Club Park, 260 S. Compo Rd. (© **203/226-4646;** www.longshore sailingschool.com), about 2 miles south of Boston Post Road (U.S. 1). Rentals are $18 to $60 per hour; small boat private lessons are $65 per hour.

WHERE TO STAY

The Westport Inn The angled, ochre-colored building housing this motor hotel has been on the scene since 1935 and provides numerous facilities and services, including an indoor pool and Laundromat. Ask for a room in the new building, and to celebrate a romantic occasion, request a room with red satin sheets scattered with rose petals at turndown. **Conte's** (© **203/254-6050**) is the in-house restaurant, presenting an Italian seafood menu. It's open for dinner only, Monday through

Saturday, with live entertainment every Friday. Guests have access to the town beach and a nearby golf course. The inn is located well east of the town center.

1595 Post Rd. E. (Rte. 1), Westport, CT 06880. (©) **203/259-5236.** Fax 203/254-8439. www.westport inn.com. 116 units. $129–$209 double. Rates include breakfast. AE, DC, DISC, MC, V. Pets accepted ($10/ night). The inn is 3 ½ miles east of Main St. and the Saugatuck River, on Rte. 1. **Amenities:** Restaurant; bar; bikes; small exercise room; heated indoor pool; sauna. *In room:* A/C, TV, hair dryer, MP3 docking station, Wi-Fi (free).

WHERE TO DINE

Acqua ★ MEDITERRANEAN/SEAFOOD A light touch does wonders with such immaculately fresh ingredients as striped bass, halibut, crab, skate, and clams. Presentations are inviting, yet without the appearance of excessive pushing and prodding in the kitchen. The decor consists of murals depicting cherubim, aged-looking tiles, and a bar facing the wood-burning oven, used to bake good designer pizzas and a customer favorite, roasted chicken. Among other possibilities are the juicy veal chop with polenta and a port wine reduction sauce, and pan-roasted *branzino* (European sea bass) with cardamom-scented broth. An express lunch in the street-level bar costs only $14, and the midday menu upstairs is far less expensive than dinner.

43 Main St. (near east end of Saugatuck Bridge). (©) **203/222-8899.** www.acquaofwestport.com. Reservations recommended on Fri-Sat. Main courses $17–$38. AE, DC, MC, V. Mon-Thurs noon-2:30pm and 5:30-9:30pm; Fri-Sat noon-2:30pm and 5:30-10:30pm.

Blue Lemon ★ NEW AMERICAN This unassuming little bistro isn't the sort of place you just stumble into. It's tucked into the corner of a U-shaped shopping square off the main downtown street. Inside, it is decidedly compact (but hardly the squeeze some quibblers insist). Bright colors and snowy tablecloths banish any gloom the space might otherwise have produced. We aren't talking trendy here, and customers are largely on the far side of 40, well-coiffed representatives of Westport gentry. Sophisticated, they are, and they appreciate food in good proportion, prepared with precision by the young chef-owner. Consider the true Dover sole, featured on Monday nights, and such inviting fabrications as shrimp and lemongrass risotto or fettuccine with braised duck, andouille sausage, white beans, and leeks.

7 Sconset Sq. (©) **203/226-2647.** www.bluelemonrestaurant.com. Reservations recommended on Fri-Sat. Main courses $18–$34. AE, MC, V. Mon-Sat 12-3:30pm and 5:30-9pm (Fri-Sat until 10:30pm); Sun 5-9pm.

Tavern on Main ★ BISTRO Westporters don't come in too many different ages, sizes, or colors, but most of them mount the Tavern's front steps with regularity. Local merchants, women who lunch, and busy executives all crowd into the clubby bar to wait for a table. The main room has fragments of the building's earliest 19th-century years—hand-hewn beams and a brick fireplace. While menu items are neither over-the-top nor overly daring, the kitchen does toy with convention. For example, the trademark lobster roll consists of warm (not cool) buttery chunks and shreds of the crustacean filling the cavity of a hollowed-out, seeded roll. Similar twists are taken with seared halibut with butternut squash risotto and sesame-crusted wasabi ahi tuna over a toss of soba noodles, red peppers, shiitake, and ponzu sauce.

146 Main St. (©) **203/221-7222.** www.tavernonmain.com. Reservations recommended. Main courses $24–$34. AE, DC, MC, V. Daily 11:30am-10pm (Fri-Sat until 11pm).

WESTPORT AFTER DARK

One of the oldest theaters on the straw-hat circuit, the **Westport Country Playhouse,** 25 Powers Court (© **203/227-4177;** www.westportplayhouse.com), had its first performance in 1931. Revitalized some years ago under the leadership of Artistic Director Joanne Woodward and other new administrators, the theater produces a full schedule of comedies, dramas, and musicals from mid-April to late September, with performances Monday through Saturday evenings and Wednesday and Saturday matinees. Single-night or short-term events take place through the winter season, as well. Famous or at least vaguely familiar actors appear in almost every production. A music series brings in acts such as Arlo Guthrie, the Preservation Hall Jazz Band, and doo-wop groups. Tickets are priced from about $15 to $48.

Ridgefield

No town in Connecticut has a grander, more imposing main street. Ridgefield's is 132 feet wide, lined with ancient elms, maples, and oaks, and bordered by massive 19th-century houses, most of them in Classical Revival and late Victorian styles. Impressive at any time of the year, the thoroughfare is in its glory during the brief blaze of the October foliage season. Only a little over an hour from New York City (58 miles northeast), the town (pop. 24,000) is nonetheless a true evocation of the New England character. The bustling shopping district has few franchise outlets.

WHAT TO SEE & DO

Aldrich Contemporary Art Museum ★★★ Larry Aldrich was a fashion designer who used his superb collection of paintings and sculptures from the second half of the 20th century to establish this museum. The original 18th-century clapboard structure in which he housed his collection soon doubled in size. But when Aldrich died in 2001, the museum took a sharp turn in another direction. It was decided that the space would become devoted exclusively to "emerging and midcareer artists" and to work no more than 5 years old. To that end, the original collection was almost completely sold off and the museum was closed for the construction of yet another building. The angular copper-roofed new structure opened in 2004. Set back from the road, it contains 12 galleries on two floors, a screening room, and performance spaces. It is a singular contribution to the cultural life of western Connecticut.

258 Main St. (near the intersection of rtes. 35 and 33 at the south end of Main St.). © **203/438-4519.** www.aldrichart.org. Admission $7 adults, $4 seniors and students, free for K-12 teachers and youths 17 and under; Tues free to all. Tues–Sun noon–5pm.

Keeler Tavern This 1713 stagecoach inn was providing sustenance to travelers between Boston and New York long before the Revolutionary War, but that conflict provided it with its object of greatest note. A British cannonball is embedded in one of its walls, presumably fired during the Battle of Ridgefield in 1777. The tavern is now a museum of Colonial life, with period furnishings and costumed guides, and listed in the National Register of Historic Places. And it has another claim to fame: It was long the summer home of architect Cass Gilbert (1849–1934), who designed the Supreme Court Building in Washington, D.C., and was a key figure in the construction of the George Washington Bridge in New York. Visits are by guided tour.

132 Main St. © **203/431-0815.** www.keelertavernmuseum.org. Admission $5 adults, $3 seniors and students, $2 children 11 and under. Feb–Dec Wed and Sat–Sun 1–4pm.

WHERE TO STAY

West Lane Inn ★★   An inn that fits most images of a romantic country getaway, this one also works for businesspeople, as it offers Internet access, voice mail, and express checkout. The two rooms with kitchenettes are ideal for longer stays. A couple of rooms have fireplaces, and all have four-poster beds. The 1849 house stands on a property blessed with giant shade trees. Take breakfast on the porch in good weather; the continental version is included, but hot a la carte dishes are extra. Snacks are available until 9pm. Bernard's (below), just across the driveway, serves lunch and dinner. The inn is smoke-free.

22 West Lane (off Rte. 35), Ridgefield, CT 06877. ⓒ **203/438-7323.** Fax 203/438-7325. www.west laneinn.com. 18 units. $180–$230 double. Rates include breakfast. AE, DC, DISC, MC, V. Free parking. Driving north from Wilton on Rte. 33, turn west on Rte. 35 at the edge of town. **Amenities:** Concierge; room service. *In room:* A/C, TV, fridge, hair dryer, Wi-Fi (free).

WHERE TO DINE

Fans of classy low brow eats will want to make a stop at **Chez Lenard ★** (no phone), on the sidewalk toward the north end of the shopping district, opposite Ballard Park. It's an open-air hot-dog stand—a bench, no tables—with foot-longs that come with such trappings as peppers and onions ("Le Hot Dog Excelsior") and cheese fondue ("Le Hot Dog Garniture Suisse"). The boss gallantly stays open right through winter.

Bernard's ★★ FRENCH   A piano in the main dining parlor is played Friday and Saturday nights and for the festive Sunday brunch, but the primary interests of the owners clearly lie in the kitchen. Imagine escargots with wild mushroom and salsify casserole braced with sautéed tomatoes and parsley coulis—and that's just to start. Main courses are about 50/50 land- and ocean-based proteins. Among the most successful are cod filets wrapped in rosemary pancetta and the herb-crusted rack of lamb with haricot verts, flageolet beans, baby carrots, and cumin sauce. Several dinner choices appear as half-priced versions at lunch, but the romantic music and lighting are reserved for evenings. Men might want to wear a jacket.

20 West Lane (near the junction with Rte. 7). ⓒ **203/438-8282.** www.bernardsridgefield.com. Reservations recommended on Fri–Sat. Main courses $26–$36. AE, DC, MC, V. Wed–Sat noon–2:30pm and 6–9pm (Fri–Sat until 10pm); Sun noon–2:30pm and 5–8pm; shorter hours after Labor Day.

The Elms Inn ★★ NEW AMERICAN   Ridgefield's oldest (1799) operating inn has 20 rooms for overnight visitors ($155–$195 double), with most of conveniences travelers expect, but the main attractions are the dining room and tavern. They are in the capable hands of Chef Brendan Walsh, who administers fresh twists on regional ingredients without masking their origins. In the main dining room, bangers and mash and *sauerbraten* are staples, and if the mixed grill of lamb, venison, and sausage is available, grab it. His food has turned toward greater simplicity of late, as with pan-fried sole with roasted fingerlings and chicken stuffed with prosciutto and fontina. The tavern serves pub grub: burgers, crab cakes, and hanger steak sandwiches.

500 Main St. (Rte. 35, at the north end of town). ⓒ **203/438-9206.** www.elmsinn.com. Reservations necessary on Fri–Sat. Main courses $21–$32. AE, DC, MC, V. Wed–Sun 11:30am–9pm.

THE LITCHFIELD HILLS ★★

When the Hamptons got too pricey, too visible, and too chichi back in the 1980s, a lot of stockbrokers, CEOs, and celebs started discovering the Litchfield Hills, arguably the most fetchingly rustic yet still sophisticated part of Connecticut.

The topography and, to an extent, the microculture of the region are defined by the river that runs through it, the Housatonic. Broad but not deep enough for vessels larger than canoes, it waters farms and villages and forests along its course, provides opportunities for recreational angling and float trips, and, over the millennia, helped to shape these foothills, which merge in the north with the Massachusetts Berkshires.

Men in overalls and CAT caps still stand on the porches of general stores, their breath steaming in the bracing autumn air. Churches hold pancake-breakfast fundraisers; neighbors squabble about development. That's one side of these bucolic hills, less than 2 hours from Manhattan.

Increasingly, the other side is fashioned by refugees from New York. These chic seekers of tranquillity and real estate fled to pre-Revolutionary saltboxes and Georgian Colonials on Litchfield's warren of back roads and brought Manhattan-bred expectations with them. Boutiques fragrant with designer coffees and cachets opened in spaces once occupied by luncheonettes and feed stores. Restaurants discovered sushi and pork belly and just how much they could get away with charging the newcomers.

Compromises and city-country conflicts aside, the Litchfield Hills remain a satisfying all-season destination for day trips and overnights from metropolitan New York and Connecticut.

Essentials

GETTING THERE   From New York City, follow the Hutchinson River Parkway to I-684 north to I-84 east, taking exit 7 onto Rte. 7 north. Continue on Rte. 7 for New Milford, Kent, West Cornwall, and Canaan. For Washington Depot, New Preston, and Litchfield, branch off onto Rte. 202 at New Milford. An especially attractive entrance into the region is Rte. 44 from the Taconic Parkway, through Millerton and into Lakeville and Salisbury.

From Boston, take the Massachusetts Turnpike west to the Lee exit, picking up Rte. 7 south from nearby Stockbridge.

VISITOR INFORMATION   The useful 112-page *Unwind* getaway planner and map is produced by the **Northwest Connecticut Convention & Visitors Bureau** (© 860/567-4506; www.litchfieldhills.com).

New Milford

A gateway to the Litchfield Hills, New Milford was founded in 1703 and functions as a commercial center for the smaller villages that surround it—Roxbury, Bridgewater, Washington, and Brookfield. It is also at the high end of a long stretch of overdeveloped Rte. 7, which is clogged with strip malls.

New Milford is a welcome stop on the drive north, if only for lunch and a short stroll. Turn right on Rte. 202 where it splits from Rte. 7 and crosses the Housatonic River and

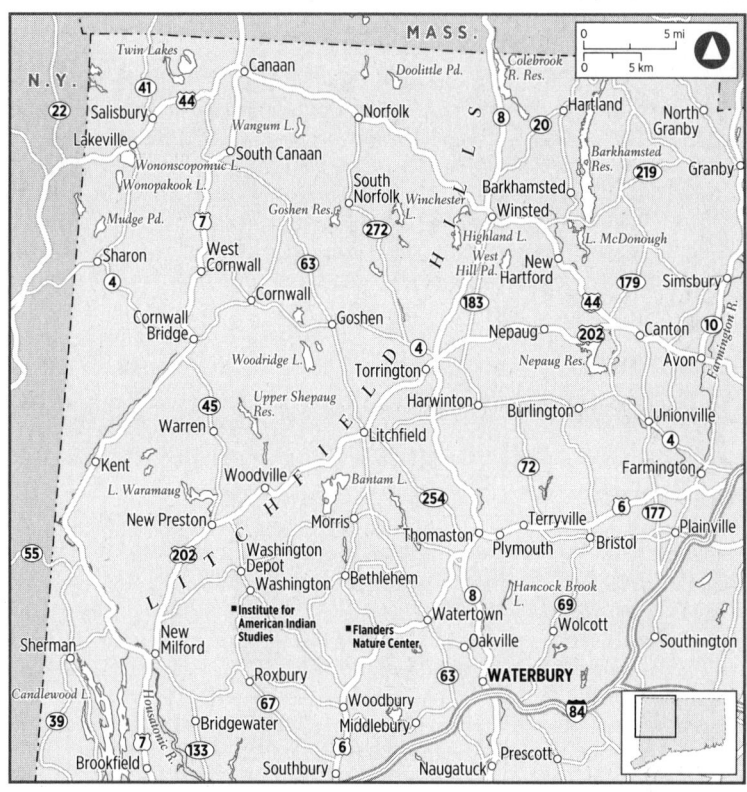

a railroad track. Up on the left is one end of the long town green. A 1902 fire destroyed many of the buildings around the green, so this isn't one of those picture-book New England settings. Rather, it is a mix of late Victoriana, early Greek Revival, and Eisenhower-era architecture, not to ignore the requisite Congregational church.

Otherwise, there are no obligatory sights, so a walk down Bank Street, west of the green and along Railroad Street, with its crafts shops, a bookstore, and an Art Moderne movie house, won't take long.

GETTING OUTSIDE

Candlewood Lake (© 860/354-6928; www.candlewoodlake.com) is the third-largest man made lake in the eastern United States. It has a finger that pokes into New Milford, but the area with the most recreational facilities is a few miles to the west. From New Milford, drive north on Rte. 7 about 2½ miles, turn west on Rte. 37 toward and through Sherman, then south on Rte. 39 to **Squantz Pond State Park** (© 203/797-4165; www.ct.gov). With over 170 acres along the lakeshore, it offers swimming, ice-skating, fishing, hiking and cycling trails, picnic grounds, rental canoes, and a boat launch.

WHERE TO DINE

There are many dining choices along Bank and Railroad streets and on Rte. 7.

The Cookhouse ★ BARBECUE   Inexplicably, Connecticut is home to some thumping-good barbecue joints. This is the current champ. It's set, appropriately enough, in a converted barn on often-tacky Rte. 7. Cast aside the diet for the day and start off with hush puppies or Nappy's Nachos, a plate piled with chips, pork, beef, jalapeños, and jack cheese. Continue, if you can, with ribs, chicken, pulled pork, or beef brisket, which are slow-smoked for 10 hours or more. They come with such sides as baked beans, collard greens, and mashed potatoes. Separate menu categories list grills, fish, and "comfort foods," the last including burritos, fajitas, macaroni and cheese, and chicken-fried steak. Live blues music is a feature of many Friday nights.

31 Danbury Rd. (Rte. 7). ☎ **860/355-4111.** www.thecookhouse.com. Main courses $15–$22. AE, DC, MC, V. Daily 11:30am–10pm (Fri–Sat until 11pm, Sun until 9pm).

Woodbury ★

The chief distinction of this attractive town strung along Rte. 6, west of Waterbury, is its over 40 high-end antiques stores. On weekends in good weather, the main road is clogged with cars full of antiquers trolling for treasures, and progress can be slow.

ANTIQUING

Shoppers are drawn here for antiques and collectibles of every sort, from funky to obscure to elegant. To winnow down the list, pick up the directory produced by the **Woodbury Antiques Dealers Association** (www.antiqueswoodbury.com) at one of the member stores.

Start off in the building at 289 Main St., at the intersection of routes 6 and 317, which contains **Jennings & Rohn Antiques** (☎ 203/263-3775). European paintings and furnishings from the 16th century to 1960 are on view, as well as lighting fixtures and some Art Deco. At **Martell & Suffin Antiques** (☎ 203/263-1913), the owners favor 18th- and early-19th-century European furniture as well as Asian works of art.

Of similar high order is the stock of **Country Loft Antiques,** 557 Main St. (☎ 203/266-4500; www.countryloftantiques.com), largely 19th-century French furnishings and *objets* displayed in a fine old barn. Wares run from biscuit tins to armoires, bolts of fabric to 18th-century dining tables. Be sure to look into the basement, outfitted as a wine cellar.

The once-popular **Woodbury Antiques & Flea Market** has ceased operation.

WHAT TO SEE & DO

Flanders Nature Center   North of Woodbury on Rte. 6, watch for Flanders Road forking to the left. Three miles along, on the right, is the office building for this 1,400-acre nature center. Yearly events include maple syrup and wreath-making, along with a fall festival. Maps of hiking trails are available.

Church Hill and Flanders Rd. ☎ **203/263-3711.** www.flandersnaturecenter.org. Free admission. Office Mon–Fri 9am–5pm; trails daily dawn to dusk.

Glebe House   About the only scrap of surviving history worth mentioning in town is this 1750 house of an Episcopal bishop, west of Rte. 6 on a street of fine 18th-century houses. A *glebe* was a property given to a preacher as partial compensation for his services. Inside are furnishings true to the period; outside is the Gertrude Jekyll Garden.

149 Hollow Rd. ℰ **203/263-2855.** www.theglebehouse.org. Admission $5 adults, $2 children ages 6-12. Apr-Oct Wed-Sun 1-4pm; Nov Sat-Sun 1-4pm.

WHERE TO STAY

Longwood Country Inn ★   South of the town center, this late-18th-century house has been a B&B since 1951. The current overseers completed thorough renovations in 2006. Three of the five units are suites, with gas fireplaces and whirlpool tubs. The food emerging from the kitchen is contemporary in aspiration and execution, and served at lunch (Wed–Sat), dinner (Tues–Sun), and Sunday brunch (reservations ℰ **203/263-7005**). Dinner entrees are priced from $22 to $35, and include cedar plank salmon with mango chutney and Long Island duck in a Grand Marnier reduction. The dining room and lounges have wood-burning fireplaces. A live combo plays here a couple of Friday evenings a month.

1204 Main St. (Rte. 6), Woodbury, CT 06798. ℰ **203/266-0800.** Fax 203/263-4479. www.longwood countryinn.com. 5 units. $225–$295 double. Rates include breakfast. AE, DC, MC, V. **Amenities:** Restaurant. *In room:* A/C, TV, Wi-Fi (free).

WHERE TO DINE

The Longwood Country Inn (see above) serves lunch and dinner and is another good dining option in town.

Good News Café ★★ NEW AMERICAN   This fun spot is one of Connecticut's best, with a cheery staff and rooms doused in ripe primary colors. The food? Make it Europe meets Asia, touching down in various parts of the Americas along the way. The results are spirited, but never bizarre, and the menu changes frequently. Examples: Red venison filet with celery root, green beans, and chestnut flan; or gemelli pasta and asparagus with capers, sage, gorgonzola, with a balsamic drizzle. Most of the entrees qualify as heart-healthy, and ingredients, whenever possible, are purchased from local farmers. Desserts, however, tend to be rich, gooey, and caloric—apple spice cake is splendiferous. Saturday nights often feature live jazz, and there's outdoor dining in summer. The walls are used for changing art exhibitions.

694 Main St. (Rte. 6). ℰ **203/266-4663.** www.good-news-cafe.com. Reservations recommended on Fri-Sat. Main courses $19–$32. AE, DC, MC, V. Wed-Mon 11:30am–10pm; Sun noon–10pm.

Washington ★★ & Washington Depot

Settled in 1734, its name changed in 1779 to honor the first American president, Washington occupies the crown of a hill beside Rte. 47. Its village green, with the impressive 1802 Congregational Meeting House surrounded by white buildings and sheltered by shade trees, is an example of a municipal arrangement found all over New England—but rarely to such near-perfection.

Adjacent Washington Depot, down the hill beside the Shepaug River, serves as the commercial center, with a bank and a small cluster of shops. Stop in at the beguiling **Hickory Stick Bookshop,** 2 Greenhill Rd. (ℰ **860/868-0525;** www.hickorystickbookshop.com), refreshingly free of the presumptions of the national bookstore chains.

Nearby **Steep Rock Reservation** (ℰ **860/868-9131;** www.steeprockassoc.org) is a wildlife and nature conservancy of 4,774 acres, a lovely spot for hiking, fly-fishing, or cross-country skiing. (Unfortunately for pet owners, dogs must be leashed.)

WHAT TO SEE & DO

Institute for American Indian Studies A worthwhile detour takes drivers down Curtis Road to this small repository of Native American crafts and artifacts. They are presented with sensitivity and, for the most part, without polemics. Down a nearby path is a re-creation of an Algonquian village. There's a picnic area on the grounds.

38 Curtis Rd. (off Rte. 199). © **860/868-0518.** www.birdstone.org. Admission $5 adults, $4.50 seniors, $3 children ages 6-16. Mon-Sat 10am-5pm; Sun noon-5pm (closed Mon-Tues Jan-Mar).

WHERE TO STAY

Mayflower Inn & Spa ★★ Galaxies of stars have already been scattered in profusion over this, one of the state's courtliest manor inns. (The breathtaking prices are the reason we have awarded only two stars, not three.) While the main building is almost entirely new, some elements survive from the original 1894 structure, the most delightful of which is the richly paneled library. Porches look out across manicured lawns to deep woods—58 acres of them. Most bedrooms have fireplaces, the bathrooms are done with tapestry rugs and mahogany wainscoting—all is as close to perfection as such an enterprise is likely to be. As might be expected, the clientele can't be described as youthful. The accomplished restaurant features top-drawer ingredients drawn from New England producers and Atlantic fisheries. The wine cellar is extensive, meticulously chosen, and pricey.

118 Woodbury Rd. (Rte. 47), Washington, CT 06793. © **860/868-9466.** Fax 860/868-1497. www.mayflower.com. 30 units. $1,040-$1,580 double; $1,420-$3,000 suite. AE, MC, V. Take Rte. 202 north 2 miles past New Preston, turn south on Rte. 47 through Washington Depot and up the hill past Washington Common. Entrance is on the left. No children 12 and under. **Amenities:** Restaurant; taproom; bikes; extensive health club; heated outdoor pool; room service; sauna; tennis court. *In room:* A/C, TV, fax, hair dryer, minibar, Wi-Fi (free).

WHERE TO DINE

One dining option is the restaurant at the **Mayflower Inn** (see above). For a more casual meal, put together a picnic from the delectable array of soups, quiches, pizzas, and salads at **The Pantry,** 5 Titus Rd., Washington Depot (© **860/868-0258**). Or, eat there at one of the dozen tables.

G. W. Tavern ★ CONTEMPORARY AMERICAN The tavern's atmospheric bar has booths and a fireplace, while the simulated attached barn is airier, with a deck that looks down on the Shepaug River. The kitchen concerns itself with interpretations of such robust Americana as crab cakes, meatloaf, chicken potpie, and fish and chips. Daily specials nearly outnumber the items on the regular menu (plus a short card of lighter fare 2:30–5:30pm). It is all quite satisfying, if hardly revelatory. Weekend brunches are especially popular; as is live jazz Thursday evenings; blues on Monday; and a variety of rock, pop, and folk performers on weekends. Find the tavern a block north of the Washington Depot shopping center.

20 Bee Brook Rd. (Rte. 47). © **860/868-6633.** www.gwtavern.com. Main courses $10-$32. AE, MC, V. Mon-Fri 11:30am-2:30pm and 5:30-10pm; Sat 11:30am-2:30pm and 5:30-11pm; Sun 11:30am-3pm and 5:30-9:30pm.

New Preston & Lake Waramaug ★★

Never more than a few houses and retailers at the junction of two country roads, the hamlet of New Preston long served primarily as a supplier for locals and, starting in the mid–19th century, the families who summered on nearby Lake Waramaug. More recently, New Preston's small grocery and hardware stores have been converted to antiques emporia of high order, and they find themselves surrounded on weekends by BMWs and Volvos. In the recent economic unpleasantness, "for sale" signs have proliferated around the rim of Lake Waramaug, long a desirable destination for buyers of weekend homes.

WHAT TO SEE & DO

At the northwest tip of the L-shaped lake, 95-acre **Lake Waramaug State Park** ★, Lake Waramaug Road (© 860/868-0220; www.ct.gov), gives the public access to a beautiful body of water that is otherwise monopolized by the private homes and inns that border it. In warmer months, canoes and paddle boats are for rent, and there's a swimming beach as well as picnic tables, a food concession, and a total of 77 camping and RV sites.

Hopkins Vineyard   A former dairy farm on a promontory above Lake Waramaug was converted into a vineyard and winery in 1979. Headquartered in a 19th-century barn across the street from the Hopkins Inn (see "Where to Stay & Dine," below), it produces about a dozen different bottlings. They won't make anyone forget Napa Valley, but prices are fair. Overlooking the lake is a wine bar, where selections of pâtés and cheese can accompany samples of the primary product. It's open Friday to Sunday from noon to 4pm (until 5pm Sat).

25 Hopkins Rd. © **860/868-7954.** www.hopkinsvineyard.com. Jan–Feb Fri–Sun 10am–5pm (from 11am Sun); Mar–Apr Wed–Sun 10am–5pm (from 11am Sun); May–Dec daily 10am–5pm (from 11am Sun).

SHOPPING

In no time, the intersecting streets that form the center of the village have gone from sleepy to spiffy. Notable among the shops is **J. Seitz & Co.,** Main Street/East Shore Road (© 860/868-0119; www.jseitz.com), featuring bedding, bath products, furniture, and clothing of the country squire variety. Two doors over is **New Preston Kitchen Goods,** 11 East Shore Rd. (© 860/868-1264; www.newprestonkitchen goods.com), selling a wide variety of high-end gadgets.

WHERE TO STAY & DINE

The Boulders ★★   This once rustic lakeside inn, with a private swimming beach, has scrambled steadily upward over the years in both price and quality, taking a great leap forward when it sold for $4.3 million in 2002. The outlying "guesthouses"—four buildings with two spacious units each plus a new carriage house—enjoy private decks, fireplaces, Jacuzzis, and refrigerators. These have contemporary furnishings, while the tone of the bedrooms in the 1895 main house is set by a massive stone fireplace, an elk horn chandelier, and country antiques and reproductions. Drinks at the handsome bar or in the large sitting room precede dinner in the main dining room or on the porch, all with lake views. A serious wine cellar complements the acclaimed cuisine that's based on seasonal and local ingredients.

E. Shore Rd. (Rte. 45), New Preston, CT 06777. © **800/455-1565** or 860/868-0541. Fax 860/868-1925. www.bouldersinn.com. 20 units. $365–$475 double. Rates include breakfast or Sun brunch, and afternoon tea. 2-night minimum on Fri–Sat. AE, DISC, MC, V. Closed Jan to early Apr except for holiday weekends. No children 12 and under. Drive north from New Preston on Rte. 45 approx. 2 miles. **Amenities:** Restaurant; small exercise room; room service; spa; tennis court; canoes and rowboats. *In room:* A/C, TV/DVD, hair dryer.

Hopkins Inn 🍴   A family named Hopkins started farming this land in 1787, and its descendants turned the farm into a vineyard and winery in 1979. The farmhouse sits atop a hill with the best views of Lake Waramaug, enhanced by meals on the dining patio. Food is the main event, as most of the guest rooms are on the spartan side, with a TV only in the two-bedroom suite in the annex. Dishes from the Swiss and Austrian Alps are served in hefty portions, with wiener schnitzel and trout bleu among the options (main courses $20–$27). The restaurant is closed from January through March, but breakfast is still served to overnight guests.

22 Hopkins Rd., New Preston, CT 06777. *©* **860/868-7295.** Fax 860/868-7464. www.thehopkinsinn. com. 13 units (2 with shared bathroom). $115–$145 double. 2-night minimum on Fri–Sat Apr–Nov. AE, DISC, MC, V. Drive north from New Preston on Rte. 45 north about 2½ miles and look for sign on left. **Amenities:** Restaurant. *In room:* A/C, TV (1 room), no phone.

Litchfield ★★

Possessed of a stately treed common reconfigured around the turn of the 20th century by the Frederick Law Olmsted landscaping firm (Olmstead designed New York's Central Park), Litchfield is testimony to the taste and affluence of the Yankee entrepreneurs who built it up in the late 18th and early 19th centuries from a Colonial farm community to an industrial center. The factories and mills were dismantled toward the end of the 19th century, and the men who built them settled back to enjoy their riches in their uncommonly large homes.

In recent decades, the town has been discovered by fashionable New Yorkers, who find it less frenetic than the Hamptons. Their influence is seen both in the quality of store merchandise and restaurant fare, as well as in the lofty prices houses command.

WHAT TO SEE & DO

Litchfield's houses and tree-lined streets reward leisurely strollers. From the stores and restaurants along West Street, walk east (to the right when facing the common), and then turn right on South Street. On the opposite corner is the recently expanded **Litchfield History Museum,** at South and East streets (*©* **860/567-4501;** www.litchfield historicalsociety.org), containing an eclectic array of local historical artifacts, including the world's largest collection of works by the 18th-century portraitist Ralph Earl. It's open from April to mid-November, Tuesday through Saturday from 11am to 5pm and Sunday from 1 to 5pm. Admission, which includes entry to the Tapping Reeve House (see below), is $5 for adults, $3 for seniors, and free for children under 14.

Walking down South Street, on the right, are the **Tapping Reeve House and Law School** (*©* **860/567-4501**). One of the few local historic houses regularly open to the public, the Reeve house was built in 1773, while the adjacent 1784 building was the earliest American law school, established before independence. It counted among its students Aaron Burr and Noah Webster. Hours are the same as those of the Litchfield History Museum, which maintains it; one ticket buys admission to both museums.

When the street starts to peter out into more modern houses, walk back toward the common and cross over to the north side. Over there on the right is the magisterial **First Congregational Church,** built in 1828. Turn left, then right on North Street, where the domestic architecture matches the quiet splendor of South Street.

Haight-Brown Vineyard Chardonnays and Merlots don't spring to mind as likely Connecticut products, but this winery, established in the 1970s, has grown and prospered, and presently offers 11 drinkable bottlings. Located a mile east of town center, its tasting room is open year-round—tastings of seven wines cost $7, or, with cheese, $12. Haight-Brown, along with Hopkins Vineyard (p. 381), Stonington Vineyards (p. 421), and Bishop's Orchards Winery (p. 402), is part of the **Connecticut Wine Trail,** an organization of 19 vineyards. A downloadable map is online at **www.ctwine.com.**

29 Chestnut Hill Rd. (at the corner of Rte. 118). © **860/567-4045.** www.haightvineyards.com. Mon–Sat 10:30am–5pm; Sun noon–5pm.

GETTING OUTSIDE

The **White Memorial Foundation,** 80 Whitehall Rd. (Rte. 202; © **860/567-0857;** www.whitememorialcc.org), is a 4,000-acre wildlife sanctuary and nature conservancy about 3 miles southwest of Litchfield. It has campsites and 35 miles of trails for hiking, cross-country skiing, and horseback riding. On the grounds is a small museum of natural history. The Holbrook Bird Observatory looks out on a landscape specifically planted to attract birds. The center's nature museum on the grounds is open year-round, Monday through Saturday from 9am to 5pm and Sunday from noon to 5pm. Admission is $5 for adults, $2.50 for children 6 to 12.

This is horse country, so consider a canter across the meadows and along the wooded trails of **Topsmead State Forest,** Buell Road (© **860/567-5694;** www.st.gov). The park has a wildlife preserve and a Tudor-style mansion that can be toured the second and fourth weekends of each month from June through October. To get here, follow Rte. 118 for a mile east of town. The grounds are open from 8am to sunset. Horses can be hired nearby at **Lee's Riding Stable,** 57 East Litchfield Rd., off Rte. 118 (© **860/567-0785;** www.windfieldmorganfarm.com/lees.html). Group trail rides cost $35 per hour per person; half-hour lessons are available for $40.

SHOPPING

Most of the interesting shops are in the row of late-19th-century brick buildings on the south side of the town green. Inserted among the galleries, antique stores, clothing shops, and the inevitable Talbot's is **Kitchenworks,** 23 West St. (© **860/567-5011;** www.kitchenworksct.com), with a good selection of cookware and tableware, as well as some nonculinary gifts.

WHERE TO DINE

The centerpiece of the **Toll Gate Hill Inn** (571 Torrington Rd./Rte. 202; © **866/567-1233** or 860/567-1233; www.tollgatehill.com) is a 1745 structure known as the Captain William Bull Tavern, listed in the National Register of Historic Places. It houses a bar and restaurant, and it's as atmospheric as all get out. (There are 20 attractive bedrooms in the outlying buildings, too.) At this writing, however, the inn is open but the restaurant is closed, so call ahead.

@ The Corner AMERICAN   It is, indeed, "at the corner," of West and South streets, a presumably desirable location that has housed in not so many previous years a pharmacy, an ice-cream shop, a nightspot, and two earlier restaurants. Whether this effort will beat the dreary odds remains to be seen, but it's trying. The spacious front dining room adjoins a fetchingly pubby bar, which attaches to a takeout shop and bakery. Ceiling fans rotate drowsily over the spacious dining room, where fresh-faced young waiters bring such alert contemporary dishes as capellini tossed with lobster chunks and portobellos and seared citrus-maple duck breast joined with roasted root vegetables. Live music is usually offered Thursday nights. It all seems to have the necessaries for long life, but with this location's history, who knows?

3 West St. ☎ **860/567-8882.** www.athecorner.com. Main courses $16–$28. AE, MC, V. Daily 11:30am–3:30pm and 4:30–9:30pm.

Patty's 🍴 BREAKFAST/BRUNCH   Breakfast lovers, Patty's has your back. Open daily, it's *the* local place for apple-sausage omelets, sweet potato pancakes, and sausage and gravy over buttermilk biscuits. It's the kind of country cafe seen in scores of other towns—a counter with stools, tables with chairs of a sort first seen sometime around Truman's election. Posh, it isn't, but don't let that stop you. Here's food with flavors and earthy panache rarely encountered in such settings, served up with a sense of humor. "Worms in Quicksand," it turns out, is mac and cheese. At lunch, one panino was composed of smoked turkey, red peppers, provolone, thin slices of red onion, leaf spinach, and pesto sauce. Expect to share the room with farmers, merchants, workmen, and weekenders, but few outsiders. Breakfast and lunch only.

499 Bantam Rd. (Rte. 202). ☎ **860/567-3335.** Most items under $10. No credit cards. Mon–Sat 6am–2pm; Sun 7am–noon.

West Street Grill ★ NEW AMERICAN   When this contemporary bistro opened about 20 years ago, local and big-city reviewers were enthralled. Known as an incubator for some of Connecticut's best chefs, several of whom went off to open their own places, it hasn't always merited the raves. But despite frequent changes and tinkering, the restaurant's fortunes have more often waxed than waned. Recently, entrees have tended toward Italianate renditions of seasonal ingredients, but that emphasis can adjust with the ever-shifting roster of chefs. Portions are substantial. It remains the trendiest spot for miles, some of its patrons bearing familiar faces from TV and newspapers. It puts out two tables on the sidewalk in warm months.

43 West St. (on the Green). ☎ **860/567-3885.** www.weststreetgrill.com. Reservations recommended for dinner, essential on Fri–Sat. Main courses $21–$38. AE, MC, V. Mon–Thurs 11:30am–3pm and 5:30–9pm; Fri–Sat 11:30am–4pm and 5:30–10:30pm.

Kent

A prominent prep school of the same name, a history as an iron-smelting center, and a continuing reputation as a gathering place of artists and writers define this town of fewer than 2,000. Noted 19th-century landscape painter George Inness helped establish that assessment, and several galleries represent the works of his creative descendants (if not his equals). They are joined by a multiplicity of antiques shops and bookstores, most of them strung along Rte. 7. South of town on the same road is the hamlet of Bull's Bridge, named for one of the two remaining covered bridges in the state that can be crossed by cars.

A super-sweet local landmark is **Belgique Pâtisserie & Chocolatier ★★**, 1 Bridge St. (☎ **860/927-3681**), which gained rapturous reviews when it was a restaurant. Unhappily, the chef-owner tired of the workload, and turned the dining room into a catering operation. All was not lost, for he then focused on his calling as a chocolatier and pastry chef. Stop in at the yellow carriage house near the intersection of routes 7 and 341 for a superb hot chocolate while examining glass cases full of the most delicate and creative tarts, cakes, mousses, chocolates, and other confections to have passed your lips. You can buy freshly baked baguettes and croissants, too. It's open Thursday to Sunday from 10am to 6pm.

Four miles northeast of Kent is **Kent Falls State Park,** on Rte. 7 (☎ **860/927-3238;** www.ct.gov). Its centerpiece, a 250-foot cascade, is clearly visible from the road, and picnic tables are set about the grounds. A path mounts the hill beside the falls. Restrooms are available. On weekends and holidays it costs $20 to park; on weekdays, parking is free.

West Cornwall

Not to be confused with Cornwall, 4 miles to the southeast, nor with Cornwall Bridge, 7 miles to the south, this tiny village is best known for its picturesque covered bridge, one of only two in the state that still permits the passage of cars. The bridge connects routes 7 and 128, crossing the Housatonic. With a state forest to the north and a state park to its immediate south, West Cornwall enjoys a piney seclusion that remains welcoming to passersby.

Housatonic Meadows State Park, on Rte. 7 (✆ 860/424-3200; www.ct.gov), is comprised of 452 acres bordering both sides of the Housatonic River immediately south of West Cornwall. With 95 campsites, it offers access to fishing, canoeing, picnicking, and cross-country skiing. **Housatonic Anglers,** Rte. 7 (✆ 860/672-4457; www.housatonicanglers.com), offers float trips, fly-fishing schools, and guided fishing trips.

Just outside Cornwall proper, off Rte. 4, is **Mohawk Mountain Ski Area,** 46 Great Hollow Rd. (✆ 860/672-6100; www.mohawkmtn.com). "Mountain" is an overstatement, but this is the state's oldest ski resort, with five lifts, 24 trails, snowmakers, and night skiing on weekends. All-day lift tickets are $50 for adults on weekends, $23 for night skiing (6–10pm). Skis and snowboards are available for rent.

WHERE TO DINE

"Exclusive" doesn't begin to describe the almost mystical reverence of the country cognoscenti for **RSVP** (7 Railroad St.; ✆ 860/676-7787), who treat the restaurant as their personal epicurean Xanadu. The exterior is indistinctive, there are only eight tables inside, and dinner is served only on Friday, Saturday, and Sunday. Reservations are as difficult to obtain as fish feathers. Take our word for it—we've never wrested one.

The Wandering Moose Café 🍴 AMERICAN   With more prior incarnations than most people can remember, this location has been serving food of one quality or another for decades. These days, the emphasis on comforting, familiar, and well-prepared meals leaves little room for innovation. Almond-crusted trout, beef stroganoff, and crab cakes are some of the best bets. Count on clam chowder, burgers, nachos, and baby back ribs, too. Most of it is quite affordable, ensuring that locals of all ages make it their HQ.

Rte. 128 (east end of the covered bridge). ✆ **860/672-0178.** www.thewanderingmoosecafe.com. Main courses $15–$26. MC, V. Tues–Fri 7am–3pm; Wed–Sat 7am–3pm and 5:30–8pm; Sat 8am–3pm and 5:30–9pm; Sun 8am–3pm and 5–8pm.

Lakeville & Salisbury

These two attractive villages share a main street lined with 19th-century houses stretching along Rte. 44. The "lake" in question is Wononscopomuc, slightly south of the town center.

The discovery in the area of a particularly pure iron ore led to the development of mines and forges as early as the mid-1700s. One of the ironworkers was the eccentric Ethan Allen, later to become the leader of the Green Mountain Boys and a hero for his capture of Fort Ticonderoga from the British in 1775.

Holley-Williams House   One wealthy forge owner, John Milton Holley, bought a 1768 mansion and doubled its size in 1808. The result is a Federal and Greek Revival mix. It contains furnishings assembled by Holley and his descendants over the 173 years the family lived there. There were a lot of them—the outhouse has seven holes.

15 Millerton Rd. (Rte. 44). ℂ **860/435-2878.** Suggested donations are $5 adults, $3 seniors and students. Visits by guided tour only. July 4 to Labor Day Sat–Sun and holidays noon–5pm; rest of year Fri noon–5pm.

WHERE TO STAY & DINE

White Hart ★   This inn's fortunes have fluctuated in its 200 years, but the white-clapboard lodging at the end of Salisbury's main street is continuing its recent rise with a thorough remodeling of every bedroom and public space. Both lunch and dinner are offered in the dining areas. Dinner entrees range from $16 to $28. The front porch is a prime summertime perch. Apart from the three suites and the large Ford Room, most of the guest rooms are on the small side. Both the **dining rooms** and the wine cellar have received excellent notices. VCRs and fridges are available for rent.

Village Green (P.O. Box 545), Salisbury, CT 06068. ℂ **800/832-0041** or 860/435-0030. Fax 860/435-0040. www.whitehartinn.com. 15 units. $140–$299 double. Rates include breakfast. AE, DC, DISC, MC, V. **Amenities:** Restaurant; cafe; bar. *In room:* A/C, TV, hair dryer.

Norfolk

Founded in 1758, Norfolk (pronounced NOR-fork) was long popular as a vacation destination for industrialists who owned mills and factories along Connecticut's rivers. At the very least, drive into the center for a look at the village green. It is highlighted by a monument that involved the participation of two of the late 19th century's most celebrated artists—sculptor Augustus Saint-Gaudens and architect Stanford White.

At the opposite corner is the 90-year-old "Music Shed," the venue for an eagerly awaited series of summer events, the **Norfolk Chamber Music Festival ★** (ℂ **860/542-3000;** www.yale.edu/norfolk). Held from July to August, it hosts performances by such luminaries as the Tokyo String Quartet and the Vermeer Quartet. A few affiliated events are scattered throughout the year.

First opened in 1883, a prominent building on the road leading into the village was recently restored and re-opened to serve as the **Infinity Music Hall & Bistro** (20 Greenwoods Rd.; ℂ **860/542-5531;** www.infinityhall.com). In its first year, the 300-seat main hall mounted a full calendar of highly varied entertainments, including live music in a range of styles—jazz, folk, rock, country, blues, zydeco—as well as comedy, poetry slams, and such nostalgia acts as the New Riders of the Purple Sage. Bigger names, such as John Mayall and Judy Collins, also stop by. Tickets for their performances run up to $75, but the majority of acts are in the $15 to $35 range, and some are even free. The attached bistro serves lunch, dinner, or simply drinks and small plates before the shows. Dinner entrees run $17 to $28.

GETTING OUTSIDE

Two prime recreational areas are near each other on Rte. 272, north of town. A mile from the village green is **Haystack Mountain State Park,** Rte. 272 (ℂ **860/482-1817;** www.ct.gov). Its chief feature is a short trail leading to a 3-story stone tower at the 1,716-foot crest. On clear days, the views from the top take in a panorama stretching from the Catskill Mountains to Long Island Sound.

Another 5 miles farther north, off Rte. 272 on the Massachusetts border, enjoy the abundant streams, rapids, and cascades at **Campbell Falls,** Rte. 272 (© **860/482-1817;** www.ct.gov). Fishing, hiking, and picnicking are all possibilities.

WHERE TO STAY

Mountain View Inn ★   This is exactly the sort of place enthusiasts imagine when planning trips to include stops at bed-and-breakfast inns. Billed by the owners as a "Gilded Age Victorian," the exterior is more simply "Large Farmhouse" than a classic example of High Victorian style. No matter. Most of the decor and furnishings inside are decidedly of the late 19th century, more than satisfying to guests seeking that atmosphere. The energetic and congenial owners set the tone by serving cookies and juice to guests on arrival. In addition to seeing after their guests' needs, they offer a boutique (hers) and an art gallery (his). The inn is in walking distance of the Infinity Music Hall & Bistro (p. 386).

67 Litchfield Rd., Norfolk, CT 06058. © **860/542.-6991.** www.mvinn.com. 7 units. $115–$235 double. Rates include breakfast. AE, DISC, MC, V. *In room:* A/C, hair dryer, Wi-Fi (free).

NEW HAVEN

81 miles NE of New York City

There has been a noticeable, positive upsurge in attitude and action in this Sound-side city in recent years, a palpable sense that things are definitely getting better. This is not to paper over the generalized afflictions of many of Connecticut's cities—nearly a quarter of its citizens live at or below the poverty line, with the attendant urban afflictions that suggests. But all along, the city has had much to offer the leisure traveler: several performing-arts centers and theaters, outstanding museums, autumnal renewals of college football rivalries that date back over 120 years, and a growing number of notable restaurants.

Much of what is worthwhile about New Haven can be credited to the presence of one of the world's most prestigious schools. Yale University both enriches its community and exacerbates the usual town-gown conflicts—a paradox with which the institution and civic authorities have struggled since the Colonial period.

Relatively little serious history has happened here, but there are a number of "firsts" that boosters love to trumpet. Yale awarded the first Doctor of Medicine degree in 1729 to a man who never practiced medicine. Noah Webster compiled his first dictionary here, Eli Whitney perfected his cotton gin, and a local man named Colt invented a revolver in 1836. The first telephone switchboard was made here, necessitated by a Reverend John E. Todd, who was the first person in the world to request telephone service. And, the first hamburger was allegedly made and sold here, as was—even less certainly—the first pizza.

Essentials

GETTING THERE   I-95 between New York and Providence skirts the shoreline of New Haven; I-91 from Springfield, Massachusetts, and Hartford, Connecticut, ends here. Connections can also be made from the south along the Merritt and Wilbur Cross parkways. Downtown traffic isn't too congested, except at the usual rush hours, and there are ample parking lots and garages near the New Haven Green and Yale University, where most visitors spend their time.

Tweed–New Haven Airport (© **203/466-8888;** www.flytweed.com; airport code HVN) primarily handles private and charter traffic. Flight schedule change frequently, but at this writing, the only commercial passenger flights are offered by **US Airways** (© **800/428-4322**), to hubs in Philadelphia and Chicago. The airport is located southeast of the city, near exits 50 and 51 off I-95.

Amtrak (© **800/USA-RAIL** [872-7245]; www.amtrak.com) runs several trains daily between Boston and New York that make stops in New Haven. To or from New York takes 1½ hours; to or from Boston, about 3 hours. **Metro North** (© **800/638-7646** or 212/532-4900; www.mta.nyc.ny.us/mnr) commuter trains make many daily trips between New Haven and New York. Metro North tickets are much cheaper than Amtrak's, but its trains take longer.

VISITOR INFORMATION   The **Greater New Haven Convention & Visitors Bureau** (© **203/777-8550;** www.visitnewhaven.com) maintains an office at 169 Orange St. **INFO New Haven,** at 1000 Chapel St. (© **203/773-9494;** www. infonewhaven.com), is open daily year-round. In addition to stocks of useful brochures, attendants can make theater and restaurant reservations, and there is a computer terminal for visitors to check their e-mail.

SPECIAL EVENTS   Important events are the **International Festival of Arts & Ideas** (www.artidea.org), held at many sites around the city in late June, and the free **Music on the Green,** in July and early August. Contact INFO New Haven (above) for dates and details.

Exploring Yale University & New Haven

Most of the major attractions are associated with Yale University and, except for the Peabody Museum, are within walking distance of one another near the **New Haven Green,** which is bounded by Elm, Church, Chapel, and College streets. The Green is divided by north-south Temple Street, with government and bank buildings, including the Gothic Revival City Hall, bordering it on its east. There's a retail district on the south and some older sections of the vast Yale campus to the north and west.

Facing Temple Street are three historic churches, all dating from the early 19th century. Next to Chapel Street is **Trinity Episcopal Church,** a brownstone Gothic Revival structure; the Georgian **First Church of Christ/Center Congregational Church;** and the essentially Federal-style **United Congregational.** The First Church of Christ is of greatest interest, built atop a crypt with tombstones inscribed as early as 1687. Tours are conducted Tuesday through Friday between 10:30am and 2:30pm.

The oldest house in New Haven is now the **Yale Visitor Center,** a Colonial-era house facing the north side of the Green at 149 Elm St., near College Street (© **203/432-2300**). While its primary mission is to familiarize prospective students and their parents with Yale on a 1-hour **guided walking tour,** the center also has an introductory video and maps for self-guided tours. It's open Monday through Friday from 9am to 4:30pm, Saturday and Sunday from 11am to 4pm. Guided tours are available weekdays at 10:30am and 2pm, Saturday and Sunday at 1:30pm.

It is impossible to imagine New Haven without Yale, so pervasive is its physical and cultural presence. After all, it helped educate our last three presidents, as well as Gerald Ford, William Howard Taft, Noah Webster, Nathan Hale, and Eli Whitney. Established in 1702 in the shoreline town now known as Clinton, the young

New Haven

CONNECTICUT

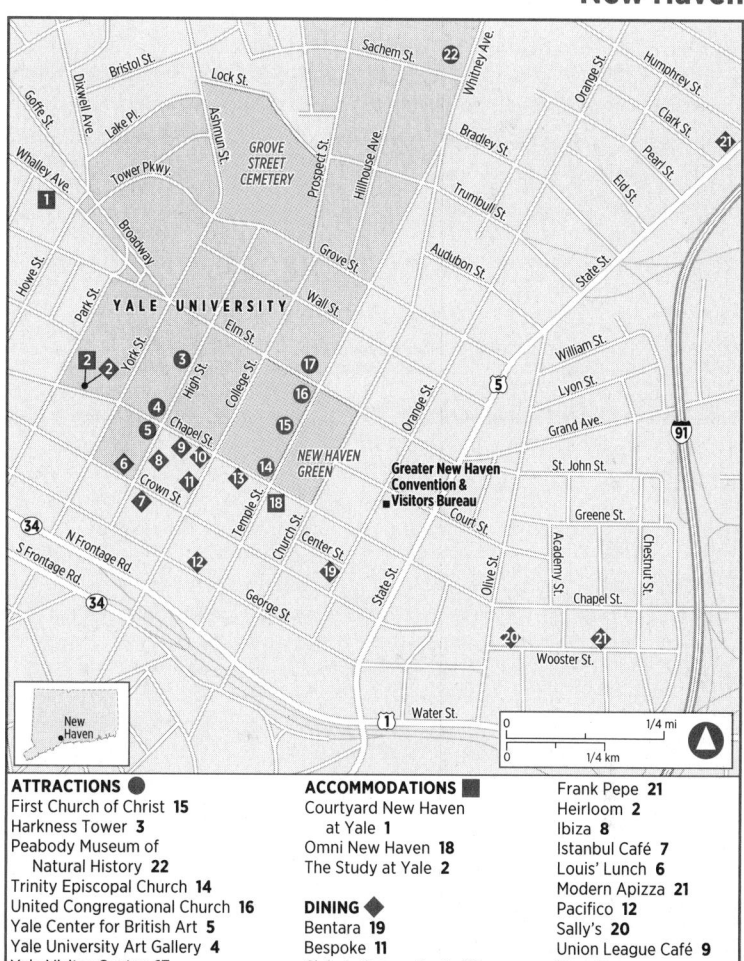

ATTRACTIONS ●

First Church of Christ **15**
Harkness Tower **3**
Peabody Museum of
    Natural History **22**
Trinity Episcopal Church **14**
United Congregational Church **16**
Yale Center for British Art **5**
Yale University Art Gallery **4**
Yale Visitor Center **17**

ACCOMMODATIONS ■

Courtyard New Haven
    at Yale **1**
Omni New Haven **18**
The Study at Yale **2**

DINING ◆

Bentara **19**
Bespoke **11**
Claire's Corner Copia **10**

Frank Pepe **21**
Heirloom **2**
Ibiza **8**
Istanbul Café **7**
Louis' Lunch **6**
Modern Apizza **21**
Pacifico **12**
Sally's **20**
Union League Café **9**
Zinc **13**

college was eventually moved here in 1718 and named for Elihu Yale, who made a
major financial contribution.

The most evocative quadrangle of the sprawling institution is the **Old Campus,**
which can be entered from College, High, or Chapel streets. Inside, the mottled
green is enclosed by Federal and Victorian Gothic buildings and dominated by
Harkness Tower, a 1920 Gothic Revival campanile that looks much older.

Peabody Museum of Natural History ★ ☺   Head to the third floor and work
your way down. At the top are dioramas with stuffed animals in various environ-
ments: bighorn sheep, Alaskan brown bears, bison, and musk oxen. On the same

floor is a small but illuminating collection of ancient Egyptian artifacts. The second floor doesn't hold much of general interest, but down on the first is a "bestiary" of large stuffed animals, which leads logically into the Great Hall of Dinosaurs. Guided tours are offered Saturday and Sunday at noon and 1pm.

170 Whitney Ave. (at Sachem St.). © **203/432-5050.** www.peabody.yale.edu. Admission $7 adults, $6 seniors, $5 children 3–18; free to all Thurs 2–5pm. Mon–Sat 10am–5pm; Sun noon–5pm.

Yale Center for British Art ★★ What looks like a parking garage from outside is a great deal more impressive inside. The museum, underwritten by Paul Mellon and designed by Louis I. Kahn, is said to be the most important repository of British art outside the United Kingdom, with holdings of more than 1,400 paintings and sculptures. Most of the paintings in the permanent collection are from the 16th through the early 19th centuries. It's a dazzling array, with canvases by such luminaries as Hogarth, Gainsborough, Hockney, and the glorious J.M.W. Turner.

1080 Chapel St. (at High St.). © **203/432-2800.** www.yale.edu/ycba. Free admission. Tues–Sat 10am–5pm; Sun noon–5pm. Open occasional evenings, usually Wed or Thurs; call for schedule.

Yale University Art Gallery ★★★ The artworks of many epochs and regions are on display, but the museum is most noted for its collections of French Impressionists and American realists of the late 19th and early 20th centuries. It's a satisfying collection for connoisseurs, and won't test the patience of reluctant museumgoers. Architect Louis I. Kahn, also responsible for the nearby Center for British Art (above), designed the largest of these three buildings, and an interior renovation markedly increased exhibition space. Take the elevator to the fourth floor and work your way down. The top floor is used primarily for special exhibitions. On the third floor are 14th- to 18th-century Gothic ecclesiastical panels and 16th-century Italian and Dutch portraits, among them paintings by Rubens and Hals. In sharp contrast are adjoining galleries of 20th-century works—Rothko and Rauschenberg as well as Picasso and Mondrian. The second floor is commanded by compelling African and Asian artworks.

1111 Chapel St. (at York St.). © **203/432-0600.** www.artgallery.yale.edu. Free admission (donations appreciated). Tues–Sat 10am–5pm (Thurs until 8pm); Sun 1–6pm.

Shopping

Atticus Bookstore/Café, 1082 Chapel St. (© **203/776-4040;** www.atticusbookstorecafe.com), could be listed under "Where to Dine," for half of this store consists of a lunch counter, tables, and a takeout section, locally famous for its scones. The rest of the space is devoted to what many call the best bookstore in town. Open daily from 8am to midnight. Much the same description might be applied to **The Book Trader,** 1140 Chapel St. (© **203/787-6147**), with its cafe serving healthy and tasty soups, sandwiches, and salads. It stock used books in good condition.

A retail time machine, **Group W Bench,** 1171 Chapel St. (© **203/624-0683**), was started in 1968 and is still packed with beads, antique toys, peace emblems, rubber chickens, and Mexican Day of the Dead dancing skeletons. You can get a nostalgia contact high just walking in the door. **Ten Thousand Villages,** 1054 Chapel St. (© **203/776-0854;** www.newhaven.tenthousandvillages.com) displays fascinating handicrafts from Third World artisans, both utilitarian and decorative. The shop endeavors to observe fair income practices, and prices are reasonable, too.

Where to Stay

New Haven lodgings are both limited and, with one notable exception, largely devoid of either charm or distinctiveness. Still, motels and hotels fill up far in advance for Yale football weekends, alumni reunions, and graduation, so reserve ahead during those periods. The former Three Chimneys Inn is now a Yale University office.

The visitor center has a **hotel reservations service** (☎ 800/332-7829).

Courtyard New Haven at Yale ★ At the edge of the older precincts of the sprawling Yale campus, this hotel covers most traveler needs without excess or frippery. The expected components of the Courtyard template are all in place: an adequate fitness room, attached covered parking, a bar, and a dining area serving complimentary hot breakfasts. Packaged snacks and bottled water are laid out and a newspaper is at the door on weekday mornings. After renovations, this is now one of the more desirable of the local chain hotels.

30 Whalley Ave. (near Howe St.), New Haven, CT 06511. ☎ **800/321-2211** or 203/777-6221. Fax 203/772-1089. www.marriott.com. 160 units. $149–$329 double. Parking $15. AE, DC, DISC, MC, V. **Amenities:** Restaurant (breakfast only); bar; modest exercise room. *In room:* A/C, TV, fridge, hair dryer, MP3 docking station, Wi-Fi (free).

Omni New Haven ★★ Its location next to the Green couldn't be improved—the Omni is within easy walking distance of theaters, much of the Yale campus, and two of the Yale museums. This is a conventional member of the reliable brand, and its 19th-floor restaurant, **John Davenport's,** offers fine views of the Green and surrounding cityscape. Some rooms are equipped with treadmills.

155 Temple St. (south of Chapel St.), New Haven, CT 06510. ☎ **888/444-6664** or 203/772-6664. Fax 203/974-6777. www.omnihotels.com. 306 units. $219–$289 double. AE, DC, DISC, MC, V. **Amenities:** Restaurant; bar; concierge; exercise room; room service. *In room:* A/C, TV, hair dryer, minibar, Wi-Fi (free).

The Study at Yale ★★★ A visit to New Haven is greatly enhanced by a stay at this distinguished new boutique hotel, a standout in a city otherwise served primarily by representatives of midlevel national hotel and motel chains. There is little about its facilities and operation that could be significantly improved. The in-house dining room, **Heirloom** (p. 393), deserves its status among the best of local restaurants. Rooms are furnished in sublimely contemporary taste, every unit equipped with stylish lamps and leather chairs. In the eight "Study" rooms, guests get an alcove with two chairs with foot stools and views over the peaked slate roofs of the ancient Yale campus.

1157 Chapel St. (btw. York and Park sts.), New Haven, CT 06511. ☎ **203/503-3900.** Fax 203/503-3901. www.studyhotels.com. 124 units. $269 double, $365 studies (junior suites). AE, DC, DISC, MC, V. **Amenities:** Restaurant; bar; concierge; 24-hour exercise room; room service. *In room:* A/C, TV, hair dryer, MP3 docking station, Wi-Fi (free).

Where to Dine

Few college towns are without at least one low-cost vegetarian restaurant, and **Claire's Corner Copia,** 1000 Chapel St., at College Street (☎ 203/562-3888), has ruled in New Haven since 1975. Options include curried couscous, veggie burgers, quesadillas, and many vegan options. Open daily. Also consider **Atticus Bookstore/Café** (p. 390).

EXPENSIVE

Bentara ★ SOUTHEAST ASIAN In business for a decade, Bentara now finds itself benefiting from a surge in gentrification to its once shabby street. Bare teak tables occupy the spare, roomy front; the back room has covered tables and a second bar. Shadow puppets hang behind opaque panels; carved fertility figures stand along one wall. Billed as Malaysian, the menu also encompasses Thai, French, and Vietnamese ingredients and techniques. Expect zippy, often fiery flavors, not for those with timid palates (nor, in all likelihood, those with nut or peanut allergies). *Nasi lemak,* for example, is spicy stir-fried beef with coconut milk basmati rice punched up with fried anchovies, peanuts, cucumber, and boiled eggs; precede it with the pan-simmered mussels in a coconut-curry sauce with slivered onions and red peppers.

76 Orange St. (at Center St.) ✆ **203/562-2511.** www.bentara.com. Main courses $15–$30. AE, DISC, MC, V. Mon–Thurs 11:30am–2:30pm and 5–9:30pm; Fri–Sat 11am–10:30pm; Sun 3–9:30pm.

Bespoke ★★★ NEW AMERICAN   This place would be comfortable in the highest echelons of Manhattan dining, and without the confiscatory tariffs. Food arrives in one dazzling display after another, brought to table by an often jovial member of the multicultural waitstaff, each of whom is prepared to explain the creations in as much detail as might be desired. The main dining area is below street level, illuminated by dozens of votive candles in wall niches. There are hints of a previous Nuevo Latino culinary passion here and there in the Bespoke menu—Cuban beer-braised pork ribs, for one—but the chef-owner ranges much farther afield these days. Porcini-dusted halibut with asparagus purée and lobster-corn emulsion was memorable, as was the pan-seared duck breast with baby bok choy. Just poke a finger at the menu in the gloom—you're unlikely to be disappointed.

266 College St. (btw. Chapel and Crown sts.). ✆ **203/562-4644.** www.bespokenewhaven.com. Main courses $26–$29. AE, DISC, MC, V. Mon–Thurs 5–9:30pm; Fri–Sat 5–10:30pm; Sun 4:30–8:30pm.

Ibiza ★★ SPANISH   This used to be Pika Tapas, but it didn't get all that much attention until the owners decided to go upmarket, introducing the newly daring modern cuisine and wines of their native Spain. Their menu includes a few traditional dishes, among them *caldo Gallego,* a potato, bean, and chorizo soup; and *codornices,* pan-roasted quail with saffron coulis. But they up the ante with vigor, as when they put together foie gras, quail eggs, kumquats, and smoked duck breast or cod confit with sautéed noodles, cockles, baby squid, and sun-dried tomatoes. To get a better idea of their range, spring for the $58 tasting menu (available Mon–Thurs). Note that lunch is served only on Friday, paella is served only at Tuesday dinner, and tapas are available at the bar Monday through Friday evenings.

39 High St. (south of Chapel St.). ✆ **203/865-1933.** www.ibizanewhaven.com. Reservations recommended. Main courses $23–$29. AE, MC, V. Mon–Thurs 5–9pm; Fri noon–2:30pm and 5–10pm; Sat 5–10pm.

Pacifico ★ NUEVO LATINO   The restaurant's name refers to the cuisines of the western coast of Latin America, but while the kitchen draws inspiration from that extended region, it doesn't engage in slavish replications of traditional dishes. In general, this means lighter, less robustly seasoned food than found in Mexico, Colombia, Peru, and Ecuador. We are offered such inventions as seared tilapia with a yucca crust and artichoke, potato, and Manchego cakes puddled in basil and yellow-tomato coulis. Pacifico's version of vegetarian paella turns out to be layered quinoa, asparagus, shiitakes, zucchini, plantain, and more packed into a round pastry basket. Presentations are pretty but unfussy. A particularly good deal is the three-course *prix fixe* lunch at $17.

220 George St. (Temple St.). ✆ **203/772-4002.** www.pacificony.com. Main courses $17–$28. AE, DC, MC, V. Daily noon–10pm (until 11pm Thurs–Sat).

Union League Café ★★ BRASSERIE   A grand salon that retains an air of the site's aristocratic origins, which date back to 1854—even the name fairly shrieks of the spot's former status as a bastion of WASP privilege, the Union League Club. Things have loosened up considerably, and denim-clad Yalies, their doting parents, and philosophizing profs are all equally comfortable here. With waiters in aprons and tables covered with butcher paper, the atmosphere is now closer to an updated French brasserie than to that of a gentlemen's sanctuary. The chef routinely tinkers with Gallic culinary tradition. Past entrees on the order of cod and sweet-potato brandade, curried lamb shank, and braised veal cheeks seemed both familiar and fresh. A daily cheese card is proffered instead of, or in addition to, dessert. The wine list is almost exclusively French. Service is informed and proficient.

1032 Chapel St. (btw. High and College sts.). © **203/562-4299.** www.unionleaguecafe.com. Main courses $21–$32. AE, DC, MC, V. Mon–Fri 11:30am–2:30pm and 5–9:30pm; Sat 5–10pm.

Zinc ★★ NEW AMERICAN   On site for over 10 years, this contemporary bistro can be fairly credited with igniting the city's restaurant renaissance, presaging all but the Union League Café (above) as a pinpoint of light in the once-dreary New Haven night. The interior is of mahogany and zinc, Manhattan-esque, but with elbow room. The chef/co-owner is adventurous without being scary. Hot sauces of many origins are frequently incorporated into dishes, as with the harissa-tinged tomato aioli that brightens the hanger steak, which also comes with black beans and honey-sweet mashed potatoes—a winner. Look, too, for the smoked duck nachos and vegetarian paella on the changing card. Zinc pays particular attention to its cheese menu, and the restaurant offers 13 wines by the glass. Owners recently opened **Kitchen Zinc,** an artisan pizza bar around back, at 966 Chapel St. (© 203/772-3002).

964 Chapel St. (opposite New Haven Green). © **203/624-0507.** www.zincfood.com. Main courses $23–$28. MC, V. Sun–Thurs 5–9pm; Fri–Sat 5–10pm.

MODERATE

Heirloom ★★ NEW AMERICAN   The new Study at Yale boutique hotel (p. 391) embellishes its high-quality image even more with this important addition to the local dining scene. The uncluttered room with a window wall softens the minimalist vibe with comfortable padded chairs. A changing menu carries through, with familiar fare ratcheted up in taste and visual appeal. Ipswich whole belly fried clams, for one example, nudges that New England standard to a new level of flavor and greaseless crunch. You may know sea scallops, but not with a balsamic glaze while floating on this puddle of sweet pea purée with mission figs. At lunch, the special mac and cheese beckons, bits of ham hock baked within. Students and locals are drawn in on otherwise slow nights by $5 burgers and $4 beers.

1157 Chapel St. (btw. Park & York sts.). © **203/503-3919.** www.studyhotels.com. Main courses $13–$33. AE, DC, MC, V. Sun–Thurs 7am–10pm; Fri–Sun 7am–11pm.

Istanbul Café ★ TURKISH   Step through the door into a room that consciously resembles a family restaurant in the eponymous city's Beyoglu market. An elaborate pewter chandelier looms overhead, Turkish ceramics hang on the walls, and mirror cloth pillows line the bench couch along the wall. The setting is right, and so's the food. Get in the mood with the starter platter of *meze*—dollops of hummus, zingy red lentil salad, creamy carrot salad, spinach yogurt, and *dolmas* (grape leaves wrapped around rice fillings). Crispy rounds of bread arrive, aromatic steam arising when they are torn open. Kabobs predominate among the entrees—chunks of chicken, lamb, and/or beef prepared in a number of traditional modes. The lamb is wonderful, especially in the Iskender kabob and Yaprak Doner kabob served only on Friday and Saturday.

245 Crown St. (at College St.). ℂ **203/787-3881**. www.istanbulcafect.com. Main courses $15–$22. AE, DC, MC, V. Mon–Fri noon–3pm and 5–10pm (until 11pm Fri); Sat–Sun noon–11pm.

INEXPENSIVE

Louis' Lunch DINER   The claim, unprovable but gaining strength as the decades roll on, is that America's very first hamburger was sold in 1900 at this little luncheonette. Although the low brick building was moved from its original location to escape demolition, not much else has changed. The wooden counter and tables are carved with the initials of a century of patrons. The beef is freshly ground each day, thrust into gas-fired ovens, and then served (medium rare, usually) on two slices of white toast. The only allowable garnishes are tomato, onion, or cheese—there's no ketchup or mustard, so don't even ask. There are no fries, either, just potato chips or potato salad. (A posted sign says, "This is not Burger King. You don't get it your way, you take it my way.") On the upside, soup is served, and, during late hours from Thursday through Saturday, franks and steak sandwiches, too . . . sometimes.

261-263 Crown St. (btw. High and College sts.). ℂ **203/562-5507**. www.louislunch.com. All items under $8. No credit cards. Tues–Wed 11am–4pm; Thurs–Sat noon–2am. Closed Aug.

New Haven After Dark

The presence of Yale and a highly educated faction of the general population ensures a cultural life in New Haven equal to that of many larger cities. A reliable source of information on cultural events and nightlife is the free weekly newspaper, the *New Haven Advocate* (www.newhavenadvocate.com).

THE PERFORMING ARTS   Within a couple of blocks of the Green, the **Shubert Performing Arts Center,** 247 College St. (ℂ **888/736-2663** or 203/562-5666; www.shubert.com), presents musicals, opera, plays, cabaret, concerts, and such touring troops as the Alvin Ailey Dance Theater. The well-regarded **Yale Repertory Theatre** (ℂ **203/432-1234;** www.yalerep.org) mounts an October-to-May season of modern productions as well as classics by Shakespeare, George Bernard Shaw, and

Tennessee Williams. It uses two venues: University Theater, 222 York St., and The Rep, 1120 Chapel St.

Away from downtown, but worth the cab fare, is the prestigious **Long Wharf Theatre,** 222 Sargent Dr. (📞 **203/787-4282;** www.longwharf.org). It's known for its success in producing new plays that often make the jump to Off-Broadway and even Broadway itself. The season runs from October to June.

Several venues on the Yale campus, including **Sprague Memorial Hall,** 470 College St., and **Woolsey Hall,** at College and Grove streets, host the performances of resident organizations, including the New Haven Symphony Orchestra, New Haven Civic Orchestra, Yale Concert Band, Yale Glee Club, Yale Philharmonia, and Yale Symphony Orchestra. For upcoming events, call the **Yale Concert Information Line** (📞 **203/432-4157**).

THE CLUB SCENE   The biggest and best venue for live rock, hip-hop, and pop is **Toad's Place,** 300 York St. (📞 **203/621-TOAD** [8623]; www.toadsplace.com), which welcomes the likes of George Clinton, The Mars Volta, and Johnny Winter, with a smattering of tribute bands and regional groups on the schedule, too. Much of the year, there are performances nightly. A mixed calendar pertains at **The Lansdowne Bar & Grill,** 179 Crown St. (📞 **203/285-3939;** www.lansdownect.com), where the schedule includes football, music jams, dance parties, costume contests, and open mic evenings.

For something less frenetic, the popular **BAR/The Brü Rm,** 254 Crown St. (📞 **203/495-1111;** www.barnightclub.com), has a lounge in front—open to the street on warm nights—and a pool table, terrace, and dance floor in back. On Sunday, listen to live jazz or blues. It's open 365 nights a year and Wednesday through Sunday for lunch. Rich beers are produced on site, and the kitchen poses a naked challenge in the eternal New Haven pizza wars. Its thinnest-crust pies are leading contenders for the crown long held by Frank Pepe's.

The gentrifying Ninth Square neighborhood has a new bar and jazz concert space, **Firehouse 12,** 45 Crown St. (📞 **203/785-0468;** www.firehouse12.com). It's open Wednesday through Saturday nights, featuring half-price drafts and free food some evenings. Combos usually appear on Friday.

HARTFORD

122 miles NE of New York City; 100 miles SW of Boston

Dissidents fleeing the rigid religious dictates of the Massachusetts Bay Colony founded Hartford in 1636. Three years later, they drafted what were called the "Fundamental Orders," the basis of a subsequent claim that Connecticut was the first political entity on Earth to have a written constitution—hence the nickname "Constitution State."

Connecticut's capital is home to several major insurance company headquarters, making the staid insurance industry the dominant employer. A third of the population is of Puerto Rican heritage, the third largest concentration of Puerto Ricans on the U.S. mainland. (For a terrific taste of Puerto Rican music, try Miguel Zenón's 2009 album, *Esta Plena,* which mixes jazz with the Afro-Caribbean tradition. Zenón teaches at the New England Conservatory in Boston.)

Downtown is a mixed bag. Dominated by the Old State House, the august Wadsworth Atheneum, and the divinely overwrought gold-domed capitol building, it also sags under what was a 40% vacancy rate in retail space in 2009. Don't plan to do any shopping here—retail has packed up and moved to outer regions. However, the city has a strong arts scene and some cosmopolitan restaurants, and there are museums worth traveling here for, including a splashy new science center for children. Most of a day trip or overnight visit can be contained within a few blocks radiating around the Old State House. The Twain and Stowe houses (below) are 1½ miles east of city center.

Essentials

GETTING THERE Interstates 84 and 91 intersect in central Hartford. The city is halfway between New York and Boston.

Bradley International (© 860/292-2000; www.bradleyairport.com; airport code BDL), in Windsor Locks, Connecticut, about 14 miles north of the city, is served by major U.S. airlines, including **American** (© 800/433-7300), **Continental** (© 800/523-3273), **Delta** (© 800/221-1212), **United** (© 800/864-8331), and **US Airways** (© 800/428-4322).

Amtrak (© 800/USA-RAIL [872-7245]; www.amtrak.com) has several trains that stop daily in Hartford.

VISITOR INFORMATION The downtown **Greater Hartford Arts Council Welcome Center,** 45 Pratt St. (© 860/2444-0253; www.letsgoarts.org/welcomecenter), is a half-block from the Old State House and open Monday through Friday from 9am to 5pm. It has great arts-centric maps for visitors.

Online information is available at **www.ctvisit.com**, the website of Connecticut's Commission on Culture & Tourism (© 888/288-4748), and includes hotel special packages and a well put together "This Weekend" page of activities. More information still is available at **www.hartford.com**, a production of the Hartford Business Improvement District.

The free weekly *Hartford Advocate* (**www.hartfordadvocate.com**) provides coverage of cultural, sports, and musical events. The daily paper, the *Hartford Courant,* is online at www.courant.com.

In addition to the regular city buses, a free "Star Shuttle" run by CT Transit (© 860/525-9181; www.cttransit.com) makes a loop past all the venues mentioned in this section except for the Twain and Stowe houses. You can print out a map of the route from the company's website.

SPECIAL EVENTS For 3 days in mid-July, the **Greater Hartford Festival of Jazz** (www.hartfordjazz.com) offers free performances at the pavilion in Bushnell Park, adjacent to the capital. In 2009, it attracted a record 55,000 fans.

What to See & Do

Free family-friendly concerts, dance performances, fireworks, and a Dragon Boat & Asian Festival (held every Aug) take place throughout the summer and fall at **Riverfront Plaza,** an area just north of the Science Center extending to the Connecticut River. Events are listed at **www.riverfront.org**. In nice weather, use the Plaza as a launching point for a riverside stroll in the refurbished Riverside Park, where you'll find 19 sculptures all related to U.S. President Abraham Lincoln (www.riverfront.org/parks/lincoln).

Connecticut Science Center ★ ☺ Open since July 2009, hopes are high for this $165-million center to be a pillar of a major economic development initiative to

Hartford

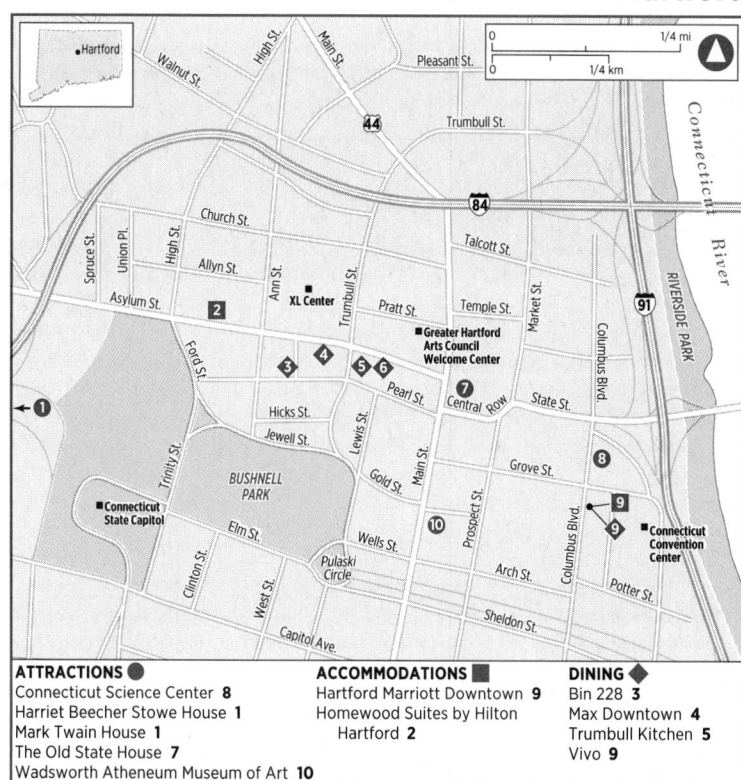

ATTRACTIONS ●
Connecticut Science Center **8**
Harriet Beecher Stowe House **1**
Mark Twain House **1**
The Old State House **7**
Wadsworth Atheneum Museum of Art **10**

ACCOMMODATIONS ■
Hartford Marriott Downtown **9**
Homewood Suites by Hilton
Hartford **2**

DINING ◆
Bin 228 **3**
Max Downtown **4**
Trumbull Kitchen **5**
Vivo **9**

remake downtown Hartford. Thanks to soaring glass walls and a swooping rooftop overhang, the building is a dramatic addition to the skyline. Inside are some 150 exhibits, mostly interactive, and a 3D theater. The center opened at an inopportune time—a depressed economy and the outbreak of the H1N1 virus made a tough one-two punch for the kid-centric venue. But kids and the adults who trail after them have given the center good marks in its opening months. It's located on the same block as the Hartford Marriott Downtown and the convention center, and is adjacent to Riverfront Plaza and the revitalized waterfront along the Connecticut River.

250 Columbus Blvd. ✆ **860/724-3623.** www.ctsciencecenter.org. Admission $17 adults, $16 seniors, $14 children 3–17, free ages 2 and under. Additional fee for 3D movie, with combo tickets available. Tues–Sun and holidays 10am–5pm. July–Aug also Mon 10am–5pm.

Harriet Beecher Stowe Center   Stowe's book *Uncle Tom's Cabin,* published in 1852, when she was 41, portrayed the physical, sexual, and emotional abuse endured by enslaved people. It became a best-seller in the United States, England, Europe, and Asia. This home was built in 1871 and is a smaller version of the adjacent Twain residence (below). Stowe and Twain moved into their respective residences within a year of each other, when Stowe was in her 60s and Twain was nearing 40. Displays illustrate 19th-century women's history, African-American history, and the changes in racial attitudes in the U.S. Seasonal and themed tours are built around African-American history, women's history, house and garden, and the activism of Nook Farm, a 19th-century artist community. A special child's tour, with storytelling and activities, is held Saturday, Sunday, and holidays at 2pm ($5 ages 5–12, $4 all others).

77 Forest St. ✆ **860/522-9258.** www.harrietbeecherstowecenter.org. Admission $9–$11 adults, $8–$9 seniors and students, $6–$8 children 5-16, free for children 4 and under. Wed–Sat 9:30am-4:30pm; Sun noon–4:30pm. June–Oct also Tues 9:30am-4:30pm. Visits by guided tour only. See Twain House (below) for directions.

Mark Twain House & Museum ★★ ☺ Samuel Clemens, whose pseudonym, Mark Twain, was a term used by Mississippi River pilots to indicate a water depth of 2 fathoms, lived here from 1874 to 1891, a period when he wrote *The Adventures of Huckleberry Finn* and *A Connecticut Yankee in King Arthur's Court*. The 19-room house is a fascinating example of the late-19th-century style sometimes known as "Picturesque Gothic," with several steeply peaked gables and brick walls whose varying patterns are highlighted by black or orange paint. The High Victorian interior was the work of distinguished designers of the time, including Louis Comfort Tiffany, who provided both advice and stained glass. Twain's enthusiasm for newfangled gadgets—*Life on the Mississippi* is said to be the first novel written on a typewriter—led to the installation of a primitive telephone in the entrance hall.

The house has been in financial trouble in recent years, struggling to service $11 million in debt from the 2003 construction of a state-of-the-art visitor center. A website note in early 2010 said, however, that the house "is turning the corner on its financial crisis" and that "a lively series of events and exhibits is bringing new visitors to the museum daily."

351 Farmington Ave. ✆ **860/247-0998.** www.marktwainhouse.org. Admission $14 adults, $12 seniors, $8 children 6-16, free for children 5 and under. Mon–Sat 9:30am-5:30pm; Sun noon-5:30pm. Closed Tues Jan-Mar. Visits by guided tour only. Take exit 46 off I-84, turn right onto Sisson Ave., then right onto Farmington Ave. From downtown, drive west on Asylum St., bearing left on Farmington Ave.

The Old State House After escaping a close call in 1975 (the city wanted to tear it down to build a parking lot), the beautiful 1796 State House was given new luster with a $12-million restoration. Visitors can walk the building by either guided or self-guided tour. Upstairs is the historic Senate chamber, complete with a full-length portrait of U.S. President George Washington by Gilbert Stuart, who produced the best-known images of the first president. Three eras of architecture are represented: Federal (Senate Chamber), Victorian (City Council Chamber), and Colonial Revival (upper hall and stairs). Also here is the "Museum of Natural and Other Curiosities," which opened in 1797. It includes a calf with two heads and the "horn of a unicorn." There are stockades in front of the building, to pose the kids for the perfect Christmas photo.

800 Main St. (at Asylum Ave.). ✆ **860/522-6766.** www.ctosh.org. Admission $6 adults; $3 seniors, students, and children 6-17; free for children 5 and under. Jan-Mar Mon–Fri 10am-5pm; Apr-Dec Tues-Sat 10am-5pm; call to confirm dates and times.

Wadsworth Atheneum Museum of Art ★★★ Opened in 1842, this was the first public art museum in the United States and it remains a repository with few equals in New England. The strength of the collection lies primarily in its American paintings, especially its 30-plus romantic landscapes of the Hudson River School of the 19th century. Also represented are Andrew Wyeth, Milton Avery, and Norman Rockwell, and canvases by abstract expressionists and pop and op artists of the 1950s and 1960s, including Willem de Kooning and Robert Rauschenberg. Through 2011, the museum is hosting a Masterpiece Series of small exhibitions to bring some of the world's greatest art to Hartford; the first series focused on Rembrandt.

600 Main St. (1 block south of the Old State House). ✆ **860/278-2670.** www.wadsworthatheneum.org. Admission $10 adults, $8 seniors, $5 students, free for children 12 and under; $5 admission first Thurs of month 5–8pm. Wed–Fri 11am–5pm; Sat–Sun 10am–5pm (until 8pm first Thurs of most months).

Where to Stay

Hartford Marriott Downtown ★★
This Marriott opened next to the Connecticut Convention Center in 2005 and immediately challenged the existing hotels on every front. Guest rooms come complete with cushy mattresses as well as MP3 docking stations and 37-inch flatscreen TVs. The main restaurant, **Vivo,** goes in for imaginative interpretations of the Mediterranean oeuvre (main courses $23–$39). The lounge, **Crush,** has white couches, a big martini card with girly concoctions such as "Gummy Bear," and DJs on Friday and Saturday nights. The hotel is entirely smoke-free. Ask for a riverside room for the best views.

200 Columbus Blvd., Hartford, CT 06103. ✆ **860/249-8000.** Fax 860/249-8181. www.hartfordmarriott. com. 409 units. $159–$349 double. Valet parking $23; self-parking $19. AE, DC, DISC, MC, V. **Amenities:** Restaurant; bar/lounge; concierge; concierge-level rooms; exercise room; Jacuzzi; indoor rooftop pool; room service; spa; Wi-Fi (free in lobby). *In room:* A/C, TV, hair dryer, MP3 docking station, Wi-Fi ($10 a day).

Homewood Suites by Hilton Hartford ★ ☺
New (since 2007), clean, and bland, this Hilton property is on a well-trafficked block downtown and is a short walk from the restaurants, museums, and nightlife listed here. All rooms are suites and have a kitchenette (at least), a pull-out couch (in all but 10 units), and either a king or queen bed. The hotel gets a lot of business travelers, visitors in for weddings or conventions (there's a ballroom on a top floor), and families who need space to spread out. Included in the rate are breakfast, no-fee weekday grocery shopping, and a light afternoon meal Monday through Thursday. In the summer months, ask for a room away from the adjacent restaurant Black-Eyed Sally's, which has an outdoor rooftop pub.

338 Asylum St., Hartford, CT 06103. ✆ **860/524-0223.** Fax 860/524-0264. www.homewoodsuites. com. 116 units. $199–$269 double. Rates include breakfast (daily) and a light afternoon meal (Mon-Thurs). AE, DC, DISC, MC, V. Self-parking $16. Pets accepted ($50 fee). **Amenities:** Restaurant (limited service); exercise room. *In room:* A/C, TV, hair dryer, kitchenette, Wi-Fi (free).

Where to Dine

In addition to the restaurants below, consider the venues listed in "Hartford After Dark" (p. 400), which all serve food, and the spacious **Vivo** (✆ **860/760-2333**), located in the Hartford Marriott (see above).

Bin 228 ★ WINE BAR
Chic, pretty, and friendly, this petite bistro seats just 24 and has a wine bar with room for about the same number. Attractive picture windows overlook a quiet downtown street, and bright paintings by local artists decorate brick walls. The menu features light fare: salads, small plates, bruschetta, *tramezzini* (small sandwiches), and panini. The grilled chicken panini is the most popular, but if you're lucky they'll be offering a more adventurous option, the prosciutto, fig, caramelized onion, and asiago cheese panini, which packs a flavor punch and was flagged by *Bon Appétit*. (The recipe is at Epicurious.com.) This is a romantic spot

with a Euro casualness, although solo eaters settle in quite comfortably alongside business folks in jeans and cashmere.

228 Pearl St. © **860/244-9463.** www.bin228winebar.com. Main courses $7.50–$14. AE, DISC, MC, V. Mon–Thurs 11:30am–11pm; Fri 11:30am–midnight; Sat 4pm–midnight. Bar open "late" most nights.

Feng Asian Bistro & Lounge ★ ASIAN FUSION   Tucked, bunkerlike, behind a windowless front punctuated by a pearlescent sign and large wooden doors, this large, modern eatery blends Japanese, Thai, and Chinese cuisines. Inside, it's dark and a little nightclubby. Feng's entrance onto the Hartford scene in 2006 was much heralded, and it immediately joined the limited ranks of urbane options in this city. The large menu ranges from sushi to steak, and the lunch maki special, with two rolls (try the eel and avocado roll and the shrimp tempura roll), plus miso soup or salad, for $9, is a good value. The main room has large tables and curved banquettes along one wall, and there's a sushi counter and a front bar for eating, too. Food is available until 1am on Friday and Saturday.

93 Asylum St. © **860/549-3364.** www.fengrestaurant.com. Main courses $13–$37; sushi $3–$28. AE, MC, V. Mon–Thurs 11:30am–midnight; Fri 11:30am–1am; Sat 5pm–1am; Sun 5–11pm.

Max Downtown ★★ NEW AMERICAN   Hartford's prime-time power lunch venue is nearly always packed with folks in suits at midday (male-to-female ratio 20:1 on a recent visit) and a lot of air-kissers at night. The main room has banquettes arrayed behind expanses of glass, with a flashy mural on the back wall. Diners are indulged with hefty chophouse favorites—"Cowboy Cut" beef rib chop with foie gras butter, perhaps?—and lighter efforts, such Georges Bank cod. Over two dozen wines are available by the glass. The adjacent piano bar is also formal, even at lunch.

A sister restaurant, **Trumbull Kitchen,** is just around the corner at 150 Trumball St. It also caters to young execs and lawyers but offers up a long menu of creative global grazing noshes. It's cheaper, with main courses from $13 to $26 at dinner and $9 to $12 at lunch, and less formal by several notches.

185 Asylum St. © **860/522-2530.** www.maxrestaurantgroup.com/downtown. Reservations recommended on Fri–Sat. Main courses $18–$37. AE, DC, MC, V. Mon–Thurs 11:30am–10pm; Fri 11:30am–11pm; Sat 5–11pm; Sun 4:30–9:30pm.

Rein's ★ DELI   Rein's is off I-84 about 15 minutes northeast of Hartford, but it's a good place to keep in mind when you're driving in the area. It is the region's wildly popular New York–style Jewish delicatessen, and it handles the large sit-down crowds with good cheer. Favorites from the large menu include whitefish salad, kasha knish of buckwheat groats, Hebrew National Kosher franks, and nine kinds of Reubens, from pastrami to turkey. Everything can be washed down with Dr. Brown's peculiar celery-flavored Cel-Ray soda or a classic chocolate egg cream. If there's a line for a table, see if any of the nine counter stools are open. Or, take a tip from those who stop here on drives between New York and Boston and call in an order to go.

435 Hartford Tpk. (Rte. 30), Vernon, CT. © **860/875-1344.** www.reinsdeli.com. Main courses $5–$13. AE, DISC, MC, V. Daily 7am–midnight. From I-84, take exit 65 to Rte. 30 north. Rein's is in a mini-mall behind the Comfort Inn.

Hartford After Dark

The **Bushnell Center for the Performing Arts,** 166 Capitol Ave. (© **888/824-2874;** www.bushnell.org), hosts a huge selection of events in its four halls, from

Broadway shows such as *In The Heights* and *Disney's The Lion King* to concerts such as Marvin Hamlisch conducting the Hartford Symphony in a tribute to Barbra Streisand. **Hartford Stage,** 50 Church St. (✆ **860/527-5151;** www.hartfordstage.org), mounts a variety of heart-warming plays such as *The Adventures of Tom Sawyer* and *Gee's Bend.*

The **XL Center,** One Civic Center Plaza (✆ **860/249-6333;** www.xlcenter. com), is the city's big sports arena. The University of Connecticut's men and women's basketball teams play here (both are powerhouses in their leagues), and so does the Hartford Wolf Pack American Hockey League team. Events such as gymnastics events, dog shows, and bridal expos fill out the schedule.

Hot Tomato's, 1 Union Place (at the corner of Asylum St.; ✆ **860/249-5100;** www.hottomatos.net), a long-popular trattoria known for its big bowls of garlicky pasta and mains such as seafood puttanesca, converted its glassed-in dining room to a lounge with attached outdoor terrace in early 2010. Plans call for occasional live music in the swank space. Hot Tomato's will continue to serve its Italian fare in the two interior rooms.

The enormous **City Steam Brewery,** 942 Main St. (✆ **860/525-1600;** www. citysteambrewerycafe.com), has seven levels over three floors—it's housed in a gorgeous 1877 building that once held the largest department store in Connecticut— and has room for hundreds of revelers. On tap are over a half-dozen of its own beers, from amber ales to Belgium white beer, to accompany a long menu of pub grub. It hosts the **Brew HA HA Comedy Club** on Thursday through Saturday nights.

Black-Eyed Sally's, 350 Asylum St. (✆ **860/278-7427;** www.blackeyedsallys. com), known for its BBQ ribs and other Southern-style treats, presents live blues bands 4 or 5 nights a week. The **Arch Street Tavern,** 85 Arch St. (✆ **860/246-7610;** www.archstreettavern.com), around the corner from the convention center, is a pub/restaurant with sports on big screens.

FROM GUILFORD TO OLD SAYBROOK

Guilford: 93 miles NE of New York City; Madison: 98 miles NE of New York City; Old Saybrook: 110 miles NE of New York City

Often ignored by vacationers making a beeline to Essex (p. 406) or Mystic (p. 411), the stretch of coast between New Haven and the Connecticut River, known simply as the Shoreline, has enough gentle pleasures to justify a short detour for lunch, a walk on a beach, or a spell of shopping.

Essentials

GETTING THERE The Shoreline can be reached from exit 57 off I-95. Pick up Rte. 1 (the Boston Post Rd.), which serves as the main street of several Shoreline towns. In the summer and fall, look for farm stands along Rte. 1.

Several daily **Amtrak** (✆ **800/USA-RAIL** [872-7245]; www.amtrak.com) trains stop at Old Saybrook. The **Shore Line East** (✆ **800/255-7433;** www.shoreline east.com) commuter line uses the same rail tracks to service towns between New Haven and New London.

VISITOR INFORMATION Information about the towns in this section is online at **www.newhavencvb.org,** the Greater New Haven website. Other good listings, special hotel packages, and a nifty "This Weekend" page of suggested activities are at **www.ctvisit.com**, the website of Connecticut's Commission on Culture & Tourism (© **888/288-4748**).

Note that the highway signs on I-95 at exit 56 for a "tourist information center" are somewhat misleading: The TA Travel Center in Branford caters primarily to truckers, with showers, a few fast-food outlets, and just a small rack of brochures.

Guilford

One of the state's oldest Colonial settlements (1639), this posh, well-kept village, 13 miles east of New Haven, is embraced by the West and East rivers. It has an uncommonly large public green with a few upscale shops along one side. Those shops include **Mix,** 29 Whitfield St. (© **203/453-0202;** www.mixdesignstore.com), a modern accessories and jewelry store with colorful items made in Sweden, Germany, and the U.S.

The town has dozens of historic houses, most of them privately owned, but a few open to the public on a limited basis, typically from June to Columbus Day. They include **Hyland House,** 84 Boston St. (www.hylandhouse.com), an early Colonial saltbox with three walk-in fireplaces and an herb garden, built around 1690, and the **Thomas Griswold House,** 171 Boston St. (© **203/453-3176;** www.guilford keepingsociety.com), with a restored blacksmith shop, built around 1774.

The Guilford visitor center is located next to the Henry Whitfield State Museum (see below). Housed in an 1870 barn, it's open May through October on Wednesday, Saturday, and Sunday from 10am to 4pm. Additional information is available from the **Guilford Chamber of Commerce** (© **203/453-9677;** www.guilfordct.com).

Bishop's Orchards This large operation features a market, a bakery, a winery, and pick-your-own fruits, including strawberries and apples, from June through October. On fall weekends, its Little Red Barn is a family destination, with maple "kettle korn," a hay maze for kids, a make-your-own-scarecrow table, mums and pumpkins for sale, and freshly made apple cider donuts. The operation has a down-country feel, perhaps because it's still owned by the family that started it in 1871. The Orchard's award-winning apple wines are tasty and make nice regional gifts. Surprisingly, the place is open year-round.

1355 Boston Post Rd. (Rte. 1). © **203/453-2338.** www.bishopsorchards.com. Free admission. Mon–Sat 8am–7pm; Sun 9am–6pm.

Henry Whitfield State Museum The Whitfield Museum bills itself as the oldest house in Connecticut and the oldest stone house in New England. Most of what you see now, though, including the leaded windows, dates from a 1930s reconstruction and not from 1639, so it is really more a museum than a historic home. It is still worth a brief visit, however, and the furnishings are authentic to the period. The low stone walls, grass fields, and grand trees of the grounds are also atmospherically evocative of the 17th century.

248 Old Whitfield St. © **203/453-2457.** www.whitfieldmuseum.com. Admission $8 adults, $6 seniors and students, $5 children 6–17, free for children 5 and under. May–Oct Wed and Sat–Sun 10am–4pm. Closed Nov–Apr.

WHERE TO DINE

The Place ★ SEAFOOD Outdoors, under a striped tent if the weather is threatening, the Place cooks its food over open wood fires. You sit on tree stumps and can buy a T-shirt that confirms that you "Put Your Rump On A Stump." What's served is, in essence, a clambake, so you are morally obligated to begin with a raft of that bivalve. Clams are roasted over smoky coals, popped open, dabbed with hot sauce, and run back over the fire as a finish. Corn cooked in the husk is another must. You can get bluefish or chicken as your main course, but this is a place for lobster. Dessert options include pecan pie and hot fudge sundaes, but the carrot cake is the winner. You will leave grinning.

901 Boston Post Rd. (Rte. 1). ☏ **203/453-9276.** Main courses $5.95–$25; most under $11. No credit cards. Mon–Fri 5–9pm; Sat 1–10pm; Sun noon–9pm. Late Apr to mid-Oct, plus Fri–Sun after mid-Oct weather permitting. The Place is opposite a shopping mall.

Whitfield's on Guilford Green ★ NEW AMERICAN Set in a restored Victorian building, Whitfield's attracts well-heeled locals to its bright, main room, which overlooks Guilford's handsome town green. In warm months, consider taking a table on the pretty back patio, which overlooks the serene Greene Art Gallery sculpture garden. Menu items at lunch include a large selection of generous salads and sandwiches with prices hovering around $12. Our favorites: the California salad, with chunks of crab meat, avocado, and Granny Smith apple; and the gooey and delicious grilled vegetable panini with zucchini, herbed goat cheese, and pesto on a unique toasted pretzel roll.

25 Whitfield St. ☏ **203/458-1300.** www.whitfieldsguilford.com. Main courses $11–$30. AE, MC, V. Mon–Sat 11:30am–3pm; Sun 9am–3pm; daily 5–9pm (until 10pm Fri–Sat).

Madison

Madison, 5 miles east of Guilford, is home to a historic architectural district that stretches west of the business district along the Boston Post Road, from the main green to the town line. It contains many examples of 18th- and 19th-century domestic styles.

The well-to-do town has gone from colony to seaside resort to year-round community, a process begun when the first house was built in 1651. Two dwellings from the early years can be visited on limited summer schedules. **Deacon John Grave House,** 581 Boston Post Rd. (☏ 203/245-4798; www.deaconjohngrave.org), dates from 1685; and the **Allis-Bushnell House,** 853 Boston Post Rd. (☏ **203/245-4567;** www.madisoncthistorical.org), from 1785. (Note that Boston Post Rd. is the main street in many of these Shoreline towns, and that the street numbers start anew each time you cross a town line.)

Off the Boston Post Road at the eastern end of Madison, and also reached from exit 62 off I-95, is **Hammonasset Beach State Park** (☏ 203/245-2785; www. ct.gov), Connecticut's largest public beach park. It's on a peninsula that juts into Long Island Sound and has a shore that's over 2 miles long. The shore, however, is narrow due to a serious erosion problem: Signs at the entrance to the beach explain that the shore is losing 1 to 2 feet of beach each year. The on-site **Meigs Point Nature Center** offers programs and activities spring through fall. From Memorial Day to Labor Day, cars with out-of-state plates are charged $20 Monday through Friday and $30 on weekends and holidays to enter and park. If that seems higher than usual it is: The state doubled the fees in October 2009.

SHOPPING

Right in downtown, stately **R. J. Julia Booksellers,** 768 Boston Post Rd. (☏ **203/245-3959;** www.rjjulia.com), holds frequent author readings. It has a cafe that's open from 10am to 8pm Monday through Saturday and 10am to 6pm on Sunday.

Five miles from downtown Madison is **Clinton Crossing,** 20-A Killingsworth Tpk. (© **860/664-0700;** www.premiumoutlets.com), an outlet mall with 70 shops, including Kenneth Cole, Barneys New York Outlet, and Saks Fifth Avenue Off 5th. Find it east on Rte. 1 and then north on Rte. 81, or directly off 1-95 at exit 63.

WHERE TO DINE

Watch the streets for an old-fashioned **Good Humor truck** in the warm months. It's original from the 1960s and sports the classic icicle logo and a side freezer door, and is run by a man who goes by the name Papa-Jo. Toasted almond ice-cream bar, anyone?

Lenny & Joe's Fish Tale ☺ SEAFOOD   At this rough-and-ready fish shack (to be honest, it feels more like a fast-food joint), seafood rules, most of it fried. And while it is sure to elevate triglyceride counts, the nutty coating on superfresh clams, oysters, shrimp, and calamari is hard to resist. Chowders and seafood rolls are good, too. **Bonus:** In summer, there's a small old-time carousel ($1 a ride, weekends only) and an ice-cream stand here, too. A second outlet 6 miles east in Westbrook, at 86 Boston Post Rd. (© **860/669-0767**), has table service and a bar, and more of a restaurant feel.

1301 Boston Post Rd. © **203/245-7289.** www.ljfishtale.com. Main courses $5–$22. DC, DISC, MC, V. Daily 11am–9pm (until 9:30pm Fri–Sat).

Old Saybrook

Its dramatic location at the mouth of the Connecticut River (35 miles east of New Haven, 26 miles west of Mystic) is Old Saybrook's principal lure.

To take a **coastal tour,** get off Rte. 1 and pick up Rte. 154 just east of the high school. The road loops for 6 miles, going down the shore, through the tony hamlet of Fenwick, and across a causeway to Saybrook Point (and the inn that's listed below) before ending up in the town's main business district and then rejoining Rte. 1.

Movie buffs will want to stop by the **Katharine Hepburn Cultural Arts Center,** 300 Main St. (© **860/510-0473;** www.katharinehepburntheater.org), which is housed in a brick Greek revival building in the center of downtown. Named for the late actress, who made her home in Old Saybrook, the facility is listed on the National Registry of Historic Places. It has a teeny boutique that sells merchandise marked "the Kate" and a small museum devoted to the actress. The boutique and museum are open during box office hours: Tuesday through Friday from 10am to 2pm, and 1 hour before show time.

WHERE TO STAY

Saybrook Point Inn & Spa ★★   Resort hotels have existed at this dramatic spot where the Connecticut River meets the ocean since the late 19th century, and the inn's current owners have the formula down pat. With an updated but old-world sophistication, the resort has one of the largest marinas along the Connecticut coast, an ingratiating restaurant (the **Terra Mar Grille** ★), a clubby bar, a summer dining terrace overlooking the water, and a spa with 12 treatment rooms. Bedrooms are spacious, decorated in 18th-century English style. All have sitting areas and most have wood-burning fireplaces and balconies with water views. The restaurant sources much of its offerings from 90 Connecticut farms, and a standout is the thick clam chowder with smoky bacon. Sunday brunch ($30) is popular. There's heavy wedding business here, often with multiple events on weekends, and the accompanying bustle and noise in high season.

2 Bridge St., Old Saybrook, CT 06475. © **800/243-0212** or 860/395-2000. www.saybrook.com. 80 units. $239–$389 double. AE, DC, DISC, MC, V. Take Rte. 154 south from Rte. 1. Pets accepted ($50 first night, $25 each additional night). **Amenities:** Restaurant; bar; bikes; health club; indoor and outdoor saltwater pools; room service; spa. *In room:* A/C, TV (DVD available), fridge, hair dryer, Wi-Fi (free).

WHERE TO DINE

Another good dining option is the **Terra Mar Grille** at the Saybrook Point Inn & Spa (see above).

Johnny Ad's SEAFOOD   On what is often described as "a patio of asphalt," this roadside clam shack is distinctive for its time-warp atmosphere. This is no faux-oldies place: Johnny Ad's has been doing business here since 1957, and music of the 1950s is piped through the simple inside rooms and onto the outdoor terrace of picnic tables next to the parking lot. The recommended options are the fried clams, the fish and chips, and the lobster salad (made with lobster and butter, no mayo). Portions are generous: A "small side order" of clam strips for $8.75, served with a lemon wedge and tarter sauce in a red-and-white cardboard box, is large enough to sate one or maybe even two people. Johnny Ad's is open year-round, unusual for a clam shack.

910 Boston Post Rd. (Rte. 1). © **860/388-4032.** Main courses $3.10–$24. No credit cards. Daily 11am–8pm (Fri-Sat until 8:30pm, Sun until 7:30pm) most of the year; in winter same hours except close at 3pm on Mon-Tues.

AN OCEAN VIEW FROM A TRAIN SEAT

Riding the Amtrak train along the Connecticut coast is an enormously satisfying way to take in gorgeous views of the state. The Regional and Acela Express Amtrak routes between New York and Boston travel the coast, and for many miles the train hugs the flat shoreline, skimming alongside inlets. If you're traveling north, get a window seat on the right and settle in for the guided tour.

The sights are rich with coastal New England geography, including small harbors dotted with sailboats and dense green woods. In Branford, the train passes a one-lane bridge where fishermen often cast rods. The view opens up to acres of marshland, where wooden perches are home to nesting birds. Passing through Guilford, travelers can catch glimpses of stone walls, then it's more marshland with canals that curve like a

drunkard's walk. In Old Saybrook, large, handsome homes come into sight.

In the stretch between Old Saybrook and New London, the train passes the sandy beaches of Old Lyme and a smattering of teeny islands, some not much bigger than a baseball infield. A red-and-white-striped tower signals the approach into the industrial zone of New London. From here, the train continues along the water to Stonington, passing what seems like thousands of sailboats, before moving inland for the trip through Rhode Island up to Massachusetts.

If you're traveling around sunset, you'll be treated to washes of orange and pink light dappling across the water. Whatever time of day, put down the book, pack away the computer, and daydream out the window. It's good for the soul.

THE CONNECTICUT RIVER VALLEY ★★

Essex: 114 miles NE of New York City; East Haddam: 124 miles NE of New York City and 132 miles SW of Boston; Old Lyme: 112 miles NE of New York City

The Connecticut River, New England's longest, originates in the far north near the Canadian border, some 407 miles from where it ends at the Long Island Sound. The river separates Vermont from New Hampshire, splits Massachusetts in half, then comes into Connecticut, takes a 45-degree turn just south of Hartford, and makes its final run to the sea.

Native Americans of the region called the river *Quinnetukut,* which, to the tin ears of the English settlers, sounded like "Connecticut." Because the river was navigable by relatively large ships as far as Hartford, its lower part became important for boat-building and industries associated with the international clipper trade. The valley retains that nautical flavor and has miraculously avoided the industrialization, development, and decay that afflict most of the region's other rivers. A book of photography, *The Connecticut River* (Wesleyan University Press, 2009), by Al Braden, shows off the beauty of the waterway today.

Given the unspoiled, upper-class, scenic atmosphere here, the valley is a popular spot for weekend getaways year-round. River cruises are obvious attractions, supplemented by a selection of worthy inns and antiques shops, rides on a steam-powered train, a venerable musical theater, and a bizarre castle on a hilltop.

Essentials

GETTING THERE Hwy. 9 runs parallel to the Connecticut River, along the west side of the valley. It connects I-91 south of Hartford to I-95 near Old Saybrook, making the valley readily accessible from all points in New England.

VISITOR INFORMATION The state's **Central Regional Tourism District** (© **800/793-4480** or 860/244-8181; www.enjoycentralct.com) is focused on the River Valley. The website of **Connecticut's Commission on Culture & Tourism** (© **888/288-4748;** www.ctvisit.com) also has a section on the River Valley region.

Essex ★★ & Ivoryton

It is difficult to imagine what improvements might be made to bring Essex, a dream of a New England waterside town, any closer to perfection. Tree-bordered streets are lined with shops and homes that retain an early-18th-century flavor, but without the frozen-in-amber quality that can afflict towns as postcard-pretty as this.

About 6,500 people live and work here, and bustle busily along Main Street, which runs down to Steamboat Dock and its flotilla of working vessels and pleasure craft that travel the Connecticut River. Many of the houses have plaques on their fronts noting their heritage, such as "Gamaliel Conklin c. 1803" (#20 Main St.) and "Uriah Hayden 1847" (#24). Some sport elaborate birdhouses on their front lawns. Streets have such names as Novelty Lane and Methodist Hill. As one writer put it, at sunset, the town is "so quiet you can hear gin splash on ice cubes in a bar three blocks away."

Ivoryton is adjacent to Essex, just to the west. It was once a center for the ivory trade, with factories fabricating piano keys and toothpicks. The village long ago subsided into residential quietude, but it perks up a bit in summer, when the **Ivoryton Playhouse,**

103 Main St. (© **860/767-7318;** www.ivorytonplayhouse.com), conducts much of its theatrical season, which runs from March to November. It's home to the estimable **Copper Beach Inn** (see below). If you drive along its Main Street, look for the large scale modern sculpture pieces featured on many of the lawns near the Inn.

Photos and up-to-date tourist information are offered at the Essex Board of Trade website, **www.essexct.com**.

WHAT TO SEE & DO

Essex is one of the prettiest, most atmospheric towns in New England to **stroll through.** Park on Main Street, head to the river, and then wander off on the side streets.

In winter, **bald eagles** come to these lower reaches of the river, and the **Connecticut Audubon Society** (© **800/996-8747;** www.ctaudubon.org) sponsors boat trips for viewing (the Audubon Society says that this area hosts the largest concentration of eagles in the Northeast). Boats run from early February to late March, generally on Tuesday, Thursday, Saturday, and Sunday. Cost is $40 per person.

Connecticut River Museum ★ The river is wide at Essex, and anglers cast lines from the museum's dock while gulls and ducks hang around hoping for a discarded tidbit. Steamboat service was fully operational here in 1823, and the existing dock dates from 1879. Designated a National Historic Site, the museum proper features model ships, marine paintings, and artifacts that relate the story of shipbuilding in the valley, which began in 1733 and helped make this a center of world trade far into the 19th century. Be sure to see the replica of America's first submarine (1776), a wooden, grenade-shaped one-man contraption called the *American Turtle.* The museum usually has walking-tour maps of Essex, too, making this a good first stop on your visit.

A **1906 schooner,** the *Mary E,* is docked alongside the museum. It takes 90-minute cruises during the day at 1:30 and 3:30pm ($20 adults, $12 children, free for children 5 and under), and 2-hour sunset cruises at 6pm ($30 per person).

Steamboat Dock (at the end of Main St.), Essex. © **860/767-8269.** www.ctrivermuseum.org. Admission $8 adults, $7 seniors, $6 students, $5 children 6–12, free children 5 and under. Daily 10am–5pm Memorial Day to Labor Day. Tues–Sun 10am–5pm rest of the year.

Essex Steam Train ☺ Take a ride on a steam locomotive from the 1920s, chugging along the river to the hamlet of Deep River. The excursion takes about an hour. The same operation also offers cruises on a beautiful **Mississippi-style riverboat** named *Becky Thatcher.* Combo train and riverboat trips are available, as are dinner trains with a four-course meal for $70.

1 Railroad Ave. (at Rte. 154 and Rte. 9), Essex. © **800/377-3987** or 860/767-0103. www.essexsteam train.com. Train and boat $26 adults, $17 children 2–11; train only $17 adults, $9 children 2–11; family packages available. Daily trips late June to early Sept; less frequently May–June and Sept–Oct; closed Nov–Apr.

Left Bank Gallery Open since 2008 and based in a former Main Street grocery store, this gallery features locally made paintings (coastal scenes, small-town life, colorful flowers), jewelry, and woodworking such as driftwood in fish shapes. The gallery's website and blog feature many of the cheery works.

10 Main St., Essex. © **860/767-0449**. www.leftbankgalleryessex.com. Mon and Wed–Thurs 11am–5pm; Fri–Sat 11am–6pm; Sun noon–5pm.

WHERE TO STAY & DINE

For a more modest meal than what's offered in the dining rooms and bars of the two properties below, check out the gourmet take-out at **Olive Oyl's,** 77 Main St. (✆ **860/767-4909;** www.oliveoylscarryout.com). You can load up on sandwiches or more regional foods such as crab cakes and stuffies (clams stuffed with spiced breadcrumbs).

Copper Beech Inn ★★   The stately Copper Beech oozes elegance and luxury, with not a single figurative hair out of place. A member of the venerated Select Registry of distinguished inns of North America, it offers 4 rooms replete with character and plenty of antiques in the 19th-century main building and 18 contemporary rooms in the Carriage House converted barn and new (open since 2009) Comstock House. The modern rooms, with plasma TVs, safes, and minibars, are designed for guests used to high-end city hotels. Unusual for a property this size, there are two dining options: the white-table-clothed, French-flavored **Cooper Beech Restaurant** (main courses $22–$35; tasting menu $39 and $75) and the bistro-style **Brasserie Pip** (mains $16–$25). The wine list, with over 500 selections and 3,500 bottles, is impressive.

46 Main St., Ivoryton, CT 06442. ✆ **888/809-2056** or 860/767-0330. Fax 860/767-7840. www.copper beechinn.com. 22 units. $150–$375 double. Rates include breakfast. AE, DC, DISC, MC, V. From Rte. 9 north, take exit 3 and head west on Main St. No children 15 and under. Pets accepted in some rooms with prior arrangement ($85 fee). **Amenities:** 2 restaurants; bar. *In room:* A/C, TV (some units), CD player, hair dryer, Wi-Fi (in main house, free).

Griswold Inn ★★   Everybody likes "the Gris." Rumpled, cluttered, folksy, and forever besieged by drop-in yachties, anglers, locals, and tourists, the main building dates to 1776. The atmospheric, mahogany-heavy taproom started life as a school-house and was moved here in 1800. There's live entertainment every night, from one man singing sea shanties to a Dixieland band. The Sunday Hunt Breakfast buffet is popular; and food in the evenings, while still hearty (think Yankee Potpie), has taken a turn toward the more innovative. A newish **wine bar** has a card of small plates, artisanal cheese from regional farms, and 50 wines by the glass. Bedrooms are bright and comfortable; some have fireplaces, and none have TVs.

36 Main St., Essex, CT 06426. ✆ **860/767-1776.** Fax 860/767-0481. www.griswoldinn.com. 30 units. $100–$180 double; suites from $160. Rates include breakfast. AE, MC, V. **Amenities:** Restaurant; 2 bars. *In room:* A/C.

Chester ★

Seven miles north of Essex, the well-turned-out riverside hamlet of Chester is teeny but justifies some savoring. Its old-fashioned Main Street and adjacent country lanes offer up enough antiques shops, art galleries, and somewhat precious boutiques to fill an hour of browsing.

Be sure to stop in at the nationally regarded **Ceramica,** 36 Main St. (✆ **800/270-0900;** www.ceramicadirect.com), the main branch of a small chain that carries uniformly gorgeous hand-painted bowls, pitchers, plates, and teapots imported from Italy. Newlyweds across the country register here to stock up on the high-end home decor.

WHERE TO DINE

River Tavern ★ NEW AMERICAN   Offering some urban panache in a bucolic setting, the high-design River Tavern is equal parts swanky, funky, and Northern

The Connecticut River Valley

CONNECTICUT

California. Undulating felt ceiling panels muffle the noise of the tall room, which is brightly decorated with orange bands of paint and abstract prints. A short menu (three fish, two meat, and one vegetarian entree when we visited) is sourced almost entirely locally, with a long list of farmers, orchards, fishermen, and other providers thanked on each day's written menu.

23 Main St. ℃ **860/526-9417**. www.rivertavernchester.net. Main courses $18–$30; 3-course prix fixe $40. AE, MC, V. Daily 11:30am–2:30pm; Mon–Thurs 5:30–9:30pm; Fri–Sat 5:30–10:30pm; Sun 4:30–9pm.

East Haddam/Hadlyme

While the town of Chester sits on the west side of the Connecticut River, East Haddam and Hadlyme (a jurisdiction of East Haddam) are directly on the east. Those eastern-side river towns wouldn't have attracted much attention if a wealthy thespian, William Gillette, hadn't decided to build his hilltop castle here (see below).

To get to the castle and surrounding state park from Chester, you need to cross the river. From April through November, take the small **Chester-Hadlyme Ferry** (℃ **860/526-2743**), at the end of Rte. 148, just 2 miles from Chester center. A ferry has operated here since 1769, and the current version can take about eight cars and walk-ons ($3 for vehicles, $1 for pedestrians and bicyclists). The pretty ride takes only a few minutes. Be sure to ask if eagles are active; they often are right here. The castle is in view from the ferry up to the left. The ferry is closed December through March, so in those months travel north on Rte. 154 to Haddam and take the (free) bridge. Either route, signs will direct you to the castle.

WHAT TO SEE & DO

There are trails on the grounds of Gillette Castle, but for more extensive hiking and bird-watching head out to **Devil's Hopyard State Park,** 366 Hopyard Rd., East Haddam (℃ **860/873-8566;** www.ct.gov). It has a reputation for some of the best birding in the state and for good brook trout stream fishing. It's located 9 miles east of Gillette Castle, 3 miles north of the intersection of routes 82 and 156.

Gillette Castle State Park ★ ☺ The Hartford-born William Gillette (1853–1937) was a successful actor and playwright known primarily for his portrayals of Sherlock Holmes. He took his money, ran to this hill rearing above the Connecticut River, and built a 24-room mansion. It's difficult to believe that he really thought the result resembled the medieval fortresses that allegedly were his inspiration: Rock gardens by roadside eccentrics in South Dakota are closer relations. The all-stone exterior has the dripping look of a sandcastle built by wet globs that fell through children's fingers. Inside, Gillette designed oddities such as a dining-room table that slides into the wall, an inexplicable space-saving effort.

But it's dramatic, and no one can argue with the location. The mansion sits atop the east bank of the Connecticut River and has superlative vistas upriver and down. Nowhere else is the blessed underdevelopment of the estuary more apparent. The expansive grounds, which are now owned and managed by the state, have picnic areas and nature trails. The park and the castle's terrace can be entered for free, making it a grand destination even to just take in the **river views** ★★.

67 River Rd., East Haddam. ℃ **860/526-2336**. www.ct.gov. Grounds free; castle admission $10 age 13 and older, $4 children 6–12, free for children 5 and under. Grounds daily 8am–sunset; castle daily 10am–4:30pm Memorial Day to Columbus Day. From the west side of the Connecticut River, take the Chester-Hadlyme Ferry (p. 409) across the river. From the east side, follow the signs from Rte. 82.

Goodspeed Opera House ★★   The dominant building in the teeny town of East Haddam is a restored 1876 Victorian of splendid proportions and white-frosting-curlicues. Located directly on the Connecticut River, it has been home to the Goodspeed Opera House since its beginning. Today, Goodspeed stages musicals on the order of *42nd Street* and *A Funny Thing Happened on the Way to the Forum.* It also helps develop new musicals and hosts a weekend of new artists every January.

6 Main St., East Haddam. *☎* **860/873-8668.** www.goodspeed.org. Tickets $30–$73.

RiverQuest ☺   This small cruise boat specializes in providing information on the birds of the Connecticut River, which include eagles, falcons, hawks, ospreys, and ducks. The boat operates most months, including February for Eagle Cruises, when the birds are particularly active. Call to confirm trips, particularly if the weather is iffy.

Eagle Landing State Park, 22 Bridge St., Haddam. *☎* **860/662-0577.** www.ctriverexpeditions.com. 90-min. cruise $20 adults and children 13 and older, $15 children 2–12; 60-min. cruise $15 adults and children 13 and older, $10 children 2–12. Daily trips July–Oct; less frequently rest of the year. The boat landing is on the west side of the river, just across from the Goodspeed Opera House.

WHERE TO DINE

Gelston House AMERICAN   Right on the banks of the Connecticut River and next door to the Goodspeed Opera House, the Gelston House has pretty views and a dining room with some old-fashioned grandeur. It offers a special *prix fixe* menu for theatergoers and a post-show late-night menu after 9pm. There are four rooms for travelers here, although they are underwhelming and pricey ($130–$225).

8 Main St., East Haddam. *☎* **860/873-1411.** www.gelstonhouse.com. Main courses $13–$28. AE, MC, V. Tues–Sat 11:30am–3pm and 4:30–9pm; Sun 11:30am–2pm and 3–9pm.

Old Lyme

Back at the most southern part of the valley, but now on the eastern side of the Connecticut River, Old Lyme (40 miles east of New Haven, 23 miles west of Mystic) is as quiet a town as the coast can claim. It was the favored residence of generations of seafarers and ship captains, and many of their 18th- and 19th-century homes have survived, some as inns and museums.

These preserved houses are best seen on **Lyme Street,** the town's main boulevard. Lyme Street north of I-95 is anchored by the Florence Griswold Museum and Bee and Thistle Inn (both below). Lyme Street south of I-95 is the heart of Old Lyme's historic district. Preservationists and community activists proudly point out this is the only main street in the region bisected by the interstate highway that continues to thrive.

WHAT TO SEE & DO

With its many tree-lined streets largely free of traffic, **biking** is an attractive option.

Florence Griswold Museum ★   After the shipbuilding and merchant trade had all but flickered out at the end of the 19th century, artists who came to be known as the "American Impressionists" took a fancy to this area. They received encouragement, patronage, and even food and shelter from "Miss Florence" (1850–1937), the wealthy daughter of a sea captain. She opened her Georgian–Federal 1817 mansion to boarders and made it a salon and country retreat for artists, with a number of painters leaving samples of their work directly on the walls of the dining room.

Among her grateful guests was Childe Hassam, considered the grand master of the American Impressionists.

Now a National Historic Landmark, the "Flo Gris" underwent extensive restoration and refurnishing in 2005 and 2006, including the installation of geothermal environmental systems that draw energy for cooling and heating from wells on the property. Visitors can stroll the mansion's property to take in its old-fashioned gardens, picnic on the banks of the small Lieutenant River, or even do some sketching.

96 Lyme St. (Rte. 1). © **860/434-5542.** www.flogris.org. Admission $9 adults, $8 seniors, $7 students, free for children 12 and under. Tues-Sat 10am–5pm; Sun 1–5pm.

GETTING OUTSIDE

Rocky Neck State Park, Rte. 156 (© **860/739-5471;** www.ct.gov), on the eastern side of Old Lyme, is one of several Connecticut parks at the edge of Long Island Sound. It has a crescent-shaped beach that's popular with families and 160 camping sites. Take I-95 to exit 72 and follow Rte. 156 south. The park is open daily from 8am to sunset.

WHERE TO STAY & DINE

Bee and Thistle Inn and Spa   On a bucolic piece of land beside the Lieutenant River, the main draws of the Bee and Thistle are the atmospheric core structure that dates from 1756 and the romantic, "English countryside" grounds and gardens for lolling about. Public areas are a jumble of antiques and collectibles, while most rooms boast four-poster beds and river views. On-site spa services include facials and massages. Dinner is served Wednesday through Saturday from 6pm to 9pm (main courses $18–$35, 3-course prix fixe for $28).

100 Lyme St. (Rte. 1), Old Lyme, CT 06371. © **800/622-4946** or 860/434-1667. Fax 860/434-3402. www.beeandthistleinn.com. 9 units. $150–$275 double. AE, DISC, MC, V. Follow signs to the Florence Griswold Museum, which is next door. **Amenities:** Restaurant (Wed-Sat dinner); exercise room; spa. *In room:* A/C, Wi-Fi (free).

MYSTIC ★★★ & THE SOUTHEASTERN COAST

New London & Groton: 127 miles NE of New York City and 106 miles SW of Boston; Mystic: 135 miles NE of New York City and 99 miles SW of Boston; Foxwoods and Mohegan Sun casinos: 134 miles NE of New York City and 106 miles SW of Boston

This section of the Connecticut shoreline, from New London east to Rhode Island, is studded with towns that still bear the stamp of their maritime pasts, a string of fishing ports and inlets that segues into the mainland beach resorts of Rhode Island. Inland are a number of still semirural villages, but their futures are uncertain due to the presence of two enormously successful and steadily expanding Indian casino complexes, Foxwoods and Mohegan Sun. They produce gushers of money that are forever altering the character of this region.

The town of Mystic and its twin attractions, Mystic Aquarium and the living museum that is Mystic Seaport, are the prime reasons for a stay—the Seaport alone can easily occupy most of a day. The town itself sustains a nautical air, with fun shops and restaurants to suit most tastes.

The tranquil neighboring village of Stonington is home to a small but active commercial fishing fleet, the last in the state, and many companies offer their vessels for whale-watching, dinner cruises, and deep-sea fishing excursions. Some enchanting inns also inhabit the area.

If at all possible, avoid visiting in July, August, and weekends from May to Columbus Day. That's when the crowds heading to Mystic Seaport can be oppressive. Restaurants are packed, and hotel rooms are often booked months in advance at very high rates.

Essentials

GETTING THERE   Take I-95 to exit 84 (New London), exit 86 (Groton), exit 90 (Mystic), or exit 91 (Stonington). If driving from the New York City area, you can avoid the heavy truck and commercial traffic of the western segment of I-95 by taking the Hutchinson River Parkway, which becomes the Merritt Parkway (Rte. 15) and merges with the Wilbur Cross Parkway. Continue to exit 54, connecting with I-95 for the rest of the trip. From Boston, take I-95 straight down.

The **Cross Sound Ferry** (© 860/443-5281; www.longislandferry.com) provides year-round service for cars between New London and Orient Point on Long Island, in New York. The one-way voyage takes about 1 hour and 20 minutes. One-way fares are $47 for a car and driver, $14 for additional adults, and $6.15 for children. Advance reservations are recommended.

Amtrak (© 800/USA-RAIL [872-7245]; www.amtrak.com) has routes between New York, Providence, and Boston, with intermediate stops at New London and Mystic.

The regional bus company **Southeast Area Transit, or SEAT** (© 860/886-2631; www.seatbus.com), connects many of the towns along the coast as well as the casinos.

VISITOR INFORMATION   A good source of information is the **Mystic Country** tourism website, **www.mysticcountry.com**. It lists, for instance, 72 inn and bed-and-breakfast options. The organization will also mail out a free **Mystic Country Vacation Guide.**

New London

New London's protected deep-draft harbor at the mouth of the Thames River was responsible for its long and influential history as a whaling port. Possessed of an architecturally interesting but largely somnolent downtown district, the city is of note to travelers primarily because it's a transit point for ferry lines connecting the mainland with three states: Rhode Island (Block Island), New York (Long Island), and Massachusetts (Martha's Vineyard).

New London is home to the **U.S. Coast Guard Academy** (www.cga.edu), whose campus is at the northern edge of the city along Rte. 32. A **full-rigged sailing vessel, the *Eagle,*** is a principal attraction. Used for training current cadets—it's the only such vessel actively commissioned in the U.S.—it is out on tour much of the year, usually from mid-April to mid-August. The *Eagle* was built in Germany in 1936 to train that country's naval cadets and was taken as a war prize after World War II.

Connecticut College (www.conncoll.edu) also has a large campus here, running between Rte. 32 and Williams Street.

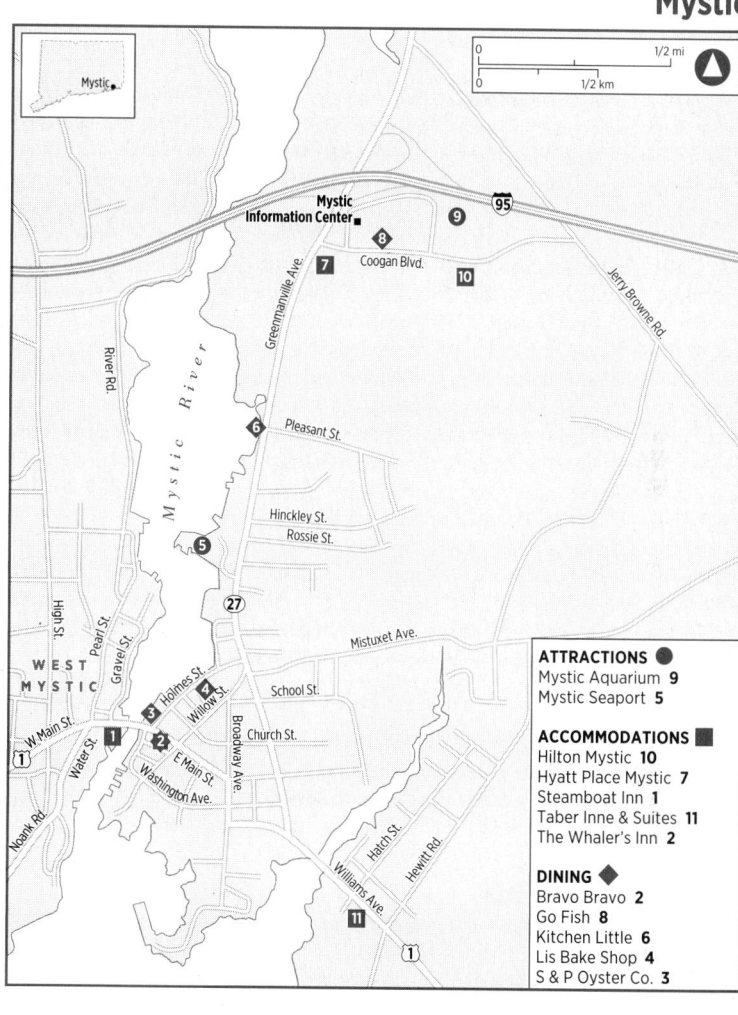

ATTRACTIONS ●
Mystic Aquarium **9**
Mystic Seaport **5**

ACCOMMODATIONS ■
Hilton Mystic **10**
Hyatt Place Mystic **7**
Steamboat Inn **1**
Taber Inne & Suites **11**
The Whaler's Inn **2**

DINING ◆
Bravo Bravo **2**
Go Fish **8**
Kitchen Little **6**
Lis Bake Shop **4**
S & P Oyster Co. **3**

10

CONNECTICUT | Mystic & The Southeastern Coast

Lyman Allyn Museum of Art   This neoclassical granite building stands on a hill looking toward the U.S. Coast Guard Academy. Its holdings are the result of the enthusiasms of private collectors and include Colonial American paintings as well as landscapes by Hudson River School artists Frederic Edwin Church and John F. Kensett. Special exhibitions bring fresh work into the venue, such as a 2009–10 show of Cuban paintings, photographs, and audio works.

625 Williams St. ✆ **860/443-2545.** www.lymanallyn.org. Admission $8 adults, $7 seniors and students, free for children 11 and under. Tues–Sat 10am–5pm; Sun 1–5pm. From exit 83 off I-95, follow signs north. The museum is at the southern edge of the Connecticut College campus.

GETTING OUTSIDE

Not far from downtown is the special **Ocean Beach Park,** at the south end of Ocean Avenue (© **800/510-7263** or 860/447-3031; www.ocean-beach-park.com), an expansive recreational facility with a broad sand beach, a boardwalk, an Olympic-size pool, a carousel and other amusement rides, an arcade, miniature golf, bath-house with lockers and showers, and concession stands. Parking is $18, which includes park admission for everyone in the car.

Both charter and open party (public) **fishing trips** are available between May and November from the Sunbeam Fleet, based at **Captain John's Sport Fishing Center,** 15 First St., Waterford (© **860/443-7259;** www.sunbeamfleet.com). Waterford is the town immediately west of New London, and the fishing center dock is next to the Niantic River Bridge (Rte. 156). Public trips last from 5½ to 9 hours and include night bass fishing from 7pm to 12:30am ($73, plus $5 rod rental; live eels included), and day blues and bass fishing departing at 1pm and, on weekends, 6am ($53 adults, $48 seniors, $33 children 12 and under, plus $5 rod rental; bait included). Check for exact days and times and reservation policies. The same company runs a handful of **lighthouse cruises** in July and August ($48 adults, $43 seniors, $29 children 12 and under), which tours past 10 lighthouses.

From late May to September, consider popping over to **Block Island** (p. 464) for a day visit. The **Block Island Express** (© **860/444-4624;** www.longislandferry.com/bif/home.htm) operates a high-speed catamaran between New London and the Old Harbor on Block Island. The passage takes about 75 minutes. Round-trip rates are $43 for ages 12 and over, $22 for ages 2 to 11. The catamaran takes passengers and bicycles only, and reservations are recommended. It operates daily July and August and less frequently in May, June, and September.

Groton

Just across the Thames River from New London, Groton is a major naval-industrial town. The U.S. Navy has a submarine base here, and the Electric Boat division of General Dynamics designs, constructs, and maintains subs here, employing 10,500 at the Groton shipyard and a hull-fabrication facility in Quonset Point, Rhode Island.

WHAT TO SEE & DO

As in New London, a number of companies in Groton offer **fishing trips.** Typical of the public boats is the 114-foot *Hel-Cat II,* 181 Thames St. (© **860/535-2066** or 860/535-3200; www.visitconnecticut.com/helcat.htm). Trips last 6 hours ($53 adults, $30 ages 12 and under as well as nonfishing adults) and 10 hours ($80 adults, $40 ages 12 and under and nonfishing adults). Tackle is available for rent. Thames Street runs along the river south of I-95, with the boat launch a half-mile south of the highway. Take exit 85, if you're driving north on I-95; or exit 87, if you're driving south.

History buffs will enjoy a stroll around **Fort Griswold Battlefield State Park,** 57 Fort St. (© **860/449-6877** in season; www.ct.gov). It was here, in 1781, that Benedict Arnold, who fought for American independence before trading allegiances, led a British force against American defenders and ruthlessly ordered the massacre of 88 prisoners after they had surrendered. The park is just off Thames Street (see directions in previous paragraph) and entrance is free.

Submarine Force Library and Museum The centerpiece of this museum at the edge of the U.S. Naval Submarine Base is the USS *Nautilus,* a 362-foot-long sub that was commissioned in 1954 and in operation until 1980. It's moored and ready for inspection, welcoming visitors to take a walk through the control rooms, attack center, galley, and sleeping quarters. The self-guided tour is aided by listening devices handed out to each visitor (and can be claustrophobic for some). Passing through, it is difficult to imagine how the sub could possibly contain a crew of 116 men, especially on its fabled 1958 cruise between Pearl Harbor and the North Pole. The museum also displays models of torpedoes, missiles, deck guns, and periscopes.

1 Crystal Lake Rd. (Naval Submarine Base). ℂ **800/343-0079** or 860/694-3174. www.submarine museum.org. Free admission. May 1–Oct 31 Wed–Mon 9am–5pm; Nov 1–Apr 30 Wed–Mon 9am–4pm. Closed 1–2 weeks in Nov for upkeep. Exit 86 from I-95, north on Rte. 12; follow signs to USS *Nautilus.*

WHERE TO DINE

Olio INTERNATIONAL Try to look past the unassuming location at the intersection of two highways. Inside, Olio is a contemporary, lounge-y space with a creative menu. Pastas (15 of them) dominate the offerings, from "open face" seafood ravioli to gnocchi with shrimp and saffron cream sauce. International standards, such as crab Rangoon spring rolls and quesadillas, fill out the menu and are tasty and quick. With bare tables and hard surfaces everywhere, it can be loud, and take the reading glasses, because the menu is written in a tiny hand and there are only guttering candles and a few dim pin lights for illumination.

33 Kings Hwy. (south of I-95 at Rte. 1). ℂ **860/445-6546.** www.ckrestaurantgroup.com/olio. Main courses $11–$24. AE, DC, DISC, MC, V. Mon–Sat 11:30am–9pm (until 10pm Fri–Sat); Sun 4:30–9pm.

Mystic ★★★

The spirit and texture of the maritime life and history of New England are captured in many ports along its indented coast, but nowhere more precisely than beside the Mystic River estuary and its harbor. This was a dynamic whaling and shipbuilding center during the Colonial period and into the 20th century, but the discontinuation of the first industry and the decline of the second haven't adversely affected the community—no derelict barges or rotting piers degrade the views or waterways.

Mystic and West Mystic are stitched together by a drawbridge, the raising of which causes regular traffic stoppages but rarely shortens tempers, except for those of visitors who don't leave their urban impatience behind. There are complaints by some that the town has been commercialized, but T-shirt shops and related tackiness is limited, and the more garish motels and attractions have been restricted to the periphery, especially up near exit 90 off I-95.

The town is home to one of New England's most singular attractions, the **Mystic Seaport** museum village (below). It's a re-created seaport of the mid-1800s, fully evoking that romantic era of clipper ships and the China trade.

The **Mystic & Shoreline Visitor Information Center** (ℂ 860/536-1641; www.mysticinfo.com) is located at the **Olde Mistick Village shopping center** (www.oldmysticvillage.com). Take exit 90 from I-95 and go south on Rte. 27. Turn left almost immediately onto Coogan Boulevard. The shopping center is on the left.

A good collection of New England history books is available in downtown Mystic at the "locally owned, fiercely independent" **Bank Square Books,** 53 W. Main St. (ℂ **860/536-3795;** www.banksquarebooks.com).

WHAT TO SEE & DO

As in New London and Groton (p. 412 and 414), several operators in Mystic offer **sailing and fishing cruises.** One of the most convenient is **Argia Mystic Cruises,** 15 Holmes St. (© 860/536-0416; www.voyagermystic.com), right in downtown Mystic. May through October, it offers trips on the *Argia,* a replica of a 19th-century schooner that docks just north of the Mystic River drawbridge. The 2½-hour sailing trips and sunset cruises (called "half-day" trips) are $42 for adults, $39 for seniors, and $33 for children under 18 (must be accompanied by an adult). Another company, **Mystic Whaler Cruises,** at City Pier, 35 Water St. (© 800/697-8420; www.mysticwhaler.com), offers similar outings on its tall ship, *Mystic Whaler.* Its **lobster dinner cruise** features a classic New England meal for $80.

Mystic Aquarium & Institute for Exploration ★★ ☺ Once you've entered this indoor/outdoor complex, you're met almost immediately by three sweet-faced beluga whales, who swim in a large specially chilled outdoor tank just feet from the walkway. Mystic is the only aquarium in New England to host the white whales, who squeal and twirl for their trainers at feeding times and can be viewed up close and even touched during a remarkable "Beluga Encounter" ($49 and $159; reservations strongly suggested). This is a very good midsize aquarium and is especially set up for children under 12, who can pet sting rays in the "touch ray" room (the rays arc up like cats to skim along children's hands) and who flock to the tank of orange-and-white-striped clownfish, better known to the younger set as "Nemo." There also are sea lion shows, a special area for penguins, and an exhibit on the *Titanic* wreck.

55 Coogan Blvd. © 860/572-5955. www.mysticaquarium.org. Admission $26 adults, $23 seniors, $19 children 3–12, free for children 2 and under. Tickets, if validated before exit, are good for 3 consecutive days. Mar–Oct daily 9am–6pm; Nov daily 9am–5pm; Dec–Feb daily 10am–5pm. Exit 90 off I-95, south on Rte. 27, left onto Coogan Blvd.

Mystic Seaport ★★★ ☺ Dubbed "the museum of America and the sea," Mystic Seaport is a re-created waterfront settlement with the look and feel of a 19th-century seafaring village. Historic buildings were transported here from all across New England, and there are whaling ships and tall ships to scramble over, too. Most visitors will be enthralled by *something* in this complex that evokes maritime's golden age, so plan to set aside at least 2 or 3 hours—if not an entire day—for exploring.

The center of the village has about 30 **shops and artifacts typical of the time,** including a cooperage (where barrels are made), a printing office, a general store, and a hand-pumped fire engine from the 1850s. In the warm months, a boathouse offers **rentals of rowboats** ($15 an hour) and small sailboats ($20).

On the left (southern) end of the village is a **working shipyard** where carpenters demonstrate historically accurate methods of production. The majestic three-masted *Charles W. Morgan,* the proudest possession of the Seaport fleet and an active whaling ship until 1921, is undergoing restoration here. Visitors can still climb aboard and walk through its insides, which date from 1841. Audio tours by cell-phone (© 860/415-0293) are available in this part of the seaport.

On the far right (northern) end of the village are many of the exhibits and activities for smaller children. There's a creepy display of wide-eyed wooden **figureheads** that might incite strange dreams. On this end, too, is a terrific exhibit called **Voyages,** which celebrates lives and transitions made on water: Cuban immigrants who arrived by small craft, tugboat operators, Navy men. Be sure to get to the top floor, where wonderful photos of the fishermen of Point Judith, Rhode Island, are housed. Photographer Markham Starr calls these men "the ocean's version of the true cowboy—independent, resourceful, and dedicated. As they wrest a living from an unforgiving sea, they ask no favors and accept the risks they take."

The seaport presents its best value in the high season, when visitors can expect the majority of exhibits to be open and the village to have an energetic buzz. It can be a bit of a ghost town in the colder months, although the docents are highly competent at the crafts they demonstrate and friendly year-round, always ready to impart as much information as visitors care to absorb.

75 Greenmanville Ave. (Rte. 27). © **888/973-2767** or 860/572-5315. www.mysticseaport.org. Admission $24 adults, $22 seniors, $15 children 6–17, free for children 2 and under. Tickets, if validated before exit, are good for a 2nd day within 7 days. AE, MC, V. Apr–Oct daily 9am–5pm; Nov daily 10am–4pm; Dec–Mar Thurs–Sun 10am–4pm. Exit 90 off I-95, south on Rte. 27.

WHERE TO STAY

Plenty of ho-hum but adequate area motels are available to soak up the area traffic at all but peak periods, meaning weekends from late spring to early fall plus weekdays in July and August. During these times, it is necessary to have reservations. The Mystic Country website, at **www.mysticcountry.com**, lists 23 hotels and B&Bs in town.

Hilton Mystic ★ ☺ Unlike most Mystic properties, the Hilton is a full-service hotel with the amenities found in its big-city cousins: indoor pool, lounge with fireplace, morning and evening room service. Renovations in 2008 warmed up the guest rooms with upscale furniture, marble or granite finishes, and the standard Hilton Serenity Bed, which features a pillow-top mattress. It's located just across the street from the Mystic Aquarium. The operation is owned by the Mashantucket Pequot tribe, which runs the Foxwoods casino, 10 miles north.

20 Coogan Blvd., Mystic, CT 06355. © **860/572-0731.** Fax 860/572-0328. www.hiltonmystic.com. 182 units. $149–$349 double. AE, DC, DISC, MC, V. Take exit 90 off I-95 and drive south, following signs to the Mystic Aquarium; the hotel is opposite. **Amenities:** Restaurant; lounge; exercise room; heated indoor pool; room service. In room: A/C, TV, hair dryer, Wi-Fi (free).

Hyatt Place Mystic ★★ ☺ The newish (since 2007) and appealing "Hyatt Place" brand offers boutique hotel stylings at chain hotel execution. All bedrooms have a food prep area (counter, sink, fridge), a desk, a sleeper-sofa couch, a 42" flatscreen TV that computers can be plugged into to watch DVDs, a sleek bath area, and a comfy pillow-top bed with an enveloping duvet. Rooms are smartly designed to allow some privacy even when several people are sharing. The downstairs feels like a Starbucks, with the front desk doubling as a casual bar that serves snacks and coffee (24 hr.) and wine and beer (until 11pm). Sure enough, people mingle on computers and with kids throughout the day, lending a nearly folksy atmosphere. Most of the year, rooms run around $169. It's walking distance from Mystic Seaport.

224 Greenmanville Ave., Mystic, CT 06355. © **860/536-9997.** Fax 860/536-9686. www.hyattplace. com. 79 units. $139–$329 double. Rates include breakfast. AE, DC, DISC, MC, V. Take exit 90 off I-95 and drive south on Rte. 27; hotel is on left directly after Coogan Blvd. **Amenities:** Restaurant (breakfast and 24-hr. snacks); bar; exercise room; heated outdoor pool (seasonal). In room: A/C, TV, fridge, hair dryer, MP3 docking station, Wi-Fi (free).

Steamboat Inn ★★ Mystic's most quietly romantic lodging is tucked around a few corners from the center of downtown. In fact, it's easily overlooked from land but readily apparent from the river, as it's perched directly on the bank of the Mystic

River. The yellow-clapboard structure has 11 large, handsome rooms, with wood-burning fireplaces (upstairs bedrooms) or kitchenettes (downstairs bedrooms). Each is decorated differently—Laura Ashley was a likely muse—and all but one have a view of the water and the sailboats that make up the traffic. Steamboat Inn has been a member of the prestigious Select Registry of distinguished inns since fall 2009.

73 Steamboat Wharf, Mystic, CT 06355. © **860/536-8300.** Fax 860/536-9528. www.steamboatinn mystic.com. 11 units. $150–$300 double. Rates include breakfast. AE, DISC, MC, V. Parking available in a gated lot. GPS users should use 15 W. Main St. for directions. Look for the sign pointing down an alley on the west bank of the Mystic River, just before the drawbridge. *In room:* A/C, TV/DVD, hair dryer, Wi-Fi (free).

Taber Inne & Suites ★   Not quite an inn but more than a motel, this ever-popular complex has something to suit most tastes and budgets. It's made up of seven buildings with basic units, hedonistic suites with fireplaces and decks, and 2-bedroom town houses. The Carriage House has a cathedral ceiling, two bedrooms, a sitting room, and a two-person Jacuzzi. Standard rooms are clean, neat, and bland. It's located a little less than a mile from town center.

66 Williams Ave. (Rte. 1), Mystic, CT 06355. © **866/822-3746** or 860/536-4904. Fax 860/572-9140. www.taberinn.com. 32 units. $149–$185 double; suites $195 and up. Rates include breakfast. 2-night minimum stay on weekends May–Oct; 3-night minimum holiday weekends. AE, MC, V. Located 2 blocks east of Rte. 27. **Amenities:** Exercise room; access to the Mystic Health Club; heated indoor pool; sauna. *In room:* A/C, TV, hair dryer, Wi-Fi (free).

The Whaler's Inn ★   Smack in the middle of all the action, Whaler's is quite literally a stone's throw from shops and restaurants. There are five buildings to stay in, including the main inn, the motel-like Stonington House, and the Hoxie House, which has the most elegant (and expensive) accommodations. There, rooms have gas fireplaces, whirlpool baths, and 600 thread-count sheets; sleigh beds and four-posters are common. More modest rooms are clean and no frills. Stonington House has long porches, although the view is of the parking lot. The restaurant Bravo Bravo, reviewed below, is on the first floor of the main inn building, and hotel guests get half-price cocktails from 4 to 6pm.

20 E. Main St., Mystic, CT 06355. © **800/243-2588** or 860/536-1506. Fax 860/572-1250. www.whalers innmystic.com. 48 units. $159–$259 double. Rates include breakfast. AE, DC, DISC, MC, V. **Amenities:** Exercise room. *In room:* A/C, TV, hair dryer, Wi-Fi (free).

WHERE TO DINE
Expensive

Bravo Bravo ★ CONTEMPORARY ITALIAN   Reserve or plan to wait, because even an expansion into the space next door only made room for more people to squeeze in. Bravo Bravo, the premium restaurant in the village, can get as noisy as a disco, aided by bare wood tables and floors, but it's a fun place for an animated night out, and it's right in the center of town. At least half the entrees involve pasta—lobster ravioli, champagne risotto, shrimp with fusilli in a sun-dried tomato vodka sauce—with options for stuffed veal medallion with a garlic spinach cheese or *osso buco.*

20 E. Main St. © **860/536-3228.** www.ckrestaurantgroup.com. Reservations recommended. Main courses $18–$35. AE, DC, DISC, MC, V. Tues–Sat 11:30am–2:30pm; Tues–Sun 5–9pm (until 10pm Fri–Sat); Mon eves in July–Aug.

Go Fish ★ SEAFOOD   Brash and boisterous, Go Fish is dominated by a sprawling granite bar at its center, often surrounded by younger drinkers and grazers. At the far end is an enclosed sushi bar, while near the front entrance is a room usually

Sustainability 101: Seafood Good for You *and* Good for the Ocean

New England has long been sensitive to the issue of overfishing—regulating fishing practices that risk depleting fish populations or destroying fish habitats. Consumers around the world have become attuned to the same things, too. It's now easier than ever to find out which wild fish are considered okay to eat because they're being managed in sustainable ways, and which are not. It's also easy to find out which wild and farmed seafood is safest to eat, as well.

On the "best" list are wild Alaskan salmon, farmed mussels and oysters, farmed rainbow trout, pink shrimp from Oregon, Dungeness or stone crab, and U.S. farmed catfish. Also okay are Maine lobster, U.S. and Canadian sea scallops, squid, U.S. farmed tilapia, wild Pacific cod, and canned light and albacore tuna from the U.S. and Canada.

On the "worst" list: Chilean sea bass, Atlantic flounder and sole, grouper, farmed salmon, yellowfin and bluefin tuna, mahimahi, and imported swordfish.

Information about fish choices and the ecosystem is available from the **Environmental Defense Fund** (www.edf. org, search for "Seafood Selector") and the **Monterey Bay Aquarium** (www. montereybayaquarium.org, search for "Seafood Watch"). Both sites offer downloadable pocket guides. Or, text the **Blue Ocean Institute**, at 30644, with the message FISH and the name of the seafood in question. They'll text back a general code (GREEN = good, YELLOW = okay, RED = bad) as well as other options.

populated by older folks and families. Local or regional seafood is employed as much as possible, including Stonington sea scallops and Noank Bluepoint Oysters. Daily specials rely on fresh catches. Portions are abundant, so you might want to skip appetizers, enticing though they are (the creamy bisque, for one). During weekday happy hour, from 4:30 to 6pm, the bar menu is half-price.

Olde Mistick Village, Coogan Blvd. at Rte. 27. © **860/536-2662.** www.gofishct.com. Main courses $9.50–$28. AE, MC, V. Mon–Thurs 11:30am–9pm; Fri–Sat 11:30am–9:30pm; Sun noon–9pm.

S&P Oyster Co ★ SEAFOOD   In the center of town (and across the street from Bravo Bravo, above), S&P's is Mystic's big fish restaurant. Its location assures that it will be busy, but the food delivers. Seafood white bean chili is a spicy blend of crawfish, scallops, and crab, served with homemade corn chips. The mixed smoked grill sampler is a heaping plate of shrimp, scallops, and tuna over polenta with a garlic lime sauce, best washed down with a Mystic Lager. The dining rooms are elegant without being too formal and look out over the Mystic River. There's good value here: Nothing's inexpensive, but the portions are generous. You'll leave satisfied.

1 Holmes St. © **860/536-2674.** www.sp-oyster.com. Main dishes $14–$32, with most under $20. AE, MC, V. Daily 11:30am–9:30pm year-round, and later on Fri–Sat and in summer. Call in advance for "priority seating," which is S&P's modified reservation system.

Moderate

Abbott's Lobster in the Rough ★ SEAFOOD   Located in the picturesque village of Noank, about 3 miles south of downtown Mystic, Abbott's is a nitty-gritty lobster venue with plenty of picnic tables and not a frill to be found—it's as if a wedge of the Maine coast had been punched into the Connecticut shore. While options include hot dogs and chicken, the classic shore dinner rules. That means clam chowder, boiled shrimp, steamed mussels, and a tasty lobster, with coleslaw, chips, and drawn butter thrown in. Abbott's doesn't have a liquor license, but you can bring your own beer or wine.

117 Pearl St., Noank. ☎ **860/536-7719.** www.abbotts-lobster.com. Main courses $5–$34. AE, DISC, MC, V. Daily late May to end of Aug noon–9pm; weekends only early May and Sept–Oct. Be prepared to ask for directions (the website has a photo of boy holding a sign: "Directions to Abbott's 10¢"). From downtown Mystic, go south on Rte. 215 and cross a railroad bridge into Noank. Immediately bear right, and then make a quick left onto Main St., then a quick right onto Pearl St.

Inexpensive

Puritan & Genesta Natural Foods, 2 Holmes St. (☎ **860/536-3537;** www. puritan-genesta.com), is a health food cafe and grocery store, good for a quick snack. It's named for the two sailboats that raced in 1885 in the first America's Cup competition.

Kitchen Little ★ DINER   Not much more than a shack by the water, this breakfast and lunch joint promising "A.M. Eggstasy" is passed every day by hundreds of tourists hurrying to Mystic Seaport. They're missing not only dozens of distinct breakfast choices (try the Portuguese fisherman plate), but also some of the coast's tastiest clam and scallop dishes. The briny, clear broth clam chowder is Southern New England style, with no milk or cream, and only found in Connecticut and Rhode Island. Expect a wait and tight quarters inside. Try to snare a table out back for views of the tall ships. It's open until 2pm weekdays and 1pm weekends.

135 Greenmanville Ave. (Rte. 27). ☎ **860/536-2122.** Main dishes $3.95–$15. No credit cards. Mon–Fri 6:30am–2pm; Sat–Sun 6:30am–1pm. Located ⅓ mile south of I-95 and ⅓ mile north of Mystic Seaport.

Lis Bake Shop BAKERY   Display trays heaped with goodies such as blueberry lemon cupcakes, gingersnap pumpkin bars, and mile-high black tuxedo cake make this cute bakery near the center of town an atmospheric stop for coffee and sweets. There's a short menu of lunch items and daily specials such as pulled pork and cheddar cheese on a butternut biscuit. You can mull over the options at a counter stool.

15 Holmes St. ☎ **860/536-9090.** All items under $8; most under $3. MC, V. Mon–Sat 7am–5pm; Sun 7:30am–3pm.

MYSTIC AFTER DARK

Maybe because its main attractions are family affairs, Mystic, unlike waterside locales such as Newport, Rhode Island, has a quiet nightlife. With Mohegan Sun 14 miles away and Foxwoods 10 miles away, some visitors just head to the casinos (p. 422). Others join locals at **Captain Daniel Packer Inne,** 32 Water St. (☎ **860/536-3555;** www.danielpacker.com), a restaurant and pub housed in a 1754 home just a few blocks from the main strip. It features music in the pub nightly.

Stonington ★ & North Stonington

These slumbering villages are only lightly brushed by the 21st century despite all the thrashing about in heavily touristed Mystic and nearby Foxwoods and Mohegan Sun gambling complexes (below). Incorporated in 1801, coastal Stonington is the oldest borough in the state. Its two lengthwise streets are lined with well-preserved Federal-style and Greek Revival homes, and the town has a pronounced maritime flavor.

It's popular for quiet weekend getaways. North Stonington, about 7 miles inland, is as peaceful a New England hamlet as can be found, with hardly any commercialization. It's listed on the National Register of Historic Places.

WHAT TO SEE & DO

Drive south in Stonington along its main **Water Street,** which is thick with boutiques and restaurants for a few blocks. At the end of Water Street is **Stonington Point,** where there's a small **town beach.** The misty blue headland across the sound is Montauk Point, the eastern extremity of New York's Long Island. At the point is the **Old Lighthouse Museum,** 7 Water St. (© 860/535-1440; www.stoningtonhistory.org). The lighthouse was built of stone in 1823, moved to its current site 300 feet away in 1840, and active until 1889. Most of the museum exhibits relate to the maritime past of the area, with scrimshaw tusks and porcelain that constituted much of the 19th-century China trade. Admission is $8 for adults, $5 for children. It's open May through October daily from 10am to 5pm.

About 7 miles north of downtown Stonington is one of the Nutmeg State's handful of wineries, **Stonington Vineyards,** 523 Taugwonk Rd., Stonington (© 860/535-1222; www.stoningtonvineyards.com), which has a tasting room in a barn beside its vineyard. There are usually five or six pressings to be sampled, with an aged-in-oak Chardonnay leading the pack. Visitors are welcome to bring a picnic, buy a bottle, and settle in at a table overlooking the vineyards or the brook that runs past. The winery is open daily year-round from at least 1 to 4pm (until 5pm in summer and fall), with a free cellar tour at 2pm. From downtown Stonington, head north on Main Street until it merges into Taugwonk Road. The vineyard is about 2½ miles after you've passed under I-95. From I-91, take exit 91 and drive north.

WHERE TO STAY

The Inn at Stonington ★★   The elegant Inn at Stonington harmonizes nicely with its neighbors on the town's stylish main street. Combining the intimacy of a small inn with the comforts of a luxury hotel, it abounds in flourishes that exceed expectations (as its membership in Select Registry would suggest). Every unit has a gas fireplace, and many have decks for taking in Stonington Harbor and Fishers Island Sound. While rooms reflect a single design sensibility, with tailored contemporary interpretations of country decor, no two are alike. The inn has a 400-foot pier with deep water for those arriving on yachts. It's so quiet here you might think you are alone—but head to the bar in the early evening to meet other guests for complimentary wine and cheese.

60 Water St., Stonington, CT 06378. © **860/535-2000.** Fax 860/535-8193. www.innatstonington.com. 18 units. $190–$445 double. Rates include breakfast and evening wine and cheese. 2-night minimum on Fri-Sat. AE, DC, MC, V. Take exit 91 off I-95; follow signs into Stonington village. No children 13 and under. *In room:* A/C, TV, hair dryer, Wi-Fi (free).

WHERE TO DINE

Milagro Cafe ★ MEXICAN   Any good BBQ restaurant knows how to slow roast a pork loin, but only an excellent Mexican place, such as Milagro, will offer that pork marinated in citrus, wrapped in banana leaves, and served with pickled onions. That dish, called *cochinita pibil,* is a house specialty. Along with the long selection of tequilas, it's a top reason to seek out this casual, colorful venue.

142 Water St. © **860/535-8178.** Main courses $13–$18. MC, V. Wed-Mon 11:30am-3pm and 5-9pm (until 10pm Fri-Sat).

Water Street Café NEW AMERICAN   Exposed pipes and industrial-type lighting contrast with rustic walls and banquettes in this cheery restaurant. The creative daily specials are often the best choices. Local oysters are consistently good, as are barbecue pork sandwiches, burgers, and lobster spring rolls.

143 Water St. ✆ **860/535-2122.** Main courses $10–$19. AE, MC, V. Daily 11:30am–2:30pm and 5–10pm (until 11pm Fri–Sat); Sat–Sun 8am–2:30pm.

The Casinos: Foxwoods Resort & Mohegan Sun

What has been wrought in the woodlands just north of the Connecticut coast in the last 2 decades is nothing less than astonishing. There was little but forest here when the Mashantucket Pequot (pronounced *Pee*-kwat) tribe received clearance to open a gambling casino on ancestral lands. Nearly overnight, the tribal bingo parlor was expanded into the **Foxwoods casino.** That was in 1992.

Foxwoods became enormously profitable, and expansion ensued—more hotels, more casino rooms, golf courses, a museum devoted to Native American culture, purchase by the tribe of adjacent lands and nearby inns and hotels.

All this wasn't lost on the Mohegan Tribe of Connecticut, which in 1996 opened its own competing casino, **Mohegan Sun.** The complexes are about 5 miles apart as the crow flies and 11 miles by car, with Mohegan Sun on the west in Uncasville nearer to Mystic, and Foxwoods on the east side of the Thames River in the town of Mashantucket. (The town is also listed as Ledyard.)

Residents of surrounding communities have been understandably ambivalent about the development. When it was learned that one of the tribe's corporate entities was to be called Two Trees Limited Partnership, a predictable query was, "Is that all you're going to leave us? Two trees?" There is a continuing danger of damage to the fragile character of this authentically picturesque corner of Connecticut. On the other hand, thousands of people have found employment here.

Foxwoods once claimed to be the largest casino in the world (complexes in China now rank higher, but it's still the biggest in the U.S.), and it does look dramatic, rising like Oz above the rolling green hills that surround it. Recent years, though, have taken some of the bloom off the rose. A *Boston Globe* story titled "The wonder, and the fall," a play on the resort's 10-year advertising campaign "The wonder of it all," reported in September 2009, that Foxwoods had $2-billion debt from all its expansion and is "now a looming threat to the tribe." In November 2009, Foxwoods failed to make full interest payment on $500 million of that debt. As of February 2010, the Mashantucket Pequot Tribal Nation was continuing to work with its lenders toward a resolution.

WHAT TO SEE & DO

Foxwoods Resort Casino   In 2009, the Foxwood complex was ranked the third largest in the world by *Business Week:* 340,000 square feet that includes 6 cavernous gambling rooms, a 3,600-seat bingo hall, and 7,600 slot machines. In addition to the gaming, the resort is home to high-end boutiques, 4 hotels—the newest, **MGM Grand at Foxwoods,** opened in 2008 (see below)—and the **MGM Grand Theater.** The theater has become one of the busiest venues in the region, with such acts as comedian Jerry Seinfeld and singer Toby Keith, and is promoted as aggressively as the gambling. Restaurant options range from unremarkable to high end; see "Where to Dine," below, for options. To remind everyone that this whole eye-popping affair is owned by the Mashantucket Pequot, a Native American tribe, the signature display is **The Rainmaker,** a glass statue of an archer shooting an arrow. As well, larger-than-life sculptures depicting Amerindians are prominent throughout the buildings.

350 Trolley Line Blvd., P.O. Box 3777, Mashantucket, CT. ✆ **800/369-9663.** www.foxwoods.com. Free admission. 24/7. Gaming areas restricted to ages 21 and older; bingo area 18 and older. Take exit 92 from I-95, then Rte. 2 west.

Mashantucket Pequot Museum & Research Center ★ $193 million from the flood of cash washing over Connecticut's resurgent Indian Nation was diverted to develop this museum, which opened in 1998. It offers a mix of film, murals, dioramas, and re-creations of scenes of Native American life. Lunch and snacks are served in a museum restaurant, and there's a gift shop with books, jewelry, and crafts. The museum website offers mountains of historical information.

110 Pequot Trail, Mashantucket, CT. ✆ **800/411-9671.** www.pequotmuseum.org. Admission $15 adults (ages 16–54), $13 seniors, $10 children 6–15, free for children 5 and under. Wed–Sat 10am–4pm.

Mohegan Sun In 1996, the barely extant Mohegan tribe opened its gambling casino, and within weeks it was drawing thousands of gamblers a day away from the nearby Foxwoods. Today, the indoor complex includes three casino wings, the **Mohegan Sun hotel** (below), and a mall of pricey shops. There also are three venues for entertainment: a **10,000-seat Arena** that hosts the **WNBA's Connecticut Sun,** a professional women's basketball team, and performers such as musician Jimmy Buffet; a 350-seat **Cabaret Theatre;** and the free **Wolf Den,** located smack dab in the center of the "Earth" casino wing, with acts such as Blue Oyster Cult. See "Where to Dine," below, for restaurant options.

The casinos bulge with eager gamblers trying their luck at Texas Hold 'em, blackjack, live-feed horse-races, and more than 6,000 slot machines. Overhead are simulated log constructions meant to suggest ancient lodge houses; it's an aesthetically pleasing space, as casinos go, although few of the avid players seem to notice. One time-warp feature stands out strongly: Unlike most public areas in Connecticut, smoking is allowed in the casino rooms, giving many areas the murky, gray haze of a 1970s nightclub.

1 Mohegan Sun Blvd., Uncasville. ✆ **888/226-7711.** www.mohegansun.com. Admission free. Daily 24 hours. Gaming areas restricted to ages 21 and older. Children 11 and under must be accompanied by an adult at all times in the complex; children 15 and under must be accompanied 11pm–7am. Take exit 79A from I-395 onto Rte. 2A east.

WHERE TO STAY

Foxwoods has four affiliated hotels at or just adjacent to the resort, including the MGM Grand, listed below. Mohegan Sun has one on-site hotel, listed below. There also are familiar chains hotels in the area, with the website for Mystic country tourism (www.mysticcountry.com) listing 37. Note that unlike in Las Vegas and other gambling centers, room rates aren't kept artificially low at the casino properties as an inducement to gamblers.

MGM Grand at Foxwoods ★★ Attached to the enormous casino complex by an indoor walkway, the MGM Grand opened in 2008, and much of the hotel still feels new and plush. The standard rooms are called deluxe, and there are two categories of suites. Many rooms in the 30-story hotel have a pretty view of the miles of evergreen woods that surround the casino, and decor is minimalist with dark earth tones. In addition to the many restaurants in the casino, the MGM Grand has in-house bars and restaurants, including celebrity chef Tom Colicchio's **Craftsteak.** Be aware that the hotel cannot guarantee a smoke-free room, and guests seem to smoke even on smoke-free floors. Many guests also warn that the minibar is managed by weight sensor, so if you even just *move* anything it's automatically added to the room bill. Review your charges when checking out.

240 MGM Grand Dr., Mashantucket, CT 06338. © **866/646-0050.** www.mgmatfoxwoods.com. 825 units. $129–$259 double. AE, MC, V. Free valet parking. **Amenities:** Many restaurants; many bars; fitness center; outdoor pool (warm months only); room service; spa w/lap pool. *In room:* A/C, TV, hair dryer, minibar, Wi-Fi (free).

Mohegan Sun Hotel ★★   The asymmetrical grouping of soaring, silver-skinned wedges that make up the on-site Mohegan Sun hotel provokes the intended "Wow!" response. The slanting columns are arrayed around a reflecting pool in abstract hom-age to woodland ponds, and the 1,200 rooms in the 34-story building are a minimum of 450 square feet each. They're conventionally attractive, many with the design and decor that was called "modern" in the 1950s. A large spa and an attractive indoor, glass-walled pool are appealing features. Escalators carry guests down to the restau-rants, shops, and gaming wings of the casino complex that envelops the hotel.

1 Mohegan Sun Blvd., Uncasville, CT 06382. © **888/777-7922.** www.mohegansun.com. 1,176 units. $150–$375 double. AE, DC, DISC, MC, V. Free valet parking. **Amenities:** Many restaurants; many bars; concierge; extensive health club; large indoor pool; room service; spa. *In room:* A/C, TV, hair dryer, high-speed Internet (free), minibar.

WHERE TO DINE

Foxwoods has more than 30 restaurants and fast-food operations situated through-out the hotel-casino complex. Unlike in Atlantic City or Vegas, there are no bargains to be found. The popular **Festival Buffet** offers an extensive all-you-can-eat spread. Otherwise, expect to pay at least $50 for dinner for two, not including drinks, taxes, and tip. The high-end options are **Paragon,** with French-influenced cuisine, **Al Dente,** which features designer pizzas and pastas, and **Cedars,** a steakhouse that grills a $50, 20-ounce, Kansas City sirloin. These three venues expect guests to be dressed for fine dining. Reservations for any of the Foxwoods restaurants can be made online or through the main number, © **800/369-9663.**

Mohegan Sun has more than 25 dining spots. Among the top venues are celebrity chef **Bobby Flay's Bar Americain** (© **860/862-8000**), **Jasper White's Summer Shack** (© **860/862-9500**), for seafood; fellow celeb **Todd English's Tuscany** (© **860/862-3238**), for contemporary Italian; and an outpost of **Michael Jordan's Steak House** (© **888/226-7711,** ext. 28600).

RHODE ISLAND

by Herbert Bailey Livesey, Leslie Brokaw & Matthew Barber

Water defines "Little Rhody" as much as mountain peaks characterize Colorado. The Atlantic Ocean borders its south-eastern side, but rather than creating one smooth coastline, the ocean fringes it, leaving a ragged edge of islands, inlets, and the large basin that is Narragansett Bay.

Providence, the state capital, lies at the northern point of that bay, 30 miles from the open ocean. The city was founded by theologian Roger Williams (1603–83). Little survives from that century, but a large section of the Providence's East Side is composed almost entirely of 18th- and 19th-century buildings.

Another group of Puritan exiles established a settlement a couple of years after Providence, on an island in the Narragansett Bay known to the Narragansett tribe as Aquidneck. Settlers thought their new home resembled the Isle of Rhodes in the Aegean, so the region's name became "Rhode Island and Providence Plantations." That moniker was subsequently applied to the entire state, and it remains the official name today.

Rhode Island's most important coastal town is Newport. It's also the best reason for an extended visit to the state.

Newport's first era of prosperity was during the Colonial period, when its ships plied new mercantile routes to China. The city also was central to the reprehensible "Triangle Trade" of rum from New England, molasses from the West Indies, and enslaved peoples from Africa. Smuggling and evading taxes brought the ship owners into conflict with their British rulers, and the occupying British army all but destroyed Newport during the American Revolution.

About a hundred years later, after the U.S. Civil War, the town began its transformation to luxury resort. Millionaires arrived and built astonishingly extravagant mansions, dubbed their summer "cottages." (Their lives spawned what authors Mark Twain and Charles Dudley Warner sneeringly described as the "Gilded Age" in their 1873 novel *The Gilded Age: A Tale of Today.*) Those mansions remain intact, and many can be visited.

The city also became a yachting destination. Sailing's most famous trophy, the America's Cup, became synonymous with Newport after the

Post-March 2010 Floods: Call Ahead to Confirm

In the spring of 2010, many of Rhode Island's rivers overflowed during the worst rains the state has seen in 200 years. Flooding took out bridges and roads and destroyed many businesses. All five counties of the state were affected, with the area south of Providence the hardest hit; more than 17,000 homeowners and businesses applied for relief from the Federal Emergency Management Agency. Call ahead to confirm operating hours and driving directions for hotels, restaurants, and attractions in the state.

racing venue was moved to the city in 1930. Newport continues to be a recreational sailing center with a packed summer cultural calendar.

The result is a city with a little of everything: Visitors who want nothing more than to listen to the surf can happily coexist with history buffs.

Finally, there is Block Island. Beloved by both year-round residents and vacationers, it's a 1-hour ferry ride from the southern coast of the state. It's a quieter and less chic summer destination than Martha's Vineyard (p. 269), the Massachusetts island about 50 miles to its east. "The Block" has few mandatory sights, leaving visitors free simply to explore its lighthouses, hike its cliffside trails, and hit the beach.

PROVIDENCE ★★

50 miles S of Boston, MA; 57 miles NE of New London, CT

Providence long delighted in the nickname "Renaissance City," but, in 2009, city officials unveiled a new marketing catchphrase: Creative Capital. Whether the ad campaign catches on or not, there's no question that the capital city has enjoyed bursts of creative energy over the past 20 years in ways that are distinct from other small and midsize New England cities.

Rivers have been uncovered to form canals and waterside walkways (and host a popular summer event called WaterFire), distressed buildings from the 1800s have been reclaimed and made into residences and office spaces, and construction has wrought new hotels and large public/private partnerships such as Providence Place, a monster mall that opened in 1999 and brought national department stores here for the first time.

Prosperity is evident in the resurgent "downcity" business center and emerging adjacent neighborhoods dubbed the Arts & Entertainment and Jewelry districts. Also on the rise is the West Side, a former industrial enclave adjoining Federal Hill, the city's traditional "Little Italy." All this new energy has attracted creative young people and restaurants, shops, bars, and various entertainments they crave.

Much of the credit for Providence's boom has gone to the ebullient and controversial six-term mayor Vincent A. "Buddy" Cianci, Jr., who served from 1975 to 1984 and again from 1991 to 2002. Although enormously popular, he also was convicted of racketeering and sent to prison after he was caught in an FBI probe into the bribery of local officials. Out of jail since 2007, he now hosts a radio talk show and makes occasional noises about getting into politics again. A 2005 documentary by Cherry Arnold, *Buddy: The Rise and Fall of America's Most Notorious Mayor,* provides a thoroughly engaging look at Cianci's audacious and extraordinary career.

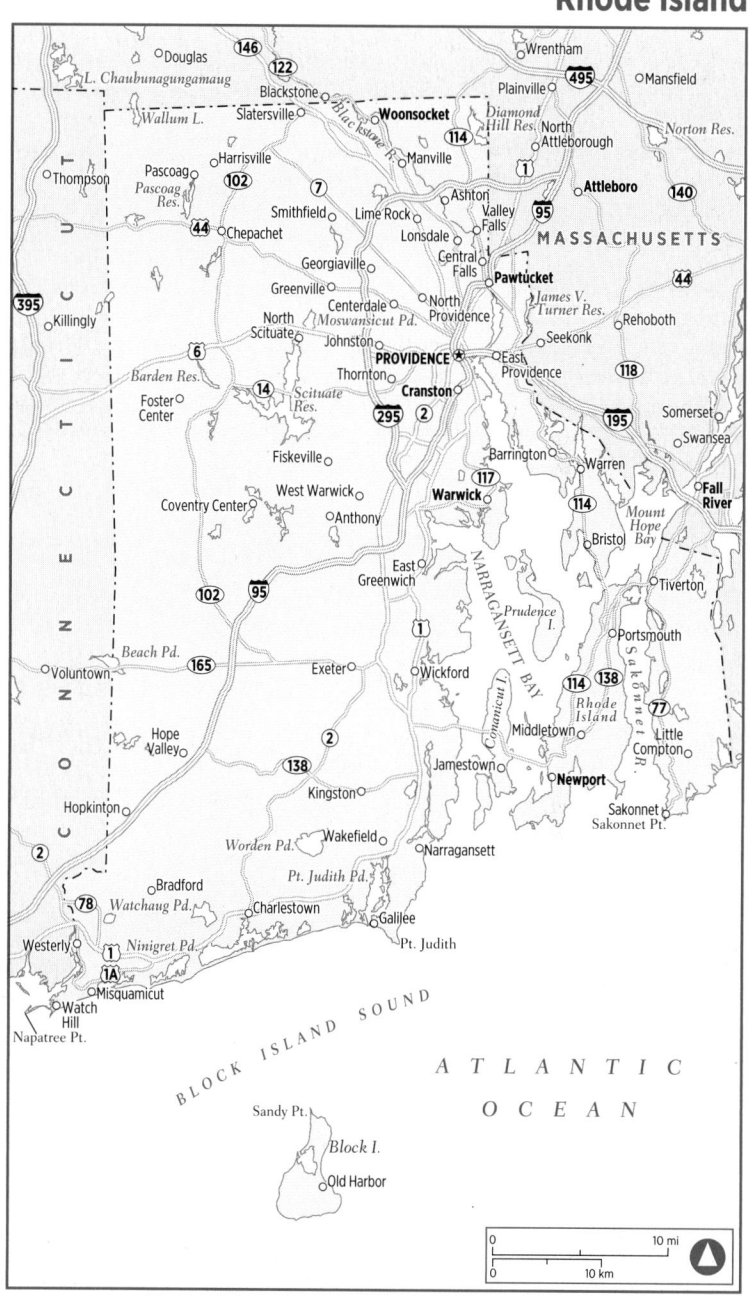

The key historic figure of the region is **Roger Williams** (1603–83), a theologian who established a colony in Providence after being banned from the Massachusetts Bay Colony in 1635 for his views on religious freedom. Admired for his fervent advocacy in the early Colonial period, he had good instincts for town building. He planted the seeds of his settlement on a steep rise overlooking a swift-flowing river at the point where it widened into a large protected harbor. That part of the city, called the East Side and dominated by the ridge now known as College Hill, is one of the most attractive city districts in New England, second only to Boston in the breadth of its cultural life and rich architectural heritage.

This is a city of manageable size—the population is about 175,000—and can easily occupy 2 or 3 days of a Rhode Island vacation. Most points of general interest are found in the East Side and College Hill. Downtown is the center for business, government, and entertainment, with City Hall, the convention center, the best large hotels, and venues for music, dance, and theatrical productions. To downtown's north, across the Woonasquatucket River, is the imposing State House, as well as the Amtrak station. To its west, on the other side of I-95, is Federal Hill, a residential area bearing a primarily Italian ethnic identity, although increasingly permeated by more recent immigrant groups.

Essentials

GETTING THERE I-95, which connects Boston and New York, runs right through the city. From Cape Cod, pick up I-195 West.

T. F. Green/Providence Airport (✆ **401/737-8222;** www.pvdairport.com; airport code: PVD) in Warwick, south of Providence (I-95, exit 13), handles national flights into the state. Major airlines flying here include **Continental** (✆ 800/523-3273), **Delta** (✆ 800/221-1212), **Southwest** (✆ 800/435-9792), **United** (✆ 800/864-8331), and **US Airways** (✆ 800/428-4322).

The **Rhode Island Public Transit Authority,** or **RIPTA** (✆ **800/244-0444** or 401/781-9400; www.ripta.com), provides transportation between the airport and the city center. Taxis are also available, costing about $25 for the 20-minute trip; shared shuttle van rides cost $11.

Amtrak (✆ **800/USA-RAIL** [872-7245];www.amtrak.com) runs several trains daily between Boston and New York that stop at the attractive station at 100 Gaspee St., near the State House.

GETTING AROUND Traffic on local streets isn't bad, even at rush hour. Taxis are not easy to come by, though; few can be found outside even the largest hotels, and when called from restaurants they can take up to an hour. The **RIPTA bus** Green and Gold Lines, which look like old-time trolleys, have routes that reach most major hotels and tourist destinations. Each ride costs $1.75.

VISITOR INFORMATION The **Providence Warwick Convention & Visitors Bureau** runs an information center in the Rhode Island Convention Center, 1 Sabin St. (✆ **800/233-1636** or 401/751-1177; www.goprovidence.com). Their website is full of good information, too, including an online form to request that a visitors guide booklet be mailed to you in advance. The center is open Monday through Saturday from 9am to 5pm.

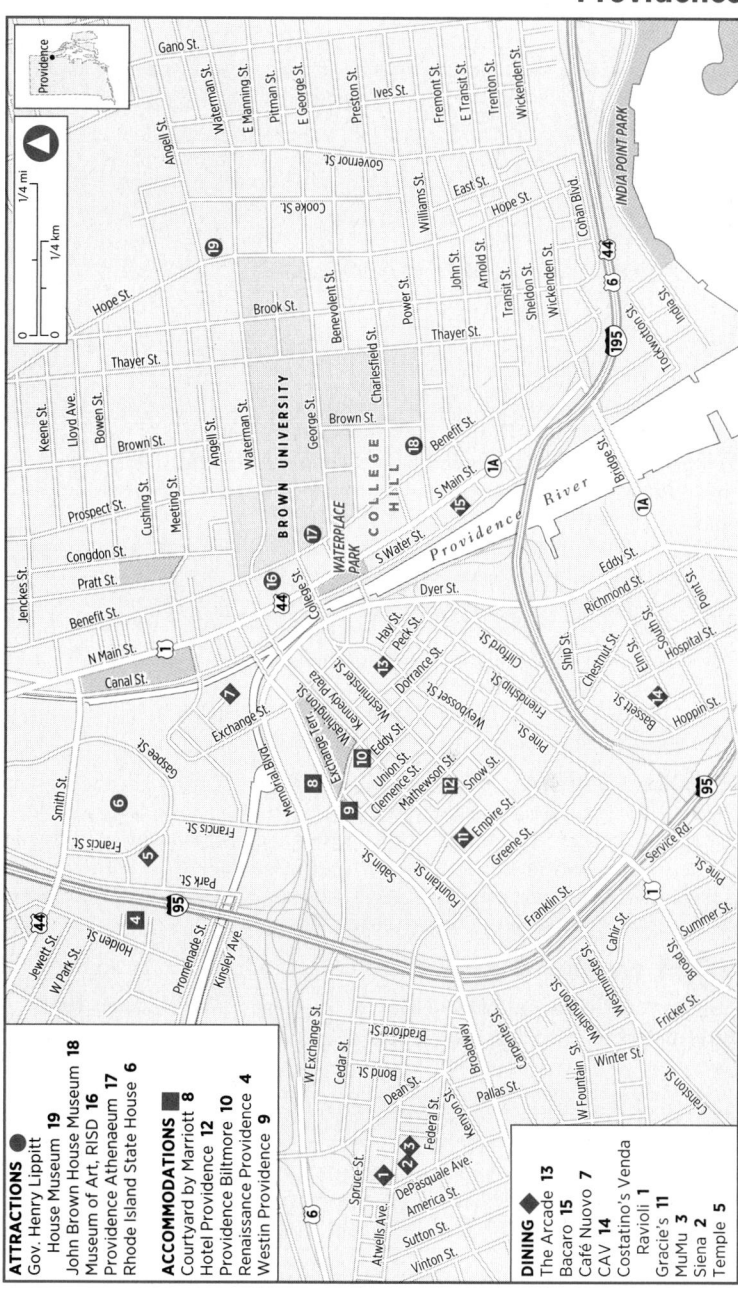

Exploring Providence

STROLL THE HISTORIC NEIGHBORHOODS

To get a sense of the city's evolution from a colony of dissidents to a contemporary center of commerce and government, take a leisurely walk from downtown (or "downcity," as it's called here) across the river toward Brown University; you'll pass most of the prominent Providence attractions.

Start at **Providence City Hall** (built in 1878), at Kennedy Plaza and Dorrance Street. Walk 1 block south, to Westminster. Turn left onto Westminster, then right in 1 block at the Arcade (see "Quick Bites," p. 437), then left onto Weybosset. Follow Weybosset until it joins Westminster, and continue along Westminster across the Providence River. Turn right, walking along the river on South Water Street as far as James Street, just before the I-195 overpass. Turn left onto James, cross South Main, and then turn left on Benefit Street.

Here on Benefit Street is the start of the so-called **Mile of History ★★**. Lined with 18th- and 19th-century houses, it is enhanced by gas streetlamps and sections of brick herringbone sidewalks. Along the way are opportunities to visit, in sequence, the 1786 **John Brown House,** the **Providence Athenaeum** (p. 431), and the **Museum of Art at the Rhode Island School of Design** (p. 431). The grand **Gov. Henry Lippitt House Museum** (p. 431) is a half-mile from the RISD museum and worth a stop if you're touring on a Friday in summer or early fall.

This area, from Benefit up to the right (east), is **College Hill ★**. It was the site of the former Rhode Island College, which started life in 1764 and was later renamed Brown University. Benefit Street is the western border of the Brown campus. College Hill is now a National Historic District and has several square miles of 18th- and 19th-century Colonial and Victorian houses lining its streets. In the middle of the Brown campus, parallel to Benefit, is Thayer Street, a funky shopping district.

The **Rhode Island Historical Society** (© **401/331-8575;** www.rihs.org) offers guided walking tours of the city's neighborhoods.

STROLL FEDERAL HILL

Federal Hill, on the west side of the city, has long been a tourist destination. It's a traditionally Italian neighborhood—the television show *Brotherhood* was filmed in the area—complete with traditional Italian eateries, but since about 1990 it has seen a rise in non-Italian restaurants and new boutiques and galleries (see "Shopping," p. 432). Atwells Avenue is the neighborhood's main artery.

What to See & Do

Boosters are understandably proud of the city's **Waterplace Park & Riverwalk ★★**, which encircles a tidal basin and borders the Woonasquatucket River down past where it joins the Moshassuck to become the Providence River. It incorporates an amphitheater, boat landings, landscaped walkways, and vaguely Venetian bridges. Summer concerts and other events are held here, including the popular **WaterFire ★★** (p. 432).

A singular attraction is **La Gondola** (© **401/421-8877;** www.gondolari.com). A faithful replica of the Venetian original, it carries up to six passengers along the Woonasquatucket and Providence rivers May through October. Especially popular for rides during the WaterFire events, its rates run from $79 to $159 for two persons—about what it would cost in the Italian city itself, minus the airfare.

In winter, an **outdoor ice skating rink** (✆ **401/331-5544;** www.kennedyplaza.org/skating-information) is set up in Kennedy Plaza. It's huge and fully utilized almost every evening in cold weather. Skate rentals, lockers, and a snack bar are on site.

Brown University   The nation's seventh-oldest college was founded in 1764 and has a reputation as the most experimental institution among its Ivy League brethren. The evidence of its pre-Revolutionary origins is seen in **University Hall,** built in 1771. Tours of the campus are intended primarily for prospective students, but anyone can join. Reservations are not necessary, but call ahead to check the schedule, which changes frequently.

Office of Admissions, 45 Prospect St. (at Angell St.). ✆ **401/863-1000.** www.brown.edu.

Gov. Henry Lippitt House Museum ★   This house is as magnificently true to its grandiose Victorian era as any residence on the Continent. Expanses of stained glass, meticulously detailed stenciling, and inlaid floors make this 1865 mansion one of the treasures of College Hill. Visits are by guided tour only, and opening hours are limited to Friday in summer and early fall.

199 Hope St. (at Angell St.). ✆ **401/453-0688.** www.preserveri.org. Admission $10. Tours May–Oct Fri 11am–3pm on the hour (last tour at 2pm); Nov–Apr by appointment only.

Museum of Art at the Rhode Island School of Design ★★   Prestigious RISD (pronounced *Riz*-dee) supports this ingratiating center of fine and decorative arts. Of the many excellent college and university museums in New England, this ranks near the top for the breadth of its collection. Holdings include textile arts and French Impressionist paintings, with works by such masters as Monet, Cézanne, Rodin, Picasso, and Matisse. But allow time for the American wing, which contains paintings by John Singleton Copley and John Singer Sargent, and the contemporary collection, which includes sculpture by Louise Bourgeois and videos by Bruce Nauman. The Gorham silver collection, which includes work by Colonial silversmith Paul Revere, is nearly worth the price of admission on its own.

224 Benefit St. (at Waterman St.). ✆ **401/454-6500.** www.risdmuseum.org. Admission $10 adults, $7 seniors, $3 children 5–18 and college students, free for children 4 and under. Free to all third Thurs of the month 5–9pm, Sun 10am–1pm, and last Sat of month. Tues–Sun 10am–5pm (3rd Thurs of the month until 9pm).

Pawtucket Red Sox Baseball at McCoy Stadium ★   Just 6 miles north of Providence is Pawtucket, a working-class city with a great attraction: the minor league ballpark for the Pawtucket Red Sox, a Triple A baseball team. As the step just before the big leagues with the Boston Red Sox, Pawtucket is the place to catch both up-and-coming stars and big name players recovering from injuries. Baseball at McCoy Stadium is old-timey American: The crowds are friendly, the prices are modest, the baseball is good, and the music is low-key. You can even get your photo taken with the mascots (Paws and Sox) for free. Fun fact: McCoy was witness to the longest game in baseball history—33 innings, played over 2 days in 1981 (the Paw Sox won).

1 Columbus Ave., Pawtucket. ✆ **401/724-7300.** www.pawsox.com. Box seats $11; general admission $7 adults, $5 senior and children 12 and under. Limited first-come, first-served free parking; otherwise, paid parking nearby. Season runs Apr–Sept. From Providence, take I-95 North to exit 27, 28, or 29 and follow signs.

Providence Athenaeum   The Providence Athenaeum commissioned this 1838 Greek Revival building to house its lending library, the fourth-oldest in the United

States. Edgar Allan Poe courted Sarah Whitman, his "Annabel Lee," among the stacks here. Glances through the old card catalog reveal handwritten cards dating well back into the 1800s; bibliophiles will lose themselves in this evocative place. Rotating exhibits of rare books and works by local artists are additional attractions. The library's financial challenges contributed to a contretemps over ways to raise funds, specifically a decision in 2003 to sell off an Audubon folio that eventually netted $5 million.

251 Benefit St. (at College St.). *C* **401/421-6970.** www.providenceathenaeum.org. Free admission. Mon–Thurs 9am–7pm; Fri 9am–5pm; Sat 1–5pm. Also Sun 1–5pm Sept–May. Closed first 2 weeks in Aug.

Rhode Island State House   Constructed of white Georgian marble that blazes in the sun, Rhode Island's capitol building dominates the city center. This near-flawless example of neoclassical governmental architecture (by McKim, Mead & White; 1885–1904) boasts one of the largest self-supported domes in the world. The gilded figure on top represents "Independent Man," the state symbol. Given pride of place inside the State Room is a portrait of George Washington, one of many depictions painted by Gilbert Stuart (1755–1828), a Rhode Island native.

82 Smith St. (at State St.). *C* **401/277-2357.** www.rilin.state.ri.us/statehousetour. Free admission. Guided tours by appointment.

Roger Williams Park Zoo ★ ☺   This zoo is divided into six habitats: Tropical America, North America, the Plains of Africa, Madagascar, Australia, and the Marco Polo Trail. Featured animals include giraffes, elephants, harbor seals, and snow leopards. Halloween brings special programs including a huge display of jack-o-lanterns and "spooky zoo" parties.

1000 Elmwood Ave. *C* **401/785-3510.** www.rogerwilliamsparkzoo.org. Admission $12 adults, $8 seniors, $6 children ages 3–12, free for children 2 and under; half-price admission Jan–Feb. Free parking. Daily 9am–4pm. From I-95 S, take exit 17; from I-95 N, take exit 16.

WaterFire Providence ★★ ☺ 📷   The signature event of the Providence summer and early fall are the WaterFire nights. Along the three rivers that run through the city, an installation of 100 floating bonfires creates a haunting glow, with world music adding to the scene. Thousands of people descend to the shores to witness the event, held a dozen times from late spring to early fall. It takes place along Memorial Boulevard and the Providence and Woonasquatucket Rivers, running for just over a half-mile from Providence Place to the Crawford Street Bridge.

Basin of Waterplace Park and along the river, downtown. *C* **401/273-1155.** www.waterfire.org. Free admission, with donations accepted at the site. Selected evenings late May to Oct, from 20 min. after sunset until midnight. Check website for the schedule.

Shopping

On the East Side of the city, **Thayer Street,** the main commercial district for Brown University, is good for browsing. The official **Brown Bookstore** is here, at no. 244 (corner of Olive St.). **Wickenden Street,** which crosses Thayer at its southern end, also has interesting shops and art galleries.

Downtown, **Providence Place,** a 170-store mall at One Providence Place (*C* **401/270-1000;** www.providenceplace.com), is home to Nordstrom, Tiffany & Co., Coach, Apple Store, J. Jill, and Build-A-Bear Workshop, among others. There's also a National Amusements IMAX movie theater. The mall's parking garage rates are reasonable for a midsized city (3–4 hr. for $5).

Foodies will want to stroll Federal Hill, the "Little Italy" area of the city, west of I-95. Head to Atwells Avenue, the main drag. Keep an eye out for **Constantino's Venda Ravioli,** 265Atwells Ave. (© **401/421-9105;** www.vendaravioli.com). It started as a retail pasta store but has expanded into a small empire of prepared foods, packaged Italian specialties, and large cheese and meat sections. There's also an espresso bar and cafe tables for noshing either inside or on a terrace.

The city has launched an I BUY ART campaign to bolster the artist community. One of the results: an influx of art galleries and upscale clothing shops along Federal Hill's Atwells Avenue and Westminster Street. For details, go to **www.buyartprovidence. com**, **www.providencefederalhill.com/shop.html**, and **www.artonthehill.org**.

Where to Stay

The Renaissance Providence, listed below, is across the street from the State House. The other four hotels recommended here are located downtown—"downcity," as it's called here.

Courtyard by Marriott Providence Downtown ★ As a midpriced entry designed primarily for businesspeople, the Marriott's rooms are equipped with well-lit desks, flatscreen TVs, and spiffed up bathrooms. It is just as comfortable for leisure travelers, with several of our recommended restaurants, the Providence Place mall, and the WaterFire installation only minutes away. While the on-site cafe doesn't serve dinner, meals can be delivered from nearby restaurants.

32 Exchange Terrace, Providence, RI 02903. © **888/887-7955** or 401/272-1191. Fax 401/272-1416. www. courtyard.com. 210 units. $159–$279 double. AE, DC, DISC, MC, V. Parking $22. **Amenities:** Cafe/bar (breakfast in the morning only, evening cocktails); exercise room; Jacuzzi; indoor pool. In room: A/C, TV, hair dryer, Wi-Fi (free).

Hotel Providence ★★ A dazzling contribution to the emerging downtown arts and entertainment district, this boutique hotel, combining two buildings, gained instant membership in the selective Small Luxury Hotels of the World marketing group. The owners filled the public areas with fine 18th- and 19th-century European antiques and artworks, and commissioned custom reproductions for the bedrooms to carry the image through. Pillow-top beds are cozy and enveloping. Guests are serenaded at 15-minute intervals by the pealing of the 16 tower bells of Grace Church, across the street, so light sleepers will want a room away from that side of the hotel.

139 Mathewson St., Providence, RI 02903. © **800/861-8990** or 401/861-8000. Fax 401/861-8002. www.thehotelprovidence.com. 80 units. $199–$239 double. AE, DC, DISC, MC, V. Valet parking $25. Small pets accepted ($75 fee). **Amenities:** Restaurant; bar; concierge; small exercise room; room service. In room: A/C, TV, hair dryer, MP3 docking station, Wi-Fi (free).

Providence Biltmore ★★ A grand staircase beneath the stunning Deco bronze ceiling dates the centrally located building to the 1920s, and a plaque in the lobby shows the nearly 7-foot-high water level reached during the villainous 1938 hurricane. From the lobby, the dramatic glass elevator shoots skyward, exiting outdoors to scoot up the side of the building. Most guest rooms are large (over half are suites averaging 600 sq. ft.), and California king beds are standard in all rooms. The in-house restaurant, McCormick & Schmick's, specializes in seafood. An **Elizabeth Arden Red Door Spa** is on-site, too (www.reddoorspas.com).

11 Dorrance St., Providence, RI 02903. © **800/294-7709** or 401/421-0700. Fax 401/455-3050. www. providencebiltmore.com. 292 units. $169–$199 double. AE, DC, MC, V. Valet parking $24. Pets accepted

($35/night). **Amenities:** Restaurant; bar; concierge; fitness center; room service. *In room:* A/C, TV, hair dryer, Wi-Fi (free).

Renaissance Providence ★★★   Here's a story: In the late 1920s, the Masons were building a neoclassical temple a couple of blocks west of the State House. But they ran out of money and construction suddenly ended, leaving the building an empty shell. There it stood for 78 years, unoccupied, a magnet for graffiti vandals and thieves. A $100-million renovation by the Marriott company transformed it into this ambitious luxury hotel, which opened in 2007. Immediately, the Renaissance Providence rivaled the best the city has to offer. A grand lobby with a fireplace welcomes guests, and **Temple,** the flashy in-house restaurant-bar, was an instant hit with locals as well as out-of-towners. Two executive-level floors have a private club/lounge with honor bar. The hotel is a 5-minute walk from the Amtrak station and across from the State House.

5 Ave. of the Arts, Providence, RI 02903. ℂ **800/468-3571** or 401/919-5000. Fax 401/276-0023. www. renaissancehotels.com. 272 units. $169–$299 double. AE, DC, DISC, MC, V. Valet parking $25. On older maps, Ave. of the Arts is called Brownell St. It's off Francis St., across from the State House. **Amenities:** Restaurant; bar; babysitting; concierge; executive-level rooms; fitness center; room service. *In room:* A/C, TV, hair dryer, minibar, Wi-Fi ($11 per day).

Westin Providence ★★   With skyway connections to the Providence Place mall and the convention center, the Westin is Providence's most prominent downtown hotel. The lobby rotunda and other public spaces have an architectural grandeur. Many of the rooms are in the 200-unit tower that was added to the main building in 2007. Bedrooms are equipped with Westin's patented Heavenly Bed mattresses and some (called WestinWORKOUT rooms) have in-room treadmills for exercising in private. **Agora,** the main dining room, gets excellent reviews and serves all meals; there's also an in-house steakhouse and wine bar called **Fleming's.** Unsettled hotel worker contract negotiations in 2009 and 2010 led to some picketing at the hotel, with service disruptions noted by some visitors on several online travel sites.

1 West Exchange St., Providence, RI 02903. ℂ **800/937-8461** or 401/598-8000. Fax 401/598-8200. www.starwoodhotels.com/westin. 564 units. $209–$314 double. AE, DC, DISC, MC, V. Valet parking $26. Pets accepted (free). **Amenities:** 2 restaurants; 2 bars; small indoor pool; fully equipped fitness center w/sauna; room service. *In room:* A/C, TV, hair dryer, Wi-Fi ($10).

Where to Dine

Providence has a sturdy Italian heritage, resulting in a profusion of tomato-sauce and pizza joints, especially on Federal Hill. That identity is starting to change, but a stroll along the main drag of the district, Atwells Avenue between Bradford and Sutton, can set off furious hunger alarms.

Another fruitful strip to explore for lower-cost dining options is that part of **Thayer Street** bordering the Brown University campus. It counts Thai, Tex-Mex, barbecue, and Indian restaurants among its possibilities.

Bacaro ★ ITALIAN   Both the readers and the editors of the *Providence Phoenix* newspaper picked this as a favorite restaurant in 2009, 2 years after it opened. What they all agreed on is that it's a standout for what may as well be called Italian tapas—small dishes that allow for a fun night of grazing and tasting. Diners choose from 30 such *cicchetti* options here, from fried smelts with lemony aioli to wild boar sausage on crispy polenta crostini served with blueberry chutney. You can also order from an expansive *salumeria* menu of cured meats and robust cheeses—ask for advice and

BIG TASTES HIDE IN LITTLE RHODY

You'd think that, in an age of instant communication, no ingratiatingly flavorful food tidbit would stay unknown for long. Regional specialties often become national staples—think Buffalo wings, Carolina blooming onions, Texas burritos. But Rhode Island's food specialties remain mysteriously secret. Even residents of neighboring states are in the dark about a lot of them. So while you're visiting, be sure to check out some of the following:

○ **Stuffies:** These come in as many versions as there are cooks. At Flo's Clam Shack (p. 459), in Newport, big quahog clams are chopped up with hot and sweet peppers and bread crumbs, packed inside the two shell halves, and shut, the whole held together by a rubber band. After they're baked, the mixture assumes the consistency of setting plaster—very tasty plaster.

○ **Rhode Island clam chowder:** This is a potato, onion, and clam (often quahog) soup of clear broth. It's neither cream-based (such as the well-known New England chowder) nor tomato-based (such as Manhattan chowder).

○ **Coffee milk and cabinets:** Obligatory Rhody beverages. Coffee milk is made with milk and sweet coffee syrup (available in any Rhode Island grocery store). Cabinets are what most of the rest of America calls a milkshake (and what some parts of New England call a frappe): milk, ice cream, and flavorings such as chocolate syrup.

○ **Johnnycakes:** Also spelled *jonnycakes,* these are breakfast fodder. Sometimes they're as thin as crepes, sometimes as thick as griddlecakes. Their primary ingredient is cornmeal. Honey is a common topping.

○ **New York System Wieners:** These have only a passing acquaintance with Big Apple franks. In Rhode Island, the wieners are short—3 or 4 inches long—served on soft steamed buns and topped (usually) with a chili-type meat sauce, minced onion, and mustard. Nobody eats just one—the typical ration is four or more.

start there. Bacaro's location on South Water Street offers views of the Providence River and is a logical destination after touring the historic east side of the city.

262 S. Water St. (near Williams St.). © **401/751-3700.** www.bacarorestaurant.net. Reservations recommended. Main courses $19–$35; cicchetti $3–$10. AE, DC, MC, V. Tues-Sat 5–10pm (Sat from 4pm).

Cafe Nuovo ★★★ INTERNATIONAL   This spacious room of glass, marble, and burnished wood occupies part of the ground floor of a downtown office tower that overlooks the confluence of the Moshassuck and Woonasquatucket rivers. (It makes an ideal overlook for the WaterFire events, p. 432.) Unlike some of its competitors, Cafe Nuovo takes reservations, is open for lunch *and* dinner, and impresses with every course, from dazzling appetizers to stunning pastries. The fare skips lightly among inspirations—Greek, Portuguese, and Japanese among them. A three-course dinner option for $30 is offered early evenings when the nearby Providence

Performing Arts Center has shows, taking the sting out of the higher-priced menu options. Restaurants come and go, but Cafe Nuovo endures, steady and embracing.

1 Citizens Plaza (access from the Steeple St. bridge). © **401/421-2525.** www.cafenuovo.com. Reservations recommended. Main courses $23–$40. AE, DC, DISC, MC, V. Mon–Fri 11:30am–3pm; Mon–Thurs 5–10:30pm; Fri–Sat 5–11pm; Sun when there's a WaterFire event.

CAV ★★ INTERNATIONAL   No corporate design drudge had a hand in *this* warehouse interior, a Jewelry District pioneer. CAV is an acronym for "Cocktails/Antiques/Victuals," and patrons are surrounded by tribal rugs, African carvings, and assorted antiques (most for sale). Turkish *kilims* under glass cover the tables. The resulting bohemian air is not unlike Greenwich Village in the 1960s. Attractive servers bring dishes prepared by folks quite accomplished at their craft. Select from such strenuous menu swings as pistachio-crusted crab cake with sriracha aioli and taro root chips to the modern comfort food that is braised lamb with poppy seed port wine demi-glace, butternut squash custard, and Israeli couscous. Consult a map or the directions at the restaurant's website before heading out.

14 Imperial Place (at Basset St.). © **401/751-9164.** www.cavrestaurant.com. Reservations recommended. Main courses $15–$32. DISC, MC, V. Mon–Thurs 11:30am–10pm; Fri 11:30am–1am; Sat 10am–10pm; Sun 10:30am–10pm.

Chez Pascal ★★ FRENCH   Located about 2 miles north on Hope Street from the Brown University campus, this warm little bistro is worth the trip. The kitchen works in the French tradition but isn't dogmatic about it. The variety of house-made pâtés and charcuterie is unusually large, from the root vegetable terrine to the pork and fennel sausage. Pascal always offers a "local pork of the day" dish, but it also caters to the desires of non-meat-eaters with a vegetarian tasting menu that often features lentil ragout with roasted sugar pumpkin. To bring in patrons on slow Tuesdays, Wednesdays, and Thursdays, there's a three-course fixed-price menu for $30. Winning desserts have included apple *galette*—a bread pudding served with cinnamon ice cream.

960 Hope St. (at 9th St.). © **401/421-4422.** www.chez-pascal.com. Reservations recommended. Main courses $25–$31. AE, DC, MC, V. Mon–Sat 5:30–9:30pm (until 10pm Fri–Sat).

Gracie's ★ NEW AMERICAN   After moving from its former Federal Hill address to the downtown Arts District across from the Trinity Repertory Company, this longtime favorite hasn't lost a smidgen of its old verve. Pin lights in the ceiling hint at the night sky, a theme carried out with rather too much enthusiasm in the proliferation of five-pointed stars scattered over the rest of the room. That aside, you're unlikely to hear any complaints about either the food or the people who bring it. The menu changes seasonally, but the first course might be house-made potato gnocchi or veal sweetbreads accompanied by a quail's egg. Carnivores will be more than sated by the lamb with hen of the woods mushrooms and grits. *Prix-fixe* menus of three, five, or seven courses are available.

194 Washington St. (1 block from Empire St.). © **401/272-7811.** www.graciesprov.com. Reservations advised. Main courses $26–$39; 3-course prix fixe $30. AE, DC, MC, V. Tues–Sat 5–10pm.

MuMu ★★ CHINESE   Smack in the middle of the busiest, most Italian part of Federal Hill is this Chinese restaurant that looks the part, with a black and scarlet color scheme, little vases of fresh flowers on each table, and a menu that goes on forever. A knowing presence is in command here: The middle-aged woman in sweater set and slacks who might welcome you is the owner of this and several other

QUICK BITES

Providence claims the invention of the diner, starting with a horse-drawn wagon transporting food down Westminster Street in 1872. The tradition is carried forward by the likes of the **Seaplane Diner,** 307 Allens Ave. (© **401/941-9547**), a silver-sided classic with table-side jukeboxes.

A bona fide National Historic Landmark is an unlikely venue for snarfing up cookies, souvlaki, and egg rolls, but **The Arcade,** 66 Weybosset St. (© **401/331-0050**), is a 19th-century progenitor of 20th-century shopping malls, an 1828 Greek Revival structure that runs between Weybosset and Westminster streets. Its main floor is given over largely to fast-food stands and snack counters of the usual kinds, while the upper floor is primarily boutiques and souvenir shops.

Another local culinary institution arrives in Kennedy Plaza on wheels every afternoon around 4:30pm. The grungy aluminum-sided **Haven Bros.** (© **401/861-7777**) is a food tractor-trailer with a counter and six stools inside and good deals on decent burgers and even better fries sold from its parking space next to City Hall. No new frontiers here, except that it hangs around until way past midnight to dampen the hunger pangs of clubgoers, lawyers, night people, and workaholic pols.

restaurants in China, Taiwan, and the U.S. She's behind the sorcery of the *xiao long bao,* pork dumplings with a tablespoon of broth *inside* (which bursts over your chin if you're not careful), and Szechuan chili ravioli, which are delectable. If you've never had Peking duck because of the advance ordering requirement at many restaurants, try it here, where it will arrive by the time you've downed your appetizer. Or make a meal of any of the six *dim sum* options.

220 Atwells Ave. (near Dean St.). © **401/369-7040.** Reservations not accepted. Main courses $6.25–$15. MC, V. Mon–Sat 11:30am–10pm (until 11pm Fri–Sat); Sun 12:30–10pm.

Siena ★ ITALIAN   Federal Hill's days as a tomato gravy and pizza destination are fading, replaced by upbeat, contemporary chefs and owners who value quality and are alert to trends. Promising "Tuscan Soul Food," Siena draws all ages (including an occasional shrieking child) and is among the hottest places in town. Waitstaff is more knowledgeable and attentive than average. Antipasti and thin, wood-grilled, upscale pizzas may distract your attention from the rest of the card, but give full consideration to the *pollo al Diavolo* (Devil's chicken), chicken breasts with an herb and hot red pepper rub; and the *aragosta cioppino,* a San Francisco fish stew of lobster, shrimp, clams, mussels, swordfish, and calamari in a spicy broth.

238 Atwells Ave. © **401/521-3311.** www.sienaprovidence.com. Reservations recommended. Main courses $14–$29. AE, DC, MC, V. Mon–Thurs 5–10pm; Fri 5–11pm; Sat 4:30–11pm; Sun 3–9pm.

Temple ★ CONTEMPORARY BISTRO   Inside the **Renaissance Providence** hotel (p. 434), this restaurant enjoys the avid interest of young professionals and older sophisticates: Walking in, you may think you've wandered through a wrong door into a disco. The music and crowd of seekers-after-companionship are in full voice. The mirrors, tiles, and other hard surfaces in the dining room ensure that the noise level restaurateurs love doesn't dip much below 70 decibels. That aside, the food has proven to be fun variations of old favorites, and cocktails include concoctions both standard and silly. A new menu focused on Mediterranean tastes debuted in spring 2010.

120 Francis St. (at Ave. of the Arts). ℃ **401/919-5050.** www.temple-downtown.com. Main courses $15-$26. Mon-Fri 6:30-10:30am, 11:30am-2pm, and 5-10pm (until 11pm Fri); Sat 7:30-10:30am, 11:30am-2pm, and 5-11pm; Sun 11:30am-2pm and 5-9pm.

Providence After Dark

This being a college town, there is no end of music options. A good source of information is the free weekly *Providence Phoenix* (www.providencephoenix.com).

THE PERFORMING ARTS   Big-ticket touring musicals on the order of *Jersey Boys* and *Rent* are showcased at the **Providence Performing Arts Center,** 220 Weybosset St. (℃ **401/421-ARTS** [2787]; www.ppacri.org). At the **Trinity Repertory Company,** 201 Washington St. (℃ **401/351-4242;** www.trinityrep.com), new plays share space with works by Shakespeare and Neil Simon.

The **Dunkin' Donuts Center,** 1 La Salle Sq. (℃ **401/331-6700;** www.dunkin donutscenter.com), hosts big-name performers, monster truck events, and NCAA basketball games.

Opera Providence (℃ **401/331-6060;** www.operaprovidence.org) stages productions at a variety of locations, including Blithewold (p. 440) in Bristol. The **Rhode Island Philharmonic** (℃ **401/248-7000;** www.ri-philharmonic.org) puts on one or two concerts a month from September through May, often at the Veterans Memorial Auditorium.

THE CLUB & MUSIC SCENE   A terrible fire at the Station rock club in nearby West Warwick killed 100 patrons and seriously injured over 200 others in 2003. Strict (and expensive) regulations requiring installation of sprinkler systems were imposed on nightclubs and other venues in the aftermath, compelling some places to suspend operations or close permanently.

One prominent survivor is the rock club **Lupo's Heartbreak Hotel,** 79 Washington St. (℃ **401/331-5876;** www.lupos.com). For jazz and blues, head to the **Hi-Hat,** 3 Davol Sq. (℃ **401/453-6500;** www.thehihat.com). It has a dinner menu, too. Find it near the west end of the Point Street bridge; the entrance is on Point Street.

At the **Trinity Brewhouse,** 186 Fountain St. (℃ **401/453-2337;** www.trinity brewhouse.com), home-brewed, award-winning beers are the main event. As the website puts it, "We sell heaven by the pint." There's often live music in the evenings.

If the bar scene doesn't appeal to you, consider heading to **AS220,** 115 Empire St. (℃ **401/831-9327;** www.as220.org), a community arts space for mostly local visual, musical, and performance artists, with events every day. Similar in mission is **Tazza Caffe,** 250 Westminster St. (℃ **401/421-3300;** www.tazzacaffe.com), an espresso bar open daily from 7am weekdays and 8am weekends to at least 11pm. It often hosts jazz, cabaret, and open-mic nights.

MOVIES   For art-house films and midnight cult movies, check the **Avon Cinema,** 260 Thayer St., at Meeting Street (℃ **401/421-AVON** [2866]; www.avoncinema. com), and the **Cable Car,** 204 S. Main St. (℃ **401/272-3970;** www.cablecar cinema.com), which has comfy sofas as a seating option.

BRISTOL

16 miles SE of Providence; 15 miles N of Newport

About halfway between Providence and Newport is Bristol, perhaps the best-kept secret in Rhode Island. First settled in 1680, this beautiful waterfront town sits on a peninsula straddling the Narragansett and Mount Hope Bays and presents a soothing excursion from the urbanity of Providence and the concentration of sights and activity that is Newport.

Bristol is best known as home to the nation's oldest 4th of July parade, which has run annually here since 1785. The parade draws up to 200,000 spectators and is the highlight of the year for what some residents call "America's Most Patriotic Town." The main boulevard, Hope Street, does away with the double yellow line in favor of a red, white, and blue band marking the 1.8-mile parade route.

Bristol's past also includes the notoriety of being the former home to the DeWolfs, the largest slave trading family in U.S. history. During much of the 1700s and the first decade of the 1800s, Rhode Island was the business epicenter of the "Triangle Trade," the trade of rum from New England, molasses from the West Indies, and enslaved peoples from Africa.

Today, though, Bristol is known for its historic homes and quaint downtown. In the past 15 years, it has undergone a gentrification from industrial town to tourist haven, with shops, a few fine dining spots, and cafes comprising a landscape of what used to be abandoned mills and fading industry.

Note that in the off season, November through April, most museums and small inns close.

Essentials

GETTING THERE   From Providence, it's fastest to take I-195 to Rte. 136, but the more scenic route is to take I-195 to exit 7, to Rte. 114 S toward Barrington. Follow Rte. 114 all the way into Bristol, and, on the way, you'll pass marinas and historic buildings and traverse scenic bridges, setting a slower pace for your visit.

VISITOR INFORMATION   The **Bristol Visitor Center** is located in the Burnside Building at 400 Hope St. (© **401/253-7000;** www.bristolri.us). It's open mid-May through October, daily from noon to 4pm.

What to See & Do

As mentioned above, July 4th is the big day of the year. Locals rent lawn chairs and spots on their lawns, and sell lemonade and cookies. Most other days, the city's quiet charm is in its well-preserved historic district, which runs along Hope Street and down side roads to Thames Street (pronounced "TH-ames"), which borders the Bristol Harbor. Start here and stroll. Homes here date back to the 1700s and 1800s. The harbor is formerly an industrial area of town that has undergone a gentrification in favor of high-end condos in converted mill buildings. There is 1- and 2-hour parking available along most streets, and a municipal parking lot on Thames.

Bristol was named one of the 2009 Dozen Distinctive Destinations in the U.S. by the National Trust for Historic Preservation, which called it a "quintessential New England waterfront town" with an "unwavering commitment" to preservation. Also cited by the Trust are town attractions Blithewold Mansion, Coggeswell Farm

Museum, Herreshoff Marine Museum and America's Cup Hall of Fame, and Colt State Park, all listed below.

Blithewold Mansion, Gardens, and Arboretum This 45-room waterfront estate was built in 1907 as a summer home to Augustus Van Wickle. Featuring beautiful gardens and landscaping, it's now a museum that feels like a rural English manor. The estate is open for tours and is preserved much as it was in the early 1900s. Garden tours are a particular treat, and in mid- to late April, thousands of daffodils on the property come into bloom, providing a magnificent scene.

101 Ferry Rd. (Rte. 114).*C* **401/253-2702.** www.blithewold.org. Admission $10 adults, $8 seniors and full-time students, $2 children 6–17, free for children 5 and under. Mid-Apr to mid-Oct Wed–Sun 10am–4pm; closed rest of the year.

Herreshoff Marine Museum and America's Cup Hall of Fame This maritime museum highlights the history of the Herreshoff Manufacturing Company, a boat builder of everything from Naval torpedo boats to championship America's Cup yachts, and once the centerpiece of industry in Bristol. The facility houses the America's Cup Hall of Fame and features a collection of 35 boats, including the famous *America³*, winner of the 1992 America's Cup race.

1 Burnside St. (off Hope St./Rte. 114).*C* **401/253-5000.** www.herreshoff.org. Admission $3. Mon–Sat 10am–5pm; Sun noon–5pm.

Mount Hope Farm and the Governor Bradford House With fields, streams, and waterfront views, this museum and inn is a National Register Historic Landmark.

250 Metacom Ave. (Rte. 136).*C* **401/254-1745.** www.mounthopefarm.com. Farm and grounds Mar–Oct. Call for days and hours of operation.

Getting Outside

The **Coggeshall Farm Museum ★**, 1 Colt Dr. (*C* **401/253-9062;** www.coggeshall farm.org), is a "living history" museum on 50 acres abutting Colt State Park (see below) in a bucolic western section of town. It is comprised of a 1790s farmhouse, several small antique farm buildings, rare breed livestock, and open fields. Costumed staff members are on site to answer questions and demonstrate farm life of the 18th century. While not the kind of museum one spends an entire day at, it's worth a visit even if just to walk around and enjoy the atmosphere of centuries-old farmland. It's open Tuesday to Sunday from 10am to 4pm year-round (though it's closed some holidays, so call in advance). Admission is $3 for adults, $2 for seniors and children. To get there, turn onto Poppasquash Road off Hope Street (Rte. 114), go 1½ miles, and turn right onto Colt Drive (an unmarked road) at the Coggeshall Farm Museum sign.

Colt State Park, Hope Street/Rte. 114 (*C* **401/253-7482;** www.riparks.com/colt.htm), was once the estate of Samuel Colt, of the same family as the famous firearms manufacturer. The state purchased the property in 1965 to preserve it as public space. Encompassing 464 acres of land, the park borders Narragansett Bay and offers stunning views over the water, especially at sunset. There are trails for biking, walking, jogging, or cycling, and bridle paths for horseback riding. In warmer months, families come for the day to barbecue, play volleyball, and otherwise enjoy the bucolic atmosphere. You'll also find anglers casting lines and kayakers paddling on the bay. Entry and parking is free, but fireplace sites and gazebos cost a fee. The park is open year-round from sunrise to sunset.

The **East Bay Bike Path** (www.riparks.com/eastbay.htm) is a 14.5-mile paved trail that runs between Bristol and Providence. It's a rail-trail, built atop a converted train track. After passing through Colt State Park, it spends much of the trip skimming Narragansett Bay. The trail is used by runners, skaters, and walkers as well as bikers. Access to the path is free.

Shopping

The most interesting shopping in Bristol is in the historic downtown area. **Jesse/ James Antiques,** 44 State St. (𝄐 **401/253-2240**), open since 1992, has notable pieces of china, glassware, and period furniture. **Harbor Bath & Body,** 251 Thames St. (𝄐 **401/396-9170;** www.harborbathandbody.com), offers a variety of natural and organic bath products, many of which are made in New England. **Thames Street Landing,** 259 Thames St. (𝄐 **401/253-2016**), is a waterfront complex that houses about a dozen businesses, from sporting goods stores to jewelry boutiques to restaurants.

Where to Stay

There are a handful of inns and bed-and-breakfasts in Bristol, but no large hotels, so plan to pay slightly more for a room here than you would at a major hotel chain. Summer months are busy, with the busiest times at the end of May—when Roger Williams University holds commencement ceremonies—and around the July 4th holiday. Make sure to book your room well in advance when planning to visit around these times, and anticipate higher rates and limited vacancies.

Bristol Harbor Inn Situated at the newly renovated Thames Street Landing complex along the waterfront, the Bristol Harbor Inn has a range of options, from standard rooms to waterfront rooms to plush suites with gas fireplaces. The least expensive units are no-frills but perfectly agreeable, while the pricier suites are more finely adorned. This is not a destination hotel but rather a fine alternative to higher-priced B&Bs nearby. If you're looking for a good, basic, affordable place to stay, this is a good bet.

259 Thames St., Bristol, RI 02809. 𝄐**866/254-1444** or 401/254-1444. Fax 401/254-1333. www.bristol harborinn.com. 40 units. Apr–Oct $135–$249 double; Nov–Mar $95–$135 double. Rates include continental breakfast. 2-night minimum Fri–Sat Apr–Oct. AE, DC, DISC, MC, V. Free parking. **Amenities:** Restaurant; pub; spa. *In room:* A/C, TV, hair dryer, Internet (free).

Rockwell House Inn Bed & Breakfast This stately 1809 Federal-style inn was once the home of Col. Giles Luther, the first recorded parade marshal for Bristol's long-running 4th of July parade. The building was also at one time the base for the Bristol District Nursing Association and town medical clinic. After being purchased in 1990 and given extensive renovations, the owners opened Rockwell House to the public in 1991. The five guest rooms are elegantly decorated, with a style that recalls the past while simultaneously providing modern comfort. You'll feel right at home when you wake up to the smell of coffee and fresh-baked pastries from the kitchen.

610 Hope St., Bristol, RI 02809. 𝄐**800/254-0040** or 401/253-0040. Fax 401/253-1811. www.rockwell houseinn.com. 5 units. May–Oct $199–$259 double; Nov–Apr $119–$199 double. Rates include full breakfast and afternoon tea by request. 2-night minimum Fri–Sat, 3-night minimum holidays. AE, DISC, MC, V. Free parking. *In room:* A/C, hair dryer, Wi-Fi (free).

Where to Dine

Once strictly home to family restaurants, sub shops, and pizza joints, Bristol has seen a number of upscale restaurants pop up in recent years. On the more modest end, an inexpensive family restaurant that's a favorite among locals is **Tweet Balzano's Family Restaurant,** 180 Mt. Hope Ave. (© **401/253-9811;** www.tweetbalzanos restaurant.com), which pulls people in primarily for the mountains of pasta and down-home New England–style seafood. The best slice of pizza in Bristol is at **Bristol House of Pizza,** 55 State St. (© **401/253-2550;** www.bristolhouseofpizza.com).

On the higher end, consider these two options in addition to those listed below: **Le Central,** 483 Hope St. (© **401/396-9965;** www.lecentralbistro.net), which serves good French bistro food at affordable prices; and **The Lobster Pot,** 119 Hope St. (© **401/253-9100;** www.lobsterpotri.com), where lobster comes boiled, broiled, grilled, or baked stuffed—it's pricey but worth every penny.

DeWolf Tavern ★ NEW AMERICAN   Located in a renovated 1818 warehouse, this interesting tavern's decor consists of the building's original stone and mortar walls and exposed wooden beams. The menu is contemporary American with a tilt toward Bristol's seafaring heritage and a dash of the East: steamed mussels in coconut milk with curry leaf and chili; tandoori marinated swordfish; *nan* (flatbread) pizzas. Be sure to order the delectable roasted Brussels sprouts and cornbread hash from the selection of side dishes.

259 Thames St.© **401/254-2005.** www.dewolftavern.com. Main courses $14–$42. AE, DISC, MC, V. Daily 11:30am–10pm (Sun until 9:30pm); bar until 12:30am Tues–Sat.

Persimmon ★★ NEW AMERICAN   Romantic, modern Persimmon is at the top of the pecking order of Bristol's restaurant scene. The menu changes seasonally—and often daily—but there is a definite trend toward seafood regardless of the time of year. Menu items on a recent visit included roast Atlantic halibut with glazed fennel and salsify; and hanger steak basted with butter, garlic, and thyme, and served with a ragout of onions, mushrooms, and potatoes, topped with a mouth-watering Bordelaise sauce.

31 State St.© **401/254-7474.** www.persimmonbristol.com. Menu priced daily; main courses generally $15–$30. AE, MC, V. Jan–June Tues–Sat 5–10pm; July–Dec Tues–Sun 5–10pm. State St. runs btw. Hope and Thames sts.

NEWPORT ★★★

71 miles S of Boston; 178 miles NE of New York City

"City by the Sea" is the unimaginative nickname an early resident unloaded on Newport. At least it was accurate, because for a time during the Colonial period Newport rivaled Boston and even New York as a center of New World trade and prosperity. It occupies the southern tip of Aquidneck Island in Narragansett Bay and is connected to the mainland by bridges and a ferry.

Wealthy industrialists, railroad tycoons, coal magnates, financiers, and robber barons were drawn to the area in the 19th century, especially between the Civil War and World War I. They bought up property at the ocean's rim to build what they called summer "cottages"—which were, in fact, mansions of immoderate design and proportions patterned after European palaces.

Immediately east and north of the business district are blocks of Colonial, Federal, and Victorian houses of the 18th and 19th centuries, many of them designated

National Historic Sites. Happily, they are not frozen in amber but are very much in use as residences, restaurants, offices, and shops. Taken together, they are as visually appealing in their own way as the 40-room cottages of the super-rich.

The principal toys of the Newport elite are extravagant pleasure yachts, and competition among them established Newport's reputation as a sailing center. In 1851, the schooner *America* defeated a British boat in a race around the Isle of Wight. The prize trophy became known as the America's Cup, which remained in the possession of the New York Yacht Club (which moved its America's Cup venue from New York to Newport in 1930) until 1983. In that shocking summer, *Australia II* snatched the Cup away from *Liberty* in the last race of a four-out-of-seven series. A San Diego–based American team regained the cup in 1987, but in 1995 a New Zealand crew took it away again. Switzerland held the cup from 2003 to 2010, but in February of 2010 it was recaptured by the U.S. by a team based at Golden Gate Yacht Club and founded by software mogul Larry Ellison. As the locations of the battles have moved to different locations around the world, Newport, nonetheless, remains a bastion of world sailing and a destination for long-distance races.

The perimeter of the city resembles a heeled boot, its toe pointing west, not unlike Italy. About where the laces of the boot would be is the downtown business and residential district. Several wharves push into the bay, providing support and mooring for flotillas of pleasure craft. Much of the strolling, shopping, eating, quaffing, and gawking is done along this waterfront and its parallel streets: America's Cup Avenue and Thames Street. (The latter used to be pronounced "Tems," in the British manner, but was Americanized to "Thaymz" after the Revolution.)

Newport has been spared the coarser intrusions that afflict so many coastal resorts. T-shirt emporia have been kept within reasonable limits—a remarkable feat, considering that some 4 million visitors come through its narrow streets every year.

Despite Newport's prevailing image as a collection of ornate mansions and regattas for the rich and famous, the city is, for the most part, middle class and not too excessively priced. Scores of inns and B&Bs ensure lodging even during festival weeks, at rates and fixtures from budget to ultraluxury level. In almost every respect, this is the "First Resort" of the New England coast.

Essentials

GETTING THERE   From New York City, take I-95 to exit 3, picking up Rte. 138 east and crossing the Newport toll bridge, which takes you slightly north of the downtown district. From Boston and the north, take Rte. 24 through Fall River, picking up Rte. 114 into town.

T. F. Green/Providence Airport (© **401/737-8222;** www.pvdairport.com; airport code: PVD) in Warwick, south of Providence (I-95, exit 13), handles national flights into the state. Major airlines serving this airport include **Continental** (© 800/523-3273), **Delta** (© 800/221-1212), **Southwest** (© 800/435-9792), **United** (© 800/864-8331), and **US Airways** (© 800/428-4322). The **Cozy Cab airport shuttle** (© **800/846-1502** or 401/846-2500; www.cozytrans.com) makes runs between the airport and the Newport area for around $25 per person each way.

The **Rhode Island Public Transit Authority,** or **RIPTA** (© **800/244-0444** or 401/781-9400; www.ripta.com), has buses that run between Providence's Kennedy Plaza and the Newport Visitor Information Center. The trip is 75 minutes and the one-way fare is $1.75.

Newport

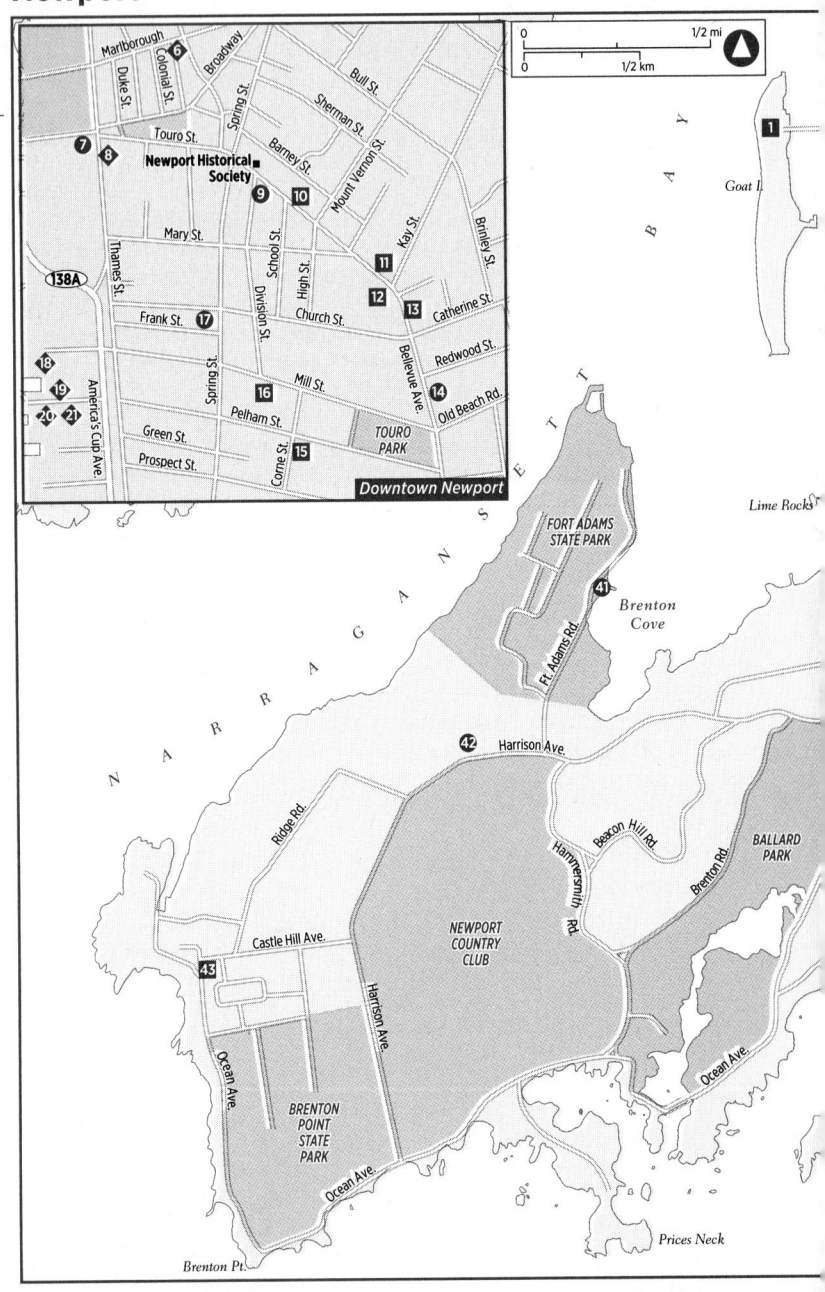

0   1/2 mi
0   1/2 km

Marlborough

Broadway

6

Colonial St.

Duke St.

Bull St.

Spring St.

Sherman St.

Touro St.

Barney St.

Mount Vernon St.

7   **8**

Newport Historical Society

9   **10**

Kay St.

Mary St.

St. Joseph's

High St.

Binney St.

11

38A

Thames St.

12   **13**

Catherine St.

Frank St.   **17**

Church St.

Division St.

Bellevue Ave.

Redwood St.

Spring St.

Mill St.

14

Old Beach Rd.

18

16

Pelham St.

19

America's Cup Ave.

Green St.

20   **21**

Corne St.

TOURO PARK

Prospect St.

15

Downtown Newport

B
A
Y

1

Goat I.

N
A
R
R
A
G
A
N
S
E
T
T

Lime Rocks

FORT ADAMS STATE PARK

41

Brenton Cove

Ft. Adams Rd.

42   Harrison Ave.

Beacon Hill Rd.

BALLARD PARK

Ridge Rd.

Hammersmith Rd.

Brenton Rd.

Castle Hill Ave.

NEWPORT COUNTRY CLUB

43

Harrison Ave.

Ocean Ave.

Ocean Ave.

BRENTON POINT STATE PARK

Ocean Ave.

Brenton Pt.

Prices Neck

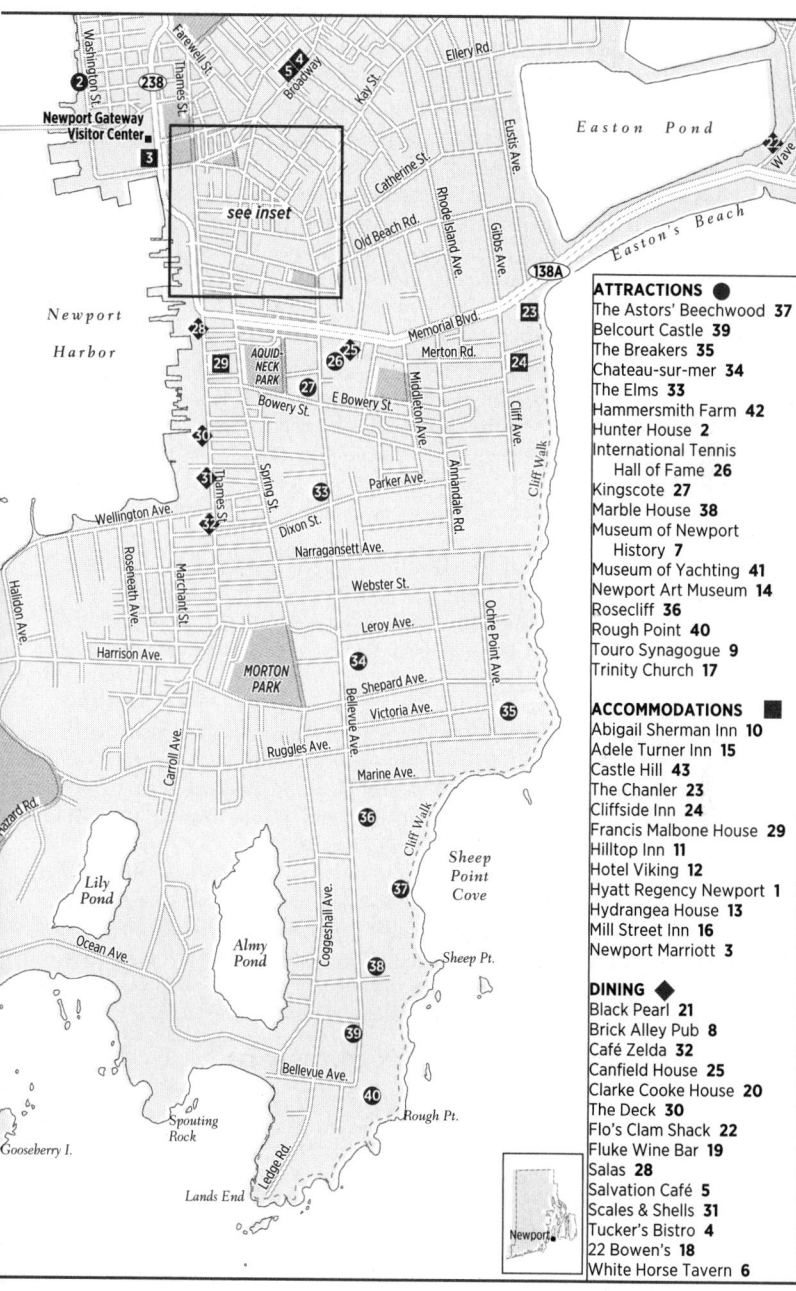

Newport Gateway Visitor Center

see inset

Newport Harbor

Washington St.

Farewell St.

Thames St.

Broadway

Ellery Rd.

Kay St.

Easton Pond

Wave

Catherine St.

Eustis Ave.

Old Beach Rd.

Rhode Island Ave.

Gibbs Ave.

Easton's Beach

Memorial Blvd.

Merton Rd.

AQUID-NECK PARK

Bowery St.

E Bowery St.

Middleton Ave.

Cliff Ave.

W. Cliff Ave.

Annandale Rd.

Parker Ave.

Spring St.

Thames St.

Dixon St.

Narragansett Ave.

Wellington Ave.

Roseneath Ave.

Marchant St.

Webster St.

Leroy Ave.

Ochre Point Ave.

Harrison Ave.

MORTON PARK

Shepard Ave.

Bellevue Ave.

Victoria Ave.

Ruggles Ave.

Marine Ave.

Carroll Ave.

Halidon Ave.

Hazard Rd.

Lily Pond

Almy Pond

Ocean Ave.

Sheep Point Cove

Sheep Pt.

Coggeshall Ave.

Bellevue Ave.

Rough Pt.

Gooseberry I.

Spouting Rock

Ledge Rd.

Lands End

Newport

ATTRACTIONS ●
The Astors' Beechwood **37**
Belcourt Castle **39**
The Breakers **35**
Chateau-sur-mer **34**
The Elms **33**
Hammersmith Farm **42**
Hunter House **2**
International Tennis
  Hall of Fame **26**
Kingscote **27**
Marble House **38**
Museum of Newport
  History **7**
Museum of Yachting **41**
Newport Art Museum **14**
Rosecliff **36**
Rough Point **40**
Touro Synagogue **9**
Trinity Church **17**

ACCOMMODATIONS ■
Abigail Sherman Inn **10**
Adele Turner Inn **15**
Castle Hill **43**
The Chanler **23**
Cliffside Inn **24**
Francis Malbone House **29**
Hilltop Inn **11**
Hotel Viking **12**
Hyatt Regency Newport **1**
Hydrangea House **13**
Mill Street Inn **16**
Newport Marriott **3**

DINING ◆
Black Pearl **21**
Brick Alley Pub **8**
Café Zelda **32**
Canfield House **25**
Clarke Cooke House **20**
The Deck **30**
Flo's Clam Shack **22**
Fluke Wine Bar **19**
Salas **28**
Salvation Café **5**
Scales & Shells **31**
Tucker's Bistro **4**
22 Bowen's **18**
White Horse Tavern **6**

VISITOR INFORMATION The **Newport Gateway Transportation and Visitor Center,** 23 America's Cup Ave. (© **800/976-5122** or 401/845-9123; www. GoNewport.com), adjacent to the bus station, is open daily from 9am to 5pm. It has attendants on duty to help with lodging and local events. The center and the website are run by the Newport & Bristol County Convention & Visitor's Bureau.

PARKING & GETTING AROUND Except for the mansions, most of Newport's attractions can be reached easily on foot, so leaving your car at your hotel or inn is wise. Parking lots aren't cheap, especially along the downtown waterfront, and many streets are narrow. The metered parking along Thames Street is closely monitored by police, and fines are steep (although Nov–Apr meter parking is free for up to 3 hr.). The Newport Visitor's Bureau has a downloadable map of parking lots at **www. citimaps.com/newport/maps/newport_parking.pdf.**

RIPTA runs a trolley in Newport (Rte. 67, also called the Yellow Line) that travels to the mansions daily year-round. In summer, the line is extended to Rough Point. Service originates at the Gateway Transportation and Visitor Center. A 24-hour pass is $5.

SPECIAL EVENTS The first big event of the summer is the June **Great Chowder Cook-Off** (© **401/846-1600;** www.newportfestivals.com), a 1-day event that includes three stages of entertainment. In the 3rd week of July, the **Black Ships Festival** (© **401/846-2720;** www.newportevents.com/Blackships) celebrates all aspects of Japanese culture with performances, sumo wrestling, sushi-, sake-, and tea-tasting.

July brings the **Newport Folk Festival** (www.newportjazzfest.net), which celebrated its 50th anniversary in 2009, and the **Newport Jazz Festival** (www. newportjazzfest.net), which started in 1954. Both are held at Fort Adams State Park and managed by George Wein, the esteemed promoter and producer who founded both festivals.

In July and early September, 10 lush private gardens are open for a **Secret Garden Tour** (© **401/847-0514;** www.secretgardentour.com). The **Newport Waterfront Irish Festival** (© **401/846-1600;** www.newportwaterfrontevents.com) arrives in early September, the **Bowen's Wharf Seafood Festival** (© **401/849-3478;** www.bowenswharf.com) later in September, and **Oktoberfest** (© **401/846-1600;** www.newportfestivals.com) on Columbus Day weekend.

Winter is quiet time. The highlight is **Christmas in Newport** (© **401/849-6454;** www.christmasinnewport.org), a city-wide celebration with events each day in December. The city has a special beauty that month, with businesses, city buildings, and residential homes all using clear and white bulbs to simulate a candle glow throughout the harbor, the wharves, and the Victorian and Colonial residential streets that line Bellevue Avenue and the Historic Hill neighborhood.

"The Cottages": Newport's Mansions

"The Cottages" is what wealthy people called the almost unimaginably sumptuous mansions they built in Newport in the era between the end of the Civil War and the beginning of World War I—the last decades before the 16th Amendment to the Constitution permitted an income tax.

Say this for the wealthy of the Gilded Age, many of whom obtained their fortunes by less than honorable means: They knew a good place to put down roots when they saw it. These are the same people who developed Florida's Palm Beach for the winter months, New York's Hudson Valley for the spring, and the Berkshires of Massachusetts (p. 336) for the autumn. Newport was for summering, and the mansion owners and their friends swept from house to luxurious house with the insouciance of a bejeweled matron dragging her sable down a grand staircase.

TICKET AND OTHER VISITOR INFORMATION

Walking the length of Bellevue Avenue to see the mansions is a serious trek for most people (from Kingscote, at #253, to Rough Point, at #680, is about 2 miles, and that's before touring any of the homes or grounds). Plan to bike or drive to the cottage district, but keep in mind that parking is limited. Narrated bus tours are also available; see p. 453. And remember that many of these residences are still privately owned (and yes, houses here do regularly come up for sale).

Amazingly, the grounds and interiors of about a dozen homes are open to the public. Details on nine are below. Six of those listed here (The Breakers, Kingscote, The Elms, Chateau-sur-Mer, Rosecliff, and Marble House) are maintained by the **Preservation Society of Newport County,** 424 Bellevue Ave. (© **401/847-1000;** www.newportmansions.org). Belcourt Castle, The Astors' Beechwood, and Rough Point are run independently.

The mansions are open by guided tour only. Tickets for the mansions run by the Preservation Society are available in a variety of combinations listed at **tickets. newportmansions.org** (text "Newport" to 82672 for Mansion updates and offers). Tickets for the most popular mansion, the Breakers (p. 448), are $18 for adults and $4.50 for children ages 6 to 17. Tickets for the Breakers plus one other mansion are $23 and $6, respectively. Tickets for any one mansion other than the Breakers are $12 and $4.50, respectively. Tickets for any five mansions are $31 and $10, respectively. Tickets for a rooftop and behind-the-scenes tour of the Elms are $15 and $4.50, respectively. Special events, such as festive Thanksgiving and Christmas celebrations, cost extra. Children age 5 and under are admitted for free, but strollers are not allowed in the properties. Parking is free at all the Society properties.

Tickets, which have no expiration date and can be used any time, can be purchased online or at any of the properties. The Preservation Society has a visitors center at its base in the middle of the district at 424 Bellevue Ave.

For the three mansions listed below that are not managed by the Preservation Society, ticket and other information is listed with their descriptions.

The Breakers and Rosecliff are fully wheelchair accessible. Marble House and the Elms are partially wheelchair accessible.

During the winter, three mansions of the Preservation Society are open, with limited hours: The Breakers, Marble House, and the Elms. In summer, the properties are all open daily. However, because of a highly variable schedule over the course of the year, confirm online or by phone which mansions are open on the day of your travel.

To learn more about the cottages, look for Michael Kathrens' *Newport Villas: The Revival Styles 1885–1935* (W. W. Norton & Company, 2009). The *Providence Journal* calls it "the most thorough and accessible guide to Newport's Gilded Age mansions yet published."

Tip: Because their sheer opulence can become numbing after a while, you might want to visit only one or two estates per day. Budget about 45 minutes to an hour for each mansion's guided tour, plus extra time for exploring the grounds.

Note: The properties are listed here in the order in which they're encountered when driving south on Bellevue Avenue, starting at Memorial Boulevard.

Kingscote ★   This mansion is a reminder that well-to-do Southern families often had second homes north of the Mason-Dixon line to avoid the sultry summers of the deep South. Architect Richard Upjohn designed the mansion in the same Gothic Revival style he used for Trinity Church in New York—romantic towers, medieval arches, and the like. Kingscote was built in 1841, nearly 40 years before the Gilded Age, but is considered one of the Newport Cottages because it was acquired in 1864 by a sea merchant who furnished it with porcelains and textiles accumulated in the China trade. The dining room is notable for its Tiffany glass panels.

253 Bellevue Ave. Maintained by the Preservation Society of Newport County; see p. 447 for ticket and other visitor information.

The Elms ★★   Architect Horace Trumbauer is said to have been inspired by the Château d'Asnières, a mid-18th-century French chateau outside Paris, and both the opulent exterior and interior details (such as those in the ornate dining room), suitable for at least a marquis, buttresses that claim. Marble hallways lead to rooms filled with Louis XIV and XV furniture, and paintings and accessories true to the late 18th century. Sunken gardens are laid out and maintained in the formal French manner.

367 Bellevue Ave. Maintained by the Preservation Society of Newport County; see p. 447 for ticket and other visitor information.

Chateau-sur-Mer ★   If you try, you may be able to imagine being one of the more than 2,000 guests who attended a "country picnic" here in 1857. This "Castle by the Sea" is High Victorian in style, which means it drew from many inspirations including Italian Renaissance and French Second Empire. It features a central atrium that reaches up three levels to a stained-glass skylight, with balconies at every level. A park designed in a style true to the period of the cottage features copper beech and weeping willows around its garden pavilion.

474 Bellevue Ave. Maintained by the Preservation Society of Newport County; see p. 447 for ticket and other visitor information.

The Breakers ★★★   If you're going to see only one of the cottages, make it this one. Architect Richard Morris Hunt was commissioned to create this replica of an Italian Renaissance palazzo, and he was unrestrained by costs: The 50×50-foot great hall has 50-foot-high ceilings and is sheathed in French marble; a room with double mirrors creates an illusion of an endless row of crystal chandeliers; a Flemish tapestry drapes along a wall above a gurgling interior fountain; and French provincial furnishings include chairs that look like red velvet thrones (all furnishings on view, by the way, are original). Bathrooms, far from common at the time, were provided with both fresh and salt running water, hot and cold.

Built over 3 years (1892–95), the team employed platoons of artisans—some 2,000—imported from Europe to apply 24-karet gold leaf to the ceilings, carve wood and marble, and provide mural-size baroque paintings. Images of oak leaves and acorns, which stand for long life and strength, are employed throughout the decor. The small family that lived here had 70 rooms in which to roam and was attended by a staff of 40 servants. The children would sled down the grand staircases on silver platters.

Such mind-numbing extravagance shouldn't really be surprising—the home was built for Cornelius Vanderbilt II, grandson of railroad tycoon Commodore Vanderbilt (and great-grandfather of CNN news anchor Anderson Cooper, whose mother is Gloria Vanderbilt). The house was passed on to Cornelius Vanderbilt II's youngest daughter, Gladys, in 1934, and purchased by the Preservation Society in 1972 from her heirs. Not surprisingly, the Breakers is designated a National Historic Landmark. The cottage sits atop a 30-foot cliff, with the Atlantic Ocean "breaking" below—hence the home's name.

44 Ochre Point Ave. Maintained by the Preservation Society of Newport County; see p. 447 for ticket and other visitor information. From Bellevue Ave. heading south, turn left on Ruggles Ave. after Chateau-sur-Mer, and then left on Ochre Point Ave. The Breakers is on the right and a parking lot on the left.

Rosecliff ★ Of all the mansions listed here, Rosecliff may be the prettiest upon first approach, glowing white across an expansive lawn. To get a preview, rent the 1974 film *The Great Gatsby*, starring Robert Redford: This mansion was used as a setting for some of that movie's scenes. Rosecliff is modeled on the garden retreat of Louis XVI at Versailles and was built for the flamboyant Tessie Fair Oelrichs, heiress to the thickest vein of silver mined in Nevada. The home has 40 rooms, a storied heart-shaped grand staircase, and the largest ballroom of all the cottages.

548 Bellevue Ave. Maintained by the Preservation Society of Newport County; see p. 447 for ticket and other visitor information.

The Astors' Beechwood Mrs. William Backhouse Astor, who liked to be called *the* Mrs. Astor, as every brochure and guide feels compelled to observe, was, during her active life in the late 1800s, the arbiter of exactly who constituted New York and Newport society. Being invited to Beechwood was absolutely critical to a social pretender's sense of self-worth, and elaborate machinations were set in motion to achieve that goal. Mrs. Astor stayed at Beechwood for 8 weeks every summer, and her annual Ball was a highlight of the Newport season. The family's money did not protect it from tragedy: A few years after Mrs. Astor's death, her son John Jacob Astor IV died on the *Titanic*.

For the past few years, the mansion has simultaneously been up for sale and enmeshed in a lawsuit over ownership. While it was open for tours during that unsettled time, it started 2010 as a wedding-only venue. Check the website for the most current status. The theatrical company that put on period plays and murder mystery shows here moved its base to Belcourt Castle (p. 447) in early 2010.

580 Bellevue Ave. ©**401/846-3772.** www.astors-beechwood.com. Not currently open for tours.

Marble House ★★★ Architect Richard Morris Hunt outdid himself for his clients William and Alva Vanderbilt, William being the younger brother of the Vanderbilts who built the Breakers (above). Some 500,000 cubic feet of marble were used both outside and in, with a lavish hand that rivals the palaces of France's Louis XIV. The mansion reaches its apogee in the ballroom, which is encrusted with three kinds of gold. Money did not buy love, however, and in 1895, 4 years after being given the house as a 39th birthday present, Alva divorced William. Adding insult to injury, she married a neighbor and moved to his Belcourt Castle (below). Alva reopened Marble House after her second husband's death and held a benefit there in 1913 to raise money for the campaign for women's right to vote. Dishes in the scullery reflect this part of her history, bearing the legend "Votes for Women."

596 Bellevue Ave. Maintained by the Preservation Society of Newport County; see p. 447 for ticket and other visitor information.

Belcourt Castle ★★   This was the only slightly less grand mansion down the road from Marble House to which Alva Vanderbilt repaired after her second marriage (see above). While the Vanderbilts were avid yachtsmen, Alva's new husband, Oliver Hazard Perry Belmont, was a fanatical horseman. His 60-room house contained extensive stables on the ground floor where his beloved steeds slept under monogrammed blankets. (The Belmonts were instrumental in building New York's famed Belmont Racetrack.) Intended to resemble a European hunting lodge, the castle has a ponderously masculine character, designed as it was for the bachelor before he won over the vivacious Alva. It contains artifacts from the medieval era through the 19th century, including stained glass, Japanese cabinetry, and a full-size replica of a gaudy Portuguese coronation carriage. Thomas Edison designed the lighting. There are 14 secret doors and a tunnel to the kitchens, which were located 2 blocks away for fear of fire. A theatrical company that puts on period plays and murder mystery shows moved its base here in early 2010. There also are evening ghost and candlelight tours (with champagne) on some nights.

657 Bellevue Ave.© **401/846-0669.** www.belcourtcastle.com. The schedule and fees for events and tours are highly variable throughout the year; call or check the website for details and reservations.

Rough Point ★★   The fabled 1887 Gothic-Tudor home of the late tobacco heiress and art collector Doris Duke made its long-awaited opening in 2000, 7 years after Duke's death. Only a portion of the 105 rooms are open for viewing, but tours do cover the entire first floor and Duke's bedroom. Watch for the ivory inset side tables bearing the marks of Catherine the Great in what is called the Yellow Room. Other highlights are her collections of Ming-dynasty vases, Flemish and French tapestries, and paintings by van Dyck and Gainsborough. Tours are wheelchair accessible and air-conditioned.

It was here in 1966 that Doris Duke's interior decorator Eduardo Tirella was killed after being crushed against the iron entrance gates by a station wagon Duke was driving. Duke said that she accidentally hit the accelerator when Tirella was opening the gates, and the police chief declared it "an unfortunate accident." After Duke died in 1993, Rough Point and its furniture were left to the Newport Restoration Foundation, which Duke had founded and used to preserve 83 homes in Newport during her lifetime. Today, the Doris Duke Charitable Foundation provides grants supporting the performing arts, environmental conservation, medical research, and the prevention of child abuse.

680 Bellevue Ave.© **401/849-7300.** www.newportrestoration.org. Admission $25. Visits at reserved times by guided tour only. Early Apr to early May Thurs–Sat 10am–2pm; early May to early Nov Tues–Sat 9:45am–3:45pm. Closed early Nov to early Apr. Parking is available.

Additional Newport Attractions

Historic Hill (also called the **Old Quarter**) is the large district of Colonial Newport that rises from America's Cup Avenue, along the waterfront, to Bellevue Avenue, the beginning of Victorian Newport. **Spring Street** ★ is the Hill's main drag, and it's a treasure trove of Colonial, Georgian, and Federal structures. Chief among its visual delights is the 1725 **Trinity Church** ★, at the corner of Church Street. The church is not open for tours, but it is a visual icon of the city. Said to have been influenced by the work of the legendary British architect Christopher Wren, it certainly reflects that inspiration in its belfry and distinctive spire, seen from all over downtown Newport and dominating Queen Anne Square, a greensward that runs to the waterfront.

International Tennis Hall of Fame & Museum On Bellevue Avenue, there was in the 1870s an exclusive men's club called the Newport Reading Room. One member was James Gordon Bennett, Jr., the wealthy publisher of the New York Herald. The story goes that Bennett persuaded a friend to ride a horse into the club, the outraged members reprimanded Bennett, Bennett had an instant snit that they hadn't enjoyed his little jest, and he went right out and bought a property on the other side of Memorial Boulevard to build his own club. Architects McKim, Mead & White produced a shingle-style edifice of lavish proportions, with turrets and verandas and an interior piazza for lawn games, equestrian shows, and a new game called tennis. In 1881, this "Newport Casino" held the first U.S. National Lawn Tennis Championships and hosted the event until it moved to Forest Hills, New York, and became known as the U.S. Open. Today, the building still has a grass lawn open for play.

194 Bellevue Ave. (at Memorial Blvd.). (©) **800/457-1144** or 401/849-3990. www.tennisfame.org. Admission $11 adults, $9 seniors, free for ages 16 and under. Daily 9:30am–5pm.

Museum of Newport History Maintained by the Newport Historical Society, this museum is in the refurbished 1772 Brick Market (not to be confused with the nearby shopping mall Brick Marketplace). It houses a printing press, boat models, antique silverware, and a ship figurehead, and shows videos on Newport history.

127 Thames St. (at Touro St.). (©)**401/841-8770.** www.newporthistorical.org. Suggested donation $4 adults, $2 children 6 and older. Daily 10am–5pm.

Newport Art Museum Exhibitions here focus on the visual arts of Newport and southeastern New England, with solo shows by contemporary artists. There also are weekly arts programs for children ages 2 to 5 and lectures on everything from stone walls in Rhode Island to the myths and reality of America's robber barons. The museum is housed in a 1862 building constructed in Victorian stick style and was the first Newport commission of Richard Morris Hunt, who went on to design many of the mansions along Bellevue Avenue.

76 Bellevue Ave. (1 block north of Memorial Blvd.). (©)**401/848-8200.** www.newportartmuseum.org. Admission $10 adults, $8 seniors, $6 students, free for children 5 and under. May–Oct Tues–Sat 10am–5pm, Sun noon–5pm; Nov–Apr Tues–Sat 10am–4pm, Sun noon–4pm.

Touro Park Opposite the Newport Art Museum (above), this small park provides a shaded respite. At its center is an Old Stone Mill. Dreamers like to believe that its eight columns were erected by Vikings. Realists say it was built by Benedict Arnold, a governor of the colony long before his great-great-grandson committed his infamous act of treason during the War of American Independence.

Bellevue Ave. (btw. Pelham and Mill sts.).

Touro Synagogue Dating from 1763, this grand building is the oldest existing synagogue in the United States. A Jewish community, largely refugees from Spain and Portugal, first arrived in Newport in 1658. Roger Williams, the dissident who had founded Providence, Rhode Island, after he was banished from the Massachusetts Bay Colony for being too committed to the concept of freedom of religion, welcomed the immigrants. The temple's congregation later received assurance from none other than President George Washington, who wrote in a letter in 1790 that the United States "gives to bigotry no sanction, to persecution no assistance." The synagogue has an active membership of 140 families and holds Shabbat services

Friday at 6pm and Saturday at 8:45am. It is orthodox, with separate seating for men and for women.

85 Touro St. (1 block from Spring St.).℗ **401/847-4794.** www.tourosynagogue.org. Admission free (donations accepted) and by guided tour only. Tours begin every half-hour. May–June Sun–Fri noon–2pm. Call or check the website for hours in spring, late summer, and fall. Closed Jan through mid-Mar.

Getting Outside

Cliff Walk ★★ offers a dramatic way to see some of the biggest highlights of Newport. The walk skirts the water's edge of the southern section of town and travels behind many of the mansions, providing even better views of many than can be seen from Bellevue Avenue. Traversing its length, high above the crashing surf, is more than a stroll but less than an arduous hike. For the full length (3.5 miles from Memorial Blvd. at the north to Lands End/Ledge Rd. at the south), start at the access point near the intersection of Memorial Boulevard and Eustis Avenue. For a shorter walk, there's an entrance/exit at the stone staircase known as Forty Steps, at the end of Narragansett Avenue. Be warned that there are some mildly rugged sections to negotiate, no facilities, and no land phones. Keep an eye out for poison ivy. The walk is open from sunrise to sunset. There are no parking lots nearby, so plan to get here by public transportation or cab. For more information, go to www.cliff walk.com and www.cliffwalkmap.com.

Biking is one of the best ways to get around town, especially out to the mansions and along **Ocean Drive ★★**. Rentals are available from **Scooters,** 476 Thames St. (℗ **401/619-0573;** www.scootersofnewport.com), open daily, with bicycles for $15 for 2 hours or $25 for a full day.

The best beach for **swimming** is **Easton's Beach ★**, 175 Memorial Blvd. (℗ **401/845-5810;** www.cityofnewport.com), just east of the Cliff Walk. It's the longest and most popular beach and has lifeguards, a boardwalk, a bathhouse, eating places, picnic areas, a carousel, bumper boat rides, chair and umbrella rentals, and the **Save the Bay Exploration Center** (℗ **401/324-6020**). The beach is open from Memorial Day to Labor Day. Parking costs $10 weekdays, $15 on weekends, $20 on holidays. There's VIP parking if you call ahead ($35 weekends), and $2 short-term parking if you're only visiting the exploration center, carousel, or food court (go to gate 2 and tell the attendant you want short-term parking and why; you'll be charged full rate but refunded most of it if you return on time and with validation).

A quieter option is **Gooseberry Beach ★**, 130 Ocean Ave. (℗ **401/847-3958**), on a beautiful stretch of Ocean Avenue just past the Rough Point mansion. Like Easton's, it has silky sand, but it's set in a cove, so the waves are smaller. It's privately owned but open to the public. Parking costs $15 Monday through Friday, $20 Saturday and Sunday. It's closed in winter.

Fort Adams State Park (℗ **401/847-2400;** www.riparks.com/fortadams.htm) is on the thumb of land that partially encloses Newport Harbor. It can be seen from the downtown docks and reached by driving or biking south on Thames Street, west on Wellington Avenue, and then west on Harrison Avenue. The park is the site of the summer jazz and folk music festivals (see "Special Events," p. 446) and of Civil War reenactments. Ocean swimming, fishing, and sailing are all possible here. The park is open year-round and entrance is free. The sprawling **1820s fort** (℗ **401/841-0707;** www.fortadams.org) for which the park is named can be viewed by guided tour only. Tours are $10 for adults, $5 for ages 6 to 17, and free for children 5 and under, and run every hour from 10am to 4pm daily Memorial Day through Columbus Day. Also on the grounds is the **Museum of Yachting** (© **401/847-1018**; www.moy.org), which puts on exhibits and restoration projects in conjunction with the International Yacht Restoration School. It's open mid-May through September daily (except Tues) from 10am to 6pm. Admission is $5 for adults, free for children 17 and younger and students with ID.

If you're driving or biking Ocean Avenue to take in the mansions and the scenery, keep in mind **Brenton Point State Park ★**. There's free parking along its Ocean Avenue edge, where you'll find grand vistas over the water—there's nothing to impede the waves rolling in and collapsing on the rock-strewn beach. You'll often see people parked here to eat lunch or just take a snooze in the late day sun.

In the winter, an **outdoor skating rink** is set up at the **Sovereign Bank Family Skating Center** (© **401/846-3018**; www.skatenewport.com), at the Newport Yachting Center, 4 Commercial Wharf, at America's Cup Avenue. The rink is open daily from about mid-November into March, depending upon weather. Admission is $7 for adults and children 12 and older, $5 for seniors and children ages 3 to 11, and free for children 2 and under. Skate rentals are available.

Organized Tours & Cruises

Bus tours of the mansions are offered by **Viking Tours** (© **401/847-6921**; www.vikingtoursnewport.com), based at the Visitor Center, 23 America's Cup Ave. Tours run daily in summer and on Saturday from November to April. The 1½-, 3-, or 4-hour tours range in cost from $24 to $51 for adults and $14 to $22 for children age 6 to 17.

Walking tours of downtown's historic Colonial neighborhoods are offered by the **Newport Historical Society,** 82 Touro St. (© **401/846-0813**; www.newport historical.org). Tours are offered year-round, with a wide variety of itineraries, including the "Pirates & Scoundrels Tour" and "Old House ABCs." Tickets are generally $5 to $12.

Options abound for getting out on the water from spring through fall. **Classic Cruises of Newport ★**, Bannister's Wharf (© **800/395-1343**; www.cruise newport.com), runs narrated 90-minute trips on its 72-foot schooner *Madeleine* and 75-minute trips aboard its classic speedboat *RumRunner II*. Rates for *Madeleine* trips are $27 for adults, $22 for children, $35 for the cocktail cruise. Rates for *Rum-Runner II* trips are $18 for adults, $13 for children, and $25 for the cocktail cruise.

Daily 90-minute cruises of the bay and harbor are also offered on the *Adirondack II ★*, Bowen's Wharf (© **401/847-0000** or 212/209-3370 for tickets; www.sail-newport.com), an 80-foot schooner. Tickets are $27 to $35, depending on time of day. Reservations must be made in advance. The same company also offers a **helicopter-and-sail package** costing $180 for two people.

Shopping

Shopping fans will find plenty to do in Newport: Much of the downtown is given over to shopping, with wharfs that have been converted to small mini malls and smaller side streets lined with local and chain operations.

Most of the shopping nearest to the waterfront seems designed entirely to sop up tourist dollars. There are outposts of chain clothing stores such as Talbots, Patagonia, and Gap, and such places as **Frazzleberries,** 475 Thames St. (© **401/841-9899**;

www.frazzleberries.com), which sells Newport-centric souvenirs such as reproductions of local beach signs and chart maps.

Interesting shopping is found in the smaller stores along **Lower Thames Street.** The **Newport Restoration Foundation Museum Store,** 415 Thames St. ((C) **401/ 324-6111;** www.newportrestoration.org/shop), carries housewares and jewelry inspired by the possessions of Doris Duke, the billionairess who restored so many Newport homes and whose Rough Point mansion (p. 450) is open for tours. Nearby **Spring** and **Franklin streets** are both noted for their antiques shops.

Where to Stay

Reserve well in advance, especially for summer weekends (2 months ahead is not too soon). Last-minute guests should stop in at the visitor center (p. 446), which has information on motels, hotels, and inns and free direct-line phones to many of them.

The properties listed here generally have wide ranges in rates depending upon seasonal demand. A $300 room on weekends in July might be half that in March. The summer season is generally Memorial Day to Columbus Day.

Most of the properties detailed below are independent inns or hotels. Newport also has a **Marriott,** located at 25 America's Cup Ave. ((C) **401/849-1000;** www. marriott.com).

VERY EXPENSIVE

Abigail Stoneman Inn ★★ A sister property to the nearby Adele Turner Inn (93 Pelham St.) and the grand Cliffside Inn (p. 455), this inn is the smallest of the group, with just two rooms and three suites. But it displays the trademark fixtures and services of its siblings, including exquisite decor, marble bathrooms with double Jacuzzis, fireplaces, full breakfast-in-bed, and extraordinary afternoon teas with scones, cakes, and finger sandwiches. The inn is walking distance from the heart of downtown but tucked enough away to ensure a quiet visit.

102 Touro St., Newport, RI 02840.(C) **800/845-1811** or 401/847-1811. www.abigailstonemaninn.com. 5 units. $250–$395 double, $330–$595 suite, with possible surcharges on Fri–Sat, holidays, or for special events. Rates include breakfast and afternoon tea. 2-night minimum Fri–Sat, 3-night minimum selected weekends. AE, DISC, MC, V. No children 12 and under. **Amenities:** Concierge; room service. In room: A/C, TV/DVD, hair dryer, MP3 docking station, Wi-Fi (most rooms; free).

Castle Hill Inn & Resort ★★★ The setting—40 oceanfront acres on a near-island bordered by the Narragansett Bay and Atlantic Ocean—is the overwhelming attraction of this, the highest-profile resort in Newport. Roof-to-foundation renovations of the 1874 Victorian mansion and its outbuildings make a visit even in foul weather a treat. There is no more enticing ritual in Newport than taking to one of the Adirondack chairs that dot the slope from the inn down toward the water, cocktail in hand, watching boats returning from the fishing grounds while the sun turns the water to gold. The best values are the Harbor Houses, which have porches overlooking the bay. Breakfast buffets are expansive, and dinners (inside or on the terrace) are among the most accomplished in Newport. If you don't stay over, consider coming for a special lunch, dinner, or Sunday brunch.

590 Ocean Dr., Newport, RI 02840.(C) **888/466-1355** or 401/849-3800. www.castlehillinn.com. 35 units. Summer from $439 double. Rates include breakfast and afternoon tea. AE, DC, MC, V. **Amenities:** Restaurant; bar. In room: A/C, TV, hair dryer, Wi-Fi (free).

The Chanler at Cliff Walk ★★ Now an elegant boutique hotel with only 20 units, this French Empire structure dates from 1873 and stands above the northern end of the Cliff Walk, overlooking the surf that rolls through the bay. All rooms have gas fireplaces, separate sitting areas, and, except for one suite, double Jacuzzis, supplemented by multinozzled shower stalls. Each is jaw-droppingly decorated to a different theme—Mediterranean, Renaissance, Tudor—but chairs, sofas, and mattresses are uniformly plush and deep. The restaurant, **Spiced Pear** (*✆ 401/847-2244*; www.spicedpear.com), has surged to elite status, using Kobe beef, foie gras emulsion, and the like. Room prices swoop up to over $1,000 a night in summer.

117 Memorial Blvd., Newport, RI 02840. *✆* **866/793-5664** or 401/847-1300. Fax 401/847-3620. www. thechanler.com. 20 units. $379–$1,399 double. Rates include breakfast. AE, DC, MC, V. **Amenities:** Restaurant; bar; concierge; room service. *In room:* A/C, TV/DVD, hair dryer, Wi-Fi (free).

EXPENSIVE

Cliffside Inn ★★ One of Newport's grandest inns. All units have at least one working fireplace, and most have whirlpool baths. Antiques are generously deployed, including Eastlake and Tiffany originals and Victorian fancies that include (in room no. 11) an amusing "bird cage" shower from 1890. A favorite unit is the Garden Suite, a duplex with private garden and big double bathroom with radiant heat beneath the Peruvian tile floors. Full breakfasts, served in the grand parlor, include crab cake Benedict and pear and pomegranate French toast, and there's an expansive afternoon tea, for guests only. The inn is walking distance from Easton's Beach (p. 452), a popular spot for swimming.

2 Seaview Ave. (left off of Cliff Ave.), Newport, RI 02840. *✆* **800/845-1811** or 401/847-1811. www. cliffsideinn.com. 16 units. $150–$575 double. Rates include breakfast and afternoon tea. 2-night minimum Fri–Sat, 3-night minimum selected weekends. AE, DISC, MC, V. **Amenities:** Room service. *In room:* A/C, TV/DVD/VCR, hair dryer, MP3 docking station, Wi-Fi (free).

Francis Malbone House ★★ In 1996, nine modern rooms were added in a wing attached to this original 1760 Colonial house. They are very nice, with king-size beds and excellent reproductions of period furniture. Four of them share two sunken gardens, and three have Jacuzzi tubs built for two. Given a choice, though, take a room in the old section, where antiques outnumber repros, Oriental rugs adorn buffed wide-plank floors, and silks and linens are deployed unsparingly. All but two units enjoy gas fireplaces. In 2000, the owners bought the adjacent Benjamin Mason House, a Colonial home from 1750, and added a suite and another guest room to their offerings. An opulent tea service is set out each afternoon. The location is good for walkers, with the most interesting parts of the waterfront right outside the property.

392 Thames St. (east of Memorial Blvd.), Newport, RI 02840. *✆* **800/846-0392** or 401/846-0392. www.malbone.com. 20 units. $265–$375 double. Rates include breakfast and afternoon tea. 2-night minimum Fri–Sat, 3-night minimum selected weekends. AE, MC, V. No children 12 and under. *In room:* A/C, TV/VCR, hair dryer, Wi-Fi (free).

Hilltop Inn ★ Owned and renovated by the innkeepers behind the Francis Malbone House (above), this 5-unit Craftsman-style inn has an excellent location at the end of Bellevue Avenue, a short uphill walk from the wharf area. If you need to avoid the climb up the long staircase, reserve the first-floor Stewart Room, which has its own porch and whirlpool tub. All but one of the rooms have king-size beds.

2 Kay St., Newport, RI 02840.© **800/846-0392.** Fax 401/619-2536. www.hilltopnewport.com. 5 units. $275–$425 double. Rates include breakfast and afternoon tea. AE, MC, V. No children 12 and under. **Amenities:** Exercise room. *In room:* A/C, TV, fridge, Wi-Fi (free).

Hyatt Regency Newport ★   The Hyatt is notable for its complete roster of hotel services, its location on an island at the northern end of Newport Harbor, and its full-service spa. You might expect such a place to be impersonal, but the staff endeavors to be pleasant. Delightful views of the harbor and town can be had from the restaurant and most of the guest rooms. Beds feature pillow-top mattresses, and newspapers are delivered to guest doors in the mornings.

1 Goat Island, Newport, RI 02840.© **401/851-1234.** Fax 401/846-7210. www.newport.hyatt.com. 257 units. $249–$449 double, plus $30 resort fee. AE, DC, DISC, MC, V. Self-parking free; valet parking $5. **Amenities:** 2 restaurants; bar; concierge; well-equipped health club and spa; indoor freshwater and outdoor saltwater pools; room service. *In room:* A/C, TV, hair dryer, Wi-Fi (free).

Hydrangea House ★   A deep violet exterior catches the eye as you enter this long-established inn. Its opulent breakfast room has one long table, beneath a crystal chandelier, where ample breakfasts are served—perhaps raspberry pancakes or scrambled eggs in puff pastry. Morning coffee can be taken on the veranda in back. Upstairs bedrooms and suites are each distinctively decorated, and all have steam showers and gas fireplaces. The inn is located in the heart of the Historic Hill district and an easy walk to downtown.

16 Bellevue Ave., Newport 02840.© **800/945-4667** or 401/846-4435. www.hydrangeahouse.com. 10 units. $295–$475 double. Rates include breakfast. 3-night minimum summer weekends. AE, MC, V. *In room:* A/C, TV, hair dryer, Wi-Fi (free).

MODERATE

Hotel Viking   On the Newport scene since 1926, this neo-Georgian sprawl of a hotel was built to accommodate the summer guests of Newport's wealthiest families. A recent renovation has sparked up many rooms and added 10 luxury suites. The Viking is less expensive than the grander options in town *and* boasts a fitness room and spa, an indoor pool, a good location, and a pleasant staff. The rooftop bar with views of the harbor is an especially outstanding feature. Be sure to ask for an updated room.

1 Bellevue Ave., Newport, RI 02840.© **800/556-7126** or 401/847-3300. www.hotelviking.com. 209 units. $199–$369 double. AE, DC, DISC, MC, V. Pets accepted ($75 fee). **Amenities:** Restaurant; bar; health club & spa; indoor pool; room service. *In room:* A/C, TV, hair dryer, Wi-Fi ($7 per day).

Mill Street Inn   Something different from most Newport inns, this is a converted 19th-century sawmill, scooped out and rebuilt from the walls in. Minimalist decor, furnishings, and service pertain, but this is an all-suite facility, where even its smallest unit has a queen-size bed and a sofa bed. The duplexes have private balconies, but everyone can use the rooftop decks, where breakfast is served on warm days. Where full breakfast and afternoon tea are included at other area properties, breakfast is relatively skimpy here. But the spacious rooms, excellent beds and bedding, and relatively modest prices compensate. There are three floors but no elevator. The inn is a member of the "Green" Hotels Association and uses resource-efficient technologies.

75 Mill St. (2 blocks east of Thames), Newport, RI 02840.© **800/392-1316** or 401/849-9500. Fax 401/848-5131. www.millstreetinn.com. 23 units. $155–$415 suite. Rates include breakfast. AE, DC, MC, V. *In room:* A/C, TV, hair dryer, minibar, Wi-Fi (free).

Where to Dine

In addition to the recommendations below, the dining rooms at **Castle Hill** (p. 454) and **The Chanler** (p. 455) are unsurpassed in this resort town. They are open to anyone unintimidated by the expenditures required. Do make reservations.

For something different, the **Newport Dinner Train,** 19 America's Cup Ave. (© 800/398-7427 or 401/841-8700; www.newportdinnertrain.com), offers meals during a 22-mile train trip along Narragansett Bay. It leaves at 6:30pm for dinner and 11:30am for lunch. Reservations are required. Fares range from $35 to $65 for adults, half-price for children. The train runs from mid-April to mid-December.

Nonsummer hours and days of operation vary considerably at Newport's restaurants, and some venues close for months between November and April. Call ahead to avoid disappointment.

EXPENSIVE

Black Pearl ★ SEAFOOD/AMERICAN   This long building near the end of the wharf has you covered. The Tavern contains an atmospheric bar and a room with marine charts on the walls. The pricier Commodore's Room is more formal, with linens, candles, and 19th-century sailing prints. And in warm months, there's a waterside patio and raw bar. Most of the preparations of fish, duck, lamb, and beef are familiar but of good quality. Don't miss the definitive clam chowder, which has been winning prizes since forever (and is for sale on their website). Other Tavern staples include the Pearlburger and chicken potpie, which arrives with a high golden-brown dome that explodes in steam when punctured. In summer, the restaurant also adds a "Hot Dog Clam Chowder Annex."

Bannister's Wharf. © **401/846-5264.** www.blackpearlnewport.com. Reservations and jackets for men required for dinner in Commodore's Room. Main courses $7–$30 in Tavern, $21–$39 in Commodore's Room. AE, MC, V. Daily 11:30am–11pm in summer; until 10pm in winter. Closed Jan to mid-Feb.

Café Zelda ★ SEAFOOD   The cafe's bar is a local favorite populated by neighborhood regulars, while the two-level dining room, where engravings of sailboats line the walls, is more often occupied by 40-plus tourists. The big deal here is the chicken-fried lobster: Lobster flesh is taken out of the shell, dipped in a pancakelike batter, and flash-fried, producing a dish resembling tempura. Another winner is the bouillabaisse, with fish and shellfish in a leek and tomato saffron broth; and the wood-grilled hanger steak with *frites* is commendable. Wash it all down with Chardonnay from Newport Vineyard. At lunch, by all means go for the Zelda burger.

528 Thomas St. © **401/849-4002.** www.cafezelda.com. Reservations recommended for dinner. Main courses $10–$35. AE, MC, V. Fri–Sun 11am–3pm; daily 5–10pm.

Clarke Cooke House ★★ NEW AMERICAN   For many, this is *the* quintessential Newport restaurant. Most of its several levels are open to the air in summer and glassed-in in winter, and several bars serve to lubricate conversation. Up on the formal third floor, you can start with a terrine of fois gras or a ceviche of sea scallops and oysters, perhaps moving on to braised short ribs. Other rooms have more casual personalities: The Bistro wraps around a fireplace and center bar; the main floor, called the Candy Store, serves full meals, snacks, sandwiches, and drinks; and the Boom Boom Room, on the lower level, is a disco with dancing on weekends from 9pm to whenever. All levels have access to the wide choices of a big wine cellar, and

457

all are seeped in nautical decor. The 19th-century structure was moved to the wharf from America's Cup Avenue in the 1970s.

1 Bannister's Wharf.© **401/849-2900.** www.clarkecooke.com. Reservations recommended on Fri–Sat in summer. Main courses $13–$44. AE, DC, DISC, MC, V. Daily 11:30am–10:30pm in summer; limited days and hours in winter; call to confirm.

Tucker's Bistro ★ BISTRO   You can't miss it at night: Cascades of tiny lights swirl around the long facade. Inside, red walls are covered with prints and mirrors in ornate gold frames and shelves are crowded with books, ceramics, and glassware—the object being to evocate a Parisian bistro of the 1930s. Lights are kept so low that the staff provides flashlights to read the menu. The food is up to the visual extravagance. Snapping taste buds to attention are the Thai shrimp nachos: crisp wontons topped with the grilled prawns, garnished with scallions and red pepper strips! Exclamation points are warranted as well for the pan-fried lobster and banana cakes with almond aioli (!) and the entree of George's Bank scallops with red beet "caviar" and apple curry vinaigrette! After these combinations, the rococo environment can look downright restrained.

150 Broadway.© **401/846-3449.** www.tuckersbistro.com. Reservations advised. Main courses $20–$33. DISC, MC, V. Daily 6–10pm (until 10:30pm Fri–Sat) in summer; Wed–Sun 6–10pm in winter.

22 Bowen's Wine Bar & Grille ★★ STEAK   On a wharf, surrounded by water and fishing boats and unlimited tureens of clam chowder—this is where the owners of the Castle Hill Inn opened this unabashed beef emporium. Their instinct was right: The restaurant has been full since the first day. The three rooms and bar have the burnished dark wood and polished brass of an old-time yacht club. Patrons are of an age and apparent income level to be comfortable with the steep prices, and possessed of sufficient knowledge to make assured choices from the extensive wine list. A $20 three-course prix fixe menu has been added on Sunday through Thursday evenings. All meats are served alone on the plate—sides are an extra $5 to $10 each. In spring and summer, there's an outdoor patio. Service is as professional as any place in Newport.

22 Bowen's Wharf.© **401/841-8884.** www.22bowens.com. Reservations recommended for dinner and weekend brunch. Main courses $23–$50; 3-course prix fixe $20 Sun–Thurs. AE, DC, MC, V. Daily 11:30am–3:30pm and 5–10pm (Fri–Sat until 11pm) in summer; Sat–Sun 11:30am–3:30pm and daily 5–9pm in winter.

MODERATE

Brick Alley Pub ★ ☺ AMERICAN   The Brick is loud, large, and good-natured, and is probably Newport's favorite hangout. Families, tourists, working stiffs, and yachtsmen squeeze through the doors into the thronged dining rooms, the bar, and the terrace. The cab of a 1938 Chevy pickup sits next to the soup-and-salad bar, with the decor also incorporating kid-size vehicles, license plates, vintage photos, and a model train. The voluminous menu is pub grub squared: stuffed clams, Cajun catfish, nachos, burgers, pizzas, steaks, stuffies, meatloaf, and squid-ink spaghetti with cream, scallops, and crabmeat. There's a children's menu for kids 10 and under, and a caution that "unattended children will be given two free puppies and a double espresso." Expect a wait.

140 Thames St.© **401/849-6334.** www.brickalley.com. Reservations recommended. Main courses $8–$30. AE, DISC, MC, V. Mon–Fri 11:30am–10pm; Sat 11:30am–10:30pm; Sun 10:30am–10pm.

Fluke Wine, Bar & Kitchen ★★★ 🏠 NEW AMERICAN   Open since 2007, the waterside Fluke is a must-dine. The second-floor houses the formal dining room, but we recommend you climb the steps to the third level. It's a happy space with a small slip of a bar and bare tables, with views of the harbor and a convivial crowd to enjoy them. Set the mood with a specialty cocktail, the Juniperotivo, perhaps (gin, pomegranate molasses, lemon juice, and fresh mint), or one of nearly a score of wines by the glass—pours are generous. The chef has a New Orleans background, so expect spicy flavors. You can make a meal of the small plates, such as the top-notch crispy potato croquettes, spicy lamb meatballs, and beet salad with pistachio *crema*. Large plates might include boar, wild mushroom risotto, or a shellfish roast.

41 Bowen's Wharf. ℂ **401/849-7778.** www.flukewinebar.com. Reservations recommended. Main courses $22–$38. AE, MC, V. Daily 5–10pm in summer; Thurs–Sun 5–10pm in winter.

Salvation Café ★ AMERICAN   About a half-mile away from the boozy water-front, this friendly, eclectically decorated cafe attracts an artsy, 30s-to-50s crowd. It's as funky-hip as Newport gets, and a gathering place so popular with locals that the tourists who discover it are barely visible. A monster Gulf sign and 1950s record covers occupy the walls. The steel-topped bar is given primarily to diners, at least in the busy early evening hours. Tables are close together, with diners elbow to elbow. Scallops with caper and raisin sauce and the spicy pad Thai with tofu are both very good, especially when washed down with Narragansett beer or glasses of red sangria. Sunday through Wednesday before 7pm, the cafe offers three main course options with a glass of sangria or Narragansett for $9. On Monday, the owners throw in a free bottle of wine to accompany any two entrees.

140 Broadway. ℂ **401/847-2620.** www.salvationcafe.com. Main courses $16–$21. AE, DC, MC, V. Daily 5–10pm (until 11pm Fri–Sat). Bar until midnight daily. Sometimes closed mid-Feb to mid-Mar; call ahead to check.

Scales & Shells ★★ SEAFOOD   The graceless name reflects the uncompromising character of this clangorous fish house: It's fish and shellfish *only* here (with one veg-etarian pasta option). Diners looking for a little elegance in the summer season should head for the upstairs room, called UpScales (it's closed in winter). On the first floor, which is open year-round, options are listed on a big blackboard next to the open kitchen, with guileless preparations that allow the natural flavors to prevail. Portions are substantial: The "large" appetizer of fried calamari is enough for four. Swordfish grilled over hardwood and topped with roasted peppers is typical. Or have linguini with your choice of clams, calamari, or shrimp. Note that credit cards aren't accepted.

527 Thames St. ℂ **401/846-3474.** www.scalesandshells.com. Reservations for patio seating only. Main courses $17–$30. No credit cards. Daily 5–9pm (until 10pm Fri–Sat) in summer; closed Mon Jan–Apr.

INEXPENSIVE

Flo's Clam Shack SEAFOOD   Just past Easton's Beach over the Newport/Mid-dletown line, this old-timer is a lopsided shanty, where you step up to the order window and choose from the handwritten menu. This is the place to get clams, on a plate or on a roll. They're cooked swiftly to order, and are as tender as any to which you might have set your teeth. This is also the place to sample "chowda" and that Rhode Island specialty, stuffies (see "Big Tastes Hide in Little Rhody," p. 435). Upstairs are a raw bar and deck even more happily ramshackle than below. There's a parking lot in back.

4 Wave Ave., Middletown.(© **401/847-8141.** www.flosclamshack.net. Main courses $5–$23. No credit cards. Daily 11am–9pm Memorial Day to Labor Day; Thurs–Sun Mar to Memorial Day and Labor Day to Dec. Closed Jan–Feb.

Newport After Dark

Many of the restaurants listed above have chummy bars for a drink and snack. The most likely places to spend a full evening lie along **Thames Street.** One of the most obvious possibilities, **The Red Parrot,** 348 Thames St., near Memorial Boulevard (© **401/847-3800;** www.redparrotrestaurant.com), has handsome windows overlooking the street and the look of an Irish pub.

A full schedule of live music is on the plate at the **Newport Blues Cafe** ★, 286 Thames St., at Green Street (© **401/841-5510;** www.newportblues.com). There's music nightly in summer, weekends in the off season. With its fireplace and dark wood, the cafe has a touch of class. (Dinner is served here nightly, with main courses such as porterhouse steak and chicken parmesan running $16–$26.)

For a warm night outside, **H2O,** 359 Thames St. (© **401/849-4466;** www.h2onewport.com), has an expansive waterfront deck with a harbor view. For DJs and dancing, check out **The Landing,** 30 Bowen's Wharf (© **401/847-4514;** www.thelandingrestaurantnewport.com).

Mudville Pub, 8 W. Marlborough St. (© **401/849-1408**), is a sports bar. It's across the street from Cardines Field, a small baseball stadium near the visitor center, where the **Newport Gulls** (www.newportgulls.com), a collegiate team, play in the summer. Fans and players alike stop in after games, and it can get packed.

NARRAGANSETT TO WATCH HILL

Narragansett: 32 miles SW of Providence; 14 miles W of Newport

Travelers rushing through the state inevitably choose I-95 to drive between Providence and the Connecticut border. They either do not have the time for a detour south of the highway or simply don't know that the nearby shore has some of the best beaches and most congenial fishing and resort villages of New England. This is called **South County,** a designation that has no official status but refers to the coast that is the southwestern edge of the state. Definitions are fuzzy, but for our purposes, South County runs from Narragansett, a coastal town almost directly due south of Providence, west to Watch Hill, a point on a slip of land nudging the Connecticut border. See the map on p. 427 to locate towns discussed in this section.

Rhode Islanders certainly know about the beguilements of the area, so try to avoid weekends in July and August, when the crush of day-trippers can turn the region's two-lane roads into parking lots.

Essentials

GETTING THERE   From I-95, take exit 9 to pick up Rte. 4. This merges with Rte. 1, arriving in Narragansett in about 20 miles. Turn east on Rte. 1A for a few miles to reach Narragansett Pier. Alternately, from Newport, take Rte. 138 to Rte. 1A south, which comes right into Narragansett Pier after 14 miles.

VISITOR INFORMATION There is a **visitor center** inside the Towers, 36 Ocean Rd. (🕿 **401/783-7121;** www.narragansettri.com/chamber). The **South County Tourism Council** (🕿 **800/548-4662** or 401/789-4422; www.south countyri.com), has a vacation planner, *South County Style,* that you can view online or request a free copy be mailed to you.

Narragansett to Point Judith

This is a good section of coastline for a drive or a swim. You'll pass some of the most desirable beaches in New England, with swaths of fine sand, relatively clean waters, and summer water temperatures that average about 70°F (21°C). When there are storms, the water kicks up enough to justify getting out the surfboard, and this is thought to be the best place in the state to catch the waves.

Traveling from east to west (you'll also be going north to south), start at **Narragansett Pier,** a village that extends inland from the shoreline. Pick up Ocean Road here. You'll pass under the **Towers,** a massive stone structure that spans the road, with cylindrical towers topped by conical roofs on either side. It is all that remains of the Gilded Age Narragansett Casino, lost in a 1900 fire. In the seaward tower is the Narragansett **visitor center** (see above).

About 3 miles after the Towers is the entrance to **Scarborough State Beach ★★** (🕿 **401/789-2324;** www.riparks.com), the most popular beach in the state. Noticeably well kept, with a row of pavilions for picnicking and changing, it has ample parking and surroundings unsullied by brash commercial enterprises. The beach is largely hard-packed sand. While the mild surf makes this a good option for families with young children, sections are often also jammed with teenagers and college students. Weekend parking costs $14 for nonresidents ($12 on weekdays, $7 for nonresident seniors).

About 2½ miles past the beach entrance is the **Point Judith Lighthouse,** 1470 Ocean Rd. (🕿 **401/789-0444**). Built in 1857 and restored in 2000, the brownstone tower is a photo op that can be approached but not entered.

Whale-watching expeditions leave from near here. Trips offered by **Frances Fleet,** 33 State St. (🕿 **800/662-2824** or 401/783-4988; www.francesfleet.com), take place in July and August, Tuesday and Thursday through Sunday, leaving at 1pm and returning at 5:30pm. Tickets are $40 for adults, $35 for seniors, and $30 for children 11 and under. If you've ever seen a monster humpback leaping from the water, you know it's unforgettable. Chances are good that a whale will show itself, although, as the company website notes, "whether or not you sight these marvelous creatures is entirely up to the whales." To get to the dock from the lighthouse, double back about 1 mile, turn left onto Point Judith Road, go two-fifths of a mile and turn left onto Galilee Escape Road, go 1 mile and turn right onto Great Island Road, and make the first left onto State Road. This is the **Port of Galilee,** where year-round ferries to **Block Island** (p. 464) depart.

WHERE TO DINE

Narragansett Beer (www.narragansettbeer.com) is a tasty New England option. Celebrating its 120th birthday in 2010, it managed to survive both Prohibition (1920–33) and sales and resales to various owners. Available in cans or longnecks, it's brewed today in Providence, Rhode Island; Pawcatuck, Connecticut; and Rochester, New York.

Coast Guard House SEAFOOD   Adjacent to the Towers (see above) is this 1888 former Coast Guard headquarters, now a restaurant that enjoys unobstructed views of the beach and breakers crashing a few feet below its windows—a diversion from the corporate-looking interior. The menu has been reworked and prices brought down (entrees top out at $27, with most under $20), with lots of appetizers and raw-bar options to enjoy on the hugely popular outdoor deck.

40 Ocean Rd., Narragansett.© **401/789-0700.** www.thecoastguardhouse.com. Main courses $15–$27. AE, DC, DISC, MC, V. Lunch and dinner only, with variable hours throughout the year; call ahead.

Crazy Burger Cafe & Juice Bar LIGHT FARE/VEGETARIAN   A funky burger joint, in business since 1995. In addition to burgers made from beef, lamb, turkey, and salmon, there are vegetarian and vegan options, including the Just Plain Nuts burger made from toasted cashews, walnuts, lentils, and zucchini. The sweet potato fries are to die for, and the ketchup is homemade. Drinks include espresso, fresh juices, and chai.

144 Boon St., Narragansett.© **401/783-1810.** www.crazyburger.com. Burgers $9–$14; other main courses $15–$25. MC, V. Daily 7am–8:30pm (Fri–Sat until 9:30pm). From the Towers on Ocean Rd., go ⅓ mile south, turn right on Rodman St., and left on Boon St.

Spain of Narragansestt ★ SPANISH   About a mile south of Scarborough Beach, this is deservedly the most popular restaurant on this stretch of shore. Partly it's the congenial staff, partly the terraces overlooking the sea. But the greatest share of credit goes to the stellar interpretations of the Spanish tapas tradition and such favorites as *paella Valenciana* (shrimp, sea scallops, clams, mussels, chicken, chorizo, calamari, saffron rice, and mild spices). Authenticity doesn't head the list of the kitchen's concerns: The irresistible fried calamari are tossed with very un-Spanish hot peppers. Do sample the *espinacas a la Catalana*—spinach sautéed with garlic, raisins, and pine nuts. The several dishes listed on the menu as "Shellfish Combinations" deserve particular consideration.

1144 Ocean Rd., Narragansett.© **401/783-9770.** www.spainri.com. Main courses $14–$33. AE, DC, DISC, MC, V. Tues–Sat 4–10pm (Fri–Sat until 11pm); Sun 1–9pm.

Watch Hill ★ & Westerly

Peacefully semirural, the Westerly township in the most southwest corner of Rhode Island is home to the peninsular resort of Watch Hill, a pretty land's-end village. Watch Hill achieved its resort status during the post–Civil War period and has retained it ever since. Many grand summer mansions and Queen Anne gingerbread houses remain from that time.

The area boasts several good public beaches. For a day trip of quiet hiking and bird-watching (hawks in the fall, especially), the best destination is **Napatree Point ★**, the long spit of land at the tip of Watch Hill that juts out into the Atlantic. It's a wildlife preserve notable for its white crescent beach and wild roses. While you can enter the Napatree preserve for free, there are no facilities, which explains its generally sparse crowds. You can't park on the point; you'll need to park in town and walk in. The 1.5-mile stroll along the shore from the Watch Hill Yacht Club to the end of the point takes about 30 minutes. Stay off the dunes to prevent dune erosion and steer clear of the grass (and wear long pants) to avoid ticks.

For swimming, eating, and nightlife, the half-mile long **Misquamicut State Beach** ★ (ⓒ **401/596-9097;** www.riparks.com/misquamicut.htm), 257 Atlantic Ave., is parallel to and south of Rte. 1. With fine-grained sand, gentle surf, and gradual drop-offs, the beach has all the amenities needed for a family day out: parking, a pavilion, a carousel, minigolf, batting cages, paddle boats, restaurants, beach stores, and DJs and live music at night. It fills up during summer days, so arrive early. The beach is open May through Labor Day, and parking is $14.

In Watch Hill on Bay Street, the small **Carousel Beach** is good for younger children. Its **Flying Horse Carousel,** which dates to 1867, is for kids only. There's shopping nearby for the adults.

Note: Parking is extremely limited in Watch Hill. Expect to pay $15 or more in a commercial lot. **Amtrak** trains traveling between Boston and New York stop in Westerly, about 6 miles north of Watch Hill on Rte. 1.

WHERE TO STAY

Shelter Harbor Inn ★   If it's time to stop for the night, for dinner, or for a spectacular Sunday brunch (reservations essential), watch for the entrance to this venerable inn just off Rte. 1, about 7 miles northeast of Watch Hill. Parts of the main building date to 1810, accounting for the creaking floorboards and doors that don't quite close. A genteel tone prevails. Several bedrooms have fireplaces, decks, or both. Furnishings are clean and simple with a touch of Ye Olde Inne, but comfortable enough. A shuttle takes guests to a private beach a mile away (or guests can drive themselves and park); a rooftop hot tub is open all year; and guests are welcome to play paddle tennis, croquet, and bocce during the summer. A creative restaurant (main courses $11–$29) and honored wine cellar round out the picture. The inn and restaurant are open 365 days a year—unusual for this area of New England.

10 Wagner Rd., Westerly, RI 02891. ⓒ**800/468-8883** or 401/322-8883. www.shelterharborinn.com. 24 units. $192–$258 double; from $96 off season. Rates include breakfast. AE, DC, DISC, MC, V. From Watch Hill, follow Rte. 1A northeast until it becomes Rte. 1; continue ⅝ miles and turn right on Wagner Rd. **Amenities:** Restaurant; bar; rooftop Jacuzzi. *In room:* A/C, TV, Wi-Fi (free).

Watch Hill Inn Apartments   Savor sunsets over the marina from this century-old clapboard lodge. Bedrooms are modern suites (they're called apartments here), based either in the main lodge or the annex building. Most have kitchenettes and/or decks, and some accommodate up to five people. The location is great: There's access to a beach, and the inn is walking distance to Napatree Point (p. 462), Carousel Beach (p. 463), and Olympia Tea Room (below). It's also just 8 miles from Mystic, Connecticut (p. 411). In summer months, meals also are offered at the in-house **Seaside Cafe,** which has a family garden patio, indoor restaurant, and sunset deck with superb views.

38–44 Bay St., Watch Hill, RI 02891. ⓒ**401/348-6300.** www.watchhillinn.com. 22 units. Summer from $280 suite. Rates include breakfast. MC, V. **Amenities:** Restaurant; bar. *In room:* A/C, TV, kitchenette (in most), Wi-Fi (free).

WHERE TO DINE

Olympia Tea Room ★ NEW AMERICAN   The genteel tone of Watch Hill is undergirded by the Olympia, long a favorite meet-and-eat retreat for wealthy locals. The layout includes a warren of wooden booths, into which the kitchen cranks out imaginative food. If available, jump for the appetizer of plump, lightly fried oysters on wilted spinach and corn salsa. The stuffies and lobster rolls are as good as you're likely to enjoy in coastal New England. Be sure to read the "Watch Hill History" in the front of the menu—it's quite entertaining. There are no highchairs, which is one way of emphasizing that this is not a venue for young children.

74 Bay St., Watch Hill.© **401/348-8211.** www.olympiatearoom.com. Main courses $20–$35. AE, MC, V. Daily 11:30am–10pm in summer and Thurs–Sun 11:30am–8pm in spring and fall. (Hours and days vary frequently; call ahead.) Closed Nov–Apr.

The Up River Cafe ★ NEW AMERICAN Six miles north of Watch Hill, in the center of the village of Westerly, this restaurant is housed in a converted old woolen mill cantilevered over the river that runs through town. The main dining room is a two-tiered affair allowing water views; the smaller adjacent room has a fireplace. It all has a North Woods look, with bare wide-board floors, carried through in the homey tavern beside the entry hall. Entrees are half sea-based, half land-based, with such surprises as the Indian-spiced lentil cakes with *saag paneer* (Indian cheese with leafy greens). Dishes utilizing the New Zealand lamb that is usually on offer are reliable, as are the sea scallops harvested by the local Stonington, Connecticut, fleet (Stonington, detailed on p. 420, is 5 miles west).

37 Main St., Westerly.© **401/348-9700.** www.theuprivercafe.net. Main courses $11–$25. AE, MC, V. Tues–Thurs 5–9pm; Sat–Sun 5–10pm; small plates served in Lounge later into the evening. From Watch Hill, take Rte. 1A north into Westerly, turn left on Broad St., and make an immediate left onto Main St.

BLOCK ISLAND ★★

Viewed from above or on a map, Block Island looks like a pork chop with a big bite taken out of the middle. Only 7 miles long and 3 miles wide, it is edged with long stretches of beach lifting at points into dramatic bluffs. The interior is dimpled with undulating hills, only rarely reaching above 150 feet in elevation. Its hollows and clefts cradle more than 350 sweet-water ponds, some no larger than a backyard swimming pool. That "bite" out of the western edge of the "chop" is **Great Salt Pond,** which almost succeeds in cutting the island in two but, as it is, serves as a fine protected harbor for fleets of pleasure boats.

The only significant concentration of houses, businesses, hotels, and people is at **Old Harbor,** on the lower eastern shore, where most of the ferries from the mainland arrive and most of the remaining fishing boats moor.

Named for Adrian Block, a Dutch explorer who briefly stepped ashore in 1641, the island's earliest European settlement was in 1661. For years, it attracted the kinds of people who nurture fierce convictions of independence: farmers, pirates, fishermen, smugglers, scavengers, and entrepreneurs, all willing to deal with the realities of isolation, lonely winters, and occasional killer hurricanes. Today it's home to about 1,000 permanent residents who love the island in all four seasons.

Vacationers are wont to describe this as paradise—and they are correct, at least if sun and sea and zephyrs are paramount considerations. Those elements transformed the island from an offshore afterthought into an accessible summer retreat for the urban middle class after the Civil War, during America's first taste of mass tourism.

Unlike other such regions throughout the country that have lost their sprawling Victorian hotels to fire or demolition, Block Island has preserved many of its buildings from that time. They crowd around Old Harbor, providing most of the lodging base. Smaller inns and B&Bs add more tourist rooms, most in converted houses built

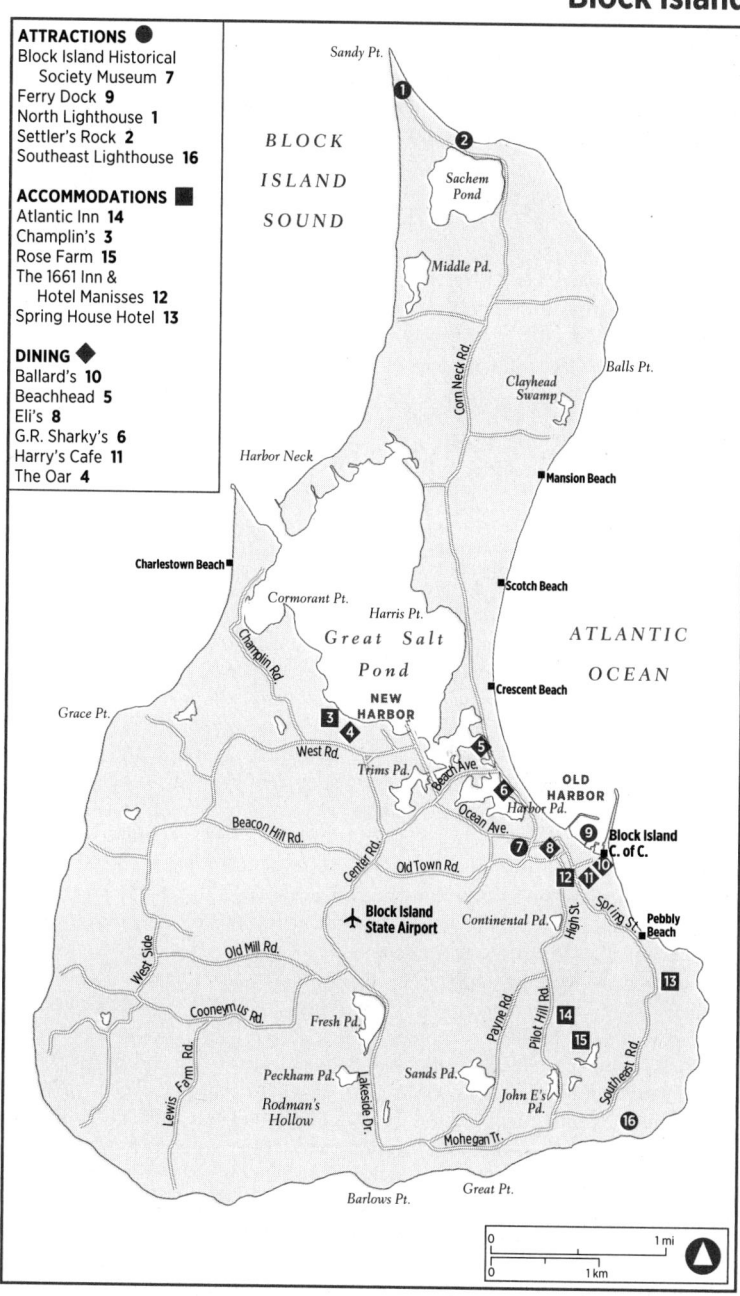

ATTRACTIONS ●
Block Island Historical
    Society Museum **7**
Ferry Dock **9**
North Lighthouse **1**
Settler's Rock **2**
Southeast Lighthouse **16**

ACCOMMODATIONS ■
Atlantic Inn **14**
Champlin's **3**
Rose Farm **15**
The 1661 Inn &
    Hotel Manisses **12**
Spring House Hotel **13**

DINING ◆
Ballard's **10**
Beachhead **5**
Eli's **8**
G.R. Sharky's **6**
Harry's Cafe **11**
The Oar **4**

Sandy Pt.

B L O C K
I S L A N D
S O U N D

Sachem
Pond

Middle Pd.

Corn Neck Rd.

Balls Pt.

Clayhead
Swamp

Harbor Neck

■ Mansion Beach

■ Charlestown Beach

Cormorant Pt.

■ Scotch Beach

Harris Pt.

A T L A N T I C

Great Salt
Pond

Champlin Rd.

O C E A N

Grace Pt.

■ Crescent Beach

NEW
HARBOR

West Rd.

Beach Ave.

Trims Pd.

OLD
HARBOR

Ocean Ave.

Harbor Pd.

Beacon Hill Rd.

Block Island
C. of C.

Central Rd.

Old Town Rd.

✈ **Block Island**
State Airport

Continental Pd.

High St.

Spring St.

■ **Pebbly**
Beach

Old Mill Rd.

West Side

Cooneymus Rd.

Fresh Pd.

Payne Rd.

Pilot Hill Rd.

Lewis Farm Rd.

Peckham Pd.

Sands Pd.

John E's
Pd.

Southeast Rd.

Lakeside Dr.

Rodman's
Hollow

Mohegan Tr.

Barlows Pt.

Great Pt.

0   1 mi
0   1 km

at the same time as the great hotels. Only a few establishments even resemble motels, and building stock is marked, with few exceptions, by tasteful Yankee understatement.

Away from the sand and surf, it is an island of peaceful pleasures and gentle observations. Police officers wear Bermuda shorts and ride bikes. Children tend lemonade stands in front of picket fences and low hedges. Clumps of hydrangeas tangle with beach roses and honeysuckle, hiding the foundations of saltboxes and Victorian farmhouses with shingles scoured gray by sea winds. No squirrels, chipmunks, possums, or raccoons live on "the Block," but the island is in the middle of a flyway for migratory birds, and egrets, ducks, goldfinches, and kingfishers are seen in abundance. The island was included on a list of the "Last Great Places" in the Western Hemisphere by the Nature Conservancy, and conservation groups created abundant walking trails throughout the island. Deer were introduced about 30 years ago, to the islanders' regret, bringing Lyme disease and the four-hoofed enthusiasm for turning flowerbeds into salad bars.

Essentials

GETTING THERE   The **Interstate Navigation Company,** Narragansett, Rhode Island (© 866/783-7996 or 401/783-7996; www.blockislandferry.com), provides most of the surface service. This includes year-round passenger-and-vehicle ferries between Point Judith and Old Harbor on the Block and passenger-only ferries on daily runs between Newport and Block Island from July 1 to September 17. The Point Judith boats depart as many as nine times daily in high season, as few as once daily in winter; sailing time is 55 minutes.

The Newport ferries leave Fort Adams at 9:15am and return from Old Harbor on Block Island at 4:45pm. Sailing time is 2 hours. While reservations aren't required for passengers, get to the dock early, as the boats tend to fill up quickly.

Round-trip fares are $19 to $23 for adults, $18 to $22 for seniors, and $6 to $9 for children. Getting a car to Block Island is something of a hassle and considerably more expensive. Passenger vehicles cost an additional $95 to $115, and there is a long list of different fees for bicycles, mopeds, and motorcycles. **Car reservations** must be made by phone at © 866/783-7996. Drivers, be prepared: You are expected to *back* your car into the close quarters of the ferry's main deck.

Given the cost of taking a car, consider parking in one of the nearby long-term lots at Point Judith or New London. Block Island is small, rental bicycles and mopeds are readily available, there are cabs for longer distances, and most hotels and inns are within a few blocks of the docks. There are even car-rental agencies on the island. If you intend to take a car anyway, understand that it's important to make ferry reservations well in advance, at © 866/783-7996 Monday through Friday between 5am and 4pm. Two months advance reservations aren't too early for weekend departures.

High-speed passenger-only service is in operation from both Point Judith and New London, Connecticut. **Island Hi-Speed Ferry,** Narragansett, Rhode Island (© 866/783-7996; www.blockislandferry.com), makes several daily round-trips from late May to early October. Sailing time is 30 minutes; round-trip passenger fare is $36 adults, $16 children. **Block Island Express,** New London, Connecticut (© 860/444-4624; www.goblockisland.com), has cut the previous average time to the Block nearly in half, to a little over an hour. Service is from late May to September; round-trip fares are $43 to $48 for adults, $22 to $24 for children.

Tip: Try to avoid the last ferry Sunday nights in summer, when boisterous weekend drunks roll on board from the bars along Water Street.

Westerly State Airport, near the Connecticut border, is the base for over a dozen regular flights to and from Block Island via **New England Airlines** (✆ **800/243-2460,** 401/596-2460 in Westerly, or 401/466-5881 on Block Island; www.block-island.com/nea). Flights depart hourly in summer, taking 12 to 15 minutes. Fares are $84 round-trip for adults, $69 for children. Make advance reservations and allow for the possibility that coastal fogs or high winds will delay or even cancel flights.

VISITOR INFORMATION The **Block Island Chamber of Commerce** has a year-round information office at the ferry landing at Old Harbor (✆ **800/383-BIRI** [2474] or 401/466-2474; www.blockislandchamber.com). Its attendants can answer questions and help visitors find lodging. In the same building are lockers for day-trippers and one of the island's few ATMs. A building at Corn Neck Road and Ocean Avenue contains the only bank, which also has an ATM.

Most streets on Block Island have no house numbers, and some roads have no names. Leave your dog at home: Hotels, inns, and B&Bs won't accept them, they are banned from the beaches, and they are supposed to be leashed at all times.

Daily newspapers from Boston, New York, and Providence are sold at the **B.I.G.** (✆ **401/466-2949**), the grocery store on Ocean Avenue (near Corn Neck Rd.). When they become available, however, depends on the ferry from Port Judith to which they are delivered each morning.

GETTING AROUND Cars are allowed on the island, but roads are narrow, winding, and without shoulders, and drivers must contend with runners and flocks of bicycles and mopeds. Unless your party includes people with mobility problems or small children, we recommend leaving your car on the mainland and joining the two-wheelers.

If you'd like to rent a car after you arrive, **Block Island Bike & Car Rental,** on Ocean Avenue (✆ **401/466-2297**), has offices near Payne's Dock and will pick you up at the ferry or airport; reserve ahead. If you decide to bring your car to the island, top off the gas tank before rolling onto the ferry. The only gas station on the island is behind G. R. Sharky's restaurant (p. 472) on Corn Neck Road.

Rental bikes and mopeds are available at several shops and stands. Convenient sources near Old Harbor include **The Moped Man,** Water Street (✆ **401/466-5444;** www.themopedman.com), on the main business street, renting bikes as well as mopeds; **Old Harbor Bike Shop,** at the ferry dock (✆ **401/466-2029**); and **Island Moped & Bikes,** Chapel Street, behind the Harborside Inn (✆ **401/466-2700**). Rates for bikes are typically $18 to $30 a day, less with widely available discount coupons. Moped rates vary but are usually from $75 to $90 for half- to full days. Bargaining often brings prices down, especially early in the week after the weekenders have left, or if your rental is for 3 or more days. Keep in mind that mopeds aren't allowed on dirt roads, which provide access to many beaches.

Some inns also rent bicycles, so a possible plan is to take a taxi from the ferry or airport to your inn, drop off luggage, and get around by bike after that. Two such inns are the **Seacrest,** 207 High St. (✆ **401/466-2882;** www.seacrestinnbi.com), and **Rose Farm,** on Roslyn Road (✆ **401/466-5925;** www.beachrosebicycles.com), but inquire about rentals when making room reservations at other places as well.

Exploring the Island

With no golf course and a lone museum that takes only 15 minutes to see, little on the island distracts from the central missions of sunning, cycling, hiking, lolling, and ingesting copious quantities of lobster, clams, chowder, and alcohol. A driving tour of every site on the list takes no more than 2 hours.

A couple of miles south of Old Harbor on what starts out as Spring Street is the **Southeast Lighthouse** (✆ **401/466-5009;** www.nps.gov). An appealing Victorian structure, built in 1874, the lighthouse's claim for attention lies primarily in the fact that it had to be moved 245 feet back from the eroding precipice in 1993. That was expensive, and now another $1 or $2 million is needed to renovate this National Historic Landmark. While a small exhibit on the ground floor can be seen for free, the admission fee to the top is $10.

Continuing along the same road, which goes through other names and soon makes a sharp right turn inland, watch for the left turn onto West Side Road. In a few hundred yards, pull over near the sign for **Rodman's Hollow,** a geological dent dug by a passing glacier. It's deeper than it looks, the bottom a few feet below sea level and laced with walking trails beneath a thick mantle of low trees. Much of what you see here, and elsewhere on the island, is designated forever wild, for the Nature Conservancy has purchased about a third of the island's surface to protect it from development. There are about 25 miles of trails, only occasionally signed with granite Greenway markers and wooden turnstiles. You can purchase a map of the trail network at the Chamber of Commerce building at the ferry landing or at the **Nature Conservancy** office (✆ **401/466-2129**) on High Street.

From Old Harbor, proceed north on Corn Neck Road, skirting Crescent Beach, on the right. If you need to get out and stretch your legs, look for the **Clay Head Trail** sign on your right and drive down the dirt road to the trail head. After a .5-mile moderate hike, the trail splits, going right to beautiful sandy beach or left up the bluff for breathtaking views high above the ocean. Watch out for unmarked grassy trails leading away from the bluff. Known as **The Maze,** they are a fun way to while away an afternoon.

Continuing along Corn Neck Road, the pavement ends at **Settler's Rock ★★★**, with a plaque naming the English pioneers who landed here in 1661. This is one of the loveliest spots on the island, with **Sachem Pond** behind the Rock and a scimitar beach curving out to **North Lighthouse** (✆ **401/466-3200**), erected in 1867. In between is a **national wildlife refuge** that is of particular interest to birders. The lighthouse, reached by a mile-long walk on the rocky beach, contains an interpretive center of local ecology and history (and the only public restroom for miles); it's open from July 5 to Labor Day daily from 10am to 4pm.

Back in Old Harbor, the **Block Island Historical Society Museum,** Old Town Road and Ocean Avenue (✆ **401/466-2481**), was an 1871 inn that now contains a miscellany of photos, ship models, and tools. Upstairs is a room set up to reflect the Victorian period. The museum is open daily from 10am to 5pm in the summer with limited hours in the spring and fall (call for schedule). Admission is $5 adults, $3 seniors and students, free for children 15 and under.

The beaches on Block Island will suit every taste. Immediately south of the Old Harbor, past the breakwater, is the northern end of **Pebbly Beach,** a section informally known as **Ballard's Beach** for the popular restaurant located there (see

"Where to Dine," below). Crowded with sunbathers and swimmers, it is one of only two on the island with lifeguards. The surf is often rough. Drinks are served at your towel. North of Old Harbor starts the 3-mile-long **Crescent Beach** (also known as Frederick J. Benson Town Beach, or simply Town Beach). The southern section, with a sandy bottom that stays shallow well out into the gentle surf, is known as **Baby Beach** because of its relative safety for children. Farther along is the main part, a broad strand served by a pavilion with a snack bar, restrooms, and showers. You can rent chairs, umbrellas, and boogie boards. The surf is higher here and rolls straight in; lifeguards are on duty. Continuing north, and with a small parking lot reached by a dirt road off Corn Neck Road, is **Scotch Beach.** Consider this grown-up and R-rated, dominated by young summer workers and residents. Still farther north is **Mansion Beach,** with a dirt road of the same name leading in from Corn Neck Road. Somewhat more secluded, it is usually less crowded than the others. On the west side of the island, running south from the jetty that marks the entrance to New Harbor, is **Charlestown Beach.** Uncrowded and relatively tranquil during the day, it draws anglers from dusk into the night surf-casting for striped bass.

Parasailing has become popular here, and chutes can be seen lifting riders up to heights of 1,200 feet above the ocean. Call **Block Island Parasail** (© 401/864-2474; www.blockislandparasail.com) with questions, but you must make reservations in person at the office near the Old Harbor ferry landing. Fares start at $75 and go up, gauged by altitude; observers are charged $20 each. The company also offers banana boat and jet boat rides, as well as dive trips.

A more old-fashioned form of transportation is provided by **Rustic Rides Farm,** on West Side Road (© 401/466-5060). A walking attendant handles the reins and protects the littlest ones on the trail. A 1-hour slow ride costs $40; a 1-hour sunset ride costs $65, and a 2-hour beach ride is $100.

Fishing, kayaking, and canoeing are popular, and one name to know is **Pond & Beyond** (© 401/578-2773). Guided tours include family paddles, kids and kay-aks, and full moon paddles. Tours last 2½ hours and cost $50 per person. **Block Island Fishworks,** Ocean Avenue (© 401/466-5392; www.bifishworks.com), sells fishing tackle and arranges charter boat outings for both inshore and deep-water angling. Another source of boat rentals is **Champlin's Resort,** on Great Salt Pond (© 401/466-7777; www.champlinsresort.com), which has bumper boats and Zodiacs as well as kayaks.

Where to Stay

Most inns are in buildings over 100 years old, so expect wavy floors, narrow hall-ways, steep staircases, and rooms of odd configuration. Air-conditioning is rare on the island, and such amenities as TV and Wi-Fi cannot be assumed. With what amounts to a 4-month year for businesses serving tourists, the differences in cost between moderate and very expensive room rates are narrow. Two- or three-night minimum stays are routinely required.

Atlantic Inn ★★   Perched on 6 rolling acres south of downtown, this 1879 Victorian hotel beguiles with its long veranda and broad views. Bedrooms are furnished mostly with antiques. Drawn by the restaurant's changing menu of special appetizers—Kobe beef carpaccio with green olives was one—people start assembling at 4pm each sum-mer day. They take up the Adirondack chairs on the sloping lawn to settle in for the spectacular sunsets, lubricated by cocktails and the most diverse beer and wine selection on the island. The kitchen is one of the two most accomplished on the Island, and you will need reservations to dine here from June to September.

High St., Box 188, Block Island, RI 02807.☎ **800/224-7422** or 401/466-5883. Fax 401/466-5678. www. atlanticinn.com. 21 units. $190–$210 double. Rates include breakfast. DISC, MC, V. Closed Nov–Apr. **Amenities:** Restaurant; bar; 2 tennis courts.

Champlin's ★★ ☺ Families are welcome at this all-inclusive resort, with 225 slips in the marina for visiting yachters. Those who are put off by the idiosyncratic adornments of Victorian inns will be pleased by the simpler lines and muted fabrics of the bedrooms here. All rooms have fridges and microwaves (another plus for families). There's live music in the bars on weekends, picnic grounds with grills, a pizza bar and ice-cream parlor, a laundry facility, and even a theater showing first-run movies. Once you've unpacked, there isn't much to compel you to leave, but the resort provides a shuttle van for trips to other parts of the island. Cars, mopeds, kayaks, and pontoon boats are available for rent.

Great Salt Pond, P.O. Box J, Block Island, RI 02807.☎ **800/762-4541** or 401/466-7777. www.champlins resort.com. 30 units. $265–$335 double. AE, MC, V. Closed mid-Oct to early May. From Old Harbor, drive west on Ocean Ave. and turn left on West Side Rd. The entrance road to Champlin's is on the right. **Amenities:** Restaurant; 2 bars; bike rentals; large outdoor pool; 2 tennis courts; watersports equipment/ rentals. *In room:* A/C, TV, fridge.

Rose Farm ★ Spot deer and pheasant on the 20 acres of the 1897 farmhouse that was the original inn. It is complemented by an additional house across the driveway. Four of the rooms feature Jacuzzis and decks. Some have canopied beds, most have ocean views, and their furnishings are often antique. Afternoon refreshments, usually iced tea and pastries, are served. Bicycles are available for rent on the property.

Roslyn Rd., Box E, Block Island, RI 02807.☎ **401/466-2034.** Fax 401/466-2053. www.rosefarminn. com. 19 units (2 with shared bathroom). $179–$309 double. Rates include breakfast. AE, DISC, MC, V. Closed Nov–Apr. From Old Harbor, drive west on High St. and turn left on paved driveway past the Atlantic Inn. Children 13 and over welcome. **Amenities:** Bike rentals. *In room:* Wi-Fi (free).

The 1661 Inn/Hotel Manisses ★★ Emus, llamas, black swans, kangaroos, lemurs, two camels, and a Scottish Highland steer graze in the meadow behind the Hotel Manisses, the most visible property of a island-wide hospitality empire. The Victorian hotel tends toward older couples. Guest rooms utilize oak antiques and lots of wicker; some have fireplaces. The Manisses parlor serves desserts and flaming coffees in the evening, and stylish dining is featured in the main dining room, with comparable fare in the more casual Gatsby Room.

At the 1661 Inn, up the hill, substantial champagne breakfast buffets and afternoon wine and cheese are served to guests of all nine of the properties. The 1661 Inn is now open year-round, although the restaurants are closed in winter.

1 Spring St., P.O. Box 1, Block Island, RI 02807.☎ **800/626-4773,** 401/466-2421, or 401/466-2063. Fax 401/466-3162. www.blockislandresorts.com. 17 units in hotel, 9 units in the inn, additional units in satellite properties. $210–$440 double. Rates include breakfast. MC, V. **Amenities:** 2 restaurants; bar; babysitting; concierge; Wi-Fi (in lobby; free). *In room:* TV/VCR, fridge, hair dryer (some rooms).

Spring House Hotel ★ Marked by its red mansard roof and wraparound porch, the island's oldest hotel (dating from 1852) has hosted Ulysses S. Grant, Mark Twain, and the Kennedy clan. The young staff is congenial, if occasionally a bit scattered.

Bedrooms in the two buildings all have queen-size or double beds, some with pull-out sofas; most are large. Formal meals are served in the all-white dining room, while a bistro menu is available in the parlor and cafe. Thursday night is martini night with live entertainment.

902 Spring St., P.O. Box 902, Block Island, RI 02807.© **800/234-9263** or 401/466-5844. www.spring househotel.com. 50 units, 4 houses, 6 condos. $275–$450 double. Rates include breakfast. AE, MC, V. Closed mid-Oct through May. **Amenities:** Restaurant; bar.

Where to Dine

Expect mostly lobsters, fried and grilled fish and chicken, and routine burgers and beef cuts. Chowders are usually surefire, especially the creamy New England version. Clam cakes appear less frequently on menus than in the past but are still a staple. Actually deep-fried fritters containing more dough than clams, they are still fun eating, especially when dipped in tartar sauce. Lobster dishes are usually sold at market prices, higher than those listed below.

Several inns and hotels have dining rooms worth noting (see "Where to Stay," above), but even there, neither jackets nor ties are required. Due to the seasonal nature of the island, its restaurants can change policies, menus, and—most important—chefs, in a twinkling. Keep that in mind if any of the observations below prove to undervalue or overstate a restaurant's virtues.

Ballard's ★ ☺ AMERICAN   Sooner rather than later, everyone winds up at Ballard's. Behind the long front porch is a warehouselike hall where a monster whale skeleton hangs, and beyond that a terrace beside a crowded beach. Several bars and frequent live bands fuel drinkers and diners from lunch until midnight. The menu is all over the map, with something for everyone and an emphasis on seafood. Complementing the lobster rolls and fish and chips are a seafood pasta with lobster, clams, scallops, and shrimp; and a salmon filet with teriyaki sauce. Kids have their own menu, and they can make as much noise and mess as they want. This place gets pricey for families, though, so you might want to go for lunch and order sandwiches.

Old Harbor.© **401/466-2231.** www.ballardsinn.com. Main courses $10–$35. AE, MC, V. Daily 11am– midnight. Closed Oct to mid-May.

The Beachead Restaurant ★ ☺ AMERICAN   The atmosphere is casual at this former tavern just across from the beach. It's a likely destination for families for lunch or dinner, and in peak season, at least, the noise level is high enough to mask childish squeals. Plenty of seating is available inside and outside on the wraparound porch. Seafood and meats are prepared in imaginative ways with an Asian flair, and the selection of beers and wines is very attractive.

Corn Neck Rd.© **401/466-2249.** www.thebeachead.com. Main courses $17–$29. MC, V. Daily 11:30am– 9pm (later in summer). Closed Dec–Apr.

Eli's ★ NEW AMERICAN   This tiny eatery is one of the island's most popular. Problem is, it can serve only 50 voracious diners at a time, and the no-reservations policy means waits of up to 2 hours. Once inside at table, tuna nachos are a popular appetizer, and marinated chicken with Thai curry fried rice is tops. Haddock is baked and herb crusted, served atop roasted potatoes with vegetables in a bacon cream broth. Such combinations are undeniably full-flavored, although the diverse

Do-It-Yourself Shore Dinners

Should you have housekeeping facilities in your lodging, you might wish to put together a New England shore dinner. Lobster is the central component, of course, and you can buy yours straight off the fishing boats. Each afternoon from about 4 to 5:30pm, boats put in at both Old Harbor and the Great Salt Pond. Depending upon their catches of the day, they charge from $6 to $8 per pound. A more reliable source is **Finn's Fish Market**, at the Old Harbor ferry landing (© **401/466-2102**). Its lobster prices are similar, and it also carries oysters, clams, shrimp, and fish.

For the other fixings—corn, tomatoes, bread, sausage, chicken—stop at either the **Block Island Grocery** (known as the B.I.G.), near Ocean Avenue and Corn Neck Road (© **401/466-2949**), a conventional supermarket; or **Block Island Depot,** Ocean Avenue (© **401/466-2403**), which carries a line of cheeses and specialty foods. The best-stocked wine and liquor store is the **Red Bird Package Store,** on Dodge Street (© **401/466-2441**), around the corner from the north end of Water Street. **Seaside Market,** toward the other end of Water Street (© **401/466-5876**), has a good wine selection and some grocery products.

ingredients are often mashed together as if in a thick stew, losing some of their individuality. Huge portions defy anyone to finish.

Chapel St. © **401/466-5230.** www.elisblockisland.com. Main courses $19–$28. DISC, MC, V. May–Oct daily 6–9pm (Sat–Sun until 10pm); Nov–Dec Sat–Sun 5:30–10pm. Closed Jan–Apr.

G. R. Sharky's AMERICAN   With its kicked-back atmosphere and pub-style menu, this entry's locale opposite Crescent Beach ensures steady business. Mounted fish, deer heads, and sports memorabilia decorate the bar. Expect the usual burgers and cheesesteak pretenders and the definitive fish and chips. Children are welcome.

Corn Neck Rd. © **401/466-9900.** Main courses $14–$27. MC, V. Daily 5–10pm. Closed late Oct to mid-May.

Harry's Café NEW AMERICAN   A former deli has been expanded into this perky eatery near the post office with side windows looking out over New Harbor. It's furnished with oak tables and bentwood chairs, and there are a few tables out on the terrace and side lawn (where the view is great). Order at the counter in front of the open kitchen, and they bring the food to you. Trust their menu when they describe their burritos as "BIG!" And expect the other choices to bounce around the continents, what with jerk scallops, ginger chicken wontons, and ravioli diablo. Most items sampled proved to be a cut or two above the island standard. Alcohol isn't served.

Water St. © **401/466-5400.** Main courses $18–$26. Daily 11am–10pm.

The Oar ★ AMERICAN   This former good-time bar is open for breakfast, lunch, and dinner, and the menu has a full range of choices from mahimahi, sirloin, and fried chicken to the standard fries, lobster rolls, and calamari. A deck and a bar with a picture window take in dramatic views of storms over the mainland and of the fleet of pleasure boats in the Great Salt Pond. Inside, the ceiling and walls are hung with scores of oars—all of them painted with cartoons, graffiti, and assorted messages of obscure or ribald intent.

West Side Rd. (Block Island Marina). © **401/466-8820.** Main courses $13–$25. MC, V. Daily 8am–midnight (bar until 1am). Closed late Oct to May.

Block Island After Dark

Nightlife isn't of the raunchy, rollicking South Florida variety, but the bars don't close at sunset, either. Among the prime candidates for a potential rockin' good time is **Captain Nick's,** on Ocean Avenue (© **401/466-5670**), opposite the Block Island Grocery. It has pool tables, three bars, and a large dance floor inside, as well as dollar beers, cheap burgers, and live music most nights in season out on the terrace. A block away, **McGovern's Yellow Kittens,** on Corn Neck Road (© **401/466-5855**), also presents live bands in summer, inside or out on the deck. Darts, pool tables, foosball, and video games help fill the winter nights. Pub food, pool tables, and foosball are also attractions at **Club Soda,** on Connecticut Avenue (© **401/466-5397**).

Ballard's (p. 471) has live rock or pop most afternoons out on the terrace and nightly inside. An occasional live-music venue is the lounge of the **National Hotel,** on Water Street (© **401/466-2901**). Yachtsmen and other sailors docked or moored at Champlin's Marina settle in on the end of the main dock at **Trader Vic's,** at New Harbor (© **401/466-2641**). The bar is downstairs, with a DJ or band out on the deck most afternoons. In addition to the sunset drinks and tapas on the front lawn of the **Atlantic Inn** (p. 469), many visitors settle in on the porch of the equally well-situated (and less expensive) **Narragansett Inn,** on Water Street (© **401/466-2626**).

Island residents try to keep **Mahogany Shoals,** on Payne's Dock at the end of Water Street (© **401/466-5572**), to themselves. What they come for is the barbed humor of Wally McDonough. He sings Irish folk ballads and banters with the audience, invariably giving better than he gets. Wally occupies his corner Wednesday through Sunday nights, assuming he feels like it. Get there around 10pm.

VERMONT

by Paul Karr

Vermont's rolling, cow-spotted hills, shaggy peaks, sugar maples, world-champion fall foliage, and quaint towns give it a distinct sense of place. This state is filled with the dairy farms, dirt roads, and small-scale enterprises that bring joy to the hearts of back-road travelers. And the towns are home to an intriguing mix of old-time Vermonters, back-to-the-landers who showed up in VW buses in the 1960s and never left (many got involved with municipal affairs or put down business roots—think Ben & Jerry); and newer, moneyed arrivals from New York or Boston who came to ski or stay at B&Bs and ended up buying second homes. Some of those second homes ended up becoming first homes.

The place captures a sense of America as it once was—because here it still *is*. Vermonters share a sense of community, and they still respect the ideals of thrift and parsimony above those of commercialism. (It took years for Walmart to get approval to build its first big-box store in Vermont.) Locals prize their villages, and understand what makes them special. That counts for a lot in an age when so many other small towns have been swallowed up by suburban creep or otherwise faded away with the changing of the times.

For travelers, Vermont remains a superb destination of country drives, mountain rambles, and overnights at country inns. A good map opens the door to back-road adventures, and it's not hard to get a taste of Vermont's way of life. The state's total population is just a shade over 600,000, making it one of only a handful of states with more senators (two) than representatives (one) in Congress. It does sometimes feel like the cows still outnumber the humans here.

Southern Vermont has mostly resisted the encroachments of progress (except at ski resorts on winter weekends), and remains a great introduction to the state. You'll find plenty of antiques shops, handsome inns, fast-flowing streams (with fish!), and inviting restaurants. The area is anchored by the towns of Bennington and Brattleboro; between them runs the spine of the Green Mountains and a national forest district, both of which reward explorers in search of Robert Frostian views and experiences. These hills also host many of the state's popular ski resorts.

Northern Vermont is different. On the region's western edge, along the shores of Lake Champlain, Burlington—the state's largest, most lively city—is ringed by fast-growing suburban communities and fun startup companies. But drive an hour east and you're deep in the Northeast Kingdom, the state's least developed, most lost-in-time region.

There are remnants of industry here—marble quarries near Rutland, converging train tracks at White River Junction, brick factories in Springfield and Bellows Falls—but mostly it's still rural living: cow pastures high in the hills, clapboard farmhouses under spreading trees, maple-sugaring operations, and the distant sound of timber being cut in woodlots. New and old co-exist here peaceably, and there are few places in America I'd rather be on a summer or fall afternoon.

BENNINGTON, MANCHESTER & ENVIRONS

Bennington: 143 miles NW of Boston; 126 miles S of Burlington. Manchester: 24 miles N of Bennington

Bennington ★

Bennington (motto: "Where Vermont Begins") is somehow Vermont's third-largest city, even though it feels a lot more like a one-stoplight town. The place owes its fame (such as it is) to a handful of eponymous moments, places, and things. There's the Battle of Bennington, fought in 1777 during the American War of Independence (which was actually fought in New York State); Bennington College, a small, prestigious liberal-arts school just outside town; and Bennington pottery, which traces its ancestry back to the original factory in 1793 and is still prized by collectors for its superb quality.

Today visitors will find a Bennington of two faces. Historic Bennington (more commonly known as **Old Bennington ★★**), with its white clapboard homes, sits atop a hill west of town off Rte. 9; look for the mini–Washington Monument obelisk and you're there. It's a gem of a neighborhood, especially if you fancy old homes and additional cows. Views materialize as you continue uphill and west from here on Rte. 7. The surrounding countryside, though defined by rolling hills, has fewer abrupt inclines and slopes than many other parts of Vermont, so go back-roading around here for a bit if you can.

Downtown Bennington, on the other hand, is a pleasant but no-frills commercial center stocked with real estate offices, plumbers, diners, coffee and sub shops, and stores that still sell things people actually need—not so much a tourist destination as a supply depot. The downtown is compact, low, and handsome, boasting a fair number of architecturally striking buildings. In particular, don't miss the stern marble Federal building (formerly the post office) with six fluted columns at 118 South St.

ESSENTIALS

GETTING THERE Bennington is at the intersection of Vermont state routes 9 and 7. If you're coming from the south, the nearest interstate access is via the New York State Thruway at Albany, about 35 miles away. (But you have to drive through the city of Troy first, which takes time; figure 45 min. or more from the Thruway to downtown Bennington.) From the east, I-91 is about 40 miles away at Brattleboro.

VISITOR INFORMATION   The **Bennington Area Chamber of Commerce,** 100 Veterans Memorial Dr. (© **800/229-0252** or 802/447-3311; www.bennington. com), maintains a **visitor center** on Rte. 7 about 1 mile north of downtown, near the veterans' complex and a small park. This office is open weekdays 9am to 5pm year-round, and also on weekends from mid-May until around mid-October. There's also a **downtown welcome center** (© **802/442-5758**) in a former blacksmith shop at South and Elm streets; look for the big blue flag. Operated by the *other* BBC—the Better Bennington Corporation, of course—it's open Monday through Friday year-round, and has a big map of the area to orient you.

EXPLORING THE TOWN

You can't miss the **Bennington Battle Monument ★★** (© **802/447-0550**) if you're passing through the area—turn off the main road (Rte. 9) in Old Bennington's little traffic circle to visit it. This 306-foot obelisk of blue limestone atop a low rise was dedicated in 1891. It resembles a shorter, paunchier Washington Monument. (This is *not* the battle site; that's about 6 miles northwest of here. This monument marks the spot where American munitions were stored.) The monument's viewing platform, which is reached by elevator, is open daily from 9am to 5pm from mid-April through October. A small fee ($2 adults, $1 children ages 6–14) is charged. On holidays and during the last 2 weeks of each year, the monument is lit up.

Near the monument, you'll find distinguished old homes lushly overarched with ancient trees. Be sure to spend a minute exploring the **old burying ground ★**, where the great poet Robert Frost and several Vermont governors are buried; see "I Had a Lover's Quarrel with the World," below. The chamber of commerce also provides a walking-tour brochure that helps you make sense of this neighborhood's formerly vibrant past.

Bennington College ★, just northwest of downtown Bennington, was founded in the 1930s as an experimental women's college. It later went co-ed and garnered a national reputation as a leading liberal-arts school with a special reputation for teaching writing: The Pulitzer Prize–winning poet W. H. Auden, novelist Bernard Malamud (*The Natural*), and novelist John Gardner all taught here. In the 1980s, Bennington produced a fresh wave of prominent young authors, including Donna Tartt, Bret Easton Ellis, and Jill Eisenstadt. The pleasant campus north of town is worth wandering; to get there, take the North Bennington Road (Rte. 67A) turnoff north of downtown (near the Bennington Square Shopping Center) and follow it about 2 miles north. There are also three attractive **covered bridges** near the college.

   "I Had a Lover's Quarrel with the World."

That's the epitaph on the tombstone of Robert Frost, who is buried in the cemetery behind the 1806 First Congregational Church where Rte. 9 makes two quick bends west of downtown and down the hill from the Bennington Monument. Signs point the way to the Frost family grave. Travelers often stop here to pay their respects to the man many still consider *the* true voice of New England. Closer to the church, look for the old tombstones—some decorated with urns and skulls—of other Vermonters who lived much less famous lives.

Vermont

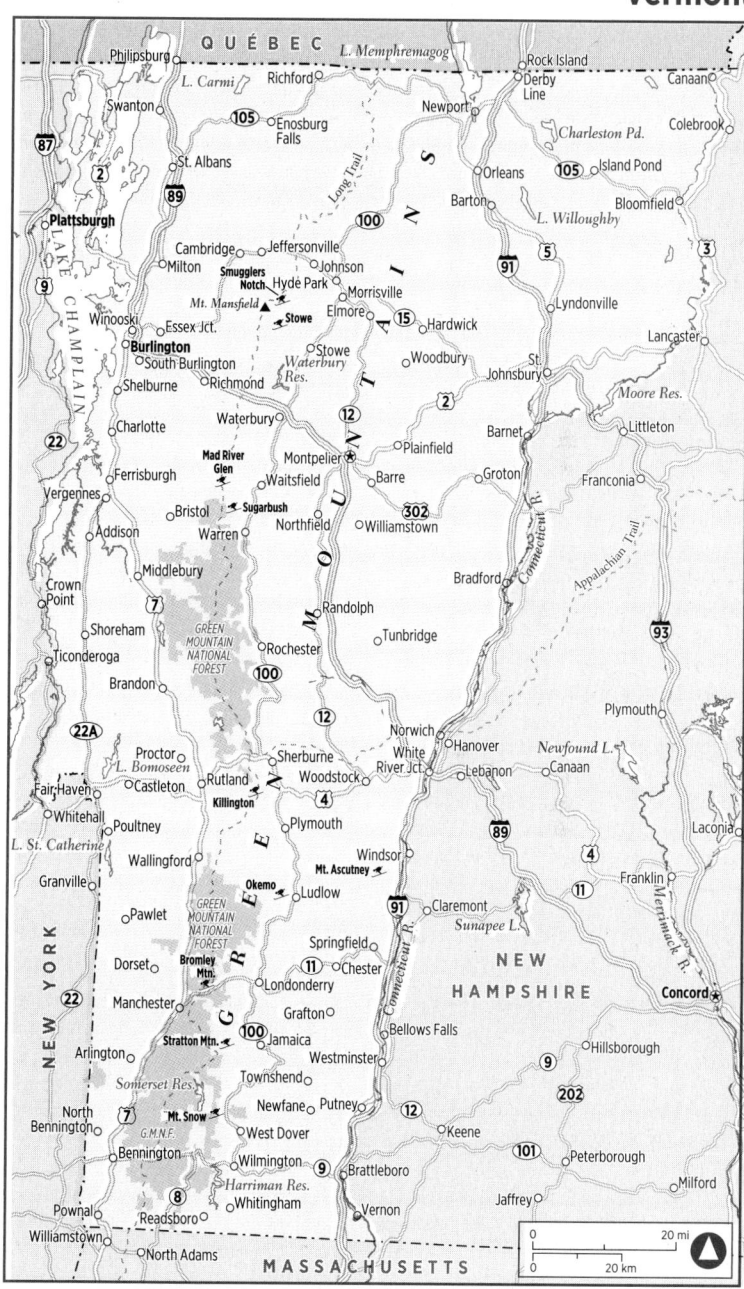

The Bennington Museum ★★ 👜 This eclectic and intriguing collection is one of the best small museums in northern New England. The museum traces its roots back to the 1850s, although it has occupied its current stone-and-column home overlooking the valley since "only" 1928. The expansive galleries here feature a range of exhibits on local arts and industry, including early Vermont furniture, glass, paintings, and Bennington pottery. Of special interest are the many colorful primitive landscapes by Grandma Moses (1860–1961), who lived much of her life nearby. (This museum has the largest collection of Moses paintings in the world.) There's also lots of American glass; a globe by James Wilson, the nation's first globe maker; a Windsor chair once owned by Ira Allen, who wrote the state's constitution; and a 1925 Martin Wasp luxury car. (Only 16 were ever made, hand-crafted in Bennington by Karl Martin between 1920 and 1925.) Rotating special exhibits bring in serious art that's sometimes unrelated to local history, such as a show of rarely shown works by Renoir, Monet, and Degas or a show of Haitian quilts. This is a great find.

75 W. Main St. (Rte. 9 btw. Old Bennington and the town center). © 802/447-1571. www.bennington museum.org. Admission $9 adults, $8 seniors and students, free for children 17 and under, $19 family. Nov–Aug Tues–Mon 10am–5pm; Sept–Oct daily 10am–5pm.

WHERE TO STAY

The Four Chimneys Inn ★★ This 1912 Colonial Revival catches your eye as you roll into Bennington from the west; it's right at the edge of Old Bennington, and the towering Bennington Monument looms just over its shoulder. Set back from Rte. 7 on a big, nicely landscaped lot, the three-story mansion features—no surprise—four prominent chimneys. Guest rooms are divided among the main inn, an ice house, and a carriage house; they're spare, whitewashed, and flower-printed rather than luxe, with rather simple furniture and dated carpeting. Still, some units sport real fireplaces burning real wood, and many have nice Jacuzzis, four-poster beds, and/or mountain views from patios. I like room no. 11 because it has its own private porch and more windows than most of the other units; the brick carriage house (room no. 9) has a cathedral-type ceiling. Upper-floor and ice-house units, on the other hand, feel a bit cramped because of the odd-angled ceilings. This place had been fading in recent years, but is improving once again under its pleasant new owners, Pete and Lynn Green (who also married at the inn).

21 West Rd. (Rte. 9, just west of downtown), Bennington, VT 05201. © 802/447-3500. Fax 802/447-3692. www.fourchimneys.com. 11 units. $125–$295 double. Rates include full breakfast. 2-night minimum stay foliage and holiday weekends. AE, DISC, MC, V. Children 12 and over accepted. **Amenities:** Dining room. *In room:* A/C, TV, hair dryer.

Paradise Inn ★ ☺ Paradise by the dashboard light? Maybe. This is perhaps Bennington's best motel, even if prices have shot up in recent years. It's clean and well managed and is walking distance to town. The tidy, generously sized accommodations are further bolstered by such surprising amenities as full kitchens in some of the suites, tennis courts, a heated pool, and a decent coffee shop. The very central location and neighborhood views aren't bad, either. Try to reserve a spot in the North Building, in spite of its dated 1980s styling—each unit has an outdoor terrace or balcony. The more up-to-date Office Building is done in Colonial Revival style. Furniture and carpeting are of the same quality/blandness as any midlevel chain business hotel.

141 W. Main St., Bennington, VT 05201. © 800/575-5784 or 802/442-8351. Fax 802/447-3889. www. theparadisemotorinn.com. 77 units. $70–$145 double; $110–$220 suite. AE, DISC, MC, V. **Amenities:**

Restaurant; exercise room; heated outdoor pool; 2 tennis courts; Wi-Fi (in lobby; free). *In room:* A/C, TV, kitchen (some units), Wi-Fi (some units; free).

South Shire Inn A locally prominent banking family hired architect William Bull in 1880 to design and build this Victorian home, with leaded glass on its bookshelves and intricate plasterwork in the main dining room. Five guest rooms in the main inn building are furnished with handsomely carved canopy or poster beds and working fireplaces (burning Duraflame logs, not wood); the two best rooms here are probably the former master bedrooms (Otto and Gold), with their king beds and tile-hearth fireplaces. Four newer, more modern guest rooms—with such names as Jim Dandy—are located in an adjacent carriage house. They each sport extra amenities and lovely exposed pine flooring (rooms in the main inn have all been carpeted). All four of these rooms have televisions with DVD players, ceiling fans, and Jacuzzis.

124 Elm St., Bennington, VT 05201. ℂ **888/201-2250** or 802/447-3839. Fax 802/442-3547. www.southshire.com. 9 units. $125–$185 double; foliage season $155–$265 double. Rates include breakfast. 2-night minimum stay during foliage season. MC, V. Not appropriate for children. *In room:* A/C, TV/DVD (some units), fridge (1 unit), hair dryer.

WHERE TO DINE

Alldays & Onions ★ AMERICAN This casual downtown eatery is named for a real company, an early-20th-century British car manufacturer (proprietors: William Alldays and John Onions). Why? I'm not sure. But I do know locals flock here to eat tasty sandwiches, salads, and soups; it's one of the town's go-to family restaurants. Expect anything from pot roast and turkey with the fixin's to seafood pasta, grilled steaks, burgers, and tortellini. More ambitious items might include a Southwestern-spiced steak or stir-fried soba noodles, but stick with traditional favorites. Breakfast, served on Saturday and Sunday only, is also good.

519 Main St. ℂ **802/447-0043.** www.alldaysandonions.com. Breakfast items $2–$8; sandwiches $3–$7; main courses $15–$19 at dinner. AE, DISC, MC, V. Mon–Wed 11am–3pm; Thurs–Fri 11am–3pm and 5–9pm; Sat 7:30am–3pm and 5–9pm; Sun 9am–1pm.

Blue Benn Diner ♪ DINER Diner fans make long pilgrimages to Vermont to eat at this 1945 Silk City classic—so classic it still has jukeboxes, and I remember the daily specials being Magic-Markered onto paper plates and hung up helter-skelter by the counter for years. (They finally got a printer to at least *print* them before hanging.) Those specials still often include vegetables, rice, soup or salad, rolls, and rice pudding with your entree. Fancy and vegetarian fare is sometimes available—think grilled portobello mushrooms on sourdough. But order any of the New England diner staples such as turkey with gravy, fried fish, yummy slabs of cornbread French toast, big delicious omelets, fruity pancakes, homemade doughnuts, or the signature dessert: butterscotch Indian pudding, served warm with a scoop of vanilla ice cream.

314 North St. (Rte. 7). ℂ **802/442-5140.** Breakfast $2–$6; sandwiches and entrees $2–$6; dinner specials $8–$10. No credit cards. Mon–Tues 6am–5pm; Wed–Fri 6am–8pm; Sat 6am–4pm; Sun 7am–4pm.

Pangaea ★★ INTERNATIONAL This upscale little culinary campus is a bit hard to find (tucked away in workaday North Bennington), but it's worth trying to locate. Chef/owner Bill Scully delivers good meals (using local and organic ingredients whenever possible) in five distinct dining spaces, including a tavern, a deli (across the street), and a fine-dining room. Start with something intriguing, such as Vermont boar-and-brie Wellington, spring rolls, or some fried oysters. Entrees could include a pan-roasted breast of Long Island duck, maple-glazed pork loin, steak frites, or seared diver scallops on a potato croquette; sauces are accented with hints of Asia and France. There's a cozy lounge next door, serving a lighter menu of burgers, pasta, cassoulet, salads, stir-fries, and beers that wouldn't be out of place in a Manhattan bar. The small card of desserts is notable, especially for the chocolate cake.

1-3 Prospect St., North Bennington. (✆**802/442-7171.** Lounge items $10–$21; main courses $19–$24. V, MC. Tues–Sun 5–9pm. From Bennington, go west on Rte. 9 a half-mile, turn right onto Rte. 67A near Hemmings, and continue 4½ miles to N. Bennington. Restaurant is in center of village.

Arlington, Manchester & Dorset ★★★

This string of closely spaced villages is Vermont at its *most* Vermont, making the area an ideal destination for a romantic getaway, antiquing trip, or even a serious outlet-shopping trip. All three towns are worth visiting, and each has its own unique charm and vibe; you can even visit all three in a single day if you sleep locally and get up early.

Arlington ★★ has a town center that borders on the microscopic. With its auto-body shop, hub-of-town gas station/convenience store, ice-cream shop, and redemption center (all remnants of a time when the main highway passed right through town), this is a real, functioning Vermont village. It also has a great riverside campground, an unusual number of good farmhouses-converted-into-inns on the surrounding roads, and Norman Rockwell. So there. It's about 8 miles south of the Manchesters, on Rte. 7A.

Manchester ★★★ (also sometimes called Manchester Village) and **Manchester Center** share a blurred town line and proximity, but maintain very different characters. The more southerly Manchester has an old-world, old-moneyed elegance and a prim, campuslike main street centered on the resplendently columned Equinox Resort. There's also a neat row of shops, a wonderful golf course, a town library, a former Lincoln home, and a fly-fishing museum. Just a mile and a half north along Main Street, Manchester Center is the major mercantile center for these parts; it almost feels like a small city, with its dozens of outlet stores (offering discounts on big-name clothing, accessories, and housewares), doughnut shop, big-box grocery store, golden-arched fast food, and surprising traffic jams at the main intersection.

Dorset ★★, an exquisitely preserved little village of white-clapboard architecture and marble sidewalks, is one last worthy visit when in the area. It's a bit farther north; to get there, follow Rte. 30 north out of Manchester Center for about 7 miles. You'll roll right into the center of town.

ESSENTIALS

GETTING THERE Arlington, Manchester, and Manchester Center all lie north of Bennington on Historic Rte. 7A, which runs parallel to and west of Rte. 7; you can take either route. Dorset is north of Manchester Center on Rte. 30, which diverges from Rte. 7A in Manchester Center.

VISITOR INFORMATION The **Manchester and the Mountains Regional Chamber of Commerce** (✆ **800/362-4144** or 802/362-2100; www.manchester vermont.net) maintains a year-round information center at 5046 Main St. (Rte. 7A N.), beside the small village green in **Manchester Center.** It's open Monday through Saturday from 10am to 5pm; from Memorial Day weekend through October, it's also open on Sundays from noon to 5pm and until 7pm on Friday and Saturday nights. If you're staying in **Arlington,** that hamlet maintains its own small self-serve visitor information center at the Stewart's gas station on Rte. 7A. Just take what you need.

For information on outdoor recreation, the **Green Mountain National Forest** maintains a district ranger office (📞 **802/362-2307**) in Manchester on Rte. 11/30, east of Rte. 7. It's open Monday through Friday from 8am to 4:30pm.

MUSEUMS & HISTORIC HOMES

American Museum of Fly Fishing ★★ 🎁 If you loved *A River Runs Through It,* you're probably crazy about fly-fishing, and you'll probably go crazy for this museum: It's home to the world's largest collection of angling art and items under one roof. The complex, which includes a gallery space, library, reading room, store, and historical resources, was specially built for the purpose. You can browse through an impressive collection of antique rods (including some owned by Daniel Webster, Ernest Hemingway, and Winslow Homer), reels, and 200-year-old flies, plus photos, instructional videos, sketchbooks, and historical items. (A Greek historian wrote of a fly-fishing-like practice in A.D. 200; who knew?) This is a surprisingly fun place to while away an hour; about the only thing missing is, well, fish. The museum is neatly positioned right between the Equinox and the Orvis fly-fishing store.

4104 Main St. (Rte. 7A), Manchester.📞 **802/362-3300.** www.amff.com. Admission $5 adults, $3 children 5-14. Tues–Sun 10am–4pm. Closed major holidays.

Hildene ★★ As you first drive up the pretty gravel road to this estate, you might not realize that you're face to face with U.S. history *and* natural history. Robert Todd Lincoln, son of the former U.S. president, summered in this stately 24-room Georgian Revival mansion between 1905 and 1926 and enjoyed showing off its remarkable features—including a sweeping staircase and a 1908 Aeolian organ with a thousand pipes (you can hear it played during the house tour). This place was built with an eye toward quality, rather than showiness or stuffiness. Lincoln also had formal gardens (designed after the patterns in a stained-glass window) planted on a gentle hill outside, with outstanding views of the flanking mountains—one of southern Vermont's most popular wedding spots every summer and fall. The home and lovely, expansive grounds can be viewed only on group tours that start at an informative visitor center; budget 2 to 3 hours for the tour plus extra time exploring the pretty grounds and diversions. (In summer, there are fun wagon rides to the Hildene farm for $1, and cross-country skiing and snowshoeing are allowed with admission to the grounds in winter.)

Historic Rte. 7A (just south of Equinox Resort), Manchester. 📞 **802/362-1788.** www.hildene.org. Admission to grounds only $5 adults, $3 children 6-14; house tours $13 adults, $5 children, free for children 5 and under. Daily 9:30am–4:30pm.

Southern Vermont Art Center ★★ This fine-art center is well worth the short detour from town to find it. Located in a striking Georgian Revival home surrounded by more than 400 hillside acres overlooking land that once belonged to fly-fishing magnate Charles Orvis, the center consists of a series of galleries displaying works from its well-regarded collection, as well as frequently changing exhibits of contemporary Vermont artists. An inventive and appealing modern building across the driveway displays even more of the permanent collection. Check the center's schedule before you arrive; you may be able to sign up for an art class or workshop while you're in town. Also, leave time to enjoy a light lunch at the **Garden Cafe** and

481

wander the lovely grounds, exploring both the sculpture garden and the woods beyond.

West Rd., Manchester. ℂ **802/362-1405.** www.svac.org. Admission $8 adults, $3 students, free for children 12 and under. Tues–Sat 10am–5pm; Sun noon–5pm. From Equinox Resort, bear left onto West Rd. at the Reluctant Panther inn, and continue approx. 1 mile.

SKIING

Bromley Mountain Ski Resort ★ ☺ Bromley is a great place to learn to ski if you don't already know how. Gentle and forgiving, the mountain features long, looping, intermediate runs that are tremendously popular with families and beginners; *SKI* magazine once named it the second-best ski destination in the entire country for families. The slopes are mostly south-facing, which means they receive the warmth of the sun and protection from the harshest winter winds. There's one ski school here for kids ("Mighty Moose"), another for adults; the base-lodge scene here is mellower than at many other resorts; and the experience is nearly guaranteed to be relaxing. Even snowboarders and telemark skiers are made to feel very welcome. This is *not* a fancy-pants resort, however, and there are no quintuple-diamond, by-the-seat-of-your-pants runs here; if you crave that, bypass Bromley.

3984 Rte. 11, Peru (P.O. Box 1130, Manchester Center, VT 05255). ℂ **866/856-2201** or 802/824-5522. www.bromley.com. Adult lift tickets $39–$68 day, $55–$58 half-day; discounts for youths and seniors.

Stratton Mountain Ski Resort ★★ Founded in the 1960s, Stratton labored in its early days under the belief that Vermont ski areas needed to be Tyrolean to be successful—hence the Swiss-chalet feel of the architecture. For awhile this mountain felt like Vail's poor country cousin. In recent years, though, Stratton has worked to shed its image as a haven of alpine quaintness. In a bid to attract a younger, edgier set, new owners spent more than $25 million in improvements, mostly in snowmaking. Now this mountain is consistently ranked among the nation's best-groomed by skiers, and also picks up big kudos for its lifts, dining choices, and customer service. The slopes here are especially popular with snowboarders; expert skiers should check out Upper Middlebrook, a twisting run off the summit.

5 Village Lodge Rd., Stratton Mountain, VT 05155. ℂ **800/787-2886** or 802/297-4000. www.stratton.com. Adult lift tickets $72–$84, $59–$71 half-day; discounts for seniors, children, and any lift tickets bought online.

OTHER OUTDOOR ACTIVITIES

HIKING & BIKING Scenic hiking trails ranging in difficulty from "very challenging" to "easy-as-an-after-dinner-stroll" can be found in the hills a short drive from town. At the Green Mountain District Ranger Station in Manchester (see "Visitor Information," above), ask for the free brochure listing hiking trails easily reached from the town.

A scenic drive 30 to 40 minutes northwest of Manchester Center takes you to the **Delaware and Hudson Rail-Trail,** approximately 20 miles of which have been built in two sections in Vermont. The southern section of the trail runs about 10 miles from **West Pawlet** to the state line at **West Rupert,** over trestles and past vestiges of former industry, such as the old Vermont Milk and Cream Co. Like most rail-trails, this one is perfect for exploring by mountain bike. You'll bike sometimes on the original ballast, other times through grassy growth. To reach the trail head, drive north on Rte. 30 from Manchester Center to Rte. 315, then continue north on Rte. 153. In **West Pawlet,** park across from the old-timey general store (a good place to pick up refreshments), then set off on the trail southward from the old

D&H freight depot across the street. The trail also passes through **Lake St. Catherine State Park** in **Poultney.**

The hills around Manchester are full of other great touring rides, too; your headquarters should be **Battenkill Sports Bicycle Shop** (*C* **800/340-2734** or 802/362-2734), at 1240 Depot St., in downtown Manchester Center. It's a wonderful little place, with free local bike maps, great bikes for sale, and a range of rentals from hybrids to touring cycles to mountain bikes ($30 per day; locks and helmets are included).

CANOEING   For a duck's-eye view of the rolling hills, stop by **BattenKill Canoe Ltd.** (*C* **800/421-5268** or 802/362-2800; www.battenkill.com) at 6328 Rte. 7A (about halfway btw. Arlington and the Equinox Resort). This friendly outfit offers daily canoe rentals for exploring the Battenkill River and surrounding areas. Trips range from 2 hours to all day, and the firm specializes in multiple-night, inn-to-inn canoe packages. The shop is open daily in season (which runs from about May–Oct) from 9am to 5:30pm, and Wednesday through Friday only during the rest of the year—but check ahead if you're coming during those months.

FLY-FISHING   Why not learn from the best? Aspiring anglers can sign up for fly-fishing classes taught by skilled instructors affiliated with **Orvis** (*C* **800/235-9763**), the famous fly-fishing supplier and manufacturer based in Manchester. The shop's 1- and 2-day classes ($235 per person per day, with occasional two-for-one deals) include instruction in knot-tying and casting, plus some catch-and-release fishing on a company pond and the Battenkill River. Classes are held from late April until mid-October. Room rate discounts are sometimes available at the Equinox Resort (see "Where to Stay," below) for visiting Orvis students.

WHERE TO STAY

The choices below mostly fall into the "luxury country inn" category, but there are plenty of other options in this valley, too.

Barnstead Inn ★ 🍴   If you're feeling shell-shocked by local room rates, consider this place within walking distance of Manchester's commercial center. Most of the guest rooms are housed in an 1830s hay barn; many are decorated in a rustic country style, some exposing the barn's burnished old beams. Expect vinyl bathroom floors, industrial carpeting (but at least it's *nice* carpeting), and a mix of motel-modern and antique furnishings in most rooms. The most interesting units include the two above the office (with two double beds, and showing off those beams) and any of the pricier suites—including the renovated Green River Suite, with a lovely fireplace of big, hand-laid stones, Persian-style rugs, a kitchenette, and a two-person Jacuzzi. A few rooms here are even priced at less than $100, which is remarkable. (On the other hand, a few of those suites nearly touch $300.) All in all, a good value and one of the closest lodgings to the outlet mall.

349 Bonnet St. (P.O. Box 988), Manchester Center, VT 05255. *C* **800/331-1619** or 802/362-1619. www.barnsteadinn.com. 15 units. $89–$165 double, $110–$299 suite; foliage-season rates higher. MC, V. Children 13 and over welcome. **Amenities:** Outdoor pool. *In room:* A/C, TV, hair dryer, Wi-Fi (free).

Barrows House ★   Within easy strolling distance of Dorset is this compound of eight Early American buildings, set on 12 landscaped acres studded with birches, firs, and maples. Built in 1784, the main house has been an inn since 1900, and its white exterior is most beautiful when the lawn is also blanketed with white snow.

The inn's primary distinctions are its historical lineage and convenience to the village; the rooms are more comfortable than elegant, with sturdy dressers, bedside tables, and the like. (Some readers have mentioned that certain buildings are not aging well.) Some units have gas or wood fireplaces, while several cottages (one of which doubles as the pool house) offer additional space and privacy for families. This place will definitely please history and Rockwell buffs; those looking for luxury amenities, though, might prefer a place in Manchester Village. The inn's superb **restaurant** (p. 487) serves a clubby menu of upscale Continental cuisine—roast duck, salmon, seared tuna, grilled steaks, lobster rolls—in a nicely glassed-in dining room.

Rte. 30, Dorset, VT 05251. Ⓒ**800/639-1620** or 802/867-4455. Fax 802/867-0132. www.barrowshouse. com. 28 units. $125–$195 double; $150–$255 suite and cottage. Rates include breakfast. MAP plans also available. 2-night minimum stay Sat–Sun and some holidays. AE, DISC, MC, V. Pets allowed in 2 cottages ($20 per night). **Amenities:** Restaurant/bar; bikes; heated outdoor pool; sauna; 2 tennis courts. *In room:* A/C, TV (some units), fridge (2 units), no phone (1 unit).

Dorset Inn ★★ Set in the center of genteel Dorset, this three-story former stage-coach stop was built in 1796 and claims to be the oldest continuously operating inn in Vermont. With more than two dozen rooms, it's large as Vermont inns go, yet very professionally run by its newest owners, the Bryants—who also own the **Mountain Top Inn & Resort** in Mendon (p. 510). Prices are surprisingly reasonable given the competition in Manchester, and the Bryants have upgraded everything from room decor to the restaurant. Guest rooms, some located in a well-crafted addition next door that dates from the 1940s, are named for famous local people and places (Frost, Saddleback, Marsh, Owls Head). They're furnished in upscale country style, in a mix of reproductions and antiques, including some canopy and sleigh beds. All units are air-conditioned, though a few still lack televisions and most don't have telephones; about one-quarter have Jacuzzi tubs, sitting rooms, and fireplaces. The excellent **restaurant and tavern** (see "Where to Dine," below) feature Chef Thom Simonetti's use of local and regional ingredients. A small, newish day spa provides treatments and pampering.

8 Church St. (at Rte. 30), Dorset, VT 05251. Ⓒ**877/367-7389** or 802/867-5500. Fax 802/867-5542. www.dorsetinn.com. 25 units. $185–$425 double. Rates include full breakfast. MAP plans available. Packages available. AE, MC, V. Pets allowed by prior permission ($25 per night). Children 6 and over welcome. **Amenities:** Restaurant; bar; spa. *In room:* A/C, TV (most units), Wi-Fi (in all but 2 units; free), no phone (most units).

The Equinox Resort & Spa ★★★ Now owned by the HEI hotel group, the venerable Equinox is changing with the times, yet it remains a longtime New England favorite. Its white clapboard and stately columns define Manchester and southern Vermont. The place's roots date to 1769, but don't be misled: This is a modern resort complete with a full-service spa, lovely indoor pool, scenic golf course, free business center, and extensive sports facilities. Rooms are moderately sized but have just been retouched by a multimillion-dollar renovation project; think earth tones, new linens, and custom-made beds. The resort also owns and has upgraded the nearby **1811 House** (which had been one of the best B&Bs in the state)—a place of cozy rooms, authentically uneven pine floors, and antique furniture—as well as the adjacent **Charles Orvis Inn.** Suites in the Orvis Inn are big and modern, and use of a private billiards room is included. The resort offers plenty of activities on its 1,300-plus acres of grounds, including skeet shooting, falconry (see "Handling Birds of a Feather," below), and guided hikes up beautiful (but steep) Mount Equinox. Of the resort's three restaurants, the **Chop House** (see "Where to Dine," below) is best, but only operates half of each week. **The Marsh Tavern** is nearly as good and opens daily, serving both pubby and formal lunches and dinners, while the **Falcon Bar** is not to be missed—an outdoor brazier has recently been added, making it a convivial place to sip drinks beneath the stars.

3567 Rte. 7A (P.O. Box 46), Manchester Village, VT 05254.© **800/362-4747** or 802/362-4700. Fax 802/362-4861. www.equinoxresort.com. 183 units. Main inn peak season $299–$449 double, $449–$849 suite; off season $169–$399 double, $399–$649 suite; Charles Orvis Inn $499–$899 suite. AE, DISC, MC, V. **Amenities:** 3 restaurants; bar; babysitting; bikes; concierge; golf course; exercise room; indoor and outdoor pools; room service; sauna; spa; 3 tennis courts. *In room:* A/C, TV, hair dryer, Wi-Fi (free).

The Inn at Manchester ★★ 👬

It looks like just another Vermont residence outside, but this is a special B&B. Built in the late 19th century, the structure was converted to an inn in 1978. It's just a half-mile from the budget shopping that draws so many to Manchester, yet also nearly within sight of the village, resort, and golf course. I've yet to ever meet anyone with a bad word to say about this place, from the location to the rooms to the amazing hospitality. Rooms are in the main inn and an adjacent carriage house dating from the mid-1800s, both decorated with art and sculpture from around the world. The public spaces are whitewashed and lovely, with fireplaces, staircases, and wingback chairs tucked throughout its various corners and angles. Most of the 18 rooms and suites have televisions (no phones, though) and some also have poster beds and/or good direct views of Mount Equinox. All units feel clean and fresh, with distinctive looks—the Sage Suite is popular for its walk-out deck, sitting room, whirlpool tub, and that Equinox view. Owners Frank and Julie Hanes are as helpful as can be; their dog, Chai, is described as a "furball of joy." Four acres of gardens and grounds, a brook, and a lazy front porch complete the peaceful experience.

3967 Main St. (Rte. 7A), Manchester Village, VT 05254.© **800/273-1793** or 802/362-1793. Fax 802/362-3218. www.innatmanchester.com. 18 units. $155–$235 double; $205–$295 suite. Rates include full breakfast. AE, DISC, MC, V. **Amenities:** Outdoor pool. *In room:* A/C, TV (most units), hair dryer, Wi-Fi (free), no phone.

Palmer House Resort Motel ★

What is a "resort motel"? Well, it's *not* a resort. But it *is* several notches above the run-of-the-mill motels that dot southern Vermont, and this place has long been surprisingly popular given the fancier and cheaper options in the valley. Owned and operated by the same family for about a half-century, its rooms are furnished with antiques and other unexpected niceties; ask for one of the somewhat larger rooms in the newer rear building if you value space. In 2000, 10 spacious suites were added, each with a king bed, sitting room, gas fireplace, two-person Jacuzzi, and private deck overlooking a trout-stocked pond and the mountains beyond—these are much more expensive than regular rooms, and somewhat bland, but they will do as a romantic retreat when the luxury inns in town are booked solid. The buildings are set on 22 nicely tended acres, and the motel even has its own small par-3 golf course. (There's no charge—just walk into the office and get some clubs.)

5383 Main St. (Rte. 7A), Manchester Center, VT 05255.© **800/917-6245** or 802/362-3600. Fax 802/362-3600. www.palmerhouse.com. 50 units. $95–$185 double; $190–$300 suite. 2-night minimum stay some weekends. AE, DISC, MC, V. Children 12 and older welcome. **Amenities:** 9-hole, par-3 golf course; exercise room; Jacuzzi; 2 pools (1 outdoor, 1 heated indoor lap); sauna; 2 tennis courts. *In room:* A/C, TV, fridge, hair dryer, Wi-Fi (free).

The Reluctant Panther ★★★ New owners took over this luxury inn, a quick walk from the Equinox, in the fall of 2005—and a month later, the historic main house burned to the ground. Unbelievably, it reopened within a year and is now a true luxury inn, where once stood a quirky B&B with a '70s vibe. Gone is the all-purple paint job; all rooms now sport a fireplace (or two), whirlpool tub, thick duvets, fluffy robes, and flatscreen TVs. In the main house, the woodsy Akwanok room is furnished with Orvis nightstand lamps and a birch headboard handcrafted in the Adirondacks, while Lady Slipper sports a claw-foot Jacuzzi and king poster bed. Other rooms are decorated according to themes, too: horses in the John Morgan Suite; flowery murals in the Florist Suite; green hues in the Fallen Spruce Suite. In the outbuildings, I like the Garden Suite's living room and see-through fireplace, as well as the expansive Panther Suite's four-poster bed, grandiose bathroom, and regal, columned Jacuzzi. The Pond View Suite, in the carriage house, is bigger than many Vermont cottages. The dining room (see "Where to Dine," below) is outstanding; a pub menu is also served on a patio (weather permitting) and in the Panther Pub.

17–39 West Rd., Manchester Village, VT 05254. ©**800/822-2331** or 802/362-2568. Fax 802/362-2586. www.reluctantpanther.com. 20 units. $179–$759 suite. Rates include full breakfast. AE, DC, DISC, MC, V. Pets allowed on limited basis ($50 per night). **Amenities:** Restaurant; pub; exercise room. *In room:* A/C, TV/DVD/CD, hair dryer, Wi-Fi (free).

West Mountain Inn ★★ Sitting atop a grassy bluff at the end of a dirt road a half-mile from Arlington center, this rambling, white-clapboard building with the stone walkway is extremely appealing when you approach it. The farmhouse dates back a century and a half, and it's a perfect spot for travelers looking to find that "real" Vermont inn. Guest rooms, named for famous Vermonters, are nicely furnished in country antiques and Victorian reproductions; they vary widely in size and shape, but even the smallest has lots of charm and character. The expansive Rockwell Kent Suite offers a four-poster canopy bed in a very wood-paneled bedroom, plus a wood-burning fireplace in a sitting room with French-style couches. A delightful little wood cottage in back has been divided up into three units (the living room is shared among guests), and three town houses have also been carved out of a former millhouse (wow, this *is* Vermont) on the grounds. These feature TVs, river views and, in one case, a kitchen. There's a hundred-year-old post-and-beam barn on the grounds, often rented for weddings and reunions, and the 150 acres of meadows are good for exploring. In addition to the included breakfast (optionally, you can skip it for a discount in the town houses), the dining room also serves hearty regional dinners nightly in a wood-paneled dining room. Nice place.

River Rd. (at Rte. 313), Arlington, VT 05250. ©**802/375-6516.** Fax 802/375-6553. www.westmountain inn.com. 20 units. $175–$310 double; town houses $185–$299. Rates include full breakfast except for town houses. MAP plans available. 2-night minimum stay Sat–Sun. AE, DISC, MC, V. **Amenities:** Restaurant. *In room:* A/C, TV (some units), kitchenette (some units), Wi-Fi (in inn units; free) , no phone.

WHERE TO DINE

In addition to the selections below, most of the inns listed above offer good to excellent dinners on site in their dining rooms, often in romantic settings. For informal dining or a beer, locals head for **Mulligan's** (© 802/362-3663), a pubby family eatery on Rte. 7A near the Equinox Resort. I also like to pick up a dozen sinkers for the trip home at **Mrs. Murphy's Donuts** (© 802/362-1874), a locals-only spot on the outlet strip.

Barrows House Restaurant ★★ CONTINENTAL Chef Lauren Wilcox delivers inn cuisine that's better than it has to be at this Dorset compound's house eatery (see "Where to Stay," above), infusing everything with Continental sensibilities. Example: You can begin with Maine crab cakes or a creamy seafood chowder full of New England veggies—but you can also start with a sweet-pea vichyssoise, Kahlúa-crusted brie, or an unusual leek crème brûlée. Daring indeed. The menu includes both small plates and entrees. The small plates (which are rather pricey) range from mini racks of lamb with a Vermont goat cheese–pistachio crust to half-servings of beef tenderloin, veal piccata, shellfish strudel, and the like. Entrees run to roasted duck, full racks of lamb, prime rib, and salmon. And watch for such great rotating seasonal specials as mushroom-cheese bisque, fruit gazpacho, diver scallops, summer lobster rolls, coconut-curried shrimp, seared tuna, salmon *en croute,* or a grilled rib-eye with a brandy and peppercorn demi-glace and buttermilk-battered onion rings.

Rte. 30, Dorset (in Barrows House).ⓒ **800/639-1620** or 802/867-4455. www.barrowshouse.com. Small plates $14–$20; main courses $22–$35. AE, MC, V. Daily 8–9:30am (to 10am Sun) and 5:30–9pm.

Chantecleer ★★★ CONTINENTAL If you enjoy top-rate Continental fare, but are put off by the stuffiness of Euro-wannabe restaurants, this is the place for you. Rustic elegance is the best description for Chantecleer, which cooks some of the best food in southern Vermont—inside a century-old dairy barn! Just outside Dorset, the restaurant's tidy exterior doesn't hint at how pleasantly romantic the interior is, even if it feels almost Pennsylvania Dutch. (Ignore the mounted cow's head above the bar; Baumann bought it at a local antiques shop.) The owner, Swiss chef Michel Baumann, changes his menu frequently. Appetizers lean toward seafood, especially shellfish (mussels, oysters, and escargot). For the main course, he might feature a pistachio-encrusted rack of Colorado lamb one night, roasted duckling with a berry sauce or medallions of duck and venison another. Whatever you eat, you must finish with Baumann's delicious "Matterhorn" sundae—Vermont ice cream shingled with toasted hazelnut nougatine and topped with Swiss and French hot fudges.

Rte. 7A (3½ miles north of Manchester Center), East Dorset.ⓒ **802/362-1616.** www.chantecleerrestaurant. com. Reservations recommended. Main courses $28–$45. AE, MC, V. Wed–Sun 6–9pm. Closed 1st 3 weeks of Nov and Apr to mid-May.

The Chop House ★★★ STEAK Truly great steakhouses are thin on the ground in Vermont (family-style restaurants, on the other hand, are everywhere). Therefore, foodies noted with interest the 2008 opening of this mostly steak restaurant in the Equinox Resort (see "Where to Stay," above) in Manchester Village, a resort that strangely had lacked a fine-dining option until now. Top chef Jeffrey Russell broils the expected porterhouses, rib-eyes, and filet mignons—get the excellent house sauce on the side—bakes potatoes, creams spinach. All good. And, smartly, he draws from the deep well of excellent cheeses and meats available from Vermont's own artisanal producers. But Russell also sets up strong appetizers that would be right at home on a Manhattan menu: chilled lobster cocktails, iceberg wedge/blue cheese salads, bisque, and one of the best mozza-tomato salads anywhere outside of Italy or New Yawk.

3567 Rte. 7A, Manchester Village (in the Equinox Resort).ⓒ **800/362-4747** or 802/362-4700. Reservations recommended. www.equinoxresort.com. Main courses $18–$65. AE, MC, V. Thurs–Sun 5–10pm.

Dorset Inn Restaurant ★★ NEW AMERICAN The Dorset Inn's (see "Where to Stay," above) restaurant and tavern are newly conceived, with a new chef and a "slow food"–themed kitchen that plays the Vermont down-home card wisely and well. This is New England home cooking, trumped up and heavily incorporating the great seasonal foods available within the state's borders. Start with smoked local pheasant with apple pâté, PEI mussels, Maine crab cakes, or a plate of locally crafted cheese. Or go off the map by ordering fries with bourbon ketchup. Entrees are solidly New England: roasted turkey croquettes with peas, mashed potatoes, gravy, and cranberry sauce; burgers of local beef; a three-meat meat loaf; slow-cooked lamb stew; chicken pappardelle; and a roasted-corn polenta with local ricotta, veggies, and red-pepper pesto. Desserts are also stellar and (mostly) regional, from maple-pumpkin cheesecake with candied walnuts to apple crumble, crème brûlée, and New England bread pudding with maple. You can even order a bowl of Ben & Jerry's. Brunch, unusually, is served from Friday through Sunday and with a Cajun accent.

8 Church St. (Rte. 30), Dorset (in the Dorset Inn). © **877/367-7389** or 802/867-5500. www.dorsetinn. com. Reservations recommended. Brunch items $12–$16, main courses $14–$28. AE, MC, V. Mon–Thurs 8–9:30am and 5–9pm; Fri–Sun 8am–2pm and 5–9pm.

Little Rooster Cafe ★ ✦ DINER   You've got to love a place where the seats are painted like birds' nests. They really take the farm motif to the extreme at this spot near the outlets and the traffic circle, but they add gourmet twists as well. Breakfast choices might include Cajun omelets, corned-beef hash (with béchamel sauce!), or flapjacks with Vermont maple syrup (natch). Lunchtime features creative sandwiches—a good roast beef sandwich with sauerkraut and a horseradish dill sauce, for instance. This is the best non-inn spot in town for eggs, pancakes, or a filling lunch, and quite affordable.

Rte. 7A S., Manchester Center. © **802/362-3496.** Breakfast and lunch items $4.50–$8.50. No credit cards. Daily 7am–2:30pm. Closed Wed in off season.

Mistral's at Toll Gate ★★ FRENCH   This place is a little hard to find, a left turn off Rte. 11/30 as you ascend east into the mountains above Manchester Center. But it's worth it. The best tables are along the windows, which overlook a lovely creek spotlighted at night. Inside the tollhouse of a long-since-bypassed byway, the restaurant is a romantic mix of modern and old. The French menu changes seasonally, with dishes that might range from fish to cannelloni stuffed with lobster to a grilled piece of filet mignon served with a Roquefort-stuffed ravioli. This kitchen is run with skill by the chef and his wife, who have been doing an admirable job since before foodies discovered Vermont; plenty of *Wine Spectator* awards testify to that.

Toll Gate Rd. (east of Manchester off Rte. 11/30), Manchester Center. © **802/362-1779.** Reservations recommended. Main courses $22–$32. AE, MC, V. July–Oct Thurs–Tues 6–9pm; Nov–June Thurs–Mon 6–9pm.

The Reluctant Panther ★★★ NEW AMERICAN   This award-winning dining room—part of the renovation of the inn by the same name (see "Where to Stay," above)—has become one of the best fine-dining options in Manchester. The handsome dining space looks out onto Mount Equinox and a small pond; waitstaff are professional; and the cuisine never disappoints. The kitchen reaches for and attains a high level with cuisine that's both New American and Continental, with flair (and plenty of wine sauces). Starters could include such things as tuna tartare with an avocado cream, hearty soups, a risotto of truffles and green peas, or a blue-cheese tart. For the main course, you might choose from a mint- and vanilla-rubbed loin of lamb, pan-seared pheasant, butter-poached Maine lobster over freshly made fettuccine, braised pork cheeks, or a sea of pan-seared diver scallops swimming around an island of cauliflower "cloud" topped with seared spinach and a truffle. Desserts are stunning and beautifully presented; the wine list is long and well chosen, though predominantly of California vintages.

17–39 West Rd., Manchester Village. © **800/822-2331** or 802/362-2568. www.reluctantpanther.com. Reservations required. Main courses $22–$32. AE, DC, DISC, MC, V. Tues–Sat 5:30–9:30pm.

SHOPPING

Manchester Center has one of the best concentrations of outlet shops in New England, both in terms of the number of shops in a compact area (it's very walkable and parkable, so you won't get tired) and the quality of the merchandise.

Among the designers and retailers with outlet shops here are: Brooks Brothers, Coach, Betsey Johnson, Cashmere Mill Shop, BCBG Max Azria, Giorgio Armani, Kate Spade, Polo Ralph Lauren, and Theory; good stuff, with something for shoppers young and old. Most of the shops are in little mini mall clusters in and around the busy little intersection at the heart of town. Hungry from shopping and window-shopping? In season there's an outdoor stand scooping **Ben & Jerry's** ice cream, and a brand new cafe serves good sandwiches, lunches, and coffee to the shopped-out masses.

If your interests include fishing or rustic, outdoorsy fashion, though, head instead for **Orvis,** the Manchester-based local company that has crafted a worldwide reputation for manufacturing top-flight fly-fishing equipment and the associated gear. The massive, wood-framed **Orvis Company Store ★★★** (© **802/362-3750**) in between Manchester and Manchester Center sells housewares, men's and women's clothing—both for daily wear and sturdy outdoor use—plus, of course, more fly-fishing equipment than you'll ever need. Two small ponds just outside the shop allow prospective customers to try the gear before buying. A sale room, with even more deeply discounted items, is directly behind the main store.

BRATTLEBORO & THE SOUTHERN GREEN MOUNTAINS

Brattleboro: 105 miles NW of Boston; 148 miles SE of Burlington

The hills and valleys around the bustling town of **Brattleboro,** in Vermont's southeast corner, have some of the state's best-hidden treasures. Driving along the main valley floors—on roads along the West or Connecticut rivers, or on Rte. 100—tends to be only moderately interesting. To really soak up the region's flavor, then, turn off the main roads and wander up and over rolling ridges into the narrow folds of mountains hiding peaceful villages. If it looks as though the landscape hasn't changed all that much in the past 2 centuries, you're right. It really hasn't.

The Wilmington / Mount Snow Region ★

Wilmington has a nice selection of antiques shops, boutiques, and pizza joints. Except on busy holiday weekends, when it's inundated by visitors driving oversized SUVs, it feels like a gracious mountain village untroubled by the times. From Wilmington, the ski resort of **Mount Snow** is easily accessible to the north via Rte. 100, which is brisk, busy, and close to impassable on sunny weekends in early October. Heading north, you'll first pass through **West Dover,** an attractive classic New England town with a prominent steeple and acres of white clapboard.

Looking for More Information?

The best source of information for this region is the big, state-operated **Guilford Welcome Center** (📞 **802/254-4593**) on I-91 just south of Brattleboro (just north of the Massachusetts border). Open 24/7/365, this attractive, cathedral-ceilinged building was inspired by Vermont's barns—it even has a weather vane on top! It's practically a tourist command post, filled with maps, brochures, and videos on activities in the region. Helpful staffers are on hand to dole out up-to-the-minute information, make reservations in a pinch, and otherwise guide you through the wonders of southern Vermont, but they're never pushy about it. The vending machines and spotless bathrooms within are an oasis for weary travelers with kids or infants; outside, there are often bake sales in good weather. One complaint: You can reach here only from the interstate, and only when coming from the south.

ESSENTIALS

GETTING THERE   Wilmington is at the junction of routes 9 and 100. Rte. 9 offers the most direct access. The Mount Snow area is north of Wilmington on Rte. 100.

VISITOR INFORMATION   The **Mount Snow Valley Chamber of Commerce** (📞 **877/887-6884;** www.visitvermont.com) maintains a visitor center on West Main Street. Open daily year-round from 10am to 5pm, the chamber offers a room-booking service, which is helpful for booking smaller inns and B&Bs; they also put together a comprehensive guide to the region. (To investigative or book on-the-mountain accommodations, however, it's best to check directly with **Mount Snow's** lodging bureau at 📞 **800/451-4211** or 800/245-7669.)

THE MARLBORO MUSIC FESTIVAL

The renowned **Marlboro Music Festival ★★★** is a series of summertime classical concerts, performed by accomplished masters as well as by highly talented younger musicians, on weekends from mid-July through mid-August in the agreeable village of **Marlboro,** east of Wilmington on Rte. 9. The musical retreat was founded in 1951 and has hosted countless noted musicians (including Pablo Casals, who participated between 1960 and 1973). Concerts take place in the 700-seat auditorium at Marlboro College, and advance ticket purchases are strongly recommended; call or write for a schedule and a ticket order form. Ticket prices usually range from about $15 to $35 per concert. Between late August and mid-June, contact the festival's winter office at 1616 Walnut St., Ste. 1600, Philadelphia, PA 19103 (📞 **215/569-4690**); in summer, write Marlboro Music at Box K, Marlboro, VT 05344, or call the box office at 📞 **802/254-2394.** The website is **www.marlboromusic.org**.

DOWNHILL SKIING

Mount Snow ★   Mount Snow is noted for its widely cut runs on the front face of the mountain (disparaged by some skiers as "vertical golf courses"), yet it still remains an excellent destination for intermediates and advanced intermediates. More advanced skiers migrate to the North Face, another world of bumps and open glades. This is also a great spot for snowboarding. Because it's the closest Vermont ski area to Boston and New York (about a 4-hr. drive from Manhattan), the mountain can get more crowded than other Vermont hills on weekends—maybe that's why the resort's lift-ticket prices have surged in recent years? But Mount Snow's village is attractively arrayed along the base of the mountain; the most imposing structure is a balconied hotel overlooking a small pond, but the overall character here is still shaped mostly by unobtrusive smaller lodges and homes. Once famed for a groovy singles scene, the hill's post-skiing activities have mellowed somewhat and embraced the baby-boomer and family markets, though 20-somethings can still find a good selection of après-ski activities.

39 Mount Snow Rd., West Dover, VT 05356.© **800/245-7669** or 802/464-3333. www.mountsnow. com. Adults $69–$75 day lift tickets, $54–$60 half-day; discounts for youths and seniors.

WHERE TO STAY

The Mount Snow area has a surfeit of lodging options, ranging from basic motels to luxury inns and slope-side condos; rates in most of them drop quite a bit in summer, when the region slips into a pleasant lethargy. In winter, though, the high prices reflect the relatively easy drive from New York and Boston.

The best phone call to make first is to **Mount Snow's lodging line (© 800/451-4211** or 800/245-7669) to ask about vacation packages and condo accommodations.

Deerhill Inn ★★   The Deerhill Inn, on a hillside above Rte. 100 in West Dover with views of the rolling mountains, was built as a ski lodge in 1954, but subsequent innkeepers have given it more of a country gloss. Though the building is aging and isn't *quite* a "luxury inn," it's trying hard and it's more than acceptable as a rustic overnight in these parts. In summer, the property features attractive gardens and a nice stonework pool; in winter, the ski slopes are just a short drive away. Guest rooms vary from the small and cozy to the spacious, some with Jacuzzis and/or flatscreen TVs; several more are located in a motel-like annex (these rooms all have balconies). The Tamarack Room features a king bed, double Jacuzzi, and attractive stone fireplace; Dahlia has a Jacuzzi, small fireplace, and walk-out private deck. The "garden" rooms are cheaper and less luxe, but maybe more Cape Cod–charming. Dining-room fare, available only to inn guests, is a highlight (the wine cellar is impressive), and all guests can use the two upstairs sitting rooms stocked with books.

14 Valley View Rd. (P.O. Box 136), West Dover, VT 05356.© **800/993-3379** or 802/464-3100. Fax 802/464-5474. www.deerhill.com. 14 units. $145–$295 double; $240–$345 suite. Rates include breakfast. 2-night minimum stay Sat–Sun. AE, MC, V. Children 8 and over welcome. **Amenities:** Dining room; bikes; outdoor pool. *In room:* TV/DVD/CD, Wi-Fi (free), no phone.

The Inn at Sawmill Farm ★★★   The Inn at Sawmill Farm is spread over 28 acres on a former dairy farm, and it was one of the very first inns in New England to cater to affluent travelers. The very impressive wine cellar is a tip-off to what's to come at the inn, which has been in the same family ever since opening 40 years ago. Buildings and guest rooms on this property, some of which date back as far as 1797, are distinctive and cohesive, yet all were updated in contemporary country styling and Colonial reproduction furniture even as the room count was gradually doubled. There are now 10 rooms in the main house, four in an adjacent farmhouse, and three in former sheep's quarters, plus an entire carriage house and two cottages you can rent entirely. Many now have flatscreen TVs and/or whirlpool tubs. Among the most interesting units are the Victorian, flowery Cider House No. 2, with its rustic beams, marble double Jacuzzi, and oversized canopy bed, and the Woodshed, a quiet wooden cottage with cathedral ceiling, whirlpool tub, small loft, plenty of windows overlooking the woods and pond, and private deck for breakfasting. The Carriage House, the most expensive unit, is a small, pond-side home with a brick wood-burning fireplace, huge sleigh bed, and a wraparound deck. Standard rooms here, though, are similar to upscale inn rooms elsewhere in Vermont: king beds and tons of flowery wallpaper and well-worn Vermont charm, without the jetted tubs or modern amenities. All rates include breakfast, afternoon tea, and outstanding five-course dinners (see "Where to Dine," below). This place is not to be missed if you can pay the freight.

7 Crosstown Rd. (P.O. Box 367), West Dover, VT 05356. *Ⓒ***800/493-1133** or 802/464-8131. Fax 802/464-1130. www.theinnatsawmillfarm.com. 20 units. Midweek $325–$425 double, $475–$625 suite; Fri-Sat $390–$525 double, $575–$750 suite plus 15% service charge. Rates include breakfast, afternoon tea service, and dinner. AE, DC, MC, V. Closed Apr–May. **Amenities:** Restaurant; exercise room; outdoor pool; tennis court. *In room:* A/C, TV (most units), hair dryer, Wi-Fi (most units; free).

Vintage Motel ★ ✎ This motel gives you a taste of the "real" Vermont: the thrifty one. A budget choice for travelers planning to spend little time in their rooms, the Vintage features basic units that are actually quite nice-looking with industrial carpeting, TVs, phones, and durable furniture. There's a common room with a microwave and VCR, and this is one of the few motels I've seen with a driving range right on-site. In winter, the place fills up with skiers and with local and visiting snowmobilers: A major trail passes through the motel's backyard.

195 Rte. 9 (P.O. Box 222), Wilmington, VT 05363. *Ⓒ***800/899-9660** or 802/464-8824. www.vintage motel.net. 17 units. $45–$85 double; $100–$200 suite. Rates include continental breakfast on weekends and holidays only. MC, V. 2-night minimum stay on Fri-Sat; 3 nights some holidays. Pets allowed in 3 units ($15 per pet). **Amenities:** Driving range; outdoor pool. *In room:* TV, fridge (some units), Wi-Fi (free).

Windham Hill Inn ★★★ Now a member of the exclusive Relais & Châteaux network, this inn is about as good as it gets if you're in search of a romantic Vermont getaway. Situated on 160 acres at the end of a dirt road in a high upland valley in West Townshend (about 20 miles/30 min. from Mount Snow), the inn was built in 1823 as a farmhouse and remained in the same family until the 1950s, when it was converted into an inn. Guest rooms are wonderfully appointed in elegant country style and floral prints, many with Jacuzzis or soaking tubs; balconies or decks; and gas fireplaces—and *all* of the rooms have good views. There isn't a bad room on the property, but especially nice are the Jesse Lawrence Room on the third floor, with its lovely modern soaking tub, plush chairs, cherry pencil-poster king bed, and gas stove; and Forget-Me-Not, on the second floor, which has a similar setup plus a window nook. An annex (the White Barn) contains eight units, the choicest of which is the great top-floor Meadowlook with lots of windows, fieldstone fireplace, soaking tub beneath a skylight, double shower—oh, and a big, open private deck. The inn's superb **dining room ★** features creative Continental and New American cooking; outside, the pastoral acreage includes 6 miles of groomed cross-country ski trails.

311 Lawrence Dr., West Townshend, VT 05359. *Ⓒ***800/944-4080** or 802/874-4080. Fax 802/874-4702. www.windhamhill.com. 21 units. $215–$295 double; $365–$465 suite. Rates include full breakfast. 2- to 3-night minimum stay Sat–Sun and some holidays. AE, DISC, MC, V. Turn uphill at West Townshend country store and continue uphill 1¼ miles to dirt road (Lawrence Dr.); turn right and continue to end. Children 12 and over welcome. **Amenities:** Restaurant; Internet (in lobby; free); outdoor heated pool; tennis court. *In room:* A/C, hair dryer.

WHERE TO DINE

Dot's ★ 🏷 DINER   Wilmington is proud of Dot's, a Main Street (literally) institution that has stubbornly remained loyal to its longtime clientele by continuing to serve good, inexpensive food in the face of the bistro-ization of the rest of the village. This is your classic Vermont diner, from the cool neon sign right down to the pine paneling, swivel stools at the counter, and checkerboard-patterned linoleum tiles. It's regionally famous for its chili (kicked up with jalapeño peppers), but other good choices include great pancakes, French toast, shakes, daily chicken specials, hot open-faced sandwiches, and the Cajun skillet: a medley of sausage, peppers, onions, and fries sautéed and served with eggs and melted Jack cheese. There's now a second, newer Dot's—known as "Dot's of Dover"—in **Dover** (**ℂ 802/464-6476**), 7 miles north on Rte. 100.

3 E. Main St., Wilmington.**ℂ 802/464-7284.** Breakfast items $3–$7, lunch and dinner items $3–$13. DISC, MC, V. Daily 5:30am–8pm (to 9pm Fri–Sat).

The Inn at Sawmill Farm ★★ CONTINENTAL   More than 20,000 bottles of wine fill the wine cellar of this top-rated inn (see "Where to Stay," above), which has earned a coveted "Grand Award" from *Wine Spectator* magazine and stocks a big selection of oh-so-fine Latours, Margaux, and various Burgundies. The wine is one of the reasons the house restaurant consistently attracts well-heeled diners. Chef/proprietor Brill Williams often incorporates game (rabbit, pheasant, venison) into the menu, in true French tradition; also look for choices like roasted poussin stuffed with shallots, a salmon filet with a sorrel cream sauce, or potato-encrusted sea bass with mushrooms—even something off-the-wall like the long-popular Indonesian curried chicken breast. The signature dessert is a sundae of dark chocolate, butter, and nut sauce. This isn't the best inn dining in the state, but it's good, and the barn/farmhouse atmosphere is romantic. Bring your wallet, though—you'll spend a lot here. (Nonguests should ask for a menu version with prices listed.)

7 Crosstown Rd., West Dover.**ℂ 800/493-1133** or 802/464-8131. www.theinnatsawmillfarm.com. Reservations recommended. Main courses $28–$39. AE, DC, MC, V. Daily 6–9:30pm. Closed Apr–May.

Brattleboro ★

Set in a scenic river valley, the commercial town of **Brattleboro** is more than just a wide place in the road to fill the gas tank and stock up on provisions (though some parts of town do lend themselves best to that). In fact, this compact, hilly former mill town has a funky, slightly dated charm; its rough brick textures have aged well, although you will note a suspiciously high concentration of ex–flower children who moved here, grew up, cut their hair, and settled in to operate many local enterprises and institutions—some with a New Age-y tinge.

ESSENTIALS

GETTING THERE   There's no airport nearby, but Brattleboro is easily accessible by car via exits 1 and 2 on **I-91.** From the east or west, Brattleboro is best reached via **Rte. 9,** which comes in from Albany and Bennington to the west and Keene, New Hampshire, to the east. From New York City via Hartford, it's about 3 hours without traffic, up to 4 hours with traffic.

Brattleboro is a stop on **Amtrak**'s (**ℂ 800/872-7245;** www.amtrak.com) oncedaily *Vermonter* service from Washington, D.C., and New York to northern Vermont. From New York's Penn Station, the ride takes about 5½ hours and costs $48 oneway; from Washington's Union Station, it's about 9 hours and $103 per person.

Brattleboro's own Union Station sits by the river in a stone building at 10 Vernon Ave. (Rte. 142), just downhill from Main Street's concentration of shops.

Greyhound (℃ **800/231-2222**; www.greyhound.com) also stops in Brattleboro, running two buses daily from New York's Port Authority bus terminal. The ride takes 5½ hours and costs $60 one-way, but as little as $44 if nonrefundable and booked online. The bus station is tucked away behind a Citgo gas station in the Rte. 5/9 traffic circle on the north side of town (about 2½ miles from the train station).

A handy, free black-and-white shuttle bus known as the **MOOver** (℃ **802/464-8487**; www.moover.com)—it's spotted to look remarkably like a cow (don't you love Vermont??)—connects the two stations two or three times a day. I repeat: This combination of dairy goodness and liberal social programming could *only happen in Vermont*. Use it.

VISITOR INFORMATION   The **Brattleboro Chamber of Commerce** office, at 180 Main St. (℃ **877/254-4565** or 802/254-4565; www.brattleborochamber.org), dispenses tourist information when it's open for business (Mon–Fri 8:30am–5pm; closed holidays).

EXPLORING THE TOWN

Here's a useful two-phase strategy for exploring Brattleboro: Park. Walk. The commercially vibrant downtown is blessedly compact, and strolling it is the best way to appreciate its human scale and handsome commercial architecture. A town of cafes, bookstores, antiques stores, and outdoor recreation shops, it invites casual browsing without an itinerary.

A good stop for kids and curious adults is the **Brattleboro Museum & Art Center** ★ (℃ **802/257-0124**; www.brattleboromuseum.org), housed inside the city's 1916 train station at 10 Vernon St. (Rte. 142), near the bridge to New Hampshire. Wonderful exhibits here highlight the history of the city and the Connecticut River Valley, and there's also plenty of both classic and contemporary sculpture and art from local and regional artists. The museum is open Thursday through Monday, 11am to 5pm (closed in Mar). Admission costs $6 for adults, $4 for seniors, $3 for students, and free for children 5 and under.

OUTDOOR PURSUITS

The **Vermont Canoe Touring Center** (℃ **802/257-5008**), open seasonally, is at the intersection of Rte. 5 and the West River north of town. This is a great spot to rent a canoe or kayak to poke around for a couple of hours, half a day, or a full day. Explore locally, or arrange for a shuttle upriver or down. The owners are helpful about providing information and maps to keep you on track. Among the best spots, especially for birders, are the marshy areas along the lower West River and a detour off the Connecticut River, known locally as "the Everglades" (insert tongue-in-cheek *here*). Get a gourmet sandwich to go at the Brattleboro Food Co-op (see "Where to Dine," below) and make a day of it.

Bike rentals and advice on day-trip destinations are available at the **Brattleboro Bicycle Shop,** 165 Main St. (℃ **800/272-8245** or 802/254-8644; www.bratbike. com). Hybrid bikes, ideal for exploring area back roads, can be rented by the day or week. It's open daily from spring through summer, closed Sundays in fall, and closed Sundays and Mondays in winter.

WHERE TO STAY

Budget-priced chain motels flank Rte. 5 north of Brattleboro, especially around the Rte. 5/9 traffic circle leading to Keene, New Hampshire. Most of these are quite impressive, more on the order of truck stops; the best choice here is probably the **Hampton Inn Brattleboro,** 1378 Putney Rd. ((© **800/426-7866** or 802/254-5700; www.hamptoninn.com). But it isn't as cheap as most of the other motel options.

Fortunately, **inns** abound in this part of Vermont, and some are priced quite affordably.

Chesterfield Inn ★★ About a 10-minute drive east of Brattleboro in New Hampshire, this attractive inn sits in a field just off the busy state highway; but inside, it's quieter and more refined than you would expect. The original farmhouse dates to the 1780s but has been expanded and modernized. Nine guest rooms are located in the main inn, plus six more in cottages nearby; all are spacious and comfortably appointed in a mix of modern and antique furniture, plus a fridge, CD player, television, and phone. The two priciest units have fireplaces, double Jacuzzis, and private decks with mountain and meadow views, but more than half of the other rooms *also* have fireplaces burning either wood or gas. The inn's chef also serves dinner 6 nights a week to guests and nonguests alike; see "Where to Dine," below, for details.

20 Cross Rd. (Rte. 9), W. Chesterfield, NH 03466.© **800/365-5515** or 603/256-3211. Fax 603/256-6131. www.chesterfieldinn.com. 15 units. $175–$345 double. Rates include breakfast. 2-night minimum stay foliage season and holidays. AE, DC, DISC, MC, V. Pets welcome in 6 back units. **Amenities:** Restaurant; babysitting. *In room:* A/C, TV, CD player, fridge, hair dryer, minibar, Wi-Fi (free).

Colonial Motel & Spa *🗲* Operated by the same family for 3 decades, this sprawling compound set back from Rte. 5 is well maintained and offers the best value in town; choose it over the chain motels back in town. Opt for the back building's larger, quieter rooms, furnished with armchairs and sofas. Free local calls are included with your room, and there's a cozy lounge and basic restaurant on-site. But this motel's best feature is its 75-foot indoor lap pool in the spa building, where there's also a sauna and a simple fitness center. A second pool is maintained outdoors for those hot summer afternoons.

Putney Rd., Brattleboro, VT 05301.© **800/239-0032** or 802/257-7733. www.colonialmotelspa.com. 68 units. $60–$85 double; $85–$140 suite. Rates include continental breakfast (Mon–Fri only). AE, DISC, MC, V. Take exit 3 off I-91; turn right and continue ½-mile. **Amenities:** Restaurant; bar; exercise room; Jacuzzi; 2 pools (1 indoor lap, 1 outdoor); sauna. *In room:* A/C, TV, Wi-Fi (free).

Latchis Hotel This downtown hotel fairly leaps out in Victorian-brick Brattleboro. Built in 1938 in understated Art Deco style at one of the city's busiest intersections (right at the foot of the commercial district), the Latchis was once the cornerstone for a small chain of hotels and theaters. It no longer has its own orchestra or commanding dining room, but the movie theater (showing great films) remains, and the place still has an authentic—if at times outdated-feeling—flair. Some units have been upgraded over the past few years, with newer furnishings and sunny art prints on the walls; other rooms and hallways, however, are badly showing their age. About two-thirds of the rooms have limited views of the river, though those views include the sounds of cars crawling down Main Street early every morning. If you need quiet, sacrifice the views and ask for a room in back. You can walk to the museum, food co-op, or shops of Main Street from here without breaking a sweat.

50 Main St., Brattleboro, VT 05301. ©**800/798-6301** or 802/254-6300. www.latchis.com. 30 units. $80–$170 double; $145–$200 suite. Rates include continental breakfast. AE, MC, V. **Amenities:** Restaurant. *In room:* A/C, TV, fridge, hair dryer, Wi-Fi (free).

WHERE TO DINE

In addition to the choices listed below, the subterranean coffee shop **Mocha Joe's** ★ (© **802/257-7794;** www.mochajoes.com), at 82 Main St., is a collection point for locals. It sports a friendly, laid-back vibe, brews a good cup of joe or espresso, and pours fresh-squeezed "-ades" in the summer. Expect a few dudes with weird beards, a few workmen, a few geeks, and some local purveyor of quartz crystals or art. Try the maple latte if you're craving something different.

Brattleboro Food Co-op ★ 📱DELI   Selling wholesome foods since 1975, this huge store also has a deli counter great for takeout meals. Grab a quick and filling lunch that won't *necessarily* be tofu and sprouts—you can also get a smoked turkey and Swiss-cheese sandwich or a crispy salad. Check out the eclectic selection of wines and cheeses as well as the natural bath products (some locally made) and the hand-cut steaks in the butcher section. Sausages are made and stuffed on premises, too, and the place is renowned for "case lot specials:" deep discounts on oversized quantities of health food. (Stash a case of organic cheese puffs in the trunk for the road.) The store section stays open until 9pm every night, a boon in early-closing Vermont. The co-op, located in a small strip mall downtown near the New Hampshire bridge, has lots of parking—though the mini mall plaza is hard to notice as you whiz downhill and around the town's main bend.

2 Main St. (in Brookside Plaza, on right at bottom of Main St. hill). ©**802/257-0236.** www.brattleboro foodcoop.com. Sandwiches $3.50–$6, prepared foods usually around $4–$5 per lb. MC, V. Mon–Sat 8am–9pm; Sun 9am–9pm.

Chesterfield Inn ★★CONTINENTAL   Chesterfield Inn chef Robert Nabstedt buys fish from the Boston market, adds local vegetables and game, and serves up dining room fare that's better than it has to be at this inn a few miles northeast of Brattleboro, just across the state line in West Chesterfield, NH.. This doesn't feel like New Hampshire at all (except for the emphasis on game, maybe). Feast on items like tea-smoked duck breast served over sesame and peanut-flavored soba noodles; grilled swordfish with a wasabi-Key lime vinaigrette; maple- and bourbon-basted barbecued shrimp over an autumn risotto; seared scallops over pappardelle; an elk *osso bucco* with ragout; herb-encrusted racks of lamb; or even a vegetarian Thanksgiving meal of baked, maple-glazed acorn squash stuffed with a cranberry-pumpkin seed stuffing. Finish with cinnamon-espresso crème brûlée, apple-berry crisp, chocolate cake, or a piece of Kentucky Derby pie.

20 Cross Rd. (Rte. 9), West Chesterfield, NH. ©**800/365-5515** or 603/256-3211. www.chesterfieldinn. com. Reservations recommended. Main courses $19–$29. MC, V. Mon–Sat 5:30–9pm.

Peter Havens Restaurant ★AMERICAN/SEAFOOD   You're likely to feel at home right away in this locally popular dining spot, which has just 10 tables. Housed in a pleasantly contemporary building, the kitchen might or might not bowl you over (quality seems uneven at times, entree to entree), but you'll be impressed by the menu of choices at least. The kitchen has perhaps moved even more in the direction of seafood than it had leaned before (though that has always been a specialty of the place) with a change in ownership; scallops, oysters, mussels, and seared tuna are now just as likely—no, more so—to be the night's star as duck or steak. The bar is convivial and popular, but make a reservation if you're visiting on a weekend: The place gets packed with a mix of locals and tourists.

32 Elliot St. ✆ **802/257-3333.** www.peterhavens.com. Reservations strongly recommended. Main courses $19–$24. MC, V. Tues–Sat 6–9pm.

T. J. Buckley's ★★ NEW AMERICAN   Brattleboro's best restaurant, little T. J. Buckley's, is housed in a classic old diner on a dim side street—but this is *far* from diner food. Instead, it's kitchen theater. Renovations such as slate floors and golden lighting have created an intimate space that seats fewer than 20 when full; no secrets exist among the chef, sous-chefs, and server, all of whom remain within a couple dozen feet of each other and you throughout the meal as they cook and serve it and you gape in awe. (The whole place—kitchen plus seating—is smaller than the kitchens of most other restaurants.) Iconoclastic chef/owner Michael Fuller's menu is always limited, with just a few entree choices each night, but the food nearly always dazzles in its execution. Expect the usual New American appetizers and entrees: beet carpaccios, wondrous pâtés, crab, seared scallops, steak, duck, and fish-of-the-day dishes—all beautifully prepared and presented, sometimes more adventurously than you might expect. (Whatever Fuller feels like making, he makes—*his* way.) **Note:** The tab for a dinner party of three or more *will* run into the hundreds, so hit a bank first (well, not in the John Dillinger sense) and bring a wad of big bills.

132 Elliot St. ✆ **802/257-4922.** Reservations strongly recommended. Main courses $27–$35. No credit cards. Winter Thurs–Sun 6–9pm; rest of year Wed–Sun 6–9pm.

Grafton ★★★

One of Vermont's most scenic and well-preserved villages, **Grafton** was founded in 1763 and soon grew into a thriving settlement. But as the agriculture and commerce shifted west and to bigger cities, Grafton became a shadow of a town—by the Depression, many of the buildings here were derelict.

Then something remarkable happened. In 1963, Hall and Dean Mathey of New Jersey created the Windham Foundation and began purchasing and restoring the dilapidated center of town, including the old hotel. This foundation eventually came to own some 55 buildings and 2,000 acres around town—even the cheese cooperative was revived. The village sprung back to life, and it's now teeming with history buffs, antiques hounds, and tourists (instead of farmers and merchants). The Windham Foundation has taken great care in preserving this gem of a village, even to the point of burying utility lines so as not to mar the village's landscape with wires.

ESSENTIALS

GETTING THERE   Take I-91 to Bellows Falls (exit 5 or 6), and follow signs to town via Rte. 5. From here, take Rte. 121 west for 12 miles to Grafton. Or for a more scenic route, follow Rte. 35 north from Townshend for about 3 miles, take the left fork, and continue 7 more miles into Grafton.

VISITOR INFORMATION   Grafton's informal **information center** is located in a gift shop inside the Grafton Inn's Daniels House, adjacent to the Daniels House Cafe (it's right behind the Old Tavern). The town also maintains a somewhat basic website at **www.graftonvermont.org**.

EXPLORING THE TOWN

Grafton is best seen at a slow pace, on foot, when the weather is welcoming. A picnic is a good idea, especially if it involves a chunk of the excellent local cheddar. Unfortunately, none of the grand (and privately owned) historic homes you see in the village are open for tours; it's a village to be enjoyed with aimless walks outdoors. Don't expect to be overwhelmed by grandeur, but keep a keen eye out for telling historical details.

Start at the **Grafton Village Cheese Co. ★** (*℃* **800/472-3866;** www.grafton villagecheese.com), a small, modern building where you can buy a snack of the great, award-winning cheese and peer through plate-glass windows to observe the cheese-making process. (No tours are allowed for sanitary reasons.) It's open daily, 10am to 5pm. Sometimes they sell big wheels of the cheese at deep discounts, too.

From the cheese shop, follow the trail over a nearby covered bridge, and then bear right on the footpath along a cow pasture to the cute **Kidder Covered Bridge.** Head into town via Water Street, and then turn onto Main Street. In the village center, white clapboard homes and shade trees abound, about as New England as it gets.

On Main Street, stop by the **Grafton Historical Society Museum ★** (*℃* **802/843-1010;** www.graftonhistory.org)—open Friday to Monday from Memorial Day through Columbus Day (and daily during foliage season)—to peruse photographs, artifacts, and memorabilia of Grafton. The suggested donation is $3 per adult. Afterward, have a look at **The Old Tavern at Grafton ★★**, the impressive building that anchors the town and has served as a social center since 1801. Partake of a beverage at the rustic Phelps Barn Lounge or a meal in one of the dining rooms. (There's also an inn here; see "Where to Stay," below.) From here, make your way back to the cheese factory by wandering along pleasant side streets. Or if you'd like to see Grafton from a different perspective, inquire at the inn about a horse-and-buggy ride.

WHERE TO STAY

If you're seeking a more luxurious experience than the two inns I've listed below, the wonderful **Windham Hill Inn** (p. 492) is only about 15 miles away in **West Townshend.** From Grafton, take either Rte. 35 S. or Rte. 121 E.; the inn is just off Windham Hill Road.

The Old Tavern at Grafton ★★ This beautiful, well-managed historic "inn" is actually a series of rooms spread throughout the village. Only about a dozen rooms are in the handsome, colonnaded main building, which dates from 1801 (and has slightly sloping corridors as a result), while the remainder are in the nearby Homestead and Windham properties across the road. All are decorated in antiques, Americana themes, and some upscale design touches (mostly; all rooms have phones, but none have televisions). These rooms are far from basic B&B digs. Room nos. 6 and 8 feature lovely, bridal-looking white canopies over the beds. Units in Windham "Cottage" are similar to those in the main building; again you find a number of snow-white canopy beds. Units in the Homestead "Cottage" (which isn't a cottage at all, but rather two historic homes joined together), on the other hand, have more of a modern, hotel-like character. Ask the hotel staff about the clock at the entrance. Finally, the Cricketers Suite is in yet another building, and has a small refrigerator, coffeemaker, and whirlpool tub where toddlers are welcome. In all, six units have suite-like layouts.

Rtes. 35 and 121 (P.O. Box 9), Grafton, VT 05146.© **800/843-1801** or 802/843-2231. Fax 802/843-2245. www.old-tavern.com. 30 units. $150–$245 double; $195–$400 suite. Rates include breakfast. MAP plan available. 2- to 3-night minimum stay on winter weekends, holidays, and in foliage season. AE, MC, V. Closed Mar to mid-Apr. Children 4 and under welcome in Homestead Cottage and Cricketers Suite. **Amenities:** Restaurant; pub; bikes; Jacuzzi; swimming pond; tennis court. *In room:* Fridge (1 unit), Wi-Fi (most units; free).

WHERE TO DINE

The Old Tavern, above, also has dining on-site.

Curtis' All American Restaurant ★ 🎁 AMERICAN   This place has all the atmosphere of a break room at an auto shop, but the great ones always do. Sarah (daughter of a southern Vermont pit master) and her partner serve up chopped pork and chicken; smoked brisket (Fri nights only); beers and wines from a bar; side dishes like loaded-up potato skins; and a weekend buffet that's all-you-can-eat. Feels like I've gone to heaven, or at least back to north Georgia. "Southern" doesn't get any better than this in the North, folks; do not miss this place if you're passing through. They even have a kids' menu.

908 Rte. 103 S., Chester.© **802/875-6999.** Main courses $4–$14. MC, V. Wed–Thurs and Sun 11am–8pm; Fri–Sat 11am–9pm.

WOODSTOCK & ENVIRONS ★

Woodstock: 16 miles W of White River Junction; 140 miles NW of Boston; 98 miles SE of Burlington

For more than a century, the resort community of **Woodstock** has been considered one of New England's most exquisite villages, and its attractiveness has benefited from the largesse of some of the country's most affluent citizens. Even the surrounding countryside is mostly unsullied—it's pretty difficult to drive here via any route that *isn't* pastoral and scenic, and by the time you're here you're already feeling as if you're in another era. Few New England villages can top Woodstock for grace and elegance; the tidy downtown is compact and neat, populated by a handful of shops, galleries, and boutiques. The lovely village green is surrounded by handsome homes, creating what amounts to a comprehensive review of architectural styles of the 19th and early 20th centuries. You could literally throw a stone (but don't) from the town center and hit a very attractive covered bridge.

In addition to Woodstock, this region also takes in nearby **White River Junction, Quechee,** and **Norwich,** three towns of distinctly different lineages along the Connecticut River on the New Hampshire border. In fact, while here you'll also want to cross that river over to **Hanover, New Hampshire** (p. 567), a lovely town that's also home to brainy, beery Dartmouth College.

Woodstock ★★

Much of Woodstock is on the National Register of Historic Places already, and—as if that weren't enough—the Rockefeller family deeded 500 acres surrounding **Mount Tom** (see "Hiking," below) to the National Park Service just to protect even *more* of it from developers. Downtown Woodstock could probably be renamed "Rockefeller National Park," for all the attention and cash that family has lavished on it. (Yes, Rockefeller money also built the faux-historic Woodstock Inn and paid to bury unsightly utility lines around town to preserve its character.)

The village, on the banks of the gently flowing Ottaquechee River, was first set-tled in 1765 and rose to prominence as a publishing center at one time: No fewer than *five* newspapers were being published in this tiny town in 1830. It soon began to attract wealthy families seeking cool solace from the big-city summers. To this day, Woodstock feels as though it should have a prestigious prep school right off the green, and it comes as a real surprise that it doesn't. A Vermont senator, in the late 19th century, said "the good people of Woodstock have less incentive than others to yearn for heaven," and that still (partly) applies today.

The town is also a center for winter outdoor recreation. In fact, the very first ski tow (a rope tow powered by, yes, an old Buick motor) in the U.S. was built in 1933 at the Woodstock Ski Hill near the present-day Suicide Six ski area. There are no huge mountains hereabouts, and maybe that's why this is no longer the center of Vermont's skiing universe (I guess Stowe is)—but that's actually a good thing. Low-key Woodstock is getting more upscale, no doubt about it, but it remains one of my 10 favorite small towns in New England: a great place in summer, winter, or fall to hike, bike, skate, cross-country ski, snowshoe, or simply window-shop or leaf-peep.

ESSENTIALS

GETTING THERE   Woodstock is located 13 miles west of White River Junction on Rte. 4 (take exit 1 off I-89). It's about 20 miles due east of Killington and Rutland, also via Rte. 4.

VISITOR INFORMATION   The **Woodstock Area Chamber of Commerce,** 18 Central St. (*©* **888/496-6378** or 802/457-3555; www.woodstockvt.com), staffs a helpful information booth on the green, open daily from June through October. If you can't make it there (but you can, really), the chamber's website is a great quick reference to all the key local sights, eats, and inns—with hyperlinks. (If you don't know what a hyperlink is, go to the green.)

EXPLORING THE TOWN

The heart of the town is the shady, elliptical **Woodstock Green.** The famous Admiral George Dewey spent his later years in Woodstock, and some local wags might try to convince you that the green was laid out in the shape of Dewey's flagship. This seems like a plausible explanation for the cigar-shaped green—but it's false. The green was already here—and shaped that way—in 1830, 7 years before Dewey was born. Oh, well. Maybe it clinched his decision to move here.

Anyway, you can learn much more about local history by wandering into the **Woodstock Historical Society ★** (*©* **802/457-1822;** www.woodstockhistorical. com) at 26 Elm St. Housed in the 1807 **Charles Dana House,** this beautiful home has rooms furnished in Federal, Empire, and Victorian styles, and has displays of dolls, costumes, and early silver and glass. The Dana House museum and adjoining buildings with more exhibits are open to the public, but only from late June through the end of October and only Friday to Sunday, noon to 4pm. Admission is $5 to the Dana House (which includes tours on the hour), or $3 to view only the gallery and barns sections, which are open the same dates but only until 3pm.

Billings Farm and Museum ★★★ ☺   This remarkable working farm offers a striking glimpse into a grander era when Vermont was still Rockwellian—as well as an introduction to the oddly interesting history of scientific farming. This farm museum was the creation of Frederick Billings, a native Vermonter who was credited

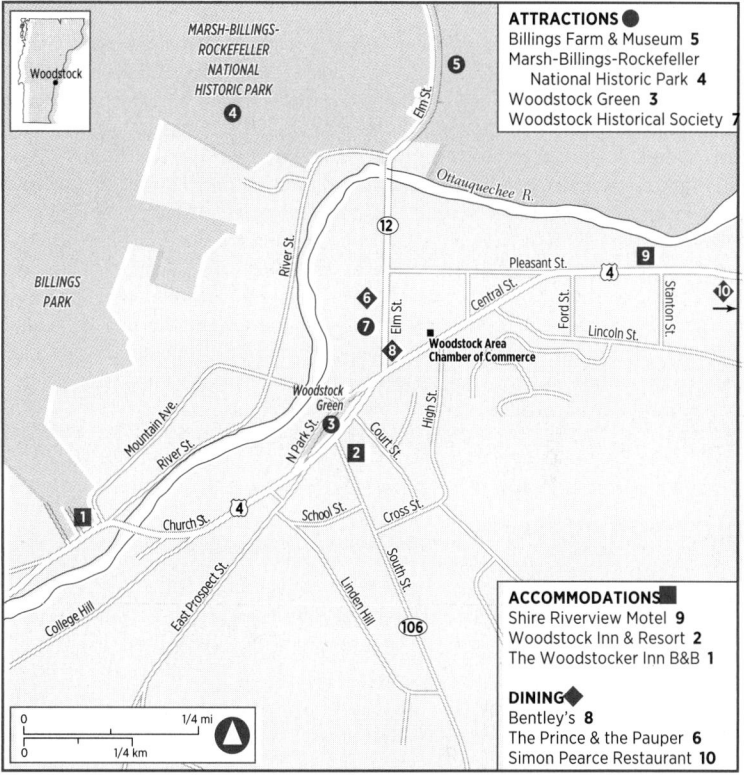

MARSH-BILLINGS-
ROCKEFELLER
NATIONAL
HISTORIC PARK
4

Woodstock

Elm St.

Ottauquechee R.

12

Pleasant St.

4

9

10

BILLINGS
PARK

River St.

6

7

Elm St.

Central St.

Ford St.

Stanton St.

Lincoln St.

■ Woodstock Area
Chamber of Commerce

8

Mountain Ave.

River St.

Woodstock
Green

3

N Park St.

Court St.

High St.

2

1

Church St.

4

School St.

Cross St.

South St.

College Hill

East Prospect St.

Linden Hill

106

0   1/4 mi
0   1/4 km

ATTRACTIONS ●
Billings Farm & Museum **5**
Marsh-Billings-Rockefeller
    National Historic Park **4**
Woodstock Green **3**
Woodstock Historical Society **7**

ACCOMMODATIONS ■
Shire Riverview Motel **9**
Woodstock Inn & Resort **2**
The Woodstocker Inn B&B **1**

DINING ◆
Bentley's **8**
The Prince & the Pauper **6**
Simon Pearce Restaurant **10**

with completing the Northern Pacific Railroad. (Billings, Montana, is named after him.) Billings returned home to create a managed forest along the principles of the pioneering ecologist George Perkins Marsh, who was born right here in Woodstock and once lived on this estate. As a 19th-century dairy farm, it was renowned for its scientific breeding of Jersey cows (and also its fine architecture, particularly its gabled 1890 Victorian farmhouse). A tour includes hands-on demonstrations of farm activities, exhibits of farm life, a look at an heirloom kitchen garden, and a visit to active milking barns. Programs for kids include wagon rides, preschool activities, and sleigh rides; there are also many holiday events. Because they're so close to each other, adults would do well to buy the 2-day combination ticket granting admission to the farm and the national historic park (see below).

River Rd. (approx. a ½-mile north of town on Rte. 12; P.O. Box 489), Woodstock. © **802/457-2355.** www.billingsfarm.org. Admission $12 adults, $11 seniors, $6 children 5–15, $3 children 3–4, free for children 2 and under; combination ticket with national historic park $17 adults, $13 seniors. May–Oct, Sat–Sun of Thanksgiving weekend, and Christmas week daily 10am–5pm; rest of the year Sat–Sun 10am–5pm.

Marsh-Billings-Rockefeller National Historic Park ★★★ Billings Farm and the National Park Service have teamed up to manage this newer park, the first and only national park focused on the history of conservation. It's more or less right across the street from the Billings Farm (see above), and is closely related. Here you'll learn more about the life of George Perkins Marsh, the author of *Man and Nature* (1864), one of the first and most influential books in the history of the environmental movement. You'll also learn more about how Woodstock native/rail tycoon Frederick Billings, who read *Man and Nature,* eventually returned and purchased Marsh's boyhood farm, putting into practice many of the principles of stewardship Marsh espoused. The property was later purchased by Mary and Laurance Rockefeller, who in 1982 established the nonprofit farm; a decade later, they donated more than 500 acres of forest land and their elaborate Victorian mansion, filled with exceptional 19th-century landscape art, to the Park Service. Visitors can tour the mansion, walk the graceful carriage roads surrounding Mount Tom, and view one of the oldest professionally managed woodlands in the nation. Mansion tours accommodate only 12 people at a time, so advance reservations are highly recommended; check in at the visitor center, located inside a carriage barn, to reserve one (or call ahead).

54 Elm St. (P.O. Box 178), Woodstock. (✆ **802/457-3368.** www.nps.gov/mabi. Free admission to grounds; mansion tour $8 adults, $4 seniors, free for children 15 and under; combination ticket with Billings Farm $16 adults, $12 seniors, $15 children 16–17. Late May to Oct daily 10am–5pm.

OUTDOOR PURSUITS

BIKING　The rolling, hilly terrain around Woodstock is ideal for exploring by road bike for those in reasonably good shape. **Start House Ski & Bike,** 28 Central St. (✆ **802-457-3377;** www.thestarthouseskiandbike.com), stocks a wide range of rides for hire and will also advise you on lovely local trips, such as one along pretty River Road.

HIKING　**Mount Tom** ★★ is the prominent hill overlooking Woodstock, and its low summit has great views over the village and to the Green Mountains. It's part of the Marsh-Billings-Rockefeller National Historic Park, but you can ascend the mountain right from the village: Start at **Faulkner Park** ★★, a town-owned park named after Mrs. Edward Faulkner, who had the oddly zigzagging trail up the mountain built to encourage locals to exercise. To reach the trail head from the green, cross the Middle Covered Bridge (visible from the green) and continue straight ahead on Mountain Avenue. The road bends left and soon arrives at the grassy park; from here, it's less than an hour to the summit. The trail winds uphill gradually, employing one of the most slowly climbing sets of switchbacks you'll ever see.

HORSEBACK RIDING　Experienced and aspiring equestrians head to the **Kedron Valley Stables** ★ (✆ **800/225-6301** or 802/457-1480; www.kedron.com), about 4½ miles south of Woodstock on Rte. 106. A full menu of riding options is available, from 1-hour beginners' lessons (about $50) to a 5-night inn-to-inn excursion (in the past, about $1,600 per person, including all meals and lodging; call for current pricing). The stables also rent out horses to experienced riders for local trail rides; offer seasonal **sleigh and carriage rides** ★; and maintain an indoor riding ring for inclement weather. In spring there's a maple-syrup operation here as well. Kedron Valley is open daily except on Thanksgiving and Christmas—but credit cards aren't accepted.

SKIING The area's best cross-country skiing is at the Woodstock Inn & Resort's **Nordic Center ★★** (*©* **802/457-6674;** www.woodstockinn.com), at the Woodstock Country Club, just south of the village center on Rte. 106. The center maintains about 38 miles of trails in two trail networks. It's not all flat, either; the high and low points along the trail system vary by some 750 feet in elevation. The ski center has a lounge and restaurant, as well as a large health and fitness center accessible via the ski trail. Lessons and tours are available. Skiing here is free if you're a Woodstock Inn guest; it costs $16 per day for nonguests (discounts for youths and half-day tickets). Skis and snowshoes can be rented on site, and there's a small discount for inn guests on the rental fees.

The ski hill **Suicide Six ★** (*©* **802/457-6661;** http://suicide6.com) has an intimidating name, but at just 650 vertical feet, it doesn't pose much of a threat. Owned and operated by the Woodstock Inn (just like the Nordic Center), this family-oriented ski resort (which opened in 1934 using a gas-powered rope tow) has a couple of double chairs, a J-bar for beginners, two dozen lifts, and a modern base lodge. Beginners, intermediates, and families with young children alike will be content here; expert skiers won't. Again, inn guests always ski free—a big boon if you're staying there. For all others, lift tickets cost $38 to $57 for adults, with discounts for seniors and youths. It's located about 2 miles north of the village, on Pomfret Road (take Rte. 12 north past the Billings Farm and Museum, and bear right).

WHERE TO STAY

Kedron Valley Inn ★★ ☺ You might recognize this inn, one of Vermont's oldest, even if you've never been here: For years, it was featured in the background of Budweiser's Christmas TV commercials (the ones with Clydesdales stomping bravely through the snow). In a complex of Greek Revival buildings at a tiny crossroads 5 miles south of Woodstock, guests rooms are beautifully furnished in antiques, reproductions, poster beds, and heirloom quilts; about three-quarters have wood-burning fireplaces, and a few even have Jacuzzis. Rooms in the newer, motel-like log building by the river are less expensive, with canopied beds, custom oak woodwork, and solid fireplaces; one (a simple two-level suite) even has a private streamside terrace and kitchenette. Unit nos. 12 and 17 in the main house, both suites reached via stairs, are among the most popular, as both have lovely period fireplaces and double Jacuzzis. There are two dining spaces, a formal dining room and a tavern, and the inn's own spring-fed pond features a sandy beach, toys for kids, and a lifeguard.

10671 South Rd. (Rte. 106), South Woodstock, VT 05071. *©* **800/836-1193** or 802/457-1473. Fax 802/457-4469. www.kedronvalleyinn.com. 26 units. $155–$195 double, $195–$245 suite; foliage season and Christmas week $195–$315 double, $370 suite. Rates include breakfast. AE, MC, V. Closed Apr and briefly prior to Thanksgiving. Pets $15 per night. **Amenities:** Restaurant; pub; swimming pond; Wi-Fi (in public rooms; free). *In room:* A/C, TV, fridge (some units), kitchenette (1 unit), no phone.

The Shire Riverview Motel ★ 🗲 The convenient Shire Motel is within walking distance of the green and the rest of the village, and with its attractive Colonial decor, it's *far* better appointed than your average motel; this is no Motel 6. Rooms are bright and have more windows than you might expect, most facing the river that runs behind and far below the property. At the end of the second-floor porch there's a veranda where you can sit on rockers overlooking the amazing view and enjoy a cup of coffee. You pay more for rooms with a similar river view; luxury-level rooms add amenities like porches, Jacuzzis, or more antique furniture. No, it's not a luxury inn—walls, plumbing, and linens won't be brand new or top-quality. But for a motel, this place offers incredible views and is both friendly and decently priced.

46 Pleasant St., Woodstock, VT 05091. ℂ **802/457-2211.** www.shiremotel.com. 42 units. $88–$228 double; foliage-season rates higher. AE, MC, V. *In room:* A/C, TV, fridge, Wi-Fi (free).

Woodstock Inn & Resort ★★★   This is possibly central Vermont's best full-scale resort. In a rambling brick building right beside the town green, this inn appears to be a venerable and long-established institution with its valet parking and apparently antique look. But it's not: It opened in 1969 (backed by Rockefeller money), though it looks centuries older and fits Woodstock like a glove. Inside, guests are greeted by a broad stone fireplace, the appealing smell of wood smoke, plenty of exposed woods, and sitting areas tucked throughout the giant open lobby. Guest rooms are tastefully decorated in country pine or a Shaker-inspired style—the best units, in the newer wing (built in 1991), have plush carpeting, refrigerators, and fireplaces. In recent years the inn has angled for a more contemporary look and younger clientele; most units have recently been refitted with new king-size bedding and added amenities like high-speed Internet in all rooms. One huge bonus here is that all guests get *free* use of the inn's downhill and **cross-country ski facilities,** all nearby (free shuttle), with discounts for golf at the golf course. The fitness center has squash courts, racquetball, and steam room, though I've found the inn's dining experiences middling. That's okay; you'll love it here anyway.

14 The Green, Woodstock, VT 05091. ℂ **800/448-7900** or 802/457-1100. Fax 802/457-6699. www. woodstockinn.com. 141 units. $149–$434 double; $360–$664 suite. 2-night minimum stay Sat–Sun. AE, MC, V. **Amenities:** 2 restaurants; bar; babysitting; bikes; concierge; golf course; putting green; health club; indoor and outdoor pools; room service; 12 tennis courts. *In room:* A/C, TV, fridge (some units), hair dryer, Wi-Fi (free).

The Woodstocker Inn B&B ★★ 📖   At the foot of Mount Tom, this 1830-built inn—so yellow it's impossible to miss—is owned by two Brits who display mighty fine hospitality and win awards for it. They also continue to do amazing renovations, including some of the best bathroom fixtures I've ever seen in a B&B. (Half the fun is figuring out how to work the various taps and contraptions.) Throughout, the lovely original pine floors are exposed, and everything is spotless. The romantic bathroom in the Westminster unit features cast-iron claw-foot tubs, side by side beneath a skylight, while the Richmond suite's big recliners face a Bose home-theater system and its bathroom sports a jetted tub and double-nozzled shower. A library, a back garden, and baskets of complimentary chocolate bars add to the comfort level, while breakfasts are a high point: Expect homemade or locally sourced yogurt, muesli, compote, sausage, bacon, and tomatoes, served in a breakfast room sporting a new woodstove and doors opening onto a patio. The inn is powered by "green" fuel and fitted in organic duvets, recycled-paper tissues, energy-efficient lighting and appliances, and natural bath products. One of my favorites.

61 River St., Woodstock, VT 05091. ℂ **802/457-3896.** Fax 802/457-3897. www.woodstockervt.com. 9 units. $130–$395 double. Rates include full breakfast. MC, V. Children not allowed. *In room:* A/C, TV, hair dryer, Wi-Fi (free), no phone.

WHERE TO DINE

Bentley's AMERICAN   Bentley's is literally and spiritually at the center of town, and it sometimes feels like the *only* dining choice in town at midday or after 9 o'clock at night. The dining room, on two levels and beyond an England-feeling bar (except for the Red Sox on the tube), affects a Victorian elegance. The kitchen here never dazzles you, though. Expect burgers and big sandwiches for lunch, while the dinner menu is more refined, leaning toward chicken, shrimp, steaks, and the like. The monster-sized chicken quesadillas are decent (if you skip the guacamole); the Caesar salads, not so much. Steak or a salad are probably safe picks. It's often very crowded here at night both at the bar and in the dining room, when it becomes the closest thing Woodstock has to a "scene." Try to reserve a table if you'll be coming on a weekend night.

3 Elm St. © **877/457-3232** or 802/457-3232. www.bentleysrestaurant.com. Reservations recommended for parties of 4 or more. Main courses $10–$15 at lunch, $8–$26 at dinner. AE, DC, DISC, MC, V. Mon–Thurs 11:30am–9:30pm; Fri–Sat 11am–10pm; Sun 11am–9pm. Later for cocktails and dancing on Fri-Sat.

The Prince and the Pauper ★★ NEW AMERICAN   It takes a bit of sleuthing to find this spot, down Dana Alley (next to the Woodstock Historical Society's Dana House), but it's worth the effort. This is one of Woodstock's best meals, in an intimate but surprisingly informal setting. Start with a drink in the taproom, and then move over to the rustic but elegant little dining room. The a la carte menu features grilled sirloin with garlic-herb butter and fries, sesame-crusted seared salmon with a Thai ginger sauce, roasted chicken with shiitake-Madeira wine sauce, panko-coated Jonah crab cakes, and smoked baby back ribs with coleslaw. But the prix-fixe menu, available daily except Saturdays and holidays, is even better. You might begin with Maine smoked salmon on toast, lobster ravioli, goat cheese soufflé, or French onion soup spiked with Vermont apple cider, then move on to five-spiced duck, boneless rack of lamb baked in puff pastry, grilled ahi tuna, or a piece of potato-encrusted Arctic char. There's also an inexpensive choice of gourmet hearth-baked pizzas, as well. Everything's good here, and it's a fairly unique venue: unfancy, yet fancy-feeling.

24 Elm St. © **802/457-1818.** www.princeandpauper.com. Reservations recommended. Bistro main courses $18–$23, prix-fixe dinners $48. AE, DISC, MC, V. Sun–Thurs 6–9pm; Fri–Sat 6-9:30pm. Lounge opens at 5pm.

Simon Pearce Restaurant ★★ NEW AMERICAN   The setting here can't be beat. Housed in a restored 19th-century woolen mill with wonderful views of a waterfall, Simon Pearce is a collage of exposed brick, pine floorboards, and handsome wooden tables and chairs. Meals are served on Simon Pearce pottery and glassware—if you like your place setting, you can buy it afterward at the sprawling retail shop in the mill. The atmosphere is a good mix of formal and informal. Chef Josh Duda's lunch menus include curried chicken salads, beef and Guinness stew, lamb burgers, shepherd's pie, a Maine lobster club sandwich, and crispy calamari with field greens. At dinner look for entrees like horseradish-crusted blue cod with crisped leeks, pan-seared salmon with Japanese vegetables and citrus-miso sauce, grilled top sirloin with Yukon gold potatoes, or roasted chicken with ancho chilies. For dessert? I've seen bittersweet chocolate pudding cake with a cappuccino semifreddo, roasted-apple tarts, blackberry cobbler, and a walnut meringue on the menu—with Vermont organic ice cream and Quechee-made sorbet for backup.

1760 Main St. (inside the Mill), Quechee. © **802/295-1470.** www.simonpearce.com. Reservations recommended for dinner (not accepted for lunch). Main courses $13–$17 at lunch, $22–$30 at dinner. AE, DC, DISC, MC, V. Daily 11:30am–9pm.

KILLINGTON & RUTLAND

Killington: 12 miles E of Rutland; 160 miles NW of Boston; 93 miles SE of Burlington

In 1937 a travel writer described the village near Killington Peak as "a church and a few undistinguished houses." The rugged, remote area was isolated from Rutland by imposing mountains, and accessible only through the daunting Sherburne Pass.

But that was before Vermont's second-highest mountain was developed into the Northeast's largest ski area, and before a wide, 5-mile-long access road was slashed through the forest right up to the mountain's base. (It was also before Rte. 4 was widened and upgraded, improving access to Rutland considerably.) Today Rte. 4 is one of the most heavily traveled routes through the Green Mountains, and a sea of condos, restaurants, and other tourist-related entities have moved in and taken possession of the pass.

So know this: **Killington** is plainly *not* the Vermont pictured on calendars and postcards. The region around the mountain boasts Vermont's most active winter scene, with loads of distractions both on and off the mountain. The area has a frenetic, where-it's-happening feel in winter. (That's *not* the case in summer, when the vast, empty parking lots trigger a mild, where-did-everybody-go panic, tempered by relief at the sinking prices of lodging.) The people happiest here are (a) skiers who like their skiing BIG; (b) singles in search of aggressive mingling on the mountain; and (c) travelers who want a wide choice of lodgings, eats, and fun stuff to do—and are willing to sacrifice a good portion of Vermont's usual charm in exchange for that.

About a dozen miles to the west, the city of **Rutland** lacks immediate charm, too. It's a working-class city with compact downtown, a rich history, and a wide array of services for travelers—most of them arrayed along two cluttered edge-city strips that inch uncomfortably close to the city center, which is too bad. But the city is also home to a huge annual state fair each fall. If you like the action of Killington but not the prices, sleeping in Rutland and then driving 25 or 30 minutes up to the ski area in the morning—or taking the local shuttle bus there—will work just fine. If you don't mind waking up to zero scenery, that is.

Killington

Killington lacks a town center, a single place that makes you feel you've arrived, and perhaps it lacks a soul as well; Killington is, basically, "wherever you parked." This town is so tied to the ski hill that it actually renamed itself after the mountain and resort in 1999; before that, it had been called Sherburne.

Since the mountain was first developed for skiing in 1958, dozens of restaurants, hotels, and stores have sprouted up along **Killington Road** (which shoots off Rte. 4 at a sudden angle) to accommodate the legions of skiers who descend upon the area during the ski season, which typically runs from October well into May, and sometimes even into June. I'll be honest: I sort of detest Killington Road. I hate the way it looks physically—strung out, clear-cut, unattractively landscaped—and the culinary offerings along its sides are very average at best. But this is the only access road in; it's a fact of life if you're skiing here. Learn to find the few diamonds in the rough.

The **ski area** itself is massive, stretching to encompass *seven* mountainsides, including Pico Peak; it's considered the biggest resort in the northeastern U.S.

ESSENTIALS

GETTING THERE **Killington Road,** the main access road to the mountain, extends southward off routes 4 and 100. (The point is still marked on some older road maps as "Sherburne.") This turnoff is about 10 or 12 miles (25 min.) east of Rutland, on your right. Coming from Woodstock to the east, the turnoff is about 20 miles west (40 min. driving time) via the same highway—but turn left.

Amtrak (☎ 800/872-7245; www.amtrak.com) offers a daily service from New York City to Rutland (the *Ethan Allen*). The ride takes a shade under 6 hours and costs $65 one-way. From Rutland there are connecting shuttles to the mountain and various resorts—or you can call a taxi.

If you're staying in Rutland, the Marble Valley Regional Transit District (☎ 802/773-3244; www.thebus.com) operates the **"Ski Bus"**—a very handy daily shuttle service between Rutland and Killington. The ride costs just $2 per person, one-way—and it's *free* for points along East Mountain Road, the other major road traversing some sections of the resort.

Some local hotels and inns also offer shuttles from tiny **Rutland airport,** from which **Cape Air** (800/352-0714; www.capeair.com) operates several daily flights to and from Boston's Logan International Airport.

VISITOR INFORMATION The **Killington Chamber of Commerce** (☎ 800/337-1928 or 802/773-4181; www.killingtonchamber.com) has information on lodging and travel packages, and staffs an information booth on Rte. 4 at the base of the access road; it's open weekdays from 9am to 5pm, shorter hours on weekends.

For information on accommodations in the area and travel to Killington, contact the resort's **lodging service** (☎ 800/621-6867) directly.

DOWNHILL SKIING

Killington ★★ A love-it or hate-it kind of place, New England's largest and most bustling ski area offers more vertical drop—and variety of experiences—than any other New England resort. It's certainly exciting. You'll find a huge choice of slope types across the seven peaks, from long, narrow, old-fashioned runs to killer moguls high on the mountains' flanks or tree-glade skiing. This is *the* Vermont choice of serious skiers. (It's also a huge operation, run with efficiency and not much personality, where tickets and passes are referred to as "products.") It's easy for kids to get separated from friends and family, and the resort seems to attract boisterous packs of young adults, so families should stick to Ramshed (the family area) or head to another resort such as Sugarbush (p. 520), Stowe (p. 528), or Suicide Six (p. 503). But for a big-mountain experience, with lots of evening activities and plenty of challenging terrain, this is still a great choice—maybe Vermont's best.

4763 Killington Rd., Killington, VT 05751. ☎ **800/621-6867** or 802/422-6200. www.killington.com. Adults $77-$82 day lift tickets; discounts for children and seniors.

CROSS-COUNTRY SKIING

Nearest to the ski resort (just east of Killington Rd. on Rte. 100/4) is **Mountain Meadows Cross Country & Snow Shoe Area** ★ (☎ 802/775-7077 or 802/775-0166; www.xcskiing.net), with more than 35 miles of trails groomed for both skating and classic skiing. The trails are largely divided into three sections, with beginner trails closest to the lodge, an intermediate area a bit farther along, and an advanced 6-mile loop farthest away. Rentals and lessons are available at the lodge.

For adults, a 1-day pass is $19, and a half-day (after 1pm) pass is $16. Kids ages 6 to 12 pay $8 per day, $6 per half-day.

The intricate network of trails at the **Mountain Top Nordic Ski & Snowshoe Center ★★** (© 802/483-6089; www.mountaintopinn.com), part of the Mountain Top Inn (p. 510), has long had a loyal local following. (It was one of the first commercial cross-country ski facilities in the East.) The 35-mile trail network offers pastoral views through mixed terrain, most of it groomed for classic and skate skiing. Trails here are often deep with snow, owing to the inn's ridge-top position high in the hills. Adults pay $20 for 1-day trail passes, $16 for half-day passes (after noon). This is challenging and picturesque terrain.

GOLF

Vermont is loaded with fine golf courses, public and private, lovely in summer and outstandingly scenic in fall. The acknowledged top course is **Green Mountain National Golf Course ★★★** (© 888/483-4653 or 802/422-4653; www.gmngc.com) on Rte. 100, about 3 miles north of the Rte. 100/Rte. 4 junction. Greens fees run from $59 to $69 per adult, not including the cost of a motorized cart (mandatory Fri–Sun and holidays). Discounts are available if you begin after 3pm. Rentals, instruction, and a driving range are also available.

A HISTORIC SITE

President Calvin Coolidge State Historic Site ★★ ☺ Even in death, the nation's most taciturn president didn't get much respect. But a trip to this historic site should restore Silent Cal's reputation once and for all among visitors, who'll get a strong sense of the man reared in this mountain village. The only president born on Independence Day, Coolidge was shaped by the strong sense of community and the harsh weather and isolation of his high upland valley. He's still a hero to Vermonters. The historic district consists of a group of about a dozen unspoiled buildings open to the public, plus a number of other private residences that can be observed from the outside only. Coolidge grew up here, and, in August 1923, in his boyhood home—the Coolidge Homestead, open for tours—Vice President Coolidge was awakened and informed that President Warren Harding had died. His own father, a notary public, administered the presidential oath of office. Coolidge is buried in the cemetery across the road, where every July 4th a wreath is laid at his simple grave in a quiet ceremony. The bright foliage in the surrounding hills is another reason to visit here.

3780 Rte. 100A, Plymouth. © **802/672-3773.** Admission $7.50 adults, $2 children 6–14, $20 family. Late May to mid-Oct daily 9:30am–5pm.

WHERE TO STAY

Skiers, especially families, headed to Killington for a week or so of skiing should also consider the **condominium** option. Talk to a representative at the **Killington Lodging Bureau** (© 800/621-6867; www.killington.com), and check online for special deals. (Killington will also help you book a stay at area inns and motels that it does *not* own.)

Blueberry Hill Inn ★★ The simple, homey Blueberry Hill Inn, dating from 1813, lies in the heart of the Moosalamoo recreation area amid 180 acres of property, about 45 minutes northwest of Killington Resort—it's halfway to Middlebury. With superb hiking, biking, canoeing, swimming, and cross-country skiing all around, it's a good stop for those who enjoy the outdoors. An inn brochure put it like this: "We offer you no radios, no televisions, no bedside phones to disturb your vacation." There are also no Jacuzzis or fancy fireplaces (and quite a few double and twin beds), surprising given the (seasonally) high room rates. Instead, you get a clean room, solid construction, plenty of wood, and lots of Americana-themed quilts. The original inn building houses four units; an attached conservatory contains three loft-style rooms, all reached via stairs, and there are four more in a pond-side 1987 addition plus one small, woody cottage. Family-style meals are served in a rustic dining room with a great stone fireplace and original wooden beams. The menu is Continental, with fusion touches—things like snapper cakes with guacamole and roasted free-range chicken. There's also a cross-country ski center on the property; a day pass is about $20.

1307 Goshen-Ripton Rd., Goshen, VT 05733. © **800/448-0707** or 802/247-6735. Fax 802/247-3983. www.blueberryhillinn.com. 12 units. $129–$189 double; foliage and holiday season $322–$414 double. Rates include breakfast. MAP rates $100 additional. MC, V. **Amenities:** Babysitting; bikes; sauna; Wi-Fi (in public areas; free). *In room:* No phone.

Inn at Long Trail ★ ☺ The Inn at Long Trail is situated in an architecturally undistinguished building (three stories of beige), poised at an ecologically important crossroads: the intersection of the highway (Rte. 4) and the Long and Appalachian trails at the Sherburne Pass. It's also only a 10-minute drive from Killington's ski slopes. More importantly, the innkeepers get high marks for sustaining a rustic experience with real hospitality; young hikers and families seem to enjoy the place. This just feels like Vermont. The interior here is far more charming than the exterior: Tree trunks support beams in the lobby, which also sports log furniture and banisters carved from birch. The oldest rooms in the inn (built in 1938 as an annex to a long-gone lodge) are furnished simply, in ski-lodge style—but more modern suites with fireplaces, telephones, TVs, and (sometimes) Jacuzzis and fireplaces are housed in a motel-like annex. Go for those. The dining room is fun, with a stone ledge that pokes right through the wall from the mountain behind the inn; it serves straight-ahead family fare plus a kids' menu. There's also a pub.

709 Rte. 4, Killington, VT 05751. © **800/325-2540** or 802/775-7181. Fax 802/747-7034. www.innat longtrail.com. 19 units. Summer and fall $79–$110 double; foliage season and holiday weekends $195–$225. All rates include breakfast; foliage and holiday rates also include dinner. 2-night minimum stay Fri–Sat and during foliage season. AE, MC, V. Closed late Apr to late June. Pets allowed with prior permission. **Amenities:** Dining room; pub; Wi-Fi (in public areas; free). *In room:* TV (some units), no phone (some units).

Killington Grand Resort Hotel ★★ ☺ This is a good (though pricey) choice for travelers seeking contemporary accommodations right on the mountain. More than half of the units have kitchen facilities, and most are quite spacious, though decorated in a generic country-condo style. There's a choice of standard queen-bedded rooms; studios; suites with sitting rooms; and two-bedroom, two-bathroom penthouses with full kitchens and gas fireplaces. Some of the units here can sleep up to eight people—this resort has really placed an emphasis on catering to families. You pay a premium for this convenience, but that convenience is hard to top during ski season. Staff here are more helpful than those at your typical big ski resort, and you can ski right onto the mountain from your room (or walk to the resort's golf course) via a special bridge. A shuttle runs you to Killington Road if you must sample the nightlife. There's a great health club here (two Jacuzzis with views, a big heated pool), plus a newer addition—the **Killington Grand Spa,** offering Swedish massage, Vichy showers, stone massages, nail care, and more.

228 E. Mountain Rd. (near Snowshed base), Killington, VT 05751. ⓒ **877/4-KTIMES** (458-4637). Fax 802-422-6881. www.killington.com. 200 units. Fall and winter $336–$395 double, suites from $508; off-peak $129–$310 double, suites from $175. 5-night minimum stay during Christmas and school holidays; 2-night minimum stay Sat–Sun. AE, DISC, MC, V. **Amenities:** 2 restaurants; 2 bars; children's programs; concierge; health club and spa; Jacuzzi; outdoor pool; room service; sauna; spa; 2 tennis courts. *In room:* A/C, TV/DVD, fridge (some units), hair dryer, kitchenette (some units), Wi-Fi (free).

The Mountain Top Inn & Resort ★★ It really *is* on top of a mountain. Situated

on 1,300 ridge-top acres, this pond-side property about 25 minutes from Killington sports one of Vermont's best inn views and a relaxing, summery feel, from the expansive front porch of Adirondack chairs to croquet games and equestrian programs. Carved out of a former turnip farm, the inn has left its heritage far behind: Even the lowest-priced rooms have been updated in woods, leathers, and tartan. Luxury rooms and suites come wonderfully outfitted with such modern amenities as flatscreen TVs, sofas, double-sided fireplaces, jetted tubs, and kitchenettes. The standard rooms are smaller and simpler but still come with fresh paint, rocking chairs, and views. Activities abound here: horse riding, clay-bird shooting, fly-fishing lessons, free canoeing and kayaking on the pond, dog-sledding (yes, really), and performances of jazz and orchestral music. The inn also rents five cabins on the grounds described as "rustic" (but they're quite nice, with TVs and big fireplaces), and can also arrange a stay in local ski chalets. The hospitality level here is very high, even if some staff are on the inexperienced side. This is among southern Vermont's most relaxing resorts. The dining room and tavern (see "Where to Dine," below) are pretty good, too.

195 Mountain Top Rd., Chittenden, VT 05737. ⓒ **800/445-2100** or 802/483-2311. Fax 802/483-6373. www.mountaintopinn.com. 55 units. $160–$445 double; $315–$545 suite; $205–$575 cabin. Resort fee of 15% additional. 2-night minimum stay Fri–Sat; 3-night minimum stay some holidays. Pets welcome in cabins only ($25 fee). AE, MC, V. **Amenities:** 2 restaurants; bar; outdoor pool. *In room:* A/C, TV, fridge (some units), kitchenette (some units).

WHERE TO DINE

Charity's 1887 Saloon & Restaurant PUB FARE Come here to drink; food is

an afterthought. Bustling and laid-back, it's a place where the grub is big and simple (wings, cheddar burgers, shrimp; rinse, repeat) and the crowd young. The barnlike interior is adorned with stained-glass lamps, spittoons, and Victorian prints, but centered around a handsome old bar that was crafted in Italy. The menu has expanded a bit over the years to take in pastas (including a Cajun version), stuffed mushroom caps, healthier sandwiches, turkey burgers, and the like; give 'em credit for that. Who was Charity? She worked an old profession in the bar's original American home. Ask a staffer if you want to know more.

Killington Rd. ⓒ **802/422-3800.** www.charitysrestaurant.com. Reservations not accepted. Main courses $7–$25 at lunch, $10–$25 at dinner. AE, MC, V. Daily 11:30am–10pm.

Choices Restaurant and Rotisserie ★ 🍴 CONTINENTAL Locals like this

unpretentious place on the access road, and indeed it's one of the best on the mountain (not saying much, but still). Full dinners come with salad or soup and bread, and they restore calories lost out on the slopes or the trail. Seafood and fresh pastas are a specialty (try the various permutations of fettuccine, most of them quite tasty), plus meats from a roaring front-and-center rotisserie. There's no theme, really, other than a Continental touch; you might just as well find curry, snails, or lamb chops on the menu as a smoked-salmon potato pancake, fish salad, nachos, or a cut of filet mignon dolled up with blue cheese. The atmosphere is nothing to write home about, and prices are higher than at the burger joints nearby, but the quality of the food and care taken in preparation are mostly ace.

Killington Rd. (at Glazebrook Center). © **802/422-4030.** Main courses $10–$28. AE, MC, V. Wed–Thurs and Sun 5–10pm; Fri–Sat 5–11pm.

Hemingway's ★★★ CONTINENAL   Killington seems an unlikely place for a culinary adventure, yet award-winning Hemingway's provides one. Set back from an arrow-flat stretch of highway (look sharp for it), Hemingway's is an elegant spot— one of the best restaurants in northern New England ever since it opened in 1982. Located in the 1860 Asa Briggs House (a former stagecoach stop), the restaurant seats guests in one of three formal areas; the two upstairs rooms are especially well appointed in linens, crystal goblets, and fresh flowers. Ted Fondulas' food draws heavily on Vermont game and produce, with lots of French and rural Italian accents. You might begin with Maine scallops, cooked three ways; a "fallen" goat cheese souf-flé with honey; good cream of garlic soup; or rabbit potpie. The splendid main courses, which change seasonally, could take in cod and Maine lobster, cooked with sweet corn, vanilla, and chives; a cut of roasted King salmon served with white beans and truffles; herbed poussin with truffled potatoes; seared breast of duck, served with pears and a duck strudel; or fennel-encrusted veal and a cheddary corn cake. Finish with a Vermont cheese plate or desserts such as apple cider "soup" with cranberry sorbet, or a peppery Florentine wafer with dark chocolate mousse and cassis berries. Dress neatly—shorts or T-shirts are out of place here.

4988 Rte. 4 (btw. Rte. 100 N. and Rte. 100 S.). © **802/422-3886.** www.hemingwaysrestaurant.com. Reservations highly recommended. Main courses $28–$34, prix-fixe and tasting menus $35–$75 per person. AE, MC, V. Wed–Sun 6–9pm; also select Mon–Tues during ski and foliage seasons (call ahead). Closed mid-Apr to mid-May and early Nov.

Highlands Dining Room ★★ NEW AMERICAN   The Mountain Top Inn & Resort's dining room delivers surprisingly sophisticated cuisine from a woodsy, folksy perch—a place where jackets are requested of gentlemen, but there are also racks of moose antlers for lighting and accouterment. Chef Shawn Casey combines influences: Meals could begin with an appetizer of tuna tartare with spicy couscous and yogurt; a Vermont cheese-and-sausage board; corn-fried calamari with fried basil and a chipotle aioli; or healthy salads of fresh produce, truffles, mozzarella, and the like. Move on to filet mignon with potato cakes, a rack of veal, pan-seared ahi tuna served over jasmine rice, or fresh ravioli stuffed with foraged wild mushrooms and Asiago cheese. The attached **Highlands Tavern** serves a simpler and lower-priced (but equally fine) menu of wings, sandwiches, burgers, chili, and (after 5pm) tasty bistro meals like chicken potpie, fish and chips, or T-bone steaks—with the big added bonus of outdoor terrace seating in front of the resort's signature pond and view. A great spot.

195 Mountain Top Rd., Chittenden, VT 05737. © **800/445-2100** or 802/483-2311. Reservations recommended. Appetizers $10–$14; main courses $24–$35. AE, DC, MC, V. Main dining room daily 6–9pm. Tavern daily noon–2pm and 5:30–9:30pm.

Wally's American Grill AMERICAN   This 1950s-retro restaurant is a festive, upbeat place—often crowded with visitors and locals who've just come off a long day on the slopes. In a strip-mallish complex near the top of Killington Road, the place's interior sets a good mood. The menu here is just diner fare, expanded for a slightly sophisticated clientele; expect omelets, malted waffles, eggs, hot cakes, and combo specials at breakfast, and check out the active orange juice. Lunch brings salads and sandwiches with Quebec-style *poutine* (fries with gravy) on the side; dinner, the usual American entrees of shrimp, pasta, lobster ravioli, salmon, and steaks. There are plenty of beers on tap here, plus cocktails and mixed drinks. Wally's is probably best as a fill-'er-up breakfast spot, not a dinner engagement.

Killington Rd. © **802/422-3177.** Breakfast items $4–$7, lunch and dinner main courses $8–$17. AE, DC, MC, V. Sun–Thurs 7am–9pm; Fri–Sat 7am–midnight.

Rutland

Rutland is a no-nonsense, blue-collar city that never had a reputation for charm or grace. Today it's undergoing a slight renaissance, new residents who enjoy the small-city atmosphere, free summer outdoor concerts, cheap real estate, and quick access to the mountains—Killington is just minutes away. But this place remains working-class at heart, and it probably always will. It's somehow the *second-largest city* in Vermont, which seems unbelievable once you've been here, but it's true (Bennington is a close third).

Rutland is the regional hub for central Vermont, with a daily newspaper and a long line of big box stores, fast-food chain restaurants, and businesses stretched out along crowded Rte. 7 both north and south of the downtown center. (The local airport is nearby, too.) At times this downtown comes perilously close to looking like one big, outdated strip mall; the concept of zoning got here too late, if it ever got here at all. Still, Rutland has the feel of a real place full of real people eating normal food—a good antidote when you've spent a little too much time in cuckoo-clock shops or the lift lines.

ESSENTIALS

GETTING THERE   It's easy to get to Rutland. From New York City, it's about a 4½-hour drive via the New York State Thruway; from Boston it's closer, about 3 hours via I-89.

The city sits right at the intersection of two old U.S. highways, routes 7 and 4. Burlington is 65 miles north and Bennington is 55 miles south, both via Rte. 7 and both about a 90-minute drive away. Woodstock is 25 miles (45 min.) east on Rte. 4, through the mountains.

Amtrak (© **800/USA-RAIL** [872-7245]; www.amtrak.com) runs one daily train to and from New York up the Hudson River Valley; the ride to Rutland takes a little less than 6 hours (arriving after dark) and costs $65 to $70 one-way.

Rutland is also served by several daily direct flights from Boston on **Cape Air** (© **800/352-0714;** www.capeair.com); the flight takes about an hour.

VISITOR INFORMATION   The **Rutland Region Chamber of Commerce,** 256 N. Main St., Rutland, VT 05701 (© **800/756-8880** or 802/773-2747; www.rutlandvermont.com), staffs an information booth at the corner of routes 7 and 4 W. from Memorial Day until Columbus Day. The chamber's main office is open year-round, weekdays from 8am to 5pm.

FESTIVALS   The **Vermont State Fair** ★ (© **802/775-5200;** www.vermontstatefair.net) has attracted fairgoers for more than a century and a half—since 1846 to be precise. Expect a conjunction of clowns, carnival rides, snacks, and live music from big-time country music acts with "The" in their names (The Gatlin Brothers, The Oakridge Boys), not to mention Bingo, cows, a demolition derby, and plenty more (but what more could you want?). Admission is $1 to $10 per adult, depending on the date, with big discounts for kids. There's also a small charge for parking (free to $3 per day). The fair is held for 10 days beginning in early September, just after Labor Day. Look for the expansive fairgrounds on Rte. 7, just south of the city center on the right-hand side as you leave town. Gates open at 8am daily.

EXPLORING THE TOWN

A stroll through Rutland's historic downtown might delight architecture buffs. Look for the detailed marblework on many of the buildings, such as the Opera House, the Gryphan's Building, and along Merchants Row. Note especially the fine marble exterior of the Chittenden Savings Bank at the corner of Merchants Row and Center Street. Nearby South Main Street (Rte. 7) also has a good selection of handsome homes built in elaborate Queen Anne style.

Another stop worth making, especially as a rainy-day diversion, is the **Chaffee Art Center ★**, at 16 S. Main St. (© 802/775-0356; www.chaffeeartcenter.org). Housed in a fairy-tale-like 1896 building with a prominent turret and mosaic floors in its archway vestibule—it's on the National Register of Historic Places, the glorious parquet floors now restored to their original luster—the arts center showcases the local talent from Rutland and the hills beyond. While it owns no permanent collections, the center does feature changing exhibits of local work, much of it for sale. It's open daily Wednesday to Saturday from 10am to 5pm, and Sunday from noon to 4pm; admission is by donation.

WHERE TO STAY & DINE

As lodging goes, Rutland is both rich and impoverished. The city's one true "inn" recently closed down, and B&Bs are not to be found. On the other hand, the city has an unusually wide selection of roadside **motels and chain hotels,** mostly clustered on or along **Rte. 7** either right downtown or just south of town, in the lower-to-middle price range for the most part. None of these is much better or different from any of the others. Check with the chamber of commerce (see "Visitor Information," above) if you need help weeding through and booking one of these, though most can easily be booked online from the comfort of your own home.

The dining scene is little better, though I fully expect culinary talents to discover this fact and move in soon; the chef at **Table 24** (see below) has already done so. If you're hankering eggs or hotcakes in the morning, though, **Clem & Co.** (© 802/747-3340) at 3 Center St.—known around town simply as "Clem's"—is a locally popular breakfast spot.

Little Harry's ★ INTERNATIONAL   Little Harry's is an offshoot of the wonderful Harry's Café outside Ludlow (p. 472). This one is located in downtown Rutland, on the first floor and in the basement of a strikingly unattractive building; yet the place itself has a wonderfully eclectic menu, just like its papa. Main courses could range from grilled steak sandwiches to jerked chicken, cioppino to duck in a hot, hot red Thai curry (there's *always* something Thai on the menu here). Appetizers are equally eclectic: Marinated olives, gazpacho, pad Thai, and hummus might make appearances. The food here spans the globe, so it's likely anyone can find something he or she likes—so long as you don't mind venturing outside America with your palate.

121 West St. (at Merchants Row). ☎ **802/747-4848.** Reservations recommended. Main courses $11–$17. AE, MC, V. Daily 5–10pm.

Table 24 ★★ AMERICAN   A welcome addition to the once-moribund Rutland dining scene, Table 24 serves up hearty lunches of soup, salad, meatloaf, chicken potpie, chicken with mashed potatoes, and burgers—you get the idea. These are cooked with a little more flair and care than your mom-and-pop diner would, though, and the restaurant uses Vermont-sourced ingredients wherever possible. Dinner is the real star—diner staples, but also things like baby back ribs, maple-glazed tenderloin, tamari-flavored trout, grilled steaks with compound butter, pan-roasted salmon, carne asada salads, and wild mushroom raviolis. Again, it's diner and bistro fare, but trumped up and better. Desserts choices include chocolate cake, ice-cream sundaes, bread pudding, and your classic banana cream pie. The high ceiling, exposed rafters, and a long, copper-top bar add to the restaurant's convivial feeling.

24 Wales St. (just off Rte. 4). ☎ **802/775-2424.** www.table24.net. Reservations recommended. Lunch items $5–$11, dinner main courses $13–$25. AE, MC, V. Mon–Sat 11:30am–9pm.

MIDDLEBURY ★★

Middlebury is 35 miles S of Burlington, 85 miles N of Bennington, and 65 miles NW of White River Junction

Middlebury is a gracious college town set among rolling hills and empty, pastoral countryside (dotted with barns and cows, it has to be added). The town center is idyllic in a New-England-as-envisioned-by-Hollywood way, and for many travelers it's *the* perfect combination of small-town charm, close access to the outdoors (the Adirondacks and Green Mountains are both pretty close at hand), and a dash of sophistication. (Foodies, rejoice.)

The worldly influence of a college (and its international student body), relocated artisans, and assorted other out-of-staters who've blown in here has led to the establishment of a natural-foods store, ethnic restaurants, a growing microbrewery, and more arts, crafts, and books than you'd expect to find in a place several times its size—especially in Vermont.

Essentials

GETTING THERE   Middlebury is on Rte. 7, almost exactly midway between **Rutland** and **Burlington,** about 30 miles (45 min.) from both of Vermont's largest cities. From New York City, it takes 5 or more hours to get here by car.

One popular route is to drive to the village of Fort Ticonderoga, then take a **cable ferry** (☎ **802/897-7999**) across Lake Champlain. Some form of ferry boat has crossed the lake here since way back in 1759; this one operates from May through October, about three times per hour from 8am until 6pm; the cost for autos is $8 one-way, $14 round-trip, but it takes just 7 minutes. In very severe weather, the ferry doesn't run, but this is Vermont: It almost always does run.

VISITOR INFORMATION   The **Addison County Chamber of Commerce,** 2 Court St. (☎ **802/388-7951;** www.addisoncounty.com), is in a handsome, historic white building just off the green, facing the Middlebury Inn. Brochures and assistance are available Monday through Friday during business hours (9am–5pm), and

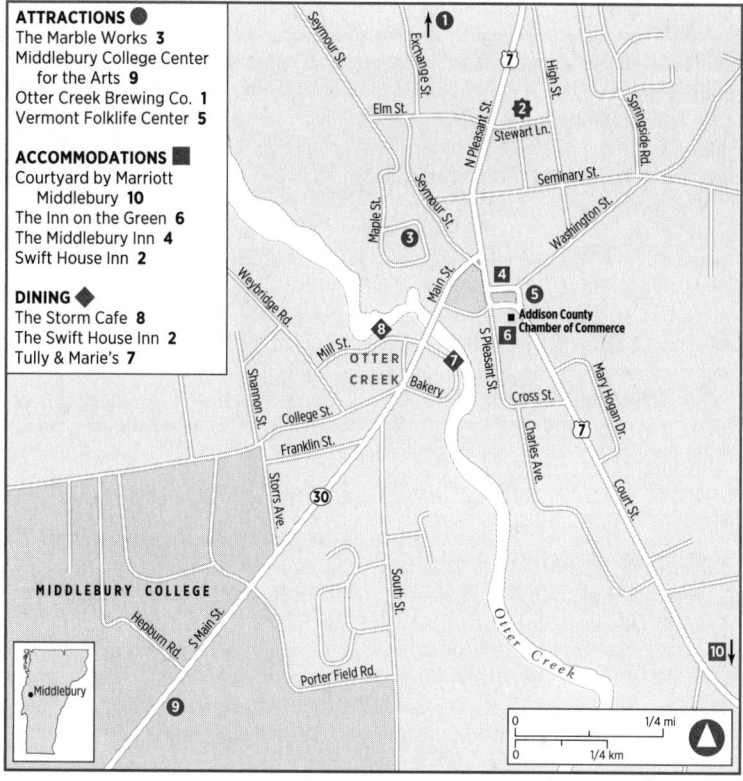

ATTRACTIONS ●
The Marble Works **3**
Middlebury College Center
  for the Arts **9**
Otter Creek Brewing Co. **1**
Vermont Folklife Center **5**

ACCOMMODATIONS ■
Courtyard by Marriott
  Middlebury **10**
The Inn on the Green **6**
The Middlebury Inn **4**
Swift House Inn **2**

DINING ◆
The Storm Cafe **8**
The Swift House Inn **2**
Tully & Marie's **7**

sometimes on Saturday and Sunday as well (early June through mid-Oct). Ask for a map and guide to downtown Middlebury, which lists local shops and restaurants and is published by the Downtown Middlebury Business Bureau.

Exploring the Town

The best place to begin a tour of Middlebury is at the Addison County Chamber of Commerce's information center (see above); be sure to request the chamber's self-guided **walking-tour** brochure.

The tiny main street has plenty of things to see—used-book shops, cafes, souvenir and stationery shops, and the like. It's a bit cutesy, but you'll find enough shopping interest to occupy an hour or two. The **Vermont Folklife Center ★** (© **802/388-4964;** www.vermontfolklifecenter.org), at 88 Main St., is a gallery of changing displays of local art from Vermont and beyond—visual art, but also music. The gift shop sells heritage books, foods, baskets, and other traditional crafts. The center is open Monday through Saturday from 10am to 5pm, Sunday 11am to 4pm; admission is by donation.

Take the footbridge over the river and find your way to **The Marble Works,** an assortment of wood and rough-marble industrial buildings on the far bank, converted to a handful of interesting shops and restaurants.

Atop a low ridge with beautiful views of the Green Mountains to the east and farmlands rolling toward Lake Champlain in the west, prestigious **Middlebury College ★** (founded in 1800) has a handsome, well-spaced campus of gray limestone and white marble buildings best explored on foot. The architecture of the college is primarily Colonial Revival, giving it a rather stern Calvinist feel. The view from the marble **Mead Memorial Chapel ★**, built in 1917 and overlooking the campus green, is especially nice.

At the edge of campus is the **Middlebury College Center for the Arts,** which opened in 1992. This architecturally engaging center houses the good little **Middlebury College Museum of Art ★★** (© 802/443-5007; http://museum.middlebury.edu), with a sampling of European and American art both old and new. Classicists will enjoy the displays of Greek painted urns, vases, and bits of stone frieze, as well as Florentine panels, a Rembrandt etching, and other Renaissance and Baroque artworks. Modern-art aficionados can check out the permanent and changing exhibits.

The museum is located on Rte. 30 (S. Main St.), and opens Tuesday through Friday from 10am to 5pm, Saturday and Sunday noon to 5pm. (It's closed during the second half of Dec and early Jan, when college is out of session.) Admission and parking are free.

Brewhounds should schedule a stop at the **Otter Creek Brewing Co. ★**, 793 Exchange St. (© 800/473-0727; www.ottercreekbrewing.com), for a quick tour and samples of the well-regarded beers, including the flagship Copper Ale, a robust Stovepipe Porter, and the organic Wolaver's line. The visitor center and gift shop are open daily; the free tours are given three times per afternoon (except Sun). Late September brings a 3-day Oktoberfest event to the brewery.

One recommended walk for people of all abilities—and especially those of literary sensibilities—is the **Robert Frost Memorial Trail ★**, dedicated to the memory of New England's poet laureate. Frost lived in a cabin on a farm across the road for 23 summers. (The cabin is now a National Historic Landmark.) It's on Rte. 125, about 6 miles east of Middlebury's village center. The trail itself is a relaxing, easy mile-long loop with excerpts of Frost's poems posted on signs all along the way—a wonderful idea. There's also information about the natural history of the trail area. This is a nice taste of the local mountains, with a pleasant poetic tint thrown in. If you have questions about the trail, call the Green Mountain National Forest's **Middlebury Ranger District office,** south of town on Rte. 7 (© 802/388-4362), which administrates it.

Where to Stay

If you're looking to save a few dollars, the outskirts of Middlebury, especially Rte. 7 south of the village green, are home to a clutch of budget motels and inns, some locally owned and some chain-run. These are frankly mostly aging and wearing out their welcomes, but they're uniformly cheap—$100 a night or less, in most cases. But buyer beware.

By far the best choice in these parts, especially for families, is the 89-room **Courtyard by Marriott Middlebury** (© 800/388-7775 or 802/388-7600) on Rte. 7 a half-mile south of the village green. Yes, it's a chain and nothing special, but it supplies the basics plus an indoor swimming pool. Some big spa suites have gas log fireplaces, Jacuzzi tubs, and fuller amenities, but all rooms come with hair dryers, coffeemakers, and free high-speed Internet access. There's also a coin-op laundry on the hotel premises.

The Inn on the Green ★★   This handsome, robin's-egg-blue village inn occupies a house that dates from 1803 (it was Victorianized with its mansard tower later in the 19th c.). It's both historic and comfortable, one of three excellent lodging experiences within shouting distance of the town green. Rooms here are furnished in a mix of solid antiques and reproductions (pencil-poster beds, sleigh daybeds, and the like). Exposed wooden floors and boldly colored walls of harvest yellow, peach, and burgundy help lighten the architectural mood of the house, and everything was freshened and renovated in the mid-1990s to upgrade with the times. The suites are most spacious, but every unit offers enough elbow room; those in the front of the house are wonderfully flooded with afternoon light. A continental breakfast (delivered to your room) is always included, though there are no Jacuzzis or fireplaces; this is not a luxury property, but rather a cozy Vermont experience.

71 S. Pleasant St., Middlebury, VT 05753. © **888/244-7512** or 802/388-7512. www.innonthegreen.com. 11 units. $119–$199 double; $199–$329 suite. Rates include continental breakfast. 2-night minimum stay Fri–Sat. AE, DC, DISC, MC, V. *In room:* A/C, TV, hair dryer, Wi-Fi (free).

The Middlebury Inn ★★   The most upscale experience in the village, the Middlebury Inn rambles along the main village square. Its impressive brick facade with a long, colonnaded front porch is as much a landmark as anything in town. The inn traces its roots to 1827, when Nathan Wood built the Vermont Hotel; the property now consists of three buildings housing 70 modern rooms. Units here are mostly on the big side, outfitted with either a sofa or upholstered chairs; Colonial-reproduction furniture; and vintage bathroom fixtures. Room nos. 116 and 246 are spacious corner units entered via foyers; no. 129, though smaller, has a four-poster bed, view of the green, and Jacuzzi. Rooms in the Porter Mansion next door also have a pleasantly historic feel, but the adjacent Courtyard annex is a standard-issue motel with double- and twin-bedded units beneath its cutesy veneer. Stick with the main inn or the mansion. An upscale **dining room/tavern** (see "Where to Dine," below) and a newish day spa ratchet up the luxury level even further, and all of the inn's guests receive complimentary passes to the nearby Vermont Sun fitness center—the best such facility in central Vermont, with an Olympic-size swimming pool and loads of workout equipment.

14 Court Sq., Middlebury, VT 05753. © **800/842-4666** or 802/388-4961. Fax 802/388-4563. www.middleburyinn.com. 70 units. Mon–Fri $88–$245 double, $240 suite; Sat–Sun $98–$270 double, $270–$375 suite. Rates include continental breakfast. AE, DC, MC, V. Pets accepted in Courtyard annex ($25 fee). **Amenities:** Restaurant; tavern; spa. *In room:* A/C, TV, hair dryer, Wi-Fi (in main inn; free).

Swift House Inn ★★   This historic complex of three whitewashed houses sits on a hillside 2 blocks from downtown Middlebury, and it was always a favorite of ours. But several waves of recent ownership have improved it with such touches as a friendly wine bar, improved pricing of the excellent **house restaurant ★★** (see "Where to Dine," below), and a "green" designation from the state of Vermont for environmentally sound practices. The five rooms in the roadside Gate House are lowest-priced and have a B&B feel, and have also been updated with newer, more upscale carpets, gorgeous wooden floors, and bathrooms. Nine units in the main Federal-style inn, built in 1814, are thoroughly imbued with the history of the place (a Vermont governor lived here at one time); inside, it's decorated in antiques and reproduction furnishings. And the carriage house's six suites are ideal for honeymooners or business travelers. They're the biggest and most luxurious, almost all of them furnished with Jacuzzis and fireplaces.

25 Stewart Lane, Middlebury, VT 05753. ⓒ **866/388-9925** or 802/388-9925. Fax 802/388-9927. www. swifthouseinn.com. 20 units. Main inn $130–$200 double; gate house $110–$150 double; carriage house $235–$270 suite. Rates include full breakfast. Packages available. 2-night minimum stay some Fri-Sat. AE, MC, V. **Amenities:** Restaurant; room service (breakfast only). *In room:* A/C, TV, hair dryer, Wi-Fi (in main inn; free).

Waybury Inn ★ Photos of Bob Newhart and "Larry, his brother Darryl, and his other brother Darryl" grace the wall behind the desk at this 1810 inn. That's because the inn was featured in the classic TV show *Newhart*—the exterior, anyway, which was painted white for television. (The interior was created on a Hollywood sound stage.) The architecturally handsome Waybury is now green on the outside, but it has loads of integrity within in a simple, farmhouse sort of way. (Poet Robert Frost was a frequent guest back in the day.) The rooms here vary in size and price, as they do in most old inns; the more you pay, the more space you get. Two of the rooms are suites, with sitting rooms, four-poster king beds, Jacuzzis, and claw-foot tubs. Romantic types will love the fact that room no. 9, the Robert Frost Suite, has a secret stash of previous guests' notes, while the New England Room features the work of local artist Warren Kimbell. Two dining spaces and a tavern serve good food, especially the **Pine Room** ★ with its inventive Continental menu. Front-facing rooms feel a bit noisy when nighttime highway traffic zooms by. This is about 5 miles southeast of Middlebury proper.

457 E. Main St. (Rte. 125, about 1½ miles past Rte. 7 S. turnoff), East Middlebury, VT 05740. ⓒ **800/348-1810** or 802/388-4015. Fax 802/382-8926. www.wayburyinn.com. 13 units (1 with detached private bathroom in the hall). $105–$190 double; $185–$285 suite. Rates include breakfast. AE, DISC, MC, V. Pets allowed with restrictions; call first ($25 fee). **Amenities:** Restaurant. *In room:* A/C, Wi-Fi (free), no phone.

Where to Dine

In addition to the eateries listed below, Middlebury possesses an abundance of delis, sandwich shops, and the like—perfect for a quick lunch or a picnic.

The Storm Cafe ★★ NEW AMERICAN This tiny, casual spot with great river views on the ground floor of a stone mill in Frog Hollow is a chef-owned restaurant popular with locals and travelers alike. The menu is simple, but great care is taken in the selection of ingredients and cooking. The salads are especially good. Interesting lunch selections include "The Berber" (pan-fried salmon in African spices on a baguette, with lemon aioli), a chicken cheesesteak with hot peppers and cheddar, and a spicy pile of Prince Edward Island mussels steamed in wine. Dinner brings appetizers and main courses of pan-seared diver scallops, duck confit sliders, beet carpaccio, grilled polenta cakes, pan-roasted chicken with liver crostini, grilled beef filets, several pasta dishes, and a daily seafood special. Desserts are killers, too—try *not* to order a Snickers blonde brownie sundae, chocolate decadence cake, banana cream pie, or crème brûlée, but I bet you'll cave in. There's a tiny wine list, too. Ultrafancy this place is not, but locals enjoy it, and for very good reasons.

3 Mill St. ⓒ **802/388-1063.** www.thestormcafe.com. Reservations recommended. Main courses $7–$9 lunch, $17–$24 dinner. MC, V. Mon 11:30am–2:30pm; Tues–Sat 11:30am–2:30pm and 5–9pm; Sun 5–9pm.

Swift House Inn ★★ CONTINENTAL   This inn restaurant consists of two dining rooms on the ground floor of the main house. It's a wonderfully homey place to
get a fancy meal right in town, in a lovely setting. Since Chef Zach Corbin came on
board, the menu has moved away from American cuisine toward French shores, yet
it remains top-notch in execution. Begin with homemade duck sausage over cassoulet beans, a lovely smoked salmon "Napoleon" of potatoes, fish, capers, and
crème fraîche; country pâté; or house salads. Main courses could run to Long Island
breast of duck with caramelized apples, grilled entrecote of beef with mashed potatoes, flounder almondine, or fresh agnolotti pasta stuffed with spinach and ricotta
cheese then topped with Parmesan cream sauce. There's also a second, bistro-style
menu here with slightly lighter entrees (and prices): Expect burgers and upscale-yet-
healthy presentations of fish. Some tables in the dining room look out onto the inn's
grounds—and, by default, sunset over the mountains to the west. Ask for one.

25 Stewart Lane. © **802/388-9925.** www.swifthouseinn.com. Reservations recommended. Main courses
$15–$21. AE, MC, V. Wed–Sun 5:30–9pm.

Tully and Marie's NEW AMERICAN/FUSION   Tully and Marie's is an Art Deco
inspired restaurant overlooking Otter Creek, in an almost-hidden location down a
narrow alley. (Try for a table perched over the water.) The menu is New American
cuisine, but with heavy influences from Asia and Mexico. At lunch expect burgers,
burritos, and an array of sandwiches and wraps filled with crab, salmon, brie, or
meat and cheese. At dinner you might find pad Thai, grilled sea scallops, house-
smoked pork barbecue, fajitas, pan-blackened salmon, jerked chicken, steak, or
curry. It's an adequate central bite.

7 Bakery Lane. © **802/388-4182.** www.tullyandmaries.com. Reservations recommended Fri–Sat. Main
courses $7–$8 at lunch, $10–$24 at dinner. AE, MC, V. Daily 11:30am–3pm and 5–9pm (to 10pm Fri–Sat).
Closed Wed in winter.

THE MAD RIVER VALLEY ★★

Warren: 3 miles S of Waitsfield; 205 miles NW of Boston; 43 miles SE of Burlington

Save a couple of telltale signs, you could drive Rte. 100 through **Warren** and **Waitsfield** and never realize you're just a couple miles downhill of some of the choicest
skiing in the entire state. There's no rampant condo or strip-mall development here,
and the valley seems to have learned from the sprawl that afflicts such resort areas
as Mount Snow and Killington. (Even the Mad River Green, a tidy strip mall on Rte.
100 just north of Rte. 17, is disguised as an old barn; it's scarcely noticeable from
the main road.) Some Vermont travelers say the valley still looks much like the Stowe
of 30 years ago. That's a good thing.

The region's character becomes less pastoral along the access road to the **Sugarbush** ski resort, however; at least the best inns and restaurants tend to be tucked
back into the forest or set along rushing streams. Make sure you get good directions
before setting out in search of accommodations or food in this valley, and try not to
do so at night unless absolutely necessary—hardly any of the roads in this part of
Vermont are lit by streetlights. (That's why you're in Vermont, remember?)

Hidden up a winding valley road, **Mad River Glen,** the area's *older* ski area, has
a pleasantly dated quality that pointedly sticks a thumb in the eye of rock-stardom
(we're looking at you, Sugarbush and Killington). It has an almost crunchy granola

sort of charm, cute and unprepossessing, and it's many Vermonters' favorite ski hill for that very reason.

Essentials

GETTING THERE   **Warren** and **Waitsfield** are closed to each other on Rte. 100, north of **Killington** and south of **Waterbury**—figure on almost an hour's drive from either Burlington or Killington. The quickest access from a major interstate is via exit 10 (Waterbury/Stowe) off I-89; then you drive about 20 miles south on Rte. 100 until you hit Waitsfield. Warren is 5 or 6 more miles down the same road.

VISITOR INFORMATION   The **Mad River Valley Chamber of Commerce** (✆ **800/828-4748** or 802/469-3409; www.madrivervalley.com) is at 4601 Main St. (that's Rte. 100) in **Waitsfield,** inside the General Wait House, which is next to the elementary school. It's open daily during regular business hours in summer, foliage season, and ski season; during slower times of the year, it sometimes closes weekends, or closes earlier.

Skiing

Mad River Glen ★★ 🎁   Mad River Glen is at once the radical dude and the Zen master of Vermont's skiing universe—a place whose motto is still "Ski it if you can!" High-speed detachable quad chairs? Forget it; up until 2007, the main lift here was a 1948 *single*-chair lift that slowly creaked its way a mile up to the summit. Snowmaking? Nope. This hill functions according to the whims of Mother Nature. Snowboarding? No, it's forbidden. Gourmet restaurants? A lodge? Toll-free number? Fancy website? No, no, no, and definitely not. Mad River long ago attained cult status among "soul skiers" (for lack of a better term), and its fans seem determined to keep it this way. Owned and operated by a cooperative since 1995, it claims to be the only cooperatively owned ski area in the country—you can even buy a small share of the resort yourself, and get discounts on tickets afterward. But don't mistake this gentler approach for easier skiing; the slopes here are twisting and narrow, hiding some of the steepest drops in New England. (Nearly half of Mad River's runs are classified as "expert.") A ski school, kids' program, and telemarking classes are all offered, and care is taken here to both preserve and explain the mountain's ecology. Tickets are pretty affordable, too, especially midweek. A renegade spirit perseveres here, even in the face of the sport's (and Vermont's) inexorable process of upscaling. If you're interested in a different skiing experience, or one that's more "ecotouristy," this is it.

PO Box 1089, Waitsfield, VT 05673. ✆ **802/496-3551.** www.madriverglen.com. Adults $39–$66 day lift tickets, $35–$51 half-day; discounts for youths and seniors.

Sugarbush ★★   Now more than a half-century old, Sugarbush is a fine intermediate-to-advanced ski resort comprising several mountains linked by a long, high-speed chairlift that crosses several ridges. (A shuttle bus offers a warmer way to traverse the hills, and the resort also recently acquired a "Snow Cat" transporter.) The number of high-speed lifts, plus the excellent snowmaking, makes this a desirable destination for serious skiers—and there have been serious improvements over the past decade. But this is not Killington. The "Bush" remains a pretty low-key area with great intermediate cruising runs on its north slopes and challenging, old-fashioned expert slopes on Castlerock Peak. Mount Ellen features a terrain pipe and half-pipe, and the resort has made "green" strides by fueling all its equipment and shuttle buses with biodiesel (vegetable oil and/or reused waste oil). This is a good choice if you seek great, exciting skiing but find Killington's sprawl a little overwhelming.

1840 Access Rd., Warren, VT 05674. © **800/537-8427** or 802/583-6300. www.sugarbush.com. Adults $77–$82 day lift tickets, $62–$67 half-day; discounts for youths and seniors.

Cycling

A rewarding 14-mile **bike trip ★★** along paved roads begins at the village of Waitsfield. Park near the covered bridge, then follow East Warren Road past the Inn at Round Barn Farm and up into hilly, farm-filled countryside. (Don't be discouraged by the long hill at the outset.) Near the village center of Warren, turn right at Brook Road to connect to Rte. 100. Return north on bustling but scenic Rte. 10 to Waitsfield, minding the traffic carefully.

Clearwater Sports, at 4147 Main St. (Rte. 100) in Waitsfield, north of the covered bridge (© **802/496-2708;** www.clearwatersports.com), has rented mountain bikes, snowshoes, kayaks, and skis out of a blue-and-white Victorian-era house since 1975; these folks are well-liked locally. Staff members are helpful, offering suggestions for routes and tours. The shop is open daily, year-round.

Where to Stay

In addition to the choices listed below, think about Sugarbush's **condos.** Call the main switchboard at © **800/537-8427** and ask for lodging services.

Inn at the Mad River Barn ✦ This classic 1960s-style ski lodge attracts a clientele that's nearly fanatical in its devotion to the place. One reason might be its charismatic (and opinionated) owner Betsy Pratt, who was co-owner of the Mad River Glen ski area before she created and sold it to the cooperative that runs the mountain now. Accommodations are in a two-story barn behind the white clapboard main house, and in an annex building (a bit fancier but with less character). *Don't* come expecting a fancy place—carpets and furniture tend toward the threadbare—but rather to relax in a ski-lodge/aunt's-home/youth-hostel-like atmosphere. It's all knotty pine and rustic Americana here; the spartan guest rooms and countrified common spaces (there's a mounted moose head by the stone fireplace, for instance) get visitors feeling at ease right away. Visitors can swim in the lovely pool a short distance away from the inn beside a grove of birches of maples.

2849 Mill Brook Rd. (Rte. 17), Waitsfield, VT 05673. © **800/631-0466** or 802/496-3310. Fax 802/496-6696. www.madriverbarn.com. 15 units. $75–$150 double; holiday and foliage-season rates higher. Rates include breakfast. 2-night minimum stay holidays and Fri–Sat in winter. AE, DISC, MC, V. **Amenities:** Exercise room; outdoor pool; sauna. *In room:* TV (most units), fridge (some units), Wi-Fi (most units; free), no phone.

Inn at the Round Barn Farm ★★ 👜 You pass through a covered bridge just off Rte. 100 to arrive at one of the most romantic and distinctive-looking B&Bs in northern New England, a regal barn and farmhouse on 235 sloping acres with views of fields all around. The centerpiece of the inn is the Round Barn, a beautiful 1910 structure used for weddings, art shows, even Sunday church services. Guest rooms are furnished in an elegant, understated country style with wingback chairs, poster beds, love seats, marble gas fireplaces, and luxe trimmings. The less expensive units in the older section of the home are comfortable, if comparatively small; the larger luxury units sport soaring ceilings beneath old log beams, and include such extras as Jacuzzis and cable televisions. There's also one suite (the Abbott), with plenty of those original beams plus CD and DVD players, a steam shower, Jacuzzi, and pull-out sofa bed. Surprisingly, no dinner is served here (there isn't even a bar); but you'll still love the place anyway.

1661 E. Warren Rd., Waitsfield, VT 05673. ℭ/fax **802/496-2276.** www.innattheroundbarn.com. 12 units. $165–$315 double; $285–$315 suite. Rates include breakfast. 3-night minimum stay during holidays and foliage season. AE, DISC, MC, V. Closed Apr 15–30. Children 15 and over welcome. **Amenities:** Indoor pool; cross-country ski center. *In room:* A/C, TV/DVD, hair dryer, Wi-Fi (most units; free), no phone (some units).

The Pitcher Inn ★★★   This inn is one of New England's most expensive, luxurious, refined—and most interesting. Set in the timeless village of Warren, the business *and* inn were rebuilt from the ground up in 1993 after a fire leveled the 19th-century home that had previously stood here; now only the barn is original. Yet architect David Sellers has created a space seamlessly blending modern convenience, whimsy, and classic New England decor while paying deep respect to the Old Vermont with "themed" rooms taking that concept to new heights. There isn't a bad room in the house; all 11 are designed with gracefulness and a sense of humor, and they've been compared to elegant puzzles—each is almost like a miniature modern art installation. The carved goose on the ceiling of the Mallard Room, for example, is attached to a weathervane on the roof; it rotates with the vane to indicate wind direction. The Trout Room feels like a riverside campground with its antique oars, a desk for fly-tying, a porch extending over a rushing steam, and a fireplace of river stones. The Mountain Room has antique snowshoes and a brick fireplace of Vermont stone. And so on. Most rooms have wood-burning or gas fireplaces, all have Jacuzzis, and most have steam showers; among the choices are a pair of 2-bedroom suites in the barn.

275 Main St. (P.O. Box 347), Warren, VT 05674. ℭ **802/496-6350.** Fax 802/496-6354. www.pitcherinn. com. 11 units. $425–$650 double; $800 suite. Rates include breakfast and afternoon tea. Packages available. 2-night minimum stay Sat–Sun; 3-night minimum on holiday weekends; 5-night minimum at Christmas. AE, MC, V. Children 15 and under accepted in suites only. **Amenities:** Restaurant; babysitting; Jacuzzi; room service; spa. *In room:* A/C, TV/VCR/CD, hair dryer, Wi-Fi (free).

West Hill House ★★ 🛏   If you go strictly by guests' comments, this is the best B&B in the entire Western world. It might not be *that,* but it's excellent—I challenge you to find someone with one bad word to say about it. Under the watchful ownership of Peter and Susan MacLaren since 2006, this is among the more relaxed inns in the valley, in part because of its quiet hillside location, in part because of the easy camaraderie among guests and hosts. Set on a lightly traveled country road, the inn offers the quintessential New England experience just a few minutes from the slopes of Sugarbush. Built in the 1850s, the farmhouse boasts three common rooms, including a bright, modern addition with a handsome fireplace for warmth in winter, an outdoor patio for summer lounging, and a game room with a pool table. Guest rooms are decorated in an updated country style, and all of them now sport air-conditioning; memory-foam mattresses on the beds; gas fireplaces or woodstoves; and steam showers or Jacuzzis. The Paris Suite, inspired by the MacLarens' time living near Versailles, is perhaps most lovely. The owners are unfailingly kind, even supplying snowshoes in winter if you wish some, while in summer they maintain lovely perennial gardens and ponds. A lovely find.

1496 W. Hill Rd., Warren, VT 05674. © **800/209-1049** or 802/496-7162. www.westhillbb.com. 8 units. $140–$200 double; $185–$250 suite. Rates include breakfast. 3-night minimum stay preferred for foliage and holiday weekends; 2-night minimum stay Fri–Sat. AE, DISC MC, V. Children 12 and over welcome. **Amenities:** Honor-system bar. *In room:* A/C, TV/VCR, hair dryer.

Where to Dine

On Friday and Saturday nights, **American Flatbread ★★** (© **802/496-8856;** www.americanflatbread.com), on Rte. 100 in Waitsfield, serves terrific-tasting, organic-flour pizzas to the public from 5:30 to 9pm. Founder George Schenk's delicious vision is pizza-as-whole food, and this was his original restaurant of what is now a small, thriving northern New England chain and frozen-pizza operation. Get there up to an hour early and put your name on the waiting list; no reservations are taken. The chef also creates inventive weekly salad and nonpizza entree specials.

You can pick up thick, inexpensive sandwiches on fresh bread at most any **country store** in the area, such as the **Warren Store** (© **802/496-3864;** www.warrenstore.com), on Main Street in Warren.

For a fancy meal, the **Pitcher Inn ★★** (see "Where to Stay," above) is superlative, and many other area inns also open their kitchens to the public.

The Common Man ★★ CONTINENTAL   It sounds like a pub, but this Common Man is anything but. Housed in a century-old barn, the interior is soaring and dramatic. Chandeliers, floral carpeting on the walls (it works), and candles on the tables create a relaxed feel. You'll be halfway through your meal before you notice there are no windows. The menu is far more ambitious than skiers' grub. Start with a Cortland-apple salad, beets with goat-cheese fondant, PEI mussels with garlic and shallots, or peppery, thin-sliced seared beef. Main courses here are solidly Continental: things like lump crab cakes with shrimp mixed in; skilled-roasted chicken breast with Gruyère cheese; grilled pork tenderloin; breast of duck; steak with blue-cheese sauce; a buttery lobster-scallop gnocchi; and a nightly fish special. You can also get plates of that great Vermont artisanal cheese. The good selection of beer and wines completes the package.

3209 German Flats Rd., Warren. © **802/583-2800.** www.commonmanrestaurant.com. Reservations recommended in peak season. Main courses $13–$24. AE, DISC, MC, V. Daily 6–9pm in ski season; Tues–Sat 6–9pm rest of year.

John Egan's Big World Pub & Grill ★ ☺ PUB FARE/INTERNATIONAL
Extreme skier John Egan starred in a bunch of Warren Miller skiing films and still teaches radical moves at Sugarbush, but he *really* took a risk when he opened this restaurant at the junction of routes 17 and 100 in Waitsfield. It has worked out well. In a 1970s-style motel dining room decorated with skiing memorabilia (including a bar made of ski sections signed by skiing luminaries), the restaurant features a wood-fired grill and serves an above-average pub menu with flair and worldliness. Sure, there are burgers and salads galore, but you can also order a rack of lamb cooked right on the wood fire; spicy Asian noodles; Thai shrimp; Hungarian goulash; boneless pork loin chops in a Dijon mustard sauce; rotisserie chicken; or a steak. (Lobsters and salmon sometimes make appearances, too.) There's a decent list of California wines and Vermont beers to wash it down with, plus a kids' menu.

Rte. 100 at Rte. 17, Waitsfield. © **802/496-3033.** www.bigworldvermont.com. Main courses $10–$28. AE, MC, V. Daily 5–9:30pm; Sun also 10am–2pm.

MONTPELIER ★★, BARRE & WATERBURY

Montpelier: 13 miles SE of Waterbury; 9 miles NW of Barre; 178 miles NW of Boston; and 39 miles SE of Burlington

Montpelier might be the most down-home, low-key state capital in the nation (and it's definitely the one with the smallest population). The glistening, iconic gold dome of Vermont's capitol building is practically the only showy or pretentious thing in the entire city; behind it, there's no cluster of mirror-sided skyscrapers, but rather a thickly forested hill. This town, it turns out, isn't a self-important center of politics, just a small town that happened to become the home of state government.

Restaurants, coffee shops, and cultural offerings have flowed here as a result, and it's an agreeable place to pass an afternoon or stay the night if you want to know how small-town Vermont ticks. The city is centered around two main boulevards: State Street, lined with handsome government buildings; and Main Street, where many of the town's stores and restaurants are found. Everything's compact here. The downtown sports a pair of hardware stores, decent small-town shopping, and one of the best art movie houses in northern New England: the **Savoy Theater** (✆ **802/229-0509** or 802/229-0598; www.savoytheater.com), where concession prices are almost criminally low.

Nearby **Barre** (pronounced "Barry") is more commercial and less charming, with a blue-collar, red-state ethos. It was once the hub of Vermont's huge granite quarrying industry, and you can still see granite curbstones lining Barre's long Main Street, not to mention signs for many businesses carved from it. Barre attracted talented stone workers from Italy and Scotland (there's a statue of Robert Burns here), who helped give the turn-of-the-20th-century town a lively, cosmopolitan flavor.

About 10 miles west of Montpelier, **Waterbury** ★ is at the junction of Rte. 100 and I-89, making it a commercial center by default if not by design. Set along the Winooski River, it has sprawled along the valley more than other Vermont towns, possibly because the flood of 1927 nearly leveled the town—or else because the town has attracted an inexplicable number of food companies (Ben & Jerry's ice-cream empire, Green Mountain Coffee's growing java business, Cold Hollow Cider Mill's cider operations) that have built factories and outlets in what were once dairy pastures. Despite its drive-through quality, Waterbury makes a decent overnight base for further explorations of the Green Mountains, Burlington (just 25 miles west), or nearby Montpelier.

Essentials

GETTING THERE Montpelier is accessible by car via exit 7 off I-89. For Barre, take exit 8; Waterbury is just south of exit 10 (the same exit as Stowe). Burlington's **airport** (code: BTV), with daily flights from New York, is about 45 miles away by car.

Amtrak (✆ **800/872-7245**; www.amtrak.com) runs one daily train (the *Vermonter*) from New York City to Montpelier. The trip takes a long 8½ hours, but costs only $56.

Greyhound (✆ **800/231-2222**; www.greyhound.com) runs buses to Montpelier, as well. From New York City, the ride takes 8 hours (change buses in White River Junction) and costs about $80 one-way; from Boston, it's a 4-hour ride costing about $55 each way.

TASTE OF SUCCESS: THE STORY OF BEN & JERRY

A clutch of doleful cows standing amid a bright green meadow on Ben & Jerry's ice-cream pints have almost become *the* symbol of Vermont, but Ben & Jerry's cows—actually, they're Vermont artist Woody Jackson's cows—also symbolize friendly capitalism (or "hippie capitalism," as some prefer).

The founding of this company is legend in small-business circles. Two friends from Long Island, Ben Cohen and Jerry Greenfield, started the company in Burlington in 1978 with $12,000 and a few mail-order lessons in ice-cream making. The pair experimented with flavor samples obtained free from salesmen, and sold their product out of an old downtown gas station.

Embracing the outlook that work should be fun, they gave away free ice cream at community events, staged outdoor movies in summer, and plowed profits back into their local community. This free-spirited approach, plus the exceptional quality of the product—their machines stir out most of the air bubbles as the ice cream freezes, creating a denser ice cream that's more expensive to manufacture—built a hugely successful corporation.

Since then, they've faced tough competition from a zillion other upstart gourmet ice-cream makers, plus a gradual national shift toward healthier diets. Yet Ben and Jerry are still at it. Though the friends sold their interest to the huge multinational food concern Unilever—a move that raised not a few eyebrows among its grass-roots investors—its heart

and soul (and manufacturing operations) remain squarely in Vermont.

The **main factory** in Waterbury might be Vermont's most popular tourist attraction. The plant is located about a mile north of I-89 on Rte. 100, and the grounds have almost a Woodstockian feel to them. During summer, crowds arrive early, milling about and making new friends while waiting for the half-hour **factory tours** to begin. Tours are first-come, first-served, and run at least every 30 minutes from 9am to 9pm from July to mid-August (last tour departs at 8pm). Tour hours are shorter the rest of the year, but they're always running from at least 9am to 5pm. The afternoon tours fill up quickly, so get there early to avoid a long wait.

Once you've got your ticket, browse the small museum (learn the long, strange history of Cherry Garcia), buy a cone of your favorite flavor at the scoop shop, or lounge along a promenade scattered with Adirondack chairs and picnic tables. Tours cost $3 for adults, $2 for kids and seniors, and free for children 11 and under. There's also a package deal where you get a tour, a T-shirt, and a pint of the good stuff for $21—only worth it if you love the T-shirt.

Kids can enjoy the "Stairway to Heaven," which leads to a playground, and a "Cow-Viewing Area," which is self-explanatory. The tours are informative and fun, and conclude with a sample of the day's featured product. For more information, call © **866/BJ-TOURS** (258-6877) or 802/882-1240.

VISITOR INFORMATION The **Central Vermont Chamber of Commerce** (© 802/229-4619; www.central-vt.com) is on Stewart Road in Montpelier, just off exit 7 of I-89. Turn left at the first light; it's a half-mile farther on the left. The chamber is open weekdays from 9am to 5pm.

Exploring Montpelier & Barre

Start your exploration of Montpelier with a visit to the gold-domed **State House ★** at 115 State St. (© 802/828-2228), guarded out front by a statue of Ethan Allen. Three capitol buildings have risen on this site since 1809; the present building retained the portico designed during the height of Greek Revival style in 1836. Modeled after the temple of Theseus in Athens, it's made of Vermont granite (of course). You can take a self-guided tour anytime the capitol is open, any weekday (except holidays) from 8am to 4pm. Free *guided* tours are offered every half-hour between July and mid-October, Monday through Friday from 10am to 3:30pm and Saturday from 11am to 2:30pm. The informative and fun tour is worthwhile if you're in the area, but not worth a major detour.

Next door to the State House is the **Vermont Historical Society Museum** (© **802/828-2291;** www.vermonthistory.org) at 109 State St. The museum is housed in a brick replica of the elegant old Pavilion Building, a once-prominent Victorian hotel, and it contains a number of Vermont artifacts such as a gun once owned by Ethan Allen, Colonial powder horns, and wood carvings. It mostly deals in Colonial history, though—there's not much on recent decades. From May through mid-October, it's open Tuesday to Saturday from 10am to 4pm. Admission is $5 for adults, $3 for students or seniors, and $12 for families. There's also a gift shop on the premises.

Where to Stay

IN MONTPELIER

Capitol Plaza Hotel ★   The favorite hotel of folks here to do business with the state government, this four-story brick hotel is centrally located (right across from the capitol) and thus makes a good base for visitors to town. The small lobby has a Colonial cast to it; guest rooms on the three upper floors adopt a light, faux-Colonial tone and have more amenities than you might expect. It has the feel of a place best suited for conventions—clean, comfortable, and convenient digs, nothing more. The more expensive rooms add wingback chairs, Ralph Lauren bedding, and high-speed Internet access, while three still-fancier suites add Jacuzzis, fridges, sofas, and bigger televisions.

100 State St., Montpelier, VT 05602. © **800/274-5252** or 802/223-5252. Fax 802/229-5427. www.capitolplaza.com. 56 units. $116–$162 double and suite; foliage season higher. AE, DISC, MC, V. **Amenities:** Restaurant. *In room:* A/C, TV, fridge (in suites), hair dryer, Wi-Fi (free).

IN WATERBURY

The Old Stagecoach Inn 🔔   This columned and gabled home, within walking distance of Waterbury's downtown, is full of interesting detailing: painted wood floors, two porches, an old library with a stamped tin ceiling, and a chessboard. Built in 1826, the house was gutted and revamped in 1890 in ostentatious period style by an Ohio millionaire. After years of disuse, it was converted to an inn in the late 1980s by owners who preserved the home's historical touches; there are still Oriental rugs, an organ, a tapestry, and a parrot. Eight guest rooms and three suites are furnished mostly in oak and pine furniture and antiques, but this building is aging and could perhaps use a touch-up; this isn't a polished, luxury-inn experience in any way. Still, the price is right if you're looking to save, and the breakfasts are good. Two third-floor rooms show off original exposed beams and skylights, while three back rooms share one bathroom and feel a bit more like paying to stay in some family's farmhouse than an actual vacation.

18 N. Main St., Waterbury, VT 05676. ℂ **800/262-2206** or 802/244-5056. Fax 802/244-6956. www. oldstagecoach.com. 11 units (3 with shared bathroom). $75–$90 double with shared bathroom; $100–$130 double with private bathroom. Rates include breakfast. 2-night minimum stay during peak periods. AE, DISC, MC, V. **Amenities:** Restaurant. *In room:* TV (some units), Wi-Fi (free).

Where to Dine

Unlike good beds, dining options in Montpelier are multiplicious. That's largely due to the influence of the wonderful **New England Culinary Institute (NECI)** campus on the edge of town. **La Brioche Bakery & Cafe** (ℂ **802/229-0443**), which is essentially NECI's pastry laboratory, occupies a key corner at State and Main streets. A deli counter here offers baked goods such as croissants and baguettes. Get them to go, or settle into a table in the afternoon sun outdoors. It's open daily from as early as 6am, usually until 6pm (to 2pm Sun).

I've also spent many an afternoon inside the cleverly named **Capitol Grounds ★**, at 27 State St. (ℂ **802/223-7800;** www.capitolgrounds.com), a stone's throw from the gold dome of the state capitol building.

IN MONTPELIER

Main Street Grill & Bar ★★ NEW AMERICAN   This modern restaurant serves as classroom and ongoing exam for students of the New England Culinary Institute. It's not unusual to see knots of students, toques at a rakish angle, walking around. You can eat in the first-level dining room, watching street life through the broad windows, or hang out in the homey bar downstairs. The menu changes often, but keeps a "farm-to-table" thread going throughout the year. Lunch might be a poached pear and Stilton salad or a bowl of clam chowder to start, followed by a hangar steak salad, grilled salmon, fried calamari, crab cakes, pulled-pork tacos, fish and chips, or something similar. Dinner is heavier, of course, and could feature a grilled leg of lamb, pan-roasted chicken, steaks, grilled venison, pasta with mussels, or a butternut squash risotto (vegetarian dishes are always on the menu). There are beer specials during the weekdays, and a popular prix-fixe Sunday brunch emphasizes fresh omelets and a meat-carving station.

The downstairs **Chef's Table ★★** dining room is a more upscale experience but is sometimes rented out for private or corporate events; call about its current status and daily specials if you're interested in trying it.

118 Main St. ℂ **802/223-3188** (Grill & Bar) or 802/229-9202 (Chef's Table). www.necidining.com. Main courses $4–$12 lunch, $12–$19 dinner. AE, DISC, MC, V. Tues–Sat 11:30am–2pm and 5:30–9pm; Sun 10am–2pm and 5:30–9pm.

Restaurant Phoebe ★ CONTINENTAL   It's simple yet fancy. Right on Montpelier's main restaurant row, Phoebe offers a combination of the familiar—pastas, local beef—and the unusual or upscale: entrees like quail, side dishes like fried artichokes. Lunch could be a burger, a piece of grilled salmon with peppers and a pesto cream sauce, or a grilled chicken panini. Dinners run to items like roasted pork loin, steaks, pan-roasted Coho salmon, and house-made fresh fettuccine, while the pastry chef is especially inventive: He turns out desserts like a flourless chocolate mascarpone torte, tequila-spiked agave cheesecake, and crème brûlée flavored with Meyer lemons and ginger.

52 State St. ✆ **802/262-3500.** www.restaurantphoebe.com. Main courses $7–$13 lunch, $12–$21 dinner. AE, MC, V. Mon 11:30am–2pm; Tues–Thurs 11:30am–2pm and 5:30–9pm; Fri–Sat 5:30–9pm.

IN WATERBURY

Hen of the Wood ★★ NEW AMERICAN   Chef Eric Warnstedt, noted in *Food & Wine* as an up-and-coming chef to watch, has made this open-kitchen concept work since opening in 2005 in a space right in downtown Waterbury. He now has a devoted local following. The menu leans on ideas borrowed from France (duck breast, a wild mushroom tartine) and Italy (a sheep's milk gnocchi), but most of the preparations are solidly New American: steamed mussels; a board of local bread, cheese, and prosciutto; seared Maine sea scallops with an olive butter; grass-fed rib-eye steaks with a tarragon-inflected aioli; and short ribs braised in red wine. There are also plenty of artisanal cheeses to sample here—the place is practically a master class in the modern art of Vermont cheesemaking (try Twig Farm's "2-Milk Round")—plus a long wine list.

92 Stowe St. ✆ **802/244-7300.** www.henofthewood.com. Reservations recommended. Main courses $16–$28. MC, V. Tues–Sat 5–9pm.

Marsala Salsa ★ 🍴 ☺ CARIBBEAN/MEXICAN   And now for something completely different. The owner of Marsala Salsa was born in the Caribbean, raised on the cuisine of India, and once worked at a Mexican restaurant. The result? A happy hybrid of international cuisines, served at very reasonable prices. The restaurant is inside a funky storefront in Waterbury's historic downtown, and has been decorated with a light touch. Mexican entrees might include carne asada, *bistec picado,* or fajitas of charbroiled chicken or sirloin with a tasty homemade avocado-lime butter. If you're more partial to Indian or Caribbean food, try the curries, vindaloo, tandoori chicken, or grilled shrimp with creamy jerk sauce. Kids get their own menu featuring a little taco pizza, minitortillas, and chicken fingers, while sweet dessert choices include deep-fried bananas, pumpkin flan, gelati, and a coconut cream caramel.

13–15 Stowe St. ✆ **802/244-1150.** Reservations recommended Sat–Sun. Main courses $10–$16. MC, V. Tues–Sat 5–9pm.

STOWE

Stowe is 10 miles N of Waterbury, 35 miles E of Burlington, and 75 miles NE of White River Junction

There's no other place in Vermont quite like **Stowe.** A wonderful destination in summer, fall, or winter—and one of Vermont's original winter-vacation resorts—it's set in beautiful hills beneath bigger mountains. Yet it's also struggling with growing pains, as condo developments and strip-mall-style restaurants have arrived en masse. The village's main street has mostly preserved its New England character and great views of the surrounding mountains and farmlands, but this is one of the few places in the state where you'll find yourself cursing out traffic as a 2-mile line snakes through the center of town on a weekend.

Most attractions are strung out along **Mountain Road** (Rte. 108), which runs from the village center all the way to the base of **Mount Mansfield** and the Stowe **ski resort**, and a **free trolley bus** connects the village with the mountain during ski season (mid-Dec to Mar). Not a skier? That's okay; you can still play. Mount Mansfield (Vermont's tallest) is a lovely driving or hiking trip, ablaze with foliage in fall to photograph and full of plenty of rewarding views in summer. **Smugglers'**

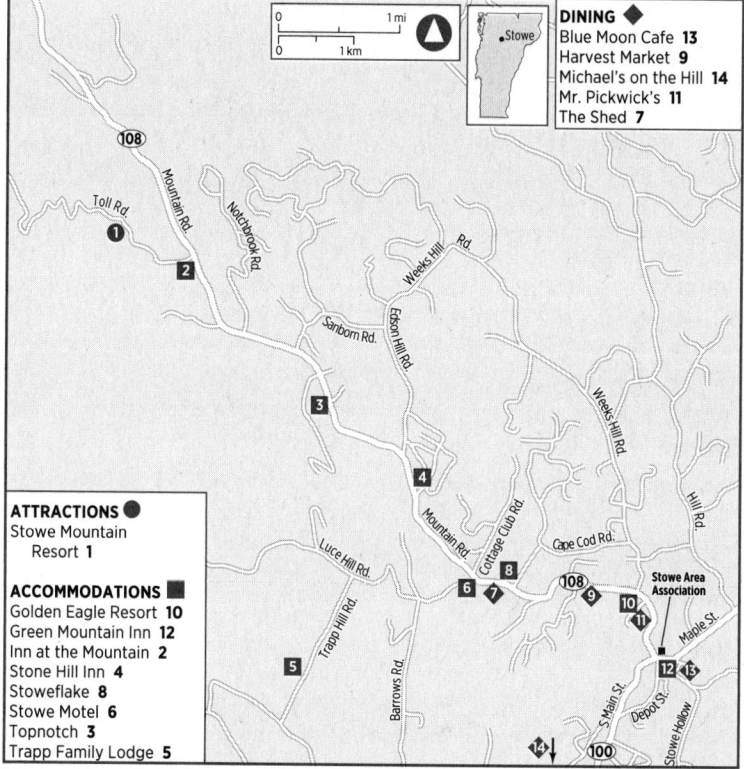

DINING ◆
Blue Moon Cafe **13**
Harvest Market **9**
Michael's on the Hill **14**
Mr. Pickwick's **11**
The Shed **7**

ATTRACTIONS ●
Stowe Mountain
  Resort **1**

ACCOMMODATIONS ■
Golden Eagle Resort **10**
Green Mountain Inn **12**
Inn at the Mountain **2**
Stone Hill Inn **4**
Stoweflake **8**
Stowe Motel **6**
Topnotch **3**
Trapp Family Lodge **5**

Notch is one of New England's most fun passes to squeeze your car through. And the concentration of **resorts** here rivals anywhere else in New England. Period.

Essentials

GETTING THERE   Stowe is on Rte. 100, about 10 miles north of Waterbury; simply take I-89 to exit 10 and head north, continuing past all the tourist stuff until you reach the village center. In summer, Stowe can also be reached from **Burlington** or **Montpelier** (after some back-roading) via Smugglers' Notch on **Rte. 108.** This scenic pass, which squeezes narrowly between rocks, is *not* recommended for RVs or trailers, but it *is* one of the state's most scenic drives. The pass is closed in winter, and absolutely packed with parked cars on both shoulders (try squeezing past *that*) in October.

Stowe has no direct train or bus service, though **Amtrak**'s (© 800/872-7245; www.amtrak.com) *Vermonter* service does make one daily run from New York City to Waterbury, 10 miles away. The ride takes nearly 9 hours and costs $56 one-way. Once there, though, you'll probably have to call a local taxi.

VISITOR INFORMATION   The **Stowe Area Association** (℃ 877/467-8693 or 802/253-7321; www.gostowe.com) maintains a great, professional **tourist information office** right in the village center at 51 Main St. It's open 9am to 8pm weekdays, plus 10am to 5pm weekends during summer, fall-foliage season, and winter ski season (during other seasons, weekend hours are more limited). The staff here can help you book a room even on short notice, give you enough maps and brochures to keep you reading all week long, and point you to a good restaurant. They also maintain clean bathrooms.

The **Green Mountain Club** (℃ 802/244-7037; www.greenmountainclub.org), a statewide association devoted to building and maintaining walking trails in the mountains, has its headquarters and **visitor center** on Rte. 100 between Waterbury and Stowe.

SPECIAL EVENTS   The weeklong **Stowe Winter Carnival** (℃ 802/253-7321; www.stowewintercarnival.com) has been held annually in January since 1921. The fest features a number of wacky events involving skis, snowshoes, and skates, as well as nighttime entertainment. Don't miss the snow-sculpture contest or snow golf, played on a snow-covered course.

Downhill Skiing

Stowe Mountain Resort ★★★   Stowe was one of the first, and one of the classiest, ski resorts in the world when it opened in the 1930s. Its regional dominance has eroded somewhat over the years since—Killington, Sunday River, and Sugarloaf, among other resorts, have snagged big shares of the New England ski market, and iconic hills like Mad River and Jay Peak carved out niches, too. But this resort still has loads of charm and plenty of excellent runs, and it's still one of the best places to get that full New England ski experience: a combination of beautiful ski trails and pastoral Vermont views. This is a tremendous challenge for advanced skiers, with winding, old-style trails—especially notable are the legendary "Front Four" trails (National, Starr, Lift Line, and Goat), which have humbled more than a handful of folks. The mountain also has several good, long lifts that go all the way from bottom to top—not the usual patchwork of shorter lifts you find at many other ski areas. For après-ski, the resort operates the very tony **Stowe Mountain Lodge** (see "Where to Stay," below) and maintains a couple of upscale restaurants with bar areas—not to mention the obligatory spa.

5781 Mountain Rd., Stowe, VT 05672. ℃ **800/253-4754** or 802/253-3000. www.stowe.com. Adults $57–$89 day lift tickets, $68–$71 half-day; discounts for youths and seniors.

Cross-Country Skiing

The **Trapp Family Lodge Nordic Ski Center** ★★ (℃ 800/826-7000 or 802/253-8511; www.trappfamily.com) on Luce Hill Road was the nation's first cross-country ski center. It remains one of the most gloriously situated in the Northeast, set atop a ridge with views across the broad valley and into the folds of mountains flanking Mount Mansfield. The center maintains some 30 miles of groomed trails (plus perhaps another 60 miles of natural backcountry trails) on 2,700 acres of rolling forestland; basically, for the cross-country ski nut, this is sheer heaven. Rates are $22 per adult for a full-day trail pass (less for kids and half-days), and $25 per day to rent skis.

Good ski touring is also enjoyed at the **Stowe Mountain Resort Cross-Country Touring Center** (© **800/253-4754** or 802/253-3000), with about 20 miles of groomed trails and 25 miles of backcountry trails at the base of Mount Mansfield. Full-day passes cost $18 to $23 for adults, about half that much for children ages 6 to 12; private and group lessons are also available here.

Summer Outdoor Pursuits

Stowe's name is synonymous with winter recreation, but it's also a great summer destination. The area's lush, rolling hills are great for hiking and biking—and all of it's towered over by craggy **Mount Mansfield,** Vermont's highest peak.

You have several options for getting to the top of Mansfield. The **auto toll road ★★** (© **802/253-3500**), part of the Stowe Mountain Resort, traces its lineage back to the 19th century, when it served horse-drawn vehicles bringing passengers to a former hotel near the mountain's crown. (That hotel was demolished in the 1960s.) Drivers now twist their way up the road and park in a lot, but there's still a ways to go to the summit. A **2-hour hike** along well-marked trails is required to get to the tippy-top, which offers unforgettable views of Lake Champlain and the Adirondacks. The toll road is open 9am to 4pm from mid-May until mid-October. The fare is a steep $24 per car, but that price covers up to six passengers (it's $6 per additional person, if you have more than six—you don't, right?). Climbing the mountain on foot is free, but bicycles and motorcycles are prohibited.

Another option is the **Stowe gondola ★** (© **802/253-3500**), which whisks visitors to the summit at the Cliff House Restaurant. Hikers can explore the rugged, open ridgeline, and then descend on the gondola before twilight. The gondola runs from mid-June to mid-October. The full round-trip costs $23 for adults, $19 for seniors, and $15 for children ages 6 to 12. There are family discounts, and you can also pay for a one-way ride. The lift is open 10am to 5pm daily in season.

The budget route up Mount Mansfield—the most rewarding, but of course the most physically demanding—is entirely **on foot ★**, with at least nine options for an ascent. This requires a good map. Ask for the *Visitor's Guide Hiking Map* at Stowe Mountain's guest-services desk, the local tourism office, your inn, or the Green Mountain Club headquarters on Rte. 100 (about 4 miles south of Stowe's village center)—it's open weekdays, and the GMC can also offer you advice on other area trails.

Another local attraction is the **Stowe Recreation Path ★★**, winding for more than 5 miles from behind the Stowe Community Church and up the valley toward the big mountain, ending behind the Topnotch Tennis Center. This appealing pathway is heavily used by local walkers, hikers, and bikers in summer; in winter it becomes an equally popular cross-country ski trail. Get onto the pathway at either end, or at points where it crosses side roads leading to Mountain Road. No motorized vehicles or skateboards are allowed.

According to the tourism office, some 300 bikes can be rented from shops near the Rec Path.

Where to Stay

Stowe is blessed with the highest concentration of **luxury resorts** in New England: there are *five* in this little village, plus several smaller inns that vault into the ultra-luxe category. There are plenty of basic **motels** of varying quality along Mountain Road serving travelers who don't want or need to stay in the resorts.

Golden Eagle Resort ★ ☺   Of the numerous lodgings lined up along Mountain Road, few are more family-friendly than this one. The Golden Eagle gets it right with a children's play area, three swimming pools, two ponds for fishing, a regulation tennis court, 80 acres of private woods laced with hiking trails, and even a small spa offering kids' massages. Adults enjoy the place, too, particularly the romantic cottages and suites with fireplaces and whirlpools behind the main building. Standard units are more basic, but some do have sitting areas or porches. The small spa area includes a popular indoor Jacuzzi, and a cafe serves breakfasts of local eggs, dairy, and bacon. Don't come if you're expecting white-glove service, valet parking, or a fancy restaurant; but the Golden Eagle is perfect for casual families. The hotel also rents out several apartment units with full kitchens and kitchenettes.

511 Mountain Rd. (P.O. Box 1090), Stowe, VT 05672. ⓒ **800/626-1010** or 802/253-4811. Fax 802-253-2561. www.goldeneagleresort.com. 94 units. $99–$199 double, $144–$299 suite; winter, holidays, and foliage season $149–$264 double, $199–$539 suite. AE, DISC, MC, V. **Amenities:** Cafe; 3 pools (2 outdoor, 1 indoor); spa; tennis court. *In room:* Fridge, Wi-Fi (some units; free).

Green Mountain Inn ★★★ 🏕   There are four true resorts on the road to Stowe Mountain, but this is the fifth—a totally different experience, because it's right in the village center. (Actually, it *is* the village center.) The handsome, historic inn is your best choice if you're seeking a New England history lesson along with your pampering. Guest rooms are spread out among several buildings old and new; rooms are tastefully decorated in an early-19th-century motif that befits the 1833 vintage of the main building. More than a dozen units have Jacuzzis and/or gas fireplaces, and the Mill House has rooms with CD players, sofas, and Jacuzzis that open into the bedrooms from behind folding wooden doors. The deluxe Mansfield House (which opened in 2000) adds double Jacuzzis, marble bathrooms, and 36-inch TVs with DVD players; all these expensive rooms are superb. Other rooms are smaller and simpler, but still offer a good taste of Vermont. The inn's restaurant, **The Whip** ★, is highly regarded by guests and locals for its Continental cooking.

18 Main St., Stowe, VT 05672. ⓒ **800/253-7302** or 802/253-7301. Fax 802/253-5096. www.green mountaininn.com. 100 units. $139–$319 double; $249–$769 suite. 2-night minimum stay summer and winter weekends and in foliage season. AE, DISC, MC, V. Pets allowed in some rooms (call ahead; $20 per night). **Amenities:** 2 restaurants; exercise room; Jacuzzi; heated outdoor pool (year-round); limited room service; sauna; steam room. *In room:* A/C, TV, hair dryer, Wi-Fi (free).

Inn at The Mountain ★   Owned and operated by Stowe Mountain Resort, this was for years the resort's "official" hotel near the base of the mountain—until the resort built the luxe Stowe Mountain Lodge, which now overshadows the Inn. Not a fancy place but rather a low-key spot, this is more like an upscale motel than an inn, though the clean, attractive rooms here are more spacious than your average motel rooms. Inside you'll find veneer furniture, small refrigerators, and tiny balconies facing the pool or the woods.

5781 Mountain Rd., Stowe, VT 05672. ⓒ **800/253-4754** or 802/253-3000. www.stowe.com. 33 units. $119–$359 double, apt. and town houses higher; holiday season rates higher. 5-night minimum stay Christmas week. AE, DC, DISC, MC, V. **Amenities:** Restaurant; exercise room; Jacuzzi; outdoor pool; limited room service; sauna; 9 tennis courts; Wi-Fi (in lobby; free). *In room:* A/C, TV, fridge.

Stone Hill Inn ★★ 🏕   With just nine rooms, the contemporary yet romantic Stone Hill Inn offers personal service and a handy location partway between Stowe village and the mountain. It's a very fancy place, with luxe amenities and furnishings in every room: four-poster king beds, Egyptian cotton towels, kindly gas fireplaces that front double Jacuzzis in the oversized bathrooms, and flatscreen TVs with DVD players and VCRs. Suite layouts are all roughly similar, yet each room somehow has a distinct color scheme and feel; fabric and wall hues of gold, purple, bordeaux, and the like put one in mind of a French chateau. The high-ceilinged common rooms sport fireplaces and billiards tables, while a guest pantry offers complimentary beverages around the clock. Breakfast is served in a bright dining room, and snacks are set out each evening. An outdoor hot tub is good for a relaxing soak, and the inn has snowshoes and a toboggan for guests to use. Stone Hill may lack history, but that's all it lacks—this is a place of quiet, luxury, and romance.

89 Houston Farm Rd. (off Mountain Rd.), Stowe, VT 05672. © **802/253-6282.** www.stonehillinn.com. 9 units. $330–$425 double. Rates include breakfast. 2-night minimum stay Sat–Sun and foliage season; 3-night minimum stay holiday weekends; 4-night minimum stay Christmas week. Closed Apr and Nov. AE, DC, DISC, MC, V. Not suitable for children. **Amenities:** Jacuzzi. *In room:* A/C, TV/DVD, hair dryer, Wi-Fi (free), no phone.

Stoweflake ★★ This resort with the cutesy name is on Mountain Road en route to the mountain, less than 2 miles from the village. It has gone on a sprucing-up program lately, adding better amenities to its most expensive rooms. As a result, the newest guest rooms are now as nice as those at Topnotch (see below)—they're regally decorated and have amenities such as two phones and wet bars. The resort has several categories of guest rooms in two wings; the "superior" rooms in the old wing are a bit cozy, okay for an overnight, but you're better off requesting "deluxe" level or better if you will be staying a few days. Many of these units have tubs with jets. The spa and fitness facilities are adequate, even if they lack the over-the-top elegance of Topnotch's (what, no waterfalls?). There's a decent-size fitness room with Cybex equipment, a squash/racquetball court, co-ed Jacuzzi, and a small indoor pool. Stoweflake also manages a small collection of fine town houses nearby. All rooms and town houses are wired for either high-speed Internet or Wi-Fi—free of charge.

1746 Mountain Rd. (P.O. Box 369), Stowe, VT 05672. © **800/253-2232** or 802/253-7355. Fax 802/253-6858. www.stoweflake.com. 95 units. Peak winter season $170–$270 double, $390 suite; holiday season $180–$290 double, $340 suite; off season $150–$250 double, $360 suite. 2-night minimum stay most weekends; 4-night minimum stay during holidays. AE, DC, DISC, MC, V. **Amenities:** 2 restaurants; babysitting; bikes; children's center; health club; indoor and outdoor pool; limited room service; spa; 2 tennis courts. *In room:* A/C, TV, fridge (some units), hair dryer, either Wi-Fi or high-speed Internet (free).

Stowe Motel ★ 🍴 This is one of the very best choices in Stowe if you're traveling on a budget. Units are spread out among three buildings; rooms are basic, but some have couches and coffee tables, and all have small fridges, air conditioners, televisions, and phones. The slightly more expensive efficiency units add two-burner stoves for in-room cooking. Surprisingly, you also get access to expansive grounds, tennis courts, a pool, hammocks, and an outdoor hot tub—a great setup for such a reasonably priced sleep. (You can often get a double room for around $100, a true steal in Stowe.) They will even rent or let you borrow snowshoes or mountain bikes. If you need more space, the motel rents out a few local houses and apartments nearby, some with hot tubs, washer/dryers, and the like. Again: a steal of a deal.

2043 Mountain Rd., Stowe, VT 05672. © **800/829-7629** or 802/253-7629. Fax 802/253-9971. www.stowemotel.com. 60 units. $75–$190 double. AE, DISC, MC, V. Pets allowed (1 per room, $10 per night). **Amenities:** Bikes; Jacuzzi; outdoor heated pool; tennis court. *In room:* A/C, TV, fridge, Wi-Fi (free).

Topnotch ★★★ The boxy, uninteresting exterior of Topnotch hides a surprisingly creative interior and upscale facility (voted one of the top resort spas in the U.S. by *Condé Nast Traveler* readers). The main lobby is in ski-lodge style, with lots of stone, wood, and a huge moose head on the wall; guest rooms are attractively appointed, mostly in country pine. Some units have wood-burning fireplaces, some have Jacuzzis, and third-floor rooms sport cathedral ceilings. The main attraction is the huge 35,000-square-foot **spa** ★, free for guests (nonguests pay a $50 fee). This spa has such nice touches as fireplaces in the locker rooms and a range of aerobics classes, weight-training programs, and revitalizing treatments for face, skin, and body. Outdoors you can ramble on 120 acres of grounds, doing anything from horseback riding to cross-country skiing. There also is indoor tennis. Three pools (2 outdoor, 1 indoor) and a Jacuzzi help loosen after-ski muscles.

4000 Mountain Rd., Stowe, VT 05672. ⓒ **800/451-8686** or 802/253-8585. Fax 802/253-9263. www. topnotchresort.com. 92 units. $180–$320 double, $315–$755 suite; holidays $380–$495 double, $500–$860 suite. 6-night minimum stay Christmas week. AE, DC, DISC, MC, V. Pets allowed. **Amenities:** 2 restaurants; concierge; exercise room; Jacuzzi; 3 pools (1 indoor, 2 outdoor); limited room service; sauna; spa; tennis courts (4 indoor, 10 outdoor). *In room:* A/C, TV, fridge, hair dryer, Wi-Fi (free).

Trapp Family Lodge ★★ Of Stowe's "big four" resorts, this one can claim the best views *and* the most history. It's a different experience from the other three, but for the outdoors enthusiast or *Sound of Music* fan, it can't be beat. You know the story: The Trapp family fled Nazi Austria under the cover of darkness and wound up on this lovely Vermont hillside, farming, singing, and eventually building a lodge. (The original burned in 1980; this is a copy.) Two of Maria's grandchildren now manage the resort and have gently tugged it into the 21st century: The newly added bakery, microbrewery, gorgeous fitness center with outdoor hot tub and indoor pool, and luxury wing testify to that. Even standard rooms are big, many with expansive balconies and views of the Green Mountains (ask about a corner unit). Family suites like no. 421 are positively huge, while a half-dozen luxury suites in the newer Millennium Wing feature touches like wood-burning fireplaces, kitchenettes, wine glasses, or stylish European-style bathrooms with Jacuzzis and open showers. You can even sleep in Maria's own room, which sports a full brick fireplace, full kitchen, four-poster bed, and the best views in the house. (Her suite also overlooks the quiet family cemetery.) Hiking, biking, and skiing trails interlace 2,000-plus acres of grounds (see "Cross-Country Skiing," p. 530), and the lodge now rents mountain bikes.

700 Trapp Hill Rd. (P.O. Box 1428), Stowe, VT 05672. ⓒ **800/826-7000** or 802/253-8511. Fax 802/253-5740. www.trappfamily.com. 120 units. $195–$585 double, $295–$880 suite. Rates include meals during holidays and foliage season. 3-night minimum stay Presidents' Day weekend and foliage season; 5-night minimum stay Christmas week. AE, DC, MC, V. Depart Stowe westward on Rte. 108; in 2 miles bear left at fork near white church; continue up hill, following signs for lodge. **Amenities:** 2 restaurants; babysitting; bikes; health club; Jacuzzi; 3 pools (1 heated indoor, 2 outdoor); limited room service; sauna; 4 tennis courts. *In room:* A/C, TV, fridge (some units), Wi-Fi (free).

Where to Dine

Packing a picnic? The **Harvest Market** ★, at 1031 Mountain Rd. (ⓒ **802/253-3800;** www.harvestatstowe.com), is a great place for picking up takeout gourmet. You can browse Vermont products and imports, or snag fresh-baked goods to bring back to the ski lodge or take for a picnic. It's open daily until 7pm.

Blue Moon Cafe ★★★ NEW AMERICAN Delectable crusty bread on the table, Frank Sinatra crooning in the background, and local art on the walls are clues that this isn't a typical ski-area restaurant in any way, shape, or form. Just a short stroll off Stowe's *real* main street, inside an older home with a contemporary interior, the Blue Moon offers what's probably the town's top fine dining—it's amazing that they're so low-key about it. The restaurant's wonderful menu changes pretty much every week, so half the fun of eating here is that you never know what's going to be on the menu until you open it. Start out with the appetizer of the moment, whether that happens to be a grilled sweet-potato-and-orange salad with frisée and pecans, some lamb skewers, a piece of smoked trout, or a preparation of Maine crab cakes. Then move on to entrees such as filet of sole with lemon, capers, and roasted potatoes; mahimahi with a mango salsa *and* a chipotle pineapple sauce; a grilled half chicken with chutney; a grilled lamb steak; or New York strip served with cognac cream and crispy fried onions. There are also a few changing small plates each week, which are even more inventive than the regular menu—rock shrimp risotto and venison burrito are two that have popped up on the menu, for instance. Finish with the popular Belgian chocolate pot, some homemade sorbet, or whichever mousse, tart, or cheese plate happens to be on the card.

35 School St. ✆ **802/253-7006.** www.bluemoonstowe.com. Reservations recommended. Small plates $13; main courses $18–$31. AE, DISC, MC, V. Sun–Thurs 6–9pm (Fri–Sat to 9:30pm).

Michael's on the Hill ★★★ NEW AMERICAN In a farmhouse on the hill and highway leading up to Stowe village, Michael's does New American like few others in the area. There are three dining spaces: a porch with plenty of windows looking out on the mountains; the elegantly arched Trout Room; and a woody-rustic, renovated barn. The menu is stunning in its new interpretations of classical Continental cuisine, Vermont-style. Appetizers might include a roasted corn soup with mint, a Maine crab cake with an asparagus tart, beer-steamed mussels, pumpkin soup with curry and local cheddar, a crab rissolé with lemon aioli, or Vermont quail. Entrees run to things like a Moroccan lamb loin chop with merguez sausage, roasted strip loin with truffled mashed potatoes and marrow, lobster ravioli, trout meunière, or riesling- and spice-braised rabbit served with polenta. This is truly an exciting place to dine. And if you're day-tripping in Waterbury village, don't miss the little cafe (✆ **802/882-2700**) at Waterbury's train station with gourmet products; it's run by the same owners.

4182 Waterbury-Stowe Rd. ✆ **802/244-7476.** www.michaelsonthehill.com. Reservations recommended. Main courses $25–$43. AE, MC, V. Wed–Mon 5–9:30pm.

Mr. Pickwick's ★★ 🎁 PUB FARE/CONTINENTAL Mr. Pickwick's is a pub and restaurant inside the Ye Old English Inne. Ignore the silly spelling and the over-the-top faux Englishness of the place, because this restaurant is actually very good. Run since 1983 with creative gusto by British ex-pats, it's an enjoyable place to eat. Begin by admiring the decor while relaxing at handsome wood tables in the booths (dubbed "pews"). Sample from among some 150 beers or 21 casks (many of them British) before studying the much-changed lunch menu—they still do fish and chips and bangers and mash here, sure, but now the food is mostly things like Caesar salads, an inventive onion soup, mulligatawny, Kobe burgers, duck confit (!), and a rocket salad of pears in wine, Stilton cheese, and fresh herbs. Dinner has become something much more interesting and upscale than it used to be, too: grilled fish, Statler chicken, delicious pasta, various steaks, prosciutto-wrapped kangaroo (yes, really) served with a chocolate plum sauce, pan-seared elk medallions, game stew, or whatever else the owners feel like finding and cooking. Anglophiles, fear not: The beef Wellington and oyster-kidney pie are still safe and sound on the menu.

433 Mountain Rd. © **802/253-7558.** www.mrpickwicks.com. Reservations accepted for parties of 6 or more. Main courses $10–$18 at lunch, $18–$36 at dinner. AE, DC, MC, V. Daily 11am–1am.

The Shed PUB FARE/BREWERY   Stowe has plenty of options for pub fare, but the Shed takes the prize for longest-running. Since it opened more than 3 decades ago, this informal place has supplied local skiers and tourists with filling food and camaraderie (join the "Hall of Foam" by ordering a microbrew sampler). A few craft brews are made right on the premise, but there are plenty more choices as well. The taproom has a pubby feel; the bright solarium in the rear is a better spot to eat Sunday brunch. Meals are pub fare and nothing special: nachos, burgers, ribs, fish and chips, chicken, shepherd's pie, sandwiches. Look for prime-rib specials on the weekends.

1859 Mountain Rd. © **802/253-4364.** Reservations recommended Fri–Sat and holidays. Main courses $8–$11 at lunch, $8–$21 at dinner. AE, DC, DISC, MC, V. Sun–Thurs 11:30am–10pm; Fri–Sat 11:30am–11pm.

BURLINGTON

Burlington: 215 miles NW of Boston; 98 miles S of Montreal; 154 miles NE of Albany, NY

Right at the doorstep of Lake Champlain, **Burlington** is Vermont's biggest city (though it isn't all *that* big). It's a vibrant college town—home to the University of Vermont, known locally as UVM—with flavors of hippie, yuppie, and vintage Vermont mashed and mixed in like a scoop of Ben & Jerry's super fudge chunk. Speaking of Ben & Jerry, they completely epitomize this place: two city hippies-gone-big-time who found the city to be their ideal testing ground. (Look for the sidewalk plaque at the corner of St. Paul and College sts. commemorating their original ice-cream shop.)

It's really no wonder that Burlington has become a magnet for those seeking an alternative to big-city life. The downtown occupies a superb position overlooking the lake and the Adirondack Mountains to the west. To the east, the Green Mountains rise dramatically, with two of their highest peaks (Mount Mansfield and Camel's Hump) stretching above an undulating ridge.

The pedestrian mall (Church St.) downtown is enjoyable, and the city's extensive bus system is absurdly cheap.

Essentials

GETTING THERE   Burlington is at the junction of I-89, Rte. 7, and Rte. 2. From New York City, it's between a 5- and 6-hour drive via either I-91 and I-89 or the New York State Thruway; from Boston, figure on 3 to 3½ hours' driving via I-93 and then I-89.

Burlington International Airport (airport code: BTV), about 3 miles east of the city center, is served daily by nonstop flights on **Continental Express** (© 800/525-0280; www.continental.com) from Newark and Cleveland; **Delta Connection** (© 800/221-1212; www.delta.com) from Atlanta and New York's JFK; **JetBlue** (© 800/538-2583; www.jetblue.com) daily from New York City's JFK and Orlando; **United** (© 800/241-6522; www.united.com) from Chicago and Washington's

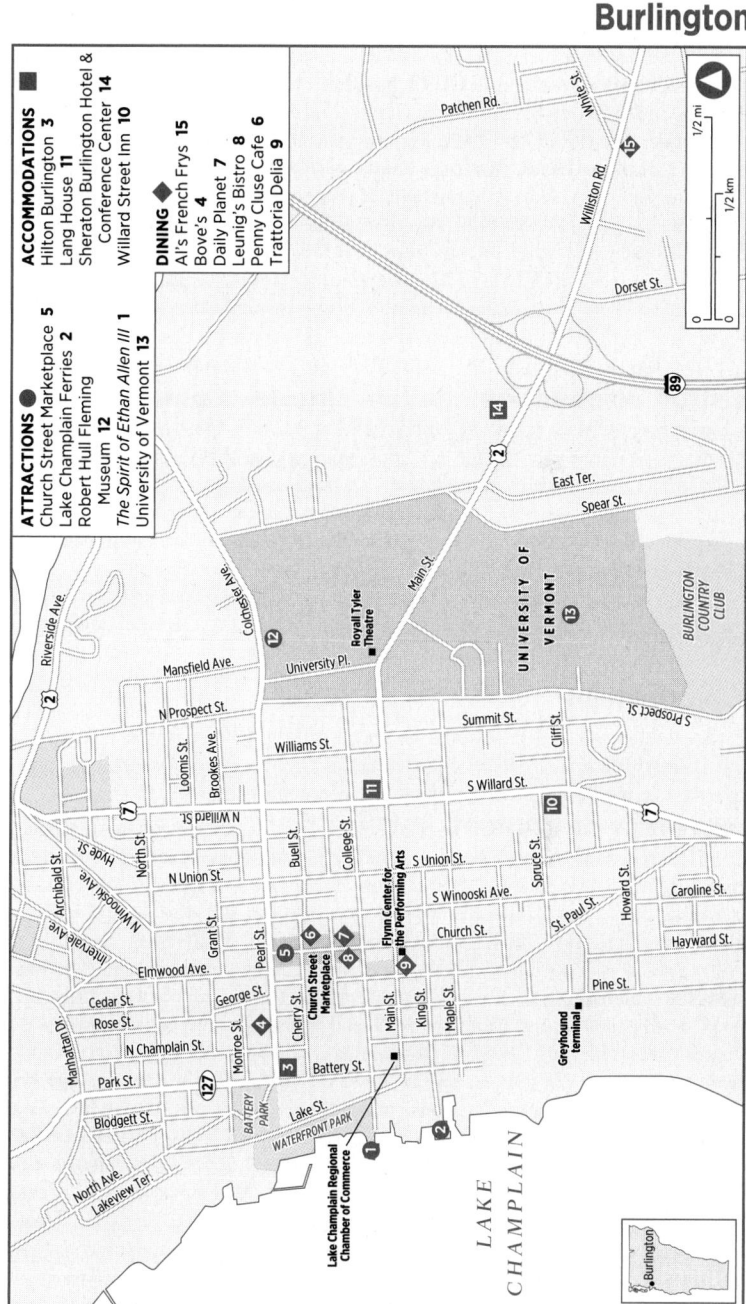

ACCOMMODATIONS ■
Hilton Burlington **3**
Lang House **11**
Sheraton Burlington Hotel &
  Conference Center **14**
Willard Street Inn **10**

DINING ◆
Al's French Frys **15**
Bove's **4**
Daily Planet **7**
Leunig's Bistro **8**
Penny Cluse Cafe **6**
Trattoria Delia **9**

ATTRACTIONS ●
Church Street Marketplace **5**
Lake Champlain Ferries **2**
Robert Hull Fleming
  Museum **12**
The Spirit of Ethan Allen III **1**
University of Vermont **13**

Patchen Rd.

White St.

Williston Rd.

Dorset St.

89

2

East Ter.

Spear St.

Main St.

UNIVERSITY OF VERMONT

BURLINGTON COUNTRY CLUB

Riverside Ave.

2

Colchester Ave.

12

Royall Tyler Theatre

University Pl.

Mansfield Ave.

N Prospect St.

S Prospect St.

Summit St.

Cliff St.

Williams St.

Loomis St.

Brookes Ave.

S Willard St.

11

10

7

7

N Willard St.

North St.

Buell St.

College St.

S Union St.

Spruce St.

St. Paul St.

Howard St.

Caroline St.

Hayward St.

Flynn Center for the Performing Arts

S Winooski Ave.

Church St.

Hyde St.

Archibald St.

N Winooski Ave.

N Union St.

Grant St.

Pearl St.

5

6

7

8

9

Intervale Ave.

Elmwood Ave.

Cedar St.

Rose St.

George St.

Cherry St.

4

Church Street Marketplace

Main St.

King St.

Maple St.

Pine St.

Greyhound terminal

Manhattan Dr.

N Champlain St.

Monroe St.

3

Park St.

Battery St.

127

BATTERY PARK

Blodgett St.

Lake St.

WATERFRONT PARK

1

2

North Ave.

Lakeview Ter.

Lake Champlain Regional Chamber of Commerce

LAKE CHAMPLAIN

15

14

2

13

1/2 mi

1/2 km

Burlington

Dulles airports; and **US Airways Express** (✆ 800/428-4322; www.usair.com) from New York City's LaGuardia, Philadelphia, and Washington's Reagan airports.

Auto rentals are available from a half-dozen national chains inside the terminal, or a bus ride into the city on a **CCTA bus** (bus no. 1; departs every 30 min., every hour on Sun) costs just $1.25.

Amtrak's (✆ 800/872-7245; www.amtrak.com) *Vermonter* service offers one daily departure to **Essex Junction** (connected by bus to downtown Burlington) from New York, New Haven, Springfield, Massachusetts, and points beyond such as Baltimore and Washington, D.C. It's a cheap ride ($56 one-way) from New York—but it also takes more than 9 hours from New York.

Greyhound (✆ 800/231-2222; www.greyhound.com) has a depot near the city center at 345 Pine St., with connections to Albany, Boston, Hartford, and New York. From New York, it's a 10- to 14-hour slog (change in Boston), costing $68 one-way; but from Boston, it takes 4½ to 5 hours and costs $56 one-way.

VISITOR INFORMATION The **Lake Champlain Regional Chamber of Commerce,** 60 Main St. (✆ 877/686-5253 or 802/863-3489; www.vermont.org), maintains an information center in a brick building near the waterfront and a short walk from Church Street Marketplace. It's open weekdays only. (On weekends, helpful maps and brochures are left in the entryway for visitors.) In summer, an information kiosk is also staffed at the Church Street Marketplace, at the corner of Church and Bank streets.

The excellent free local weekly paper, *Seven Days* (www.7dvt.com), carries great local articles and dining reviews plus a very good listing of local events, exhibits, and happenings.

Orientation

Burlington basically comprises three distinct areas: the **UVM campus** on top of the hill, a **downtown** area centered on the active Church Street Marketplace, and a thin strip of **waterfront** running along Lake Champlain.

UNIVERSITY OF VERMONT Founded in 1791 (funded by a state donation of 29,000 acres of forest land), Vermont's public university has since grown to accommodate nearly 10,000 undergraduates, more than a thousand graduate students, and a few hundred medical students. The campus is set on 400 acres atop a small hill overlooking downtown Burlington and Lake Champlain to the west; it also has a pretty good view of the Green Mountains to the east. The campus is large, with more than 400 buildings, many of which were designed by noted architectural firms such as H. H. Richardson and McKim, Mead, and White. A controversial new student center opened in 2007, dwarfing surrounding buildings with both its size and its boxy design, but it's here to stay. What UVM *doesn't* have is the usual college strip of beery bars, bagel shops, and bookstores adjacent to campus. Downtown serves that function, 5 blocks away; College Street connects the two, as does the free **College Street Shuttle** (it looks like an old-fashioned trolley). The shuttle runs between Burlington's waterfront boathouse and the UVM campus year-round, every 15 to 30 minutes from 11am until 9pm. Use it.

CHURCH STREET Downtown centers around the largely traffic-free Church Street Marketplace, a pedestrian corridor that jumps with activity most of the year—it's most fun in summer, obviously. This is the place to wander without purpose, people-watching and snacking. While the shopping and grazing are excellent here, don't overlook the superb historic commercial architecture that graces much of the area. A number of side streets radiate out from Church Street, too, with a mix of restaurants, shops, and offices.

THE WATERFRONT   The waterfront has benefited from a multimillion-dollar renovation, which included new construction of buildings such as the **Wing Building** (a quirky structure of brushed steel and other nontraditional materials). Next door is the **Cornerstone Building,** with a restaurant and offices (and better views of the lake thanks to its higher vantage point). Nearby, the city's **Community Boathouse** is a good destination on a hot summer day. Bear in mind that Burlingtonians accept a fairly liberal definition of the adjective "lakeside," though; in some cases, it can mean a shop or restaurant that's actually 300 ft. away and with no sight of water.

Exploring Burlington

Frankly speaking, there are not a ton of attractions in Burlington; instead the chief attractions are the lovely natural setting, the lakefront (which is mostly hidden from view), and the city's vibrant culture and counterculture. So if it's attractions you want, think about striking out into the countryside to nearby country towns like **Charlotte, Shelburne, Colchester, Underhill,** and **Jericho,** which hold some of the best sights.

Ethan Allen Homestead Museum   A quiet retreat on one of the most idyllic, least-developed stretches of the Winooski River, this museum just north of the city center is a shrine to Vermont's favorite son; even today, centuries later, he and his Green Mountain Boys remain larger-than-life figures in this state. Though Allen wasn't actually born in Burlington, he settled here later in life on property confiscated from a British sympathizer during the Revolution. Inside this red reconstruction of a farmhouse, an orientation center gives an intriguing multimedia account of Allen's life, plus info about regional history. The admissions fees have recently been jacked up quite a bit (more than double, in some cases), for some reason.

Rte. 127, Colchester. (C) **802/865-4556.** www.ethanallenhomestead.org. Admission $7 adults, $3 children 3–6, seniors $5, $25 per family. Mid-May to mid-Oct Thurs–Sat 10am–4pm; Sun 1–4pm. From city center, follow Pearl St. (at the northern end of Church St. Marketplace) to Rte. 127, and then continue about 2 miles north. From I-89, take exit 17 to North Ave., or exit 15 to Rte. 15.

Lake Champlain Ferries ★★   Car ferries chug across the often placid, sometimes turbulent waters of Lake Champlain from Burlington to Port Kent, New York, between late May and early October, and it's a good way to cut out miles of driving if you're heading west toward the Adirondacks. It's also a great way to see the lake, leaves, and mountains on a pleasant, inexpensive 1-hour cruise. Reservations are taken for the Burlington route only, which operates 10 to 20 times per day when it's running. Travelers are advised to make reservations at least a day in advance. Two other ferries also cross the lake—much more quickly, in just 12 to 20 minutes—linking Grande Isle, Vermont, with Plattsburgh, New York; and Charlotte, Vermont, with Essex, New York (note that credit cards are not accepted for fares on these two shorter rides). Between June and mid-October, narrated, musically accompanied, or dinner-inclusive lake cruises are also offered by the ferry company; call (C) **802/864-9669** for details. Note that these three ferries are unaffiliated with the "cable ferry" at Ticonderoga, New York, a fourth Champlain crossing.

King St. Dock. ☎ **802/864-9804.** www.ferries.com. Burlington–Port Kent $18 one-way car and driver, $4.95 additional adults, $2.20 children 6–12; Charlotte–Essex and Grande Isle–Cumberland Head $9.50 one-way for car and driver, $3.75 additional adults, $1.50 children 6–12; all round-trip fares slightly discounted. No credit cards for Charlotte or Grande Isle ferries.

Robert Hull Fleming Museum ★   This University of Vermont facility houses a collection of art and anthropological displays, with permanent holdings of African, ancient Egyptian, Asian, and Middle Eastern art. A selection of paintings by 20th-century Vermont artists is also on permanent display, and changing exhibitions reflect various cultures around the globe. Call or check the museum website for the schedule of lectures and other special events, as well. (Note that if you drive to the museum on weekdays, you must feed the museum's parking meters 75¢ per hour and also obtain a pass from the reception desk; on weekends, there's a free parking lot nearby.)

61 Colchester Ave. (UVM campus). ☎ **802/656-0750.** www.flemingmuseum.org. Admission $5 adults, $3 seniors and students, $10 family. Labor Day to Apr Tues–Fri 9am–4pm (Wed to 8pm), Sat–Sun 1–5pm; May to Labor Day Tues–Fri noon–4pm, Sat–Sun 1–5pm.

Shelburne Museum ★★★   Established in 1947 by one Electra Havemeyer Webb, the Shelburne houses one of the nation's best collections of American folk and decorative art. The museum occupies three dozen buildings spread out across 45 rolling acres, about 7 miles south of Burlington, and no less than the *New York Times* has opined that "there is nothing like Shelburne in the museum universe." The holdings total some 150,000 items in all—the expected quilts, tools, duck decoys, and weather vanes, but also entire *buildings* gathered from around New England and New York, which are a highlight. The structures include an 1890 railroad station, an entire lighthouse, a stagecoach inn, an Adirondack lodge, and a Vermont round barn. Even a 220-foot steamship is eerily landlocked on the museum's grounds. More recent additions include a 1950s ranch house (furnished in '50s style) and the engaging Kalkin House, creatively constructed of prefab metal structures and other materials. Rotating special exhibits highlight specific aspects of Americana such as Shaker design, African-American quilt work, the art of John James Audubon, and similar topics. As if this weren't enough, there's an annual summer festival here highlighting Vermont cheeses, wines, and beers known as the Vermont Cheesemakers Festival.

Rte. 7 (P.O. Box 10), Shelburne. ☎ **802/985-3346.** www.shelburnemuseum.org. Summer admission $18 adults, $9 children 6–18; discounted rates after 3pm. Late May to mid-Oct daily 10am–5pm; selected buildings also Apr to late May and mid-Oct to Dec 31 (call for information).

The Spirit of Ethan Allen III ★   The vistas of Lake Champlain and the Adirondacks haven't changed much since Samuel de Champlain first explored the area in 1609—but travel sure has. This tour ship, holding 500 passengers on three decks (it's much larger than its predecessor), offers a more genteel touring alternative to taking a ferry ride. The enclosed decks are air-conditioned, and food and drink are served from a deli and cash bar. In addition to four-times-daily narrated tours (1½ hr.; sunset cruise more expensive than the others), there are many specialty trips involving lunch, brunch, dinner, music, or even a murder (dramatically, for mystery buffs; not a real one). Parking is available at an additional cost.

Burlington Boathouse. ☎ **802/862-8300.** www.soea.com. Narrated 90-min. tours $15–$20 adults, $6–$13 children 3–11; meal and specialty cruises $23–$48 adults, $12–$31 children 3–11. Narrated cruises daily mid-May to mid-Oct; specialty cruises mid-June to mid-Oct.

Where to Stay

Several excellent resort properties are located within a half-hour's drive of the city. If those are too rich for your blood, a number of chain motels cluster along Rte. 7 (Shelburne Rd.) in South Burlington, about a 5- to 10-minute drive from downtown. While they lack even a trace of New England charm, they're mostly clean, modern, and reliable.

Basin Harbor Club ★★ ☺ This is one of Vermont's most peaceful resorts if your goal is to kick back and enjoy lake breezes and lovely scenery. The property is well integrated into its fine natural setting on the shores of Lake Champlain. Indeed, the best units aren't in the main inn but rather are the various cottages facing out onto the lake from their wooded, cliff-top perches; they feel wonderfully isolated, yet many sport fireplaces, comfy beds, work desks, sofas, and Jacuzzis. You won't find televisions here, so borrow or rent bikes, kayaks, canoes, or a speedboat; hit the little golf course; or grab a tennis racquet (lessons are available) and head to the clay courts. A good program of events and activities, including art classes and lectures, supplements your own walks in the nice gardens and lounging in the bright, Adirondack chairs on the lawn. Dining is at three good restaurants of various types—you choose from among B&B, MAP, or full dining plans in spring and fall, while all meals are included in summer rates—and the excellent kids' program completes the sense of having stepped into an upscale summer camp from another century. Summertime bonus: Thursday nights bring lobster dinners and live jazz to the beach.

4800 Basin Harbor Rd., Vergennes, VT 05491. ☏ **800/622-4000** or 802/475-2311. Fax 802/475-6545. www.basinharbor.com. 123 units. $147–$521 double; $262–$780 cottage. Rates include breakfast, lunch, and dinner mid-June to early Sept only. Rates do not include 18% service fee. B&B and MAP plans and rates also available. 2-night minimum stay some weekends. MC, V. Closed mid-Oct to mid-May. From Burlington, follow Rte. 7 south about 20 miles, turn right onto Rte. 27A and follow into Vergennes; just after bridge, turn right onto Panton Rd. (watch for Basin Harbor signs), then bear right after 1½ miles onto Basin Harbor Rd.; continue about 5 more miles to resort. "Well-behaved" pets allowed in cottages ($10 per pet per night). **Amenities:** 3 restaurants; babysitting; bikes; children's programs; concierge; golf course; exercise room; outdoor pool; 5 tennis courts; watersports equipment/rentals. *In room:* A/C, fridge (some units), hair dryer, Wi-Fi (free; extra charge for larger bandwidth).

The Essex ★ This inn, just outside the fringe of Burlington's exurban sprawl, bills itself as "Vermont's Culinary Resort"—a big claim, given that there are so many great eats and wonderful inns in the state. It isn't quite up to the luxury level of the top-rank Vermont inns yet. True, the setting (20 acres of hillside) is majestic, the fitness center and rock-climbing course are great, and the cooking classes are a fun option. And some rooms—particularly the suites outfitted for longer stays, built with full kitchens (including Hearthstone gas stoves)—are nice, gussied up with fireplaces, CD players, Jacuzzis, four-poster beds, and the like. Other units, though, are fairly ordinary for the high prices. A **spa** was added in 2009, there's an airport shuttle and kids' play area, and the property offers several dining options (see "Where to Dine," below). This is a work in progress.

70 Essex Way, Essex, VT 05452. ☏ **800/727-4295** or 802/878-1100. Fax 802/878-0063. www.vt culinaryresort.com. 120 units. May–Oct $219–$349 double; $249–$579 suite; Nov–Apr $189–$289 double, $219–$489 suite. AE, DC, MC, V. **Amenities:** 2 restaurants; bikes; exercise room; golf course; heated outdoor pool; room service; spa. *In room:* A/C, TV, fridge (some units), Wi-Fi (free).

Hilton Burlington ★ This nine-story Hilton hotel—formerly a Radisson and then a Wyndham—has great views if you spend extra for a lakeside room. It's a sleek glass box built in 1976; renovations have kept the aging process mostly at bay. It's the most centrally located of any hotel in the city, tucked right between the waterfront and Church Street Marketplace, but otherwise nothing special. Rooms are standard chain-hotel fare. A few "cabana" units by the pool area are convenient for families, while executive-floor rooms add duvets and more amenities. The airport shuttle is a plus, and the staff is friendly and competent. I'd eat elsewhere, though—the breakfast and dining are middling at best.

60 Battery St., Burlington, VT 05401. ☎ **800/445-8667** or 802/658-6500. Fax 802/658-4659. www. hilton.com. 257 units. Summer $159–$269 double; winter $139–$179 double. AE, DISC, MC, V. Self-parking in garage $5.50 per day. **Amenities:** Restaurant; babysitting; concierge; exercise room; Jacuzzi; indoor pool; room service. *In room:* A/C, TV, hair dryer, Wi-Fi ($9.95 per day).

The Inn at Shelburne Farms ★★ The numbers behind this elaborate mansion on the shore of Lake Champlain tell the story: 60 rooms, 10 chimneys, 1,400 acres. It's a whimsical house, a tourist attraction in and of itself (in fact, there's an admission charge to the extensive farms on the property; see "Exploring Burlington," above). Yet from May through October, you can sleep here and pretend it's all yours. Built in 1899, the sprawling Edwardian "farmhouse" is a place to fantasize about the lifestyles of the rich and famous. Famous architect Frederick Law Olmsted helped design the grounds—the concept was an "agricultural estate" complete with grazing cows on the lawns and a sustainable dairy operation, but also super-plush (for the time) bedrooms and fittings. Today the property is aging, but looks fairly luxurious if a bit dated; expect French design touches, floral wallpapers, and a spare, white-washed elegance to the rooms. Units here vary considerably in decor and amenities: About a quarter of the rooms share hallway bathrooms with other rooms, for example (the Oak Room is probably best of these)—but you can also rent luxurious digs like Overlook, the original master bedroom of owner Lila Webb, with its frilly draperies, big king bed, and views of the lake, meadows, and grounds. The Louis XVI room was furnished with whitewashed furniture when the home was built in 1899, and that furniture is still here, complemented by a design scheme popular at that time.

1611 Harbor Rd., Shelburne, VT 05482. ☎ **802/985-8498.** www.shelburnefarms.org. 26 units (7 with shared bathrooms). $155–$220 double with shared bathroom; $260–$465 double with private bath-room; $260–$380 cottage. 2-night minimum stay Sat–Sun. AE, DC, DISC, MC, V. Closed mid-Oct to early May. **Amenities:** Restaurant; babysitting; tennis court. *In room:* Kitchenette (2 units), Wi-Fi (in some main floor rooms; free).

Lang House ★ This stately, walk-up Queen Anne mansion (1881) sits on the hillside between downtown and the University of Vermont. It's appointed with rich cherry and maple woodwork. Rooms vary in size, though most have smallish bathrooms and quite small TVs, and are perhaps a bit on the pricey side for what you get. Two of the best rooms are corner units: no. 101 on the first floor, and no. 202 on the second floor with a sitting area tucked into the turret. Breakfast is good, and the owners have a liquor license, so they can sell you a bottle of wine or beer. All in all, a good experience. Only cautions? There's no elevator, and you're sleeping practically right on a big university campus with a national reputation for its parties. So you might *hear* some of that partying late at night.

360 Main St., Burlington, VT 05401. © **877/919-9799** or 802/652-2500. Fax 802/651-8717. www.langhouse. com. 11 units. $165–$245 double. Rates include breakfast. AE, DISC, MC, V. *In room:* A/C, TV, Wi-Fi (free).

Sheraton Burlington Hotel & Conference Center ★   Perhaps the largest conference facility in Vermont, the Sheraton also does a decent job catering to travelers and their families. A sprawling and modern complex, it's just off the interstate a few minutes' drive east of downtown, on the strip leading to Burlington's airport (handy if you're flying in or out). Some units are more traditional-looking (furnished in wrought-iron beds or hardwood furniture), while others are more modern (flatscreen TVs in the club rooms, for instance), but all are more than adequate. There are plenty of business-hotel amenities here, too, like a nice indoor pool, a free fitness center, a business center, and a free airport-shuttle center—families take note. Ask for a room facing east if you want views of Mount Mansfield and the Green Mountains.

870 Williston Rd., Burlington, VT 05403. © **800/866-6117** or 802/865-6600. Fax 802/865-6670. www.starwoodhotels.com/sheraton. 309 units. $89–$229 double. AE, DC, DISC, MC, V. **Amenities:** Restaurant; lounge; exercise room; 2 Jacuzzis; indoor pool; Wi-Fi (free in public areas). *In room:* A/C, TV, hair dryer, Wi-Fi ($11 per day).

Willard Street Inn ★★ 🛏   This impressive and historic inn is housed in a splendid 1881 Queen Anne–style brick mansion a few minutes' walk from the university campus, and surely belongs in some sort of glossy "beautiful homes" magazine. All rooms are exceptionally well decorated in genuine and reproduction antiques. Some have down comforters and fireplaces, and many have interesting slopes, angles, and eaves; four-poster beds and handsome, not-too-frilly decor are the norm here. Among the best units are the third-floor Tower Room (in the turret), which boasts a small sitting area (with wicker furniture!) and the best views of the lake; and Champlain Lookout, on the second floor, with its spacious bedroom and bathroom and more great lake views. I like the antique tub in Nantucket, too. Walk down the marble staircase and check out the marble-floored solarium, green lawns, and English gardens. This inn's owners really go the extra mile to ensure guests' satisfaction—breakfasts are universally raved about.

349 S. Willard St. (2 blocks south of Main St.), Burlington, VT 05401. © **800/577-8712** or 802/651-8710. Fax 802/651-8714. www.willardstreetinn.com. 14 units (1 with private bathroom across hall). $140–$250 double. Rates include full breakfast. 2-night minimum stay Sat–Sun. AE, DISC, MC, V. Children 12 and older welcome. *In room:* A/C, TV, Wi-Fi (free).

Where to Dine

Al's French Frys ★ 🛏 FAST FOOD   Ignore the spelling. Al's is where *the* Ben and Jerry go to satisfy their french-fry cravings, so why shouldn't you? It's a must-hit roadside joint when you're in the neighborhood of the Burlington airport or driving through on the interstate. Al's is both fun and efficient, and the fries here (which you can order by the cup, pint, or even quart) draw locals back time and again. Other offerings—hamburgers, dogs, wraps, chicken strips, and grilled cheese sandwiches (for less than a buck)—are okay, nothing special. But you're here for the fries—add a side order of cheese or chili sauce if you want to get experimental with them. There's no beer here, but you can order cola, shakes (in five flavors), or—this being Vermont—a cup of plain or chocolate milk.

1251 Williston Rd. (Rte. 2, just east of I-89), South Burlington. ✆ **802/862-9203.** www.alsfrenchfrys. com. Fries $1–$4, sandwiches and burgers $2–$5. No credit cards. Mon–Thurs 10:30am–11pm; Fri–Sat 10:30am–midnight; Sun 11am–11pm.

Bove's ★ 🍴 ITALIAN   A Burlington landmark since 1941, Bove's is a classic red-sauce-on-spaghetti joint a couple blocks from the Church Street Marketplace. It's got real character, and only one or two items on the entire menu here cost more than 10 bucks—amazing. Grab a seat at a vinyl-upholstered booth, and sit down to a plate of spaghetti with butter sauce, meat sauce, sausage, meatballs, or a few other things. Choose any sauce and you can't go wrong: The red sauce is tangy, the vodka-cream sauce rich, the garlic sauce super-garlicky. These sauces are also now a thriving side operation, in case you want to take a jar home. Not hungry for pasta? Bove's also offers grinders (that's New Hampshire/Vermont lingo for a sub sandwich), veal cutlets, and fried clams, plus simple, sweetish desserts and daily specials like manicotti, stuffed peppers, lasagna, and chicken cacciatore. Takeout is no problem—they specialize in it.

68 Pearl St. ✆ **802/864-6651.** www.boves.com. Sandwiches $2–$6, dinner items $7–$10. No credit cards. Tues–Thurs 2–8:45pm; Fri–Sat 11am–8:45pm.

Butler's Restaurant and Tavern ★ REGIONAL/CONTINENTAL   The house restaurant at the Essex (see "Where to Stay," above), Butler's is also a sort of auxiliary campus of the Montpelier-based New England Culinary Institute. On the tavern menu, expect slightly fancy takes on nachos, burgers, fish and chips, sandwiches, and chili—the BLT, to take just one example, is made of maple-glazed bacon and put together with truffled mayonnaise. The restaurant offers a more intimate experience and more ambitious fare: Entrees might run to homemade gnocchi, pan-seared diver scallops, porcini-dusted beef tenderloin with cheddar-flavored mashed potatoes, or a grilled top sirloin steak.

70 Essex Way, Essex Junction. ✆ **802/764-1413.** www.vtculinaryresort.com. Reservations recommended at Butler's (not necessary in tavern). Tavern menu $6–$15; restaurant menu $14–$23. AE, DC, DISC, MC, V. Restaurant daily 11:30am–10pm. Tavern daily 2–11pm.

The Daily Planet ★ 🍴 INTERNATIONAL   Named for Superman alter-ego Clark Kent's day-job newspaper (I think), this popular spot often fills with college students and/or downtown folks getting out of work. It's central (on Central St.) and feels cutting-edge, even though it's been here more than 20 years. The mild chaos in the dining room only adds to the experience, which begins with a fun, eclectic menu—better than you might expect given the pubby look to the place and its largely college-age clientele. Look for smoked-salmon tostadas, green chili polenta with chèvre, pork carnitas, or Vietnamese beef sandwiches on the bar menu; lemon-poached tuna, cider-brined pork chops, rack of lamb with chimichurri sauce, and shrimp in yellow curry on the more substantial dinner menu. The vegetarian entrees here are among the very best in town. Desserts are creative and tempting, too—choices might include a lavender crème brûlée, a praline sundae, or a hazelnut-topped cheesecake. Don't forget to check the specialty martini menu (which includes a kicky chocolate mole version employing chipotle-flavored tequila) and the rotating art exhibitions.

15 Center St. ✆ **802/862-9647.** www.dailyplanet15.com. Reservations recommended for parties of 5 or more. Main courses $3–$13 at lunch, $9–$19 at dinner. AE, DISC, MC, V. Daily 5–11pm (until midnight Fri–Sat).

Leunig's Bistro ★ CONTINENTAL   What an intriguing place for a meal Leunig's is. Named for an Australian cartoonist, this fun spot right on the Church Street mall (in a former A&W Root Beer shop) has a retro feel with its washed walls, marble bar, crystal chandeliers, and oversized posters. The inventive menu uses regional ingredients, prepared with a Continental (usually a French) hand. An upscale brunch is served Saturday and Sunday, with seasonally changing items such as gravlax crepes, eggs Benedict, and the like; weekday lunches run to good, upscale bistro-style sandwiches and soups (you can add truffled fries or foie gras to any lunch, if that gives you a sense of it). But dinner is where things *really* get cranked up and daring: On the nightly menu, you might find a grilled rack of lamb, a neat vegetable Napoleon, a filet mignon, a piece of pear-and-cardamom stuffed pork, a rack of wild boar, lamb shanks, or skate wings cooked in parchment paper. The side dishes, salads, and cheese plates here are also outstanding. (Truly adventurous foodies might want to try the $100 tasting menu for two: a little bit of everything.) Leunig's claims to offer "the panache of Paris, and the value of Vermont," and they just might be right about that.

115 Church St. ⓒ **802/863-3759.** www.leunigsbistro.com. Reservations recommended. Main courses $6–$15 at lunch, $18–$26 at dinner. AE, DISC, MC, V. Mon–Thurs 11am–10pm; Fri 11am–11pm; Sat 9am–11pm; Sun 9am–10pm.

Penny Cluse Cafe ★ CAFE   The Penny Cluse gets most local foodies' votes for "best breakfast" in the city, and they do indeed serve a mostly breakfast-centric menu. Just a block off the Church Street Marketplace, it's a casual, bright spot decorated in a vaguely Southwestern motif. Among the many excellent breakfast items here: pancakes made from buttermilk or gingerbread; banana bread with maple cream cheese; breakfast sandwiches; a "tofu scram;" and the Zydeco breakfast of eggs, black beans, andouille sausage, and corn muffins. Lunch plates range to chorizo tacos, chicken and biscuits, a smoked-salmon plate, and good sandwiches—including some terrific veggie options. The breakfast prices are at the high end of the usual Vermont price scale for that meal, but they leave you satisfied, so you might not mind. Good coffees and teas abound, too.

169 Cherry St. ⓒ **802/651-8834.** www.pennycluse.com. Breakfast and lunch items $5–$10. MC, V. Mon–Fri 6:45am–3pm; Sat–Sun 8am–3pm.

Trattoria Delia ★★ 🍴 ITALIAN   Serving the best Italian food in Burlington, Lori and Tom Delia's eatery is in a low-traffic location, almost hidden through a speakeasy-like door beneath a large building. But Burlingtonites (Burlingtonians?) know exactly where it is—be sure to reserve ahead if you're coming on a summer weekend. Inside the place is culinary magic; genuinely Italian entrees like veal shanks, red-wine-braised wild boar, filet mignon in white-truffle butter, sirloin sautéed in chianti, seafood stew, and pasta dishes predominate. Go for bruschetta, tagliatelle alla Bolognese, spaghetti and Gulf shrimp baked in a parchment paper, then choose from the selection of dessert wines and desserts such as gelati, torte, tiramisu, and panna cotta. The wine list is good, as evidenced by a raft of *Wine Spectator* awards. This is real Italian food, upscale and delicious.

152 Saint Paul St. ⓒ **802/864-5253.** www.trattoriadelia.com. Reservations recommended. Main courses $15–$28. DC, MC, V. Daily 5–10pm.

THE NORTHEAST KINGDOM

Vermont's Northeast Kingdom has a wilder, more remote character than the rest of the state. Consisting of Orleans, Essex, and Caledonia counties, the region was given its memorable nickname in 1949 by Vermont Sen. George Aiken. What gives this region its character is its stubborn, old-fashioned insularity. It looks and feels *much* more like hardscrabble parts of neighboring New Hampshire (which it faces across the Connecticut River) than the farmhouses and malls of Manchester, country stores of the Mad River Valley, or ski hills of Stowe. You won't find any designer fly-fishing shops in *these* parts.

The landscape here is open and spacious, its dairy pastures ending abruptly at the hard edge of dense boreal forests. The leafy woodlands of the south quickly give way to spiky woods of spruce and fir. Accommodations and services for visitors aren't plentiful or easy to find here, but a growing number of inns are sprouting up in these hills.

Even if your time is limited, stop in **St. Johnsbury,** which holds two excellent attractions. Also try to cruise through at least a couple of small towns here before heading elsewhere. The fall foliage can be brilliant, although it arrives a bit earlier here (from late Sept to very early Oct, usually) than elsewhere in New England.

The entire tour described below, from Hardwick to St. Johnsbury by way of Newport, Derby Line, and Lake Willoughby, is about 90 miles by car. Allow at least a full day for it if you plan to hike, bike, or photograph in the region.

Visitor information is available from the **Northeast Kingdom Chamber of Commerce** (© **800/639-6379** or 802/748-3678; www.nekchamber.com), at 51 Depot Sq., in downtown St. Johnsbury.

DRIVING TOUR: THE NORTHEAST KINGDOM

START:	**Hardwick**
FINISH:	**St. Johnsbury**
TIME:	**One full day**

Begin in Hardwick at the intersection of routes 14 and 15, about 23 miles NW of St. Johnsbury and 26 miles NE of Montpelier:

1 Hardwick

A small town with rough edges set on the Lamoille River, Hardwick has a single main street with some intriguing shops, a couple of casual, family-style restaurants, and one of Vermont's best natural-foods stores (the Buffalo Mountain Food Co-op). A 2005 fire claimed part of this downtown block, but it has since been rebuilt.

From Hardwick, head north 7 miles on Rte. 14 to the turnoff to Craftsbury and:

2 Craftsbury Common ★★

An uncommonly graceful village, Craftsbury Common is home to a small academy and a large number of historic homes and buildings spread along a central green and the village's main street. The town occupies a wide upland ridge and

The Northeast Kingdom

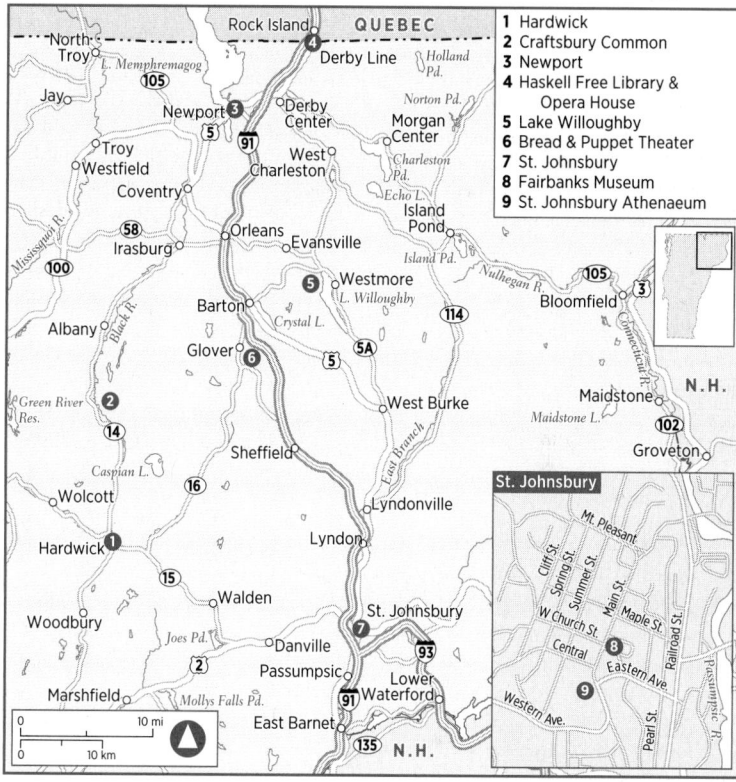

1 Hardwick
2 Craftsbury Common
3 Newport
4 Haskell Free Library &
   Opera House
5 Lake Willoughby
6 Bread & Puppet Theater
7 St. Johnsbury
8 Fairbanks Museum
9 St. Johnsbury Athenaeum

offers sweeping views to the east and west; be sure to stop by the old cemetery on the south side of town, too, where you can wander among historic tombstones of pioneers—they date back to the 1700s. Craftsbury is an excellent destination for mountain biking and cross-country skiing.

From Craftsbury, continue north to reconnect to Rte. 14. Pass through the towns of Albany and Irasburg as you head north. At the village of Coventry, veer north on Rte. 5 to the lakeside town of:

3 Newport

This commercial (and commercial-looking) outpost is set on the southern shores of big Lake Memphremagog, a stunning 27-mile-long lake that's just 2 miles wide at its broadest point (the bulk of it actually lies across the border in Canada). From Newport, continue north on Rte. 5 (crossing under I-91) about 7 miles more to the border town of Derby Line. This outpost has a handful of restaurants and antiques shops; if you've got your passport, you can also park and walk across the bridge to poke around the Quebec town of Rock Island.

Back in Derby Line, look for the:

4 Haskell Free Library & Opera House ★

At the corner of Caswell Avenue and Church Street, this handsome neoclassical building (© **802/873-3022;** www.haskellopera.org) contains a public library on the first floor and an elegant opera house on the second, which is modeled after the old Boston Opera House. The theater opened in 1904 with advertisements promoting a minstrel show featuring "new songs, new jokes, and beautiful electric effects." It's a beautiful theater, with a scene of Venice painted on the drop curtain and carved cherubim adorning the balcony.

What's coolest about this building, though, is that it lies half in Canada and half in the United States. (The Haskell family donated the building jointly to the towns of Derby Line and Rock Island.) A thick, black line runs right beneath the seats of the opera house, marking the border between nations. Because the stage portion is set entirely in Canada, legends abound of frustrated U.S. marshals sitting in the audience watching fugitives perform on stage, free as birds. (Those stories are almost certainly false.) More recently, the theater has been used for an occasional extradition hearing. Performances still take place here. Tours are also available, from May through October, anytime during regular library hours; a $3 per person donation is suggested. (The library is open Tues–Sat.)

From Derby Line, retrace your path south on Rte. 5 to Derby Center and the junction of Rte. 5A. Continue south on Rte. 5A to the town of Westmore, on the shores of:

5 Lake Willoughby ★★

This underappreciated lake might be one of the most scenic in Vermont—it almost looks like something from Switzerland. Carved out by glaciers and set in an unpopulated area, the lake is best viewed from the north, where its shimmering sheet of water appears to be pinched between the base of two low mountains at its southern end. Rte. 5A as it runs along the lake's eastern shore is lightly traveled, thus good for biking or walking.

Head southwest on Rte. 16, which branches off Rte. 5A just north of the lake. Follow Rte. 16 through the peaceful villages of Barton and Glover. About 1 mile south of Glover, turn left on Rte. 122. On your left, look for the farmstead that serves as home to the:

6 Bread & Puppet Theater

For nearly 3 decades, Polish artist and performer Peter Schumann's Bread & Puppet Theater staged an elaborate annual summer pageant at this farm, attracting thousands of attendees who gaped at the theater's brightly painted puppets (crafted of fabric and papier-mâché, they could be an amalgam of Ralph Nader and Hieronymus Bosch). The huge puppets marched around the farm grounds, acting out dramas that typically featured rebellion against tyranny of one sort or another. It was like Woodstock, minus the music.

Alas, the event became too popular—and attracted drifters of questionable character. In 1998, a murder at an adjacent campground prodded Schumann to shut down the circus for a while. His troupe still designs and builds puppets here, however, and periodically takes its unique shows on the road—or offers live performances in Glover. (For the latest schedules, check the troop's website, **www.breadandpuppet.org.**)

Between June and October, you can still visit the venerable, slightly tottering barn, home of the **Bread & Puppet Museum ★** (℃ **802/525-3031** or 802/525-1271), which preserves many of the puppets from past events. This remarkable display shouldn't be missed if you're near the area. Downstairs, in former cow-milking stalls, smaller displays include mournful washerwomen doing laundry and King Lear addressing his daughters. Upstairs, the vast hayloft is filled with soaring, haunting puppets, some up to 20 feet tall. Admission is free, though donations are encouraged. It's open daily 10am to 6pm from spring through November.

From Glover, continue south through farmlands to Lyndonville, where you pick up Rte. 5 South to:

7 St. Johnsbury

This is by far the largest community in the Kingdom, and its major center of commerce. First settled in 1786, the town enjoyed a buoyant prosperity in the 19th century, largely stemming from the success of platform scales (which were invented right here in 1830 by Thaddeus Fairbanks, and are still manufactured here). The place hasn't yet been overtaken by sprawl, outlet shops, boutiques, or brewpubs, and the downtown features an abundance of commercial architecture in two distinct neighborhoods connected by steep Eastern Avenue.

The commercial part of town lies along Railroad Street (Rte. 5) at the base of the hill, while the most visually pleasing section of town runs along Main Street at the top of the hill. There you'll find the local library (with its fine art museum), the St. Johnsbury Academy, and a second museum. This northern end of Main Street is also notable for its grand residential architecture.

In St. Johnsbury, at the corner of Main and Prospect streets, find the:

8 Fairbanks Museum ★★

This imposing Romanesque red-sandstone structure was constructed in 1889 to hold the accumulations of obsessive amateur collector Franklin Fairbanks, grandson of the inventor of the platform scale. Fairbanks was once described as "the kind of little boy who came home with his pockets full of worms." Some of his collections now displayed here include four stuffed bears, a huge moose with full antlers, art from Asia, and 4,500 stuffed native and exotic birds—just the tip of the iceberg. (In fact, it's sort of surprising there isn't an *actual* iceberg here as well.)

The soaring, barrel-vaulted main hall, which is reminiscent of an old-fashioned train station, embodies Victorian grandeur. Amid the assorted clutter, look for the, er, unique mosaics of John Hampson, who depicted famous moments in American history (Washington bidding his troops farewell and the like) entirely from mounted insects. In the Washington scene, iridescent green beetles form the epaulets, and the regal great coat was made using hundreds of purple moth wings. These works alone are worth the price of admission, and capture the peculiar oddity of the place.

The museum (℃ **802/748-2372;** www.fairbanksmuseum.org) is open Tuesday through Saturday from 9am to 5pm, and Sunday from 1 to 5pm; from April to October, it's also open Monday from 9am to 5pm. Admission is $6 for adults, $5 for seniors and children ages 5 to 17, and $18 per family (maximum of 2 adults). There's a planetarium ★ here as well—the only one in Vermont.

Also on Main Street, just south of the museum at 1171 Main St., find the:

9 St. Johnsbury Athenaeum ★★

Inside a brick building with a blunt mansard tower and prominent keystones over the windows, St. Johnsbury's public library houses an extraordinary little art gallery dating to 1873. It claims to be the oldest unadulterated art gallery in the nation.

Your first view of the gallery is spectacular. After winding through the cozy library and past a ticking regulator clock, you round a corner and find yourself gazing across Yosemite National Park—or, at least, a pretty good facsimile. The luminous 10×15-foot oil painting of the park here, *The Domes of the Yosemite* ★★★, was made by painter Albert Bierstadt in 1867, just 3 years after President Lincoln created the California park. Horace Fairbanks later bought it and built this gallery specifically for the painting. (Not everyone was happy about that. "Now *The Domes* is doomed to the seclusion of a Vermont town, where it will astonish the natives," groused the *Boston Globe*.) Natural light from a skylight only enhances the painting, and there's a viewing gallery at the opposite end of the hall.

That's not all there is here. Another 100 or so works fill the remaining walls of the museum. Most are copies, but there are a few originals from Hudson River School painters such as Asher B. Durand, Thomas Moran, and Jasper Cropsey.

The Athenaeum (© 802/748-8291; www.stjathenaeum.org) is open weekdays from 10am to 5pm and Saturdays 9:30am to 4pm. Admission is free, but donations are encouraged.

Downhill Skiing

Jay Peak ★★ 📷 Just south of the Canada border, Jay Peak is a great choice for those who prefer to avoid the glitz and clutter of modern-looking ski resorts. Though some condo development has taken place at the base of this mountain, Jay still has the feel of a remote, isolated destination, accessible only via a winding road through thick woods—something you just can't find in the U.S. anymore. Thanks to its staggering snowfall (an average of about 30 ft. annually, more than anywhere else in New England), there's extensive glade skiing between the trees here, with views of nothing but trees and mountains. (They also make snow here if Mother Nature decides to take a break from it.) The resort's ski school specializes in training you to run the glades, so it's a good place for intermediate-to-advanced skiers to learn how to navigate the peak's exciting, challenging trails. In summer, there's a golf course, aerial tram (similar to a gondola), and swimming pool for families to enjoy. Be aware that lodging and dining are limited to what's on the mountain, and après-ski is nonexistent.

4850 Rte. 242, Jay, VT 05859. © **800/451-4449** or 802/988-2611. www.jaypeakresort.com. Adults $67 day lift tickets, $49 half-day; discounts for youths, students, seniors, and VT residents.

Cross-Country Skiing

The **Craftsbury Outdoor Center** maintains more than 50 miles of cross-country trails through the gentle hills surrounding the village of Craftsbury. These forgiving, old-fashioned trails, maintained by the center's **Nordic Center** ★★ division (© 802/586-7767; www.craftsbury.com), emphasize landscape over speed. They even guarantee skiable snow from January until the second Sunday in March. A trail pass costs $10 per person per day, while a full setup of rental equipment costs just $15 per day more—an outstanding value, given the local scenery.

Another option is the **Highland Lodge Ski Touring Center** ★ (© 802/533-2647; www.highlandlodge.com), on Caspian Lake in Greensboro, with more than 30 miles of roller-packed trails (some of which are further groomed) through rolling woodlands and fields. When you stay at the lodge (see "Where to Stay," below), you ski for free.

Where to Stay & Dine

Also don't miss the **P&H Truck Stop** ★ (© 802/429-2141) in Wells River, right at exit 17 off I-91. It's a must-stop on the way to Jay Peak or St. Johnsbury.

Comfort Inn & Suites ★   This big chain hotel is about a mile south of St. Johnsbury's downtown district, up on a hill right where Rte. 5 crosses under the interstate. Built in 2000, it consists of more than 100 units and has a number of nice business-hotel touches, such as granite vanity counters, high-backed desk chairs, small fridges in every room, and a free continental breakfast. Rooms are pleasantly appointed, more like an inn than a chain motel, and the basement houses an appealing small pool, fitness center, and game room outfitted with air hockey and a billiards table. It's a good pick when you're tired of driving or with a family.

703 Rte. 5 S., St. Johnsbury, VT 05819. © **866/464-2408** or 802/748-1500. Fax 802/748-1243. 107 units. $89–$149 double; $139–$399 suite. Rates include continental breakfast. AE, DISC, MC, V. From I-91, take exit 20. **Amenities:** Exercise room; indoor pool; sauna. *In room:* A/C, TV, fridge, hair dryer, Wi-Fi (free).

Highland Lodge ★   Built in the mid–19th century, this all-inclusive lodge has been accommodating guests since 1926. Just across the road from lovely Caspian Lake, it has 11 rooms furnished in a comfortable country style, plus 11 nearby cottages, most equipped with kitchenettes. A stay here is supremely relaxing: Summer activities include swimming, boating on the lake, cycling, and playing tennis on a clay court. In winter, the lodge maintains its own cross-country ski area (see "Cross-Country Skiing," above) with miles of packed and groomed trails. Behind the lodge is an attractive nature preserve for exploration. Rates here always include breakfast, dinner, and free use of the canoes, kayaks, and most of the other equipment scattered about the property (there's a charge for skis, snowshoes, mountain bikes, and sailboats). You can even get a single room here for a fair price—about 60% of the double-occupancy rates. But children and teens are charged an extra fee, depending on their age—from $100 for an 18-year-old to $40 for a 2-year-old. (Infants are not charged.)

1608 Craftsbury Rd., Greensboro, VT 05841. © **802/533-2647.** Fax 802/533-7494. www.highland lodge.com. 22 units. $237–$330 double. Rates include breakfast, dinner, and 15% service charge. Extra charge per child ages 2–20. DISC, MC, V. Closed mid-Mar to May and mid-Oct to Christmas. From Hardwick, take Rte. 15 east 2 miles to Rte. 16, and then drive 2 miles north to East Hardwick. Follow signs 6 miles to inn. **Amenities:** Dining room; babysitting; bikes; children's program; tennis court; watersports equipment/rentals; Wi-Fi (entire main inn and some cottages; free). *In room:* No phone.

WilloughVale Inn ★★   An elegant inn on a low rise at the north end of Lake Willoughby, the WilloughVale offers stunning views across the water to the twin mountains bracketing the southern end of the lake. It's ideal for a quiet retreat with some books or a bicycle; Robert Frost stayed here in 1909 and even wrote a poem about it ("A Servant to Servants"). Rooms in the main lodge are tastefully appointed, much of their furniture crafted right here in Vermont. Some have private sections of porch and have been thoroughly updated with Jacuzzis, big-screen satellite televisions, gas fireplaces, and similar touches. The cottages—four right on the lake with kitchenettes (including the one Frost stayed in), plus three others nearby with lake views—give off a rustic, Adirondack-lodge feeling, albeit with modern comforts. All these cottages now have wall-unit air-conditioning and televisions, and some have fireplaces or Jacuzzis, yet still feel rustic thanks to their exposed woodwork. Note that this inn's restaurant is seasonal, opening in spring and closing in fall; it serves good food with a superb view of the lake, but in winter you'll have to hunt for other options.

793 Rte. 5A S., Westmore, VT 05860. © **888/594-9102** or 802/525-4123. Fax 802/525-4514. www.willoughvale.com. 13 units. $115–$240 double; $180–$320 cottage. Weekly rates available (summer only). Rates include continental breakfast. 2-night minimum stay in cottages, and in lodge during July, Aug, and fall-foliage season. AE, MC, V. Closed Jan to mid-June. Small dogs sometimes accepted ($20 per night; call ahead). **Amenities:** Restaurant; tavern; bikes; watersports equipment/rentals. *In room:* A/C, TV/DVD, fridge (some units), Wi-Fi (free).

NEW HAMPSHIRE

by Paul Karr

New Hampshire gets a bad rap from the national press and late-night comedy. Some of it is deserved, but not all of it. No, it's not quite as postcard-worthy as Vermont, and no, it's nowhere near as lobster-obsessed as Maine. Yes, the state charges everyone, even residents, an annoying $2 to traverse a measly 15 miles of interstate highway. Beaches are practically nonexistent. The fields are too full of rocks, winter is much too long. That "Live Free or Die" license plate? It's for real: Granite Staters still mostly regard government as an annoyance, and zoning as a grand conspiracy to undermine their Constitutional property rights.

The last time I checked, the state still did not have any bottle-return laws, bills banning billboards, or legislation requiring motorcyclists to wear helmets, and no sales or income tax. Longtime New Hampshire resident Robert Frost once famously stated that "Good fences make good neighbors," and—even if things are changing with new arrivals from out of state—folks here still mostly agree with that proclamation.

Yet that's what makes this state so wonderful to visit: its authenticity. You'll hear *real* accents and see *real* ingenuity in action, not some fake Hollywood or historical-park version. (Remember, these are the same folks who took up arms against King George.)

The Granite State's rebellious attitude has had consequences, of course. Public services are partly funded by lottery sales and through a stiff "tourist tax" on meals and hotels, and through high local property taxes that have hit residents hard. Legislators could create income and sales taxes—but they won't, not in this lifetime. That would be political suicide.

Get beyond New Hampshire's stubbornness, though, and it's a very good place to take vacation—especially if you like incredible views, fall-foliage drives, and maple syrup. Sure, you'll still find plenty of pickup trucks, pancake houses, hunting caps, and country-rock music here, but it's not *all* about flannel shirts and rifle racks anymore. Granite Staters do know how to have fun—the band Aerosmith formed in **New London,** and comedian Adam Sandler was born in **Manchester.** They've got Dartmouth College in the lovely small town of **Hanover,** too.

It's also a state blessed with the huge peaks of the **White Mountains** (p. 572), lovely lakes like **Lake Winnipesaukee,** outstanding foliage in the **Mount Monadnock** area, and increasingly good resorts and restaurants. You can toss a Frisbee on a beach; ride bikes along country lanes; or canoe or boat on a placid lake. Need a little city culture? **Portsmouth** is a great 1- or 2-day stop, a sort of miniature Boston with seafood, music, and history, while **Manchester** has a gritty Franco-industrial heritage.

First-time travelers to New Hampshire are often surprised to learn that it isn't landlocked—it actually has a coastline. Granted, it isn't much of one (just 18 miles long), but this little strip manages to pack in a lot of variety (and real-estate value). The coastline has honky-tonk beach towns, eye-popping mansions in blue-blood villages, old forts, the odd fishing village, vest-pocket state parks with swaths of sand, and one historic seaport city with a vibrant maritime history and culture. Ecologically speaking, you can find sand dunes, hardwood forests, bird-friendly tidal inlets, and a complex system of salt marshes that has prevented development from overtaking the seacoast entirely by rendering the ground unstable for big buildings in those areas.

The inns in New Hampshire are getting better, and local fare is always easy to find in diners and family restaurants. Most of all, you'll get a strong sense of the wily independence that has always defined New England.

PORTSMOUTH ★★

Portsmouth: 11 miles N of Hampton; 10 miles NE of Exeter; 55 miles N of Boston; 54 miles S of Portland

Portsmouth is a civilized little seaside city of bridges, brick, and seagulls, and is quite a gem. Filled with elegant architecture that's more intimate than intimidating, this bonsai-size city projects a strong, proud sense of its heritage without being overly precious. Part of the city's appeal is its variety: Upscale coffee shops and art galleries stand alongside old-fashioned barbershops and tattoo parlors. Despite a steady influx of money in recent years, the town still retains an earthiness that serves as a tangy vinegar for more saccharine coastal spots. Portsmouth's humble waterfront must actually be sought out; when found, it's rather understated.

This city's history runs deep, a fact that's evident on even a quick stroll through town. For 3 centuries, Portsmouth has been the hub of the coastal Maine/New Hampshire region's maritime trade. In the 1600s, Strawbery Banke (it wasn't called Portsmouth until 1653) was a major center for the export of wood and dried fish to Europe. Later it prospered as a regional center for trade. Just across the Piscataqua River in Maine (so important a connection that there are four bridges from Portsmouth to that state), the Portsmouth Naval Shipyard—founded back in 1800—evolved into a prominent base for the building, outfitting, and repairing of U.S. Navy submarines.

Today Portsmouth's maritime tradition continues with a lively trade in bulk goods; look for the scrap metal and minerals along the shores of the river on Market Street. The city's *de facto* symbol is the tugboat, one or two of which are almost always tied up in or near the waterfront's picturesque "tugboat alley."

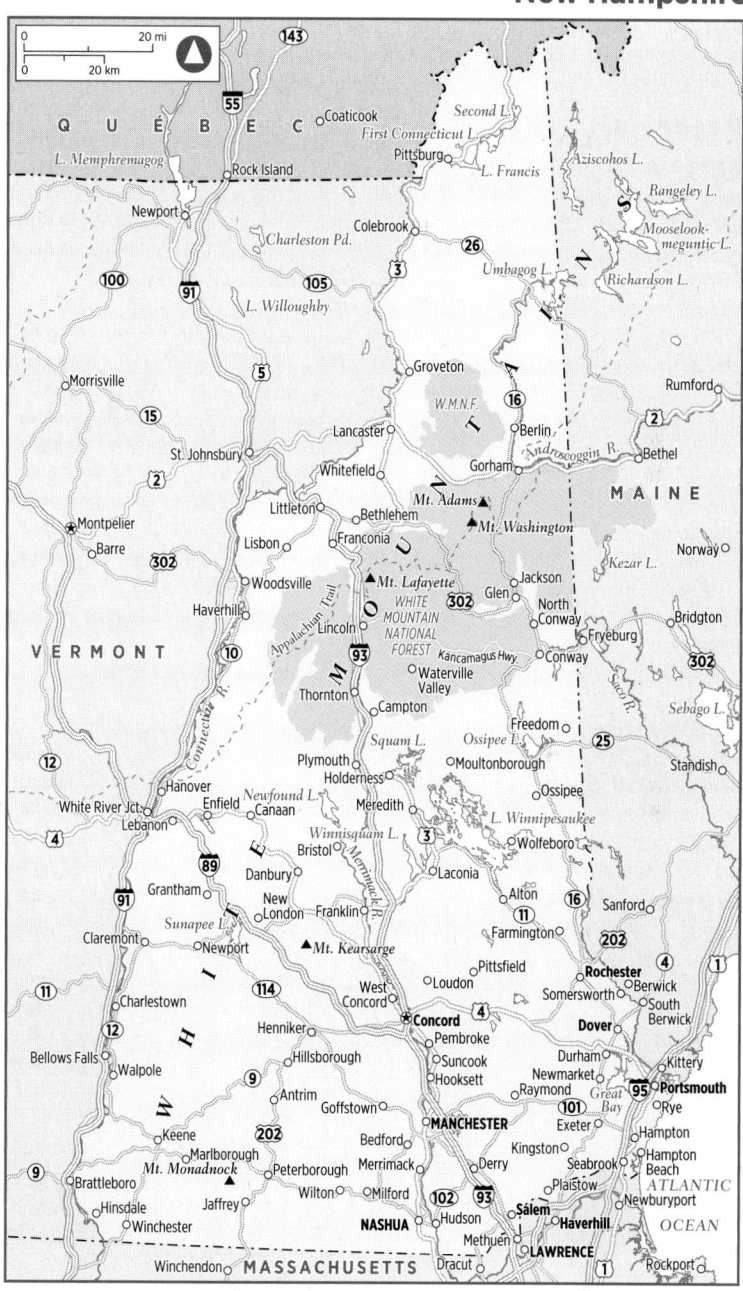

Visitors to Portsmouth will discover a surprising number of experiences in such a small space—good shopping in the boutiques that now occupy much of the historic downtown; good eating at many small restaurants and bakeries; great coffee; and plenty of history to explore in the form of historic homes, parks, gardens, and museums. As if that weren't enough, ocean beaches are just a couple of minutes away.

Essentials

GETTING THERE Portsmouth is on exits 3 through 7 on I-95. The most direct route to downtown is via Market Street (exit 7), the last New Hampshire exit just before the bridge that crosses the river into Maine. Take that exit, and then bear right (coming from the south) or left (from the north). From Boston's Logan Airport, Portsmouth is about a 1-hour drive via I-95; from Portland Jetport or Manchester airport, the trip is an hour at most.

The bus is a viable option to Portsmouth, as well. **Greyhound** (© **800/231-2222;** www.greyhound.com) and **C&J** (© **800/258-7111** or 603/430-1100; www.ridecj.com) each run about five buses daily from Boston's South Station directly to Portsmouth (trip time: 1¼ hr.); C&J also runs trips from Boston's Logan Airport. Greyhound is probably the better choice, because it drops you off right in Market Square, while C&J calls at a modern but distant bus station about 5 miles south of the city. (There's a 50¢ "trolley" [bus] shuttle from the station into and back from the city about once an hour—though *no* shuttle on Sun. Otherwise, you'll need to call a taxi or have a rental car outfit pick you up.)

A ticket from South Station costs $18 each way; the trip from Logan Airport costs $24 one-way on C&J. From New York City, a one-way Greyhound ticket to Portsmouth costs about $48, and the ride takes about 6½ hours.

It's also possible to get here by train—sometimes. **Amtrak** (© **800/872-7245;** www.amtrak.com) runs five trains daily from Boston's North Station to downtown Dover, New Hampshire, about 12 miles from Portsmouth; a one-way ticket is $19 per person, and the trip takes about 90 minutes. So far, so good. You can then take a no. 2 **COAST bus** (© **603/743-5777;** www.coastbus.org) from Dover station to the center of downtown Portsmouth, a 45-minute trip that costs $1.50. However, this bus runs on a very limited schedule on Saturday, and not at *all* on Sunday, making this route impractical for weekend travel.

VISITOR INFORMATION The **Greater Portsmouth Chamber of Commerce,** 500 Market St. (© **603/610-5510;** www.portsmouthchamber.org), has an information center on the road into town from exit 7—it's on the right, across from the piles of scrap metal. From Memorial Day to Columbus Day, it's open daily until at least 5pm every day (later Thurs–Fri). The rest of the year, the info center is open weekdays only. During summer a staffed information hut opens in Market Square in front of the Breaking New Grounds coffee shop.

Historic Buildings

John Paul Jones House ★ This yellow, three-story 1758 home is easy to miss, simply because it's parked right at one of Portsmouth's busiest traffic intersections a few blocks down State Street from the Market Square area. Yet it's worth finding—and near several excellent restaurants. Scottish Revolutionary War hero Jones ("I have not yet begun to fight") didn't build it; he's believed (we're not sure) to have

Portsmouth

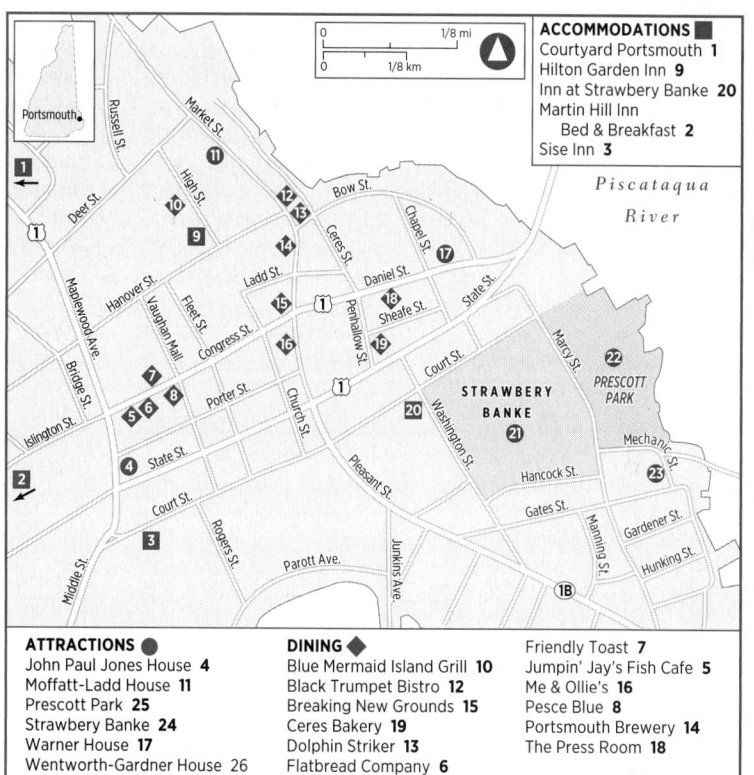

ACCOMMODATIONS ■
Courtyard Portsmouth **1**
Hilton Garden Inn **9**
Inn at Strawbery Banke **20**
Martin Hill Inn
    Bed & Breakfast **2**
Sise Inn **3**

Piscataqua River

ATTRACTIONS ●
John Paul Jones House **4**
Moffatt-Ladd House **11**
Prescott Park **25**
Strawbery Banke **24**
Warner House **17**
Wentworth-Gardner House **26**

DINING ◆
Blue Mermaid Island Grill **10**
Black Trumpet Bistro **12**
Breaking New Grounds **15**
Ceres Bakery **19**
Dolphin Striker **13**
Flatbread Company **6**
Friendly Toast **7**
Jumpin' Jay's Fish Cafe **5**
Me & Ollie's **16**
Pesce Blue **8**
Portsmouth Brewery **14**
The Press Room **18**

lived in it during the war while here to oversee construction of his sloop, the *Ranger* (probably the first ship ever to sail under the U.S. flag; a model is on display). The house is immaculately restored and maintained by the Portsmouth Historical Society, which formed in 1917 to protect it from the wrecking ball. Jones sailed out of Portsmouth the next year and never returned.

43 Middle St. (corner of State St.). ℂ **603/436-8420.** Admission $6 adults, free for children. Memorial Day to Oct daily 11am–5pm (last tour at 4:30pm). Closed Nov to mid-May.

Moffatt-Ladd House & Garden ★★ Built for a family of prosperous merchants and traders, this 1763 home is as notable for its elegant gardens as it is for the home's great hall and elaborate carvings. Now a National Historic Landmark, it belonged to a single family from 1763 until 1913, when it became a museum. As a result, many of the furnishings here have never left the premises; aficionados of Early American furniture and painting, take note.

154 Market St. ℂ **603/436-8221.** www.moffattladd.org. Admission to house and gardens $6 adults, $2.50 children 11 and under; gardens only $2 per person. Tours mid-June to mid-Oct Mon–Sat 11am–5pm; Sun 1–5pm (last tour at 4:30pm). Closed mid-Oct to mid-June.

Strawbery Banke ★★★   In 1958, the city of Portsmouth was finalizing plans to raze this neighborhood (which was settled in 1653!) to make way for "urban renewal." A group of local citizens resisted the move, and they prevailed, establishing an outdoor history museum that's become one of the largest and best in New England. Today the attraction consists of 10 downtown acres and more than 40 historic buildings, some restored with period furnishings, others featuring historic exhibits. (The remainder can be viewed only from the outside, but are mostly well restored.) The focus is on the buildings, architecture, and history. The neighborhood surrounds an open lawn (formerly an inlet) and has a settled, picturesque quality; several working crafts shops demonstrate Colonial skills and craftwork. The most intriguing home might be the Drisco House, half of which depicts life in the 1790s and half of which shows life in the 1950s—nicely demonstrating how houses grow and adapt to each era.

Visitor center at 14 Hancock St. (at Marcy St.) ✆ **603/433-1100.** www.strawberybanke.org. Summer admission $15 adults, $10 children 5-17, free for children 4 and under, $40 per family; winter rates discounted. May–Oct daily for self-guided tours 10am–5pm; Nov–Apr 90-min. guided tours on the hour Sat–Sun only 10am–2pm; extra tours in Dec. Look for directional signs posted around town.

Warner House ★ 🏛   This house, built in 1716 for a merchant and ship owner, was later the New Hampshire governor's mansion during the mid–18th century (when Portsmouth was the state capital). After a period as a private home, it was opened to the public in the 1930s. The brick structure with Georgian architectural elements is a favorite of architectural historians for its wall murals (said to be the oldest such murals still in place in the U.S.), early wall marbleizing, and white-pine paneling. It is a bit hard to find, although it's very close to Market Square—from the square, walk past the post office toward Memorial Bridge; look to your left for a brick house with dormers and a white picket fence.

150 Daniel St. ✆ **603/436-5909.** www.warnerhouse.org. Admission $5 adults, $4 seniors, $2.50 children 7-12, free for children 6 and under. Mid-June to mid-Oct Tues and Thurs–Sat noon–4pm. Closed mid-Oct to mid-June.

Wentworth-Gardner House ★★   Arguably one of the best-looking mansions in the Seacoast region, this is considered one of the nation's prime examples of Georgian architecture. The yellow 1760 home features many period elements, including pronounced *quoins* (blocks on the building's corners), pedimented window caps, plank sheathing (to make the home appear as if made of masonry), an elaborate doorway with Corinthian pilasters, a broken scroll, and a paneled door topped with a pineapple (even then, the symbol of hospitality). Perhaps most memorable is its scale—though a grand home of the Colonial era, it's fairly modest in size. Once again, you need to look carefully for this house; it's wedged between Prescott Park and Geno's Chowder Shop on Mechanic Street. Walk down the street that juts off from the base of the little bridge beside the park.

50 Mechanic St. (at Gardner St.). ✆ **603/436-4406.** www.wentworthgardnerandlear.org. Admission $5 adults, $2 children 6-14, free for children 5 and under. Mid-June to mid-Oct Thurs–Sun noon–4pm. Closed mid-Oct to mid-June. From the Prescott Park rose gardens (across from Strawbery Banke), walk 1 block and make a left toward the bridge. Take right onto Mechanic St. just before crossing the bridge; house is 2 blocks farther on right, at corner of Gardner St. and before Hunking St.

Where to Stay

Downtown accommodations are preferable, as everything is within walking distance, but prices tend to be high. The fairly new **Courtyard Portsmouth** (✆ **603/436-2121**), at 1000 Market St., is big and modern, with business amenities and comfortable beds. The **Hilton Garden Inn** (☎ 603/431-1499) is in a very central downtown location, with a nice indoor pool.

In addition to the options listed below, also see the **Portsmouth Harbor Inn and Spa** in chapter 14; it's just across the river in Kittery.

Inn at Strawbery Banke ★ This little inn is tucked away in a simple but old (built in 1814) home on Court Street, a very central base for exploring Portsmouth: Strawbery Banke is just a block away, and Market Square is just 2 blocks away. The owner has done a nice job of taking an antique home and making it comfortable for modern guests. Though rooms are tiny and simply furnished, they're brightened by stenciling, pencil-poster beds, wooden shutters, and beautifully preserved pine floors (one has a private bathroom down the hall). Two sitting rooms are stocked with TVs, phones (there are none in the rooms), and plenty of books; breakfast is served in the dining room. Note that stairs to upper-floor rooms are a bit steep.

314 Court St., Portsmouth, NH 03801. ☎ **800/428-3933** or 603/436-7242. www.innatstrawberybanke. com. 7 units (1 with detached bathroom). Mar–Oct $160–$170 double; Nov–Feb $100–$115 double. Rates include full breakfast. 2-night minimum stay Sat–Sun in Aug and Oct. AE, DISC, MC, V. Children 10 and over welcome. *In room:* A/C, no phone.

Martin Hill Inn Bed & Breakfast ★ This B&B is in a residential neighborhood a half-mile west of Market Square, and consists of two attractive buildings: a main house (built around 1815) plus a guesthouse built 35 years later. Rooms have queen-size beds, writing tables, and sofas or sitting areas, and are appointed in handsome wallpapers, antiques, and four-poster or brass beds; some even have private porches. There are no televisions in this inn's rooms, however. A stone pathway leads to a small water garden. The full breakfast here might consist of johnnycakes, "golden-rod" eggs, quiche, nutty waffles, or cooked fruit—a good start to the day. There are a number of rules at the inn, however: Check-in is limited to 4–6pm; there's a mandatory $3 charge for housekeepers' tips on your first night; children 11 and under aren't accepted; and so forth.

404 Islington St., Portsmouth, NH 03801. ☎ **603/436-2287.** www.martinhillinn.com. 7 units. May–Nov $140–$210 double; rest of year $105–$160 double. 2-night minimum stay summer and holiday weekends. Rates include full breakfast. MC, V. Children 12 and over welcome. *In room:* A/C, Wi-Fi (free).

Sise Inn ★ This Queen Anne–style home in the downtown district was built for a prominent merchant in 1881; the hotel section was added a century later. The effect is mostly harmonious, though, as the antique stained glass and oak trim mesh with the contemporary design elements. Some rooms have antique armoires, updated Victorian styling, or whirlpool or soaking tubs. I like no. 302, a bi-level, two-bedroom suite with a claw-foot tub; no. 406, a suite with soaking tub and private sitting room; no. 120, with its private patio; and no. 216 (in the carriage house), with a working sauna, two-person whirlpool, and lovely natural light.

40 Court St. (at Middle St.), Portsmouth, NH 03801. ☎ **877/747-3466** or 603/433-1200. Fax 603/431-0200. www.siseinn.com. 34 units. $119–$199 double; $159–$279 suite. Rates include continental breakfast. AE, DISC, MC, V. *In room:* Wi-Fi (free).

Wentworth by the Sea ★★★ The reopening of this historic resort in 2003 was a major event. A photogenic grand hotel of white paint and red accents, it was built on a lovely spot on New Castle Island in 1874 but later shut down. Today it's operated jointly by a Maine firm and Marriott in professional, luxurious fashion. As befits an old hotel, rooms vary in size, but most are spacious, with good views of ocean or harbor; especially interesting are the suites that occupy the three turrets. Some units have gas-powered fireplaces or private balconies in addition to the spruced-up bathroom fixtures, detailing, and furnishings. The luxury suites beside the water are truly outstanding: They have water views, modern kitchens, and marble bathrooms with Jacuzzis—plus access to a private dock-side pool. A full-service spa offers a range of treatments, and there's a handsome lounge area as well as an excellent **dining room ★** in the main building; in summer a seasonal deck grill opens adjacent to the Marina Suites. You can also golf at the lovely 18-hole Wentworth golf course (a 5-min. walk down the road), even though it's a private club and separately owned.

588 Wentworth Rd. (P.O. Box 860), New Castle, NH 03854. © **866/240-6313** or 603/422-7322. Fax 603/422-7329. www.wentworth.com. 161 units. Peak season $259–$459 double, $439–$559 suite, $599–$899 marina suite; off season $179–$229 double, $259–$329 suite, $359–$599 marina suite. AE, DISC, MC, V. From downtown, take Rte. 1A (Miller Ave.) 1½ miles south; turn left onto Rte. 1B and continue 1½ miles to hotel. **Amenities:** 2 restaurants; bar; 2 pools (1 indoor, 1 outdoor); spa. *In room:* A/C, TV, hair dryer, Internet (free), kitchenette (some units).

Where to Dine

Beyond the options listed below, you could visit the dining room or grill at the **Wentworth by the Sea** resort (see "Where to Stay," above), on Rte. 1B a few miles south of the city—Chef Daniel Dumont's Continental fare is outstanding, served beneath a remarkable (and original) frescoed dome. The resort's **Latitudes** grill has a simpler menu but offers something the main inn doesn't—an outdoor patio, softly lit at night.

Downtown Portsmouth's casual dining scene got a shot in the arm with the opening of a branch of the terrific **Flatbread Company** (© **603/436-7888;** www. flatbreadcompany.com) pizzeria, at 138 Congress St. It's *the* place to eat a terrific organic-wheat crust pizza.

Black Trumpet Bistro ★★ BISTRO Formerly known as Lindbergh's Crossing, this bistro changed ownership in 2007—to Lindbergh's chef, Evan Mallett, who has settled in nicely. He cooks exotically spiced comfort food in an intimate, two-story building within a former warehouse. The menu, composed of small plates, medium plates, and full entrees, is influenced by the south of France, Spain, Africa, and Latin America. You can partake of starters like saffron Provençal fish soup, octopus with chorizo, bacalao salad, mussels steamed in porter, or a Moroccan-spice beet soup. Among the entrees, try something like wild mushroom and ricotta crepes; bison short ribs; roasted chicken; or fish with a sauce, such as habanero-banana cream. The side dishes are uniformly inventive and healthy, wild-foraged mushrooms make frequent appearances, and the wine list is strong. If you don't have reservations and they're full, sit at the bar.

29 Ceres St. © **603/431-0887.** www.blacktrumpetbistro.com. Reservations recommended. Small plates $6–$15; main courses $20–$27. AE, DC, MC, V. Sun–Thurs 5:30–9:30pm; Fri–Sat 5:30–10pm.

Blue Mermaid Island Grill ★★ 🍴 GLOBAL The Blue Mermaid is a Portsmouth favorite as much for its good food as for its refusal to take itself too seriously. A short stroll west of Market Square, in a historic area called the Hill, it's unpretentious—folk tunes play in the background, and service is casual yet professional. The menu is adventurous in a low-key, global way, leaning toward the Caribbean—but they really run the table. You might try a burrito, tortilla pizza, or sesame-crusted seared cod sandwich for lunch, or a dinner of braised beef short ribs in guava-soy sauce served with corn bread; Bimini-style grilled chicken with bananas and walnuts

Portsmouth: Coffee Capital

Portsmouth has perhaps the best cafe scene in northern New England. There are numerous places in the compact downtown alone where you can get a decent-to-very-good cup of coffee and better-than-average baked goods. My favorite spots to quaff a coffee drink or pot of tea with a book include **Breaking New Grounds,** 14 Market Sq. (© **603/436-9555**), with outstanding espresso shakes, good tables out on the square, and late hours; the tie-dyed **Friendly Toast,** 113 Congress St. (© **603/430-2154;** www.thefriendlytoast.net), serving a fun variety of eggs and other breakfast dishes all day long; and **Me and Ollie's,** 10 Pleasant St. (© **603/436-7777;** www.meandollies.com), known locally for its good bread, sandwiches, and homemade granola. And there are several *more* bakeries and coffee shops within shouting distance of Market Square. The funky **Ceres Bakery,** 51 Penhallow St. (© **603/436-6518;** www.ceresbakery.com), on a side street off the main square, has a handful of tiny interior tables; grab a sandwich, cookie, or slice of cake to go and walk to the waterfront rose gardens nearby.

in a bourbon-coconut (!) sauce; paella; barbecued mahimahi with mole sauce; or spicy "rasta pasta" (saw that one coming). Or, for fun, you can also make a dinner out of several of the funky small-plate offerings, like chicken-and-jack-cheese wontons, lobster quesadillas, Jamaican beef patties, and veggie spring rolls. They also cook steaks and seafood on a wood-fired grill, plus burgers, pasta, and pizzas. Libations include local draft brews, of course, but also a wine list and a menu of tropical mixed drinks, fun margaritas, and martinis. A fascinating place—try it out.

409 The Hill (at Hanover and High sts., facing the municipal parking garage). © **603/427-2583.** www.bluemermaid.com. Reservations recommended for parties of 6 or more. Main courses $6–$12 at lunch, $16–$24 at dinner. AE, DISC, MC, V. Mon–Fri 11:30am–9pm; Sat noon–10pm; Sun noon–9pm.

Dolphin Striker ★ SEAFOOD/AMERICAN   In an old brick warehouse down on one of Portsmouth's most charming streets, the Dolphin serves traditional New England seafood dishes—some of them dressed up in new ways, such as a mushroom-crusted filet of cod or a piece of salmon "lacquered" in tomato-y balsamic vinaigrette and then grilled. But the Maine lobster potpie hasn't changed since, well, probably 1700, and you can also get pan-seared scallops, curried monkfish, bouillabaisse, and other fishy dishes. Seafood avoiders can find refuge in the beef Wellington, steak au poivre, chicken carbonara, or grilled pork chop. The main dining room here has a rustic, public-house atmosphere with wide pine-board floors and wooden furniture; downstairs is a comfortable pub known as the Spring Hill Tavern, with quite good acoustic acts. There's also a lighter, tavern-style menu of burgers, sandwiches, fish and chips, lobster rolls, and the like.

15 Bow St. © **603/431-5222.** www.dolphinstriker.com. Reservations recommended. Main courses $18–$27. AE, DC, DISC, MC, V. Daily 5–11pm.

Jumpin' Jay's Fish Café ★★ 🎒 SEAFOOD   One of Portsmouth's best-loved eateries, Jay McSharry's signature eatery is the place for anyone who wants to eat a fish cooked in something other than a deep-fryer. A sleek and spare dining room dotted with splashes of color and white Corian tabletops, it features an open kitchen and a polished-steel bar. People seem to have fun eating here, one reason Jay's attracts a younger, more culinary-attuned clientele than most other spots in town. The fresh catch of the day is posted on the blackboards; you pick your fish and the way you want it cooked, and then pair it with one of the sauces, such as an orange-sesame glaze, a lobster velouté, a citrusy mustard sauce, a butter sauce, or simply olive oil with herbs. (Up to a half-dozen fish make it onto the menu on a given night, depending on what's fresh.) Starters include escargots, fish stews, crab cakes, and fried oysters; a few pasta dishes are also available. The food here is great, and the attention to detail by the kitchen and waitstaff is admirable. This is one of Portsmouth's iconic spots, a place that wouldn't feel right anywhere else.

150 Congress St. ✆ **603/766-3474.** www.jumpinjays.com. Reservations recommended. Main courses $16–$21. AE, DISC, MC, V. Mon–Thurs 5:30–9pm (summer to 9:30pm), Fri–Sat 5–10pm; Sun 5–9pm.

Pesce Blue ★★ SEAFOOD/ITALIAN Another excellent seafood eatery in downtown Portsmouth? Indeed. Here James Walter serves with a strong Italian accent. Lunch might be a piece of grilled flatbread topped with smoked salmon; a "salad" of mussels, San Marzano tomatoes, marinated olives, and capers; or a cut of pan-roasted haddock with baccala-whipped potatoes and ramps. Plenty of antipasti are available as well. Dinners run to crisp pieces of sockeye salmon, lasagna made from the house lamb sausage, oil-poached halibut, mixed seafood grills, great small plates of things such as tuna tartare with pickled apples and capers, or an entire salt-baked branzino. Don't overlook the pastas, either—seasonal pumpkin gnocchi in a nutmeg cream sauce, orecchiette with Bolognese sauce, or spaghetti with clam sauce. Desserts have included mascarpone cheesecake, fennel panna cotta, molten chocolate cake, and olive oil–orange cake topped with vanilla cream. On Sunday, the kitchen serves an upscale brunch of truffled lobster frittatas, buttermilk pancakes, poached eggs, lobster rolls, Niçoise salads, and the like.

103 Congress St. ✆ **603/430-7766.** www.pesceblue.com. Main courses $9–$21 at lunch, $14–$26 at dinner. AE, DISC, MC, V. Mon–Fri noon–2pm and 5:30–9pm; Sat 5:30–9:30pm; Sun 10am–2pm.

Portsmouth Brewery ★ PUB FARE In the heart of the historic district (look for the tipping tankard suspended over the sidewalk), New Hampshire's first brewpub opened here in 1991 and still draws a loyal clientele with its superb beers and fun atmosphere. The tin-ceiling, brick-wall dining room is open, airy, echoey, and redolent of hops. Brews are made in 200-gallon batches and include specialties such as Old Brown Dog ale and a delightfully creamy Black Cat Stout—plus some cool offbeat styles like cream ale, "California common," Flanders Red (a Dutch-style red ale), a "braggot" (a medieval style), and plenty more. The eclectic menu complements the beers and holds it own; it includes the expected pizzas, burgers, fish and chips, and sandwiches (including a "steak bomb"), of course, but also offers a changing selection of specials that trot the globe adventurously—things like Asian rice noodles in a coconut broth, oven-baked ziti, and a meatloaf spiked with chipotle peppers.

56 Market St. ✆ **603/431-1115.** www.portsmouthbrewery.com. Reservations accepted for parties of 10 or more. Main courses $9–$26. AE, DC, DISC, MC, V. Daily 11:30am–12:30am.

The Press Room AMERICAN Locals flock here for the good atmosphere, live music, and easy-on-the-budget prices rather than fancy cuisine. A downtown favorite since 1976, the restaurant boasts that it was first in the area to serve Guinness beer—and, indeed, the interior has a rustic, Gaelic sort of charm. On cold days, a fire burns in the woodstove while drinkers throw darts beneath heavy wooden beams. Choose from a menu of inexpensive selections such as quesadillas, nachos, salads, burgers, wraps, and stir-fries, or order a heavier (but still cheap) meal of blackened haddock, steak tips, or jambalaya. The live jazz here is justifiably popular (see "Portsmouth After Dark," below).

77 Daniel St. ✆ **603/431-5186.** www.pressroomnh.com. Reservations not accepted. Sandwiches $4–$7, main courses $7–$13. AE, DISC, MC, V. Sun–Thurs 5–11pm; Fri–Sat 11:30am–11pm.

PORTSMOUTH AFTER DARK
Performing Arts

The Music Hall ★★   This historic theater near Market Square dates to 1878 and was more recently restored to its former glory. A variety of shows are staged here, from lots of film to comedy revues, *The Nutcracker,* and concerts by visiting pop artists. Call or check the website for a current calendar. 28 Chestnut St. ✆ **603/436-2400.** www.themusichall.org.

The Press Room ★   A popular local pub and eatery (see "Where to Dine," above), the Press Room also offers casual entertainment almost every night, either upstairs or down. It's best known locally for copious amounts of live jazz; the club brings in quality performers from Boston and beyond. You might hear beat poetry or blues on occasion, too. 77 Daniel St. ✆ **603/431-5186.** www.pressroomnh.com. Cover varies.

Spring Hill Tavern   Quality acoustic noodling, live jazz, classical guitar, and/or low-key rock are on top most nights of the week here in the pub located right downstairs from the popular Dolphin Striker seafood restaurant (see "Where to Dine," above). Expect anything from a seasoned New Orleans–style blues band to a local singer-songwriter's nascent efforts. There are also sometimes fun free-form jam sessions. 15 Bow St. ✆ **603/431-5222.** www.dolphinstriker.com. Cover varies.

THE MOUNT MONADNOCK REGION ★

Peterborough: 71 miles NW of Boston; 38 miles SW of Manchester, NH

New Hampshire's southwestern corner is a pretty region of rolling hills, small villages, rustic farms, winding back roads, and amazing fall foliage. What the area lacks in major attractions, it makes up for in peacefulness and bucolic charm—plus one good-sized mountain. The inns here tend to be more basic and less luxurious than those in southern Vermont, but their prices do appeal to budget travelers. This is also becoming a popular area for Bostonians seeking a respite from city life, and in fall thousands of them stream north to the region for the excellent leaf-peeping, which is by all accounts some of the best in New England.

There aren't many museums or fancy restaurants around here. The preferred activities are woodland strolls, back-road cycling trips, afternoons reading on the porch, and obscure country-store exploration.

Peterborough ★★

Peterborough, settled in 1749 in a river valley at the confluence of two local rivers, is a town that has successfully pulled off the economic transition from the Colonial and industrial eras to the modern one without sacrificing its soul. That's a neat trick, one that much of small-town New England still hasn't quite figured out how to perform. The town and its neighbors have carved out a new identity for themselves as centers of publishing and light technology—the *Old Farmer's Almanac* and *Yankee Magazine* are both published in nearby Dublin, and the outdoor-gear manufacturer Eastern Mountain Sports is based here.

ESSENTIALS

GETTING THERE Peterborough is situated between **Keene** and **Nashua** on Rte. 101; reach it from Boston (about 90 min. away) via Rte. 3 or I-93 to Nashua. From New York and Hartford, take I-91 north to Brattleboro, Vermont; exit and cross the river on Rte. 9 to Keene; and continue east on Rte. 101 to Peterborough—it takes about 4 hours in all.

A decent map is *essential* for exploring the many fine little villages and towns nearby, as the winding state and county roads have no rhyme or reason to them.

VISITOR INFORMATION The **Greater Peterborough Chamber of Commerce** (*©* **603/924-7234;** www.greater-peterborough-chamber.com) provides advice over the phone or at a year-round information center at 10 Wilton Rd. (just east of the intersection of Rte. 101 and Rte. 202). The center is always open weekdays during business hours, and it's also open on Saturday from 10am to 3pm during the peak tourist season, from mid-June through the end of October.

OUTDOOR PURSUITS

Mount Monadnock ★★ rises impressively above the gentler hills of southern New Hampshire. Though only 3,165 feet high (about half the height of Mt. Washington in northern New Hampshire), it has a solitary grandeur. Its knobby peak was scaled by such New England literary luminaries as Ralph Waldo Emerson and Henry David Thoreau back in the day, when ascents were still rare. Today, though, more than 100,000 hikers follow their lead and head for the summit each year. It's *not* a place for solitary walks. Some 40 miles of trails (30% of which can be cross-country skied) lace the patchwork of public and private lands on the various slopes of the mountain.

The most popular and best-marked trails leave from near the entrance to **Monadnock State Park ★★** (*©* **603/532-8862**), about 4 miles northwest of Jaffrey Center off Rte. 124. (Head west on Rte. 124; after 2 miles, follow the park signs to the north). A round-trip hike up and down the most direct, crowded routes (the **White Dot** and **White Cross** trails, which begin at the end of a paved road) should take someone in decent shape 3 to 4 hours—keep your eyes on the trail and be careful, as some sections are steep and some involve broken-up rock or ledges.

The final ascent is pretty steep; if you're afraid of heights, stop at one of the overlooks on the way up and snap pictures. You can just see Boston and bits of all the New England states from the top, if you know where to look. The state park is open year-round (a ranger is on duty in summer). Admission costs $4 for adults, $2 for children 12 and over. No pets are allowed in this park. There's also camping at about two dozen sites in a small camping area, some available by reservation only; the sites cost $25 per night, and there are no water or electrical hookups.

WHERE TO STAY

Benjamin Prescott Inn Col. Benjamin Prescott fought at the Battle of Bunker Hill before retiring to Jaffrey in 1775. This three-story farmhouse built by his sons dates from 1853, a handsome yellow Greek Revival building on an (often busy) road about 2 miles east of Jaffrey's town center. Throughout the inn, there's a strong sense of history and a connection to the past. All 10 rooms have ceiling fans and phone jacks (phones are provided on request), while the two suites are air-conditioned; otherwise, rooms are simply furnished—cranberry-hued Col. Prescott's Room is furnished with two armchairs and a desk, Susannah's Suite has a narrow brass bed and a sitting room with a couch. Guests can wander the farmlands beyond the inn or hike Monadnock, just a short drive down the road.

433 Turnpike Rd. (Rte. 124), Jaffrey, NH 03452. ⓒ **888/950-6637** or 603/532-6637. Fax 603/532-1142. www.benjaminprescottinn.com. 10 units. $95–$160 double; peak season $120–$195 double. Rates include full breakfast. 2-night minimum some holidays and peak-season weekends. AE, MC, V. Children 12 and over welcome. *In room:* A/C (2 units), Wi-Fi (free), no phone.

Birchwood Inn 🗲 This quiet retreat offers rooms at affordable prices and a thoroughly British experience. Thoreau visited the inn during one of his many rambles through New England; neither the town nor the inn seems to have changed much since. A handsome, historic brick farmhouse with a white-clapboard ell, it's in the middle of the crossroads town of Temple near the town grange and a park with three war memorials. (It's also an easy stroll to a historic cemetery with headstones dating back to the 18th c.) The inn itself is decorated in an informal country style and operated by a pair of affable guys; all its rooms and suites are named for cities in England, each with a different theme (musical instruments, train memorabilia, country-store) bordering on the kitschy. Rooms have small TVs with DVD players, there's Wi-Fi access throughout, and an on-site tavern opens 5 nights a week, serving actual English-style pub food and beer.

340 Rte. 45 (P.O. Box 23), Temple, NH 03084. ⓒ **603/878-3285.** Fax: 603/878-2159. www.thebirchwood inn.com. 5 units. $89–$139 double. Rates include full breakfast. 2-night minimum stay during foliage season. No credit cards. Drive 1½ miles south on Rte. 101. Children 11 and over welcome. **Amenities:** Restaurant; pub. *In room:* TV/DVD, Wi-Fi (free), no phone.

Hancock Inn ★★ The Hancock Inn, built in 1789, claims to be New Hampshire's oldest. You'll find classic Americana inside, from creaky floors and braided oval rugs to guest rooms appointed in understated Colonial decor. The Rufus Porter Room has an evocative full-length wall mural from the inn's early days, plus two fireplaces, while the Ballroom has a high, vaulted ceiling (it really used to be the ballroom) and Jacuzzi. The Bell Tower Room comes furnished with a cannonball king-size bed, gas fireplace, and Jacuzzi—it overlooks the garden. And the Moses Eaton Room features the designs of Eaton, a famed stencil artist who lived in this town for a time. This inn has the same historical charm as other historic inns in this area, but with more upscale rooms. The food is good, too.

33 Main St., Hancock, NH 03449. ⓒ **800/525-1789** or 603/525-3318. www.hancockinn.com. 14 units. $150–$260 double; $260–$290 suite. Rates include breakfast. AE, DC, DISC, MC, V. Pets accepted in 1 unit (free). **Amenities:** Restaurant. *In room:* A/C, TV, hair dryer, Wi-Fi (most units; free).

Monadnock Inn In the middle of one of New Hampshire's most gracious villages, this lovely, architecturally eclectic inn (formerly called the Inn at Jaffrey Center) was built around 1830. After years of decline, it got a much-needed makeover in 2000, when all its rooms were updated in traditional New England style—some with four-poster or canopy beds. Units that formerly shared a bathroom all got their own bathrooms, and fixtures such as aging claw-foot tubs were refurbished.

The building is definitely showing its age, but it's still a conveniently placed sleep in a pretty village. Some rooms have TVs; all have goose-down comforters. The lawns and porches are attractive, and the inn's friendly innkeepers serve better meals than you'd expect in the **restaurant ★★** and pub. The village's churches and lanes are within walking distance.

379 Main St. (P.O. Box 484), Jaffrey Center, NH 03452. ☎ **877/510-7019** or 603/532-7800. Fax 603/532-7900. www.theinnatjaffreycenter.com. 11 units. $110–$160 double. Rates include continental breakfast. Minimum stays required during foliage and holiday weekends. MC, V. **Amenities:** Restaurant; pub. *In room:* Wi-Fi (most units; free), no phone.

WHERE TO DINE

Three of the four inns listed above maintain restaurants serving dinner to both their own guests and the public, and they're actually quite good.

Acqua Bistro ★★★ BISTRO Acqua Bistro is the Monadnock region's best gourmet meal for miles, hands down. Hidden off Peterborough's main streets, near Twelve Pine and the Sharon Arts Center, it's in a modern, agreeable dining space overlooking a little stream. The kitchen offers fusion twists on Continental fare. Small plates and entrees could run to tea-smoked duck, ginger-crusted scallops, rib-eye steaks, salmon, seared tuna, grilled organic chicken breast, duck, or a gourmet burger. There's always something intriguing on the menu for vegetarians, as well as creative thin-crust pizzas with alternative toppings like chicken sausage, shrimp with wasabi cream, and chipotle barbecue baked in a stone oven. There's a good wine list, house cocktails, a full martini menu—you can order a cheese plate or other light meal from a special bar menu if you're not overly hungry. Sunday mornings feature a great, stylish brunch.

9 School St. (in Depot Sq.), Peterborough. ☎ **603/924-9905.** www.acquabistro.com. Reservations accepted for parties of 5 or more. Main courses $14–$25. MC, V. Tues-Sat 4-10pm; Sun 11am-10pm; off-season hours may be shorter.

Peterborough Diner ☺ DINER This classic throwback to the 1940s is hidden on a side street, but it's worth finding. Behind the faded exterior is a cozy diner of wood, aluminum, tile, and ceiling fans, plus a jukebox. The meals are just as you'd expect: filling, cheap, basic. Look for hot-oven grinders sided with fries, plates of hot turkey with cranberry sauce, and veal parmigiana. A few fancier items like chicken cordon bleu, are also on the menu, but you don't come for those—you come for milkshakes and banana splits. Or order a "belly buster," which is three of everything: eggs, slices of bacon, slices of toast, sausage patties, pancakes, and slices of French toast. Keep your doctor on speed-dial.

10 Depot St., Peterborough. ☎ **603/924-6710.** www.peterboroughdiner.com. Breakfast items $2-$6, lunch and dinner items $4-$8. AE, DISC, MC, V. Mon-Fri 6am-9pm (to 8pm in winter), Sat-Sun 7am-8pm.

Twelve Pine ★ 📷 DELI This inviting deli and market, in a former railroad building behind Peterborough's main street, has been here since 1996. It's a great spot to nosh and linger; select a premade meal or sandwich from a deli counter, bring it to a table, eat, repeat. Sandwiches are made with homemade bread and heaping fillings; cheeses are available by the pound, and fresh juices and gourmet coffees round out the meal. On your way out, stock up on gourmet foods to go in the market and wine shop. In an age of megalithic whole-foods stores, it's refreshing to see a home-grown version still holding its own—and then some.

11 School St. (in Depot Sq.), Peterborough. ℂ **877/412-7463** or 603/924-6140. www.twelvepine.com. Sandwiches around $6, other items priced per lb. MC, V. Mon–Fri 8am–7pm; Sat 9am–5pm; Sun 9am–4pm.

Hanover ★★

If your idea of a perfect New England experience involves a big green park surrounded by old brick buildings and smart people, visit **Hanover,** a university town in the Connecticut River Valley about a half-hour's drive north of **Cornish** and right across the river from **Norwich.** Settled in 1765, the town was first home to early colonists who were granted a charter by King George III to establish a college here. That school was named for the second Earl of Dartmouth, its first trustee, and ever since has had a profound impact in shaping the town.

The handsome village green marks the border between college and town. In summer, it's a great place for strolling or lounging. The best way to explore Hanover is on foot, anyway, so your first job is to park your car—which can be trying during peak seasons (fall, plus whenever school is in session or there's a football game). Try the municipal lots west of Main Street if you can't find a meter. The chief attraction is the pretty campus of **Dartmouth College** itself, but downtown also offers plenty of fine restaurants, galleries, bookstores, and pubs.

ESSENTIALS

GETTING THERE Hanover is a bit off the interstate. From Boston, Concord, or Manchester to the south, take I-93 to I-89 N. From Brattleboro or St. Johnsbury, Vermont, take I-91. From Montpelier or Burlington, Vermont, take I-89 S. to I-91 N. in White River Junction, head north a few miles, then exit for Norwich and cross the river.

Amazingly, there is daily direct bus service to Hanover from both Boston and New York. **Dartmouth Coach** (ℂ 800/637-0123; www.dartmouthcoach.com) travels to and from Boston at least a half-dozen times per day, an easy 2½-hour ride costing $50 round-trip. From New York City, there's one Dartmouth Coach trip daily ($149 round-trip, 5 hr.)—it departs from the Yale Club, on Vanderbilt Avenue beside Grand Central Terminal.

Amtrak (ℂ 800/872-7245; www.amtrak.com) also runs one train daily (7 hr.; $56 one-way) from New York City to **White River Junction,** Vermont, about 4½ miles away. From there, you'll need to take a cab—or, I suppose, you could go on foot (a 90-min. to 2-hr. walk), but I would never recommend doing that after dark.

VISITOR INFORMATION Dartmouth College alumni and local chamber of commerce volunteers maintain an **information center** right on the town green daily from June through September. During the off season, head for the offices of the **Hanover Area Chamber of Commerce** (ℂ 603/643-3115; www.hanover chamber.org) at 47 S. Main St., across from the town post office. It's open weekdays only, during normal business hours. Bonus: The chamber's members include businesses across the river in Norwich, Vermont, too.

SPECIAL EVENTS In early to mid-February, look for the fantastic and intricate ice sculptures marking the return of the annual **Dartmouth Winter Carnival.** Call Dartmouth College's student affairs office at ℂ 603/646-3399 for more information on this traditionally beer-soaked event.

EXPLORING HANOVER & THE VICINITY

Hanover is a great town to explore on foot, by bike, or even by *canoe*. Start by picking up a map of the **Dartmouth campus** at the college's information center on the green (summer and fall only), or at the Hanover Inn (see "Where to Stay," below) across the street. Free guided tours of the campus are also offered during summer, and the expansive, leafy neighborhood is a delight to walk through—especially the fraternity district, believe it or not, which is full of grand old homes (the nonfraternities, I mean), ponds, and a golf course.

On the south side of the green, next door to the Hanover Inn, is the modern **Hopkins Center for the Arts** ★★ (© **603/646-2422**). Locally known as "The Hop," the center attracts national acts to its 900-seat concert hall and stages top-notch dance and theatrical performances in its Moore Theater. Wallace Harrison, the architect who later went on to fame for designing Lincoln Center in New York, designed this building. You can find a comprehensive schedule of upcoming events at the Hop at its website, **http://hop.dartmouth.edu**.

Enfield Shaker Museum ★ A cluster of historic buildings on Lake Mascoma about a 20-minute drive southeast of Hanover, "The Chosen Vale" (as its first inhabitants called this valley) was founded in 1793. During the mid-1800s, this Shaker community counted 350 members and held 3,000 acres; today, however, the museum is state-owned. Dominating the village is the Great Stone Dwelling, an austere but gracious granite five-plus-story structure erected between 1837 and 1841. (At the time, it was the tallest building north of Boston.) A self-guided walking tour of the surrounding village—check out the Stone Mill Building, too—is free with admission.

447 Rte. 4A, Enfield. © **603/632-4346.** www.shakermuseum.org. Admission $7.50 adults, $6.50 seniors, $5 college students, $3 children 10–17, free for children 9 and under. Mon–Sat 10am–5pm; Sun noon–5pm (last tour 4pm).

Hood Museum of Art ★★ 👪 Often overlooked by visitors to Hanover (maybe because it's not even visible from the street, but rather set back behind other buildings), this modern, open structure beside the Hopkins Center houses one of the oldest college museums in the country. The permanent collection holds some 65,000 items, including a superb selection of 19th-century American landscapes; significant holdings of African, African-American, and Native American art and artifacts; and six stone reliefs dating from 900 B.C. Assyria. Special exhibits are frequent and high-quality—for one show, artist Fred Wilson arranged hidden and neglected items from the permanent collection in thought-provoking, sometimes disturbing ways. A 2009 exhibit highlighted the work of legendary mixed-media artist Robert Rauschenberg, who was an artist-in-residence at the college in 1963.

Wheelock St. © **603/646-2808.** http://hoodmuseum.dartmouth.edu. Free admission. Tues–Sat 10am–5pm (Wed to 9pm); Sun noon–5pm. From the Hanover green, facing the Hopkins Center, cross Wheelock St. and take the footpath to the left of the Hopkins Center.

Ledyard Canoe Club ★ One idyllic way to spend a lazy afternoon in Hanover is by drifting along the Connecticut River in a canoe—assuming you know how to paddle one safely, that is. Dartmouth's historic boating club is just downhill from the campus at the river's bank. While much of the club's focus is on competitive racing, it's also a place where travelers can rent a boat for a few hours and explore the tree-lined river. Life jackets must be carried at all times, and worn by children and non-swimmers. The club is open daily from spring through mid-October.

GARDENS OF stone

There was a seriously thriving artists' colony in the little village of **Cornish,** about 20 miles south of Hanover, in the early 20th century; today, the chief relic of those heady days is the **Saint-Gaudens National Historic Site ★★** (☎ **603/675-2175;** www.nps.gov/saga) off Rte. 12A, a remarkable little spot. The Irish-born sculptor Augustus Saint-Gaudens arrived here in 1885, having received an important commission to create a statue of Abraham Lincoln. His friend Charles Beaman, a Manhattan lawyer who owned several homes in the area, assured him he could find a plenty of "Lincoln-shaped men" in the area. Saint-Gaudens came, found them, and stayed for the rest of his life, creating work that today fills American museums, cemeteries, and parks. (He even designed a U.S. coin, the lovely "double eagle").

Saint-Gaudens' hillside home and studio Aspet—named for the village in Ireland where he was raised—are superb places to learn more about the artist. Grounds are open year-round, while the buildings open to the public daily from late May through October, 9am to 4:30pm. Admission is $5 for adults, free for children 16 and under during that season. There's no charge to visit the grounds during the off season.

Off W. Wheelock St. ☎ **603/643-6709.** www.dartmouth.edu/-lcc. Canoe and kayak rentals $10 per hr., $20 per day Mon–Fri, $30 per day Sat–Sun. Summer Mon–Fri 10am–8pm, Sat–Sun 9am–8pm; spring and fall Mon–Fri noon–6pm, Sat–Sun 10am–6pm. Open whenever river temperature is higher than 50°F (10°C), generally mid-May to mid-Oct. Turn upstream at the bottom of the hill west of the bridge; follow signs to the clubhouse.

WHERE TO STAY

There are plenty of midpriced chain hotel and motel properties clumped together along a strip just off the interstate in **West Lebanon,** 5 miles south of Hanover. Take exit 20 off I-89 to find them.

The Hanover Inn ★★   The venerable white-and-brick Hanover Inn is one of the oldest lodgings in the region, yet it's also the Upper Valley's best-managed and most up-to-date luxury hotel—perfectly situated for exploring both the Dartmouth campus and the compact downtown. (The inn is located directly across Hanover's big central green from the college.) Built in 1780, most of the present-day five-story structure you see today was actually added in successive stages—in 1924, 1939, and, finally, 1968. This inn offers professional service, attractive rooms, fine dining, and subterranean walkways connecting you to the college's Hood Museum of Art and its Hopkins Center for the Arts. Rooms are trim and solid, as you'd expect; most have canopy or four-poster beds and down comforters, and some even overlook the pretty green. Going all out? The Baker Tower Suite features a wet bar, sitting space, and the best views. The inn's dining options include a fancy dining room (see "Where to Dine," below), a terrace of outdoor tables fronting the green, and a wine bistro (see below).

Wheelock St. (P.O. Box 151), Hanover, NH 03755. ☎ **800/443-7024** or 603/643-4300. Fax 603/643-4433. www.hanoverinn.com. 92 units. From $259 double; from $309 suite. AE, DISC, MC, V. Valet parking $12 per day. Pets accepted ($15 per night). **Amenities:** 3 restaurants; 2 bars; babysitting; limited room service. *In room:* A/C, TV, hair dryer, Wi-Fi (free).

SIDE TRIP: NEWPORT, SUNAPEE & NEW LONDON

While visiting the Hanover, Concord, or Cornish areas, don't forget to side-trip over to the Newport–Lake Sunapee region. The commercial center of the area is **Newport ★★**, a mill town with grit, character, and substantial history in a pretty valley setting. This town produced Sarah Josepha Hale, author of the children's poem "Mary Had a Little Lamb" and creator of the Thanksgiving holiday—President Lincoln was sufficiently impressed by her persistence to make it official. Hale was also one of the first American women to serve as editor of a national publication (*Godey's Lady's Book*). Yet she's only one of the famous folks who grew up here.

The town's historical attractions include a quilt project documenting Newport's industrial past (including healthy numbers of Finn, Polish, Greek, and Italian immigrants); an antique 1815 Hunnemen "handtub," a wheeled apparatus built by an apprentice of Paul Revere and once used by firemen to pump water while fighting blazes (it's on display inside the Lake Sunapee Bank, at 9 Main St.); and a wooden **covered bridge ★★**, painstakingly built by a local craftsman to replicate the priceless original, which was sadly torched by an arsonist in 1993.

Drop by the town's **Richards Free Library ★** (*✆* **603/863-3430**), at 58 N. Main St., to get oriented; for my money, it's one of the best small-town libraries in New England. (Tantalizing historical tidbit: President Kennedy was supposed to accept a writing award at this library on the night of Nov 22, 1963. He politely declined, due to commitments in Dallas.) You'll find a few restaurants on Main Street as well. For more details, contact the helpful Newport Area Chamber of Commerce (*✆* **603/863-1510**). A good, volunteer-run **info kiosk** is open on the town "common" (big green space) during the summer.

Six miles away, big **Lake Sunapee ★★** is said to be one of the purest in the nation, and it's much deeper than it looks. Sunapee is a longtime favorite summer resort of Bostonians, and offers excellent swimming, boating, and fishing.

WHERE TO DINE

A good spot for a quick bite or drink is **Zins winebistro ★**, an informal bistro serving about 35 wines by the glass (plus 25 beers) off the lobby of the regal Hanover Inn (see above) on Wheelock Street. It's open daily, serving light meals of sandwiches, salads, burgers, and grilled fish with the wine. Helpfully, they also offer a short menu of kids' meals.

Daniel Webster Room ★★ AMERICAN The main dining room in the Hanover Inn will appeal to anyone looking for fine dining in a formal New England atmosphere. The Colonial Revival–style room is reminiscent of a 19th-century resort hotel, with big fluted columns, floral carpeting, and regally upholstered chairs. Inn chef Jason Merrill has unveiled a new, much more contemporary New American/fusion-oriented menu in recent years: gingered tuna loin with wasabi rice cake and ponzu sauce, pappardelle with ragout made from local lamb, and a changing daily vegetable dish depending on what's being harvested—the heavy resort fare that used to fill the menu is mostly out. (They'll still grill you up a nice strip steak and side it

The short, steep mountain across the way—which, together with the beach, forms **Mount Sunapee State Park** (𝄞 **603/763-5561**)—is a fine place to hike or catch a gondola ride for expansive foliage and lake views. There's a $4 charge ($2 for kids) to enter either the beach or mountain portions of the park; the ski hill itself is operated by the family-owned **Mount Sunapee Resort** (𝄞 **603/763-3500;** www.mount sunapee.com).

Early August brings one outstanding arts event to the park, the 9-day **Craftsman's Fair ★** (𝄞 **603/224-3375;** www. nhcrafts.org). Expect high-quality handcrafted art pieces and great demonstrations and workshops (soap carving, pottery, and the like). Two-day admission tickets cost about $10 per adult, $8 per senior or student; children 11 and under are admitted for free.

The main harbor for the lake, **Sunapee Harbor,** is a few miles away at the junction of routes 103B and 11. This is the place to put in your boat, grab an ice-cream cone, or watch a sunset. You might see a famous face with your cone, too; members of the band Aerosmith own homes in the harbor area.

On the back side of the lake, pretty **New London ★★** is an attractive college town with lots of fine homes, a few good restaurants, and an outstanding summer musical theater. Without ever straying off Main Street, you can settle down for a full meal at the tony **Millstone** (𝄞 **603/526-4201;** www.millstone restaurant.com); relax over coffee and sandwiches at **Ellie's Cafe** (𝄞 **603/526-2448;** http://elliescafeanddeli.com); or go British-pub-style with a shared "board" of bread, cheeses, sliced meats, and beer at **Peter Christian's Tavern** (𝄞 **603/526-4042;** www.peterchristianstavern. com). The **New London Barn Playhouse** (New London, NH; 𝄞 **603/526-6710;** www.nlbarn.org) is the place to head in New Hampshire if you like musical theater. Drawing on the local pool of acting talent, shows like *Hairspray, Hello, Dolly!,* and *Carousel* take over the house from June through August.

with mashed potatoes, though, if you wish.) Tasty small-plate choices include items like shrimp-and-crab fritters, small grilled flatbread pizzas, crispy tofu with cashews, and pan-roasted day-boat scallops. At lunch, go low (chowder, a salad) or high (the lobster club); either way, it's excellent. Yes, the inn serves great breakfasts, too—New England classics (buttermilk pancakes with real maple syrup), but also bagels with lox, poached eggs, and a cinnamon brioche French toast.

Wheelock St. (in the Hanover Inn). 𝄞 **603/643-4300.** www.hanoverinn.com. Reservations recommended. Main courses $7–$21 at lunch, $12–$27 at dinner. AE, DISC, MC, V. Mon 7–10:30am and 11:30am–1:30pm; Tues–Fri 7–10:30am, 11:30am–1:30pm, and 6–9pm; Sat 7–10:30am and 6–9pm; Sun 11am–1:30pm.

Lou's 🍴 BAKERY/DINER   Lou's has been a Hanover institution since the 1940s, attracting hordes of students for breakfast on the weekends and a steady local clientele of working folk during the week. This is no-frills New Hampshire, just a black-and-white-checkerboard linoleum floor, maple-and-vinyl booths, and a harried yet efficient crew of waiters. Breakfast is served all day (real maple syrup on your pancakes costs extra, though), and the sandwiches, served on freshly baked bread, are huge. Locals know to pop in after the diner closes in the late afternoon; while the staff preps for the next morning's rush, you can buy the day's remaining baked goods (if any are left) until 5pm.

30 S. Main St. © **603/643-3321.** http://lousrestaurant.net. Breakfast items $3–$7; lunch items $5–$8. AE, MC, V. Mon–Fri 6am–3pm; Sat–Sun 7am–3pm (opens 8am Sun in winter). Bakery daily to 5pm.

THE WHITE MOUNTAINS ★★★

The White Mountain range is northern New England's outdoor recreation capital. This high range of peaks is a sprawling, rugged playground that calls out to legions of intrepid kayakers, mountaineers, rock climbers, thrill-seeking skiers, mountain bikers, bird-watchers, and backpacking hikers.

The **White Mountain National Forest** organizes and administrates most of this vast landscape, nearly 800,000 acres of rocky, forested terrain, more than 100 waterfalls, dozens of backcountry lakes, miles of clear brooks and cascading streams—you get the idea. An elaborate network of hiking trails (more than 1,000 miles' worth) dates back to the 19th century, when city folk took to these mountains to build character and experience nature first-hand. Pathways ranging from easy to vertical lace the forests, trade the rivers, and traverse knifelike ridgelines where the weather can change so quickly and dramatically it can do you in, if you're not ready for it.

The heart of the White Mountains is 6,288-foot **Mount Washington,** an ominous, brooding peak that's often cloud-capped and mantled with snow both early and late in the season. It's so big, you can see it from Portland, Maine, 100 miles away. An often-blustery peak, it's accessible by cog railway, car, and foot, making it one of the more popular destinations in the region. You won't find untouched wilderness here, but you will find abundant natural drama.

Flanking Washington is the brawny **Presidential Range,** a series of similarly wind-blasted granite peaks which are similarly named for U.S. presidents and offering similarly eye-popping views. Beyond this range, plenty of lesser-known ridges also beckon hikers seeking an elemental test, too.

But even if your idea of fun *doesn't* involve scary cliffs, near-vertical ski runs, and icy plunges into mountain streams, you can still enjoy the scenery around here via spectacular drives. The most scenic is the **Kancamagus Highway** between Conway and Lincoln, offering plenty of pullouts to picnic and snap great photos.

Towns are few and far between: **North Conway** is the lodging capital, with hundreds of motel units and strip-mall and outlet shopping. **Loon Mountain** and **Waterville Valley** are condo villages attached to ski resorts. And **Bethlehem, Jackson,** and the **Franconia and Crawford notches** offer genteel main streets and old-style (or sometimes just old) hotels and inns.

Backcountry Fees

The White Mountain National Forest requires anyone using the backcountry—for hiking, mountain biking, picnicking, skiing, or any other activity—to pay a recreation fee. Anyone parking at a trail head must display a backcountry permit on the car dashboard; those lacking a permit face a fine. Permits are available at ranger stations and many stores in the region. An annual permit costs $20, and a 7-day pass is $5. You can also buy a day pass for $3, but it covers only one site: the spot you bought it at. (If you drive anywhere else on the mountain later in the afternoon and park

The White Mountains

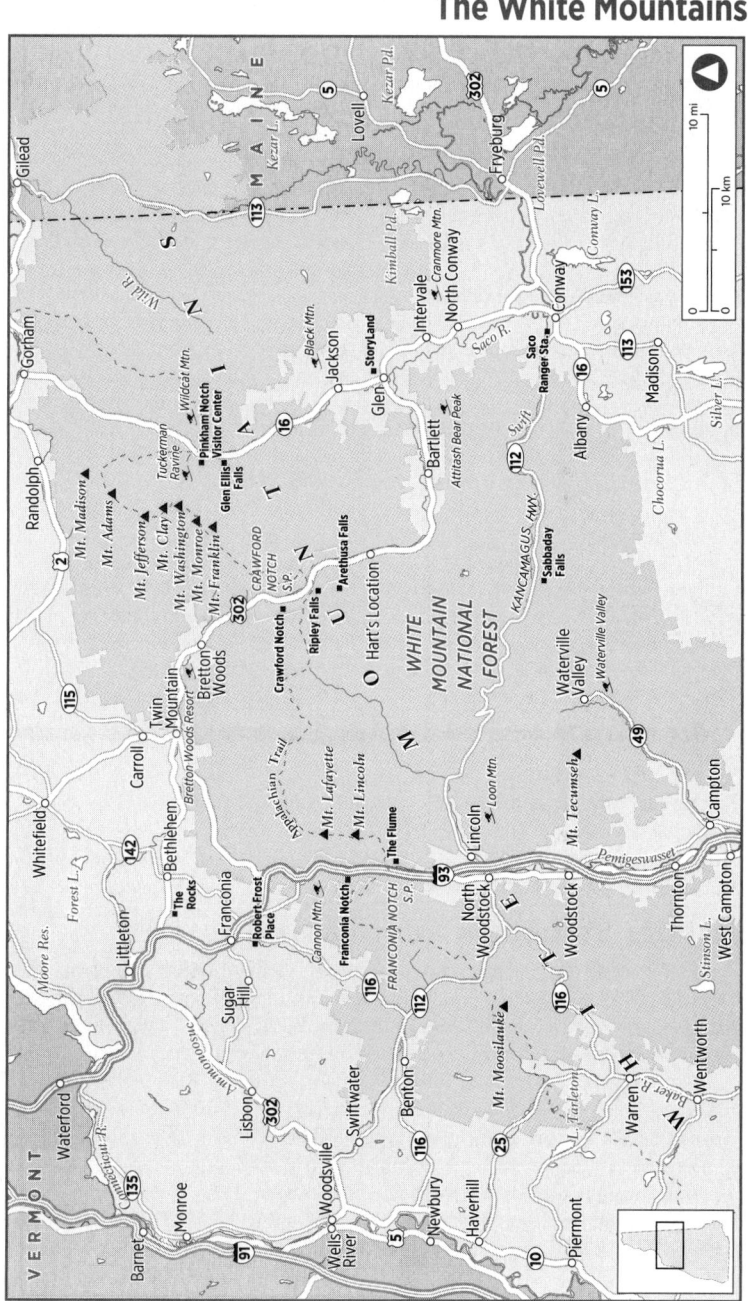

ACTIVITIES IN THE WHITE MOUNTAINS

Backpacking The White Mountains have some of the most challenging and scenic backpacking in the eastern U.S. The best trails are within the huge White Mountain National Forest, which encompasses several 5,000-plus-foot peaks and more than 100,000 acres of designated wilderness. The trails range from easy walks along bubbling streams to demanding ridgeline paths buffeted by fierce winds.

The **Appalachian Mountain Club** (© 603/466-2727; www.amc-nh.org) is an excellent source of general information about the region's outdoors offerings. It's a major supplier of lodging, too. Eight sturdy **mountain huts** ★ (small cabins) offer bare-bones, bunk-room-style shelter and great campfire conviviality in dramatic settings; hearty breakfasts and dinners are included with your rates, which are about $90 per adult, less for kids. The AMC maintains a clutch of other cabins and lodges in the mountains, too, such as the 16-bed

Shapleigh Bunkhouse in Crawford Notch (a bunk plus breakfast costs $40 to $65 per non-AMC member) and the Joe Dodge Lodge, in Pinkham Notch, which has some four-person family rooms.

The **Appalachian Trail** ★★★ passes through New Hampshire, entering the state at Hanover and running along the highest peaks of the White Mountains before exiting into Maine along the scenic, tough-to-climb **Mahoosuc Range** ★★ northeast of Gorham. The trail is well maintained in these stretches, though it tends to attract teeming crowds along the highest elevations in summer.

Everything you could possibly need for a day or overnight hike, including sleeping bags and pads, tents, and backpacks, is available at **Eastern Mountain Sports** (© 603/356-5433), at a brand-spanking-new location taking a run at L.L.Bean–type greatness. It's located in the Settlers' Crossing mall (don't confuse it with Settlers'

again, you'll have to pay the $3 all over again.) You're much better off with the 7-day or annual pass.

For more information, contact the **Forest Service's White Mountains office** (© **603/536-6100;** www.fs.fed.us/r9/white).

Ranger Stations & Information

The Forest Service's brand new **White Mountain National Forest headquarters** are located at 71 White Mountain Dr. in Campton (take exit 27 from I-93 and follow signs to reach it). The facility houses the Forest Supervisor's Office, Pemigewasset Ranger District staff, and a handy visitor center that's open daily, year-round, 8am to 4:30pm.

There are two more stations in the mountains: the **Saco Ranger Station,** at 33 Kancamagus Hwy., 300 feet west of Rte. 16 in Conway (© **603/447-5448**); and the **Androscoggin Ranger Station,** at 300 Glen Rd. in Gorham (© **603/466-2713**).

The National Parks Service also maintains two helpful year-round visitor centers. The **Gateway Visitor Center** ★ (© 603/745-3816) is just off exit 32 of I-93, well stocked and in a good position en route to many attractions. It's open daily 8:30am to 4pm. Then there's the **Lincoln Woods Visitor Center** (© 603/630-5190), about 5 miles east of Lincoln right on the Kancamagus Highway. There's a **suspension**

Green, a *different* mall) on Rte. 16/302 between Conway and North Conway (though closer to Conway). The store is open daily.

Hiking The essential guide to hiking in this region is the Appalachian Mountain Club's *White Mountain Guide*, which contains up-to-date and detailed descriptions of every trail in the area. The guide is available at most bookstores and outdoor shops (even at some gas stations) in the region.

Skiing The best downhill ski areas in the White Mountains are Cannon Mountain, Loon Mountain, Waterville Valley, Wildcat, and Attitash Bear Peak, with vertical drops of 2,000 feet and all the services one would expect of a professional ski resort. See below in this chapter for details on these ski hills.

The state also boasts some two dozen cross-country ski centers. The state's premier cross-country destination is **Jackson ★★** (✆ 800/927-6697 or 603/383-9355; www.jacksonxc.com), whose town cross-country association maintains more than 50 miles of lovely trails in and around the scenic village (near the base of Mt. Washington). A trail pass at Jackson costs $19 per adult ($10 if you're only snowshoeing), $8 per child.

Two more good Nordic ski centers are located at **Bretton Woods Resort** (✆ 800/314-1752 or 603/278-3322; www.brettonwoods.com)—anchored by that huge, red-and-white hotel at the western entrance to Crawford Notch—and the spectacularly remote **Balsams/ Wilderness** cross-country ski center (✆ 800/255-0600 or 603/255-3400; www.thebalsams.com) operated by the Balsams resort in the northerly reaches of the state. Adults will pay $15 to $17 per day to ski the trails at any of these facilities (with big discounts for kids and seniors), and any of them can rent you a set of good skis to get you on your way.

bridge very near this visitor center, too, accessible via a footpath. The visitor center is open daily 8am to 5pm.

Info and advice are also available at the **AMC's Pinkham Notch Visitor Center** (✆ 603/466-2721), on Rte. 16 between Jackson and Gorham. The center is open daily, year-round, from 6am to 10pm. It has a cafe and a travel store, too.

Camping

The White Mountain National Forest maintains about two dozen drive-in campsites scattered throughout the region, from small to large. Campsites mostly cost in the $16 to $20 range per night. Online reservations are accepted at many of these campsites through the **National Recreation Reservation Service** (✆ 877/444-6777; www.recreation.gov). Most of the mountains' campsites are rather basic—in fact, some have only pit toilets—but all of them are pretty well maintained. Remember that some sites require reservations at least a week in advance (in other words, no walk-ins), and 2- to 3-night minimum stays are enforced on certain Saturdays and Sundays during peak season.

Of all these **national-forest campgrounds,** the biggest (and least personal) is **Dolly Copp Campground** (✆ 603/466-2713), near the base of Mount Washington.

Still, it has a superior location and great views from the open sites. Along the Kancamagus Highway, many travelers enjoy **Covered Bridge Campground** (℡ 603/447-2166), about 6 miles west of Conway and adjacent to an 1858 covered bridge. (It's also a short drive to some delightful river swimming at the Rocky Gorge Scenic Area.) Both of these campgrounds are open only seasonally, from around mid-May until mid-October.

Backcountry tent camping is free throughout the White Mountains, and no permit is needed. (You *will* need to purchase a parking permit to leave your car at the trail head, however; see "Backcountry Fees," above.) Check with a ranger station and the forest-service website about updated camping rules. Three-sided log lean-tos are also scattered throughout the backcountry, providing overnight shelter. Some of these are free; at others, a backcountry manager will collect a small fee from you. Again, contact any of the three ranger stations (see "Ranger Stations & Information," above) for details and locations of these campgrounds.

There are also 10 **state parks offering camping** in northern New Hampshire, including four in the White Mountains; most of them are pretty nice. Consult the state parks division's website (www.nhstateparks.org), or call them at ℡ **603/271-3628** for rates, reservations, and details. You can also now reserve these state campgrounds through the online system at **www.reserveamerica.com**.

North Conway ★

North Conway is 150 miles N of Boston and 62 miles NW of Portland

North Conway is the commercial heart of the White Mountains. Outdoor purists abhor the place—except, maybe, when seeking a post-hike pizza and beer. Shoppers, on the other hand, are drawn magnetically to the outlets and other accoutrements of commerce perched along routes 302 and 16, the two highways that overlap in town. On rainy weekends and during foliage season, the road can resemble a linear parking lot. There's so much clutter here you often forget to look *up*—which is where the peaks of the Whites are standing quietly.

Sprawl notwithstanding, North Conway is beautifully situated along the eastern edge of the broad and fertile Saco River valley (here usually called the Mt. Washington Valley). Gentle, forest-covered mountains, some with sheer cliffs that could be distant cousins of those in Yosemite, border the bottomlands. Northward up the valley, hills rise in a triumphant crescendo to the blustery, tempestuous heights of Mount Washington.

But the central village is trim and attractive (if often congested), with an open green, some colorful shops, Victorian frontier-town commercial architecture, and a little train station. It's a good place to park, stretch your legs, and get a cup of coffee or a snack.

ESSENTIALS

GETTING THERE North Conway and the Mount Washington Valley sit on routes 16 and 302. Rte. 16 connects to the Spaulding Turnpike, then to I-95 to Boston and New York; Rte. 302 zigzags from Maine to Vermont. Traffic can be vexing in this valley on holiday weekends in summer, and it gets *really* bad on foliage weekends in fall, when backups several miles long are common. Try to plan around these busy times to preserve your sanity.

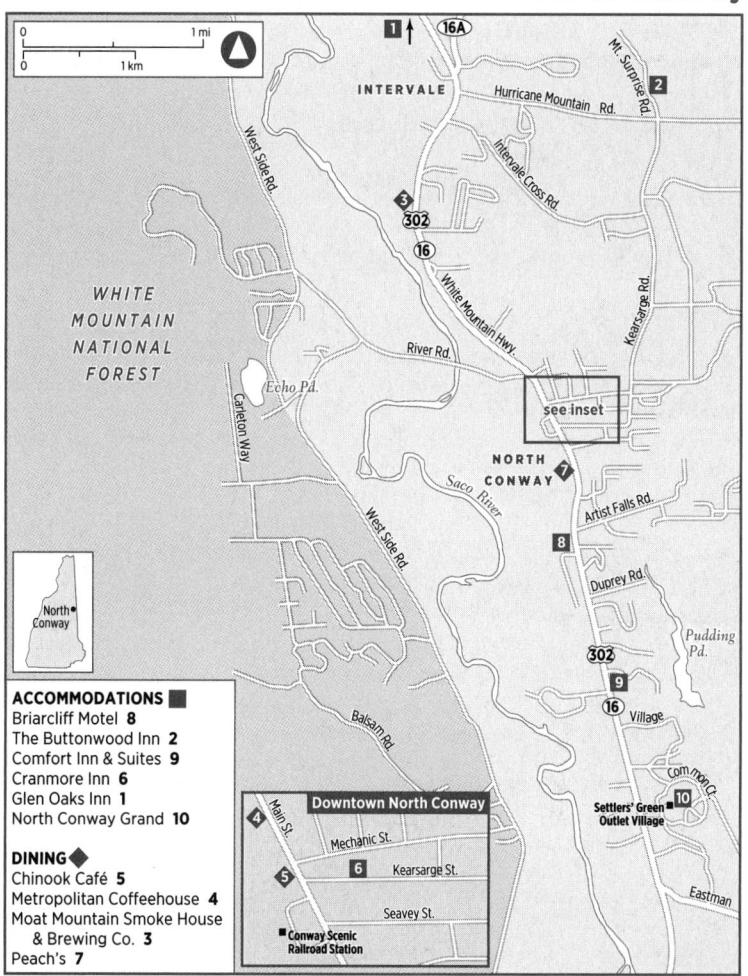

0   1 mi
0   1 km

INTERVALE

WHITE
MOUNTAIN
NATIONAL
FOREST

Echo Pd.

North
Conway

ACCOMMODATIONS ■
Briarcliff Motel **8**
The Buttonwood Inn **2**
Comfort Inn & Suites **9**
Cranmore Inn **6**
Glen Oaks Inn **1**
North Conway Grand **10**

DINING ◆
Chinook Café **5**
Metropolitan Coffeehouse **4**
Moat Mountain Smoke House
& Brewing Co. **3**
Peach's **7**

16A

INTERVALE

Hurricane Mountain Rd.

Mt. Surprise Rd.

Intervale Cross Rd.

302

16

White Mountain Hwy.

Kearsarge Rd.

River Rd.

Carleton Way

see inset

NORTH
CONWAY

Saco River

Artist Falls Rd.

West Side Rd.

Duprey Rd.

Pudding
Pd.

302

West Side Rd.

Balsam Rd.

16 Village

Common Ct.

Settlers' Green ■
Outlet Village

Eastman

Downtown North Conway

Main St.

Mechanic St.

6 Kearsarge St.

Seavey St.

■ Conway Scenic
Railroad Station

13

NEW HAMPSHIRE | The White Mountains

Concord Coach (✆ 800/639-3317; www.concordcoachlines.com) runs two daily buses from Boston's South Station and Logan Airport, picking up and dropping off in **North Conway** at the Eastern Slope Inn (Rte. 16/302) and in **Conway** at the First Stop Market gas station on West Main Street (across from the high school). The cost is $30 one-way, $56 round-trip to South Station—a few dollars more each way for the airport—and takes about 4 hours.

VISITOR INFORMATION   Contact the **Mount Washington Valley Chamber of Commerce** (✆ 877/948-6867; www.mtwashingtonvalley.org), which operates year-round offices and a seasonal information booth, both opposite the village green. Staff can help arrange for local accommodations. The info booth is open daily in summer, weekends only in winter.

DOWNHILL SKIING

Cranmore Mountain Resort ★ 🏷️
Mount Cranmore claims to be the oldest operating ski area in New England, and ski pioneer Hannes Schneider did in fact practically single-handedly bring a new form of downhill skiing to America here, beginning in 1939. (The resort was also famous, for half a century, for its tracked ski lift, known as the Skimobile—now sadly gone by the wayside.) Cranmore's slopes are unrepentantly old-fashioned, but the mountain has restyled itself as a snow-sports mecca—look for snow tubing, snow scooters, and ski bikes. These slopes aren't likely to challenge advanced skiers, but they delight many beginners and intermediates, as well as those who enjoy diversion with the ski toys. It's ideal for families, thanks to the relaxed attitude, range of activities, and not-outrageous ticket prices.

1 Skimobile Rd. (P.O. Box 1640), North Conway, NH 03850. 📞 **800/786-6754.** www.cranmore.com. Adults $55 day lift tickets; discounts for youths and seniors.

WHERE TO STAY

In addition the choices I've listed below, **Rte. 16** in North Conway is packed to the gills with basic motels (many family-run), which are affordably priced in the off season—you can sometimes find a room for as low as $50 per night in spring or late fall—but disappointingly expensive during peak travel times (summer, ski-season weekends, fall-foliage season). They vary wildly in upkeep from place to place, though, and some, frankly, are just awful.

Briarcliff Motel 🏷️ Of North Conway's dozens of roadside motels, the Briarcliff is one of the best choices. Located about a half-mile south of the village center, this is your basic U-shaped motel with standard-size rooms, but all its units have been redecorated in rich colors, much like B&B rooms. You have to pay extra for a room with a "porch" and mountain view—and the porches are actually part of a long enclosed sitting area, each unit separated from its neighbor by cubicle-height partitions. So think twice about doing so. Need a soda, an iron, a microwave, a ski locker? Head for the common room; rooms don't have any of these things. But this is still a bargain, and well kept up.

Rte. 16 (P.O. Box 504), North Conway, NH 03860. 📞 **800/338-4291** or 603/356-5584. www.briarcliff motel.com. 30 units. Summer and fall $99–$179 double; rest of the year $69–$189 double. 2-night minimum stay holidays and foliage season. AE, DISC, MC, V. **Amenities:** Outdoor pool. *In room:* A/C, TV, fridge, Wi-Fi (free).

The Buttonwood Inn ★ Just a few minutes' drive from the outlets and restaurants, the Buttonwood has more of a classic country-inn feel than most other North Conway inns. It's set on 17 acres (with cross-country ski trails) on the side of Mount Surprise in an 1820s-era home, with a tastefully appointed interior inspired by Shaker style. Most rooms are smallish and cozy, though two common rooms (one with a television, one with a fireplace) allow guests plenty of space to unwind. Two units have gas fireplaces, one has a Murphy bed, and one has a large Jacuzzi (it's also wheelchair accessible). The hosts are helpful with the planning of day trips, no matter your interests. Breakfasts are a hit.

64 Mt. Surprise Rd., North Conway, NH 03860. 📞 **800/258-2625** or 603/356-2625. Fax 603/356-3140. www.buttonwoodinn.com. 10 units (2 with detached private bathroom). $99–$299 double. Rates

include breakfast. 2- to 3-night minimum stay Sat–Sun and holidays. AE, DISC, MC, V. Closed Apr. "Well-behaved" children 10 and over welcome. **Amenities:** Outdoor heated pool. *In room:* A/C, TV (some units), hair dryer, Wi-Fi (free).

Comfort Inn & Suites ★ ☺ This tidy chain hotel consists entirely of "suites" (big rooms with low partitions; not separate rooms) spread out among three stories, giving travelers a bit more elbowroom than the other motels in town. It's a good choice for families, because it's close to outlet shopping and near a pirate-themed miniature golf course. A few rooms have gas fireplaces. For a chain property, it's uncommonly well run.

2001 White Mountain Hwy. (Rte. 16), North Conway, NH 03860. ✆ **877/424-6423** or 603/356-8811. Fax 603/356-7770. www.comfortinn.com. 59 units. $99–$199 double; executive suites to $249. Rates include continental breakfast. AE, DISC, MC, V. **Amenities:** Exercise room; heated indoor pool. *In room:* A/C, TV, fridge, hair dryer, Wi-Fi (free).

Cranmore Inn ★ ☺ The Cranmore Inn has the feel of a 19th-century boarding-house—which is appropriate, because that's what it is. Open since 1863, this three-story Victorian home is a short walk from North Conway's village center. Its heritage—it claims to be the oldest continuously operating hotel in town—adds charm and quirkiness, but comes with occasional old-house drawbacks such as uneven water pressure and hallway bathrooms. Still, it offers good value, thanks to its handy location, the hospitality of the innkeepers, and the nice rooms. Interestingly, some of the 16 units in the main inn consist of two bedrooms, connected in the middle by a private hallway bathroom; these are very family-friendly. Three big "kitchen units" are housed in an annex; these suites come with their own kitchens, gas woodstoves, separate dining rooms, living rooms, and even personal computers (but they don't include breakfast).

80 Kearsarge St. (P.O. Box 1349), North Conway, NH 03860. ✆ **800/526-5502** or 603/356-5502. www.cranmoreinn.com. 19 units (some with private bathroom across hall). June–Mar $89–$210 double; Apr–May $65–$155 double. Rates include full breakfast (except kitchenette units). 2-night minimum stay weekends, holidays, and in foliage season. DISC, MC, V. **Amenities:** Jacuzzi; outdoor pool. *In room:* TV (some units), kitchenette (some units).

Glen Oaks Inn ★ Just 10 minutes north of North Conway is a spur road that leads through the little village of Intervale, with several lodges and a feeling of being removed from the clutter of outlet shops. Glen Oaks was built here in 1850, and a mansard-roofed third floor was added when the home became an inn in 1890. Typical for the era, the rooms are small to medium-sized, and are decorated mostly with reproductions and some country Victorian antiques. Some rooms have private bathrooms across the hallways; some have fireplaces. The best units might be the two in nearby stone cottages—the Cottle Room has a wood-burning fireplace, wing chairs, and a small porch with Adirondack chairs, while the newer Forest Cottage has a two-person Jacuzzi and small refrigerator.

Rte. 16A (P.O. Box 37), Intervale, NH 03845. ✆ **877/854-6535** or 603/356-9772. Fax 603/356-5652. www.glenoaksinn.com. 11 units. $99–$219 double. Rates include full breakfast. 2-night minimum stay most weekends and holidays. AE, DISC, MC, V. Children 6 and over welcome. **Amenities:** Outdoor pool. *In room:* A/C, TV/VCR, fridge (some units), Wi-Fi (free).

North Conway Grand ★★ ☺ If you're looking for convenience, amenities, and easy access to outlet shopping, this former Sheraton is a safe bet. Built on the site of North Conway's former airfield, it's a four-story, gabled hotel with a pond, adjacent (and architecturally similar) to Settlers' Green, one of the town's key shopping complexes. The hotel offers clean comfortable rooms with the usual chain-hotel furnishings. Recently, the hotel's amenities have been ramped up, including now-year-round access to an outdoor heated pool and Jacuzzi (the patio is heated); there's another brick-terraced pool inside with his-and-her saunas, plus a newly constructed outdoor kiddy pool and play area featuring spray jets and other fun features. Some suites have Jacuzzis, but even the simplest room has a full flight of business-hotel amenities and a video-game setup for the kids.

Rte. 16 at Settlers' Green (P.O. Box 3189), North Conway, NH 03860. © **800/655-1452** or 603/356-9300. Fax 603/356-6028. www.northconwaygrand.com. 200 units. Summer $109–$219 double; off season $79–$149 double. AE, DC, DISC, MC, V. **Amenities:** Restaurant; children's programs; exercise room; Jacuzzi; 3 pools (1 indoor; 2 outdoor); sauna; 4 tennis courts. *In room:* A/C, TV/DVD, fridge, hair dryer, Wi-Fi (free).

WHERE TO DINE

North Conway is a hub of family-style restaurants, fast-food chains, and bars that happen to also serve food. If you want more refined dining, you're better off heading for The Inn at Thorn Hill in Jackson, about 10 minutes north (see "Mount Washington & Environs," below). Or check with your inn or hotel—it might serve decent resort fare (a smaller B&B won't offer dinner service, though).

For a good breakfast or lunch, look for the peach-colored house on Rte. 16 in North Conway—it's a wildly popular local breakfast and lunch spot called, naturally, **Peach's ★** (© **603/356-5860;** www.peachesnorthconway.com). Expect eggs, Belgian waffles, sandwiches, and sweets. It's open daily from 7am until 2:30pm. The **Metropolitan Coffee House** (© **603/356-2332;** http://metcoffeehouse.com) is another good bet on Main Street. The free Wi-Fi, purple couches, and world music might keep you (or your teenager) there all day. It's open daily from 7am until 9pm.

There's also **Flatbread Company** (© **603/356-4470;** www.flatbreadcompany. com), an organic-pizza place inside the Eastern Slope Inn on Rte. 16, just north of the village center.

Chinook Café ★ CAFE/VEGETARIAN   Located in Conway, a pretty village about a 10-minute drive south of North Conway, the Chinook Café serves healthy, vaguely gourmet fare for breakfast (polenta with goat cheese, oatmeal pancakes) and lunch (smoked salmon and white-bean-and-portobello sandwiches), with a good selection of vegetarian items, too. There are changing daily specials, and the homemade baked goods are a fitting conclusion to a hike.

80 Main St. (across from fire station), Conway. © **603/447-6300.** Breakfast and lunch items $5–$7. MC, V. Daily 7:30am–3pm.

Moat Mountain Smokehouse and Brewing Co. ★ 📋 BARBECUE/PUB FARE   In a town starved for good eats, a lot of people end up at Moat Mountain—the place in the valley for fresh, on-site brewed beer, smoked meats, and wood-fired pizza. It's casual and relaxed. Though this isn't nearly as good as barbecue cooked in the South (the real South, I mean, not southern New Hampshire), you can still choose from quite a selection of smoky barbecued items—brisket and ribs are especially popular. Other menu choices include burgers, sliders (miniburgers), quesadillas, and nachos—including a version with chicken and a mango-pineapple salsa. About a dozen beers are on tap most nights, many of them brewed in-house; these beers are the highlight of a trip here.

3378 White Mountain Hwy. (Rte. 16), North Conway (approx. 1 mile north of the village). ℂ **603/356-6381.** www.moatmountain.com. Reservations not accepted. Main courses $7–$20. AE, MC, V. Daily 11:30am–9pm (until 10pm Fri–Sat).

Mount Washington & Environs ★★

One of two gateway villages to **Mount Washington ★★★** and its massive surrounding peaks, **Jackson ★★** is a quiet place in a picturesque valley off Rte. 16. It's only about a 15-minute drive north of North Conway—yet this is a world apart. The compact village center, approached via a single-lane covered bridge, has retained its old-world elegance—reminders of a time when Jackson was the favored destination of the East Coast upper-middle-class types, who migrated in summer from East Coast cities to grand hotels and summer homes here.

Today, thanks to its revamped golf course and one of the most elaborate, well-maintained cross-country ski networks in the nation, Jackson has found renewed purpose as a resort in summer *and* winter. It's no longer undiscovered, but it does still feels a bit out of the mainstream, especially compared to the busy scene just to the south, in the Conways.

ESSENTIALS

GETTING THERE Jackson is just off Rte. 16, about 11 miles north of North Conway. Heading north, look for the covered bridge on the right.

Surprisingly, **Concord Coach** (ℂ **800/639-3317** or 603/228-3300; www.concordcoachlines.com) offers one daily bus to Jackson from Boston. Wait at the covered bridge and wave down the driver for the return trip. The trip takes 4 hours one-way and costs about $60 round-trip.

VISITOR INFORMATION The **Jackson Area Chamber of Commerce** (ℂ **800/866-3334** or 603/383-9356; www.jacksonnh.com), based in offices at the Jackson Falls Marketplace on Rte. 16B, can answer questions about area attractions and make lodging reservations.

EXPLORING MOUNT WASHINGTON ★★★

Mount Washington, just north of Jackson in the heart of the White Mountain National Forest, is often described with impressive facts and figures that don't always succeed at evoking the windblown, hellishly scenic peak. But here are a few anyway.

At 6,288 feet, Washington is *the* highest mountain in the Northeast. It's also said to have some of the worst weather in the world, and it still holds the world's record for the highest surface wind speed ever recorded—231 mph in 1934, a record some Granite Staters take a perverse pride in. Winds topping 150 mph are routinely recorded here, a result of the mountain's position at the confluence of three major storm tracks.

Strangely, this is also the New England mountain with the most options for getting to its summit. Visitors can ascend via a special **cog railway** (see "Crawford Notch," later in this chapter); by car, along a snaky **toll road** to the summit; in an all-terrain vehicle (ATV), using the same road; in a guide-driven van; or **on foot.** You can even climb **by bike,** though only twice a year—during two annual thigh-punishing races to the summit. The grade increases steeply to 22% near the top, where even pros have flipped over backwards trying to downshift in time.

The best place to learn about Mount Washington and its approaches is rustic **Pinkham Notch Visitor Center** (ℂ **603/466-2721**), operated by the Appalachian Mountain Club. At the crest of Rte. 16 between Jackson and Gorham, the center offers overnight accommodations and meals at the adjacent Joe Dodge Lodge (see "Where to Stay," below), maps, a limited selection of outdoor supplies, and plenty of advice from its helpful staff. A number of hiking trails also depart from here, with several loops and side trips. It's open year-round.

About a dozen **trails** lead to the mountain's summit, ranging in length from about 4 to 15 miles. (Detailed information is available at the visitor center.) The most direct and dramatic way is via the **Tuckerman Ravine Trail ★★★**, which departs right from Pinkham Notch. It's a true full-day's endeavor. Healthy hikers should allow 4 to 5 hours for the ascent, 2 to 4 hours for the return trip. Be sure to allow enough time to enjoy the dramatic glacial cirque of Tuckerman Ravine, which attracts extreme skiers to its sheer drops as late as June, and often holds patches of snow well into the summer.

The **Mount Washington Auto Road ★★** (✆ 603/466-3988; www.mount washingtonautoroad.com) opened in 1861 as a carriage road and has since remained a wildly popular attraction. The steep, winding 8-mile road (with an *average* grade of 12%) is partly paved and incredibly dramatic; your breath will be taken away at one curve after another. The ascent will test your iron will; the descent will test your car's brakes. This trip is not worth doing, though, if the summit is in the clouds—wait for a **clear day.**

Located on Rte. 16 just north of Pinkham Notch, the road is open daily from early May until late October from 8am to 5pm (hours may be slightly different early or late in the season). The cost is $23 per vehicle and driver, plus $8 for each additional adult ($6 per child age 5–12); it's $14 for a motorcycle and its operator. This price includes an audiocassette or CD narration pointing out sights along the way (available in English, French, or German) and the famous bumper sticker.

No trailers, RVs, or mopeds are allowed, which makes sense. But management has also imposed some other slightly curious vehicle restrictions to protect against breakdowns and logjams; for example, Acuras, Hondas, Saturns, Sterlings, and Jaguars with automatic transmissions must show a "1," "L," or "S" on the shifter to be allowed on the road; only H-3 version Hummers can ascend; and no Lincoln Continentals from 1969 or earlier are permitted. (Dang!) But most taxis and police cars are okay, so long as the first gear is operational.

If you'd prefer to leave the driving to someone else—or it's winter—**van tours** ascend throughout the day in safe weather, allowing you to relax, enjoy the views, and learn about the mountain from informed guides. The cost is $29 for adults, $25 for seniors, and $12 for children ages 5 to 12, and includes a short stay on the summit.

One additional note: The average temperature atop the mountain is 30°F (–1°C). (The record low was –43°F/–42°C, and the warmest temperature ever recorded atop the mountain, in August, was 72°F/22°C.) Even in August, bring backup just in case blustery, cold weather moves in suddenly. Wearing only shorts and a T-shirt, with nothing else as backup, is a bad idea.

EXPLORING PINKHAM NOTCH ★★★

The AMC's Pinkham Notch Visitor Center is at the height of land on Rte. 16. Just south of the center, look for signs to **Glen Ellis Falls ★★**, which is worth a quick stop because it's such an easy walk. From the parking area, you pass through a pedestrian tunnel and walk along the Glen Ellis River for less than 10 minutes until the path suddenly seems to drop off the face of the earth. The stream plummets 65 feet down a cliff here; observation platforms are situated at the top and near the bottom of the falls, some of this area's most impressive after a heavy rain. From the parking lot to the base of the falls is less than a half-mile walk.

From the same AMC visitor center, it's about 2.5 miles up to **Hermit Lake** and **Tuckerman Ravine ★★★** via the Tuckerman Ravine Trail (see above). Even if you're not planning to continue on to the summit, the ravine—with its sheer sides and lacey cataracts—might be the most dramatic destination in the White Mountains. If you're in good shape, it's well worth the 2-hour hike in anything except miserable weather. The trail is wide and only moderately demanding. Bring a picnic and lunch on the massive boulders that litter the ravine's floor.

In summer, an enclosed gondola known as the **Wildcat Express ★** at the Wildcat Mountain ski area (see "Downhill Skiing," below) hauls passengers up the mountain for views of Tuckerman Ravine and Mount Washington's summit. The lift operates Saturday and Sunday from Memorial Day to mid-June, then daily through mid-October. The ski resort's base lodge is just north of Pinkham Notch on Rte. 16. It costs $15 per adult to ride the gondola, with discounts for seniors and kids, but it doesn't run in bad weather. There's now also a "ziprider," a zipline ride down a similar track—it costs $5 extra, and you must be between 75 and 275 lbs., and between 4'4" and 6'8".

Too crazy for you? There's also **Frisbee golf** on the mountain ($10–$15 per person, depending on whether you brought your own disc or not).

CROSS-COUNTRY SKIING

Jackson ranks among the top cross-country ski resorts in the nation. The reason is the nonprofit **Jackson Ski Touring Foundation** (☎ **800/927-6697** or 603/383-9355; www.jacksonxc.com), which created and maintains the extensive trail network. The terrain is wonderfully varied; many trails are rated "most difficult," which will keep advanced skiers from getting bored. But novice and intermediate skiers also have plenty of good options spread out along the valley floor.

Start at the base lodge, near the Wentworth Resort in the center of Jackson. There's parking here, and you can ski right through the village and into the hills. Gentle trails traverse the valley floor, with more advanced trails winding up the mountains. One-way ski trips with shuttles back to Jackson are available; ask if you're interested. Given how extensive and well maintained the trails are, passes are a good value at $19 for adults, $15 for seniors, and $8 for children ages 10 to 15. Rentals are available at the ski center (ticket/rental packages are available); snowshoes can be rented, too—there are specifically groomed trails for snowshoers.

DOWNHILL SKIING

Black Mountain ★★ ✈ ☺ Dating back to the 1930s, Black Mountain was one of the White Mountains' pioneering ski areas. It hasn't gone all modern like many of New England's other ski hills; no, it remains a quintessential family mountain—modest in size, nonthreatening, ideal for beginners—though there's also glade skiing for more advanced skiers. A day here feels a bit like you've trespassed in some farmer's unused hayfield, which actually adds to the charm; this place isn't even on the radar of the Aspen set. The views of the Presidentials are very good, and a lift ticket is surprisingly inexpensive compared with the other resorts in the area—on a weekday, an adult can ski for less than $30, and that's just criminal. Bonus: Most of the 44 trails are pointed due south, so no frigid north winds blast your face. The resort also offers two compact terrain parks for snowboarders, as well as lessons, rentals, a day-care center for small kids, a ski school, and a base lodge with a cafeteria and pub. Nice place.

1 Black Mountain Rd. (P.O. Box B), Jackson, NH 03846. © **800/475-4669** or 603/698-4490. www.blackmt.com. Adults $29–$39 day lift ticket; $26 half-day; discounts for seniors and youths.

Wildcat ★★   Set high in Pinkham Notch, Wildcat combines a rich heritage as a venerable ski resort with the best views of any ski area in the White Mountains. This mountain offers a bountiful supply of intermediate trails, as well as some challenging expert terrain. It's skiing the way it used to be—no base-area clutter, just a single lodge with an unpretentious cafeteria and a pub. That also means there are no on-slope hotels, condos, or other accommodations, but there are plenty of lodging options within an easy 15-minute drive of the mountain. Ask about ticket packages combining your lift ticket with downhill ski rentals and, if you need some, lessons.

Rte. 16, Pinkham Notch, NH 03846. © **888/754-9453** or 603/466-3326. www.skiwildcat.com. Adults $65 day lift tickets, $45 half-day; discounts for seniors, teens, and children 6–12.

ESPECIALLY FOR KIDS

Parents with young children (age 10 and under) can buy peace of mind at **Story Land ★★**, at the northern junction of routes 16 and 302 (© **603/383-4186;** www.storylandnh.com). This old-fashioned (mid-1950s) fantasy village is filled with 30 acres of improbably leaning buildings, magical rides, cuckoo clocks, minitrains, fairy-tale creatures, a swan boat, and plenty of other enchanted beings. It's open weekends from 9am to 5pm from Memorial Day to mid-June; daily 9am to 6pm from mid-June to Labor Day; and again weekends only from 9am to 5pm through Columbus Day. Admission is about $25 per person for all visitors ages 4 and over; children 3 and under enter free.

WHERE TO STAY

Eagle Mountain House ★   The white wooden Eagle Mountain House is a handsome relic that has survived the ravages of time, fire, and the fickle tastes of tourists. Built in 1916, the classic, five-story hotel is set in an idyllic valley above Jackson. Guest rooms are furnished in a country-pine look with stenciled blanket chests, armoires, and feather comforters. You pay more for rooms with mountain views, though it's not really necessary to spend the extra cash—just plan to spend most of your free time lounging on the long, wide wraparound porch with views across the hotel's golf course out to the mountains beyond.

179 Carter Notch Rd. (P.O. Box E), Jackson, NH 03846. © **800/966-5779** or 603/383-9111. Fax 603/383-0854. www.eaglemt.com. 93 units. $69–$199 double; $129–$239 suite. 2-night minimum some weekends and peak periods. MAP plans available. AE, DISC, MC, V. Pets accepted in 4 units ($35 per night). **Amenities:** 2 restaurants; tavern; exercise room; Jacuzzi; outdoor pool; sauna; 2 tennis courts. *In room:* TV, fridge ($5 fee), Wi-Fi (some units; free).

The Inn at Thorn Hill ★   This elegant inn is a good choice for a romantic getaway. The classic shingle-style home (now swathed in light-yellow siding) was designed by famed architect Stanford White in 1895, just outside Jackson's village center and surrounded by wooded hills. Inside, the place has a comfortable Victorian feel. Rooms are luxuriously appointed—every room in the main house has a two-person Jacuzzi. There are also three cottages, done up in French country style, with air-conditioning and porches, and a half-dozen rooms in an adjacent carriage house.

Some of the nicest units include the Katherine Suite, with a fireplace and two-person Jacuzzi, and the little yellow Notch View Cottage with its classic screened front porch and double Jacuzzi with a forest view. The hospitality here is excellent, and the **dining room**'s ★★ three-course dinners (see "Where to Dine," below) are among the best in the valley. There's also quite a lovely spa area with a wooden sauna, whirlpool-like tubs, and a menu of services from hydrotherapy and facials to massages and yoga.

Thorn Hill Rd. (P.O. Box A), Jackson, NH 03846. ☏ **800/289-8990** or 603/383-4242. www.innatthorn hill.com. 25 units. $169–$400 double; $309–$440 suite. Rates include full breakfast, afternoon tea, and dinner. 2- to 3-night minimum stay Sat–Sun and some holidays. AE, DISC, MC, V. Children 8 and over welcome. **Amenities:** 3 restaurants; bar; babysitting; Jacuzzi; limited room service; outdoor pool; spa. *In room:* A/C, TV/DVD, hair dryer, Wi-Fi ($6 per day).

Joe Dodge Lodge at Pinkham Notch ★ 🏨 Guests come to the Joe Dodge Lodge more for the camaraderie than for the accommodations, yet they seem to always go away smiling; fresh air and good service will do that for you. Situated spectacularly at the base of Mount Washington, far from commercial clutter and with easy access to many hiking and skiing trails, the lodge is operated by the Appalachian Mountain Club somewhat like a tightly run youth hostel. Guests share bunkrooms, dormitory-style bathrooms, and optional meals at family-style tables in the main lodge. (A few private rooms provide double beds and family accommodations, with breakfast and dinner included in the prices, but you should try to book these ahead if possible.) The festive atmosphere is wonderful, as is the can't-be-beat location. You can also buy a trail lunch to-go in the cafeteria.

Rte. 16, Pinkham Notch, NH. (Mailing address: AMC, P.O. Box 298, Gorham, NH 03581.) ☏ **603/466-2721.** www.outdoors.org. 108 beds in bunkrooms of 2, 3, and 4 beds (all with shared bathroom). Private rooms $130–$150 double, including breakfast and dinner. Bunkrooms peak season $51 per adult, $28 per child 15 and under (discount for AMC members); off season $43 per adult, $25 per child. MAP also available. Holiday rates higher. MC, V. Children 3 and over welcome. **Amenities:** Cafeteria. *In room:* Wi-Fi (free), no phone.

Wentworth Resort Hotel ★★ The venerable Wentworth sits in the middle of Jackson Village, all turrets, eaves, and awnings. Built in 1869, this Victorian shingled inn once consisted of a campuslike setting of 39 buildings (including a dairy and an electrical plant), but it had edged to the brink of deterioration by the mid-1980s. Then the remaining buildings were refurbished, with a number of condominium clusters added around a refreshed golf course. Regular rooms are decorated with Victorian-inspired furnishings; suites (all with king-size beds) are stocked with such amenities as propane fireplaces, whirlpools, outdoor hot tubs, and claw-foot tubs. Visitors of stout constitution can stroll up the road and plunge into the icy waters of Jackson Falls; others can hang out in the hotel and eat in the very good **dining room** ★. Bear in mind that this building is aging, so some rooms have seen better days, but the 2009 addition of a luxury cottage ("Fairlawn") was a very positive sign: All eight expansive suites here have steam showers, either a whirlpool tub or an outdoor hot tub, multiple flatscreen TVs, a gas fireplace, and a sitting room.

1 Carter Notch Rd. (P.O. Box M), Jackson, NH 03846. ☏ **800/637-0013** or 603/383-9700. Fax 603/383-4265. www.thewentworth.com. 76 units. Peak season $214–$245 double, $314–$354 suite; off season $158–$168 double, $238–$278 suite. Rates include full breakfast and dinner. B&B and no-meals plans also available. AE, DC, DISC, MC, V. **Amenities:** Restaurant; golf course; outdoor pool; tennis court. *In room:* A/C, TV/DVD (some units), fridge (some units), Wi-Fi (free).

WHERE TO DINE

Most of the inns in town offer some form of dinner service and/or a pubby tavern right on their premises, though the quality level of food at these inns does vary. Check the write-ups above for more details.

The Inn at Thorn Hill ★★ NEW AMERICAN   The romantic Inn at Thorn Hill is one of the best choices for a meal in the valley. The dining room faces the forested hill behind the inn. Start with a glass of wine from the wine list (the restaurant has won *Wine Spectator* awards of excellence), then browse the menu, which has leaned away from Asian accent to more solidly Continental and New American fare of late. A new chef, Peter Belmonte, joined the inn in 2009, so we'll see what direction he takes; so far, appetizers include things like saffrony mussel soup, chèvre tarts (yum), crab-and-melon salads with crème fraîche, and cucumber soup with toasted anise. Entrees could be a Maine lobster with a potato cake and fava beans; roasted chicken with a green pea risotto; steak frites with Bordelaise; or rack of lamb with a carrot puree. Desserts are great—in the past, they've included choices like a chèvre cheesecake, sour-cream panna cotta, and chocolate pavé. There's also a simpler "lounge menu" of burgers, fondue, salads, and the like. Wine-themed dinners are held throughout the year at the inn, and they're well worth attending.

Thorn Hill Rd., Jackson. (C) **603/383-4242.** www.innatthornhill.com. Reservations recommended. Main courses $24–$36. AE, DISC, MC, V. Daily 6–9pm.

Thompson House Eatery ★ AMERICAN   This friendly, old-fashioned spot in a 19th-century Cape-style "plank" farmhouse sits at the edge of Jackson's golf course. It attracts crowds for the fare, which is pricier than it used to be. You can dine both indoors and (in good weather) out. Elbow up at a communal table and meet fellow travelers while awaiting service and food; for lunch, expect a variety of fun deli-style sandwiches, plus turkey, meatloaf, BLTs, and a few salads. For dinner, prices spike upward and the fare becomes somewhat more refined—barbecue-spiced pork tenderloin, a seafood mélange cooked in sherry, lamb chops with mint jelly, bronzed duck breast, and even some vegetarian items like a Parmesan-crusted eggplant layered with smoked cheddar and portobello mushrooms. (You can also order lighter fare, like scallops or a mushroom dish called, I kid you not, "Fungus Among Us.") Desserts and martinis are excellent; there's also a bar with its own substantial menu.

193 Main St. (off Rte. 16A, near intersection with Rte. 16), Jackson. (C) **603/383-9341.** www.thompson houseatery.com. Reservations recommended for dinner. Main courses $8–$13 at lunch, $17–$31 at dinner. AE, DISC, MC, V. Thurs–Mon 11:30am–3pm and 5:30–9pm; Tues–Wed 5:30–9pm.

Crawford Notch ★★

Crawford Notch is a wild, rugged mountain valley that angles right through the heart of the White Mountains. There's a surplus of history here. For years after its discovery by European settlers in 1771, this was an impenetrable wilderness—literally a barrier to commerce, because it blocked trade between the upper Connecticut River Valley and the busy harbors of Portland and Portsmouth. Eventually some plucky bunch got through the pass, and it finally developed into an important route.

By the way, don't get confused by directions and maps referring to the towns of **Twin Mountain** and **Bretton Woods.** Those two are the very *same* village; it simply has two different names.

ESSENTIALS

GETTING THERE   Rte. 302 runs right through Crawford Notch for approximately 25 miles between the towns of **Bartlett** and **Twin Mountain.** From Portland, Maine, it's 2 hours or less of driving; from Boston, take Rte. 16 from Portsmouth (about 3 hr.). Or from New York City, take I-91 to exit 17 (Wells River, Vermont) and crawl east along Rte. 302, a trip of about 6 hours one-way. Already in New Hampshire? From the central part of the state, take I-93 to exit 40 (Bethlehem) and head east.

VISITOR INFORMATION   The **Twin Mountain–Bretton Woods Chamber of Commerce** (© 800/245-8946; www.twinmountain.org) provides general information and lodging referrals from a booth near the intersection of routes 302 and 3. It's open from late May through mid-October.

HIKING

The Appalachian Mountain Club's **Highland Center at Crawford Notch ★★** (© 603/278-4453), on Rte. 302 in Bretton Woods, is a multipurpose facility on 26 acres of AMC-owned land. It's a great headquarters for hikes into the surrounding mountains. Under one roof, you can book a tour, hike the path that passes nearby (two AMC huts are each a short hike away), bunk down for the night in the Highland Lodge, eat communal dinners, and use L.L.Bean gear for free (yes, really). It's open year-round.

From late spring through fall, the center is also the hub for two AMC-operated **hiker shuttles** (© 603/466-2727). These vans cruise the mountains daily from June through mid-September, and then on weekends through mid-October, depositing and picking up hikers; they're useful, though pricey—but if you haven't brought a car, this is really your only option. Rides cost $18 one-way, regardless of length; AMC members get a $2 discount.

SKIING

Attitash ★★   This is one of New England's most scenic ski areas, and Attitash is also a good mountain for families and skiers at the intermediate-to-advanced level. The resort consists of 70 or so trails across two peaks: 1,750-foot Attitash and adjacent Bear Peak. Dotted with rugged rock outcroppings and full of sweeping views of Mount Washington and the Presidential Range (there's also an observation tower on the main summit), this is an eye-popping place—with excellent skiing. Look for great cruising runs and a handful of challenging drops. Snowboarders can hone their skills at the terrain park. You can stay right on the mountain in the 143-unit summit hotel. As with many of these New Hampshire ski hills, though, the base area is sleepy at night; if you're looking for a beer or some live music, pile into the car and drive about 15 minutes to North Conway, where you'll find both of those things.

Rte. 302 (P.O. Box 308), Bartlett, NH 03812. © **877/677-7669** or 603/374-2600. www.attitash.com. Adults $62–$69 day lift tickets, $48–$55 half-day; discounts for seniors, students, and children.

Bretton Woods (Mount Washington Resort) ★★ ☺   In terms of sheer acreage, Bretton Woods/Mount Washington is New England's biggest ski resort; it's also possibly the most family-friendly. And it's at the foot of Mount Washington. What else could you ask for? The resort continues to do an award-winning job taking care of kids—there are tons of programs for the little ones here, and *SKI* magazine annually ranks it among the nation's best family ski areas. The low-key attitude is a big part of that. Accommodations are available both on the mountain and nearby, notably at the grand, red-roofed Mount Washington Resort (see "Where to Stay & Dine," below), though nightlife here mostly consists of a hot tub in your room or catching the late news on TV. Trails feature plenty of glades and wide cruising runs, perfect for beginners and families, as well as a few more challenging options for advanced skiers—they're not up to the most radical slopes in Vermont and Maine, though. There's also night skiing; four freestyle (snowboard) terrain parks; and—for those so inclined—an excellent cross-country ski center nearby. This is a great New Hampshire experience.

Rte. 302, Bretton Woods, NH 03575. (✆ **800/314-1752** or 603/278-1000. www.brettonwoods.com. Adults $66–$74 day lift tickets ($10 discount for Mt. Washington Resort guests); $50–$56 half-day; discounts for teens, young children, and seniors.

A HISTORIC RAILWAY

Mount Washington Cog Railway ★★   Mount Washington's Cog Railway was a marvel of engineering when it opened in 1869, and it remains so today. Part moving museum, part slow-motion roller-coaster ride, the Cog Railway steams to the mountain's summit at a determined, "I think I can" pace of about 4 mph. But you'll still get some adrenaline thrills, especially when the train crosses Jacob's Ladder, a rickety-seeming trestle 25 feet high that angles upward at a grade of more than (!) 37%. Holy smokin' transmission, Batman! Passengers enjoy the expanding views on the 3-hour round-trip, which includes important stops to add water to the steam engine, check the track switches, and allow other trains to ascend or descend. A 20-minute stop at the summit gives you a little time to poke around. *Caveats:* This ride is noisy, breezy, sulfurous, and a little sooty; *don't* wear white. Dress warmly in a jacket and sweater that you don't mind getting a little dirty, and you'll be okay. There's now also a shorter, 1-hour ride, operating twice daily all winter, through the lovely, snow-covered vistas.

Base Rd., Bretton Woods. (✆ **800/922-8825** or 603/278-5404. www.thecog.com. Fare $59 adults, $54 seniors, $39 children 4–12, free for children 3 and under; winter fares lower. MC, V. Memorial Day to late Oct daily (and Sat–Sun in May) usually on the hour 9am to 3 or 4pm (check website or call for schedule). Reservations recommended. From Rte. 302, turn onto Base Rd. at Fabyan's Station Restaurant and continue 6 miles to railway base station.

WHERE TO STAY & DINE

If the Mount Washington Resort (see below) is full, there are two more adjacent properties owned by the same group offering affordable lodgings and comparable views: the **Bretton Arms Inn** (next door to the big main hotel) and the more modern, motel-like **The Lodge ★** across the highway. Call the resort's reservation line at (✆ **800/314-1752** or 603/278-1000 to book either property.

In addition to the choices below, the **Dry River Campground** ((✆ **603/374-2272**) inside Crawford Notch State Park offers three dozen campsites in the notch for $18 to $25 per night.

Mount Washington Resort ★★ ☺   At the foot of New Hampshire's highest peak, this five-story resort, with gleaming white clapboards and a cherry-red roof, almost looks like a Bavarian castle appearing out of the mist. Built in 1902, it once drew luminaries like Babe Ruth, Thomas Edison, and Woodrow Wilson. I love the 900-foot-long back porch, which looks directly up at the massive mountain and down onto the resort's golf course, pool, and tennis court. Guest rooms vary in size and decor, but many have grand views. Meals are taken in an impressive, lost-in-time octagonal dining room while an orchestra plays. There are lots of family and kids' programs and activities (such as fly-casting lessons), and new management (it's now owned by the Omni chain) is making overdue improvements. Though the hotel can still feel a bit unfinished at times, it remains a classic New England resort in an unbeatable setting—and service is improving with the management change.

Rte. 302, Bretton Woods, NH 03575. ✆ **800/314-1752** or 603/278-1000. www.mtwashington.com. 200 units. $145–$525 double; $910–$1,750 suite. Rates include breakfast and dinner. Minimum stay during holidays. AE, DISC, MC, V. **Amenities:** 2 restaurants; babysitting; bikes; children's programs (summer); concierge; 2 golf courses; Jacuzzi; 2 pools (1 indoor, 1 outdoor); room service; sauna. *In room:* TV, Wi-Fi (free).

Notchland Inn ★★   Off Rte. 302 on a wild section of Crawford Notch, this inn looks like a bit spooky at first glance, like that hotel in *The Shining*. Fear not; built of hand-cut granite in the mid-1800s, the Notchland is classy yet informal, perfectly situated for exploring the surrounding mountains. The front parlor was designed by Gustav Stickley, a founder of the Arts & Crafts movement, in a suitably wood-heavy style; check out the unique fireplace. Guest rooms are big and beautiful, outfitted with antiques, wood-burning fireplaces (all units), high ceilings, and thermostats. Most of the five suites have Jacuzzis and/or private decks; two are located in an adjacent former schoolhouse (the one upstairs has a wonderful soaking tub), and there are two newish cottages with modern touches like kitchens or wet bars. The optional five-course dinner is probably worth signing on for—any other food is a long, dark drive away. (Nonguests can dine here, as well.) And the foliage here is amazing in fall. But you'll pay for the location and experience: This is one of the pricier choices in the Whites. Note that the innkeepers own two dogs, who peaceably roam the property.

2 Morey Rd. (just off Rte. 302), Hart's Location, NH 03812. ✆ **800/866-6131** or 603/374-6131. www.notchland.com. 15 units. $195–$228 double; $280–$380 cottage and suite. Rates include full breakfast. 2- to 3-night minimum stay Sat–Sun, foliage season, and some holidays. AE, DISC, MC, V. Children 12 and over welcome. **Amenities:** Dining room; babysitting; Jacuzzi. *In room:* A/C (some units), CD player, kitchenette (some units), hair dryer, Wi-Fi (free), no phone.

Franconia Notch ★★

Franconia Notch *is* New Hampshire. As travelers drive north on I-93, the Kinsman Range to the west and the Franconia Range to the east begin converging, and the two mountain ranges press inward on either side like a closing book, forming "the Notch." This narrow defile offers little in the way of civilization or services, but a whole lot of natural drama. Plan on a leisurely ride through the notch, allowing extra time to get out of your car and explore the local forests, peaks, and eateries. Too bad the Old Man of the Mountain isn't here anymore—then this drive would rank even higher on my "must-do" list of places in northern New England.

Interestingly, the area around the notch is just as developed for recreation—or more so—as equally rugged and much more famous Crawford Notch to the northeast (see above). Outdoorsy types may enjoy it here more, as a result. **Warning:** You won't be alone. Day-trippers *have* discovered this place.

ESSENTIALS

GETTING THERE   I-93 runs right through the Notch, narrowing from four lanes to two (and becoming the Franconia Notch Pkwy.) in its most scenic parts. Several scenic roadside pull-offs dot the route. The notch is about 2¼ hours by car from Boston via I-93, or about 5½ hours from New York City via I-84 and I-93.

Concord Coach (© **800/639-3317** or 603/228-3300; www.concordcoachlines. com) runs two daily buses from Boston, a 3½-hour trip that costs about $30 each way. There is no ticket office in Franconia; wait at Mac's Market, right off I-93 at exit 38.

VISITOR INFORMATION Information on the park and surrounding area is available at the **Flume Gorge & Gilman Visitor Center** (© **603/745-8391**), in the notch at exit 34A of I-93.

North of the notch, the **Franconia Notch Chamber of Commerce** (© **603/ 823-5661** in summer or 603/823-3450 in winter; www.franconianotch.org) maintains a helpful little hut of visitor information on Main Street next to the town hall, open spring through fall.

EXPLORING FRANCONIA NOTCH STATE PARK ★

Franconia Notch State Park's (© **603/745-8391**) 8,000 acres, nestled within the much bigger White Mountain National Forest, host an array of scenic attractions easily accessible from I-93 and the Franconia Notch Parkway.

The Flume ★★ is a rugged 800-foot gorge through which the Flume Brook tumbles. A popular attraction as far back as the mid–19th century, it's 800 feet long, 90 feet deep, and as narrow as 20 feet at the bottom; visitors explore it by using a series of boardwalks and bridges on a 2-mile-long walk. If you're looking for an easy, quick hit of nature with the kids, this is worth the money. (But if you'll be in town for awhile, set off on one of the local hiking trails instead and seek your own sights without the crowds or cost.) The Flume is open daily 9am to 5pm from early May through mid-October, weather permitting—it stays open a half-hour later in July and August. Admission costs $13 for adults, $9 for children ages 6 to 12, and is free for younger children. You can walk or snowshoe the grounds for free in the off season.

Echo Lake ★★ is a picturesquely situated recreation area with a 28-acre lake, handsome swimming beach (with lifeguards), and picnic tables scattered about—all within view of the peaks of Cannon Mountain and Mount Lafayette. It's a great place to bring the kids, even if no pets are allowed; and Lance Armstrong wannabes will appreciate the 8-mile bike path that runs alongside the lake and meanders up and down the notch. The beach is open daily from mid-June through early September 10:30am to 5:30pm—admission costs $4 per adult, $2 for children age 6 to 11, and is free for younger kids. Inexpensive canoe and kayak rentals are also available at the beach (last rental at 4:30pm); to find the lake, take exit 34C off I-93.

For a high-altitude view of the region, set off for the alpine ridges on the **Cannon Mountain Aerial Tramway** ★★ (© **603/823-8800**). This old-fashioned cable car serves the ski hill (see "Downhill Skiing," below) in winter; in summer, it whisks up to 80 travelers at a time to the summit of the 4,180-foot mountain. Once up top, you can strike out on foot along the Rim Trail for superb views. Be prepared for cool, gusty winds, though. The tramway usually operates from mid-May through mid-October, and costs $13 round-trip for adults, $10 for children ages 6 to 12.

DOWNHILL SKIING

Cannon Mountain ★★ During downhill skiing's formative years, this state-run ski area was *the* place to ski in the East. One of New England's very first ski mountains, Cannon remains famed for its challenging runs and exposed faces, and the mountain still attracts skiers who are serious about getting down the hill in style. (The scenery is knockout-gorgeous, too—ranked second-best in the Eastern U.S. by *SKI* magazine.) Many of the old-fashioned New England–style trails here are narrow and fun (but sometimes icy, because they're constantly scoured by the notch's winds), and the enclosed tramway is an elegant way to get to the summit. There's no base lodge scene to speak of, though.

Franconia Notch Pkwy., Franconia, NH 03580. ✆ **603/823-8800** or 603/823-7771. www.cannonmt.com. Adults $66 day lift tickets, $44 half-day; discounts for seniors, teens, and youths.

LITERARY HISTORY

The Frost Place ★★ Robert Frost lived in New Hampshire from the time he was 10 until he was 45. The Frost Place is a smallish, humble farmhouse where the poet once came with his family to escape the ravages of hay fever; it's one of several northern New England abodes he inhabited during his career. Today his former farmhouse is a quietly respectful tribute in the form of an arts center and gathering place for local writers. Walking the grounds, it's not hard to see how his granite-edged poetry evolved here at the fringes of the White Mountains. First editions of Frost's works are on display; a nature trail in the woods nearby is posted with excerpts from some of his poems. In early July every year, there's a Frost Day celebration with readings from resident poets and lectures. Pay the suggested donation; this is a special place.

Ridge Rd. (P.O. Box 74), Franconia. ✆ **603/823-5510.** www.frostplace.org. Admission free; suggested donation $5 adults, $4 seniors, $3 students 6–18. Late May to June Sat–Sun 1–5pm; July to early Oct Wed–Mon 1–5pm. Closed mid-Oct to mid-May. From center of town, travel south 1 mile on Rte. 116 to Ridge Rd. (a gravel road); turn and follow signs a short way to the house, parking in lot below the house.

WHERE TO STAY

Franconia Inn ★ This inn is set on a quiet road in a bucolic valley about 2 miles from the village of Franconia. Built in 1934 after a fire destroyed the previous 1886 structure, the inn has an informal feel, with wingback chairs around a fireplace in one common room, and puzzles and books in a paneled library. Guest rooms are appointed in a relaxed country fashion; a few have gas fireplaces, a few have Jacuzzis. The inn is a haven for cross-country skiers—about 40 miles of groomed trails begin right outside the front door—and walkers will enjoy exploring the hundred-plus acres of grounds, as well. Other activities include horseback and glider rides, badminton, tennis, and croquet. **Breakfast** ★★ is delicious, with plenty of gourmet choices available; it's served in a pretty, French-doored breakfast room.

1172 Easton Rd., Franconia, NH 03580. ✆ **800/473-5299** or 603/823-5542. www.franconiainn.com. 34 units. $115–$241 double and suite. Rates usually include breakfast. MAP rates also available. 3-night minimum stay on holiday weekends. AE, MC, V. Closed Apr to mid-May. **Amenities:** Restaurant; bar; bikes; Jacuzzi; heated outdoor pool; sauna; 4 clay tennis courts; Wi-Fi (in public areas; free). *In room:* No phone.

Sugar Hill Inn ★★★ This classic New England inn, with wraparound porch and sweeping mountain panoramas occupying 16 acres on lovely Sugar Hill, is as welcoming and comfortable a spot as you'll find in the Whites. A new owner purchased the inn in 2006, and so far he has improved the property substantially with central air-conditioning; an in-ground pool, the inn's first; a cottage; and a raft of new luxurious rooms. Rooms are graciously appointed in country style; many also have gas

Vermont Castings stoves for heat and atmosphere, and some of the suites and cottage units have double Jacuzzis. The dining room ★★, one of the area's best, serves upscale eclectic dinners in a cozy, fire-lit-tavern setting (see "Where to Dine," below). There's even a simple 9-hole golf course (unaffiliated with the inn) with a knockout view of the mountains right across the road. This was a good place before; now it's becoming a great one.

116 Rte. 117, Sugar Hill, NH 03586. ℂ **800/548-4748** or 603/823-5621. www.sugarhillinn.com. 12 units. $125–$265 double; $210–$410 suite and cottage. Rates include full breakfast. 2- to 3-night minimum stay in foliage season and holiday weekends. AE, MC, V. Closed Apr. Children 12 and over welcome. **Amenities:** Restaurant; outdoor pool; spa. *In room:* A/C (most units), hair dryer, Wi-Fi (in main inn; free), no phone.

WHERE TO DINE

In addition to the fun, cost-conscious eatery listed below, the two inns described above each serve gourmet dinners in dining rooms to their own guests and the general public. Both kitchens are very good to excellent.

The **Sugar Hill Inn**'s dining room ★★ is a point of pride for the inn's latest owner, who himself received culinary training at the prestigious French Culinary Institute in New York (though he employs an executive chef). The four-course, prix-fixe (about $50 per person) dinners run to entrees such as maple-cured grilled pork, breast of duck, crispy sockeye salmon, and beef tenderloin. Salads and desserts are excellent as well.

The **Franconia Inn**'s candlelit dining room ★ serves classically resort-appropriate meals of crab, lamb, salmon, lobster bisque, and the like.

Polly's Pancake Parlor ★★ 🍴 ☺ This family-style eatery, in a shaggy wood-sided building dating from around 1830, a few miles uphill from the little village of Sugar Hill, is one of my favorite breakfast stops in New England (or anywhere). And the folks at the James Beard Foundation apparently agree: They awarded the pancake house a medal in 2006! Besides possessing possibly the best views of any pancake shop in the Western world, the restaurant serves a wonderful assortment of pancakes (order a combo of three; I like the chocolate chip and cornmeal versions). Of course, all are served with real New Hampshire maple syrup and maple sugar from the "sugar farm" on which Polly's sits. Kids love this place, and there's also a good gift shop for adults that doubles as a display for antique farm implements. They also serve sandwiches and salads (which is not why you're here), plus maple-inflected desserts (which *is*). Breakfast and American-road-food aficionados shouldn't miss it. It's open only from spring through foliage season, but you can mail-order the syrup by phone year-round.

672 Rte. 117, Sugar Hill, NH 03586. ℂ **800/432-8972** or 603/823-5575. www.pollyspancakeparlor.com. Most items $4–$10. May to late Oct Mon–Fri 7am–2pm; Sat–Sun 7am–3pm.

MAINE

by Paul Karr

Humor columnist Dave Barry once suggested that Maine's state motto should be changed to "Cold, but damp."

That's cute, but it's also sort of true. Spring tends to last just a few blustery days. November features bitter winds alternating with gray sheets of rain. And the winter brings a mix of blizzards and ice storms—and it sometimes lasts 6 months.

But summer and fall are the big payoff for your year-long patience. You can drink in a huge dose of tranquillity during these seasons in Maine, and it's almost like medicine to city-jangled nerves.

Summer in Maine brings the smell of salt air; osprey diving for fish off wooded points; puffy cumulus clouds and fog banks building over the sea; and the haunting whoop of loons. It brings long, lazy days when the sun rises over the beaches and the Atlantic Ocean very early, well before travelers do—by 8 o'clock in the morning, it already feels like noon. It brings a special, haze-tinted coastal light that can't be described (but has been painted by some wonderful artists down through history). And summer brings lobsters!

Autumn is every bit as nice: brilliant foliage against rippling, blue bay waters; tart apples ripening in the orchards; the wonderful smell of wood smoke.

The trick is finding the *right* spot in which to enjoy the coast. The main road along Maine's coast, Rte. 1, is for long stretches an amalgam of convenience stores, fast-food restaurants, and shops selling slightly tacky souvenirs. And traffic isn't restricted to Rte. 1, either: Even the most beautiful places on this coast—the loop road, beaches, and most popular mountain peaks in Acadia National Park, for instance—can get pretty crowded in summer. Arriving without a room reservation in high season is just a bad idea.

On the other hand, Maine's remote position and size *can* work to your advantage sometimes. This state has an amazing 5,500 miles of coastline, plus 3,000 or so coastal islands. With a little homework, you can find that perfect little cove or island, book a room in advance, and enjoy coastal Maine's extremely lovely scenery without battling traffic jams, lines, or rising blood pressures.

Getting to know the locals here is fun, too. Their ancestors were mostly fishermen (as opposed to the farmers who colonized the rest of New England) and other seafaring folk; and today, coastal Mainers—even transplanted ones—still exhibit a wry sense of humor and gregariousness. Need proof? There's a Bait's Motel—complete with worm-hanging-off-a-hook-shaped sign—in Searsport; a tiny street called Fitz Hugh Lane in Somesville; and an oil company called Midnight Oil in Newcastle. Take the time to get to know these local folks. You'll be glad you did.

For even more detailed coverage of this gorgeous coastline, pick up my other two books on the region, *Frommer's Maine Coast* and *Frommer's Maine Coast: Day by Day*, to supplement your travels. They're great resources for enjoying this region in even greater detail.

THE SOUTHERN MAINE COAST ★★

York is 45 miles SW of Portland, 10 miles NE of Portsmouth, and 65 miles NE of Boston

Maine's southern coast runs roughly from the state line at Kittery to Portland, and this stretch is the primary destination of most travelers to the state. While it takes some work to find privacy or remoteness here, there are at least two excellent reasons to come: long, sandy beaches and a sense of history in the coastal villages (some of them, anyway).

Nearly all of Maine's best sand beaches lie along this stretch of coastline. Whether you prefer dunes, the lulling sound of breaking waves, or a carnival-like atmosphere in a beach town, you can find what you need here. The weather is highly variable, though: During a good Northeast blow (say, a 3-day winter storm), waves pound the shores, rise above the roads, and threaten beach houses built decades ago. But during balmy midsummer days, the sea can be as gentle as a pond, waves lapping timidly at the shore as the tide creeps in, inch by inch, covering tidal pools full of crabs, snails, and starfish.

One thing all the beaches here share in common is that they're all washed by the chilly Gulf of Maine, which makes for invigorating swimming—but I never fail to get in the water at least once, no matter how cold. (The salty water feels almost like a spa treatment.) Though the "beach" season here is brief and intense, running only from around July 4th until Labor Day (the first week of Sept), some towns are making an effort to stretch their tourist seasons into fall. However, this idea hasn't fully taken hold yet—the frigid waters might have something to do with that—and once Labor Day weekend is finished, these oceanside communities mostly slow down to a crawl.

Kittery ★ & The Yorks ★★

For travelers driving into Maine from the south, **Kittery** is the first town to appear after crossing the big bridge spanning the Piscataqua River from New Hampshire. Once famous for its (still operating) naval yard, Kittery is now better known for its dozens of factory outlets.

"The Yorks," just to the north, are three towns that share a name, but little else. In fact, it's rare to find three such well-defined and diverse New England archetypes within such a compact area. **York Village ★** is full of 17th-century American history and architecture in a compact area and has a good library. **York Harbor ★★** reached its zenith during America's late Victorian era, when wealthy urbanites constructed cottages at the ocean's edge; it's the most relaxing and scenic of the three. Finally, **York Beach ★★** is a fun beach town with amusements, taffy shops, a small

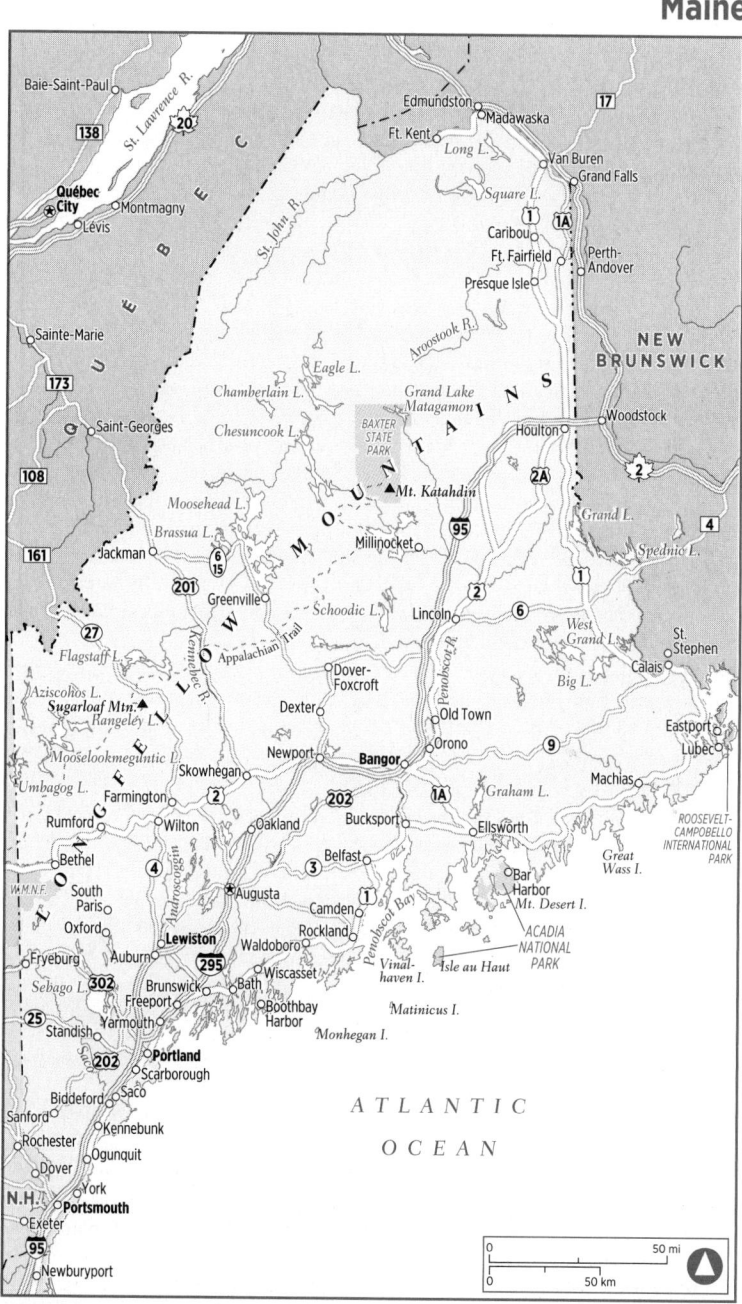

zoo, gabled summer homes set in crowded enclaves, a great lighthouse, and two excellent beaches with sun, sand, rocks, surf, surfers, and fried-fish stands.

ESSENTIALS

GETTING THERE   Kittery is accessible from either **I-95** or **Rte. 1,** with well-marked exits. Coming from the south, the Yorks are reached most easily by taking I-95 N. toward (but not onto) the Maine Turnpike; exit just south of the turnpike entrance, and turn right. Coming from the north, pay your toll exiting the turnpike and then take the first exit, an immediate right. Go around the hairpin turn and you'll be pointing right into town.

Amtrak (*©* **800/872-7245;** www.amtrak.com) operates five trains daily from Boston's North Station (which does *not* connect directly to Amtrak's national rail network; you must take a subway or taxi from Boston's South Station first) into southern Maine. The station is outside Wells, about 10 miles away from the Yorks, and inland—not on the beach. A one-way ticket from Boston costs $19; the trip takes 1¼ hours. From Wells, you'll then need to call a local taxi or arrange for a pickup to get to your final destination on the beach.

No bus lines serve the stretch of southern Maine coastline between Kittery and Portland. However, two bus lines run regular buses daily from Boston's South Station to downtown **Portsmouth,** New Hampshire, which is so close to Kittery that you can actually walk over a bridge into Maine from Portsmouth. The lines are **Greyhound** (*©* **800/231-2222;** www.greyound.com) and **C&J** (*©* **800/258-7111** or 603/430-1100; www.ridecj.com). A bus from New York City's Port Authority to Portsmouth costs about $48 one-way and takes about 6½ hours; from Boston, figure a fare of $18 to $24 one-way and a bit more than a 1-hour ride.

VISITOR INFORMATION   The **Maine State Visitor Information Center** (*©* **207/439-1319**) is at a well-marked rest area on I-95. It's full of info and helpful staff; it has a pet exercise area and copious vending machines; and it's open daily from 8am to 6pm in summer, from 9am to 5:30pm the rest of the year. (The vending machines and restrooms are open 24 hr.)

The **Greater York Region Chamber of Commerce** (*©* **207/363-4422;** www. gatewaytomaine.org) also operates another helpful **visitor center,** one that mirrors the shape of a stone cottage. It's across Rte. 1 from the Maine Turnpike access road (right beside the Stonewall Kitchen headquarters and cafe) on Stonewall Lane. In peak season, it's open Monday to Saturday from 9am to 5pm and Sunday from 10am to 4pm; from Labor Day through June, it's open Monday to Friday 9am to 4pm and Saturday from 10am to 2pm.

EXPLORING KITTERY

Kittery has no true town center, but is instead made of several disconnected villages (all of them quite old) and a long, skinny shopping strip.

On the waterfront, such as it is, the historic **Portsmouth Naval Shipyard** faces Portsmouth, New Hampshire. This shipyard isn't open to the public, for security reasons (they fix nuclear submarines here; cut 'em some slack), but you can visit the engaging displays at the **Kittery Historical & Naval Museum** (*©* **207/439-3080;** www.kitterymuseum.com) nearby to learn a bit about the history of subs, the shipyard's specialty. It's open daily from June through October 10am to 4pm and charges a small admission fee. Find it by taking Rte. 1 to the Kittery traffic circle, then exiting at Rte. 236 S. (Rogers Rd.) and continuing onto Rogers Road Extension.

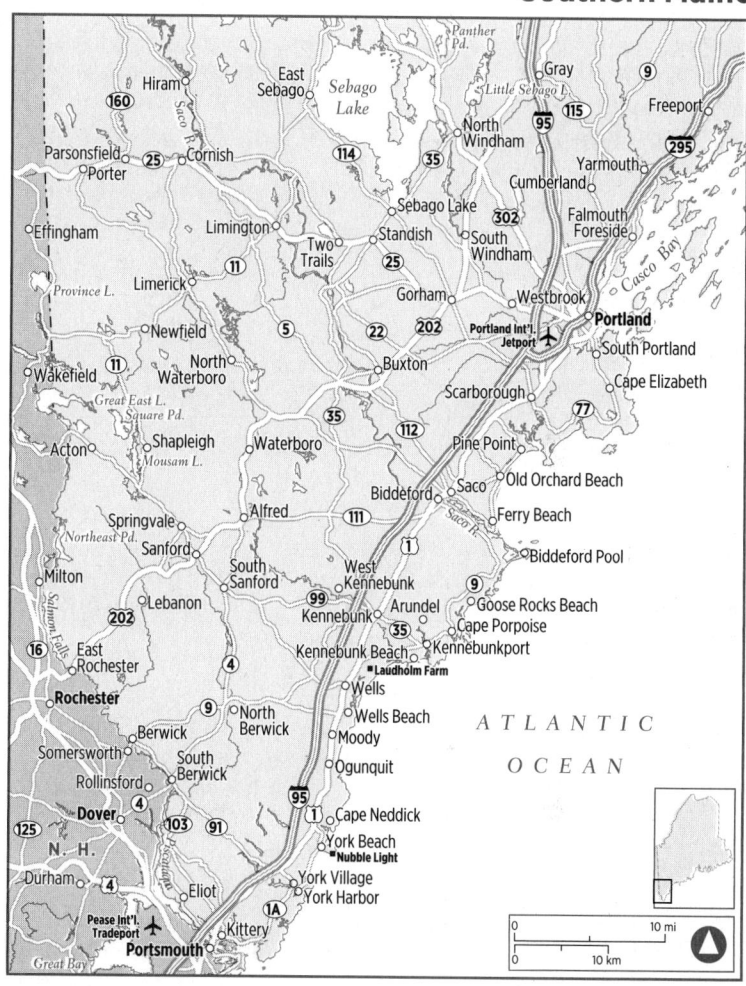

From Kittery, it's easy to take Rte. 1 north to York. But it's much prettier to follow winding **Rte. 103 ★**. This quiet road passes through the historic, lost-in-time village of **Kittery Point,** where homes seem to be just inches from the roadway and there are not one but *two* historic forts; both are parks open to the public.

EXPLORING YORK

York is split into several village centers, described above; the best for walking around in is **York Village ★★**, a fine destination for those curious about early American history. First settled in 1624, the village opens several homes to the public.

From late June through the end of August, daily except Saturday, a trackless "trolley"—a bus gussied up to *look* like an old-fashioned trolley, basically—links the two beaches (**Short Sands** and **Long Sands**) in York. The ride costs $2.50 each way. Hop on at any of the well-marked stops. There's also now a shuttle out to **Nubble Light,** a scenic point too far for most folks to walk to (or take good pictures of) from the beaches; that ride costs $1 each way.

Old York Historical Society ★★★   York's local historical society oversees the bulk of the town's collection of historic buildings, some of which date to the early 18th century, and most of which are astonishingly well preserved or restored. Tickets are available to eight Old York–operated properties in all; one good place to start is at the barn-red **Old Gaol ★★**, which still has its (now-musty) dungeons and was built in 1719 as a jail to hold criminals, debtors, and other miscreants. It's the oldest surviving public building in the United States. Next, cross the street to the yellow **Jefferds Tavern ★**, near the **old burying ground ★**. Inside, changing exhibits document various facets of early life. A 10-minute walk along Lindsay Road brings you to **Hancock Wharf,** next door to the **George Marshall Store.** (Also nearby is the **Elizabeth Perkins House,** with its well-preserved Colonial Revival interiors.) Finally, just down the hill from the jail is the **Emerson-Wilcox House ★**, built in the mid-1700s and periodically added onto through the years; it's a virtual catalog of architectural styles and early decorative arts.

207 York St., York. (207/363-4974. www.oldyork.org. Admission per building $5 adults, $4 seniors, $3 children 3-15; pass to all buildings $10 adults, $9 seniors, $5 children 4-15, $20 families. Museum and Old Gaol June to mid-Oct Mon–Sat 10am–5pm; some properties shorter hours.

BEACHES

York Beach actually consists of *two* beaches, **Long Sands Beach ★★** and **Short Sands Beach ★**, separated by a rocky headland. Both have plenty of room for sunning and Frisbees when the tide is out. (When the tide is in, though, both become narrow and cramped.)

Short Sands fronts the honky-tonk town of **York Beach,** and it offers candlepin bowling, taffy-pulling machines, and video arcades. It's a better pick for families traveling with kids who have short attention spans. Long Sands runs along Rte. 1A, directly across from a line of motels, summer homes, and convenience stores. Parking at *both* beaches is metered from mid-May through mid-October; pay heed, as enforcement is strict and you must pay from 8am until 10pm, 7 days a week. (In the off season, they decapitate the meters—literally—and parking is then free and plentiful until spring.)

SHOPPING

Kittery has become a shopping mecca ever since the arrival of little clusters of factory outlet shopping malls along both sides of Rte. 1. The lineup begins about 4 miles south of York. More than 100 of these outlets now flank the highway, in more than a dozen strip malls—not the prettiest sight in Maine, but if you're looking to score a deal, you just might find it beautiful.

Name-brand retailers with factory shops here purveying cut-rate designer stuff include Coach, Orvis, Samsonite, Gap, Adidas, Eddie Bauer, Banana Republic, Calvin Klein, Brookstone, and Polo Ralph Lauren, among many others. On rainy summer days, hordes of disappointed beachgoers head here and swarm the aisles; at those times, parking is especially tight.

Information on current outlets is available from the **Kittery Outlet Association.** Call 🕽 **888/548-8379,** or visit the website at www.thekitteryoutlets.com.

Stonewall Kitchen's flagship store (🕽 **207/351-2712**) is in York, on Stonewall Lane (behind the huge tourist information center on Rte. 1). Sample the company's jams before buying; the store is open daily until 8pm.

WHERE TO STAY

Besides the properties listed below, York Beach is stocked with plenty of condo and house rentals and motel rooms right on Long Sands Beach, plus a bunch more on Short Sands. The quality of these places is highly variable, though, as all the properties are individually owned. (At least all of them can truthfully boast that you can literally walk across the street to the beach.)

No matter where you stay, try to book ahead during high season. Failing that, turn up at the York visitor center (see "Visitor Information," above) and ask about vacancies, if you have arrived without a room—which, in summer, is usually a bad idea.

In Kittery

Portsmouth Harbor Inn and Spa ★★   This handsome 1899 home is just across the river from downtown Portsmouth, New Hampshire (p. 554), a pleasant, half-mile walk across a drawbridge. Rooms are tastefully restored and furnished in eclectic antiques, and though some are on the small side, all are boldly furnished and fun. Valora has ruby-red walls, harbor views, attractive antiques, and an above-average-size bathroom with historic accents. King George comes with a king-size bed (of course) and kingly skyline and bridge views. Dido's two single beds, meanwhile, can be adapted into an extra-long king. The whimsically decorated sitting room has two couches on which you can sprawl and browse through intriguing books. Spa services in an annex building are quite popular with guests.

6 Water St., Kittery, ME 03904. 🕽 **207/439-4040.** Fax 207/438-9286. www.innatportsmouth.com. 5 units. Mon–Fri $120–$190 double; Sat–Sun $120–$200 double. Rates include full breakfast. 2-night minimum sometimes required. MC, V. Not recommended for children 11 and under. **Amenities:** Jacuzzi; spa. *In room:* A/C, TV/DVD, hair dryer, Wi-Fi (free).

In The Yorks

Dockside Guest Quarters ★   David and Harriette Lusty established this quiet retreat in 1954, but more recent additions and new management (son David and his wife) haven't changed the friendly, maritime flavor of the place. Situated on an island connected to the mainland by a small bridge, the inn occupies nicely landscaped grounds shaded with maples and white pines. A few of the rooms are in the cozy main house, built in 1885, but the bulk of the accommodations are in small, shared, town-house-style cottages down by the water, added between 1968 and 1998. These are simply furnished, but bright and airy; most have private decks overlooking the entrance to York Harbor. Several also have woodstoves, fireplaces, and/or kitchenettes (though you do pay quite a bit extra for the kitchenette units and suites). The inn also maintains a simple restaurant (run by yet another son), and offers personalized boat tours of the harbor from its own private dock in addition to rowboats for guest use.

22 Harris Island Rd., York, ME 03909. 🕽 **888/860-7428** or 207/363-2868. www.docksidegq.com. 25 units. $117–$265 double; $236–$312 suite. Rates include breakfast. 2-night minimum stay in summer. DISC, MC, V. Closed Jan–Apr and Mon–Fri in May, Nov, and Dec. From Rte. 1A in York Harbor, turn onto Rte. 103 and cross bridge over York River; make an immediate left and follow signs to end of road. **Amenities:** Restaurant; bikes. *In room:* A/C, TV, kitchenette (some units), Wi-Fi (in main house; free).

Union Bluff Hotel ★★   With its turrets, dormers, and porches, the Union Bluff looks like a 19th-century beach hotel—except it was actually built in 1989, replacing the previous version (ca. 1870) of the hotel, which had burned in a fire. Inside, the hotel is modern if bland; but rooms have oak furniture, wall-to-wall carpeting, and small refrigerators, and the place seems to be getting better over time, not deteriorating like most beachside hotels do. There are about 20 rooms in an annex next door, but the main inn's rooms and views are better—the best units are the suites on the top floor and have beach vistas (and some have Jacuzzis, fireplaces, and decks overlooking the sea). It's amazing how low rates plummet here midweek and off season, when the hotel becomes among the most inexpensive places to stay in all of southern Maine; but weekends, even before and after summer, are quite expensive. Step outside and you're a half-block from Short Sands Beach, downtown T-shirt and shell shops, and the bowling alley and arcade. The hotel assigns one parking spot for each room, a boon because parking is very tight in Short Sands. But if you've brought an RV or a second car, you'll need to use the big parking lot adjacent to the hotel—bring lots of quarters.

8 Beach St. (P.O. Box 1860), York Beach, ME 03910. © **800/833-0721** or 207/363-1333. www.unionbluff.com. 61 units. Mid-June to Aug $179–$279 double, $229–$379 suite; rest of year $59–$169 double, $89–$289 suite. AE, DISC, MC, V. **Amenities:** Restaurant; pub. *In room:* A/C, fridge (some units), Wi-Fi (free).

WHERE TO DINE

Bob's Clam Hut ★ ▮▮ SEAFOOD   Operating since 1956, Bob's manages to retain its old-fashioned feel—despite being surrounded on all sides by outlet malls, and with prices that have escalated way out of the "budget eats" category. The cooks still fry up heaps of clams and other seafood, toss them with fries and coleslaw into baskets, and send them out with tremendous efficiency. Order at the window, get a soda from the machine, and stake out a table inside or a picnic table out on the deck (with its lovely/unlovely view of marshes and busy Rte. 1) while waiting for your number to be called. The food is surprisingly light, cooked in cholesterol-free vegetable oil; the onion rings are pretty good, but it's the plump clams that have inspired generations of fans to make return visits every summer. You can also get fish and chips quite cheaply, if you're not a fan of big, pricey fried-shellfish baskets. Continuing with the unhealthy-yet-so-tasty theme, Bob's scoops up New Hampshire–made Annabelle's ice cream from an adjacent window—now that's overkill.

315 Rte. 1 (west side of Rte. 1, just south of outlets), Kittery. © **207/439-4233.** www.bobsclamhut.com. Sandwiches $4–$13, dinner items $8–$29. AE, MC, V. Mon–Thurs 11am–7pm; Fri–Sat 11am–8pm; Sun 11am–7pm.

Goldenrod Restaurant ☺ DINER   Follow the neon to this seasonal beach-town classic, which is *the* place in York Beach for local color—it has been a summer institution here since 1896. Visitors and their kids love gawking through the plate-glass windows at ancient taffy machines hypnotically churning out taffy in volume (millions of candies a year). The restaurant, right behind the candy-making operation, is low on frills—it feels like long-gone New England, even if the food isn't all that impressive. Diners sit on stout oak furniture around a stone fireplace or elbow-to-elbow at an antique soda fountain; breakfasts are your basic New England diner standards, while for lunch and dinner you eat soups, burgers, and too-pricey sandwiches. But what saves the place is the **candy counter ★**, where you can line up to buy boxes of wax-wrapped taffy "kisses" (check the striping or coloring on the candy to know its flavor; I like the molasses and peppermint ones), almond-pocked birch bark, and other penny-candy treats. The shakes, malts, and sundaes are on the sweet side, but not bad.

2 Railroad Ave. (at Ocean Ave.), York Beach. (©) **207/363-2621.** www.thegoldenrod.com. Breakfast items $2–$6, most lunch and dinner items $5–$8. MC, V. Memorial Day to Labor Day daily 8am–10pm (until 9pm in June); Labor Day to Columbus Day Wed–Sun 8am–3pm. Closed Columbus Day to Memorial Day.

Lobster Cove ★ ☺ SEAFOOD   Right across the street from the pounding surf of Long Sands Beach, dependable Lobster Cove is a good choice when the family is too tired to cook or drive off the beach. A "feed" is what you'll get here: Breakfast consists of standard diner choices like omelets, pancakes, and eggs Benedict, while lunch runs to burgers and sandwiches. But dinner is prime time, when cars with out-of-state plates pack into the little dirt lot and the shore dinner of lobster, corn on the cob, clam chowder, and steamed clams is hefty, popular, and good. Lobster pie is another old-fashioned New England favorite on the menu, and they also do lobster rolls, clam rolls, steaks, steamed clams with butter, and broiled seafood, too. Old-timey Maine dessert choices include a wild blueberry pie (a must-order, in season) or warmed bread pudding with whiskey sauce. They've got a liquor license and a long cocktail menu, as well. Inoffensive and unfancy it may be, but it fits the bill in certain situations.

756 York St. (south end of Long Sands Beach), York Harbor. (©) **207/351-1100.** www.lobstercoverestaurant. com. Main courses $7–$21. AE, MC, V. Daily 8am–9pm.

Stonewall Kitchen Café ★★ CAFE   Stonewall Kitchen's York-based gourmet-foods operation took a step forward when it opened this quality, inexpensive cafe, smartly located right at its York headquarters next to the local tourist information office. The cafe serves simple, hearty items such as fish chowder, soups, lobster rolls, lobster BLTs, muffulettas (a New Orleans–style olive-salami sandwich), turkey wraps with cranberry spread, and many more; check the board to find out what's being served that day. Finish with a dessert such as lemon squares, brownies, or fresh-baked cookies. The cafe kitchen also prepares gourmet meals to go, and will do so up to an hour after the table service concludes. There's an espresso machine here, too.

2 Stonewall Lane (set back from Rte. 1), York. (©) **207/351-2719.** www.stonewallkitchen.com. Sandwiches and salads $7–$11. AE, DC, DISC, MC, V. Mon–Sat 8am–3pm, Sun 9am–3pm; takeout available until 4pm.

Union Grill ★ AMERICAN/SEAFOOD   Surprisingly, there aren't many upscale dining choices in the Yorks, so the Union Hotel's stab at "fancy" is a welcome development. Seafood predominates, though the menu wanders around. Start with a lobster corn dog, duck wings, calamari, or oysters on the half shell; then move on to a gourmet flatbread pizza (topped with Kobe short ribs, for instance) or entrees like a crusted lobster "mignon," seared scallops with dumplings, line-caught cod, or organic salmon. Landlubbers can go for a wild boar chop with béarnaise, crispy chicken with sweet potatoes, or a venison burger. Desserts are sweetish: a molten lava cake, a huge cookie, warmed bread pudding, or an oversized banana split with three gelati. It will be very interesting to see whether this place's lofty aspirations and high price point can make it in Short Sands—a place still so lowbrow, there's a gypsy palm reader on the main street.

8 Beach St. (in the Union Bluff Hotel), York Beach. (©) **800/833-0721** or 207/363-1333. www.unionbluff. com. Main courses $11–$30. MC, V. Reservations recommended. Mid-May to mid-Oct daily 7–11am and 5–9:30pm; off season Thurs–Sun only. Pub daily 11:30am–10pm year-round.

Ogunquit ★★

Ogunquit (oh-GUN-quit) is a bustling little beachside town that has attracted vacationers and artists for more than a century. Though certainly notable for its abundant and elegant summer-resort architecture and nightlife, Ogunquit is *most* famous for its 3½-mile white-sand beach, backed by grassy dunes and serviced by a beautiful seaside walking path, one of Maine's best. This beach is the town's front porch, and almost everyone ends up here at least once a day if the sun is shining.

Despite its architectural gentility and overall civility, the town can become over-run with tourists and cars during summer weekends. If you despise crowds and the processes of jockeying for parking spots and beach space, visit during the off season or during summer weekdays instead.

ESSENTIALS

GETTING THERE Ogunquit is on Rte. 1, about halfway between York and Wells. It's accessible from both exit 7 (the Yorks) and exit 19 (Wells) of the Maine Turnpike, though you'll have to drive awhile from either exit.

Turn seaward at the confusing intersection at the center of town and follow Shore Road—the southernmost of the two spurs—to reach Perkins Cove and the best shops, accommodations, and restaurants. (For the best beach access, take the *other* prong of the intersection to Beach St.) Expect traffic to creep along Rte. 1 during summer weekends.

VISITOR INFORMATION The **Ogunquit Welcome Center** (*©* **207/646-2939;** www.ogunquit.org) is easy to miss: It's on the east side of Rte. 1, just south of the main intersection. The center is open daily from Memorial Day through Columbus Day (until 8pm during summer weekends), and daily except Sunday dur-ing the off season. Yes, it has restrooms.

GETTING AROUND Ogunquit's entrance is a horrid three-way intersection that seems intentionally designed to cause massive traffic tie-ups. Parking in and around the village is tight and relatively expensive for small-town Maine ($6–$15 per day in various lots). My advice? The town is best navigated on foot, by bike, or by using the local shuttle bus (see "Trolley Ho!," below).

EXPLORING OGUNQUIT

The village center is good for an hour or two of browsing among the boutiques, or sipping a cappuccino at one of the several coffee emporia.

From the village, you can walk to scenic Perkins Cove along **Marginal Way ★★**, a mile-long oceanside pathway that departs across from the Seacastles Resort on Shore Road. It passes tide pools, pocket beaches, and rocky, fissured bluffs, all worth exploring. The seascape can be spectacular, even if Marginal Way can get quite crowded with walkers during fair-weather weekends. Do like the regulars and locals do: Head out in the early morning for your walk.

Perkins Cove ★, accessible either from Marginal Way or by driving south along Shore Road and then veering left at the Y intersection, is a small, well-protected harbor that attracts lots of visitors (sometimes too many). A handful of galleries, restaurants, and T-shirt shops cater to tourists here. Also at the cove, an intriguing pedestrian drawbridge is operated by whoever happens to be handy.

Not far from the cove is the **Ogunquit Museum of American Art ★★★**, 543 Shore Rd. (*©* **207/646-4909;** www.ogunquitmuseum.org), one of the best small art museums in the nation. (That's not just me talking; the director of New York's

Ogunquit

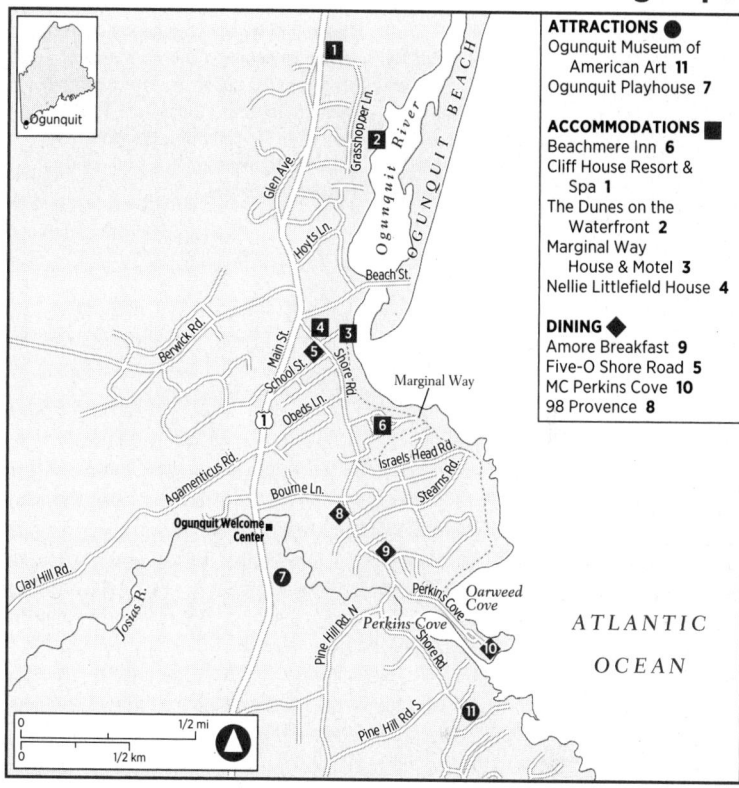

ATTRACTIONS ●
Ogunquit Museum of
American Art **11**
Ogunquit Playhouse **7**

ACCOMMODATIONS ■
Beachmere Inn **6**
Cliff House Resort &
Spa **1**
The Dunes on the
Waterfront **2**
Marginal Way
House & Motel **3**
Nellie Littlefield House **4**

DINING ◆
Amore Breakfast **9**
Five-O Shore Road **5**
MC Perkins Cove **10**
98 Provence **8**

Metropolitan Museum of Art said so, too.) It's open only in summer and early fall, however. Set back from the road in a grassy glen overlooking the rocky shore, the museum has a spectacular view that initially overwhelms the artwork as visitors walk through the door. But stick around for a few minutes—the changing exhibits in this architecturally engaging modern building of cement block, slate, and glass will get your attention soon enough; its curators have a track record of staging superb shows and attracting national attention, and the permanent collection holds work by sea-scape master Marsden Hartley and many members of the Ogunquit Colony, including Charles H. Woodbury, Hamilton Easter Field, and Robert Laurent.

The museum is open from July to October, Monday to Saturday from 10:30am to 5pm and Sunday from 1 to 5pm. Admission costs $7 for adults, $5 for seniors, and $4 for students; it's free for children 11 and under.

For evening entertainment, head for the **Ogunquit Playhouse ★★** (© 207/ **646-2402;** www.ogunquitplayhouse.org), a 750-seat summer stock theater right on Rte. 1 (just south of the main intersection) with an old-style look that has garnered a solid reputation for its careful, serious attention to stagecraft. The theater has

Trolley Ho! Taking the Ogunquit Trolley

A number of trackless "trolleys" (📞 **207/646-1411**; www.ogunquittrolley. com)—actually buses—with names like *Dolly* and *Ollie* (you get the idea) run all day from mid-May to Columbus Day between Perkins Cove and the Wells town line to the north, with detours to the sea down Beach and Ocean streets.

These trolleys are very handy, and they stop everywhere. (There's a map of stops posted online at **www.ogunquit. com/trolley.cfm.**) Rides cost $1.50 one-way (free for children); it's worth the expense to avoid driving and parking hassles and limits.

entertained Ogunquit since 1933, attracting noted actors such as Bette Davis, Tallulah Bankhead, Sally Struthers . . . er, and Lorenzo Lamas. Performances run from mid-May through mid-October, and tickets generally cost in the range of $30 to $45 per person.

WHERE TO STAY

In addition to the selections below, there are loads of family-owned budget- to moderately priced motel operations around town. Simply cruising Rte. 1 can yield dividends (don't forget your AAA card, if you're a member).

Beachmere Inn ★★ ☺   In a town of motels, simple B&Bs, and condos, the Beachmere excels. Operated by the same family since 1937, this quiet, well-run cliff-top inn sprawls across a scenic lawn where repeat visitors have reclined for decades. Nearly every unit gives you an amazing look up or down the beach, and all have kitchenettes. The original Victorian section dates from the 1890s and is the most fun; it's all turrets, big porches, angles, and bright, beachy interiors. Next door is the modern Beachmere South, with spacious rooms and plenty of private balconies or patios—those on the end have absolutely knockout views. A new wing (Beachmere West) was added in 2008, with a small but nice little hot tub, exercise room, and children's play area; units in this wing have sitting rooms and bigger bathrooms. The adjacent Marginal Way footpath (see "Exploring Ogunquit," above) is terrific for walks and beach access, and groups can inquire about several off-property cottages a short walk away. The inn is now open year-round: You can rent snowshoes in winter to (carefully) stroll the path.

62 Beachmere Place, Ogunquit, ME 03907. 📞 **800/336-3983** or 207/646-2021. Fax 207/646-2231. www.beachmereinn.com. 53 units. June–Aug $175–$250 double, $275–$380 suite, $460 cottage; May and Sept to mid-Oct $105–$220 double, $195–$265 suite, $270–$305 cottage; Apr and mid-Oct to early May $95–$160 double, $155–$195 suite, $235 cottage. Rates include continental breakfast. 3-night minimum stay in summer. AE, DC, DISC, MC, V. **Amenities:** Lounge; children's play room; Jacuzzi. *In room:* A/C, TV/DVD, kitchenettes (some units), Wi-Fi (in main inn; free).

Cliff House Resort and Spa ★★   This complex of modern buildings replaced a grand hotel and now offers some of the best hotel-room ocean views in Maine—nearly a 360-degree panorama, in some cases. The rooms come in a number of styles, most with comforts such as digital televisions and recliners; other updates include new beds and furniture in the Cliffscape wing and a covered corridor linking all terraces and guest rooms with the dining areas. A vanishing-edge pool fronting the sea does indeed seem to disappear into the blue yonder, and there's an upscale restaurant with knockout vistas. The state-of-the-art **spa** and fitness facility dispenses a wide range of treatments and exercise programs.

Shore Rd. (P.O. Box 2274), Ogunquit, ME 03907. ℭ **207/361-1000.** Fax 207/361-2122. www.cliffhouse maine.com. 200 units. July–Aug $265–$310 double, $335–$360 spa room and suite; mid-Apr to June and Sept–Nov $175–$255 double, $225–$310 and suite. Meal plans available. 3-night minimum stay July–Aug and holiday weekends; 2-night minimum other weekends. AE, DISC, MC, V. Closed Dec to mid-Apr. No children in spa-room units. **Amenities:** Restaurant; bar; health club; Jacuzzi; 3 pools (1 indoor, 2 outdoor); room service. *In room:* A/C, TV, hair dryer, Wi-Fi ($9.95 per day).

The Dunes on the Waterfront ★★   This classic motor court (built around 1936) somehow manages to be rustic yet elegant. It has made the transition into the modern luxury age more gracefully than just about other vintage motel I've ever seen. The complex consists of a motel-like main building, but most guests come to stay in one of the 19 gabled cottages (painted white and trimmed in green shutters) scattered about the 12-acre grounds. Plenty of old-fashioned charm remains in here, as they've been decked out in vintage maple furnishings, oval braided rugs, maple floors, knotty pine paneling, and louvered doors. These cottages all have full kitchens, and many have wood-burning fireplaces as well. The complex is wedged between busy Rte. 1 and the ocean, but it somehow stays quiet and peaceful; Adirondack chairs overlook a lagoon, and guests can borrow a rowboat to get across to the sandy beach without having to pay for parking.

518 Rte. 1 (P.O. Box 917), Ogunquit, ME 03907. ℭ **888/295-3863.** www.dunesonthewaterfront.com. 36 units. Summer $140–$345 double, $235–$435 cottage; spring and fall $95–$225 double, $160–$335 cottage. July–Aug 1-week minimum stay in cottages, 3-night minimum stay in motel. MC, V. Closed Nov to late Apr. **Amenities:** Outdoor pool; watersports equipment/rentals. *In room:* A/C, TV, fridge.

Marginal Way House and Motel ★   This simple, old-fashioned compound centers on a four-story, mid-19th-century guesthouse with summery, basic rooms and white-painted furniture. The whole complex is plunked down on a large, grassy lot on a quiet cul-de-sac, and it's hard to believe you're smack in the middle of busy Ogunquit. But you are: The beach and village are each just a few minutes' walk away. Room no. 7, despite its skinny twin beds, has a private porch and canopy and ocean views. The main building is surrounded by four more contemporary buildings that lack charm, but rooms here are mostly comfortable and bright. The "motel" building has only rooms with double beds, but the Wharf House has a cool quietude about it, enhanced by white linens and shady trees. Some units have little decks with views; all rooms have refrigerators and televisions, but none have phones. The property also maintains some one- and two-bedroom efficiency apartments (some have minimum stays); inquire when booking.

22-24 Wharf Lane (P.O. Box 697), Ogunquit, ME 03907. ℭ **207/646-8801.** www.marginalwayhouse. com. 30 units (1 with private bathroom down hall). Early June to Labor Day $86–$208 double; mid-Apr to early June and early Sept to Oct $49–$146 double. $15 extra charge for more than 2 people (except kids age 2 and under). Minimum-stay requirements some weekends. MC, V. Closed Nov to mid-Apr. Pets accepted in off season only ($15 per night); advance notice required. *In room:* A/C (most units), TV, fridge, Wi-Fi (in most; free), no phone.

Nellie Littlefield House ★★ 🛏   Of the many B&Bs and boardinghouses filling downtown Ogunquit, this might be the friendliest. The handsome 1889 home stands at the edge of the town's compact commercial district and features elegant Queen Anne–style detailing. All rooms are carpeted and feature a mix of modern and antique reproduction furnishings; several have refrigerators. Rooms to the rear have private decks, although views are limited—mostly looking out on a motel next door. The most spacious room is the third-floor J. H. Littlefield suite, with two televisions and a Jacuzzi, and the most unique unit is probably the circular Grace Littlefield room in the upper turret, overlooking the street. The basement features a compact fitness room. Hospitality remains a strong selling point here.

27 Shore Rd. (P.O. Box 1341), Ogunquit, ME 03907. © 207/646-1692. www.nellielittlefieldhouse.com. 8 units. June–Sept $108–$230 double; Mar–May and Oct–Dec to $85–$170 double; holiday rates higher. Rates include full breakfast. 3-night minimum stay on high-season weekends and holidays. DISC, MC, V. Closed Jan–Feb. Children 13 and over are welcome. **Amenities:** Small exercise room. *In room:* A/C, TV, fridge (some units).

WHERE TO DINE

Amore Breakfast ★★ ♦ BREAKFAST Newly relocated down the village's main street in the Perkins Cove district, Amore is a breakfast-only place—but what a breakfast it is. (This is *not* a place for weight-watchers. But you're on vacation, right?) Look for numerous variations on the eggs Benedict theme (including a popular one with a big hunk of lobster on top), plus good Belgian waffles, a calorific bananas-Foster-style French toast with pecans outside and cream cheese inside, French toast topped with blueberries, and more than a dozen tasty variations on an omelet. Coffee is from a small-batch San Diego coffee roaster. And they've got heart, too: Annual benefit meals are held, with the proceeds going to care packages for a Dominican orphanage. Italian owner Leanne Cusimano deserves (and gets local) kudos.

309 Shore Rd. © 866/641-6661 or 207/646-6661. www.amorebreakfast.com. Breakfast items $5–$14. MC, V. Summer daily 7am–1pm; off season closed Wed–Thurs. Also closed mid-Dec to Apr.

Arrows ★★★ NEW AMERICAN When owners Mark Gaier and Clark Frasier opened Arrows in a gray farmhouse outside town in 1988, they quickly put Ogunquit on the national culinary map. They've done so not only by creating an elegant and intimate atmosphere, but also by serving up some of the freshest, most innovative cooking in New England. The emphasis is on local products—often very local. The salad greens are grown in gardens on the grounds, and much of the rest is produced or raised locally. The food transcends traditional New England fare and is deftly prepared with exotic twists and turns. The menu changes nightly, but among the more popular recurring appetizers is a house-cured prosciutto—hams are hung in the restaurant to cure in the off season. Entrees might include roasted chicken stuffed with a sourdough-and-foie-gras stuffing; roasted halibut; tenderloin of pork with yam puree and pork dumplings; Maine-caught sole with a champagne glaze; or "surf and turf" (roasted rib-eye au poivre plus a chilled lobster cocktail). The wine list is top-rate. Note that there is a moderate dress code: Jackets are preferred for men, and shorts aren't allowed.

41 Berwick Rd. © 207/361-1100. www.arrowsrestaurant.com. Reservations strongly recommended. Main courses $41–$43, tasting menus $95–$135. MC, V. June to Columbus Day Wed–Sun 6–9pm; late Oct to Dec and mid-Apr to May Thurs–Sun 6–9pm. Closed Jan to mid-Apr. Turn onto Berwick Rd. at Key Bank in the village center; restaurant is 2 miles along road, on right.

Five-O Shore Road ★★ SEAFOOD/FUSION A fine choice if you're looking for a more casual alternative to the more formal restaurants listed, Five-O is one of those spots where just reading the menu is a decent evening's entertainment. The formerly Caribbean-inspired menu has been transformed into one that veers all over the map. And the fun thing about eating here is that you can mix-and-match small plates, tapas-style, if nightly main courses like baby back ribs, rack of lamb, Delmonico steaks, quail, or fish, don't grab you. Instead, you could eat some rope-grown Maine mussels, almond-crusted fried duck tenders, escargot with shallots, wild salmon poached in lobster-saffron bullion, molé-spiced pork, pâté, a cheese plate, or some hand-made onion rings with barbecue sauce. (Or just order a fresh Maine lobster in season, perhaps served over a bed of mussels steamed with blue cheese, sweet cream, and cracked pepper.) Five-O also has a cool cocktail lounge and club, and a strong wine list. Is this Maine or Manhattan? Either way, it's still a winner.

50 Shore Rd. ℂ **207/646-5001.** www.five-oshoreroad.com. Reservations strongly recommended in summer. Small plates $8–$13, main courses $14–$32. AE, DISC, MC, V. Valet parking. Memorial Day to Labor Day Mon–Fri 5–9pm, Sat–Sun 11am–2pm and 5–9pm; call for hours outside peak season.

MC Perkins Cove ★★★ SEAFOOD/NEW AMERICAN   Chef-partners Mark Gaier and Clark Frasier (the M and C in MC) of Arrows (see above) have opened this bistro, which manages to be fun rather than stuffy. (Well, no bathing suits are allowed in the dining room, but still.) Expect big food, even on the "small" plates: Chopped salads, fried calamari, and oysters on half shells give way to more sophisticated starters like mussels steamed in a red-curry sauce, rustic pizzas of ham and apple, or house-cured smoked salmon with dill. For your entree, choose a main dish such as a steamed lobster; a piece of sesame-encrusted, deep-fried trout; a Kobe burger; some grilled tuna; a hanger steak; or a piece of plank-roasted fish—then add aioli or another sauce and one of the so-called "evil carbos" (french fries, onion rings, and so on). Desserts might be best of all: Finish with a brown-butter brownie with vanilla ice cream, burnt orange caramel, and candied orange peel; mini whoopee pies; apple-blueberry turnovers with a mulled cider reduction; a bittersweet chocolate cake with chocolate sauce and pistachio crème anglaise; or peppermint-stick ice cream with cookies.

111 Perkins Cove Rd. ℂ **207/646-6263.** www.mcperkinscove.com. Reservations recommended. Main courses $8–$19 at lunch, $19–$31 at dinner. DC, DISC, MC, V. Late May to mid-Oct daily 11:30am–2pm and 5:30–11pm; rest of year closed Tues. Also closed Jan.

98 Provence ★★★ FRENCH   How many good meals can you eat in one town? Find out. At this bistro, Chef Pierre Gignac incorporates fresh, local ingredients (such as lobster) in a menu that changes thrice yearly to reflect the seasons but never gets too fusion-minded; instead, it's solidly French throughout. Start with lobster cooked in puff pastry with a sherried honey-ginger cream; Provençal fish stew; escargots with a Parmesan crisp and black trumpet mushrooms; rabbit fricassee; or the daily soup or mussel dish. (Yes, they have a daily, changing mussel dish.) Then move on to veal with wild mushrooms; a grilled boar chop with a chestnut croquette and pomegranate sauce; braised beef short ribs; a cassoulet of duck confit, lamb shoulder, and pork sausage; rack of lamb roasted with cumin and garlic; or the catch of the day. There's also now a daily bistro prix-fixe menu with lighter items (and prices)—the trio might be vichyssoise, stewed chicken, and lemon tart, for instance, or soft-shell crab with halibut confit and Provence-style nougat, served frozen. The summery, classy interior decor is about as close as you'll get in New England to a Provençal feel. Outstanding place.

262 Shore Rd. ℂ **207/646-9898.** www.98provence.com. Reservations recommended. Main courses $23–$28, prix-fixe menus $29–$39. AE, MC, V. Summer Wed–Mon 5:30–9:30pm; off season Thurs–Mon 5:30–9pm.

The Kennebunks ★★

"The Kennebunks" consist of the side-by-side villages of **Kennebunk** and **Kennebunkport,** both situated along the shores of small rivers and both claiming a very scenic section of the rocky coast.

The region was first colonized in the mid-1600s, and it flourished after the American Revolution when ship captains, boat builders, and prosperous merchants constructed imposing, solid homes in both towns. The Kennebunks are each famed for their striking historical architecture, shopping, dining, fine inns and hotels, ocean views (the Bush family owns a summer home here), and long, sandy beaches. Be sure to take time to explore both towns.

ESSENTIALS

GETTING THERE   Kennebunk is just off exit 25 of the Maine Turnpike; turn left after the ramp, and follow signs east into town. You can also get here by taking Rte. 1 north from York and Ogunquit.

To reach Kennebunkport, take the exit for Kennebunk and continue through town on Port Road (Rte. 35) for about 3½ miles. At the traffic light, turn left and cross the small bridge.

VISITOR INFORMATION   The helpful **Kennebunk-Kennebunkport Chamber of Commerce** (© 800/982-4421 or 207/967-0857; www.visitthekennebunks. com) can answer questions year-round by phone or in person at its offices at 17 Western Ave. (Rte. 9), beside the H.B. Provisions general store.

GETTING AROUND   Several higher-end inns in these two towns offer shuttle services to the downtown areas. Otherwise, a local **trolley** (actually a bus that looks like a trolley) makes several convenient stops in and around the Kennebunks, and also serves the best local beaches; it picks up about once per hour from 10am until 4pm (3pm in spring and fall). But it's *expensive:* Your fare comes in the form of a day pass, and that costs $15 per adult or $5 per child ages 3 to 17. The upside? One ticket allows you unlimited jumping on and off all day long.

Call © 207/967-3686 for details, or check the trolley's schedule online at **www. intowntrolley.com**.

EXPLORING KENNEBUNK

Kennebunk's downtown is inland, just off the turnpike, and is a dignified, compact commercial center of clapboard and brick.

If you're a history buff, the **Brick Store Museum ★**, 117 Main St. (© 207/985-4802; www.brickstoremuseum.org), should be your very first stop in town. The museum hosts showings of historical art and artifacts throughout summer, switching to contemporary art exhibits in the off season. And they've got extensive local historic archives, too. The museum is housed in a former brick store plus three adjacent buildings renovated to a polish. Admission is free (though a $5 per person donation is suggested), and tours cost $5 per person. The museum opens Tuesday to Friday from 10am to 4:30pm, and Saturday from just 10am until 1pm.

The $5, 1½-hour **walking tours ★** of Kennebunk's historic district (Maine's first) that set out from the museum are a must-do if you love history.

When en route to or from the coast, be sure to note the extraordinary homes that line Port Road (Rte. 35). This includes the famously elaborate **Wedding Cake House ★**, which you should be able to identify all on your own.

EXPLORING KENNEBUNKPORT

Dock Square has a bustling feel to it, with low buildings of mixed vintages and styles. The boutiques in the area are attractive, and many feature creative artworks and crafts, but sometimes they're a bit crowded. Kennebunkport's real attraction is found in the surrounding blocks, though, where side streets are lined with one of the nation's richest collections of Early American homes.

Many of the beautiful Federal-style houses here have been converted to B&Bs (see "Where to Stay," below). And the amazing meetinghouse-style **South Congregational Church ★★**, the one with the big clock faces just off Dock Square at North and Temple streets, is well worth the short detour.

Ocean Drive (marked by a post in Dock Sq.) runs out to and beyond the Bush compound at **Walkers Point ★**, and the route is lined with opulent summer homes. Take a quick look at the presidential palace, snap a pic, and move on—there's plenty more to see out here, including outstanding ocean and shore views.

BEACHES

The coastal area around Kennebunkport is home to several of the state's best beaches. Southward across the river (technically, this is Kennebunk, though it's much closer to Kennebunkport) are **Gooch's Beach ★★** and **Kennebunk Beach ★★**. Head eastward from the intersection of routes 9 and 35 along—yes—Beach Street past the White Barn Inn (see "Where to Stay," below), and, in a few minutes, you'll arrive at the ocean and a handsome row of eclectic, shingled summer homes.

The narrow road continues to twist past sandy strands and rocky headlands for a few miles, and this portion is well worth exploring, too. It can get congested in summer, though; avoid gridlock by parking and wandering on foot or by bike. (Also take note of local parking regulations: Only local residents are permitted to park along some stretches of these beaches. Check with your hotel reception desk if you're in doubt.)

WHERE TO STAY

Beach House Inn ★★ This is a good choice if you'd like to be close to the people-watching, dog-walking action on and above Kennebunk Beach. The inn was built in 1891 but has been extensively modernized and expanded. The rooms here aren't necessarily historic, but most have Victorian furnishings and accents, plus nice framed photographs of beach landscapes. Suites have lovely panoramic views of the ocean across the road. But the main draw here is the lovely front porch, where you can stare out at the water and watch passing walkers and cyclists. The inn has bikes and canoes for guests to use, and provides beach chairs and towels, too.

211 Beach Ave., Kennebunk, ME 04043. (✆) **207/967-3850.** Fax 207/967-4719. www.beachhseinn.com. 35 units. Late June to mid-Sept $255–$390 double; early June to late June and mid-Sept to Oct $185–$399 double; Nov–Dec $155–$300 double. Rates include continental breakfast and afternoon tea. 2-night minimum Sat–Sun. AE, MC, V. Closed Jan–May. **Amenities:** Babysitting; bikes; canoes. *In room:* A/C, TV/VCR/CD, hair dryer, Wi-Fi (free).

The Colony Hotel ★★ One of a handful of oceanside resorts that has actually preserved the classic New England vacation experience without fading into oblivion, this mammoth white Georgian Revival inn (ca. 1914) lords over the ocean at the mouth of the river on the Kennebunkport side. All rooms in the three-story main inn have been renovated; they're bright and cheery, simply furnished in summer-cottage antiques. Rooms in two of the three outbuildings carry over the feeling of the main hotel; the exception is the East House, a 1950s-era motel at the back edge of the property with uninteresting rooms. Staff encourages guests to socialize in the lobby, on the porch, on the putting green, even at a shuffleboard court that's lighted for nighttime play. Yes, the building is aging, and no—most rooms still don't have televisions. But if you're coming for proximity to the ocean, quiet, and casual elegance, you can still find them here.

140 Ocean Ave. (P.O. Box 511), Kennebunkport, ME 04046. ℂ **800/552-2363** or 207/967-3331. Fax 207/967-8738. www.thecolonyhotel.com/maine. 123 units. Summer $149–$549 double; spring and fall $99–$399 double. Rates include breakfast. 3-night minimum stay summer weekends and holidays. AE, MC, V. Closed Nov to mid-May. Pets accepted ($30 per pet per night). **Amenities:** Restaurant; lounge; bikes; heated saltwater pool; room service. *In room:* A/C (some units), TV (some units), Wi-Fi (free).

Old Fort Inn ★★   The Old Fort tops some of the much better-known B&Bs in town. A sophisticated little inn, it sits on 15 acres in a quiet, picturesque neighborhood of late-19th-century summer homes 2 blocks from the ocean. Guests check in at a tidy antiques shop and park around back at the large carriage house, an interesting amalgam of stone, brick, shingle, and stucco. Rooms and suites here all have creature comforts yet retain the charm of yesteryear: They are solidly wrought and delightfully decorated with antiques and reproductions. About half the rooms have in-floor heated tiles in the bathrooms; all have such welcome amenities as plush robes, refrigerators, Aveda bath products, discreet self-serve snack bars, microwaves, and sinks. There are two large suites in the main house—light-filled no. 216 faces east, overlooking the attractive pool, for instance. A good, very full buffet breakfast is served in the main building daily; a free hour of tennis on a carefully kept court is included with your rate; and the inn now also offers massage and other spa services.

Old Fort Rd. (P.O. Box M), Kennebunkport, ME 04046. ℂ **800/828-3678** or 207/967-5353. Fax 207/967-4547. www.oldfortinn.com. 16 units. $125–$245 double; $295–$390 suite. Rates include full breakfast and 1 hr. free tennis. 2-night minimum stay weekends; 3-night minimum holiday weekends. AE, DC, DISC, MC, V. **Amenities:** Heated outdoor pool; tennis court. *In room:* A/C, TV, fridge, hair dryer, microwave, minibar, Wi-Fi (free).

White Barn Inn ★★★   As it has long done, the exclusive White Barn goes the extra mile to pamper its guests to no end, and it remains the state's best inn (with arguably its best dining room; see "Where to Dine," below). Upon checking in, guests are shown to a parlor and served a drink while valets gather luggage and park cars. The atmosphere here is distinctly European, with an emphasis on service and a polished international staff. Rooms are individually decorated in an upscale country style recently recast to emphasize simple, sea-inspired pastel colors. The biggest main-house unit, no. 8, feels most "New England-y" with its mix of the modern (double Jacuzzi, thick robes) and the classic: a two-sided fireplace, folding screens in the enormous bathroom, prints on the walls. Suites in the adjacent May's Cottage outbuilding are spectacular—each has a unique color theme, most have flatscreen TVs and/or whirlpools, and a few have great front porches. Across the road, several cottages on the Kennebunk River at a private marina offer cozy escapes, yet they're equipped with modern kitchens and bathrooms to go with their full river and harbor views. There are plenty of extra touches here, from fresh flowers to daily tea and scones, a new spa, a secluded outdoor pool behind a gate, and a pedicab whisking guests into the nearby town. And Chef Jonathan Cartwright's resort cuisine? Sublime.

37 Beach Ave. (¼ mile east of junction of routes 9 and 35; P.O. Box 560-C), Kennebunk, ME 04043. ℂ **207/967-2321.** Fax 207/967-1100. www.whitebarninn.com. 25 units, 4 cottages. $310–$620 double;

$540–$925 cottage and suite. Rates include continental breakfast and afternoon tea. 2-night minimum Sat–Sun; 3-night minimum holiday weekends. AE, MC, V. Free valet parking. **Amenities:** Bikes; concierge; outdoor heated pool; limited room service. *In room:* A/C, TV, Wi-Fi (free).

The Yachtsman Lodge & Marina ★★   The White Barn Inn took over this riverfront motel in 1997 and made it over into a much more appealing base for exploring the Kennebunkport side of the river. Within walking distance of Dock Square, its nice touches abound: down comforters, granite-topped vanities, high ceilings, CD players, and French doors that open onto patios just above the river. While the rooms here are all motel-size and all on one level, their simple, classical styling and fine amenities are far superior to anything you'd ever find at a roadside or even chain motel. (Room rates here are higher than you might expect, as a consequence of that.)

Ocean Ave. (P.O. Box 2609), Kennebunkport, ME 04046. (℃) **207/967-2511.** Fax 207/967-5056. www.yachtsmanlodge.com. 30 units. $189–$369 double. Rates include continental breakfast. AE, MC, V. 2-night minimum stay Sat–Sun and holidays. **Amenities:** Bikes; canoes. *In room:* A/C, TV/VCR/CD, fridge, hair dryer, Wi-Fi (free).

WHERE TO DINE

Federal Jack's Restaurant and Brew Pub ★ AMERICAN   This light, airy, and modern restaurant, named after a schooner built at Cape Porpoise a century ago, is tucked back from the bridge in a retail complex sitting oddly amid boatyards lining the south bank of the Kennebunk River. From the second-floor perch (look for a seat on the spacious three-season deck in warmer weather), you can gaze across the river toward the shops of Dock Square. The restaurant is best known for its Kennebunkport Brewing Co. ales, lagers, and porters, which they've been brewing here beneath the pub since 1992. An upscale menu to accompany your beer features the expected hamburgers, seafood, wings, calamari, and pizza, plus some nods to and twists on regional fare—glazed salmon, a lobster feed. Keep an eye on the menu, which might include something as upscale as a grilled-crab-and-havarti sandwich, lamb burger, or plate of tuna sashimi, or as downscale as a bowl of Texas chili and a simple hummus wrap. Yes, they have a kids' menu, and Sunday brunch is served from 11:30am to 2pm.

8 Western Ave., Lower Village (south bank of Kennebunk River), Kennebunk. (℃) **207/967-4322.** www.federaljacks.com. Main courses $2.95–$16, lobster dinners priced to market. AE, DISC, MC, V. Daily 11:30am–1am (late-night menu only after 9pm Sun–Thurs and after 10pm Fri–Sat).

Hurricane ★★ AMERICAN   Brooks and Luanne MacDonald's Hurricane remains the best place in downtown Kennebunkport for a gourmet lunch or dinner. Its windows on the river and casual, maritime decor are perfect for a sea town where millionaires wander around in jeans and boat shoes. Lunch might start with a cup of lobster chowder, the "Ice Cube" (a block of iceberg lettuce with blue-cheese dressing, toasted pecans, roasted pears, and croutons), a lobster Cobb salad, a bento box of Maine seafood, or a salad; the main course could be a Cubano sandwich, a grilled tuna burger, or a three-cheese tortellini. Dinner entrees run to such items as a Mediterranean stew of Maine lobster and other local seafood; pan-roasted chicken with a pecorino macaroni-and-cheese; grilled beef tenderloin; brined pork chop with honeyed sweet potatoes; baked lobster stuffed with scallops, crab, and shrimp; or a slowly cooked rack of lamb. Finish with a dessert like vanilla-bean crème brûlée, Key lime tart with coconut rum sauce, panna cotta, toffee-flavored bread pudding, or a course of cheeses—or, if it's around Christmas, ask if the eggnog cheesecake is on the menu.

29 Dock Sq., Kennebunkport. © **207/967-9111.** www.hurricanerestaurant.com. Reservations recommended. Small plates $8–$25, main courses $19–$45. AE, DC, DISC, MC, V. Daily 11:30am–10:30pm (winter to 9:30pm).

Pier 77 Restaurant ★ REGIONAL   Long a tony restaurant with a wonderful ocean view, Pier 77 was recently renovated and renamed by husband-and-wife team Peter and Kate Morency. The food, drawing on Peter's training at the Culinary Institute of America and 20 years in top kitchens in Boston and San Francisco, is more contemporary and skillful than almost anything else in Maine. Lunches run to comfort food: barbecued pork, spaghetti and meatballs, cheddar burgers, fried clams. The dinner menu leans toward traditional American favorites (pastas, steaks, lobster) as well, but there are also some slightly more adventurous dishes: A trio of duck courses and a tomato-y seafood stew have landed on the menu, for instance. The restaurant has earned *Wine Spectator*'s awards of excellence since 1993. A more casual section known as the Ramp Bar & Grill stays open all day, even between the lunch and dinner services.

77 Pier Rd., Cape Porpoise (Kennebunkport). © **207/967-8500.** www.pier77restaurant.com. Reservations recommended. Main courses $9–$18 at lunch, $18–$30 at dinner. AE, MC, V. Restaurant daily 11:30am–2:30pm and 5–9pm. Ramp Bar & Grill 11:30am–9pm. Closed Tues Oct–Dec.

White Barn Inn ★★★ REGIONAL/NEW AMERICAN   The White Barn Inn's (see "Where to Stay," above) classy dining room—carved out of a former barn, naturally, attached to the inn—attracts gourmands from across the nation. The barn itself is half the fun, with its cathedral-like space and an eclectic collection of country antiques displayed in the old hayloft; window displays are changed with the seasons. Chef Jonathan Cartwright's menu also changes frequently, nearly always incorporating local ingredients. You might start with his signature lobster spring roll (daikon radish, carrots, snow peas, and Thai sauce accent the lobster meat), or locally caught pan-seared diver scallops; glide through an *intermezzo* course of fruit soup or sorbet; then graduate to a pan-seared filet of salmon, a grilled chicken breast over creamed spinach, or a simply steamed lobster over fettuccine with cognac coral-butter sauce. Cartwright's special tasting menus run to seasonal items such as variations of oyster, sautéed smoked haddock rarebit, Quebec foie gras roulade, or peekytoe crab with a roast pineapple salad. And the table service is astonishingly attentive and knowledgeable, capping the experience. It's no surprise at all to learn this is often selected one of America's top inn restaurants by readers of top travel magazines; it's simply Maine's best.

37 Beach Ave., Kennebunkport. © **207/967-2321.** www.whitebarninn.com. Reservations recommended. Fixed-price dinner $91, tasting menu $125 per person. AE, MC, V. Mon–Thurs 6:30–9:30pm; Fri 5:30–9:30pm. Closed 2 weeks in Jan.

PORTLAND ★★

Portland: 106 miles N of Boston

Maine's largest city, salty **Portland** sits on a hammerhead-shaped peninsula extending into scenic Casco Bay. It's easy to drive right past the place on I-295, admiring the skyline at 60 miles an hour, on your way to the villages, islands, and rocky points farther up the coast. People don't usually think about an urban experience while packing for a vacation in Maine.

Portland

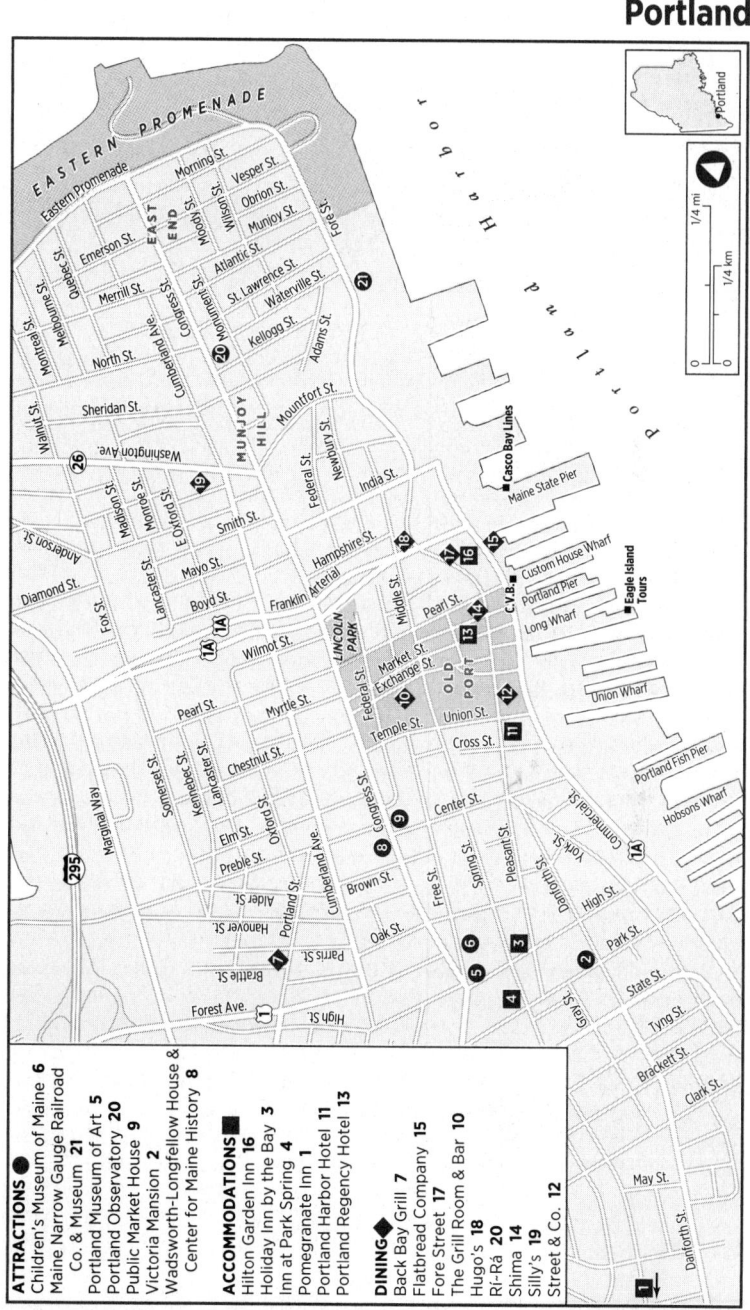

ATTRACTIONS ●
Children's Museum of Maine **6**
Maine Narrow Gauge Railroad
  Co. & Museum **21**
Portland Museum of Art **5**
Portland Observatory **20**
Public Market House **9**
Victoria Mansion **2**
Wadsworth-Longfellow House &
  Center for Maine History **8**

ACCOMMODATIONS ■
Hilton Garden Inn **16**
Holiday Inn by the Bay **3**
Inn at Park Spring **4**
Pomegranate Inn **1**
Portland Harbor Hotel **11**
Portland Regency Hotel **13**

DINING ◆
Back Bay Grill **7**
Flatbread Company **15**
Fore Street **17**
The Grill Room & Bar **10**
Hugo's **18**
Ri-Rá **20**
Shima **14**
Silly's **19**
Street & Co. **12**

But I can speak from direct experience: Portland is *well* worth an afternoon's detour, or even a whole weekend. This historic city has plenty of charm—not only in its renovated, touristy Old Port (a place of brick sidewalks, cobblestone streets, and fish)—but also throughout its lovely residential neighborhoods, some of which look out onto Casco Bay.

You can catch a 20-minute ferry to quiet offshore islands; drive 20 minutes to terrific lighthouses and beaches; browse through good antiques and boutique shops; drink excellent coffee and eat top-flight baked goods; photograph an amazing variety of historic mansions, churches, and other architectural treasures; and dine better than you can anywhere else in northern New England.

Essentials

GETTING THERE   Coming from the south by car, downtown Portland is most easily reached by taking exit 44 off the Maine Turnpike (I-95), and then following I-295 (which is free) into the city. Exit onto Franklin Arterial (exit 7), and continue straight downhill to the city's ferry terminal. Turn right onto Commercial Street, and continue a few blocks to parking meters and the visitor center on the right (see below). Get oriented there.

Amtrak (✆ **800/872-7245**; www.amtrak.com) runs a daily *Downeaster* service from Boston's North Station to Portland (passengers from other cities must change stations from South Station to North Station in Boston by taxi or subway). The train makes five round-trips daily (2½ hr. one-way), and a ticket costs $24 each way. From the station, downtown is a short city-bus ride, or a drab 30- to 45-minute walk, away.

The regional line **Concord Coach** (✆ **800/639-3317** or 207/228-3300; www.concordcoachlines.com) connects Portland to Boston, with more than a dozen buses daily from Boston's bus station and Logan Airport. The trip takes about 2 hours and costs $21 to $26 one-way, $35 to $44 round-trip. Its bus terminal is set on Thompson Point Road (a 30- to 45-min. walk from downtown) next to the Amtrak station; from there, you can walk, but it's difficult. City buses and taxis also serve the terminal.

Greyhound (✆ **800/231-2222**; www.greyhound.com) provides bus service into Portland from both Boston and New York City. Several buses daily make the trip from Boston, which takes about 2 hours and costs $21 each way; from New York, there's only one bus per day (7 hr.), costing $47 each way. Greyhound's bus terminal is at 950 Congress St., about a mile downhill from, and south of, the downtown core—walking distance, though a long way.

Portland International Jetport (✆ **207/874-8877**; www.portlandjetport.org), airport code PWM, is the largest airport in Maine. It's served by flights from **AirTran** (✆ 800/247-8726; www.airtran.com), **Continental** (✆ 800/523-3273; www.continental.com), **Delta/Northwest** (✆ 800/221-1212; www.delta.com), **JetBlue** (✆ 800/538-2583; www.jetblue.com), **United Express** (✆ 800/864-8331; www.ual.com), and **US Airways** (✆ 800/428-4322; www.usair.com). The airport has grown by fits and starts in recent years but is still easily navigated. Many hotels in the city offer free shuttles to and from the airport; inquire when booking your hotel.

Car rentals are available from a half-dozen chain outfits at the terminal. Also, the no. 5 **Metro city bus** ($1.25) passes nearby about twice per hour (but once per hour, for shorter hours, on Sun); limos and vans can be called to pick you up; and a taxi into the city center costs about $20, tip included.

VISITOR INFORMATION The **Convention and Visitors Bureau of Greater Portland** (www.visitportland.com) maintains *four* information centers in and around the city. The **main info center** (© 207/772-5800) is located on the new Ocean Gateway Pier, at the far-northern end of Commercial Street past the Casco Bay Ferry docks. Most of the time, it's open Monday to Saturday; in July and August, it also opens on Sunday, and it's closed the last two weeks of February.

You'll also find tourist information kiosks at the **Portland International Jetport** (© 207/775-5809), near the baggage claim, open daily year-round; in **Deering Oaks Park** at the Forest Avenue exit of I-295, open at least 6 days a week year-round (closed Sun in Sept and June); and one ad hoc kiosk that opens up outside the **cruise-ship terminal** on Commercial Street for 4 hours after any cruise ship arrives.

Portland also has a free weekly newspaper, the *Portland Phoenix* (www.thephoenix.com/portland), offering good listings of local events, films, nightclub performances, and the like. Copies are widely available at restaurants, bars, convenience stores, and in newspaper boxes on the curb.

Exploring the City

Visitors to Portland usually begin with a quick stroll around the historic **Old Port ★**. Bounded by Commercial, Congress, Union, and Pearl streets, this area near the waterfront has some of the city's best commercial architecture, a clutch of boutiques, some of the state's best restaurants (seafood is a special strength here), and one of the densest concentrations of bars on the eastern seaboard. **Exchange Street** is the spiritual heart of the Old Port, with the most boutiques, eateries, and coffee shops.

The city's finest harborside stroll is along the **Eastern Prom Pathway ★★**, which wraps for about a mile along the waterfront beginning at the Casco Bay Lines ferry terminal at the corner of Commercial and Franklin streets. This paved pathway is suitable for walking or biking and offers expansive views of the islands and sailboats in the harbor. The pathway skirts the lower edge of the **Eastern Promenade ★★**, a 68-acre hillside park with broad, grassy slopes extending down to the water. There's also a tiny beach here, though it's often off-limits for swimming. The pathway continues on to Back Cove Pathway, a 3.5-mile loop around tidal Back Cove.

Atop **Munjoy Hill,** above the Eastern Promenade, you'll find a cluster of good restaurants, grocers, and a coffee shop, not to mention the distinctive **Portland Observatory** (© 207/774-5561) at 138 Congress St.: a quirky, shingled tower built in 1807 to signal the arrival of ships into port. Exhibits inside the tower provide a quick glimpse of Portland's past, but the real reason people come is for the great views from the top. It's open daily (when flags are flying from the cupola) from Memorial Day through Columbus Day, with guided tours from 10am until 5pm; the last tour leaves at 4:30pm. (In the middle of summer, the observatory stays open until 8pm for sunset viewing from on high.) Admission to the tower is $7 for adults, $4 for children ages 6 to 16.

Children's Museum of Maine ★ ☺

The centerpiece exhibit in Portland's kids' museum—a stout, columned downtown building next to the art museum—is its *camera obscura,* a room-size "camera" on the top floor. Children gather around a white table in a dark room, where they see magically projected images that include cars driving by on streets, boats plying the harbor, and seagulls flapping by. This never fails to enthrall, providing a memorable lesson in the workings of lenses. That's just one attraction; there are plenty more, from a simulated supermarket checkout counter to a firehouse pole to a mock space shuttle that kids pilot from a high cockpit.

142 Free St. (next to the Portland Museum of Art). ✆ **207/828-1234.** www.childrensmuseumofme.org. Admission $6; free 5–8pm 1st Fri of the month. AE, MC, V. Mon–Sat 10am–5pm; Sun noon–5pm. Closed Mon Nov–Apr.

Maine Narrow Gauge Railroad Co. & Museum ☺ During the late 19th century, Maine was home to several narrow-gauge railways, operating on rails that were just 2 feet apart. Most of these trains have disappeared, but this nonprofit organization is dedicated to preserving some of the few examples that remain. The small admission fee to the museum is waived if you purchase a more expensive ticket for the short ride on a little train that putters along Casco Bay at the foot of the Eastern Promenade. Views of the islands are great; the ride is slow and yawn-inducing, but young kids enjoy it.

58 Fore St. ✆ **207/828-0814.** www.mngrr.org. Museum admission $2 adults, $1 seniors and children 3–12; train fare (includes museum admission) $10 adults, $9 seniors, $6 children 3–12, free for children 2 and under. Memorial Day to Columbus Day daily 10am–4pm (trains run on the hour); rest of the year Mon–Fri 10am–4pm. From I-295, take Franklin Arterial exit to Fore St.; turn left and continue to museum on right.

Portland Head Light & Museum ★★★ A short drive from downtown Portland, this 1794 lighthouse has been called one of the most picturesque in the nation. It's certainly one of the most-photographed; you'll possibly recognize it from advertisements, calendars, postcards, or posters. It was the first constructed in the new United States, commissioned by President George Washington; it began warning ships in 1791 and was manned by a keeper until 1989, when it was automated and the graceful keeper's house converted into a small museum focusing on the history of navigation. The lighthouse itself is still active, thus it's closed to the public. But you can stop by the museum, browse for lighthouse-themed gifts in a gift shop, and wander the lawns, cliffs, and other grounds of adjacent **Fort Williams Park,** which is a great place for a picnic, tossing around a Frisbee, strumming a guitar, or peering out to sea through the looking-glasses on the cliff-top.

1000 Shore Rd. (in Ft. Williams Park), Cape Elizabeth. ✆ **207/799-2661.** www.portlandheadlight.com. Free admission for grounds; museum $2 adults, $1 children 6–18. Park grounds daily year-round sunrise-sunset (until 8:30pm in summer); museum daily Memorial Day to Columbus Day 10am–4pm, Sat-Sun only mid-Apr to mid-May and mid-Oct to late Dec. From Portland, follow State St. across bridge to South Portland; bear left on Broadway. At 3rd light, turn right on Cottage Rd. (Rte. 77), which becomes Shore Rd.; follow several more miles to park on left.

Portland Museum of Art ★★★   Portland's top-rate art museum announces itself boldly with a high, thin, brick front wall, and indeed it was designed by the famous firm of I.M. Pei & Partners in 1983. Its holdings are superb, with art drawn from its own fine collections plus a parade of touring exhibits. (Summer exhibits are usually targeted at a broader audience and include the work of internationally famous painters.) The holdings are particularly strong in terms of American artists with Maine connections, such as Winslow Homer, Andrew Wyeth, and Edward Hopper; it also hosts fine displays of Early American furniture and crafts. The museum also shares the Joan Whitney Payson Collection with Colby College (the college borrows it for one semester every 2 years), which include wonderful work by Renoir, Degas, and Picasso, among other titans. Special exhibitions have brought in the landscape paintings of Frederic Church, art by Native American high-school students from northern Maine, and a mysterious *Mona Lisa* that may have been a preparatory study for the famous work; who knows? Guided tours are given once daily at 2pm.

7 Congress Sq. (corner of Congress and High sts.). ℂ **207/775-6148.** www.portlandmuseum.org. Admission $10 adults, $8 seniors, $4 students 6–17; free admission Fri 5–9pm. Tues–Sun 10am–5pm (Fri to 9pm); Memorial Day to mid-Oct also Mon 10am–5pm.

Victoria Mansion ★★★ 📖   Widely regarded as one of the most elaborate Victorian brownstone homes ever built in the U.S., this mansion (also known as the Morse-Libby House, but rarely called that) is oft-mentioned in books on American architecture. It's a remarkable piece of high Victoriana. Built between 1858 and 1863 for a Maine businessman who had made his fortune in New Orleans, the towering, slightly foreboding home is a prime example of Italianate style. Inside, craftsmen and artisans went to town with murals and other details; the decor is somber, yet the home offers an engaging look into a bygone era. It's a must for architecture buffs—or just snap a photo of the exterior from the sidewalk, if you're pressed for time or don't want to buy the pricey admission ticket. The weeks leading up to Christmas bring special events and extra tours.

109 Danforth St. ℂ **207/772-4841.** www.victoriamansion.org. Admission $15 adults, $14 seniors, $5 children 6–17, $35 family, free for children 5 and under. May–Oct Mon–Sat 10am–4pm, Sun 1–5pm; late Nov to Dec daily 11am–5pm. Tours (45 min.) twice per hour. Closed Jan–Apr and Nov until day after Thanksgiving. From the Old Port, head west on Fore St., and veer right on Danforth St. at light (beside Yosaku sushi restaurant); proceed 3 blocks to the mansion on right, at corner of Park St.

Wadsworth-Longfellow House & Center for Maine History ★★   The Maine Historical Society's self-described "history campus" includes three buildings lined up along busy Congress Street in downtown Portland. Most local residents never give these buildings a second thought, but they're important. The austere brick Wadsworth-Longfellow House dates from 1785 and was built by Gen. Peleg Wadsworth, father of the noted poet Henry Wadsworth. It's furnished in an early-19th-century style, with many samples of Longfellow family furniture on display. Adjacent to the home is the Maine History Gallery, in a garish postmodern building (formerly a bank). Changing exhibits here explore the rich texture of Maine history. And just behind the Longfellow house is the library of the Maine Historical Society, a popular destination for amateur genealogists and Portland buffs. You have to be a history nerd to appreciate this place, but it's gold if you are.

Take Me Out to the Sea Dogs

The Portland Sea Dogs are a minor league Double-A team affiliated with the Boston Red Sox (a perfect marriage in baseball-crazy northern New England). They play through summer at Hadlock Field (271 Park Ave.; (C) 800/936-3647 or 207/879-9500; www.seadogs.com), a small stadium near downtown that still retains an old-time feel despite aluminum benches and other updating. Activities are geared toward families, with lots of entertainment between innings and a selection of food that's a couple of notches above basic hot dogs and hamburgers. You might even catch future pro stars. The season runs from April to Labor Day.

489 Congress St. (C) **207/774-1822.** www.mainehistory.org. Admission $8 adults, $7 seniors and students, $3 children 5-17. Wadsworth-Longfellow House May-Oct and Dec Mon-Sat 10:30am-4pm and Sun noon-4pm; tours on the hour. Closed Jan-Apr and Nov. History museum Mon-Sat 10am-5pm; Sun noon-5pm. Research library normally Tues-Sat 10am-4pm but hours vary.

Where to Stay

If you're looking for something central, the **Hilton Garden Inn** at 65 Commercial St. ((C) **207/780-0780;** www.hiltongardeninn.hilton.com) is right across from the city's ferry dock. It's convenient to all the Old Port's restaurants, bakeries, and pubs—not to mention the islands of Casco Bay. You'll pay for the privilege of being in the heart of the waterfront, though: Double rooms mostly run from about $189 up to $369 per night.

The **Holiday Inn by the Bay,** 88 Spring St. ((C) **800/345-5050** or 207/775-2311; www.innbythebay.com), offers great views of the harbor from about half the rooms, along with the usual chain-hotel creature comforts. Peak-season rates are approximately $180 for a double. Budget travelers seeking chain hotels typically head toward the area around the Maine Mall in South Portland, about 8 miles south of the attractions of downtown.

Inn at Park Spring ★ This small, tasteful B&B is located on a busy downtown street in a historic brick home that dates back to 1835. It's well located for exploring the city on foot, and well kept by friendly owners John and Nancy Gonsalves. Guests can linger or watch TV in the front parlor, or chat at the dining table in the adjacent room (communal breakfasts here are a highlight—unless you're shy). The accommodations are all corner rooms, and most are bright and sunny. Especially nice is the Spring Room, with its queen sleigh bed, hardwood flooring, and wonderful views of the historic row houses along Park Street; and crimson-hued Gables, on the third (top) floor, which gets plenty of afternoon light and is furnished with a king bed, big sitting room, and nice bathroom. The Portland Museum of Art is only 2 blocks away, the Old Port about 10 minutes away, and great restaurants are within an easy walk.

135 Spring St., Portland, ME 04101. (C) **800/437-8511** or 207/774-1059. www.innatparkspring.com. 6 units. Mid-Apr to Oct and holidays $129-$205 double; Nov to mid-Apr $99-$165 double. 2-night minimum stay Sat-Sun. Rates include full breakfast. AE, MC, V. No children 9 and under. *In room:* A/C, hair dryer, Wi-Fi (free).

Pomegranate Inn ★★ Housed in a dove-gray, 1884 Italianate home in Portland's lovely West End, this winning B&B is decorated with whimsy and elegance.

Look for bold wall paintings by a local artist and eclectic antique furniture collected and tastefully arranged throughout. Each of the eight rooms is distinct, with painted floors and faux-marble woodwork. Most have gas fireplaces; the best room might be the one in the carriage house, which comes with its own private terrace (sliding doors lead out to a little garden) and a fireplace. Sit-down breakfasts are served in a cheery dining room.

49 Neal St., Portland, ME 04102. (C) **800/356-0408** or 207/772-1006. Fax 207/773-4426. www. pomegranateinn.com. 8 units. Memorial Day to Oct $185–$295 double; rest of the year $140–$225 double. Rates include full breakfast. 2-night minimum stay summer weekends and holidays. AE, DISC, MC, V. On-street parking. Take Spring St. to Neal St. and turn right. Children 16 and over welcome. *In room:* A/C, TV, Wi-Fi (free).

Portland Harbor Hotel ★★ Adjacent to Portland's bar scene on the corner of Fore and Union streets, this semicircular, town-house-like structure was designed to fit in with the much older brick facades that prevail in the surrounding Old Port. Yet it's quite modern inside, with many amenities and a boutique feel. An interior courtyard throws off European ambience; big, exquisite rooms are furnished with comfy queen- and king-size beds and spacious work desks. Even standard rooms are outfitted with armoires, duvets, two-line phones, large televisions, and deep bathtubs in granite-faced bathrooms, while deluxe rooms and suites add Jacuzzis and sitting areas. The house restaurant, **Eve's at the Garden,** serves gourmet meals, and the front desk rents bicycles and helmets to aid your sightseeing.

468 Fore St., Portland, ME 04101. (C) **888/798-9090** or 207/775-9090. Fax 207/775-9990. www.portland harborhotel.com. 100 units. Mid-May to mid-Oct $229–$249 double, $329 suite; off season $159–$179 double, $259 suite. AE, DC, DISC, MC, V. Valet parking in garage $16 per day. **Amenities:** Dining room; bar; babysitting; bikes; concierge; exercise room; room service. *In room:* A/C, TV, hair dryer, Wi-Fi (free).

Portland Regency Hotel ★★ Centrally located on a cobblestone courtyard right in the middle of the Old Port, the Regency boasts one of the city's premier hotel locations. And it's got more than location—this is also one of the most architecturally striking luxury hotels in southern Maine. Housed in an 1895 brick armory, the hotel is thoroughly modern and offers attractive rooms, appointed and furnished with all the expected amenities. You can choose from several types of rooms and suites, each fitted to the place's unique architecture; for a splurge, ask about a luxurious corner room with a handsome (nonworking) fireplace, sitting area, city views out the big windows, and a Jacuzzi. The small health club is among the best in town (it includes a sauna and hot tub), and the basement level conceals both a restaurant (Twenty Milk Street) and the small **Armory Lounge** ★, a great, quiet place to sip a drink.

20 Milk St., Portland, ME 04101. (C) **800/727-3436** or 207/774-4200. Fax 207/775-2150. www.theregency. com. 95 units. Early July to late Oct $249–$269 double, $289–$389 suite; off season $159–$219 double, $209–$329 suite. AE, DISC, MC, V. Valet parking $12 per day. **Amenities:** Restaurant; bar; babysitting; health club; Jacuzzi; limited room service; sauna; spa. *In room:* A/C, TV, minibar, Wi-Fi (free).

Where to Dine
EXPENSIVE

Back Bay Grill ★★ NEW AMERICAN Back Bay Grill has long been one of Portland's best restaurants, with an upscale, contemporary ambience; the only trouble is finding it (it's near the city's main post office, far from most other sights). The menu, revamped seasonally, emphasizes local produce and meats as much as possible. Diners might start with some kicky Maine crab cakes, a saffrony mussel chowder, beef tartare with truffle flavors, foie gras served with crispy polenta, house-cured gravlax salmon, or local mussels steamed in white wine. Among the main courses, look for such dishes as filet mignon with gnocchi, breast of duck, salmon with couscous, Casco Bay cod in a tomato-lemongrass broth, two versions of lamb, or agnolotti stuffed with goat's-milk ricotta and spinach. Finish with crème brûlée, caramel ice cream with bourbon sauce, vanilla panna cotta, or a walnut-and-lemon crepe with mead-and-caramel sauce.

65 Portland St. ☏ **207/772-8833.** www.backbaygrill.com. Reservations recommended. Main courses $18–$35. AE, DC, DISC, MC, V. Mon–Thurs 5:30–9:30pm; Fri–Sat 5:30–10pm. From Congress St., take High St. downhill to Park Ave. and turn right (becomes Portland St.); continue 4 blocks to Parris St.

Fore Street ★★ CONTEMPORARY GRILL Fore Street has emerged as one of northern New England's most celebrated restaurants. Chef Sam Hayward gets pro-filed in magazines like *Saveur* and *House Beautiful,* his restaurant was often in *Gourmet*'s 100 Best, and so forth. Hayward's secret is simplicity: Local and organic ingredients are used where possible, and the kitchen avoids fussy presentations. The dining space centers on a busy open kitchen where a team of chefs constantly stoke the wood-fired brick oven and grill, which feature prominently in the culinary phi-losophy here. The menu changes nightly, but entrees might run to spit-roasted pork loin, grilled duckling, grilled marinated hanger steak, or a piece of pan-seared blue-fish; the wood-roasted mussels are also a big hit. Finish with a dessert such as chocolate soufflé, hand-dipped chocolates, or gelati—these are often accented in summer by seasonal Maine berries or fruits. Though it can be difficult to snag a reservation here on summer weekends, managements always sets aside a few tables every night for walk-ins. Get there early and grab one.

288 Fore St. ☏ **207/775-2717.** www.forestreet.biz. Reservations recommended. Main courses $13–$29. AE, MC, V. Sun–Thurs 5:30–10pm (May–Oct Sun to 9:30pm); Fri–Sat 5:30–10:30pm.

Hugo's ★★★ NEW AMERICAN A decade ago, this place was fading fast, but Chef Rob Evans and partner Nancy Pugh bought the place and changed all that. Now it's arguably the most exciting place to eat in northern New England. Trained in star kitchens (French Laundry, the Inn at Little Washington), Evans brought a philosophy of using local ingredients and crafting unusual, exciting menus. (He was named "best chef in the Northeast" by the James Beard Foundation in 2009.) Evans offers a small-plate style of service of midsized, constantly changing portions of everything from sweetbreads with peanut and cilantro flavors to goat-cheese ravioli with molé sauce; raw Maine sea urchin over sticky rice; pan-fried Arctic Char; local cod baked in parchment paper; a combo plate of rib-eye, short ribs, potato puree, and onions; or crisped pork belly with fried pig's tail and a jalapeño marmalade. A nightly "blind" tasting menu (you don't find out what you ate until the end) expands the journey to six courses, and chef's menus (by advance reservation only) run to even more flights. Dessert could be a very upscale take on peanut-butter cups, ice-cream floats, or an apple turnover jacked up with dates, bacon, pralines, and home-made butter ice cream. A good tapas menu (charcuterie, cheese plates) is served at the bar, and the same partners also run a Belgian fries-and-shakes shop, Duckfat, down the block.

88 Middle St. ☏ **207/774-8538.** www.hugos.net. Reservations strongly recommended. Plates $10–$25, tasting menus $75 and up. AE, MC, V. Tues–Thurs 5:30–9pm; Fri–Sat 5:30–9:30pm.

Street & Co. ★★ SEAFOOD   Dana Street's intimate brick-walled bistro specializes in seafood, and it's possibly the city's best place to eat fish. You pass the open
kitchen as you're seated in one of the two halves of a quirky dining room, then watch
the talented chefs perform their magic in the tiny space. The fish is as fresh as can
be (the docks are a block away), and they do lobster in interesting configurations
(such as grilled and served over linguine in a buttery garlic sauce). Other fine choices
include tuna, mussels, or the grilled catch of the day. Reservations are definitely
recommended, although some tables are set aside for walk-ins; it can't hurt to check
if you're strolling down Wharf Street and get hungry (try toward opening, rather than
toward the middle of the service). During summer, outdoor seating is available at a
few choice alfresco tables on a cobblestone alley: plain but atmospheric.

33 Wharf St. ② 207/775-0887. www.streetandcompany.net. Reservations recommended. Main
courses $14–$24. AE, MC, V. Mon–Thurs 5:30–9:30pm; Fri–Sat 5:30–10pm. Lounge opens 30 min. earlier.

MODERATE

Beale Street BBQ ★★ 🏮 BARBECUE   Beale Street BBQ owner Mark Quigg
once operated a takeout grill on Rte. 1 near Freeport, but author Stephen King got
wind of his cooking; soon Quigg was catering movie shoots and opening a restaurant.
Of all the barbecue joints in Maine, this is probably my favorite. It's got an appealing
roadhouse atmosphere, friendly staff, and great smoked meats. Check the board for
daily specials, which usually include a fish entree as well as Creole and Cajun offerings. But I nearly always stick to the barbecue sampler (from the menu: "AKA All
You Really Need to Know About BBQ"): You get your choice of pulled pork, chicken,
or beef brisket; sweet, crunchy corn bread; a half slab of ribs; a quarter chicken;
spicy smoked links; and a mound of barbecued beans and coleslaw. Two people can
comfortably split it, and it's just $24.

725 Broadway, S. Portland. ② 207/767-0130. www.mainebbq.com. Reservations not accepted. Main
courses $9–$18. MC, V. Daily 11:30am–10pm. From Portland waterfront, cross Casco Bay Bridge (Rte. 77)
and turn right onto Broadway; continue approx. ⅓ mile to restaurant.

Benkay ★ 🍤 SUSHI   Among Portland's sushi restaurants, Benkay is hippest,
usually teeming with a lively local crowd lured by the affordable menus. Chef Seiji
Ando trained in Osaka and Kyoto; his sashimi, and maki rolls deliver a lot for the
price, and there's a wide range of choices and combinations. Standard Japanese bar-
food items such as tempura (deep-fried vegetables), *gyoza* (dumplings), teriyaki,
katsu (fried chicken or pork cutlets), and udon (thick noodles) are also served. It
stays open pretty late, too—until midnight on Friday and Saturday, which is handy
in early-closing Portland. For dessert, consider the green tea ice cream: deliciously
bitter . . . and good for you. Sort of.

2 India St. (at Commercial). ② 207/773-5555. www.sushiman.com. Reservations not accepted. Main
courses $7.95–$17. AE, MC, V. Mon–Thurs 11:30am–2pm and 5–9:30pm; Fri 11:30am–2pm and 5pm–midnight; Sat 5pm–midnight; Sun 5–9pm.

Flatbread Company ★★ 😊 PIZZA   This upscale pizzeria—an offshoot of the
original Flatbread Company in Vermont, with a serious hippie tinge—might have the
best waterfront location in town. It sits on a slip overlooking the Casco Bay Lines
terminal, so you can watch fishermen and ferries while you eat. The inside brings to
mind a Phish concert, with quirky decor and bearded staffers stoking wood-fired
ovens, slicing nitrate-free pepperoni and organic vegetables, and the like. The laid-back,

wood-smoky, family-fun atmosphere makes the place fun to enter; but the pizza is excellent and will keep you coming back. Organic salads are also available.

72 Commercial St. (C) **207/772-8777.** www.flatbreadcompany.com. Reservations accepted for large parties only. Most pizzas $12–$15. AE, MC, V. Daily 11:30am–10pm.

The Grill Room & Bar ★★ AMERICAN   It replaced the popular Natasha's in this same space, but the Grill Room—the place with the bull for a sign—didn't miss a stride: good food, served unpretentiously. Chef Harding Lee Smith, a Portland native, left Back Bay Grill to open this mecca to meat. Most items are cooked out on the open kitchen's wood-fired grills, but there's more than just cow here: yummy seared-tuna sandwiches on ciabatta and thin-crust pizzas, for example. Of course, you can always get a slab of steak (porterhouse, rib-eye, sirloin; the works) or a piece of grilled fish or chicken, and you're encouraged to do so. Choose from a card of tasty sauces ranging in description from "zippy" to "brandy cream," and you're good to go. The outdoor tables in Tommy's Park are ideal in summer, but my favorite feature of this place is its bar area with personable barkeeps, good beers on tap, and Red Sox on the tube. This is fast becoming a favorite local bite.

84 Exchange St. (C) **207/774-2333.** www.thefrontroomrestaurant.com. Appetizers and pizzas $7–$12, main courses $13–$27. AE, DISC, MC, V. Daily 11am–2:30pm and 5–10pm (Sun to 9pm).

Rí-Rá ★ PUB FARE   This Old Port eatery is styled after an Irish pub, though it's somewhat fancier than *real* Irish pubs. (Patriots and Red Sox are on the TV instead of soccer—sorry, "footie.") They've got the decor right, at least: The doors were imported from a pub in Kilkenny, and the back bar and counter are from other public drinking houses in County Louth. Upstairs beyond the pub is a dining room with a view of the docks; look for smoked turkey wraps, fish and chips, meatloaf, shepherd's pie, and Guinness bread pudding, plus a few more upscale dishes such as crab-filled salmon, Derrybeg pork (which is glazed with apricot, mustard, and cider), and *broxty*, a scallion-potato pancake topped with parsley sauce and meat.

72 Commercial St. (C) **207/761-4446.** www.rira.com. Main courses $9–$20. AE, MC, V. Mon–Sat 11:30am–10pm; Sun 11am–10pm.

INEXPENSIVE

Shima ★ 🍴 FRENCH/JAPANESE/SUSHI   Just around the corner from the Regency hotel, Shima (Japanese for "island," and also the chef's last name) opened in the fall of 2009 and is run by a Japanese-Hawaiian sushi chef who also trained in France. You can tell this guy comes from these diverse backgrounds: The huge, creative menu features the expected sushi rolls, pork belly, and *omakase* (chef's choice) service that any self-respecting sushi joint or *izakaya* (bar) in Tokyo would. But it also veers off on interesting Hawaiian tangents (pineapples, bigeye), and employs creamy French sauces in more than a few spots. (Don't be surprised if a duck entree pops up, either.) The biggest surprise here is the price point: Nothing's outright expensive, and many items feel like a steal. Yet the quality is very good for a just-opened place. Hip music plays in the background, and service is on two levels—upstairs is my preference, though it's sometimes harder to snag a table there than on street level. Good debut.

339 Fore St. (C) **207/773-8389.** Main courses $8–$20. DISC, MC, V. Mon–Fri 11:30am–3pm and 5:30–10pm, Sat noon–11pm.

Silly's ★ 🎒 ☺ INTERNATIONAL   Silly's has long been the favored cheap-eats joint of hip Portlanders. Situated on a busy commercial street near the Eastern Promenade, the interior is informal, bright, and funky, with mismatched 1950s dinettes and a hodgepodge back patio beneath trees. There's also a weird fascination with Einstein here, and, like Einstein, the menu is creative. The place is noted for its roll-ups ("Abdullahs"), a series of tasty fillings piled into soft tortillas; try one with shish kabob and feta, or a "Diesel," made with pulled pork and coleslaw. Newer menu additions include a slop "bucket," which has a messy, layered-burrito feel. The fries are hand-cut, the burgers big and juicy, and there's beer on tap. Don't overlook the dessert menu of cookies, pies, ice creams, cakes, and big milkshakes—Silly's whips its shakes up with peanut butter, tahini, bananas, malt, or almost anything else you could imagine, plus a few things (cranberry sauce? marshmallow crispies? check) you couldn't have.

40 Washington Ave. ✆ **207/772-0360.** www.sillys.com. Most items $5–$13; pizzas to $18. MC, V. Tues–Sun 11am–9pm.

MIDCOAST MAINE

Bath: 33 miles NE of Portland; Boothbay Harbor: 23 miles E of Bath; 41 miles SW of Rockland

Veteran Maine travelers contend that the rocky, central stretch of the coast, long known as the "Midcoast," is both its most lovely *and* the part that's fastest losing its native charm—it's becoming too commercial, they say, too developed, too tacky, too fancy. These grousers have a point, especially along Rte. 1.

But get off the main roads and you'll swiftly find another Maine, full with some of the most pastoral, picturesque meadows, mountains, peninsulas, and harbors in the entire state.

The coast is best reached via Rte. 1, which you catch in **Brunswick** by taking exit 28 off I-295. Traveling north, highlights of this coastal route include the shipbuilding town of **Bath,** pretty little **Wiscasset,** and the Boothbay region on the southern end of the Midcoast; the lovely Pemaquid peninsula; lost-in-time **Monhegan Island;** and finally, the power trio of **Camden, Rockland,** and **Rockport** at the northern end of the Midcoast (which are covered in the next section, "Penobscot Bay").

Beyond local tourist huts and chambers of commerce, the best source of information for the Midcoast region in general is found at the **Maine State Information Center** (✆ **207/846-0833**), just off exit 17 of I-295 in Yarmouth, which isn't yet in the Midcoast—but you'll almost certainly pass through here to get there, so stock up. This state-run center is crammed with glossy brochures, and it's staffed with a helpful crew who can provide information about the entire state but is particularly well informed about the middle reaches of coast. It's open daily, year-round; and even when it's closed, the attached restroom facilities are open.

Freeport ★

If **Freeport** were a mall, L.L.Bean would be the anchor store. It's the business that launched this town to prominence, elevating its status from just another Maine fishing village near the interstate to one of the state's major tourist draws for the outlet centers that sprang up here in Bean's wake.

Freeport still has the look of a classic Maine village today, but it's a village that's been largely taken over by those outlet shops; most of the old historic homes and stores here have been converted into upscale stores purveying name-brand clothing and housewares at cut-rate prices. Banana Republic occupies an exceedingly handsome brick Federal-style home; a Carnegie library became an Abercrombie & Fitch, pumping club music (oh, the inhumanity); and even the McDonald's is housed in a tasteful, understated Victorian farmhouse, for crying out loud—you really have to look to find the arches.

Still, strict planning guidelines have managed to preserve most of the town's local charm, at least in the downtown section. (Huge parking lots are hidden from view off the main drag.) As a result, Freeport is one of the more aesthetically pleasing places to shop in New England—though even with these large lots, parking can be scarce during the peak season.

Expect crowds. Seeking out the real Maine? Ask directions off the main road to **South Freeport,** which consists of a boat dock, a general store, and a good lobster shack (see "Where to Dine," p. 627) on a point of land.

Seeking a bargain? You've come to the right place.

ESSENTIALS

GETTING THERE   Freeport is on Rte. 1, about 16 miles north of Portland. The downtown is reached by taking I-295 north to either exit 20 or 22, then following signs.

VISITOR INFORMATION   The **Freeport Merchants Association** (✆ **207/ 865-1212** or 800/865-1994 [automated]; www.freeportusa.com) at 23 Depot St. is the closest thing to a local tourist office here. The association publishes a map and directory of businesses, restaurants, and overnight accommodations that's widely available around town.

SHOPPING

Freeport crams more than 140 retail shops between exit 20 of I-295 (at the far lower end of Main St.) and Mallet Road, the access road to exit 22 at the northern end of the main street. The bulk of these are "factory" or "outlet" stores, offering cut-rate prices on samples, seconds, and styles that never quite caught on. If you don't want to miss a single shop, get off at exit 17 and drive north on Rte. 1.

The bargains can vary from extraordinary to "huh?" Plan on wearing out some shoe leather and taking at least a half-day if you're really intent on finding the best deals. The rotation of national chains here currently includes Abercrombie & Fitch, Banana Republic, Gap, Calvin Klein, Patagonia, North Face, Nike, Chaudier, Mikasa, Nine West, Timberland, and Maidenform, among many others.

Stores in Freeport are typically open daily 9am to 9pm during the busy summer and close much earlier (5 or 6pm) in other seasons; between Thanksgiving and Christmas, they remain open late once more.

Cuddledown   Cuddledown started producing down comforters in 1973 and now makes a whole line of products much appreciated in northern climes and beyond. Some of the down pillows are made right in the outlet shop, which also carries a variety of European goose-down comforters in all sizes and weights. Look for linens, blankets, moccasins, and home furnishings, too. 475 Rte. 1 (btw. exits 17 and 20). ✆ **888/235-3696.** www.cuddledown.com.

Freeport Knife Co. ★   This store sports a wide selection of knives for kitchen and camp alike, including blades from Germany, Switzerland, and Japan. Look for their custom line, or just bring in your dull blade for a sharpening. They also sell

Midcoast Maine

Key locations shown on map: South China, Liberty, Threemile Pd., Sheepscot Pd., Maranacook L., Manchester, Augusta, Winthrop, Hallowell, Androscoggin L., Turner, Cobbosseecontee L., Gardiner, Randolph, Union, Jefferson, Greene, Litchfield, Damariscotta L., Waldoboro, Thomaston, Lewiston, Auburn, Richmond, Nobleboro, Cushing, St. George, Lisbon Falls, Wiscasset, Newcastle, Damariscotta, Friendship, Topsham, Woolwich, Edgecomb, Bristol, Port Clyde, Brunswick, Bowdoin College, Bath, Ft. William Henry, New Harbor, Burnt I., Allen I., Freeport, Boothbay Harbor, Phippsburg, Southport, Christmas Cove, Pemaquid Point, Yarmouth, Cumberland, South Harpswell, Orrs Island, Sebasco, Newagen, Damariscove I., Monhegan I., Monhegan, Bailey Island, Small Point, Portland, South Portland, Cape Elizabeth, ATLANTIC OCEAN

replacement parts and do repairs on all brands of knives. 181 Lower Main St. ☎ **207/865-0779.** www.freeportknife.com.

L.L.Bean ★★★ ☺   Monster outdoor retailer L.L.Bean traces its roots from the day Leon Leonwood Bean decided that what the world really needed was a good weatherproof hunting shoe. He joined a watertight gum shoe to a laced leather upper; hunters liked it; the store grew; an empire was born. Today L.L.Bean sells millions of dollars' worth of clothing and outdoor goods nationwide through its well-respected catalogs, and it continues to draw hundreds of thousands of customers through its doors to a headquarters building and several offshoots around town. The modern, multilevel main store is about the size of a regional mall, but it's very taste-fully done with its own indoor trout pond and lots of natural wood. Selections include Bean's own trademark clothing, along with home furnishings, books, shoes, and plenty of outdoor gear for camping, fishing, and hunting (a particularly good section). The staff is incredibly knowledgeable—Bean's encourages staff to take the gear home and try it out so as to better serve customers. 95 Main St. (at Bow St.). ☎ **877/755-2326.** www.llbean.com.

Mangy Moose A souvenir shop with a twist: Virtually everything in this place is moose-related. Really. There are moose wineglasses, moose trivets, moose cookie cutters, and (of course) moose T-shirts. Somehow this merchandise is a notch above what you'll find in most other souvenir shops around the state. 112 Main St. ✆ **800/606-6517** or 207/865-6414. www.themangymoose.com.

Thos. Moser Cabinetmakers ★★ Classic furniture reinterpreted in lustrous wood and leather is the focus at this shop, which—thanks to a steady parade of ads in the *New Yorker* and a Madison Avenue branch—has become nearly as representative of Maine as L.L.Bean. Shaker, mission, and modern styles are wonderfully reinvented by Tom Moser and his designers and woodworkers, who produce heirloom-quality signed pieces. Nationwide delivery is easy to arrange. There's a good selection of knotted rugs made by an independent artisan, and a good gallery of rotating Maine-made art on-site. Finally, don't miss the "Special Opportunity Room" and its samples, prototypes, and refurbished pieces; you can save big bucks here. 149 Main St. ✆ **800/708-9041** or 207/865-4519. www.thomasmoser.com.

WHERE TO STAY

Reservations are strongly recommended in Freeport during peak summer season; the opening of a clutch of mid-range chain hotels and motels just south of town on Rte. 1 (around the interstate exit, and then for the next few miles south of it) has helped alleviate the summer crush somewhat. Head there if you're stuck for a room.

Harraseeket Inn ★★ The Harraseeket is a large, modern hotel a short walk north of L.L.Bean on Freeport's main street. Despite its size, a traveler could drive right past and not even notice it—which a good thing. A 19th-century home is the soul of the hotel, though most rooms are in annexes added 1989 and 1997. Guests can relax in the dining room, read the paper in a common room while the baby-grand player piano plays, or sip a cocktail in the homey Broad Arrow Tavern (with its wood-fired oven and grill, it serves lunch and dinner). Guest rooms are large and tastefully furnished, with quarter-canopy beds and a mix of contemporary and antique furnishings; some have gas or wood-burning fireplaces, more than half now have whirlpools, and some are even done up with wet bars and refrigerators. The big second-floor Thomas Moser Room is a nod to the local furniture craftsman, with a pencil-post bed, writing desk, dresser, and flatscreen TV in the bedroom, plus a sitting room with a modern sofa, lounge chair, coffee table, Bose stereo, and stone fireplace. And a soaking tub. This inn is especially pet-friendly, with doggy beds and treats for four-footed guests.

162 Main St., Freeport, ME 04032. ✆ **800/342-6423** or 207/865-9377. Fax 207/865-1684. www.harraseeket inn.com. 84 units. $120–$295 double; $245–$315 suite. All rates include full breakfast and afternoon tea. MAP rates available. AE, DC, DISC, MC, V. Take exit 22 off I-295 and turn left; continue to Main St. Pets accepted ($25 per pet per night). **Amenities:** 2 restaurants; bar; concierge; indoor pool; room service. *In room:* A/C, TV, fridge (some units), hair dryer (some units), Wi-Fi (free).

Maine Idyll Motor Court ★ 🍃 Talk about a throwback to a happier time: This motel, 2 short miles north of Freeport's busy Main Street, doesn't take credit cards—but they *will* take your personal check. This 1930s "motor court" is a Maine classic, a cluster of 20 cottages scattered around a grove of oak and beech trees. It could have faded into oblivion, yet it hasn't: The place is still good enough for a simple night's sleep. Most cottages come with a tiny porch, wood-burning fireplace (birch logs are provided), television, modest kitchen facilities (no ovens), and dated furniture. These cabins aren't especially large, but they're comfortable enough and kept clean; some have showers, while others have bathtubs, and a good number of the cottages have two bedrooms (one even has three bedrooms). Ask for a cottage with air-conditioning if that's important—a few units have it. Kids like the swing set and play area, dog-walkers head for nature trails accessible from the property, while picnickers fire up grill sets. The only interruption is the occasional drone of traffic: I-295 is just through the trees to one side, and Rte. 1 is on the other side. Get past that traffic sandwich, though, and this place is a good value. They even have free Wi-Fi access.

1411 Rte. 1, Freeport, ME 04032. (✆) 207/865-4201. www.maineidyll.com. 20 units. May–Oct $63–$110 double. Rates include continental breakfast. No credit cards. Closed Nov–Apr. Pets on leashes accepted ($4 per pet per night). *In room:* A/C (some units), TV, kitchenette, Wi-Fi (free), no phone.

WHERE TO DINE

Gritty McDuff's ★ BREWPUB   Spacious, informal, and air-conditioned in summer, Gritty's is an offshoot of Portland's original brewpub. It's a short drive south of Freeport's village center and is best known for a varied selection of house-brewed beers, like the unfiltered Black Fly Stout. The pub offers a wide-ranging bar menu of reliable salads, burgers, steaks, stone-oven pizzas, cheesesteak sandwiches, quesadillas, and pub classics such as shepherd's pie and fish and chips. There's a kids' menu as well.

187 Rte. 1 (Lower Main St.). (✆) 207/865-4321. www.grittys.com. Reservations not accepted. Main courses $10–$17. AE, DISC, MC, V. Daily 11:30am–11pm.

Harraseeket Lunch & Lobster ★ 🏠 LOBSTER   Next to a boatyard on the Harraseeket River, about a 10-minute drive from Freeport's busy shopping district, this lobster pound's picnic tables get crowded on sunny days—although, with its little heated dining room, it's a worthy destination anytime. Point and pick out a lobster, then take in river views from the dock as you wait for your number to be called. Advice? Come in late afternoon to avoid the lunch and dinner hordes—and don't wear your nicest clothes. This is roll-up-your-sleeves eating. You can also order fried fish, burgers, chowder, or ice cream from the window.

36 Main St., South Freeport. (✆) 207/865-4888. www.harraseeketlunchandlobster.com. Lobsters market price (typically $8–$15). No credit cards. Mid-June to Labor Day daily 11am–8:45pm; May to mid-June and early Sept to mid-Oct daily 11am–7:45pm. Closed mid-Oct to Apr. From Freeport, take South St. (off Bow St.) to South Freeport and turn left at stop sign.

Jameson Tavern ★ AMERICAN   In a farmhouse right in the shadow of L.L.Bean (on the north side), Jameson Tavern touts itself as the birthplace of Maine. And it really is: In 1820, papers were signed here legally separating Maine from Massachusetts. Mainers still appreciate that pen stroke today. The historic Tap Room is to the left, a compact spot of beer and pubby food. The rest of the house contains the main dining room, decorated in a more formal, country-Colonial style. Meals here are hearty: filet mignon wrapped in bacon, poached salmon, baked haddock, fresh pastas, and seafood salads. What's new in this old place? A nice porch, open about half of the year (not in winter, obviously) for dining semi-alfresco.

115 Main St. (✆) 207/865-4196. www.jamesontavern.com. Reservations recommended. Main courses $7–$18 in taproom and dining room at lunch, $15–$26 in dining room at dinner. AE, DC, DISC, MC, V. Taproom daily 11am–11pm. Dining room Sun–Thurs 11:30am–9pm; Fri–Sat 11:30am–10pm.

Pemaquid Peninsula ★★

Pemaquid Peninsula is an irregular, rocky wedge driven deep into the Gulf of Maine. Far less commercial than Boothbay Peninsula across the Damariscotta River, it's much more suited to relaxed exploration and nature appreciation than its cousin. Rugged and rocky **Pemaquid Point,** at the extreme southern tip of the peninsula, is one of the most dramatic destinations in Maine when the ocean surf pounds the shore.

ESSENTIALS

GETTING THERE The peninsula and point are accessible from the south and west by taking Rte. 1 to Damariscotta, then turning south down Rte. 130 and driving south; it's about 15 miles to land's end. Coming from the north or northeast, take Rte. 1 through Waldoboro, then turn south down Rte. 32 just south of town and continue about 20 miles to the point.

VISITOR INFORMATION The **Damariscotta Region Chamber of Commerce** (*②* **207/563-8340;** www.damariscottaregion.com) is a good source of local information and maintains a seasonal information booth just off Rte. 1 during the summer months. To get to its office at 15 Courtyard St. in Damariscotta, follow Rte. 27 south, branching off from Rte. 1 just east (across the bridge) of **Wiscasset.**

EXPLORING THE PEMAQUID PENINSULA

The Pemaquid Peninsula invites slow driving and frequent stops. South on Rte. 129 toward Walpole is **Damariscotta,** a sleepy head-of-the-harbor village. On the left is the austerely handsome Walpole Meeting House, dating from 1772. Usually not open to the public, services are held here during the summer, and the public is welcome.

Then head down Rte. 129 to picturesque **Christmas Cove,** so named because Capt. John Smith (of Pocahontas fame) anchored here on Christmas Day in 1614. While wandering about, look for the rustic **Coveside Bar and Restaurant** (*②* **207/644-8282;** www.covesiderestaurant.com), a popular marina with a pennant-bedecked lounge and basic dining room.

About 5 miles north of South Bristol, turn right on Pemaquid Road, which will take you to Rte. 130. Continue south on Rte. 130 to the village of New Harbor, then look for signs to **Colonial Pemaquid** (*②* **207/677-2423**). Open daily from Memorial Day to Labor Day, this state historic site has exhibits on the original 1625 settlement here; archaeological digs take place in the summertime. The $2 admission charge (free for children age 11 and under) includes a visit to stout **Fort William Henry,** a 1907 replica of a supposedly impregnable fortress. Nearby **Pemaquid Beach** is good for a (chilly) ocean dip or a picnic with the family.

Pemaquid Point ★★ (*②* **207/677-2494**), owned by the town of **Bristol,** is the place to while away an afternoon. Bring a picnic and a book, and find a spot on the dark, fractured rocks to settle in. The ocean views are superb, and the only distractions are the tenacious seagulls that might take a profound interest in your lunch.

Head back north along Rte. 32 from **New Harbor,** the most scenic way to leave the peninsula, if you plan on continuing northeast along Rte. 1 to places like Camden and Rockland. Along the way, look for the sign pointing to the **Rachel Carson Salt Pond Preserve ★★**, a Nature Conservancy property. The noted naturalist Rachel Carson studied these roadside tide pools extensively while researching her 1956 bestseller *The Edge of the Sea,* and it's still a good spot for budding naturalists and experts alike. At low tide, you can see starfish, green crabs, periwinkles, and other creatures in the tidal pools and among the rocks.

WHERE TO STAY

Bradley Inn ★ This quiet, thrown-back-in-time inn in a remote location is within hiking or biking distance of Pemaquid's point, but there are reasons to lag behind at the inn, as well. Wander the landscaped grounds, settle in for a game of cards in the pub, or sink into a massage in the seaside spa. Rooms are tastefully appointed with four-poster cherry beds (no televisions, though). Third-floor rooms are the best, despite the hike up the stairs, thanks to distant glimpses of John's Bay. A high-ceilinged second-floor suite occupying the entire floor is equipped with a full kitchen and dining room, while the separate Garden Cottage has a lofty ceiling, fieldstone fireplace, and Jacuzzi. Breakfasts are good. The inn is popular for summer weddings, so ask if it's booked with one if you're seeking solitude and quiet.

3063 Bristol Rd. (Rte. 130), New Harbor, ME 04554. (© **800/942-5560** or 207/677-2105. Fax 207/677-3367. www.bradleyinn.com. 17 units. Apr–Dec $155–$250 double; $175–$375 suite and cottage. Rates include full breakfast and afternoon tea. AE, MC, V. Closed Jan–Mar. **Amenities:** Dining room; pub; bikes; room service; spa. *In room:* Kitchen (1 unit), Wi-Fi (free).

Hotel Pemaquid ☕ This 1889 inn isn't directly on the water—but it's just a minute's walk from the Point. The main house has the flavor of an old-time boardinghouse, while outbuildings are (slightly) more modern. The place remains steadfastly old-fashioned: no credit cards accepted whatsoever, narrow hallways, and some bathrooms are shared. And the halls and walls are filled with antiques, including a fine collection of old radios and phonographs. The two- and three-bedroom suites here—one with a sun porch, one with a kitchen—are decent choices for traveling families, and cottages and a carriage house are available by the week.

3098 Bristol Rd. (Rte. 130), New Harbor, ME 04554. (© **207/677-2312.** www.hotelpemaquid.com. 23 units (4 with shared bathrooms). $85–$95 double with private bathroom; $70–$80 double with shared bathroom; $90–$205 suite and bungalow; cottages and carriage house $825–$1,400 weekly. 2-night minimum stay Sat–Sun. No credit cards. Closed mid-Oct to mid-Apr. *In room:* TV (some units), no phone.

WHERE TO DINE

Shaw's Fish and Lobster Wharf ★ LOBSTER   Shaw's attracts hordes of tourists, and it's no trick to figure out why: It's one of the best-situated lobster pounds, with postcard-perfect views of the working harbor. You can stake out a seat on the open deck or the indoor dining room (go for the deck), or order up some appetizers from the raw bar. This is one of the few lobster joints in Maine with a full liquor license.

129 Rte. 32, New Harbor. (© **207/677-2200.** Main courses $10–$25; lobster market price. MC, V. Mid-May to mid-Oct daily 11am–9pm. Closed mid-Oct to mid-May.

PENOBSCOT BAY

Camden: 230 miles NE of Boston; 8 miles N of Rockland; 18 miles S of Belfast

Traveling east along the Maine coast, you might suddenly discover (if you use a compass or GPS) that you're abruptly heading almost due north as you approach **Rockland.** The culprit behind this turn toward Canada is none other than **Penobscot Bay,** a big bite out of the coastline that forces you to make a lengthy northern detour to cross the head of the bay (where the Penobscot River flows in at **Bucksport**).

You'll find some of Maine's most distinctive coastal scenery in this bay's region, which is dotted with broad offshore islands and high hills rising above its mainland shores. Though the mouth of the bay is occupied by two large islands, its waters still churn up when the winds and tides are right.

The bay's western shore gets a heavy stream of tourist traffic, especially along the stretch of Rte. 1 passing through Rockland and lovely **Camden.** Nevertheless, it offers some of the best moments on the Maine coast wedged between the gourmet bakeries and T-shirt shops: moments like sitting on a grassy knoll in Camden watching tall ships in the harbor and waiting for a concert to begin, for instance.

Services for travelers are abundant here, though during peak season you need a small miracle to find a weekend bed at the last minute. This region's quiet beauty is no secret.

Rockland & Environs

On the southwestern edge of Penobscot Bay, **Rockland** has long been proud of its blue-collar waterfront. Built around the fishing and shipbuilding industries, Rockland only dabbled in tourism for centuries, but with the decline of fisheries and the rise of Maine's tourist economy, the balance has begun shifting. Now the city is being swiftly colonized by creative restaurateurs, innkeepers, artisans, and other types slowly transforming the place from a one-trick pony (as in, fish processing) to a genuinely diverse place—and the arts capital of the Midcoast. Pretty amazing.

The city's waterfront has a small park from which windjammers come and go, but even more appealing is Rockland's downtown—basically, one long street lined with historic brick architecture. If you're seeking picturesque harbor towns, head instead for nearby **Camden, Rockport, Port Clyde,** or **Stonington.** Rockland itself is best as a local base for exploring a beautiful coastal region—especially if you like your towns to be a bit rough and salty around the edges—and luckily there are a few luxury B&Bs, inns, and resorts in town in which you can sequester yourself.

ESSENTIALS

GETTING THERE   By car, Rte. 1 passes directly through the center of Rockland. It's about a 3½-hour drive here from Boston via I-95 and Rte. 1, nearly a 7-hour drive from New York City.

Concord Coach (✆ **800/639-3317** or 603/228-3300; www.concordcoachlines. com) runs two to three daily buses from Portland and Boston to Rockland; the ride takes 4½ hours from Boston and costs $57 to $62 round-trip.

From mid-May through late October, the **Maine Eastern Railroad** (✆ **866/637-2457;** www.maineeasternrailroad.com) runs excursion trains between Brunswick and Rockland. Round-trip fares are $40 per adult, $35 for seniors, and $20 for children ages 5 to 15.

VISITOR INFORMATION   The **Penobscot Bay Regional Chamber of Commerce** (✆ **800/562-2529** or 207/596-0376; www.therealmaine.com) staffs an information desk in the city's Harbor Park. It's open daily from Memorial Day through Labor Day, on weekdays the rest of the year.

SPECIAL EVENTS   The **Maine Lobster Festival** (✆ **800/562-2529** or 207/596-0376; www.mainelobsterfestival.com) takes place at Harbor Park during the first weekend in August (plus the preceding Thurs–Fri). Entertainers and vendors, plus all sorts of Maine products, fill the waterfront parking lot for thousands of

Penobscot Bay

festival-goers who enjoy the steamy (sorry) atmosphere. Admission is $8 per day ($2 for children), or $32 for a 4-day pass (but there's a discount for buying online in advance). Food, of course, costs extra—as do reserved tickets for certain musical performances.

MUSEUMS

Farnsworth Art Museum ★★★   Rockland, for all its rough edges, has long and historic ties to the arts. Noted sculptor Louise Nevelson grew up in Rockland; and, in 1935, philanthropist Lucy Farnsworth bequeathed a fortune to establish the Farnsworth Art Museum, which has since become one of the most respected little art museums in New England. Located right downtown, the Farnsworth has a superb collection of paintings and sculptures by renowned American artists with connections to Maine—not only Nevelson, but also three generations of Wyeths (N. C., Andrew, and Jamie), plus Rockwell Kent, Childe Hassam, and Maurice Prendergast. The exhibit halls are modern, spacious, and well designed, and shows are professionally prepared. Equally interesting is the museum-owned **Olson House ★**, a 25-minute drive away, in the village of Cushing; it's perhaps Maine's most well-known home, immortalized in Andrew Wyeth's famous painting *Christina's World.*

16 Museum St., Rockland. © **207/596-6457.** www.farnsworthmuseum.org. Museum $10 adults, $8 seniors and students 18 and older, free for children 17 and under (includes admission to Olson House and Farnsworth Victorian Homestead); Olson House only $4 per person. MC, V. Memorial Day to Columbus Day daily 10am–5pm; rest of year Tues–Sun 10am–5pm.

Owls Head Transportation Museum ★ 📖 You don't need to be a car or plane buff to enjoy this museum—though it helps. Founded in 1974 and located 3 miles south of Rockland on Rte. 73, the museum has an extraordinary collection of cars, motorcycles, bicycles, and planes, nicely displayed in a tidy, hangarlike building at the edge of the Knox County Airport. Look for an early Harley-Davidson motorcycle and a sleek Rolls-Royce Phantom dating from the Roaring Twenties.

117 Museum St., Owls Head. © **207/594-4418.** www.ohtm.org. Admission $8 adults, $7 seniors, $5 children 5–17, $20 families. Apr–Oct daily 10am–5pm; Nov–Mar daily 10am–4pm.

WINDJAMMER TOURS ★★★

During the transition from sail to steam, captains of fancy new steamships belittled old-fashioned sailing ships as "windjammers." The term stuck; through a curious metamorphosis, the name evolved into one of adventure and romance.

Today windjammer vacations combine adventure with limited creature comforts—like lodging at a backcountry cabin floating on the water. Guests typically bunk in small, two-person cabins with cold running water, a porthole to let in fresh air, and not much else. You know it's not going to be a luxe experience when a ship's brochure boasts its cabins are all "at least 6 feet by 8 feet."

Maine is the windjammer cruising capital of the U.S., and the two most active Maine harbors are here in **Rockland** and **Camden.** Cruises last from 3 days to a week, during which these handsome, creaky vessels poke around tidal inlets and small coves that ring the beautiful bay. It's a superb way to explore the coast the way it's historically always been explored—from out on the water, looking in. Rates might run between $120 and $150 per person per night (in other words, $300–$1,000 per person for the entire trip); you'll find that rates are most affordable early and late in the season.

More than a dozen windjammers cruise the bay region during summer (some migrate south to the Caribbean for the winter); the ships vary widely in size and vintage, and accommodations range from cramped and rustic to fairly spacious and well appointed. Schedules can vary, too, if the weather is tricky, although captains have become much more organized in recent years.

A "standard" cruise *usually* features a stop at one or more spruce-studded islands in the bay (perhaps with a lobster bake onshore, prepared by the captain); breakfasts served at tables below decks (or perched cross-legged on the deck); and a real sense of getting away from it all as the ship plows through frothy waters.

Ideally, you'll get a chance to look at a couple of ships in person on the harbor to find one that suits you. If you can't do that, contact the **Maine Windjammer Association ★** (© **800/807-9463;** www.sailmainecoast.com), or check its good website for a listing of a dozen member ships—it's easy to comparison-shop, because prices, specifications, schedules, and even the captains' identities are clearly laid out on the site.

If you're trying to book a *last-minute* windjammer cruise, though, it's better to drop by the tourist office on the Rockland waterfront (see "Visitor Information," above) and inquire about open berths.

WHERE TO STAY

Captain Lindsey House Inn ★   The three-story brick Captain Lindsey House is a couple minutes' walk from the Farnsworth Museum, a nice advantage over farther-out digs. It was built in 1835 by a sea captain and then went through several subsequent incarnations (including one as headquarters of the Rockland Water Co.). Guests enter through a doorway a few steps off Main Street into an opulent first-floor common area done up in rich tones, dark-wood paneling, and a mix of antique and contemporary furniture. Upstairs rooms are decorated in simple country style with old-style wooden beds, coffee tables, rocking chairs, and desks; rooms on the third floor have attractive exposed pine floors and Oriental carpets. All the beds are covered with feather duvets, though only a few rooms have tubs. This isn't the most luxurious inn in town (which is no knock on the place; it's plenty comfy enough), but it does have a good dose of throwback-Maine character and some of the friendliest inn owners on the entire Midcoast.

5 Lindsey St., Rockland, ME 04841. *©* **800/523-2145** or 207/596-7950. Fax 207/596-2758. www.lindsey house.com. 9 units. $136–$211 double. Rates include breakfast. AE, DISC, MC, V. *In room:* A/C, TV, hair dryer, Wi-Fi (free).

LimeRock Inn ★★   This turreted, Queen Anne–style inn sits sleepily on a quiet side street just 2 blocks off Rockland's main drag, yet it's one of the best lodging options in town. Attention has been paid to detail throughout, from the kingly choices of country Victorian furniture to the Egyptian cotton bed sheets. All eight guest rooms are welcoming; among the best are the Island Cottage Room, a bright and airy south-of-France-like chamber wonderfully converted from an old shed (it has a private deck and a Jacuzzi); the Turret Room, with a canopy bed, cherry daybed, and French doors leading into a bathroom with a claw-foot tub and shower; and the elegant Grand Manan Room, with a big four-poster mahogany king bed, fireplace, and double Jacuzzi that puts one in mind of a Southern plantation home.

96 Limerock St., Rockland, ME 04841. *©* **800/546-3762** or 207/594-2257. www.limerockinn.com. 8 units. $119–$239 double. Rates include full breakfast. DISC, MC, V. *In room:* Hair dryer, Wi-Fi (free).

Samoset Resort ★★   Established in 1889 on a scenic hill outside Rockland, the Samoset was meant as a grown-up summer camp for the wealthy. This is not the original building—the original was shuttered, auctioned off, and destroyed by fire decades ago. But the place has bounced back, big-time, as a noted golf resort and luxury property thanks to a number of exciting recent upgrades. Most recently, in 2009, a new heated pool and hot tub were added on the hill's highest point, with sweeping views of the bay, plus a tiki bar serving frozen drinks and light meals; it's a huge hit already. Rooms vary in position and view, but many have balconies or porches with grand Penobscot Bay views; all have rich wood-leather headboards, flatscreen TVs, and marble vanities. Bathrooms are extra-big, some with whirlpool tubs. The golf course remains one of the most scenic in New England, while the quiet local roads are perfect for strolling, and there's even a minilighthouse adjacent to the property. Check out the good health club before heading to dinner—your options include seasonal **Marcel's** (see "Where to Dine," below), serving excellent resort fare, and the Breakwater Grill, serving lighter fare year-round. All in all, a great luxury comeback.

220 Warrenton St., Rockport, ME 04856. *©* **800/341-1650** or 207/594-2511. www.samoset.com. 178 units. Early July to late Aug $259–$289 double, $369 suite, $539–$769 cottage; May to early July and late Aug to Nov $179–$289 double, $259–$289 suite, $539–$769 cottage. MAP rates available. AE, DC,

DISC, MC, V. **Amenities:** 3 restaurants; babysitting; children's programs; concierge; Jacuzzi; 2 pools (1 indoor, 1 heated outdoor); room service; sauna; 4 tennis courts. *In room:* A/C, TV, hair dryer, Wi-Fi (free).

WHERE TO DINE

In addition to the choices listed below, locals often drop by the unpretentious **Brown Bag** (✆ 207/596-6372; www.thebrownbagrockland.com), at 606 Main St. in Rockland, for lunch or breakfast. This place has occupied its simple no-frills storefront for decades; breakfasts are better than lunches, but it's still a decent quick sandwich or picnic option when you're on the road.

Cafe Miranda ★★ 🎁 CONTEMPORARY AMERICAN Even a 2007 fire couldn't stop this place, which offers one of the best values/craziest menus in New England. Hidden on a side street, it's a tiny, contemporary restaurant with a huge, ever-morphing menu of big flavors and hip attitude. "We do not serve the food of cowards," owner/chef Kerry Altiero says right on top of the menu, and he's right. I could write a whole book on the regularly changing menu here—and probably should—but suffice to say you never know what you'll get 'til you get there. Small plates and entrees could include things like grilled lamb patties with parsley and garlic; "50 MPH tomatoes" deep-fried and served with spicy ranch dressing; a "squash-o'-rama" (roasted squash with cheese); fire-roasted feta with sweet peppers, tomatoes, "really good" olives, and herbs; a Portuguese seafood combo of mussels, shrimp, clams, fish, and sausage steamed in wine and pummeled with parsley; or, of course, the immortal "Pitch a Tent"—sausage, gravy, onions, garlic, and mushrooms beneath a "tent" of pasta. Share everything with your fellow diner(s), because you'll never eat at a place this original again. Altiero, again: "It's comfort food for whatever planet you're from." Amen.

15 Oak St., Rockland. ✆ **207/594-2034.** www.cafemiranda.com. Reservations strongly recommended. Small plates $9–$14, main courses $19–$27. DISC, MC, V. Daily 5–9:30pm.

Cod End Cookhouse ★ 🎁 ☺ SEAFOOD Half the allure of Cod End is its hidden, scenic location—it's as though you'd stumbled upon a secret place. Situated between the Town Landing and the East Wind Inn in little Tenants Harbor, this is a classic lobster pound with fine views of a working harbor from its deck. To get to the cookhouse, you walk through a fish market first (where you can buy fish or lobster to go), then place your order at an outdoor shack. Steamed lobsters are the main draw, obviously, but there's actually a lot more to eat here, too—everything from chowders, stews, and lobster bisque to seafood pastas, charbroiled salmon, clam and haddock rolls, and a simple kids' menu of burgers, dogs, and sandwiches (including a classic PB&J). Yes, you probably do want to sample the sweetish blueberry cake for dessert.

Commercial St. (next to the town dock), Tenants Harbor. ✆ **207/372-6782.** www.codend.com. Main courses $5–$10 at lunch, $8–$15 at dinner. DISC, MC, V. Memorial Day to Sept daily 11am–8:30pm. Closed Sept to Memorial Day.

Marcel's ★★ AMERICAN This upper-crust (but never too stuffy) seasonal eatery on the ground level of the Samoset resort (see "Where to Stay," above) is a great place for a fancy bite in the Midcoast. In a room with big windows looking out on the water, Chef Tim Pierce employs astounding creativity within the confines of his classic American resort fare (think steak Diane, lobster thermidor, filet mignon, and bisque). The menu changes annually, but you can always start with a Caesar salad prepared tableside (as it has been for decades); a lobster stew rich with cream and sherry; or inventive, summery salads such as one of grilled watermelon, spinach, and shallot "onion" rings. Pan-seared scallops in a knockout citrus cream are ever-popular, as are the annual permutation of lobster and steak. Pierce has even begun sneaking some Asian influences into the menu, such as tuna tataki and yuzu sauce. Desserts run to sundaes, cakes, and ice creams—no molecular experiments here, just summery classics. Great spot; be sure to dress up (gentlemen should wear a jacket).

220 Warrenton St., Rockport. ℂ **800/341-1650** or 207/594-2511. www.samoset.com. Reservations required. Main courses $24–$36. AE, MC, V. June to mid-Sept Thurs–Tues 5:30–9pm.

Primo ★★★ MEDITERRANEAN/NEW AMERICAN   Primo is one of northern New England's top eats. The restaurant occupies two nicely decorated floors of a century-old home located a short drive south of Rockland's downtown. Owner/chef Melissa Kelly graduated first in her class at the Culinary Institute of America and won a James Beard Foundation award for "best chef in the Northeast" in the 1990s. Her Italian-inflected menu reflects the seasons and draws from local products wherever available. Start with an appetizer such as wood-fired pizza with artisanal mushrooms, planked octopus with chickpea salad, antipasti, or fried and roasted local oysters paired with rémoulade sauce and house-cured Tasso ham. Entrees might run to seared diver scallops with fettuccine, local halibut over a white-bean puree, monkfish medallions with peekytoe-crab-and-risotto cakes, grilled steak or duck, or chicken with lavender-and-honey-roasted figs and a sweet ricotta gnocchi. Finish with one of co-owner/pastry chef Price Kushner's inventive desserts: warm Belgian chocolate cake, an espresso float, a rhubarb-strawberry tartlet with vanilla gelato and strawberry sauce, or a bowl of hot *zeppole* (small Italian doughnuts) tossed in cinnamon and sugar. The wine list is outstanding. It's hard to get a last-minute table here during summer; failing that, order off the menu from the cozy upstairs bar.

2 S. Main St. (Rte. 173), Rockland. ℂ **207/596-0770**. www.primorestaurant.com. Reservations highly recommended. Appetizers $9–$18, main courses $25–$42. AE, DC, DISC, MC, V. Summer daily 5:30–9pm; call for hours in off season.

Camden ★★

A quintessential coastal Maine town at the foot of wooded Camden Hills, the affluent village of **Camden** sits on a picturesque harbor no Hollywood movie set could ever improve upon. The village has been attracting wealthy travelers from the East Coast for more than a century, and the mansions of the moneyed still dominate the shady side streets (though many have since been converted into B&Bs). Simply put, Camden is possessed of a grace and sophistication that eludes many other coastal towns.

The best way to enjoy this town is to park your car—and that might require driving a block or two off of busy Rte. 1, which runs right through the center of town. Camden is of a perfect scale to explore on foot, with plenty of boutiques and galleries. Don't miss the scenic, bowl-shaped **town park ★★** on the hill behind the town library: It was designed by the firm of Frederick Law Olmsted, the famed landscape architect who designed New York City's Central Park.

Yes, there are T-shirt shops and throngs of tourists here now. Yes, prices have escalated. Yes, on a summer weekend, you'll need to elbow your way past the crowds to get anywhere. But so long as you don't expect it to be a pristine, undiscovered fishing village, Camden is pretty enjoyable.

ESSENTIALS

GETTING THERE   Camden is on Rte. 1. Coming from the south, however, it's easier to get here by turning left onto Rte. 90 about 6 miles north of **Waldoboro,** thus bypassing the busy downtown streets of Rockland.

Concord Coach (*©* **800/639-3317** or 603/228-3300; www.concordcoachlines. com) runs two to three daily buses from Boston. See "Getting There," under "Rockland & Environs," earlier in this chapter, for more details.

VISITOR INFORMATION   The **Camden-Rockport-Lincolnville Chamber of Commerce** (*©* **800/223-5459** or 207/236-4404; www.camdenme.org) dispenses helpful information from its tourist office down at Camden's **Public Landing** (by the harbor), where there's also free parking (although spaces are very scarce in summer). The office is open year-round Monday to Saturday; in summer it's also open Sunday.

EXPLORING CAMDEN

Camden Hills State Park ★★ (*©* **207/236-3109**), one of the Midcoast's best parks, is about a mile north of the village center on Rte. 1. This 6,500-acre park has an oceanside picnic area, camping at more than 100 sites, a toll road winding up 800-foot **Mount Battie** with spectacular bay views from the summit, and a variety of well-marked hiking trails. The day-use fee is $4.50 for adults, $1 for children ages 5 to 11. It's open from mid-May to mid-October, sunrise to sunset.

If hikes and mild heights don't bother you, you might climb to the ledges of **Mount Megunticook ★★,** preferably early in the morning before the crowds have amassed (and while mists still linger in the valleys). Leave from near the state park's campground—the trail head is clearly marked—and follow the well-maintained path to open ledges, where you should step carefully. The hike takes only 30 to 45 minutes; spectacular views of the harbor await, plus glimpses of smaller hills and valleys. Depending on your stamina level, you can keep walking on the park's trail network to Mount Battie, or into lesser-traveled woodlands on the east side of the Camden Hills.

The Camden area is great to explore by bike. One nice loop several miles long takes you from Camden into the cute little village of **Rockport ★,** which has an equally scenic harbor and fewer tourists than Camden. There's a boat landing, park, and art galleries (see "Rocking It in Rockport," below). The Camden-Rockport Historical Society has drawn up a 9-mile bike (or car) tour, with brief descriptions of some of the historic properties along this route. The brochure is free; check for it at the chamber of commerce at the town's Public Landing (see "Visitor Information," above). The brochure also includes a 2-mile walking tour of downtown Camden.

If you want to cycle the area, bike rentals ($20 per day), repairs, maps, and local riding advice are available at **Bikesenjava** (*©* **207/596-1004;** www.haybikesenjava. com), located at 481 Main St. in Rockland. As you might have guessed, they also serve coffee.

WHERE TO STAY

Camden vies mightily with Kennebunkport (p. 608), and Manchester, Vermont (p. 480), for the title of "bed-and-breakfast capital of northern New England." B&Bs are everywhere in this town. The two stretches of **Rte. 1** just north and south of the village center—called Elm Street and High Street, respectively—are virtual bed-and-breakfast alleys of handsome homes converted to lodgings. (Others are tucked away on side streets.)

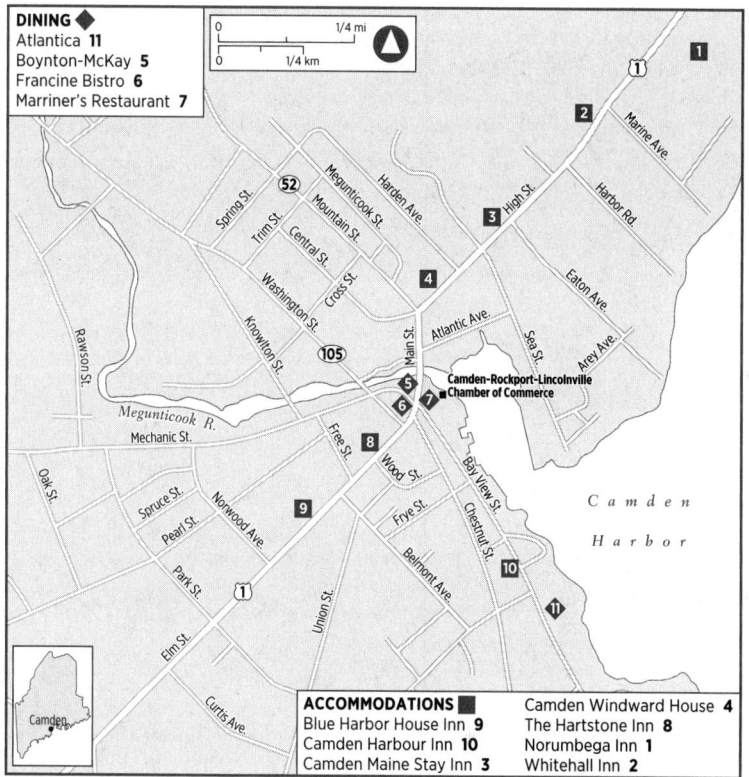

Camden

DINING ◆
Atlantica **11**
Boynton-McKay **5**
Francine Bistro **6**
Marriner's Restaurant **7**

0 | 1/4 mi
0 | 1/4 km

Camden-Rockport-Lincolnville
■ Chamber of Commerce

Megunticook R.
Mechanic St.

C a m d e n

H a r b o r

Camden

14

MAINE | Penobscot Bay

ACCOMMODATIONS ■
Blue Harbor House Inn **9**
Camden Harbour Inn **10**
Camden Maine Stay Inn **3**

Camden Windward House **4**
The Hartstone Inn **8**
Norumbega Inn **1**
Whitehall Inn **2**

Despite the preponderance of B&Bs, summer or fall weekends can still get tight. It's best to reserve well in advance. Failing to snag a room, you might try **Camden Accommodations** (✆ **800/344-4830** or 207/236-6090; www.camdenac.com), which provides assistance year-round with anything from booking a room at a local B&B to finding cottages for seasonal rentals or extended stays.

Also check out the village of **Lincolnville,** about 6 miles north of town on Rte. 1. You can find anything from a family-owned motel (rooms $50 a night in the off season) to a plush resort at ocean's edge with a balcony and a Jacuzzi.

And there's good camping at **Camden Hills State Park** (see "Exploring Camden," above), which is open from mid-May until mid-October. Sites cost $25 to $38 per night for non-Maine residents in summer ($10 discount for residents), depending on whether or not you need electric and water hookups; from mid-September until the park closes the price dips to just $18 per site.

Blue Harbor House Inn ★★   On busy Rte. 1 just south of town, this pale-blue 1810 farmhouse has been an inn since 1978 and is decorated throughout with a feminine country look. Rooms and suites vary in size; some are smallish, with slanting angles and low ceilings, but you can expect touches such as four-poster beds, claw-foot tubs, wicker furniture, Jacuzzis, writing desks, and slipper chairs. And the exposed wood floors are absolutely lovely. The best rooms are the carriage-house suites, with their private entrances and extra amenities—two of them, Captains Quarters and Bali Hai, share a private outdoor patio. The early evening hours feature a nice cocktail service, with cocktails made to order and lovely hors d'oeuvres for a small extra charge. (**Fun fact:** One of the owners used to work as a cocktail bartender on the real *Love Boat* cruise ship. Gopher, Isaac, and Julie would be proud.)

67 Elm St., Camden, ME 04843. ℂ **800/248-3196** or 207/236-3196. Fax 207/236-6523. www.blueharbor house.com. 11 units. $95–$155 double; $145–$185 suite. Rates include full breakfast. AE, DISC, MC, V. Closed mid-Oct to mid-May. **Amenities:** Dining room. *In room:* A/C, TV, fridge (some units), hair dryer.

Camden Harbour Inn ★★★ 🏨 This 1871 mansion sits in a quiet neighborhood on a rise with a view of the sea and mountains beyond, on the way to Rockport—think of it as Camden's "quiet side." This had been just another fusty, Victorian-era hotel until 2007, when it got a complete makeover from the two Dutchmen who bought it. No longer a creaky place of floral wallpaper or simple antiques, it's now a luxury inn with a spa, gourmet restaurant, even a wine refrigerator in every room. The place is all about modern design. All rooms have private bathrooms and flatscreen TVs, of course, but most also sport water views, fireplaces, and/or terraces. The New Amsterdam Suite is one of the poshest in town, with its king-size featherbed and two private decks; other suites are designed in Taiwanese, Thai, and Mauritian themes. The inn is within walking distance of downtown, and there's an excellent French restaurant, **Natalie's ★**, as well.

83 Bayview St., Camden, ME 04843. ℂ **800/236-4266** or 207/236-4200. Fax 207/236-7063. www. camdenharbourinn.com. 22 units. Mid-June to mid-Oct $175–$375 double; $235–$700 suite. Rates include full breakfast. 2-night minimum stay in peak season. AE, DISC, MC, V. Closed Dec–Apr. Children 12 and over welcome. **Amenities:** Restaurant; bar; spa. *In room:* A/C, TV, hair dryer, Wi-Fi (free).

Camden Maine Stay Inn ★ The Maine Stay is one of Camden's friendliest bed-and-breakfasts. In a home dating from 1802 (later expanded in Greek Revival style in 1840), it's your classic slate-roofed New England manse in a shady yard, within walking distance of both downtown *and* Camden Hills State Park. Guest rooms, spaced out over three floors, have ceiling fans (only a few have televisions); each is distinctively furnished in antiques; things are mostly frilly and floral, but the wooden floors are often exposed as a sort of counterpoint. Note that top-floor rooms have foreshortened ceilings with intriguing angles. The downstairs Carriage House Room unit, away from the buzz of Rte. 1, is popular; its French doors lead to a private stone patio, while a Vermont Castings stove keeps things toasty inside.

22 High St., Camden, ME 04843. ℂ **207/236-9636.** Fax 207/236-0621. www.mainestay.com. 8 units. $110–$240 double; $170–$270 suite. Rates include full breakfast. AE, MC, V. Children 12 and over welcome. **Amenities:** Dining room. *In room:* TV (some units), kitchenette (1 unit), Wi-Fi (free).

Camden Windward House ★★ One of the big complaints from travelers staying on Camden's High Street is the noise from passing traffic. The Windward's owners solved that problem by installing double windows on their historic 1854 home; as a result, when you close the door, the village feels miles away. Welcoming common rooms are decorated with a light Victorian hand and cranberry glass. Rooms vary in size and decor—some are quite frilly, some rather solid and plain—but all have flatscreen TVs, phones, and air-conditioning; some suites add gas fireplaces,

Jacuzzis, claw-foot tubs, decks, or canopy beds. The Chart Room's white canopy bed is lovely and bridal-looking; the expansive Quarterdeck suite features exposed beam-work, skylights, and a Jacuzzi; and even the simple, elegant Brass Room has a private deck. Guests choose from plenty of hot breakfast entrees, served in a pleasant dining room of maple tables, and you can order an in-room massage—rare at a B&B. This place is better and friendlier than you might expect.

6 High St., Camden, ME 04843. ℂ **877/492-9656** or 207/236-9656. www.windwardhouse.com. 8 units. Peak season $190–$280 double; off season $99–$240 double. Rates include full breakfast and after-noon tea. AE, MC, V. Children 12 and over welcome. **Amenities:** Bar. *In room:* A/C, TV/DVD, hair dryer, Wi-Fi (some units; free).

The Hartstone Inn ★★★ 🏨 Among the many great inns in the Camden area, this one's just a little more special. Chef/innkeeper Michael Salmon draws raves for his cooking at this downtown inn, and the accommodations in the early-19th-cen-tury Victorian home owned by him and his wife are top-rate, too. The Hartstone's rooms are designed with grace, furnished in lovely antiques and some of the most beautiful decor in the Midcoast; all suites here include Jacuzzis, Wi-Fi access, fridges, fireplaces, and other luxe touches, but even the smaller rooms are plenty comfort-able, with MP3 docking stations and flatscreen TVs (and some Jacuzzis and canopy beds). The full breakfasts here are wonderful, as are five-course **dinners ★★** marrying local Maine seafood with Caribbean chilies, spices, and cooking tech-niques—lobster with vanilla *beurre blanc,* for instance. (The chef cooked at resorts in Aruba prior to coming to Maine.) It's a unique experience on a coastline already full of good inns, and the small spa and cooking school here are cappers to the experience.

41 Elm St., Camden, ME 04843. ℂ **800/788-4823** or 207/236-4259. www.hartstoneinn.com. 14 units (1 with bathroom across hall). $135–$190 double; $175–$275 suite. Rates include full breakfast. MC, V. Closed late Nov to late Apr. **Amenities:** Dining room; spa. *In room:* A/C, TV/DVD, MP3 docking station, fridge (some units), Wi-Fi (some units; free).

Norumbega Inn ★★ You'll have no problem at all finding the Norumbega: Just head north out of town and look for the castle on the right. Well, it's actually a man-sion (built of stone by telegraph-system inventor Joseph Stearns in 1886), but it *looks* like a castle. Wonderfully eccentric and full of curves, turrets, angles, and rich materials, this hotel is on the National Historic Registry. There's extravagant carved-oak woodwork in the lobby, a stunning oak-and-mahogany inlaid floor, and a kingly downstairs billiards room. New management is currently updating all furnishings, but some "king" beds still consist of two twin beds pushed together. Still, all units have robes, some have fireplaces, most have air-conditioning, and three ground-level units sport private decks. The two suites here rank among the finest in northern New England: the bright and airy Library suite, in the original two-story library (so big it has an *interior* balcony), and the sprawling Penthouse with its superlative bay views, king-size bed, and huge oval tub. And if you're the sort of traveler who goes gaga over Sherlock Holmes, Hercule Poirot, Angela Lansbury, or the board game Clue, don't miss Norumbega's "Murder Mystery" weekends—be the first to solve the mystery, and you win a free stay. No lie.

63 High St., Camden, ME 04843. ℂ **877/363-4646** or 207/236-4646. www.norumbegainn.com. 12 units. June–Oct $195–$525 double and suite; Nov to mid-Feb and mid-Apr to May $105–$345 double, $275–$525 suite. All rates include full breakfast. 2-night minimum stay in summer Sat–Sun, and holi-days. AE, DISC, MC, V. Closed mid-Feb to mid-Apr. Children age 7 and over welcome. **Amenities:** Concierge. *In room:* A/C (most units), TV, fridge (1 unit), hair dryer, Wi-Fi (most units; free).

Whitehall Inn ★ 🍴 Set at the edge of town on busy Rte. 1, the Whitehall is a venerable Camden institution thanks partly to its association with local poet Edna St. Vincent Millay, who was "discovered" here by a guest who went on to fund Edna's college education. The room where the discovery happened still has a 1904 Steinway piano that Edna played. As for the three-story inn, it's all columns, gables, a long roofline, and atmospherically winding staircases. The antique furnishings—including a handsome Seth Thomas clock, Oriental carpets, and cane-seated rockers on the front porch—are well cared for. Guest rooms are simple yet appealing, and have recently been updated with important additions like flatscreen TVs (previously, there were *no* TVs in many rooms), though the "economy" rooms still share hallway bathrooms just as they did in olden days. The only drawback? That traffic—try to get a room in back.

52 High St., Camden, ME 04843. © **800/789-6565** or 207/236-3391. www.whitehall-inn.com. 45 units (some with shared bathroom). July–Oct $129–$199 double; mid-May to June $99–$159 double. Rates include full breakfast. AE, MC, V. Closed Nov to mid-May. **Amenities:** 2 restaurants; babysitting; tennis court. *In room:* TV, no phone (some units).

WHERE TO DINE

In addition to its fine-dining options, downtown Camden has a wealth of places to nosh, snack, lunch, and brunch.

Some great doughnuts, for instance, are fried up at **Boynton-McKay ★** (© **207/236-2465;** www.boynton-mckay.com) at 30 Main St.—a former pharmacy that's now a prime spot for lunch, coffee, a quick sandwich, or a blue-plate special. Just up the street, pick up a bag of gourmet groceries at **French & Brawn** (© **207/236-3361**), on Main Street at the corner of Elm.

Atlantica ★★ SEAFOOD/BISTRO Atlantica gets high marks for its menu, always well prepared under the management of Chef Ken Paquin, a graduate of the Culinary Institute of America (and former top dog at the Equinox in Vermont). On the waterfront with a small indoor seating area and an equally small deck, Paquin cooks subtly creative fare that leans toward seafood and takes in Asian and French influences: seared day-boat scallops over lemon risotto with a steamed lobster; roasted breast of duck; porcini-dusted bass; local oysters baked with spinach and Pernod; Maine shrimp in an Asian egg-drop soup; tournedos of beef with a shallot confit and shiitake mushrooms; and grilled lamb chops. All good. Plus there's that great harbor view. At press time, the restaurant was for sale, so eat there while you can.

1 Bayview Landing. © **888/507-8514** or 207/236-6011. www.atlanticarestaurant.com. Reservations recommended. Main courses $12–$24. AE, MC, V. Thurs–Mon 5–9pm. Closed Jan–Mar.

Francine Bistro ★★ FRENCH This place feels more like a French brasserie in Manhattan's Meatpacking District than a coastal seafood joint—and that's a good thing. A meal from chef/owner Brian Hill (long ago, of the seminal Boston alternative-rock band Heretix, but I digress) might begin with fish, onion, or lentil soup; a ceviche of halibut, serrano chilies, and red onions; mussels in bordeaux and shallots; or skewers of grilled lamb with white pesto, orange, and endive—nice to see in a state dominated by fried fish and lobster. Entrees might run to roast chicken with a chèvre gratin or a cauliflower-cheese hash; duck a l'orange; a crispy skate wing with Jerusalem artichokes; roasted sea bass in caramelized garlic sauce; seared halibut with shrimp; haddock stuffed with scallops; or some reliable steak frites. Hill cut his teeth in some truly great kitchens around the country, and it shows.

55 Chestnut St., Camden. ☎ **207/230-0083.** www.francinebistro.com. Reservations recommended. Main courses $17–$25. MC, V. Tues–Sat 5:30–10pm.

Marriner's Restaurant DINER "The last local luncheonette" is how Marriner's sums itself up, and it has used a sign with the legend DOWN HOME, DOWN EAST, NO FERNS, NO QUICHE to also get its message across: namely, that this is a no-frills affair, so don't expect snootiness or fancy food. The space is done up in a nautical theme of pine booths and vinyl seats, and the kitchen has been spooning up filling breakfasts and lunches for locals since 1942. It's a good place for early risers to get a quick start on the day and check out some local characters. Go for pancakes, chowders, or the lobster and crab rolls—and don't miss the homemade pies, either.

35 Main St., Camden. ☎ **207/236-4949.** Most breakfast items $4–$6, lunch items $4–$12 (most under $7). MC, V. Daily 6am–2pm.

THE BLUE HILL PENINSULA ★★

Blue Hill is 136 miles NE of Portland, 23 miles N of Stonington, and 14 miles SW of Ellsworth

Forming the eastern boundary of Penobscot Bay—though you must drive north and then *south* to get there, diverging from Rte. 1 by a good 15 miles or more—the **Blue Hill Peninsula** is a little piece of back-roads paradise. The roads are hilly, winding, and narrow, passing through sprucey forests, past old saltwater farms, and over bridges, touching down at the edges of inlets and boatyards from time to time. And the light is nearly always a special, misty color of yellow.

The essayist E.B. White recognized a special quality here: He bought a farm and memorialized the experience in great little books like *One Man's Meat* and *Charlotte's Web.* (White's ashes are buried in a village cemetery on the peninsula.) While they may take a little extra time to find, the island of **Deer Isle** and villages like **Brooklin** and **Blue Hill** are well worth building into any Maine-coast itinerary.

There's also a strong countercultural streak running through the area; somehow, though, the boat-builders, fishermen, artists, and ex-hippies all get along just fine. Together they've create a unique blend of quiet water views, hand-painted boats, small-town churches and general stores, tiny art galleries, organic produce, and grassroots radio: a place that could only happen in Maine.

Deer Isle ★★

The island known as **Deer Isle** is well off the beaten path, yet worth the long detour from Rte. 1. Looping, winding roads cross through forest and farmland, and travelers are rewarded with sudden glimpses of hidden coves. An occasional settlement even crops up now and again. This island doesn't cater exclusively to tourists the way many coastal towns and islands do; it's still largely occupied by fifth- or sixth-generation fishermen, farmers, second-home owners, and artists who prize their seclusion here.

The main village—**Stonington,** on the island's southern tip—is still a rough-hewn sea town. This village does now have a handful of inns and galleries, but its primary focus is to serve locals and summer residents, not travelers. *Outside* magazine once named this one of America's 10 best towns to live in if you're an extreme/outdoorsy type.

Well, maybe if you don't mind living hours removed from the nearest significant population center and airport. I've yet to see a lobsterman kayaking on his downtime, either—they're too busy working—though I suppose it does happen.

Be that as it may, this is a great island on which to simply relax, smell the salt air, and watch the changing landscapes.

ESSENTIALS

GETTING THERE The island of Deer Isle is connected to the mainland via a high, narrow, **suspension bridge** built in 1938—still a bit scary to cross during high winds. You get to the bridge via one of several winding roads that split off of Rte. 1.

Coming from the south or west (Portland or Camden), turn onto Rte. 175 in Orland, then connect to Rte. 15 and continue to Deer Isle. From the east (Mount Desert Isle or Canada), head south on Rte. 172 to Blue Hill, where you can also pick up Rte. 15.

VISITOR INFORMATION The **Deer Isle–Stonington Chamber of Commerce** (© **207/348-6124;** www.deerislemaine.com) staffs a seasonal information booth just beyond the bridge on Little Deer Isle. This booth is normally open daily during summer, but its hours depend on the availability of volunteer staffers. Call or check the website first.

EXPLORING DEER ISLE

With its network of narrow roads leading nowhere, Deer Isle is ideal for rambling around on—by car or bike. Especially tranquil is the narrow road between Deer Isle and the village of **Sunshine** (yes, really) to the east. Plan to stop and explore the various coves and inlets en route. To get here, follow Rte. 15—then, south of Deer Isle, turn east toward **Stinson Neck,** continuing about 10 scenic miles over bridges and causeways.

Stonington ★, at the southern end of the island, consists of one commercial street that wraps along harbor's edge. While B&Bs and boutiques have made inroads here in recent years, it's still a bit of a rough-and-tumble waterfront town—a good place for taking pictures and eating fish.

WHERE TO STAY

Inn on the Harbor ★ 🌴 This quirky waterfront inn has the best location in town, right on Stonington's main street. After a makeover, the guest rooms (more than half of which overlook the harbor) are now nicely appointed with antiques and carpets. The most inexpensive rooms are a real bargain, in or out of season (when rates plummet), especially so because every unit in the place has a phone, television, and Wi-Fi access. This is a good spot for resting up before or after a local kayaking expedition, or as a base for day trips out to Isle au Haut (which is part of Acadia National Park).

45 Main St. (P.O. Box 69), Stonington, ME 04681. © **800/942-2420** or 207/367-2420. Fax 207/367-5165. www.innontheharbor.com. 14 units. Mid-May to mid-Oct $139–$225 double; mid-Oct to mid-May $65–$135 double. Rates include continental breakfast mid-May to mid-Oct only. AE, DISC, MC, V. Children 12 and over welcome. *In room:* TV, kitchenette (1 unit), no phone (1 unit), Wi-Fi (free).

Pilgrim's Inn ★★ Set between an open bay and a mill pond, Pilgrim's is a historic, handsomely renovated inn with a few adjacent cottages. The home was built in 1793 by Ignatius Haskell, a prosperous sawmill owner; his granddaughter later opened the home to boarders, and it has housed summer guests ever since. The interior is tastefully decorated in a style that's informed by early Americana: Think exposed wooden floors, woody canopy beds, flowery bed prints, and rugs and quilts galore. The rooms are also appointed in antiques and painted in muted Colonial colors. (Especially intriguing are the units on the top floor, which show off the home's impressive diagonal beams.) Other accents include private staircases, antique tubs, woodstoves, and fireplaces. Breakfasts here are big and fancy: goat-cheese pancakes, eggs Benedict, smoked salmon, and the like. Three nearby cottages are also rented by the inn (and two of them stay open year-round, unlike the main inn), and allow pets inside. The inn maintains a tavern-style dining room with several intriguing spaces; expect typical American resort fare like steaks, fish, lobsters, and rack of lamb.

20 Main St. (P.O. Box 69), Deer Isle, ME 04627. ℂ **888/778-7505** or 207/348-6615. Fax 207/348-7769. www.pilgrimsinn.com. 15 units. $109–$209 double; $179–$249 cottage. Rates include full breakfast. MC, V. Closed mid-Oct to mid-May (2 cottages year-round). Pets accepted in cottages only ($50 fee). Children 10 and over welcome in inn, all children welcome in cottages. **Amenities:** Restaurant; pub; bikes. *In room:* Kitchenette (1 room), Wi-Fi (free).

WHERE TO DINE

Fish and shellfish completely dominate the menus of the restaurants on this island, just as you'd expect.

If you don't end up eating on the dock at the Fishermen's Friend (see below), you're probably eating at the **Maritime Café ★** (ℂ **207/367-2600**), a short block away on Main Street. The cafe serves a lunch menu of hearty sandwiches (organic sausage, turkey, lobster and crab rolls), and dinners of steamed lobsters, pan-seared scallops over linguine, crab cakes, crab-stuffed haddock filets, and grilled rib-eye steaks plus beer, wine, and espresso.

Fisherman's Friend ★ 🍴 SEAFOOD Just one dock over from the Isle au Haut ferry and attached to a general store, this seasonal seafood eatery is a locals' sort of place: lively, crowded, and completely unpretentious. The menu features home-cooked meals, including a range of broiled and fried fresh fish. But many people come for lobsters—the owners boast that they prepare it 30 different ways here, and those permutations include baked and stuffed, baked with spinach and cream, steamed, stir-fried, buttered, champagne-poached (!), cooked in a pie, thin-sliced and placed in crepes, or served with other sauces ranging from coconut curry to tomato. The popular lobster stew brims with meaty chunks. There's even a wine list, a selection of pastas, and a dessert menu of typical seasonal New England favorites like blueberry pie, strawberry-rhubarb pie, strawberry shortcake, raspberry crisp, and tollhouse pie.

5 Atlantic Ave. (off Main St., at end of dock), Stonington. ℂ 207/367-2442. www.stoningtonharbor. com. Reservations recommended in summer. Lobster dishes market-priced; main courses $13–$20 at dinner. DISC, MC, V. Mid-May to mid-Oct daily 11am–9pm (Fri–Sat to 10pm); Mid-Oct to mid-May call for hours.

Blue Hill ★★

Blue Hill, population 2,400, is very easy to find—just look for the dome of Blue Hill itself, which lords over the northern end of Blue Hill Bay. You can see it from miles away, looming like a whaleback.

Set between the hill and the bay is a quiet and historic town, clustered compactly along the shore. There's not much going on here, a quality which curiously seems to attract repeat summer guests who love the place. The village center offers an old-fashioned general store, art galleries, boats on a harbor, a fried-seafood joint, and a couple of choices for both lodging and fine dining. It's a good place for a (very) quiet break.

ESSENTIALS

GETTING THERE   Blue Hill is southeast of **Ellsworth,** at the junction of routes 15 and 172. From **Bar Harbor,** follow Rte. 3 through Ellsworth, cross the bridge and follow Rte. 172 about 14 miles to Blue Hill. Coming from the south (from **Rockland** or Belfast) on Rte. 1, turn south onto Rte. 15 about 5 miles east of **Bucksport** and continue about 12 miles to Blue Hill.

VISITOR INFORMATION   It's tiny, so Blue Hill doesn't maintain a true visitor information office or kiosk. Instead, look for the town's brochure and map at state information centers, or contact the **Blue Hill Peninsula Chamber of Commerce** (✆ **207/374-3242;** www.bluehillpeninsula.org), located at 107 Main St. Locals are also often willing to answer strangers' questions.

EXPLORING BLUE HILL

One good way to start your exploration of this area is to climb to the open summit of **Blue Hill ★★**, from which you can get good views of the bay and the bald mountaintops of nearby Mount Desert Island.

The trail is free. To reach the trail head from the center of the village, drive north on Rte. 172 about 1½ miles, then turn west (left) on Mountain Road at the Blue Hill Fairgrounds. Drive another ¾ mile and look for the well-marked trail on the right; park on either shoulder of the road. The moderate ascent is about a mile long and takes about 45 minutes; there are no tricky, death-defying stretches along the way, and you'll know you've arrived when you spy the fire tower. Bring a picnic lunch, but don't dump your leftover food on the trail afterward—bears have occasionally been sighted around here.

Blue Hill has traditionally attracted lots of writers, artists, and potters; you can't throw a stone without hitting a gallery or studio here. Family-run **Rackliffe Pottery ★** (✆ **888/631-3321** or 207/374-2297; www.rackliffepottery.com), on Rte. 172 (Ellsworth Rd.), uses native clay and lead-free glazes for its works, for instance. Visitors are welcome to watch the potters at work, and it's open year-round.

The best "museum" in town is the **Parson Fisher House ★★** (✆ **207/374-2459;** www.jonathanfisherhouse.org), on routes 176 and 15, a half-mile west of the village. Fisher, Blue Hill's first permanent minister, was a small-town Renaissance man when he settled here in 1796. Educated at Harvard, Fisher not only delivered sermons in six different languages (including Aramaic), but was also a writer, painter, and inventor of boundless energy. On a tour of this home, which he built himself in 1814, you can view a clock with wooden works and a camera obscura that Fisher made, plus pictures he painted and books he wrote, published, and bound by hand. Outside, the property's owners are slowly recreating Fisher's original orchard.

The house is open from July to mid-October Thursday through Saturday from 1 to 4pm. Admission is by donation; $5 per person is suggested.

WHERE TO STAY

Blue Hill Farm Country Inn   Comfortably situated on 48 acres about 2 miles north of the Blue Hill's village center, this inn (not to be confused with its similar-named neighbor; see below) has some of the most relaxing and comfortable common areas in the region. The first floor of a big barn was converted into a spacious living room, with sitting areas arrayed so that you can opt for either privacy or the company of others. Guest rooms are small and lightly furnished, though—none come with anything larger than a double bed. The more modern rooms are upstairs in the barn loft and are decorated in a country-farmhouse style, though they're a bit motel-like. The seven older rooms in the farmhouse have more character—but they share a single bathroom with a small tub and hand-held shower head.

Rte. 15 (P.O. Box 437), Blue Hill, ME 04614. ☎ **207/374-5126.** www.bluehillfarminn.com. 14 units (7 with shared bathroom). $115 double with private bathroom; $95 double with shared bathroom. Rates include continental breakfast. AE, MC, V. *In room:* No phone.

Blue Hill Inn ★★   The Blue Hill Inn has been hosting travelers since 1840 on one of the village's main streets, within walking distance of everything. It's a Federal-style inn, decorated in a Colonial American motif; creaky wooden floors stamp it with authenticity. The innkeepers have pleasantly furnished all rooms with antiques and down comforters; a few units in the main house have wood-burning fireplaces (these rooms are open only from mid-May through Oct), while a large contemporary suite in an adjacent, free-standing building has a cathedral ceiling, fireplace, full kitchen, living room, and deck (and it's open year-round). Breakfasts here are very good.

40 Union St. (P.O. Box 403), Blue Hill, ME 04614. ☎ **800/826-7415** or 207/374-2844. Fax 207/374-2829. www.bluehillinn.com. 12 units. $155–$205 double; $175–$275 suite. Rates include full breakfast and afternoon pastries. 2-night minimum stay in summer. DISC, MC, V. Main inn closed Dec to mid-May, suite open year-round. Children 13 and over are welcome. **Amenities:** Dining room. *In room:* A/C, TV (1 unit), kitchenette (1 unit), no phone (most units).

WHERE TO DINE

The **Fish Net** (☎ 207/374-5240), at the north end of Main Street (near the junction of rtes. 172 and 177), is the place locals go for quick meals of fried fish, lobster rolls, clam baskets, and ice-cream cones. It's open seasonally. There's also a bakery, **Blue Hill Hearth** (☎ 207/610-9696), at 58 Main St., serving sandwiches, pizzas, and soups.

Arborvine ★★ SEAFOOD/FUSION   The Arborvine gives this sleepy town a top-flight eatery. In a beautifully renovated Cape Cod–style house, the restaurant's interior is warm and inviting—think rough-hewn timbers, polished wooden floors, and a cozy bar area. The owners are careful to use locally procured ingredients, such as Bagaduce River oysters on the half shell as an appetizer. The intriguing nightly main courses change but might run to haddock niçoise, broiled Stonington halibut with grilled polenta, coriander-crusted ahi with seaweed and Japanese flavorings, or seared local scallops in a garlicky saffron broth. The nonseafood choices are equally exciting: a rack of lamb in pine nuts and basil, beef medallions over a dollop of Vermont chèvre, crispy roast duckling with a quince glaze, or just a simple boneless rib-eye with duxelle sauce. Yummy desserts could include a Grand Marnier–spiked chocolate mousse; chocolate cake with raspberry ganache; a lemon mousse Napoleon; a gingery vanilla crème brûlée; or a Bartlett pear in puff pastry sided with macadamia-nut-flavored cream, pomegranate sauce, and a bit of cinnamon ice cream.

Main St. ☎ **207/374-2119.** www.arborvine.com. Main courses $27–$31. MC, V. Summer daily 5:30–8:30pm; off season Fri–Sun 5:30–8:30pm.

MOUNT DESERT ISLAND ★★★

Bar Harbor: 270 miles NE of Boston, 160 miles NE of Portland

Mount Desert Island is home to spectacular **Acadia National Park,** and for many visitors, these two places are one and the same. Yet the park's holdings are only *part* of the appeal of this wonderful island, which is connected to the mainland by a short causeway. Besides the parklands, you'll find scenic harborside fishing villages and remote backcountry roads aplenty, lovely B&Bs and fine restaurants, oversize 19th-century summer "cottages," and the historic tourist town of **Bar Harbor.**

Mount Desert Island is split almost precisely in two by a deep inlet known as Somes Sound. Most of the parklands are on the eastern lobe of the island, though it does take in some large tracts, campgrounds, and mountains on the isle's western flank, too.

The eastern side is much more heavily developed. **Bar Harbor** is the center of commerce and entertainment, a once-charming resort now in danger of being swallowed whole by all its T-shirt and trinket shops. The western side has a quieter, more settled air and teems with more wildlife than tourists; the villages are mostly filled with fishermen and second-homers, rather than actual businesses.

This island isn't huge—it's only about 15 miles from the causeway to the southernmost tip at Bass Harbor Head—yet you can do an awful lot of adventuring within this compact space. And you can see many different kinds of villages and landscapes, too. The best strategy is to take it slowly, exploring on foot, by bicycle, even by canoe or kayak. Give yourself a week if you have that much time to spare. You'll be glad you did.

Acadia National Park ★★★

It's not hard to understand why Acadia is one of the crown jewels of the National Park system. (It draws the second-most visitors, annually, of any of the U.S. national parks.) The landscape here is a rich tapestry of rugged cliffs, pounding ocean surf, fishing and leisure boats lolling in harbors, and quiet forest paths.

Acadia's terrain, like so much of the rest of northern New England, was shaped by the cutting action of the last great glaciers moving into and then out of the region about 18,000 years ago. A mile-high ice sheet rumbled slowly over the land, scouring valleys into deep U-shapes, rounding many once-jagged peaks, and depositing boulders at odd places in the landscape—including the famous 10-foot-tall Bubble Rock, which appears perched precariously on the side of South Bubble Mountain.

 Fjord Tough

Mount Desert Island is divided deeply right down the middle into two lobes (almost like a brain) by **Somes Sound,** a tidal inlet that is also the only true fjord—that is, a valley carved out by a glacier and then subsequently filled in with rising ocean water—in the entire lower 48 states. No, it's not nearly as scenic as the ones in Norway and Alaska, but when you drive over that little bridge from one side to the other, you can truthfully report to friends back home that you crossed a fjord this morning. Pretty cool.

Mount Desert Island & Acadia National Park

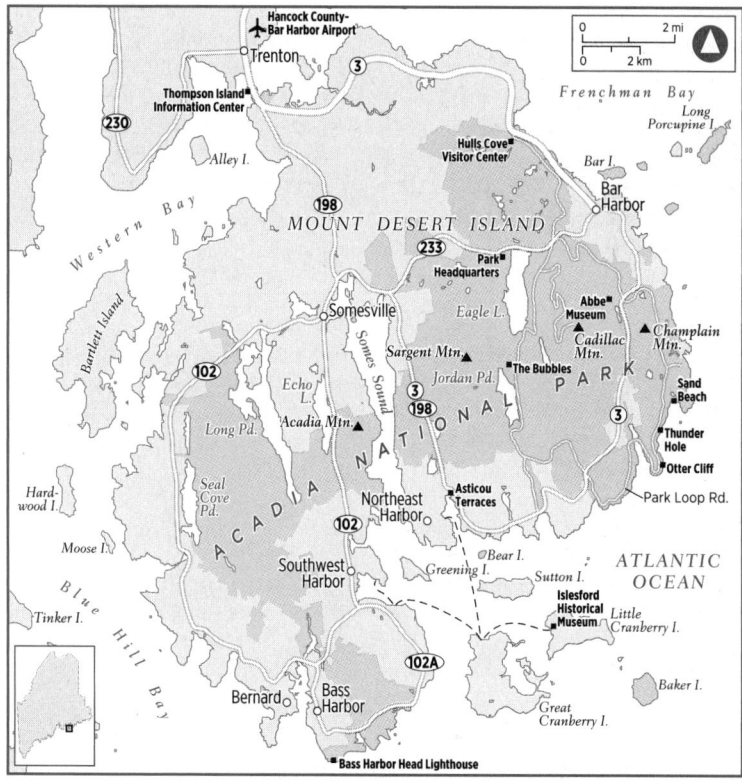

In the 1840s, Hudson River School painter Thomas Cole brought his sketchbooks and easels to remote Mount Desert Island, which was then home to a small number of fishermen and boat-builders. His stunning renditions of the coast were displayed in New York City museums and galleries, triggering a tourism rush as urbanites flocked to the island to "discover" nature and "rusticate" in wood-beamed lodges and Victorian inns. By 1872, national magazines were touting Eden (the town of Bar Harbor's name before 1919) as a summer getaway. It attracted the attention of wealthy industrialists and soon became the summer home of Carnegies, Rockefellers, Astors, and Vanderbilts, who built massive "cottages" (mansions, really, in the shingle style of the time) with dozens of bedrooms.

By the early 1900s, the island's popularity and growing development began to concern people. Textile heir George Dorr and Harvard president Charles Eliot, aided by the largesse of John D. Rockefeller, Jr., began acquiring and protecting large tracts of the island for the public to enjoy. These parcels were eventually donated to the U.S. government, and in 1919, the land was designated Lafayette National Park—the first national park east of the Mississippi—after the French general.

Renamed Acadia National Park in 1929, the park has now grown to encompass nearly half the island in piecemeal holdings. It is a world-class destination for those who enjoy outdoors adventure. In parts, the park seems to share more in common with Alaska than New England: You can see bald eagles soaring overhead, whales breaching below, cliffs and fir-topped mountains at nearly every turn.

In between, you'll find remote coves perfect for beach picnics; lovely offshore islands accessible only by sea kayak; clear ponds and lakes with nary a boat in them; and uncrowded mountaintops with views of it all and outstanding foliage in fall.

ESSENTIALS

GETTING THERE   Acadia National Park is near Ellsworth. Normally travelers take Rte. 1 to Ellsworth from southern Maine, but you can avoid coastal congestion by taking the Maine Turnpike to Bangor, then picking up I-395 to Rte. 1A and continuing south into Ellsworth. Though this is longer in terms of miles, it's the quicker route in summer.

From Ellsworth, bear right onto Rte. 3 (Rte. 1 doesn't go there) and continue about 15 minutes to the island causeway in **Trenton.** Cross the bridge, and you're on the island. Consult a map carefully to determine which route to take from here; there are three possible choices, all leading to very different destinations—routes 3 and 233 go to Bar Harbor, Rte. 198 goes to Northeast Harbor, and Rte. 102 leads to Southwest Harbor.

Year-round there are several flights daily from Boston on small planes to the **Hancock County–Bar Harbor airport** (airport code BHB; www.bhbairport.com) in Trenton, just across the causeway from Mount Desert Island; for more information contact **U.S. Airways Express** (✆ **800/428-4322;** www.usairways.com). From here, call a taxi, rent a car, or—best of all—ride the **free shuttle bus** (see below) to downtown Bar Harbor from late June through mid-October.

GETTING AROUND   A **free summer shuttle-bus service** ★★, known as the *Island Explorer* (www.exploreacadia.com), was inaugurated in 1999 as part of an effort to reduce the number of cars on the island's roads. It's working: The propane-powered buses—equipped with racks for bikes—serve multiple routes covering nearly the entire island and will stop anywhere you request outside the village centers, including trail heads, ferries, small villages, and campgrounds. (Bring a book, though; there are lots of stops.)

All routes begin or end at the central **Village Green** in Bar Harbor, but you can and should pick up the bus almost anywhere else to avoid parking hassles in town. Route no. 3 runs from Bar Harbor along much of the Park Loop, offering easy, free access to some of the park's best hiking trails. The buses operate from late June through mid-October; ask for a schedule at island information centers, in shops, or at any hotel or campground.

GUIDED TOURS   **Acadia National Park Tours** (✆ **207/288-0300;** www.acadia tours.com) offers 2½-hour park tours from mid-May through October, departing twice daily (10am and 2pm) from downtown Bar Harbor. The bus tour includes three stops (Sieur De Monts Springs, Thunder Hole, and Cadillac Mountain) and plenty of park trivia, courtesy of the driver. This is an easy way for first-time visitors to get a quick introduction to the park before setting out on their own side trips. Tickets are available at Testa's Restaurant (53 Main St.) in Bar Harbor; the cost is $28 for adults, $15 for children 12 and under.

Packing a Picnic for Acadia

Before you set out to explore, pack a lunch and keep it handy. Once you get inside the park, you'll find very few places (other than the Jordan Pond House; see "Where to Dine," below) to stop for lunch or snacks. Having drinks and snacks at hand will prevent you from having to backtrack into Bar Harbor or elsewhere midday to fend off starvation.

ENTRY POINTS & FEES   Entrance fees to the park are collected at several gates and points from May through October; the rest of the year, entrance is free—one of this nation's great outdoor bargains either way. A 1-week pass, which includes unlimited trips on the Park Loop Road (closed in winter), costs $20 per car from late June through early October and $10 per car in spring and fall; there's no additional charge per passenger once you've bought the pass. Hikers, cyclists, and anyone else traveling without a vehicle (that is, motorcyclists or boaters) must pay a $5-per-person fee.

You can enter the park at several points in the interwoven network of park and town roads—a glance at a park map, available free at the visitor center, will make these access points self-evident. The main point of entry to Park Loop Road, the park's most scenic byway, is near the official park visitor center at **Hulls Cove** (on Rte. 3 just north of Bar Harbor); the entry fee is collected at a tollbooth on the loop road, a half-mile north of Sand Beach.

VISITOR CENTERS & INFORMATION   Acadia staffs two visitor centers. The **Thompson Island Information Center** (© **207/288-3411**), on Rte. 3, is the first you'll pass as you enter Mount Desert Island. This center is maintained by the local chambers of commerce, but park personnel are often on hand to answer inquiries. Open daily at 6am mid-May through mid-October (its closing hours vary depending on staff), it's a good first stop for general lodging and restaurant information.

If you're interested primarily in information about the park itself, continue on Rte. 3 to the National Park Service's **Hulls Cove Visitor Center,** about 7½ miles beyond Thompson Island. This attractive, stone-walled center has professionally prepared park-service displays, such as a large relief map of the island, natural-history exhibits, and a short introductory film. You can also request free brochures about hiking trails and the carriage roads, or purchase postcards and more detailed guidebooks. The center is open daily from mid-April through the end of October.

And information is available year-round, by phone or in person, at the **park headquarters** (© **207/288-3338**), on Rte. 233 between Bar Harbor and Somesville, open daily (but closed weekends in summer). You can also ask questions online at their website, **www.nps.gov/acad**.

SEASONS   Spring is forgettable in Acadia, but summer is the peak season. The weather in July and August is perfect for just about any outdoor activity. Most days are warm (in the 70s or 80s Fahrenheit/low to mid-20s Celsius), with afternoons frequently cooler than mornings owing to the sea breezes. (Fog occasionally rolls in from the southeast on a hot day, which gives the landscape a magical quality.) While sun seems to be the norm, come prepared for rain; it's not uncommon at all. Once or twice every summer, a heat wave somehow settles onto the island, producing temperatures

14

MAINE | Mount Desert Island

in the 90s Fahrenheit (30s Celsius), dense haze, and stifling humidity, but this rarely lasts more than a few days. Enjoy summer: Soon enough (sometimes even during late Aug), a brisk north wind will blow in from the Canadian Arctic, forcing visitors into sweaters at night. You'll smell the approach of autumn, with winter not far behind.

Fall here is wonderful. Between Labor Day and the foliage season in early October, days are often warm and clear, nights have a crisp tang, and you can avoid the congestion, crowds, and pesky insects of summer. It's not that the park is empty in September; bus tours seem to proliferate at this time, which can mean periodic crowds and backups at the most popular sites (such as Thunder Hole). Not to worry: If you walk a minute or two off the road, you can find solitude and an agreeably peaceful walk or perch. Hikers and bikers will have the trails and carriage roads to themselves.

Winter is an increasingly popular time to travel to Acadia, especially among those who enjoy cross-country skiing the carriage roads. Be aware, though, that snow along the coast is inconsistent, and services—including most restaurants and many inns—are often closed down in winter. Expect to stay in either a really cheap motel or an expensive resort, and to eat what locals do: pizza, burgers, and sandwiches.

RANGER PROGRAMS   Frequent ranger programs are offered throughout the year. These include talks at campground amphitheaters and tours of island locales and attractions. Examples include an Otter Point nature hike, walks across the carriage roads' stone bridges, cruises on Frenchman Bay (rangers provide commentary on many trips), and discussions of the changes in Acadia's landscape. Ask for a schedule of events and more information at any visitor center or campground.

DRIVING TOUR: DRIVING THE PARK LOOP ROAD

The 20-mile **Park Loop Road** ★★ is to Acadia what Half Dome is to Yosemite—the park's premier attraction, but also a magnet for crowds. This remarkable road starts near the Hulls Cove Visitor Center and runs along ridges high above Bar Harbor before dropping down along the rocky coast. Here spires of spruce and fir cap dark granite ledges, making a sharp contrast with the white surf and blue-black sea. After following the picturesque coast and touching upon several coves, the road loops back inland along Jordan Pond and Eagle Lake, with a detour to the summit of the island's highest peak, Cadillac Mountain.

Ideally, visitors should try to make two circuits of the loop road. The first time, get the lay of the land. On the second circuit (one pass gets you all-day access), plan to stop frequently and poke around on foot, setting off on trails or scrambling along the coastline and taking photos. (Scenic pull-offs are strategically staggered at intervals.) The two-lane road is one-way along some of its coastal sections; in these cases, the right-hand lane is set aside for parking, so you can stop wherever you'd like, admire the vistas from the shoulder, and click away.

From about 10am until 4pm every good-weather day in July and August, anticipate big crowds along the loop road. Parking lots often fill up and close their gates early at the most popular destinations, such as Sand Beach, Thunder Hole, and the Cadillac Mountain summit—so try to visit these spots early or late in the day. Alternatively, on cloudy or drizzly days, you'll practically have the loop road to yourself.

From the Hulls Cove Visitor Center, the Park Loop initially runs atop:

1 Paradise Hill

Our tour starts with sweeping views eastward over Frenchman Bay. You'll see the town of Bar Harbor far below, and just beyond it the Porcupines, a cluster of islands that look like, well, porcupines. Sort of.

Following the Park Loop Road clockwise, you'll dip into a wooded valley and come to:

2 Sieur de Monts Spring

Here you'll find a rather uninteresting natural spring, unnaturally encased, along with a botanical garden with some 300 species showcased in 12 habitats. The original **Abbe Museum** (© **207/288-3519**) is here, featuring a small but select collection of Native American artifacts. It's open daily late May to early October from 9am to 4pm; admission is $3 for adults, $1 for children ages 6 to 15. (A larger and more modern branch of the museum in Bar Harbor features more and better-curated displays; a ticket here gets you a discount there. See "Exploring Bar Harbor," below, for details.)

The Tarn is the main reason to stop here; a few hundred yards south of the springs via a footpath, it's a slightly medieval-looking and forsaken pond sandwiched between steep hills. Departing from the south end of the Tarn is the fine **Dorr Mountain Ladder Trail** (see "Hiking," below).

Continue the clockwise trip on the loop road; views eastward over the bay soon resume, almost uninterrupted, until you get to:

3 The Precipice Trail

The park's most dramatic walking track, the **Precipice Trail ★★** ascends sheer rock faces on the eastern side of **Champlain Mountain.** Only about .75 mile to the summit, it's nevertheless a rigorous climb and involves scrambling up iron rungs and ladders in exposed places (those with a fear of heights and those under 5 ft. tall should *avoid* this trail). The trail is often closed midsummer to protect nesting peregrine falcons, and at these times rangers are often on hand at the trail-head parking lot to suggest alternative hikes.

Between the Precipice Trail and the next stop is a tollbooth where visitors pay the park's **entrance fee.**

Picturesquely set between the arms of a rocky cove is:

4 Sand Beach

Sand Beach ★★ is virtually the only sand beach on the island, although swimming these cold waters (about 50°F/10°C) is best enjoyed on extremely hot days or by those with hardy constitutions. When it's sunny out, the sandy strand is crowded midday with picnickers, tanners, tide-pool combers, and book readers.

Two worthwhile hikes begin near the beach. **The Beehive Trail** overlooks Sand Beach (see "Hiking," below); it starts from a trail head across the loop road. From the east end of Sand Beach, look for the start of the **Great Head Trail,** a loop of about 2 miles that follows on the bluff overlooking the beach, then circles back along the shimmering bay before cutting through the woods back to Sand Beach.

About a mile south of Sand Beach is:

5 Thunder Hole

Thunder Hole ★ is a shallow oceanside cave into which the ocean surges, compresses, and bursts out violently like a thick cannon shot of foam. (A road-side walking trail allows you to leave your car parked at the Sand Beach lot and hike to this point.)

If the sea is quiet—as it sometimes is on midsummer days—don't bother visiting this attraction; there'll be nothing to see. But on days when the seas are rough, and big swells are rolling in all the way from the Bay of Fundy, this is a must-see, three-star attraction; you can feel the ocean's power and force. The best viewing time is **3 hours before high tide;** check tide tables, available at local hotels, restaurants, and info kiosks, to figure out when that is.

Just before the road curves around Otter Point, you'll be driving atop:

6 Otter Cliffs

This set of 100-foot-high precipices is capped with dense stands of spruce trees. From the top, look for spouting whales in summer. In early fall, thousands of eider ducks can sometimes be seen floating in big, raftlike flocks just offshore. A footpath traces the edge of the crags.

At Seal Harbor, the loop road veers north and inland back toward Bar Harbor. On the route is:

7 Jordan Pond

Jordan Pond ★★ is a small but beautiful body of water encased by gentle, forested hills. A 3-mile hiking loop follows the pond's shoreline (see "Hiking," below), and a network of splendid carriage roads converges at the pond. After a hike or mountain-bike excursion, spend some time at a table on the lawn of the Jordan Pond House restaurant (see "Where to Dine," below).

Shortly before the loop road ends, you'll pass the entrance to:

8 Cadillac Mountain

Reach this **mountain** ★ by car, ascending an early carriage road. At 1,528 feet, it's the highest peak touching the Atlantic Ocean between Canada and Brazil. During much of the year, it's also the first place on U.S. soil touched by the rays of sunrise. But because this is the only mountaintop in the park accessible by car (and also because it's the island's highest point), the parking lot at the summit often gets jammed.

Views are undeniably great, even if the shopping-mall-at-Christmas crowds can put a serious crimp in your enjoyment of the place. Luckily, some lovely peaks accessible only by foot—such as Acadia and Champlain mountains—have equally excellent views and far fewer crowds.

GETTING OUTSIDE

CARRIAGE RIDES ★★   Several types of carriage rides are offered by the official concessionaire, **Carriages of Acadia** (© 877/276-3622; www.carriagesofacadia.com), from the park's stables about a half-mile south of the Jordan Pond House (just north and inland from **Seal Harbor**). These 1- to 2-hour tours depart daily in season, and might take in sweeping ocean views from a local mountaintop, a ramble through the Rockefeller bridges, or a stop by the Jordan Pond House for tea and popovers. Check for current pricing; reservations are recommended. (You can also rent a stall at the stables and ride the trails yourself—*if* you've brought your own horse.)

GOLF   Mount Desert Island has two good golf courses. The **Kebo Valley Golf Club** (© **207/288-3000;** www.kebovalleyclub.com) is one of the oldest in America, open since 1888. The **Northeast Harbor Golf Club** (© **207/276-5335;** www. nehgc.com) is another good choice. Greens fees at both are $85 per person for 18 holes during peak summer season (July through Labor Day); these rates dip considerably, however, during the shoulder seasons of spring and fall.

HIKING   Hiking is the quintessential Acadia activity, and it should be experienced by everyone at least once. The park has perhaps 120 miles of hiking trails (which are well maintained *and* well marked), plus nearly 60 more miles of carriage roads, which are also good for easy strolling. Some of these trails traverse the sides or faces of the island's low "mountains," and almost all of their summits have good, unimpeded views of the Atlantic far below. Many of these pathways were crafted by stonemasons or others with aesthetic intentions, so the routes aren't always direct—instead, they're incredibly scenic, taking advantage of natural fractures in the rocks, picturesque ledges, and sudden vistas that open up as you round certain bends.

The Hulls Cove Visitor Center has a brief chart summarizing area hikes; combined with the park map, it's all you need to find a trail and start exploring. Try stringing together several hikes to make your walk more varied, and be sure to plan your hiking according to the weather: If it's damp or foggy, you'll stay drier and warmer strolling the carriage roads; if it's clear and dry, head for the high peaks (Cadillac Mountain, the **Bubbles**) with the best views.

MOUNTAIN BIKING   The 57 miles of gravel **carriage roads ★★★** built by Rockefeller are among this park's hidden treasures. These were maintained by Rockefeller until his death in 1960, after which they became somewhat shaggy and overgrown. A major restoration effort was launched in 1990, though, and today the roads are superbly restored and maintained—and wide open. With their hard-packed surfaces, gentle grades, and good signage, they make for excellent mountain biking. (Note that bikes are allowed onto the island's free shuttle buses; see "Getting Around," above.)

A useful map of the carriage roads is available free at any visitor center on the island; more detailed guides can be purchased at area bookshops, but they really aren't necessary. Remember that anywhere carriage roads cross private land (mostly btw. **Seal Harbor** and **Northeast Harbor**), they're *closed* to mountain bikes, which are also banned from hiking trails.

Mountain bikes can be rented along Cottage Street in Bar Harbor, with rates running around $20 for a full day, or $12 to $15 for a half-day (which is 4 hr. in the bike-rental universe). Most bike shops include locks and helmets as basic equipment, but ask what's included before you rent. Also ask about closing times, as you'll be able to squeeze in a couple of extra hours of biking in early summer (it stays light until 9pm) with a late-closing shop. The **Bar Harbor Bicycle Shop** (© **207/288-3886;** www.barharborbike.com) at 141 Cottage St., gets many people's vote for most convenient and friendliest. Or you could try **Acadia Bike** (© **800/526-8615;** www. acadiabike.com) at 48 Cottage St., also very good.

14

MAINE

Mount Desert Island

CAMPING

The National Park Service maintains two campgrounds in the park. Both are quite popular; during July and August, expect both to fill by early to midmorning.

The more popular of the two is **Blackwoods ★★** (© **207/288-3274**), on the island's eastern side, with about 300 sites. To get there, follow Rte. 3 about 5 miles south out of Bar Harbor; bikers and pedestrians have easy access to the loop road from the campground via a short trail, and the Island Explorer bus stops here as well. This campground has no public showers or electrical hookups, but an enterprising business just outside the campground entrance provides clean showers for a modest fee. Camping fees at Blackwoods are $20 per night from May through October, $10 per site in April and November. Advance **reservations** can be made to Blackwoods by calling © **877/444-6777** between 10am and midnight (until 10pm in winter), or by using a new reservations system online at **www.recreation.gov**. An Acadia pass (see "Entry Points & Fees," above) is also required for campground entry.

The **Seawall ★** (© **207/244-3600**) campground is located over on the quieter, western half of the island, near the tiny fishing village of Bass Harbor (one of the Island Explorer shuttle-bus lines also stops here). Seawall has about 215 sites, and it's a good base for cyclists or those wishing to explore several short coastal hikes within easy striking distance. However, it's quite a ways from Bar Harbor and Sand Beach on the other side of the island; for families, it might not be the best choice. The campground is open mid-May through the end of September, but they *do not take reservations*. It's first come, first served all the way—and the lines form early. In general, if you get here by 9 or 10am, you're pretty much assured of a campsite, especially if you want a walk-in site.

Camping fees at Seawall are $14 to $20 per night, depending on whether you want to drive to your site, or can pack a tent in for a distance of up to 150 yards. There are also no electrical or water hookups here, and (as it is with Blackwoods) prior acquisition of an Acadia entrance pass is required to stay at the campground.

WHERE TO DINE

Jordan Pond House ★★ 🍴 AMERICAN   The secret to the Jordan Pond House? Location, location, location. The restaurant traces its roots from 1847, when a farm was established on this picturesque property at the southern tip of Jordan Pond looking north toward The Bubbles, a pair of glacially sculpted mounds. In 1979, the original structure and its birch-bark dining room were destroyed by fire. A more modern, two-level dining room was built in its place—less charm, but it still has one of the island's best dining locations, on a nice lawn spread out before the pond. Afternoon tea with popovers and jam is a hallowed tradition here. The lobster stew is expensive but very good. Dinners include classic entrees like prime rib, steamed lobster, pasta, and lobster stew; the prix-fixe meal special is a deal.

Park Loop Rd. (near Seal Harbor), Acadia National Park. © **207/276-3316.** www.jordanpond.com. Reservations recommended. Main courses $12–$17 at lunch, $15–$23 at dinner. AE, DISC, MC, V. Mid-May to late Oct daily 11:30am–8pm (until 9pm July–Aug).

Bar Harbor ★

Bar Harbor provides most of the meals and beds to travelers coming to Mount Desert Island, and it has done so since the grand resort era of the late 19th century, when wealthy vacationers first discovered this region. Sprawling hotels and

Bar Harbor

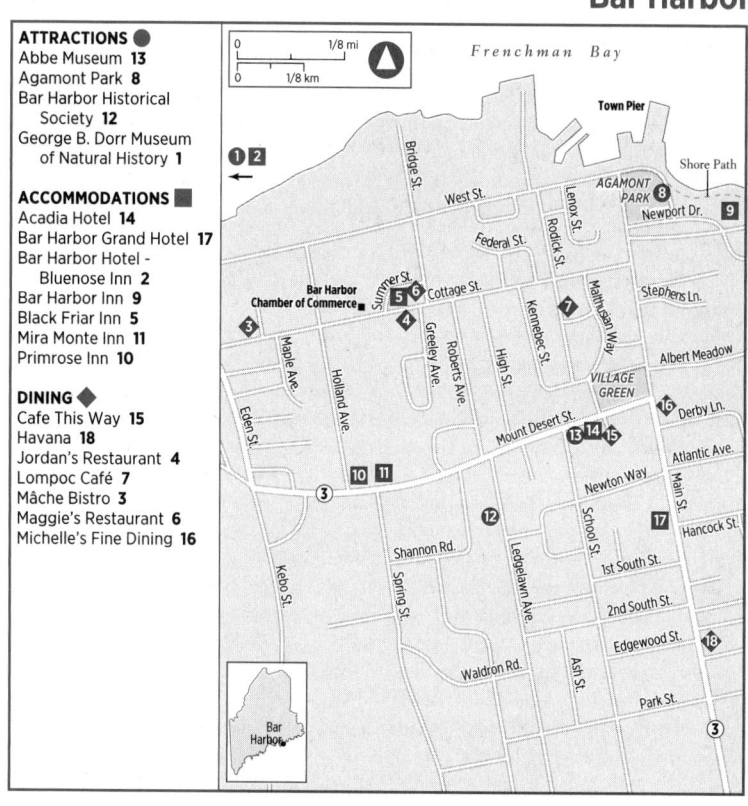

ATTRACTIONS ●
Abbe Museum **13**
Agamont Park **8**
Bar Harbor Historical
    Society **12**
George B. Dorr Museum
    of Natural History **1**

ACCOMMODATIONS ■
Acadia Hotel **14**
Bar Harbor Grand Hotel **17**
Bar Harbor Hotel -
    Bluenose Inn **2**
Bar Harbor Inn **9**
Black Friar Inn **5**
Mira Monte Inn **11**
Primrose Inn **10**

DINING ◆
Cafe This Way **15**
Havana **18**
Jordan's Restaurant **4**
Lompoc Café **7**
Mâche Bistro **3**
Maggie's Restaurant **6**
Michelle's Fine Dining **16**

boardinghouses once cluttered the shores and hillsides here, as a newly affluent middle class arrived by steamboat and rail car from the city in droves to find out what all the fuss was about.

The tourist trade continued to boom through the early 1900s—until it all but collapsed from the double hit of the Great Depression and the advent of car travel. The town was dealt yet another blow in 1947, when an accidental fire spread rapidly and leveled many of the opulent cottages in town (as well as a large portion of the rest of the island).

In recent years, Bar Harbor has bounced back with a vengeance, revived and rediscovered by visitors and entrepreneurs alike. Some see the place as a tacky place of T-shirt vendors, ice-cream cones, and souvenir shops, plus crowds spilling off the sidewalks into the street and appalling traffic. That is all true. Yet the town's history, distinguished architecture, and location on Frenchman Bay still make it a desirable base for exploring the island, and by far, it has the best selection of lodging, meals, supplies, and services on the isle. (If you want to shop, fine-dine, or go out at night, you've pretty much *got* to stay here.) Otherwise, if quiet is what you're seeking, consider bunking elsewhere on the island (see "Where to Stay," below).

ESSENTIALS

GETTING THERE Bar Harbor is on Rte. 3, about 10 miles southeast of the causeway leading onto Mount Desert Island.

VISITOR INFORMATION The **Bar Harbor Chamber of Commerce** (*©* **800/345-4617;** www.barharborinfo.com), stockpiles a huge arsenal of information about local attractions, both at its offices on 1 West St. (at the pier) and in a welcome center on Rte. 3 in Trenton, just before the bridge onto the island. Write, call, or e-mail in advance for a directory of area lodging and attractions. The chamber's website is chock-full of information and helpful links, too.

EXPLORING BAR HARBOR

The best water views in town are from the foot of Main Street at grassy (and free) **Agamont Park ★★**, which overlooks the town pier and Frenchman Bay. From here, stroll past The Bar Harbor Inn on the **Shore Path ★★**, a wide, winding trail that follows the shoreline for half a mile along a public right of way. The pathway also passes in front of many elegant summer homes (some converted into inns), offering a superb vantage point from which to view the area's architecture.

The **Abbe Museum ★**, 26 Mount Desert St. (*©* **207/288-3519;** www.abbemuseum.org), opened in 2001 as an in-town extension of the smaller, simpler museum at the Sieur de Monts spring in the national park (see the driving tour, above), showcasing a top-rate collection of Native American artifacts. A 17,000-square-foot gallery, this downtown branch has an orientation center and a glass-walled lab where visitors can see archaeologists at work preserving artifacts, along with changing exhibits and videos that focus largely on Maine and other New England tribes. From late May through October, it opens daily from 10am to 6pm; the rest of the year, it's open Thursday to Sunday only. Admission costs $6 for adults, $2 for children ages 6 to 15, and is free for younger children.

A short stroll around the corner from the Abbe Museum is the **Bar Harbor Historical Society,** 33 Ledgelawn Ave. (*©* **207/288-0000** or 207/288-3807). Housed in a 1918 former convent, the historical society showcases artifacts of life in the old days—dishware and photos from those grand old hotels that once dotted the town, exhibits on the noted landscape architect Beatrix Farrand, and so forth. Scrapbooks document the devastating 1947 fire, too. The museum is open from June through October Monday to Saturday from 1 to 4pm; admission is free. Even during the off season, entrance can sometimes be arranged.

Just at the northern edge of the town, on Rte. 3 with a spectacular bay view, is the campus of the **College of the Atlantic** (*©* **207/288-5015**), a school founded in 1969 with an emphasis on environmental education. The college's campus, a blend of old and new buildings, features the **George B. Dorr Museum of Natural History** (*©* **207/288-5395;** www.coamuseum.org) at 105 Eden St. It features exhibits that focus on interactions among island residents, from the two-legged to the four-legged, finny, and furry. It's open Tuesday through Saturday from 10am to 5pm; admission is by donation, though I'd toss in at least $3 per adult and $1 per child (more if you're deeply appreciative of the place).

WHERE TO STAY

Bar Harbor is the bedroom community for Mount Desert Island, with hundreds of hotel, motel, and inn rooms. They're invariably filled during the busy days of summer, and even the most basic rooms can be quite expensive in July and August. It's essential to reserve as early in advance as possible.

Expensive

Bar Harbor Grand Hotel ★ Bar Harbor's newest big hotel (it opened in 2003) fills a gap between quaint, expensive inns and B&Bs and the island's family-owned motels, hotels, and cottages. The hotel's blocky, two-tower design faithfully copies the style of the Rodick House, a now-defunct 19th-century lodging in Bar Harbor that could once boast of being Maine's largest hotel. The Grand, however, does the former one better with spacious rooms and bathrooms and, of course, all-modern fixtures. Rooms and suites are decked out in the same floral bedspreads and curtains you'd expect in any upscale business hotel, and the access to downtown Bar Harbor and the nearby ocean are big pluses. Concessions to business and tourist travelers include a guest laundry facility, gift shop, and Wi-Fi. Not surprisingly, they're getting a lot of tour groups here. Expect comfort, rather than island character.

269 Main St., Bar Harbor, ME 04609. ℂ **888/766-2529** or 207/288-5226. Fax 207/288-8548. www.bar harborgrand.com. 70 units. May–Oct $119–$229 double, $209–$279 suite; Apr and mid-Oct to early Nov $89–$109 double, $139–$195 suite. Rates include continental breakfast. DISC, MC, V. Closed mid-Nov to Mar. **Amenities:** Exercise room; Jacuzzi; heated outdoor pool. *In room:* A/C, TV/DVD, fridge, Wi-Fi (free).

The Bar Harbor Inn ★★ The Bar Harbor Inn, just off Agamont Park, nicely mixes traditional style with contemporary touches. On shady grounds just a moment's stroll from Bar Harbor's downtown, this property offers both convenience and charm. The shingled main inn, which dates from the turn of the 19th century, has a settled, old-money feel with its semicircular dining room and buttoned-down lobby. Guest rooms, located in the main building and two outbuildings, are much more contemporary: Units in the Oceanfront Lodge and main inn both offer spectacular bay views, and many have private balconies. (The less expensive Newport Building lacks views but is still comfortable and up-to-date.) The inn also has a **spa** with Vichy showers, aromatherapy, heated-stone treatments, and facial treatments, while the somewhat formal **Reading Room** dining room serves resort meals with the best dining-room views in town.

Newport Dr., Bar Harbor, ME 04609. ℂ **800/248-3351** or 207/288-3351. www.barharborinn.com. 153 units. Mid-May to mid-Oct $119–$379 double; mid-Mar to mid-May and mid-Oct to Nov $79–$215 double. Rates include continental breakfast. AE, DISC, MC, V. Closed Dec to mid-Mar. **Amenities:** Dining room; exercise room; Jacuzzi; heated outdoor pool; limited room service; spa. *In room:* A/C, TV, hair dryer, Wi-Fi ($8.95 per day).

Bluenose Inn ★ This resort-style complex—situated in two buildings—offers stunning views of the surrounding terrain. Facilities here are more modern, too: Expect spacious carpeted rooms with huge bathrooms, small refrigerators, and balconies, as well as a good fitness center, indoor and outdoor pools, and one of the town's best hotel dining rooms, the **Rose Garden** ★. The two buildings are slightly different in character, but in either case upper-floor rooms with sea views are worth the extra cost, especially if the weather is good. The staff here is professional and friendly.

90 Eden St., Bar Harbor, ME 04609. ℂ **800/445-4077** or 207/288-3348. www.barharborhotel.com. 97 units. Mid-June to mid-Oct $179–$369 double, $349–$499 suite; spring and late fall $139–$219 double, $259–$279 suite. AE, DC, DISC, MC, V. Closed Nov–Apr. **Amenities:** Restaurant; exercise room; Jacuzzi; 2 pools (1 indoor, 1 outdoor); spa. *In room:* A/C, TV, fridge, hair dryer, Wi-Fi (free).

Moderate

Acadia Hotel ★ 🔖   The simple, seasonal Acadia Hotel is nicely situated overlooking Bar Harbor's village green, easily accessible to in-town activities and the free shuttle buses running around the island. A handsome, simple home dating from the late 19th century, the hotel features a wraparound porch; guest rooms are plain but decorated in nice floral motifs. Units vary widely in size and amenities, however—some have simple whirlpool tubs, phones, or king beds; one has a kitchenette; and about half have small refrigerators. Others are as basic as it comes. It's a no-frills place, clean and well run—all things considered, a good value in an expensive town.

20 Mt. Desert St., Bar Harbor, ME 04609. ℂ **888/876-2463** or 207/288-5721. www.acadiahotel.com. 11 units. July to mid-Oct $129–$169 double; May–June $59–$109 double. Packages available. Closed late Oct to Apr. AE, MC, V. *In room:* A/C, TV, fridge (some units), Wi-Fi (free), no phone (some units).

Black Friar Inn ★ 🔖   The seasonal Black Friar, tucked on a Bar Harbor side street overlooking a parking lot, is a yellow-shingled home with quirky pediments and an eccentric air. A former owner "collected" interiors and installed them throughout the home, including a replica of a pub in London with elaborate carved-wood paneling (it's now a common room); stamped-tin walls (look in the breakfast room); and a doctor's office (now one of the guest rooms). Rooms are carpeted and furnished in a mix of antiques; most are smallish, though the big suite features nice paneling, a sofa, wingback chair, private porch, and gas fireplace. Other rooms sport such touches as rose-tinted stained-glass windows and brass beds. The least expensive units are the two garret rooms on the third floor. The inn features a small restaurant and a pub when it's open.

10 Summer St., Bar Harbor, ME 04609. ℂ **207/288-5091.** Fax 207/288-4197. www.blackfriarinn.com. 6 units. $65–$175 double; $100–$175 suite. Rates include full breakfast. 2-night minimum stay required most of year. MC, V. Closed Dec–Apr. Children 12 and over welcome. **Amenities:** Restaurant; pub. *In room:* A/C, Wi-Fi (free).

Mira Monte Inn ★   A stay at this Italianate home (built in 1864), a few minutes' walk from Bar Harbor's restaurants and attractions and open year-round, used to feel like a trip to your grandmother's house. It's gotten a lot more contemporary lately (TVs, phones, and Wi-Fi are all fairly recent additions), even if the common rooms are still furnished in a country Victorian style. The grounds are nicely landscaped, and a nice brick terrace off the street is a good place to enjoy breakfast in warm weather. Most rooms have a balcony, fireplace, or both, and some now even have Jacuzzis. Others have the feel of a spare country farmhouse. If you're a light sleeper, avoid rooms facing Mount Desert Street; those facing the gardens in the rear are much quieter. Families should ask about booking a suite in the adjacent outbuilding: These have better amenities, and some have double Jacuzzis.

69 Mount Desert St., Bar Harbor, ME 04609. ℂ **800/553-5109.** www.miramonte.com. 12 units. $95–$244 double; $105–$290 suite. Rates include full breakfast. 2-night minimum stay in midsummer. AE, DISC, MC, V. Most units closed late Oct to mid-May. *In room:* A/C, TV/CD, hair dryer, Wi-Fi (free).

Primrose Inn ★★   This Victorian stick–style inn, built in 1878, is one of the most notable properties on the "mansion row" along Mount Desert Street. Its distinctive architecture has been preserved, and was perhaps even enhanced during a 1987 addition of rooms, private bathrooms, and balconies. This inn is comfortable, furnished with "functional antiques" and modern reproductions; many of the spacious rooms have a floral theme, thick carpets, marble vanities, canopy beds, sitting or reading rooms, and handsome daybeds. (Two newer "premium" rooms also have private entrances and are stocked with king beds, gas fireplaces, and such other amenities as a porch or whirlpool tub.) The owners have gone ahead and added flatscreen TVs and Wi-Fi access, too, while the 24/7 free soft-drinks fridge remains. Breakfasts of eggs Florentine, Belgian waffles, blueberry pancakes, and the like are a hit, and the innkeepers can furnish you with a GPS unit if you'll be driving around the island and worry about getting lost.

73 Mount Desert St., Bar Harbor, ME 04609. © **877/846-3424** or 207/288-4031. www.primroseinn. com. 13 units. Late June to Aug $159–$229 double; late May to mid-June and Sept–Oct $99–$209 double. Rates include full breakfast and afternoon tea. 2-night minimum stay summer and fall. AE, DISC, MC, V. Closed Nov to mid-May. *In room:* A/C, TV/DVD, hair dryer, Wi-Fi (free).

WHERE TO DINE

In addition to the selections listed below, you can get good local pizza at **Rosalie's** (© **207/288-5666;** www.rosaliespizza.com) on Cottage Street; eat upstairs or down, or take out a pie to go. There's also a superb natural-foods market, **Alternative ★** (© **207/288-8225**), on Mount Desert Street right across from the Village Green.

And the owners of the island's best vegetarian eatery, **Eden Vegetarian Café,** took a hiatus in 2009 but will likely re-open in 2010 in a new location. Ask at the tourist office if you're interested in dining there.

Cafe This Way ★★ CONTEMPORARY AMERICAN   Cafe This Way is the kind of place where they know how to do wonderful Asian and Mediterranean things with simple ingredients. It has the feel of a hip coffeehouse, yet it's much more airy and creative than that. Bookshelves line one wall, and there's a small bar tucked into a nook; oddly, they serve breakfast and dinner but no lunch. Breakfasts are excellent though mildly sinful—it's more like brunch. Go for the burritos, corned beef hash with eggs, a range of omelets (build your own if you like), or the calorific Café Monte Cristo: a French toast sandwich stuffed with fried eggs, ham, and cheddar cheese, served with fries and syrup. Yikes. Dinners are equally appetizing, with tasty starters that might run to Maine crab cakes in tequila-lime sauce, grilled chunks of Cyprus cheese, or lobster spring rolls. The main-course offerings of the night could include anything from lobster cooked in sherry cream, or stewed in spinach and Gruyère cheese, to sea scallops in vinaigrette, grilled lamb and steaks, peach-flavored pork chops, or the Korean stir-fry dish known as *bibimbap*. You'll always find a tasty vegetarian option, as well.

14½ Mount Desert St. © **207/288-4483.** www.cafethisway.com. Reservations recommended for dinner. Breakfast items $5–$8, main courses $15–$26. MC, V. Mid-Apr to Oct Mon–Sat 7–11am and 5:30–9pm; Sun 8am–1pm and 5:30–9pm.

Havana ★★ 🎁 LATIN AMERICAN/FUSION   Havana excited foodies all over Maine when it opened in 1999 in what was then a town of fried fish and baked haddock. The spare decor in an old storefront is as classy as anything you'll find in Boston, and the menu can hold its own in the big city, too. Chef/owner Michael Boland's menu is inspired by Latino fare, which he melds nicely with New American ideas. Expect items like appetizers of crab cakes, duck empanadas, fig-and-blue-cheese tarts, or spicy beef and pork skewers dusted with cinnamon and vanilla. Entrees could include choices as adventurous as a lobster poached in butter served with a saffrony potato empanada; paella made with local lobsters and mussels; breast of duck with a blueberry glaze; broiled filet mignon with ancho gravy; pork tenderloin stuffed with cranberry and chorizo stuffing; seared black cod; or coconut-encrusted tuna steaks with a plum-red chili jam. Finish with an equally dazzling dessert, such as a chocolate lava cake with cinnamon churros; apple empanadas; caramel and cream; *dulce de leche* cheesecake with guava sauce; a maple carrot cake; or spicy pumpkin crème brûlée kicked up with jalapeño peppers.

318 Main St. ℂ **207/288-2822.** www.havanamaine.com. Reservations recommended. Main courses $24–$32. AE, DC, DISC, MC, V. Daily 5–10pm. Sometimes closed in late fall.

Jordan's Restaurant 🍴 DINER   This unpretentious breakfast-and-lunch joint has been dishing up filling fare since 1976 and offers a glimpse of the old Bar Harbor. It's a popular haunt of local working folks and retirees, but the staff is also friendly to tourists. Diners can settle into a pine booth or at a laminated table and order off the place-mat menu, choosing from basic fare such as grilled cheese sandwiches with tomato or slim burgers. The soups and chowders are all homemade, and there are some crab dishes (though no lobster). But breakfast is the star here, with a broad selection of three-egg omelets, muffins, and pancakes made with plenty of those great wild Maine blueberries (best when they're in season). With its "seniors-at-coffee-klatch" atmosphere and its rock-bottom prices, this is *not* a gourmet experience, but fans of big breakfasts, Americana-style cuisine, and diners will enjoy it.

80 Cottage St. ℂ **207/288-3586.** Breakfast and lunch items $3–$13. MC, V. Daily 4:30am–2pm. Closed Feb–Mar.

Lompoc Café ★ AMERICAN   The Lompoc Café has a well-worn, neighborhood-bar feel to it—waiters and other workers from around Bar Harbor congregate here after-hours. The cafe consists of three sections: the original bar, a tidy beer garden just outside (try your hand at bocce), and a small and open barnlike structure at the garden's edge to handle the overflow. Most of the beers are local (ask for a sample before ordering a full glass of blueberry ale). Bar menus are normally yawn-inducing, but this one has some surprises—lamb meatballs in mint, good salads, Vietnamese-style *bahn mi* sandwiches, or a BLT using fried green tomatoes. There's also quite a little wine list and some house cocktails, like the lemony "Blonde with an Attitude." The outdoor tables are fun, and live music acts often play here.

36 Rodick St. ℂ **207/288-9392.** www.lompoccafe.com. Reservations not accepted. Sandwiches and salads $7–$12. MC, V. Daily 11:30am–1am.

Mâche Bistro ★★ NEW AMERICAN   Little Mâche Bistro has developed a devoted local following; its soothing, plain decor conceals a sophisticated kitchen—you wouldn't expect an imported-cheese course offered in a place with plywood floors, but there is one here. Chef Kyle Yarborough's menu changes monthly; appetizers could include local crab with aioli, fish chowder, excellent house antipasti, or a wine-poached pear with Maytag blue cheese. Main courses, now more New American than French bistro, might run to herb-encrusted haddock over garlic mashed potatoes, slow-roasted pork with chorizo and vegetables, grilled hanger steak with a blue-cheese butter, seared duck over white beans, or a grilled portobello stuffed with goat cheese and caramelized onions.

135 Cottage St. ℂ **207/288-0447.** www.machebistro.com. Reservations recommended. Main courses $16–$23. AE, MC, V. Tues–Sun 5:30–9pm (closed Sun in winter).

Maggie's Restaurant ★★ SEAFOOD   The slogan for Maggie's is "Notably fresh seafood," and the place invariably delivers on that understated promise. (Only locally caught fish is used.) It's a casually elegant spot, good for a romantic evening while you enjoy the soothing music, attentive service, and excellent seafood. Appetizers could run to cheesy potatoes with lobster, grilled clams in wine sauce, a kid-sized pizza, or a simple salad; main courses might include "bronzed" cod with a lime-tartar sauce, lobster crepes, Gulf shrimp with feta and olives over rice, pan-seared scallops, or salmon seared in Indian spices and served with cucumber-mint salsa. They also do nice steaks and chicken, though that's not why you come here. Desserts are homemade, and it's also worth leaving room for them: blueberry pie, lemon curd, and dark chocolate pudding cakes, and a rotating menu of gourmet ice-cream sundaes—the island's best.

6 Summer St. ⓒ **207/288-9007.** www.maggiesbarharbor.com. Reservations recommended July–Aug. Main courses $16–$24. MC, V. Mon–Sat 5–9:30pm.

Michelle's Fine Dining ★★ FRENCH/SEAFOOD   Michelle's, located inside the Ivy Manor Inn, supplies one of the island's best dinner experiences. The three dining rooms are elegant, plus there's outside seating when the weather's good. The extensive menu elaborates on traditional French cuisine with New England twists. Nightly appetizers might include lobster bisque, French onion soup, crab cakes, or steak tartare. Main courses—divided into seafood and nonseafood entrees—are even more elaborate, with dishes such as chateaubriand for two (carved tableside); roasted rack of lamb; seared salmon with a pine-nut crisp; two versions of duck; Cornish hen; and a bouillabaisse for two of lobster, mussels, clams, and scallops. Finish with a cheese plate, one of several soufflés, the crème brûlée, or Michelle's unique "bag of chocolate": It comes with berries and is served in an edible chocolate bag. This place is expensive but worth it.

194 Main St. ⓒ **888/670-1997** or 207/288-2138. www.michellesfinedining.com. Reservations required during peak season. Main courses $24–$54. AE, DISC, MC, V. Daily 6–9pm. Closed late Oct to early May.

Elsewhere on the Island ★★

You'll find plenty to explore outside Acadia National Park and Bar Harbor, too. Quiet fishing villages, deep woodlands, and unexpected ocean views are among the jewels you can turn up once you get beyond Bar Harbor town limits.

ESSENTIALS

GETTING AROUND   The eastern half of the island is best navigated using Rte. 3, which forms a rough loop from Bar Harbor through **Seal Harbor** and past **Northeast Harbor,** then runs up along the eastern shore of Somes Sound. Routes 102 and 102A provide access to the island's western half. If you don't have a car, use the free **Island Explorer shuttle** (p. 648).

VISITOR INFORMATION   The Thompson Island Information Center as you enter the island is a great info source. Locally, the **Southwest Harbor–Tremont Chamber of Commerce** (ⓒ **800/423-9264** or 207/244-9264; www.acadiachamber. com) in Southwest Harbor and the **Mount Desert Chamber of Commerce** (ⓒ **207/276-5040;** www.mountdesertchamber.org) in Northeast Harbor can also help.

EXPLORING THE REST OF THE ISLAND

Down one peninsula of the eastern lobe of the island is the staid, prosperous village of **Northeast Harbor ★★**, long a favorite retreat of well-heeled folks. You can see shingled palaces poking out from the forest and shore, but the village itself (which consists of just one short main street and a marina) is also worth investigating for its art galleries, restaurants, and general store.

One of the best, least-publicized places for enjoying views of the harbor is from the understated, wonderful **Asticou Terraces ★★**. Finding the parking lot can be tricky: Head a half-mile east (toward Seal Harbor) on Rte. 3 from the junction with Rte. 198, and look for the small gravel lot on the water side of the road with a sign reading ASTICOU TERRACES. Park here, cross the road on foot, and set off up a magnificent path made of local rock that ascends the sheer hillside, with expanding views of the harbor and the town.

When leaving Northeast Harbor, think about a quick detour out to Sargent Drive. This one-way route runs through Acadia National Park along the shore of Somes Sound, affording superb views of the glacially carved inlet. On the far side of Somes Sound, there's good hiking. The nearby towns of **Southwest Harbor ★★** and **Bass Harbor** are both home to fishermen and boat-builders, and though the character of these towns is changing, they're still far more humble than Northeast and Seal harbors.

WHERE TO STAY

In addition to the hotels and inns described below, there are also a number of excellent **campgrounds** on the island, including two (Seawall and Blackwoods) that are part of the national park—see p. 654 for more details on both sites. Also consider tenting at one of the many privately owned campgrounds dotting the island; you can obtain a complete listing and guide from any tourist office on Mount Desert Island.

Just remember that some campgrounds fill up ahead of time or by midday; and advance booking, if possible, is always better.

The Claremont ★★   Early prints of the venerable Claremont show an austere, four-story wooden building overlooking Somes Sound from a grassy rise. It hasn't changed much since. The place offers classic New England grace. (It's somehow appropriate that the state's largest croquet tournament is held here each Aug.) Common areas are pleasantly appointed in country style—the library, with its fireplace, is popular. Most of the guest rooms are bright and airy, outfitted in antiques, old furniture, and modern bathrooms. There's also a set of 14 cottages of varied vintages and styles in the woods and on the water, all with fireplaces and kitchenettes; they sleep from two to seven people each. Outdoor amenities include the aforementioned croquet lawn, plus rowboats, a tennis court, and bicycles for guest use. The dining room, **Xanthus ★**, offers fabulous views of the fjord and an upscale menu of lobster, crab cakes, fish, scallops, pork, and steaks.

P.O. Box 137, Southwest Harbor, ME 04679. ✆ **800/244-5036** or 207/967-2321. www.theclaremont hotel.com. 44 units. July-Aug $170–$275 double, $200–$335 cottage; late May to June and Sept to mid-Oct $125–$190 double, $155–$235 cottage. Room (not cottage) rates include breakfast. 15% service fee for cottages. 3-night minimum stay in cottages. MC, V. Closed mid-Oct to late May. From center of Southwest Harbor, follow Clark Point Rd. almost to end and turn left on Claremont Rd. **Amenities:** Dining room; lounge; babysitting; bikes; tennis court. *In room:* Kitchenette (some units).

Inn at Southwest ★ There's a late-19th-century feel to this mansard-roofed Victorian home, which thankfully stays spare rather than frilly. All guest rooms, named for Maine lighthouses, are outfitted simply in contemporary and antique furniture, and all have ceiling fans and down comforters. Among the most pleasant rooms is Blue Hill Bay on the third floor, with its yellow-and-blue color scheme, big bathroom, sturdy oak bed and bureau, and glimpses of the harbor. The Pumpkin Island unit features a sleigh bed and rosewood sofa. The lone suite (Winter Harbor) has a pencil-poster canopy bed, French doors, and a gas-log fireplace. Breakfasts give you good incentive to rise early: The changing entrees could include Belgian waffles with raspberry sauce, poached pears, or blueberry French toast.

371 Main St. (P.O. Box 593), Southwest Harbor, ME 04679. © **207/244-3835.** www.innatsouthwest. com. 7 units. $105–$185 double. Rates include full breakfast. DISC, MC, V. Closed Nov to late Apr. *In room:* Wi-Fi (free), no phone.

Kingsleigh Inn ★★ In a 1904 Queen Anne–style home on Southwest Harbor's bustling Main Street, the Kingsleigh has long been a reliable place to bunk down in the area. Its living room features a wood-burning fireplace and fine art, while sitting and breakfast rooms offer further refuge. All guest rooms are outfitted with sound machines (to drown out the ambient "noise"), wineglasses, and robes; some also have air conditioners. Prints and wallpapers are flowery in the rooms, most of which are small to moderate size, though a few have private decks. The huge third-floor penthouse suite—by far the most expensive room here—has outstanding views (plus a telescope to see them better with); the inn's only TV (with VCR and DVD players); a fireplace; and a king-size bed. Three-course breakfasts are filling and genuinely artistic—expect choices such as asparagus frittata, crepes, Belgian waffles, and French toast. Other nice touches include walking sticks for guests and all-day, self-service espresso.

373 Main St. (P.O. Box 1426), Southwest Harbor, ME 04679. © **207/244-5302.** Fax 207/244-7691. www. kingsleighinn.com. 8 units. $110–$195 double; $225–$305 suite. Rates include full breakfast. AE, MC, V. Closed Nov–Mar. Children 13 and over welcome. *In room:* A/C (some units), TV/DVD (1 unit), hair dryer, Wi-Fi (free), no phone.

Lindenwood Inn ★★ 🏠 Australian innkeeper Jim King gave up cabinetmaking to open a string of successful B&Bs in Southwest Harbor, and his latest is his best; it feels like renting a home with friends. In a handsome Queen Anne–style captain's home built in 1904 over harbor's edge, King has modernized the rooms in simple, bold colors and accented them with items from his collections of African and aboriginal art—a strikingly unique interior and feel you can't find anywhere else in New England. Most units have balconies and plenty of windows; some have fireplaces, French doors, and/or private porches or decks; and all possess comfy beds. The public areas remain funky and appealing, and the heated in-ground pool and Jacuzzi are wonderful in summer. There's a small honor bar for fixing a late-night cocktail upstairs, plus a lounge in the basement with a pool table, darts, and a big-screen TV. The biggest draws, however, are the outstanding hospitality, great decor, yummy breakfasts, and laid-back vibe.

118 Clark Point Rd., Southwest Harbor, ME 04679. © **800/307-5335** or 207/244-5335. www.lindenwood inn.com. 8 units. $95–$215 double; $145–$295 suite. Rates include full breakfast. AE, MC, V. **Amenities:** Lounge; Jacuzzi; heated outdoor pool. *In room:* TV, kitchenette (1 unit), fridge (2 units), no phone.

WHERE TO DINE

In addition to the choices listed here, you'll find ice-cream, pizza, sandwich, and takeout-seafood shops scattered about the island. Even most of the village grocery stores offer good prepared sandwiches or meals.

Beal's Lobster Pound ★ LOBSTER   Some say Beal's is among the best lobster shacks in Maine, and it's certainly got the right atmosphere: Creaky picnic tables sit on a plain concrete pier overlooking a working-class harbor, right next to a Coast Guard base. (Don't wear a jacket and tie.) You go inside to pick out lobster from a tank, pay by the pound, choose some side dishes (corn on the cob, slaw, steamed clams), then pop coins in a soda machine outside while you wait for your number to be called. The food will arrive on Styrofoam and paper plates, but who cares? These lobsters are good. There's also a takeout window across the deck serving fries, fried clams, and fried fish (sensing a theme?), plus ice cream.

182 Clark Point Rd., Southwest Harbor. ✆ **207/244-7178** or 207/244-3202. www.bealslobster.com. Lobsters market-priced. AE, DISC, MC, V. Summer daily 9am–8pm; after Labor Day 9am–5pm. Closed Columbus Day to Memorial Day.

The Burning Tree ★★ 🍴 SEAFOOD   Located on a busy straightaway of Rte. 3 between Bar Harbor and Otter Creek, the Burning Tree is an easy restaurant to blow right past—but that would be a mistake. This low-key place, with its bright, open, and sometimes noisy dining room, is a find: It serves up some of the best and freshest seafood dinners on the island, with New American twists. Much of the produce and herbs comes from the restaurant's own gardens, while the rest of the ingredients are bought locally whenever possible. Everything's prepared with imagination and skill; expect unusual preparations like a New Orleans–style lobster, lobster fritters (great idea), and mixed seafood over noodles and cream, plus old standards like salmon and halibut (served with inventive and tasty sauces). The seafood stew is good, too, but desserts are middling at best. Don't miss the bartender's house cocktails, made with local fruits and berries when possible.

Rte. 3, Otter Creek. ✆ **207/288-9331.** Reservations recommended. Main courses $18–$23. DISC, MC, V. Wed–Mon 5–10pm. Closed Columbus Day to late May.

Fiddlers' Green ★★ NEW AMERICAN   Island-native Chef Derek Wilbur's bistro is a big hit in these seafaring parts. Begin with something from the cold seafood bar: oysters on the half shell or a trio of smoked fish and shellfish, for instance. Or start with one of Wilbur's small plates, like Thai-curried shrimp with coconut milk, fried catfish filet with a Cajun rémoulade, grilled merguez, or smoked baby back ribs. You'll always find steaks and pasta dishes (such as lobster strozzapreti with a *vinho verde* cream sauce) on the menu, but seafood is the true star: tempura-fried scallops, lobster potpie, or a good old steamed lobster. There's an extensive wine list, too, and martini drinkers should take note: Wilbur's bar serves a long list of classic and obscure versions. Desserts run to chocolate cakes, a Mayan-style fruit-and-chocolate soup, ice creams, cheese with figs, and caramel crepes filled with mascarpone cream and local blueberries.

411 Main St., Southwest Harbor. ✆ **207/244-9416.** www.fiddlersgreenrestaurant.com. Reservations recommended. Main courses $16–$32. AE, DISC, MC, V. Tues–Sun 5:30–9pm. Closed Columbus Day to Memorial Day.

Redbird Provisions ★★ CONTINENTAL/SEAFOOD Redbird opened in 2007 in a renovated cottage right on Northeast Harbor's cute main street, and it has been an unqualified winner so far. The kitchen cooks up local seafood and other main courses with a talented hand, using Asian, French, and Italian accents in a no-pretenses dining room. Lunches run to harvest-style soups and extremely inventive flatbreads, sandwiches, and salads (the smoked-trout salad niçoise is especially good). Dinnertime sees a broadening of the menu's scope to include appetizers like truffled cauliflower soup and ricotta-stuffed squash blossoms; pasta dishes such as risotto or a saffrony homemade orecchiette with clams and lemon confit; and main courses like organic Scottish salmon with white bean ragout and roasted figs, loin of lamb, or a strip streak served with a Yukon potato gratin. The small, porch-side outdoor dining space is nice in warmer weather.

11 Sea St., Northeast Harbor. ✆ **207/276-3006.** www.redbirdprovisions.com. Reservations recommended. Main courses $9–$22 at lunch, $25–$34 at dinner. DISC, MC, V. Tues–Sat 11:30am–2pm and 6–9pm; Sun 6–9pm. Closed late Oct to late May.

WESTERN MAINE ★

Bethel is 70 miles NW of Portland, 135 miles NE of Concord, and 180 miles N of Boston

Maine's western mountains make up a rugged, brawny region that stretches northeast between the White Mountains and the Carrabassett Valley. Yes, the Whites are higher, and the Maine coast is a lot more picture-postcard and convenient for travelers. But you can find natural wonders here in western Maine that those other places can't touch: huge azure lakes and sparkling little ponds; forests thick with spruce and fir; mossy, mossy woods (to borrow from Thoreau); and more mountains and foothills than you could tramp through in a lifetime.

Bethel ★★

Until somewhat recently, **Bethel** was a sleepy resort town with one of those family-oriented ski areas that seemed destined for mothballs. But then the **Sunday River** ski area (7 miles north of town) changed hands; a brash entrepreneur dusted it off and polished it up, and it eventually became what it is today, which is one of New England's most vibrant and challenging ski destinations.

With the rise of Sunday River, the sturdy town of Bethel itself has been dragged into the modern era, yet without taking on the artificial, packaged flavor of many other ski towns (there are no outlet malls here). This village is still defined by the stoic buildings of the respected Gould Academy prep school; a broad, green village common; and the Bethel Inn, a sprawling, old-fashioned resort that's managed to stay ahead of the tide by adding condos without ever losing its pleasant, timeworn character or lovely appearance.

ESSENTIALS

GETTING THERE Downtown Bethel is a simple turnoff from the intersection of two busy roads, routes 26 and 2. Get there from Portland or Boston via the Maine Turnpike (I-95), taking exit 63 ("Gray") and heading west on Rte. 26 for about an hour. From New Hampshire, drive east of Gorham on Rte. 2 for 20 to 30 minutes.

In fall and winter, there's a helpful free shuttle called the **Mountain Explorer ★** (✆ **207/784-9335**), which runs between downtown Bethel and one or the other of the ski resorts' base lodges about once per hour. The catch? The bus operates weekends only from Thanksgiving until mid-December, then daily from mid-December through mid-April (from around 6:30am until around midnight). When the snows melt, though, the bus disappears until the following winter.

VISITOR INFORMATION   The **Bethel Area Chamber of Commerce** (✆ **800/ 442-5826** or 207/824-2282; www.bethelmaine.com) has offices at 30 Cross St. (also referred to as Station Place), behind the movie theater. It's open Monday to Saturday from 9am to 5pm and Sunday from noon to 5pm; during off season it sometimes closes weekends, so it's best to call ahead.

GRAFTON NOTCH STATE PARK

Grafton Notch State Park ★★ straddles Rte. 26 as it angles northwest from Bethel into New Hampshire. This 33-mile drive, one of my favorites in the state, is both picturesque and dramatic, and unlike the Kancamangus Highway, it's never stop-and-go (there are no services along the way; gas up and buy food in Bethel). You begin by passing through fertile farmlands in a broad river valley before ascending through bristly forests to a glacial notch hemmed in by rough, gray cliffs on the hillsides above.

Foreboding **Old Speck Mountain** ★★ towers to the south; views of **Lake Umbagog** ★★ open to the north as you continue into New Hampshire. The foliage is excellent in early October most years. This route attracts few crowds, but it's popular with thoroughgoing Canadian tourists *and* Canadian logging rigs loaded up with Maine timber (drive carefully and yield the road if necessary) headed for the Maine coast or I-95.

Public access to the park consists of a handful of roadside parking lots near scenic areas. The best of the bunch is **Screw Auger Falls** ★, where the Bear River drops through several small cascades before tumbling dramatically into a narrow, corkscrewing gorge carved long ago by glacial runoff through granite bedrock. Picnic tables dot the forested banks upriver of the falls, and kids seem inexorably drawn to splash and swim in the smaller pools on warm days.

This is as good a state park as you'll find in northern New England, yet it's incredibly affordable. From mid-May through mid-October, access to the 3,000-acre parks costs $3 per nonresident ($1 for kids and seniors); get a pass at the self-pay station in any of the parking lots.

DOWNHILL SKIING

Sunday River Ski Resort ★★★   Sunday River has grown at stunning speed, to swiftly become one of the best ski mountains in New England with great, well-maintained terrain. Unlike ski areas that developed around a single tall peak, Sunday River expanded along an undulating ridge 3 miles wide that encompasses *seven* peaks—so simply traversing the resort, stitching a run together via the various chairlift rides, can take an hour or more. As a result, you're rarely bored. The descents offer something for everyone, from deviously steep and bumpy runs to wide, wonderful intermediate trails. Sunday River is also blessed with plenty of river water for snowmaking and makes tons of the fluffy stuff. The superb skiing conditions are, alas, offset by an uninspiring base area; the lodges and condos here tend to be architecturally dull, and there's little nightlife save a brewpub (see "Where to Dine," below). Anyway, you won't care, because the trails here are usually so good that they're often crowded all weekend even though there isn't a town or city of signifi-cant size for many tens of miles. Come on a weekday, though, and you'll pretty much have the place to yourself. There's good night skiing, with good discounts to match, and they'll even *refund* your ticket if you don't like the day's snow conditions and ask for your money back by 10am.

Skiway Rd., Newry, ME 04261. © **207/824-3000.** www.sundayriver.com. Adults $77–$79 day lift tick-ets; discounts for seniors, youths, and night skiing. Turn off rtes. 2/5/26 at brewpub onto Sunday River Rd.; after 2½ miles, bear left onto Skiway Rd.

OTHER OUTDOOR PURSUITS

BIKING   An easy, scenic route for touring cycles follows winding **Sunday River Road ★** several miles into the foothills of the Mahoosuc mountain range. Start at the Sunday River ski resort (see above); follow the same directions, but continue past the resort and west alongside the river through a tranquil scene marked by a little cemetery and a covered bridge. Eventually, you head into forested hills (the road turns to dirt). This dead-end road is lightly traveled beyond the resort, and views from the valley are rewarding throughout. Ask locally, or consult a local cyclists' hangout (such those listed just below) for a map.

Serious mountain bikers should head for the **Sunday River Mountain Bike Park ★★** (© 207/824-3000) at the ski area, with 28 trails (of every skill level) covering more than 25 miles open during summer and fall weekends. Experienced riders will enjoy taking their bikes by chairlift to the summit, then careening back down on service roads and ski trails. Visit the South Ridge Lodge first for your rental, and then hit the slopes. An adult trail pass costs $10 per day; an adult pass including all-day chairlift rides costs $27 (about half-price for children 12 and under). Cycle rentals—a bit pricey—are also available. The park is open from spring through mid-October, Friday through Sunday only.

Bethel Outdoor Adventure ★★ (© 800/533-3607 or 207/824-4224; www.betheloutdooradventure.com), on Rte. 2 in Bethel, rents off-road bikes for $25 per day, in addition to its steady business renting out canoes and kayaks and leading fishing tours locally. The center is located right where Rte. 2 crosses the Androscoggin River, on the way from Bethel to Sunday River.

BOATING   Canoe rentals and shuttles for exploring the Androscoggin River can be arranged by **Bethel Outdoor Adventure** (see "Biking," above). You can also hire a guide here to take you out by canoe or kayak, or sign up for a 2-hour lesson to brush up on skills before heading out on your own.

GOLF   Bethel has two excellent courses. Bethel Inn's **Country Club ★** (© 207/824-6276; www.bethelinn.com) is an unusually scenic 18-hole golf course right next to the inn; the course is somewhat flat but undeniably attractive. Greens fees for 18 holes are $50 per person; twilight rates are about half-price. Clubs and golf carts can be rented, and the club also has a driving range. Tee times are not manda-tory, but they're strongly recommended in high season, which includes fall, when the setting borders on the spectacular. The course is open early May through late Octo-ber, weather permitting.

Sunday River also maintains a **golf course ★★** (www.sundayriver.com/golf), with its own obviously splendid views and some lovely mountainside golfing. It's expensive: Greens fees range from $95 to $120 per person (cart included and required). Twilight rates are 70% to 75% cheaper for a pair of golfers playing together, though.

14

MAINE | Western Maine

HIKING   The **Appalachian Trail ★★★** crosses the Mahoosuc Range northwest of Bethel. Many who have hiked the entire 2,000-mile trail say this stretch is both the most demanding and the most strangely beautiful. The trail doesn't forgive here; it gives up switchbacks in favor of sheer, rocky ascents and descents. (It's also hard to find water along this part of the trail during the high summer months.) Still, it's worth the effort for serious hikers.

One stretch of the trail crosses **Old Speck Mountain ★★**, which, at 4,170 feet, is (surprisingly) Maine's third-highest peak. Even weekend walkers can tackle this hike. Look for the well-signed parking lot where Rte. 26 intersects the trail to the state park; park, pay, strap on boots (some parts are muddy), and join the A.T. right from the parking lot. In just .1 mile, you'll intersect the Eyebrow Trail—this moderately difficult side trail ascends an 800-foot cliff called The Eyebrow, but don't walk it if you're afraid of heights. Otherwise, stay on the main trail and continue up past several great notch overlooks, over rushing streams and past mild cascades, and into increasing views of the valley foliage. The summit is wooded, so there are no views from the top, but you can keep walking down into a bowl containing **Old Speck Lake** and a primitive campsite. (I don't usually recommend this, though, because the total walking time might leave you out on the trail after dark; stop at the summit, unless you're camping overnight at the lake.)

You can also take a walk on the A.T. *east* up **Baldpate Mountain ★**, the cliff whose face and top show patches of open ledge right across Rte. 26 from Old Speck, on the way to distant Mount Katahdin (p. 673). The trail continues across the highway. Baldpate is higher than you might think: Its summit is only about 400 feet lower than Old Speck's. Check trail books if you're trying to decide which trail to hike. The Appalachian Mountain Club's *Maine Mountain Guide* contains information about these and other area walks; pick up a copy before arriving in the Notch—shops in Bethel should carry it—if you're a serious walker.

WHERE TO STAY

Just outside Grafton State Park's boundaries, there's camping at the **Grafton Notch Campground** (© **207/824-2292;** www.campgrafton.com) for $25 per night. It's not part of the park, but privately owned. Find it on the west (left) side of Rte. 26, a mile or two before the entrance to the park.

There's also a less-wild campground on Rte. 2 at the headquarters of **Bethel Outdoor Adventure** (© **800/533-3607** or 207/824-4224; www.betheloutdoor adventure.com). RVs and tenters are both welcome; call for current site rates.

The Bethel Inn Resort   A classic, old-fashioned resort set on 200 acres right in the village, Bethel's signature inn has a quiet and settled air—appropriate, as it was built to house the patients of one Dr. John Gehring, who put Bethel on the map by treating nervous disorders here through a regimen of healthy country living. (The town was once known as "the resting place of Harvard" for the legions of faculty who were treated here.) The rambling white inn's rooms are quainter than spacious—tired, even. Rooms and suites added to an outbuilding in the late 1990s are more modern, with amenities such as DVD players, Jacuzzis, and air-conditioning (which the main inn still lacks). You might also be placed in the row of condo units down by the golf course, but again the condition is slipping. Some spa services are available; there's a fitness center on the grounds; and the **cross-country ski center ★** and **golf course** (see above) are scenic—yet this property seems to have really lost

its footing of late. Stay for the history if you must, but don't expect a [cut off]
experience that matches the very high prices; if you want that, look elsewhe[cut off]

21 Broad St. (on the Common), Bethel, ME 04217. © **800/654-0125** or 207/824-2175. www.beth[cut off]
com. 150 units. Summer $198–$418 double; winter $158–$454 double. Rates include breakfast and di[cut off]
ner. 2- to 3-night minimum stay ski season and weekends in summer. AE, DISC, MC, V. Pets accepted
($10 per night). **Amenities:** 2 restaurants; bar; babysitting; golf course; health club; Jacuzzi; heated
outdoor pool; sauna; tennis court; watersports equipment/rentals. *In room:* A/C (some units), TV, hair
dryer, Wi-Fi (free).

Jordan Grand Resort Hotel ★★ ☺

The anchor for expanded development in the far-flung Jordan Bowl area, this hotel feels miles away from the rest of the Sunday River resort of which it's part, mostly because it *is* far away—even staff joke about its remoteness. A modern, sprawling hotel, it manages to be family-friendly, clean, and shipshape enough, and is a positively great hotel for (experienced) skiers who want to ski out the door and be first on untracked slopes every morning. Owing to the quirky terrain, parking is inconvenient; you might have to walk quite a long distance to your room (opt for the valet parking). Rooms are simply furnished in a durable condo style, many quite spacious and most with balconies and/or washers and dryers; all now have custom-made Boyne beds, too. This hotel has become a popular destination for ski-happy families—possibly because it has day care and kitchenettes—so it wouldn't be the best choice in town for a couple seeking a quiet, romantic getaway. Otherwise, it's very good. The two hotel restaurants serve food that's a notch above ski-hill pub fare.

Sunday River Rd. (P.O. Box 450), Bethel, ME 04217. © **800/543-2754** or 207/824-5300. Fax 207/824-2111. www.sundayriver.com. 195 units. Ski season $140–$210 double, $275–$460 suite; rest of year $119 double, $235 suite. AE, DC, DISC, MC, V. **Amenities:** 2 restaurants; babysitting; children's center; concierge; exercise room; Jacuzzi; outdoor pool; limited room service; sauna; spa; steam room; Wi-Fi (in public areas; free). *In room:* A/C, TV, kitchenette (some units).

The Victoria Inn ★★

Built in 1895 and damaged by lightning some years back, the homey Victoria was restored in 1998 with antique lighting fixtures, period furniture, and the original, formidable oak doors. It's a good sleeper pick when you want to get away from resortville. Guest rooms have a William Morris feel, with patterned, flowery wallpaper, canopylike beds, and handmade duvet covers. (If you enjoy sleek, modern hotel rooms, though, skip this place.) Room no. 1 is a luxurious master suite with a turret window and sizable bathroom, but most intriguing are the four "loft" rooms in the attached carriage house, each with a gas fireplace, Jacuzzi, and soaring ceilings revealing some of the building's rugged original beams. These suites have small second-story sleeping lofts and sleep up to eight guests each. The dining room serves the best fancy meal in the area (see "Where to Dine," below).

32 Main St., Bethel, ME 04217. © **888/774-1235** or 207/824-8060. www.thevictoria-inn.com. 15 units. $109–$179 double; $149–$309 suite. Rates include full breakfast. 2-night minimum stay Sat-Sun and holidays. AE, MC, V. Pets sometimes accepted ($30 per night). **Amenities:** Restaurant. *In room:* A/C, TV, hair dryer, Wi-Fi (free).

WHERE TO DINE

Bethel is pretty short on good eats, even if most hotels and inns in the area serve dinners to the public as well as their own guests.

The **Sunday River** ski resort is your best bet for a casual meal: It offers a total of *nine* different dining experiences at last count, including a crepe shop, the Foggy and several pubs. Of them all, those inside the resort's two ~~mmit Resort~~ **mmit Resort** and the **Jordan Grand Resort**—are best for

~~llent~~ little natural-foods store, the **Good Food Store ★★** ~~vw.goodfoodbethel.com~~), on Rte. 2 west of downtown Bethel ~~o~~ Sunday River and Grafton Notch. It's very convenient for ~~g a vite~~ pre-hike or post-ski; the local beers, baked goods, ice creams, produce, meats, and other items are excellent.

Sunday River Brewing Company BREWPUB This modern brewpub, on prime real estate at the corner of Rte. 2 and the Sunday River access road, is a good choice if your objective is to quaff locally brewed ales and porters. Its motto? "Eat Food. Drink Beer. Have Fun." That about says it. The beers are good; the food (burgers, nachos, wings, pork sandwiches) doesn't strive for culinary heights. Come early if you're looking for a quiet bite, as it gets louder when bands take the stage.

29 Sunday River Rd. (at Rte. 2), Bethel. © 207/824-4253. www.sundayriverbrewpub.com. Main courses $8–$16. AE, MC, V. Mon–Thurs 11:30am–9:30pm; Fri–Sun 11:30am–11:30pm.

Victoria Restaurant ★★ 🏠 CONTINENTAL One of Bethel's best inns, the Victoria (see "Where to Stay," above), also operates one of its best eateries 6 nights a week. The predictably Continental menu is prepared with skill. Start with chowder, crostini with goat cheese and eggplant, or some smoked Maine salmon tartine, and then move on to main courses like lobster in a champagne butter sauce (served over pappardelle), grilled rib-eyes, bacon-wrapped filet mignon, grilled rack of lamb, chicken piccata, pork tenderloin, shrimp fra diavola, or salmon. Not many surprises, but again, it's all quite well done. Desserts run to items like chocolate cake with a cappuccino filling, Key lime pie, and a maple-flavored take on that New England favorite, apple crisp. Much better than you'd expect in a small mountain town.

32 Main St., Bethel, ME 04217. © 888/774-1235 or 207/824-8060. www.thevictoria-inn.com. Main courses $18–$28. MC, V. Mon–Sat 5:30–9:30pm.

BAXTER STATE PARK & ENVIRONS ★★★

Baxter State Park is one of Maine's crown jewels, even more spectacular in some ways than **Acadia National Park.** This 200,000-plus-acre park in the remote north-central part of the state is unlike any other state park in New England—don't look for fancy bathhouses or groomed picnic areas. When you enter Baxter State Park, you're entering near-wilderness.

Former Maine governor and philanthropist Percival Baxter single-handedly created this park, using his inheritance and investment profits to buy up the land and donate it to the state in 1930. Baxter stipulated that it remain "forever wild," and caretakers have done a great job fulfilling his wishes: You won't find any paved roads or electrical hookups at the campgrounds, and strict vehicle-size restrictions keep all RVs out, too. You *will* find rugged backcountry and remote lakes. You'll also find **Mount Katahdin,** a granite monolith that rises above all the sparkling lakes and boreal forests around it.

Essentials

GETTING THERE   Baxter State Park is 85 miles farther north past the city of **Bangor,** and the local tourism office says it takes about 5½ hours to drive here from Boston, about 10 hours from New York. To find the park, take I-95 to **Medway** (exit 244), then head west 11 miles on Rte. 11/157 to the mill town of **Millinocket,** the last major stop for supplies. Go through town and follow signs to Baxter State Park.

Another, lesser-used entrance is in the park's northeast corner. Follow I-95 to exit 259, and then take Rte. 11 north through **Patten** and west on Rte. 159 to the park. The speed limit throughout the park is 20 mph, and neither motorcycles nor ATVs are allowed inside its boundaries. (No pets are allowed inside, either.)

VISITOR INFORMATION   Baxter State Park provides maps and information from a **park headquarters** at 64 Balsam Dr. in **Millinocket** (✆ **207/723-5140;** www.baxterstateparkauthority.com).

For information on canoeing and camping *outside* Baxter State Park, contact **North Maine Woods, Inc.,** 92 Main St. (P.O. Box 425), Ashland, ME 04732 (✆ **207/435-6213;** www.northmainewoods.org). This group is not an environmental group, but rather a consortium of the paper companies, logging companies, other North Woods landowners, and various concerned individuals who control and manage nearly all recreational access to private parcels of the Maine woods. They can answer all your questions about fees, campgrounds, access rights, rules, and the like.

For help in finding cottages, rentals, and tour outfitters in the region, contact the **Katahdin Area Chamber of Commerce,** 1029 Central St., Millinocket, ME 04462 (✆ **207/723-4443;** www.katahdinmaine.com), usually open for a half-day every weekday until early afternoon.

FEES   Baxter State Park visitors driving cars with out-of-state license plates into the park are charged a flat fee of $13 per car per day. (It's *free* for Maine residents, as well as to any occupants of a rental car bearing Maine plates.) This fee is charged only once per stay if you're coming to camp; otherwise, you need to pay each day you enter the park. You can cut your costs by buying a **seasonal pass** for $39 at the gate. There's no running water inside the park during winter.

Outdoor Pursuits

BACKPACKING   The park maintains about 180 miles of backcountry hiking trails and a few dozen backcountry campsites, some of them accessible only by canoe. Most hikers coming to the park are intent on ascending **Mount Katahdin** (see "Hiking," below), Maine's highest peak. But dozens of other peaks here are also worth scaling—heck, even simply walking through the deep woods here is a sublime (and sublimely quiet) experience. Reservations are required for backcountry camping; many of the best spots fill up quickly in early January, when reservations open for the calendar year (see "Camping," below).

En route to Mount Katahdin, the Appalachian Trail winds through the "100-Mile Wilderness," a remote and bosky stretch where the trail crosses few roads and passes no settlements. It's the quiet habitat of loons and moose. Trail descriptions are available from the **Appalachian Trail Conservancy,** 799 Washington St. (P.O. Box 807), Harpers Ferry, WV 25425 (✆ **304/535-6331;** www.appalachiantrail.org).

Grinning and Bearing It in Baxter

A few dozen black bears dwell in Baxter State Park, and while they're not interested in eating you, they do get ornery when disturbed (it's a mamabear protective thing). And they get *very* hungry at night. The park has published the following tips to help you keep a safe distance from the bears:

o Put food and anything else with an odor (toothpaste, repellant, soap, deodorant, perfume) **in a sealed bag or container** and keep it in your car.

o If you're camping in the backcountry without a car, put all your food, dinner leftovers, and other "smelly" things in a bag and **hang it between two trees** (far from your tent, not close to it) so that a bear can't reach it easily.

o *Never* keep food **inside your tent.**

o **Take all trash** with you from the campsite when you check out.

o **Don't toss food** on the trail.

o Finally, do I really need to say this? **Do not feed the bears,** or any other animals in the park, for that matter; they might bite the hands that feed them.

CAMPING Baxter State Park has a clutch of **campgrounds** accessible by car, plus a few backcountry camping areas that must be walked into; most are open summer only, from mid-May until mid-October. Some bunkhouses are open year-round.

But don't count on finding a spot if you show up without reservations in midsummer—the park starts processing requests on a first-come, first-served basis the first week in January, and dozens of die-hard campers traditionally spend a cold night outside headquarters to secure the best spots. **Call well in advance** (as in, during the previous year) for the forms you'll need to mail in.

Camping inside the park is charged per person (minimum charge $20), and the cabins and bunkhouses cost $11 to $27 per person. Reservations can be made by mail, in person at the headquarters in Millinocket (see "Visitor Information," above), and (sometimes) by phone—but *only* less than 14 days from arrival. Don't call them about any other dates.

North Maine Woods, Inc. (see "Visitor Information," above) also maintains a small network of **primitive campsites** on its 2-million-acre holdings. While you may have to drive through massive clear-cuts to reach them, some are positioned on secluded coves or picturesque points. A map showing logging-road access and campsite locations is available for a small fee plus postage from the North Maine Woods headquarters. Daily camping fees are minimal, though you must also pay an access fee to the lands.

CANOEING The state's premier canoe trip is the **Allagash River ★★**, starting west of Baxter State Park and running northward for nearly 100 miles, finishing at the village of Allagash. The **Allagash Wilderness Waterway** (© **207/941-4014**) was the first state-designated wild and scenic river in the country, protected from development since 1970. Most travelers spend between 7 and 10 days making the trip from Chamberlain Lake to Allagash. The trip begins on a chain of lakes involving light portaging. At Churchill Dam, a stretch of Class I to II white water runs for about 9 miles, and then it's back to lakes and a mix of flat water and mild rapids.

Toward the end, there's a longish portage (about 450 ft.) around picturesque Allagash Falls before finishing up above the village of Allagash.

About 80 simple campsites are scattered along the route; most have outhouses, fire rings, and picnic tables. There's a small nightly fee to use them.

HIKING With 180 miles of maintained backcountry trails and 46 peaks (including 18 that are higher than 3,000 ft.), Baxter State Park is a serious destination for serious hikers. The most imposing peak is 5,267-foot **Mount Katahdin ★★★**, the northern terminus of the **Appalachian Trail.** An ascent up this rugged, glacially scoured mountain is a trip you'll not soon forget. The raw drama and grandeur of the rocky, windswept summit is equal to anything you'll find in the White Mountains.

Allow at least 8 hours for the round-trip, and abandon your plans if the weather takes a turn for the worse while you're en route. The most popular route departs from **Roaring Brook Campground;** in fact, it's popular enough that it's often closed to day hikers—when the parking lot fills, hikers are shunted off to other trails. You ascend first to dramatic **Chimney Pond,** which is set like a jewel in a glacial cirque, and then continue upward toward Katahdin's summit via one of two trails. (The **Saddle Trail** is the most forgiving, the **Cathedral Trail ★** the most dramatic.) From here, descent begins along the aptly named **Knife Edge,** a narrow, rocky spine between Baxter Peak and Pamola Peak. *Do not take this trail if you are afraid of heights.* In spots, the trail narrows to 2 or 3 feet with a drop of hundreds of feet on either side. Obviously, it's also not the spot to be if high winds move in or thunderstorms are threatening. From the Knife Edge, the trail follows a long and gentle ridge back down to Roaring Brook.

Katahdin draws the biggest crowds, but there are numerous other trails in the park where you'll find more solitude and wildlife than on the main peak. One pleasant day hike is to the summit of **South Turner Mountain,** which offers wonderful views across to Mount Katahdin and blueberries for picking (in late summer). This trail also departs from Roaring Brook Campground, and requires about 3 to 4 hours for a round-trip. To the north, more good hikes begin at the **South Branch Pond Campground.**

My advice for picking the best hike for yourself? Talk to rangers, and buy a trail map at park headquarters when you first enter Baxter.

WHITE-WATER RAFTING One unique way to view Mount Katahdin is by rafting the West Branch of the **Penobscot River.** Flowing along the park's southern border, this wild river has some of the most technically challenging white water in the East. At least a dozen rafting companies operate trips on the Penobscot, with prices in the neighborhood of $100 or $120 per person, including a lunch.

Among the outfitters in the area is the **New England Outdoor Center** (✆ 800/ 766-7238; www.neoc.com), on a stretch of the river southeast of Millinocket. Its **River Drivers Restaurant ★** (✆ 207/723-5438) is among the best eateries in the vicinity of Baxter. The same owners also run nearby **Twin Pine Camps Cabins,** a rustic lodge on the shores of Millinocket Lake with stellar views of Katahdin (cabins for two start at around $120), as well as another facility near **Caratunk** on the **Kennebec River.**

FAST FACTS: NEW ENGLAND

Area Codes **Massachusetts** is divided into a number of area codes: 617 and 857 for Boston; 781 and 339 for a suburban ring surrounding Boston; 508, 978, 774, and 351 for central Massachusetts and Cape Cod; and 413 for western Massachusetts.

Connecticut uses 860 and 959 for Hartford and northern and eastern parts of the state, and 203 and 475 for roughly the southwestern quarter of the state (the part closest to New York City).

Rhode Island's area code is 401. **Vermont's** is 802. **New Hampshire**'s is 603. **Maine**'s is 207.

Automobile Organizations Auto clubs can supply useful maps, suggested routes, guidebooks, accident and bail-bond insurance, and emergency road service. The **American Automobile Association (AAA)** is the major auto club in the United States. If you belong to a motor club in your home country, inquire about AAA reciprocity before you leave. You may be able to join AAA even if you're not a member of a reciprocal club; to inquire, call AAA (℄ **800/222-4357;** www.aaa.com). Call the same number for AAA nationwide emergency road service.

Business Hours Banks are generally open Monday to Friday 9am to 3pm. Drive-through teller hours are longer. Shops are usually open Monday to Friday from 9am to 6pm, Saturday from 10am to 6 or 7pm, and Sunday from noon until 5 or 6pm. In bigger cities or in shopping-mall or outlet-shop areas, these hours will be somewhat extended, as late as 9pm during peak summer shopping season.

Drinking Laws The legal age for purchase and consumption of alcoholic beverages is 21; proof of age is required and often requested at bars, night-clubs, and restaurants, so it's always a good idea to bring ID when you go out.

Do not carry open containers of alcohol in your car or any public area that isn't zoned for alcohol consumption. The police can fine you on the spot. And don't even think about driving while intoxicated.

Electricity The United States uses 110 to 120 volts AC (60 cycles), the same as in Canada and Japan but different from the 220 to 240 volts AC (50 cycles) used in most of Europe, Australia, and New Zealand. Downward converters that change 220 to 240 volts to 110 to 120 volts are difficult to find in the United States, so bring one with you.

If you're coming from Europe, bring a connection kit of the right power and phone adapters, a spare phone cord, and a spare Ethernet network cable—or find out whether your hotel supplies them to guests.

Embassies & Consulates All embassies are located in the nation's capital, Washington, D.C. Some consulates are located in major U.S. cities, and most nations have a mission to the United Nations in New York City. If your country isn't listed below, call for directory information in Washington, D.C. (☏ **202/555-1212**) or check **www.embassy.org/embassies**.

The embassy of **Australia** is at 1601 Massachusetts Ave. NW, Washington, DC 20036 (☏ **202/797-3000;** usa.embassy.gov/au).

The embassy of **Canada** is at 501 Pennsylvania Ave. NW, Washington, DC 20001 (☏ **202/682-1740;** www.canadainternational.gc.ca/washington). Other Canadian consulates are in Buffalo (New York), Detroit, Los Angeles, New York, and Seattle.

The embassy of **Ireland** is at 2234 Massachusetts Ave. NW, Washington, DC 20008 (☏ **202/462-3939;** www.embassyofireland.org). Irish consulates are in Boston, Chicago, New York, San Francisco, and other cities. See website for complete listing.

The embassy of **New Zealand** is at 37 Observatory Circle NW, Washington, DC 20008 (☏ **202/328-4800;** www.nzembassy.com). New Zealand consulates are in Los Angeles, Salt Lake City, San Francisco, and Seattle.

The embassy of the **United Kingdom** is at 3100 Massachusetts Ave. NW, Washington, DC 20008 (☏ **202/588-6500;** http://ukinusa.fco.gov.uk). Other British consulates are in Atlanta, Boston, Chicago, Cleveland, Houston, Los Angeles, New York, San Francisco, and Seattle.

Emergencies   For fire, police, and ambulance, find any phone and dial ☏ **911.** If this fails, dial ☏ **0** (zero) and report an emergency.

Gasoline (Petrol)   New England's gas prices are a bit higher than the U.S. average; at press time, the price was somewhere around $2.70 per gallon. There are very few "full-service" gas stations in New England, and, if you do find one, you'll often pay up to 10¢ extra per gallon for the privilege of letting someone else pump the gas and maybe clean your windshield. Taxes are always included in the listed per-gallon price of gas in the U.S. International travelers should note that 1 U.S. gallon equals 3.8 liters or .85 imperial gallons.

Holidays   Banks, government offices, post offices, and many stores, restaurants, and museums are closed on the following legal national holidays: January 1 (New Year's Day), the third Monday in January (Martin Luther King, Jr., Day), the third Monday in February (Presidents' Day), the last Monday in May (Memorial Day), July 4 (Independence Day), the first Monday in September (Labor Day), the second Monday in October (Columbus Day), November 11 (Veterans' Day/Armistice Day), the fourth Thursday in November (Thanksgiving Day), and December 25 (Christmas). The Tuesday after the first Monday in November is Election Day, a federal government holiday in presidential-election years (held every 4 years, and next in 2012).

Some states have their own special state holidays, too. Maine and Massachusetts celebrate **Patriots' Day** on a Monday in mid-April; Vermont observes **Town Meeting Day** on the first Tuesday in March and also **Bennington Battle Day** in mid-August. All state offices are closed on these days. Most state offices remain closed on the day after Thanksgiving, which changes annually.

For more information on holidays, see "Calendar of Events," in chapter 3.

Hospitals   All large and small cities in New England maintain good hospital facilities, and some smaller towns have them, too. The quality of service is very good here. If health is a serious issue for you, check ahead with your accommodations (or consult the phone book when you arrive) about the nearest emergency-room service or 24-hour clinic.

Insurance   For information on traveler's insurance, trip-cancellation insurance, and medical insurance while traveling, please visit **www.frommers.com/planning.**

Internet Access **Internet cafes** are scattered throughout New England, though they're getting less common; these days, most travelers find a coffee shop or hotel equipped for Wi-Fi access instead. You'll need a card or antenna in your laptop to access Wi-Fi, plus a password for the local network. Some, but not all, cafes and hotels charge a fee for this service.

Many **public libraries** in the New England states—even those in small towns—offer free Internet access via free terminals. You'll probably need to surrender a piece of picture ID when you sign up, but you'll get it back when you sign out.

Legal Aid If you are "pulled over" for a minor infraction (such as speeding), never attempt to pay the fine directly to a police officer; this could be construed as attempted bribery, a much more serious crime. Pay fines by mail, or directly into the hands of the clerk of the court. If accused of a more serious offense, say and do nothing before consulting a lawyer. Here, the burden is on the state to prove a person's guilt beyond a reasonable doubt, and everyone has the right to remain silent, whether he or she is suspected of a crime or actually arrested. Once arrested, a person can make one telephone call to a party of his or her choice. International visitors should call their embassy or consulate.

Mail At press time, domestic postage rates were 28¢ for a postcard and 44¢ for a letter scheduled to go up to 46¢ in 2011. For international mail, a first-class letter of up to 1 ounce costs 98¢ (75¢ to Canada and 79¢ to Mexico); a first-class postcard costs the same as a letter. For more information, go to **www.usps.com**.

If you aren't sure what your address will be in the United States, mail can be sent to you, in your name, c/o General Delivery at the main post office of the city or region where you expect to be. (Call ✆ **800/275-8777** for information on the nearest post office.) The addressee must pick up mail in person and must produce proof of identity (driver's license, passport, and so forth). Most post offices will hold your mail for up to 1 month, and are open Monday to Friday from 8am to 6pm, and Saturday from 9am to 3pm.

Always include zip codes when mailing items in the U.S. If you don't know the zip code, visit the post office website **www.usps.com/zip4**.

Maps All New England states offer free maps at well-stocked visitor information centers; ask at the counter if you don't see them. For incredibly detailed maps, consider purchasing one or more of the **DeLorme** atlases, which depict every road and stream, along with many hiking trails and access points for canoes. DeLorme's headquarters and map store (✆ **800/561-5105** or 800/642-0970) are in Yarmouth, Maine, but their products are available at bookstores and convenience stores throughout the region.

Passports See "Embassies & Consulates," above, for whom to contact if you lose your document while traveling in the U.S. For other information, please contact the following agencies:

For Residents of Australia Contact the **Australian Passport Information Service** at ✆ **131-232,** or visit the government website at www.passports.gov.au.

For Residents of Canada Contact the central **Passport Office,** Department of Foreign Affairs and International Trade, Ottawa, ON K1A 0G3 (✆ **800/567-6868;** www.ppt.gc.ca).

For Residents of Ireland Contact the **Passport Office,** Setanta Centre, Molesworth Street, Dublin 2 (✆ **01/671-1633;** www.dfa.ie).

For Residents of New Zealand Contact the **Passports Office** at ✆ **0800/225-050** in New Zealand or 04/474-8100, or log on to www.passports.govt.nz.

For Residents of the United Kingdom Visit your nearest passport office, major post office, or travel agency, or contact the **United Kingdom Passport Service** at ✆ **0870/521-0410** or search its website at www.ukpa.gov.uk.

For Residents of the United States To find your regional passport office, either check the U.S. Department of State website (http://travel.state.gov) or call the **National Passport Information Center** toll-free number (℃ **877/487-2778**) for automated information.

Police For police, dial ℃ **911**. If this fails, dial ℃ **0** (zero) and report the emergency.

Smoking Smoking is banned in all public places (restaurants, bars, offices, hotel lobbies) in all six New England states.

Taxes The United States has no value-added tax (VAT) or other indirect tax at the national level. However, states, counties, and cities can add local taxes to purchases—including hotel bills, restaurant checks, and airline tickets. These taxes will *not* appear as part of the quoted prices; they'll be added when you pay. (Some items, such as food, clothing, and footwear, are often exempt from these state sales taxes up to a point, but policies vary from state to state.)

The **sales, dining, and lodging taxes** in New England, as of 2010, are as follows: **Connecticut** charges 6% on sales and 12% on lodging, but no local taxes. **Maine** charges a 5% sales tax in stores, 7% at hotels and restaurants, and 10% for auto rentals. **Massachusetts** charges 6.25% on sales (plus various local taxes such as Boston's city and airport taxes on hotels). **New Hampshire** charges *no* sales tax in stores, but an 8% tax on lodging and dining. **Rhode Island** charges 7% on sales, 8% for restaurant meals, and 12% on lodging. **Vermont** charges a 6% sales tax on purchases, 9% tax on hotel rooms and restaurant meals, and 10% tax on alcohol purchased in restaurants. Vermont towns and cities can (and mostly do) also add an additional 1% local tax to meals, lodgings, and purchases.

Telephones Pay phones are becoming extinct in northern New England, but you do still sometimes find them on main streets and inside shopping malls. Local calls usually cost 50¢ for a few minutes of talk time; you need to deposit more coins for more time or longer-distance calls.

For additional information on using telephones, calling cards, and cellphones in this region, see "Staying Connected," in chapter 3.

Time The continental United States is divided into **four time zones:** Eastern Standard Time (EST), Central Standard Time (CST), Mountain Standard Time (MST), and Pacific Standard Time (PST). Alaska and Hawaii have their own zones. For example, when it's 9am in Los Angeles (PST), it's 7am in Honolulu (HST), 10am in Denver (MST), 11am in Chicago (CST), noon in New York City (EST), 5pm in London (GMT), and 2am the next day in Sydney.

All New England states are in the **Eastern time zone** (the same zone as NY) and 5 to 6 hours behind the time in London. Why 5 to 6? Because **daylight saving time** is in effect from 1am on the second Sunday in March to 1am on the first Sunday in November, except in Arizona, Hawaii, the U.S. Virgin Islands, and Puerto Rico. Daylight saving time moves the clock 1 hour ahead of standard time.

Tipping In hotels, tip **bellhops** at least $1 per bag ($2–$3 if you have a lot of luggage) and tip the **chamber staff** $1 to $2 per day (more if you've left a disaster area to clean up). Tip the **doorman** or **concierge** if he or she has provided you with some useful service (for example, calling a cab for you or obtaining difficult-to-get theater tickets). Tip a **valet-parking attendant** a few dollars any time you get your car.

In restaurants, bars, and nightclubs, tip **service staff** and **bartenders** 15% to 20% of the check (assuming the service was decent), tip **coatroom attendants** $1 per garment, tip **taxi drivers** 15% of tour fare. Tip **skycaps** at airports at least $1 per bag ($2–$3 if you have a lot of luggage). And tip **hair stylists** and **barbers** 15% to 20%, too.

Toilets You won't find public toilets or "restrooms" on the streets in most U.S. cities, but they can be found in hotel lobbies, bars, restaurants, museums, department stores, railway and bus stations, and service stations. Large hotels and fast-food restaurants are often the best bets for clean facilities. Restaurants and bars in resorts or heavily visited areas may reserve their restrooms for patrons.

Visas For information about U.S. visas, go to **http://travel.state.gov** and click on "Visas." Or go to one of the following websites:

Australian citizens can obtain up-to-date visa information from the **U.S. Embassy Canberra,** Moonah Place, Yarralumla, ACT 2600 (☏ **02/6214-5600**), or by checking the U.S. Diplomatic Mission's website at **http://canberra.usembassy.gov/visas**.

British subjects can obtain up-to-date visa information by calling the **U.S. Embassy Visa Information Line** (☏ **9042/450-100**), or by visiting the "Visas to the U.S." section of the American Embassy London's website at **www.usembassy.org.uk**.

Irish citizens can obtain up-to-date visa information through the **Embassy of the USA Dublin,** 42 Elgin Rd., Dublin 4, Ireland (☏ **353/1-668-8777**), or by checking the "Visas to the U.S." section of the website at **http://dublin.usembassy.gov**.

Citizens of **New Zealand** can obtain up-to-date visa information by contacting the **U.S. Embassy New Zealand,** 29 Fitzherbert Terrace, Thorndon, Wellington (☏ **644/462-6000**), or get the information directly from the website at **http://newzealand. usembassy.gov**.

Visitor Information All New England states maintain excellent tourism information offices and kiosks throughout their key areas. Call or e-mail these offices in advance and ask for information to be mailed to you before departure, or collect it online. Local tourism and chamber of commerce addresses and phone numbers are also provided in state-specific chapters.

Here's contact information for each state's tourism authority:

○ **Connecticut Commission on Culture & Tourism,** 1 Constitution Plaza, 2nd Floor, Hartford, CT 06103 (☏ **888/288-4748** or 860/256-2800; www.ctvisit.com).

○ **Maine Office of Tourism,** 59 State House Station, Augusta, ME 04333 (☏ **888/624-6345** or 207/287-5711; www.visitmaine.com).

○ **Massachusetts Office of Travel and Tourism,** 10 Park Plaza, Ste. 4510, Boston, MA 02116 (☏ **888/227-6277** or 207/973-8500; www.massvacation.com).

○ **New Hampshire Division of Travel and Tourism Development,** 172 Pembroke Rd. (P.O. Box 1856), Concord, NH 03302 (☏ **800/386-4664** or 603/271-2665; www.visitnh.gov).

○ **Rhode Island Tourism Division,** 315 Iron Horse Way, Ste. 101, Providence, RI 02908 (☏ **800/250-7384;** www.visitrhodeisland.com).

○ **Vermont Department of Tourism and Marketing,** National Life Building, Sixth Floor, Montpelier, VT 05620 (☏ **800/837-6668** or 802/828-3237; www. travel-vermont.com).

If you're going back-roading or backcountry hiking, consider purchasing one or more of the **DeLorme atlases,** which depict every road and stream in these states, plus many hiking trails and access points for canoes. DeLorme's headquarters and map store (☏ **800/561-5105** or 800/642-0970) are in Yarmouth, Maine, open daily, and their products are also available at many bookstores, gas stations, and convenience stores in the region.

Travel blogging hasn't really developed in this region yet—there are hundreds of microbloggers writing about local travel, news, or dining, but none is considered authoritative or universally followed yet. It's best to follow the blogs of local newspaper reporters in the region or of the official tourism agencies listed above.

AIRLINE WEBSITES

MAJOR AIRLINES

Air France
www.airfrance.com

Air New Zealand
www.airnewzealand.com

Alitalia
www.alitalia.com

American Airlines
www.aa.com

British Airways
www.british-airways.com

Cape Air
www.flycapeair.com

Continental Airlines
www.continental.com

Delta Air Lines
www.delta.com

Frontier Airlines
www.frontierairlines.com

Icelandair
www.icelandair.com

Japan Airlines
www.jal.co.jp

Lufthansa
www.lufthansa.com

Nantucket Airlines
www.nantucketairlines.com

Qantas Airways
www.qantas.com

South African Airways
www.flysaa.com

Swiss Air
www.swiss.com

United Airlines
www.united.com

US Airways
www.usairways.com

Virgin America
www.virginamerica.com

Virgin Atlantic Airways
www.virgin-atlantic.com

BUDGET AIRLINES

AirTran Airways
www.airtran.com

Frontier Airlines
www.frontierairlines.com

JetBlue Airways
www.jetblue.com

Southwest Airlines
www.southwest.com

Spirit Airlines
www.spiritair.com

15

FAST FACTS: NEW ENGLAND | Airline Websites

Index

T